Beginning ASP.NET 2.0 in C# 2005

From Novice to Professional

Matthew MacDonald

Apress®

Beginning ASP.NET 2.0 in C# 2005: From Novice to Professional

ISBN-13 (pbk): 978-1-59059-572-5

ISBN-10 (pbk): 1-59059-572-6

Printed and bound in the United States of America 9 8 7 6 5 4 3

Contributor of Chapter 27: Julian Templeman
Lead Editor: Jonathan Hassell
Technical Reviewer: Ronald Landers
Editorial Board: Steve Anglin, Dan Appleman, Ewan Buckingham, Gary Cornell, Jason Gilmore, Jonathan Hassell, Chris Mills, Dominic Shakeshaft, Jim Sumser
Project Manager and Production Director: Grace Wong
Copy Edit Manager: Nicole LeClerc
Copy Editor: Kim Wimpsett
Assistant Production Director: Kari Brooks-Copony
Production Editor: Kelly Winquist
Compositor: Pat Christenson
Proofreader: Nancy Riddiough
Indexer: Michael Brinkman
Artist: Kinetic Publishing Services, LLC
Cover Designer: Kurt Krames
Manufacturing Director: Tom Debolski

Distributed to the book trade worldwide by Springer-Verlag New York, Inc., 233 Spring Street, 6th Floor, New York, NY 10013. Phone 1-800-SPRINGER, fax 201-348-4505, e-mail `orders-ny@springer-sbm.com`, or visit `http://www.springeronline.com`.

For information on translations, please contact Apress directly at 2560 Ninth Street, Suite 219, Berkeley, CA 94710. Phone 510-549-5930, fax 510-549-5939, e-mail `info@apress.com`, or visit `http://www.apress.com`.

The source code for this book is available to readers at `http://www.apress.com` in the Source Code section. You will need to answer questions pertaining to this book in order to successfully download the code.

For my loving wife, Faria

Contents at a Glance

PART 4 ■■■ Website Security

PART 5 ■■■ Web Services

PART 6 ■■■ Advanced ASP.NET

Contents

PART 2 ■■■ Developing ASP.NET Applications

PART 3 Working with Data

PART 4 Website Security

PART 5 ■■■ Web Services

PART 6 Advanced ASP.NET

About the Author

MATTHEW MACDONALD is an author, educator, and MCSD developer. He's a regular contributor to programming journals and the author of more than a dozen books about .NET programming, including *Pro ASP.NET 2.0 in C# 2005* (Apress, 2005), *Microsoft .NET Distributed Applications* (Microsoft Press, 2003), *Programming .NET Web Services* (O'Reilly, 2002), and *ASP.NET: The Complete Reference* (Osborne McGraw-Hill, 2002). In a dimly remembered past life, he studied English literature and theoretical physics. You can read about his new books at `http://www.prosetech.com`.

About the Technical Reviewer

RONALD LANDERS is the president and senior technical consultant for IT Professionals (ITP), a Los Angeles, California–based IT staffing, development, and project services company. Mr. Landers has worked in the IT field for the past 20 years specializing in database design and implementation, application architecture and development, business process engineering, and web-based technologies that include web services, electronic commerce, and web portals.

In addition to his work at ITP, Mr. Landers has been teaching IT classes at UCLA Extension for the past 13 years. Currently, his courses include beginning and advanced classes in SQL Server, ASP.NET, web services, and object-oriented programming.

Acknowledgments

No author could complete a book without a small army of helpful individuals. I'm deeply indebted to the whole Apress team, including Grace Wong and Kelly Winquist, who helped everything move swiftly and smoothly; Kim Wimpsett, who performed the copy edit; Ronald Landers, who performed the most recent round of technical review; Julian Templeman, who contributed Chapter 27; and many other individuals who worked behind the scenes indexing pages, drawing figures, and proofreading the final copy. I owe a special thanks to Gary Cornell, who always offers invaluable advice about projects and the publishing world. He has helped build a truly unique company with Apress.

I'd also like to thank those who were involved with previous editions of this book. This includes Emma Acker and Jane Brownlow at Osborne McGraw-Hill and previous tech reviewers Gavin Smyth, Tim Verycruysse, and Julian Skinner. I also owe a hearty thanks to all the readers who caught errors and took the time to report problems and ask good questions. Keep sending in the feedback—it helps make better books!

Finally, I'd never write *any* book without the support of my wife and these special individuals: Nora, Razia, Paul, and Hamid. Thanks, everyone!

Introduction

ASP (Active Server Pages) is a relatively new technology that's already leapt through several stages of evolution. It was introduced about seven years ago as an easy way to add dynamic content to ordinary web pages. Since then, it's grown into something much more ambitious: a platform for creating advanced web applications, including e-commerce shops, data-driven portal sites, and just about anything else you can find on the Internet.

ASP.NET 2.0 is the latest version of ASP, and it represents the most dramatic change yet. With ASP.NET, developers no longer need to paste together a jumble of HTML and script code in order to program the Web. Instead, you can create full-scale web applications using nothing but code and a design tool such as Visual Studio 2005. The cost of all this innovation is the learning curve. Not only do you need to learn how to use an advanced design tool (Visual Studio) and a toolkit of objects (the .NET Framework), you also need to master a programming language such as C#.

Beginning ASP.NET 2.0 in C# 2005 assumes you want to master ASP.NET, starting from the basics. Using this book, you'll build your knowledge until you understand the concepts, techniques, and best practices for writing sophisticated web applications. The journey is long, but it's also satisfying. At the end of the day, you'll find that ASP.NET allows you to tackle challenges that are simply out of reach on many other platforms. You'll also become part of the fast-growing ASP.NET developer community.

About This Book

This book explores ASP.NET, which is a core part of Microsoft's .NET Framework. The .NET Framework is not a single application—it's actually a collection of technologies bundled into one marketing term. The .NET Framework includes languages such as C# and VB .NET, an engine for hosting programmable web pages and web services (ASP.NET), a model for interacting with databases (ADO.NET), and a class library stocked with tools for everything from writing files to reading XML. To master ASP.NET, you need to learn about each of these ingredients.

This book covers all these topics from the ground up. As a result, you'll find yourself learning many techniques that will interest any .NET developer, even those who create Windows applications. For example, you'll learn about component-based programming, you'll discover structured error handling, and you'll see how to access files, XML, and relational databases. You'll also learn the key topics you need for web programming, such as state management, web controls, and web services. By the end of this book, you'll be ready to create your own rich web applications and make them available over the Internet.

Note This book has a single goal: to be as relentlessly practical as possible. I take special care not to leave you hanging in the places where other ASP.NET books abandon their readers. For example, when encountering a new technology, you'll not only learn how it works but also why (and when) you should use it. I also highlight common questions and best practices with tip boxes and sidebars at every step of the way. Finally, if a topic is covered in this book, it's covered *right*. This means you won't learn how to perform a task without learning about potential drawbacks and the problems you might run into—and how you can safeguard yourself with real-world code.

Who Should Read This Book

This book is aimed at anyone who wants to create dynamic websites with ASP.NET. Ideally, you have experience with a previous version of a programming language such as C or Java. If not, you should be familiar with basic programming concepts (loops, conditional structures, arrays, and so on), whether you've learned them in Java, C, Pascal, Turing, or a completely different programming language. This is the only requirement for reading this book. Understanding HTML helps, but it's not required. ASP.NET works at a higher level, allowing you to deal with full-featured web controls instead of raw HTML. You also don't need any knowledge of XML, because Chapter 17 covers it in detail.

This book will also appeal to programmers who have some experience with C# and .NET but haven't worked with ASP.NET in the past. However, if you've used a previous version of ASP.NET, you'll probably be more interested in a faster-paced look with a book such as *Pro ASP.NET 2.0 in C# 2005* (Apress, 2005) instead.

Note This book begins with the fundamentals: C# syntax, the basics of object-oriented programming, and the philosophy of the .NET Framework. If you've never worked with C#, you can spend a little more time with the syntax review in Chapter 2 to pick up everything you need to know. If you aren't familiar with the ideas of object-oriented programming, Chapter 3 fills in the blanks with a quick, but comprehensive, review of the subject. The rest of the book builds on this foundation, from ASP.NET basics to advanced examples that show the techniques you'll use in real-world web applications.

What You Need to Use This Book

The main prerequisite for this book is a computer with Visual Studio 2005. You can also use the scaled-down Visual Studio Web Developer 2005 Express Edition, but you'll run into a few minor limitations. Most significantly, you can't use Visual Studio Web Developer to create class libraries (separate components), a technique discussed in Chapter 24. (However, you still use the sample code directly in your web projects.)

To run ASP.NET pages, you need Windows 2000 Professional, Windows XP Professional, Windows 2000 Server, or Windows Server 2003. You also need to install IIS (Internet Information Services), the web hosting software that's part of the Windows operating system, if you want to try web services or test deployment strategies.

Finally, this book includes several examples that use SQL Server. You can use any version of SQL Server to try these, including SQL Server 2005 Express Edition, which is included with some versions of Visual Studio. If you use other relational database engines, the same concepts will apply; you will just need to modify the example code.

Code Samples

To master ASP.NET, you need to experiment with it. One of the best ways to learn ASP.NET is to try the code samples for this book, examine them, and dive in with your own modifications. To obtain the sample code, surf to `http://www.prosetech.com` or the publisher's website at `http://www.apress.com`. You'll also find some links to additional resources and any updates or errata that affect the book.

Chapter Overview

This book is divided into six parts. Unless you've already had experience with the .NET Framework, the most productive way to read this book is in order from start to finish. Chapters later in the book sometimes incorporate features that were introduced earlier in order to create more well-rounded and realistic examples. On the other hand, if you're already familiar with the .NET platform, C#, and object-oriented programming, you'll make short work of the first part of this book.

Part 1: Introducing .NET

You could start coding an ASP.NET application right away by following the examples in the second part of this book. But to really master ASP.NET, you need to understand a few fundamental concepts about the .NET Framework.

Chapter 1 sorts through the Microsoft jargon and explains what the .NET Framework really does and why you need it. Chapter 2 introduces you to C# with a comprehensive language reference, and Chapter 3 explains the basics of modern object-oriented programming. Chapter 4 introduces the Visual Studio design environment.

Part 2: Developing ASP.NET Applications

The second part of this book delves into the heart of ASP.NET programming and introduces its new event-based model. In Chapters 5 and 6, you learn how to program a web page's user interface through a layer of objects called *server controls*.

Next, you'll explore the fundamentals of ASP.NET programming. Chapter 7 presents different techniques for handling errors, and Chapter 8 introduces some of the most remarkable ASP.NET controls, such as the input validators. Chapter 9 describes different strategies for state management. Chapter 10 shows how you can standardize the appearance of an entire website with master pages, and Chapter 11 shows you how to add navigation to a website. Finally, Chapter 12 walks you through the steps for deploying your application to a web server. Taken together, these chapters contain all the core concepts you need to design web pages and create a basic ASP.NET website.

Part 3: Working with Data

Almost all software needs to work with data, and web applications are no exception. In Chapter 13, you begin exploring the world of data by considering ADO.NET—Microsoft's new technology for interacting with relational databases. Chapters 14 and 15 explain how to use data binding and the advanced ASP.NET data controls to create web pages that integrate attractive, customizable data displays with automatic support for paging, sorting, and editing.

Chapter 16 moves out of the database world and considers how to interact with files. Chapter 17 broadens the picture even further and describes how ASP.NET applications can use the XML support that's built into the .NET Framework.

Part 4: Website Security

Every public website needs to deal with security—making sure that sensitive data cannot be accessed by the wrong users. In Chapter 18, you'll start out learning how ASP.NET provides different authentication systems for dealing with users. You can write your own custom logic to verify user names and passwords, or you can use existing Windows account information on your web server. In Chapter 19, you'll learn about a new model that extends the basic authentication system with prebuilt security controls and objects that automate common tasks. If you want, you can even get ASP.NET to create and manage a database with user information automatically. Finally, Chapter 20 deals with another add-on—the profiles model that lets you store information for each user automatically, without writing any database code.

Part 5: Web Services

Web services are a new feature of ASP.NET and are one of Microsoft's most heavily promoted new technologies. Using web services, you can share pieces of functionality on your web server with other applications on other computers. Best of all, the whole process works with open standards such as XML, ensuring that applications written in different programming languages and running on different operating systems can interact without a hitch.

Chapter 21 presents an overview of web service technology. Chapter 22 shows how to create a basic web service and use it in a client. Chapter 23 shows you how to enhance your web service with caching, security, and transactions.

Part 6: Advanced ASP.NET

This part includes the advanced topics you can use to take your web applications that extra step. Chapters 24 and 25 cover how you can create reusable components and web controls for ASP.NET applications. Chapter 26 demonstrates how careful use of caching can boost the performance of almost any web application. Chapter 27 introduces the new model for building advanced portal sites, called *Web Parts*.

Feedback

This book has the ambitious goal of being the best tutorial and reference for ASP.NET. Toward that end, your comments and suggestions are extremely helpful. You can send complaints, adulation, and everything in between directly to `apress@prosetech.com`. I can't solve your ASP.NET problems or critique your code, but I do benefit from information about what this book did right and wrong (and what it may have done in an utterly confusing way). You can also send comments about the website support for this book.

PART 1

Introducing .NET

CHAPTER 1

Introducing the .NET Framework

Microsoft has a time-honored reputation for creating innovative technologies and wrapping them in buzzwords that confuse everyone. Now that developers are finally sorting out ActiveX, COM (Component Object Model), and Windows DNA (Distributed interNet Architecture), Microsoft has a whole new technology called .NET, with a whole new set of technical jargon. So, exactly what does it all mean?

This chapter examines the technologies that underlie .NET. First, you'll take a quick look at the history of web development and learn why the .NET Framework was created. Next, you'll get a high-level overview of the different parts of .NET and see how ASP.NET fits into the wider world of development. Finally, you'll see what new frills and features ASP.NET adds to the programmer's toolkit with version 2.0.

The Evolution of Web Development

The Internet began in the late 1960s as an experiment. Its goal was to create a truly resilient information network—one that could withstand the loss of several computers without preventing the others from communicating. Driven by potential disaster scenarios (such as nuclear attack), the U.S. Department of Defense provided the initial funding.

The early Internet was mostly limited to educational institutions and defense contractors. It flourished as a tool for academic collaboration, allowing researchers across the globe to share information. In the early 1990s, modems were created that could work over existing phone lines, and the Internet began to open up to commercial users. In 1993, the first HTML browser was created, and the Internet revolution began.

HTML and HTML Forms

It would be difficult to describe early websites as web applications. Instead, the first generation of websites often looked more like brochures, consisting mostly of fixed HTML pages that needed to be updated by hand.

A basic HTML page is a little like a word-processing document—it contains formatted content that can be displayed on your computer, but it doesn't actually *do* anything. The following example shows HTML at its simplest, with a document that contains a heading and single line of text:

```
<html>
    <head>
        <title>Sample Web Page</title>
    </head>
    <body>
        <h1>Sample Web Page Heading</h1>
        <p>This is a sample web page.</p>
    </body>
</html>
```

An HTML document has two types of content: the text and the tags that tell the browser how to format it. The tags are easily recognizable, because they occur inside angled brackets (< >). HTML defines tags for different levels of headings, paragraphs, hyperlinks, italic and bold formatting, horizontal lines, and so on. For example, <h1>Some Text</h1> tells the browser to display *Some Text* in the Heading 1 style, which uses a large, bold font. Figure 1-1 shows the simple HTML page in a browser.

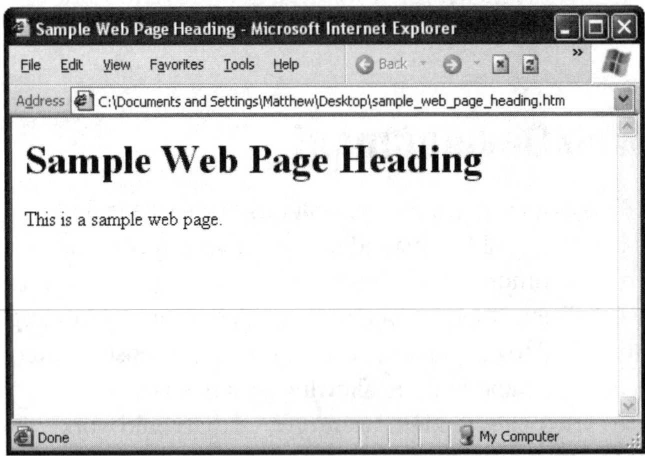

Figure 1-1. *Ordinary HTML: the "brochure" site*

Tip You don't need to master HTML to program ASP.NET web pages, although it's often useful. For a quick introduction to HTML, refer to one of the excellent HTML tutorials on the Internet, such as `http://www.w3schools.com/html` or `http://archive.ncsa.uiuc.edu/General/Internet/WWW/HTMLPrimer.html`.

HTML 2.0 introduced the first seed of web programming with a technology called *HTML forms.* HTML forms expand HTML so that it includes not only formatting tags but also tags for graphical widgets, or *controls.* These controls include common ingredients such as drop-down lists, text boxes, and buttons. Here's a sample web page created with HTML form controls:

```
<html>
    <body>
        <form>
            <input type="checkbox">This is choice #1<br>
            <input type="checkbox">This is choice #2<br><br>
            <input type="submit" value="Submit">
        </form>
    </body>
</html>
```

In an HTML form, all controls are placed between the <form> and </form> tags. The preceding example includes two check boxes (represented by the <input type="checkbox"> tags) and a button (represented by the <input type="submit"> tag). In a browser, this page looks like Figure 1-2.

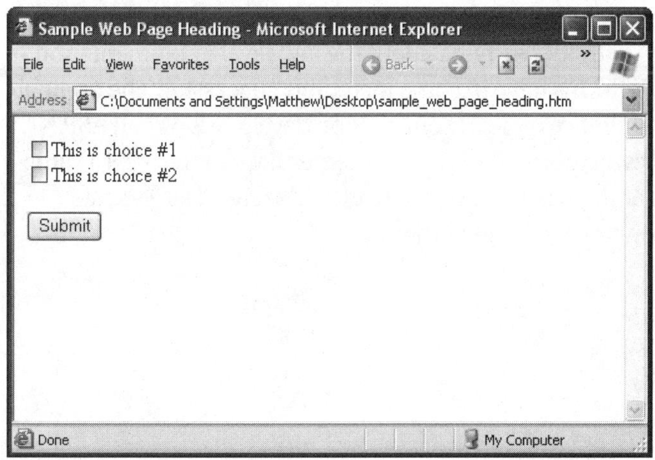

Figure 1-2. *An HTML form*

HTML forms allow web application developers to design standard input pages. When the user clicks the Submit button on the page shown in Figure 1-2, all the data in the input controls (in this case, the two check boxes) is patched together into one long string and sent to the web server. On the server side, a custom application receives and processes the data. Amazingly enough, the controls that were created for HTML forms more than ten years ago are still the basic foundation that you'll use to build dynamic ASP.NET pages! The difference is the type of application that runs on the server side. In the past, when the user clicked a button on a form page, the information might have been e-mailed to a set account or sent to an application on the server that used the challenging CGI (Common Gateway Interface) standard. Today, you'll work with the much more capable and elegant ASP.NET platform.

Server-Side Programming

To understand why ASP.NET was created, it helps to understand the problems of other web development technologies. With the original CGI standard, for example, the web server must launch a completely separate instance of the application for each web request. If the website is popular, the web server must struggle under the weight of hundreds of separate copies of the application, eventually becoming a victim of its own success.

To counter this problem, Microsoft developed ISAPI (Internet Server Application Programming Interface), a higher-level programming model. ISAPI solved the performance problem but at the cost of significant complexity. Even after ISAPI developers master the tricky C++ programming language, they still lie awake at night worrying about confounding issues such as multithreading. ISAPI programming is definitely not for the fainthearted.

ISAPI never really went away. Instead, Microsoft used it to build higher-level development platforms, such as ASP and ASP.NET. Both of these technologies allow developers to program dynamic web pages without worrying about the low-level implementation details. For that reason, both platforms have become incredibly successful. The original ASP platform garnered a huge audience of nearly one million developers. When ASP.NET was first released, it generated even more interest as the centerpiece of the .NET Framework. In fact, ASP.NET 1.0 was enthusiastically put to work in dozens of large-scale commercial websites even when it was only in late beta.

Despite having similar underpinnings, ASP and ASP.NET are radically different. ASP is a script-based programming language that requires a thorough understanding of HTML and a good deal of painful coding. ASP.NET, on the other hand, is an object-oriented programming model that lets you put together a web page as easily as you would build a Windows application. In many respects, it's easier to learn ASP.NET than to master ASP, even though ASP.NET is far more powerful.

■ **Tip** Don't let the version numbers confuse you. ASP.NET 1.*x* and ASP.NET 2.0 share the same underlying plumbing and use essentially the same technology. Although they run on different versions of the .NET Framework, the changes are evolutionary, not revolutionary. This similarity doesn't hold for classic ASP, which is based on older Microsoft technologies such as COM.

Client-Side Programming

At the same time that server-side web development was moving through an alphabet soup of technologies, a new type of programming was gaining popularity. Developers began to experiment with the different ways they could enhance web pages by embedding multimedia and miniature applets built with JavaScript, DHTML (Dynamic HTML), and Java code. These client-side technologies don't involve any server processing. Instead, the complete application is downloaded to the client browser, which executes it locally.

The greatest problem with client-side technologies is that they aren't supported equally by all browsers and operating systems. One of the reasons that web development is so popular in the first place is because web applications don't require setup CDs, downloads, and other tedious (and error-prone) deployment steps. Instead, a web application can be used on any computer that has Internet access. But when developers use client-side technologies, they encounter a few familiar headaches. Suddenly, cross-browser compatibility becomes a problem. Developers are forced to test their websites with different operating systems and browsers, and they might even need to distribute browser updates to their clients. In other words, the client-side model sacrifices some of the most important benefits of web development.

For that reason, ASP.NET is designed as a server-side technology. All ASP.NET code executes on the server. When the code is finished executing, the user receives an ordinary HTML page, which can be viewed in any browser. Figure 1-3 shows the difference between the server-side and client-side model.

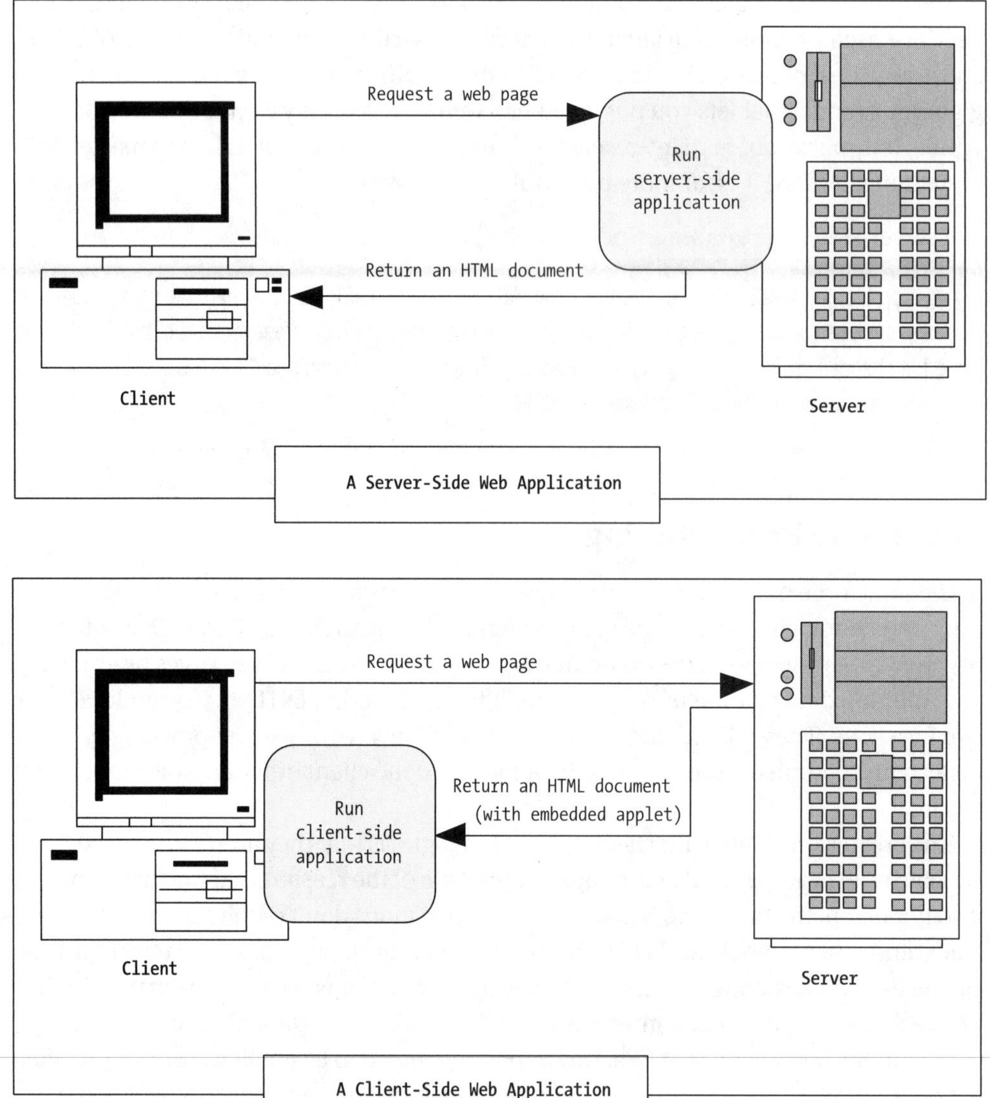

Figure 1-3. *Server-side and client-side web applications*

These are some other reasons for avoiding client-side programming:

Isolation: Client-side code can't access server-side resources. For example, a client-side application has no easy way to read a file or interact with a database on the server (at least not without running into problems with security and browser compatibility).

Security: End users can view client-side code. And once malicious users understand how an application works, they can often tamper with it.

Thin clients: As the Internet continues to evolve, web-enabled devices such as mobile phones, palmtop computers, and PDAs (personal digital assistants) are appearing. These devices can communicate with web servers, but they don't support all the features of a traditional browser. Thin clients can use server-based web applications, but they won't support client-side features such as JavaScript.

In some cases, ASP.NET allows you to combine the best of client-side programming with server-side programming. For example, the best ASP.NET controls can intelligently detect the features of the client browser. If the browser supports JavaScript, these controls will return a web page that incorporates JavaScript for a richer, more responsive user interface. However, no matter what the capabilities of the browser, *your* code is always executed on the server.

The Problems with ASP

The original ASP became more popular than even Microsoft anticipated, and it wasn't long before it was being wedged into all sorts of unusual places, including mission-critical business applications and highly trafficked e-commerce sites. Because ASP hadn't been designed with these uses in mind, a number of problems began to appear. What began as a simple solution for creating interactive web pages became a complicated discipline that required knowledge in several fields as well as some painful experience.

If you've programmed with ASP before, you may already be familiar with some or all of these problems:

Scripting limitations: ASP applications rely on the VBScript language, which suffers from a number of limitations, including poor performance. To overcome these problems, developers usually need to add separately developed components, which add a new layer of complexity. In ASP.NET, web pages are designed in a modern .NET language, not a scripting language.

No application structure: ASP code is inserted directly into a web page along with the HTML markup. The resulting tangle of code and HTML has nothing in common with today's modern, object-oriented languages. As a result, web form code can rarely be reused or modified without hours of effort.

Headaches with deployment and configuration: If you want to update a component used in an ASP website, you often need to manually stop and restart the server. This process just isn't practical on a live website. Changing configuration options can be just as ugly. Thankfully, ASP.NET includes a slew of features that allow websites to be dynamically updated and reconfigured.

State limitations: To ensure optimum performance, the Web is built on *stateless* protocols, which means as soon as a page is sent to a user, the connection is closed and any user-specific information is discarded. ASP includes a session state feature that allows programmers to work around this problem. Using session state, a web application can retain temporary information about each client in server memory. However, session state is useless in scenarios where a website is hosted by several separate web servers. In this scenario, a client might access server B while its session information is trapped on server A and essentially abandoned. ASP.NET corrects this problem by allowing state to be stored in a central repository, such as a separate process or a database that all servers can access.

ASP.NET deals with these problems (and many more) by introducing a completely new model for web pages. This model is based on a remarkable piece of technology called the .NET Framework.

The .NET Framework

You should understand that the .NET Framework is really a cluster of several technologies:

The .NET languages: These include C# and VB .NET (Visual Basic .NET), the object-oriented and modernized successor to Visual Basic 6.0; these languages also include JScript .NET (a server-side version of JavaScript), J# (a Java clone), and C++ with Managed Extensions.

The CLR (Common Language Runtime): The CLR is the engine that executes all .NET programs and provides automatic services for these applications, such as security checking, memory management, and optimization.

The .NET Framework class library: The class library collects thousands of pieces of prebuilt functionality that you can "snap in" to your applications. These features are sometimes organized into technology sets, such as ADO.NET (the technology for creating database applications) and Windows Forms (the technology for creating desktop user interfaces).

ASP.NET: This is the engine that hosts web applications and web services, with almost any feature from the .NET class library. ASP.NET also includes a set of web-specific services.

Visual Studio: This optional development tool contains a rich set of productivity and debugging features. The Visual Studio setup CDs (or DVD) include the complete .NET Framework, so you won't need to download it separately.

Sometimes the division between these components isn't clear. For example, the term *ASP.NET* is sometimes used in a narrow sense to refer to the portion of the .NET class library used to design web pages. On the other hand, ASP.NET also refers to the whole topic of .NET web applications, which includes .NET languages and many fundamental pieces of the class library that aren't web-specific. (That's generally the way we use the term in this book. Our exhaustive examination of ASP.NET includes .NET basics, the C# language, and topics that any .NET developer could use, such as component-based programming and database access.)

Figure 1-4 shows the .NET class library and CLR—the two fundamental parts of .NET.

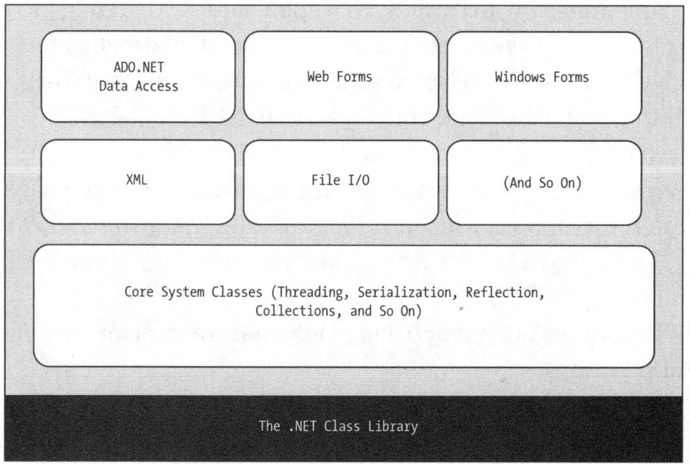

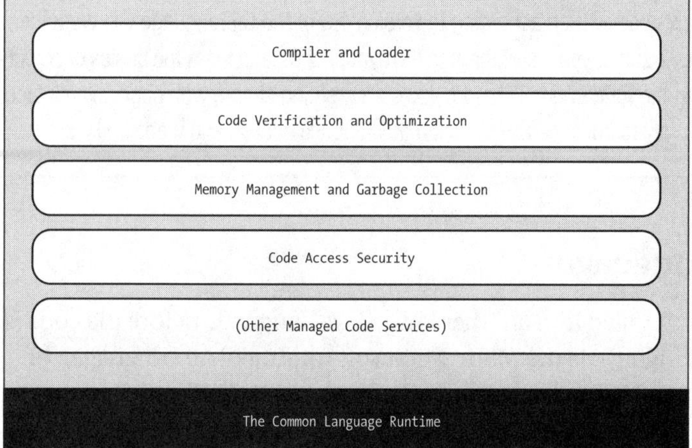

Figure 1-4. *The .NET Framework*

C#, VB .NET, and the .NET Languages

This book uses C#, Microsoft's .NET language of preference. C# is a new language that was designed for .NET 1.0. It resembles Java and C++ in syntax, but no direct migration path exists from Java or C++.

The other language that's commonly used to create ASP.NET applications is Visual Basic (VB). Somewhat schizophrenically, Microsoft renamed VB twice, calling it VB .NET when .NET 1.0 hit the scene and renaming it as VB 2005 in .NET 2.0.[1] These name changes can't hide that the .NET versions of VB are dramatically different from the language that classic VB 6 developers know. In fact, VB .NET is a redesigned language that improves on traditional VB 6 and breaks compatibility with existing VB 6 applications. Migrating to VB .NET is a stretch—and a process of discovery for the most seasoned VB developer.

Interestingly, C# and VB .NET are actually far more similar than Java and C# or than VB 6 and VB .NET. Though the syntax is different, both C# and VB .NET use the .NET class library and are supported by the CLR. In fact, almost any block of C# code can be translated, line by line, into an equivalent block of VB .NET code. An occasional language difference pops up (for example, C# supports a language feature called *anonymous methods,* while VB .NET doesn't), but for the most part, a developer who has learned one .NET language can move quickly and efficiently to another.

In short, both C# and VB .NET are elegant, modern languages that are ideal for creating the next generation of web applications.

■ **Note** .NET 1.0 introduced completely new languages. However, the changes in the .NET 2.0 languages are much more subtle. Both C# 2005 and VB 2005 add a few new features, but most parts of these languages remain unchanged. As a result, any code written according to version 1.0 of the C# language will work identically with version 2.0. In Chapters 2 and 3, you'll sort through the syntax of C# and learn the basics of object-oriented programming. By learning the fundamentals before you start creating simple web pages, you'll face less confusion and move more rapidly to advanced topics such as database access and web services.

The Intermediate Language

All the .NET languages are compiled into another lower-level language before the code is executed. This lower-level language is the MSIL (Microsoft Intermediate Language), or just IL. The CLR, the engine of .NET, uses only IL code. Because all .NET languages are designed based on IL, they all have profound similarities. This is the reason that the C# and VB .NET languages provide essentially the same features and performance. In fact,

1. This chapter uses *VB .NET* to refer to the .NET versions of the VB language (either VB .NET 1.*x* or VB 2005).

the languages are so compatible that a web page written with C# can use a VB .NET component in the same way it uses a C# component, and vice versa.

The .NET Framework formalizes this compatibility with something called the CLS (Common Language Specification). Essentially, the CLS is a contract that, if respected, guarantees that a component written in one .NET language can be used in all the others. One part of the CLS is the CTS (common type system), which defines data types such as strings, numbers, and arrays that are shared in all .NET languages. The CLS also defines object-oriented ingredients such as classes, methods, events, and quite a bit more. For the most part, .NET developers don't need to think about how the CLS works, even though they rely on it every day.

Figure 1-5 shows how the .NET languages are compiled to IL. Every EXE or DLL file that you build with a .NET language contains IL code. This is the file you deploy to other computers.

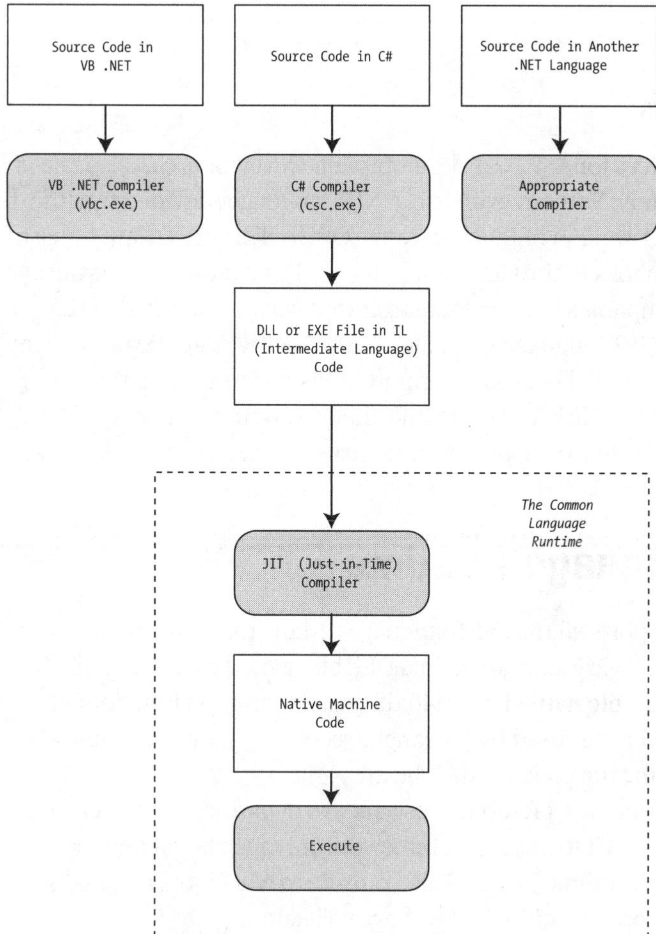

Figure 1-5. *Language compilation in .NET*

The CLR runs only IL code, which means it has no idea which .NET language you originally used. Notice, however, that the CLR actually performs another compilation step—it takes the IL code and transforms it to native machine language code that's appropriate for the current platform. This step occurs when the application is launched, just before the code is actually executed. In an ASP.NET application, these machine-specific files are cached while the web application is running so that they can be reused, ensuring optimum performance.

■ **Note** You might wonder why .NET compilers don't compile straight to machine code. The reason is that the machine code depends on several factors, including the CPU. For example, if you create machine code for a computer with an Intel processor, the compiler may be able to use Hyper-Threading to produce enhanced code. This machine-specific version isn't suitable for deployment to other computers, because no guarantee exists that they're using the same processor.

Other .NET Languages

C# and VB aren't the only choices for ASP.NET development. Developers can also use J# (a language with Java-like syntax). You can even use a .NET language provided by a third-party developer, such as a .NET version of Eiffel or even COBOL. This increasing range of language choices is possible thanks to the CLS, which defines basic requirements and standards that allow other companies to write languages that can be compiled to IL.

Although you can use any .NET language to create an ASP.NET web application, some of them do not provide the same level of design support in Visual Studio, and most ASP.NET developers use C# or VB .NET. For more information about third-party .NET languages, check out the website `http://www.dotnetlanguages.net`.

The Common Language Runtime

The CLR is the engine that supports all the .NET languages. Many modern languages use runtimes. In VB 6, the runtime logic is contained in a DLL file named msvbvm60.dll. In C++, many applications link to a file named mscrt40.dll to gain common functionality. These runtimes may provide libraries used by the language, or they may have the additional responsibility of executing the code (as with Java).

Runtimes are nothing new, but the CLR represents a radical departure from Microsoft's previous strategy. For starters, the CLR and .NET Framework are much larger and more ambitious than the VB 6 or C++ runtime. The CLR also provides a whole set of related services such as code verification, optimization, and garbage collection.

■ **Note** The CLR is the reason that some developers have accused .NET of being a Java clone. The claim is fairly silly. It's true that .NET is quite similar to Java in key respects (both use a special managed environment and provide features through a rich class library), but it's also true that every programming language "steals" from and improves on previous programming languages. This includes Java, which adopted parts of the C/C++ language and syntax when it was created. Of course, in many other aspects .NET differs just as radically from Java as it does from VBScript.

All .NET code runs inside the CLR. This is true whether you're running a Windows application or a web service. For example, when a client requests an ASP.NET web page, the ASP.NET service runs inside the CLR environment, executes your code, and creates a final HTML page to send to the client.

The implications of the CLR are wide-ranging:

Deep language integration: C# and VB .NET, like all .NET languages, compile to IL. In other words, the CLR makes no distinction between different languages—in fact, it has no way of knowing what language was used to create an executable. This is far more than mere language compatibility; it's language *integration*.

Side-by-side execution: The CLR also has the ability to load more than one version of a component at a time. In other words, you can update a component many times, and the correct version will be loaded and used for each application. As a side effect, multiple versions of the .NET Framework can be installed, meaning that you're able to upgrade to new versions of ASP.NET without replacing the current version or needing to rewrite your applications.

Fewer errors: Whole categories of errors are impossible with the CLR. For example, the CLR prevents many memory mistakes that are possible with lower-level languages such as C++.

Along with these truly revolutionary benefits, the CLR has some potential drawbacks. Here are three issues that are often raised by new developers but aren't always answered:

Performance: A typical ASP.NET application is much faster than a comparable ASP application, because ASP.NET code is compiled natively. However, other .NET applications probably won't match the blinding speed of well-written C++ code, because the CLR imposes some additional overhead. Generally, this is a factor only in a few performance-critical high-workload applications (such as real-time games). With high-volume web applications, the potential bottlenecks are rarely processor-related but are usually tied to the speed of an external resource such as a database or the web server's file system. With ASP.NET caching and some well-written database code, you can ensure excellent performance for any web application.

Code transparency: IL is much easier to disassemble, meaning that if you distribute a compiled application or component, other programmers may have an easier time determining how your code works. This isn't much of an issue for ASP.NET applications, which aren't distributed but are hosted on a secure web server.

Questionable cross-platform support: No one is entirely sure whether .NET will be adopted for use on other operating systems and platforms. Ambitious projects such as Mono (a free implementation of .NET on Linux, Unix, and Windows) are currently underway (see `http://www.go-mono.com`). However, .NET will probably never have the wide reach of a language such as Java because it incorporates too many different platform-specific and operating system–specific technologies and features.

■ **Tip** Although implementations of .NET are available for other platforms, they aren't supported by Microsoft, and they provide only a subset of the total range of features. The general consensus is that these implementations aren't ideal for mission-critical business systems.

The .NET Class Library

The .NET class library is a giant repository of classes that provide prefabricated functionality for everything from reading an XML file to sending an e-mail message. If you've had any exposure to Java, you may already be familiar with the idea of a class library. However, the .NET class library is more ambitious and comprehensive than just about any other programming framework. Any .NET language can use the .NET class library's features by interacting with the right objects. This helps encourage consistency among different .NET languages and removes the need to install numerous components on your computer or web server.

Some parts of the class library include features you'll never need to use in web applications (such as the classes used to create desktop applications with the Windows interface). Other parts of the class library are targeted directly at web development, such as those used for web services and web pages. Still more classes can be used in various programming scenarios and aren't specific to web or Windows development. These include the base set of classes that define common variable types and the classes for data access, to name just a few.

You'll explore the .NET Framework throughout this book. In the meantime, here are some general characteristics of the .NET Framework:

Open standards: Microsoft currently provides programming tools that allow you to work with many open standards, such as XML (Extensible Markup Language). In .NET, however, many of these standards are "baked in" to the framework. For example, ADO.NET (Microsoft's data access technology) uses XML natively, behind the scenes. Similarly, web services work automatically through XML and HTTP (Hypertext Transfer Protocol). This deep integration of open standards makes cross-platform work much easier.

Emphasis on infrastructure: Microsoft's philosophy is that it will provide the tedious infrastructure so that application developers need only to write business-specific code. For example, the .NET Framework automatically handles files, databases, and transactions. You just add the logic needed for your specific application.

Performance and scalability: The .NET Framework emphasizes distributed and Internet applications. Technologies such as ADO.NET are designed from the ground up to be scalable even when used by hundreds or thousands of simultaneous users.

Visual Studio

The last part of .NET is the optional Visual Studio development tool, which provides a rich environment where you can rapidly create advanced applications. Some of the features of Visual Studio include the following:

Page design: You can create an attractive page with drag-and-drop ease using Visual Studio's integrated web form designer. You don't need to understand HTML.

Automatic error detection: You could save hours of work when Visual Studio detects and reports an error before you run your application. Potential problems are underlined, just like the "spell-as-you-go" feature found in many word processors.

Debugging tools: Visual Studio retains its legendary debugging tools, which allow you to watch your code in action and track the contents of variables. And you can test web applications just as easily as any other application type, because Visual Studio has a built-in web server that works just for debugging.

IntelliSense: Visual Studio provides statement completion for recognized objects and automatically lists information such as function parameters in helpful tooltips.

You don't need to use Visual Studio to create web applications. In fact, you might be tempted to use the freely downloadable .NET Framework and a simple text editor to create ASP.NET web pages and web services. However, in doing so you'll multiply your work, and you'll have a much harder time debugging, organizing, and maintaining your code. Chapter 4 provides a comprehensive look at the latest version of Visual Studio—Visual Studio 2005.

.NET 2.0

ASP.NET is a resoundingly successful platform. Thousands of websites used it while it was still in early beta, and today more than 50,000 public web servers rely on it every day.[2] As a result of its dramatic rise, ASP.NET websites overtook JSP (Java Server Pages) websites in a single year.

With .NET version 2.0, Microsoft aims to continue its success by refining and enhancing ASP.NET. The good news is that Microsoft hasn't removed features, replaced functionality, or reversed direction. Instead, almost all the changes add higher-level features that can make your programming much more productive.

■ Note Officially, ASP.NET 2.0 is backward compatible with ASP.NET 1.0. In reality, 100 percent backward compatibility is impossible, because correcting bugs and inconsistencies in the language can change how existing code works. Microsoft maintains a list of the breaking changes (most of which are obscure) at `http://www.gotdotnet.com/team/changeinfo/Backwards1.1to2.0`. However, you're unlikely to ever run into a problem when migrating an ASP.NET 1.*x* project to ASP.NET 2.0. It's much more likely that you'll find some cases where the old way of solving a problem still works, but ASP.NET 2.0 introduces a much better approach. In these cases, it's up to you whether to defer the change or try to reimplement your web application to take advantage of the new features.

The following sections introduce some of the most important changes in the different parts of the .NET Framework.

C# 2.0

C# adds several new language features in version 2.0. Some of these are exotic features that only a language aficionado will love, while others are more generally useful. All of them are fairly technical, and you'll need to sort through the language overview in Chapter 2 before you're ready to tackle them.

---

2. All numbers come from the Internet research firm Netcraft. See `http://www.netcraft.com`.

The new features include the following:

Partial classes: Partial classes allow you to split a C# class into two or more source code files. This feature is primarily useful for hiding messy details you don't need to see. Visual Studio uses partial classes in some project types to tuck automatically generated code out of sight.

Generics: Generics allow you to create classes that are flexible enough to work with different class types but still support strong type checking. For example, you could code a collection class using generics that can store any type of object. When you create an instance of the collection, you "lock it in" to the class of your choice so that it can store only a single type of data. The important part in this example is that the locking in happens when you *use* the collection class, not when you code it.

Anonymous methods: Anonymous methods allow you to define a block of code on the fly, inside another method. You can use this technique to quickly hook up an event handler.

Iterators: Iterators give you an easy way to create classes that support *enumeration*, which means you can loop through the values they contain using the C# foreach statement.

Chapter 3 describes partial classes and generics. Anonymous methods and iterators are more specialized and aren't described at all in this book (although you can learn more about both language features by reading the article at `http://www.ondotnet.com/pub/a/dotnet/2004/04/05/csharpwhidbeypt1.html`).

ASP.NET 2.0

With ASP.NET 2.0, Microsoft set a bold goal—to help web developers dramatically reduce the amount of code they need to write. To accomplish this, ASP.NET 2.0 introduces new features for security, personalization, and data display. But instead of changing the existing features, ASP.NET 2.0 adds new, higher-level features that are built on top of the existing infrastructure.

For the most part, this book won't distinguish between the features that are new in ASP.NET 2.0 and those that have existed since ASP.NET 1.0. However, here are highlights of some of the new features:

Navigation: ASP.NET has a new higher-level model for creating site maps that describe your website. Once you create a site map, you can use it with new navigation controls to let users move comfortably around your website (see Chapter 11).

Master pages: Need to implement a consistent look across multiple pages? With master pages, you can define a template and reuse it effortlessly. On a similar note, ASP.NET themes let you define a standardized set of appearance characteristics for controls, which you can apply across your website for a consistent look. Both features appear in Chapter 10.

Data providers: Tired of managing the retrieval, format, and display of your data? With the new data provider model, you can extract information from a database and control how it's displayed without writing a single line of code. ASP.NET 2.0 also adds new data controls that are designed to show information with much less hassle (either in a grid or in a browser view that shows a single record at a time). You'll learn more in Part 3.

Membership and profiles: ASP.NET adds a handful of new controls for managing security, allowing users to log in, register, and retrieve passwords without needing any custom code. Instead, you use the higher-level membership classes that ASP.NET provides (see Chapter 19). Profiles offer a similar high-level approach to help you store and retrieve user-specific information in your database, without writing any database code (see Chapter 20).

Portals: One common type of web application is the portal, which centralizes different information using separate panes on a single web page. Although you could create a portal website in ASP.NET 1.*x*, you needed to do it by hand. In ASP.NET 2.0, a new Web Parts feature makes life dramatically easier (see Chapter 27).

Administration: To configure an application in ASP.NET 1.*x*, you needed to edit a configuration file by hand. Although this process wasn't too difficult, ASP.NET 2.0 streamlines it with the WAT (Website Administration Tool), which works through a web page interface. You'll be introduced to the WAT in Chapter 5.

And of course, ASP.NET 2.0 also contains bug fixes, performance improvements, and a slew of minor enhancements you'll learn about throughout the book.

Visual Studio 2005

Microsoft provided two separate design tools for creating web applications with ASP.NET 1.*x*—the full-featured Visual Studio .NET and the free Web Matrix. Professional developers strongly favored Visual Studio .NET, but Web Matrix offered a few innovative features of its own. Because Web Matrix included its own scaled-down web server, programmers could create and test web applications without needing to worry about configuring virtual directories on their computer using IIS (Internet Information Services).

With .NET 2.0, Web Matrix disappears, but Visual Studio steals some of its best features, including the integrated web server, which lets you get up and running with a test website in no time.

Another welcome change in Visual Studio 2005 is the support for different coding models. While Visual Studio .NET 2003 locked developers into one approach, Visual Studio 2005 supports a range of different coding models, making it a flexible, all-purpose design tool. That means you can choose to put your HTML tags and event handling code in the same file or in separate files without compromising your ability to use Visual Studio and benefit from helpful features such as IntelliSense. You'll learn about this distinction in Chapter 5.

Visual Studio 2005 is available in several editions. The Standard Edition has all the features you need to build any type of application (Windows or web). The Professional Edition and the Team Edition increase the cost and pile on more tools and frills (which aren't discussed in this book). For example, they incorporate features for managing source code that's edited by multiple people on a development team and running automated tests.

The scaled-down Visual Web Developer 2005 Express Edition is much cheaper than any other Visual Studio edition, but it also has a few significant limitations. It gives you full support for developing web applications, but it doesn't support any other type of application. This means you can't use it to develop separate components for use in your applications or to develop Windows applications that interact with web services. However, rest assured that Visual Web Developer is a bona fide version of Visual Studio, with a similar set of features and development interface.

The Last Word

This chapter presented a high-level overview that gave you your first taste of ASP.NET and the .NET Framework. You also looked at how web development has evolved, from the basic HTML forms standard to the latest changes in .NET 2.0.

In the next chapter, you'll get a comprehensive overview of the C# language.

CHAPTER 2

Learning the C# Language

Before you can create an ASP.NET application, you need to choose a .NET language in which to program it. If you're an ASP or VB developer, the natural choice is VB 2005. If you're a longtime Java programmer or old-hand C coder, or you just want to learn the official language of .NET, C# 2005 will suit you best.

This chapter presents an overview of the C# language. You'll learn about the data types you can use, the operations you can perform, and the code you'll need to define functions, loops, and conditional logic. This chapter assumes you've programmed before and you're already familiar with most of these concepts—you just need to see how they're implemented in C#.

If you've programmed with a similar language such as Java, you might find that the most beneficial way to use this chapter is to browse through it without reading every section. This approach will give you a general overview of the C# language. You can then return to this chapter later as a reference when needed. But remember, though you can program an ASP.NET application without mastering all the language details, this deep knowledge is often what separates the casual programmer from the legendary programming guru.

Note The examples in this chapter show individual lines and code snippets. You won't actually be able to use these code snippets in an application until you've learned about objects and .NET types. But don't despair—the next chapter builds on this information, fills in the gaps, and presents an ASP.NET example for you to try.

The .NET Languages

The .NET Framework 2.0 ships with three core languages that are commonly used for building ASP.NET applications: C#, VB, and J#. These languages are, to a large degree, functionally equivalent. Microsoft has worked hard to eliminate language conflicts in the .NET Framework. These battles slow down adoption, distract from the core framework features, and make it difficult for the developer community to solve problems together and share solutions. According to Microsoft, choosing to program in VB instead of C# is just a lifestyle choice and won't affect the performance, interoperability, feature set, or development time of your applications. Surprisingly, this ambitious claim is essentially true.

.NET also allows other third-party developers to release languages that are just as feature rich as C# or VB. These languages (which already include Eiffel, Pascal, Python, and even COBOL) "snap in" to the .NET Framework effortlessly. In fact, if you want to install another .NET language, all you need to do is copy the compiler to your computer and add a line to register it in the machine.config configuration file (which is found in a directory like c:\Windows\Microsoft.NET\Framework\v2.0.40607\Config). Typically, a setup program would perform these steps for you automatically. Once installed, the new compiler can transform your code creations into a sequence of IL (Intermediate Language) instructions, just like the VB and C# compilers do with VB and C# code.

IL is the only language that the CLR (Common Language Runtime) recognizes. When you create the code for an ASP.NET web form, it's changed into IL using the C# compiler (csc.exe), the VB compiler (vbc.exe), or the J# compiler (vjc.exe). You can perform the compilation manually or let ASP.NET handle it automatically when a web page is requested, as you'll learn in Chapter 5.

C# Language Basics

New C# programmers are sometimes intimidated by the quirky syntax of the language, which includes special characters such as semicolons (;), curly braces {}, and backward slashes (\). Fortunately, once you get accustomed to C#, these details will quickly melt into the background. In the following sections, you'll learn about four general principles you need to know about C# before you learn any other concepts.

Case Sensitivity

Some languages are case-sensitive, while others are not. Java, C, and C# are all examples of case-sensitive languages. VB .NET is not. This difference can frustrate former VB programmers who don't realize that keywords, variables, and functions must be entered with the proper case. For example, if you try to create a conditional statement by entering *If* instead of *if*, your code will not be recognized, and the compiler will flag it with an error when you try to build your application.

C# also has a definite preference for lowercase words. Keywords—such as if, for, foreach, while, typeof, and so on—are always written in lowercase letters. When you define your own variables, it makes sense to follow the conventions used by other C# programmers and the .NET Framework class library. That means you should give private variables names that start with a lowercase letter and give public variables names that start with an initial capital letter. For example, you might name a private variable MyNumber in VB and myNumber in C#. Of course, you don't need to follow this style as long as you make sure you use the same capitalization consistently.

■ **Note** If you're designing code that other developers might see (for example, you're creating components that you want to sell to other companies), coding standards are particularly important. The MSDN Help has information about coding standards, and you can also get an excellent summary of best practices in a white paper by Juval Lowy at `http://www.idesign.net`.

Commenting

Comments are descriptive text that is ignored by the compiler. C# provides two basic types of comments. The first type is the single-line comment. In this case, the comment starts with two slashes and continues for the entire current line. Optionally, C# programmers can also use multiple-line comments using the /* and */ comment brackets. This trick is often used to quickly comment out an entire block of code. This way the code won't be executed, but it will still remain in your source code file if you need to refer to it or use it later:

```
// A C# comment.
/* A multiline
   C# comment. */
```

C# also includes an XML-based commenting syntax that you can use to describe your code in a standardized way. With XML comments, you use special tags that indicate whether your comment applies to a class, method, parameter, and so on. Here's an example of a comment that provides a summary for an entire application:

```
/// <summary>
/// This application provides web pages
/// for my e-commerce site.
/// </summary>
```

XML comments always start with three slashes. The benefit of XML-based comments is that automated tools (including Visual Studio) can extract the comments from your code and use them to build help references and other types of documentation. For more information about XML comments, you can refer to an excellent MSDN article at `http://msdn.microsoft.com/msdnmag/issues/02/06/XMLC`. And if you're new to XML syntax in general, you'll learn about it in detail in Chapter 17.

Line Termination

C# uses a semicolon (;) as a line-termination character. Every line of C# code must end with this semicolon, except when you're defining a block structure such as a method, a conditional statement, or a looping construct. By omitting this semicolon, you can easily split a line of code over multiple physical lines.

The following code snippet demonstrates four equivalent ways to perform the same operation (adding three numbers together):

```
// A code statement split over two lines.
myValue = myValue1 + myValue2 +
          myValue3;

// A code statement split over three lines.
myValue = myValue1 +
          myValue2 +
          myValue3;

// A code statement on a single line.
myValue = myValue1 + myValue2 + myValue3;

// Two code statements in a row.
myValue = myValue1 + myValue2;
myValue = myValue + myValue3;
```

As you can see in this example, the line-termination character gives you a wide range of freedom to split your line in whatever way you want. The general rule of thumb is to make your code as readable as possible. Thus, if you have a long line, split it so it's easier to read. On the other hand, if you have a complex code statement that performs several operations at once, you can split the line or separate your logic into multiple code statements to make it clearer.

Block Structures

The C#, Java, and C languages all rely heavily on curly braces—parentheses with a little more attitude: {}. You can find the curly braces to the right of most keyboards (next to the P key); they share a key with the square brackets: [].

Curly braces group multiple code statements together. Typically, the reason you'll want to group code statements together is because you want them to be repeated in a loop, executed conditionally, or grouped into a function. You'll see all these techniques in this chapter. But in each case, the curly braces play the same role, which makes C# simpler and more concise than other languages that need a specialized syntax for each type of block structure:

```
{
    // Code statements go here.
}
```

Variables and Data Types

As with all programming languages, you keep track of data in C# using *variables*. Variables can store numbers, text, dates, and times, and they can even point to full-fledged objects.

When you declare a variable, you give it a name, and you specify the type of data it will store. To declare a local variable, you start the line with the data type, followed by the name you want to use. A final semicolon ends the statement:

```
// Create an integer variable named errorCode.
int errorCode;

// Create a string variable named myName.
string myName;
```

■ **Note** Remember, in C# the variables *name* and *Name* aren't equivalent! To confuse matters even more, C# programmers sometimes use this fact to their advantage—by using multiple variables that have the same name but with different capitalization. Avoid this technique unless you have a good reason for using it.

Every .NET language uses the same variable data types. Different languages may provide slightly different names (for example, a VB Integer is the same as a C# int), but the CLR makes no distinction—in fact, they are just two different names for the same base data type. This design allows for deep language integration. Because languages share the same core data types, you can easily use objects written in one .NET language in an application written in another .NET language. No data type conversions are required.

■ **Note** The reason all .NET languages have the same data types is because they all adhere to the CTS (common type system), a Microsoft-designed ECMA standard that sets out the ground rules that all .NET languages must follow when dealing with data.

To create this common data type system, Microsoft needed to iron out many of the inconsistencies that existed between VBScript, VB 6, C++, and other languages. The solution was to create a set of basic data types, which are provided in the .NET class library. Table 2-1 lists these core data types.

Table 2-1. *Common Data Types*

Class Library Name	VB Name	C# Name	Contains
Byte	Byte	byte	An integer from 0 to 255.
Int16	Short	short	An integer from –32,768 to 32,767.
Int32	Integer	int	An integer from –2,147,483,648 to 2,147,483,647.
Int64	Long	long	An integer from about –9.2e18 to 9.2e18.
Single	Single	float	A single-precision floating point number from approximately –3.4e38 to 3.4e38.
Double	Double	double	A double-precision floating point number from approximately –1.8e308 to 1.8e308.
Decimal	Decimal	decimal	A 128-bit fixed-point fractional number that supports up to 28 significant digits.
Char	Char	char	A single 16-bit Unicode character.
String	String	string	A variable-length series of Unicode characters.
Boolean	Boolean	bool	A true or false value.
DateTime	Date	*	Represents any date and time from 12:00:00 AM, January 1 of the year 1 in the Gregorian calendar, to 11:59:59 PM, December 31 of the year 9999. Time values can resolve values to 100 nanosecond increments. Internally, this data type is stored as a 64-bit integer.
TimeSpan	*	*	Represents a period of time, as in ten seconds or three days. The smallest possible interval is 1 *tick* (100 nanoseconds).
Object	Object	object	The ultimate base class of all .NET types. Can contain any data type or object.

* *If the language does not provide an alias for a given type, you can just use the .NET class name.*

You can also define a variable by using the type name from the .NET class library. This approach produces identical variables. It's also a requirement when the data type doesn't have an alias built into the language. For example, you can rewrite the earlier example that used C# data type names with this code snippet that uses the class library names:

```
System.Int32 errorCode;
System.String myName;
```

This code snippet uses fully qualified type names that indicate that the Int32 type is found in the System namespace (along with all the most fundamental types). In Chapter 3, you'll learn about types and namespaces in more detail.

Assignment and Initializers

Once you've created your variable, you canfreely assign values to them, as long as these values have the correct data type. Here's the code that shows this two-step process:

```
// Define variables.
int errorCode;
string myName;

// Assign values.
errorCode = 10;
myName = "Matthew";
```

You can also assign a value to a variable in the same line that you create it. This example compresses four lines of code into two:

```
int errorCode = 10;
string myName = "Matthew";
```

C# safeguards you from errors by restricting you from using uninitialized variables. This means the following code will not succeed:

```
int number;               // Number is uninitialized.
number = number + 1;      // Error.
```

The proper way to write this code is to explicitly initialize the number variable to 0 before using it:

```
int number = 0;           // Number now contains 0.
number = number + 1;      // Number now contains 1.
```

C# also deals strictly with data types. For example, the following code statement won't work as written:

```
decimal myDecimal = 14.5;
```

The problem is that the literal 14.5 is automatically interpreted as a double, and you can't convert a double to a decimal without using casting syntax, which is described later in this chapter. To get around this problem, C# defines a few special characters that you can append to literal values to indicate their data type so that no conversion will be required. These are as follows:

- M (decimal)
- D (double)
- F (float)
- L (long)

For example, you can rewrite the earlier example using the decimal indicator as follows:

```
decimal myDecimal = 14.5M;
```

Strings and Escaped Characters

C# treats text a little differently than other languages such as VB. It interprets any embedded backslash (\) as the start of a special character escape sequence. For example, \n means add a new line (carriage return). The most useful character literals are as follows:

- \" (double quote)
- \n (new line)
- \t (horizontal tab)
- \\ (backward slash)

You can also insert a special character based on its hex code using the syntax \x123. This inserts a single character with hex value 123.

WHAT'S IN A NAME? NOT THE DATA TYPE!

You'll notice that the preceding examples don't use variable prefixes. Most C and VB programmers are in the habit of adding a few characters to the start of a variable name to indicate its data type. In .NET, this practice is discouraged, because data types can be used in a much more flexible range of ways without any problem, and most variables hold references to full objects anyway. In this book, variable prefixes aren't used, except for web controls, in which it helps to distinguish lists, text boxes, buttons, and other common user interface elements. In your own programs, you should follow a consistent (typically companywide) standard that may or may not adopt a system of variable prefixes.

Note that in order to specify the actual backslash character (for example, in a directory name), you require two slashes. Here's an example:

```
// A C# variable holding the
// c:\MyApp\MyFiles path.
path = "c:\\MyApp\\MyFiles";
```

Alternatively, you can turn off C# escaping by preceding a string with an @ symbol, as shown here:

```
path = @"c:\MyApp\MyFiles";
```

Arrays

Arrays allow you to store a series of values that have the same data type. Each individual value in the array is accessed using one or more index numbers. It's often convenient to picture arrays as lists of data (if the array has one dimension) or grids of data (if the array has two dimensions). Typically, arrays are laid out contiguously in memory.

All arrays start at a fixed lower bound of 0. This rule has no exceptions. When you create an array in C#, you specify the number of elements. Because counting starts at 0, the highest index is actually one less than the number of elements. (In other words, if you have three elements, the highest index is 2.)

```
// Create an array with four strings (from index 0 to index 3).
// You need to initialize the array with the
// new keyword in order to use it.
string[] stringArray = new string[4];

// Create a 2x4 grid array (with a total of eight integers).
int[,] intArray = new int[2, 4];
```

By default, if your array includes simple data types, they are all initialized to default values (0 or false), depending on whether you are using some type of number or a Boolean variable. You can also fill an array with data at the same time that you create it. In this case, you don't need to explicitly specify the number of elements, because .NET can determine it automatically:

```
// Create an array with four strings, one for each number from 1 to 4.
string[] stringArray = {"1", "2", "3", "4"};
```

The same technique works for multidimensional arrays, except that two sets of curly brackets are required:

```
// Create a 4x2 array (a grid with four rows and two columns).
int[,] intArray = {{1, 2}, {3, 4}, {5, 6}, {7, 8}};
```

Figure 2-1 shows what this array looks like in memory.

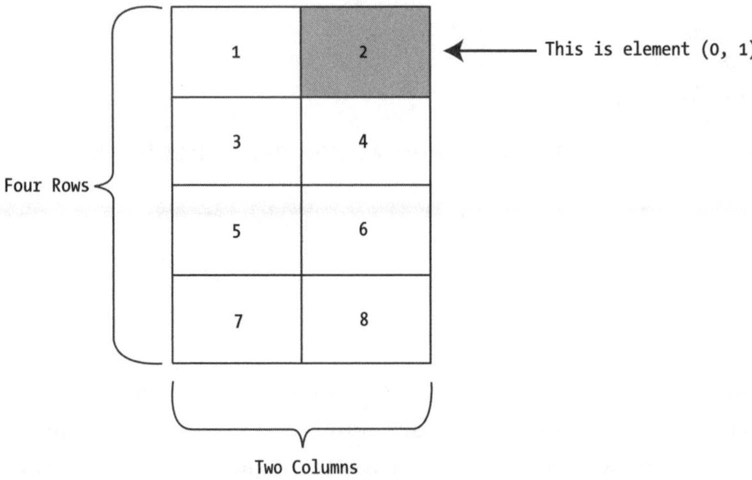

Figure 2-1. *A sample array of integers*

To access an element in an array, you specify the corresponding index number in square brackets: []. Array indices are always zero-based. That means that myArray[0] accesses the first cell in a one-dimensional array, myArray[1] accesses the second cell, and so on:

```
// Access the value in row 0 (first row), column 1 (second column).
int element;
element = intArray[0, 1];     // Element is now set to 2.
```

The ArrayList

C# arrays do not support redimensioning. This means that once you create an array, you can't change its size. Instead, you would need to create a new array with the new size and copy values from the old array to the new, which would be a tedious process. However, if you need a dynamic arraylike list, you can use one of the collection classes provided to all .NET languages through the .NET class library. One such class is the ArrayList, which always allows dynamic resizing. Here's a snippet of C# code that uses an ArrayList:

```
// Create the ArrayList. It's an object, not an array,
// so the syntax is slightly different.
ArrayList dynamicList = new ArrayList();
```

```
// Add several strings to the list.
// The ArrayList is not strongly typed, so you can add any data type.
dynamicList.Add("one");
dynamicList.Add("two");
dynamicList.Add("three");

// Retrieve the first string. Notice that the object must be converted to a
// string, because there's no way for .NET to be certain what it is.
string item = Convert.ToString(dynamicList[0]);
```

You'll learn more about the ArrayList and other collections in Chapter 3.

■ **Tip** In many cases, it's easier to dodge counting issues and use a full-fledged collection rather than an array. Collections are generally better suited to modern object-oriented programming and are used extensively in ASP.NET. The .NET class library provides many types of collection classes, including simple collections, sorted lists, key-indexed lists (dictionaries), and queues. You'll see examples of collections throughout this book.

Enumerations

An enumeration is a group of related constants, each of which is given a descriptive name. Every enumerated value corresponds to a preset integer. In your code, however, you can refer to an enumerated value by name, which makes your code clearer and helps prevent errors. For example, it's much more straightforward to set the border of a label to the enumerated value BorderStyle.Dashed rather than the obscure numeric constant 3. In this case, Dashed is a value in the BorderStyle enumeration, and it represents the number 3.

■ **Note** Just to keep life interesting, the word *enumeration* actually has more than one meaning. As described in this section, enumerations are sets of constant values. However, programmers often talk about the process of *enumerating*, which means to loop, or *iterate*, over a collection. For example, it's common to talk about enumerating over all the characters of a string (which means looping through the string and examining each character in a separate pass).

Here's an example of an enumeration that defines different types of users:

```
// Define an enumeration called UserType with three possible values.
enum UserType
{
    Admin,
    Guest,
    Invalid
}
```

Now you can use the UserType enumeration as a special data type that is restricted to one of three possible values. You assign or compare the enumerated value using the dot notation shown in the following example:

```
// Create a new value and set it equal to the UserType.Admin constant.
UserType newUserType = UserType.Admin;
```

Internally, enumerations are maintained as numbers. In the preceding example, 0 is automatically assigned to Admin, 1 to Guest, and 2 to Invalid. You can set a number directly in an enumeration variable, although this can lead to an undetected error if you use a number that doesn't correspond to one of the defined values.

In some scenarios, you might want to control what numbers are used for various values in an enumeration. This technique is typically used when the number has some specific meaning or corresponds to some other piece of information. For example, the following code defines an enumeration that represents the error code returned by a legacy component:

```
enum ErrorCode
{
    NoResponse = 166,
    TooBusy = 167,
    Pass = 0
}
```

Now you can use the ErrorCode enumeration, which was defined earlier, with a function that returns an integer representing an error condition, as shown here:

```
ErrorCode err;

err = DoSomething();
if (err == ErrorCode.Pass)
{
    // Operation succeeded.
}
```

Clearly, enumerations create more readable code. They also simplify coding, because once you type in the enumeration name (ErrorCode) and add the dot (.), Visual Studio will pop up a list of possible values using IntelliSense.

■ **Tip** Enumerations are widely used in .NET. You won't need to create your own enumerations to use in ASP.NET applications, unless you're designing your own components. However, the concept of enumerated values is extremely important, because the .NET class library uses it extensively. For example, you set colors, border styles, alignment, and various other web control styles using enumerations provided in the .NET class library.

Variable Operations

You can use all the standard types of variable operations in C#. When working with numbers, you can use various math symbols, as listed in Table 2-2. C# follows the conventional order of operations, performing exponentiation first, followed by multiplication and division and then addition and subtraction. You can also control order by grouping subexpressions with parentheses:

```
int number;

number = 4 + 2 * 3;
// Number will be 10.

number = (4 + 2) * 3;
// Number will be 18.
```

Table 2-2. *Arithmetic Operations*

Operator	Description	Example
+	Addition	1 + 1 = 2.
–	Subtraction (and to indicate negative numbers)	5 – 2 = 3.
*	Multiplication	2 * 5 = 10.
/	Division	5 / 2 = 2.5.
%	Gets the remainder left after integer division	7 % 3 = 1.

When dealing with strings, you can use the addition operator (+) to join two strings:

```
// Join three strings together.
myName = firstName + " " + lastName;
```

In addition, C# also provides special shorthand assignment operators. Here are a few examples:

```
// Add 10 to myValue. This is the same as myValue = myValue + 10;
myValue += 10;

// Multiple myValue by 3. This is the same as myValue = myValue * 3;
myValue *= 3;

// Divide myValue by 12. This is the same as myValue = myValue / 12;
myValue /= 12;
```

Advanced Math

In the past, every language has had its own set of keywords for common math operations such as rounding and trigonometry. In .NET languages, many of these keywords remain. However, you can also use a centralized Math class that's part of the .NET Framework. This has the pleasant side effect of ensuring that the code you use to perform mathematical operations can easily be translated into equivalent statements in any .NET language with minimal fuss.

To use the math operations, you invoke the methods of the System.Math class. These methods are *static*, which means they are always available and ready to use. (The next chapter explores the difference between static and instance members in more detail.)

The following code snippet shows some sample calculations that you can perform with the Math class:

```
int myValue;
myValue = Math.Sqrt(81);            // myValue = 9
myValue = Math.Round(42.889, 2);    // myValue = 42.89
myValue = Math.Abs(-10);            // myValue = 10
myValue = Math.Log(24.212);         // myValue = 3.18.. (and so on)
myValue = Math.PI;                  // myValue = 3.14..
```

The features of the Math class are too numerous to list here in their entirety. The preceding examples show some common numeric operations. For more information about the trigonometric and logarithmic functions that are available, refer to the MSDN Help reference for the Math class.

Type Conversions

Converting information from one data type to another is a fairly common programming task. For example, you might retrieve text input for a user that contains the number you want to use for a calculation. Or, you might need to take a calculated value and transform it into text you can display in a web page.

Conversions are of two types: widening and narrowing. *Widening* conversions always succeed. For example, you can always convert a number into a string, or you can convert a 32-bit integer into a 64-bit integer. You won't need any special code:

```
int mySmallValue;
long myLargeValue;

mySmallValue = Int32.MaxValue;

// This always succeeds. No matter how large mySmallValue is,
// it can be contained in myLargeValue.
myLargeValue = mySmallValue;
```

On the other hand, *narrowing* conversions may or may not succeed, depending on the data. If you're converting a 32-bit integer to a 16-bit integer, you could encounter an error if the 32-bit number is larger than the maximum value that can be stored in the 16-bit data type. All narrowing conversions must be performed explicitly. C# uses an elegant method for explicit type conversion. To convert a variable, you simply need to specify the type in parentheses before the expression you're converting.

The following code shows how to change a 32-bit integer to a 16-bit integer:

```
int count32 = 1000;
short count16;

// Convert the 32-bit integer to a 16-bit integer.
// If count32 is large, this could cause a problem.
count16 = (short)count32;
```

If you don't use an explicit cast when you attempt to perform a narrowing conversion, you'll receive an error when you try to compile your code. However, even if you perform an explicit conversion, you could still end up with a problem. For example, consider the code shown here, which causes an overflow:

```
int mySmallValue;
long myLargeValue;

myLargeValue = Int32.MaxValue;
myLargeValue++;

// This will appear to succeed, but your data will be incorrect
// because mySmallValue cannot hold a value this large.
mySmallValue = (int)myLargeValue;
```

The .NET languages differ in how they handle this problem. In VB, you'll always receive an error that you must intercept and respond to. In C#, however, you'll simply wind up with incorrect data in mySmallValue. To avoid this problem, you should either check that your data is not too large before you attempt a conversion (which is always a good idea) or use the checked block. The checked block enables overflow checking for a portion of code. If an overflow occurs, you'll automatically receive an error, just like you would in VB:

```
checked
{
    // This will cause an exception to be thrown.
    mySmallValue = (int)myLargeValue;
}
```

■ **Tip** Usually, you won't use the checked block, because it's inefficient. The checked blocked catches the problem (preventing a data error), but it throws an exception, which you need to handle using error handling code, as explained in Chapter 7. Overall, it's easier just to perform your own checks with any potentially invalid numbers before you attempt an operation. However, the checked block *is* handy in one situation—debugging. That way, you can catch unexpected errors while you're still testing your application and resolve them immediately.

In C#, you can't use casting to convert numbers to strings, or vice versa. In this case, the data isn't just being moved from one variable to another—it needs to be translated to a completely different format. Thankfully, .NET has a number of solutions for performing advanced conversions. One option is to use the static methods of the Convert class, which support many common data types such as strings, dates, and numbers:

```
int count;
string countString = "10";

// Convert the string "10" to the numeric value 10.
count = Convert.ToInt32(countString);

// Convert the numeric value 10 into the string "10".
countString = Convert.ToString(count);
```

The second step (turning a number into a string) will always work. The first step (turning a string into a number) won't work if the string contains letters or other non-numeric characters, in which case an error will occur. Chapter 7 discusses error handling.

The Convert class is a good all-purpose solution, but you'll also find other static methods that can do the work, if you dig around in the .NET class library. The following code uses the static Int32.Parse() method to perform the same task:

```
int count;
string countString = "10";

// Convert the string "10" to the numeric value 10.
count = Int32.Parse(countString);
```

You'll also find that you can use object methods to perform some conversions a little more elegantly. The next section demonstrates this approach with the ToString() method.

Object-Based Manipulation

.NET is object-oriented to the core. In fact, even ordinary variables are really full-fledged objects in disguise. This means that common data types have the built-in smarts to handle basic operations (such as counting the number of letters in a string). Even better, it means you can manipulate strings, dates, and numbers in the same way in C# and in VB. This wouldn't be true if developers used special keywords that were built into the C# or VB language.

As an example, every type in the .NET class library includes a ToString() method. The default implementation of this method returns the class name. In simple variables, a more useful result is returned: the string representation of the given variable. The following code snippet demonstrates how to use the ToString() method with an integer:

```
string myString;
int myInteger = 100;

// Convert a number to a string. myString will have the contents "100".
myString = myInteger.ToString();
```

To understand this example, you need to remember that all int variables are based on the Int32 class in the .NET class library. The ToString() method is built into the Int32 class, so it's available when you use an integer in any language.

The next few sections explore the object-oriented underpinnings of the .NET data types in more detail.

The String Class

One of the best examples of how class members can replace built-in functions is found with strings. In the past, every language has defined its own specialized functions for string manipulation. In .NET, however, you use the methods of the String class, which ensures consistency between all .NET languages.

The following code snippet shows several ways to manipulate a string using its object nature:

```
string myString = "This is a test string        ";
myString = myString.Trim();                // = "This is a test string"
myString = myString.Substring(0, 4);       // = "This"
myString = myString.ToUpper();             // = "THIS"
myString = myString.Replace("IS", "AT");   // = "THAT"

int length = myString.Length;              // = 4
```

The first few statements use built-in methods, such as Trim(), Substring(), ToUpper(), and Replace(). These methods generate new strings, and each of these statements replaces the current myString with the new string object. The final statement uses a built-in Length property, which returns an integer that represents the number of letters in the string.

■ **Tip** A method is just a function or procedure that's hardwired into an object. A property is similar to a variable—it's a piece of data that's associated with an object. You'll learn more about methods and properties in the next chapter.

Note that the Substring() method requires a starting offset and a character length. Strings use zero-based counting. This means that the first letter is in position 0, the second letter is in position 1, and so on. You'll find this standard of zero-based counting throughout the .NET Framework for the sake of consistency. You've already seen it at work with arrays.

You can even use the string methods in succession in a single (rather ugly) line:

```
myString = myString.Trim().SubString(0, 4).ToUpper().Replace("IS", "AT");
```

Or, to make life more interesting, you can use the string methods on string literals just as easily as string variables:

```
myString = "hello".ToUpper(); // Sets myString to "HELLO"
```

Table 2-3 lists some useful members of the System.String class.

Table 2-3. *Useful String Members**

Member	Description
Length	Returns the number of characters in the string (as an integer).
ToUpper() and ToLower()	Returns a copy of the string with all the characters changed to uppercase or lowercase characters.
Trim(), TrimEnd(), and TrimStart()	Removes spaces or some other characters from either (or both) ends of a string.
PadLeft() and PadRight()	Adds the specified character to either side of a string, the number of times you indicate. For example, PadLeft(3, " ") adds three spaces to the left side.
Insert()	Puts another string inside a string at a specified (zero-based) index position. For example, Insert(1, "pre") adds the string *pre* after the first character of the current string.
Remove()	Removes a specified number of characters from a specified position. For example, Remove(0, 1) removes the first character.
Replace()	Replaces a specified substring with another string. For example, Replace("a", "b") changes all *a* characters in a string into *b* characters.
Substring()	Extracts a portion of a string of the specified length at the specified location (as a new string). For example, Substring(0, 2) retrieves the first two characters.
StartsWith() and EndsWith()	Determines whether a string ends or starts with a specified substring. For example, StartsWith("pre") will return either true or false, depending on whether the string begins with the letters *pre* in lowercase.
IndexOf() and LastIndexOf()	Finds the zero-based position of a substring in a string. This returns only the first match and can start at the end or beginning. You can also use overloaded versions of these methods that accept a parameter that specifies the position to start the search.
Split()	Divides a string into an array of substrings delimited by a specific substring. For example, with Split(".") you could chop a paragraph into an array of sentence strings.
Join()	Fuses an array of strings into a new string. You can also specify a separator that will be inserted between each element.

* *Remember, all the string methods that appear to change a string actually return a copy of the string that has the changes.*

The DateTime and TimeSpan Types

The DateTime and TimeSpan data types also have built-in methods and properties. These class members allow you to perform three useful tasks:

- Extract a part of a DateTime (for example, just the year) or convert a TimeSpan to a specific representation (such as the total number of days or total number of minutes).
- Easily perform date calculations.
- Determine the current date and time and other information (such as the day of the week or whether the date occurs in a leap year).

For example, the following block of code creates a DateTime object, sets it to the current date and time, and adds a number of days. It then creates a string that indicates the year that the new date falls in (for example, 2006):

```
DateTime myDate = DateTime.Now;
myDate = myDate.AddDays(100);
string dateString = myDate.Year.ToString();
```

The next example shows how you can use a TimeSpan object to find the total number of minutes between two DateTime objects:

```
DateTime myDate1 = DateTime.Now;
DateTime myDate2 = DateTime.Now.AddHours(3000);

TimeSpan difference;
difference = myDate2.Subtract(myDate1);

double numberOfMinutes;
numberOfMinutes = difference.TotalMinutes;
```

These examples give you an idea of the flexibility .NET provides for manipulating date and time data. Tables 2-4 and 2-5 list some of the more useful built-in features of the DateTime and TimeSpan objects.

Table 2-4. *Useful DateTime Members*

Member	Description
Now	Gets the current date and time.
Today	Gets the current date and leaves time set to 00:00:00.
Year, Date, Day, Hour, Minute, Second, and Millisecond	Returns one part of the DateTime object as an integer. For example, Month will return 12 for any day in December.
DayOfWeek	Returns an enumerated value that indicates the day of the week for this DateTime, using the DayOfWeek enumeration. For example, if the date falls on Sunday, this will return DayOfWeek.Sunday.
Add() and Subtract()	Adds or subtracts a TimeSpan from the DateTime.
AddYears(), AddMonths(), AddDays(), AddHours(), AddMinutes(), AddSeconds(), AddMilliseconds()	Adds an integer that represents a number of years, months, and so on, and returns a new DateTime. You can use a negative integer to perform a date subtraction.
DaysInMonth()	Returns the number of days in the month represented by the current DateTime.
IsLeapYear()	Returns true or false depending on whether the current DateTime is in a leap year.
ToString()	Changes the current DateTime to its string representation. You can also use an overloaded version of this method that allows you to specify a parameter with a format string.

Table 2-5. *Useful TimeSpan Members*

Member	Description
Days, Hours, Minutes, Seconds, Milliseconds	Returns one component of the current TimeSpan. For example, the Hours property can return an integer from 0 to 23.
TotalDays, TotalHours, TotalMinutes, TotalSeconds, TotalMilliseconds	Returns the total value of the current TimeSpan, indicated as a number of days, hours, minutes, and so on. For example, the TotalDays property might return a number like 234.342.
Add() and Subtract()	Combines TimeSpan objects together.
FromDays(), FromHours(), FromMinutes(), FromSeconds(), FromMilliseconds()	Allows you to quickly specify a new TimeSpan. For example, you can use TimeSpan.FromHours(24) to define a TimeSpan object exactly 24 hours long.
ToString()	Changes the current TimeSpan to its string representation. You can also use an overloaded version of this method that allows you to specify a parameter with a format string.

The Array Class

Arrays also behave like objects in the new world of .NET. For example, if you want to find out the size of an array, you can use the Array.GetUpperBound() method in any language. The following code snippet shows this technique in action:

```
int[] myArray = {1, 2, 3, 4, 5};
int bound;

// Zero represents the first dimension of an array.
bound = myArray.GetUpperBound(0);    // bound = 4
```

Arrays also provide a few other useful methods, which allow you to sort them, reverse them, and search them for a specified element. Table 2-6 lists some useful members of the System.Array class.

Table 2-6. *Useful Array Members*

Member	Description
Length	Returns an integer that represents the total number of elements in all dimensions of an array. For example, a 3×3 array has a length of 9.
GetLowerBound() and GetUpperBound()	Determines the dimensions of an array. As with just about everything in .NET, you start counting at zero (which represents the first dimension).
Clear()	Empties an array's contents.
IndexOf() and LastIndexOf()	Searches a one-dimensional array for a specified value and returns the index number. You cannot use this with multidimensional arrays.
Sort()	Sorts a one-dimensional array made up of comparable data such as strings or numbers.
Reverse()	Reverses a one-dimensional array so that its elements are backward, from last to first.

Conditional Structures

In many ways, conditional logic—deciding which action to take based on user input, external conditions, or other information—is the heart of programming.

All conditional logic starts with a *condition*: a simple expression that can be evaluated to true or false. Your code can then make a decision to execute different logic depending on the outcome of the condition. To build a condition, you can use any combination of literal values or variables along with *logical operators*. Table 2-7 lists the basic logical operators.

Table 2-7. *Logical Operators*

Operator	Description
==	Equal to
!=	Not equal to
<	Less than
>	Greater than
<=	Less than or equal to
>=	Greater than or equal to
&&	And (evaluates to true only if both expressions are true)
||	Or (evaluates to true if either expression is true)

You can use all the comparison operators with any numeric types. With string data types, you can use only the equality operators (== and !=). C# doesn't support other types of string comparison operators—instead, you need to use the String.Compare() method. The String.Compare() method deems that a string is "less than" another string if it occurs earlier in an alphabetic sort. Thus, *apple* is less than *attach*. The return value from String.Compare is 0 if the strings match, 1 if the first supplied string is greater than the second, and –1 if the first string is less than the second. Here's an example:

```
int result;
result = String.Compare("apple", "attach");  // result = -1
result = String.Compare("apple", "all");     // result = 1
result = String.Compare("apple", "apple");   // result = 0

// Another way to perform string comparisons.
string word = "apple";
result = word.CompareTo("attach");           // result = -1
```

The if Block

The if block is the powerhouse of conditional logic, able to evaluate any combination of conditions and deal with multiple and different pieces of data. Here's an example with an if block that features two conditions:

```
if (myNumber > 10)
{
    // Do something.
}
```

```
else if (myString == "hello")
{
    // Do something.
}
else
{
    // Do something.
}
```

Keep in mind that the if block matches one condition at most. For example, if myNumber is greater than 10, the first condition will be met. That means the code in the first conditional block will run, and no other conditions will be evaluated. Whether myString contains the text *hello* becomes irrelevant, because that condition will not be evaluated.

An if block can have any number of conditions. If you test only a single condition, you don't need to include any else blocks.

The switch Block

C# also provides a switch block that you can use to evaluate a single variable or expression for multiple possible values. The only limitation is that the variable you're evaluating must be an int, bool, char, string, or enumeration. Other data types aren't supported.

In the following code, each case examines the myNumber variable and tests whether it's equal to a specific integer:

```
switch (myNumber)
{
    case 1:
        // Do something.
        break;
    case 2:
        // Do something.
        break;
    default:
        // Do something.
        break;
}
```

You'll notice that the C# syntax inherits the convention of C programming, which requires that every conditional block of code is ended by a special break keyword. If you omit this keyword, the compiler will alert you and refuse to build your application. The only exception is if you choose to stack multiple case statements directly on top of each other with no intervening code. This allows you to write one segment of code that handles more than one case. Here's an example:

```
switch (myNumber)
{
    case 1:
    case 2:
        // This code executes if myNumber is 1 or 2.
        break;
    default:
        // Do something.
        break;
}
```

Unlike the if block, the switch block is limited to evaluating a single piece of information at a time. However, it provides a leaner, clearer syntax than the if block for situations in which you need to test a single variable.

Loop Structures

Loop structures allow you to repeat a segment of code multiple times. C# has three basic types of loops. You choose the type of loop based on the type of task you need to perform. Your choices are as follows:

- You can loop a set number of times with a for loop.
- You can loop through all the items in a collection of data using a foreach loop.
- You can loop until a certain condition is met, using a while loop.

The for and foreach blocks are ideal for chewing through sets of data that have known, fixed sizes. The while block is a more flexible construct that allows you to continue processing until a complex condition is met. The while block is often used with repetitive tasks or calculations that don't have a set number of iterations.

The for Block

The for block is a basic ingredient in many programs. It allows you to repeat a block of code a set number of times, using a built-in counter. To create a for loop, you need to specify a starting value, an ending value, and the amount to increment with each pass. Here's one example:

```
for (int i = 0; i < 10; i++)
{
    // This code executes ten times.
    System.Diagnostics.Debug.Write(i);
}
```

You'll notice that the for loop starts with brackets that indicate three important pieces of information. The first portion, (int i = 0), creates the counter variable (i) and sets its initial value (0). The third portion, (i++), increments the counter variable. In this example, the counter is incremented by 1 after each pass. That means i will be equal to 0 for the first pass, equal to 1 for the second pass, and so on. The middle portion, (i < 10), specifies the condition that must be met for the loop to continue. This condition is tested at the start of every pass through the block. If i is greater than or equal to 10, the condition will evaluate to false, and the loop will end.

If you run this code using a tool such as Visual Studio, it will write the following numbers in the Debug window:

```
0 2 3 4 5 6 7 8 9
```

It often makes sense to set the counter variable based on the number of items you're processing. For example, you can use a for loop to step through the elements in an array by checking the size of the array before you begin. Here's the code you would use:

```
string[] stringArray = {"one", "two", "three"};

for (int i = 0; i <= stringArray.GetUpperBound(0); i++)
{
    System.Diagnostics.Debug.Write(stringArray[i] + " ");
}
```

This code produces the following output:

```
one two three
```

BLOCK-LEVEL SCOPE

If you define a variable inside some sort of block structure (such as a loop or a conditional block), the variable is automatically released when your code exits the block. That means you will no longer be able to access it. The following code demonstrates the problem:

```
int tempVariableA;
for (int i = 0; i < 10; i++)
{
    int tempVariableB;
    tempVariableA = 1;
    tempVariableB = 1;
}
// You cannot access tempVariableB here.
// However, you can still access tempVariableA.
```

This change won't affect many programs. It's really designed to catch a few more accidental errors. If you do need to access a variable inside and outside of some type of block structure, just define the variable *before* the block starts.

The foreach Block

C# also provides a foreach block that allows you to loop through the items in a set of data. With a foreach block, you don't need to create an explicit counter variable. Instead, you create a variable that represents the type of data for which you're looking. Your code will then loop until you've had a chance to process each piece of data in the set.

The foreach block is particularly useful for traversing the data in collections and arrays. For example, the next code segment loops through the items in an array using foreach. This code is identical to the previous example but is a little simpler:

```
string[] stringArray = {"one", "two", "three"};

foreach (string element in stringArray)
{
    // This code loops three times, with the element variable set to
    // "one", then "two", and then "three".
    Debug.Write(element + " ");
}
```

In this case, the foreach loop examines each item in the array and tries to convert it to a string. Thus, the foreach loop defines a string variable named element. If you used a different data type, you'd receive an error.

The foreach block has one key limitation: it's read-only. For example, if you wanted to loop through an array and change the values in that array at the same time, foreach code wouldn't work. Here's an example of some flawed code:

```
int[] intArray = {1,2,3};

foreach (int num in intArray)
{
    num += 1;
}
```

In this case, you would need to fall back on a basic for block with a counter.

The while Block

Finally, C# supports a while structure that tests a specific condition after each pass through the loop. When this condition evaluates to false, the loop is exited.

Here's an example that loops ten times. At the beginning of each pass, the code evaluates whether the counter (i) has exceeded a set value:

```
int i = 0;
while (i < 10)
{
    i += 1;
    // This code executes ten times.
}
```

You can also place the condition at the end of the loop using the slightly different do...while syntax. In this case, the condition is tested at the end of each pass through the loop:

```
int i = 0;
do
{
    i += 1;
    // This code executes ten times.
}
while (i < 10);
```

Both of these examples are equivalent, unless the condition you're testing is false to start. In that case, the while loop will skip the code entirely. The do...while loop, on the other hand, will always execute the code at least once, because it doesn't test the condition until the end.

■ **Tip** Sometimes you need to exit a loop in a hurry. In C#, you can use the break statement to exit any type of loop.

Methods

Methods are the most basic building block you can use to organize your code. Ideally, each method will perform a distinct, logical task. By breaking your code down into methods, you not only simplify your life, but you also make it easier to organize your code into classes and step into the world of object-oriented programming.

The first decision you need to make when creating a method is whether you want to return any information. A method can return, at most, one piece of data. When you declare a method in C#, the first part of the declaration specifies the data type of the return value, and second part indicates the method name. If your method doesn't return any information, you should use the void keyword instead of a data type at the beginning of the declaration.

Here are two examples:

```
// This method doesn't return any information.
void MyMethodNoData()
{
    // Code goes here.
}

// This method returns an integer.
int MyMethodReturnsData()
{
    // As an example, return the number 10.
    return 10;
}
```

Notice that the method name is always followed by parentheses, even if the method doesn't accept parameters. This allows Visual Studio to recognize that it's a method.

In this example, the methods don't specify their accessibility. This is just a common C# convention. You're free to add an accessibility keyword (such as public or private) as follows:

```
private void MyMethodNoData()
{
    // Code goes here.
}
```

The accessibility determines how different classes in your code can interact. Private methods are hidden from view and are available only locally, whereas public methods can be called by any other class in your application. The next chapter discusses accessibility in more detail.

■ **Tip** If you don't specify accessibility, the method is always private. The examples in this book always include accessibility keywords, because they improve clarity. Most programmers agree that it's a good approach to explicitly spell out the visibility of your code.

Invoking your methods is straightforward—you simply type the name of method, followed by parentheses. If your method returns data, you have the option of using the data it returns or just ignoring it:

```
// This call is allowed.
MyMethodNoData();

// This call is allowed.
MyMethodReturnsData();

// This call is allowed.
int myNumber;
myNumber = MyMethodReturnsData();

// This call isn't allowed.
// MyMethodNoData() does not return any information.
myNumber = MyMethodNoData();
```

Parameters

Methods can also accept information through parameters. Parameters are declared in a similar way to variables. By convention, parameter names always begin with a lowercase letter in any language.

Here's how you might create a function that accepts two parameters and returns their sum:

```
private int AddNumbers(int number1, int number2)
{
    return (number1 + number2);
}
```

When calling a method, you specify any required parameters in parentheses or use an empty set of parentheses if no parameters are required:

```
// Call a method with no parameters.
MyMethodNoData();

// Call a method that requires two integer parameters.
MyMethodNoData2(10, 20);

// Call a method with two integer parameters and an integer return value.
int returnValue = AddNumbers(10, 10);
```

Method Overloading

C# supports method *overloading*, which allows you to create more than one function or method with the same name, but with a different set of parameters. When you call the method, the CLR automatically chooses the correct version by examining the parameters you supply.

This technique allows you to collect different versions of several functions together. For example, you might allow a database search that returns an author name. Rather than create three functions with different names depending on the criteria, such as GetNameFromID(), GetNameFromSSN(), and GetNameFromBookTitle(), you could create three versions of the GetCustomerName() function. Each function would have the same name but a different *signature*, meaning it would require different parameters.

This example provides two overloaded versions for the GetProductPrice() method:

```
private decimal GetProductPrice(int ID)
{
    // Code here.
}
```

```
private decimal GetProductPrice(string name)
{
    // Code here.
}

// And so on...
```

Now you can look up product prices based on the unique product ID or the full product name, depending on whether you supply an integer or string argument:

```
decimal price;

// Get price by product ID (the first version).
price = GetProductPrice(1001);

// Get price by product name (the second version).
price = GetProductPrice("DVD Player");
```

You cannot overload a function with versions that have the same signature—that is, the same number of parameters and parameter data types—because the CLR will not be able to distinguish them from each other. When you call an overloaded function, the version that matches the parameter list you supply is used. If no version matches, an error occurs.

■ **Note** .NET uses overloaded methods in most of its classes. This approach allows you to use a flexible range of parameters while centralizing functionality under common names. Even the methods you've seen so far (such as the String methods for padding or replacing text) have multiple versions that provide similar features with various options.

Delegates

Delegates allow you to create a variable that "points" to a method. You can use this variable at any time to invoke the method. Delegates help you write flexible code that can be reused in many situations. They're also the basis for events, an important .NET concept that you'll consider in the next chapter.

The first step when using a delegate is to define its signature. A delegate variable can point only to a method that matches its specific signature. In other words, it must have the same return type and the same parameter types. For example, if you have a method that accepts a single string parameter and another method that accepts two string parameters, you'll need to use a separate delegate type for each method.

DELEGATES ARE THE BASIS OF EVENTS

Wouldn't it be nice to have a delegate that could refer to more than one function at once and invoke them all? This would allow the client application to have multiple "listeners" and notify the listeners all at once when something happens.

In fact, delegates do have this functionality, but you're more likely to see it in use with .NET events. Events, which are described in the next chapter, are based on delegates but work at a slightly higher level. In a typical ASP.NET program, you'll use events extensively, but you'll probably never work directly with delegates.

To consider how this works in practice, assume your program has the following function:

```
private string TranslateEnglishToFrench(string english)
{
    // Code goes here.
}
```

This function returns a string and accepts a single string argument. With those two details in mind, you can define a delegate type that matches this signature. Here's how you would do it:

```
private delegate string StringFunction(string in);
```

Notice that the name you choose for the parameters and the name of the delegate don't matter. The only requirement is that the data types for the return value and parameters match exactly.

Once you've defined a type of delegate, you can create and assign a delegate variable at any time. Using the StringFunction delegate type, you could create a delegate variable like this:

```
StringFunction functionReference;
```

Once you have a delegate variable, the fun begins. Using your delegate variable, you can point to any method that has the matching signature. In this example, the StringFunction delegate type requires one string parameter and returns a string. Thus, you can use the functionReference variable to store a reference to the TranslateEnglishToFrench() function you saw earlier. Here's how to do it:

```
functionReference = TranslateEnglishToFrench;
```

■ **Note** When you assign a delegate in C#, you don't use brackets after the function name. This indicates that you are *referring* to the function, not attempting to execute it. If you added the brackets, the CLR would attempt to run your function and convert the return value to the delegate type, which wouldn't work (and therefore would generate a compile-time error).

Now that you have a delegate variable that references a function, you can invoke the function *through* the delegate. To do this, you just use the delegate variable name as though it were the function name:

```
string frenchString;
frenchString = functionReference("Hello");
```

In the previous code example, the procedure that the functionReference delegate points to will be invoked with the parameter value "Hello", and the return value will be stored in the frenchString variable.

The following code shows all these steps—creating a delegate variable, assigning a method, and calling the method—from start to finish:

```
// Create a delegate variable.
StringFunction functionReference;

// Store a reference to a matching method in the delegate.
functionReference = TranslateEnglishToFrench;

// Run the method that functionReference points to.
// In this case, it will be TranslateEnglishToFrench().
string frenchString = functionReference("Hello");
```

The value of delegates is in the extra layer of flexibility they add. It's not apparent in this example, because the same piece of code creates the delegate variable and uses it. However, in a more complex application one method would create the delegate variable, and another method would use it. The benefit in this scenario is that the second method doesn't need to know where the delegate points. Instead, it's flexible enough to use any method that has the right signature. In the current example, imagine a translation library that could translate between English and a variety of different languages, depending on whether the delegate it uses points to TranslateEnglishToFrench(), TranslateEnglishToSpanish(), TranslateEnglishToGerman(), and so on.

The Last Word

It's impossible to do justice to an entire language in a single chapter. However, if you've programmed before, you'll find that this chapter provides all the information you need to get started with the C# language. As you work through the full ASP.NET examples in the following chapters, you can refer to this chapter to clear up any language issues.

In the next chapter, you'll learn about more important language concepts and the object-oriented nature of .NET.

CHAPTER 3

Types, Objects, and Namespaces

Object-oriented programming has been a popular buzzword over the last several years. In fact, one of the few places that object-oriented programming *wasn't* emphasized was in ordinary ASP pages. With .NET, the story changes considerably. Not only does .NET allow you to use objects, it demands it. Almost every ingredient you'll need to use to create a web application is, on some level, really a kind of object.

So how much do you need to know about object-oriented programming to write pages in .NET? It depends on whether you want to follow existing examples and cut and paste code samples or have a deeper understanding of the way .NET works and gain more control. This book assumes that if you're willing to pick up a thousand-page book, then you're the type of programmer who excels by understanding how and why things work the way they do. It also assumes you're interested in some of the advanced ASP.NET programming tasks that *will* require class-based design, such as designing custom controls (see Chapter 25) and creating your own components (see Chapter 24).

This chapter explains objects from the point of view of the .NET Framework. It won't rehash the typical object-oriented theory, because countless excellent programming books cover the subject. Instead, you'll see the types of objects .NET allows, how they're constructed, and how they fit into the larger framework of namespaces and assemblies.

The Basics About Classes

As a developer, you've probably already created classes or at least heard about them. *Classes* are the code definitions for objects. The nice thing about a class is that you can use it to create as many objects as you need. For example, you might have a class that represents an XML file, which can be used to read some data. If you want to access multiple XML files at once, you can create several instances of your class, as shown in Figure 3-1. These instances are called *objects*.

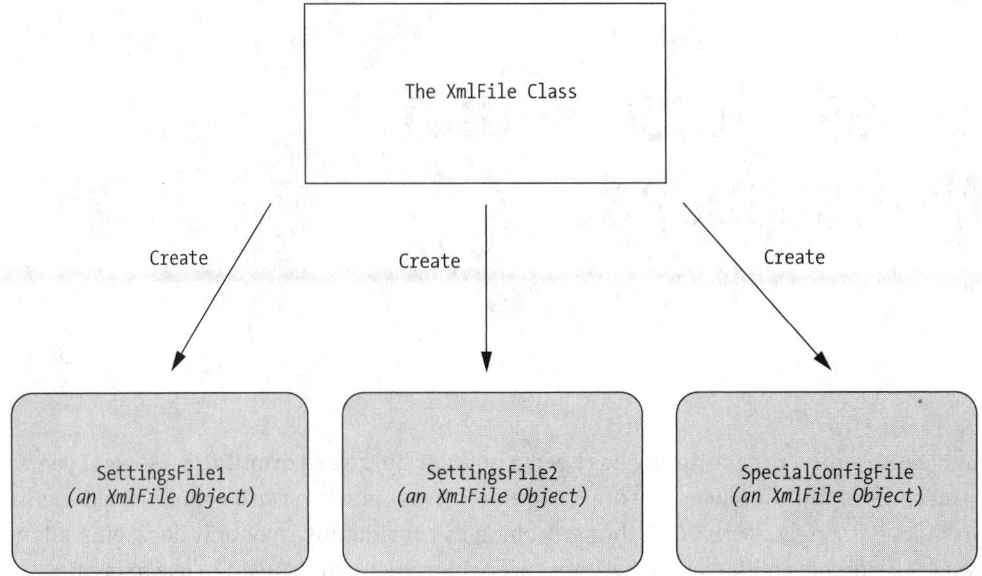

Figure 3-1. *Classes are used to create objects.*

Classes interact with each other with the help of three key ingredients:

- *Properties*: Properties allow you to access an object's data. Some properties may be read-only, so they cannot be modified, while others can be changed. For example, the previous chapter demonstrated how you can use the read-only Length property of a String object to find out how many characters are in a string.
- *Methods*: Methods allow you to perform an action with an object. Unlike properties, methods are used for actions that perform a distinct task or may change the object's state significantly. For example, to open a connection to a database, you might call an Open() method in a Connection object.
- *Events*: Events provide notification that something has happened. If you've ever programmed an ordinary desktop application in Visual Basic, you know how controls can fire events to trigger your code. For example, if a user clicks a button, the Button object fires a Click event, which your code can react to. ASP.NET controls also provide events.

In addition, classes contain their own code and internal set of private data. Classes behave like *black boxes,* which means that when you use an object, you shouldn't waste any time wondering how it works or what low-level information it's using. Instead, you need to worry only about the public interface of a class, which is the set of properties, methods, and events that are available for you to use. Together, these elements are called class *members.*

In ASP.NET, you'll create your own custom classes to represent individual web pages. In addition, you'll create custom classes if you design separate components. For the most part, however, you'll be using prebuilt classes from the .NET class library, rather than programming your own.

Static Members

One of the tricks about .NET classes is that you really use them in two ways. You can use some class members without creating an object first. These are called *static* members, and they're accessed by class name. For example, you can use the static property DateTime.Now to retrieve a DateTime object that represents the current date and time. You don't need to create a DateTime object first.

On the other hand, the majority of the DateTime members require a valid instance. For example, you can't use the AddDays() method or the Hour property without a valid object. These *instance* members have no meaning without a live object and some valid data to draw on.

The following code snippet uses static and instance members:

```
// Get the current date using a static method.
// Note that you need to use the class name DateTime.
DateTime myDate = DateTime.Now;

// Use an instance method to add a day.
// Note that you need to use the object name myDate.
myDate = myDate.AddDays(1);

// The following code makes no sense.
// It tries to use the instance method AddDays with the class name DateTime!
myDate = DateTime.AddDays(1);
```

Both properties and methods can be designated as static. Static methods are a major part of the .NET Framework, and you will use them frequently in this book. Remember, some classes may consist entirely of static members (such as the Math class shown in the previous chapter), and some may use only instance members. Other classes, like DateTime, provide a combination of the two.

The next example, which introduces a basic class, will use only instance members. This is the most common design and a good starting point.

A Simple Class

To create a class, you must define it using a special block structure:

```
public class MyClass
{
    // Class code goes here.
}
```

You can define as many classes as you need in the same file. However, good coding practices suggest that in most cases you use a single file for each class.

Classes exist in many forms. They may represent an actual thing in the real world (as they do in most programming textbooks), they may represent some programming abstraction (such as a rectangle or color structure), or they may just be a convenient way to group related functionality (like with the Math class). Deciding what a class should represent and breaking down your code into a group of interrelated classes are part of the art of programming.

Building a Basic Class

In the next example, you'll see how to construct a .NET class piece by piece. This class will represent a product from the catalog of an e-commerce company. The Product class will store product data, and it will include the built-in functionality needed to generate a block of HTML that displays the product on a web page. When this class is complete, you'll be able to put it to work with a sample ASP.NET test page.

Once you've defined a class, the first step is to add some basic data. The next example defines three member variables that store information about the product, namely, its name, price, and a URL that points to an image file:

```
public class Product
{
    private string name;
    private decimal price;
    private string imageUrl;
}
```

A local variable exists only until the current procedure ends. On the other hand, a *member variable* (or *field*) is declared as part of a class. It's available to all the procedures in the class, and it lives as long as the containing object lives.

When you create a member variable, you need to explicitly set its *accessibility*. The accessibility determines whether other parts of your code will be able to read and alter this variable. For example, if ObjectA contains a private variable, ObjectB will not be able to read or modify it. Only ObjectA will have that ability. On the other hand, if ObjectA has a public variable, any other object in your application is free to read and alter the information it contains. Local variables don't support any accessibility keywords, because they can never be made available to any code beyond the current procedure. Generally, in a simple ASP.NET application, most of your variables will be private because the majority of your code will be self-contained in a single web page class. As you start creating separate components to reuse functionality, however, accessibility becomes much more important. Table 3-1 explains the access levels you can use.

Table 3-1. *Accessibility Keywords*

Keyword	Accessibility
public	Can be accessed by any other class
private	Can be accessed only by code procedures inside the current class
internal	Can be accessed by code procedures in any of the classes in the current assembly (the compiled code file)
protected	Can be accessed by code procedures in the current class or by any class that inherits from this class
protected internal	Can be accessed by code procedures in the current application or by any class that inherits from this class

The accessibility keywords don't just apply to variables. They also apply to methods, properties, and events, all of which will be explored in this chapter.

■ **Tip** By convention, all the public pieces of your class (the class name, public events, properties and procedures, and so on) should use *Pascal case*. This means the name starts with an initial capital. (The function name DoSomething() is one example of Pascal case.) On the other hand, private members can use any case you want. Usually, private members will adopt *camel case*. This means the name starts with an initial lowercase letter. (The variable name myInformation is one example of camel case.) Some developers begin all private member names with _ or m_ (for member), although this is purely a matter of convention.

Creating a Live Object

When creating an object, you need to specify the new keyword. The new keyword *instantiates* the object, which means it creates a copy of the class in memory. If you define an object but don't instantiate it, you'll receive the infamous "null reference" error when you try to use the object. That's because the object doesn't actually exist yet, meaning your reference points to nothing at all.

The following code snippet creates an object based on the Product class and then releases it:

```
Product saleProduct = new Product();

// Optionally you could do this in two steps:
// Product saleProduct;
// saleProduct = new Product();

// Now release the class from memory.
saleProduct = null;
```

In .NET, you almost never need to use the last line, which releases the object. That's because objects are automatically released when the appropriate variable goes out of scope. Objects are also released when your application ends. In an ASP.NET web page, your application is given only a few seconds to live. Once the web page is rendered to HTML, the application ends, and all objects are automatically released.

■ **Tip** Just because an object is released doesn't mean the memory it uses is immediately reclaimed. The CLR uses a long running service (called *garbage collection*) that periodically scans for released objects and reclaims the memory they hold.

In some cases, you will want to define an object variable without using the new keyword to create it. For example, you might want to assign an instance that already exists to your object variable. Or you might receive a live object as a return value from a function. The following code shows one such example:

```
// Define but don't create the product.
Product saleProduct;

// Call a function that accepts a numeric product ID parameter,
// and returns a product object.
saleProduct = FetchProduct(23);
```

In these cases, when you aren't actually creating the class, you shouldn't use the new keyword.

Adding Properties

The simple Product class is essentially useless because your code cannot manipulate it. All its information is private and unreachable. Other classes won't be able to set or read this information.

To overcome this limitation, you could make the member variables public. Unfortunately, that approach could lead to problems because it would give other objects free access to change everything, even allowing them to apply invalid or inconsistent data. Instead, you need to add a "control panel" through which your code can manipulate Product objects in a safe way. You do this by adding *property accessors.*

Accessors usually have two parts. The get accessor allows your code to retrieve data from the object. The set accessor allows your code to set the object's data. In some cases, you might omit one of these parts, such as when you want to create a property that can be examined but not modified.

Accessors are similar to any other type of procedure in that you can write as much code as you need. For example, your property set accessor could raise an error to alert the client code of invalid data and prevent the change from being applied. Or, your property set accessor could change multiple private variables at once, thereby making sure the object's internal state remains consistent. In the Product class example, this sophistication isn't required. Instead, the property accessors just provide straightforward access to the private variables.

Property accessors, like any other public piece of a class, should start with an initial capital. This allows you to give the same name to the property accessor and the underlying private variable, because they will have different capitalization, and C# is a case-sensitive language. (This is one of the rare cases where it's acceptable to differentiate between two elements based on capitalization.) Another option would be to precede the private variable name with an underscore.

```
public class Product
{
    private string name;
    private decimal price;
    private string imageUrl;

    public string Name
    {
        get
        { return name; }
        set
        { name = value; }
    }
```

```
    public decimal Price
    {
        get
        { return price; }
        set
        { price = value; }
    }
    public string ImageUrl
    {
        get
        { return imageUrl; }
        set
        { imageUrl = value; }
    }
}
```

The client can now create and configure the class by using its properties and the familiar dot syntax. For example, if the object is named SaleProduct, you can set the product name using the SaleProduct.Name property. Here's an example:

```
Product saleProduct = new Product();
saleProduct.Name = "Kitchen Garbage";
saleProduct.Price = 49.99M;
saleProduct.ImageUrl = "http://mysite/garbage.png";
```

You'll notice that the C# example uses an *M* to indicate that the literal number 49.99 should be interpreted as a decimal value, not a double.

Adding a Basic Method

The current Product class consists entirely of data. This type of class is often useful in an application. For example, you might use it to send information about a product from one function to another. However, it's more common to add functionality to your classes along with the data. This functionality takes the form of *methods*.

Methods are simply procedures that are built into your class. When a method is called on an object, your code responds to do something useful, such as return some calculated data. In this example, we'll add a GetHtml() method to the Product class. This method will return a string representing a formatted block of HTML based on the current data in the Product object. You could then take this block of HTML and place it on a web page to represent the product:

```
public class Product
{
    // (Variables and properties omitted for clarity.)
```

```
    public string GetHtml()
    {
        string htmlString;
        htmlString = "<h1>" + name + "</h1><br />";
        htmlString += "<h3>Costs: " + price.ToString() + "</h3><br />";
        htmlString += "<img src=" + imageUrl + ">";
        return htmlString;
    }
}
```

All the GetHtml() method does is read the private data and format it in some attractive way. This really targets the class as a user interface class rather than as a pure data class or "business object."

Adding a Constructor

Currently, the Product class has a problem. Ideally, classes should ensure that they are always in a valid state. However, unless you explicitly set all the appropriate properties, the Product object won't correspond to a valid product. This could cause an error if you try to use a method that relies on some of the data that hasn't been supplied. To solve this problem, you need to equip your class with one or more *constructors*.

A constructor is a method that automatically runs when the class is first created. In C#, the constructor always has the same name as the name of the class. Unlike a normal method, the constructor doesn't define any return type, not even void.

The next code example shows a new version of the Product class. It adds a constructor that requires the product price and name as arguments:

```
public class Product
{
    // (Additional class code omitted for clarity.)

    public Product(string name, decimal price)
    {
        // These parameters have the same name as the internal variables.
        // The "this" keyword refers to the class variables.
        // "this" refers to the current instance of the Product class.
        this.name = name;
        this.price = price;
    }
}
```

Here's an example of the code you need to create an object based on the new Product class, using its constructor:

```
Product saleProduct = new Product("Kitchen Garbage", 49.99M);
```

The preceding code is much leaner than the code that was required to create and initialize the previous version of the Product class. With the help of the constructor, you can create a Product object and configure it with the basic data it needs in a single line.

If you don't create a constructor, .NET supplies a default public constructor that does nothing. If you create at least one constructor, .NET will not supply a default constructor. Thus, in the preceding example, the Product class has exactly one constructor, which is the one that is explicitly defined in code. To create a Product class, you *must* use this constructor. This restriction prevents a client from creating an object without specifying the bare minimum amount of data that's required:

```
// This will not be allowed, because there is
// no zero-argument constructor.
Product saleProduct = new Product();
```

Most of the classes you use will have constructors that require parameters. As with ordinary methods, constructors can be overloaded with multiple versions, each providing a different set of parameters. When creating an object, you can choose the constructor that suits you best based on the information that you have available. The .NET Framework classes use overloaded constructors extensively.

Adding a Basic Event

Classes can also use events to notify your code. To define an event in C#, you must first create a delegate that defines the signature for the event you're going to use. Then you can define an event based on that delegate using the event keyword.

As an illustration, the Product class example has been enhanced with a NameChanged event that occurs whenever the Name is modified through the property procedure. This event won't fire if code inside the class changes the underlying private name variable without going through the property procedure:

```
public class Product
{
    // (Additional class code omitted for clarity.)
```

```
    // Define the delegate that represents the event.
    public delegate void NameChangedEventHandler();

    // Define the event.
    public event NameChangedEventHandler NameChanged;

    public string Name
    {
        get
        { return name; }
        set
        {
            name = value;

            // Fire the event, provided there is at least one listener.
            if (NameChanged != null)
            {
                NameChanged();
            }
        }
    }
}
```

To fire an event, you just call it by name. However, before firing an event, you must check that at least one subscriber exists by testing whether the event reference is null. If it isn't null, it's safe to fire the event.

It's quite possible that you'll create dozens of ASP.NET applications without once defining a custom event. However, you'll be hard-pressed to write a single ASP.NET web page without *handling* an event. To handle an event, you first create a subroutine called an *event handler*. The event handler contains the code that should be executed when the event occurs. Then, you connect the event handler to the event.

To handle the Product class, you need to begin by creating an event handler in another class. The event handler needs to have the same syntax as the event it's handling. In the Product example, the event has no parameters, so the event handler would look like the simple subroutine shown here:

```
public void ChangeDetected()
{
    // This code executes in response to the NameChanged event.
}
```

The next step is to hook up the event handler to the event. First, you create a delegate that points to the event handler method. Then, you attach this delegate to the event using the += operation:

```
Product saleProduct = new Product();

// This connects the saleProduct.NameChanged event to an event handling
// procedure called ChangeDetected.
// Note that ChangedDetected needs to match the NameChangedEventHandler
// delegate.
saleProduct.NameChanged += new NameChangedEventHandler(ChangeDetected);

// Now the event will occur in response to this code:
saleProduct.Name = "Kitchen Garbage";
```

It's worth noting that if you're using Visual Studio, you won't need to manually hook up event handlers for web controls at all. Instead, Visual Studio can add the code you need to connect all the event handlers you create.

ASP.NET uses an *event-driven* programming model, so you'll soon become used to writing code that reacts to events. But unless you're creating your own components, you won't need to fire your own custom events. For an example where custom events make sense, refer to Chapter 25, which discusses how you can build your own controls.

Testing the Product Class

To learn a little more about how the Product class works, it helps to create a simple web page. This web page will create a Product object, get its HTML representation, and then display it in the web page. To try this example, you'll need to use the three files that are provided with the online samples in the Chapter03 directory:

- *Product.cs*: This file contains the code for the Product class. It's in the App_Code subdirectory, which allows ASP.NET to compile it automatically (a trick you'll learn more about in Chapter 5).
- *Garbage.jpg*: This is the image that the Product class will use.
- *Default.aspx*: This file contains the web page code that uses the Product class.

The easiest way to test this example is to use Visual Studio, because it includes an integrated web server. Without Visual Studio, you would need to create a virtual directory for this application using IIS, which is much more awkward.

Here are the steps you need to perform the test:

1. Start Visual Studio.
2. Select File ➤ Open ➤ Web Site from the menu.
3. In the Open Web Site dialog box, browse to the Chapter03 directory, select it, and click Open. This loads your project into Visual Studio.
4. Choose Debug ➤ Start Without Debugging to launch the website. Visual Studio will open a new window with your default browser and navigate to the Default.aspx page.

When the Default.aspx page executes, it creates a new Product object, configures it, and uses the GetHtml() method. The HTML is written to the web page using the Response.Write() method. Here's the code:

```
<%@ Page Language="CS" %>
<script runat="server">
    private void Page_Load(object sender, EventArgs e)
    {
        Product saleProduct = new Product("Kitchen Garbage", 49.99M);
        saleProduct.ImageUrl = "garbage.jpg";
        Response.Write(saleProduct.GetHtml());
    }
</script>

<html>
    <head runat="server">
        <title>Product Test</title>
    </head>
</html>
```

The <script> block holds a subroutine named Page_Load. This subroutine is triggered when the page is first created. Once this code is finished, the HTML is sent to the client. Figure 3-2 shows the web page you'll see.

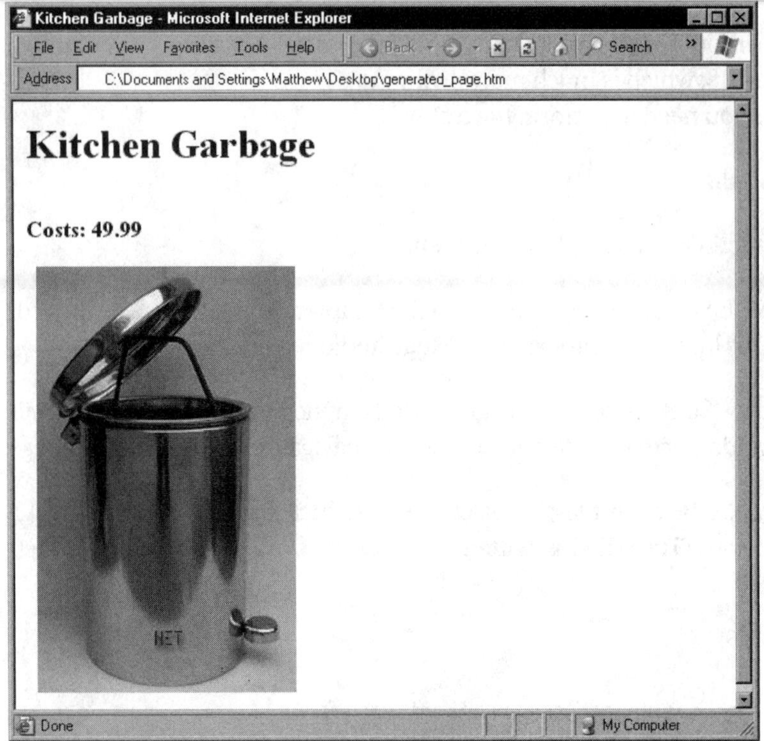

Figure 3-2. *Output generated by a Product object*

Interestingly, the GetHtml() method is that it's similar to how an ASP.NET web control works, but on a much cruder level. To use an ASP.NET control, you create an object (explicitly or implicitly) and configure some properties. Then ASP.NET automatically creates a web page by examining all these objects and requesting their associated HTML (by calling a hidden GetHtml() method or by doing something conceptually similar[1]). It then sends the completed page to the user. The end result is that you work with objects, instead of dealing directly with raw HTML code.

When using a web control, you see only the public interface made up of properties, methods, and events. However, understanding how class code actually works will help you master advanced development.

Now that you've seen the basics of classes and a demonstration of how you can use a class, it's time to introduce a little more theory about .NET objects and revisit the basic data types introduced in the previous chapter.

1. Actually, the ASP.NET engine calls a method named Render() in every web control.

Value Types and Reference Types

In Chapter 2, you learned how simple data types such as strings and integers are actually objects created from the class library. This allows some impressive tricks, such as built-in string handling and date calculation. However, simple data types differ from more complex objects in one important way. Simple data types are *value types*, while classes are *reference types*.

This means a variable for a simple data type contains the actual information you put in it (such as the number 7). On the other hand, object variables actually store a reference that points to a location in memory where the full object is stored. In most cases, .NET masks you from this underlying reality, and in many programming tasks you won't notice the difference. However, in three cases you will notice that object variables act a little differently than ordinary data types: in assignment operations, in comparison operations, and when passing parameters.

Assignment Operations

When you assign a simple data variable to another simple data variable, the contents of the variable are copied:

```
integerA = integerB;  // integerA now has a copy of the contents of integerB.
                      // There are two duplicate integers in memory.
```

Objects work a little differently. Copying the entire contents of an object could slow down an application, particularly if you were performing multiple assignments. With objects, the default is to just copy the reference in an assignment operation:

```
objectA = objectB;    // objectA and objectB now both point to the same thing.
                      // There is one object and two ways to access it.
```

In the preceding example, if you modify objectB by setting a property, objectA will be automatically affected. In fact, objectA *is* objectB. To override this behavior, you would need to manually create a new object and initialize its information to match the existing object. Some objects provide a Clone() method that allows you to easily copy the object. One example is the DataSet, which is used to store information from a database.

Equality Testing

A similar distinction between objects and simple data types appears when you compare two variables. When you compare simple variables, you're comparing the contents:

```
if (integerA == integerB)
{
    // This is true as long as the integers have the same content.
}
```

When you compare object variables, you're actually testing whether they're the same instance. In other words, you're testing whether the references are pointing to the same object in memory, not if their contents match:

```
if (objectA == objectB)
{
    // This is true if both objectA and objectB point to the same thing.
    // This is false if they are separate, yet identical, objects.
}
```

■ **Note** This rule has a special exception. When classes override the == operator, they can change what type of comparison it performs. The only significant example of this technique in .NET is the String class. For more information, read the sidebar "Would the Real Reference Types Please Stand Up?" later in this chapter.

Passing Parameters by Reference and by Value

You can create three types of procedure parameters. The standard type is *pass-by-value.* When you use pass-by-value parameters, the procedure receives a copy of the parameter data. That means that if the procedure modifies the parameter, this change won't affect the calling code. By default, all parameters are pass-by-value.

The second type of parameter is *pass-by-reference.* With pass-by-reference, the procedure accesses the parameter value directly. If a procedure changes the value of a pass-by-reference parameter, the original variable is also modified.

To get a better understanding of the difference, consider the following code, which shows a procedure that uses a parameter named number. This code uses the ref keyword to indicate that number should be passed by reference. When the procedure modifies this parameter (multiplying it by 2), the calling code is also affected:

```
private void ProcessNumber(ref int number)
{
    number *= 2;
}
```

The following code snippet shows the effect of calling the ProcessNumber procedure. Note that you need to specify the ref keyword when you define the parameter in the function and when you call the function. This indicates that you are aware that the parameter value may change:

```
int num = 10;
ProcessNumber(ref num);        // Once this call completes, Num will be 20.
```

This behavior is straightforward when you're using value types, such as integers. However, if you use reference types, such as a Product object or an array, you won't see this behavior. The reason is because the entire object isn't passed in the parameter. Instead, it's just the *reference* that's transmitted. This is much more efficient for large objects (it saves having to copy a large block of memory), but it doesn't always lead to the behavior you expect.

One notable quirk occurs when you use the standard pass-by-value mechanism. In this case, pass-by-value doesn't create a copy of the object, but a copy of the *reference*. This reference still points to the same in-memory object. This means that if you pass a Product object to a procedure, for example, the procedure will be able to alter your Product object, regardless of whether you use pass-by-value or pass-by-reference.

OUTPUT PARAMETERS

C# also supports a third type of parameter: the output parameter. To use an output parameter, precede the parameter declaration with the keyword out. Output parameters are commonly used as a way to return multiple pieces of information from a single procedure.

When you use output parameters, the calling code can submit an uninitialized variable as a parameter, which is otherwise forbidden. This approach wouldn't be appropriate for the ProcessNumber() procedure, because it reads the submitted parameter value (and then doubles it). If, on the other hand, the procedure used the parameter just to return information, you could use the out keyword, as shown here:

```
private void ProcessNumber(int number, out int double, out int triple)
{
    double = num * 2;
    triple = num * 3;
}
```

Remember, output parameters are designed solely for the procedure to return information to your calling code. In fact, the procedure won't be allowed to retrieve the value of an out parameter, because it may be uninitialized. The only action the procedure can take is to set the output parameter.

Here's an example of how you can call the revamped ProcessNumber() procedure:

```
int num = 10;
int double, triple;
ProcessNumber(num, out double, out triple);
```

Reviewing .NET Types

So far, the discussion has focused on simple data types and classes. The .NET class library is actually composed of *types,* which is a catchall term that includes several objectlike relatives:

Classes: This is the most common type in .NET Framework. Strings and arrays are two examples of .NET classes, although you can easily create your own.

Structures: Structures, like classes, can include properties, methods, and events. Unlike classes, they are value types, which alters the way they behave with assignment and comparison operations. Structures also lack some of the more advanced class features (such as inheritance) and are generally simpler and smaller. Integers, dates, and chars are all structures.

Enumerations: An enumeration defines a set of integer constants with descriptive names. Enumerations were introduced in the previous chapter.

Delegates: A delegate is a function pointer that allows you to invoke a procedure indirectly. Delegates are the foundation for .NET event handling and were introduced in the previous chapter.

Interfaces: They define contracts to which a class must adhere. Interfaces are an advanced technique of object-oriented programming, and they're useful when standardizing how objects interact. You'll learn about interfaces with custom control programming in Chapter 25.

WOULD THE REAL REFERENCE TYPES PLEASE STAND UP?

Occasionally, a class can override its behavior to act more like a value type. For example, the String type is a full-featured class, not a simple value type. (This is required to make strings efficient, because they can contain a variable amount of data.) However, the String type overrides its equality and assignment operations so that these operations work like those of a simple value type. This makes the String type work in the way that programmers intuitively expect. Arrays, on the other hand, are reference types through and through. If you assign one array variable to another, you copy the reference, not the array (although the Array class also provides a Clone() method that returns a duplicate array to allow true copying).

Table 3-2 sets the record straight and explains a few common types.

Table 3-2. *Common Reference and Value Types*

Data Type	Nature	Behavior
Int32, Decimal, Single, Double, and all other basic numeric types	Value Type	Equality and assignment operations work with the variable contents, not a reference.
DateTime, TimeSpan	Value Type	Equality and assignment operations work with the variable contents, not a reference.
Char, Byte, and Boolean	Value Type	Equality and assignment operations work with the variable contents, not a reference.
String	Reference Type	Equality and assignment operations appear to work with the variable contents, not a reference.
Array	Reference Type	Equality and assignment operations work with the reference, not the contents.

Understanding Namespaces and Assemblies

Whether you realize it at first, every piece of code in .NET exists inside a .NET type (typically a class). In turn, every type exists inside a namespace. Figure 3-3 shows this arrangement for your own code and the DateTime class. Keep in mind that this is an extreme simplification—the System namespace alone is stocked with several hundred classes. This diagram is designed only to show you the layers of organization.

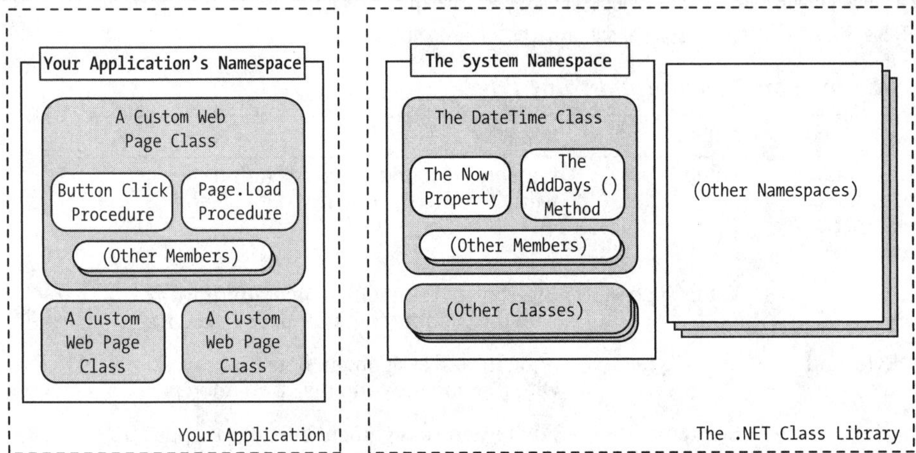

Figure 3-3. *A look at two namespaces*

Namespaces can organize all the different types in the class library. Without namespaces, these types would all be grouped into a single long and messy list. This sort of organization is practical for a small set of information, but it would be impractical for the thousands of types included with .NET.

Many of the chapters in this book introduce new .NET classes and namespaces. For example, in the chapters on web controls, you'll learn how to use the objects in the System.Web.UI namespace. In the chapters about web services, you'll study the types in the System.Web.Services namespace. For databases, you'll turn to the System.Data namespace. In fact, you've already learned a little about one namespace: the basic System namespace that contains all the simple data types explained in the previous chapter.

To continue your exploration after you've finished the book, you'll need to turn to the MSDN reference, which painstakingly documents the properties, methods, and events of every class in every namespace (see Figure 3-4). If you have Visual Studio installed, you can view the MSDN Help by selecting Start ➤ Programs ➤ Microsoft Visual Studio 2005 ➤ Microsoft Visual Studio 2005 Documentation (the exact path depends on the version of Visual Studio you've installed). You can find class reference information, grouped by namespace, under the .NET Development ➤ .NET Framework SDK ➤ Class Library Reference node.

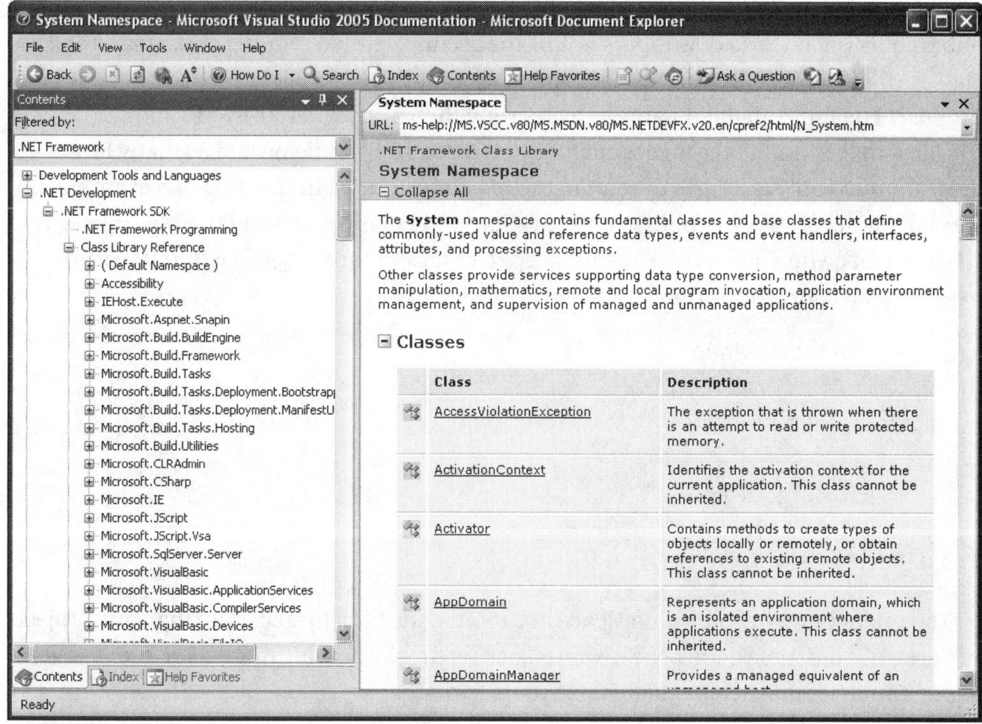

Figure 3-4. *The MSDN Class Library reference*

Using Namespaces

Often when you write ASP.NET code, you'll just use the namespace that Visual Studio creates automatically. If, however, you want to organize your code into multiple namespaces, you can define the namespace using a simple block structure, as shown here:

```
namespace MyCompany
{
    namespace MyApp
    {
        public class Product
        {
            // Code goes here.
        }
    }
}
```

In the preceding example, the Product class is in the namespace MyCompany.MyApp. Code inside this namespace can access the Product class by name. Code outside it needs to use the fully qualified name, as in MyCompany.MyApp.Product. This ensures that you can use the components from various third-party developers without worrying about a name collision. If those developers follow the recommended naming standards, their classes will always be in a namespace that uses the name of their company and software product. The fully qualified name of a class will then almost certainly be unique.

Namespaces don't take an accessibility keyword and can be nested as many layers deep as you need. Nesting is purely cosmetic—for example, in the previous example, no special relationship exists between the MyCompany namespace and the MyApp namespace. In fact, you could create the namespace MyCompany.MyApp without using nesting at all using this syntax:

```
namespace MyCompany.MyApp
{
    public class Product
    {
        // Code goes here.
    }
}
```

You can declare the same namespace in various code files. In fact, more than one project can even use the same namespace. Namespaces are really nothing more than a convenient, logical container that helps you organize your classes.

■ **Tip** If you're using Visual Studio, all your code will automatically be placed in a projectwide namespace. By default, this namespace has the same name as your project. For more information, refer to Chapter 4, which tackles Visual Studio in detail.

Importing Namespaces

Having to type long, fully qualified names is certain to tire your fingers and create overly verbose code. To tighten code up, it's standard practice to import the namespaces you want to use. When you import a namespace, you don't need to type the fully qualified name. Instead, you can use the object as though it were defined locally.

To import a namespace, you use the using statement. These statements must appear as the first lines in your code file, outside of any namespaces or block structures:

```
using MyCompany.MyApp;
```

Consider the situation without importing a namespace:

```
MyCompany.MyApp.Product salesProduct = new MyCompany.MyApp.Product();
```

It's much more manageable when you import the MyCompany.MyApp namespace. Once you do, you can use this syntax instead:

```
Product salesProduct = new Product();
```

Importing namespaces is really just a convenience. It has no effect on the performance of your application. In fact, whether you use namespace imports, the compiled IL code will look the same. That's because the language compiler will translate your relative class references into fully qualified class names when it generates an EXE or DLL file.

Assemblies

You might wonder what gives you the ability to use the class library namespaces in a .NET program. Are they hardwired directly into the language? The truth is that all .NET classes are contained in *assemblies*. Assemblies are the physical files that contain compiled code. Typically, assembly files have the extension .exe if they are stand-alone applications or .dll if they're reusable components.

■Tip The .dll extension is also used for code that needs to be executed (or *hosted*) by another type of program. When your web application is compiled, it's turned into a DLL file, because your code doesn't represent a stand-alone application. Instead, the ASP.NET engine executes it when a web request is received.

A strict relationship doesn't exist between assemblies and namespaces. An assembly can contain multiple namespaces. Conversely, more than one assembly file can contain classes in the same namespace. Technically, namespaces are a *logical* way to group classes. Assemblies, however, are a *physical* package for distributing code.

The .NET classes are actually contained in a number of assemblies. For example, the basic types in the System namespace come from the mscorlib.dll assembly. Many ASP.NET types are found in the System.Web.dll assembly. In addition, you might want to use other, third-party assemblies. Often, assemblies and namespaces have the same names. For example, you'll find the namespace System.Web in the assembly file System.Web.dll. However, this is a convenience, not a requirement.

When compiling an application, you need to tell the language compiler what assemblies the application uses. By default, a wide range of .NET assemblies is automatically supported by the compiler. (Technically, these default assemblies are defined in a web.config configuration file that applies settings for the entire computer and is found in a directory like c:\Windows\Microsoft.NET\Framework\v2.0.40607\Config, depending on the version of the .NET Framework you have installed.) If you need to use additional assemblies, you need to define them in a configuration file for your website. Visual Studio makes this process seamless, letting you add assembly references to the configuration file with a couple of quick mouse clicks.

Advanced Class Programming

Part of the art of object-oriented programming is determining class relations. For example, you could create a Product object that contains a ProductFamily object or a Car object that contains four Wheel objects. To create this sort of class relationship, all you need to do is define the appropriate variable or properties in the class. This type of relationship is called *containment.*

For example, the following code shows a ProductCatalog class, which holds an array of Product objects:

```
public class ProductCatalog
{
    private Product[] products;

    // (Other class code goes here.)
}
```

In ASP.NET programming, you'll find special classes called *collections* that have no purpose other than to group various objects. Some collections also allow you to sort and retrieve objects using a unique name. In the previous chapter, you saw an example with the ArrayList, which provides a dynamically resizable array. Here's how you might use the ArrayList to modify the ProductCatalog class:

```
public class ProductCatalog
{
    private ArrayList products = new ArrayList();

    // (Other class code goes here.)
}
```

This approach has benefits and disadvantages. It makes it easier to add and remove items from the list, but it also removes a useful level of error checking, because the ArrayList supports any type of object. You'll learn more about this issue later in this chapter (in the "Generics" section).

In addition, classes can have a different type of relationship known as *inheritance.*

Inheritance

Inheritance is a form of code reuse. It allows one class to acquire and extend the functionality of another class. For example, you could create a class called TaxableProduct that inherits from Product. The TaxableProduct class would gain all the same methods, properties, and events of the Product class. You could then add additional members that relate to taxation:

```
public class TaxableProduct : Product
{
    private decimal taxRate = 1.15M;

    public decimal TotalPrice
    {
        get
        {
            // The code can access the Price property because it's
            // a public part of the base class Product.
            // The code cannot access the private price variable, however.
            return (Price * taxRate);
        }
    }
}
```

This technique appears much more useful than it really is. In an ordinary application, most classes use containment and other relationships instead of inheritance, which can complicate life needlessly without delivering many benefits. Dan Appleman, a renowned .NET programmer, once described inheritance as "the coolest feature you'll almost never use."

In all honesty, you'll see inheritance at work in ASP.NET in one place. Inheritance allows you to create a custom class that inherits the features of a class in the .NET class library. For example, when you create a custom web form, you actually inherit from a basic Page class to gain the standard set of features. Similarly, when you create a custom web service, you inherit from the WebService class. You'll see this type of inheritance throughout the book.

There are many more subtleties of class-based programming with inheritance. For example, you can override parts of a base class, prevent classes from being inherited, or create a class that must be used for inheritance and can't be directly created. However, these topics aren't covered in this book, and they aren't required to build ASP.NET applications.

Static Members

The beginning of this chapter introduced the idea of static properties and methods, which can be used without a live object. Static members are often used to provide useful functionality related to an object. The .NET class library uses this technique heavily (as with the System.Math class explored in the previous chapter).

Static members have a wide variety of possible uses. Sometimes they provide basic conversions and utility functions that support a class. To create a static property or method, you just need to use the static keyword right after the accessibility keyword.

The following example shows a TaxableProduct class that contains a static TaxRate property and private variable. This means there is one copy of the tax rate information, and it applies to all TaxableProduct objects:

```
public class TaxableProduct : Product
{
    // (Other class code omitted for clarity.)

    private static decimal taxRate = 1.15M;

    // Now you can call TaxableProduct.TaxRate, even without an object.
    public static decimal TaxRate
    {
        get
        { return taxRate; }
        set
        { taxRate = value; }
    }
}
```

You can now retrieve the tax rate information directly from the class, without needing to create an object first:

```
// Change the TaxRate. This will affect all TotalPrice calculations for any
// TaxableProduct object.
TaxableProduct.TaxRate = 1.24M;
```

Static data isn't tied to the lifetime of an object. In fact, it's available throughout the life of the entire application. This means static members are the closest thing .NET programmers have to global data.

A static member can't access an instance member. To access a nonstatic member, it needs an actual instance of your object.

■ **Tip** You can create a class that's entirely composed of static members. Just add the static keyword to the declaration, as in the following:

```
public static class TaxableUtil
```

When you declare a class with the static keyword, you ensure that it can't be instantiated.

Casting Objects

Objects can be converted with the same syntax that's used for simple data types. However, an object can be converted only into three things: itself, an interface that it supports, or a base class from which it inherits. You can't convert an object into a string or an integer. Instead, you will need to call a conversion method, if it's available, such as ToString() or Parse().

For example, you could convert a TaxableProduct object into a Product object. You wouldn't actually lose any information, but you would no longer be able to access the TotalPrice property—unless you converted the reference back to a TaxableProduct object. This underscores an important point: when you convert an object, you don't actually change that object. The same object remains floating as a blob of binary data somewhere in memory. What you change is the way you access that object. In other words, you don't change the object; you change the way your code "sees" that object.

For example, if you have a Product variable that references a TaxableProduct object, your object really *is* a TaxableProduct object. However, you can use only the properties and methods that are defined in the Product class. This is one of the subtleties of manipulating objects, and it's demonstrated in the next example.

The following example creates a TaxableProduct object, converts it to a Product reference, and then checks whether the object can be safely transformed back into a TaxableProduct (it can). You'll notice that the actual conversion uses the syntax introduced in the previous chapter, where the data type is placed in parentheses before the variable that you want to convert:

```
// Define two empty variables (don't use the new keyword).
Product theProduct;
TaxableProduct theTaxableProduct;

// This works, because TaxableProduct derives from Product.
theProduct = new TaxableProduct();
```

```
// This will be true.
if (theProduct is TaxableProduct)
{
    // Convert the object, and assign to the other variable.
    theTaxableProduct = (TaxableProduct)theProduct;
}

decimal totalPrice;

// This works.
totalPrice = theTaxableProduct.TotalPrice;

// This won't work, even though theTaxableProduct and theProduct are the same
// object. The Product class doesn't provide a TotalPrice property.
totalPrice = theProduct.TotalPrice;
```

At this point, it might seem that being able to convert objects is a fairly specialized technique that will be required only when you're using inheritance. This isn't always true. Object conversions are also required when you use some particularly flexible classes.

One example is the ArrayList class introduced in the previous chapter. The ArrayList is designed in such a way that it can store any type of object. To have this ability, it treats all objects in the same way—as instances of the root System.Object class. (Remember, all classes in .NET inherit from System.Object at some point, even if this relationship isn't explicitly defined in the class code.) The end result is that when you retrieve an object from an ArrayList collection, you need to cast it from a System.Object to its real type, as shown here:

```
// Create the ArrayList.
ArrayList products = new ArrayList();

// Add several Product objects.
products.Add(product1);
products.Add(product2);
products.Add(product3);

// Retrieve the first item, with casting.
Product retrievedProduct = (Product)products[0];

// This works.
Respose.Write(retrievedProduct.GetHtml());
```

```
// Retrieve the first item, as an object. This doesn't require casting,
// but you won't be able to use any of the Product methods or properties.
Object retrievedObject = products[0];

// This generates a compile error. There is no Object.GetHtml() method.
Respose.Write(retrievedObject.GetHtml());
```

As you can see, if you don't perform the casting, you won't be able to use the methods and properties of the object you retrieve. You'll find many cases like this in .NET code, where your code is handed one of several possible object types and it's up to you to cast the object to the correct type in order to use its full functionality.

Partial Classes

Partial classes give you the ability to split a single class into more than one source code (.cs) file. For example, if the Product class became particularly long and intricate, you might decide to break in into two pieces, as shown here:

```
// This part is stored in file Product1.cs.
public partial class Product
{
    private string name;
    private decimal price;
    private string imageUrl;

    public string Name
    {
        get
        { return name; }
        set
        { name = value; }
    }

    public decimal Price
    {
        get
        { return price; }
        set
        { price = value; }
    }
```

```
    public string ImageUrl
    {
        get
        { return imageUrl; }
        set
        { imageUrl = value; }
    }

    public Product(string name, decimal price)
    {
        // These parameters have the same name as the internal variables.
        // The "this" keyword refers to the class variables.
        // "this" refers to the current instance of the Product class.
        this.name = name;
        this.price = price;
    }
}

// This part is stored in file Product2.cs.
public partial class Product
{
    public string GetHtml()
    {
        string htmlString;
        htmlString = "<h1>" + name + "</h1><br>";
        htmlString += "<h3>Costs: " + price.ToString() + "</h3><br>";
        htmlString += "<img src=" + imageUrl + ">";
        return htmlString;
    }
}
```

A partial class behaves the same as a normal class. This means every method, property, and variable you've defined in the class is accessible everywhere, no matter which source file contains it. When you compile the application, the compiler tracks down each piece of the Product class and assembles it into a complete unit. It doesn't matter what you name the source code files, so long as you keep the class name consistent.

Partial classes don't offer much in the way of solving programming problems, but they can be useful if you have extremely large, unwieldy classes. The real purpose of partial classes in .NET is to hide automatically generated designer code by placing it in a separate file from your code. Visual Studio uses this technique when you create web pages for a web application and forms for a Windows application.

Generics

Generics are a more subtle and powerful feature than partial classes. Generics allow you to create classes that are parameterized by type. In other words, you create a class template that supports any type. When you instantiate that class, you specify the type you want to use, and from that point on, your object is "locked in" to the type you chose.

To understand how this works, it's easiest to consider some of the .NET classes that support generics. In the previous chapter, you learned how the ArrayList class allows you to create a dynamically sized collection that expands as you add items and shrinks as you remove them. The ArrayList has one weakness, however—it supports any type of object. This makes it extremely flexible, but it also means you can inadvertently run into an error. For example, imagine you use an ArrayList to track a catalog of products. You intend to use the ArrayList to store Product objects, but there's nothing to stop a piece of misbehaving code from inserting strings, integers, or any arbitrary object in the ArrayList. Here's an example:

```
// Create the ArrayList.
ArrayList products = new ArrayList();

// Add several Product objects.
products.Add(product1);
products.Add(product2);
products.Add(product3);

// Notice how you can still add other types to the ArrayList.
products.Add("This string doesn't belong here.");
```

The solution is a new List collection class. Like the ArrayList, the List class is flexible enough to store different objects in different scenarios. But because it supports generics, you can lock it into a specific type whenever you instantiate a List object. To do this, you specify the class you want to use in angled brackets after the class name, as shown here:

```
// Create the List for storing Product objects.
List<Product> products = new List<Product>();
```

Now you can add only Product objects to the collection:

```
// Add several Product objects.
products.Add(product1);
products.Add(product2);
products.Add(product3);

// This line fails. In fact, it won't even compile.
products.Add("This string can't be inserted.");
```

To figure out whether a class uses generics, look for the angled brackets. For example, the List class is listed as List<T> in the .NET Framework documentation to emphasize that it takes one type parameter. You can find this class, and many more collections that use generics, in the System.Collections.Generics namespace. (The original ArrayList resides in the System.Collections namespace.)

■ **Note** Now that you've seen the advantage of the List class, you might wonder why .NET includes the ArrayList at all. In truth, the ArrayList is still useful if you really do need to store different types of objects in one place (which isn't terribly common). However, the real answer is that generics weren't implemented in .NET until version 2.0, so many existing classes don't use them because of backward compatibility.

You can also create your own classes that are parameterized by type, like the List collection. Creating classes that use generics is beyond the scope of this book, but you can find a solid overview at `http://www.ondotnet.com/pub/a/dotnet/2004/04/12/csharpwhidbeypt2.html` if you're still curious.

The Last Word

At its simplest, object-oriented programming is the idea that your code should be organized into separate classes. If followed carefully, this approach leads to code that's easier to alter, enhance, debug, and reuse. Now that you know the basics of object-oriented programming, you can take a tour of the premier ASP.NET development tool: Visual Studio 2005.

CHAPTER 4

Introducing Visual Studio 2005

Before .NET was released, ASP developers overwhelmingly favored simple text editors such as Notepad for programming web pages. Other choices were available, but each suffered from its own quirks and limitations. Tools such as Visual InterDev and web classes for Visual Basic were useful for rapid development, but often they made deployment more difficult or obscured important features. The standard was a gloves-off approach of raw HTML with blocks of code inserted wherever necessary.

Visual Studio changes all that. First, it's extensible and can even work in tandem with other straight HTML editors such as Microsoft FrontPage or Macromedia Dreamweaver. Second, it inherits the best features from other code editors, such as the ability to drag and drop web page interfaces into existence and troubleshoot misbehaving code. In its latest release, Visual Studio gets even better—by finally allowing developers to create and test websites without worrying about web server settings.

This chapter provides a lightning-fast tour that shows how to create a web application in the Visual Studio environment. You'll also learn how IntelliSense can dramatically reduce the number of errors you'll make and how to use the renowned single-step debugger that lets you look under the hood and "watch" your program in action.

The Promise of Visual Studio

All .NET applications are built from plain-text source files. C# code is stored in .cs files and VB code is stored in .vb files, regardless of whether this code is targeted for the Windows platform or the Web. Despite this fact, you'll rarely find C# or VB developers creating Windows applications by hand in a text editor. The process is not only tiring, but it also opens the door to a host of possible errors that could be easily caught at design time. The same is true for ASP.NET programmers. Although you can write your web page classes and code your web page controls manually, you'll spend hours developing and testing your code.

Visual Studio is an indispensable tool for developers on any platform. It provides several impressive benefits:

Integrated error checking: Visual Studio can detect a wide range of problems, such as data type conversion errors, missing namespaces or classes, and undefined variables. As you type, errors are detected, underlined, and added to an error list for quick reference.

The web form designer: To create a web page in Visual Studio, you simply drag ASP.NET controls to the appropriate location, resize them, and configure their properties. Visual Studio does the heavy lifting: automatically creating the underlying .aspx template file for you with the appropriate tags and attributes and adding the control variables to your code-behind file.

An integrated web server: To host an ASP.NET web application, you need web server software such as IIS (Internet Information Services), which waits for web requests and serves the appropriate pages. Setting up your web server isn't difficult, but it is inconvenient. Thanks to the integrated development web server in Visual Studio, you can run a website directly from the design environment.

Productivity enhancements: Visual Studio makes coding quick and efficient, with a collapsible code display, automatic statement completion, and color-coded syntax. You can even create sophisticated macro programs that automate repetitive tasks.

Fine-grained debugging: Visual Studio's integrated debugger allows you to watch code execution, pause your program at any point, and inspect the contents of any variable. These debugging tools can save endless headaches when writing complex code routines.

Easy deployment: When you start an ASP.NET project in Visual Studio, all the files you need are generated automatically, including a sample web.config configuration file. When you compile the application, all your page classes are compiled into one DLL for easy deployment.

Complete extensibility: You can add your own add-ins, controls, and dynamic help plug-ins to Visual Studio and customize almost every aspect of its appearance and behavior.

The latest version of Visual Studio is Visual Studio 2005.

■ **Note** Almost all the tips and techniques you learn in this chapter will work equally well with the Standard Edition, Professional Edition, and Team Edition of Visual Studio 2005 as well as Visual Web Developer 2005 Express Edition.

Creating a Website

You start Visual Studio by selecting Start ➤ Programs ➤ Microsoft Visual Studio 2005 ➤ Microsoft Visual Studio 2005. When the IDE (integrated development environment) first loads, it shows an initial start page. You can access various user-specific options from this page and access online information such as recent MSDN articles.

To create your first Visual Studio application, follow these steps:

1. Select File ➤ New Web Site from the Visual Studio menu. The New Web Site dialog box (shown in Figure 4-1) will appear.

2. Next, you need to choose the type of application. In the New Web Site dialog box, select the ASP.NET Web Site template.

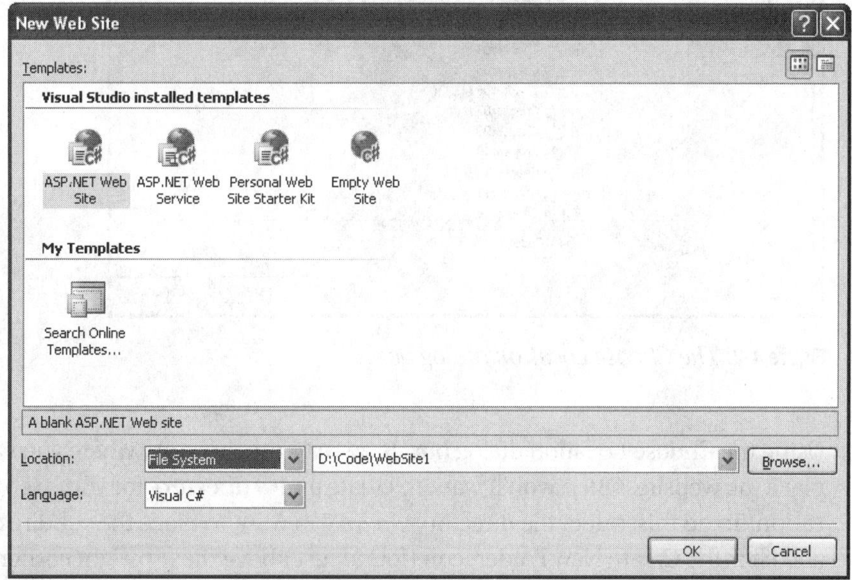

Figure 4-1. *The New Web Site dialog box*

Note Visual Studio supports two types of basic ASP.NET applications: web applications and web service applications. These applications are actually compiled and executed in the same way. In fact, you can add web pages to a web service application and web services to an ordinary web application. The only difference is the files that Visual Studio creates by default. In a web application, you'll start with one sample web page in your project. In a web service application, you'll start with a sample web service. Additionally, Visual Studio includes more sophisticated templates for specific types of sites, with preconfigured pages.

---

3. Next, you need to choose a location for the website. The location specifies where the website files will be stored. Typically, you'll choose File System and then use a folder on the local computer (or a network path). You can type in a directory by hand in the Location text box and skip straight to step 5. Alternatively, you can click the Browse button, which shows the Choose Location dialog box (see Figure 4-2).

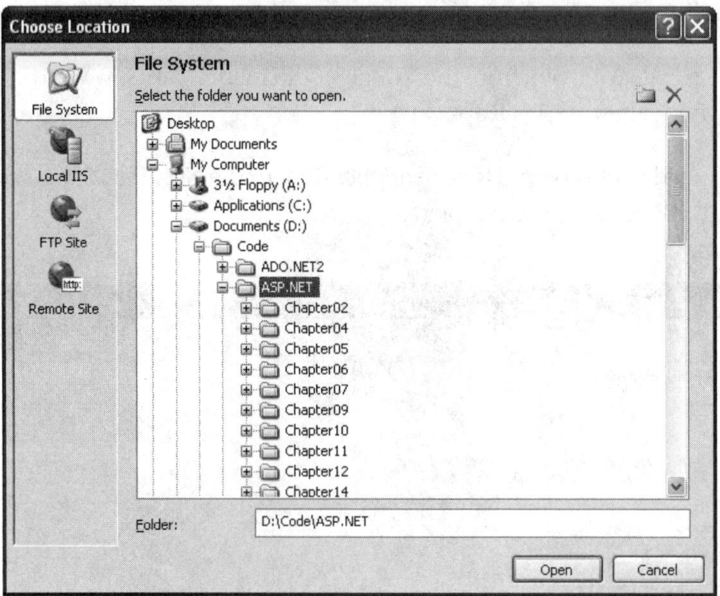

Figure 4-2. *The Choose Location dialog box*

4. Using the Choose Location dialog box, browse to the directory where you want to place the website. Often, you'll want to create a new directory for your web application. To do this, select the directory where you want to place the subdirectory, and click the Create New Folder icon (found just above the top-right corner of the directory tree). Either way, once you've selected your directory, click Open. The Choose Location dialog box also has options (represented by the buttons on the left) for creating a web application on an IIS virtual directory or a remote web server. You can ignore these options for now. In general, it's easiest to develop your web application locally and upload the files once they are perfect.

Tip Remember, the location where you create your website probably isn't where you'll put it when you deploy it. Don't worry about this wrinkle—in Chapter 12 you'll learn how to take your development website and put in on a live web server so it can be accessible to others over a network or the Internet.

5. Click OK to create the website. At this point, Visual Studio generates an empty website with one web page—a Default.aspx page. This page is the entry point for your website.

Unlike previous versions of Visual Studio, Visual Studio 2005 doesn't create project and solution files to track the contents of your projects. Instead, Visual Studio does its best to keep the website directory clean and uncluttered, with only the files you actually need. This change simplifies deployment, and it's especially handy if you're developing with a team of colleagues, because you can each work on separate pages without needing to synchronize other project or solution files.

Occasionally, Visual Studio will prompt you to let it create additional files and directories if they're needed. To see one example, select Debug ➤ Start Debugging to launch your website, and then surf to the default page using your computer's web browser (typically Internet Explorer). Before Visual Studio completes this step, it will inform you that you need to add a configuration file that specifically allows debugging or modify the existing configuration file (see Figure 4-3). When you click OK, Visual Studio will create a new file named web.config and add it to the web application directory. (You'll learn about the web.config file in Chapter 5.)

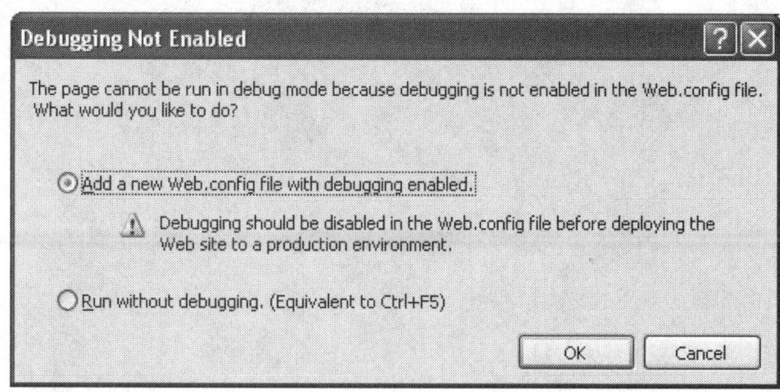

Figure 4-3. *Creating other files when needed*

When you run a web application, Visual Studio starts its integrated web server. Behind the scenes, ASP.NET compiles the code in the Default.aspx page, runs it, and then returns the final HTML to the browser. Of course, seeing as you haven't added anything to this page, all you'll see is a blank web page!

■ **Note** When you run a web page, you'll notice that the URL in the browser includes a port number. For example, if you run a web application in a folder named OnlineBank, you might see a URL like `http://localhost:4235/OnlineBank/Default.aspx`. This URL indicates that the web server is running on your computer (localhost), so its requests aren't being sent over the Internet. It also indicates that all requests are being transmitted to port number 4235. That way, the requests won't conflict with any other applications that might be running on your computer and listening for requests. Every time Visual Studio starts the integrated web server, it randomly chooses an available port.

The Solution Explorer

To take a high-level look at your website, you can use the Solution Explorer—the window at the top-right corner of the design environment that lists all the files in your web application directory (see Figure 4-4). The Solution Explorer reflects *everything* that's in the web application directory—no files are hidden. This means if you add a plain HTML file, graphic, or a subdirectory in Windows Explorer, the next time you fire up Visual Studio you'll see the new contents in the Solution Explorer. (If you add these same ingredients while Visual Studio is open, you won't see them right away, because Visual Studio scans the directory only when you first open the project.)

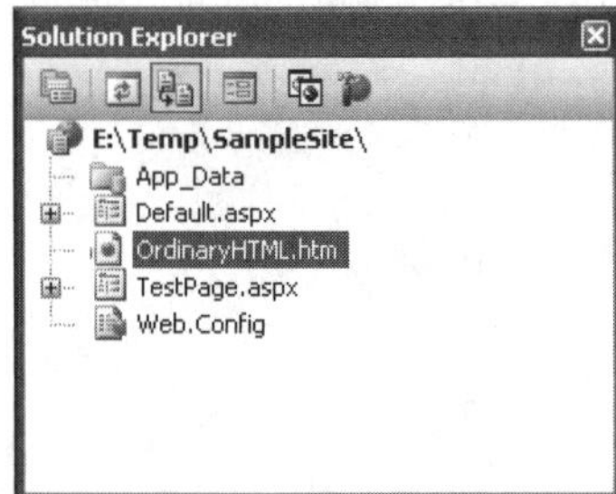

Figure 4-4. *The Solution Explorer*

Of course, the whole point of the Solution Explorer is to save you from resorting to using Windows Explorer. Instead, it allows you to perform a variety of file management tasks within Visual Studio. You can rename, delete, or copy files with a simple right-click. And, of course, you can add new items by choosing Website ➤ Add New Item.

You can add various types of files to your project, including web forms, web services, stand-alone components, resources you want to use such as bitmaps and text files, and even ordinary HTML files. Visual Studio event provides some basic designers that allow you to edit these types of files directly in the IDE. Figure 4-5 shows some of the file types you can add to a web application.

■ **Tip** In the downloadable samples, you'll find that many of the web pages use a style sheet named Styles.css. This style sheet applies the Verdana font to all elements of the web page. To learn more about the CSS (Cascading Style Sheets) standard, you can refer to the tutorial at `http://www.w3schools.com/css`. CSS is a standard supported by almost all browsers.

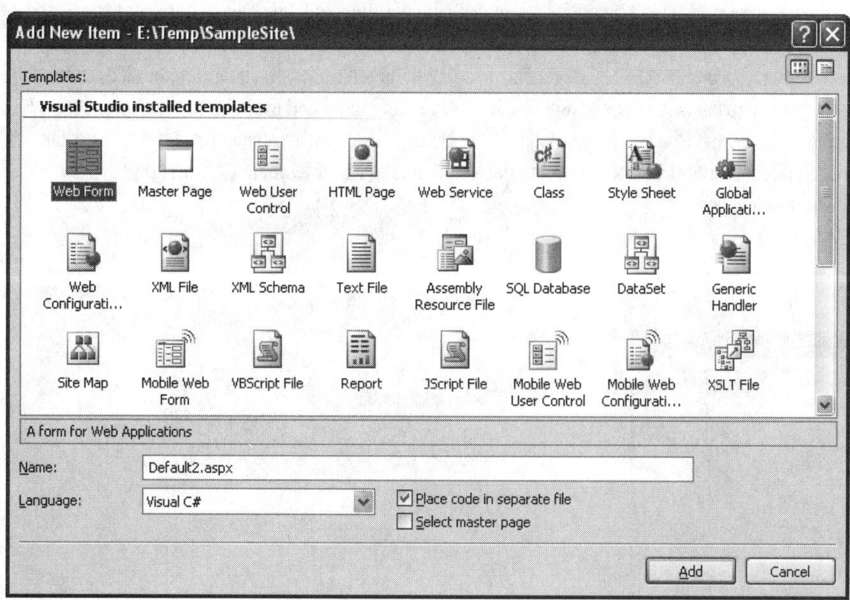

Figure 4-5. *Supported file types*

When you add a new web form, Visual Studio gives you the choice of two coding models. You can place all the code for the file in the same file as the HTML and control tags, or you can separate these into two distinct files, one with the markup and the other with your C# code. This second model is closest to earlier versions of Visual Studio, and it's what you'll use in this book. The key advantage of splitting the two components of a web page into separate files is that it's more manageable when you need to work with complex pages. However, both approaches give you the same performance and functionality.

In Chapter 5, you'll explore the two code models in more detail. But for now, just select the Place Code in Separate File check box in the Add New Item dialog box when you're creating a web page. Your project will end up with two files for each web page: a page that includes the HTML control tags (with the file extension .aspx) and a source code file (with the same name and a file extension of .aspx.cs). To make the relationship clear, the Solution Explorer displays the code file underneath the .aspx file (see Figure 4-6).

MIGRATING AN OLDER VISUAL STUDIO .NET PROJECT

If you have an existing web application created with Visual Studio .NET 2002 or 2003, you can open the project or solution file using the File ➤ Open Project command. When you do, Visual Studio opens a conversion wizard.

The conversion wizard is exceedingly simple. It prompts you to choose whether to create a backup and, if so, where it should be placed. If this is your only copy of the application, a backup is a good idea in case some aspects of your application can't be converted successfully. Otherwise, you can skip this option.

When you click Finish, Visual Studio performs an *in-place conversion*, which means it overwrites your web page files with the new versions. This conversion won't change the code you've written, but it does modify the web pages and code classes to use Visual Studio's new code model and event handling approach. Any errors and warnings are added to a conversion log, which you can display when the conversion is complete. A typical conversion doesn't produce any errors but generates a long list of warnings informing you of the changes that were made.

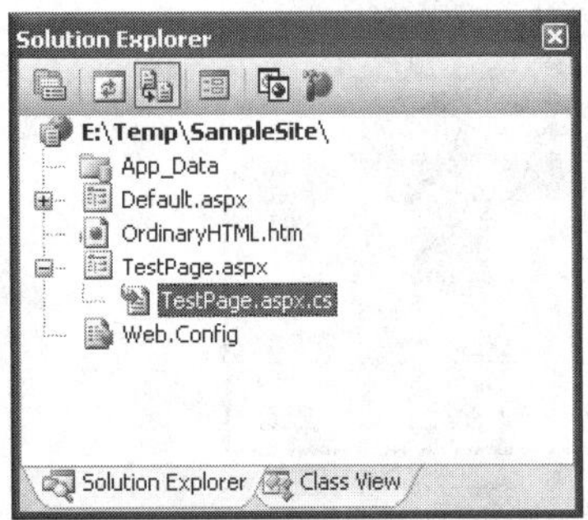

Figure 4-6. *A code file for a web page*

You can also add files that already exist by selecting Add ➤ Add Existing Item. You can use this technique to copy files from one project into another. Visual Studio leaves the original file alone and simply creates a copy in your web application directory. However, don't use this approach with a web page that has been created in an older version of Visual Studio. Instead, refer to the sidebar "Migrating an Older Visual Studio .NET Project."

Designing a Web Page

Now that you understand the basic organization of Visual Studio, you can begin designing a simple web page. To start, double-click the web page you want to design. (Start with Default.aspx if you haven't added any additional pages.) A blank designer page will appear.

Adding Web Controls

To add a web control, drag the control you want from the Toolbox on the left and drop it onto your web page. The controls in the Toolbox are grouped in numerous categories based on their functions, but you'll find basic ingredients such as buttons, labels, and text boxes in the Standard tab.

■Tip By default, the Toolbox is enabled to automatically hide itself when your mouse moves away from it, somewhat like the AutoHide feature for the Windows taskbar. This behavior is often exasperating, so you may want to click the pushpin in the top-right corner of the Toolbox to make it stop in its fully expanded position.

In a web form, controls are positioned line by line, like in a word processor document. To add a control, you need to drag and drop it to an appropriate place. To organize several controls, you'll probably need to add spaces and carriage returns to position elements the way you want them. Figure 4-7 shows an example with a TextBox, Label, and Button control.

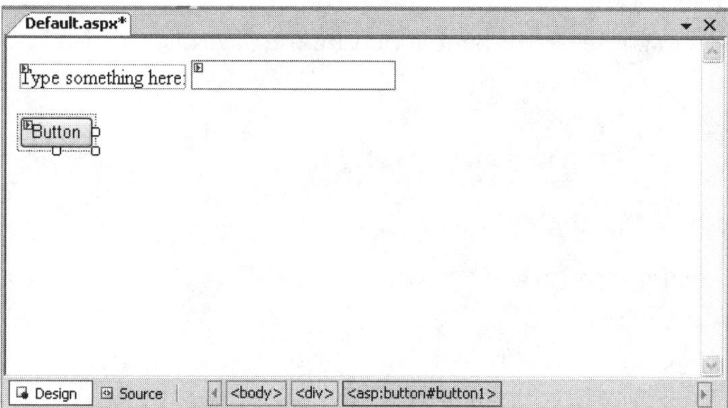

Figure 4-7. *The Design view for a page*

You'll find that some controls can't be resized. Instead, they grow or shrink to fit the amount of content in them. For example, the size of a Label control depends on how much text you enter in it. On the other hand, you can adjust the size of a Button or TextBox control by clicking and dragging in the design environment.

As you add web controls Visual Studio automatically adds the corresponding control tags to your .aspx file. You can even look at the .aspx code or add server control tags and HTML tags manually by typing them in. To switch your view, click the Source button at the bottom of the web designer. You can click Design to revert to the graphical web form designer.

THE MISSING GRID LAYOUT FEATURE

If you've used previous versions of Visual Studio .NET, you may remember a feature called *grid layout*, which allowed you to position elements with absolute coordinates by dragging them where you want them. Although this model seems convenient, it really isn't suited to most web pages because controls can't adjust their positioning when the web page content changes. This leads to inflexible layouts (such as controls that overwrite each other). To gain more control over layout, most web developers use tables.

That said, Visual Studio 2005 has a backdoor way to use grid layout. All you need to do is add a style attribute that uses CSS to specify absolute positioning. This attribute will already exist in any pages you've created with a previous version of Visual Studio .NET in grid layout mode.

Here's an example:

```
<asp:Button id="cmd" style="POSITION: absolute; left: 100px; top: 50px;"
 runat="server"  ... />
```

Once you've made this change, you're free to drag the button around the window at will. Of course, you shouldn't go this route just because it seems closer to the Windows model. Few great Web pages rely on absolute positioning, because it's just too awkward and inflexible.

Figure 4-8 shows what you might see in the Source view for the page displayed in Figure 4-7.

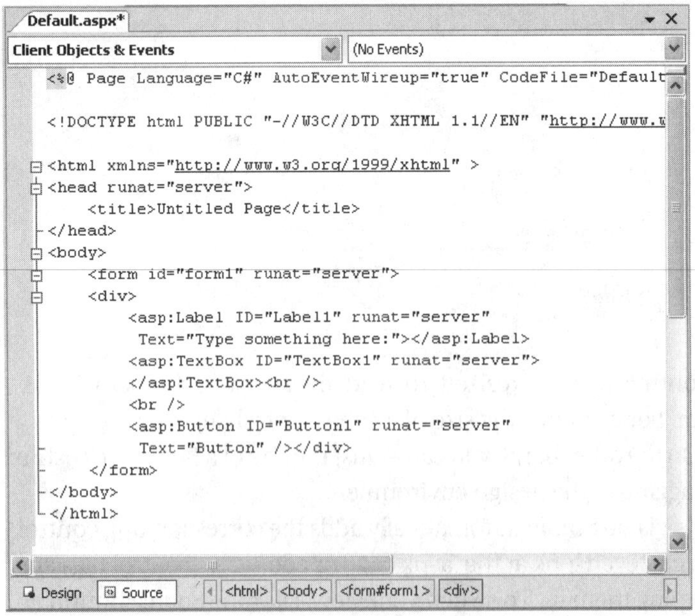

```
Default.aspx*
Client Objects & Events        (No Events)
<%@ Page Language="C#" AutoEventWireup="true" CodeFile="Default

<!DOCTYPE html PUBLIC "-//W3C//DTD XHTML 1.1//EN" "http://www.w

<html xmlns="http://www.w3.org/1999/xhtml" >
<head runat="server">
    <title>Untitled Page</title>
</head>
<body>
    <form id="form1" runat="server">
    <div>
        <asp:Label ID="Label1" runat="server"
         Text="Type something here:"></asp:Label>
        <asp:TextBox ID="TextBox1" runat="server">
        </asp:TextBox><br />
        <br />
        <asp:Button ID="Button1" runat="server"
         Text="Button" /></div>
    </form>
</body>
</html>
Design  Source  <html> <body> <form#form1> <div>
```

Figure 4-8. *The Source view for a page*

Using the Source view, you can manually add attributes or rearrange controls. In fact, Visual Studio even provides IntelliSense features that automatically complete opening tags and alert you if you use an invalid tag. Whether you use the Design view or the Source view is entirely up to you—Visual Studio keeps them both synchronized.

The Properties Window

To configure a control in Design view, you must first select it on the page or choose it by name from the drop-down list at the top of the Properties window. Then, you can modify any of its properties. Good ones to try include Text (the content of the control), ID (the name you use to interact with the control in your code), and ForeColor (the color used for the control's text).

Every time you make a selection in the Properties window, Visual Studio translates your change to the corresponding ASP.NET control tag attribute. Visual Studio even provides special "choosers" that allow you to select extended properties. For example, you can select a color from a drop-down list that shows you the color (see Figure 4-9), and you can configure the font from a standard font selection dialog box.

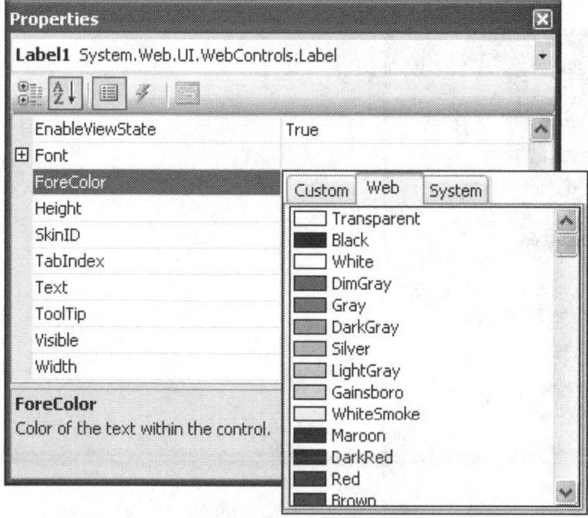

Figure 4-9. *Setting the Color property*

Finally, you can select one object in the Properties window that needs some explanation—the DOCUMENT object, which represents the web page itself. These settings have different effects. Using this object, you can set various options for the entire, page, including the title that will be displayed in the browser, linked style sheets, and support for other features that are discussed later in this book (such as tracing and session state).

Adding Ordinary HTML

Not everything in your web page needs to be a full-fledged web control. You can also add the familiar HTML tags, such as paragraphs, headings, lists, divisions, and so on. To add an HTML element, you can type it in using the Source view, or you can drag the element you want from the HTML tab of the Toolbox.

Visual Studio also provides an indispensable style builder for formatting any static HTML element. To test it, add a Div to your web page from the HTML tab of the Toolbox. Then, right-click the panel, and choose Style. The Style Builder window (shown in Figure 4-10) will appear, with options for configuring the colors, font, layout, and border for the element. As you configure these properties, the web page HTML will be updated to reflect your settings.

■ **Note** A Div is a <div> tag, or division, which is an all-purpose HTML container. A <div> doesn't have any default representation in HTML. However, it's commonly used in conjunction with styles. Using a <div>, you can group together several other elements. You can also specify a default font or color that will be applied to all of them or add a border that will be displayed around that entire section of your web page.

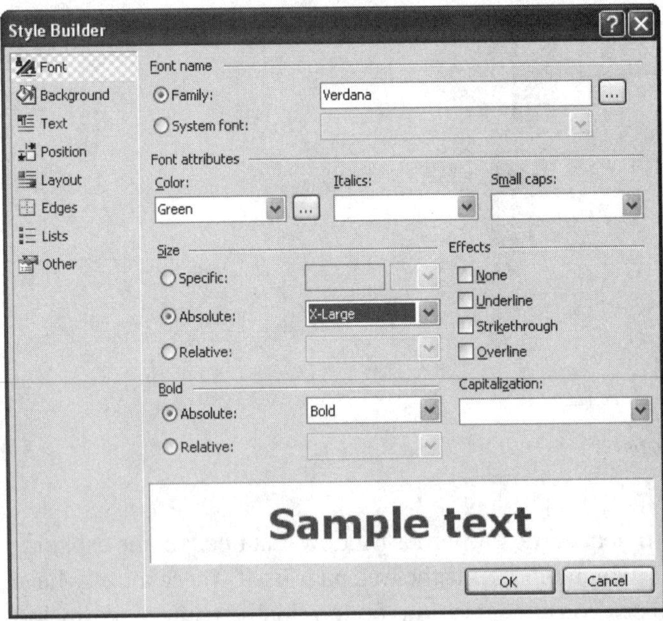

Figure 4-10. *Building styles*

With the right changes, you can transform a <div> tag into a nicely shaded and bordered box, as shown in Figure 4-11. You're then free to add other HTML and web controls inside this box. This is a technique you'll see in the examples throughout this book.

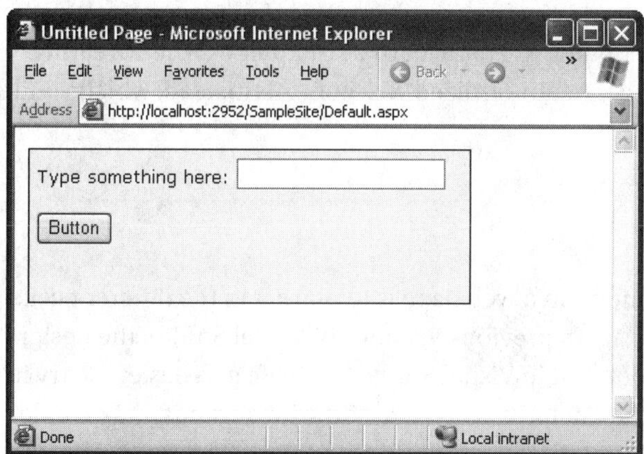

Figure 4-11. *Using a styled division*

Here's the style that was built in the style builder for the example in Figure 4-10. Note that the style attribute is split over several lines in a way that isn't legal in HTML, just to fit the bounds of the printed page.

```
<div style="border-right: 1px solid; padding-right: 5px; border-top: 1px solid;
 padding-left: 5px; font-size: smaller; padding-bottom: 5px;
 border-left: 1px solid; width: 318px; padding-top: 5px;
 border-bottom: 1px solid;
 font-family: Verdana; height: 100px; background-color: #ffffcc">

    <asp:Label ID="Label1" runat="server"
     Text="Type something here:" Width="144px"></asp:Label>
    <asp:TextBox ID="TextBox1" runat="server">
    </asp:TextBox><br />
    <br />
    <asp:Button ID="Button1" runat="server"
     Text="Button" />

</div>
```

Visual Studio also allows you to convert HTML elements into server controls. If you want to configure the element as a server control so that you can handle events and interact with it in code, you .need to right-click it and select Run As Server Control. This adds the required runat="server" attribute to the control tag. Alternatively, you could switch to Source view and type this in on your own. Keep in mind that HTML server controls are really designed for backward compatibility, as you'll learn in Chapter 6. When creating new interfaces, you're better off using the standardized web controls instead, which you'll find on the Standard tab of the Toolbox.

HTML Tables

One convenient way to organize content in a web page is to place it in the different cells of an HTML table using the <table> tag. In previous versions of Visual Studio, the design-time support for this strategy was poor. But in Visual Studio 2005, life gets easier. To try it, drag a table from the HTML tab of the Toolbox. You'll start off with a standard 3×3 table, but you can quickly transform it using editing features that more closely resemble a word processor than a programming tool. Here are some of the tricks you'll want to use:

- To move from one cell to another in the table, press the Tab key or use the arrow keys. The current cell is highlighted with a blue border. Inside each cell you can type in static HTML or drag and drop controls from the Toolbox.
- To add new rows and columns, right-click inside a cell, and choose from one of the many options in the Insert submenu to insert rows, columns, and individual cells.
- To resize a part of the table, just click and drag away.
- To format a cell, right-click inside it, and choose Style. This shows the same style builder you saw in Figure 4-10.
- To work with several cells at once, hold down Ctrl while you click each cell. You can then right-click to perform a batch formatting operation.
- To merge cells together (in other words, change two cells into one cell that spans two columns), just select the cells, right-click, and choose Merge Cells.

Figure 4-12 shows a table in Visual Studio, complete with several controls in different cells of the first row.

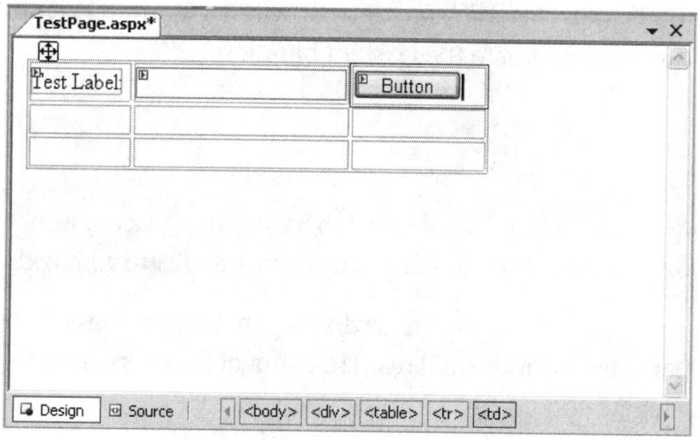

Figure 4-12. *Using an HTML table*

Once you get the hang of these conveniences, you might never need to resort to a design tool such as Macromedia Dreamweaver or Microsoft FrontPage.

Writing Code

Many of Visual Studio's most welcome enhancements appear when you start to write the code that supports your user interface. To start coding, you need to switch to the code-behind view. To switch back and forth, you can use two buttons that appear just above the Solution Explorer window. The tooltips identify these buttons as View Code and View Designer, respectively. Another approach that works just as well is to double-click either the .aspx page in the Solution Explorer (for the designer) or the .aspx.cs page (for the code view). The "code" in question is the C# code, not the HTML markup in the .aspx file.

When you switch to code view, you'll see the page class for your web page. Just before your page class, Visual Studio imports a number of core .NET namespaces. These namespaces give you easy access to many commonly used ASP.NET classes:

```
using System;
using System.Data;
using System.Configuration;
using System.Web;
using System.Web.Security;
using System.Web.UI;
using System.Web.UI.WebControls;
using System.Web.UI.WebControls.WebParts;
using System.Web.UI.HtmlControls;
```

Inside your page class are methods, most of which are directly wired to control events. The following section explains how you can create these event handlers.

Adding Event Handlers

Most of the code in an ASP.NET web page is placed inside event handlers that react to web control events. Using Visual Studio, you have three ways to add an event handler to your code:

Type it in manually: In this case, you add the subroutine directly to the page class. You must specify the appropriate parameters, and you'll need to connect the event handler to the event using your own delegate code.

Double-click a control in Design view: In this case, Visual Studio will create an event handler for that control's default event, if it doesn't already exist. For example, if you double-click the page, it will create a Page.Load event handler. If you double-click a button or input control, it will create an event handler for the Click or Change event.

Choose the event from the Properties window: Just select the control, and click the lightning bolt in the Properties window. You'll see a list of all the events provided by that control. Double-click next to the event you want to handle, and Visual Studio will automatically generate the event handler in your page class. Alternatively, if you've already created the event handler, just select the event in the Properties window, and click the drop-down arrow at the right. You'll see a list that includes all the methods in your class that match the signature this event requires. You can then choose a method from the list to connect it. Figure 4-13 shows an example where the Button.Click event is connected to the Button1_Click method in the page class.

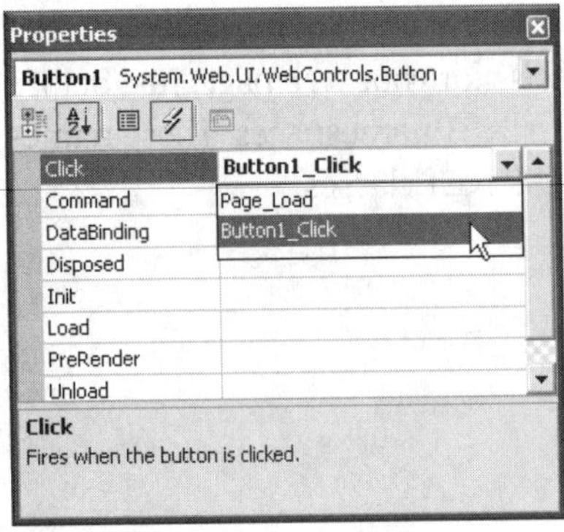

Figure 4-13. *Creating or attaching an event handler*

For example, when you double-click a Button control, Visual Studio creates an event handler like this:

```
protected void Button1_Click(object sender, EventArgs e)
{
    // Your code for reacting to the button click goes here.
}
```

When you use Visual Studio to attach or create an event handler, it adjusts the control tag so that it's linked to the appropriate event:

```
<asp:button ID="Button1" runat="server" text="Button" OnClick="Button1_Click" />
```

Inside your event handler, you can interact with any of the control objects on your web page using their IDs. For example, if you've created a TextBox control named TextBox1, you can set the text using the following line of code:

```
protected void Button1_Click(object sender, EventArgs e)
{
    TextBox1.Text = "Here is some sample text.";
}
```

This creates a simple event handler that reacts when Button1 is clicked by updating the text in TextBox1. You'll learn much more about the ASP.NET web form model in the next two chapters.

IntelliSense and Outlining

Visual Studio provides a number of automatic time-savers through its IntelliSense technology. They are similar to features such as automatic spell checking and formatting in Microsoft Office applications. We introduce most of these features in this chapter, but you'll need several hours of programming before you'll become familiar with all of Visual Studio's time-savers. We don't have enough space to describe advanced tricks such as the intelligent search-and-replace features and Visual Studio's programmable macros. These features could occupy an entire book of their own!

Outlining

Outlining allows Visual Studio to "collapse" a method, class, structure, namespace, or region to a single line. It allows you to see the code that interests you while hiding unimportant code. To collapse a portion of code, click the minus (–) symbol next to the first line. Click the box again, which will now have a plus (+) symbol, to expand it (see Figure 4-14).

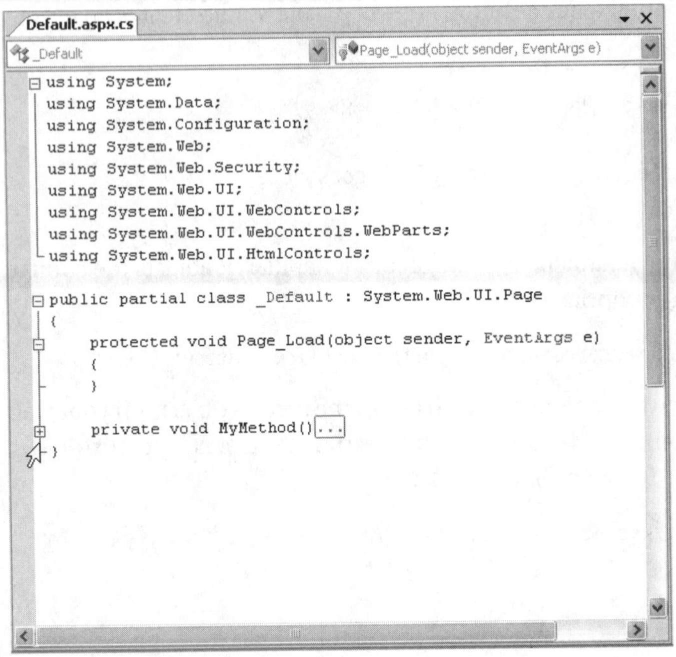

```
Default.aspx.cs
_Default                                  Page_Load(object sender, EventArgs e)
using System;
using System.Data;
using System.Configuration;
using System.Web;
using System.Web.Security;
using System.Web.UI;
using System.Web.UI.WebControls;
using System.Web.UI.WebControls.WebParts;
using System.Web.UI.HtmlControls;

public partial class _Default : System.Web.UI.Page
{
    protected void Page_Load(object sender, EventArgs e)
    {
    }

    private void MyMethod()...
}
```

Figure 4-14. *Collapsing code*

You can hide any section of code you want. Simply select the code, right-click the selection, and choose Outlining ➤ Hide Selection.

Member List

Visual Studio makes it easy for you to interact with controls and classes. When you type a class or object name, it pops up a list of available properties and methods (see Figure 4-15). It uses a similar trick to provide a list of data types when you define a variable or to provide a list of valid values when you assign a value to an enumeration.

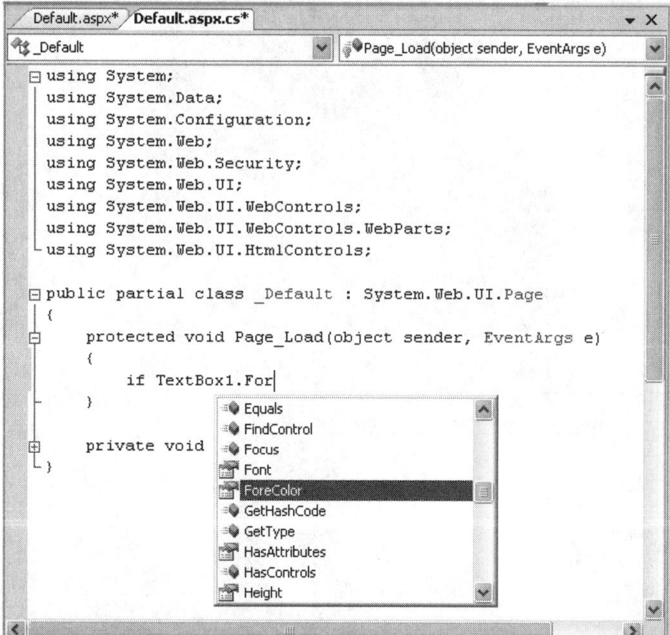

Figure 4-15. *IntelliSense at work*

■Tip Forgotten the names of the controls in your web page? You can get IntelliSense to help you. Just type the this keyword followed by the dot operator (.) Visual Studio will pop up a list with all the methods and properties of the current form class, including the control variables.

Visual Studio also provides a list of parameters and their data types when you call a method or invoke a constructor. This information is presented in a tooltip above the code and appears as you type. Because the .NET class library uses function overloading a lot, these methods may have multiple versions. When they do, Visual Studio indicates the number of versions and allows you to see the method definitions for each one by clicking the small up and down arrows in the tooltip. Each time you click the arrow, the tooltip displays a different version of the overloaded method (see Figure 4-16).

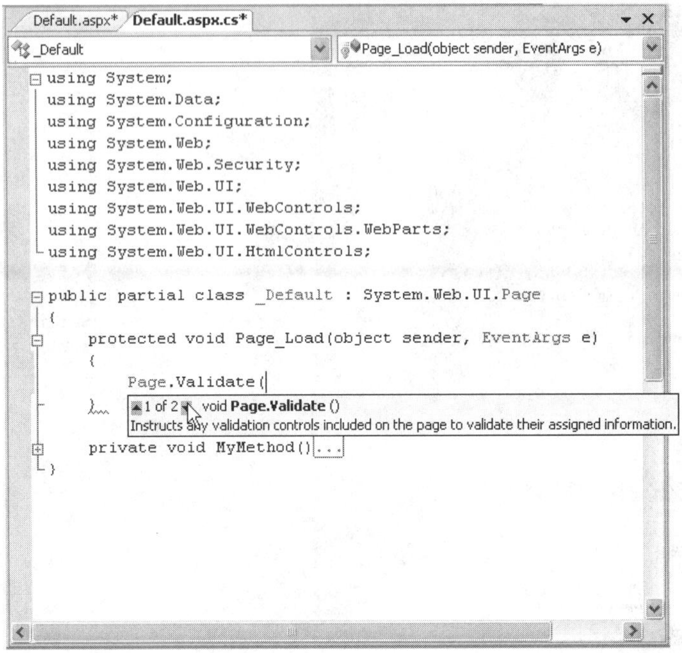

Figure 4-16. *IntelliSense with overloaded methods*

Error Underlining

One of the code editor's most useful features is error underlining. Visual Studio is able to detect a variety of error conditions, such as undefined variables, properties, or methods; invalid data type conversions; and missing code elements. Rather than stopping you to alert you that a problem exists, the Visual Studio editor underlines the offending code. You can hover your mouse over an underlined error to see a brief tooltip description of the problem (see Figure 4-17).

Visual Studio won't necessarily flag your errors immediately. But when you try to run your application (or just compile it), Visual Studio will quickly scan through the code, marking all the errors it finds. If your code contains at least one error, Visual Studio will ask you whether it should continue. At this point, you'll almost always decide to cancel the operation and fix the problems Visual Studio has discovered. (If you choose to continue, you'll actually wind up using the last compiled version of your application, because Visual Studio can't build an application that has errors.)

Whenever you attempt to build an application that has errors, Visual Studio will display the Error List window with a list of all the problems it detected, as shown in Figure 4-18. You can then jump quickly to a problem by double-clicking it in the list.

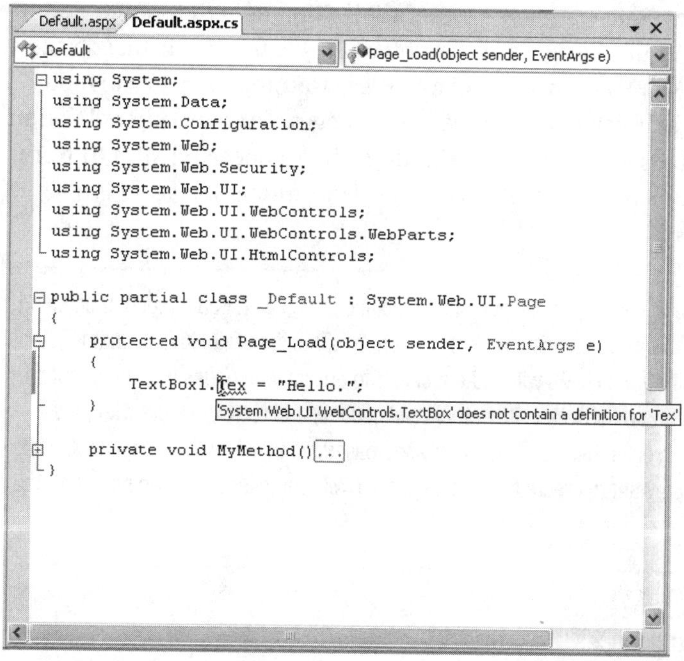

```
using System;
using System.Data;
using System.Configuration;
using System.Web;
using System.Web.Security;
using System.Web.UI;
using System.Web.UI.WebControls;
using System.Web.UI.WebControls.WebParts;
using System.Web.UI.HtmlControls;

public partial class _Default : System.Web.UI.Page
{
    protected void Page_Load(object sender, EventArgs e)
    {
        TextBox1.Tex = "Hello.";
    }

    private void MyMethod()...
}
```

'System.Web.UI.WebControls.TextBox' does not contain a definition for 'Tex'

Figure 4-17. *Highlighting errors at design time*

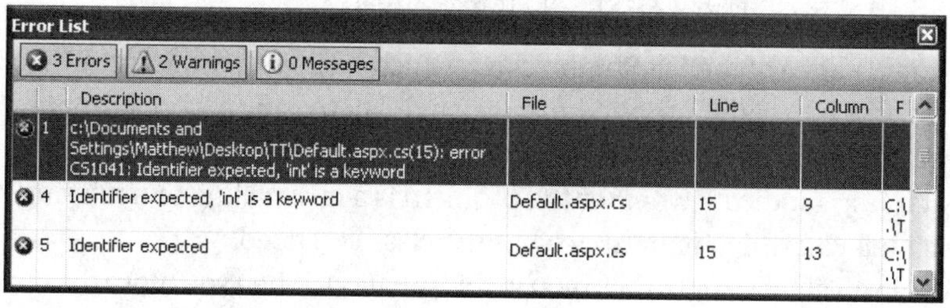

Error List

3 Errors | 2 Warnings | 0 Messages

	Description	File	Line	Column
1	c:\Documents and Settings\Matthew\Desktop\TT\Default.aspx.cs(15): error CS1041: Identifier expected, 'int' is a keyword			
4	Identifier expected, 'int' is a keyword	Default.aspx.cs	15	9
5	Identifier expected	Default.aspx.cs	15	13

Figure 4-18. *Build errors in the Error List*

You may find that as you fix errors and rebuild your project, you discover more problems. That's because Visual Studio doesn't check for all types of errors at once. When you try to compile your application, Visual Studio scans for basic problems such as unrecognized class names. If these problems exist, they can easily mask other errors. On the other hand, if your code passes this basic level of inspection, Visual Studio checks for more subtle problems such as trying to use an unassigned variable.

Visual Studio may also generate warnings for the HTML content in the Source view of your web pages. By default, Visual Studio will warn you when you use HTML that deviates from the strict rules of XHTML. You can safely ignore these warnings, or you can hide them altogether by switching the validation mode of your pages. To change the validation mode, choose View ➤ Toolbars ➤ HTML Source Editing. Then, choose HTML 4.01 from the drop-down box in the toolbar instead of XHTML 1.0 Transitional.

■ **Note** XHTML is a stricter form of HTML that will eventually replace it. You won't gain much, if anything, by using XHTML today. However, some companies and organization mandate the use of XHTML, namely, with a view to future standards. In the future, XHTML will make it easier to design web pages that are adaptable to a variety of different platforms, can be processed by other applications, and are extensible with new markup features. (For example, you could use XSLT, another XML-based standard, to transform an XHTML document into another form.) If you want to create pages that are XHTML-compliant, you can start with the XHTML tutorial at `http://www.w3schools.com/xhtml`.

Automatically Importing Namespaces

Sometimes, you'll run into an error because you haven't imported a namespace that you need. For example, imagine you type a line of code like this:

```
FileStream fs = new FileStream("newfile.txt", FileMode.Create);
```

This line creates an instance of the FileStream class, which resides in the System.IO namespace. However, if you haven't imported the System.IO namespace, you'll run into a compile-time error. Unfortunately, the error simply indicates no known class named FileStream exists—it doesn't indicate whether the problem is a misspelling or a missing import, and it doesn't tell you which namespace has the class you need.

Visual Studio offers an invaluable tool to help you in this situation. When you move the text cursor to the unrecognized class name (FileStream in this example), a small box icon appears underneath. If you hover over that location with the mouse, a page icon appears. Click the page icon, and a drop-down list of autocorrect options appear (see Figure 4-19). Using these options, you can convert the line to use the fully qualified class name or add the required namespace import to the top of your code file, which is generally the cleanest option (particularly if you use classes from that namespace more than once in the same page).

The only case when this autocorrect feature won't work is if Visual Studio can't find the missing class. This might happen if the class exists in another assembly, and you haven't added a reference to that assembly yet.

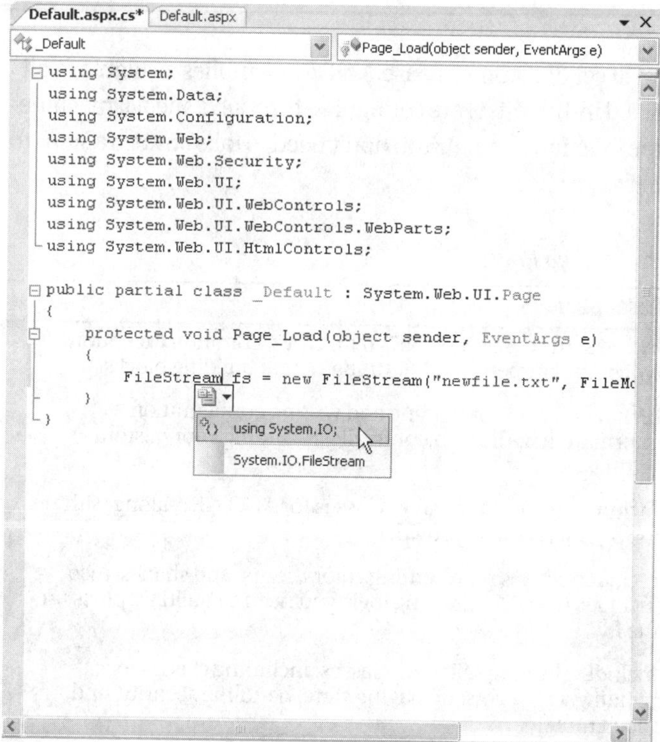

Figure 4-19. *Build errors in the Error List*

Auto Format and Color

Visual Studio also provides some cosmetic conveniences. It automatically colors your code, making comments green, keywords blue, and normal code black. The result is much more readable code. You can even configure the colors Visual Studio uses by selecting Tools ➤ Options and then choosing the Environment ➤ Fonts and Colors section.

In additional, Visual Studio is configured by default to automatically format your code. This means you can type your code lines freely without worrying about tabs and positioning. As soon as you insert a closing brace (the curly bracket: }), Visual Studio applies the "correct" indenting. Fortunately, if you have a different preference, you can configure this behavior—just select Tools ➤ Options, make sure the Show All Settings check box is checked, and then find the Text Editor ➤ C# ➤ Formatting group of settings.

Assembly References

By default, ASP.NET makes a small set of commonly used .NET assemblies available to all web pages. These assemblies (listed in Table 4-1) are configured through a special machine-wide configuration file (called the machine.config). You don't need to take any extra steps to use the classes in these assemblies.

Table 4-1. *Assemblies Available to All Web Pages*

Assembly	Description
mscorlib.dll and System.dll	Includes the core set of .NET data types, common exception types, and numerous other fundamental building blocks.
System.Configuration.dll	Includes classes for reading and writing configuration information in the web.config file, including your custom settings.
System.Data.dll	Includes the data container classes for ADO.NET, along with the SQL Server data provider.
System.Drawing.dll	Includes classes representing colors, fonts, and shapes. Also includes the GDI+ drawing logic you need to build graphics on the fly.
System.Web.dll	Includes the core ASP.NET classes, including classes for building web forms, managing state, handling security, and much more.
System.Web.Services.dll	Includes classes for building web services—units of code that can be remotely invoked over HTTP.
System.Xml.dll	Includes .NET classes for reading, writing, searching, transforming, and validating XML.
System.EnterpriseServices.dll	Includes .NET classes for COM+ services such as transactions.
System.Web.Mobile.dll	Includes .NET classes for the mobile web controls, which are targeted for small devices such as web-enabled cell phones.

■ **Note** Remember, assemblies can contain more than one namespace: For example, the System.Web.dll assembly includes classes in the System.Web namespace, the System.Web.UI namespace, and many more related namespaces.

If you want to use additional features or a third-party component, you may need to import more assemblies. For example, if you want to use an Oracle database, you need to add a reference to the System.Data.OracleClient.dll assembly.

To add a reference, follow these steps:

1. Right-click your web application in the Solution Explorer, and choose Add Reference. This shows the Add Reference dialog box, with a list of assemblies that are registered with Visual Studio.

2. In the Add Reference window, select the component you want to use. If the component isn't located in the centralized component registry on your computer (known as the GAC, or global assembly cache), you'll need to click the Browse tab and find the DLL file from the appropriate directory.

3. Once you've selected the DLL, click OK to add the reference to your web application.

When you add a reference, Visual Studio modifies the web.config file to indicate that you use this assembly. If you add a reference to an assembly that isn't stored in the GAC, Visual Studio will create a Bin subdirectory in your web application and copy the DLL into that directory so it's readily available. This step isn't required for assemblies in the GAC because they are shared with all the .NET applications on the computer. You'll learn more about this model in Chapter 5.

Adding a reference isn't the same as importing the namespace with the using statement. The using statement allows you to use the classes in a namespace without typing the long, fully qualified class names. However, if you're missing a reference, it doesn't matter what using statements you include—the classes won't be available. For example, if you import the System.Web.UI namespace, you can write Page instead of System.Web.UI.Page in your code. But if you haven't added a reference to the System.Web.dll assembly that contains these classes, you still won't be able to access the classes in the System.Web.UI namespace.

■ **Tip** You can create your own component assemblies. This technique allows you to share functionality between several web applications or between several types of .NET applications. You'll learn more about this feat in Chapter 24.

Visual Studio Debugging

Once you've created an application, you can compile and run it by choosing Debug ➤ Start Debugging from the menu or by clicking the Start Debugging button on the toolbar. Visual Studio launches your default web browser and requests the page that's currently selected in the Solution Explorer. This is a handy trick—if you're in the middle of coding SalesPage1.aspx, you'll see SalesPage1.aspx appear in the browser, not the Default.aspx home page.

Visual Studio's built-in web server also allows you to retrieve a file listing. This means if you create a web application named MyApp, you can request in the form http://localhost:port/MyApp (omitting the page name) to see a list of all the files in your web application folder (see Figure 4-20). Then, just click the page you want to test.

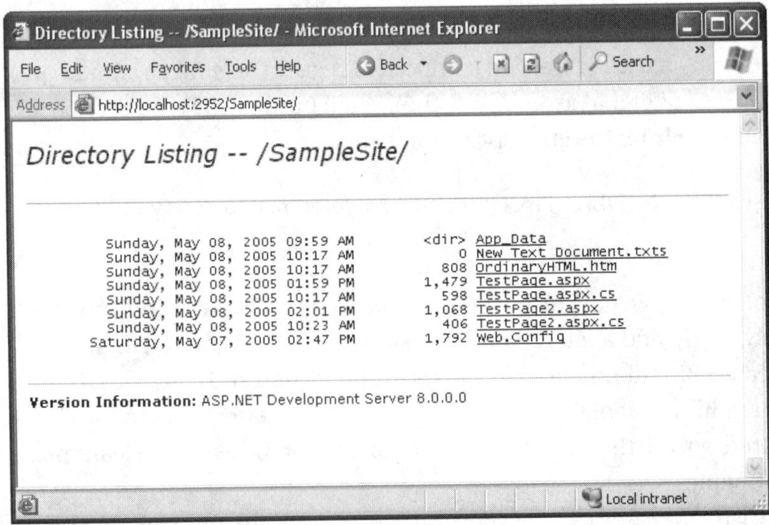

Figure 4-20. *Choosing from a list of pages*

This trick won't work if you have a Default.aspx page. If you do, any requests that don't indicate the page you want are automatically redirected to this page.

Single-Step Debugging

Single-step debugging allows you to test your assumptions about how your code works and see what's really happening under the hood of your application. It's incredibly easy to use. Just follow these steps:

1. Find a location in your code where you want to pause execution, and start single-stepping. (You can use any executable line of code but not a variable declaration, comment, or blank line.) Click in the margin next to the line code, and a red breakpoint will appear (see Figure 4-21).

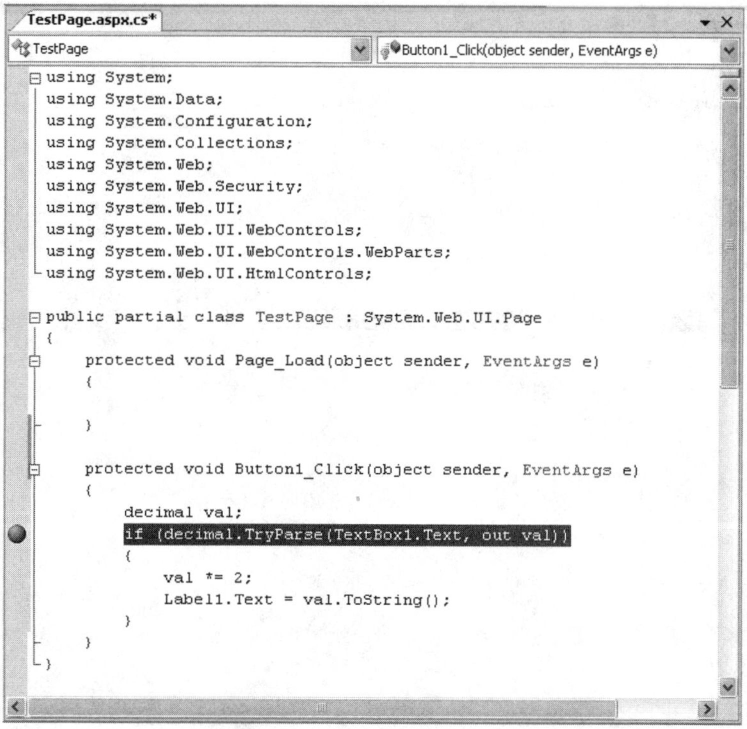

```
TestPage.aspx.cs*
TestPage                                  Button1_Click(object sender, EventArgs e)
using System;
using System.Data;
using System.Configuration;
using System.Collections;
using System.Web;
using System.Web.Security;
using System.Web.UI;
using System.Web.UI.WebControls;
using System.Web.UI.WebControls.WebParts;
using System.Web.UI.HtmlControls;

public partial class TestPage : System.Web.UI.Page
{
    protected void Page_Load(object sender, EventArgs e)
    {

    }

    protected void Button1_Click(object sender, EventArgs e)
    {
        decimal val;
        if (decimal.TryParse(TextBox1.Text, out val))
        {
            val *= 2;
            Label1.Text = val.ToString();
        }
    }
}
```

Figure 4-21. *Setting a breakpoint*

2. Now start your program as you would ordinarily (by pressing the F5 key or using the Start button on the toolbar). When the program reaches your breakpoint, execution will pause, and you'll be switched to the Visual Studio code window. The breakpoint statement won't be executed.

3. At this point, you have several options. You can execute the current line by pressing F11. The following line in your code will be highlighted with a yellow arrow, indicating that this is the next line that will be executed. You can continue like this through your program, running one line at a time by pressing F11 and following the code's path of execution.

4. Whenever the code is in break mode, you can hover over variables to see their current contents (see Figure 4-22). This allows you to verify that variables contain the values you expect.

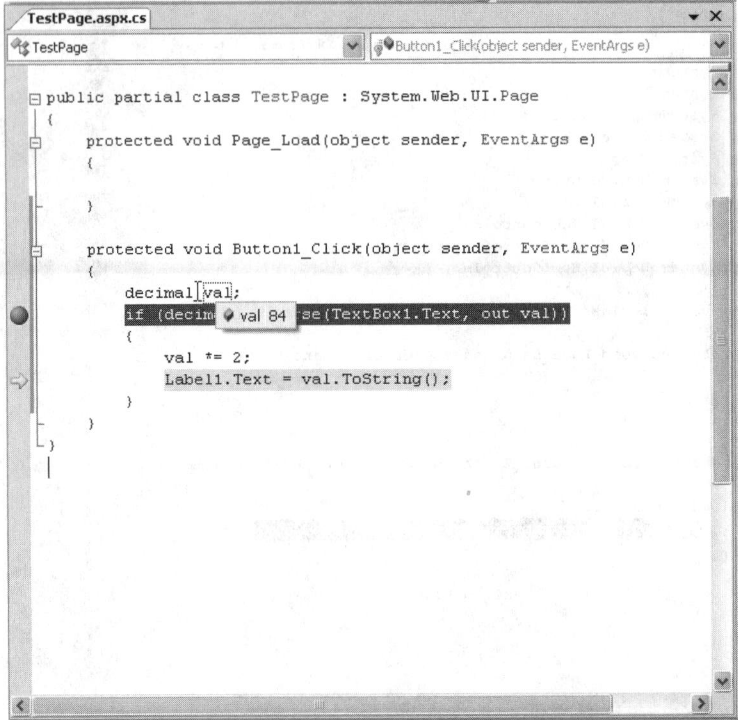

Figure 4-22. *Viewing variable contents in break mode*

5. You can also use any of the commands listed in Table 4-2 while in break mode. These commands are available from the context menu by right-clicking the code window or by using the associated hot key.

Table 4-2. *Commands Available in Break Mode*

Command (Hot Key)	Description
Step Into (F11)	Executes the currently highlighted line and then pauses. If the currently highlighted line calls a procedure, execution will pause at the first executable line inside the method or function (which is why this feature is called stepping *into*).
Step Over (F10)	The same as Step Into, except it runs procedures as though they are a single line. If you select Step Over while a procedure call is highlighted, the entire procedure will be executed. Execution will pause at the next executable statement in the current procedure.
Step Out (Shift-F11)	Executes all the code in the current procedure and then pauses at the statement that immediately follows the one that called this method or function. In other words, this allows you to step "out" of the current procedure in one large jump.

Command (Hot Key)	Description
Continue (F5)	Resumes the program and continues to run it normally, without pausing until another breakpoint is reached.
Run to Cursor	Allows you to run all the code up to a specific line (where your cursor is currently positioned). You can use this technique to skip a time-consuming loop.
Set Next Statement	Allows you to change the path of execution of your program while debugging. This command causes your program to mark the current line (where your cursor is positioned) as the current line for execution. When you resume execution, this line will be executed, and the program will continue from that point. Although this technique is convenient for jumping over large loops and simulating certain conditions, it's easy to cause confusion and runtime errors by using it recklessly.
Show Next Statement	Brings you to the line of code where Visual Studio is currently halted. (This is line of code that will be executed next when you continue.) This line is marked by a yellow arrow. The Show Next Statement command is useful if you lose your place while editing.

You can switch your program into break mode at any point by clicking the Pause button in the toolbar or selecting Debug ➤ Break All. This might not stop your code where you expect, however, so you'll need to rummage around to get your bearings.

Advanced Breakpoints

Choose Debug ➤ Windows ➤ Breakpoints to see a window that lists all the breakpoints in your current project. The Breakpoints window provides a hit count, showing you the number of times a breakpoint has been encountered (see Figure 4-23). You can jump to the corresponding location in code by double-clicking a breakpoint. You can also use the Breakpoints window to disable a breakpoint without removing it. That allows you to keep a breakpoint to use in testing later, without leaving it active. Breakpoints are automatically saved with the Visual Studio project files, although they aren't used when you compile the application in release mode.

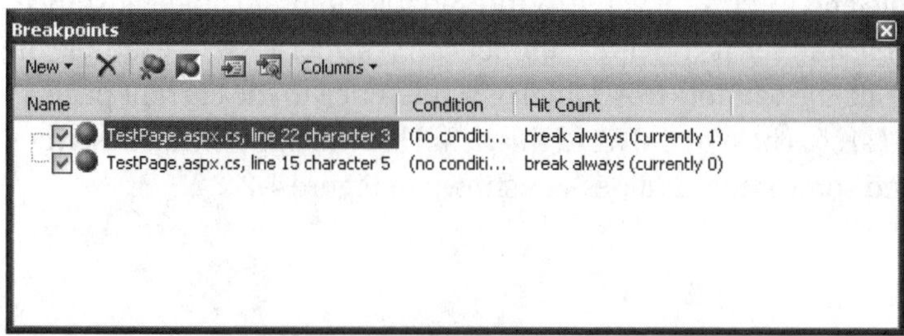

Figure 4-23. *The Breakpoints window*

Visual Studio allows you to customize breakpoints so that they occur only if certain conditions are true. To customize a breakpoint, right-click it, and select Breakpoint Properties. In the window that appears, you can take one of the following actions:

- Click the Condition button to set an expression. You can choose to break when this expression is true or when it has changed since the last time the breakpoint was hit.
- Click the Hit Count button to create a breakpoint that pauses only after a breakpoint has been hit a certain number of times (for example, at least twenty) or a specific multiple of times (for example, every fifth time).

Variable Watches

In some cases, you might want to track the status of a variable without switching into break mode repeatedly. In this case, it's more useful to use the Autos, Locals, and Watch windows, which allow you to track variables across an entire application. Table 4-3 describes these windows.

Table 4-3. *Variable Watch Windows*

Window	Description
Autos	Automatically displays variables that Visual Studio determines are important for the current code statement. For example, this might include variables that are accessed or changed in the previous line.
Locals	Automatically displays all the variables that are in scope in the current procedure. This offers a quick summary of important variables.
Watch	Displays variables you have added. Watches are saved with your project, so you can continue tracking a variable later. To add a watch, right-click a variable in your code, and select Add Watch; alternatively, double-click the last row in the Watch window, and type in the variable name.

Each row in the Autos, Locals, and Watch windows provides information about the type or class of the variable and its current value. If the variable holds an object instance, you can expand the variable and see its private members and properties. For example, in the Locals window you'll see the variable this, which is a reference to the current page class. If you click the plus (+) sign next to the word this, a full list will appear that describes many page properties (and some system values), as shown in Figure 4-24.

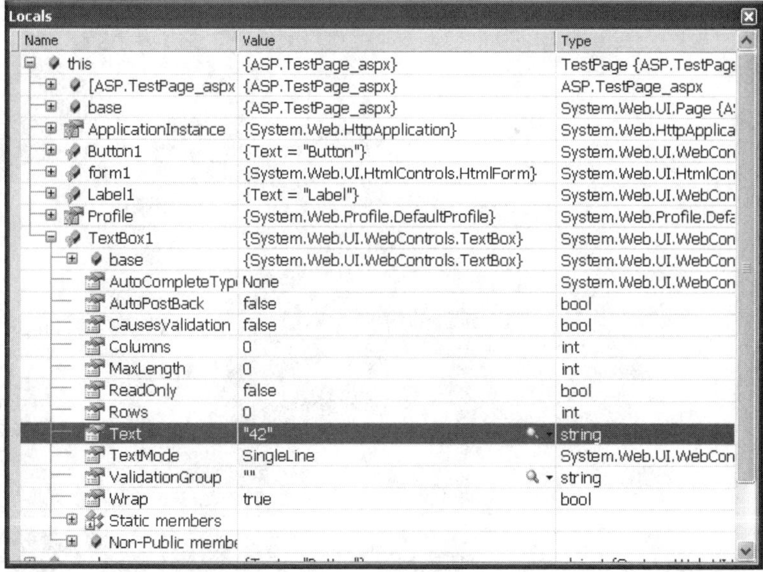

Figure 4-24. *Viewing the current page class in the Locals window*

If you are missing one of the Watch windows, you can show it manually by selecting it from the Debug ➤ Windows submenu.

■ **Tip** The Autos, Locals, and Watch windows allow you to change simple variables while your program is in break mode. Just double-click the current value in the Value column, and type in a new value. This allows you to simulate scenarios that are difficult or time-consuming to re-create manually and allows you to test specific error conditions.

The Last Word

In this chapter, you took a quick look at Visual Studio 2005. If you've programmed with earlier versions of Visual Studio, you'll appreciate the new cleaner project model, which refrains from generating extra files you won't want to manage. You'll also appreciate the new built-in web server, which makes debugging a website painless on any computer.

In the next chapter, you'll start building simple web applications with Visual Studio.

PART 2

Developing ASP.NET Applications

CHAPTER 5

Web Form Fundamentals

ASP.NET introduces a remarkable new model for creating web pages. In old-style ASP development, programmers had to master the quirks and details of HTML markup before being able to design dynamic web pages. Pages had to be carefully tailored to a specific task, and additional content could be generated only by outputting raw HTML tags.

In ASP.NET, you can use a higher-level model of server-side web controls. These controls are created and configured as objects and automatically provide their own HTML output. Even better, ASP.NET allows web controls to behave like their Windows counterparts by maintaining state and even raising events that you can react to in code.

In this chapter, you'll learn some of the core topics that every ASP.NET developer must master. You'll learn what makes up an ASP.NET application and what types of files it can include. You'll also learn how server controls work and how you can use them to build dynamic web pages.

The Anatomy of an ASP.NET Application

It's sometimes difficult to define exactly what a web application is. Unlike a traditional desktop program (which users start by running a stand-alone EXE file), ASP.NET applications are almost always divided into multiple web pages. This division means a user can enter an ASP.NET application at several different points or follow a link from the application to another part of the website or another web server. So, does it make sense to consider a website as an application?

In ASP.NET, the answer is yes. Every ASP.NET application shares a common set of resources and configuration settings. Web pages from other ASP.NET applications don't share these resources, even if they're on the same web server. Technically speaking, every ASP.NET application is executed inside a separate *application domain*. Application domains are isolated areas in memory, and they ensure that even if one web application causes a fatal error, it's unlikely to affect any other application that is currently running on the same computer. Similarly, application domains restrict a web page in one application from accessing the in-memory information of another application. Each web application is maintained separately and has its own set of cached, application, and session data.

The standard definition of an ASP.NET application describes it as a combination of files, pages, handlers, modules, and executable code that can be invoked from a virtual directory (and, optionally, its subdirectories) on a web server. In other words, the virtual directory is the basic grouping structure that delimits an application. Figure 5-1 shows a web server that hosts four separate web applications.

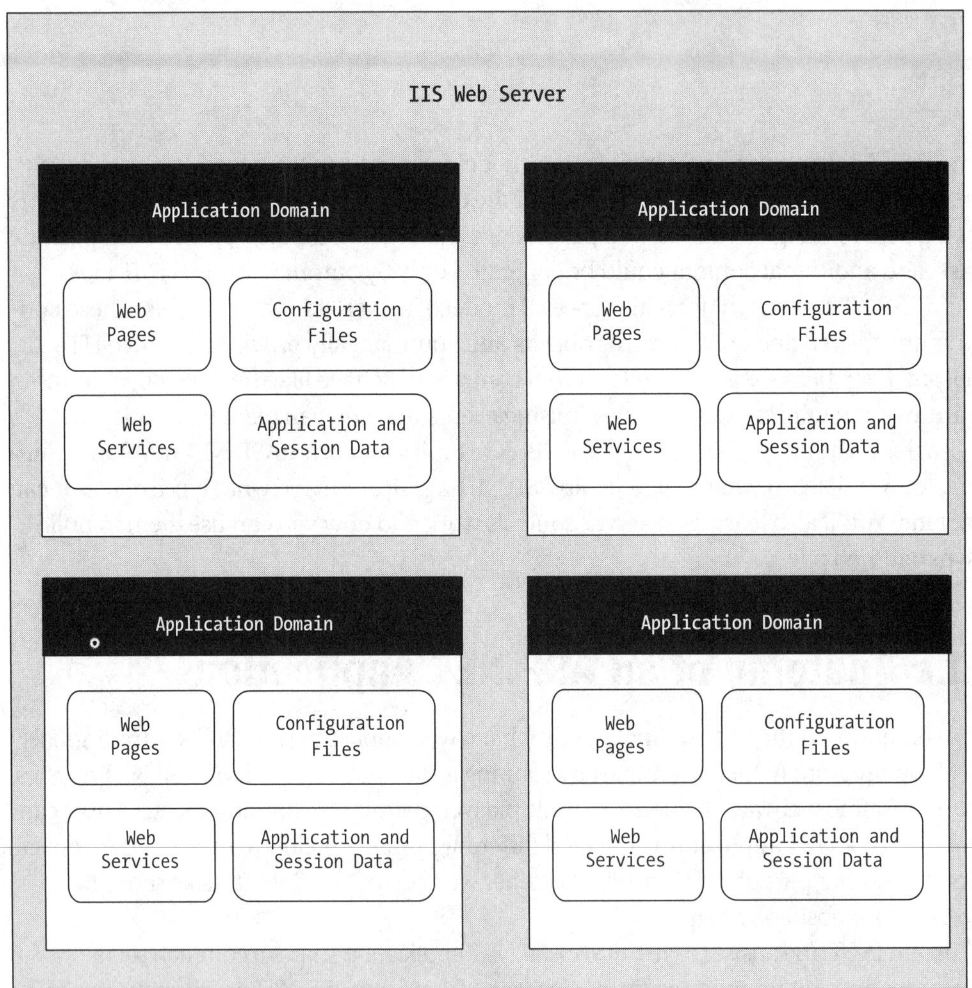

Figure 5-1. *ASP.NET applications*

ASP.NET File Types

ASP.NET applications can include many types of files. Table 5-1 introduces the essential ingredients.

Table 5-1. *ASP.NET File Types*

File Name	Description
Ends with .aspx	These are ASP.NET web pages (the .NET equivalent of the .asp file in an ASP application). They contain the user interface and, optionally, the underlying application code. Users request or navigate directly to one of these pages to start your web application.
Ends with .ascx	These are ASP.NET user controls. User controls are similar to web pages, except that they can't be accessed directly. Instead, they must be hosted inside an ASP.NET web page. User controls allow you to develop a small piece of user interface and reuse it in as many web forms as you want without repetitive code. You'll learn about user controls in Chapter 25.
Ends with .asmx	These are ASP.NET web services, which are described in Part 5 of this book. Web services work differently than web pages, but they still share the same application resources, configuration settings, and memory.
web.config	This is the XML-based configuration file for your ASP.NET application. It includes settings for customizing security, state management, memory management, and much more. This file is referred to throughout the book.
global.asax	This is the global application file. You can use this file to define global variables (variables that can be accessed from any web page in the web application) and react to global events (such as when a web application first starts).
Ends with .cs	These are code-behind files that contain C# code. They allow you to separate the Application logic from the user interface of a web page. We'll introduce the code-behind model in this chapter and use it extensively in this book.

In addition, your web application can contain other resources that aren't special ASP.NET files. For example, your virtual directory can hold image files, HTML files, or CSS files. These resources might be used in one of your ASP.NET web pages, or they might be used independently. A website could even combine static HTML pages with dynamic ASP.NET pages.

Most of the file types in Table 5-1 are optional. You can create a legitimate ASP.NET application with a single web page (.aspx file) or web service (.asmx file).

WHAT ABOUT ASP FILES?

ASP.NET doesn't use any of the same files as ASP (such as .asp pages and the global.asa file). If you have a virtual directory that contains both .aspx and .asp files, you really have two applications: an ASP.NET web application and a legacy ASP application.

In fact, the process that manages and renders .asp files and the ASP.NET service that compiles and serves .aspx files are two separate programs that don't share any information. This design has a couple of important implications:

- You can't share state information between ASP and ASP.NET applications. The Session and Application collections, for example, are completely separate.
- You specify ASP and ASP.NET configuration settings in different ways. If you specify an ASP setting, it won't apply to ASP.NET, and vice versa.

Generally, you should keep ASP and ASP.NET files in separate virtual directories to avoid confusion. However, if you're migrating a large website, you can safely use both types of files as long as they don't try to share resources.

ASP.NET Application Directories

Every web application should have a well-planned directory structure. For example, you'll probably want to store images in a separate folder from where you store your web pages. Or, you might want to put public ASP.NET pages in one folder and restricted ones in another so you can apply different security settings based on the directory. (See Chapter 18 for more about how to create authorization rules like this.)

Along with the directories you create, ASP.NET also uses a few specialized subdirectories, which it recognizes by name (see Table 5-2). Keep in mind that you won't see all these directories in a typical application. Visual Studio will prompt you to create them as needed.

Table 5-2. *ASP.NET Directories*

Directory	Description
Bin	Contains all the compiled .NET components (DLLs) that the ASP.NET web application uses. For example, if you develop a custom database component (see Chapter 24), you'll place the component here. ASP.NET will automatically detect the assembly, and any page in the web application will be able to use it. This seamless deployment model is far easier than working with traditional COM components, which must be registered before they can be used (and often reregistered when they change).

Directory	Description
App_Code	Contains source code files that are dynamically compiled for use in your application. You can use this directory in a similar way to the Bin directory; the only difference is that you place source code files here instead of compiled assemblies.
App_GlobalResources	This directory stores global resources that are accessible to every page in the web application. This directory is used in localization scenarios, when you need to have a website in more than one language. Localization isn't covered in this book, although you can refer to *Pro ASP.NET 2.0 in C#* (Apress, 2005) for more information.
App_LocalResources	This directory serves the same purpose as App_GlobalResources, except these resources are accessible to a specific page only.
App_WebReferences	Stores references to web services that the web application uses. You'll learn about web services in Part 5.
App_Data	This directory is reserved for data storage, including SQL Server 2005 Express Edition database files and XML files. Of course, you're free to store data files in other directories.
App_Browsers	This directory contains browser definitions stored in XML files. These XML files define the capabilities of client-side browsers for different rendering actions. Although ASP.NET defines different browsers and their capabilities in a computerwide configuration file, this directory allows you to distinguish browsers according to different rules for a single application.
App_Themes	Stores the themes that are used by your web application. You'll learn about themes in Chapter 10.

Application Updates

One of the most useful features of ASP.NET has nothing to do with new controls or enhanced functionality. Instead, the so-called zero-touch deployment and application updating means you can modify your ASP.NET application easily and painlessly without needing to restart the server.

Page Updates

If you modify a code file or a web form, ASP.NET automatically recompiles an updated version for the next client request. This means new client requests always use the most recent version of the page. ASP.NET even compiles the page automatically to native machine code and caches it to improve performance.

Component Updates

You can replace any assembly in the Bin directory with a new version, even if it's currently in use. The file will never be locked (except for a brief moment when the application first starts). As a result, you can also add or delete assembly files without any problem. ASP.NET continuously monitors the Bin directory for changes. When a change is detected, it creates a new application domain and uses it to handle any new requests. Existing requests are completed using the old application domain, which contains a cached copy of all the old versions of the components. When all the existing requests are completed, the old application domain is removed from memory.

This automatic rollover feature, sometimes called *shadow copy*, allows you to painlessly update a website without taking it offline, even if it uses separate components.

Configuration Changes

In the somewhat painful early days of ASP programming, configuring a web application was no easy task. You needed to either create a script that modified the IIS metabase or use IIS Manager. Once a change was made, you would often need to stop and start the IIS web service (again by using IIS Manager or the iisreset utility). Sometimes you would even need to reboot the server before the modification would take effect.

Fortunately, these administrative headaches are no longer required for ASP.NET, which manages its own configuration independently from IIS. The configuration of an ASP.NET web application is defined using the web.config file. The web.config file stores information in a plain-text XML format so that you can easily edit it with a tool such as Notepad. If you change a web.config setting, ASP.NET uses the same automatic rollover as it does when you update a component. Existing requests complete with the original settings and new requests are served by a new application domain that uses the new web.config settings. Once again, modifying live sites is surprisingly easy in ASP.NET. You'll learn more about ASP.NET configuration and the web.config file later in the "ASP.NET Configuration" section.

A Simple One-Page Applet

The first example you'll see demonstrates how server-based controls work using a single-page applet. This type of program, which combines user input and the program output on the same page, is used to provide popular tools on many sites. Some examples include calculators for mortgages, taxes, health or weight indices, and retirement savings plans; single-phrase translators; and stock-tracking utilities.

The page shown in Figure 5-2 allows the user to convert a number of U.S. dollars to the equivalent amount of euros.

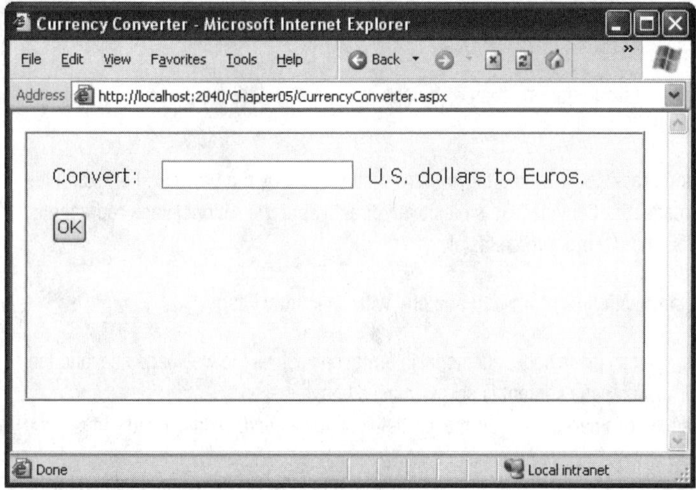

Figure 5-2. *A simple currency converter*

The following listing shows the HTML for this page. To make it as clear as possible, we've omitted the style attribute of the <div> tag used for the border. This page has two <input> tags: one for the text box and one for the submit button. These elements are enclosed in a <form> tag, so they can submit information to the server when the button is clicked. The rest of the page consists of static text:

```
<html>
  <head>
    <title>Currency Converter</title>
  </head>
  <body>
    <form method="post">
      <div>
        Convert:  
        <input type="text">  U.S. dollars to Euros.
        <br /><br />
        <input type="submit" value="OK">
      </div>
    </form>
  </body>
</html>
```

As it stands, this page looks nice but provides no functionality. It consists entirely of the user interface (HTML tags) and contains no code.

THE LEAST YOU NEED TO KNOW ABOUT HTML

If your HTML is a little rusty, a few details in the previous web page might look a little perplexing. To help understand it, review the basic rules of HTML:

- Anything enclosed in angled brackets (< >) is a tag, which is interpreted by the browser. For example, in the currency converter page, the Convert text is displayed directly, but the <input> tags represents something else—a text box and a button, respectively.
- HTML documents always start with an <html> tag and end with an </html> tag.
- Inside the HTML document, you can place code, additional information such as the web page title, and the actual web page content. The web page content is always placed between <body> and </body> tags. The web page title is part of the information between the <head> and </head> tags.
- Controls, the graphical widgets that users can click and type into, must always be placed inside a form. Otherwise, you won't be able to access the information the user enters. In ASP.NET, every control needs to go inside the <form> tag.
- The <div> tag, on its own, doesn't do anything. However, it's useful to use a <div> tag to group portions of your page that you want to format in a similar way (for example, with the same font, background color, or border). That way, you can apply style settings to the <div> tag, and they'll cascade down into every tag it contains. (The <div> formatting isn't shown in this example, because it's too long. However, you can check out the online currency converter example to see the full list of style settings.)
- Whitespace is ignored in HTML. This means spaces, line breaks, and so on, are collapsed. If you need to explicitly insert additional spaces, you can use the character entity   (which stands for nonbreaking space). To insert line breaks, you can use the break tag: <br />.

Technically, you don't need to understand HTML to program ASP.NET web pages—although having some basic HTML knowledge certainly helps you get up to speed. For a quick primer, you can refer to one of the excellent HTML tutorials on the Internet, such as `http://www.w3schools.com/html` or `http://archive.ncsa.uiuc.edu/General/Internet/WWW/HTMLPrimer.html`.

The ASP Solution—and Its Problems

In many older web programming platforms, you'd add the currency conversion functionality to this page by examining the posted form values and manually writing the result to the end of the page. In classic ASP, you'd write this dynamic information using the Response.Write() command.

This approach works well for a simple page, but it encounters the following difficulties as the program becomes more sophisticated:

"Spaghetti" code: You need to generate the page output in the order it appears, which often isn't the natural order in your code. If you want to tailor different parts of the output based on a single condition, you'll need to reevaluate that condition at several places in your code.

Lack of flexibility: Once you've perfected your output, it's difficult to change it. If you decide to modify the page several months later, you have to read through the code, follow the logic, and try to sort out numerous details.

Combining content and formatting: Depending on the complexity of your user interface, you may need to add HTML tags and style attributes on the fly. This encourages programs to tangle formatting and content details together, making it difficult to change just one or the other at a later date.

Complexity: Your code becomes increasingly intricate and disorganized as you add different types of functionality. For example, it could be extremely difficult to track the effects of different conditions and different rendering blocks if you created a combined tax/mortgage/interest calculator. Before you know it, you'll be forced to write the application using separate web pages.

Quite simply, an old-style ASP application that needs to create a sizable portion of interface using Response.Write() commands encounters the same dilemmas that a Windows program would find if it needed to manually draw its text boxes and command buttons on an application window in response to every user action.

The ASP.NET Solution: Server Controls

In ASP.NET, you can still use Response.Write() to create a dynamic web page. But ASP.NET provides a better approach. It allows you to turn static HTML tags into objects—called *server controls*—that you can program on the server.

ASP.NET provides two sets of server controls:

HTML server controls: These are server-based equivalents for standard HTML elements. These controls are ideal if you're a seasoned web programmer who prefers to work with familiar HTML tags (at least at first). They are also useful when migrating existing ASP pages to ASP.NET, because they require the fewest changes. You'll learn about HTML server controls throughout this chapter.

Web controls: These are similar to the HTML server controls, but they provide a richer object model with a variety of properties for style and formatting details. They also provide more events and more closely resemble the controls used for Windows development. Web controls also feature some user interface elements that have no direct HTML equivalent, such as the GridView, Calendar, and validation controls. You'll learn about web controls in the next chapter.

HTML Server Controls

HTML server controls provide an object interface for standard HTML elements. They provide three key features:

They generate their own interface: You set properties in code, and the underlying HTML tag is updated automatically when the page is rendered and sent to the client.

They retain their state: Because the Web is stateless, ordinary web pages need to go to a lot of work to store information between requests. For example, every time the user clicks a button on a page, you need to make sure every control on that page is refreshed so that it has the same information the user saw last time. With ASP.NET, this tedious task is taken care of for you. That means you can write your program the same way you would write a traditional Windows program.

They fire events: Your code can respond to these events, just like ordinary controls in a Windows application. In ASP code, everything is grouped into one block that executes from start to finish. With event-based programming, you can easily respond to individual user actions and create more structured code. If a given event doesn't occur, the event handler code won't be executed.

The easiest way to convert the currency converter to ASP.NET is to start by generating a new web form in Visual Studio. To do this, select Website ➤ Add New Item. In the Add New Item dialog box, choose Web Form (the first item in the list), type a name for the new page (such as CurrencyConverter.aspx), and click OK to create the page. Finally, copy all the content from the original HTML page into the new ASP.NET web form.

When you paste your HTML content, this should overwrite everything that's currently in the page, except the *page directive*. The page directive gives ASP.NET basic information about how to compile the page. It indicates the language you're using for your code and the way you connect your event handlers. If you're using the code-behind approach, which is recommended, the page directive also indicates where the code file is located and the name of your custom page class.

Here's the web form, with the page directive (in bold) followed by the HTML content that's copied from the original page:

```
<%@ Page Language="C#" AutoEventWireup="true"
    CodeFile="CurrencyConverter.aspx.cs" Inherits="CurrencyConverter" %>
<html>
  <head>
    <title>Currency Converter</title>
  </head>
  <body>
    <form method="post">
      <div>
        Convert:  
        <input type="text">  U.S. dollars to Euros.
        <br /><br />
        <input type="submit" value="OK">
      </div>
    </form>
  </body>
</html>
```

Now you need to add the attribute runat="server" to each tag that you want to transform into a server control. You should also add an id attribute to each control that you need to interact with in code. The id attribute assigns the unique name that you'll use to refer to the control in code.

■ **Tip** The quickest way to add the runat="server" attribute is to use Visual Studio. First, add your HTML page to a website. Then, select each HTML tag separately on the design surface of the page. Right-click, and choose Run As Server Control from the menu to transform it into a server control.

In the currency converter application, you can change the input text box and submit button into server controls. In addition, the <form> element must also be processed as a server control to allow ASP.NET to access the controls it contains, as shown here:

```
<%@ Page Language="C#" AutoEventWireup="true"
    CodeFile="CurrencyConverter.aspx.cs" Inherits="CurrencyConverter" %>
<html>
  <head>
    <title>Currency Converter</title>
  </head>
  <body>
    <form method="post" runat="server">
      <div>
        Convert:  
        <input type="text" id="US" runat="server">
          U.S. dollars to Euros.
        <br /><br />
        <input type="submit" value="OK" id="Convert" runat="server">
      </div>
    </form>
  </body>
</html>
```

Note ASP.NET controls are always placed inside the <form> tag of the page. The <form> tag is a part of the standard for HTML forms, and it allows the browser to send information to the web server.

The web page still won't do anything when you run it, because you haven't written any code. However, now that you've converted the static HTML elements to HTML server controls, you're ready to work with them.

View State

To try this page, launch it in Visual Studio. Then, select View ➤ Source in your browser to look at the HTML that ASP.NET sent your way.

The first thing you'll notice is that the HTML that was sent to the browser is slightly different from the information in the .aspx file. First, the runat="server" attributes are stripped out (because they have no meaning to the client browser, which can't interpret them). Second, and more important, an additional hidden field has been added to the form, as shown here:

```
<html>
  <head>
    <title>Currency Converter</title>
  </head>
  <body>
    <form method="post">
      <input type="hidden" name="__VIEWSTATE" value="dDw3NDg2NTI5MDg7Oz4=" />
      <div>
        Convert:  
        <input type="text" id="US">  U.S. dollars to Euros.
        <br /><br />
        <input type="submit" value="OK" id="Convert">
      </div>
    </form>
  </body>
</html>
```

This hidden field stores information, in a compressed format, about the state of every control in the page. It allows you to manipulate control properties in code and have the changes automatically persisted. This is a key part of the web forms programming model. Thanks to view state, you can often forget about the stateless nature of the Internet and treat your page like a continuously running application.

Even though the currency converter program doesn't yet include any code, you'll already notice one change. If you enter information in the text box and click the submit button to post the page, the refreshed page will still contain the value you entered in the text box. (In the original example that uses ordinary HTML elements, the value will be cleared every time the page is posted back.) This change occurs because ASP.NET controls automatically retain state.

The HTML Control Classes

Before you can continue any further with the currency converter, you need to know about the control objects you've created. All the HTML server controls are defined in the System.Web.UI.HtmlControls namespace. Each kind of control has a separate class. Table 5-3 describes the basic HTML server controls and shows you the related HTML element.

Table 5-3. *The HTML Server Control Classes*

Class Name	HTML Tag Represented	Description
HtmlAnchor	<a>	A hyperlink that the user clicks to jump to another page.
HtmlButton	<button>	A button that the user clicks to perform an action. This is not supported by all browsers, so HtmlInputButton is usually used instead. The key difference is that the HtmlButton is a container element. As a result, you can insert just about anything inside it, including text and pictures. The HtmlInputButton, on the other hand, is strictly text-only.
HtmlForm	<form>	The form wraps all the controls on a web page. Controls that appear inside a form will send their data to the server when the page is submitted.
HtmlImage	<img>	A link that points to an image, which will be inserted into the web page at the current location.
HtmlInputButton, HtmlInputSubmit, and HtmlInputReset	<input type="button">, <input type="submit">, and <input type="reset">	A button that the user clicks to perform an action (often it's used to submit all the input values on the page to the server).
HtmlInputCheckBox	<input type="checkbox">	A check box that the user can check or clear. Doesn't include any text of its own.
HtmlInputFile	<input type="file">	A Browse button and text box that can be used to upload a file to your web server, as described in Chapter 16.
HtmlInputHidden	<input type="hidden">	Contains text-based information that will be sent to the server when the page is posted back but won't be visible to the user.
HtmlInputImage	<input type="image">	Similar to the <img> tag, but it inserts a "clickable" image that submits the page.
HtmlInputRadioButton	<input type="radio">	A radio button that can be selected in a group. Doesn't include any text of its own.
HtmlInputText and HtmlInputPassword	<input type="text"> and <input type="password">	A single-line text box where the user can enter information. Can also be displayed as a password field (which displays asterisks instead of characters to hide the user input).
HtmlSelect	<select>	A drop-down or regular list box, where the user can select an item.
HtmlTable, HtmlTableRow, and HtmlTableCell	<table>, <tr>, <th>, and <td>	A table that displays multiple rows and columns of static text.

Class Name	HTML Tag Represented	Description
HtmlTextArea	<textarea>	A large text box where the user can type multiple lines of text.
HtmlGenericControl	Any other HTML element.	This control can represent a variety of HTML elements that don't have dedicated control classes.
HtmlHead and HtmlTitle	<head> and <title>	Represents the header information for the page. You can use this to dynamically change the title or connect style sheets (as explained in Chapter 10).

So far, the currency converter defines three controls, which are instances of the Html-Form, HtmlInputText, and HtmlInputButton classes, respectively. It's important that you know the class names, because you need to define each control class in the code-behind file if you want to interact with it. (Visual Studio simplifies this task: whenever you add a control using its web designer, the appropriate tag is added to the .aspx file, and the appropriate variables are defined in the code-behind class.) Table 5-4 gives a quick over-view of some of the most important control properties.

Table 5-4. *Important HTML Control Properties*

Control	Most Important Properties
HtmlAnchor	Href, Target, Title
HtmlImage and HtmlInputImage	Src, Alt, Width, and Height
HtmlInputCheckBox and HtmlInputRadioButton	Checked
HtmlInputText	Value
HtmlSelect	Items (collection)
HtmlTextArea	Value
HtmlGenericControl	InnerText

To actually add some functionality to the currency converter, you need to add some ASP.NET code. Web forms are event-driven, which means every piece of code acts in response to a specific event. In the simple currency converter page example, the most useful event occurs when the user clicks the submit button (named Convert). The HtmlInputButton allows you to react to this action by handling the ServerClick event.

Before you continue, it makes sense to add another control that can display the result of the calculation. In this case, you can use a <div> tag named Result. The <div> tag is one way to insert a block of formatted text into a web page. Here's the line of HTML that you'll need:

```
<div style="font-weight: bold" id="Result" runat="server">
```

The style attribute applies the CSS properties used to format the text. In this example, it merely applies a bold font.

The example now has the following four server controls:

- A form (HtmlForm object). This is the only control you do not need to access in your code-behind class.
- An input text box named US (HtmlInputText object).
- A submit button named Convert (HtmlInputButton object).
- A <div> tag named Result (HtmlGenericControl object).

Listing 5-1 shows the revised web page (CurrencyConverter.aspx), and Listing 5-2 shows the code-behind class (CurrencyConverter.aspx.cs), which calculates the currency conversion and displays the result.

Listing 5-1. *CurrencyConverter.aspx*

```
<%@ Page Language="C#" AutoEventWireup="true"
    CodeFile="CurrencyConverter.aspx.cs" Inherits="CurrencyConverter" %>
<html>
  <head>
    <title>Currency Converter</title>
  </head>
  <body>
    <form method="post" runat="server">
      <div>
        Convert:  
        <input type="text" id="US" runat="server">  U.S. dollars to Euros.
        <br /><br />
        <input type="submit" value="OK" id="Convert" runat="server"
         OnServerClick="Convert_ServerClick">
        <br /><br />
        <div style="font-weight: bold" id="Result" runat="server"></div>
      </div>
    </form>
  </body>
</html>
```

Listing 5-2. *CurrencyConverter.aspx.cs*

```
using System;
using System.Web;
using System.Web.UI;
using System.Web.UI.WebControls;
using System.Web.UI.HtmlControls;

public partial class CurrencyConverter : System.Web.UI.Page
{
    protected void Convert_ServerClick(Object sender, EventArgs e)
    {
        decimal USAmount = decimal.Parse(US.Value);
        decimal euroAmount = USAmount * 0.85M;
        Result.InnerText = USAmount.ToString() + " U.S. dollars = ";
        Result.InnerText += euroAmount.ToString() + " Euros.";
    }
}
```

The code-behind class is a typical example of an ASP.NET page. You'll notice the following conventions:

- It starts with several using statements. This provides access to all the important namespaces. This is a typical first step in any code-behind file.

- The page class is defined with the partial keyword. That's because your class code is merged with another code file that you never see. This extra code, which ASP.NET generates automatically, defines all the server controls that are used on the page. This allows you to access them by name in your code.

- The page defines a single event handler. This event handler retrieves the value from the text box, multiplies it by a preset conversion ratio (which would typically be stored in another file or a database), and sets the text of the <div> tag. You'll notice that the event handler accepts two parameters (sender and e). This is the .NET standard for all control events. It allows your code to identify the control that sent the event (through the sender parameter) and retrieve any other information that may be associated with the event (through the e parameter). You'll see examples of these advanced techniques in the next chapter, but for now, it's important to realize that you won't be allowed to handle an event unless your event handler has the correct, matching signature.

- The event handler is connected to the control event using the OnServerClick attribute in the <input> tag for the button. You'll learn more about how this hookup works in the next section.
- The event handler uses ToString() to convert the decimal value to text. Remember, C# is notoriously strict about data type conversions. Before you can display your information in the page, you need to convert the decimal value to a string so that it can be added to the InnerText property.

You can launch this page to test your code. When you enter a value and click the OK button, the page is resubmitted, the event handling code runs, and the page is returned to you with the conversion details (see Figure 5-3).

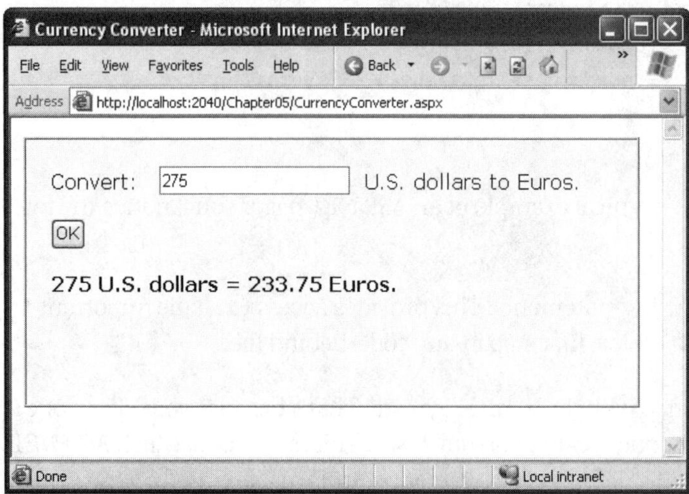

Figure 5-3. *The ASP.NET currency converter*

Event Handling

This example works using a technique called *automatic event wireup.* To use this approach, you use an attribute in the control tag to connect your event handler.

For example, if you want to handle the ServerClick method of the Convert button, you simply need to set the OnServerClick attribute in the control tag with the name of the event handler you want to use:

```
<input type="submit" value="OK" id="Convert"
 OnServerClick="Convert_ServerClick" runat="server">
```

ASP.NET controls always use this syntax and give the attribute the event name preceded by the word On. For example, if you want to handle an event named ServerChange, you'd set an attribute in the control tag named OnServerChange. You don't need to connect a small set of page events through a control tag, such as Page.Load event. Everything else is hooked up using the control tag. When you double-click a control in Visual Studio, this change takes place automatically, so you never need to hook up your event handlers manually.

ASP.NET allows you to use another technique, called *manual event wireup*, which was used in previous versions of Visual Studio .NET. With manual event wireup, every event handler is connected with code that uses delegates, just as you saw in Chapter 3.

For example, here's the delegate code that's required to hook up the ServerClick event of the Convert button using manual event wireup:

```
Convert.ServerClick += new EventHandler(this.Convert_ServerClick);
```

Essentially, this code creates a new delegate using the EventHandler type and attaches it to the ServerClick event. The EventHandler delegate defines the signature that the ServerClick event handler must match. As you'll see later, some events pass additional information to your event handlers and have a different signature. In this case, you need to use a different delegate.

Seeing as Visual Studio handles event wireup, why should ASP.NET 2.0 developers care that they have two ways to hook up an event handler? Well, most of the time you won't worry about it. But the manual event wireup technique is useful in certain circumstances. The most common example is if you want to create a control object and add it to a page dynamically at runtime. In this situation, you can't hook up the event handler through the control tag, because there isn't a control tag. Instead, you need to create the control and attach its event handlers using code. (The next chapter has an example of how you can use dynamic control creation to fill in a table.)

Behind the Scenes with the CurrencyConverter

So, what really happens when ASP.NET receives a request for the CurrencyConverter.aspx page? The process actually unfolds over several steps:

1. First, the request for the page is sent to the web server. If you're running a live site, the web server is almost certainly IIS, which you'll learn more about in Chapter 12. If you're running the page in Visual Studio, the request is sent to the built-in test server.

2. The web server determines that the .aspx file extension is registered with ASP.NET and passes it to the ASP.NET worker process. If the file extension belonged to another service (as it would for .asp files), ASP.NET would never get involved.

3. If this is the first time a page in this application has been requested, ASP.NET automatically creates the application domain and a special application object (technically, an instance derived from the .NET class System.Web.HttpApplication).

4. ASP.NET considers the specific .aspx file. If it has never been executed, ASP.NET compiles and caches the page in the directory c:\[WinDir\Microsoft.NET\Framework\[Version]\Temporary ASP.NET Files, where [Version] is the version number of the .NET Framework. If this task has already been performed (for example, someone else has already requested this page) and the file hasn't been changed, ASP.NET will use the compiled version.

5. The compiled CurrencyConverter acts like a miniature program. It starts firing events (most notably, the Page.Load event). However, you haven't created an event handler for that event, so no code runs. At this stage, everything is working together as a set of in-memory .NET objects.

6. When the code is finished, ASP.NET asks every control in the web page to render itself into the corresponding HTML tags.

■ **Tip** In fact, ASP.NET performs a little sleight of hand and may customize the output with additional client-side JavaScript or DHTML if it detects that the client browser supports it. In the case of CurrencyConverter.aspx, the output of the page is too simple to require this type of automatic tweaking.

---

7. The final page is sent to the user, and the application ends.

The description is lengthy, but it's important to start with a good understanding of the fundamentals. When you click a button on the page, the entire process repeats itself. However, in step 5 the ServerClick event fires for HtmlInputButton right after the Page.Load event, and your code runs.

Figure 5-4 illustrates the stages in a web page request.

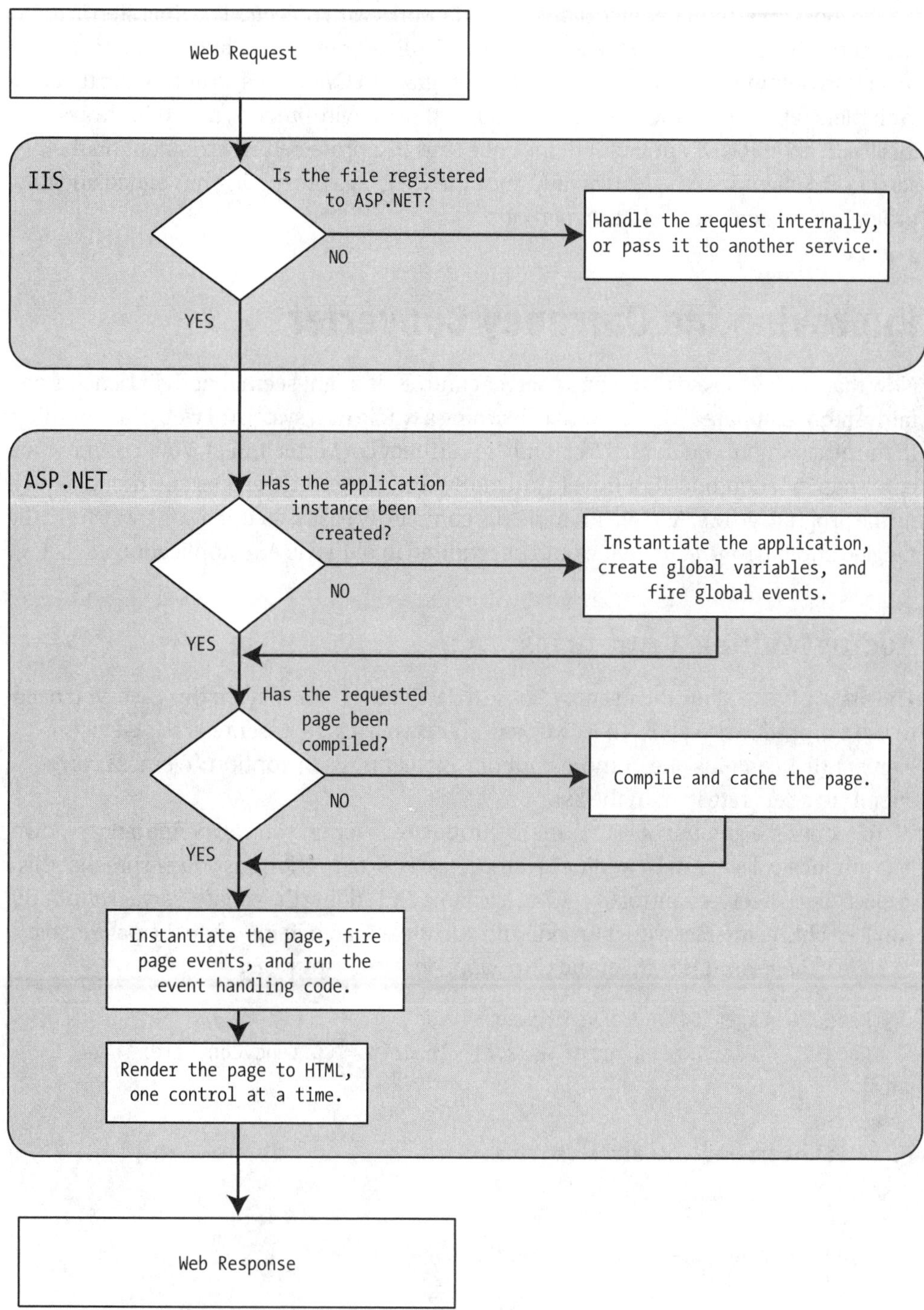

Figure 5-4. *The stages in an ASP.NET request*

The most important detail is that your code works with objects. The final step is to transform these objects into the appropriate HTML output. A similar conversion from objects to output happens with a Windows program in C#, but it's so automatic that programmers rarely give it much thought. Also, in those environments, the code always runs locally. In an ASP.NET application, the code runs in a protected environment on the server. The client sees the results only once the web page processing has ended and the program has been released from memory.

Improving the Currency Converter

Now that you've looked at the basic server controls, it might seem that their benefits are fairly minor compared with the cost of learning a whole new system of web programming. In the next section, you'll start to extend the currency converter applet. You'll see how you can "snap in" additional functionality to the existing program in an elegant, modular way. As the program grows, ASP.NET handles its complexity easily, steering you away from the tangled and intricate code that would be required in old-style ASP applications.

Adding Multiple Currencies

The first task is to allow the user to choose a destination currency. In this case, you need to use a drop-down list box. In HTML, a drop-down list is represented by a <select> element that contains one or more <option> elements. Each <option> element corresponds to a separate item in the list.

To reduce the amount of HTML in the currency converter, you can define a drop-down list without any list items by adding an empty <select> tag. As long as you ensure that this <select> tag is a server control (by giving it a name and adding the runat="server" attribute), you'll be able to interact with it in code and add the required items when the page loads.

Here's the revised HTML for the CurrencyConverter.aspx page:

```
<%@ Page Language="C#" AutoEventWireup="true"
    CodeFile="CurrencyConverter.aspx.cs" Inherits="CurrencyConverter" %>
<html>
  <head>
    <title>Currency Converter</title>
  </head>
  <body>
    <form method="post" runat="server">
      <div>
        Convert:  
        <input type="text" id="US" runat="server">  U.S. dollars to  
        <select id="Currency" runat="server"></select>
```

```
        <br /><br />
        <input type="submit" value="OK" id="Convert"
         OnServerClick="Convert_ServerClick" runat="server">
        <br /><br />
        <div style="font-weight: bold" id="Result" runat="server"></div>
      </div>
    </form>
  </body>
</html>
```

The currency list can now be filled using code at runtime. In this case, the ideal event is the Page.Load event, because this is the first event that occurs when the page is executed. Here's the code you need to add to the CurrencyConverter page class:

```
protected void Page_Load(Object sender, EventArgs e)
{
    if (this.IsPostBack == false)
    {
        Currency.Items.Add("Euro");
        Currency.Items.Add("Japanese Yen");
        Currency.Items.Add("Canadian Dollar");
    }
}
```

Dissecting the Code...

This example illustrates two important points:

- You can use the Items property to get items in a list control. This allows you to append, insert, and remove <option> elements. Remember, when generating dynamic content with a server control, you set the properties, and the control creates the appropriate HTML tags.
- Before adding any items to this list, you need to make sure this is the first time the page is being served. Otherwise, the page will continuously add more items to the list or inadvertently overwrite the user's selection every time the user interacts with the page. To perform this test, you check the this.IsPostBack property. The this keyword points to the current instance of the page class. In other words, IsPostback is a property of the CurrencyConverter class, which CurrencyConverter inherited from the generic Page class. If IsPostBack is false, the page is being created for the first time, and it's safe to initialize it.

Storing Information in the List

Of course, if you're a veteran HTML coder, you know that a select list also provides a value attribute that you can use to store additional information. Because the currency converter uses a short list of hard-coded values, this is an ideal place to store the conversion rate.

To set the value tag, you need to create a ListItem object and add that to the HtmlInputSelect control. The ListItem class provides a constructor that lets you specify the text and value at the same time that you create it, thereby allowing condensed code like this:

```
protected void Page_Load(Object sender, EventArgs e)
{
    if (this.IsPostBack == false)
    {
        // The HtmlInputSelect control accepts text or ListItem objects.
        Currency.Items.Add(new ListItem("Euros", "0.85"));
        Currency.Items.Add(new ListItem("Japanese Yen", "110.33"));
        Currency.Items.Add(new ListItem("Canadian Dollars", "1.2"));
    }
}
```

To complete the example, you must rewrite the calculation code to take the selected currency into account, as follows:

```
protected void Convert_ServerClick(object sender, EventArgs e)
{
    decimal amount = Decimal.Parse(US.Value);

    // Retrieve the select ListItem object by its index number.
    ListItem item = Currency.Items[Currency.SelectedIndex];

    decimal newAmount = amount * Decimal.Parse(item.Value);
    Result.InnerText = amount.ToString() + " U.S. dollars = ";
    Result.InnerText += newAmount.ToString() + " " + item.Text;
}
```

Figure 5-5 shows the revamped currency converter.

All in all, this is a good example of how you can store information in HTML tags using the value attribute. However, in a more sophisticated application, you probably wouldn't store the currency rate. Instead, you would just store some sort of unique identifying ID value. Then, when the user submits the page, you would retrieve the corresponding conversion rate from a database or some other storage location (such as an in-memory cache).

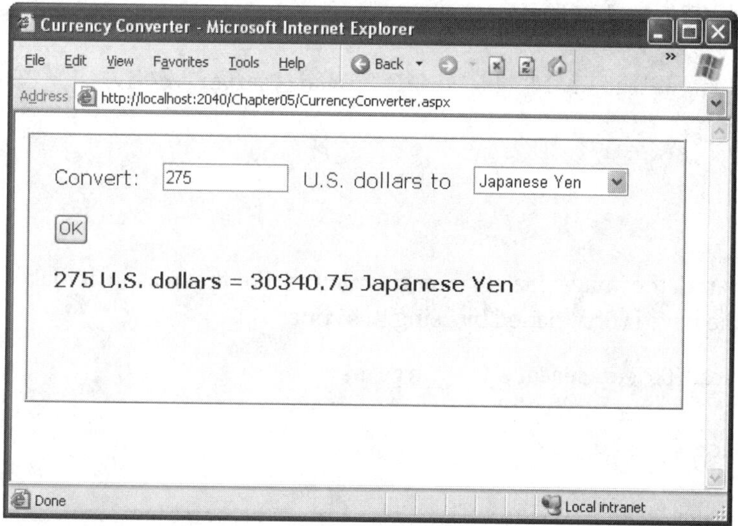

Figure 5-5. *The multicurrency converter*

Adding Linked Images

Adding other functionality to the currency converter is just as easy as adding a new button. For example, it might be useful for the utility to display a currency conversion rate graph. To provide this feature, the program would need an additional button and image control.

Here's the revised HTML:

```
<%@ Page Language="C#" AutoEventWireup="true"
    CodeFile="CurrencyConverter.aspx.cs" Inherits="CurrencyConverter" %>
<html>
  <head>
    <title>Currency Converter</title>
  </head>
  <body>
    <form method="post" runat="server">
      <div>
        Convert:  
        <input type="text" id="US" runat="server">  U.S. dollars to  
        <select id="Currency" runat="server"></select>
        <br /><br />
        <input type="submit" value="OK" id="Convert"
         OnServerClick="Convert_ServerClick" runat="server">
        <input type="submit" value="Show Graph" id="ShowGraph" runat="server">
        <br /><br />
```

```
            <img id="Graph" runat="server">
            <br /><br />
            <div style="font-weight: bold" id="Result" runat="server"></div>
        </div>
    </form>
  </body>
</html>
```

As it's currently declared, the image doesn't refer to a picture. For that reason, it makes sense to hide it when the page is first loaded by using this code:

```
protected void Page_Load(Object sender, EventArgs e)
{
    if (this.IsPostBack == false)
    {
        // The HtmlInputSelect control accepts text or ListItem objects.
        Currency.Items.Add(new ListItem("Euros", "0.85"));
        Currency.Items.Add(new ListItem("Japanese Yen", "122.33"));
        Currency.Items.Add(new ListItem("Canadian Dollars", "1.48"));
    }
    Graph.Visible = false;
}
```

Interestingly, when a server control is hidden, ASP.NET omits it from the final HTML page.

Now you can handle the click event of the new button to display the appropriate picture. The currency converter has three possible picture files—pic0.png, pic1.png, and pic2.png—depending on the selected currency:

```
protected void ShowGraph_ServerClick(Object sender, EventArgs e)
{
    Graph.Src = "Pic" + Currency.SelectedIndex.ToString() + ".png";
    Graph.Alt = "Currency Graph";
    Graph.Visible = true;
}
```

You need to make sure you link to the event handler through the button:

```
<input type="submit" value="Show Graph" id="ShowGraph"
 OnServerClick="ShowGraph_ServerClick" runat="server">
```

Already the currency converter is beginning to look more interesting, as shown in Figure 5-6.

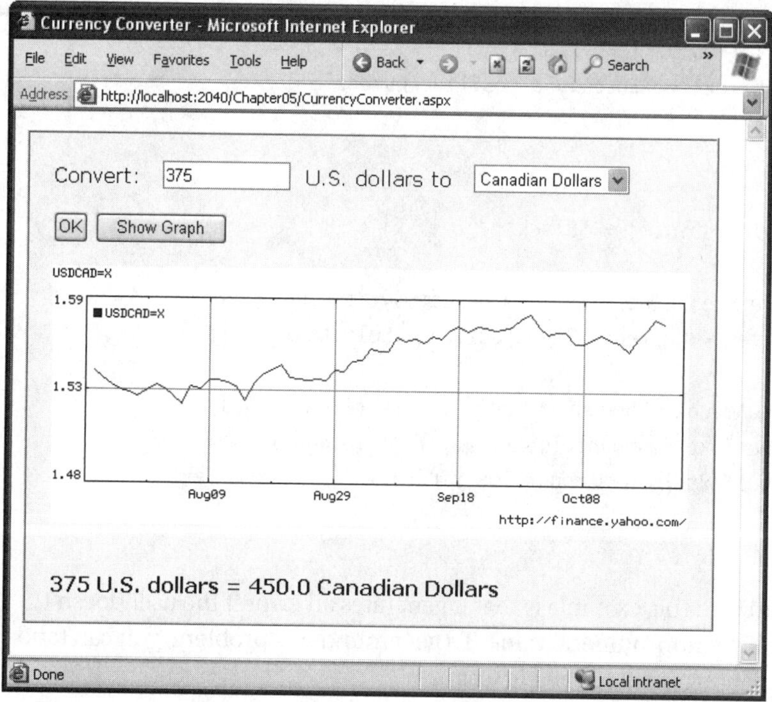

Figure 5-6. *The currency converter with an image control*

Setting Styles

In addition to a limited set of properties, each HTML control also provides access to the CSS style attributes through its Style collection. To use this collection, you need to specify the name of the CSS style attribute and the value you want to assign to it. Here's the basic syntax:

```
ControlName.Style["AttributeName"] = "AttributeValue";
```

For example, you could use this technique to emphasize an invalid entry in the currency converter with the color red. In this case, you'll also need to reset the color to its original value for valid input, because the control uses view state to remember all its settings, including its style properties:

```
protected void Convert_ServerClick(object sender, EventArgs e)
{
    decimal amount = Decimal.Parse(US.Value);

    if (amount <= 0)
```

```
    {
        Result.Style["color"] = "Red";
        Result.InnerText = "Specify a positive number";
    }
    else
    {
        Result.Style["color"] = "Black";

        // Retrieve the select ListItem object by its index number.
        ListItem item = Currency.Items[Currency.SelectedIndex];

        decimal newAmount = amount * Decimal.Parse(item.Value);
        Result.InnerText = amount.ToString() + " U.S. dollars = ";
        Result.InnerText += newAmount.ToString() + " " + item.Text;
    }
}
```

The only problem with this example is that it generates an error if the user doesn't cooperate and types in a non-numeric value. To get around this problem, you can (and should) use error handling, as described in Chapter 7.

■ **Tip** The Style collection sets the style attribute in the HTML tag with a list of formatting options such as font family, size, and color. But if you aren't familiar with CSS styles, you don't need to learn them now. Instead, you should use the web control equivalents, which provide higher-level properties that allow you to configure their appearance and automatically create the appropriate style attributes. You'll learn about web controls in the next chapter.

This concludes the simple currency converter applet, which now boasts automatic calculation, linked images, and dynamic formatting. In the following sections, you'll look at the building blocks of ASP.NET interfaces more closely.

A Deeper Look at HTML Control Classes

Related classes in the .NET Framework use inheritance to share functionality. For example, every HTML control inherits from the base class HtmlControl. The HtmlControl class provides essential features every HTML server control uses. Figure 5-7 shows the inheritance diagram.

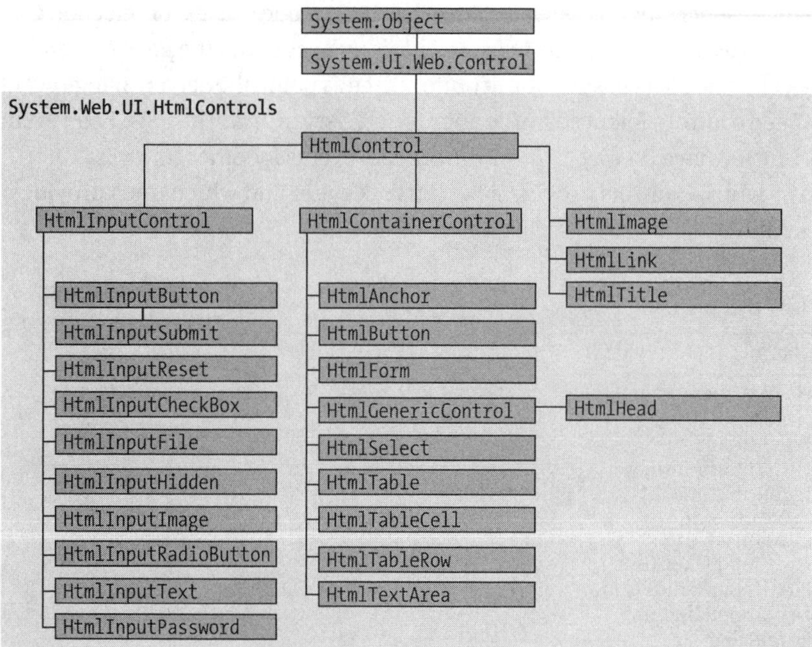

Figure 5-7. *HTML control inheritance*

The next few sections dissect the ASP.NET classes that are used for HTML server controls. You can use this material to help understand the common elements that are shared by all HTML controls. For the specific details about each HTML control, you can refer to the class library reference in the Visual Studio Help.

HTML server controls generally provide properties that closely match their tag attributes. For example, the HtmlImage class provides Align, Alt, Border, Src, Height, and Width properties. For this reason, users who are familiar with HTML syntax will find that HTML server controls are the most natural fit. Users who aren't as used to HTML will probably find that web controls (described in the next chapter) have a more intuitive set of properties.

HTML Control Events

HTML server controls also provide one of two possible events: ServerClick or ServerChange. The ServerClick is simply a click that is processed on the server side. It's provided by most button controls, and it allows your code to take immediate action. This action might override the expected behavior. For example, if you intercept the click event of a hyperlink control (the <a> element), the user won't be redirected to a new page unless you provide extra code to forward the request.

The ServerChange event responds when a change has been made to a text or selection control. This event isn't as useful as it appears because it doesn't occur until the page is posted back (for example, after the user clicks a submit button). At this point, the ServerChange event occurs for all changed controls, followed by the appropriate ServerClick. The Page.Load event is the first to fire, but you have no way to know the order of events for other controls.

Table 5-5 shows which controls provide a ServerClick event and which ones provide a ServerChange event.

Table 5-5. *HTML Control Events*

Event	Controls That Provide It
ServerClick	HtmlAnchor, HtmlInputReset, HtmlButton, HtmlInputButton, HtmlInputImage
ServerChange	HtmlInputText, HtmlInputCheckBox, HtmlInputRadioButton, HtmlInputHidden, HtmlSelect, HtmlTextArea

Advanced Events with the HtmlInputImage Control

Chapter 4 introduced the .NET event standard, which dictates that every event should pass exactly two pieces of information. The first parameter identifies the object (in this case, the control) that fired the event. The second parameter is a special object that can include additional information about the event.

In the examples you've looked at so far, the second parameter (e) has always been used to pass an empty System.EventArgs object. This object doesn't contain any additional information—it's just a glorified placeholder. Here's one such example:

```
protected void Convert_ServerClick(Object sender, EventArgs e)
{ ... }
```

In fact, only one HTML server control sends additional information: the HtmlInputImage control. It sends an ImageClickEventArgs object (from the System.Web.UI namespace) that provides X and Y properties representing the location where the image was clicked. You'll notice that the definition for the HtmlInputImage.ServerClick event handler is a little different from the event handlers used with other controls:

```
protected void ImgButton_ServerClick(Object sender, ImageClickEventArgs e)
{ ... }
```

Using this additional information, you can replace multiple button controls and image maps with a single, intelligent HtmlInputImage control. The sample ImageTest.aspx page shown in Figure 5-8 puts this feature to work with a simple graphical button. Depending on whether the user clicks the button border or the button surface, a different message is displayed.

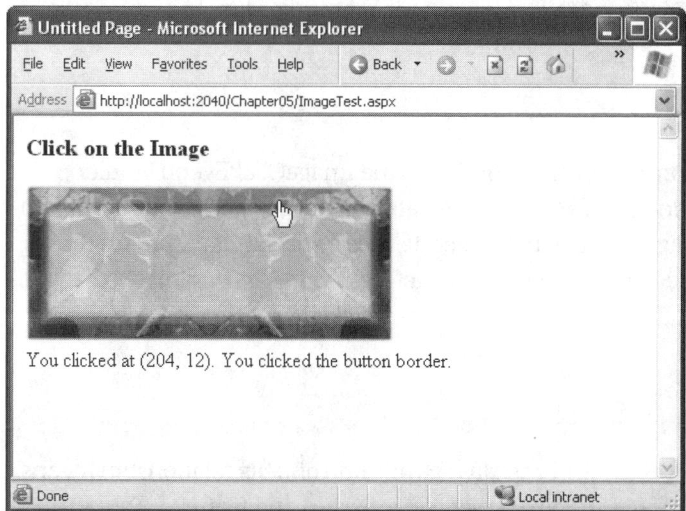

Figure 5-8. *Using an HtmlInputImage control*

The page code examines the click coordinates provided by the ImageClickEventArgs object and displays them in another control. Here's the page code you need:

```
using System;
using System.Web;
using System.Web.UI;
using System.Web.UI.WebControls;
using System.Web.UI.HtmlControls;

public partial class ImageTest : System.Web.UI.Page
{
    protected void ImgButton_ServerClick(Object sender,
      ImageClickEventArgs e)
    {
        Result.InnerText = "You clicked at (" + e.X.ToString() +
                           ", " + e.Y.ToString() + "). ";
```

```
        if ((e.Y < 100) && (e.Y > 20) && (e.X > 20) && (e.X < 275))
        {
            Result.InnerText += "You clicked on the button surface.";
        }
        else
        {
            Result.InnerText += "You clicked the button border.";
        }
    }
}
```

Note that the InitializeComponent() method uses the ImageClickEventHandler delegate instead of the generic EventHandler delegate when it connects your event handler. That's because the ImageClickEventHandler defines a special signature for the ImageClick event. This signature includes the ImageClickEventArgs parameter that contains the additional information about where the user clicked.

The HtmlControl Base Class

Every HTML control inherits from the base class HtmlControl. This relationship means that every HTML control will support a basic set of properties and features. Table 5-6 shows these properties.

Table 5-6. *HtmlControl Properties*

Property	Description
Attributes	Provides a collection of all the tag attributes and their values. Rather than setting an attribute directly, it's better to use the corresponding property. However, this collection is useful if you need to add or configure a custom attribute or an attribute that doesn't have a corresponding property.
Controls	Provides a collection of all the controls contained inside the current control. (For example, a <div> server control could contain an <input> server control.) Each object is provided as a generic System.Web.UI.Control object so that you may need to cast the reference to access control-specific properties.
Disabled	Set this to true to disable the control, thereby ensuring that the user cannot interact with it and its events will not be fired.
EnableViewState	Set this to false to disable the automatic state management for this control. In this case, the control will be reset to the properties and formatting specified in the control tag every time the page is posted back. If this is set to true (the default), the control uses a hidden input field to store information about its properties, thereby ensuring that any changes you make in code are remembered.

Property	Description
Page	Provides a reference to the web page that contains this control as a System.Web.UI.Page object.
Parent	Provides a reference to the control that contains this control. If the control is placed directly on the page (rather than inside another control), it will return a reference to the page object.
Style	Provides a collection of CSS style properties that can be used to format the control.
TagName	Indicates the name of the underlying HTML element (for example, img or div).
Visible	When set to false, the control will be hidden and will not be rendered to the final HTML page that is sent to the client.

The HtmlControl class also provides built-in support for data binding, which you'll examine in Chapter 14.

The HtmlContainerControl Class

Any HTML control that requires a closing tag also inherits from the HtmlContainer control. For example, elements such as <a>, <form>, and <div> always use a closing tag, because they can contain other HTML elements. On the other hand, <img> and <input> are used only as stand-alone tags. Thus, the HtmlAnchor, HtmlForm, and HtmlGenericControl classes inherit from HtmlContainerControl, while HtmlImage and HtmlInput do not.

The HtmlContainer control adds two properties, as described in Table 5-7.

Table 5-7. *HtmlContainerControl Properties*

Property	Description
InnerHtml	The HTML content between the opening and closing tags of the control. Special characters that are set through this property will not be converted to the equivalent HTML entities. This means you can use this property to apply formatting with nested tags such as <b>, <i>, and <h1>.
InnerText	The text content between the opening and closing tags of the control. Special characters will be automatically converted to HTML entities and displayed like text (for example, the less-than character (<) will be converted to < and will be displayed as < in the web page). This means you can't use HTML tags to apply additional formatting with this property. The simple currency converter page used the InnerText property to enter results into a <div> tag.

PROPERTIES CAN BE SET IN CODE OR IN THE TAG

To set the initial value of a property, you can configure the control in the Page.Load event handler, or you can adjust the control tag in the .aspx file by adding special attributes. Note that the Page.Load event occurs after the page is initialized with the default values and the tag settings. This means your code can override the properties set in the tag (but not vice versa).

The following HtmlImage control is an example that sets properties through attributes in the control tag. The control is automatically hidden, and won't appear in the rendered page.

```
<img Visible="False" id="Graph" runat="server">
```

Remember, if you set control properties in the Properties window, you are using the control tag approach. As you make your changes, Visual Studio updates the control tag in the .aspx file.

The HtmlInputControl Class

This control defines some properties (shown in Table 5-8) that are common to all the HTML controls that are based on the <input> tag, including the <input type="text">, <input type="submit">, and <input type="file"> elements.

Table 5-8. *HtmlInputControl Properties*

Property	Description
Type	Provides the type of input control. For example, a control based on <input type="file"> would return *file* for the type property.
Value	Returns the contents of the control as a string. In the simple currency converter, this property allowed the code to retrieve the information entered in the text input control.

The Page Class

One control we haven't discussed in detail yet is the Page class. As explained in the previous chapter, every web page is a custom class that inherits from System.Web.UI.Page. By inheriting from this class, your web page class acquires a number of properties that your code can use. These include properties for enabling caching, validation, and tracing, which are discussed throughout this book.

Table 5-9 describes some of the more fundamental properties, including the traditional built-in objects that ASP developers often used, such as Response, Request, and Session.

Table 5-9. *Basic Page Properties*

Property	Description
Application and Session	These collections hold state information on the server. Chapter 9 discusses this topic.
Cache	This collection allows you to store objects for reuse in other pages or for other clients. Chapter 26 discusses caching.
Controls	Provides a collection of all the controls contained on the web page. You can also use the methods of this collection to add new controls dynamically.
EnableViewState	When set to false, this overrides the EnableViewState property of the contained controls, thereby ensuring that no controls will maintain state information.
IsPostBack	This Boolean property indicates whether this is the first time the page is being run (false) or whether the page is being resubmitted in response to a control event, typically with stored view state information (true). This property is often used in the Page.Load event handler, thereby ensuring that basic setup is performed only once for controls that maintain view state.
Request	Refers to an HttpRequest object that contains information about the current web request, including client certificates, cookies, and values submitted through HTML form elements. It supports the same features as the built-in ASP Request object.
Response	Refers to an HttpResponse object that allows you to set the web response or redirect the user to another web page. It supports the same features as the built-in ASP Response object, although it's used much less in .NET development.
Server	Refers to an HttpServerUtility object that allows you to perform some miscellaneous tasks, such as URL and HTML encoding. It supports the same features as the built-in ASP Server object.
User	If the user has been authenticated, this property will be initialized with user information. Chapter 18 describes this property in more detail.

The Controls Collection

The Page.Controls collection includes all the controls on the current web form. You can loop through this collection and access each control. For example, the following code writes the name of every control on the current page to a server control called Result:

```
Result.InnerText = "List of controls: ";
foreach (Control ctrl in this.Controls)
{
    Result.InnerText += " " + ctrl.ID;
}
```

You can also use the Controls collection to add a dynamic control. The following code creates a new button with the caption Dynamic Button and adds it to the bottom of the page:

```
HtmlButton ctrl = new HtmlButton();
ctrl.InnerText = "Dynamic Button";
ctrl.ID = "DynamicButton";
this.Controls.Add(ctrl);
```

The best place to generate new controls is in the Page.Load event handler. This ensures that the control will be created each time the page is served. In addition, if you're adding an input control that uses view state, the view state information will be restored to the control after the Page.Load event fires. This means a dynamically generated text box will retain its text over multiple postbacks, just like a text box that is defined in the .aspx file. Dynamically created controls are difficult to position, however. By default, they appear at the bottom of the page. The only way to change this behavior is to create a container control that acts as a placeholder, such as a server-side <div> tag. You can then add the dynamic control to the Controls collection of the container control.

The HttpRequest Class

The HttpRequest class encapsulates all the information related to a client request for a web page. Most of this information corresponds to low-level details such as posted-back form values, server variables, the response encoding, and so on. If you're using ASP.NET to its fullest, you'll almost never dive down to that level. Other properties are generally useful for retrieving information, particularly about the capabilities of the client browser. Table 5-10 provides a quick look at its most frequently used properties.

Table 5-10. *HttpRequest Properties*

Property	Description
ApplicationPath and PhysicalPath	ApplicationPath gets the ASP.NET application's virtual directory (URL), while PhysicalPath gets the "real" directory.
Browser	Provides a link to an HttpBrowserCapabilities object that contains properties describing various browser features, such as support for ActiveX controls, cookies, VBScript, and frames. This replaces the BrowserCapabilities component that was sometimes used in ASP development.
ClientCertificate	An HttpClientCertificate object that gets the security certificate for the current request, if there is one.

Property	Description
Cookies	Gets the collection of cookies sent with this request. Chapter 9 discusses cookies in more detail.
Headers and ServerVariables	Provides a name/value collection of HTTP headers and server variables. You can get the low-level information you need if you know the corresponding header or variable name.
IsAuthenticated and IsSecureConnection	Returns true if the user has been successfully authenticated and if the user is connected over SSL (also known as the Secure Sockets Layer).
QueryString	Provides the parameters that were passed along with the query string. Chapter 9 discusses how you can use the query string to transfer information between pages.
Url and UrlReferrer	Provides a Uri object that represents the current address for the page and the page where the user is coming from (the previous page that linked to this page).
UserAgent	A string representing the browser type. Internet Explorer provides the value MSIE for this property.
UserHostAddress and UserHostName	Gets the IP address and the DNS name of the remote client. You could also access this information through the ServerVariables collection.
UserLanguages	Provides a sorted string array that lists the client's language preferences. This can be useful if you need to create multilingual pages.

The HttpResponse Class

The HttpResponse class allows you to send information directly to the client. In traditional ASP development, the Response object was used heavily to create dynamic pages. Now, with the introduction of the new server-based control model, these relatively crude methods are no longer needed.

The HttpResponse does still provide some important functionality, namely, caching support, cookie features, and the Redirect() method, which allows you to transfer the user to another page:

```
// You can redirect to a file in the current directory.
Response.Redirect("newpage.aspx");

// You can redirect to another website.
Response.Redirect("http://www.prosetech.com");
```

Table 5-11 lists the most commonly used members of the HttpResponse class.

Table 5-11. *HttpResponse Members*

Member	Description
BufferOutput	When set to true (the default), the page isn't sent to the client until it's completely rendered and ready, as opposed to being sent piecemeal.
Cache	References an HttpCachePolicy object that allows you to configure how this page will be cached. Chapter 26 discusses caching.
Cookies	The collection of cookies sent with the response. You can use this property to add cookies, as described in Chapter 9.
Write(), BinaryWrite(), and WriteFile()	These methods allow you to write text or binary content directly to the response stream. You can even write the contents of a file. These methods are de-emphasized in ASP.NET and shouldn't be used in conjunction with server controls.
Redirect()	This method transfers the user to another page in your application or a different website.

The HttpServerUtility Class

The HttpServerUtility class provides some miscellaneous helper methods, as listed in Table 5-12.

Table 5-12. *ServerUtility Methods*

Method	Description
CreateObject()	Creates an instance of the COM object that is identified by its programmatic ID (progID). This is included for backward compatibility, because it will generally be easier to interact with COM objects using the .NET Framework services.
HtmlEncode() and HtmlDecode()	Changes an ordinary string into a string with legal HTML characters and back again.
UrlEncode() and UrlDecode()	Changes an ordinary string into a string with legal URL characters and back again.
MapPath()	Returns the physical file path that corresponds to a specified virtual file path on the web server.
Transfer()	Transfers execution to another web page in the current application. This is similar to the Response.Redirect() method but is slightly faster. It cannot be used to transfer the user to a site on another web server or to a non-ASP.NET page (such as an HTML page or a ASP page).

Out of these methods, the most commonly used are UrlEncode()/UrlDecode() and HtmlEncode()/HtmlDecode(). These functions change a string into a representation that can safely be used as part of a URL or displayed in a web page. For example, imagine you want to display this text on a web page:

```
Enter a word <here>
```

If you try to write this information to a page or place it inside a control, you end up with this instead:

```
Enter a word
```

The problem is that the browser has tried to interpret the <here> as an HTML tag. A similar problem occurs if you actually use valid HTML tags. For example, consider this text:

```
To bold text use the <b> tag.
```

Not only will the text <b> not appear, but the browser will interpret it as an instruction to make the text that follows bold. To circumvent this automatic behavior, you need to convert potential problematic values to their special HTML equivalents. For example, < becomes < in your final HTML page, which the browser displays as the < character.

You can perform this transformation on your own, or you can circumvent the problem by using the InnerText property. When you set the contents of a control using InnerText, any illegal characters are automatically converted into their HTML equivalents. However, this won't help if you want to set a tag that contains a mix of embedded HTML tags and encoded characters. It also won't be of any use for controls that don't provide an InnerText property, such as the Label web control you'll examine in the next chapter. In these cases, you can use the HtmlEncode() method to replace the special characters. Here's an example:

```
// Will output as "Enter a word &lt;here&gt;" in the HTML file, but the
// browser will display it as "Enter a word <here>".
ctrl.InnerHtml = Server.HtmlEncode("Enter a word <here>");
```

Or consider this example, which mingles real HTML tags with text that needs to be encoded:

```
ctrl.InnerHtml = "To <b>bold</b> text use the ";
ctrl.InnerHtml += Server.HtmlEncode("<b>") + " tag.";
```

Figure 5-9 shows the results of successfully and incorrectly encoding special HTML characters. You can refer to the HtmlEncodeTest.aspx page included with the examples for this chapter.

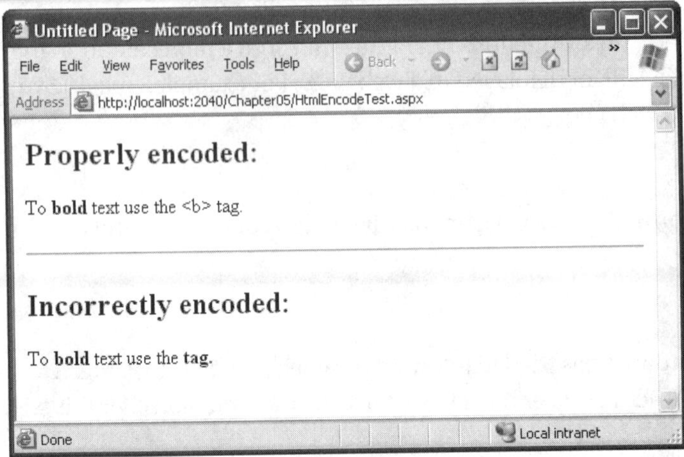

Figure 5-9. *Encoding special HTML characters*

The HtmlEncode() method is particularly useful if you're retrieving values from a database and you aren't sure whether the text is valid HTML. You can use the HtmlDecode() method to revert the text to its normal form if you need to perform additional operations or comparisons with it in your code. Table 5-13 lists some special characters that need to be encoded.

Table 5-13. *Common HTML Special Characters*

Result	Description	Encoded Entity
	Nonbreaking space	
<	Less-than symbol	<
>	Greater-than symbol	>
&	Ampersand	&
"	Quotation mark	"

Similarly, the UrlEncode() method changes text into a form that can be used in a URL. Generally, this allows information to work as a query string variable, even if it contains spaces and other characters that aren't allowed in a URL. You'll see this technique demonstrated in Chapter 9.

ASP.NET Configuration

The last topic you'll consider in this chapter is the ASP.NET configuration file system.

Every web server starts with some basic settings that are defined in two configuration files in the c:\[WinDir]\Microsoft.NET\Framework\[Version]\Config directory, where [Version] is the version number of the .NET Framework. These two files are machine.config and web.config. Generally, you won't edit either of these files manually, because they affect the entire computer. Instead, you'll create a web.config in your web application folder. Using that file, you can set additional settings or override the defaults that are configured elsewhere.

The .config files have several advantages over traditional ASP configuration:

They are never locked: As described in the beginning of this chapter, you can update web.config settings at any point, and ASP.NET will smoothly transition to a new application domain.

They are easily accessed and replicated: Provided you have the appropriate network rights, you can change a web.config file from a remote computer. You can also copy the web.config file and use it to apply identical settings to another application or another web server that runs the same application in a web farm scenario.

The settings are easy to edit and understand: The settings in the web.config file are human-readable, which means they can be edited and understood without needing a special configuration tool. As a result, you can easily add or modify settings using a text editor such as Notepad.

■ **Note** With ASP.NET, you don't need to worry about the IIS metabase. However, you still can't perform a few tasks with a web.config file. For example, you can't create or remove a virtual directory. Similarly, you can't change file mappings. If you want the ASP.NET service to process requests for additional file types (such as HTML or a custom file type you define), you must use IIS Manager, as described in Chapter 12.

The web.config File

The web.config file uses a predefined XML format. The entire content of the file is nested in a root <configuration> element. This element contains a <system.web> element, which is used for ASP.NET settings. Inside the <system.web> element are separate elements for each aspect of configuration.

Here's the basic skeletal structure of the web.config file:

```
<?xml version="1.0" encoding="utf-8" ?>
<configuration>
    <system.web>
        <!-- Configuration sections go here. -->
    </system.web>
</configuration>
```

This example adds a comment in the place where you'd normally find additional settings. XML comments are bracketed with the <!-- and --> character sequences, as shown here:

```
<!-- This is the format for an XML comment. -->
```

■ **Tip** To learn more about XML, the format used for the web.config file, you can refer to Chapter 17.

You can include as few or as many configuration sections as you want. For example, if you need to specify special error settings, you could add just the <customErrors> group. Note that the web.config file is case-sensitive, like all XML documents, and starts every setting with a lowercase letter. This means you cannot write <CustomErrors> instead of <customErrors>.

If you want an at-a-glance look at all the available settings, head to the c:\[WinDir]\Microsoft.NET\Framework\[Version]\Config directory, and look at the web.config.comments file. This file consists of XML comments that show the available options for every possible setting. You can also look up individual tag names in the index of the MSDN Help. We'll describe individual configuration sections in this book when discussing the related topic. For example, in Chapter 9, we'll describe the settings in the <sessionState> group.

Nested Configuration

ASP.NET uses a multilayered configuration system that allows you to use different settings for different parts of your application. To use this technique, you need to create additional subdirectories inside your virtual directory. These subdirectories can contain their own web.config files with additional settings.

Subdirectories inherit web.config settings from the parent directory. For example, imagine you create a website in the directory c:\ASP.NET\TestWeb. Inside this directory, you create a folder named Secure. Pages in the c:\ASP.NET\TestWeb\Secure directory can acquire settings from three files, as shown in Figure 5-10.

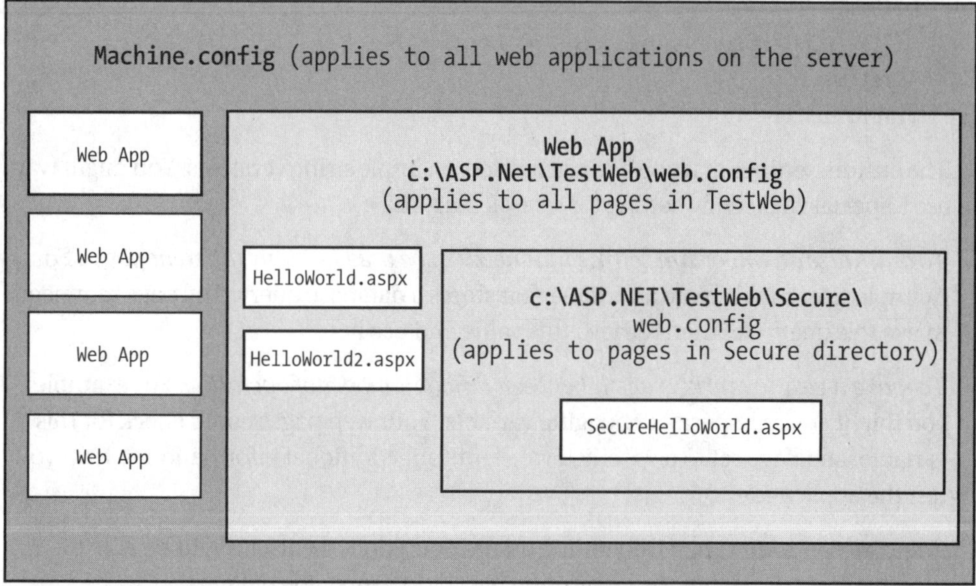

Figure 5-10. *Configuration inheritance*

Any machine.config or web.config settings that aren't explicitly overridden in the c:\ASP.NET\TestWeb\Special\web.config file will still apply to the SecureHelloWorld.aspx page. In this way, subdirectories can specify just a small set of settings that differ from the rest of the web application. One reason you might want to use multiple directories in an application is to apply different security settings. Files that need to be secured would then be placed in a dedicated directory with a web.config file that defines more stringent security settings.

Storing Custom Settings in the web.config File

ASP.NET also allows you to store your own settings in the web.config file, in an element called <appSettings>. Note that the <appSettings> element is nested in the root <configuration> element, not the <system.web> element, which contains the other groups of predefined settings. Here's the basic structure:

```
<?xml version="1.0" encoding="utf-8" ?>
<configuration>
    <appSettings>
        <!-- Custom application settings go here. -->
    </appSettings>
```

```
    <system.web>
        <!-- Configuration sections go here. -->
    </system.web>
</configuration>
```

The custom settings that you add are written as simple string variables. You might want to use a special web.config setting for several reasons:

To centralize an important setting that needs to be used in many different pages: For example, you could create a variable that stores a database query. Any page that needs to use this query can then retrieve this value and use it.

To make it easy to quickly switch between different modes of operation: For example, you might create a special debugging variable. Your web pages could check for this variable, and if it's set to a specified value, output additional information to help you test the application.

To set some initial values: Depending on the operation, the user might be able to modify these values, but the web.config file could supply the defaults.

You can enter custom settings using an <add> element that identifies a unique variable name (key) and the variable contents (value). The following example adds two special variables, one that contains a database connection string and one that defines a suitable SQL statement for retrieving sales records:

```
<?xml version="1.0" encoding="utf-8" ?>
<configuration>
  <appSettings>
    <add key="ConnectionString"
     value="Data Source=localhost;Initial Catalog=Pubs;User ID=sa"/>
    <add key="SelectSales" value="SELECT * FROM Sales"/>
  </appSettings>

  <system.web>
      <!-- Configuration sections go here. -->
  </system.web>
</configuration>
```

■ **Note** It's a good idea to always use the same database connection string in all your pages, because this ensures that SQL Server can reuse connections for different clients. (The technical term for this performance-enhancing feature is *connection pooling*.) This design is so important that ASP.NET actually defines a <connectionStrings> section in the web.config file, which you can use as an alternative to creating a custom application setting. You'll see this technique in action in Chapter 13.

You can create a simple test page to query this information and display the results, as shown in the following example (which is provided with the sample code as ShowSettings.aspx and ShowSettings.aspx.cs). You retrieve custom application settings from web.config by key name, using the WebConfigurationManager class, which is found in the System.Web.Configuration namespace. This class provides a static property called AppSettings with a collection of application settings.

```
using System.Web.UI;
using System.Web.UI.WebControls;
using System.Web.Configuration;

public partial class ShowSettings : System.Web.UI.Page
{
    protected void Page_Load()
    {
        lblTest.Text = "This app will connect with";
        lblTest.Text += "the connection string:<br /><b>";
        lblTest.Text +=
          WebConfigurationManager.AppSettings["ConnectionString"];
        lblTest.Text += "</b><br /><br />";
        lblTest.Text += "And will execute the SQL Statement:<br />";
        lblTest.Text += "<b>";
        lblTest.Text += WebConfigurationManager.AppSettings["SelectSales"];
        lblTest.Text += "</b>";
    }
}
```

Dissecting the Code...

This example introduces a few new details:

- The System.Web.Configuration namespace is imported to make it easier to access the WebConfigurationManager class.
- The += operator is used to quickly add information to the label. This is equivalent to writing lblTest.Text = lblText.Text + "[extra content]".
- A few HTML tags are added to the label, including bold tags (<b>) to emphasize certain words and a line break (<br />) to split the output over multiple lines.

Later, in Part 3 of this book, you'll learn how to use connection strings and SQL statements with a database. For now, the simple application just displays the custom web.config settings, as shown in Figure 5-11.

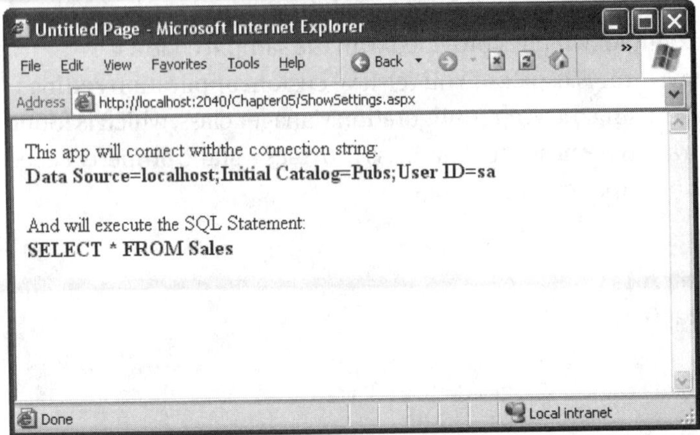

Figure 5-11. *Displaying custom application settings*

Developers commonly ask whether the web.config file constitutes a potential security risk. Unlike code files, the web.config file can't be deployed in a compiled form. For that reason, it might seem like a potential security risk to store information such as a database access password in plain text. However, ASP.NET is configured, by default, to deny any requests for .config files. This means a remote user will not be able to access the file through IIS. Instead, they'll receive the error message shown in Figure 5-12.

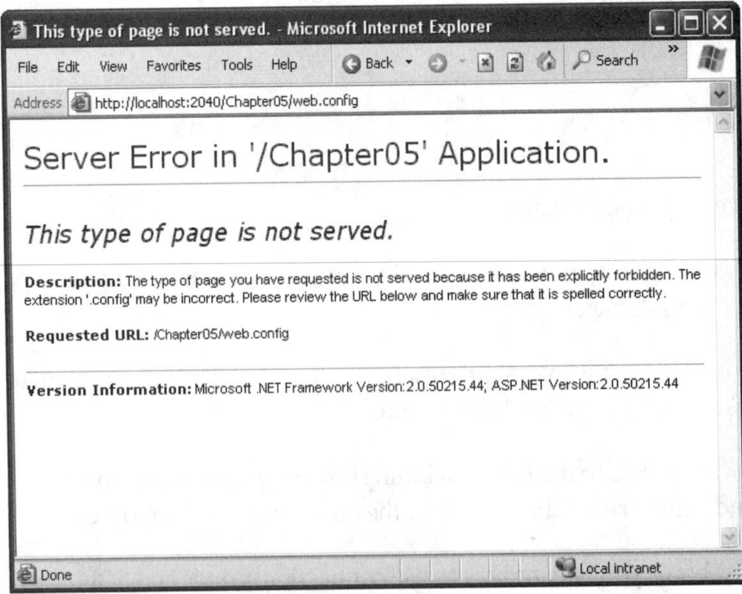

Figure 5-12. *Requests for web.config are denied.*

Modifying web.config Settings Programmatically

ASP.NET also allows you to change configuration file settings (including custom application settings and any other configuration detail).

However, you need to think twice before you use these features. The web.config file is *never* a good solution for state management. Instead, it makes sense as a way to occasionally update a setting that, under normal circumstances, almost never changes. That's because changing a configuration setting has a significant cost. In web server terms, file access is slow, especially when multiple people could be updating the web.config at once (using the same page simultaneously). However, the real problem is that every time a web application's configuration settings change, an entirely new application domain is created, as discussed at the beginning of this chapter. Not only does this add overhead, it also dumps out useful optimization information, such as cached data (which you'll learn about in Chapter 26) and application state (Chapter 9). As a rule of thumb, never store frequently changed values in a configuration file—instead, use a database or one of the state management techniques in Chapter 9.

Now that you know not to abuse this feature, you're ready to see it in action. However, to make it work, you need to use a slightly more complex approach. First, you need to use the WebConfigurionManager.OpenWebConfiguration() method to retrieve a Configuration object for the current web application. Then, you can use this object to read or change values. When you want to commit your changes, you simply call Configuration.Save().

Here's some code that rewrites the application setting example shown earlier so that it updates one of the settings after reading it:

```
protected void Page_Load(object sender, EventArgs e)
{
    lblTest.Text = "This app will connect with";
    lblTest.Text += "the connection string:<br /><b>";
    lblTest.Text +=
      WebConfigurationManager.AppSettings["ConnectionString"];
    lblTest.Text += "</b><br /><br />";
    lblTest.Text += "And will execute the SQL Statement:<br />";
    lblTest.Text += "<b>";
    lblTest.Text += WebConfigurationManager.AppSettings["SelectSales"];
    lblTest.Text += "</b>";

    // Get the configuration information for this web application.
    Configuration config =
      WebConfigurationManager.OpenWebConfiguration(Request.ApplicationPath);
```

```
    // Make the change.
    config.AppSettings.Settings["SelectSales"].Value =
      "SELECT Price FROM Sales";

    // Save all the changes you've made since retrieving the configuration
    // information.
    config.Save();
}
```

Notice that when you use OpenWebConfiguration(), you supply a path. You get the configuration information for this path. In this example, the code gets the configuration for the root web application directory, because it uses the Request.ApplicationPath property when calling the OpenWebConfiguration() method.

The first time you request this page, you'll see the initial setting "SELECT * FROM Sales". However, the web page has already updated this value. The second time you request the page, you'll see the new setting "SELECT Price FROM Sales". You'll notice that the second request takes a little longer, because the page needs to be compiled and cached all over again; the effect of changing a setting in the web.config file has forced the application domain to restart.

The Website Administration Tool (WAT)

You might wonder why the ASP.NET team went to all the trouble of creating a sophisticated tool like the WebConfigurationManager that performs too poorly to be used in a typical web application. The reason is because the WebConfigurationManager isn't really intended to be used in your web pages. Instead, it's designed to allow developers to build custom configuration tools that simplify the work of configuring web applications. ASP.NET even includes a graphical configuration tool that's entirely based on the WebConfigurationManager, although you'd never know it unless you dived into the code.

This tool is called the WAT (Website Administration Tool), and it lets you configure various parts of the web.config file using a web page interface. To run the WAT to configure the current web project in Visual Studio, select Website ➤ ASP.NET Configuration. A web browser window will appear (see Figure 5-13). Internet Explorer will automatically log you on under the current Windows user account, allowing you to make changes.

You can use the WAT to automate the web.config changes you made in the previous example. To try this, click the Application tab. Using this tab, you can edit or remove application settings (select the Manage Application Settings link) or create a new setting (click the Create Application Settings link). Figure 5-14 shows how you can edit the application settings you added by hand in the previous example.

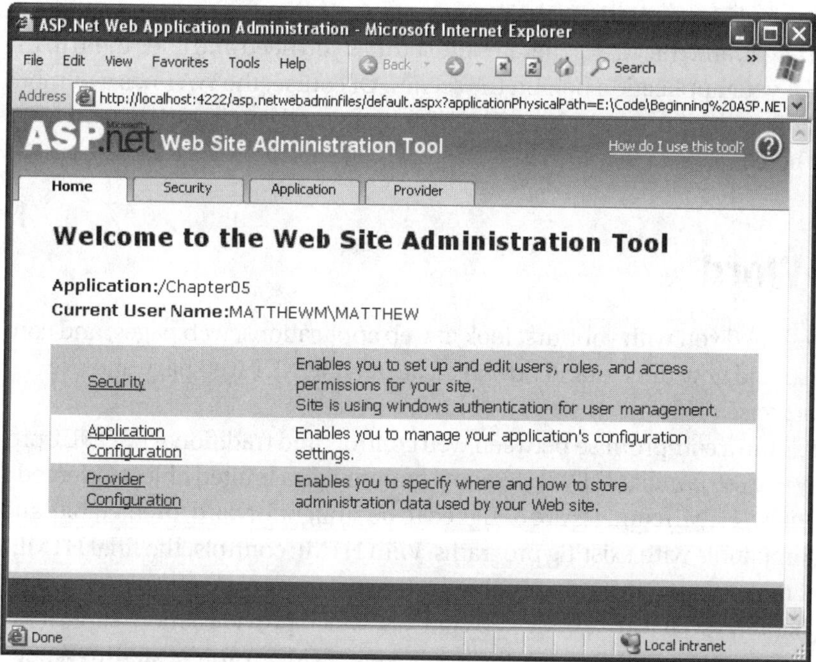

Figure 5-13. *Running the WAT*

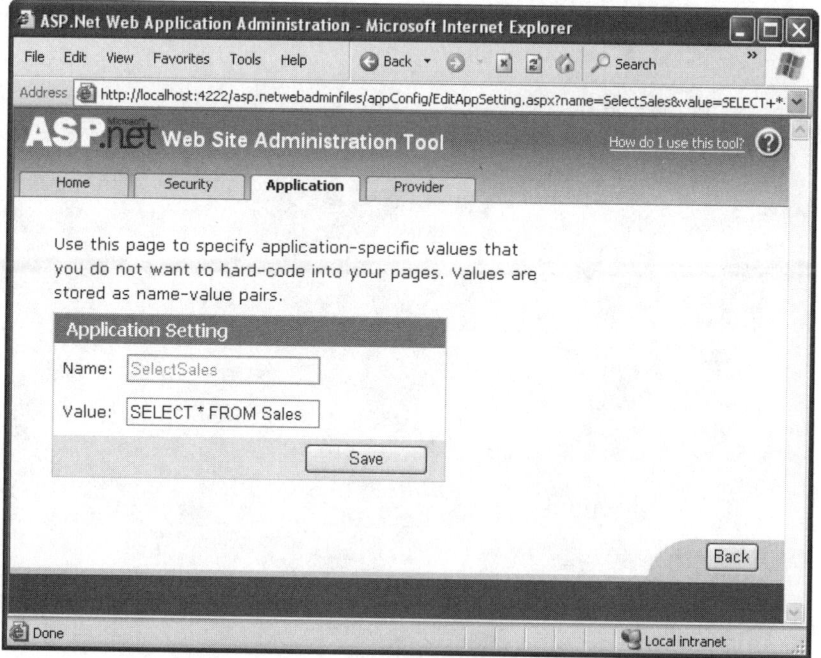

Figure 5-14. *Editing an application setting with the WAT*

This is the essential idea behind the WAT. You make your changes using a graphical interface (a web page), and the WAT generates the settings you need and adds them to the web.config file for your application behind the scenes. Of course, the WAT has a number of settings for configuring more complex ASP.NET settings, and you'll see it at work throughout this book.

The Last Word

This chapter presented you with your first look at web applications, web pages, and configuration. You should now understand how to create an ASP.NET web page and use HTML server controls.

HTML controls are a compromise between web controls and traditional ASP.NET programming. They use the familiar HTML elements but provide a limited object-oriented interface. Essentially, HTML controls are designed to be straightforward, predictable, and automatically compatible with existing programs. With HTML controls, the final HTML page that is sent to the client closely resembles the original .aspx page.

In the next chapter, you'll learn about web controls, which provide a more sophisticated object interface that abstracts away the underlying HTML. If you're starting a new project or need to add some of ASP.NET's most powerful controls, web controls are the best option.

CHAPTER 6

Web Controls

The previous chapter introduced the event-driven and control-based programming model of ASP.NET. This model allows you to create programs for the Web using the same object-oriented, modern code you would use to write a Windows application.

However, HTML server controls really show only a glimpse of what is possible with ASP.NET's new server control model. To see some of the real advantages, you need to dive into the richer and more extensible web controls. In this chapter, you'll explore the basic web controls and their class hierarchy. You'll also delve deeper into ASP.NET's event handling, learn the details of the web page life cycle, and put your knowledge to work by creating a web page for designing greeting cards.

Stepping Up to Web Controls

Now that you've seen the new model of server controls, you might wonder why you need additional web controls. But in fact, HTML controls are much more limited than server controls need to be. For example, every HTML control corresponds directly to an HTML tag, meaning you're bound by the limitations and abilities of HTML. Web controls, on the other hand, have no such restriction. They emphasize the future of web design.

These are some of the reasons you should switch to web controls:

They provide a rich user interface: A web control is programmed as an object but doesn't necessarily correspond to a single element in the final HTML page. For example, you might create a single Calendar or GridView control, which will be rendered as dozens of HTML elements in the final page. When using ASP.NET programs, you don't need to know anything about HTML. The control creates the required HTML tags for you.

They provide a consistent object model: HTML is full of quirks and idiosyncrasies. For example, a simple text box can appear as one of three elements, including <textarea>, <input type="text">, and <input type="password">. With web controls, these three elements are consolidated as a single TextBox control. Depending on the properties you set, the underlying HTML element that ASP.NET renders may differ. Similarly, the names of properties don't follow the HTML attribute names. For example, controls that display text, whether it's a caption or a text box that can be edited by the user, expose a Text property.

They tailor their output automatically: ASP.NET server controls can detect the type of browser and automatically adjust the HTML code they write to take advantage of features such as support for JavaScript. You don't need to know about the client because ASP.NET handles that layer and automatically uses the best possible set of features.

They provide high-level features: You'll see that web controls allow you to access additional events, properties, and methods that don't correspond directly to typical HTML controls. ASP.NET implements these features by using a combination of tricks.

Throughout this book, you'll see examples that use the full set of web controls. To master ASP.NET development, you need to become comfortable with these user-interface ingredients and understand all their abilities. HTML server controls, on the other hand, are less important for web development, unless you need to have fine-grained control over the HTML code that will be generated and sent to the client. They are de-emphasized in .NET.

Basic Web Control Classes

If you've ever created a Windows application before, you're probably familiar with the basic set of standard controls, including labels, buttons, and text boxes. ASP.NET provides web controls for all these standbys. (And if you've created .NET Windows applications, you'll notice that the class names and properties have many striking similarities, which are designed to make it easy to transfer the experience you acquire in one type of application to another.)

Table 6-1 lists the basic control classes and the HTML elements they generate. Some controls (such as Button and TextBox) can be rendered as different HTML elements. In this case, ASP.NET uses the element that matches the properties you've set. Also, some controls have no real HTML equivalent. For example, the CheckBoxList and RadioButtonList controls output as a <table> that contains multiple HTML check boxes or radio buttons. ASP.NET exposes them as a single object on the server side for convenient programming, thus illustrating one of the primary strengths of web controls.

Table 6-1. *Basic Web Controls*

Control Class	Underlying HTML Element
Label	<span>
Button	<input type="submit"> or <input type="button">
TextBox	<input type="text">, <input type="password">, or <textarea>
CheckBox	<input type="checkbox">

Control Class	Underlying HTML Element
RadioButton	<input type="radio">
Hyperlink	<a>
LinkButton	<a> with a contained <img> tag
ImageButton	<input type="image">
Image	<img>
ListBox	<select size="X"> where X is the number of rows that are visible at once
DropDownList	<select>
CheckBoxList	A list or <table> with multiple <input type="checkbox"> tags
RadioButtonList	A list or <table> with multiple <input type="radio"> tags
BulletedList	An <ol> ordered list (numbered) or <ul> unordered list (bulleted).
Panel	<div>
Table, TableRow, and TableCell	<table>, <tr>, and <td> or <th>

This table omits some of the more specialized controls used for data, navigation, security, and web portals. You'll see these controls as you learn about the corresponding feature throughout this book.

The Web Control Tags

ASP.NET tags have a special format. They always begin with the prefix asp: followed by the class name. If there is no closing tag, the tag must end with />. (This syntax convention is borrowed from XML, which you'll learn about in much more detail in Chapter 17.) Each attribute in the tag corresponds to a control property, except for the runat="server" attribute, which signals that the control should be processed on the server.

The following, for example, is an ASP.NET TextBox:

```
<asp:TextBox id="txt" runat="server" />
```

When a client requests this .aspx page, the following HTML is returned. The name is a special attribute that ASP.NET uses to track the control.

```
<input type="text" name="ctrl" />
```

Alternatively, you could place some text in the TextBox, set its size, make it read-only, and change the background color. All these actions have defined properties. For example, the TextBox.TextMode property allows you to specify SingleLine (the default), MultiLine (for a textarea type of control), or Password (for an input control that displays all asterisks when the user types in a value). You can adjust the color using the BackColor and

ForeColor properties. And you can tweak the size of the TextBox using the Rows property. Here's an example of a customized TextBox:

```
<asp:TextBox id="txt" BackColor="Yellow" Text="Hello World"
 ReadOnly="true" TextMode="MultiLine" Rows="5" runat="server" />
```

The resulting HTML uses the textarea element and sets all the required style attributes. Figure 6-1 shows it in the browser.

```
<textarea name="txt" rows="5" readonly="readonly" id="txt"
 style="background-color:Yellow;">Hello World</textarea>
```

Figure 6-1. *A customized text box*

Clearly, it's easy to create a web control tag. It doesn't require any understanding of HTML. However, you *will* need to understand the control class and the properties that are available to you.

CASE-SENSITIVITY IN ASP.NET FORMS

The .aspx layout portion of a web page tolerates different capitalization for tag names, property names, and enumeration values. For example, the following two tags are equivalent, and both will be interpreted correctly by the ASP.NET engine, even though their case differs:

```
<asp:Button id="Button1" runat="server"
  Enabled="False" Text="Button" Font-Size="XX-Small" />
<asp:button id="Button2" runat="server"
  Enabled="false" tExT="Button" font-size="xx-SMALL" />
```

This design was adopted to make .aspx pages behave more like ordinary HTML web pages, which ignore case completely. However, you can't use the same looseness in your C# code or in the tags that apply settings in the web.config file or the machine.config file. Here, case must match *exactly*.

Web Control Classes

Web control classes are defined in the System.Web.UI.WebControls namespace. They follow a slightly more tangled object hierarchy than HTML server controls, as shown in Figure 6-2.

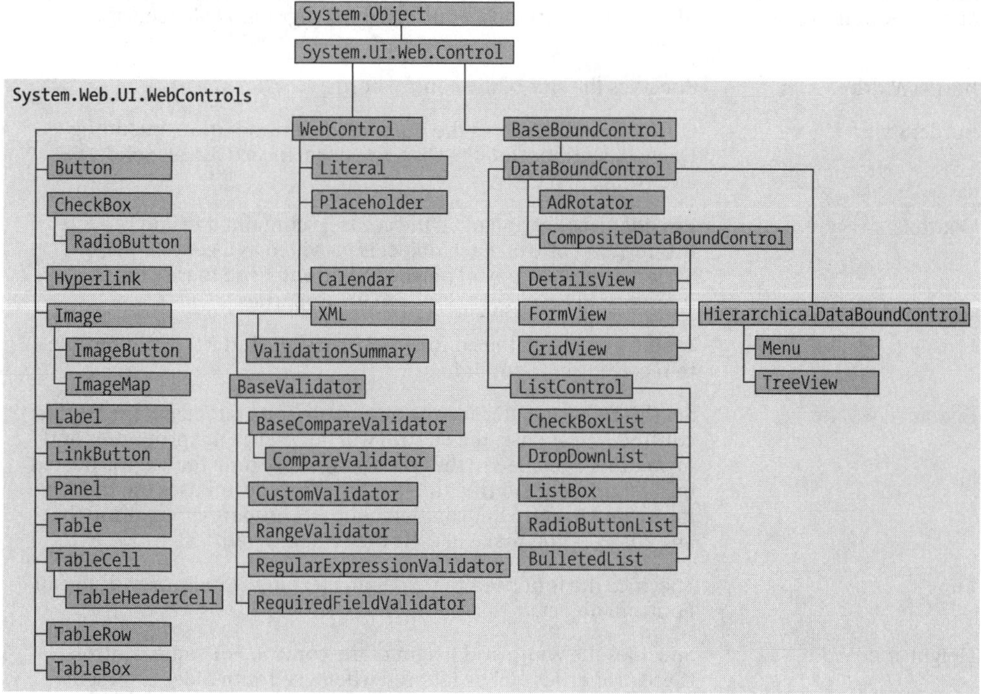

Figure 6-2. *The web control hierarchy*

This inheritance diagram includes some controls that you won't study in this chapter, including the data controls, such as the GridView and DetailsView, and the validation controls. You'll explore these controls in later chapters.

The WebControl Base Class

All web controls begin by inheriting from the WebControl base class. This class defines the essential functionality for tasks such as data binding and includes some basic properties that you can use with any control, as described in Table 6-2.

Table 6-2. *WebControl Properties*

Property	Description
AccessKey	Specifies the keyboard shortcut as one letter. For example, if you set this to Y, the Alt+Y keyboard combination will automatically change focus to this web control. This feature is supported only on Internet Explorer 4.0 and higher.
BackColor, BorderColor, and ForeColor	Sets the colors used for the background, foreground, and border of the control. In most controls, the foreground color sets the text color.
BorderWidth	Specifies the size of the control border.
BorderStyle	One of the values from the BorderStyle enumeration, including Dashed, Dotted, Double, Groove, Ridge, Inset, Outset, Solid, and None.
Controls	Provides a collection of all the controls contained inside the current control. Each object is provided as a generic System.Web.UI.Control object, so you will need to cast the reference to access control-specific properties.
Enabled	When set to false, the control will be visible, but it will not be able to receive user input or focus.
EnableViewState	Set this to false to disable the automatic state management for this control. In this case, the control will be reset to the properties and formatting specified in the control tag every time the page is posted back. If this is set to true (the default), the control uses the hidden input field to store information about its properties, ensuring that any changes you make in code are remembered.
Font	Specifies the font used to render any text in the control as a special FontInfo object.
Height and Width	Specifies the width and height of the control. For some controls, these properties will be ignored when used with older browsers.
Page	Provides a reference to the web page that contains this control as a System.Web.UI.Page object.
Parent	Provides a reference to the control that contains this control. If the control is placed directly on the page (rather than inside another control), it will return a reference to the page object.
TabIndex	A number that allows you to control the tab order. The control with a TabIndex of 0 has the focus when the page first loads. Pressing Tab moves the user to the control with the next lowest TabIndex, provided it is enabled. This property is supported only in Internet Explorer 4.0 and higher.
ToolTip	Displays a text message when the user hovers the mouse above the control. Many older browsers don't support this property.
Visible	When set to false, the control will be hidden and will not be rendered to the final HTML page that is sent to the client.

The next few sections describe some of the common concepts you'll use with almost any web control, including how to set properties that use units and enumerations and how to use colors and fonts.

Units

All the properties that use measurements, including BorderWidth, Height, and Width, require the Unit structure, which combines a numeric value with a type of measurement (pixels, percentage, and so on). This means when you set these properties in a control tag, you must make sure to append px (pixel) or % (for percentage) to the number to indicate the type of unit.

Here's an example with a Panel control that is 300 pixels wide and has a height equal to 50 percent of the current browser window:

```
<asp:Panel Height="300px" Width="50%" id="pnl" runat="server" />
```

If you're assigning a unit-based property through code, you need to use one of the static methods of the Unit type. Use Pixel() to supply a value in pixels, and use Percentage() to supply a percentage value:

```
// Convert the number 300 to a Unit object
// representing pixels, and assign it.
pnl.Height = Unit.Pixel(300);

// Convert the number 50 to a Unit object
// representing percent, and assign it.
pnl.Width = Unit.Percentage(50);
```

You could also manually create a Unit object and initialize it using one of the supplied constructors and the UnitType enumeration. This requires a few more steps but allows you to easily assign the same unit to several controls:

```
// Create a Unit object.
Unit myUnit = new Unit(300, UnitType.Pixel);

// Assign the Unit object to several controls or properties.
pnl.Height = myUnit;
pnl.Width = myUnit;
```

Enumerated Values

Enumerations are used heavily in the .NET class library to group a set of related constants. For example, when you set a control's BorderStyle property, you can choose one of several predefined values from the BorderStyle enumeration. In code, you set an enumeration using the dot syntax:

```
ctrl.BorderStyle = BorderStyle.Dashed;
```

In the .aspx file, you set an enumeration by specifying one of the allowed values as a string. You don't include the name of the enumeration type, which is assumed automatically.

```
<asp:Label BorderStyle="Dashed" Text="Border Test" id="ctrl"
 runat="server" />
```

Figure 6-3 shows the label with the altered border.

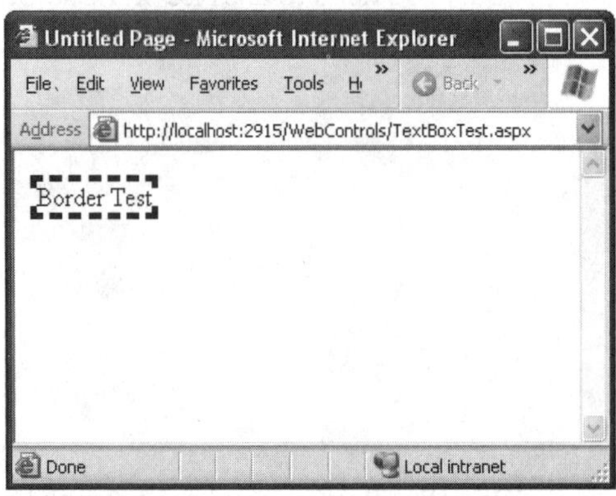

Figure 6-3. *Modifying the border style*

Colors

The Color property refers to a Color object from the System.Drawing namespace. You can create color objects in several ways:

Using an ARGB (alpha, red, green, blue) color value: You specify each value as an integer from 0 to 255. The alpha component represents the transparency of a color, and usually you'll use 255 to make the color completely opaque.

Using a predefined .NET color name: You choose the correspondingly named read-only property from the Color class. These properties include the 140 HTML color names.

Using an HTML color name: You specify this value as a string using the ColorTranslator class.

To use any of these techniques, you must import the System.Drawing namespace, as follows:

```
using System.Drawing;
```

The following code shows several ways to specify a color in code:

```
// Create a color from an ARGB value
int alpha = 255, red = 0, green = 255, blue = 0;
ctrl.ForeColor = Color.FromARGB(alpha, red, green, blue);

// Create a color using a .NET name
ctrl.ForeColor = Color.Crimson;

// Create a color from an HTML code
ctrl.ForeColor = ColorTranslator.FromHtml("Blue");
```

When defining a color in the .aspx file, you can use any one of the known color names:

```
<asp:TextBox ForeColor="Red" Text="Test" id="txt" runat="server" />
```

The HTML color names that you can use are listed in the MSDN Help. Alternatively, you can use a hexadecimal color number (in the format #<red><green><blue>) as shown here:

```
<asp:TextBox ForeColor="#ff50ff" Text="Test"
     id="txt" runat="server" />
```

Fonts

The Font property actually references a full FontInfo object, which is defined in the System.Web.UI.WebControls namespace. Every FontInfo object has several properties that define its name, size, and style (see Table 6-3).

Table 6-3. *FontInfo Properties*

Property	Description
Name	A string indicating the font name (such as Verdana).
Size	The size of the font as a FontUnit object. This can represent an absolute or relative size.
Bold, Italic, Strikeout, Underline, and Overline	Boolean properties that apply the given style attribute.

In code, you can assign a font by setting the various font properties using the familiar dot syntax:

```
ctrl.Font.Name = "Verdana";
ctrl.Font.Bold = true;
```

You can also set the size using the FontUnit type:

```
// Specifies a relative size.
ctrl.Font.Size = FontUnit.Small;

// Specifies an absolute size of 14 pixels.
ctrl.Font.Size = FontUnit.Point(14);
```

In the .aspx file, you need to use a special "object walker" syntax to specify object properties such as Font. The object walker syntax uses a hyphen (-) to separate properties. For example, you could set a control with a specific font (Tahoma) and font size (40 point) like this:

```
<asp:TextBox Font-Name="Tahoma" Font-Size="40" Text="Size Test" id="txt"
 runat="server" />
```

Or you could set a relative size like this:

```
<asp:TextBox Font-Name="Tahoma" Font-Size="Large" Text="Size Test"
 id="txt" runat="server" />
```

Figure 6-4 shows the altered TextBox in this example.

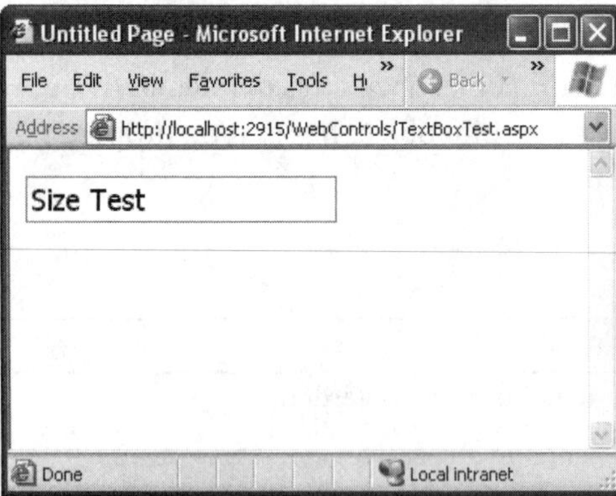

Figure 6-4. *Modifying a control's font*

Focus

Unlike HTML server controls, every web control provides a Focus() method. The Focus() method affects only input controls (controls that can accept keystrokes from the user). When the page is rendered in the client browser, the user starts in the focused control.

For example, if you have a form that allows the user to edit customer information, you might call the Focus() method on the first text box in that form. That way, the cursor appears in this text box immediately when the page first loads in the browser. If the text box is partway down the form, the page even scrolls down to it automatically. The user can then move from control to control using the time-honored Tab key.

If you're a seasoned HTML developer, you know there isn't any built-in way to give focus to an input control. Instead, you need to rely on JavaScript. This is the secret to ASP.NET's implementation. When your code is finished processing and the page is rendered, ASP.NET adds an extra block of JavaScript code to the end of your page. This JavaScript code simply sets the focus to the last control that used the Focus() method. If you haven't called Focus() at all, this code isn't added to the page. If you've called it for more than one control, the JavaScript code set the focus to the last control that called Focus().

Rather than call the Focus() method programmatically, you can set a control that should always be focused by setting the DefaultFocus property of the <form> tag:

```
<form id="Form1" DefaultFocus="TextBox2" runat="server">
```

You can override the default focus by calling the Focus() method in your code.

Another way to manage focus is using access keys. For example, if you set the AccessKey property of a TextBox to A, pressing Alt+A focus will switch to the TextBox. Labels can also get into the game, even though they can't accept focus. The trick is to set the Label.AssociatedControlID property to specify a linked input control. That way, the label transfers focus to a nearby control.

For example, the following label gives focus to TextBox2 when the keyboard combination Alt+2 is pressed:

```
<asp:Label AccessKey="2" AssociatedControlID="TextBox2" runat="server">
 TextBox2:</asp:Label><asp:TextBox runat="server" ID="TextBox2" />
```

Focusing and access keys are also supported in non-Microsoft browsers, including Firefox.

The Default Button

Along with control focusing, ASP.NET also allows you to designate a default button on a web page. The default button is the button that is "clicked" when the user presses the Enter key. For example, if your web page includes a form, you might want to make the submit button into a default button. That way, if the user hits Enter at any time, the page is posted back and the Button.Click event is fired for that button.

To designate a default button, you must set the HtmlForm.DefaultButton property with the ID of the respective control, as shown here:

```
<form id="Form1" DefaultButton="cmdSubmit" runat="server">
```

The default button must be a control that implements the IButtonControl interface. The interface is implemented by the Button, LinkButton, and ImageButton web controls but not by any of the HTML server controls.

In some cases, it makes sense to have more than one default button. For example, you might create a web page with two groups of input controls. Both groups may need a different default button. You can handle this by placing the groups into separate panels. The Panel control also exposes the DefaultButton property, which works when any input control it contains gets the focus.

List Controls

The list controls include the ListBox, DropDownList, CheckBoxList, RadioButtonList, and BulletedList. They all work in essentially the same way but are rendered differently in the browser. The ListBox, for example, is a rectangular list that displays several entries, while the DropDownList shows only the selected item. The CheckBoxList and RadioButtonList are similar to the ListBox, but every item is rendered as a check box or option button, respectively. Finally, the BulletedList is the odd one out—it's the only list control that isn't selectable. Instead, it renders itself as a sequence of numbered or bulleted items.

All the selectable list controls provide a SelectedIndex property that indicates the selected row as a zero-based index (just like the HtmlSelect control you used in the previous chapter). For example, if the first item in the list is selected, the SelectedIndex will be 0. Selectable list controls also provide an additional SelectedItem property, which allows your code to retrieve the ListItem object that represents the selected item. The ListItem object provides three important properties: Text (the displayed content), Value (the hidden value from the HTML markup), and Selected (true or false depending on whether the item is selected).

In the previous chapter, you used code like this to retrieve the selected ListItem object from an HtmlSelect control called Currency, as follows:

```
ListItem item;
item = Currency.Items[Currency.SelectedIndex];
```

With a web control, you can simplify this with a clearer syntax:

```
ListItem item;
item = Currency.SelectedItem;
```

Multiple-Select List Controls

Some list controls can allow multiple selections. This isn't allowed for the DropDownList or RadioButtonList, but it is supported for a ListBox, provided you have set the SelectionMode property to the enumerated value ListSelectionMode.Multiple. The user can then select multiple items by holding down the Ctrl key while clicking the items in the list. With the CheckBoxList, multiple selections are always possible.

If you have a list control that supports multiple selections, you can find all the selected items by iterating through the Items collection of the list control and checking the ListItem.Selected property of each item. Figure 6-5 shows a simple web page example. It provides a list of computer languages and indicates which selections the user made when the OK button is clicked.

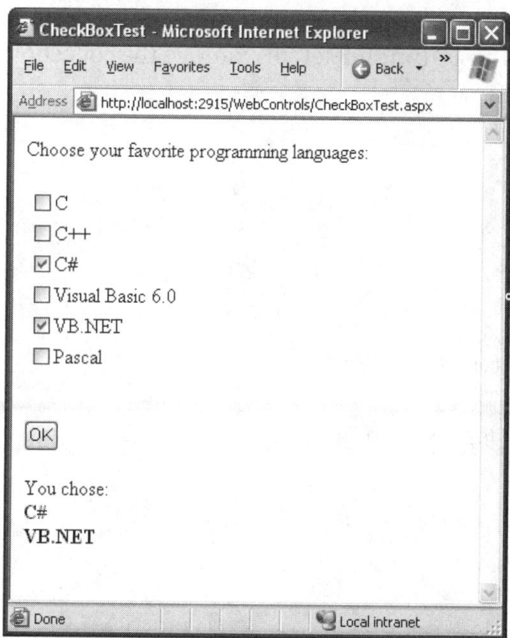

Figure 6-5. *A simple CheckListBox test*

The .aspx file for this page defines CheckListBox, Button, and Label controls, as shown here:

```
<%@ Page Language="C#" AutoEventWireup="true"
    CodeFile="CheckListTest.aspx.cs" Inherits="CheckListTest" %>
<html>
<head runat="server">
  <title>CheckBoxTest</title>
</head>
<body>
  <form method="post" runat="server">
    Choose your favorite programming languages:<br /><br />
    <asp:CheckBoxList id="chklst" runat="server" /><br /><br />
    <asp:Button id="cmdOK" Text="OK" OnClick="cmdOK_Click" runat="server" />
    <br /><br />
    <asp:Label id="lblResult" runat="server" />
  </form>
</body>
</html>
```

The code adds items to the CheckListBox at startup and iterates through the collection when the button is clicked:

```
using System;
using System.Web;
using System.Web.UI;
using System.Web.UI.WebControls;
using System.Web.UI.HtmlControls;

public partial class CheckBoxTest : System.Web.UI.Page
{
    protected void Page_Load(object sender, System.EventArgs e)
    {
        if (!this.IsPostBack)
        {
            chklst.Items.Add("C");
            chklst.Items.Add("C++");
            chklst.Items.Add("C#");
            chklst.Items.Add("Visual Basic 6.0");
            chklst.Items.Add("VB.NET");
            chklst.Items.Add("Pascal");
        }
    }
```

```
    protected void cmdOK_Click(object sender, System.EventArgs e)
    {
        lblResult.Text = "You chose:<b>";

        foreach (ListItem lstItem in chklst.Items)
        {
            if (lstItem.Selected == true)
            {
                // Add text to label.
                lblResult.Text += "<br />" + lstItem.Text;
            }
        }
        lblResult.Text += "</b>";
    }
}
```

CONTROL PREFIXES

When working with web controls, it's often useful to use a three-letter lowercase prefix to identify the type of control. The preceding example (and those in the rest of this book) follows this convention to make user interface code as clear as possible. Some recommended control prefixes are as follows:

- Button: cmd
- CheckBox: chk
- Image: img
- Label: lbl
- List control: lst
- Panel: pnl
- RadioButton: opt
- TextBox: txt

If you're a veteran programmer, you'll also notice that this book doesn't use prefixes to identify data types. This is in keeping with the new philosophy of .NET, which recognizes that data types can often change freely and without consequence and that variables often point to full-featured objects instead of simple data variables.

The BulletedList Control

The BulletedList control is a server-side equivalent of the <ul> (unordered list) and <ol> (ordered list) elements. As with all list controls, you set the collection of items that should be displayed through the Items property. Additionally, you can use the properties in Table 6-4 to configure how the items are displayed.

Table 6-4. *Added BulletedList Properties*

Property	Description
BulletStyle	Determines the type of list. Choose from Numbered (1, 2, 3...), LowerAlpha (a, b, c...) and UpperAlpha (A, B, C...), LowerRoman (i, ii, iii...) and UpperRoman (I, II, III...), and the bullet symbols Disc, Circle, Square, or CustomImage (in which case you must set the BulletStyleImageUrl property).
BulletStyleImageUrl	If the BulletStyle is set to Custom, this points to the image that is placed to the left of each item as a bullet.
FirstBulletNumber	In an ordered list (using the Numbered, LowerAlpha, UpperAlpha, LowerRoman, and UpperRoman styles), this sets the first value. For example, if you set FirstBulletNumber to 3, the list might read 3, 4, 5 (for Numbered) or C, D, E (for UpperAlpha).
DisplayMode	Determines whether the text of each item is rendered as text (use Text, the default) or a hyperlink (use HyperLink).

If you choose to set the DisplayMode to use hyperlinks, you can react to the Button.Click event to determine which item was clicked. Here's an example:

```
protected void BulletedList1_Click(object sender, BulletedListEventArgs e)
{
    string itemText = BulletedList1.Items[e.Index].Text;
    Label1.Text = "You choose item" + itemText;
}
```

Figure 6-6 shows all the DisplayMode values that the BulletList supports. When you click one of the items, the list is changed to use that DisplayMode. You can try this example page with the sample WebControls project for this chapter.

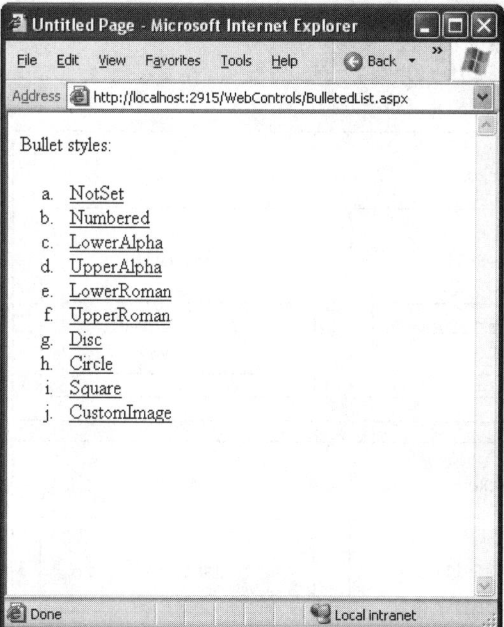

Figure 6-6. *Various BulletedList styles*

Table Controls

Essentially, the Table control is built out of a hierarchy of objects. Each Table object contains one or more TableRow objects. In turn, each TableRow object contains one or more TableCell objects. Each TableCell object contains other ASP.NET controls of HTML content that displays information. If you're familiar with the HTML table tags, this relationship (shown in Figure 6-7) will seem fairly logical.

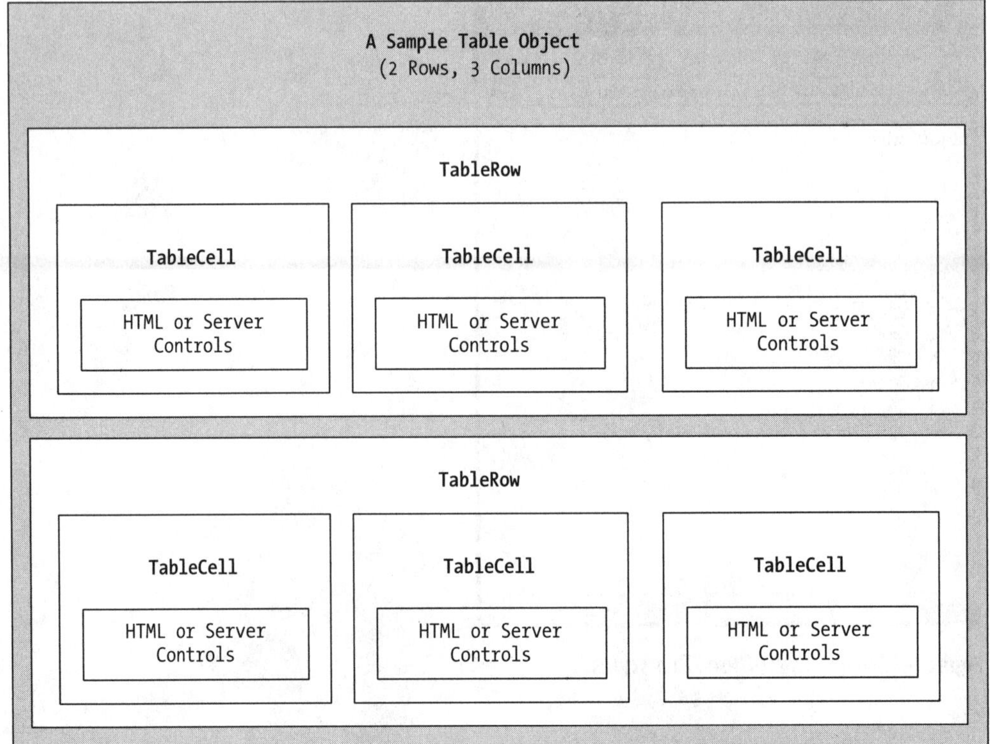

Figure 6-7. *Table control containment*

To create a table dynamically, you follow the same philosophy as you would for any other web control. First, you create and configure the necessary ASP.NET objects. Then, ASP.NET converts these objects to their final HTML representation before the page is sent to the client.

Consider the example shown in Figure 6-8. It allows the user to specify a number of rows and columns as well as whether cells should have borders.

Table Test - Microsoft Internet Explorer
File Edit View Favorites Tools Help
Back
Address http://localhost:1405/WebControls/TablePictures.aspx
Rows: 4
Cols: 3
Put Border Around Cells
Create
Done
Local intranet

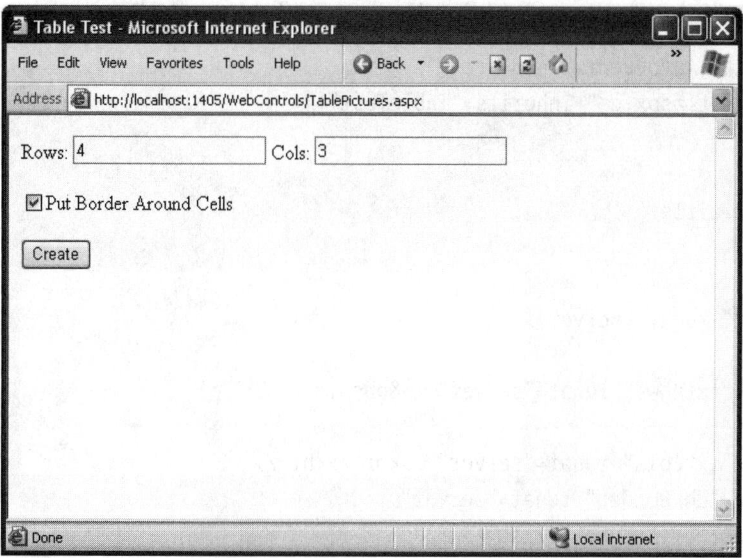

Figure 6-8. *The table test options*

When the user clicks the create button, the table is filled dynamically with sample data according to the selected options, as shown in Figure 6-9.

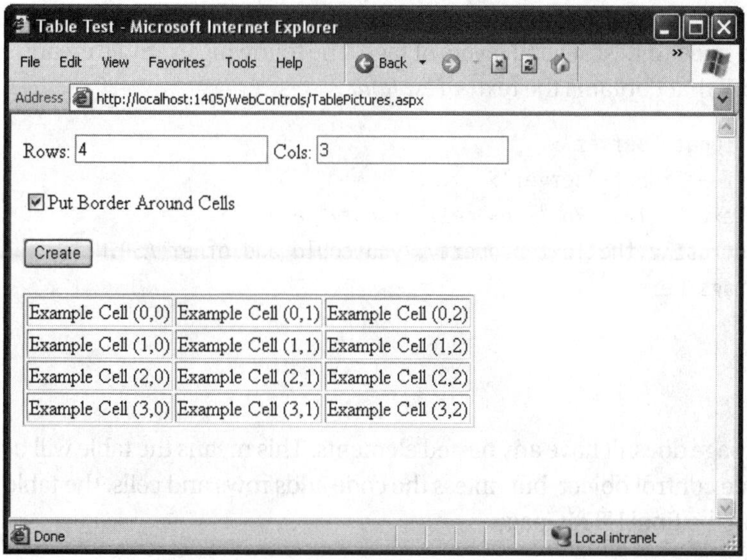

Table Test - Microsoft Internet Explorer
File Edit View Favorites Tools Help
Back
Address http://localhost:1405/WebControls/TablePictures.aspx
Rows: 4
Cols: 3
Put Border Around Cells
Create
Example Cell (0,0)
Example Cell (0,1)
Example Cell (0,2)
Example Cell (1,0)
Example Cell (1,1)
Example Cell (1,2)
Example Cell (2,0)
Example Cell (2,1)
Example Cell (2,2)
Example Cell (3,0)
Example Cell (3,1)
Example Cell (3,2)
Done
Local intranet

Figure 6-9. *A dynamically generated table*

The .aspx code creates the TextBox, CheckBox, Button, and Table controls:

```
<%@ Page Language="C#" AutoEventWireup="true"
    CodeFile="TableTest.aspx.cs" Inherits="TableTest" %>
<html>
<head runat="server">
  <title>Table Test</title>
</head>
<body>
  <form method="post" runat="server">
    Rows:
    <asp:TextBox id="txtRows" runat="server" /> 
    Cols:
    <asp:TextBox id="txtCols" runat="server" /><br /><br />
    <asp:CheckBox id="chkBorder" runat="server"
         Text="Put Border Around Cells" />
    <br /><br />
    <asp:Button id="cmdCreate" OnClick="cmdCreate_Click" runat="server"
     Text="Create" /><br /><br />
    <asp:Table id="tbl" runat="server" />
  </form>
</body></html>
```

You'll notice that the Table control doesn't contain any actual rows or cells. To make a valid table, you would need to nest several layers of tags. The following example creates a table with a single cell that contains the text *A Test Row*:

```
<asp:Table id="tbl" runat="server">
  <asp:TableRow id="row" runat="server">
    <asp:TableCell Text="A Test Row" id="cell" runat="server">
      <!-- Instead of using the Text property, you could add other ASP.NET
           control tags here. -->
    </asp:TableCell>
  </asp:TableRow>
</asp:Table>
```

The table test web page doesn't have any nested elements. This means the table will be created as a server-side control object, but unless the code adds rows and cells, the table will not be rendered in the final HTML page.

The TableTest class uses two event handlers. When the page is first loaded, it adds a border around the table. When the button is clicked, it dynamically creates the required TableRow and TableCell objects in a loop:

```
using System;
using System.Web;
using System.Web.UI;
using System.Web.UI.WebControls;
using System.Web.UI.HtmlControls;

public partial class TableTest : System.Web.UI.Page
{
    protected void Page_Load(object sender, System.EventArgs e)
    {
        // Configure the table's appearance.
        // This could also be performed in the .aspx file
        // or in the cmdCreate_Click event handler.
        tbl.BorderStyle = BorderStyle.Inset;
        tbl.BorderWidth = Unit.Pixel(1);
    }

    protected void cmdCreate_Click(object sender, System.EventArgs e)
    {
        // Remove all the current rows and cells.
        // This is not necessary if EnableViewState is set to false.
        tbl.Controls.Clear();

        int rows = Int32.Parse(txtRows.Text);
        int cols = Int32.Parse(txtCols.Text);
        TableCell cellNew = null;
        for (int row = 0; row < rows; row++)
        {
            // Create a new TableRow object.
            TableRow rowNew = new TableRow();

            // Put the TableRow in the Table.
            tbl.Controls.Add(rowNew);
```

```
                for (int col = 0; col < cols; col++)
                {
                    // Create a new TableCell object.
                    cellNew = new TableCell();

                    cellNew.Text = "Example Cell (" + row.ToString() + ",";
                    cellNew.Text += col.ToString() + ")";

                    if (chkBorder.Checked)
                    {
                        cellNew.BorderStyle = BorderStyle.Inset;
                        cellNew.BorderWidth = Unit.Pixel(1);
                    }

                    // Put the TableCell in the TableRow.
                    rowNew.Controls.Add(cellNew);
                }
            }
        }
    }
```

This code uses the Controls collection to add child controls. Every container control provides this property. You could also use the TableCell.Controls collection to add web controls to each TableCell. For example, you could place an Image control and a Label control in each cell. In this case, you can't set the TableCell.Text property. The following code snippet uses this technique, and Figure 6-10 displays the results:

```
// Create a new TableCell object.
cellNew = new TableCell();

// Create a new Label object.
Label lblNew = new Label();
lblNew.Text = "Example Cell (" + row.ToString() + "," + col.ToString() +
  ")<br />";

System.Web.UI.WebControls.Image imgNew = new System.Web.UI.WebControls.Image();
imgNew.ImageUrl = "cellpic.png";
```

```
// Put the label and picture in the cell.
cellNew.Controls.Add(lblNew);
cellNew.Controls.Add(imgNew);

// Put the TableCell in the TableRow.
rowNew.Controls.Add(cellNew);
```

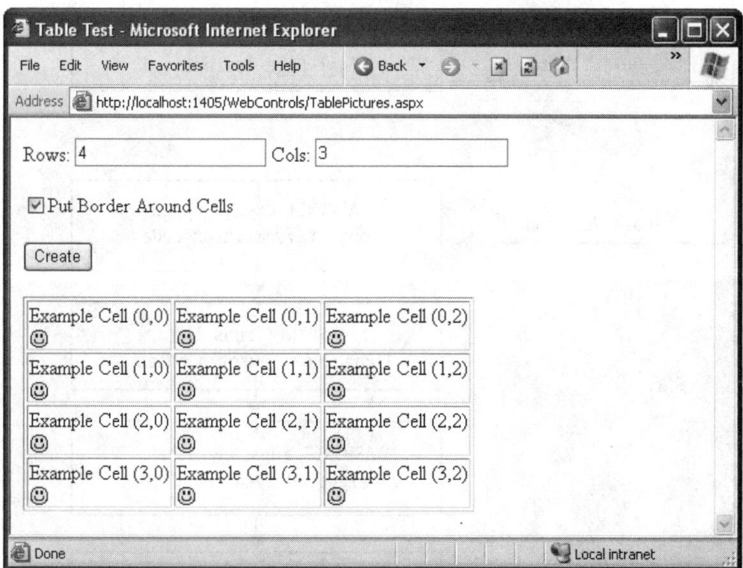

Figure 6-10. *A table with contained controls*

The real flexibility of the table test page is that each Table, TableRow, and TableCell is a full-featured object. If you want, you can give each cell a different border style, border color, and text color by setting the corresponding properties.

AutoPostBack and Web Control Events

The previous chapter explained that one of the main limitations of HTML server controls is their limited set of useful events—they have exactly two. HTML controls that trigger a postback, such as buttons, raise a ServerClick event. Input controls provide a ServerChange event that doesn't actually fire until the page is posted back.

Server controls are really an ingenious illusion. You'll recall that the code in an ASP.NET page is processed on the server. It's then sent to the user as ordinary HTML. Figure 6-11 illustrates the order of events in page processing.

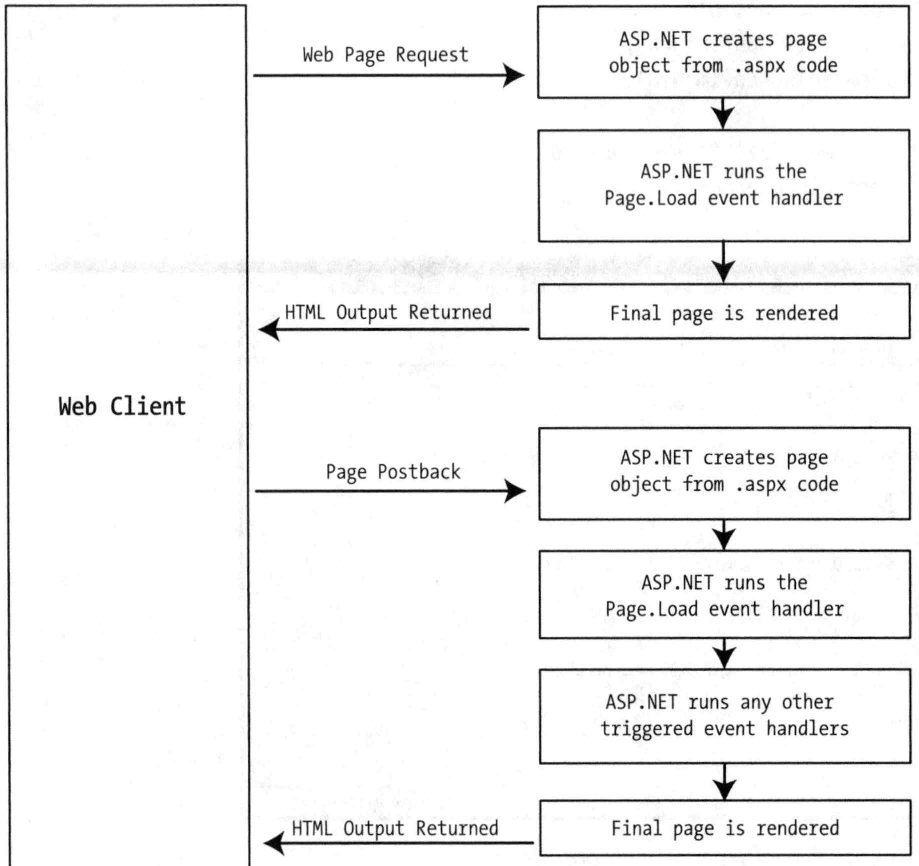

Figure 6-11. *The page processing sequence*

This is the same in ASP.NET as it was in traditional ASP programming. The question is, how can you write server code that will react immediately to an event that occurs on the client? The answer is a new innovation called the *automatic postback*.

The automatic postback submits a page back to the server when it detects a specific user action. This gives your code the chance to run again and create a new, updated page. Controls that support automatic postbacks include almost all input web controls. Table 6-5 provides a basic list of web controls and their events.

Table 6-5. *Web Control Events*

Event	Web Controls That Provide It
Click	Button, ImageButton
TextChanged	TextBox (fires only after the user changes the focus to another control)
CheckChanged	CheckBox, RadioButton
SelectedIndexChanged	DropDownList, ListBox, CheckBoxList, RadioButtonList

If you want to capture a change event (like TextChanged, CheckChanged, or SelectedIndexChanged) immediately, you need to set the control's AutoPostBack property to true. This means that when the user clicks a radio button or check box, the page will be resubmitted to the server. The server examines the page, loads all the current information, and then allows your code to perform some extra processing before returning the page back to the user. Depending on the result you want, you could have a page that has some controls that post back automatically, and others that don't.

In other words, every time you need to update the web page, it's actually being sent to the server and re-created (see Figure 6-12). However, ASP.NET makes this process so transparent that your code can treat your web page like a continuously running program that fires events.

This postback system isn't ideal for all events. For example, some events that you may be familiar with from Windows programs, such as mouse movement events or key press events, aren't practical in an ASP.NET application. Resubmitting the page every time a key is pressed or the mouse is moved would make the application unbearably slow and unresponsive.

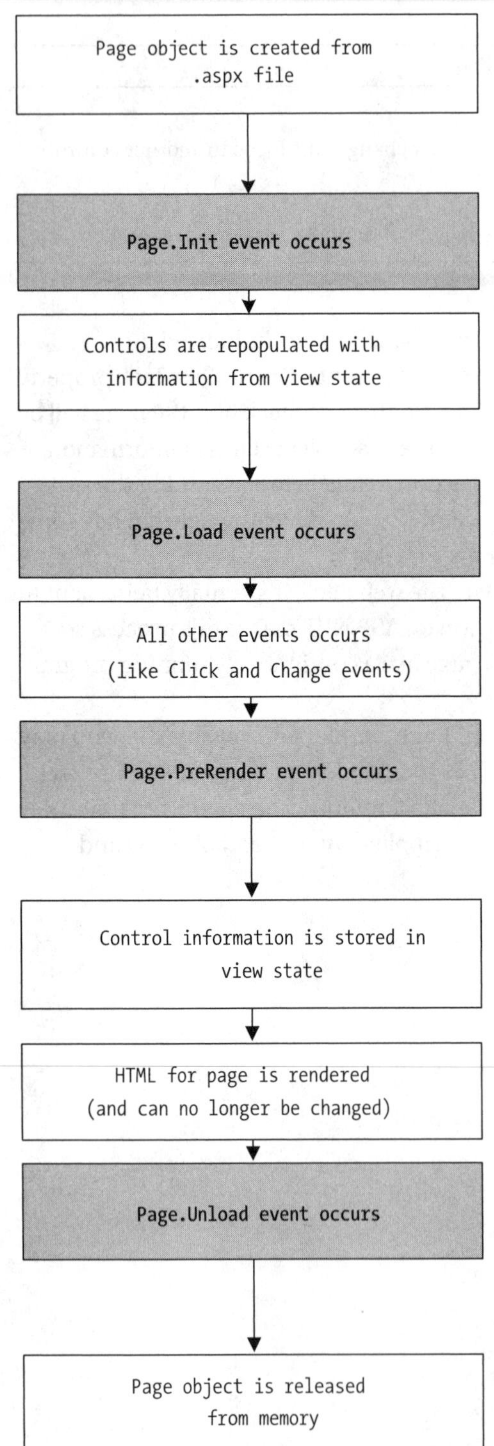

Figure 6-12. *The postback processing sequence*

How Postback Events Work

Chapter 1 explained that not all types of web programming use server-side code like ASP.NET. One common example of client-side web programming is JavaScript, which uses simple code that's limited in scope and is executed by the browser. ASP.NET uses the client-side abilities of JavaScript to bridge the gap between client-side and server-side code.

Here's how it works: If you create a web page that includes one or more web controls that are configured to use AutoPostBack, ASP.NET adds a special JavaScript function to the rendered HTML page. This function is named __doPostBack(). When called, it triggers a postback, sending data back to the web server.

ASP.NET also adds two additional hidden input fields that are used to pass information back to the server. This information consists of the ID of the control that raised the event and any additional information that might be relevant. These fields are initially empty, as shown here:

```
<input type="hidden" name="__EVENTTARGET" value="" />
<input type="hidden" name="__EVENTARGUMENT" value="" />
```

The __doPostBack() function has the responsibility for setting these values with the appropriate information about the event and then submitting the form. A sample __doPostBack() function is shown here:

```
<script language="javascript">
<!--
    function __doPostBack(eventTarget, eventArgument) {
        var theform = document.Form1;
        theform.__EVENTTARGET.value = eventTarget;
        theform.__EVENTARGUMENT.value = eventArgument;
        theform.submit();
    }
// -->
</script>
```

Remember, ASP.NET generates the __doPostBack() function automatically, provided at least one control on the page uses automatic postbacks. This code grows lengthier as you add more AutoPostBack controls to your page, because the event data must be set for each control.

Finally, any control that has its AutoPostBack property set to true is connected to the __doPostBack() function using the onclick or onchange attributes. These attributes indicate what action the browser should take in response to the client-side JavaScript events onclick and onchange.

The following example shows the tag for a list control named lstBackColor, which posts back automatically. Whenever the user changes the selection in the list, the client-side onchange event fires. The browser then calls the __doPostBack() function, which sends the page back to the server.

```
<select id="lstBackColor" onchange="__doPostBack('lstBackColor','')"
 language="javascript">
```

In other words, ASP.NET automatically changes a client-side JavaScript event into a server-side ASP.NET event, using the __doPostBack() function as an intermediary. Figure 6-13 shows this process.

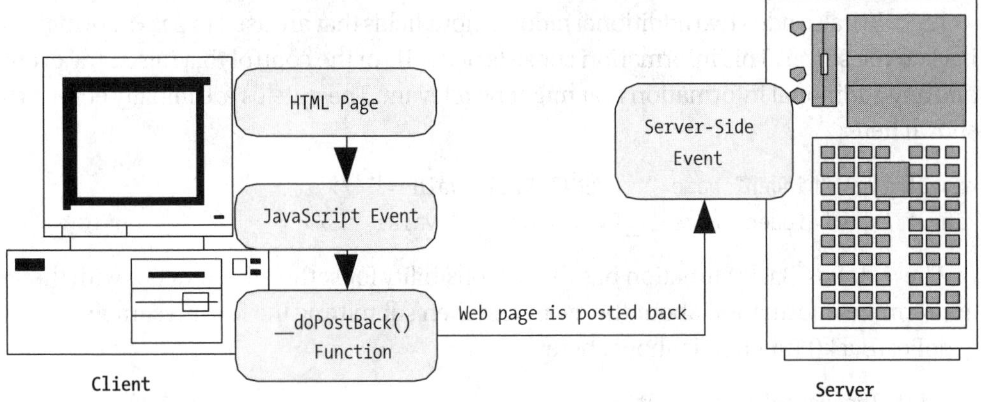

Figure 6-13. *An automatic postback*

If you're a seasoned ASP developer, you may have manually created a solution like this for traditional ASP web pages. ASP.NET handles these details for you automatically, simplifying life a great deal.

The Page Life Cycle

To understand how web control events work, you need to have a solid understanding of the page life cycle. Consider what happens when a user changes a control that has the AutoPostBack property set to true:

1. On the client side, the JavaScript __doPostBack event is invoked, and the page is resubmitted to the server.

2. ASP.NET re-creates the Page object using the .aspx file.

3. ASP.NET retrieves state information from the hidden view state field and updates the controls accordingly.

4. The Page.Load event is fired.

5. The appropriate change event is fired for the control. (If more than one control has been changed, the order of change events is undetermined.)

6. The Page.Unload event fires, and the page is rendered (transformed from a set of objects to an HTML page).

7. The new page is sent to the client.

To watch these events in action, it helps to create a simple event tracker application (see Figure 6-14). All this application does is write a new entry to a list control every time one of the events it's monitoring occurs. This allows you to see the order in which events are triggered.

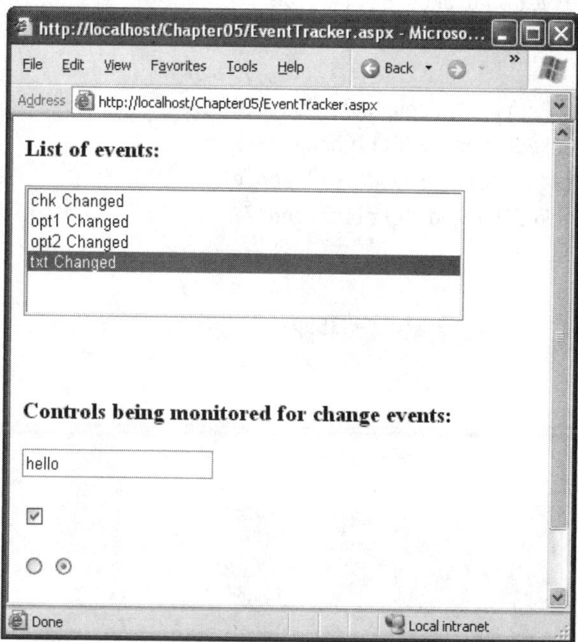

Figure 6-14. *The event tracker*

Listing 6-1 shows the markup code for the event tracker, and Listing 6-2 shows the code-behind class that makes it work.

Listing 6-1. *EventTracker.aspx*

```
<%@ Page Language="C#" AutoEventWireup="true"
    CodeFile="EventTracker.aspx.cs" Inherits="EventTracker" %>
<html>
<head runat="server">
  <title>Event Tracker</title>
</head>
<body>
  <form method="post" runat="server">
    <h3>Controls being monitored for change events:</h3>
    <asp:TextBox id=txt runat="server" AutoPostBack="true"
     OnTextChanged="CtrlChanged" />
    <br /><br />
    <asp:CheckBox id=chk runat="server" AutoPostBack="true"
     OnCheckedChanged="CtrlChanged"/>
    <br /><br />
    <asp:RadioButton id=opt1 runat="server" GroupName="Sample"
         AutoPostBack="true" OnCheckedChanged="CtrlChanged"/>
    <asp:RadioButton id=opt2 runat="server" GroupName="Sample"
         AutoPostBack="true" OnCheckedChanged="CtrlChanged"/>
    <br /><br /><br />
    <h3>List of events:</h3>
    <asp:ListBox id=lstEvents runat="server" Width="355px"
         Height="505px" /><br />
  </form>
</body></html>
```

Listing 6-2. *EventTracker.cs*

```
using System;
using System.Web;
using System.Web.UI;
using System.Web.UI.WebControls;
using System.Web.UI.HtmlControls;
```

```
public partial class EventTracker : System.Web.UI.Page
{
    protected void Page_Load(object sender, System.EventArgs e)
    {
        Log("<< Page_Load >>");
    }

    protected void EventTracker_PreRender(object sender, System.EventArgs e)
    {
        // When the Page.UnLoad event occurs, it is too late
        // to change the list.
        Log("Page_PreRender");
    }

    protected void CtrlChanged(Object sender, EventArgs e)
    {
        // Find the control ID of the sender.
        // This requires converting the Object type into a Control class.
        string ctrlName = ((Control)sender).ID;
        Log(ctrlName + " Changed");
    }

    private void Log(string entry)
    {
        lstEvents.Items.Add(entry);

        // Select the last item to scroll the list so the most recent
        // entries are visible.
        lstEvents.SelectedIndex = lstEvents.Items.Count - 1;
    }
}
```

Dissecting the Code...

The following points are worth noting about this code:

- The code writes to the ListBox using a private Log() subroutine. The Log() subroutine adds the text and automatically scrolls to the bottom of the list each time a new entry is added, thereby ensuring that the most recent entries remain visible.
- All the change events are handled by the same subroutine, CtrlChanged(). The event handling code uses the source parameter to find out what control sent the event, and it incorporates that information in the log string.

A Simple Web Page Applet

Now that you've had a whirlwind tour of the basic web control model, it's time to put it to work with the second single-page utility. In this case, it's a simple example for a dynamic e-card generator. You could extend this sample (for example, allowing users to store e-cards to the database or using the techniques in Chapter 16 to mail notification to card recipients), but even on its own, this example demonstrates basic control manipulation with ASP.NET.

The web page is divided into two regions. On the left is an ordinary <div> tag containing a set of web controls for specifying card options. On the right is a Panel control (named pnlCard), which contains two other controls (lblGreeting and imgDefault) that are used to display user-configurable text and a picture. This text and picture represents the greeting card. When the page first loads, the card hasn't yet been generated and the right portion is blank (as shown in Figure 6-15).

■ **Tip** The <div> tag is useful when you want to group text and controls and apply a set of formatting properties (such as a color or font) to all of them. The <div> tag is used in many of the examples in this book, but it can safely be omitted—the only change will be the appearance of the formatted page.

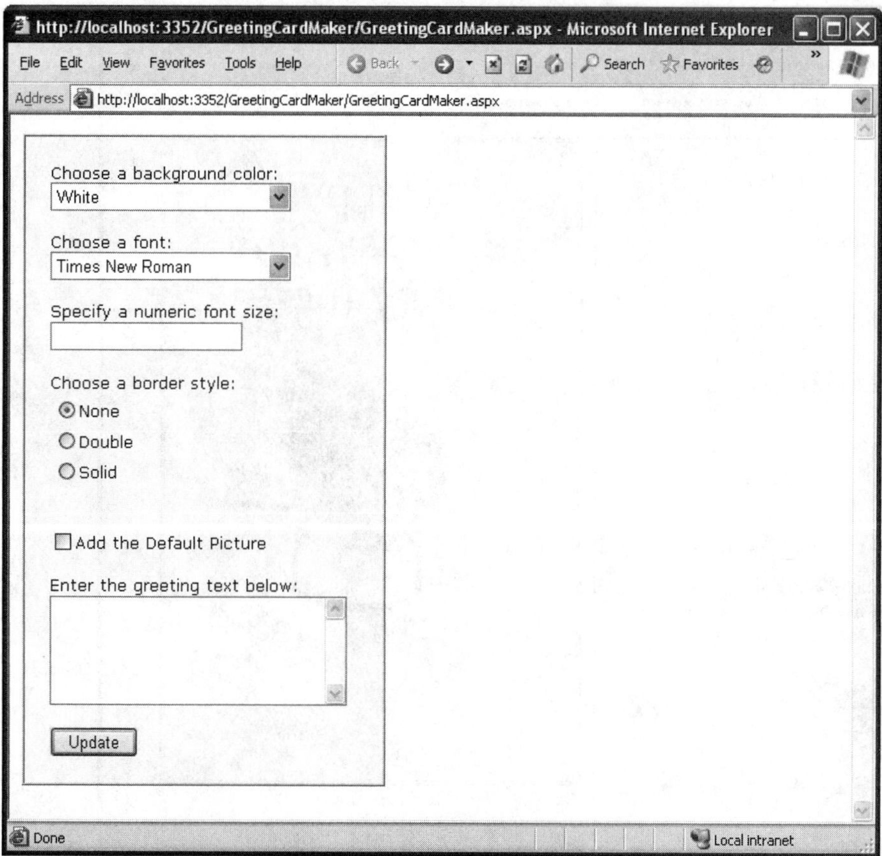

Figure 6-15. *The e-card generator*

Whenever the user clicks the OK button, the page is posted back and the "card" is updated (see Figure 6-16).

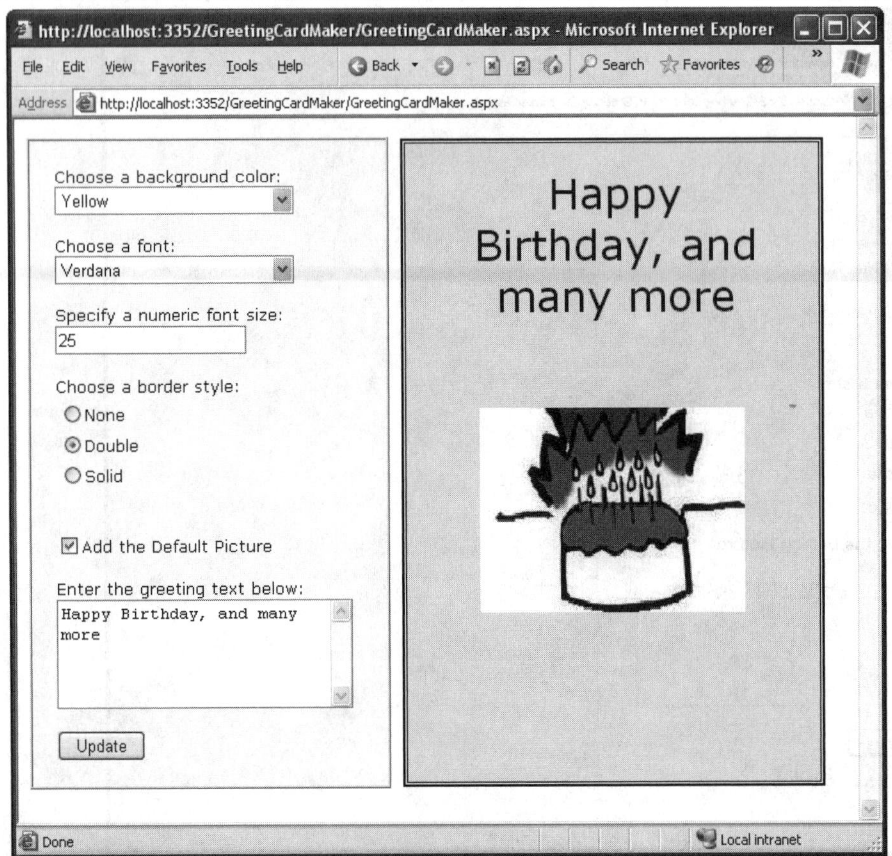

Figure 6-16. *A user-configured greeting card*

The .aspx layout code is straightforward. Of course, the sheer length of it makes it difficult to work with efficiently. This is an ideal point to start considering Visual Studio, which will handle the .aspx details for you automatically and won't require you to painstakingly format and organize the user interface markup tags. Here's the code:

```
<%@ Page Language="C#" AutoEventWireup="true"
    Inherits="GreetingCardMaker" CodeFile="GreetingCardMaker.aspx.cs" %>
<html>
<head runat="server">
    <title>Greeting Card Maker</title>
</head>
```

```
<body>
  <form method="post" runat="server">
    <!-- div style attribute left out for clarity. -->
    <div>
      <!-- Here are the controls: -->
      Choose a background color:<br />
      <asp:DropDownList id="lstBackColor" runat="server" Width="194px"
        Height="22px"/><br /><br />
      Choose a font:<br />
      <asp:DropDownList id="lstFontName" runat="server" Width="194px"
        Height="22px" /><br /><br />
      Specify a numeric font size:<br />
      <asp:TextBox id="txtFontSize" runat="server" /><br /><br />
      Choose a border style:<br />
      <asp:RadioButtonList id="lstBorder" runat="server" Width="177px"
        Height="59px" /><br /><br />
      <asp:CheckBox id="chkPicture" runat="server"
        Text="Add the Default Picture"></asp:CheckBox><br /><br />
      Enter the greeting text below:<br />
      <asp:TextBox id="txtGreeting" runat="server" Width="240px" Height="85px"
        TextMode="MultiLine" /><br /><br />
      <asp:Button id="cmdUpdate" OnClick="cmdUpdate_Click"
        runat="server" Width="71px" Height="24px" Text="Update" />
    </div>

    <!-- Here is the card: -->
    <asp:Panel id="pnlCard" style="Z-INDEX: 101; LEFT: 313px; POSITION:
absolute;
      TOP: 16px" runat="server" Width="339px" Height="481px"
      HorizontalAlign="Center"><br /> 
    <asp:Label id="lblGreeting" runat="server" Width="256px"
      Height="150px" /><br /><br /><br />
    <asp:Image id="imgDefault" runat="server" Width="212px"
      Height="160px" />
    </asp:Panel>
  </form>
</body></html>
```

The code follows the familiar pattern with an emphasis on two events: the Page.Load event, where initial values are set, and the Button.Click event, where the card is generated.

The using statements are omitted from the following listing, because the basic set of required namespaces should be familiar to you by now:

```
public partial class GreetingCardMaker : System.Web.UI.Page
{
    protected void Page_Load(object sender, System.EventArgs e)
    {
        if (!this.IsPostBack)
        {
            // Set color options.
            lstBackColor.Items.Add("White");
            lstBackColor.Items.Add("Red");
            lstBackColor.Items.Add("Green");
            lstBackColor.Items.Add("Blue");
            lstBackColor.Items.Add("Yellow");

            // Set font options.
            lstFontName.Items.Add("Times New Roman");
            lstFontName.Items.Add("Arial");
            lstFontName.Items.Add("Verdana");
            lstFontName.Items.Add("Tahoma");

            // Set border style options by adding a series of
            // ListItem objects.
            ListItem item = new ListItem();

            // The item text indicates the name of the option.
            item.Text = BorderStyle.None.ToString();

            // The item value records the corresponding integer
            // from the enumeration. To obtain this value, you
            // must cast the enumeration value to an integer,
            // and then convert the number to a string so it
            // can be placed in the HTML page.
            item.Value = ((int)BorderStyle.None).ToString();

            // Add the item.
            lstBorder.Items.Add(item);
```

```
        // Now repeat the process for two other border styles.
        item = new ListItem();
        item.Text = BorderStyle.Double.ToString();
        item.Value = ((int)BorderStyle.Double).ToString();
        lstBorder.Items.Add(item);

        item = new ListItem();
        item.Text = BorderStyle.Solid.ToString();
        item.Value = ((int)BorderStyle.Solid).ToString();
        lstBorder.Items.Add(item);

        // Select the first border option.
        lstBorder.SelectedIndex = 0;

        // Set the picture.
        imgDefault.ImageUrl = "defaultpic.png";
    }
}

protected void cmdUpdate_Click(object sender, System.EventArgs e)
{
    // Update the color.
    pnlCard.BackColor = Color.FromName(lstBackColor.SelectedItem.Text);

    // Update the font.
    lblGreeting.Font.Name = lstFontName.SelectedItem.Text;

    if (Int32.Parse(txtFontSize.Text) > 0)
    {
        lblGreeting.Font.Size =
          FontUnit.Point(Int32.Parse(txtFontSize.Text));
    }

    // Update the border style. This requires two conversion steps.
    // First, the value of the list item is converted from a string
    // into an integer. Next, the integer is converted to a value in
    // the BorderStyle enumeration.
    int boderValue = Int32.Parse(lstBorder.SelectedItem.Value);
    pnlCard.BorderStyle = (BorderStyle)borderValue;
```

```
        // Update the picture.
        if (chkPicture.Checked)
        {
            imgDefault.Visible = true;
        }
        else
        {
            imgDefault.Visible = false;
        }

        // Set the text.
        lblGreeting.Text = txtGreeting.Text;
    }
}
```

As you can see, this example limits the user to a few preset font and color choices. The code for the BorderStyle option is particularly interesting. The lstBorder control has a list that displays the text name of one of the BorderStyle enumerated values. You'll remember from the introductory chapters that every enumerated value is really an integer with a name assigned to it. The lstBorder also secretly stores the corresponding number so that the code can retrieve the number and set the enumeration easily when the user makes a selection and the cmdUpdate_Click event handler fires.

Improving the Greeting Card Applet

ASP.NET pages have access to the full .NET class library. With a little exploration, you'll find classes that might help the greeting-card maker, such as tools that let you retrieve all the known color names and all the fonts installed on the web server.

For example, you can fill the lstFontName control with a list of fonts using the special System.Drawing.Text.InstalledFontCollection class. Here's the code you'll need:

```
// Get the list of available fonts, and add them to the font list.
System.Drawing.Text.InstalledFontCollection fonts;
fonts = new System.Drawing.Text.InstalledFontCollection();
foreach (FontFamily family in fonts.Families)
{
    lstFontName.Items.Add(family.Name);
}
```

Figure 6-17 shows the resulting font list.

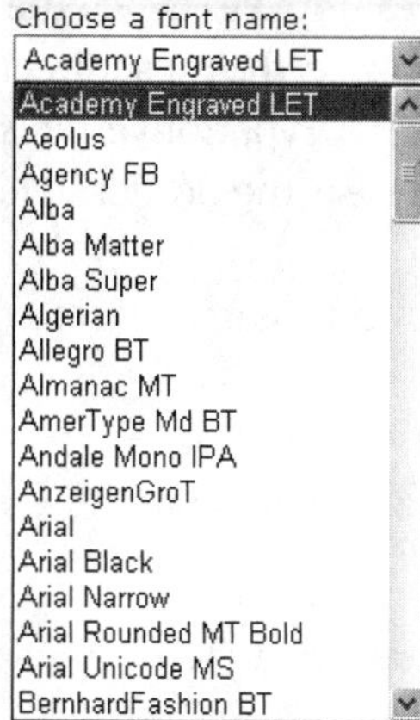

Figure 6-17. *The font list*

You can also get a list of color names from the System.Drawing.KnownColor enumeration. To do this, you use one of basic enumeration features: the static Enum.GetNames() method, which inspects an enumeration and provides an array of strings, with one string for each value in the enumeration. A minor problem with this approach is that it includes system environment colors (for example, Active Border) in the list. It may not be obvious to the user what colors these values represent. Still, this approach works well for this simple application.

```
// Get the list of colors.
string[] colorArray = Enum.GetNames(typeof(System.Drawing.KnownColor));
lstBackColor.DataSource = colorArray;
lstBackColor.DataBind();
```

This web page can then use data binding to automatically fill the list control with information from the ColorArray. You'll explore data binding in much more detail in Chapter 14.

You can use a similar technique to fill in BorderStyle options:

```
// Set border style options.
string[] borderStyleArray = Enum.GetNames(typeof(BorderStyle));
lstBorder.DataSource = borderStyleArray;
lstBorder.DataBind();
```

This code raises a new challenge: how do you convert the value that the user selects into the appropriate constant for the enumeration? When the user chooses a border style from the list, the SelectedItem property will have a text string like "Groove". But to apply this border style to the control, you need a way to determine the enumerated constant that matches this text.

You can handle this problem in a few ways. (Earlier, you saw an example in which the enumeration integer was stored as a value in the list control.) In this case, the most direct approach involves using an advanced feature called a TypeConverter. A TypeConverter is a special class that is able to convert from a specialized type (in this case, the BorderStyle enumeration) to a simpler type (such as a string), and vice versa.

To access this class, you need to import the System.ComponentModel namespace:

```
using System.ComponentModel;
```

You can then add the following code to the cmdUpdate_Click event handler:

```
// Find the appropriate TypeConverter for the BorderStyle enumeration.
TypeConverter cnvrt = TypeDescriptor.GetConverter(typeof(BorderStyle));

// Update the border style using the value from the converter.
pnlCard.BorderStyle = cnvrt.ConvertFromString(
  lstBorder.SelectedItem.Text);
```

Don't worry if this example introduces a few features that look entirely alien! These features are more advanced (and aren't tied specifically to ASP.NET). However, they show you some of the flavor that the full .NET class library can provide for a mature application.

Generating the Cards Automatically

The last step is to use ASP.NET's automatic postback events to make the card update dynamically every time an option is changed. The OK button could now be used to submit the final, perfected greeting card, which might then be e-mailed to a recipient or stored in a database.

To configure the controls so they automatically trigger a page postback, simply add the AutoPostBack="true" attribute to each user input control. An example is shown here:

```
Choose a background color:<br />
<asp:DropDownList id="lstBackColor" AutoPostBack="true" runat="server"
    Width="194px" Height="22px"/><br /><br />
```

Next, you need to create an event handler that can handle the change events. To save a few steps, you can use the same event handler for all the input controls. All the event handler needs to do is call the update routine that regenerates the greeting card.

```
protected void ControlChanged(object sender, System.EventArgs e)
{
    // Refresh the greeting card (because a control was clicked).
    UpdateCard();
}
```

```
protected void cmdUpdate_Click(object sender, System.EventArgs e)
{
    // Refresh the greeting card (because the button was clicked).
    UpdateCard();
}

protected void UpdateCard()
{
    // (The code that draws the greeting card goes here.)
}
```

Next, alter the control tags so that the changed event of each input control is connected to the ControlChanged event handler. You'll notice that the name of the change event depends on the control. For example, the TextBox provides a TextChanged event, the ListBox provides a SelectedIndexChanged event, and so on.

With these changes, it's easy to perfect the more extensive card-generating program shown in Figure 6-18. The full code for this application is provided with the online samples.

■ **Tip** Automatic postback isn't always best. Sometimes an automatic postback can annoy a user, especially when the user is working over a slow connection or when the server needs to perform a time-consuming option. For that reason, it's sometimes best to use an explicit submit button and not enable AutoPostBack for most input controls.

A WORD ABOUT CONVENTIONS

From this point on, the examples will adopt a few conventions designed to make code examples more concise and readable:

- The .aspx layout file is rarely shown with an example, unless it requires special coding (such as the creation of a template or data-binding syntax, two topics you'll explore in Part 3 of this book). The .aspx files are really nothing more than an ordering of standard control tags.
- The using statements in the code-behind file are omitted, unless they reference an unusual namespace that hasn't been identified. Generally, you'll reuse the same standard block of using statements for each code-behind file.

These changes won't affect you if you're using an IDE such as Visual Studio, which generates the .aspx file, control variables, and most using statements automatically. And if you want to see the full details, you'll find them in the downloadable code.

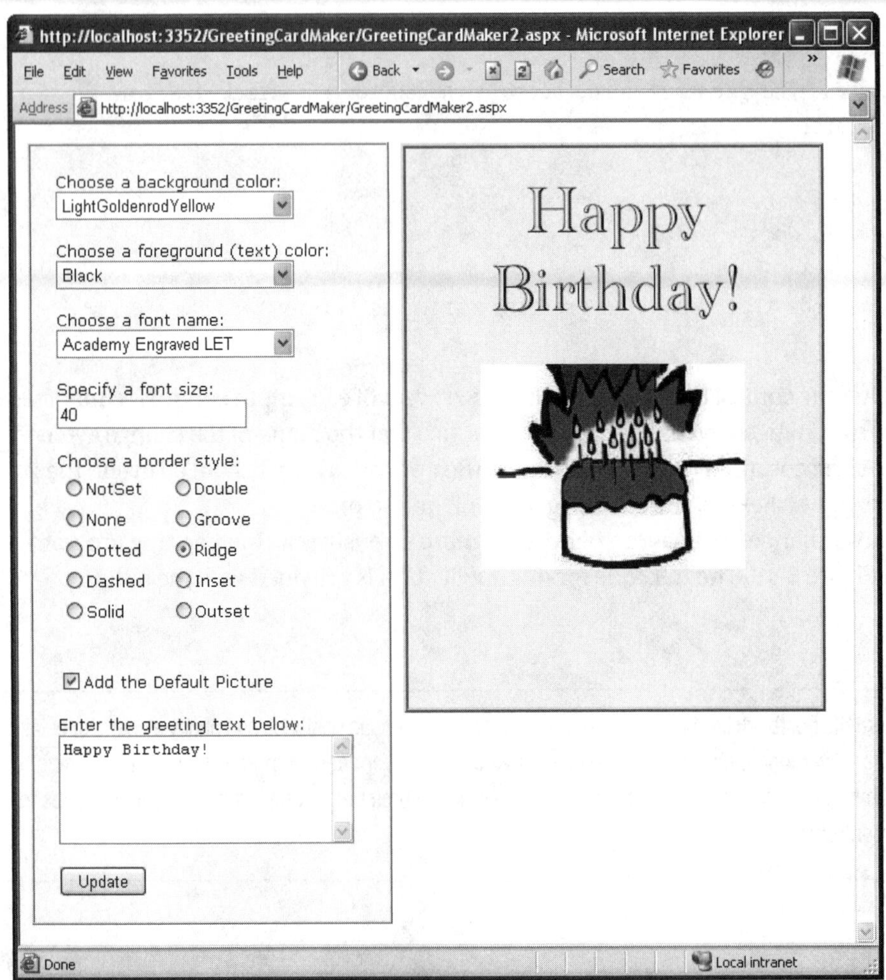

Figure 6-18. *A more extensive card generator*

The Last Word

This chapter introduced you to web controls and their object interface. As you continue through this book, you'll learn more about the web controls. The following highlights are still to come:

- In Chapter 8, you'll learn about advanced controls such as the AdRotator, the Calendar, and the validation controls. You'll also learn about specialized container controls, like the MultiView and Wizard.
- In Chapter 11, you'll learn about navigation controls like the TreeView and Menu.
- In Chapter 15, you'll learn about the GridView, DetailsView, and FormView—high-level web controls that let you manipulate a complex table of data from any data source.
- In Chapter 25, you'll learn how you can use .NET inheritance to create your own customized web controls.

For a good reference that shows each web control and lists its important properties, refer to the MSDN Help.

CHAPTER 7

Tracing, Logging, and Error Handling

No software can run free from error, and ASP.NET applications are no exception. Sooner or later your code will be interrupted by a programming mistake, invalid data, unexpected circumstances, or even hardware failure. Novice programmers spend sleepless nights worrying about errors. Professional developers recognize that bugs are an inherent part of software applications and code defensively, testing assumptions, logging problems, and writing error handling code to deal with the unexpected.

In this chapter, you'll learn the error handling and debugging practices that can defend your ASP.NET applications against common errors, can track user problems, and can help you solve mysterious issues. You'll learn how to use structured exception handling, how to use logs to keep a record of unrecoverable errors, and how to configure custom web pages for common HTTP errors. You'll also learn how to use page tracing to see diagnostic information about ASP.NET pages.

Common Errors

Errors can occur in a variety of situations. Some of the most common causes of errors include attempts to divide by zero (usually caused by invalid input or missing information) and attempts to connect to a limited resource such as a file or a database (which can fail if the file doesn't exist, the database connection times out, or the code has insufficient security credentials).

Another infamous type of error is the *null reference exception*, which usually occurs when a program attempts to use an uninitialized object. As a .NET programmer, you'll quickly learn to recognize and resolve this common but annoying mistake. The following code example shows the problem in action:

```
SqlConnection conOne;
...
// The next line will fail and generate a null reference exception.
// You cannot modify a property (or use a method) of an object that
// doesn't exist!
conOne.ConnectionString = "...";

SqlConnection conTwo = new SqlConnection();
...
// This works, because the object has been initialized
// with the new keyword.
conTwo.ConnectionString = "...";
```

When an error occurs in your code, .NET checks to see whether any active error handlers appear in the current scope. If the error occurs inside a function, .NET searches for local error handlers and then checks for any active error handlers in the calling code. If no error handlers are found, the page processing is aborted, and an error page is displayed in the browser. Depending on whether the request came from the local computer or a remote client, the error page may show a detailed description (as shown in Figure 7-1) or a generic message. You'll explore this topic a little later in the "Error Pages" section of this chapter.

Even if an error is the result of invalid input or the failure of a third-party component, an error page can shatter the professional appearance of any application. The application users end up with a feeling that the application is unstable, insecure, or of poor quality—and they're at least partially correct.

If an ASP.NET application is carefully designed and constructed, an error page will almost never appear. Errors may still occur because of unforeseen circumstances, but they will be caught in the code and identified. If the error is a critical one that the application cannot solve on its own, it will report a more useful (and user-friendly) page of information that might include a link to a support e-mail or phone number where the customer can receive additional assistance. You'll look at those techniques in this chapter.

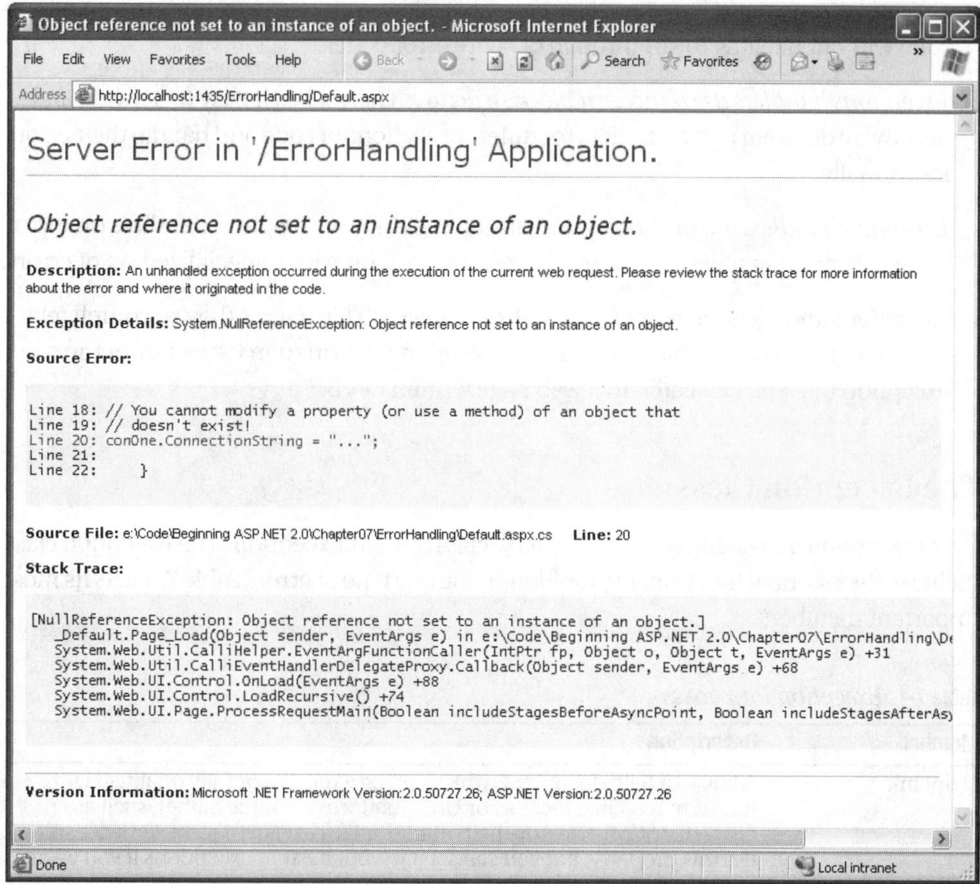

Figure 7-1. *A sample error page*

Exception Handling

Most .NET languages support *structured exception handling*. Essentially, when an error occurs in your application, the .NET Framework creates an exception object that represents the problem. You can catch this object using an exception handler. However, if you fail to use an exception handler, your code will be aborted, and the user will see an error page.

Structured exception handling provides several key features:

Exceptions are object-based: Each exception provides a significant amount of diagnostic information wrapped into a neat object, instead of a simple message and error code. These exception objects also support an InnerException property that allows you to wrap a generic error over the more specific error that caused it. You can even create and throw your own exception objects.

Exceptions are caught based on their type: This allows you to streamline error handling code without needing to sift through obscure error codes.

Exceptions handlers use a modern block structure: This makes it easy to activate and deactivate different error handlers for different sections of code and handle their errors individually.

Exception handlers are multilayered: You can easily layer exception handlers on top of other exception handlers, some of which may check only for a specialized set of errors.

Exceptions are a generic part of the .NET Framework: This means they're completely cross-language compatible. Thus, a .NET component written in C# can throw an exception that you can catch in a web page written in VB.

The Exception Class

Every exception object derives from the base class System.Exception. The Exception class includes the essential functionality for identifying any type of error. Table 7-1 lists its most important members.

Table 7-1. *Exception Properties*

Member	Description
HelpLink	A link to a help document, which can be a relative or fully qualified URL (uniform resource locator) or URN (uniform resource name), such as file:///C:/ACME/MyApp/help.html#Err42. The .NET Framework doesn't use this property, but you can set it in your custom exceptions if you want to use it in your web page code.
InnerException	A nested exception. For example, a method might catch a simple file IO (input/output) error and create a higher-level "operation failed" error. The details about the original error could be retained in the InnerException property of the higher-level error.
Message	Contains a text description with a significant amount of information describing the problem.
Source	The name of the assembly where the exception was raised.
StackTrace	A string that contains a list of all the current method calls on the stack, in order of most to least recent. This is useful for determining where the problem occurred.
TargetSite	A reflection object (an instance of the System.Reflection.MethodBase class) that provides some information about the method where the error occurred. This information includes generic method details such as the procedure name and the data types for its parameter and return value. It doesn't contain any information about the actual parameter values that were used when the problem occurred.
GetBaseException()	This method is useful for nested exceptions that may have more than one layer. It retrieves the original (deepest nested) exception by moving to the base of the InnerException chain.

When you catch an exception in an ASP.NET, it won't be an instance of the generic System.Exception class. Instead, it will be an object that represents a specific type of error. This object will be based on one of the many classes that inherit from System.Exception. These include diverse classes such as DivideByZeroException, ArithmeticException, System.IO.IOException, System.Security.SecurityException, and many more. Some of these classes provide additional details about the error in additional properties.

Visual Studio provides a useful tool to browse through the exceptions in the .NET class library. Simply select Debug ➤ Exceptions from the menu (you'll need to have a project open in order for this work). The Exceptions dialog box will appear. Expand the Common Language Runtime Exceptions group, which shows a hierarchical tree of .NET exceptions arranged by namespace (see Figure 7-2).

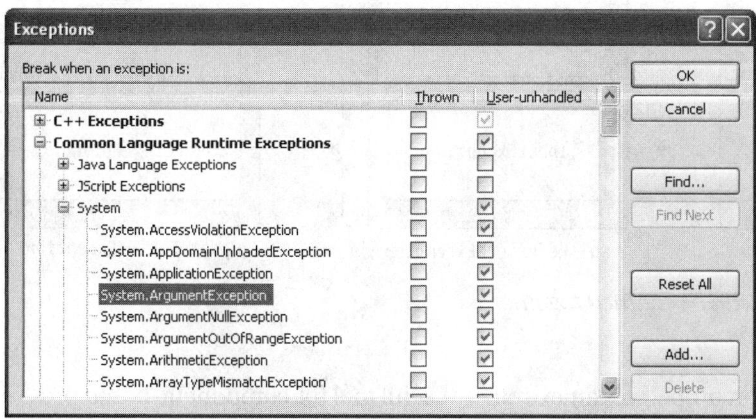

Figure 7-2. *Visual Studio's exception viewer*

The Exceptions dialog box allows you to specify what exceptions should be handled by your code when debugging and what exceptions will cause Visual Studio to enter break mode immediately. That means you don't need to disable your error handling code to troubleshoot a problem. For example, you could choose to allow your program to handle a common FileNotFoundException (which could be caused by an invalid user selection) but instruct Visual Studio to pause execution if an unexpected DivideByZero exception occurs.

To set this up, add a check mark in the Thrown column next to the entry for the DivideByZero exception. This way, you'll be alerted as soon as the problem occurs. If you don't add a check mark to the Thrown column, your code will continue, run any exception handlers it has defined, and try to deal with the problem. You'll be notified only if an error occurs and no suitable exception handler is available.

The Exception Chain

Figure 7-3 shows how the InnerException property works. In this case, a FileNotFoundException led to a NullReferenceException, which led to a custom UpdateFailedException. The code returns an UpdateFailedException that references the NullReferenceException, which references the original FileNotFoundException.

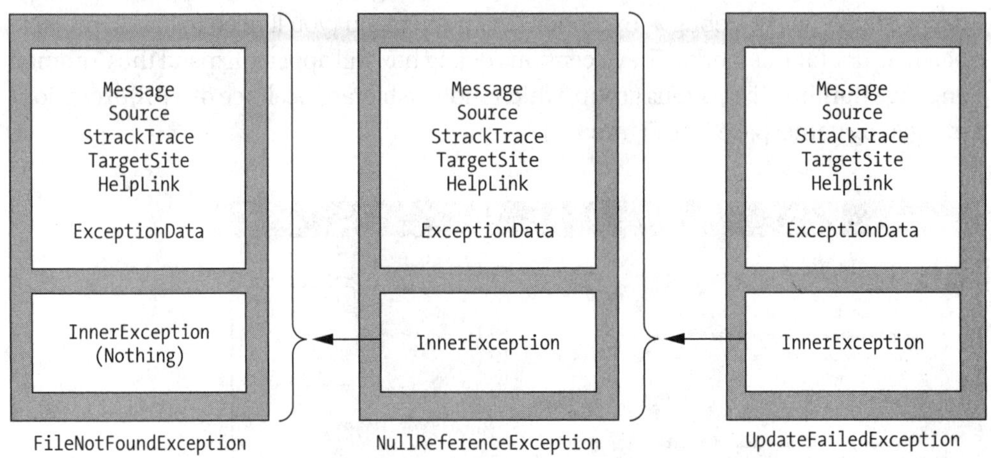

Figure 7-3. *Exceptions can be chained together.*

The InnerException property is an extremely useful tool for component-based programming. Generally, it's not much help if a component reports a low-level problem such as a null reference or a divide-by-zero error. Instead, it needs to communicate a more detailed message about which operation failed and what input may have been invalid. The calling code can then often correct the problem and retry the operation.

On the other hand, sometimes you're debugging a bug that lurks deep inside the component itself. In this case, you need to know precisely what caused the error—you don't want to replace it with a higher-level exception that could obscure the root problem. Using an exception chain handles both these scenarios: you receive as many linked exception objects as needed, which can specify information from the least to the most specific error condition.

Handling Exceptions

The first line of defense in an application is to check for potential error conditions before performing an operation. For example, a program can explicitly check whether the divisor is 0 before performing a calculation or if a file exists before attempting to open it:

```
if (divisor != 0)
{
    // It's safe to divide some number by divisor.
}

if (System.IO.File.Exists("myfile.txt"))
{
    // You can now open the myfile.txt file.
    // However, you should still use exception handling because a variety of
    // problems can intervene (insufficient rights, hardware failure, etc.).
}
```

Even if you perform this basic level of "quality assurance," your application is still vulnerable. For example, you have no way to protect against all the possible file access problems that occur, including hardware failures or network problems that could arise spontaneously in the middle of an operation. Similarly, you have no way to validate a user ID and password for a database before attempting to open a connection—and even if there were, that technique would be subject to its own set of potential errors. In some cases, it may not be practical to perform the full range of defensive checks, because they may impose a noticeable performance drag on your application. For all these reasons, you need a way to detect and deal with errors when they occur.

The solution is structured exception handling. To use structured exception handling, you wrap potentially problematic code in the special block structure shown here:

```
try
{
    // Risky code goes here (such as opening a file or
    // connecting to a database).
}
catch
{
    // An error has been detected. You can deal with it here.
}
finally
{
    // Time to clean up, regardless of whether there was an error or not.
}
```

The try statement enables error handling. Any exceptions that occur in the following lines can be "caught" automatically. The code in the catch block will be executed when an error is detected. And either way, whether a bug occurs or not, the finally section of the code will be executed last. This allows you to perform some basic cleanup, such as closing a database connection. The finally code is important because it will execute even if an error has occurred that will prevent the program from continuing. In other words, if an unrecoverable exception halts your application, you'll still have the chance to release resources.

The act of catching an error neutralizes it. If all you want to do is render a specific error harmless, you don't even need to add any code in the catch block of your error handler. Usually, however, this portion of the code will be used to report the error to the user or log it for future reference. In a separate component (such as a business object), this code might handle the exception, perform some cleanup, and then rethrow it to the calling code, which will be in the best position to remedy it or alert the user. Or, it might actually create a new exception object with additional information and throw that.

Catching Specific Exceptions

Structured exception handling is particularly flexible because it allows you to catch specific types of exceptions. To do so, you add multiple catch statements, each one identifying the type of exception (and providing a new variable to catch it in), as follows:

```
try
{
    // Risky database code goes here.
}
catch (System.Data.SqlException err)
{
    // Catches common problems like connection errors.
}
catch (System.NullReferenceException err)
{
    // Catches problems resulting from an uninitialized object.
}
```

An exception will be caught as long as it's of the same class or if it's derived from the indicated class. In other words, if you use this statement:

```
catch (Exception err)
```

you will catch any exception, because every exception object is derived from the System.Exception base class.

Exception blocks work a little like the switch block structure. This means as soon as a matching exception handler is found, the appropriate catch code is invoked. Therefore, you should organize your catch statements from most specific to least specific:

```
try
{
    // Risky database code goes here.
}
catch (System.Data.SqlException err)
{
    // Catches common problems like connection errors.
}
catch (System.NullReferenceException err)
{
    // Catches problems resulting from an uninitialized object.
}
catch (System.Exception err)
{
    // Catches any other errors.
}
```

Ending with a catch statement for the generic Exception class is often a good idea to make sure no errors slip through. However, in component-based programming, you should make sure you intercept only those exceptions you can deal with or recover from. Otherwise, it's better to let the calling code catch the original error.

Nested Exception Handlers

When an exception is thrown, .NET tries to find a matching catch statement in the current procedure. If the code isn't in a local structured exception block, or if none of the catch statements matches the exception, the CLR will move up the call stack one level at a time, searching for active exception handlers.

Consider the example shown here, where the Page.Load event handler calls a private DivideNumbers() function:

```
protected void Page_Load(Object sender, EventArgs e)
{
    try
    {
        DivideNumbers(5, 0);
    }
    catch (DivideByZeroException err)
    {
        // Report error here.
    }
}

private decimal DivideNumbers(decimal number, decimal divisor)
{
    return number/divisor;
}
```

In this example, the DivideNumbers() function lacks any sort of exception handler. However, the DivideNumbers() function call is made inside an exception handler, which means the problem will be caught further upstream in the calling code. This is a good approach because the DivideNumbers() routine could be used in a variety of circumstances (or if it's part of a component, in a variety of different types of applications). It really has no access to any kind of user interface and can't directly report an error. Only the calling code is in a position to determine whether the problem is a serious or minor one, and only the calling code can prompt the user for more information or report error details in the web page.

You can also overlap exception handlers in such a way that different exception handlers filter out different types of problems. Here's one such example:

```
protected void Page_Load(Object sender, EventArgs e)
{
    try
    {
        decimal average = GetAverageCost(DateTime.Now);
    }
    catch (DivideByZeroException err)
    {
        // Report error here.
    }
}
```

```
private decimal GetAverageCost(Date saleDate)
{
    try
    {
        // Use Database access code here to retrieve all the sale records
        // for this date, and calculate the average.
    }
    catch (SqlException err)
    {
        // Handle a database related problem.
    }
    finally
    {
        // Close the database connection.
    }
}
```

Dissecting the Code...

You should be aware of the following points:

- If an SqlException occurs during the database operation, it will be caught in the GetAverageCost() function.
- If a DivideByZeroException occurs (for example, the function attempts to calculate an average based on a DataSet that contains no rows), the exception will be caught in the calling Page.Load event handler.
- If another problem occurs (such as a null reference exception), no active exception handler exists to catch it. In this case, .NET will search through the entire call stack without finding a matching catch statement in an active exception handler and will generate a runtime error, end the program, and return a page with exception information.

Exception Handling in Action

You can use a simple program to test exceptions and see what sort of information is retrieved. This program allows a user to enter two values and attempts to divide them. It then reports all the related exception information in the page (see Figure 7-4).

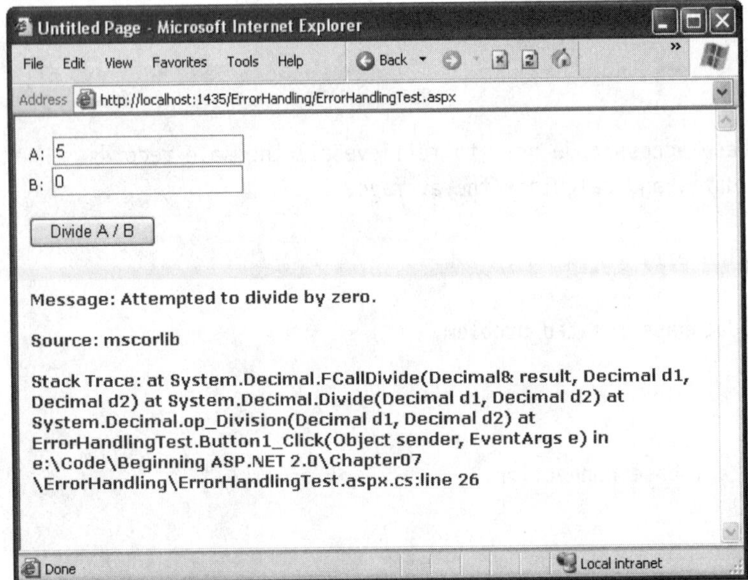

Figure 7-4. *Catching and displaying exception information*

Obviously, you can easily avoid this problem with extra code-safety checks or elegantly resolve it using the validation controls. However, this code provides a good example of how you can deal with the properties of an exception object. It also gives you a good idea about what sort of information will be returned.

Here's the page class code for this example:

```
public partial class ErrorHandlingTest : Page
{
    protected void cmdCompute_Click(Object sender, EventArgs e)
    {
        try
        {
            decimal a, b, result;
            a = Decimal.Parse(txtA.Text);
            b = Decimal.Parse(txtB.Text);
            result = a / b;
            lblResult.Text = result.ToString();
            lblResult.ForeColor = Color.Black;
        }
        catch (Exception err)
```

```
        {
            lblResult.Text = "<b>Message:</b> " + err.Message;
            lblResult.Text += "<br /><br />";
            lblResult.Text += "<b>Source:</b> " + err.Source;
            lblResult.Text += "<br /><br />";
            lblResult.Text += "<b>Stack Trace:</b> " + err.StackTrace;
            lblResult.ForeColor = Color.Red;
        }
    }
}
```

Note that as soon as the error occurs, execution is transferred to an exception handler. The code in the try block isn't completed. It's for that reason that the result for the label is set in the try block. These lines will be executed only if the division code runs error-free.

You'll see many more examples of exception handling throughout this book. The data access chapters in Part 3 of this book show the best practices for exception handling when accessing a database.

Mastering Exceptions

Keep in mind these points when working with structured exception handling:

Break down your code into multiple try/catch blocks: If you put all your code into one exception handler, you'll have trouble determining where the problem occurred. You have no way to "resume" the code in a try block. This means that if an error occurs at the beginning of a lengthy try block, you'll skip a large amount of code. The rule of thumb is to use one exception handler for one related task (such as opening a file and retrieving information).

Use ASP.NET's error pages during development: During development, you may not want to implement portions of your application's error handling code because it may mask easily correctable mistakes in your application.

Don't use exception handlers for every statement: Simple code statements (assigning a constant value to a variable, interacting with a control, and so on) may cause errors during development testing but will not cause any future problems once perfected. Error handling should be used when you're accessing an outside resource or dealing with supplied data that you have no control over (and thus may be invalid).

Throwing Your Own Exceptions

You can also define and create your own exception objects to represent special error conditions. All you need to do is create an instance of the appropriate exception class and then use the throw statement.

The next example introduces a modified DivideNumbers() function. It explicitly checks whether the specified divisor is 0 and then manually creates and throws an instance of the DivideByZeroException class to indicate the problem, rather than attempt the operation. Depending on the code, this pattern can save time by eliminating some unnecessary steps, or it can prevent a task from being initiated if it can't be completed successfully.

```
protected void Page_Load(Object sender, EventArgs e)
{
    try
    {
        DivideNumbers(5, 0);
    }
    catch DivideByZeroException err
    {
        // Report error here.
    }
}

private decimal DivideNumbers(decimal number, decimal divisor)
{
    if (divisor == 0)
    {
        DivideByZeroException err = new DivideByZeroException();
        throw err;
    }
    else
    {
        return number/divisor;
    }
}
```

Alternatively, you can create a .NET exception object and specify a custom error message by using a different constructor:

```
private decimal DivideNumbers(decimal number, decimal divisor)
{
    if (divisor == 0)
    {
        DivideByZeroException err = new DivideByZeroException(
          "You supplied 0 for the divisor parameter. You must be stopped.");
        throw err;
    }
    else
    {
        return number/divisor;
    }
}
```

In this case, any ordinary exception handler will still catch the DivideByZeroException. The only difference is that the error object has a modified Message property that contains the custom string. Figure 7-5 shows the resulting exception.

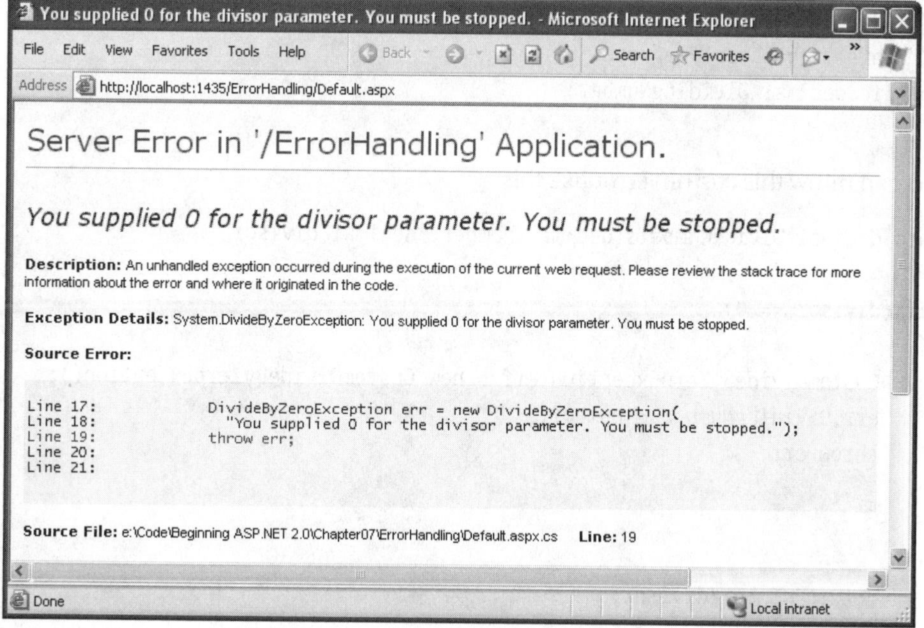

Figure 7-5. *Standard exception, custom message*

Throwing an error is most useful in component-based programming. In component-based programming, your ASP.NET page is creating objects and calling methods from a class defined in a separately compiled assembly. In this case, the class in the component needs to be able to notify the calling code (the web application) of any errors. The component should handle recoverable errors quietly and not pass them up to the calling code. On the other hand, if an unrecoverable error occurs, it should always be indicated with an exception and never through another mechanism (such as a return code). For more information about component-based programming, refer to Chapter 24.

If you can find an exception in the class library that accurately reflects the problem that has occurred, you should throw it. If you need to return additional or specialized information, you can create your own custom exception class.

Custom exception classes should always inherit from System.ApplicationException, which itself derives from the base Exception class. This allows .NET to distinguish between two broad classes of exceptions—those you create and those that are native to the .NET Framework.

When you create an exception class, you can add properties to record additional information. For example, here is a special class that records information about the failed attempt to divide by zero:

```
public class CustomDivideByZeroException : ApplicationException
{
    // Add a variable to specify the "other" number.
    // This might help diagnose the problem.
    public decimal DividingNumber;
}
```

You can throw this custom error like this:

```
private decimal DivideNumbers(decimal number, decimal divisor)
{
    if (divisor == 0)
    {
        CustomDivideByZeroException err = new CustomDivideByZeroException();
        err.DividingNumber = number;
        throw err;
    }
    else
    {
        return number/divisor;
    }
}
```

To perfect the custom exception, you need to supply it with the three standard constructors. This allows your exception class to be created in the standard ways that every exception supports:

- On its own, with no arguments
- With a custom message
- With a custom message and an exception object to use as the inner exception

These constructors don't actually need to contain any code. All these constructors need to do is forward the parameters to the base class (the constructors in the inherited ApplicationException class) using the base keyword, as shown here:

```
public class CustomDivideByZeroException : ApplicationException
{
    // Add a variable to specify the "other" number.
    decimal DividingNumber;

    public CustomDivideByZeroException() : base()
    {}

    public CustomDivideByZeroException(string message) : base(message)
    {}

    public CustomDivideByZeroException(string message, Exception inner) :
      base(message, inner)
    {}
}
```

The third constructor is particularly useful for component programming. It allows you to set the InnerException property with the exception object that caused the original problem. The next example shows how you could use this constructor with a component class called ArithmeticUtility:

```
public class ArithmeticUtilityException : ApplicationException
{
    public ArithmeticUtilityException() : base()
    {}

    public ArithmeticUtilityException(string message) : base(message)
    {}
```

```
    public ArithmeticUtilityException(string message, Exception inner) :
      base(message, inner)
    {}
}

public class ArithmeticUtility
{
    private decimal Divide(decimal number, decimal divisor)
    {
        try
        {
            return number/divisor;
        }
        catch (Exception err)
        {
            // Create an instance of the specialized exception class,
            // and place the original error in the InnerException property.
            ArithmeticUtilityException errNew =
              new ArithmeticUtilityException("Divided by zero", err);

            // Now "rethrow" the new exception.
            throw errNew;
        }
    }
}
```

Remember, custom exception classes are really just a standardized way for one class to communicate an error to a different portion of code. If you aren't using components or your own utility classes, you probably don't need to create custom exception classes.

Logging Exceptions

In many cases, it's best not only to detect and catch errors but to log them as well. For example, some problems may occur only when your web server is dealing with a particularly large load. Other problems might recur intermittently, with no obvious causes. To diagnose these errors and build a larger picture of site problems, you need to log errors automatically so they can be reviewed later.

The .NET Framework provides a wide range of logging tools. When certain errors occur, you can send an e-mail, add a database record, or create and write to a file. We describe many of these techniques in other parts of this book. However, you should keep your logging code as simple as possible. For example, you'll probably run into trouble if you try to log a database error to another table in the database.

One of the best logging tools is provided in the Windows event logs. To view these logs, select Settings ➤ Control Panel ➤ Administrative Tools ➤ Event Viewer from the Start menu. By default, you'll see three logs, as shown in Figure 7-6. You can right-click a log to clear the events in the log, save log entries, and import an external log file. Table 7-2 describes the logs.

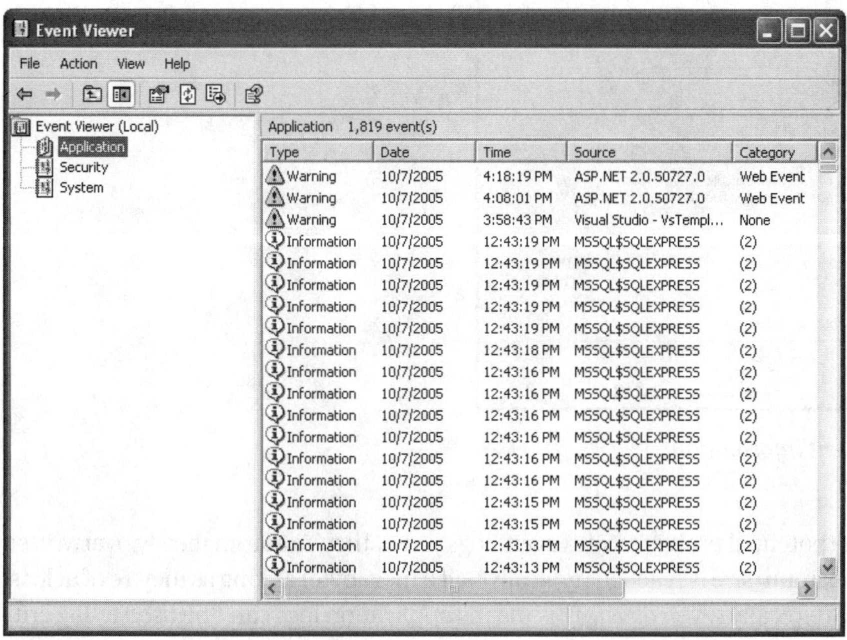

Figure 7-6. *The Event Viewer*

Table 7-2. *Windows Event Logs*

Log Name	Description
Application log	Used to track errors or notifications from any application. Generally, you'll use this log or create your own.
Security log	Used to track security-related problems but generally used exclusively by the operating system.
System log	Used to track operating system events.

Each event record identifies the source (generally, the application or service that created the record), the type of notification (error, information, warning), and the time it was left. You can also double-click a record to view additional information such as a text description. Figure 7-7 shows an example with an unhandled error that occurred in an ASP.NET page, which ASP.NET chooses to log.

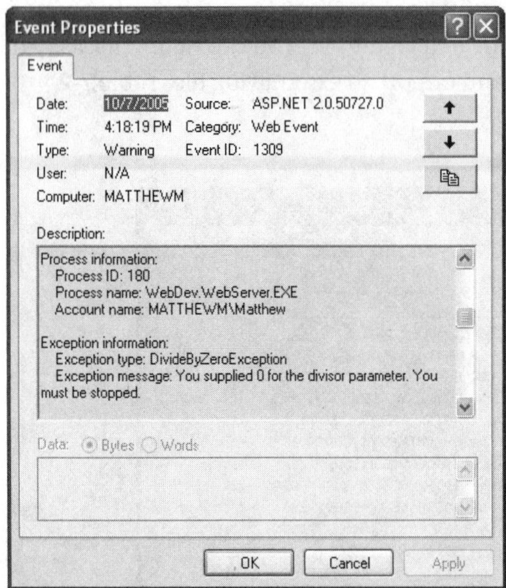

Figure 7-7. *Event information*

One of the potential problems with event logs is that they're automatically overwritten when the maximum size is reached (typically half a megabyte) as long as they're of at least a certain age (typically seven days). This means application logs can't be used to log critical information that you need to retain for a long period of time. Instead, they should be used to track information that is valuable only for a short amount of time. For example, you can use event logs to review errors and diagnose strange behavior immediately after it happens, not a month later.

You do have some ability to configure the amount of time a log will be retained and the maximum size it will be allowed to occupy. To configure these settings, right-click the application log, and select Properties. You'll see the Application Properties window shown in Figure 7-8.

Generally, you should not disable automatic log deletion, because it could cause a large amount of wasted space and slow performance if information isn't being regularly removed. Instead, if you want to retain more log information, set a larger disk space limit.

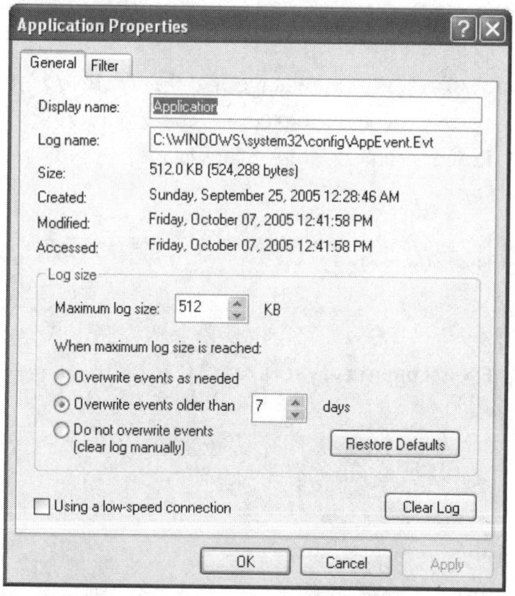

Figure 7-8. *Log properties*

Using the EventLog Class

You can interact with event logs in an ASP.NET page by using the classes in the System.Diagnostics namespace. Import the namespace at the beginning of your code-behind file:

```
using System.Diagnostics;
```

The following example rewrites the simple ErrorTest page to use event logging:

```
public partial class ErrorTestLog : Page
{
    protected void cmdCompute_Click(Object sender, EventArgs e)
    {
        try
        {
            decimal a, b, result;
            a = Decimal.Parse(txtA.Text);
            b = Decimal.Parse(txtB.Text);
            result = a / b;
            lblResult.Text = result.ToString();
            lblResult.ForeColor = Color.Black;
        }
```

```
        catch (Exception err)
        {
            lblResult.Text = "<b>Message:</b> " + err.Message + "<br /><br />";
            lblResult.Text += "<b>Source:</b> " + err.Source + "<br /><br />";
            lblResult.Text += "<b>Stack Trace:</b> " + err.StackTrace;
            lblResult.ForeColor = Color.Red;

            // Write the information to the event log.
            EventLog log = new EventLog();
            log.Source = "DivisionPage";
            log.WriteEntry(err.Message, EventLogEntryType.Error);
        }
    }
}
```

EVENT LOG SECURITY

This logging code will run without a hitch when you try it in Visual Studio. However, when you deploy your application to a web server (as described in Chapter 12), you might not be so lucky. The problem is that the ASP.NET service runs under a Windows account that has fewer privileges than an average user. If you're using IIS 5, this user is the account named ASPNET, which ordinarily won't have the permissions to create event log entries.

To remedy this problem, you can use a different account (as explained in Chapter 12), or you can grant the required permissions to the account that ASP.NET is already using (like the ASPNET account). To do the latter, you need to modify the registry as described in these steps:

1. Run regedit.exe, either by using a command-line prompt or by choosing Run from the Start menu.
2. Browse to the HKEY_Local_Machine\SYSTEM\CurrentControlSet\Services\EventLog section of the registry.
3. Select the EventLog folder if you want to give ASP.NET permission to all areas of the event log. Or, select a specific folder that corresponds to the event log ASP.NET needs to access.
4. Choose Security ➤ Permissions.
5. Add the account that ASP.NET is using to the list. If you're using IIS 5, this is the ASPNET account. To add it, click the Add button, type in **ASPNET**, and then click OK.
6. Give the ASPNET account Full Control for this section of the registry by selecting the Allow check box next to Full Control.

The event log record will now appear in the Event Viewer utility, as shown in Figure 7-9. Note that logging is intended for the system administrator or developer. It doesn't replace the code you use to notify the user and explain that a problem has occurred.

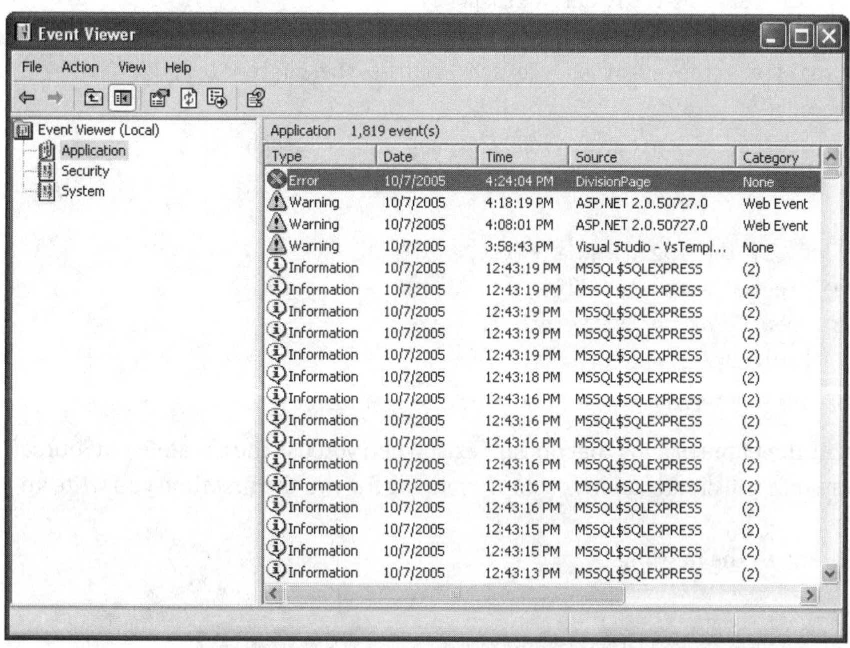

Figure 7-9. *A custom event*

Custom Logs

You can also log errors to a custom log. For example, you could create a log with your company name and add records to it for all your ASP.NET applications. You might even want to create an individual log for a particularly large application and use the Source property of each entry to indicate the page (or web service method) that caused the problem.

Accessing a custom log is easy—you just need to use a different constructor for the EventLog class to specify the custom log name. You also need to register an *event source* for the log. This initial step needs to be performed only once—in fact, you'll receive an error if you try to create the same event source. Typically, you'll use the name of the application as the event source.

Here's an example that uses a custom log named ProseTech and registers the event source DivideByZeroApp:

```
// Register the event source if needed.
if (!EventLog.SourceExists("DivideByZeroApp"))
{
    // This registers the event source and creates the custom log,
    // if needed.
    EventLog.CreateEventSource("DivideByZeroApp", "ProseTech");
}

// Open the log. If the log doesn't exist,
// it will be created automatically.
EventLog log = new EventLog("ProseTech");
log.Source = "DivideByZeroApp";
log.WriteEntry(err.Message, EventLogEntryType.Error);
```

If you specify the name of a log that doesn't exist when you use the CreateEventSource() method, the system will create a new, custom event log for you the first time you write an entry.

Figure 7-10 shows the new log.

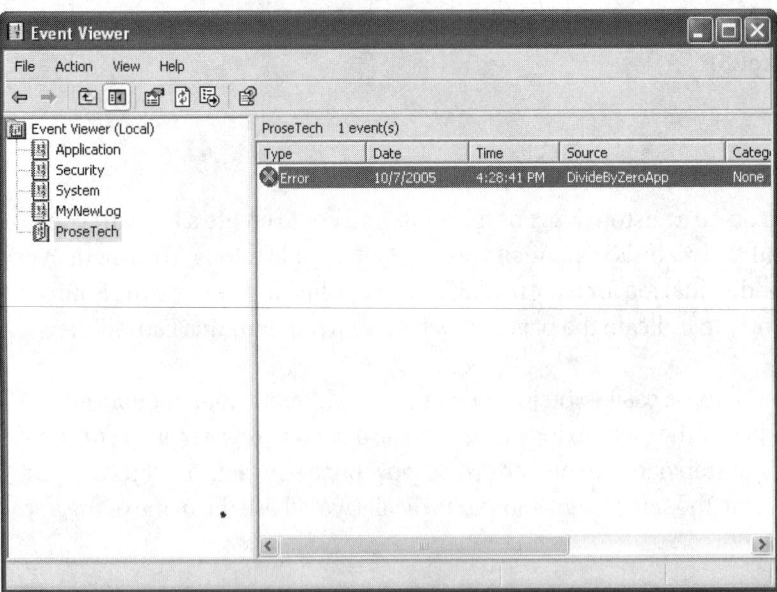

Figure 7-10. *A custom log*

■ **Tip** Event logging uses disk space and takes processor time away from web applications. Don't store unimportant information, large quantities of data, or information that would be better off in another type of storage (such as a relational database). Generally, you should use an event log to log unexpected conditions or errors, not customer actions or performance-tracking information.

Retrieving Log Information

One of the disadvantages of the event logs is that they're tied to the web server. This can make it difficult to review log entries if you don't have a way to access the server (although you can read them from another computer on the same network). This problem has several possible solutions. One interesting technique involves using a special administration page. This ASP.NET page can use the EventLog class to retrieve and display all the information from the event log.

The following example retrieves all the entries that were left by the ErrorTestCustomLog page and displays them in a simple web page (shown in Figure 7-11). The results are shown using a label in a scrollable panel (a Panel control with the Scrollbars property set to Vertical). A more sophisticated approach would use similar code but one of the data controls discussed in Chapter 15 instead.

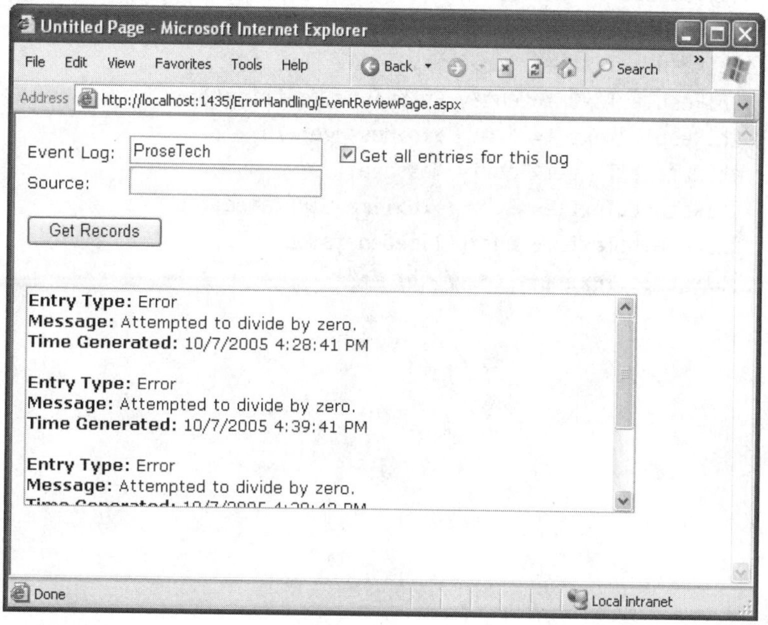

Figure 7-11. *A log viewer page*

Here's the web page code you'll need:

```
public partial class EventReviewPage : Page
{
    protected void cmdGet_Click(Object sender, EventArgs e)
    {
        lblResult.Text = "";

        // Check if the log exists.
        if (!EventLog.Exists(txtLog.Text))
        {
            lblResult.Text = "The event log " + txtLog.Text ;
            lblResult.Text += " doesn't exist.";
        }
        else
        {
            EventLog log = new EventLog(txtLog.Text);
            foreach (EventLogEntry entry in log.Entries)
            {
                // Write the event entries to the page.
                if (chkAll.Checked ||
                  entry.Source == txtSource.Text)
                {
                    lblResult.Text += "<b>Entry Type:</b> ";
                    lblResult.Text += entry.EntryType.ToString();
                    lblResult.Text += "<br /><b>Message:</b> ";
                    lblResult.Text += entry.Message;
                    lblResult.Text += "<br /><b>Time Generated:</b> ";
                    lblResult.Text += entry.TimeGenerated;
                    lblResult.Text += "<br /><br />";
                }
            }
        }
    }
```

```
    protected void chkAll_CheckedChanged(Object sender,
      EventArgs e)
    {
        // The chkAll control has AutoPostback = true.
        if (chkAll.Checked)
        {
            txtSource.Text = "";
            txtSource.Enabled = false;
        }
        else
        {
            txtSource.Enabled = true;
        }
    }
}
```

If you choose to display all the entries from the application log, the page will perform slowly. Two factors are at work here. First, it takes time to retrieve each event log entry, and a typical application log can easily hold several thousand entries. Second, the code used to append text to the Label control is inefficient. Every time you add a new piece of information to the Label.Text property, .NET needs to generate a new string object. A better solution is to use the specialized System.Text.StringBuilder class, which is designed to handle intensive string processing with a lower overhead by managing an internal buffer or memory.

Here's the more efficient way you could write the string processing code:

```
// For maximum performance, join all the event
// information into one large string using the
// StringBuilder.
System.Text.StringBuilder sb = new System.Text.StringBuilder();

EventLog log = new EventLog(txtLog.Text);
foreach (EventLogEntry entry in log.Entries)
{
    // Write the event entries to the StringBuilder.
    if (chkAll.Checked ||
      entry.Source == txtSource.Text)
```

```
        {
            sb.Append("<b>Entry Type:</b> ");
            sb.Append(entry.EntryType.ToString());
            sb.Append("<br /><b>Message:</b> ");
            sb.Append(entry.Message);
            sb.Append("<br /><b>Time Generated:</b> ");
            sb.Append(entry.TimeGenerated);
            sb.Append("<br /><br />");
        }
    }
    // Copy the complete text to the web page.
    lblResult.Text = sb.ToString();
```

■ **Tip** You can get around some of the limitations involved with the event log by using your own custom logging system. All the ingredients you need are built into the common class library. For example, you could store error information in a database using the techniques described in Chapter 13.

Error Pages

As you create and test an ASP.NET application, you'll become familiar with the rich information pages that are shown to describe unhandled errors. These pages are extremely useful for diagnosing problems during development, because they contain a wealth of information. Some of this information includes the source code where the problem occurred (with the offending line highlighted), the type of error, and a detailed error message describing the problem. Figure 7-12 shows a sample rich error page.

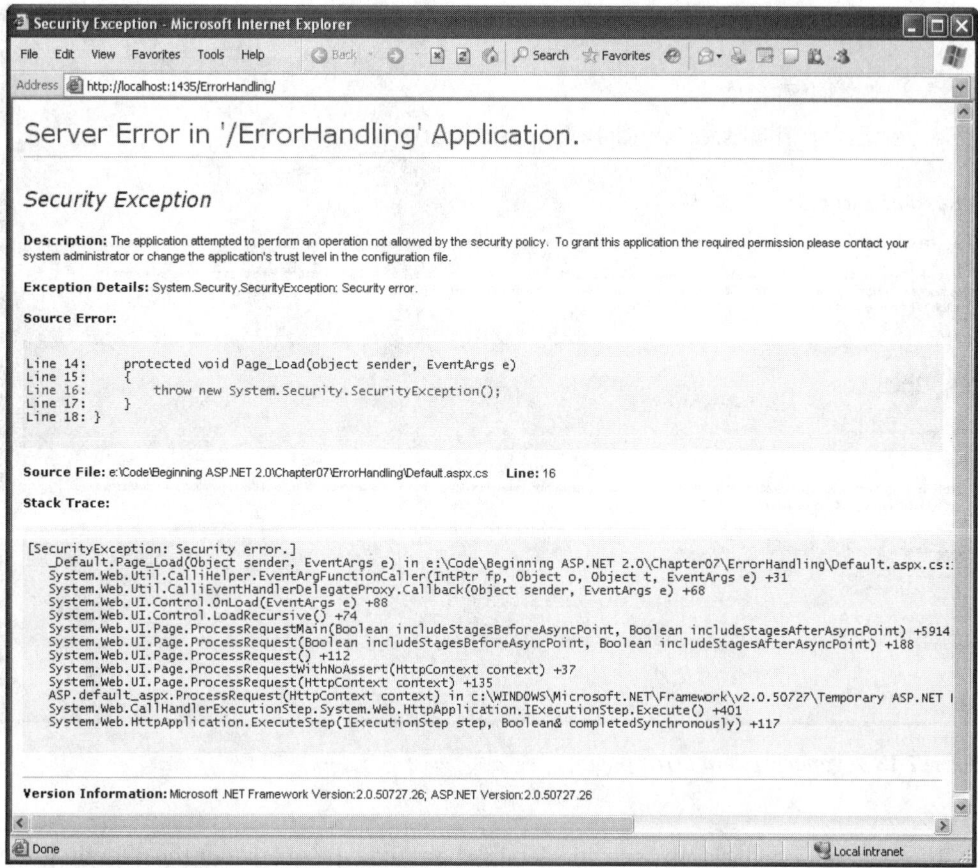

Figure 7-12. *A rich ASP.NET error page*

This error page is shown only for local requests that access the ASP.NET application through the `http://localhost` domain. (This domain always refers to the current computer, regardless of its actual server name or Internet address.) ASP.NET doesn't create a rich error page for requests from other computers, which receive the rather unhelpful generic page shown in Figure 7-13.

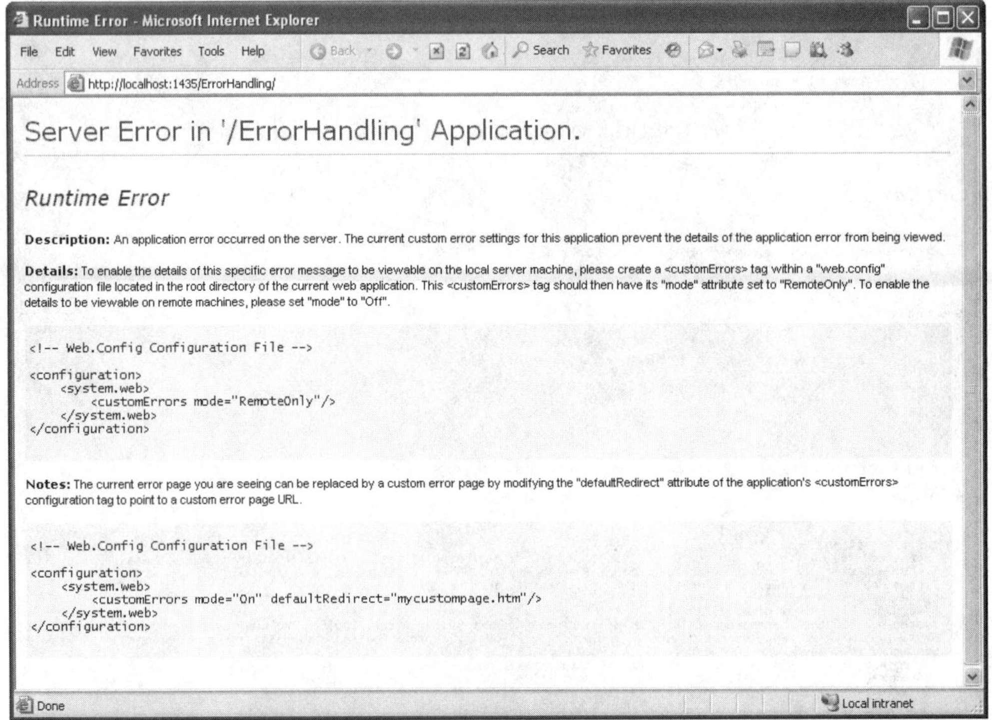

Figure 7-13. *A generic client error page*

This generic page lacks any specific details about the type of error or the offending code. Sharing this information with end users would be a security risk (potentially exposing sensitive details about the source code), and it would be completely unhelpful, because clients are never in a position to modify the source code themselves. Instead, the page includes a generic message explaining that an error has occurred and describing how to enable remote error pages.

Error Modes

Remote error pages remove this restriction and allow ASP.NET to display detailed information for problems regardless of the source of the request. Remote error pages are intended as a testing tool. For example, in the initial rollout of an application beta, you might use field testers. These field testers would need to report specific information about application errors to aid in the debugging process. Similarly, you could use remote error pages if you're working with a team of developers and testing an ASP.NET application from a live web server. In this case, you might follow the time-honored code/compile/upload pattern.

To change the error mode, you need to modify the <customErrors> section in the web.config file. By default, Visual Studio creates a web.config with this section but comments it out. However, the default settings are equivalent to this:

```
<configuration>
  <system.web>
    <customErrors mode="RemoteOnly" />
    ...
  </system.web>
</configuration>
```

Table 7-3 lists the options for the mode attribute.

Table 7-3. *Error Modes*

Error Mode	Description
RemoteOnly	This is the default setting, which uses rich ASP.NET error pages only when the developer is accessing an ASP.NET application on the current machine.
Off	This configures rich error pages (with source code and stack traces) for all unhandled errors, regardless of the source of the request. This setting is helpful in many development scenarios but should not be used in a deployed application.
On	ASP.NET error pages will never be shown. When an unhandled error is encountered, a corresponding custom error page will be shown if one exists. Otherwise, ASP.NET will show the generic message explaining that application settings prevent the error details from being displayed and describing how to change the configuration.

A Custom Error Page

In a deployed application, you should use the On or RemoteOnly error mode. Any errors in your application should be dealt with through error handling code, which can then present a helpful and user-oriented message (rather than the developer-oriented code details in ASP.NET's rich error messages).

However, it isn't possible to catch every possible error in an ASP.NET application. For example, a hardware failure could occur spontaneously in the middle of an ordinary code statement that could not normally cause an error. More commonly, the user might encounter an HTTP error by requesting a page that doesn't exist. ASP.NET allows you to handle these problems with custom error pages.

You can implement custom error pages in two ways. You can create a single generic error page and configure ASP.NET to use it by modifying the web.config file as shown here:

```
<configuration>
  <system.web>
    <customErrors defaultRedirect="DefaultError.aspx" />
  </system.web>
</configuration>
```

ASP.NET will now exhibit the following behavior:

- If ASP.NET encounters an HTTP error while serving the request, it will forward the user to the DefaultError.aspx web page.
- If ASP.NET encounters an unhandled application error and it isn't configured to display rich error pages, it will forward the user to the DefaultError.aspx. Remote users will never see the generic ASP.NET error page.
- If ASP.NET encounters an unhandled application error and it is configured to display rich developer-targeted error pages, it will display the rich error page instead.

■Note What happens if an error occurs in the error page itself? If an error occurs in a custom error page (in this case, DefaultError.aspx), ASP.NET will not be able to handle it. It will not try to reforward the user to the same page. Instead, it will display the normal client error page with the generic message.

Specific Custom Error Pages

You can also create error pages targeted at specific types of HTTP errors (such as the infamous 404 Not Found error, or Access Denied). This technique is commonly used with websites to provide friendly equivalents for common problems. Figure 7-14 shows how one site handles this issue.

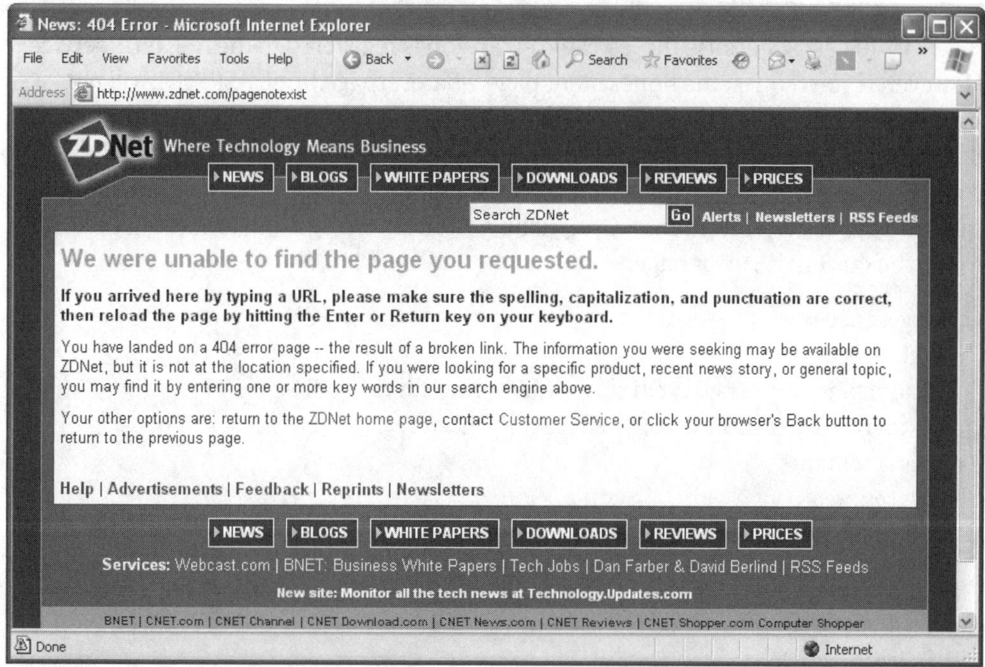

Figure 7-14. *A sample custom error page*

To define an error-specific custom page, you add an <error> element to the <customErrors> element. The <error> element identifies the HTTP error code and the redirect page.

```
<configuration>
  <system.web>
    <customErrors defaultRedirect="DefaultError.aspx">
      <error statusCode="404" redirect="404.aspx" />
    <customErrors>
  </system.web>
</configuration>
```

In this example, the user will be redirected to the 404.aspx page when requesting an ASP.NET page that doesn't exist. This custom error page may not work exactly the way you expect, because it comes into effect only if ASP.NET is handling the request.

For example, if you request the nonexistent page whateverpage.aspx, you'll be redirected to 404.aspx, because the .aspx file extension is registered to the ASP.NET service. However, if you request the nonexistent page whateverpage.html, ASP.NET will not process the request, and the default redirect setting specified in IIS will be used. Typically, this means the user will see the page c:\[WinDir]\Help\IISHelp\common\404b.htm. You could change the set of registered ASP.NET file types to include .html and .htm files, but this will slow down performance. Optionally, you could change your ASP.NET application to use the custom IIS error page:

```
<configuration>
  <system.web>
    <customErrors defaultRedirect="/defaulterror.aspx">
      <error statusCode="404" redirect="/Errors/404b.htm" />
    <customErrors>
  </system.web>
</configuration>
```

When an error occurs that isn't specifically addressed by a custom <error> element, the default error page will be used.

Page Tracing

ASP.NET's detailed error pages are extremely helpful when you're testing and perfecting an application. However, sometimes you need more information to verify that your application is performing properly or to track down logic errors, which may produce invalid data but no obvious exceptions. In traditional ASP development, programmers often resorted to using Response.Write() to display debug information directly on the web page. Unfortunately, this technique is fraught with problems:

Code entanglement: It's difficult to separate the ordinary code from the debugging code. Before the application can be deployed, you need to painstakingly search through the code and remove or comment out all the Response.Write() statements.

No single point of control: If problems occur later down the road, you have no easy way to "reenable" the write statements. Response.Write() statements are tightly integrated into the code.

User interface problems: Response.Write() outputs information directly into the page. Depending on the current stage of page processing, the information can appear in just about any location, potentially scrambling your layout.

You can overcome these problems with additional effort and some homegrown solutions. However, ASP.NET provides a far more convenient and flexible method built into the framework services. It's called *tracing*.

Enabling Tracing

To use tracing, you need to explicitly enable it. There are several ways to switch on tracing. One of the easiest ways is by adding an attribute to the Page directive in the .aspx portion of your page:

```
<%@ Page Trace="true" ... %>
```

You can also enable tracing using the built-in Trace object (which is an instance of the System.Web.TraceContext class). Here's an example of how you might turn tracing on in the Page.Load event handler:

```
protected void Page_Load(Object sender, EventArgs e)
{
    Trace.IsEnabled = true;
}
```

This technique is particularly useful because it allows you to enable or disable tracing for a page programmatically. For example, you could examine the query string collection and enable tracing only if a special Tracing variable is received. This could allow developers to run tracing diagnostics on deployed pages, without revealing that information for normal requests from end users.

```
protected void Page_Load(Object sender, EventArgs e)
{
    if (Request.QueryString("Tracing") == "On")
    {
        Trace.IsEnabled = true;
    }
}
```

Note that by default, once you enable tracing it will only apply to local requests. That prevents actual end users from seeing the tracing information. If you need to trace a web page from an offsite location, you should use a technique like the one shown previously (for query string activation). You'll also need to change some web.config settings to enable remote tracing. Information about modifying these settings is found at the end of this chapter, in the "Application-Level Tracing" section.

WHAT ABOUT VISUAL STUDIO?

Visual Studio provides a full complement of debugging tools that allow you to set breakpoints, step through code, and view the contents of variables while your program executes. Though you can use Visual Studio in conjunction with page tracing, you probably won't need to do so. Instead, page tracing will become more useful for debugging problems after you have deployed the application to a web server. Chapter 4 discussed Visual Studio debugging.

Tracing Information

ASP.NET tracing automatically provides a lengthy set of standard, formatted information. For example, Figure 7-15 shows a rudimentary ASP.NET page with a label and button.

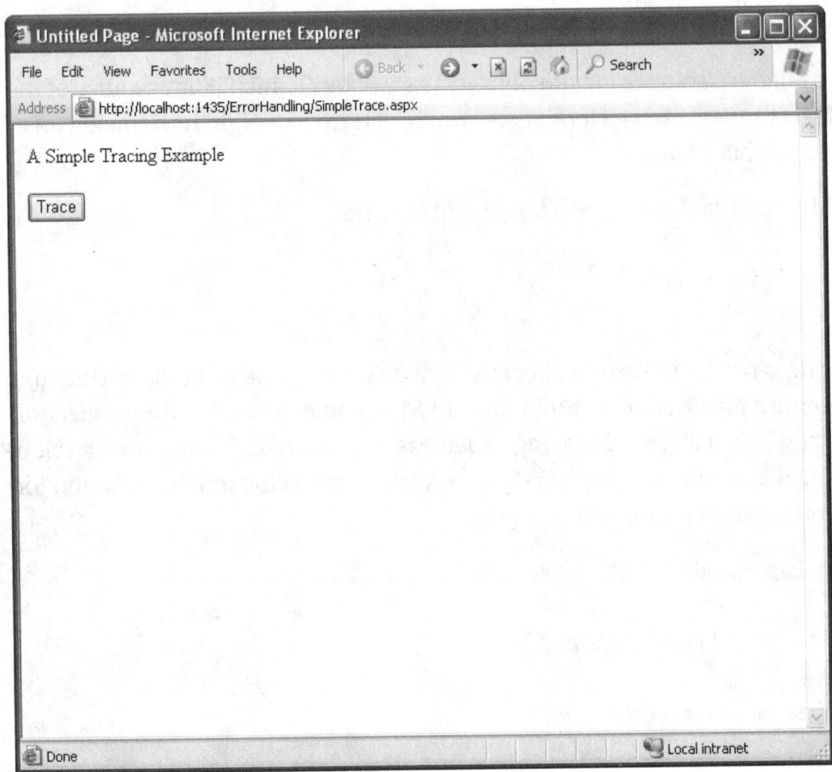

Figure 7-15. *A simple ASP.NET page*

On its own, this page does very little, displaying a single line of text. When you click the button to enable tracing, however, you end up with a lot of extra diagnostic information, as shown in Figure 7-16.

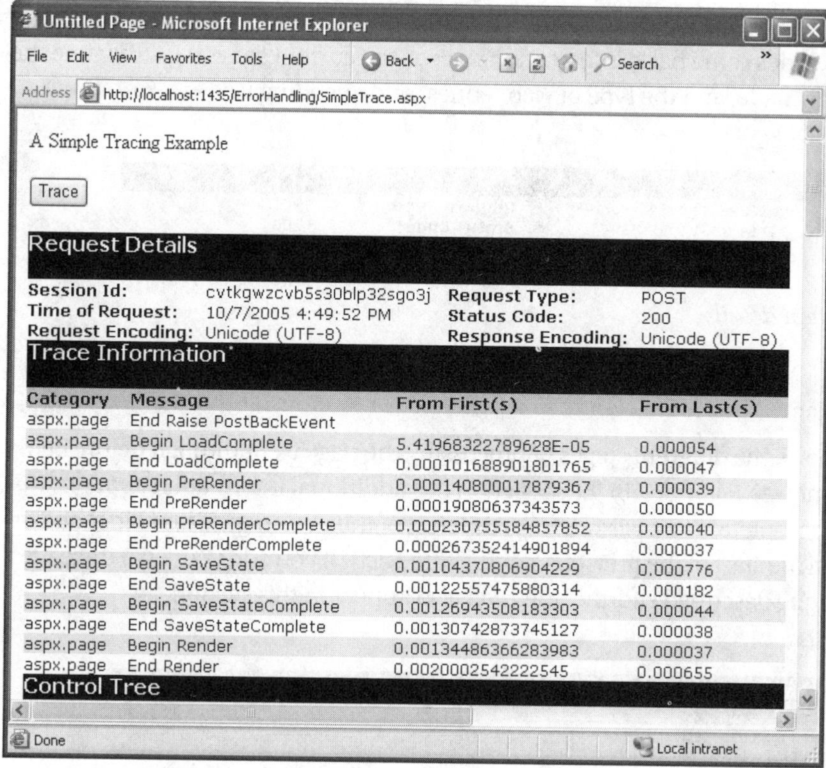

Figure 7-16. *Tracing the simple ASP.NET page*

Tracing information is provided in several different categories, which are described in the following sections. Depending on your page, you may not see all the sections. For example, if the page request didn't supply any query string parameters, you won't see the QueryString collection. Similarly, if there's no data currently being held in application or session state, you won't see those sections either.

■ **Tip** If you're using style sheets, your rules may affect the formatting and layout of the trace information, potentially making it difficult to read. If this becomes a problem, you can use application-level tracing, as described later in this chapter (see the "Application-Level Tracing" section).

Request Details

This section includes some basic information such as the current session ID, the time the web request was made, and the type of web request and encoding (see Figure 7-17).

Request Details			
Session Id:	vqa22245szjcs545kripra45	**Request Type:**	POST
Time of Request:	11-12-2001 6:49:35 PM	**Status Code:**	200
Request Encoding:	Unicode (UTF-8)	**Response Encoding:**	Unicode (UTF-8)

Figure 7-17. *Request details*

Trace Information

This section shows the different stages of processing the page went through before being sent to the client (see Figure 7-18). Each section has additional information about how long it took to complete, as a measure from the start of the first stage (From First) and as a measure from the start of the previous stage (From Last). If you add your own trace messages (a technique described shortly), they will also appear in this section.

Category	Message	From First(s)	From Last(s)
aspx.page	Begin ProcessPostData Second Try		
aspx.page	End ProcessPostData Second Try	0.000164	0.000164
aspx.page	Begin Raise ChangedEvents	0.000320	0.000156
aspx.page	End Raise ChangedEvents	0.000455	0.000134
aspx.page	Begin Raise PostBackEvent	0.000586	0.000131
aspx.page	End Raise PostBackEvent	0.003737	0.003152
aspx.page	Begin PreRender	0.004063	0.000326
aspx.page	End PreRender	0.004235	0.000173
aspx.page	Begin SaveViewState	0.007149	0.002914
aspx.page	End SaveViewState	0.007771	0.000621
aspx.page	Begin Render	0.007975	0.000204
aspx.page	End Render	0.011350	0.003375

Figure 7-18. *Trace information*

Control Tree

The control tree shows you all the controls on the page, indented to show their hierarchy (which controls are contained inside other controls), as shown in Figure 7-19. In this simple page example, the only explicitly created controls are the label (lblMessage) and the web page. However, ASP.NET adds literal controls automatically to represent spacing and any other static elements that aren't server controls (such as text or ordinary HTML tags). One useful feature of this section is the Viewstate column, which tells you how many bytes of space are required to persist the current information in the control. This can help you gauge whether enabling control state is detracting from performance, particularly when working with data-bound controls such as the GridView.

Control Tree			
Control Id	Type	Render Size Bytes (including children)	Viewstate Size Bytes (excluding children)
__PAGE	ASP.TraceExample_aspx	1691	24
ctrl0	System.Web.UI.ResourceBasedLiteralControl	427	0
Form1	System.Web.UI.HtmlControls.HtmlForm	1236	0
ctrl1	System.Web.UI.LiteralControl	137	0
cmdWrite	System.Web.UI.WebControls.Button	201	0
ctrl2	System.Web.UI.LiteralControl	2	0
Label1	System.Web.UI.WebControls.Label	113	0
ctrl3	System.Web.UI.LiteralControl	2	0
cmdWriteCategory	System.Web.UI.WebControls.Button	232	0
ctrl4	System.Web.UI.LiteralControl	2	0
cmdError	System.Web.UI.WebControls.Button	203	0
ctrl5	System.Web.UI.LiteralControl	2	0
cmdSession	System.Web.UI.WebControls.Button	171	0
ctrl6	System.Web.UI.LiteralControl	14	0
ctrl7	System.Web.UI.LiteralControl	28	0

Figure 7-19. *Control tree*

Session State and Application State

These sections display every item that is in the current session or application state. (Figure 7-20 shows the Session State section.) Each item in the appropriate state collection is listed with its name, type, and value. If you're storing simple pieces of string information, the value is straightforward—it's the actual text in the string. If you're storing an object, .NET calls the object's ToString() method to get an appropriate string representation. For complex objects that don't override ToString() to provide anything useful, the result may just be the class name.

Session State		
Session Key	Type	Value
Test	System.String	This is just a string
MyDataSet	System.Data.DataSet	System.Data.DataSet

Figure 7-20. *Session state*

Cookies Collection

This section displays all the cookies that are sent with the response and the content and size of each cookie in bytes (see Figure 7-21). Even if you haven't explicitly created a cookie, you'll see the ASP.NET_SessionId cookie, which contains the current session ID. If you're using forms-based authentication, you'll also see the security cookie.

Cookies Collection		
Name	Value	Size
ASP.NET_SessionId	vqa22245szjcs545kripra45	42

Figure 7-21. *Cookies collection*

Headers Collection

This section lists all the HTTP headers (see Figure 7-22). Generally, you don't need to use this information, although it can be useful for troubleshooting unusual network problems.

Headers Collection	
Name	**Value**
Cache-Control	no-cache
Connection	Keep-Alive
Content-Length	68
Content-Type	application/x-www-form-urlencoded
Accept	image/gif, image/x-xbitmap, image/jpeg, image/pjpeg, application/vnd.ms-excel, application/msword, application/pdf, */*
Accept-Encoding	gzip, deflate
Accept-Language	en-us
Host	fariamat
Referer	http://fariamat/ASP.NET/Chapter11/ErrorHandling/TraceExample.aspx
User-Agent	Mozilla/4.0 (compatible; MSIE 6.0; Windows NT 5.1; .NET CLR 1.0.2914)

Figure 7-22. *Headers collection*

Form Collection

This section lists the posted-back form information (see Figure 7-23).

Form Collection	
Name	**Value**
__VIEWSTATE	dDwtMjA5NDAxOTA1OTs7Pg==
cmdSession	Add Session Item

Figure 7-23. *Form collection*

Query String Collection

This section lists the variables and values submitted in the query string (see Figure 7-24). Generally, you'll be able to see this information directly in the address box in the browser, so you won't need to refer to the information here.

Querystring Collection	
Name	Value
search	cat
style	full

Figure 7-24. *Query string collection*

Server Variables

This section lists all the server variables and their contents. You don't generally need to examine this information. Note also that if you want to examine a server variable programmatically, you can do so by name with the built-in Request.ServerVariables collection or by using one of the more useful higher-level properties from the Request object.

Writing Trace Information

The default trace log provides a set of important information that can allow you to monitor some important aspects of your application, such as the current state contents and the time taken to execute portions of code. In addition, you'll often want to generate your own tracing messages. For example, you might want to output the value of a variable at various points in execution so you can compare it with an expected value. Similarly, you might want to output messages when the code reaches certain points in execution so you can verify that various procedures are being used (and are used in the order you expect).

To write a custom trace message, you use the Write() method or the Warn() method of the built-in Trace object. These methods are equivalent. The only difference is that Warn() displays the message in red lettering, which makes it easier to distinguish from other messages in the list. Here's a code snippet that writes a trace message when the user clicks a button:

```
protected void cmdWrite_Click(Object sender, EventArgs e)
{
    Trace.Write("About to place an item in session state.");
    Session["Test"] = "Contents";
    Trace.Write("Placed item in session state.");
}
```

These messages appear in the trace information section of the page, along with the default messages that ASP.NET generates automatically (see Figure 7-25).

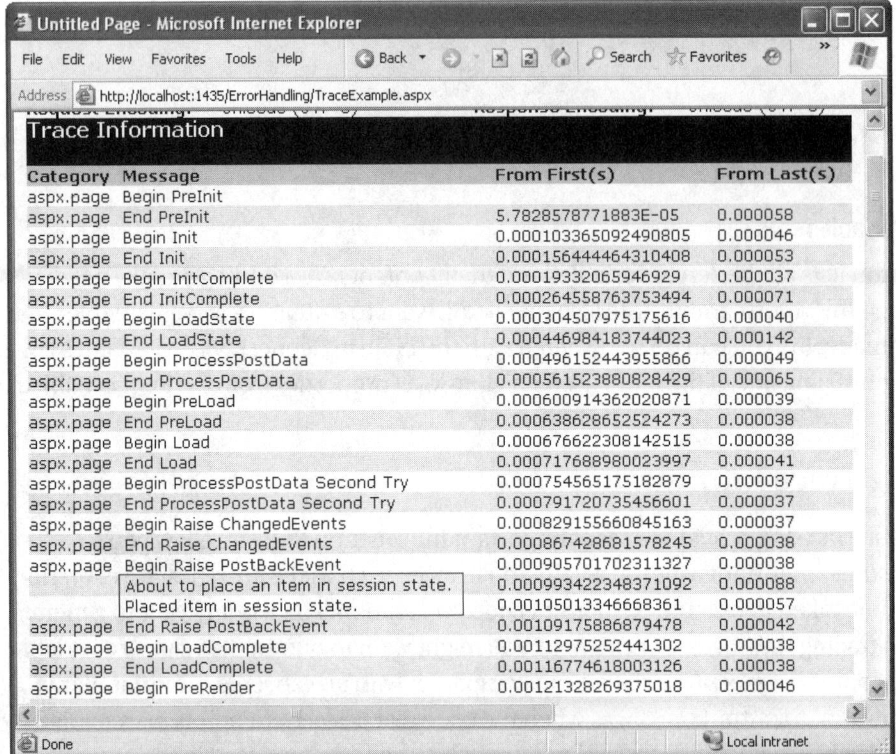

Figure 7-25. *Custom trace messages*

You can also use an overloaded method of Write() or Warn() that allows you to specify the category. A common use of this field is to indicate the current procedure, as shown in Figure 7-26.

```
protected void cmdWriteCategory_Click(Object sender, EventArgs e)
{
    Trace.Write("Page_Load", "About to place an item in session state.");
    Session["Test"] = "Contents";
    Trace.Write("Page_Load", "Placed item in session state.");
}
```

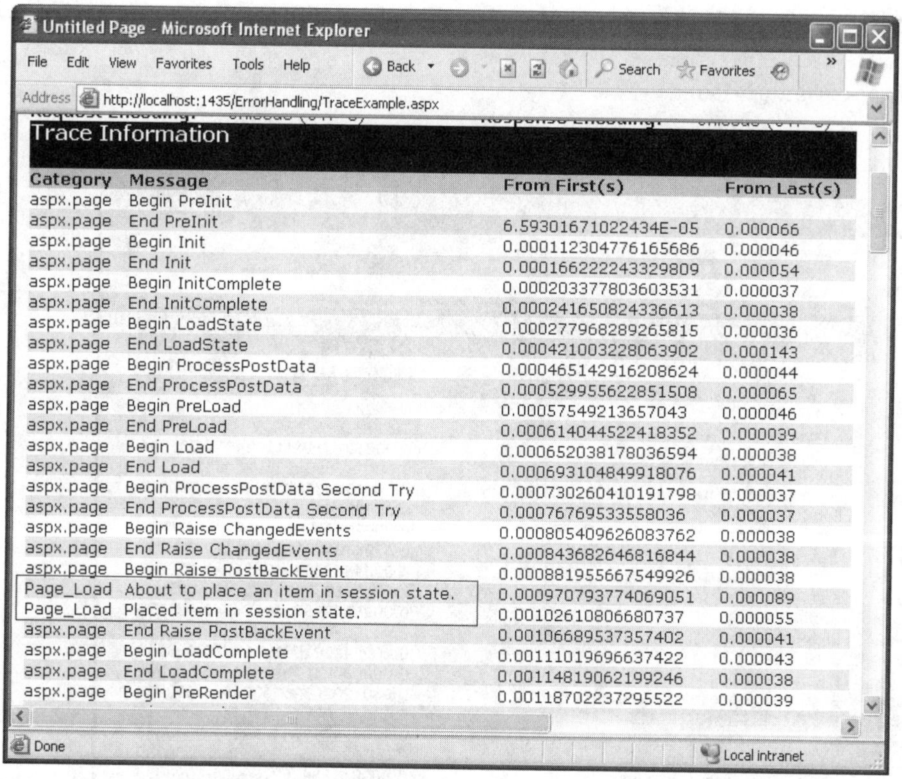

Untitled Page - Microsoft Internet Explorer

http://localhost:1435/ErrorHandling/TraceExample.aspx

Trace Information

Category	Message	From First(s)	From Last(s)
aspx.page	Begin PreInit		
aspx.page	End PreInit	6.59301671022434E-05	0.000066
aspx.page	Begin Init	0.000112304776165686	0.000046
aspx.page	End Init	0.000166222243329809	0.000054
aspx.page	Begin InitComplete	0.000203377803603531	0.000037
aspx.page	End InitComplete	0.000241650824336613	0.000038
aspx.page	Begin LoadState	0.000277968289265815	0.000036
aspx.page	End LoadState	0.000421003228063902	0.000143
aspx.page	Begin ProcessPostData	0.000465142916208624	0.000044
aspx.page	End ProcessPostData	0.000529955622851508	0.000065
aspx.page	Begin PreLoad	0.00057549213657043	0.000046
aspx.page	End PreLoad	0.000614044522418352	0.000039
aspx.page	Begin Load	0.000652038178036594	0.000038
aspx.page	End Load	0.000693104849918076	0.000041
aspx.page	Begin ProcessPostData Second Try	0.000730260410191798	0.000037
aspx.page	End ProcessPostData Second Try	0.00076769533558036	0.000037
aspx.page	Begin Raise ChangedEvents	0.000805409626083762	0.000038
aspx.page	End Raise ChangedEvents	0.000843682646816844	0.000038
aspx.page	Begin Raise PostBackEvent	0.000881955667549926	0.000038
Page_Load	About to place an item in session state.	0.000970793774069051	0.000089
Page_Load	Placed item in session state.	0.00102610806680737	0.000055
aspx.page	End Raise PostBackEvent	0.00106689537357402	0.000041
aspx.page	Begin LoadComplete	0.00111019696637422	0.000043
aspx.page	End LoadComplete	0.00114819062199246	0.000038
aspx.page	Begin PreRender	0.00118702237295522	0.000039

Done | Local intranet

Figure 7-26. *A categorized trace message*

Alternatively, you can supply category and message information with an exception object that will automatically be described in the trace log, as shown in Figure 7-27:

```
protected void cmdError_Click(Object sender, EventArgs e)
{
    try
    {
        DivideNumbers(5, 0);
    }
    catch (Exception err)
    {
        Trace.Warn("cmdError_Click", "Caught Error", err);
    }
}
```

```
private decimal DivideNumbers(decimal number, decimal divisor)
{
    return number/divisor;
}
```

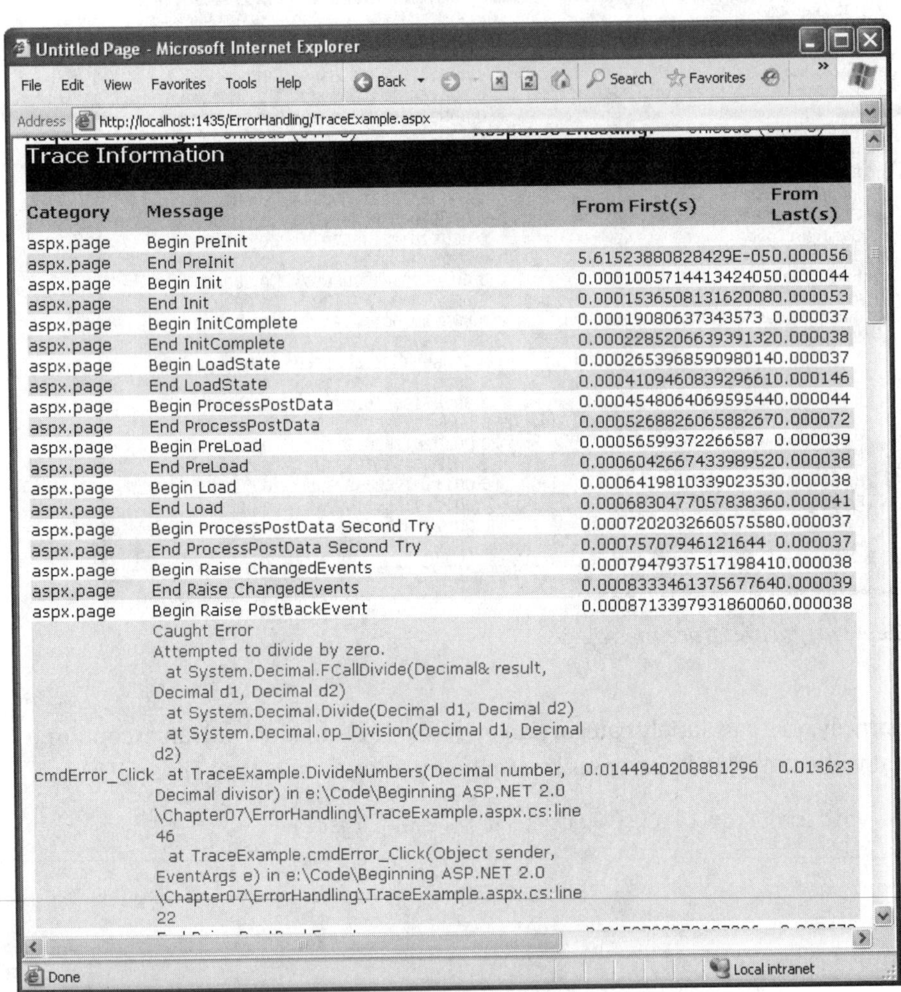

Figure 7-27. *An exception trace message*

By default, trace messages are listed in the order they were written by your code. Alternatively, you can specify that messages should be sorted by category using the TraceMode attribute in the Page directive:

```
<%@ Page Trace="true" TraceMode="SortByCategory" %>
```

or the TraceMode property of the Trace object in your code:

```
Trace.TraceMode = TraceMode.SortByCategory;
```

Reading Trace Information

ASP.NET also allows you to interact with the trace messages programmatically. This feature isn't used too often, but it can be useful if you want to capture the trace information and log it to another source (such as a database or the event log). You could save the entire trace log or search for important trace messages.

Trace messages aren't available at any time. If you want to access them, you need to wait until the trace log is completed. At this point, the Trace object fires a TraceFinished event, which you can handle. Here's a sample event handler that loops through all the trace messages and writes them to page with no additional formatting:

```
private void OnTraceFinished(object sender, TraceContextEventArgs e)
{
    foreach (TraceContextRecord r in e.TraceRecords)
    {
        Response.Write(r.Category + ": " + r.Message + "<br />");
    }
}
```

It's up to you to hook up your trace event handler. One good place to perform this task is in the Page.Load event handler. Here's an example:

```
protected void Page_Load(object sender, EventArgs e)
{
    Trace.TraceFinished += new TraceContextEventHandler(OnTraceFinished);
}
```

Application-Level Tracing

Application-level tracing allows you to enable tracing for an entire application. To do this, you need to modify settings in the web.config file, as shown here:

```
<configuration>
  <system.web>
    <trace enabled="true" requestLimit="10" pageOutput="false"
     traceMode="SortByTime" localOnly="true" />
  </system.web>
</configuration>
```

Table 7-4 lists the tracing options.

Table 7-4. *Tracing Options*

Attribute	Values	Description
Enabled	true, false	Turns application-level tracing on or off.
requestLimit	Any integer (for example, 10)	This is the number of HTTP requests for which tracing information will be stored. Unlike page-level tracing, this allows you collect a batch of information from multiple requests. When the maximum is reached, the information for the oldest request is abandoned every time a new request is received.
pageOutput	true, false	Determines whether tracing information will be displayed on the page (as it is with page-level tracing). If you choose false, you'll still be able to view the collected information by requesting trace.axd from the virtual directory where your application is running.
traceMode	SortByTime, SortByCategory	Determines the sort order of trace messages.
localOnly	true, false	Determines whether tracing information will be shown only to local clients (clients using the same computer) or can be shown to remote clients as well. By default, this is true and remote clients cannot see tracing information.
mostRecent	true, false	If true, ASP.NET keeps only the most recent trace messages. When the requestLimit maximum is reached, the information for the oldest request is abandoned every time a new request is received. If false (the default), ASP.NET stops collecting new trace messages when the limit is reached.

To view tracing information, you request the trace.axd file in the web application's root directory. This file doesn't actually exist; instead, ASP.NET automatically intercepts the request and interprets it as a request for the tracing information. It will then list the most recent collected requests, provided you're making the request from the local machine or have enabled remote tracing (see Figure 7-28).

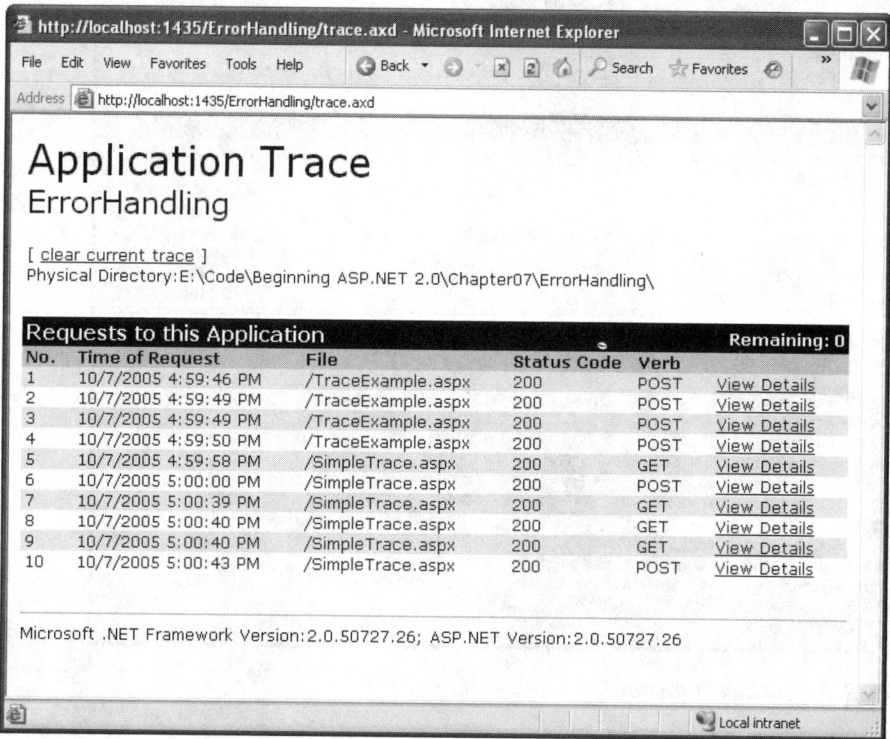

Figure 7-28. *Traced application request*

You can see the detailed information for any request by clicking the View Details link. This provides a useful way to store tracing information for a short period of time and allows you to review it without needing to see the actual pages (see Figure 7-29).

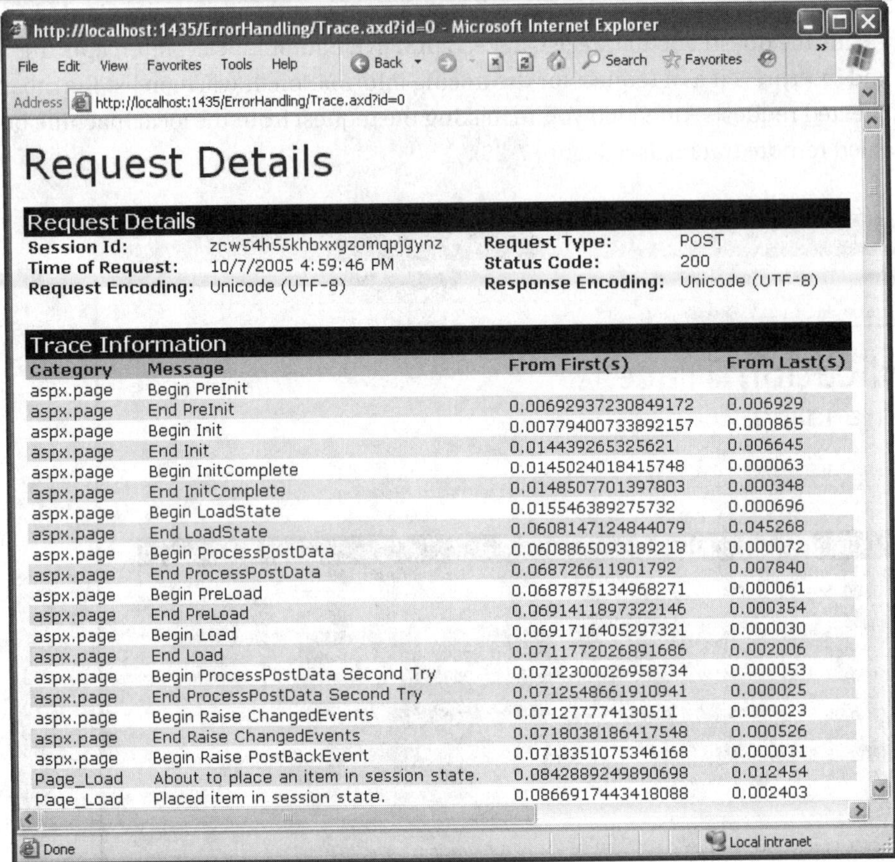

Request Details

Request Details

Session Id:	zcw54h55khbxxgzomqpjgynz	**Request Type:**	POST
Time of Request:	10/7/2005 4:59:46 PM	**Status Code:**	200
Request Encoding:	Unicode (UTF-8)	**Response Encoding:**	Unicode (UTF-8)

Trace Information

Category	Message	From First(s)	From Last(s)
aspx.page	Begin PreInit		
aspx.page	End PreInit	0.00692937230849172	0.006929
aspx.page	Begin Init	0.00779400733892157	0.000865
aspx.page	End Init	0.014439265325621	0.006645
aspx.page	Begin InitComplete	0.0145024018415748	0.000063
aspx.page	End InitComplete	0.0148507701397803	0.000348
aspx.page	Begin LoadState	0.015546389275732	0.000696
aspx.page	End LoadState	0.0608147124844079	0.045268
aspx.page	Begin ProcessPostData	0.0608865093189218	0.000072
aspx.page	End ProcessPostData	0.068726611901792	0.007840
aspx.page	Begin PreLoad	0.0687875134968271	0.000061
aspx.page	End PreLoad	0.0691411897322146	0.000354
aspx.page	Begin Load	0.0691716405297321	0.000030
aspx.page	End Load	0.0711772026891686	0.002006
aspx.page	Begin ProcessPostData Second Try	0.0712300026958734	0.000053
aspx.page	End ProcessPostData Second Try	0.0712548661910941	0.000025
aspx.page	Begin Raise ChangedEvents	0.071277774130511	0.000023
aspx.page	End Raise ChangedEvents	0.0718038186417548	0.000526
aspx.page	Begin Raise PostBackEvent	0.0718351075346168	0.000031
Page_Load	About to place an item in session state.	0.0842889249890698	0.012454
Page_Load	Placed item in session state.	0.0866917443418088	0.002403

Figure 7-29. *Request trace information*

The Last Word

The difference between an ordinary website and a professional web application is often in how it deals with errors. In this chapter, you learned the different lines of defense you can use in .NET, including structured error handling, logging, custom error pages, and tracing.

In the next chapter, you'll tackle some of ASP.NET's most interesting web controls.

CHAPTER 8

Validation and Rich Controls

This chapter looks at some of the real promise of ASP.NET and the web control model. First, you'll learn about ASP.NET's validation controls. These controls take a previously time-consuming and complicated task—verifying user input and reporting errors—and automate it with an elegant, easy-to-use collection of validators. You'll learn how to add these controls to an existing page and use regular expressions, custom validation functions, and manual validation. And as usual, you'll peer under the hood to see how ASP.NET implements these features.

Next, you'll consider two controls that have no equivalent in the ordinary HTML world: the Calendar and AdRotator controls. These controls demonstrate how the web control model can invent new types of web page user interfaces without breaking browser compatibility. The Calendar and AdRotator controls are only two of several rich controls included with ASP.NET; you'll explore the others throughout this book.

Finally, you'll consider how you can create more sophisticated pages with multiple views using advanced container controls such as the MultiView and Wizard controls. These controls allow you to pack a miniature application into a single page. Using them, you can handle a multistep task without redirecting the user from one page to another.

Validation

As a seasoned developer, you probably realize users will make mistakes. What's particularly daunting is the range of possible mistakes that users can make, such as the following:

- Users might ignore an important field and leave it blank.
- Users might try to type a short string of nonsense to circumvent a required field check, thereby creating endless headaches on your end, such as invalid e-mail addresses that cause problems for your automatic mailing programs.

- Users might make an honest mistake, such as entering a typing error, entering a nonnumeric character in a number field, or submitting the wrong type of information. They might even enter several pieces of information that are individually correct but when taken together are inconsistent (for example, entering a MasterCard number after choosing Visa as the payment type).

A web application is particularly susceptible to these problems, because it relies on basic HTML input controls that don't have all the features of their Windows counterparts. For example, a common technique in a Windows application is to handle the KeyPress event of a text box, check to see whether the current character is valid, and prevent it from appearing if it isn't. This technique is commonly used to create text boxes that accept only numeric input.

In web applications, however, you don't have that sort of fine-grained control. To handle a KeyPress event, the page would have to be posted back to the server every time the user types a letter, which would slow down the application hopelessly. Instead, you need to perform all your validation at once when a page (which may contain multiple input controls) is submitted. You then need to create the appropriate user interface to report the mistakes. Some websites report only the first incorrect field, while others use a special table, list, or window that describes them all. By the time you have perfected your validation routines, a considerable amount of fine-tuned effort has gone into writing validation code.

ASP.NET aims to save you this trouble and provide you with a reusable framework of validation controls that manages validation details by checking fields and reporting on errors automatically. These controls can even use client-side DHTML and JavaScript to provide a more dynamic and responsive interface while still providing ordinary validation for older browsers (often referred to as *down-level* browsers).

The Validation Controls

ASP.NET provides five validator controls, which are described in Table 8-1. Four are targeted at specific types of validation, while the fifth allows you to apply custom validation routines.

Table 8-1. *Validator Controls*

Control Class	Description
RequiredFieldValidator	Validation succeeds as long as the input control doesn't contain an empty string.
RangeValidator	Validation succeeds if the input control contains a value within a specific numeric, alphabetic, or date range.
CompareValidator	Validation succeeds if the input control contains a value that matches the value in another, specified input control.

Control Class	Description
RegularExpressionValidator	Validation succeeds if the value in an input control matches a specified regular expression.
CustomValidator	Validation is performed by a user-defined function.

Each validation control can be bound to a single input control. In addition, you can apply more than one validation control to the same input control to provide multiple types of validation.

If you use the RangeValidator, CompareValidator, or RegularExpressionValidator, validation will automatically succeed if the input control is empty, because there is no value to validate. If this isn't the behavior you want, you should add a RequiredFieldValidator to the control. This ensures that two types of validation will be performed, effectively restricting blank values.

Like all other web controls, you add a validator as a tag in the form <asp:ControlClassName />. The other validation control, ValidationSummary, doesn't perform any actual control checking. Instead, you can use it to provide a list of all the validation errors for the entire page.

The Validation Process

You can use the validator controls to verify a page automatically when the user submits it or manually in your code. The first approach is the most common.

When using automatic validation, the user receives a normal page and begins to fill in the input controls. When finished, the user clicks a button to submit the page. Every button has a CausesValidation property, which can be set to true or false. What happens when the user clicks the button depends on the value of the CausesValidation property:

- If CausesValidation is false, ASP.NET will ignore the validation controls, the page will be posted back, and your event handling code will run normally.

- If CausesValidation is true (the default), ASP.NET will automatically validate the page when the user clicks the button. It does this by performing the validation for each control on the page. If any control fails to validate, ASP.NET will return the page with some error information, depending on your settings. Your click event handling code may or may not be executed—meaning you'll have to specifically check in the event handler whether the page is valid.

Based on this description, you'll realize that validation happens automatically when certain buttons are clicked. It doesn't happen when the page is posted back because of a change event (such as choosing a new value in an AutoPostBack list) or if the user clicks a button that has CausesValidation set to false. However, you can still validate one or more controls manually and then make a decision in your code based on the results. You'll learn about this process in more detail a little later (see the "Manual Validation" section).

■ **Note** Many other buttonlike controls that can be used to submit the page also provide the CausesValidation property. Examples include the LinkButton, ImageButton, and BulletedList.

Client-Side Validation

In most modern browsers (including Internet Explorer 5 or later and any version of Firefox), ASP.NET automatically adds JavaScript code for client-side validation. In this case, when the user clicks a CausesValidation button, the same error messages will appear without the page needing to be submitted and returned from the server. This increases the responsiveness of the application.

However, even if the page validates successfully on the client side, ASP.NET still revalidates it when it's received at the server. This is because it's easy for an experienced user to circumvent client-side validation. For example, a malicious user might delete the block of JavaScript validation code and continue working with the page. By performing the validation at both ends, ASP.NET makes sure your application can be as responsive as possible while also remaining secure.

The Validator Classes

The validation control classes are found in the System.Web.UI.WebControls namespace and inherit from the BaseValidator class. This class defines the basic functionality for a validation control. Table 8-2 describes its properties.

Table 8-2. *Properties of the BaseValidator Class*

Property	Description
ControlToValidate	Identifies the control that this validator will check. Each validator can verify the value in one input control.
ErrorMessage, ForeColor, and Display	If validation fails, the validator control can display a text message (set by the ErrorMessage property). The Display property allows you to configure whether this error message will be added dynamically as needed (Dynamic) or whether an appropriate space will be reserved for the message (Static). Static is useful when the validator is in a table and you don't want the width of the cell to collapse when no message is displayed.

Property	Description
IsValid	After validation is performed, this returns true or false depending on whether it succeeded or failed. Generally, you'll check the state of the entire page by looking at its IsValid property instead to find out if all the validation controls succeeded.
Enabled	When set to false, automatic validation will not be performed for this control when the page is submitted.
EnableClientScript	If set to true, ASP.NET will add JavaScript and DHTML code to allow client-side validation on browsers that support it.

When using a validation control, the only properties you need to implement are ControlToValidate and ErrorMessage. In addition, you may need to implement the properties that are used for your specific validator. Table 8-3 outlines these properties.

Table 8-3. *Validator-Specific Properties*

Validator Control	Added Members
RequiredFieldValidator	None required
RangeValidator	MaximumValue, MinimumValue, Type
CompareValidator	ControlToCompare, Operator, Type, ValueToCompare
RegularExpressionValidator	ValidationExpression
CustomValidator	ClientValidationFunction, ServerValidate event

Later in this chapter (in the "A Validated Customer Form" section), you'll see a customer form example that demonstrates each type of validation.

A Simple Validation Example

To understand how validation works, you can create a simple web page. This test uses a single Button web control, two TextBox controls, and a RangeValidator control that validates the first text box. If validation fails, the RangeValidator control displays an error message, so you should place this control immediately next to the TextBox it's validating. Figure 8-1 shows the appearance of the page after a failed validation attempt.

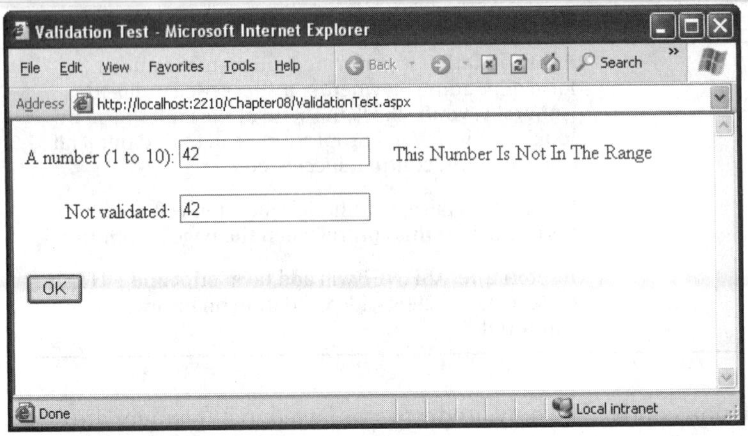

Figure 8-1. *Failed validation*

In addition, place a Label control at the bottom of the form. This label will report when the page has been successfully posted back and the event handling code has executed. Disable its EnableViewState property to ensure that it will be cleared every time the page is posted back.

The layout code defines a RangeValidator control, sets the error message, identifies the control that will be validated, and requires an integer from 1 to 10. These properties are set in the .aspx file, but they could also be configured in the event handler for the Page.Load event. The Button automatically has its CauseValidation property set to true, because this is the default.

```
<html><body>
  <form method="post" runat="server">
    A number (1 to 10):
    <asp:TextBox id=txtValidated runat="server" />
    <asp:RangeValidator id="RangeValidator" runat="server"
         ErrorMessage="This Number Is Not In The Range"
         ControlToValidate="txtValidated"
         MaximumValue="10" MinimumValue="1"
         Type="Integer" />
    <br /><br />
    Not validated:
    <asp:TextBox id=txtNotValidated runat="server" /><br /><br />
    <asp:Button id=cmdOK runat="server" Text="OK" /><br /><br />
    <asp:Label id=lblMessage runat="server"
         EnableViewState="false" />
  </form>
</body></html>
```

Finally, here is the code that responds to the button click:

```
protected void cmdOK_Click(Object sender, EventArgs e)
{
    lblMessage.Text = "cmdOK_Click event handler executed.";
}
```

If you're testing this web page in a modern browser (such as Internet Explorer 5 or later), you'll notice an interesting trick. When you first open the page, the error message is hidden. But if you type an invalid number (remember, validation will succeed for an empty value) and press the Tab key to move to the second text box, an error message will appear automatically next to the offending control. This is because ASP.NET adds a special JavaScript function that detects when the focus changes. This code uses the special WebUIValidation.js script library file that is installed on your server with the .NET Framework (in the c:\Inetpub\wwwroot\aspnet_client\system_web\[Version] directory) and is somewhat complicated. However, ASP.NET handles all the details for you automatically. If you try to click the OK button with an invalid value in txtValidated, your actions will be ignored, and the page won't be posted back.

These features are relatively high-level, because they combine DHTML and JavaScript. Clearly, not all browsers will support this client-side validation. To see what will happen on a down-level browser, set the RangeValidator.EnableClientScript property to false, and rerun the page. Now error messages won't appear dynamically as you change focus. However, when you click the OK button, the page will be returned from the server with the appropriate error message displayed next to the invalid control.

The potential problem in this scenario is that the click event handling code will still execute, even though the page is invalid. To correct this problem and ensure that your page behaves the same on modern and older browsers, you must specifically abort the event code if validation hasn't been performed successfully.

```
protected void cmdOK_Click(Object sender, EventArgs e)
{
    // Abort the event if the control isn't valid.
    if (!RangeValidator.IsValid) return;
    lblMessage.Text = "cmdOK_Click event handler executed.";
}
```

This code solves the current problem, but it isn't much help if the page contains multiple validation controls. Fortunately, every web form provides its own IsValid property. This property will be false if *any* validation control has failed. It will be true if all the validation controls completed successfully or if validation was not performed (for example, if the validation controls are disabled or if the button has CausesValidation set to false).

```
protected void cmdOK_Click(Object sender, EventArgs e)
{
    // Abort the event if the page isn't valid.
    if (!this.IsValid) return;
    lblMessage.Text = "cmdOK_Click event handler executed.";
}
```

Remember, client-side validation is just nice frosting on top of your application. Server-side validation will always be performed, ensuring that crafty users can't "spoof" pages.

Other Display Options

In some cases, you might have already created a carefully designed form that combines multiple input fields. Perhaps you want to add validation to this page, but you can't reformat the layout to accommodate all the error messages for all the validation controls. In this case, you can save some work by using the ValidationSummary control.

To try this, set the Display property of the RangeValidator control to None. This ensures the error message will never be displayed. However, validation will still be performed and the user will still be prevented from successfully clicking the OK button if some invalid information exists on the page.

Next, add the ValidationSummary in a suitable location (such as the bottom of the page):

```
<asp:ValidationSummary id="Errors" runat="server" />
```

When you run the page, you won't see any dynamic messages as you enter invalid information and tab to a new field. However, when you click the OK button, the ValidationSummary will appear with a list of all error messages, as shown in Figure 8-2. In this case, it retrieves one error message (from the RangeValidator control). However, if you had a dozen validators, it would retrieve all their error messages and create a list.

The ValidationSummary control also provides some useful properties you can use to fine-tune the error display. You can set the HeaderText property to display a special title at the top of the list (such as *Your page contains the following errors:*). You can also change the ForeColor and choose a DisplayMode. The possible modes are BulletList (the default), List, and SingleParagraph.

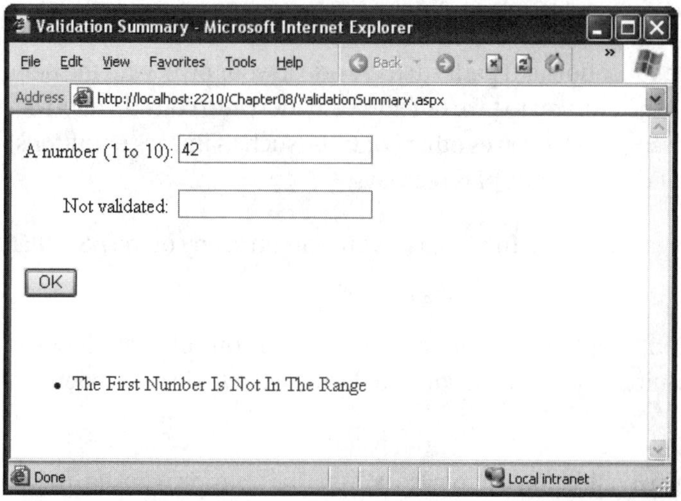

Figure 8-2. *The validation summary*

Finally, you can choose to have the validation summary displayed in a pop-up dialog box instead of on the page (see Figure 8-3). This approach has the advantage of leaving the user interface of the page untouched, but it also forces the user to dismiss the error messages by closing the window before being able to modify the input controls. If users will need to refer to these messages while they fix the page, the inline display is better.

To show the summary in a dialog box, set the ValidationSummary.ShowMessageBox property to true.

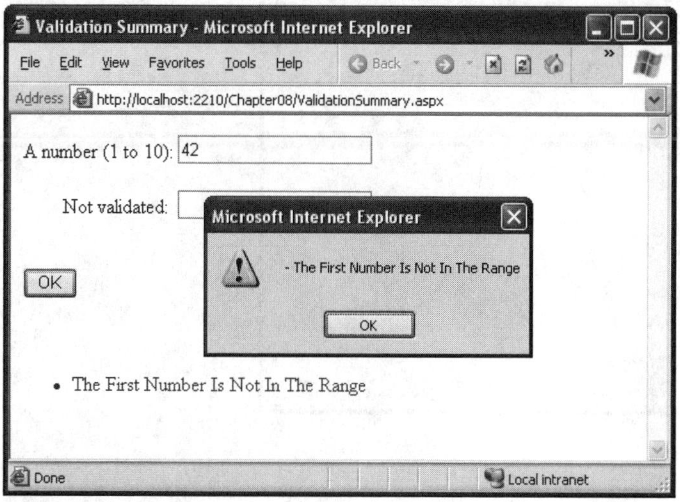

Figure 8-3. *A message box summary*

Manual Validation

Your final option is to disable validation and perform the work on your own, with the help of the validation controls. This allows you to take other information into consideration or create a specialized error message that involves other controls (such as images or buttons).

You can create manual validation in one of three ways:

- Use your own code to verify values. In this case, you won't use any of the ASP.NET validation controls.
- Disable the EnableClientScript property for each validation control. This allows an invalid page to be submitted, after which you can decide what to do with it depending on the problems.
- Add a button with CausesValidation set to false. When this button is clicked, manually validate the page by calling the Page.Validate method. Then examine the IsValid property, and decide what to do.

The next example uses the second approach. Once the page is submitted, it examines all the validation controls on the page by looping through the Page.Validators collection. Every time it finds a control that hasn't validated successfully, it retrieves the invalid value from the input control and adds it to a string. At the end of this routine, it displays a message that describes which values were incorrect, as shown in Figure 8-4.

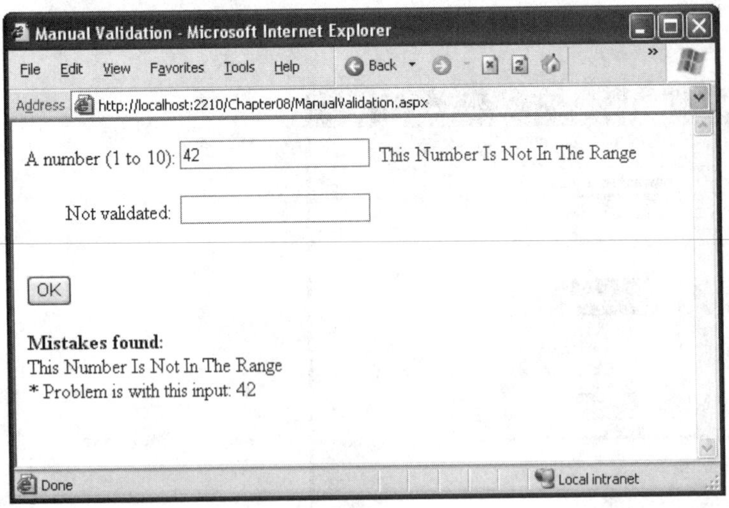

Figure 8-4. *Manual validation*

This technique adds a feature that wouldn't be available with automatic validation, which uses the ErrorMessage property. In that case, it isn't possible to include the actual incorrect values in the message.

Here's the event handler that checks for invalid values:

```
protected void cmdOK_Click(Object sender, EventArgs e)
{
    string errorMessage = "<b>Mistakes found:</b><br />";

   // Create a variable to represent the input control.
   TextBox ctrlInput;

    // Search through the validation controls.
    foreach (BaseValidator ctrl in this.Validators)
    {
        if (!ctrl.IsValid)
        {
            errorMessage += ctrl.ErrorMessage + "<br />";

            // Find the corresponding input control, and change the
            // generic Control variable into a TextBox variable.
            // This allows access to the Text property.
            ctrlInput = (TextBox)this.FindControl(ctrl.ControlToValidate);
            errorMessage += " * Problem is with this input: ";
            errorMessage += ctrlInput.Text + "<br />";
        }
    }
    lblMessage.Text = errorMessage;
}
```

This example uses an advanced technique: the Page.FindControl() method. It's required because the ControlToValidate property is just a string with the name of a control, not a reference to the actual control object. To find the control that matches this name (and retrieve its Text property), you need to use the FindControl() method. Once the code has retrieved the matching text box, it can perform other tasks such as clearing the current value, tweaking a property, or even changing the text box color. Note that the FindControl() method returns a generic Control reference, because you might search any type of control. To access all the properties of your control, you need to cast it to the appropriate type (such as TextBox in this example).

Understanding Regular Expressions

Regular expressions are an advanced tool for matching patterns. They have appeared in countless other languages and gained popularity as an extremely powerful way to work with strings. In fact, Visual Studio even allows programmers to perform a search-and-replace operation in their code using a regular expression (which may represent a new height of computer geekdom).

Regular expressions can almost be considered an entire language of their own. How to master all the ways you can use regular expressions—including pattern matching, back references, and named groups—could occupy an entire book (and several books are dedicated to just that subject). Fortunately, you can understand the basics of regular expressions without nearly that much work.

Literals and Metacharacters

All regular expressions consist of two kinds of characters: literals and metacharacters. Literals are not unlike the string literals you type in code. They represent a specific defined character. For example, if you search for the string literal "l", you'll find the character *l* and nothing else.

Metacharacters provide the true secret to unlocking the full power of regular expressions. You're probably already familiar with two metacharacters from the DOS world (? and *). Consider the command-line expression shown here:

```
Del *.*
```

The expression *.* contains one literal (the period) and two metacharacters (the asterisks). This translates as "delete every file that starts with any number of characters and ends with an extension of any number of characters (or has no extension at all)." Because all files in DOS implicitly have extensions, this has the well-documented effect of deleting everything in the current directory.

Another DOS metacharacter is the question mark, which means "any single character." For example, the following statement deletes any file named hello that has an extension of exactly one character.

```
Del hello.?
```

The regular expression language provides many flexible metacharacters—far more than the DOS command line. For example, \s represents any whitespace character (such as a space or tab). \d represents any digit. Thus, the following expression would match any string that started with the numbers 333, followed by a single whitespace character and any three numbers. Valid matches would include 333 333 and 333 945 but not 334 333 or 3334 945.

```
333\s\d\d\d
```

One aspect that can make regular expressions less readable is that they use special metacharacters that are more than one character long. In the previous example, \s represents a single character, as does \d, even though they both occupy two characters in the expression.

You can use the plus (+) sign to represent a repeated character. For example, 5+7 means "one or more occurrences of the character 5, followed by a single 7." The number 57 would match, as would 555557. You can also use parentheses to group a subexpression. For example, (52)+7 would match any string that started with a sequence of 52. Matches would include 527, 52527, 5252527, and so on.

You can also delimit a range of characters using square brackets. [a-f] would match any single character from *a* to *f* (lowercase only). The following expression would match any word that starts with a letter from *a* to *f*, contains one or more "word" characters (letters), and ends with *ing*—possible matches include *acting* and *developing*.

```
[a-f]\w+ing
```

The following is a more useful regular expression that can match any e-mail address by verifying that it contains the @ symbol. The dot is a metacharacter used to indicate any character except newline. However, some invalid e-mail addresses would still be allowed, including those that contain spaces and those that don't include a dot (.). You'll see a better example a little later in the customer form example.

```
.+@.+
```

Finding a Regular Expression

Clearly, picking the perfect regular expression may require some testing. In fact, numerous reference materials (on the Internet and in paper form) include useful regular expressions for validating common values such as postal codes. To experiment, you can use the simple RegularExpressionTest page included with the online samples, which is shown in Figure 8-5. It allows you to set a regular expression that will be used to validate a control. Then you can type in some sample values and see whether the regular expression validator succeeds or fails.

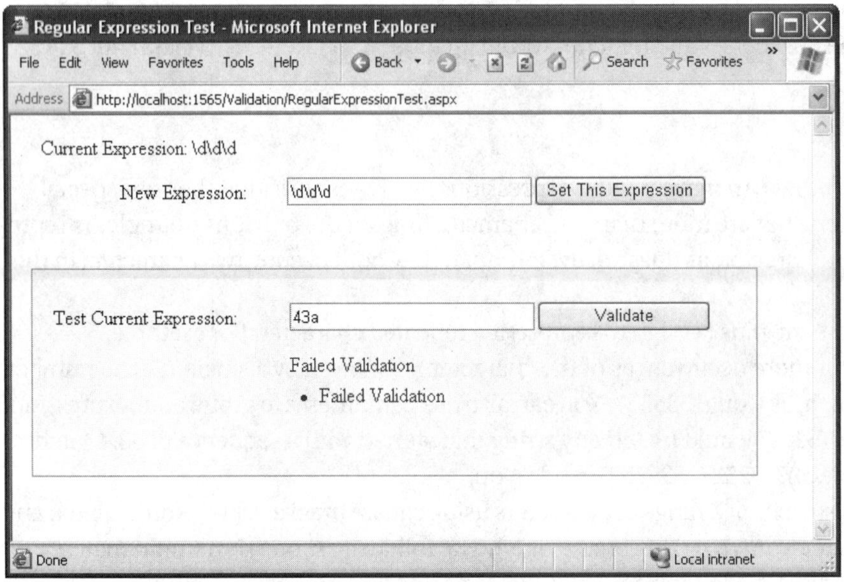

Figure 8-5. *A regular expression test page*

The code is quite simple. The Set This Expression button assigns a new regular expression to the RegularExpressionValidator control (using whatever text you have typed). The Validate button simply triggers a postback, which causes ASP.NET to perform validation automatically. If an error message appears, validation has failed. Otherwise, it's successful.

```
public partial class RegularExpressionTest : Page
{
    protected void cmdSetExpression_Click(Object sender, EventArgs e)
    {
        TestValidator.ValidationExpression = txtExpression.Text;
        lblExpression.Text = "Current Expression: ";
        lblExpression.Text += txtExpression.Text;
    }
}
```

Table 8-4 shows some of the fundamental regular expression building blocks. If you need to match a literal character with the same name as a special character, you generally precede it with a \ character. For example, *hello* matches *hello* in a string, because the special asterisk (*) character is preceded by a slash (\).

Table 8-4. *Regular Expression Characters*

<table>
<tr><th>Character</th><th>Description</th></tr>
<tr><td>*</td><td>Zero or more occurrences of the previous character or subexpression. For example, 7*8 matches 7778 or just 8.</td></tr>
<tr><td>+</td><td>One or more occurrences of the previous character or subexpression. For example, 7+8 matches 7778 but not 8.</td></tr>
<tr><td>( )</td><td>Groups a subexpression that will be treated as a single element. For example, (78)+ matches 78 and 787878.</td></tr>
<tr><td>|</td><td>Either of two matches. For example, 8|6 matches 8 or 6.</td></tr>
<tr><td>[ ]</td><td>Matches one character in a range of valid characters. For example, [A-C] matches A, B, or C.</td></tr>
<tr><td>[^]</td><td>Matches a character that isn't in the given range. For example, [^A-B] matches any character except A and B.</td></tr>
<tr><td>.</td><td>Any character except newline. For example, .here matches where and there.</td></tr>
<tr><td>\s</td><td>Any whitespace character (such as a tab or space).</td></tr>
<tr><td>\S</td><td>Any nonwhitespace character.</td></tr>
<tr><td>\d</td><td>Any digit character.</td></tr>
<tr><td>\D</td><td>Any character that isn't a digit.</td></tr>
<tr><td>\w</td><td>Any "word" character (letter, number, or underscore).</td></tr>
</table>

Table 8-5 shows a few of common (and useful) regular expressions.

Table 8-5. *Commonly Used Regular Expressions*

Content	Regular Expression	Description
E-mail address*	\S+@\S+\.\S+	Check for an at (@) sign and dot (.) and allow nonwhitespace characters only.
Password	\w+	Any sequence of word characters (letter, space, or underscore).
Specific-length password	\w{4,10}	A password that must be at least four characters long but no longer than ten characters.
Advanced password	[a-zA-Z]\w{3,9}	As with the specific length password, this regular expression will allow four to ten total characters. The twist is that the first character must fall in the range of a–z or A–Z (that is to say it must start with a nonaccented ordinary letter).

Continued

Table 8-5. *Continued*

Content	Regular Expression	Description
Another advanced password	[a-zA-Z]\w*\d+\w*	This password starts with a letter character, followed by zero or more word characters, a digit, and then zero or more word characters. In short, it forces a password to contain a number somewhere inside it. You could use a similar pattern to require two numbers or any other special character.
Limited-length field	\S{4,10}	Like the password example, this allows four to ten characters, but it allows special characters (asterisks, ampersands, and so on).
Social Security number	\d{3}-\d{2}-\d{4}	A sequence of three, two, then four digits, with each group separated by a dash. You could use a similar pattern when requiring a phone number.

* *You have many different ways to validate e-mail addresses with regular expressions of varying complexity. See* `http://www.4guysfromrolla.com/webtech/validateemail.shtml` *for a discussion of the subject and numerous examples.*

Some logic is much more difficult to model in a regular expression. An example is the Luhn algorithm, which verifies credit card numbers by first doubling every second digit, then adding these doubled digits together, and finally dividing the sum by ten. The number is valid (although not necessarily connected to a real account) if there is no remainder after dividing the sum. To use the Luhn algorithm, you need a CustomValidator control that runs this logic on the supplied value. (You can find a detailed description of the Luhn algorithm at `http://en.wikipedia.org/wiki/Luhn_formula`.)

A Validated Customer Form

To bring together these various topics, you'll now see a full-fledged web form that combines a variety of pieces of information that might be needed to add a user record (for example, an e-commerce site shopper or a content site subscriber). Figure 8-6 shows this form.

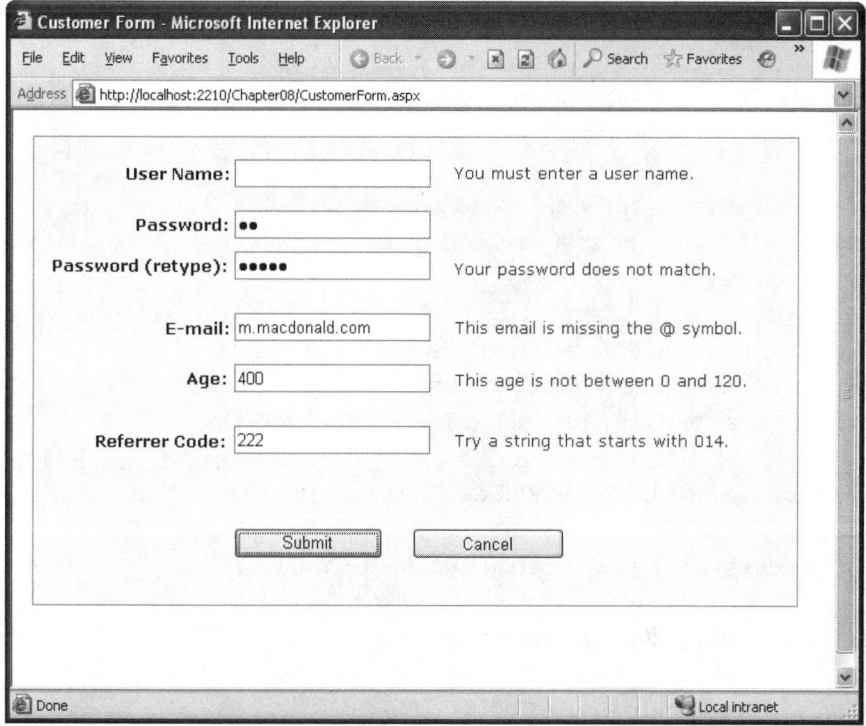

Figure 8-6. *A sample customer form*

Several types of validation are taking place on the customer form:

- Two RequiredFieldValidator controls make sure the user enters a user name and a password.
- A CompareValidator ensures that the two versions of the masked password match.
- A RegularExpressionValidator checks that the e-mail address contains an at (@) symbol.
- A RangeValidator ensures the age is a number from 0 to 120.
- A CustomValidator performs a special validation on the server of a "referrer code." This code verifies that the first three characters make up a number that is divisible by 7.

The tags for the validator controls are as follows:

```
<asp:RequiredFieldValidator id="vldUserName" runat="server"
    ErrorMessage="You must enter a user name."
    ControlToValidate="txtUserName" />

<asp:RequiredFieldValidator id="vldPassword" runat="server"
    ErrorMessage="You must enter a password."
    ControlToValidate="txtPassword" />

<asp:CompareValidator id="vldRetype" runat="server"
    ErrorMessage="Your password does not match."
    ControlToCompare="txtPassword" ControlToValidate="txtRetype" />

<asp:RegularExpressionValidator id="vldEmail" runat="server"
    ErrorMessage="This email is missing the @ symbol."
    ValidationExpression=".+@.+" ControlToValidate="txtEmail" />

<asp:RangeValidator id="vldAge" runat="server"
    ErrorMessage="This age is not between 0 and 120." Type="Integer"
    MaximumValue="120" MinimumValue="0"
    ControlToValidate="txtAge" />

<asp:CustomValidator id="vldCode" runat="server"
    ErrorMessage="Try a string that starts with 014."
    ControlToValidate="txtCode" />
```

The form provides two validation buttons—one that requires validation and one that allows the user to cancel the task gracefully. Here's the event handling code:

```
protected void cmdSubmit_Click(Object sender, EventArgs e)
{
    if (!this.IsValid) return;
    lblMessage.Text = "This is a valid form.";
}

protected void cmdCancel_Click(Object sender, EventArgs e)
{
    lblMessage.Text = "No attempt was made to validate this form.";
}
```

The only form-level code that is required for validation is the custom validation code. The validation takes place in the event handler for the CustomValidator.ServerValidate event. This method receives the value it needs to validate (e.Value) and sets the result of the validation to true or false (e.IsValid).

```
protected void vldCode_ServerValidate(Object source, ServerValidateEventArgs e)
{
    try
    {
        // Check whether the first three digits are divisible by seven.
        int val = Int32.Parse(e.Value.Substring(0, 3));
        if (val % 7 == 0)
        {
            e.IsValid = true;
        }
        else
        {
            e.IsValid = false;
        }
    }
    catch
    {
        // An error occurred in the conversion.
        // The value is not valid.
        e.IsValid = false;
    }
}
```

This example also introduces one new detail: error handling. This error handling code ensures that potential problems are caught and dealt with appropriately. Without error handling, your code may fail, leaving the user with nothing more than a cryptic error page. The reason this example requires error handling code is because it performs two steps that aren't guaranteed to succeed. First, the Int32.Parse() method attempts to convert the data in the text box to an integer. An error will occur during this step if the information in the text box is nonnumeric (for example, if the user entered the characters 4G). Similarly, the String.Substring() method, which extracts the first three characters, will fail if fewer than three characters appear in the text box. To guard against these problems, you can specifically check these details before you attempt to use the Parse() and Substring() methods, or you can use error handling to respond to problems after they occur. (Another option is to use the TryParse() method, which returns a Boolean value that tells you whether the conversion succeeded.)

■ **Tip** In some cases, you might be able to replace custom validation with a particularly ingenious use of a regular expression. However, you can use custom validation to ensure that validation code is executed only at the server. That prevents users from seeing your regular expression template (in the rendered JavaScript code) and using it to determine how they can outwit your validation routine. For example, a user may not have a valid credit card number, but if they know the algorithm you use to test credit card numbers, they can create a false one more easily.

The CustomValidator has another quirk. You'll notice that your custom server-side validation isn't performed until the page is posted back. This means that if you enable the client script code (the default), dynamic messages will appear informing the user when the other values are incorrect, but they will not indicate any problem with the referral code until the page is posted back to the server.

This isn't really a problem, but if it troubles you, you can use the CustomValidator.ClientValidationFunction property. Add a client-side JavaScript or VBScript validation function to the .aspx portion of the web page. (Ideally, it will be JavaScript for compatibility with browsers other than Internet Explorer.) Remember, you can't use client-side ASP.NET code, because C# and VB .NET aren't recognized by the client browser.

Your JavaScript function will accept two parameters (in true .NET style), which identify the source of the event and the additional validation parameters. In fact, the client-side event is modeled on the .NET ServerValidate event. Just as you did in the ServerValidate event handler, in the client validation function, you retrieve the value to validate from the Value property of the event argument object. You then see the IsValid property to indicate whether validation succeeds or fails.

The following is the client-side equivalent for the code in the ServerValidate event handler. You'll notice that the JavaScript code resembles C# superficially.

```
<script language="JavaScript">
<!--
function MyCustomValidation(objSource, objArgs)
{
    // Get value.
    var number = objArgs.Value;

    // Check value and return result.
    number = number.substr(0, 3);
    if (number % 7 == 0)
```

```
    {
        objArgs.IsValid = true;
    }
    else
    {
        objArgs.IsValid = false;
    }
}
// -->
</script>
```

Once you've added the function, set the ClientValidationFunction property of the CustomValidator control to the name of the function. You can add this information manually or by using the Properties window in Visual Studio.

```
<asp:CustomValidator id="vldCode" runat="server"
     ErrorMessage="Try a string that starts with 014."
     ControlToValidate="txtCode"
     ClientValidationFunction="MyCustomValidation" />
```

ASP.NET will now call this function on your behalf when it's required.

■ **Tip** Even when you use client-side validation, you must still include the ServerValidate event handler, both to provide server-side validation for clients that don't support the required JavaScript and DHTML features and to prevent clients from circumventing your validation by modifying the HTML page they receive.

By default, custom validation isn't performed on empty values. However, you can change this behavior by setting the CustomValidator.ValidateEmptyText property to true. This is a useful approach if you create a more detailed JavaScript function (for example, one that updates with additional information) and want it to run when the text is cleared.

YOU CAN VALIDATE LIST CONTROLS

The examples in this chapter have concentrated exclusively on validating text entry, which is the most common requirement in a web application. While you can't validate RadioButton or CheckBox controls, you can validate most single-select list controls.

When validating a list control, the value that is being validated is the Value property of the selected ListItem object. Remember, the Value property is the special hidden information attribute that can be added to every list item. If you don't use it, you can't validate the control (validating the text of the selection isn't a supported option).

Validation Groups

In more complex pages, you might have several distinct groups of pages, possibly in separate panels. In these situations, you may want to perform validation separately. For example, you might create a form that includes a box with login controls and a box underneath it with the controls for registering a new user. Each box includes its own submit button, and depending on which button is clicked, you want to perform the validation just for that section of the page.

This scenario is possible thanks to a feature called *validation groups*. To create a validation group, you need to put the input controls and the CausesValidation button controls into the same logical group. You do this by setting the ValidationGroup property of every control with the same descriptive string (such as "Form1" or "Login"). Every control that provides a CausesValidation property also includes the ValidationGroup property.

For example, the following page defines two validation groups, named Group1 and Group2. The controls for each group are placed into separate Panel controls.

```
<form id="form1" runat="server">
    <asp:Panel ID="Panel1" runat="server">
        <asp:TextBox ID="TextBox1" ValidationGroup="Group1" runat="server" />
        <asp:RequiredFieldValidator ID="RequiredFieldValidator1"
         ErrorMessage="*Required" ValidationGroup="Group1"
         runat="server" ControlToValidate="TextBox1" />
        <asp:Button ID="Button1" Text="Validate Group1"
         ValidationGroup="Group1" runat="server" />
    </asp:Panel>
    <br />
    <asp:Panel ID="Panel2" runat="server">
        <asp:TextBox ID="TextBox2" ValidationGroup="Group2"
         runat="server" />
        <asp:RequiredFieldValidator ID="RequiredFieldValidator2"
         ErrorMessage="*Required" ValidationGroup="Group2"
         ControlToValidate="TextBox2" runat="server" />
        <asp:Button ID="Button2" Text="Validate Group2"
         ValidationGroup="Group2" runat="server" />
    </asp:Panel>
</form>
```

If you click the button in the topmost Panel, only the first text box is validated. If you click the button in the second Panel, only the second text box is validated (as shown in Figure 8-7).

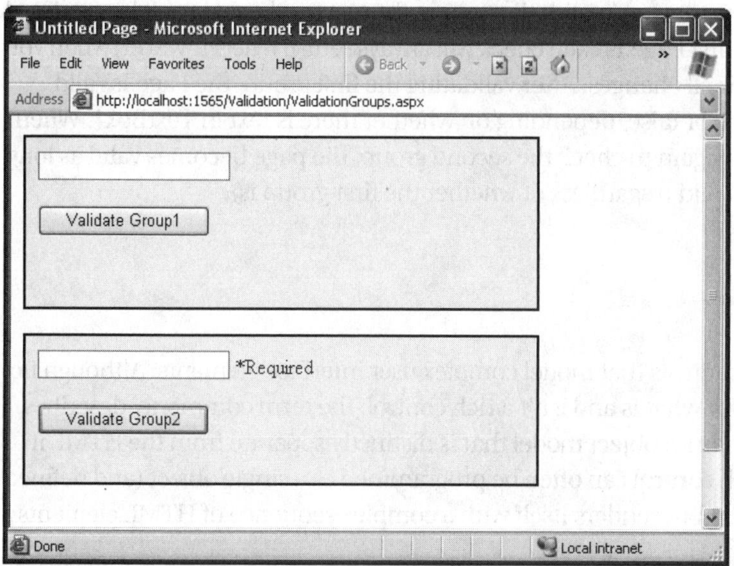

Figure 8-7. *Grouping controls for validation*

What happens if you add a new button that doesn't specify any validation group? In this case, the button validates every control that isn't explicitly assigned to a named validation group. In the current example, no controls fit the requirement, so the page is posted back successfully and deemed to be valid.

If you want to make sure a control is always validated, regardless of the validation group of the button that's clicked, you'll need to create multiple validators for the control, one for each group (and one with no validation group). Alternatively, you might choose to manage complex scenarios like these using server-side code, as shown in the following example.

You can use an overloaded version of the Page.Validate() method to validate just a specific group. You specify the name of the group you want to validate. For example, using the previous page, you could create a button that has no validation group assigned and respond to the Button.Click event with this code:

```
protected void cmdValidateAll_Click(object sender, EventArgs e)
{
    Label1.Text = "Valid: " + Page.IsValid.ToString();
    Page.Validate("Group1");
    Label1.Text += "<br />Group1 Valid: " + Page.IsValid.ToString();
    Page.Validate("Group2");
    Label1.Text += "<br />Group2 Valid: " + Page.IsValid.ToString();
}
```

Because this button isn't in any validation group, the two text boxes won't be validated automatically, and the first Page.IsValid check will always return true. However, when you call Page.Validate(), this all changes. After validating the first group, the Page.IsValid property will return true or false, depending on whether there is text in TextBox1. When you call Page.Validate() again to check the second group, the page becomes valid as long as the second group is valid (regardless of whether the first group is).

Rich Controls

Rich controls are web controls that model complex user interface elements. Although no strict definition exists for what is and isn't a rich control, the term commonly describes web controls that provide an object model that is distinctly separate from the HTML it generates. A typical rich control can often be programmed as a single object (and defined with a single control tag) but renders itself with a complex sequence of HTML elements and may even use client-side JavaScript.

ASP.NET includes numerous rich controls that are discussed elsewhere in this book, including data-based list controls, security controls, and controls tailored for web portals. The following list identifies the rich controls that don't fall into any specialized category. The rich controls in this list all appear in the Standard tab of the Visual Studio Toolbox.

AdRotator: A banner ad that displays one of a set of images based on a predefined schedule that's saved in an XML file.

Calendar: A calendar that displays and allows you to move through months and days and to select a date or a range of days.

MultiView, View, and Wizard: You can think of these controls as more advanced panels that let you switch between groups of controls on a page. These controls are described later in this chapter (in the section "Pages with Multiple Views").

TreeView and Menu: These are two of the most impressive rich controls. Both allow you to show multilayered data, such as a menu with multiple levels or a hierarchical tree. They're often used for website navigation (see Chapter 11).

Xml: This takes an XML file and an XSLT style sheet file as input and displays the resulting HTML in a browser. You'll learn about the Xml control in Chapter 17.

One of the best features of ASP.NET's control model is that other developers can create their own rich controls, which can then be incorporated into any ASP.NET application. You'll get a taste of this in Chapter 25, when you learn to create your own controls. Even without this knowledge, however, you can already start to use some of these advanced third-party controls. These controls provide features unlike any HTML element—including advanced grids, charting tools, and menus.

ASP.NET custom controls act like web controls in every sense. Your web page interacts with the appropriate control object, and the final output is rendered automatically every time the page is sent to the client as HTML. That means the controls need to be installed only on your server, and any client can benefit from them.

■ **Tip** The Internet contains many hubs for control sharing. One such location is Microsoft's own `http://www.asp.net`, which provides a control gallery where developers can submit their own ASP.NET web controls. Some of these controls are free (at least in a limited version), and others require a purchase.

In the following sections, you'll learn about two ASP.NET rich controls: the Calendar and the AdRotator.

The Calendar Control

The Calendar control is one of the most impressive web controls. It's commonly called a rich control because it can be programmed as a single object (and defined in a single simple tag) but rendered in dozens of lines of HTML output.

```
<asp:Calendar id="Dates" runat="server" />
```

The Calendar control presents a single-month view, as shown in Figure 8-8. The user can navigate from month to month using the navigational arrows, at which point the page is posted back and ASP.NET automatically provides a new page with the correct month values. You don't need to write any additional event handling code to manage this process. When the user clicks a date, the date becomes highlighted in a gray box. You can retrieve the selected day in your code as a DateTime object from the Calendar.SelectedDate property.

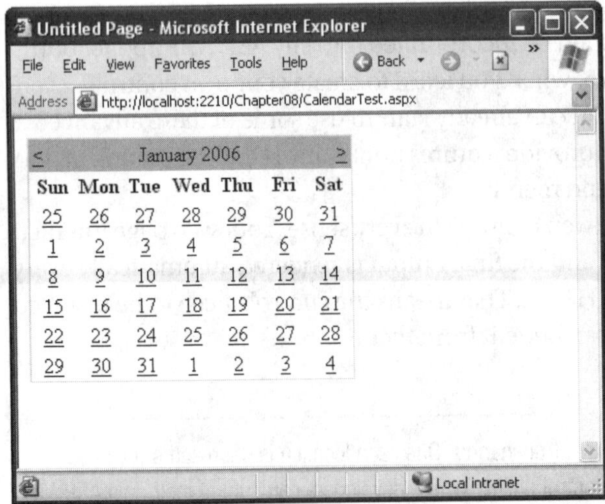

Figure 8-8. *The default Calendar*

This basic set of features may provide everything you need in your application. Alternatively, you can configure different selection modes to allow users to select entire weeks or months or to render the control as a static calendar that doesn't allow selection. The only fact you must remember is that if you allow month selection, the user can also select a single week or a day. Similarly, if you allow week selection, the user can also select a single day.

You set the type of selection through the Calendar.SelectionMode property. You may also need to set the Calendar.FirstDayOfWeek property to configure how a week is selected. (For example, set FirstDayOfWeek to the enumerated value Monday, and weeks will be selected from Monday to Sunday.)

When you allow multiple date selection, you need to examine the SelectedDates property, which provides a collection of all the selected dates. You can loop through this collection using the foreach syntax. The following code demonstrates this technique:

```
lblDates.Text = "You selected these dates:<br />";

foreach (DateTime dt in MyCalendar.SelectedDates)
{
    lblDates.Text += dt.ToLongDateString() + "<br />";
}
```

Figure 8-9 shows the resulting page after this code has been executed.

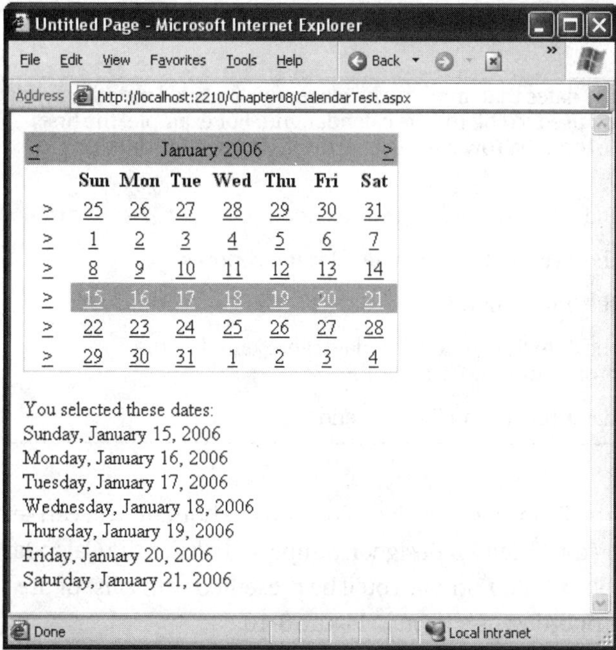

Figure 8-9. *Selecting multiple dates*

Formatting the Calendar

The Calendar control provides a whole host of formatting-related properties. You can set various parts of the Calendar, like the header, selector, and various day types, by using one of the style properties (for example, WeekendDayStyle). Each of these style properties references a full-featured TableItemStyle object that provides properties for coloring, border style, font, and alignment. Taken together, they allow you to modify almost any part of the Calendar's appearance.

Table 8-6 lists the style properties that the Calendar control provides.

Table 8-6. *Properties for Calendar Styles*

Member	Description
DayHeaderStyle	The style for the section of the Calendar that displays the days of the week (as column headers).
DayStyle	The default style for the dates in the current month.
NextPrevStyle	The style for the navigation controls in the title section that move from month to month.

Continued

Table 8-6. *Continued*

Member	Description
OtherMonthDayStyle	The style for the dates that aren't in the currently displayed month. These dates are used to "fill in" the calendar grid. For example, the first few cells in the topmost row may display the last few days from the previous month.
SelectedDayStyle	The style for the selected dates on the Calendar.
SelectorStyle	The style for the week and month date selection controls.
TitleStyle	The style for the title section.
TodayDayStyle	The style for the date designated as today (represented by the TodaysDate property of the Calendar).
WeekendDayStyle	The style for dates that fall on the weekend.

You can adjust each style using the Properties window. For a quick shortcut, you can set an entire related color scheme using the Calendar designer. Simply right-click the Calendar control on your design page, and select Auto Format. You'll be presented with a list of predefined formats that set the style properties, as shown in Figure 8-10.

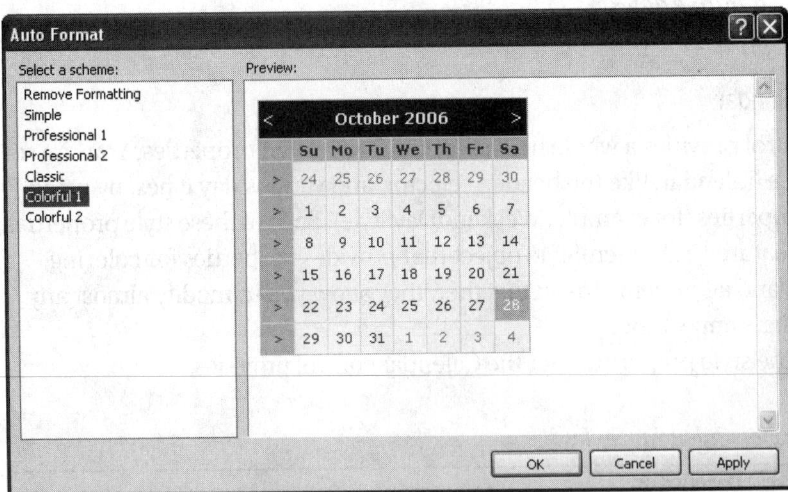

Figure 8-10. *Calendar styles*

You can also use additional properties to hide some elements or configure the text they display.

Restricting Dates

In most situations where you need to use a calendar for selection, you don't want to allow the user to select any date in the calendar. For example, the user might be booking an appointment or choosing a delivery date—two services that are generally provided only on set days. The Calendar control makes it surprisingly easy to implement this logic. In fact, if you've worked with the date and time controls on the Windows platform, you'll quickly recognize that the ASP.NET versions are far superior.

The basic approach to restricting dates is to write an event handler for the Calendar. DayRender event. This event occurs when the Calendar is about to create a month to display to the user. This event gives you the chance to examine the date that is being added to the current month (through the e.Day property) and decide whether it should be selectable or restricted.

The following code makes it impossible to select any weekend days or days in years greater than 2010:

```
protected void DayRender(Object source, DayRenderEventArgs e)
{
    // Restrict dates after the year 2010 and those on the weekend.
    if (e.Day.IsWeekend || e.Day.Date.Year > 2010)
    {
        e.Day.IsSelectable = false;
    }
}
```

The e.Day object is an instance of the CalendarDay class, which provides various useful properties, as described in Table 8-7.

Table 8-7. *CalendarDay Properties*

Property	Description
Date	The DateTime object that represents this date.
IsWeekend	True if this date falls on a Saturday or Sunday.
IsToday	True if this value matches the Calendar.TodaysDate property, which is set to the current day by default.
IsOtherMonth	True if this date doesn't belong to the current month but is displayed to fill in the first or last row. For example, this might be the last day of the previous month or the next day of the following month.
IsSelectable	Allows you to configure whether the user can select this day.

The DayRender event is extremely powerful. Besides allowing you to tailor what dates are selectable, it also allows you to configure the cell where the date is located through the e.Cell property. (The Calendar is really a sophisticated HTML table.) For example, you could highlight an important date or even add information. Here's an example that highlights a single day—the fifth of May:

```
protected void DayRender(Object source, DayRenderEventArgs e)
{
    // Check for May 5 in any year, and format it.
    if (e.Day.Date.Day == 5 && e.Day.Date.Month == 5)
    {
        e.Cell.BackColor = System.Drawing.Color.Yellow;

        // Add some static text to the cell.
        Label lbl = new Label();
        lbl.Text = "<br />My Birthday!";
        e.Cell.Controls.Add(lbl);
    }
}
```

Figure 8-11 shows the resulting calendar display.

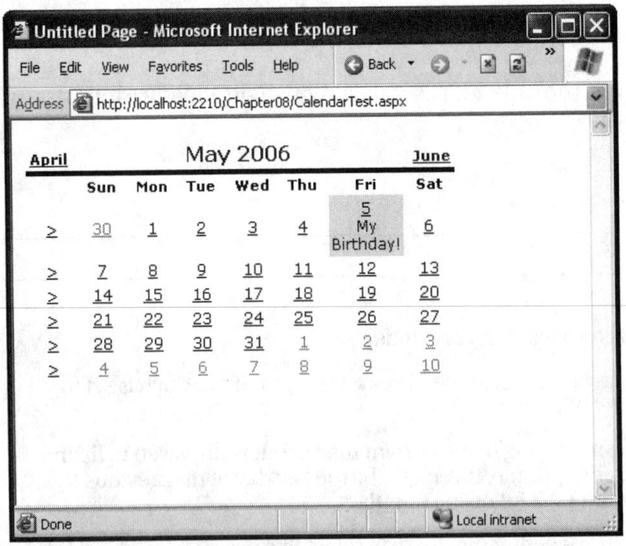

Figure 8-11. *Highlighting a day*

The Calendar control provides two other useful events: SelectionChanged and VisibleMonthChanged. These occur immediately after a change but before the page is returned to the user. You can react to these events and update other portions of the web page to correspond to the current calendar month. For example, you might want to set a corresponding list of times in a list control. The following code demonstrates this approach, using a different set of time values if a Monday is selected in the Calendar:

```
protected Sub SelectionChanged(Object source, EventArgs e)
{
    lstTimes.Items.Clear();

    switch (MyCalendar.SelectedDate.DayOfWeek)
    {
        case DayOfWeek.Monday:
            // Apply special Monday schedule.
            lstTimes.Items.Add("10:00");
            lstTimes.Items.Add("10:30");
            lstTimes.Items.Add("11:00");
        break;
        default:
            lstTimes.Items.Add("10:00");
            lstTimes.Items.Add("10:30");
            lstTimes.Items.Add("11:00");
            lstTimes.Items.Add("11:30");
            lstTimes.Items.Add("12:00");
            lstTimes.Items.Add("12:30");
            break;
    }
}
```

To try these features of the Calendar control, run the Appointment.aspx page from the online samples. This page provides a formatted Calendar control that restricts some dates, formats others specially, and updates a corresponding list control when the selection changes.

Table 8-8 gives you an at-a-glance look at almost all the members of the Calendar control class.

Table 8-8. *Calendar Members*

Member	Description
Caption and CaptionAlign	Gives you an easy way to add a title to the Calendar. By default, the caption appears at the top of the title area, just above the month heading. However, you can control this to some extent with the CaptionAlign property. Use Left or Right to keep the caption at the top but move it to one side or the other, and use Bottom to place the caption under the Calendar.
CellPadding	ASP.NET creates a date in a separate cell of an invisible table. CellPadding is the space, in pixels, between the border of each cell and its contents.
CellSpacing	The space, in pixels, between cells in the same table.
DayNameFormat	Determines how days are displayed in the Calendar header. Valid values are Full (as in Sunday), FirstLetter (S), FirstTwoLetters (Su), and Short (Sun), which is the default.
FirstDayOfWeek	Determines which day is displayed in the first column of the calendar. The values are any day name from the FirstDayOfWeek enumeration (such as Sunday).
NextMonthText and PrevMonthText	Sets the text that the user clicks to move to the next or previous month. These navigation links appear at the top of the Calendar and are the greater-than (>) and less-than (<) signs by default. This setting is applied only if NextPrevFormat is set to Custom.
NextPrevFormat	Sets the text that the user clicks to move to the next or previous month. This can be FullMonth (for example, December), ShortMonth (Dec), or Custom, in which case the NextMonthText and PrevMonthText properties are used. Custom is the default.
SelectedDate and SelectedDates	Sets or gets the currently selected date as a DateTime object. You can specify this in the control tag in a format like this: "12:00:00 AM, 12/31/2005" (depending on your computer's regional settings). If you allow multiple date selection, the SelectedDates property will return a collection of DateTime objects, one for each selected date. You can use collection methods such as Add, Remove, and Clear to change the selection.
SelectionMode	Determines how many dates can be selected at once. The default is Day, which allows one date to be selected. Other options include DayWeek (a single date or an entire week) or DayWeekMonth (a single date, entire week, or entire month). You have no way to allow the user to select multiple noncontiguous dates. You also have no way to allow larger selections without also including smaller selections. (For example, if you allow full months to be selected, you must also allow week selection and individual day selection.)

Member	Description
SelectMonthText and SelectWeekText	The text shown for the link that allows the user to select an entire month or week. These properties don't apply if the SelectionMode is Day.
ShowDayHeader, ShowGridLines, ShowNextPrevMonth, and ShowTitle	These Boolean properties allow you to configure whether various parts of the calendar are shown, including the day titles, gridlines between every day, the previous/next month navigation links, and the title section. Note that hiding the title section also hides the next and previous month navigation controls.
TitleFormat	Configures how the month is displayed in the title area. Valid values include Month and MonthYear (the default).
TodaysDate	Sets which day should be recognized as the current date and formatted with the TodayDayStyle. This defaults to the current day on the web server.
VisibleDate	Gets or sets the date that specifies what month will be displayed in the Calendar. This allows you to change the Calendar display without modifying the current date selection.
DayRender event	Occurs once for each day that is created and added to the currently visible month before the page is rendered. This event gives you the opportunity to apply special formatting, add content, or restrict selection for an individual date cell.
SelectionChanged event	Occurs when the user selects a day, a week, or an entire month by clicking the date selector controls.
VisibleMonthChanged event	Occurs when the user clicks the next or previous month navigation controls to move to another month.

The AdRotator

The basic purpose of the AdRotator is to provide a banner-type graphic on a page (often used as an advertisement link to another site) that is chosen randomly from a group of possible banners. In other words, every time the page is requested, a different banner could be chosen and displayed, which is the "rotation" indicated by the name AdRotator.

In ASP.NET, it wouldn't be too difficult to implement an AdRotator type of design on your own. You could react to the Page.Load event, generate a random number, and then use that number to choose from a list of predetermined image files. You could even store the list in the web.config file so that it can be easily modified separately as part of the application's configuration. Of course, if you wanted to enable several pages with a random banner, you would have to either repeat the code or create your own custom control. The AdRotator provides these features for free.

The Advertisement File

The AdRotator stores its list of image files in a special XML file. This file uses the format shown here:

```
<Advertisements>
  <Ad>
    <ImageUrl>prosetech.jpg</ImageUrl>
    <NavigateUrl>http://www.prosetech.com</NavigateUrl>
    <AlternateText>ProseTech Site</AlternateText>
    <Impressions>1</Impressions>
    <Keyword>Computer</Keyword>
  </Ad>
</Advertisements>
```

This example shows a single possible advertisement. To add more advertisements, you would create multiple <Ad> elements and place them all inside the root <Advertisements> element:

```
<Advertisements>
  <Ad>
    <!-- First ad here. -->
  </Ad>

  <Ad>
    <!-- Second ad here. -->
  </Ad>
</Advertisements>
```

Each <Ad> element has a number of other important properties that configure the link, the image, and the frequency, as described in Table 8-9.

Table 8-9. *Advertisement File Elements*

Element	Description
ImageUrl	The image that will be displayed. This can be a relative link (a file in the current directory) or a fully qualified Internet URL.
NavigateUrl	The link that will be followed if the user clicks the banner.
AlternateText	The text that will be displayed instead of the picture if it cannot be displayed. This text will also be used as a tooltip in some newer browsers.

Element	Description
Impressions	A number that sets how often an advertisement will appear. This number is relative to the numbers specified for other ads. For example, a banner with the value 10 will be shown twice as often as the banner with the value 5.
Keyword	A keyword that identifies a group of advertisements. You can use this for filtering. For example, you could create ten advertisements and give half of them the keyword Retail and the other half the keyword Computer. The web page can then choose to filter the possible advertisements to include only one of these groups.

The AdRotator Class

The actual AdRotator class provides a limited set of properties. You specify both the appropriate advertisement file in the AdvertisementFile property and the type of window that the link should follow (the Target window). The target can name a specific frame, or it can use one of the values defined in Table 8-10.

Table 8-10. *Special Frame Targets*

Target	Description
_blank	The link opens a new unframed window.
_parent	The link opens in the parent of the current frame.
_self	The link opens in the current frame.
_top	The link opens in the topmost frame of the current window (so the link appears in the full window).

Optionally, you can set the KeywordFilter property so that the banner will be chosen from a specific keyword group. This is a fully configured AdRotator tag:

```
<asp:AdRotator id="Ads" runat="server" AdvertisementFile="MainAds.xml"
    Target="_blank" KeywordFilter="Computer" />
```

■ **Tip** In Visual Studio, you can't link to an advertisement file unless you have added it to the current project.

Additionally, you can react to the AdRotator.AdCreated event. This occurs when the page is being created and an image is randomly chosen from the file. This event provides you with information about the image that you can use to customize the rest of your page. For example, you might display some related content or a link, as shown in Figure 8-12.

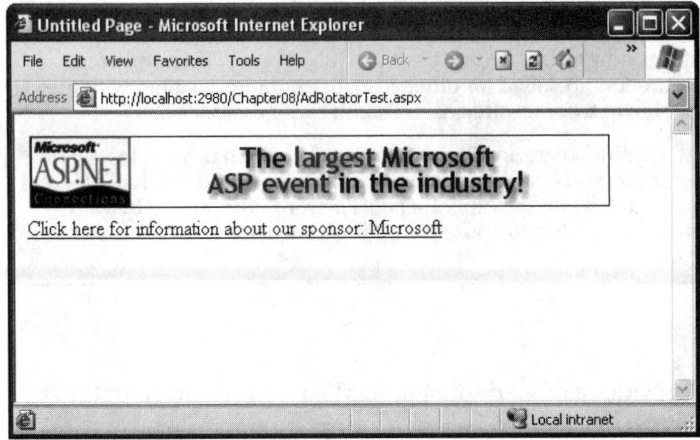

Figure 8-12. *An AdRotator with synchronized content*

The event handling code for this example simply configures the HyperLink control based on the randomly selected advertisement:

```
protected void Ads_AdCreated(Object sender, AdCreatedEventArgs e)
{
    // Synchronize the Hyperlink control.
    lnkBanner.NavigateUrl = e.NavigateUrl;

    // Syncrhonize the text of the link.
    lnkBanner.Text = "Click here for information about our sponsor: ";
    lnkBanner.Text += e.AlternateText;
}
```

As you can see, rich controls such as the Calendar and AdRotator don't just add a sophisticated HTML output, they also include an event framework that allows you to take charge of the control's behavior and integrate it into your application.

Pages with Multiple Views

In a typical website, you'll surf through many separate pages. For example, if you want to add an item to your shopping cart and take it to the checkout in an e-commerce site, you'll need to jump from one page to another. This design has its advantages—namely, it lets you carefully separate different tasks into different code files. It also presents some challenges; for example, you need to come up with a way to transfer information from one page to another (a topic that's covered in detail in Chapter 9).

However, in some cases it makes more sense to create a single page that can handle several different tasks. For example, you might want to provide several views of the same data (such as a grid-based view and a chart-based view) and allow the user to switch from one view to the other without leaving the page. Or, you might want to handle a small multistep task in one place (such as supplying user information for an account sign-up process). In these examples, you need a way to create dynamic pages that provide more than one possible view. Essentially, the page hides and shows different controls depending on which view you want to present.

The simplest way to understand this technique is to create a page with several Panel controls. Each panel can hold a group of ASP.NET controls. For example, imagine you're creating a simple three-step wizard. You'll start by adding three panels to your page, one for each step—say, panelStep1, panelStep2, and panelStep3. Then, you'll place the appropriate controls inside each panel. To start, the Visible property of each panel should be false, except for panelStep1, which appears the first time the user request the page.

■ **Note** When you set the Visible property of a control to false, the control won't appear in the page at runtime—in fact, no HTML will be generated for it. Any controls inside an invisible panel are also hidden from sight. However, the control will still appear in the Visual Studio design surface so that you can still select it and configure it.

Finally, you'll add one or more navigation buttons. For example, the following code handles the click of a Next button. It checks which step the user is currently on, hides the current panel, and shows the following panel. This way the user is moved to the next step.

```
protected void cmdNext_Clicked(object sender, EventArgs e)
{
    if (panelStep1.Visible)
    {
        // Move to step 2.
        panelStep1.Visible = false;
        panelStep2.Visible = true;
    }
    else if (panelStep2.Visible)
    {
        // Move to step 3.
        panelStep2.Visible = false;
        panelStep3.Visible = true;
```

```
        // Change text of button from Next to Finish.
        cmdNext.Text = "Finish";
    }
    else if (panelStep3.Visible)
    {
        // The wizard is finished.
        panelStep3.Visible = false;

        // Add code here to perform the appropriate task
        // with the information you've collected.
        lblInfo.Text = "Wizard Finished.";
    }
}
```

This approach works relatively well. Even when the panels are hidden, you can still interact with all the controls on each panel and retrieve the information they contain. The problem is that you need to write all the code for controlling which panel is visible. If you make your wizard much more complex—for example, you want to add a button for returning to a previous step—it becomes more difficult to keep track of what's happening. At best, this approach clutters your page with the code for managing the panels. At worst, you'll make a minor mistake and end up with two panels showing at the same time.

Fortunately, ASP.NET gives you a more robust option. You can use two controls that are designed for the job—the MultiView and the Wizard. In the following sections, you'll see how you can use both of these controls with the GreetingCardMaker example developed in Chapter 6.

The MultiView Control

The MultiView is the simpler of the two multiple-view controls. Essentially, the MultiView gives you a way to declare multiple views and show only one at a time. It has no default user interface—you get only whatever HTML and controls you add. The MultiView is equivalent to the custom panel approach explained earlier.

Creating a MultiView is suitably straightforward. You add the <asp:MultiView> tag to your .aspx page file and then add one <asp:View> tag inside it for each separate view:

```
<asp:MultiView ID="MultiView1" runat="server">
  <asp:View ID="View1" runat="server">...</asp:View>
  <asp:View ID="View2" runat="server">...</asp:View>
  <asp:View ID="View3" runat="server">...</asp:View>
</asp:MultiView>
```

In Visual Studio, you create these tags by first dropping a MultiView control onto your form and then using the Toolbox to add as many View controls inside it as you want. The View control plays the same role as the Panel control in the previous example, and the MultiView takes care of coordinating all the views so that only one is visible at a time.

Inside each view, you can add HTML or web controls. For example, consider the GreetingCardMaker example demonstrated in Chapter 6, which allows the user to create a greeting card by supplying some text and choosing colors, a font, and a background. As the GreetingCardMaker grows more complex, it requires more controls, and it becomes increasingly difficult to fit all those controls on the same page. One possible solution is to divide these controls into logical groups and place each group in a separate view.

Creating Views

Here's the full markup for a MultiView that splits the greeting card controls into three views named View1, View2, and View3:

```
<asp:MultiView id="MultiView1" runat="server" >

  <asp:View ID="View1" runat="server">
    Choose a foreground (text) color:<br />
    <asp:DropDownList ID="lstForeColor" runat="server" AutoPostBack="True"
     OnSelectedIndexChanged="ControlChanged" />
    <br /><br />
    Choose a background color:<br />
    <asp:DropDownList ID="lstBackColor" runat="server" AutoPostBack="True"
     OnSelectedIndexChanged="ControlChanged" />
  </asp:View>

  <asp:View ID="View2" runat="server">
    Choose a border style:<br />
    <asp:RadioButtonList ID="lstBorder" runat="server" AutoPostBack="True"
     OnSelectedIndexChanged="ControlChanged" RepeatColumns="2" />
    <br />
    <asp:CheckBox ID="chkPicture" runat="server" AutoPostBack="True"
     OnCheckedChanged="ControlChanged" Text="Add the Default Picture" />
  </asp:View>

  <asp:View ID="View3" runat="server">
    Choose a font name:<br />
    <asp:DropDownList ID="lstFontName" runat="server" AutoPostBack="True"
     OnSelectedIndexChanged="ControlChanged" />
    <br /><br />
    Specify a font size:<br />
```

```
    <asp:TextBox ID="txtFontSize" runat="server" AutoPostBack="True"
     OnTextChanged="ControlChanged" />
    <br /><br />
    Enter the greeting text below:<br />
    <asp:TextBox ID="txtGreeting" runat="server" AutoPostBack="True"
     OnTextChanged="ControlChanged" TextMode="MultiLine" />
  </asp:View>

</asp:MultiView>
```

Visual Studio shows all your views at design time, one after the other (see Figure 8-13). You can edit these regions in the same way you design any other part of the page.

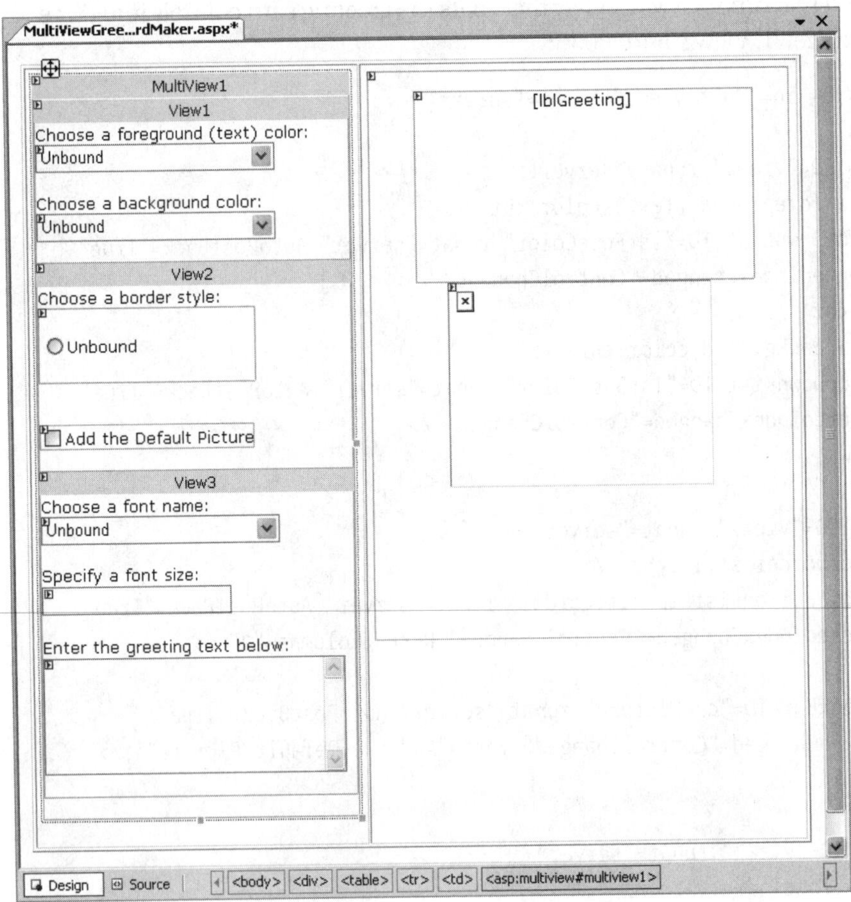

Figure 8-13. *Designing multiple views*

Showing a View

If you run this example, you won't see what you expect. The MultiView will appear empty on the page, and all the controls in all your views will be hidden.

The reason this happens is because the MultiView.ActiveViewIndex property is, by default, set to –1. The ActiveViewIndex property determines which view will be shown. If you set the ActiveViewIndex to 0, however, you'll see the first view. Similarly, you can set it to 1 to show the second view, and so on. You can set this property using the Properties window or using code:

```
// Show the first view.
MultiView1.ActiveViewIndex = 0;
```

This example shows the first view (View1) and hides whatever view is currently being displayed, if any.

■ **Tip** To make more readable code, you can create an enumeration that defines a name for each view. That way, you can set the ActiveViewIndex using the descriptive name from the enumeration rather than an ordinary number. Refer to Chapter 3 for a refresher on enumerations.

You can also use the SetActiveView() method, which accepts any one of the view objects you've created. This may result in more readable code (if you've chosen descriptive IDs for your view controls), and it ensures that any errors are caught earlier (at compile time instead of runtime).

```
MultiView.SetActiveView(View1);
```

This gives you enough functionality that you can create previous and next navigation buttons. However, it's still up to you to write the code that checks which view is visible and changes the view. This code is a little simpler, because you don't need to worry about hiding views any longer, but it's still less than ideal.

Fortunately, the MultiView includes some built-in smarts that can save you a lot of trouble. Here's how it works: The MultiView recognizes buttons controls with specific command names. (Technically, a button control is any control that implements the IButtonControl interface, including the Button, ImageButton, and LinkButton.) If you add a button control to the view that uses one of these recognized command names, the button gets some automatic functionality. Using this technique, you can create navigation buttons without writing any code.

Table 8-11 lists all the recognized command names. Each command name also has a corresponding static field in the MultiView class, so you can easily get the right command name if you choose to set it programmatically.

Table 8-11. *Recognized Command Names for the MultiView*

Command Name	MultiView Field	Description
PrevView	PrevViewCommandName	Moves to the previous view.
NextView	NextViewCommandName	Moves to the next view.
SwitchViewByID	SwitchViewByIDCommandName	Moves to the view with a specific ID (string name). The ID is taken from the CommandArgument property of the button control.
SwitchViewByIndex	SwitchViewByIndexCommandName	Moves to the view with a specific numeric index. The index is taken from the CommandArgument property of the button control.

To try this, add this button to the first view:

```
<asp:Button ID="Button1" runat="server" CommandArgument="View2"
CommandName="SwitchViewByID" Text="Go to View2" />
```

When clicked, this button sets the MultiView to show the view specified by the CommandArgument (View2).

Rather than create buttons that take the user to a specific view, you might want a button that moves forward or backward one view. To do this, you use the PrevView and NextView command names. Here's an example that defines previous and next buttons:

```
<asp:Button ID="Button1" runat="server" Text="< Prev" CommandName="PrevView" />
<asp:Button ID="Button2" runat="server" Text="Next >" CommandName="NextView" />
```

Once you add these buttons to your view, you can move from view to view easily. Figure 8-14 shows the previous example with the second view currently visible.

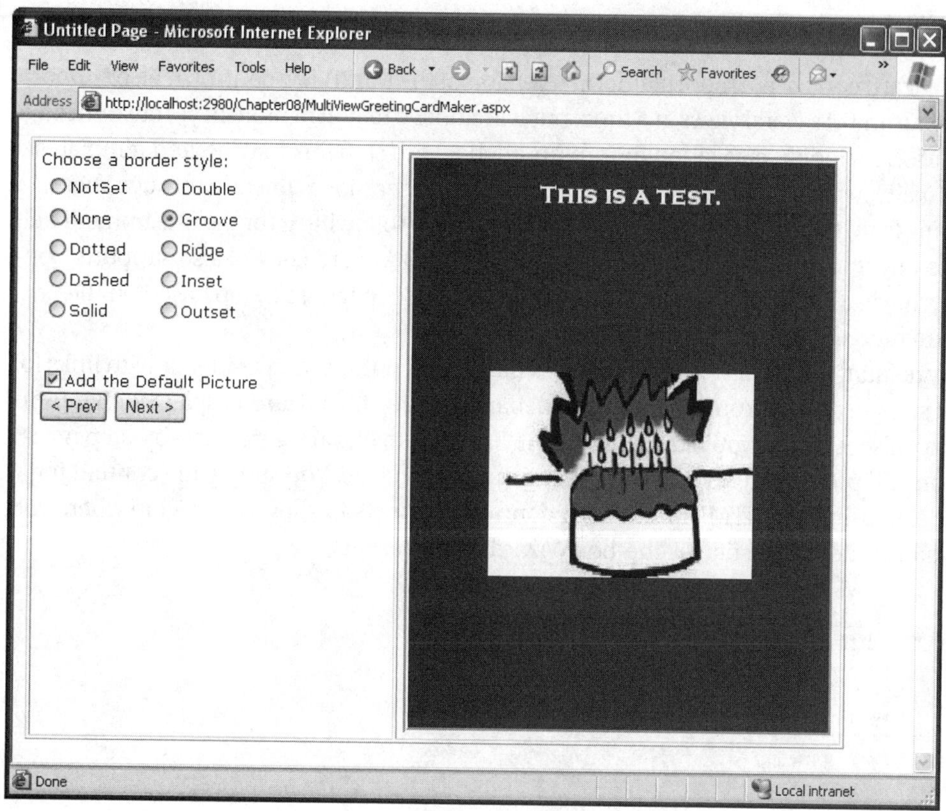

Figure 8-14. *Moving from one view to another*

■ **Tip** Be careful how many views you cram into a single page. When you use the MultiView control, the entire control model—including the controls from every view—is created on every postback and persisted to view state. For the most part, this won't be a significant factor. However, it increases the overall page size, especially if you're tweaking controls programmatically (which increases the amount of information they need to store in view state).

The Wizard Control

The Wizard control is a more glamorous version of the MultiView control. It also supports showing one of several views at a time, but it includes a fair bit of built-in yet customizable behavior, including navigation buttons, a sidebar with step links, styles, and templates.

Usually, wizards represent a single task, and the user moves linearly through them, moving from the current step to the one immediately following it (or the one immediately preceding it in the case of a correction). The ASP.NET Wizard control also supports non-linear navigation, which means it allows you to decide to ignore a step based on the information the user supplies.

By default, the Wizard control supplies navigation buttons and a sidebar with links for each step on the left. You can hide the sidebar by setting the Wizard.DisplaySideBar property to false. Usually, you'll take this step if you want to enforce strict step-by-step navigation and prevent the user from jumping out of sequence. You supply the content for each step using any HTML or ASP.NET controls. Figure 8-15 shows the region where you can add content to an out-of-the-box Wizard instance.

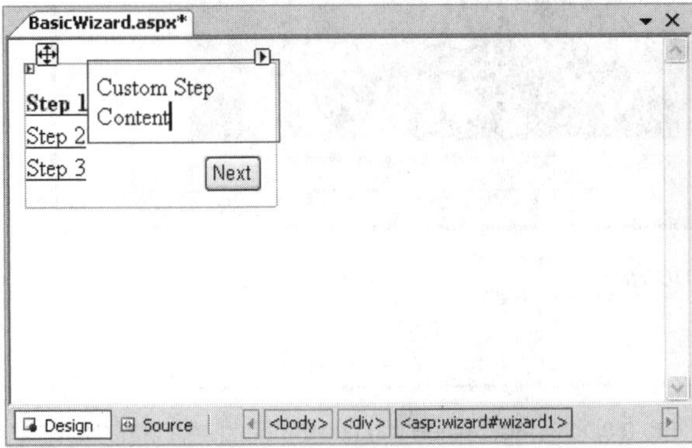

Figure 8-15. *The region for step content*

Wizard Steps

To create a wizard in ASP.NET, you simply define the steps and their content using <asp:WizardStep> tags. Each step takes a few basic pieces of information, as listed in Table 8-12.

Table 8-12. *WizardStep Properties*

Property	Description
Title	The descriptive name of the step. This name is used for the text of the links in the sidebar.
StepType	The type of step, as a value from the WizardStepType enumeration. This value determines the type of navigation buttons that will be shown for this step. Choices include Start (shows a Next button), Step (shows Next and Previous buttons), Finish (shows a Finish and Previous button), Complete (show no buttons and hides the sidebar, if it's enabled), and Auto (the step type is inferred from the position in the collection). The default is Auto, which means the first step is Start, the last step is Finish, and all other steps are Step.
AllowReturn	Indicates whether the user can return to this step. If false, once the user has passed this step, the user will not be able to return. The sidebar link for this step will have no effect, and the Previous button of the following step will either skip this step or be hidden completely (depending on the AllowReturn value of the preceding steps).

To see how this works, consider a wizard that again uses the GreetingCardMaker example. It guides the user through four steps. The first three steps allow the user to configure the greeting card, and the final step shows the generated card.

```
<asp:Wizard ID="Wizard1" runat="server" ActiveStepIndex="0"
 BackColor="LemonChiffon" BorderStyle="Groove" BorderWidth="2px"
CellPadding="10">

  <WizardSteps>
    <asp:WizardStep runat="server" Title="Step 1 - Colors">
      Choose a foreground (text) color:<br />
      <asp:DropDownList ID="lstForeColor" runat="server" />
      <br />
      Choose a background color:<br />
      <asp:DropDownList ID="lstBackColor" runat="server" />
    </asp:WizardStep>

    <asp:WizardStep runat="server" Title="Step 2 - Background">
      Choose a border style:<br />
      <asp:RadioButtonList ID="lstBorder" runat="server" RepeatColumns="2" />
      <br /><br />
      <asp:CheckBox ID="chkPicture" runat="server"
       Text="Add the Default Picture" />
    </asp:WizardStep>
```

```
    <asp:WizardStep runat="server" Title="Step 3 - Text">
      Choose a font name:<br />
      <asp:DropDownList ID="lstFontName" runat="server" />
      <br /><br />
      Specify a font size:<br />
      <asp:TextBox ID="txtFontSize" runat="server" />
      <br /><br />
      Enter the greeting text below:<br />
      <asp:TextBox ID="txtGreeting" runat="server"
        TextMode="MultiLine" />
    </asp:WizardStep>

    <asp:WizardStep runat="server" StepType="Complete" Title="Greeting Card">
      <asp:Panel ID="pnlCard" runat="server" HorizontalAlign="Center">
        <br /> 
        <asp:Label ID="lblGreeting" runat="server" />
        <asp:Image ID="imgDefault" runat="server" Visible="False" />
      </asp:Panel>
    </asp:WizardStep>
  </WizardSteps>

</asp:Wizard>
```

If you look carefully, you'll find a few differences from the original page and the MultiView-based example. First, the controls aren't set to automatically post back. That's because the greeting card isn't rendered until the final step, at the conclusion of the wizard. (You'll learn more about how to handle this event in the next section.) Another change is that no navigation buttons exist. That's because the wizard adds these details automatically based on the step type. For example, you'll get a Next button for the first two steps, a Previous button for steps 2 and 3, and a Finish button for step 4. The final step, which shows the complete card, doesn't provide any navigation links because the StepType is set to Complete. Figure 8-16 shows the wizard steps.

Unlike the MultiView control, you can see only one step at a time in Visual Studio. To choose which step you're currently designing, select it from the smart tag, as shown in Figure 8-17. But be warned—every time you do, Visual Studio changes the Wizard.ActiveStepIndex property to the step you choose. Make sure you set this back to 0 before you run your application so it starts at the first step.

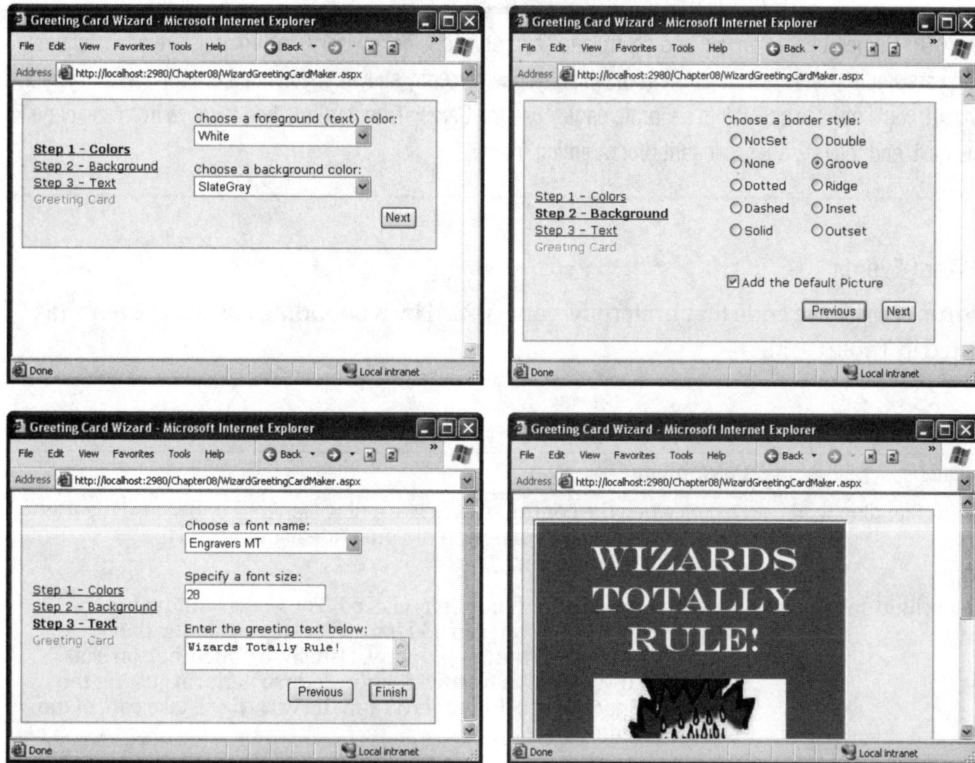

Figure 8-16. *A wizard with four steps*

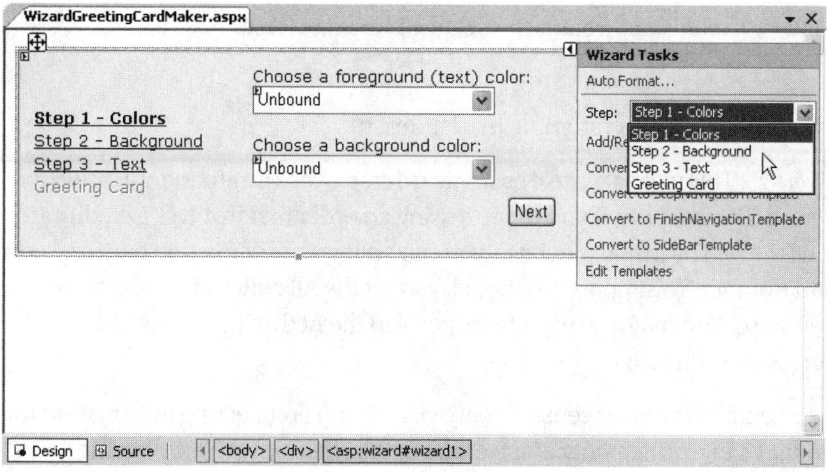

Figure 8-17. *Designing a step*

■ **Note** Remember, when you add controls to separate steps on a wizard, the controls are all instantiated and persisted in view state, regardless of which step is currently shown. If you need to slim down a complex wizard, you'll need to split it into separate pages, use the Server.Transfer() method to move from one page to the next, and tolerate a less elegant programming model.

Wizard Events

You can write the code that underpins your wizard by responding to several events (as listed in Table 8-13).

Table 8-13. *Wizard Events*

Event	Description
ActiveStepChanged	Occurs when the control switches to a new step (either because the user has clicked a navigation button or your code has changed the ActiveStepIndex property).
CancelButtonClick	Occurs when the Cancel button is clicked. The Cancel button is not shown by default, but you can add it to every step by setting the Wizard.DisplayCancelButton property. Usually, a Cancel button exits the wizard. If you don't have any cleanup code to perform, just set the CancelDestinationPageUrl property, and the wizard will take care of the redirection automatically.
FinishButtonClick	Occurs when the Finish button is clicked.
NextButtonClick and PreviousButtonClick	Occurs when the Next or Previous button is clicked on any step. However, because there is more than one way to move from one step to the next, it's better to handle the ActiveStepChanged event.
SideBarButtonClick	Occurs when a button in the sidebar area is clicked.

On the whole, two wizard programming models exist:

Commit-as-you-go: This makes sense if each wizard step wraps an atomic operation that can't be reversed. For example, if you're processing an order that involves a credit card authorization followed by a final purchase, you can't allow the user to step back and edit the credit card number. To support this model, you set the AllowReturn property to false on some or all steps. You may also want to respond to the ActiveStepChanged event to commit changes for each step.

Commit-at-the-end: This makes sense if each wizard step is collecting information for an operation that's performed only at the end. For example, if you're collecting user information and plan to generate a new account once you have all the information, you'll probably allow a user to make changes midway through the process. You execute your code for generating the new account when the wizard ends by reacting to the FinishButtonClick event.

To implement commit-at-the-end with the current example, just respond to the FinishButtonClick event. For example, to implement the greeting card wizard, you simply need to respond to this event to call Update(), the private method that refreshes the greeting card:

```
protected void Wizard1_FinishButtonClick(object sender,
  WizardNavigationEventArgs e)
{
    Update();
}
```

For the complete code, refer to Chapter 6 (or check out the downloadable sample code). If you decide to use the commit-as-you go model, you would respond to the ActiveStepChanged event and call Update() at that point to refresh the card every time the user moves from one step to another. This assumes the greeting card is always visible. (In other words, it's not contained in the final step of the wizard.) The commit-as-you-go model is similar to the previous example that used the MultiView.

Formatting the Wizard

Without a doubt, the Wizard control's greatest strength is the way it lets you customize its appearance. This means if you want the basic model (a multistep process with navigation buttons and various events), you aren't locked into the default user interface.

Depending on how radically you want to change the wizard, you have several options. For less dramatic modifications, you can set various top-level properties. For example, you can control the colors, fonts, spacing, and border style, as you can with any ASP.NET control. You can also tweak the appearance of every button. For example, to change the Next button, you can use the following properties: StepNextButtonType (use a button, link, or clickable image), StepNextButtonText (customize the text for a button or link), StepNextButtonImageUrl (set the image for an image button), and StepNextButtonStyle (use a style from a style sheet). You can also add a header using the HeaderText property.

More control is available through styles. You can use styles to apply formatting options to various portions of the Wizard control just as you can use styles to format parts of rich data controls such as the GridView. Table 8-14 lists all the styles you can use. As with other style-based controls, more specific style settings (such as SideBarStyle) override more general style settings (such as ControlStyle) when they conflict. Similarly, StartNextButtonStyle overrides NavigationButtonStyle on the first step.

Table 8-14. *Wizard Styles*

Style	Description
ControlStyle	Applies to all sections of the Wizard control
HeaderStyle	Applies to the header section of the wizard, which is visible only if you set some text in the HeaderText property
SideBarStyle	Applies to the sidebar area of the wizard
SideBarButtonStyle	Applies to just the buttons in the sidebar
StepStyle	Applies to the section of the control where you define the step content
NavigationStyle	Applies to the bottom area of the control where the navigation buttons are displayed
NavigationButtonStyle	Applies to just the navigation buttons in the navigation area
StartNextButtonStyle	Applies to the Next navigation button on the first step (when StepType is Start)
StepNextButtonStyle	Applies to the Next navigation button on intermediate steps (when StepType is Step)
StepPreviousButtonStyle	Applies to the Previous navigation button on intermediate steps (when StepType is Step)
FinishPreviousButtonStyle	Applies to the Previous navigation button on the last step (when StepType is Finish)
CancelButtonStyle	Applies to the Cancel button, if you have Wizard.DisplayCancelButton set to true

■ **Note** The Wizard control also supports templates, which gives you a more radical approach to formatting. If you can't get the level of customization you want through properties and styles, you can use templates to completely define the appearance of each section of the Wizard control, including the headers and navigation links. Templates require data binding expressions and are discussed in Chapter 14 and Chapter 15.

The Last Word

This chapter showed you how validation controls, the rich Calendar and AdRotator controls, and the MultiView and Wizard controls can go far beyond the limitations of ordinary HTML elements.

Throughout this book, you'll consider some more examples of rich controls and learn how to use them to create rich web applications that are a world apart from HTML basics. Some of the most exciting rich controls that are still ahead include the navigation controls (Chapter 11) and the data controls (Chapter 15).

CHAPTER 9

State Management

The most significant difference between programming for the Internet and programming for the desktop is *state management*—in other words, how you retain information for the current user. In a traditional Windows application, state is managed automatically. Memory is plentiful and always available. In a web application, it's a different story. Thousands of users might simultaneously run the same application on the same computer (the web server), each one communicating over the stateless HTTP of the Internet. These conditions make it impossible to program a web application like a traditional Windows program.

Understanding these state limitations is the key to creating efficient, robust web applications. In this chapter, you'll learn why state is no trivial issue in the world of Internet programming, and you'll see how you can use ASP.NET's state management features to store and manage information carefully and consistently. You'll explore different state options, including view state, session state, and custom cookies, and consider how to transfer information from page to page using cross-page posting and the query string. You'll also look at how you can react to application events with the global.asax file.

The Problem of State

In a traditional Windows program, users interact with a continuously running application. A portion of memory on the desktop computer is allocated to store the current set of working information.

In a web application, the story is quite a bit different. A professional ASP.NET site might look like a continuously running application, but it's really just a clever illusion. Web applications use a highly efficient disconnected access pattern. In a typical web request, the client connects to the web server and requests a page. When the page is delivered, the connection is severed, and the web server abandons any information it has about the client. By the time the user receives a page, the "application" has already stopped running.

Because clients need to be connected for only a few seconds at most, a web server can handle thousands of requests without a performance hit. However, if you need to retain information between user actions (and you almost always do), you need to take additional steps.

View State

In the previous chapters, you learned how ASP.NET controls use *view state* to remember their state. View state information is maintained in a hidden field and automatically returned to the server with every postback. However, view state isn't limited to server controls. Your web page code can add bits of information directly to the view state collection of the containing page and retrieve it later after the page is posted back. The type of information you can store includes simple data types and your own custom objects.

The ViewState property of the page provides the view state collection. This property is an instance of the StateBag collection class. To add and remove items in this class, you use a dictionary-based syntax, where every item has a unique string name.

For example, consider this code:

```
// The this keyword refers to the current Page object. It's optional.
this.ViewState["Counter"] = 1;
```

This places the value 1 (or rather, an integer that contains the value 1) into the view state collection and gives it the descriptive name Counter. If currently no item has the name Counter, a new item will be added automatically. If an item is already indexed under the name Counter, it will be replaced.

When retrieving a value, you use the key name. You also need to cast the retrieved value to the appropriate data type using the casting syntax you saw in Chapter 2 and Chapter 3. This extra step is required because the ViewState collection stores all items as generic objects, which allows it to handle many different data types.

Here's the code that retrieves the counter from view state and converts it to an integer:

```
int counter;
counter = (int)this.ViewState["Counter"];
```

■ **Note** ASP.NET provides many collections that use the same dictionary syntax. This includes the collections you'll use for session and application state, as well as those used for caching and cookies. You'll see several of these collections in this chapter.

A View State Example

The following example is a simple counter program that records how many times a button is clicked. Without any kind of state management, the counter will be locked perpetually at 1. With careful use of view state, the counter works as expected.

```
public partial class SimpleCounter : Page
{
    protected void cmdIncrement_Click(Object sender, EventArgs e)
    {
        int counter;
        if (ViewState["Counter"] == null)
        {
            counter = 1;
        }
        else
        {
            counter = (int)ViewState["Counter"] + 1;
        }

        ViewState["Counter"] = counter;
        lblCount.Text = "Counter: " + counter.ToString();
    }
}
```

The code checks to make sure the item exists in view state before it attempts to retrieve it. Otherwise, you could easily run into problems such as the infamous null reference exception.

Figure 9-1 shows the output for this page.

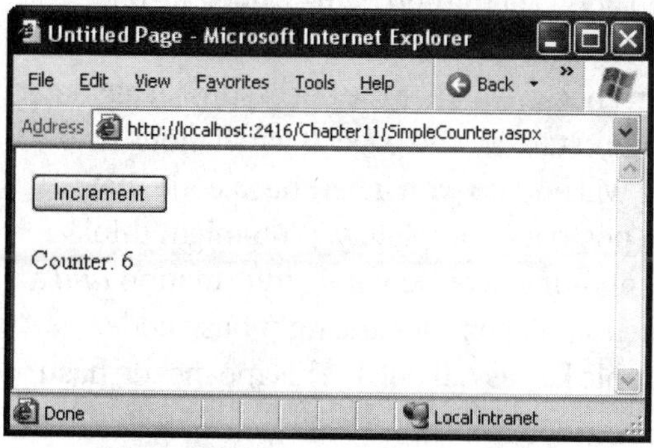

Figure 9-1. *A simple view state counter*

You have other ways to solve the state management problem with the simple counter example. For example, you could enable view state for the Label control and use the label to store the counter. Every time the Increment button is clicked, you could then retrieve the current value from the label text and convert it to an integer. However, this technique isn't always appropriate. For example, you might create a program that tracks button clicks but doesn't display them on the screen. In this case, you could still store this information in a web control, but you would have to make it hidden. That, of course, is exactly what view state does: it stores information automatically in a special hidden field in the page. Because ASP.NET handles these lower-level details for you, your code becomes clearer and more concise.

Making View Sate Secure

You probably remember from Chapter 5 that view state information is stored in a single jumbled string that looks like this:

```
<input type="hidden" name="__VIEWSTATE" value="dDw3NDg2NTI5MDg7Oz4="/>
```

As you add more information to view state, this value can become much longer. Because this value isn't formatted as clear text, many ASP.NET programmers assume that their view state data is encrypted. It isn't. Instead, the view state information is simply patched together in memory and converted to a Base64 string. A clever hacker could reverse-engineer this string and examine your view state data in a matter of seconds.

If you want to make view state more secure, you have two choices. First, you can make sure the view state information is tamper-proof by instructing ASP.NET to use a *hash code.*

A hash code is sometimes described as a cryptographically strong checksum. The idea is that ASP.NET examines all the data in your view state and runs it through a hashing algorithm (with the help of a secret key value). The hashing algorithm creates a short segment of data, which is the hash code. This code is then added at the end of the view state data.

When the page is posted back, ASP.NET examines the view state data and recalculates the hash code using the same process. It then checks whether the checksum it calculated matches the hash code that is stored in the view state for the page. If a malicious user changes part of the view state data, ASP.NET will end up with a new hash code that doesn't match. At this point, it will reject the postback completely. (You might think a really clever user could get around this by generating fake view state information *and* a matching hash code. However, malicious users can't generate the right hash code, because they don't have the same cryptographic key as ASP.NET. This means the hash codes they create won't match.)

Hash codes are actually enabled by default, so if you want this functionality, you don't need to take any extra steps. Occasionally, developers choose to disable this feature to prevent problems in a web farm where different servers have different keys. (The problem occurs if the page is posted back and handled by a new server, which won't be able to verify the view state information.) To disable hash codes, you can use the enableViewStateMac attribute of the <pages> element in the web.config or machine.config file, as shown here:

```
<configuration xmlns="http://schemas.microsoft.com/.NetConfiguration/v2.0">
  <system.web>
    <pages enableViewStateMac="false" />
    ...
  </system.web>
</configuration>
```

Of course, a better way to solve this problem is configure multiple servers to use the same key, thereby removing any problem. Chapter 12 describes this technique.

Even when you use hash codes, the view state data will still be readable by the user. In many cases, this is completely acceptable—after all, the view state tracks information that's often provided directly through other controls. However, if your view state contains some information you want to keep secret, you can enable view state *encryption*.

You can turn on encryption for an individual page using the ViewStateEncryption-Mode property of the Page directive:

```
<%@Page ViewStateEncryptionMode="Always"%>
```

Or you can set the same attribute in a configuration file:

```
<configuration xmlns="http://schemas.microsoft.com/.NetConfiguration/v2.0">
  <system.web>
    <pages viewStateEncryptionMode="Always" />
    ...
  </system.web>
</configuration>
```

Either way, this enforces encryption. You have three choices for your view state encryption setting—always encrypt (Always), never encrypt (Never), or encrypt only if a control specifically requests it (Auto). The default is Auto, which means a control must call the Page.RegisterRequiresViewStateEncryption() method to request encryption. If no control calls this method to indicate it has sensitive information, the view state is not encrypted, thereby saving the encryption overhead. On the other hand, a control doesn't have absolute power—if it calls Page.RegisterRequiresViewStateEncryption() and the encryption mode is Never, the view state won't be encrypted.

■ **Tip** Don't encrypt view state data if you don't need to do so. The encryption will impose a performance penalty, because the web server needs to perform the encryption and decryption with each postback.

Retaining Member Variables

You have probably noticed that any information you set in a member variable for an ASP.NET page is automatically abandoned when the page processing is finished and the page is sent to the client. (The Counter variable in the previous code listing is an example.) Interestingly, you can work around this limitation using view state.

The basic principle is to save all member variables to view state when the Page.PreRender event occurs and retrieve them when the Page.Load event occurs. Remember, the Load event happens every time the page is created. In the case of a postback, the Load event occurs first, followed by any other control events.

The following example uses this technique with a single member variable (named Contents). The page provides a text box and two buttons. The user can choose to save a string of text and then restore it at a later time (see Figure 9-2). The Button.Click event handlers store and retrieve this text using the Contents member variable. These event handlers don't need to save or restore this information using view state, because the PreRender and Load event handlers perform these tasks when page processing starts and finishes.

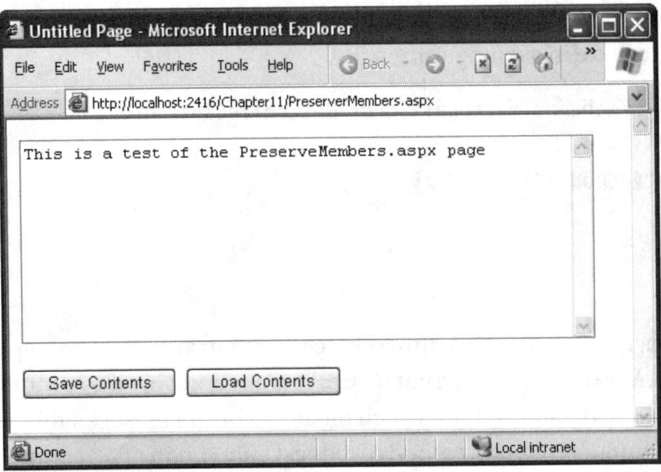

Figure 9-2. *A page with state*

```
public partial class PreserveMembers : Page
{
    // A member variable that will be cleared with every postback.
    private string contents;
```

```
    protected void Page_Load(Object sender, EventArgs e)
    {
        if (this.IsPostBack)
        {
            // Restore variables.
            contents = (string)ViewState["contents"];
        }
    }

    protected void Page_PreRender(Object sender, EventArgs e)
    {
        // Persist variables.
        ViewState["contents"] = contents;
    }

    protected void cmdSave_Click(Object sender, EventArgs e)
    {
        // Transfer contents of text box to member variable.
        contents = txtValue.Text;
        txtValue.Text = "";
    }

    protected void cmdLoad_Click(Object sender, EventArgs e)
    {
        // Restore contents of member variable to text box.
        txtValue.Text = contents;
    }
}
```

The logic in the Load and PreRender event handlers allows the rest of your code to work more or less as it would in a desktop application. However, you must be careful not to store needless amounts of information when using this technique. If you store unnecessary information in view state, it will enlarge the size of the final page output and can thus slow down page transmission times. Another disadvantage with this approach is that it hides the low-level reality that every piece of data must be explicitly saved and restored. When you hide this reality, it's more likely that you'll forget to respect it and design for it.

If you decide to use this approach to save member variables in view state, use it *exclusively.* In other words, refrain from saving some view state variables at the PreRender stage and others in control event handlers, because this is sure to confuse you and any other programmer who looks at your code.

■ **Tip** The previous example reacted to the Page.PreRender event, which occurs just after page processing is complete and just before the page is rendered in HTML. This is an ideal place to store any leftover information that is required. You cannot store view state information in an event handler for the Page.Unload event. Though your code will not cause an error, the information will not be stored in view state, because the final HTML page output is already rendered.

Storing Custom Objects

You can store your own objects in view state just as easily as you store numeric and string types. However, to store an item in view state, ASP.NET must be able to convert it into a stream of bytes so that it can be added to the hidden input field in the page. This process is called *serialization*. If your objects aren't serializable (and by default they're not), you'll receive an error message when you attempt to place them in view state.

To make your objects serializable, you need to add a [Serializable] attribute before your class declaration. For example, here's an exceedingly simple Customer class:

```
[Serializable]
public class Customer
{
    public string FirstName;
    public string LastName;

    public Customer(string firstName, string lastName)
    {
        FirstName = firstName;
        LastName = lastName;
    }
}
```

Because the Customer class is marked as serializable, it can be stored in view state:

```
// Store a customer in view state.
Customer cust = new Customer("Marsala", "Simons");
ViewState["CurrentCustomer"] = cust;
```

Remember, when using custom objects, you'll need to cast your data when you retrieve it from view state.

```
// Retrieve a customer from view state.
Customer cust;
cust = (Customer)ViewState["CurrentCustomer"];
```

Once you understand this principle, you'll also be able to determine which .NET objects can be placed in view state. You simply need to find the class information in the MSDN Help. You can view the MSDN Help library by selecting Start ➤ Programs ➤ Microsoft Visual Studio 2005 ➤ Microsoft Visual Studio 2005 Documentation (the exact shortcut depends on your version of Visual Studio). Once you've loaded the help, you can find class reference information grouped by namespace under the .NET Development ➤ .NET Framework SDK ➤ Class Library Reference node. Find the class you're interested in, and examine the documentation. If the class declaration is preceded with the [Serializable] attribute, the object can be placed in view state. If the [Serializable] attribute isn't present, the object isn't serializable, and you won't be able to store it in view state. However, you will still be able to use other types of state management, such as session state, which is described later in this chapter (see the "Session State" section).

Transferring Information

One of the most significant limitations with view state is that it's tightly bound to a specific page. If the user navigates to another page, this information is lost. This problem has several solutions, and the best approach depends on your requirements.

In the following sections, you'll learn two basic techniques to transfer information between pages: cross-page posting and the query string.

Cross-Page Posting

One approach that's new in ASP.NET 2.0 is to trigger a postback to another page. This technique sounds conceptually straightforward, but it's a potential minefield. If you're not careful, it can lead you to create pages that are tightly coupled to others and difficult to enhance and debug.

The infrastructure that supports cross-page postbacks is a new property named PostBackUrl, which is defined by the IButtonControl interface and turns up in button controls such as ImageButton, LinkButton, and Button. To use cross-posting, you simply set PostBackUrl to the name of another web form. When the user clicks the button, the page will be posted to that new URL with the values from all the input controls on the current page.

Here's an example—a page named CrossPage1.aspx that defines a form with two text boxes and a button. When the button is clicked, it posts to a page named CrossPage2.aspx.

```
<%@ Page Language="C#" AutoEventWireup="true" CodeFile="CrossPage1.aspx.cs"
    Inherits="CrossPage1" %>
<html>
<head runat="server">
    <title>CrossPage1</title>
```

```
</head>
<body>
    <form id="form1" runat="server" >
     First Name:<asp:TextBox ID="txtFirstName" runat="server" />
      <br />
     Last Name:<asp:TextBox ID="txtLastName" runat="server" />
      <br /><br />
     <asp:Button runat="server" ID="cmdPost"
     PostBackUrl="CrossPage2.aspx" Text="Cross-Page Postback" />
    </form>
</body>
</html>
```

The CrossPage1.aspx page doesn't include any code. Figure 9-3 shows how it appears in the browser.

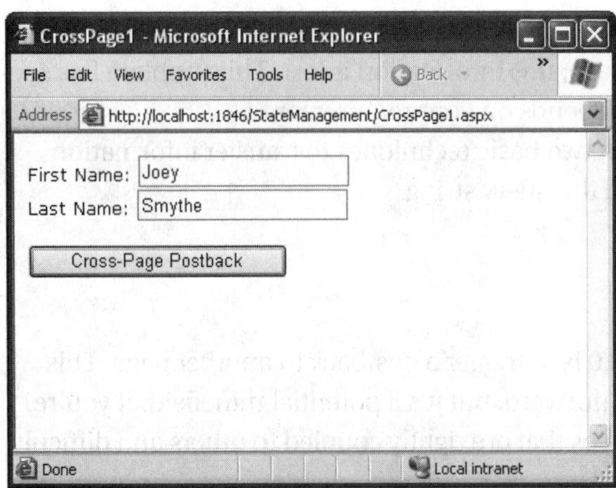

Figure 9-3. *The source of a cross-page postback*

Now if you load this page and click the button, the page will be posted back to CrossPage2.aspx. At this point, the CrossPage2.aspx page can interact with CrossPage1.aspx using the Page.PreviousPage property. Here's an event handler that grabs the title from the previous page and displays it:

```
public partial class CrossPage2 : System.Web.UI.Page
{
    protected void Page_Load(object sender, EventArgs e)
    {
        if (PreviousPage != null)
```

```
        {
            lblInfo.Text = "You came from a page titled " +
              PreviousPage.Header.Title;
        }
    }
}
```

Note that this page checks for a null reference before attempting to access the PreviousPage object. If it's false, no cross-page postback took place. This means CrossPage2.aspx was requested directly, or CrossPage2.aspx posted back to itself. Either way, no PreviousPage object is available.

Figure 9-4 shows what you'll see when CrossPage1.aspx posts to CrossPage2.aspx.

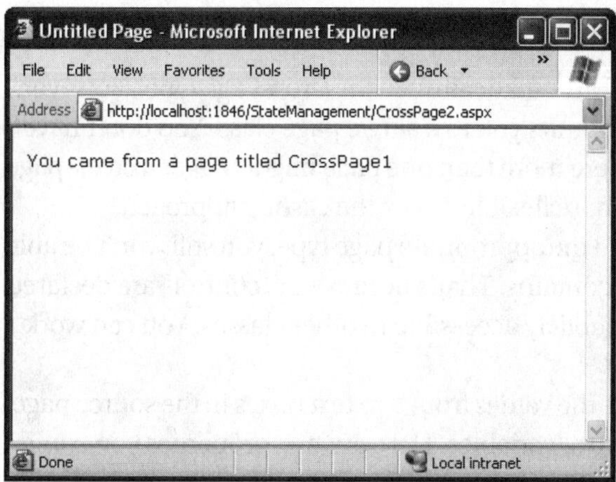

Figure 9-4. *The target of a cross-page postback*

Getting More Information from the Source Page

The previous example shows an interesting initial test, but it doesn't really allow you to transfer any useful information. After all, you're probably interested in retrieving specific details (such as the text in the text boxes of CrossPage1.aspx) from CrossPage2.aspx. The title alone isn't very interesting.

To get more specific details, such as control values, you need to cast the PreviousPage reference to the appropriate page class (in this case it's the CrossPage1 class). Here's an example that handles this situation properly, by checking first whether the PreviousPage object is an instance of the expected class:

```
protected void Page_Load(object sender, EventArgs e)
{
    if (PreviousPage != null)
```

```
    {
        CrossPage1 prevPage = PreviousPage as CrossPage1;
        if (prevPage != null)
        {
            // (Read some information from the previous page.)
        }
    }
}
```

You can also solve this problem in another way. Rather than casting the reference manually, you can add the PreviousPageType directive to the .aspx page, right after the Page directive. The PreviousPageType directive indicates the expected type of the page initiating the cross-page postback. Here's an example:

```
<%@ PreviousPageType VirtualPath="CrossPage1.aspx" %>
```

Now, the PreviousPage property will automatically use the CrossPage type. However, this approach is more fragile because it limits you to a single page class. You don't have the flexibility to deal with situations where more than one page might trigger a cross-page postback. For that reason, it's usually more flexible to use the casting approach.

Once you've cast the previous page to the appropriate page type, you still won't be able to directly access the control objects it contains. That's because the controls are declared as protected members, so they aren't publicly accessible to other classes. You can work around this by using properties.

For example, if you wanted to expose the values from two text boxes in the source page, you might add properties wrap the control variables. Here are two properties you could add to the CrossPage1 class to expose its TextBox controls:

```
public TextBox FirstNameTextBox
{
    get { return txtFirstName; }
}
public TextBox LastNameTextBox
{
    get { return txtLastName; }
}
```

However, this usually isn't the best approach. The problem is that it exposes too many details, giving the target page the freedom to read everything from the text in the text box to its fonts and colors. If you need to change the page later to use different input controls, it will be difficult to maintain these properties. Instead, you'll probably be forced to rewrite code in both pages.

A better choice is to define specific, limited methods that extract just the information you need. For example, you might decide to add a FullName() property that retrieves just the text from the two text boxes. Here's the full page code for CrossPage1.aspx with this property:

```
public partial class CrossPage1 : System.Web.UI.Page
{
    public string FullName
    {
        get { return txtFirstName.Text + " " + txtLastName.Text; }
    }
}
```

This way, the relationship between the two pages is clear, simple, and easy to maintain. You can probably change the controls in the source page (CrossPage1) without needing to change other parts of your application. For example, if you decided to use different controls for name entry in CrossPage1.aspx, you would be forced to revise the code inside the FullName property. However, your changes would be confined to CrossPage1.aspx, and you wouldn't need to modify CrossPage2.aspx at all.

Here's how you can rewrite the code in CrossPage2.aspx to display the information from CrossPage1.aspx:

```
protected void Page_Load(object sender, EventArgs e)
{
    if (PreviousPage != null)
    {
        lblInfo.Text = "You came from a page titled " +
            PreviousPage.Header.Title + "<br />";

        CrossPage1 prevPage = PreviousPage as CrossPage1;
        if (prevPage != null)
        {
            lblInfo.Text += "You typed in this: " + prevPage.FullName;
        }
    }
}
```

Figure 9-5 shows the new result.

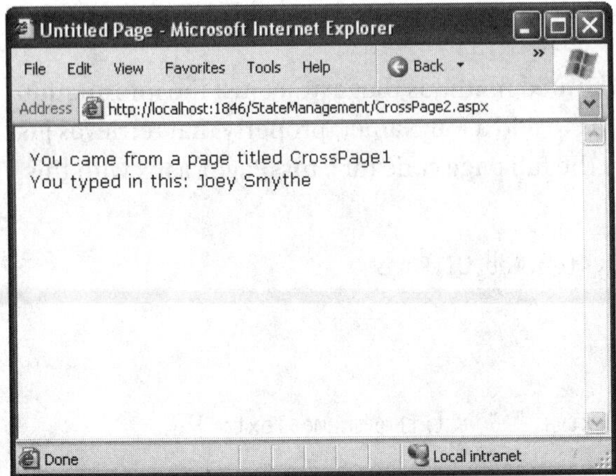

Figure 9-5. *Retrieving specific information from the source page*

■ **Note** Cross-page postbacks are genuinely useful, but they can lead the way to more complicated pages. If you allow multiple source pages that post to the same destination page, it's up to you to code the logic that figures out which page it came from and then acts accordingly. To avoid these headaches, it's easiest to perform cross-page postbacks between two specific pages only.

ASP.NET uses some interesting sleight of hand to make cross-page postbacks work. The first time the second page accesses Page.PreviousPage, ASP.NET needs to create the previous page object. To do this, it actually starts the page processing but interrupts it just before the PreRender stage, and it doesn't let the page render any HTML output.

However, this still has some interesting side effects. For example, all the page events of the previous page are fired, including Page.Load and Page.Init, and the Button.Click event also fires for the button that triggered the cross-page post back. ASP.NET fires these events because they might be needed to initialize the source page.

The Query String

Another common approach is to pass information using a query string in the URL. This approach is commonly found in search engines. For example, if you perform a search on the Google website, you'll be redirected to a new URL that incorporates your search parameters. Here's an example:

```
http://www.google.ca/search?q=organic+gardening
```

The query string is the portion of the URL after the question mark. In this case, it defines a single variable named q, which contains the string *organic+gardening*.

The advantage of the query string is that it's lightweight and doesn't exert any kind of burden on the server. However, it also has several limitations:

- Information is limited to simple strings, which must contain URL-legal characters.
- Information is clearly visible to the user and to anyone else who cares to eavesdrop on the Internet.
- The enterprising user might decide to modify the query string and supply new values, which your program won't expect and can't protect against.
- Many browsers impose a limit on the length of a URL (usually from 1KB to 2KB). For that reason, you can't place a large amount of information in the query string and still be assured of compatibility with most browsers.

Adding information to the query string is still a useful technique. It's particularly well suited in database applications where you present the user with a list of items that correspond to records in a database, like products. The user can then select an item and be forwarded to another page with detailed information about the selected item. One easy way to implement this design is to have the first page send the item ID to the second page. The second page then looks that item up in the database and displays the detailed information. You'll notice this technique in e-commerce sites such as Amazon.

To store information in the query string, you need to place it there yourself. Unfortunately, you have no collection-based way to do this. Typically, this means using a special HyperLink control or a special Response.Redirect() statement such as the one shown here:

```
// Go to newpage.aspx. Submit a single query string argument
// named recordID, and set to 10.
Response.Redirect("newpage.aspx?recordID=10");
```

You can send multiple parameters as long as they're separated with an ampersand (&):

```
// Go to newpage.aspx. Submit two query string arguments:
// recordID (10) and mode (full).
Response.Redirect("newpage.aspx?recordID=10&mode=full");
```

The receiving page has an easier time working with the query string. It can receive the values from the QueryString dictionary collection exposed by the built-in Request object:

```
string ID = Request.QueryString["recordID"];
```

Note that information is always retrieved as a string, which can then be converted to another simple data type. Values in the QueryString collection are indexed by the variable name.

Note Unlike view state, information passed through the query string is clearly visible and unencrypted. Don't use the query string for information that needs to be hidden or made tamper-proof.

A Query String Example

The next program presents a table of entries. When the user chooses an item by clicking the appropriate hyperlink, the user is forwarded to a new page. This page displays the received ID number. This provides a quick and simple query string test. In a sophisticated application, you would want to combine some of the data control features that are described later in this book in Part 3.

The first page provides a list of items, a check box, and a submission button (see Figure 9-6).

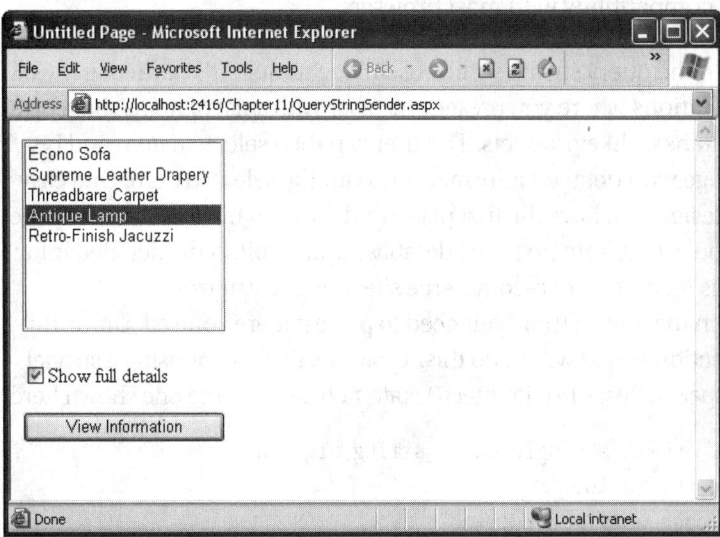

Figure 9-6. *A query string sender*

Here's the code for the first page:

```
public partial class QueryStringSender : Page
{
    protected void Page_Load(Object sender, EventArgs e)
    {
        // Add sample values.
        lstItems.Items.Add("Econo Sofa");
        lstItems.Items.Add("Supreme Leather Drapery");
        lstItems.Items.Add("Threadbare Carpet");
        lstItems.Items.Add("Antique Lamp");
        lstItems.Items.Add("Retro-Finish Jacuzzi");
    }

    protected void cmdGo_Click(Object sender, EventArgs e)
    {
        if (lstItems.SelectedIndex == -1)
        {
            lblError.Text = "You must select an item.";
        }
        else
        {
            // Forward the user to the information page,
            // with the query string data.
            string url = "QueryStringRecipient.aspx?";
            url += "Item=" + lstItems.SelectedItem.Text + "&";
            url += "Mode=" + chkDetails.Checked.ToString();
            Response.Redirect(url);
        }
    }
}
```

One interesting aspect of this example is that it places information in the query string that really isn't valid—namely, the space that appears in the item name. When you run the application, you'll notice that ASP.NET encodes the string for you automatically, converting spaces to the valid %20 equivalent escape sequence. The recipient page reads the original values from the QueryString collection without any trouble. Figure 9-7 shows the recipient page.

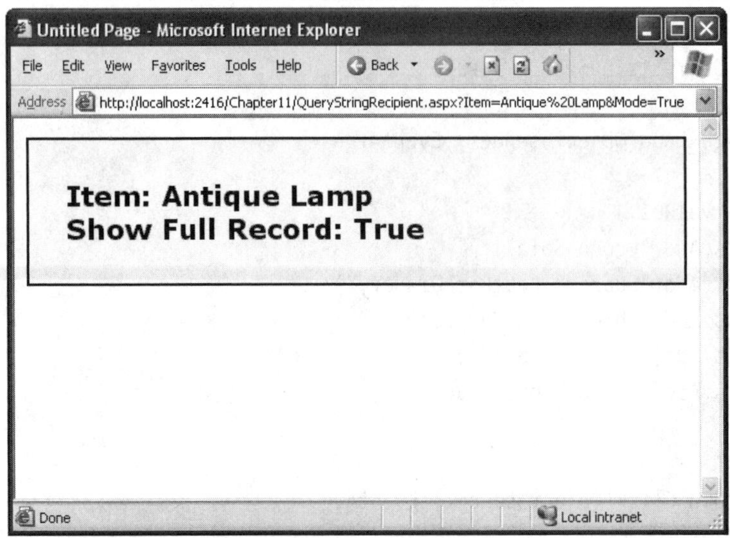

Figure 9-7. *A query string recipient*

```
public partial class QueryStringRecipient : Page
{
    protected void Page_Load(Object sender, EventArgs e)
    {
        lblInfo.Text = "Item: " + Request.QueryString["Item"];
        lblInfo.Text += "<br />Show Full Record: ";
        lblInfo.Text += Request.QueryString["Mode"];
    }
}
```

Custom Cookies

Custom cookies provide another way that you can store information for later use. Cookies are small files that are created on the client's hard drive (or, if they're temporary, in the web browser's memory). One advantage of cookies is that they work transparently without the user being aware that information needs to be stored. They also can be easily used by any page in your application and even be retained between visits, which allows for truly long-term storage. They suffer from some of the same drawbacks that affect query strings—namely, they're limited to simple string information, and they're easily accessible and readable if the user finds and opens the corresponding file. These factors make them a poor choice for complex or private information or large amounts of data.

Some users disable cookies on their browsers, which will cause problems for web applications that require them. For the most part, cookies are widely adopted because so many sites use them. However, they can limit your potential audience, and they aren't suited for the embedded browsers used with mobile devices. Also, a user might manually delete a cookie file that is stored on their hard drive.

A good rule of thumb is to use cookies to retain preference-related information, such as a customer's last order item or e-mail address. You can then use this information to provide a richer experience. However, you shouldn't require the use of cookies or assume that they'll always be present.

Cookies are fairly easy to use. Both the Request and Response objects (which are provided through Page properties) provide a Cookies collection. The important trick to remember is that you retrieve cookies from the Request object, and you set cookies using the Response object.

To set a cookie, just create a new HttpCookie object. You can then fill it with string information (using the familiar dictionary pattern) and attach it to the current web response:

```
// Create the cookie object.
HttpCookie cookie = new HttpCookie("Preferences");

// Set a value in it.
cookie["LanguagePref"] = "English";

// Add it to the current web response.
Response.Cookies.Add(cookie);
```

A cookie added in this way will persist until the user closes the browser and will be sent with every request. To create a longer-lived cookie, you can set an expiration date:

```
// This cookie lives for one year.
cookie.Expires = DateTime.Now.AddYears(1);
```

You retrieve cookies by cookie name using the Request.Cookies collection:

```
HttpCookie cookie = Request.Cookies["Preferences"];

// Check to see whether a cookie was found with this name.
// This is a good precaution to take,
// because the user could disable cookies,
// in which case the cookie will not exist.
```

```
string language;
if (cookie != null)
{
  language = cookie["LanguagePref"];
}
```

The only way to remove a cookie is by replacing it with a cookie that has an expiration date that has already passed. This code demonstrates the technique:

```
HttpCookie cookie = new HttpCookie("LanguagePref");
cookie.Expires = DateTime.Now.AddDays(-1);
Response.Cookies.Add(cookie);
```

A Cookie Example

The next example shows a typical use of cookies to store a customer name. If the name is found, a welcome message is displayed, as shown in Figure 9-8.

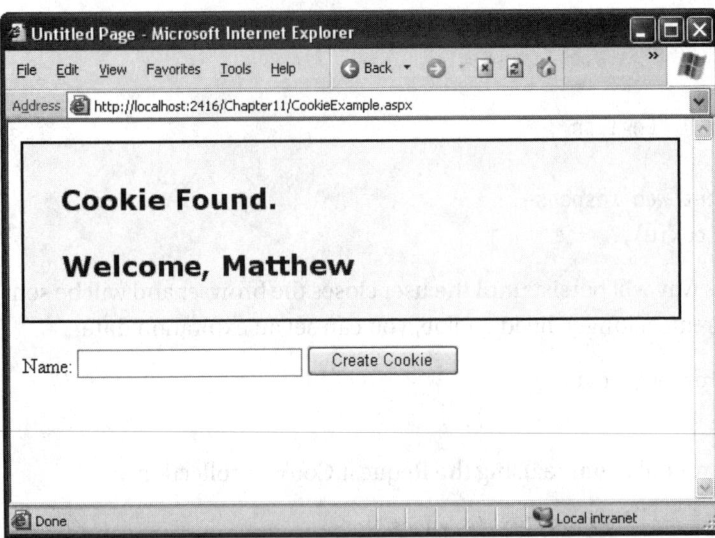

Figure 9-8. *Displaying information from a custom cookie*

Here's the code for this page:

```
public partial class CookieExample : Page
{
    protected void Page_Load(Object sender, EventArgs e)
    {
        HttpCookie cookie = Request.Cookies["Preferences"];
```

```
        if (cookie == null)
        {
            lblWelcome.Text = "<b>Unknown Customer</b>";
        }
        else
        {
            lblWelcome.Text = "<b>Cookie Found.</b><br /><br />";
            lblWelcome.Text += "Welcome, " + cookie["Name"];
        }
    }

    protected void cmdStore_Click(Object sender, EventArgs e)
    {
        // Check for a cookie, and only create a new one if
        // one doesn't already exist.
        HttpCookie cookie = Request.Cookies["Preferences"];
        if (cookie == null)
        {
            cookie = new HttpCookie("Preferences");
        }

        cookie["Name"] = txtName.Text;
        cookie.Expires = DateTime.Now.AddYears(1);
        Response.Cookies.Add(cookie);

        lblWelcome.Text = "<b>Cookie Created.</b><br /><br />";
        lblWelcome.Text += "New Customer: " + cookie["Name"];
    }
}
```

■ **Note** You'll find that some other ASP.NET features use cookies. Two examples are session state (which allows you to temporarily store user-specific information in server memory) and forms security (which allows you to restrict portions of a website and force users to access it through a login page). Chapter 18 discusses forms security, and the next section of this chapter discusses session state.

Session State

There comes a point in the life of most applications when they begin to have more sophisticated storage requirements. An application might need to store and access complex information such as custom data objects, which can't be easily persisted to a cookie or sent through a query string. Or the application might have stringent security requirements that prevent it from storing information on the client in view state or a custom cookie. In these situations, you can use ASP.NET's built-in session state facility.

Session state management is one of ASP.NET's premiere features. It allows you to store any type of data in memory on the server. The information is protected, because it is never transmitted to the client, and it's uniquely bound to a specific session. Every client that accesses the application has a different session and a distinct collection of information. Session state is ideal for storing information such as the items in the current user's shopping basket when the user browses from one page to another.

Session Tracking

ASP.NET tracks each session using a unique 120-bit identifier. ASP.NET uses a proprietary algorithm to generate this value, thereby guaranteeing (statistically speaking) that the number is unique and it's random enough that a malicious user can't reverse-engineer or "guess" what session ID a given client will be using. This special ID is the only piece of information that is transmitted between the web server and the client. When the client presents the session ID, ASP.NET looks up the corresponding session, retrieves the serialized data from the state server, converts it to live objects, and places these objects into a special collection so that they can be accessed in code. This process takes place automatically.

For this system to work, the client must present the appropriate session ID with each request. You can accomplish this in two ways:

Using cookies: In this case, the session ID is transmitted in a special cookie (named ASP.NET_SessionId), which ASP.NET creates automatically when the session collection is used. This is the default, and it's also the same approach that was used in earlier versions of ASP.

Using modified URLs: In this case, the session ID is transmitted in a specially modified (or *munged*) URL. This is a new feature in ASP.NET that allows you to create applications that use session state with clients that don't support cookies.

Session state doesn't come for free. Though it solves many of the problems associated with other forms of state management, it forces the server to store additional information in memory. This extra memory requirement, even if it is small, can quickly grow to performance-destroying levels as hundreds or thousands of clients access the site.

In other words, you must think through any use of session state. A careless use of session state is one of the most common reasons that a web application can't scale to serve a large number of clients. Sometimes, a better approach is to use caching, as described in Chapter 26.

Using Session State

You can interact with session state using the System.Web.SessionState.HttpSessionState class, which is provided in an ASP.NET web page as the built-in Session object. The syntax for adding items to the collection and retrieving them is basically the same as for adding items to a page's view state.

For example, you might store a DataSet in session memory like this:

```
Session["dsInfo"] = dsInfo;
```

You can then retrieve it with an appropriate conversion operation:

```
dsInfo = (DataSet)Session["dsInfo"];
```

■ **Note** Chapter 13 explores the DataSet.

Session state is global to your entire application for the current user. However, session state can be lost in several ways:

- If the user closes and restarts the browser.
- If the user accesses the same page through a different browser window, although the session will still exist if a web page is accessed through the original browser window. Browsers differ on how they handle this situation.
- If the session times out due to inactivity. More information about session timeout can be found in the configuration section.
- If the programmer ends the session in code.

In the first two cases, the session actually remains in memory, because the web server has no idea that the client has closed the browser or changed windows. The session will linger in memory, remaining inaccessible, until it eventually expires.

Table 9-1 describes the methods and properties of the HttpSessionState class.

Table 9-1. *HttpSessionState Members*

Member	Description
Count	The number of items in the current session collection.
IsCookieless	Identifies whether this session is tracked with a cookie or using modified URLs.
IsNewSession	Identifies whether this session was just created for the current request. If currently no information is in session state, ASP.NET won't bother to track the session or create a session cookie. Instead, the session will be re-created with every request.
Mode	Provides an enumerated value that explains how ASP.NET stores session state information. This storage mode is determined based on the web.config configuration settings discussed in the "Session State Configuration" section later in this chapter.
SessionID	Provides a string with the unique session identifier for the current client.
Timeout	The current number of minutes that must elapse before the current session will be abandoned, provided that no more requests are received from the client. This value can be changed programmatically, giving you the chance to make the session collection longer term when required for more important operations.
Abandon()	Cancels the current session immediately and releases all the memory it occupied. This is a useful technique in a logoff page to ensure that server memory is reclaimed as quickly as possible.
Clear()	Removes all the session items but doesn't change the current session identifier.

A Session State Example

The next example uses session state to store several Furniture data objects. The data object combines a few related variables and uses a special constructor so that it can be created and initialized in one easy line. Rather than use full property procedures, the class takes a shortcut and uses public member variables.

```
public class Furniture
{
    public string Name;
    public string Description;
    public decimal Cost;

    public Furniture(string name, string description,
      decimal cost)
```

```
    {
        Name = name;
        Description = description;
        Cost = cost;
    }
}
```

Three Furniture objects are created the first time the page is loaded, and they're stored in session state. The user can then choose from a list of furniture piece names. When a selection is made, the corresponding object will be retrieved, and its information will be displayed, as shown in Figure 9-9.

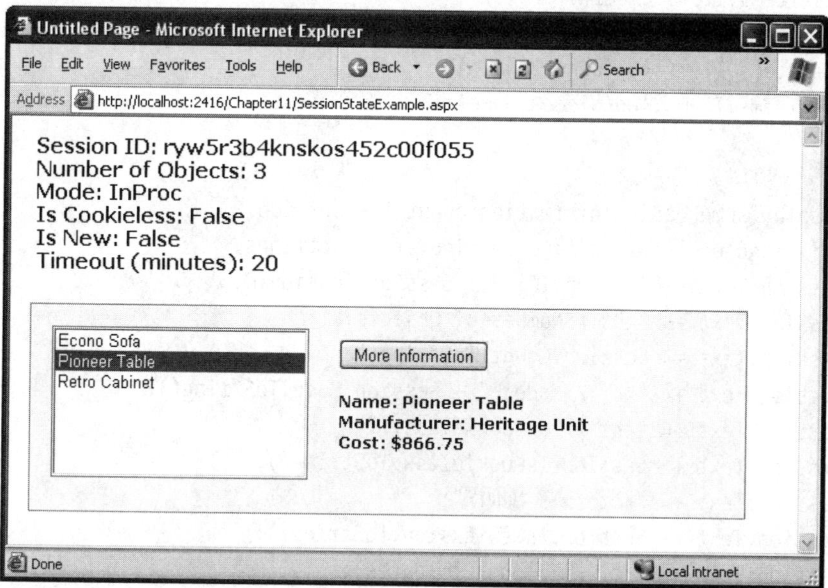

Figure 9-9. *A session state example with data objects*

```
public partial class SessionStateExample : Page
{
    protected void Page_Load(Object sender, EventArgs e)
    {
        if (!this.IsPostBack)
        {
            // Create Furniture objects.
            Furniture piece1 = new Furniture("Econo Sofa",
                                        "Acme Inc.", 74.99M);
```

```
            Furniture piece2 = new Furniture("Pioneer Table",
                                             "Heritage Unit", 866.75M);
            Furniture piece3 = new Furniture("Retro Cabinet",
                                             "Sixties Ltd.", 300.11M);

            // Add objects to session state.
            Session["Furniture1"] = piece1;
            Session["Furniture2"] = piece2;
            Session["Furniture3"] = piece3;

            // Add rows to list control.
            lstItems.Items.Clear();
            lstItems.Items.Add(piece1.Name);
            lstItems.Items.Add(piece2.Name);
            lstItems.Items.Add(piece3.Name);
        }

        // Display some basic information about the session.
        // This is useful for testing configuration settings.
        lblSession.Text = "Session ID: " + Session.SessionID;
        lblSession.Text += "<br />Number of Objects: ";
        lblSession.Text += Session.Count.ToString();
        lblSession.Text += "<br />Mode: " + Session.Mode.ToString();
        lblSession.Text += "<br />Is Cookieless: ";
        lblSession.Text += Session.IsCookieless.ToString();
        lblSession.Text += "<br />Is New: ";
        lblSession.Text += Session.IsNewSession.ToString();
        lblSession.Text += "<br />Timeout (minutes): ";
        lblSession.Text += Session.Timeout.ToString();
    }

    protected void cmdMoreInfo_Click(Object sender, EventArgs e)
    {
        if (lstItems.SelectedIndex == -1)
        {
            lblRecord.Text = "No item selected.";
        }
        else
```

```
        {
            // Construct the right key name based on the index.
            string key = "Furniture" +
                (lstItems.SelectedIndex + 1).ToString();

            // Retrieve the Furniture object from session state.
            Furniture piece = (Furniture)Session[key];

            // Display the information for this object.
            lblRecord.Text = "Name: " + piece.Name;
            lblRecord.Text += "<br />Manufacturer: ";
            lblRecord.Text +=  piece.Description;
            lblRecord.Text += "<br />Cost: $" + piece.Cost.ToString();
        }
    }
}
```

It's also a good practice to add a few session-friendly features in your application. For example, you could add a logout button to the page that automatically cancels a session using the Session.Abandon() method. This way, the user will be encouraged to terminate the session rather than just close the browser window, and the server memory will be reclaimed faster.

MAKING SESSION STATE MORE SCALABLE

When web developers need to store a large amount of state information, they face a confounding problem. They can use session state and ensure excellent performance for a small set of users, but they risk poor scalability for large numbers. Alternatively, they can use a database to store temporary session information. This allows them to store large amount of session information for long times (potentially weeks or months instead of mere minutes). However, it also slows performance because the database must be queried for almost every page request.

The compromise involves caching. The basic approach is to create a temporary database record with session information and store its unique ID in session state. This ensures that the in-memory session information is always minimal, but your web page code can easily find the corresponding session record. To reduce the number of database queries, you'll also add the session information to the cache (indexed under the session identifier). On subsequent requests, your code can check for the session information in the cache first. If the information is no longer in the cache, your code can retrieve it from the database as a last resort. This process becomes even more transparent if you create a custom component that provides the session information and performs the required cache lookup for you.

For more information, read about custom components in Chapter 24 and caching in Chapter 26.

Session State Configuration

You configure session state through the web.config file for your current application (which is found in the same virtual directory as the .aspx web page files). The configuration file allows you to set advanced options such as the timeout and the session state mode. If you're creating your web application in Visual Studio, your project will include an automatically generated web.config file.

The following is a typical web.config file, with the most important attributes you can use to configure session state:

```
<?xml version="1.0" encoding="utf-8" ?>
<configuration>
    <system.web>
        <!-- Other settings omitted. -->

        <sessionState
            cookieless="UseCookies" cookieName="ASP.NET_SessionId"
            regenerateExpiredSessionId="false"
            timeout="20"
            mode="InProc"
            stateConnectionString="tcpip=127.0.0.1:42424"
            stateNetworkTimeout="10"
            sqlConnectionString="data source=127.0.0.1;Integrated Security=SSPI"
            sqlCommandTimeout="30" allowCustomSqlDatabase="false"
            customProvider=""
        />
    </system.web>
</configuration>
```

The following sections describe these settings.

Cookieless

You can set the cookieless setting to one of the values defined by the HttpCookieMode enumeration, as described in Table 9-2.

Table 9-2. *HttpCookieMode Values*

Value	Description
UseCookies	Cookies are always used, even if the browser or device doesn't support cookies or they are disabled. This is default. If the device does not support cookies, session information will be lost over subsequent requests, because each request will get a new ID.
UseUri	Cookies are never used, regardless of the capabilities of the browser or device. Instead, the session ID is stored in the URL.
UseDeviceProfile	ASP.NET chooses whether to use cookieless sessions by examining the BrowserCapabilities object. The drawback is that this object indicates what the device should support—it doesn't take into account that the user may have disabled cookies in a browser that supports them.
AutoDetect	ASP.NET attempts to determine whether the browser supports cookies by attempting to set and retrieve a cookie (a technique commonly used on the Web). This technique can correctly determine whether a browser supports cookies but has them disabled, in which case cookieless mode is used instead.

Here's an example that forces cookieless mode (which is useful for testing)

```
<sessionState cookieless="UseUri" ... />
```

In cookieless mode, the session ID will automatically be inserted into the URL. When ASP.NET receives a request, it will remove the ID, retrieve the session collection, and forward the request to the appropriate directory. Figure 9-10 shows a munged URL.

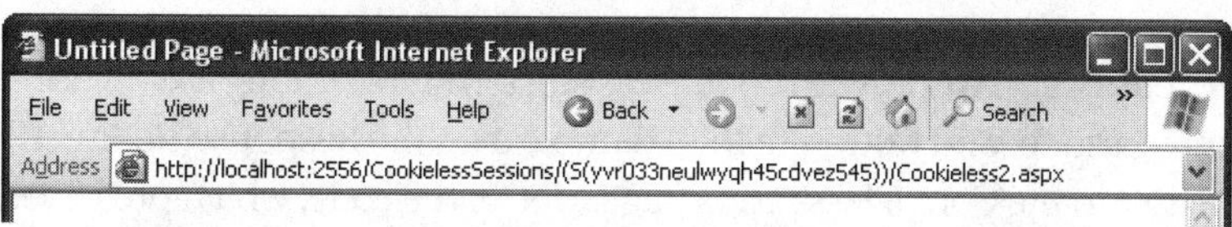

Figure 9-10. *A munged URL with the session ID*

Because the session ID is inserted in the current URL, relative links also automatically gain the session ID. In other words, if the user is currently stationed on Page1.aspx and clicks a relative link to Page2.aspx, the relative link includes the current session ID as part of the URL. The same is true if you call Response.Redirect() with a relative URL, as shown here:

```
Response.Redirect("Page2.aspx");
```

Figure 9-11 shows a sample website (included with the online samples in the CookielessSessions directory) that tests cookieless sessions. It contains two pages and uses cookieless mode. The first page contains a HyperLink control and two buttons. The HyperLink's NavigateUrl property is set to the relative path Cookieless2.aspx. If you click this link, the session ID is retained, and the session information can be retrieved on the new page.

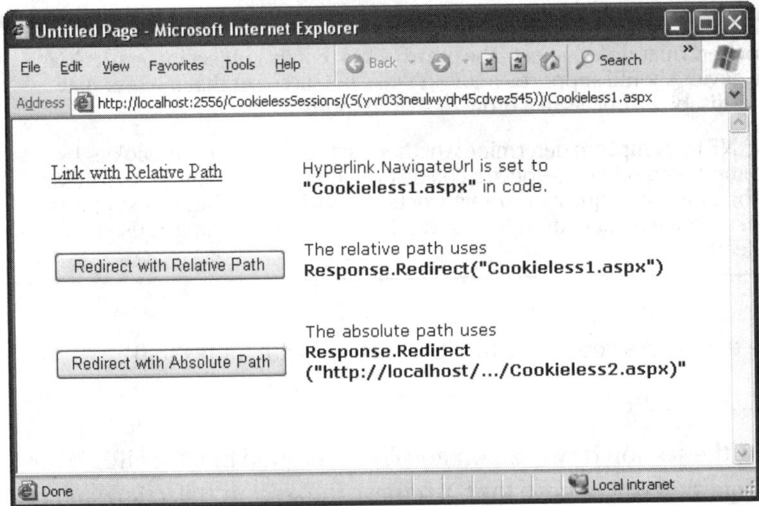

Figure 9-11. *Three tests of cookieless sessions*

Even programmatic redirection works with cookieless session state, as long as you use a relative path. For example, the second button in this example uses the Response.Redirect() method to forward the user to the Cookieless2.aspx page. Here's the code, which preserves the munged URL with no extra steps required:

```
protected void cmdLink_Click(Object sender, EventArgs e)
{
    Response.Redirect("Cookieless2.aspx");
}
```

The only real limitation of cookieless state is that you cannot use absolute links, because ASP.NET cannot insert the session ID into them. For example, if you use the third command button, the current session will be abandoned. The code is as follows, and Figure 9-12 shows the result of this code:

```
protected void cmdLinkAbsolute_Click(Object sender, EventArgs e)
{
    string url;
    url = "http://localhost/Code/ASP.NET/Chapter09/CookielessSessions/";
```

```
    url += "Cookieless2.aspx";
    Response.Redirect(url);
}
```

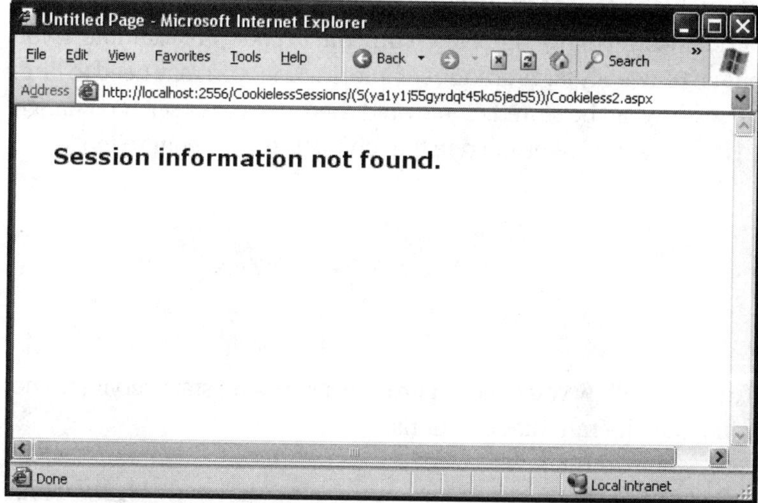

Figure 9-12. *A lost session*

By default, ASP.NET allows you to reuse a session identifier. For example, if you make a request and your query string contains an expired session, ASP.NET creates a new session and uses that session ID. The problem is that a session ID might inadvertently appear in a public place—such as in a results page in a search engine. This could lead to multiple users accessing the server with the same session identifier and then all joining the same session with the same shared data.

To avoid this potential security risk, you should include the optional regenerateExpiredSessionId attribute and set it to true whenever you use cookieless sessions. This way, a new session ID will be issued if a user connects with an expired session ID. The only drawback is that this process also forces the current page to lose all view state and form data, because ASP.NET performs a redirect to make sure the browser has a new session identifier.

Timeout

Another important session state setting in the web.config file is the timeout. This specifies the number of minutes that ASP.NET will wait, without receiving a request, before it abandons the session.

```
<sessionState
    timeout="20" />
```

This setting represents one of the most important compromises of session state. A difference of minutes can have a dramatic effect on the load of your server and the performance of your application. Ideally, you will choose a timeframe that is short enough to allow the server to reclaim valuable memory after a client stops using the application but long enough to allow a client to pause and continue a session without losing it.

You can also programmatically change the session timeout in code. For example, if you know a session contains an unusually large amount of information, you may need to limit the amount of time the session can be stored. You would then warn the user and change the timeout property. Here's a sample line of code that changes the timeout to ten minutes:

```
Session.Timeout = 10;
```

Mode

The other session state settings allow you to configure special session state services. The next few sections describe the different mode options.

■ **Note** If you're hosting ASP.NET using more than one web server (which is affectionately known as a *web farm*), you'll also need to take some extra configuration steps to make sure all the web servers are in sync. Otherwise, one server might encode information in session state differently than another, which will cause a problem if the user is routed from one server to another during a session. The solution is to modify the <machineKey> section of the machine.config file so that it's consistent across all servers. For more information, refer to Chapter 12.

InProc

For the default mode (InProc), the other two settings have no effect. They are just included as placeholders to show you the appropriate format. InProc is similar to how session state was stored in previous versions of ASP. It instructs information to be stored in the same process as the ASP.NET worker threads, which provides the best performance but the least durability. If you restart your server, the state information will be lost.

InProc is the default option, and it makes sense for most small websites. In a web farm scenario, though, it won't work. To allow session state to be shared between servers, you must use the out-of-process or SQL Server state service. Another reason you might want to avoid InProc mode is if you find that your users are losing session state information at unpredictable times. In ASP.NET, application domains can be restarted for a variety of reasons, including configuration changes, updated pages, and when certain thresholds are met (regardless of whether an error has occurred). If you find that you're losing sessions *before* the timeout limit, you may want to experiment with a more durable mode.

■ **Note** When using the StateServer and SqlServer modes, the objects you store in session state must be serializable. Otherwise, ASP.NET will not be able to transmit the object to the state service or store it in the database. Earlier in this chapter, you learned how to create a serializable Customer class for storing in view state.

Off

This setting disables session state management for every page in the application. This can provide a slight performance improvement for websites that are not using session state.

StateServer

With this setting, ASP.NET will use a separate Windows service for state management. This service runs on the same web server, but it's outside the main ASP.NET process, which gives it a basic level of protection if the ASP.NET process needs to be restarted. The cost is the increased time delay imposed when state information is transferred between two processes. If you frequently access and change state information, this can make for a fairly unwelcome slowdown.

When using the StateServer setting, you need to specify a value for the stateConnectionString setting. This string identifies the TCP/IP address of the computer that is running the StateServer service and its port number (which is defined by ASP.NET and doesn't usually need to be changed). This allows you to host the StateServer on another computer. If you don't change this setting, the local server will be used (set as address 127.0.0.1).

Of course, before your application can use the service, you need to start it. The easiest way to do this is to use the Microsoft Management Console (MMC). Select Start ➤ Programs ➤ Administrative Tools ➤ Computer Management. (You can also access the Administrative Tools group through the Control Panel.) Then select the Services and Applications ➤ Services node. Find the service called ASP.NET State Service in the list, as shown in Figure 9-13.

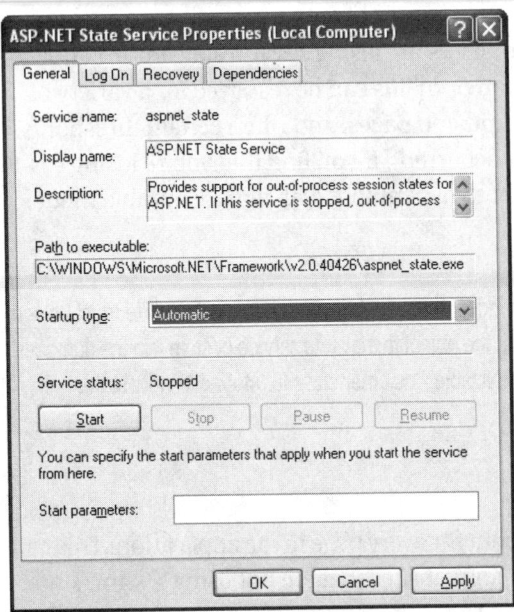

Figure 9-13. *The ASP.NET state service*

Once you find the service in the list, you can manually start and stop it by right-clicking it. Generally, you'll want to configure Windows to automatically start the service. Right-click it, select Properties, and modify the Startup Type setting it to Automatic, as shown in Figure 9-14.

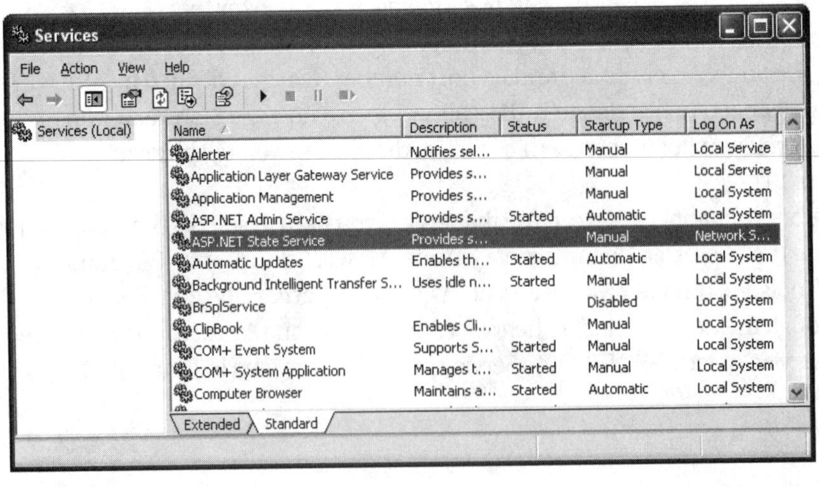

Figure 9-14. *Service properties*

■ Note When using StateServer mode, you can also set an optional stateNetworkTimeout attribute that specifies the maximum number of seconds to wait for the service to respond before canceling the request. The default value is 10 (seconds).

SqlServer

This setting instructs ASP.NET to use an SQL Server database to store session information, as identified by the sqlConnectionString attribute. This is the most resilient state store but also the slowest by far. To use this method of state management, you'll need to have a server with SQL Server installed.

When setting the sqlConnectionString attribute, you follow the same sort of pattern you use with ADO.NET data access. Generally, you'll need to specify a data source (the server address) and a user ID and password, unless you're using SQL integrated security.

In addition, you need to install the special stored procedures and temporary session databases. These stored procedures take care of storing and retrieving the session information. ASP.NET includes a Transact-SQL script for this purpose called InstallSqlState.sql. It's found in the C:\[WinDir]\Microsoft.NET\Framework\[Version] directory. You can run this script using an SQL Server utility such as OSQL.exe or Query Analyzer. It needs to be performed only once.

Ordinarily, the state database is always named ASPState. As a result, the connection string in the web.config file doesn't explicitly indicate the database name. Instead, it simply reflects the location of the server and the type of authentication that will be used:

```
<sessionState sqlConnectionString="data source=127.0.0.1;Integrated
Security=SSPI"
... />
```

If you want to use a different database (with the same structure), simply set allowCustomSqlDatabase to true, and make sure the connection string includes the Initial Catalog setting, which indicates the name of the database you want to use:

```
<sessionState allowCustomSqlDatabase="true" sqlConnectionString=
"data source=127.0.0.1;Integrated Security=SSPI;Initial Catalog=CustDatabase"
... />
```

When using the SqlServer mode, you can also set an optional sqlCommandTimeout attribute that specifies the maximum number of seconds to wait for the database to respond before canceling the request. The default is 30 seconds.

Custom

When using custom mode, you need to indicate which session state store provider to use by supplying the customProvider attribute. The customProvider attribute points to the name of a class that's part of your web application in the App_Code directory or in a compiled assembly in the Bin directory or the GAC.

Creating a custom state provider is a low-level task that needs to be handled carefully to ensure security, stability, and scalability. Custom state providers are also beyond the scope of this book. However, other vendors may release custom state providers you want to use. For example, Oracle may provide a custom state provider that allows you to store state information in an Oracle database.

Application State

Application state allows you to store global objects that can be accessed by any client. Application state is based on the System.Web.HttpApplicationState class, which is provided in all web pages through the built-in Application object.

Application state is similar to session state. It supports the same type of objects, retains information on the server, and uses the same dictionary-based syntax. A common example with application state is a global counter that tracks how many times an operation has been performed by all the web application's clients.

For example, you could create a global.asax event handler that tracks how many sessions have been created or how many requests have been received into the application. Or you can use similar logic in the Page.Load event handler to track how many times a given page has been requested by various clients. Here's an example of the latter:

```
protected void Page_Load(Object sender, EventArgs e)
{
    int count = (int)Application["HitCounterForOrderPage"];
    count++;
    Application["HitCounterForOrderPage"] = count;
    lblCounter.Text = count.ToString();
}
```

Once again, application state items are stored as objects, so you need to cast them when you retrieve them from the collection. Items in application state never time out.

They last until the application or server is restarted, or the application domain refreshes itself (because of automatic process recycling settings or an update to one of the pages or components in the application).

Application state isn't often used, because it's generally inefficient. In the previous example, the counter would probably not keep an accurate count, particularly in times of heavy traffic. For example, if two clients requested the page at the same time, you could have a sequence of events like this:

1. User A retrieves the current count (432).
2. User B retrieves the current count (432).
3. User A sets the current count to 433.
4. User B sets the current count to 433.

In other words, one request isn't counted because two clients access the counter at the same time. To prevent this problem, you need to use the Lock() and Unlock() methods, which explicitly allow only one client to access the Application state collection at a time.

```
protected void Page_Load(Object sender, EventArgs e)
{
    // Acquire exclusive access.
    Application.Lock();

    int count = (int)Application["HitCounterForOrderPage"];
    count++;
    Application["HitCounterForOrderPage"] = count;

    // Release exclusive access.
    Application.Unlock();

    lblCounter.Text = count.ToString();
}
```

Unfortunately, all other clients requesting the page will now be stalled until the Application collection is released. This can drastically reduce performance. Generally, frequently modified values are poor candidates for application state. In fact, application state is rarely used in the .NET world because its two most common uses have been replaced by easier, more efficient methods:

- In the past, application state was used to store application-wide constants, such as a database connection string. As you saw in Chapter 5, this type of constant can be stored in the web.config file, which is generally more flexible because you can change it easily without needing to hunt through web page code or recompile your application.
- Application state can also be used to store frequently used information that is time-consuming to create, such as a full product catalog that requires a database lookup. However, using application state to store this kind of information raises all sorts of problems about how to check whether the data is valid and how to replace it when needed. It can also hamper performance if the product catalog is too large. Chapter 26 introduces a similar but much more sensible approach—storing frequently used information in the ASP.NET cache. Many uses of application state can be replaced more efficiently with caching.

An Overview of State Management Choices

Each state management choice has a different lifetime, scope, performance overhead, and level of support. Table 9-3 and Table 9-4 show an at-a-glance comparison of your state management options.

Table 9-3. *State Management Options Compared (Part 1)*

	View State	Query String	Custom Cookies
Allowed Data Types	All serializable .NET data types.	A limited amount of string data.	String data.
Storage Location	A hidden field in the current web page.	The browser's URL string.	The client's computer (in memory or a small text file, depending on its lifetime settings).
Lifetime	Retained permanently for postbacks to a single page.	Lost when the user enters a new URL or closes the browser. However, this can be stored in a bookmark.	Set by the programmer. Can be used in multiple pages and can persist between visits.
Scope	Limited to the current page.	Limited to the target page.	The whole ASP.NET application.

	View State	Query String	Custom Cookies
Security	By default it's tamper-proof but easy to read. You can issue the Page directive to enforce encryption.	Clearly visible and easy for the user to modify.	Insecure, and can be modified by the user.
Performance Implications	Storing a large amount of information will slow transmission, but will not affect server performance.	None, because the amount of data is trivial.	None, because the amount of data is trivial.
Typical Use	Page-specific settings.	Sending a product ID from a catalog page to a details page.	Personalization preferences for a website.

Table 9-4. *State Management Options Compared (Part 2)*

	Session State	Application State
Allowed Data Types	All .NET data types.	All .NET data types.
Storage Location	Server memory.	Server memory.
Lifetime	Times out after a predefined period (usually 20 minutes, but can be altered globally or programmatically).	The lifetime of the application (typically, until the server is rebooted).
Scope	The whole ASP.NET application.	The whole ASP.NET application. Unlike other methods, application data is global to all users.
Security	Very secure, because data is never transmitted to the client.	Very secure, because data is never transmitted to the client.
Performance Implications	Storing a large amount of information can slow down the server severely, especially if there are a large number of users at once, because each user will have a separate copy of session data.	Storing a large amount of information can slow down the server, because this data will never time out and be removed.
Typical Use	Store items in a shopping basket.	Storing any type of global data.

■ **Note** ASP.NET has another, more specialized type of state management called *profiles*. Profiles allow you to store and retrieve user-specific information from a database. The only catch is that you need to authenticate the user in order to get the right information. You'll learn about profiles in Chapter 20.

The Global.asax Application File

The global.asax file allows you to write code that responds to global application events. These events fire at various points during the lifetime of a web application, including when session are created. This makes the global.asax file useful in conjunction with the state management features you've learned about so far. For example, you could use the global.asax file to preinitialize a set of objects that you store in application state for the duration of your application. Of course, you can also use these events to perform other tasks. For example, you can run some logging code that runs every time a request is received, no matter what page handles the request.

The global.asax file looks similar to a normal .aspx file, except that it can't contain any HTML or ASP.NET tags. Instead, it contains event handlers. For example, the following global.asax file reacts to the Application.EndRequest event, which happens just before the page is sent to the user:

```
<script language="c#" runat="server">
    protected void Application_OnEndRequest()
    {
        Response.Write("<hr />This page was served at " +
          DateTime.Now.ToString());
    }
</script>
```

This event handler uses the Write() method of the built-in Response object to write a footer at the bottom of the page with the date and time that the page was created (see Figure 9-15).

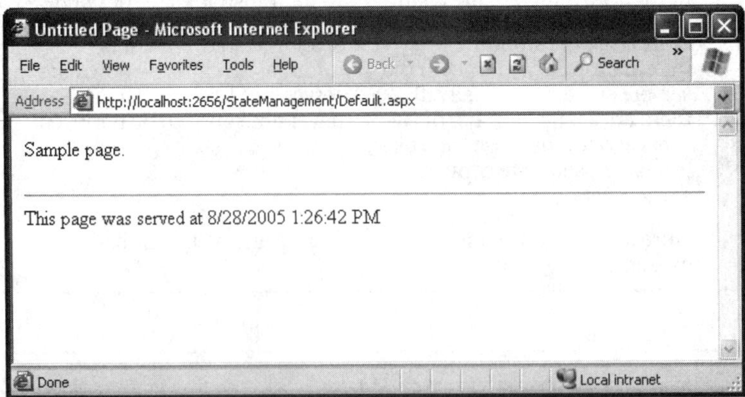

Figure 9-15. *HelloWorld.aspx with an automatic footer*

Each ASP.NET application can have one global.asax file. Once you place it in the appropriate virtual directory, ASP.NET recognizes it and uses it automatically. For example, if you if you place the global.asax shown previously into a virtual directory, every web page in that application will include a footer.

■ **Tip** To add a global.asax file to an application in Visual Studio, choose Website ➤ Add New Item, and select the Global Application Class file type.

Generally, adding an automatic footer is not a useful function for a professional website. A more typical use might be writing an entry to a database log. That way, usage information would be tracked automatically. However, the global.asax file is a minor ingredient, and many web applications won't use it at all.

The global.asax file supports the code-behind model, which allows you to split the code into a separate class in a .cs file. However, you don't really need to take this step, because you won't add any controls or markup to the global.asax file. If you create the global.asax file in Visual Studio, it won't use the code-behind model.

Application Events

Application.EndRequest is only one of more than a dozen events you can respond to in your code. To create a different event handler, you simply need to create a subroutine with the defined name. Table 9-5 lists some of the most common application events that you'll use.

Table 9-5. *Basic Application Events*

Method Name	Description
Application_Start	Occurs when the application starts, which is the first time it receives a request from any user. It doesn't occur on subsequent requests. This event is commonly used to create or cache some initial information that will be reused later.
Application_End	Occurs when the application is shutting down, generally because the web server is being restarted. You can insert cleanup code here.
Application_BeginRequest	Occurs with each request the application receives, just before the page code is executed.
Application_EndRequest	Occurs with each request the application receives, just after the page code is executed.

Continued

Table 9-5. *Continued*

Method Name	Description
Session_Start	Occurs whenever a new user request is received and a session is started.
Session_End	Occurs when a session times out or is programmatically ended.
Application_Error	Occurs in response to an unhandled error. You can find more information about error handling in Chapter 7.

The Last Word

State management is the art of retaining information between requests. Usually, this information is user-specific (such as a list of items in a shopping cart, a user name, or an access level), but sometimes it's global to the whole application (such as usage statistics that track site activity). Because ASP.NET uses a disconnected architecture, you need to explicitly store and retrieve state information with each request. The approach you choose to store this data can dramatically affect the performance, scalability, and security of your application. Remember to consult Table 9-3 and Table 9-4 to help evaluate different types of state management and determine what is best for your needs.

CHAPTER 10

Master Pages and Themes

Using the techniques you've learned so far, you can create polished web pages and let users surf from one page to another. However, to integrate your web pages into a unified, consistent website, you need a few more tools. In this chapter, you'll consider two of the most important: master pages and themes.

Essentially, a *master page* is a blueprint for part of your website. Using a master page, you can define web page layout, complete with all the usual details such as headers, menu bars, and ad banners. Once you've perfected a master page, you can use it to create *content pages*. Each content page automatically acquires the layout and the content of the linked master page. Using this technique, you can make sure all your content pages will have a standardized look and feel.

Another feature for standardizing websites is *themes*, which let you define a group of formatting presets for virtually any ASP.NET control. With themes, you don't need to worry about painstakingly formatting the controls on every web page. Instead, you can apply a premade theme to your page to effortlessly update the appearance of all the controls it contains. Best of all, once you've standardized on a specific theme and applied it to multiple pages, you can give your entire website a face-lift just by changing the definition for that theme.

Master Page Basics

The best websites don't look like a series of web pages—instead, they give the illusion of a continuously running application. For example, try ordering a book on Amazon. While you search, click through the links, and then head to your shopping cart, you'll always see a continuous user interface with a common header at the top and set of navigation links on the left.

Creating something as polished with ASP.NET is possible, but it isn't as easy as it seems. For example, what if you want a navigation bar on every web page? Not only do you need to copy the same user interface markup to each page, you also need to make sure it ends up in the same place. An offset of a couple of pixels will completely ruin the illusion, making it obvious that the pages aren't really integrated. And even if you copy your markup perfectly, you're still left with an extremely brittle design. If you decide to update your navigation bar later, you'll need to modify every web page to apply the same change.

So, how can you deal with the complexity of different pages that need to look and act the same? One option is to subdivide the page into *frames*. Frames are an HTML feature that lets the browser show more than one web page alongside another. Unfortunately, frames have problems of their own, including that each frame is treated as a separate document and requested separately by the browser. This makes it difficult to create code that communicates between frames. A better choice is to use ASP.NET's master pages feature, which allows you to define page templates and reuse them across your website.

■ **Note** Frames are also out of favor because they limit your layout options. That's because each frame occupies a separate, fixed portion of a window. When you scroll one frame, the other frames remain fixed in place. To create frames that work properly, you need to make assumptions about the target device and its screen size. Most popular websites (think Google, Amazon, and eBay) don't use frames.

Master pages are similar to ordinary ASP.NET pages. Like ordinary pages, master pages are text files that can contain HTML, web controls, and code. However, master pages have a different file extension (.master instead of .aspx), and they can't be viewed directly by a browser. Instead, master pages must be used by other pages, which are known as *content pages*. Essentially, the master page defines the page structure and the common ingredients. The content pages adopt this structure and just fill it with the appropriate content.

For example, if a website such as `http://www.amazon.com` had been created using ASP.NET, a single master page might define the layout for the entire site. Every page would use that master page, and as a result every page would have the same basic organization and the same title, footer, and so on. However, each page would also insert its specific information, such as product descriptions, book reviews, or search results, into this template.

A Simple Master Page and Content Page

To see how this works, it helps to create a simple example. To create a master page in Visual Studio, select Website ➤ Add New Item from the menu. Select Master Page, give it a file name, and click OK.

When you create a new master page in Visual Studio, you start with a blank page that includes a single ContentPlaceHolder control (see Figure 10-1). The ContentPlaceHolder is the portion of the master page that a content page can change. Or, to look at it another way, everything else in a master page is unchangeable. If you add a header, that header appears in every content page. If you want to give the content page the opportunity to supply content in a specific section of the page, you need to add a ContentPlaceHolder.

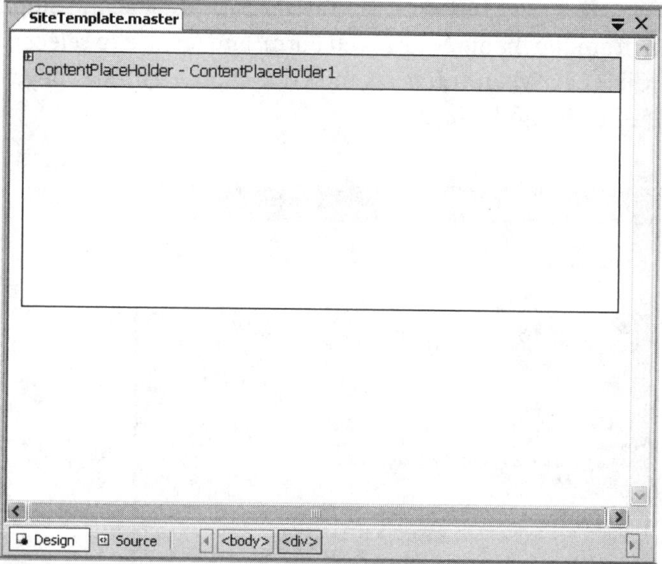

Figure 10-1. *A new master page*

When you first create a master page, you'll start with nothing more than a single ContentPlaceHolder. To make the example more practical, try adding a header before the ContentPlaceHolder and a footer after it, as shown in Figure 10-2.

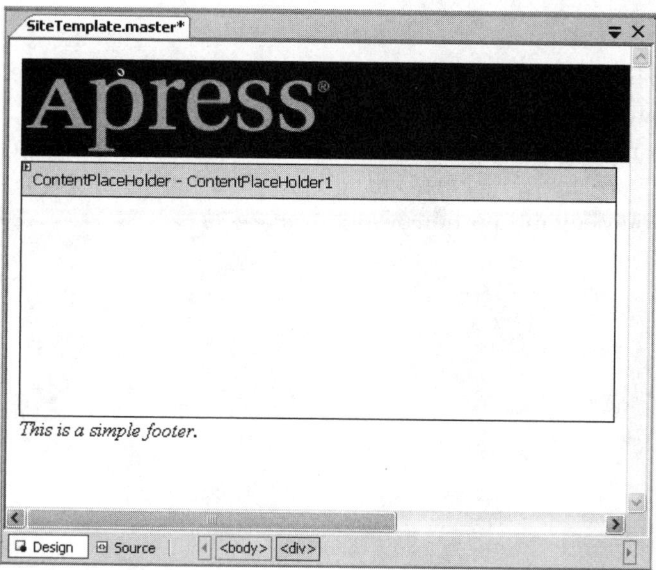

Figure 10-2. *A simple master page with a header and footer*

Now you're ready to create a content page based on this master page. To take this step, select Website ➤ Add New Item from the menu. Select Web Form, and choose to select a master page (see Figure 10-3). Click OK. When you're prompted to choose a master page, use the one you created with the header and footer.

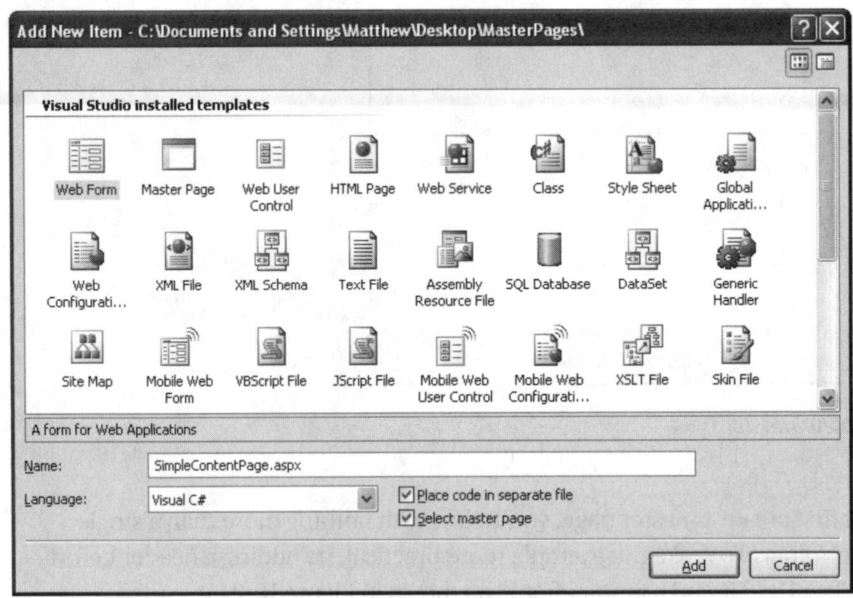

Figure 10-3. *Creating a content page*

Now you'll see something a little more interesting. Your content page will have all the elements of the master page, but the elements will be shaded in gray, indicating you can't select or change them in any way. However, you can add content or drag and drop new controls into the ContentPlaceHolder region to create a page like the one shown in Figure 10-4. In fact, this is the only editable portion of your page.

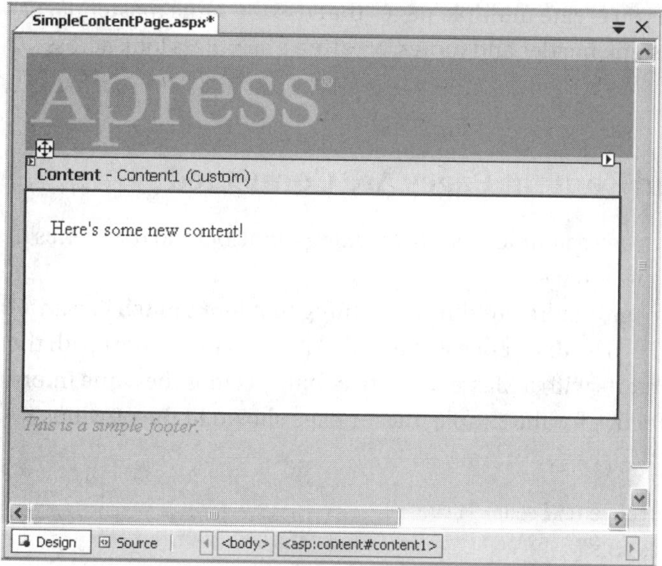

Figure 10-4. *A simple content page at design time*

The design-time representation is a little misleading. That's because when you run the page, the ContentPlaceHolder section will expand or collapse to fit the content you place in it. If you've added volumes of text, the footer won't appear until the end. And if you've included only a single line of text, you'll see something more compact, as in Figure 10-5.

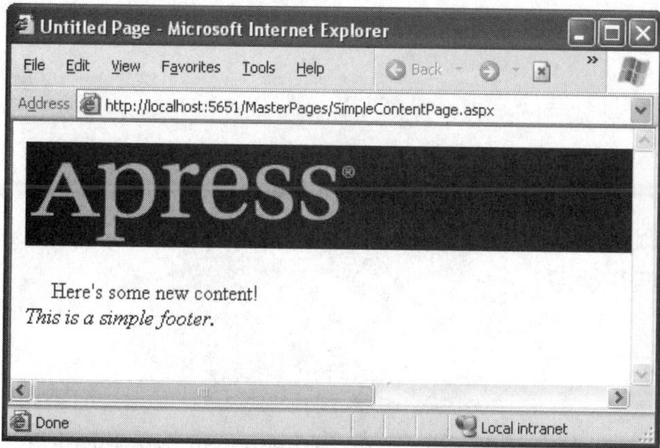

Figure 10-5. *A simple content page at runtime*

The real magic starts when you create multiple pages that use the same master page. Now, each page will have the same header and footer, creating a seamless look across your entire website.

How Master Pages and Content Pages Are Connected

Now that you've seen a master page example, it's worth taking a look behind the scenes to see how you implement the master page.

When you create a master page, you're building something that looks much like an ordinary ASP.NET web form. The key difference is that although web forms start with the Page directive, a master page starts with a Master directive that specifies the same information. Here's the Master directive for the simple master page shown in the previous example:

```
<%@ Master Language="C#" AutoEventWireup="true"
CodeFile="SiteTemplate.master.cs"
    Inherits="SiteTemplate" %>
```

The ContentPlaceHolder is less interesting. You declare it like any ordinary control. Here's the complete code for the simple master page:

```
<%@ Master Language="C#" AutoEventWireup="true"
CodeFile="SiteTemplate.master.cs"
    Inherits="SiteTemplate" %>
<head runat="server">
    <title>Untitled Page</title>
</head>
<body>
    <form id="form1" runat="server">
        <img src="apress.jpg" /><br />
        <asp:ContentPlaceHolder id="ContentPlaceHolder1" runat="server">
        </asp:ContentPlaceHolder>
        <i>This is a simple footer.</i>
    </form>
</body>
</html>
```

When you create a content page, ASP.NET links your page to the master page by adding an attribute to the Page directive. This attribute, named MasterPageFile, indicates the associated master page. Here's what it looks like:

```
<%@ Page Language="C#" MasterPageFile="~/SiteTemplate.master"
    AutoEventWireup="true" CodeFile="SimpleContentPage.aspx.cs"
    Inherits="SimpleContentPage" Title="Untitled Page" %>
```

Notice that the MasterPageFile attribute begins with the path ~/ to specify the root website folder. If you specify just the filename, ASP.NET checks a predetermined subfolder (named MasterPages) for your master page. If you haven't created this folder or your master page isn't there, ASP.NET checks the root of your web folder next. Using the ~/ syntax is better, because it indicates unambiguously where ASP.NET can find your master page.

Note You can use the ~/ characters to create a *root-relative path*—a path that always starts from the root folder of your web application. This is a special syntax understood by ASP.NET and its server controls. You can't use this syntax with ordinary HTML. For example, this syntax won't work in an ordinary hyperlink that isn't a server control (such as the <a> tag).

The Page directive has another new attribute—Title. That's because the master page, as the outermost shell of the page, always defines the <head> section of the page, which includes its title. Remember, your content page can't modify anything that's in the master page. However, this is an obvious shortcoming with the title information, so to circumvent it ASP.NET adds the Title attribute, which you can set to override the title specified in the master page with something more appropriate. This system works as long as the master page has the runat="server" attribute in the <head> tag, which is the default.

The rest of the content page looks a little different from an ordinary web form. That's because the content page can't define anything that's already provided in the master page, including the <head> section, the root <html> element, the <body> element, and so on. In fact, the content page can do only one thing—it can supply a Content tag that corresponds to the ContentPlaceHolder in the master page. This is where you insert the content for this page. As a result, your content pages are a little bit simpler than ordinary web pages.

Here's the complete code for the simple content page, with a single line of text and two line breaks added:

```
<%@ Page Language="C#" MasterPageFile="~/SiteTemplate.master"
    AutoEventWireup="true" CodeFile="SimpleContentPage.aspx.cs"
    Inherits="SimpleContentPage" Title="Untitled Page" %>
<asp:Content ID="Content1" ContentPlaceHolderID="ContentPlaceHolder1"
  runat="Server">
    <br />
    Here's some new content!
    <br />
</asp:Content>
```

For ASP.NET to process this page successfully, the ContentPlaceHolderID attribute in the <Content> tag must match the ContentPlaceHolder specified in the master page exactly. This is how ASP.NET knows where it should insert your content in the master page template.

■ **Tip** If a master page defines a ContentPlaceHolder but your content page doesn't define a corresponding Content control, you'll see a black box in its place when you design the page in Visual Studio. To add the required Content control, right-click that section of the page, and choose Create Custom Content.

You should realize one important fact by looking at the content page markup. Namely, the content from the master page (the address bar and the footer) *isn't* inserted into the content file. Instead, ASP.NET grabs these details from the master page when it processes the page. This has an important effect. It means that if you want to change the header or footer that's used in all your content pages, you need to change only one file—the master page. When you make this change, it will appear in all content pages automatically. In other words, master pages don't just let you reuse standard elements; they also make it easy to update these details later.

■ **Tip** Now that you understand how to hook up master pages and child pages, you can easily take an existing page and modify it to use your master page. However, you'll need to remove some of the basic boilerplate tags, such as <html>, <head>, and <body>, and wrap all the content in one or more <Content> tags. Visual Studio won't add the Content control automatically except when you're creating a new content page from scratch.

A Master Page with Multiple Content Regions

Master pages aren't limited to one ContentPlaceHolder. Instead, you can insert as many as you need to give the client the ability to intersperse content in various places. All you need to do is add multiple ContentPlaceHolder controls and arrange them appropriately.

Figure 10-6 shows a master page that needs more careful consideration. It includes an initial ContentPlaceHolder where the user can insert content and then a shaded box (created by a <div> tag) that contains a heading (*OTHER LINKS*) and second ContentPlaceHolder. The idea here is that the page is split into two logical sections. In the content page, you won't need to worry about how to format each section or how to position the other links box. Instead, you simply supply content for each portion, and ASP.NET will insert it into the correct location in the master page.

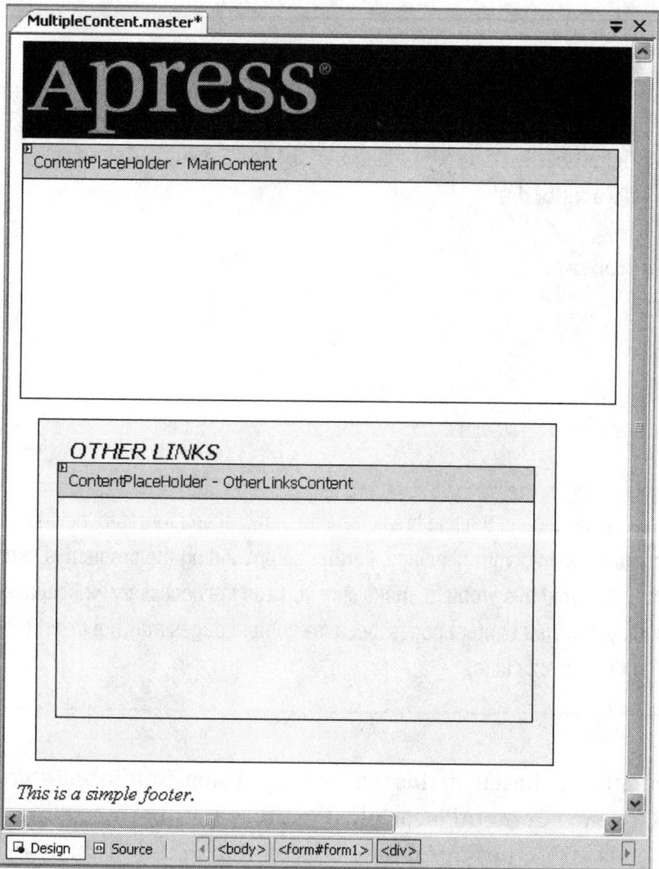

Figure 10-6. *A master page with two content regions*

Here's the code for the master page (with the style portion of the <div> tag omitted to save space):

```
<%@ Master Language="C#" AutoEventWireup="true"
    CodeFile="MultipleContent.master.cs" Inherits="MultipleContent" %>
<html xmlns="http://www.w3.org/1999/xhtml" >
<head id="Head1" runat="server">
    <title>Untitled Page</title>
</head>
<body>
    <form id="form1" runat="server">
        <img src="apress.jpg" /><br />
        <asp:ContentPlaceHolder id="MainContent" runat="server">
        </asp:ContentPlaceHolder>
```

```
        <i>
            <div style="...">
                <b>OTHER LINKS</b>
                <br />
                <asp:ContentPlaceHolder id="OtherLinksContent" runat="server">
                </asp:ContentPlaceHolder>
            </div>
            This is a simple footer.
        </i>
    </form>
</body>
</html>
```

■ **Tip** The most underrated part of a master page is the line break, or <br /> tag. If you forget to include it, you can easily end up having child content run into your headings. Further compounding the problem is that this isn't always obvious at design time. To avoid this problem, make sure you add the necessary whitespace in your master page. Never rely on adding it in your content pages, because content pages may not insert the correct amount of space (or insert it in the correct place).

When you create a new content page based on this master page, Visual Studio will start you with one Content control for each ContentPlaceHolder in the master page, making your life easy. All you need to do is insert the appropriate information. Here's a slightly shortened example:

```
<%@ Page Language="C#" MasterPageFile="~/MultipleContent.master"
    AutoEventWireup="true" CodeFile="MultipleContentPage.aspx.cs"
    Inherits="MultipleContentPage" Title="Untitled Page" %>
<asp:Content ID="Content1" ContentPlaceHolderID="MainContent" runat="Server">
    This is the generic content for this page. Here you might provide some site
    specific text ... </asp:Content>
<asp:Content ID="Content2" ContentPlaceHolderID="OtherLinksContent"
  runat="Server">
    Here's a <a href="http://www.prosetech.com">link</a>.<br />
    ...
</asp:Content>
```

Figure 10-7 shows the final result. Notice how the two content sections flow into their designated locations seamlessly.

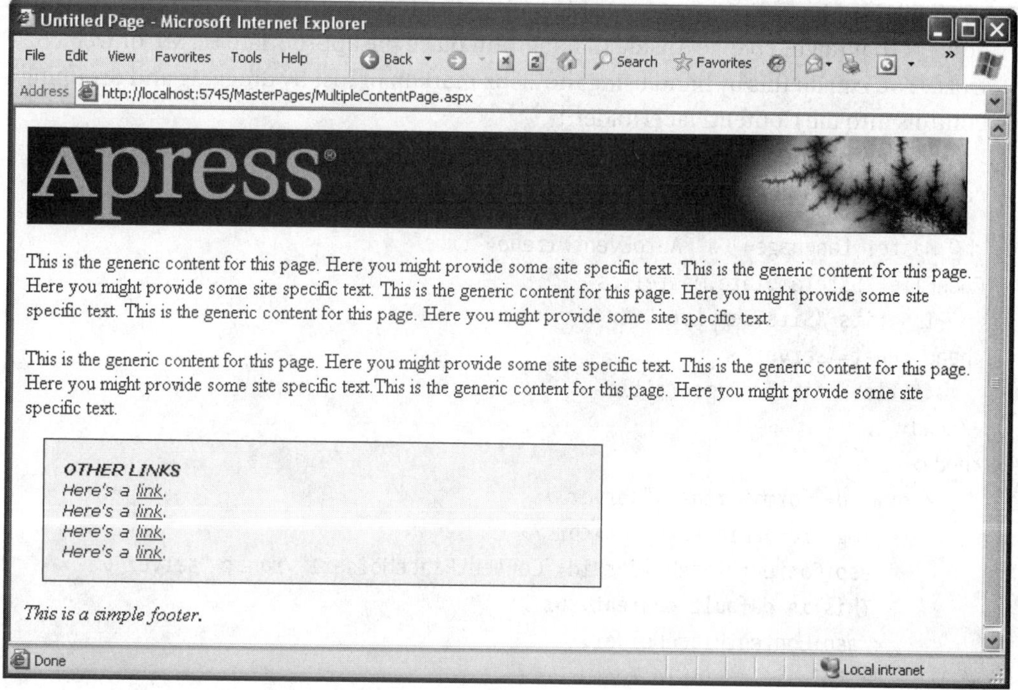

Figure 10-7. *Using the multiple content master page*

Another important trick is at work in this example. The master page doesn't just define the structure of the web page; it also supplies some important style characteristics (such as a default font and background color) through the <div> tag. This is another handy trick to offload the formatting work to the master page, which allows you to maintain it and modify it much more easily. In the second half of this chapter, you'll find out about themes, which give you another way to reuse formatting in a website.

■ **Caution** If you create a master page without a single ContentPlaceHolder, content pages won't be able to supply any content at all, and they'll always show the master page exactly!

Default Content

So far, you've seen master page examples with two types of content: fixed content and page-supplied content. However, in some cases your situation might not be as clear-cut. You might have some content that the content page may or may not want to replace. You can deal with this using default content.

Here's how it works: You create a master page and create a ContentPlaceHolder for the content that might change. Inside that tag, you place the appropriate HTML or web controls. (You can do this by hand using the .aspx markup or just by dragging and dropping controls into the ContentPlaceHolder.)

For example, here's a version of the simple header-and-footer master page shown earlier, with default content:

```
<%@ Master Language="C#" AutoEventWireup="true"
CodeFile="SiteTemplate.master.cs"
    Inherits="SiteTRemplate" %>
<head runat="server">
    <title>Untitled Page</title>
</head>
<body>
    <form id="form1" runat="server">
        <img src="apress.jpg" /><br />
        <asp:ContentPlaceHolder id="ContentPlaceHolder1" runat="server">
         This is default content.<br />
        </asp:ContentPlaceHolder>
        <i>This is a simple footer.</i>
    </form>
</body>
</html>
```

So, what happens when you create a content page based on this master page? If you use Visual Studio, you won't see any change. That's because Visual Studio automatically creates a <Content> tag for each ContentPlaceHolder. When a content page includes a <Content> tag, it automatically overrides the default content.

However, something interesting happens if you delete the <Content> tag. Now when you run the page, you'll see the default content. In other words, default content appears only when the content page chooses not to specify any content for that placeholder.

You might wonder whether the content pages can use *some* of the default content or just edit it slightly. This isn't possible because the default content is stored only in the master page, not in the content page. As a result, you need to decide between using the default content as is or replacing it completely.

Master Pages and Relative Paths

One quirk that can catch unsuspecting developers is the way that master pages handle relative paths. If all you're using is static text, this issue won't affect you. However, if you add <img> tags or any other HTML tag that points to another resource, problems can occur.

The problem shows up if you place the master page in a different directory from the content page that uses it. This is a recommended best practice for large websites. In fact, Microsoft encourages you to use a dedicated folder for storing all your master pages. However, if you're not suitably careful, this can cause problems when you use relative paths.

For example, imagine you put a master page in a subfolder named MasterPages and add the following <img> tag to the master page:

```
<img src="banner.jpg" />
```

Assuming the file \MasterPages\banner.jpg exists, this appears to work fine. The image will even appear in the Visual Studio design environment. However, if you create a content page in another subfolder, the image path is interpreted relative to that folder. If the file doesn't exist there, you'll get a broken link instead of your graphic. Even worse, you could conceivably get the wrong graphic if another image has the same file name.

This problem occurs because the <img> tag is ordinary HTML. As a result, ASP.NET won't touch it. Unfortunately, when ASP.NET processes your content page, the relative path in this tag is no longer appropriate. The same problem occurs with <a> tags that provide relative links to other pages.

To solve your problem, you could try to think ahead and write your URL relative to the content page where you want to use it. But this creates confusion and limits where your master page can be used. A better fix is to turn your <img> tag into a server-side control, in which case ASP.NET will fix the mistake:

```
<img src="banner.jpg" runat="server"/>
```

This works because ASP.NET uses this information to create an HtmlImage server control. This object is created after the Page object for the master page is instantiated. At this point, ASP.NET interprets all the paths relative to the location of the master page.

And as with all server-side controls, you can further clear things up by using the ~/ characters to create a root-relative path. Here's an example that clearly points to a picture in an Images folder in the root web application folder:

```
<img src="~/Images/banner.jpg" runat="server"/>
```

Remember, the ~/ syntax is understood only by ASP.NET controls, so you can't use this trick with an <img> tag that doesn't include the runat="server" attribute.

Advanced Master Pages

Using what you've learned, you can create and reuse master pages across your website. However, still more tricks and techniques can help you take master pages to the next level and make them that much more practical. In the following sections, you'll look at how tables can help you organize your layout and how your content pages can interact with the master page class in code.

Table-Based Layouts

For the most part, HTML uses a flow-based layout. That means as more content is added, the page is reorganized and other content is bumped out of the way. This layout can make it difficult to get the result you want with master pages. For example, what happens if you craft the perfect layout, only to have the structure distorted by a huge block of information that's inserted into a <Content> tag?

Although you can't avoid this problem completely, master pages can use HTML tables to help control the layout. With an HTML table, a portion of your page is broken into columns and rows. You can then add a ContentPlaceHolder in a single cell, ensuring that the other content is aligned more or less the way you want. However, you'll need to type the HTML table tags into the .aspx portion of the master page by hand, as Visual Studio doesn't provide any way to design an HTML table at design time.

For a good example, consider a traditional web application with a header, footer, and navigation bar. Figure 10-8 shows how this structure is broken up into a table.

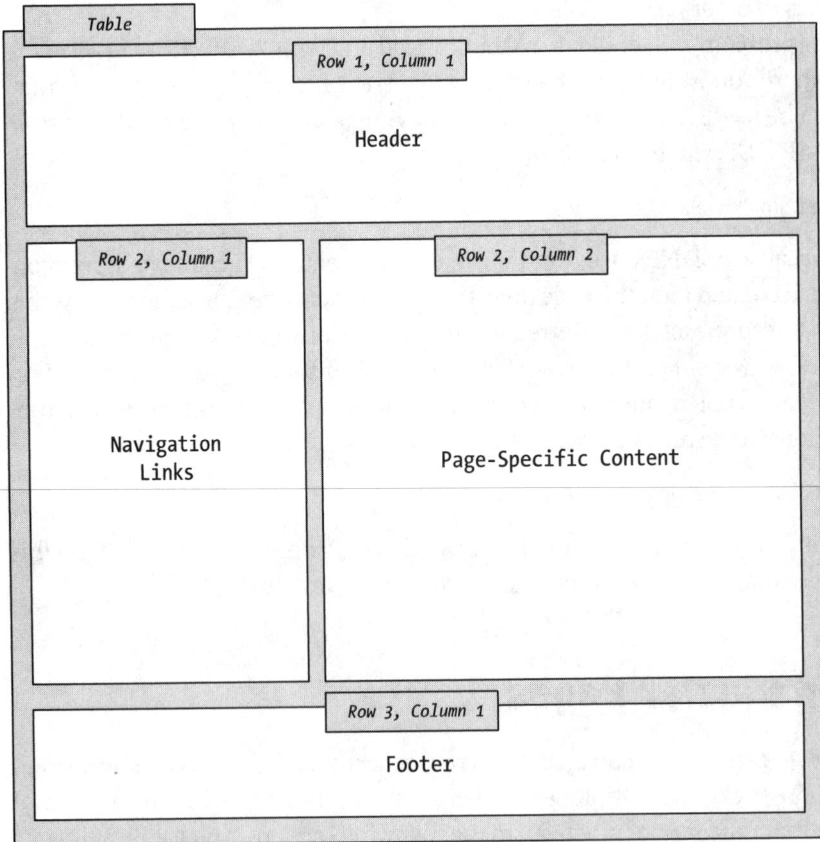

Figure 10-8. *A table-based layout*

In HTML, tables are delineated with the <table> tag. Each row is defined with a nested <tr> tag, and inside each row you can place a <td> tag for each cell. You place the content inside the various <td> tags. Content can include any combination of HTML or web controls.

The number of <td> tags you add in a <tr> defines the number of columns in your table. If you aren't consistent (and usually you won't be), the table takes the dimensions of the row with the most cells.

To create the table shown in Figure 10-8, you start by creating a table and giving it a width of 100% so it fills the browser window:

```
<table width="100%">
  ...
</table>
```

The next step is to add your first row. However, you can use a trick here. The complete table actually has two columns, but the first row (with the header) and the last row (with the footer) need to fill the full width of the table. To accomplish this, you add the colspan attribute and set it to 2, indicating that the header spans two columns:

```
<table width="100%">
  <tr><td colspan="2">My Header</td></tr>
  ...
</table>
```

You can fill in the rest of the table in a similar fashion. The second row has two columns. The first column holds the navigation links (or, in this example, the text *Navigation Controls*) and has a fixed width of 150 pixels. The second column, which fills the remaining space, holds a ContentPlaceHolder where the content page can supply information.

The following code shows the complete table, with some added formatting and background colors that make it easier to distinguish the different sections of the table. Also, the text in the navigation controls section has been replaced with a TreeView.

```
<table width="100%">
    <tr>
        <td colspan="2" bgcolor="#ffccff">
            <h1>My Header</h1>
        </td>
    </tr>
    <tr>
        <td width="150px" bgcolor="#ffffcc">
            <asp:TreeView ID="tree" runat="server" Width="150px">
            </asp:TreeView>
        </td>
```

```
        <td>
            <asp:ContentPlaceHolder id="ContentPlaceHolder1" runat="server">
            </asp:ContentPlaceHolder>
        </td>
    </tr>
    <tr>
        <td colspan="2" bgcolor="#ccff33"><i>My Footer</i></td>
    </tr>
</table>
```

■ **Tip** To learn more about HTML tables and how to specify borders, cell sizes, alignment, and more, refer to the examples at `http://www.w3schools.com/html/html_tables.asp`.

Figure 10-9 shows the resulting master page and a content page that uses the master page (both in Visual Studio).

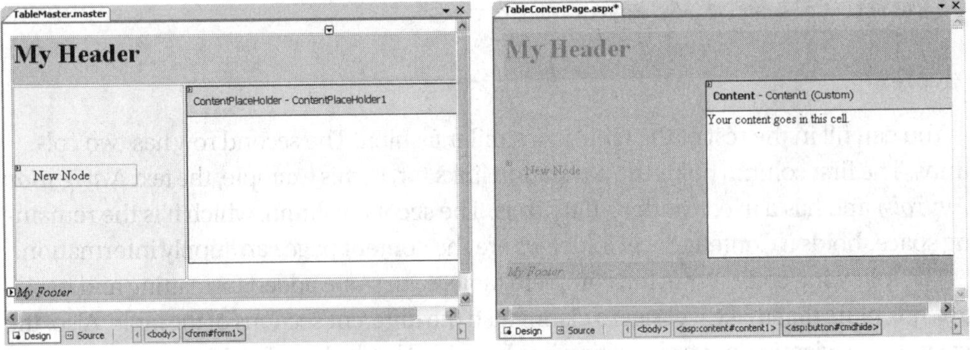

Figure 10-9. *A master page and content page using a table*

To convert this example into something more practical, just replace the static text in the master page with the actual header, navigation controls, and footer you really want. (For example, you may want to use the site map features described in Chapter 11.) All the child pages will acquire these features automatically. This is the first step to defining a practical structure for your entire website.

NESTING MASTER PAGES

You can nest master pages so that one master page uses another master page. This is not used too often, but it could allow you to standardize your website to different degrees. For example, you might have two sections of your website. Each section might require its own navigation controls. However, both sections may need the same header. In this case, you could create a top-level master page that adds the header. Then, you would create a second master page that uses the first master page (through the MasterPageFile attribute). This second master page would get the header and could add the navigation controls. You would create two versions of this second master page, one for each section of your website. Finally, your content pages would use one of the two second-level master pages to standardize their layout.

Be careful when implementing this approach—although it sounds like a nifty way to make a modular design, it can tie you down more than you realize. For example, you'll need to rework your master page hierarchy if you decide later that the two website sections need similar but slightly different headers. Another problem is that Visual Studio doesn't support nested master pages, so you'll need to code them by hand (not graphically). For these reasons, it's usually better to use only one level of master pages and copy the few elements that are in common. In most cases, you won't be creating many master pages, so this won't add a significant amount of duplication.

Code in a Master Page

In all the examples in this chapter, master pages have provided static layout. However, just like a web page, master pages also include a code portion that can respond to events in the page life cycle or the constituent controls. For example, you could respond to the Page.Load event to initialize a master page using code, or you could handle clicks in a set of navigation controls to direct a user to the right page.

Interacting with a Master Page Programmatically

A master control isn't limited to event handling code. It can also provide methods that the content page can trigger as needed or provide properties that the content page can set according to its needs. This allows the content page to interact with the master page.

For example, imagine you want to give the user the ability to collapse the cell with the navigation controls to have more room to see the page content. You don't want to implement this feature in the master page, because you want it to be available only on certain pages. However, the content page obviously can't implement this feature on its own, because it involves modifying a fixed portion of the master page. The solution is to create a way for the content page to interact with the master page so that it can politely ask the master page to collapse or hide the navigation controls as needed.

One good way to implement this design is by adding a new CollapseNavigationControls property to the master page class. This property, when set to true, could then automatically hide the navigation controls. Here's the property you need to add to the master page class:

```
public bool ShowNavigationControls
{
    set
    {
        Treeview1.Visible = value;
    }
    get
    {
        return Treeview1.Visible;
    }
}
```

You should notice a few important facts about this property. First, it's public so that other classed (and therefore other pages) can access it. Second, it just wraps the Visible property in the TreeView control on the master page. Whatever value is passed to CollapseNavigationControls is simply applied to TreeView.Visible. This is useful because ordinarily the TreeView.Visible property isn't directly accessible to the content page.

To access this page, the content page uses the built-in Page.Master property. This page always returns the linked object for the master page. However, you can't access the ShowNavigationControls property directly as Page.Master.ShowNavigationControls, because .NET doesn't know you've added this property. Instead, you need to cast the Page.Master object to the appropriate type. Only then can you call the ShowNavigationControls method.

Here's the button handling code for a content page that hides or shows the navigation controls depending on whether a Hide or Show button is clicked:

```
protected void cmdHide_Click(object sender, EventArgs e)
{
    TableMaster_master master = (TableMaster)this.Master;
    master.ShowNavigationControls = false;
}

protected void cmdShow_Click(object sender, EventArgs e)
{
    TableMaster_master master = (TableMaster)this.Master;
    master.ShowNavigationControls = true;
}
```

Figure 10-10 shows this content page in action.

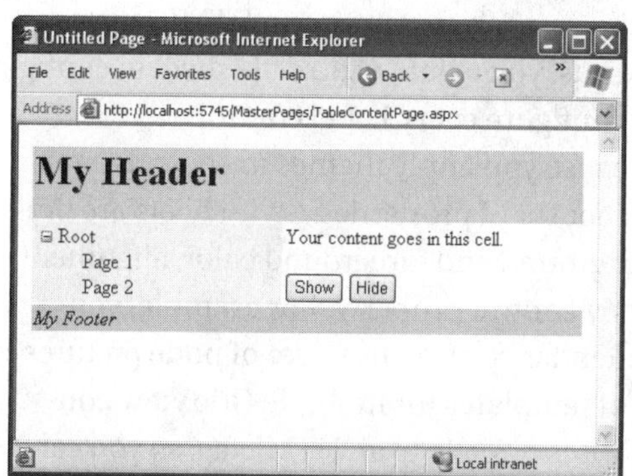

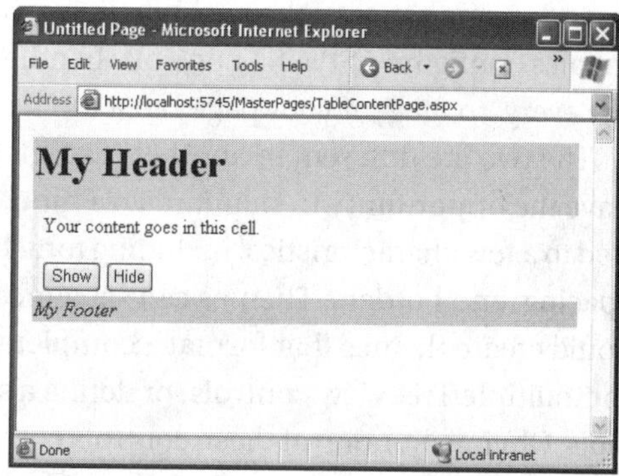

Figure 10-10. *A content page that interacts with its master page*

Note that when you navigate from page to another, all the web page objects are re-created. Even if you move to another content page that uses the same master page, ASP.NET creates a different instance of the master page object. As a result, the TreeView.Visible property of the navigation controls is reset to its default value (true) every time the user navigates to a new page. If this isn't the effect you want, you would need to store the setting somewhere else (such as in a cookie or in session state). Then you could write code in the master page that always checks the last saved value. Chapter 9 has more about the ways you can store information for longer.

Themes

Master pages are a great way to enforce a consistent layout across all your web pages. However, once you make sure your content ends up in the right place, you're still faced with another challenge: formatting. Even though your content pages use the same layout, they won't necessarily adopt the same formatting rules, which means fonts, colors, and other formatting details are sure to clash.

ASP.NET addresses this problem with themes. Here's how it works: You define all the style characteristics for your controls in a separate file. For example, if you want all your check boxes to have bold text and a light-gray background, you define this in your theme file. If you want all your radio buttons to match, you define that in your theme file as well. You can then link your theme file to a web page, which automatically applies all the formatting options to all the check boxes and radio buttons in that page. Best of all, you maintain the style information in themes separately from the page (as with master pages). This means once themes are in place, you can revamp your entire website by modifying the information in your theme.

If you are savvy with HTML, you may recognize that theming sounds a lot like CSS (Cascading Style Sheets), a standard for formatting web pages. However, a significant difference exists between the two. Whereas style sheets apply formatting to HTML elements, themes configure ASP.NET controls. In other words, you would use a style sheet to configure every <p> tag on your page but a theme to configure every Label control.

The two are different in another respect. Because you apply themes to controls, you have the opportunity to standardize a much richer set of properties. Style sheets are limited to a few characteristics, including font, background and foreground color, alignment, spacing, and borders. Themes can set almost any control property. For example, you could create themes that format a complete Calendar control, use a set of node pictures for multiple TreeView controls, or define a set of templates for multiple GridView controls. Obviously, none of these controls corresponds directly to an HTML tag, so you can't get anywhere near this functionality with style sheets.

■ **Note** Unlike style sheets, themes are applied by ASP.NET on the server. As a result, you don't have to worry that your page won't display correctly on a different browser because it implements CSS differently.

How Themes Work

All themes are application-specific. To use a theme in a web application, you need to create a folder that defines it. This folder needs to be placed in a folder named App_Themes, which must be placed inside the top-level directory for your web application. In other words, a web application named SuperCommerce might have a theme named FunkyTheme in the folder SuperCommerce\App_Themes\FunkyTheme. An application can contain definitions for multiple themes, as long as each theme is in a separate folder. Only one theme can be active on a given page at a time.

To actually make your theme accomplish anything, you need to create at least one *skin* file in the theme folder. A *skin file* is a text file with the .skin extension. ASP.NET never serves skin files directly—instead, they're used behind the scenes to define a theme.

A skin file is essentially a list of control tags—with a twist. The control tags in a skin file don't need to completely define the control. Instead, they need to set only the properties that you want to standardize. For example, if you're trying to apply a consistent color scheme, you might be interested in setting only properties such as ForeColor and BackColor. When you add a control tag for the ListBox, it might look like this:

```
<asp:ListBox runat="server" ForeColor="White" BackColor="Orange"/>
```

The runat="server" portion is always required. Everything else is optional. You should avoid setting the ID attribute in your skin, because the page that contains the ListBox needs to define a unique name for the control.

It's up to you whether you create multiple skin files or place all your control tags in a single skin file. Both approaches are equivalent, because ASP.NET treats all the skin files in a theme directory as part of the same theme definition. Often, it makes sense to put the control tags for complex controls (such as the data controls) in separate skin files. Figure 10-11 shows the relationship between themes and skins in more detail.

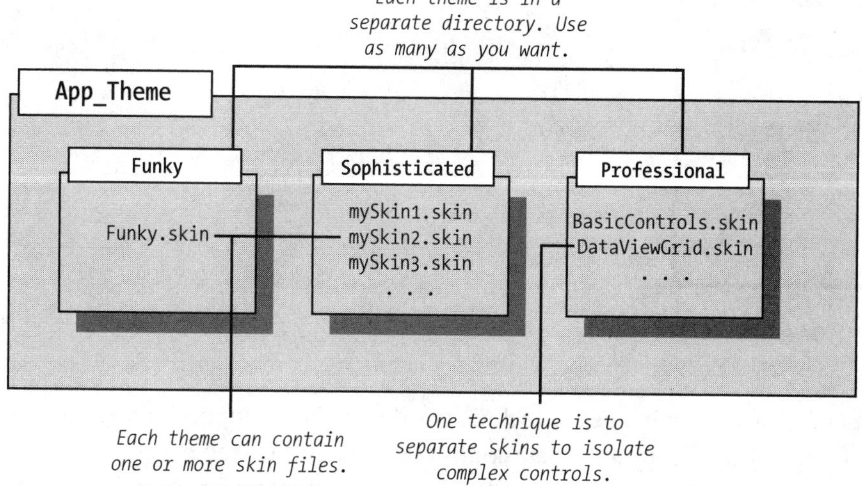

Figure 10-11. *Themes and skins*

ASP.NET also supports global themes. These are themes you place in the c:\Inetpub\wwwroot\aspnet_client\system_web\[Version]\Themes folder. However, it's recommended that you use local themes, even if you want to create more than one website that has the same theme. Using local themes makes it easier to deploy your web application, and it gives you the flexibility to introduce site-specific differences in the future.

If you have a local theme with the same name as a global theme, the local theme takes precedence, and the global theme is ignored. The themes are *not* merged together.

■ **Tip** ASP.NET doesn't ship with any predefined themes. This means you'll need to create your own from scratch or download sample themes from websites such as `http://www.asp.net`.

Applying a Simple Theme

To add a theme to your project, select Website ➤ Add New Item, and choose Skin File. Visual Studio will warn you that skin files need to be placed in a subfolder of the App_Themes folder and ask you whether that's what you intended. If you choose Yes, Visual Studio will create a folder with the same name as your theme file. You can then rename the folder and the file to whatever you'd like to use. Figure 10-12 shows an example with a theme that contains a single skin file.

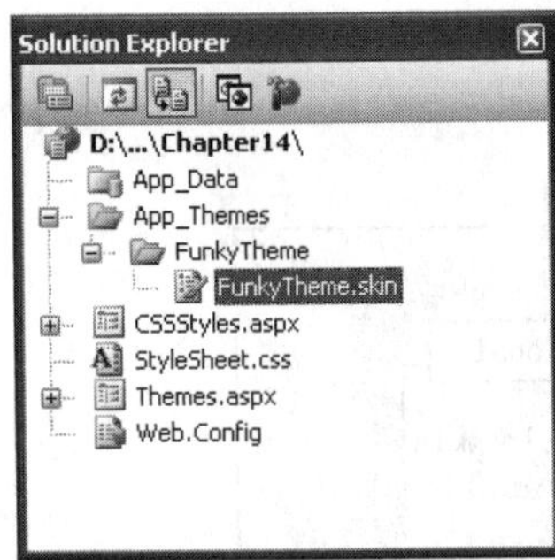

Figure 10-12. *A theme in the Solution Explorer*

Unfortunately, Visual Studio doesn't include any design-time support for creating themes, so it's up to you to copy and paste control tags from other web pages.

Here's a sample skin that sets background and foreground colors for several common controls:

```
<asp:ListBox runat="server" ForeColor="White" BackColor="Orange"/>
<asp:TextBox runat="server" ForeColor="White" BackColor="Orange"/>
<asp:Button runat="server" ForeColor="White" BackColor="Orange"/>
```

To apply the theme in a web page, you need to set the Theme attribute of the Page directive to the folder name for your theme. (ASP.NET will automatically scan all the skin files in that theme.)

```
<%@ Page Language="C#" AutoEventWireup="true" ... Theme="FunkyTheme" %>
```

You can make this change by hand, or you can select the DOCUMENT object in the Properties window at design time and set the Theme property (which provides a handy drop-down list of all your web application's themes). Visual Studio will modify the Page directive accordingly.

When you apply a theme to a page, ASP.NET considers each control on your web page and checks your skin files to see whether they define any properties for that control. If ASP.NET finds a matching tag in the skin file, the information from the skin file overrides the current properties of the control.

Figure 10-13 shows the result of applying the FunkyTheme to a simple page. You'll notice that conflicting settings (such as the existing background for the list box) are overwritten. However, changes that don't conflict (such as the custom font for the buttons) are left in place.

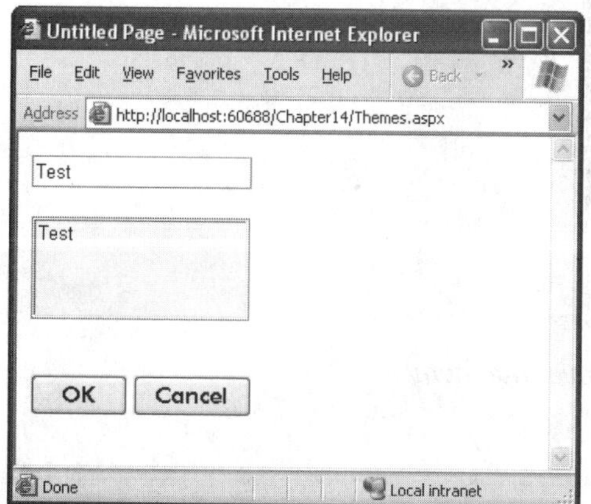

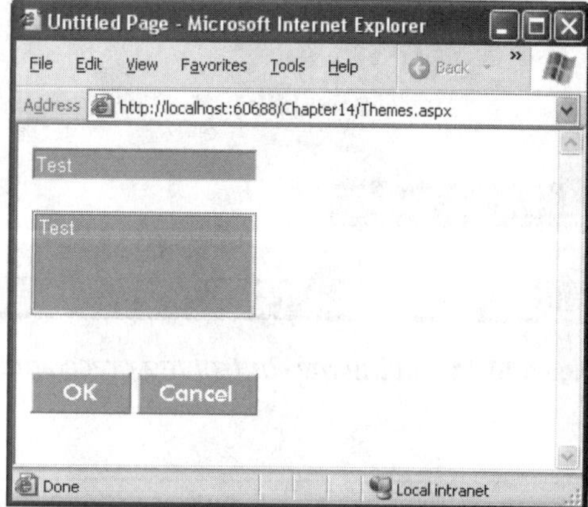

Figure 10-13. *A simple page before and after theming*

Handling Theme Conflicts

As you've seen, when properties conflict between your controls and your theme, the theme wins. However, in some cases you might want to change this behavior so that your controls can fine-tune a theme by specifically overriding certain details. ASP.NET gives you this option, but it's an all-or-nothing setting that applies to all the controls on the entire page.

To make this change, just use the StyleSheetTheme attribute instead of the Theme attribute in the Page directive. (The StyleSheet designation indicates that this setting works more like CSS.) Here's an example:

```
<%@ Page Language="C#" AutoEventWireup="true" ... StyleSheetTheme="FunkyTheme" %>
```

Now the custom yellow background of the ListBox control takes precedence over the background color specified by the theme. Figure 10-14 shows the result—and a potential problem. Because the foreground color has been changed to white, the lettering is now difficult to read. Overlapping formatting specifications can cause glitches like this, which is why it's often better to let your themes take complete control by using the Theme attribute.

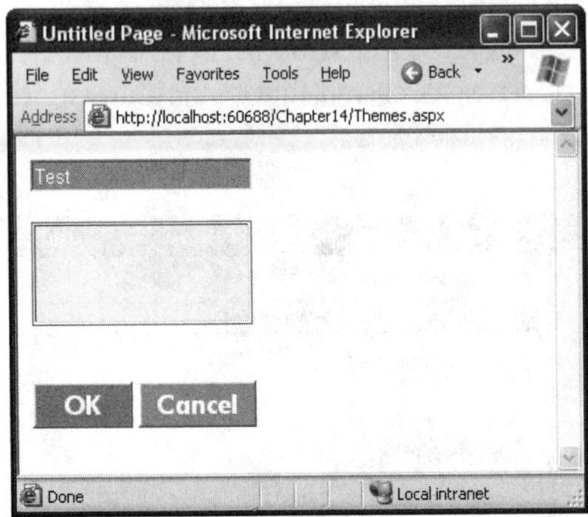

Figure 10-14. *Giving the control tag precedence over the theme*

■ **Note** It's possible to use both the Theme attribute and the StyleSheetTheme attribute at the same time so that some settings are always applied (those in the Theme attribute) and others are applied only if they aren't already specified in the control (those in the StyleSheetTheme attribute). However, in practice this design is terribly confusing and not recommended.

Another option is to configure specific controls so they opt out of the theming process entirely. To do this, simply set the EnableTheming property of the control to false. ASP.NET will still apply the theme to other controls on the page, but it will skip over the control you've configured.

```
<asp:Button ID="Button1" runat="server" ... EnableTheming="false" />
```

APPLYING A THEME TO AN ENTIRE WEBSITE

Using the Page directive, you can bind a theme to a single page. However, you might decide that your theme is ready to be rolled out for the entire web application. The cleanest way to apply this theme is by configuring the <pages> element in the web.config file for your application, as shown here:

```
<configuration>
  <system.web>
    <pages Theme="FunkyTheme" />
  </system.web>
</configuration>
```

If you want to use the style sheet behavior so that the theme doesn't overwrite conflicting control properties, use the StyleSheetTheme attribute instead of Theme:

```
<configuration>
  <system.web>
    <pages styleSheetTheme="FunkyTheme" />
  </system.web>
</configuration>
```

Either way, when you specify a theme in the web.config file, the theme will be applied throughout all the pages in your website, provided these pages don't have their own theme settings. If a page specifies the Theme attribute, the page setting will take precedence over the web.config setting. If your page specifies the Theme attribute with a blank string (Theme=""), no theme will be applied at all.

Using this technique, it's just as easy to apply a theme to part of a web application. For example, you can create a separate web.config file for each subfolder and use the <pages> setting to configure different themes.

Creating Multiple Skins for the Same Control

Having each control locked into a single format is great for standardization, but it's probably not flexible enough for a real-world application. For example, you might have several types of text boxes that are distinguished based on where they're used or what type of data they contain. Labels are even more likely to differ, depending on whether they're being used for headings or body text. Fortunately, ASP.NET allows you to create multiple declarations for the same control.

Ordinarily, if you create more than one theme for the same control, ASP.NET will give you a build error stating that you can have only a single default skin for each control. To get around this problem, you need to create a named skin by supplying a SkinID attribute. Here's an example:

```
<asp:ListBox runat="server" ForeColor="White" BackColor="Orange" />
<asp:TextBox runat="server" ForeColor="White" BackColor="Orange" />
<asp:Button runat="server" ForeColor="White" BackColor="Orange" />
<asp:TextBox runat="server" ForeColor="White" BackColor="DarkOrange"
 Font-Bold="True" SkinID="Dramatic"/>
<asp:Button runat="server" ForeColor="White" BackColor="DarkOrange"
 Font-Bold="True" SkinID="Dramatic"/>
```

The catch is that named skins aren't applied automatically like default skins. To use a named skin, you need to set the SkinID of the control on your web page to match. You can choose this value from a drop-down list that Visual Studio creates based on all your defined skin names, or you can type it in by hand:

```
<asp:Button ID="Button1" runat="server" ... SkinID="Dramatic" />
```

If you don't like the opt-in model for themes, you can make all your skins named. That way, they'll never be applied unless you set the control's SkinID.

ASP.NET is intelligent enough to catch if you try to use a skin name that doesn't exist, in which case you'll get a build warning. The control will then behave as though you set EnableTheming to false, which means it will ignore the corresponding default skin.

■ **Tip** The SkinID doesn't need to be unique. It just has to be unique for each control. For example, imagine you want to create an alternate set of skinned controls that use a slightly smaller font. These controls match your overall theme, but they're useful on pages that display a large amount of information. In this case, you can create new Button, TextBox, and Label controls, and give each one the same skin name (such as Smaller).

Skins with Templates and Images

So far, the theming examples have applied relatively simple properties. However, you could create much more detailed control tags in your skin file. Most control properties support theming. If a property can't be declared in a theme, you'll receive a build error when you attempt to launch your application.

For example, many controls support styles that specify a range of formatting information. The data controls are one example, and the Calendar control provides another. Here's how you might define Calendar styles in a skin file to match your theme:

```
<asp:Calendar ID="Calendar1" runat="server" BackColor="White" ForeColor="Black"
 BorderColor="Black" BorderStyle="Solid" CellSpacing="1"
 Font-Names="Verdana" Font-Size="9pt" Height="250px" Width="500px"
 NextPrevFormat="ShortMonth" SelectionMode="Day">
  <SelectedDayStyle BackColor="DarkOrange" ForeColor="White" />
  <DayStyle BackColor="Orange" Font-Bold="True" ForeColor="White" />
  <NextPrevStyle Font-Bold="True" Font-Size="8pt" ForeColor="White" />
  <DayHeaderStyle Font-Bold="True" Font-Size="8pt" ForeColor="#333333"
   Height="8pt" />
  <TitleStyle BackColor="Firebrick" BorderStyle="None" Font-Bold="True"
   Font-Size="12pt" ForeColor="White" Height="12pt" />
  <OtherMonthDayStyle BackColor="NavajoWhite" Font-Bold="False"
   ForeColor="DarkGray" />
</asp:Calendar>
```

This skin defines the font, colors, and styles of the Calendar control. It also sets the selection mode, the formatting of the month navigation links, and the overall size of the calendar. As a result, all you need to use this formatted calendar is the following streamlined tag:

```
<asp:Calendar ID="Calendar1" runat="server" />
```

■Caution When you create skins that specify details such as sizing, be careful. When these settings are applied to a page, they could cause the layout to change with unintended consequences. If you're in doubt, set a SkinID so that the skin is applied only if the control specifically opts in.

Another powerful technique is to reuse images by making them part of your theme. For example, imagine you perfect an image that you want to use for OK buttons throughout your website and another one for all Cancel buttons. The first step to implement this design is to add the images to your theme folder. For the best organization, it makes sense to create one or more subfolders just for holding images. In this example, the images are stored in a folder named ButtonImages (see Figure 10-15).

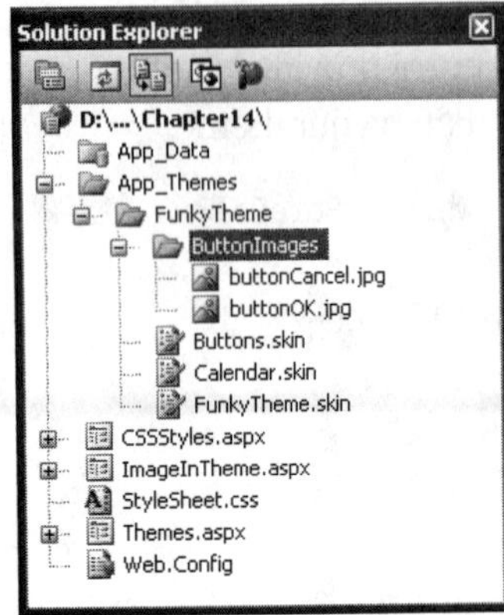

Figure 10-15. *Adding images to a theme*

Now, you need to create the skins that use these images. In this case, both of these tags should be named skins. That's because you're defining a specific type of standardized button that should be available to the page when needed. You *aren't* defining a default style that should apply to all buttons.

```
<asp:ImageButton runat="server" SkinID="OKButton"
 ImageUrl="ButtonImages/buttonOK.jpg" />
<asp:ImageButton runat="server" SkinID="CancelButton"
 ImageUrl="ButtonImages/buttonCancel.jpg" />
```

When you add a reference to an image in a skin file, always make sure the image URL is relative to the theme folder, not the folder where the page is stored. When this theme is applied to a control, ASP.NET automatically inserts the App_Themes\ThemeName portion at the beginning of the URL.

APPLYING THEMES DYNAMICALLY

In some cases, themes aren't used to standardize website appearance but to make that appearance configurable for each user. All you need to do to implement this design is to simply set the Page.Theme or Page.StyleSheet property dynamically in your code. For example, set Page.Theme to the string "FunkyTheme" to apply the theme in the FunkyTheme directory. The only caveat is that you need to complete this step in the Page.Init event stage. After this point, attempting to set the property causes a compilation error. Similarly, you can also set the SkinID property of a control dynamically to attach it to a different named skin. But be careful—if a theme or skin change leads to a control specifying a skin name that doesn't exist in the current theme, an exception will be thrown.

Now to apply these images, simply create an ImageButton in your web page that references the corresponding skin name:

```
<asp:ImageButton ID="ImageButton1" runat="server" SkinID="OKButton" />
<asp:ImageButton ID="ImageButton2" runat="server" SkinID="CancelButton" />
```

You can use the same technique to create skins for other controls that use images. For example, you can standardize the node pictures of a TreeView, the bullet image used for the BulletList control, or the icons used in a GridView.

The Last Word

Building a professional web application involves much more than designing individual web pages. You also need the tools to integrate your web pages in a complete, unified website. In this chapter, you considered two new ASP.NET features that let you do that. Master pages allow you to standardize the layout of your website. Themes effortlessly apply groups of formatting settings. Both features make it easy to bring your pages together into a well-integrated web application.

The Last Word

CHAPTER 11

■ ■ ■

Website Navigation

You've already learned simple ways to send a website visitor from one page to another. For example, you can add HTML links (or HyperLink controls) to your page to let users surf through your site. If you want to perform page navigation in response to another action, you can call the Response.Redirect() method or the Response.Transfer() method in your code. But in professional web applications, the navigation requirements are more intensive. These applications need a system that allows users to surf through a hierarchy of pages, without forcing you write the same tedious navigation code in every page.

Fortunately, ASP.NET includes a navigation model that makes it easy to let users surf through your web applications. Before you can use this model, you need to determine the hierarchy of your website—in other words, how pages are logically organized into groups. You then define that structure in a dedicated file and bind that information to specialized navigation controls. Best of all, these navigation controls include nifty widgets such as the TreeView and Menu.

In this chapter, you'll learn everything you need to know about the new site map model and the navigation controls that work with it.

Site Maps

If your website has more than a handful of pages, you'll probably want some sort of navigation system to let users move from one page to the next. Obviously, you can use the ASP.NET toolkit of controls to implement almost any navigation system, but this requires that *you* perform all the hard work. Fortunately, ASP.NET has a set of navigation features that can simplify the task dramatically.

As with all the best ASP.NET features, ASP.NET navigation is flexible, configurable, and pluggable. It consists of three components:

- A way to define the navigational structure of your website. This part is the XML site map, which is (by default) stored in a file.
- A convenient way to read the information in the site map file and convert it to an object model. The SiteMapDataSource control and the XmlSiteMapProvider perform this part.
- A way to use the site map information to display the user's current position and give the user the ability to easily move from one place to another. This part takes place through the navigation controls you bind to the SiteMapDataSource control, which can include breadcrumb links, lists, menus, and trees.

You can customize or extend each of these ingredients separately. For example, if you want to change the appearance of your navigation controls, you simply need to bind different controls to the SiteMapDataSource. On the other hand, if you want to read site map information from a different type of file or from a different location, you need to change your site map provider.

Figure 11-1 shows how these pieces fit together.

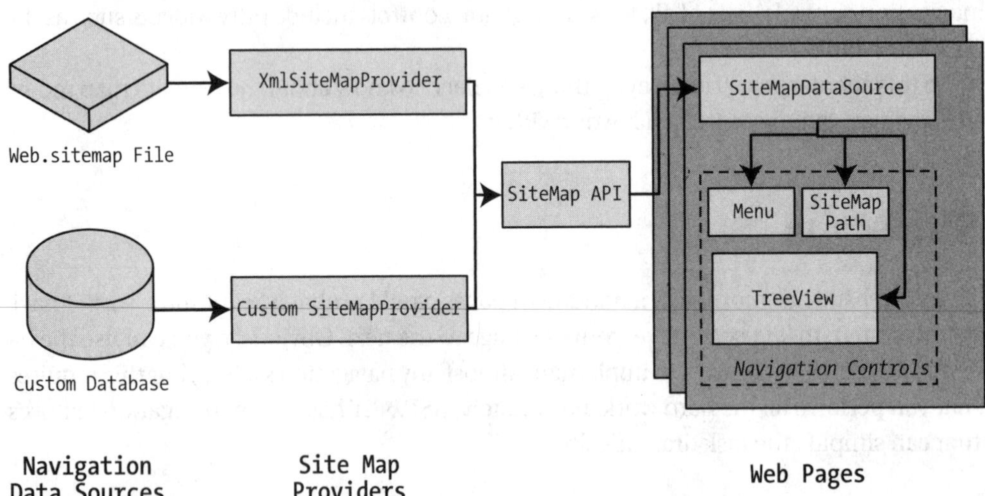

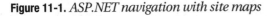

Figure 11-1. *ASP.NET navigation with site maps*

Defining a Site Map

The starting point in site map–based navigation is the site map provider. ASP.NET ships with a single site map provider, named XmlSiteMapProvider, which is able to retrieve site map information from an XML file. If you want to retrieve a site map from another location or in a custom format, you'll need to create your own site map provider or look for a third-party solution on the Web.

The XmlSiteMapProvider looks for a file named Web.sitemap in the root of the virtual directory. Like all site map providers, the task of the XmlSiteMapProvider is to extract the site map data and create the corresponding SiteMap object. This SiteMap object is then made available to the SiteMapDataSource, which you place on every page that uses navigation. The SiteMapDataSource provides the site map information to navigation controls, which are the final link in the chain.

You can create a site map using a text editor such as Notepad, or you can create it in Visual Studio by selecting Website ➤ Add New Item and then choosing the Site Map option. Either way, it's up to you to enter all the site map information by hand. The only difference is that if you create it in Visual Studio, the site map will start with a basic structure that consists of three nodes.

Before you can fill in the content in your site map file, you need to understand the rules that all ASP.NET site maps must follow. The following sections break these rules down piece by piece.

■ **Note** Before you begin creating site maps, it helps to have a basic understanding of XML, the format that's used for the site map file. You should understand what an element is, how to start and end an element, and why exact capitalization is so important. If you're new to XML, you may find that it helps to refer to Chapter 17 for a quick introduction before you read this chapter.

Rule 1: Site Maps Begin with the <siteMap> Element

Every Web.sitemap file begins by declaring the <siteMap> element and ends by closing that element. You place the actual site map information between the start and end tag (where the three dots are shown):

```
<siteMap xmlns="http://schemas.microsoft.com/AspNet/SiteMap-File-1.0">
    ...
</siteMap>
```

Rule 2: Each Page Is Represented by a <siteMapNode> Element

So, what does the site map content look like? Essentially, every site map defines an organization of web pages. To insert a page into the site map, you add the <siteMapNode> element with some basic information. Namely, you need to supply the title of the page (which appears in the navigation controls), a description (which you may or may not choose to use), and the URL (the link for the page). You add these three pieces of information using three attributes. The attributes are named title, description, and url, as shown here:

```
<siteMapNode title="Home" description="Home" url="~/Default.aspx" />
```

Notice that this element ends with the characters />. This indicates it's an *empty element* that represents a start tag and an end tag in one. Empty elements (an XML concept described in Chapter 17) never contain other nodes.

And here's a complete, valid site map file that uses this page to define a website with exactly one page:

```
<siteMap xmlns="http://schemas.microsoft.com/AspNet/SiteMap-File-1.0">
    <siteMapNode title="Home" description="Home" url="~/Default.aspx" />
</siteMap>
```

Notice that the URL for each page begins with the ~/ character sequence. This is quite important. The ~/ characters represent the root folder of your web application. In other words, the URL ~/Default.aspx points to the Default.aspx file in the root folder. This style of URL isn't required, but it's strongly recommended, because it makes sure you always get the right page. If you were to simply enter the URL Default.aspx without the ~/ prefix, ASP.NET would look for the Default.aspx page in the *current* folder. If you have a web application with pages in more than one folder, you'll run into a problem.

For example, if the user browses into a subfolder and clicks the Default.aspx link, ASP.NET will look for the Default.aspx page in that subfolder instead of in the root folder. Because the Default.aspx page isn't in this folder, the navigation attempt will fail with a 404 Not Found error.

Rule 3: A <siteMapNode> Element Can Contain Other <siteMapNode> Elements

Site maps don't consist of simple lists of pages. Instead, they divide pages into groups. To represent this in a site map file, you place one <siteMapNode> inside another. Instead of using the empty element syntax shown previously, you'll need to split your <siteMapNode> element into a start tag and an end tag:

```
<siteMapNode title="Home" description="Home" url="~/Default.aspx">
    ...
</siteMapNode>
```

Now you can slip more nodes inside. For example, here's an example where a Home group contains two more pages:

```
<siteMapNode title="Home" description="Home" url="~/Default.aspx">
    <siteMapNode title="Products" description="Our products"
      url="~/Products.aspx">
    <siteMapNode title="Hardware" description="Hardware choices"
      url="~/Hardware.aspx" />
</siteMapNode>
```

Essentially, this represents the hierarchical group of links shown in Figure 11-2.

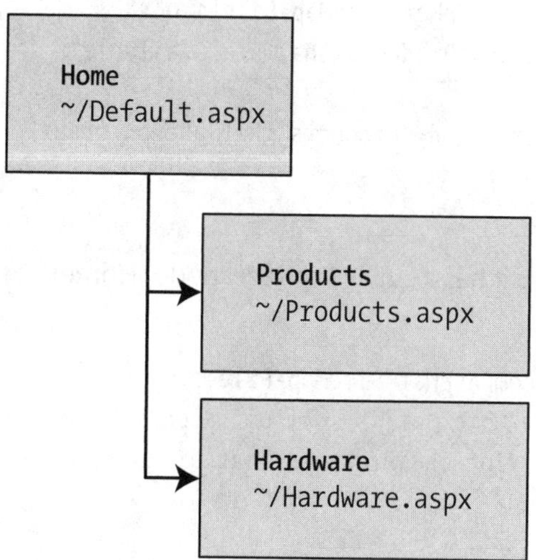

Figure 11-2. *Three nodes in a site map*

In this case, all three nodes are links. This means the user could surf to one of three pages. However, when you start to create more complex groups and subgroups, you might want to create nodes that serve only to organize other nodes but aren't themselves as links. In this case, just omit the url attribute, as shown here with the Products node:

```
<siteMapNode title="Products" description="Products">
    <siteMapNode title="In Stock" description="Products that are available"
      url="~/instock.aspx">
    <siteMapNode title="Not In Stock" description="Products that are on order"
      url="~/outofstock.aspx" />
</siteMapNode>
```

When you show this part of the site map in a web page, the Products node will appear as ordinary text, not a clickable link.

No limit exists to how many layers deep you can nest group and subgroups. However, it's a good rule to go just two or three levels deep; otherwise, it may be difficult for users to grasp the hierarchy when they see it in a navigation control. If you find that you need more than two or three levels, you may need to reconsider how you are organizing your pages into groups.

Rule 4: Every Site Map Begins with a Single <siteMapNode>

Another rule applies to all site maps. A site map always must have a single root node. All the other nodes must be contained inside this root-level node.

That means the following is *not* a valid site map, because it contains two top-level nodes:

```
<siteMap xmlns="http://schemas.microsoft.com/AspNet/SiteMap-File-1.0">
    <siteMapNode title="In Stock" description="Products that are available"
      url="~/instock.aspx">
    <siteMapNode title="Not In Stock" description="Products that are on order"
      url="~/outofstock.aspx" />
</siteMap>
```

However, the following one is valid, because it has a single top-level node (Home), which then contains two more nodes:

```
<siteMap xmlns="http://schemas.microsoft.com/AspNet/SiteMap-File-1.0">
    <siteMapNode title="Home" description="Home" url="~/default.aspx">
        <siteMapNode title="In Stock" description="Products that are available"
          url="~/instock.aspx">
        <siteMapNode title="Not In Stock"
          description="Products that are on order"
          url="~/outofstock.aspx" />
    </siteMapNode>
</siteMap>
```

As long as you use only one top-level node, you can nest nodes as deep as you want, in groups as large or as small as you want.

Rule 5: Duplicate URLs Are Not Allowed

You cannot create two site map nodes with the same URL. This might seem to present a bit of a problem in cases where you want to have the same link in more than one place—and it does. However, it's a requirement because the default SiteMapProvider included with ASP.NET stores nodes in a collection, with each item indexed by its unique URL.

This limitation doesn't prevent you from creating more than one URL that points to the same page but has a minor difference. For example, the following two nodes are acceptable, even though they lead to the same page (products.aspx). That's because the two URLs have different query string arguments at the end.

```
<siteMapNode title="In Stock" description="Products that are available"
  url="~/products.aspx?stock=1">
<siteMapNode title="Not In Stock" description="Products that are on order"
  url="~/products.aspx?stock=0" />
```

As a general rule of thumb, you shouldn't use this technique just to create multiple entries that point to the same page. However, if you really do use the query string argument in your page code, this is a valid technique. For example, you might use this approach to tell a single page to display different information, depending on which link the user clicks. Chapter 9 describes the query string in more detail.

Seeing a Simple Site Map in Action

A typical site map can be a little overwhelming at first glance. However, if you keep the five rules described previously in mind, you'll be able to sort out exactly what's taking place.

The following is an example that consists of seven nodes. (Remember, each *node* is a link to an individual page or a heading used to organize a group of pages.) The example defines a simple site map for a company named RevoTech.

```
<siteMap xmlns="http://schemas.microsoft.com/AspNet/SiteMap-File-1.0">
    <siteMapNode title="Home" description="Home" url="~/default.aspx">

        <siteMapNode title="Information" description="Learn about our company">
            <siteMapNode title="About Us" description="How RevoTech was founded"
              url="~/aboutus.aspx" />
            <siteMapNode title="Investing"
              description="Financial reports and investor analysis"
              url="~/financial.aspx" />
        </siteMapNode>

        <siteMapNode title="Products" description="Learn about our products">
            <siteMapNode title="RevoStock"
              description="Investment software for stock charting"
              url="~/product1.aspx" />
            <siteMapNode title="RevoAnalyze"
              description="Investment software for yield analysis"
              url="~/product2.aspx" />
        </siteMapNode>

    </siteMapNode>
</siteMap>
```

■ **Note** The URL in the site map is not case-sensitive.

In the following section, you'll bind this site map to the controls in a page, and you'll see its structure emerge.

Binding an Ordinary Page to a Site Map

Once you've defined the Web.sitemap file, you're ready to use it in a page. First, it's a good idea to make sure you've created all the pages that are listed in the site map file, even if you leave them blank. Otherwise, you'll have trouble testing whether the site map navigation actually works.

The next step is to add the SiteMapDataSource control to your page. You can drag and drop it from the Data tab of the Toolbox. It creates a tag like this:

```
<asp:SiteMapDataSource ID="SiteMapDataSource1" runat="server" />
```

The SiteMapDataSource control appears as a gray box on your page in Visual Studio, but it's invisible when you run the page.

The last step is to add controls that are linked to the SiteMapDataSource. Although you can use any of the data controls described in Part 3, in practice you'll find that you'll get the results you want only with the three controls that are available in the Navigation tab of the Toolbox. That's because these controls support hierarchical data (data with multiple nested levels), and the site map is an example of hierarchical data. In any other control, you'll see only a single level of the site map at a time, which is impractical.

These are the three navigation controls:

TreeView: The TreeView displays a "tree" of grouped links that shows your whole site map at a glance.

Menu: The Menu displays a multilevel menu. By default, you'll see only the first level, but other levels pop up (thanks to some nifty JavaScript) when you move the mouse over the subheadings.

SiteMapPath: The SiteMapPath is the simplest navigation control—it displays the full path you need to take through the site map to get to the current page. For example, it might show Home > Products > RevoStock if you're at the product1.aspx page. Unlike the other navigation controls, the SiteMapPath is useful only for moving up the hierarchy.

To connect a control to the SiteMapDataSource, you simply need to set its DataSourceID property to match the name of the SiteMapDataSource. For example, if you added a TreeView, you should tweak the tag so it looks like this:

```
<asp:TreeView ID="TreeView1" runat="server" DataSourceID="SiteMapDataSource1" />
```

Figure 11-3 shows the result—a tree that displays the structure of the site, as defined in the website. Notice that the TreeView doesn't use the description information; instead, it displays only the node titles.

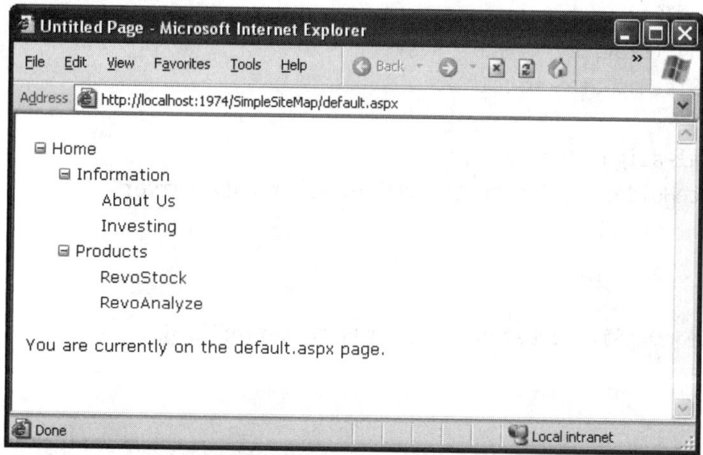

Figure 11-3. *A site map in the TreeView*

Best of all, this tree is created automatically; as long as you link it to the SiteMapDataSource control, you don't need to write any code.

When you click one of the nodes in the tree, you'll automatically be taken to the page you defined in the URL. Of course, unless that page also includes a navigation control such as the TreeView, the site map will disappear from sight. The next section shows a better approach.

Binding a Master Page to a Site Map

Website navigation works best when combined with another ASP.NET feature—master pages. That's because you'll usually want to show the same navigation controls on every page. The easiest way to do this is to create a master page that includes the SiteMapDataSource and the navigation controls. You can then reuse this template for every other page on your site.

Here's how you might define a basic structure in your master page that puts navigation controls on the left:

```
<%@ Master Language="C#" AutoEventWireup="true"
  CodeFile="MasterPage.master.cs" Inherits="MasterPage" %>
<html>
<head runat="server">
  <title>Navigation Test</title>
</head>
```

```
<body>
<form id="form1" runat="server">
  <table>
    <tr>
      <td style="width: 226px;vertical-align: top;">
        <asp:TreeView ID="TreeView1" runat="server"
         DataSourceID="SiteMapDataSource1" />
      </td>
      <td style="vertical-align: top;">
        <asp:ContentPlaceHolder id="ContentPlaceHolder1" runat="server" />
      </td>
    </tr>
  </table>
  <asp:SiteMapDataSource ID="SiteMapDataSource1" runat="server" />
</form>
</body>
</html>
```

Then, create a child with some simple static content:

```
<%@ Page Language="C#" MasterPageFile="~/MasterPage.master"
AutoEventWireup="true"
  CodeFile="default.aspx.cs" Inherits="_default" Title="Untitled Page" %>
<asp:Content ID="Content1" ContentPlaceHolderID="ContentPlaceHolder1"
  runat="Server">
    <br />
    <br />
    You are currently on the default.aspx page (Home).
</asp:Content>
```

In fact, while you're at it, why not create a second page so you can test the navigation between the two pages?

```
<%@ Page Language="C#" MasterPageFile="~/MasterPage.master"
AutoEventWireup="true" CodeFile="product1.aspx.cs"
Inherits="product1" Title="Untitled Page" %>
<asp:Content ID="Content1" ContentPlaceHolderID="ContentPlaceHolder1"
  runat="Server">
    <br />
    <br />
    You are currently on the product1.aspx page (RevoStock).
</asp:Content>
```

Now you can jump from one page to another using the TreeView (see Figure 11-4). Because both pages use the same master, and the master page includes the TreeView, the site map always remains visible.

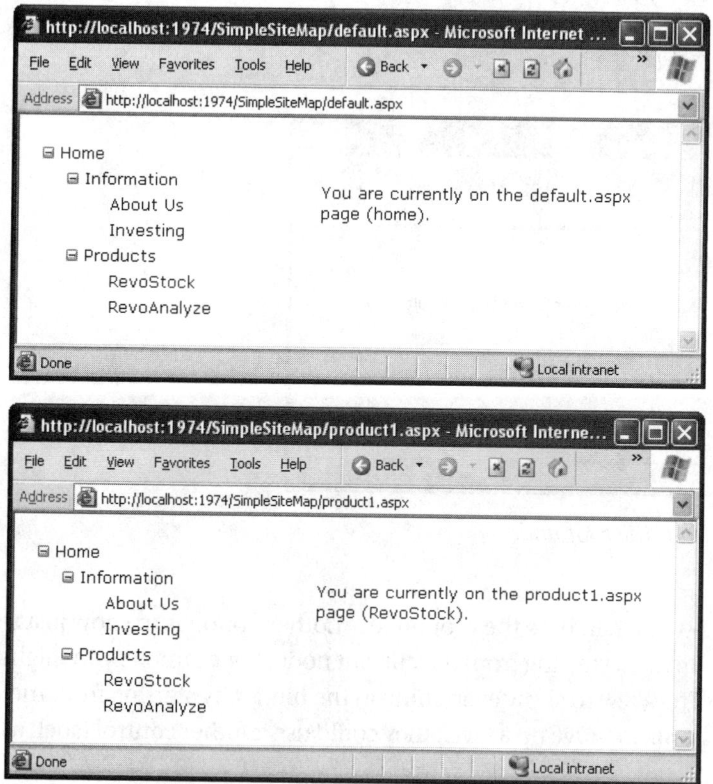

Figure 11-4. *Navigating from page to page with the TreeView*

You can do a lot more to customize the appearance of your pages and navigation controls. You'll consider these topics in the following sections.

Binding Portions of a SiteMap

In the current example, the TreeView shows the structure of the site map file *exactly*. However, this isn't always what you want. For example, you might not like the way the Home node sticks out because of the XmlSiteMapProvider rule that every site map must begin with a single root.

One way to clean this up is to configure the properties of the SiteMapDataSource. For example, you can set the ShowStartingNode property to false to hide the root node:

```
<asp:SiteMapDataSource ID="SiteMapDataSource1" runat="server"
  ShowStartingNode="false" />
```

Figure 11-5 shows the result.

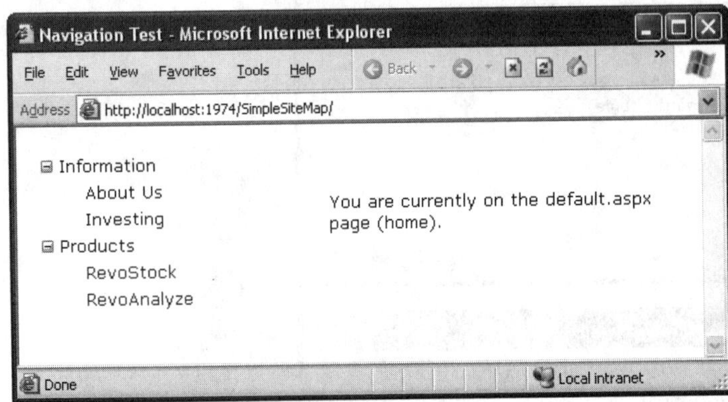

Figure 11-5. *A site map without the root node*

This example shows how you can hide the root node. Another option is to show just a portion of the complete site map, starting from the current node. For example, you might use a control such as the TreeView to show everything in the hierarchy starting from the current node. If the user wants to move up a level, they could use another control (such as the SiteMapPath).

Showing Subtrees

By default, the SiteMapDataSource shows a full tree that starts with the root node. However, the SiteMapDataSource has several properties that can help you configure the navigation tree and limit the display to just a specific branch. Typically, this is useful if you have a deeply nested tree. Table 11-1 describes the full set of properties.

Table 11-1. *SiteMapDataSource Properties*

Property	Description
ShowStartingNode	Set this property to false to hide the first (top-level) node that would otherwise appear in the navigation tree. The default is true.
StartingNodeUrl	Use this property to change the starting node. Set this value to the URL of the node that should be the first node in the navigation tree. This value must match the url attribute in the site map file exactly. For example, if you specify a StartingNodeUrl of "~/home.aspx", then the first node in the tree is the Home node, and you will see nodes only underneath that node.
StartFromCurrentNode	Set this property to true to set the current page as the starting node. The navigation tree will show only pages beneath the current page (which allows the user to move down the hierarchy). For this to work, the site map provider must be able to find a node that matches the current page in the site map file.
StartingNodeOffset	Use this property to shift the starting node up or down the hierarchy. It takes an integer that instructs the SiteMapDataSource to move from the starting node down the tree (if the number is positive) or up the tree (if the number is negative). The actual effect depends on how you combine this property with other SiteMapDataSource properties. For example, if StartFromCurrentNode is false, you'll use a positive number to move down the tree from the starting node toward the current node. If StartFromCurrentNode is true, you'll use a negative number to move up the tree away from the current node and toward the starting node.

Figuring out these properties can take some work, and you might need to do a bit of experimenting to decide the right combination of SiteMapDataSource settings you want to use. To make matters more interesting, you can use more than one SiteMapDataSource on the same page. This means you could use two navigation controls to show different sections of the site map hierarchy.

Before you can see this in practice, you need to modify the site map file used for the previous few examples into something a little more complex. Currently, the site map has three levels, but only the first level (the Home node) and the third level (the individual pages) have URL links. The second-level groupings (Information and Products) are just used as headings, not links. To get a better feel for how the SiteMapDataSource properties work with multiple navigation levels, modify the Product node as shown here:

```
<siteMapNode title="Products" description="Learn about our products"
  url="~/products.aspx">
```

And change the Information node:

```
<siteMapNode title="Products" description="Learn about our company"
  url="~/information.aspx">
```

Next, create the products.aspx and information.aspx pages.

The interesting feature of the Products node is that not only is it a navigable page, but it's a page that has other pages both above it and below it in the navigation hierarchy. This makes it ideal for testing the SiteMapDataSource properties. For example, you can create a SiteMapDataSource that shows pages only below the current page like this:

```
<asp:SiteMapDataSource ID="SiteMapDataSource1" runat="server"
   StartFromCurrentNode = "true" />
```

And you can create one that always shows pages under the Information group like this:

```
<asp:SiteMapDataSource ID="SiteMapDataSource2" runat="server"
  StartingNodeUrl = "~/information.aspx"  />
```

■ **Note** For this technique to work, ASP.NET must be able to find a page in the Web.sitemap file that matches the current URL. Otherwise, it won't know where the current position is, and it won't provide any navigation information to the bound controls.

Now, just bind two navigation controls. In this case, one TreeView is linked to each SiteMapDataSource:

```
Pages under the current page:
<asp:TreeView ID="TreeView1" runat="server"
  DataSourceID="SiteMapDataSource1" />
<br />
The Information group of pages:<br />
<asp:TreeView ID="TreeView2" runat="server"
  DataSourceID="SiteMapDataSource2" />
```

Figure 11-6 shows the result as you navigate from products.aspx down the tree to products1.aspx. The first TreeView shows the portion of the tree under the current page, and the second TreeView is always fixed on the Information group.

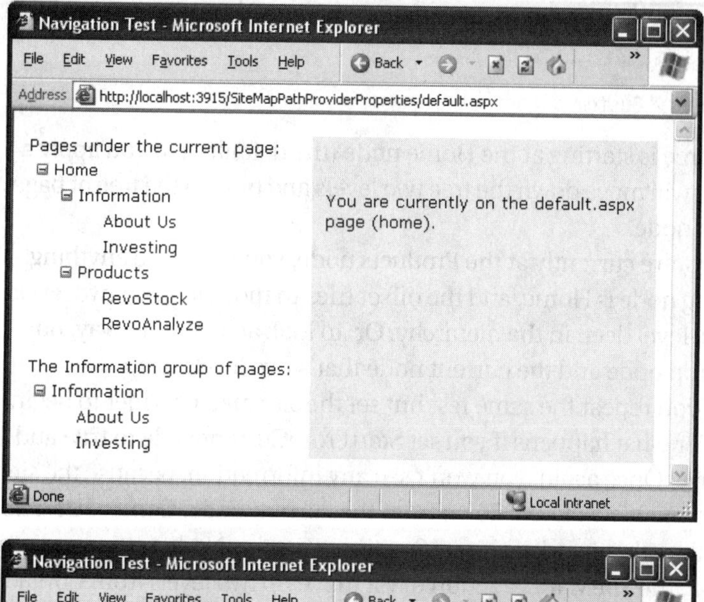

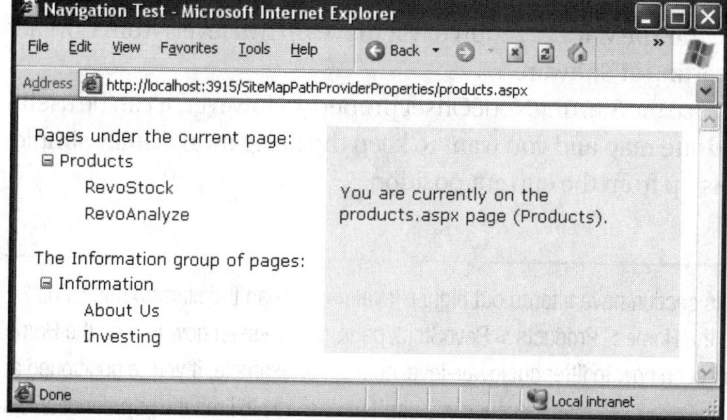

Figure 11-6. *Showing portions of the site map*

You'll need to get used to the SiteMapDataSource.StartingNodeOffset property. It takes an integer that instructs the SiteMapDataSource to move that many levels down the tree (if the number is positive) or up the tree (if the number is negative). An important detail that's often misunderstood is that when the SiteMapDataSource moves down the tree, it moves *toward* the current node. If it's already at the current node, or your offset takes it beyond the current node, the SiteMapDataSource won't know where to go, and you'll end up with a blank navigation control.

To understand how this works, it helps to consider an example. Imagine you're at this location in a website:

```
Home > Products > Software > Custom > Contact Us
```

If the SiteMapDataSource is starting at the Home node (the default) and you apply a StartingNodeOffset of 2, it will move down the tree two levels and bind to the tree of pages that starts at the Software node.

On the other hand, if you're currently at the Products node, you won't see anything! That's because the starting node is Home, and the offset tries to move it down two levels. However, you're only one level deep in the hierarchy. Or, to look at it another way, no node exists between the top node and the current node that's two levels deep.

Now, what happens if you repeat the same test but set the site map provider to begin on another node? Consider what happens if you set StartFromCurrentNode to true and surf to the Contact Us page. Once again, you won't see any information, because the site map provider attempts to move two levels down from the current node, Contact Us, and it has nowhere to go. On the other hand, if you set StartFromCurrentNode to true and use a StartingNodeOffset of -2, the SiteMapDataSource will move *up* two levels from Contact Us and bind the subtree starting at Software.

Overall, you won't often use the StartingNodeOffset property. However, it can be useful if you have a deeply nested site map and you want to keep the navigation display simple by showing just a few levels up from the current position.

■ **Note** All the examples in this section have filtered out higher-level nodes than the starting node. For example, if you're positioned at the Home > Products > RevoStock page, you've seen how to hide the Home and Products levels. You haven't seen how to filter out lower-level nodes. For example, if you're positioned at the Home page, you'll always see the full site map, because you don't have a way to limit the number of levels you see below the starting node. You have no way to change this behavior with the SiteMapDataSource, but later you'll explore the TreeView control (in the section "The TreeView Control") and see that the TreeView.MaxDataBindDepth property serves this purpose.

Using Different Site Maps in the Same File

Imagine you want to have a dealer section and an employee section on your website. You might split this into two structures and define them both under different branches in the same file, like this:

```
<siteMap xmlns="http://schemas.microsoft.com/AspNet/SiteMap-File-1.0" >
  <siteMapNode title="Root" description="Root" url="~/">
    <siteMapNode title="Dealer Home" description="Home" url="~/default.aspx">
      ...
    </siteMapNode>
```

```
    <siteMapNode title="Employee Home" description="Home" url="~/
default_emp.aspx">
      ...
    </siteMapNode>
  </siteMapNode>
</siteMap>
```

Now, to bind the menu to the dealer view, you set the StartingNodeUrl property to "~/default.aspx". You can do this programmatically or, more likely, by creating an entirely different master page and implementing it in all your dealer pages. In your employee pages, you set the StartingNodeUrl property to "~/default_emp.aspx". This way, you'll show only the pages under the Dealer Home branch of the site map.

You can even make your life easier by breaking a single site map into separate files using the siteMapFile attribute, like this:

```
<siteMap xmlns="http://schemas.microsoft.com/AspNet/SiteMap-File-1.0" >
  <siteMapNode title="Root" description="Root" url="~/">
    <siteMapNode siteMapFile="Dealers.sitemap" />
    <siteMapNode siteMapFile="Employees.sitemap" />
  </siteMapNode>
</siteMap>
```

Even with this technique, you're still limited to a single site map tree, and it always starts with the Web.sitemap file. However, you can manage your site map more easily because you can factor some of its content into separate files.

However, this seemingly nifty technique is greatly limited because the site map provider doesn't allow duplicate URLs. This means you have no way to reuse the same page in more than one branch of a site map. Although you can try to work around this problem by creating different URLs that are equivalent (for example, by adding query string parameters on the end), this raises more headaches. Sadly, this problem has no solution with the default site map provider that ASP.NET includes.

Navigating Programmatically

You aren't limited to no-code data binding in order to display navigation hierarchies. You can interact with the navigation information programmatically. This allows you to retrieve the current node information and use that to configure details such as the page heading and title. All you need to do is interact with the objects that are readily available through the Page class.

The site map API is remarkably straightforward. To use it, you need to work with two classes from the System.Web namespace. The starting point is the SiteMap class, which provides the static properties CurrentNode (the site map node representing the current page) and RootNode (the root site map node). Both of these properties return a SiteMapNode object. Using the SiteMapNode object, you can retrieve information from the site map, including the title, description, and URL values. You can branch out to consider related nodes using the navigational properties in Table 11-2.

■ **Note** You can also search for nodes using the methods of the current SiteMapProvider object, which is available through the SiteMap.Provider static property. For example, the SiteMap.Provider.FindSiteMapNode() method allows you to search for a node by its URL.

Table 11-2. *SiteMapNode Navigational Properties*

Property	Description
ParentNode	Returns the node one level up in the navigation hierarchy, which contains the current node. On the root node, this returns a null reference.
ChildNodes	Provides a collection of all the child nodes. You can check the HasChildNodes property to determine whether child nodes exist.
PreviousSibling	Returns the previous node that's at the same level (or a null reference if no such node exists).
NextSibling	Returns the next node that's at the same level (or a null reference if no such node exists).

To see this in action, consider the following code, which configures two labels on a page to show the heading and description information retrieved from the current node:

```
protected void Page_Load(object sender, EventArgs e)
{
    lblHead.Text = SiteMap.CurrentNode.Title;
    lblDescription.Text = SiteMap.CurrentNode.Description;
}
```

The next example is a little more ambitious. It implements a Previous/Next set of links, allowing the user to traverse an entire set of subnodes. The code checks for the existence of sibling nodes, and if there aren't any in the required position, it simply hides the links.

```
protected void Page_Load(object sender, EventArgs e)
{
    if (SiteMap.CurrentNode.NextSibling != null)
```

```
    {
        lnkNext.NavigateUrl = SiteMap.CurrentNode.NextSibling.Url;
        lnkNext.Visible = true;
    }
    else
    {
        lnkNext.Visible = false;
    }
}
```

Figure 11-7 shows the result.

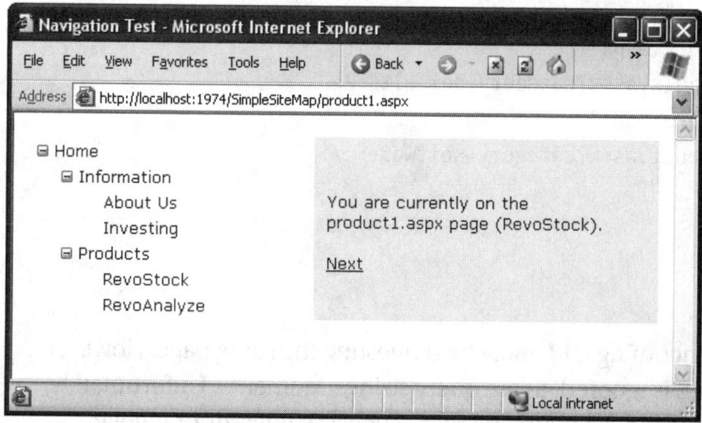

Figure 11-7. *Creating a Next page link*

Mapping URLs

In some situations, you might want to have several URLs lead to the same page. This might be the case for a number of reasons—maybe you want to implement your logic in one page and use query string arguments but still provide shorter and easier-to-remember URLs to your website users (often called *friendly* URLs). Or maybe you have renamed a page, but you want to keep the old URL functional so it doesn't break user bookmarks. Although web servers sometimes provide this type of functionality, ASP.NET includes its own URL mapping feature.

The basic idea behind ASP.NET URL mapping is that you map a request URL to a different URL. The mapping rules are stored in the web.config file, and they're applied before any other processing takes place. Of course, for ASP.NET to apply the remapping, it must be processing the request, which means the request URL must use a file type extension that's mapped to ASP.NET. (See Chapter 12 for more information about how to configure ASP.NET to handle file extensions that it wouldn't ordinarily handle.)

You define URL mapping in the <urlMappings> section of the web.config file. You supply two pieces of information—the request URL (as the attribute url) and the new destination URL (mappedUrl). Here's an example:

```
<configuration xmlns="http://schemas.microsoft.com/.NetConfiguration/v2.0">
  <system.web>
    <urlMappings enabled="true">
      <add url="~/Category.aspx"
       mappedUrl="~/Default.aspx?category=default" />
      <add url="~/Software.aspx"
       mappedUrl="~/Default.aspx?category=software" />
    </urlMappings>
    ...
  </system.web>
</configuration>
```

To make a match, the incoming URL must be requesting the same page. However, the case of the request URL is ignored, as are query string arguments. Unfortunately, ASP.NET doesn't support advanced matching rules, such as wildcards or regular expressions.

When you use URL mapping, the redirection takes place in the same way as the Server.Transfer() method, which means no round-trip happens and the URL in the browser will still show the original request URL, not the new page. In your code, the Request.Path and Request.QueryString properties reflect the new (mapped) URL. The Request.RawUrl property returns the original, friendly request URL.

This can introduce some complexities if you use it in conjunction with site maps—namely, does the site map provider try to use the original request URL or the destination URL when looking for the current node in the site map? The answer is both. It begins by trying to match the request URL (provided by the Request.RawUrl property), and if no value is found, it then uses the Request.Path property instead. This is the behavior of the XmlSiteMapProvider, so you could change it in a custom provider if desired.

The SiteMapPath Control

The TreeView shows the available pages, but it doesn't indicate where you're currently positioned. To solve this problem, it's common to use the TreeView in conjunction with the SiteMapPath control. Because the SiteMapPath is always used for displaying navigational information (unlike the TreeView, which can also show other types of data), you don't even need to explicitly link it to the SiteMapDataSource:

```
<asp:SiteMapPath ID="SiteMapPath1" runat="server" />
```

The SiteMapPath provides *breadcrumb navigation*, which means it shows the user's current location and allows the user to navigate up the hierarchy to a higher level using links. Figure 11-8 shows an example with a SiteMapPath control when the user is on the product1.aspx page. Using the SiteMapPath control, the user can return to the default.aspx page. (If a URL were defined for the Products node, you would also be able to click that portion of the path to move to that page.) Once again, the SiteMapPath has been added to the master page, so it appears on all the content pages in your site.

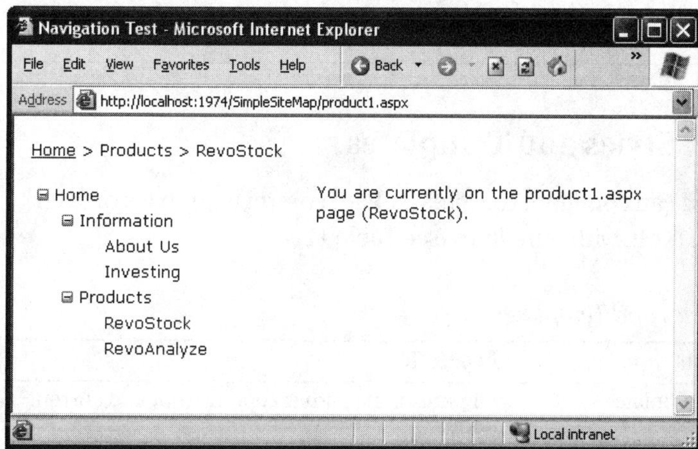

Figure 11-8. *Breadcrumb navigation with SiteMapPath*

The SiteMapPath control is useful because it provides both an at-a-glance view that shows the current position and a way to move up the hierarchy. However, you always need to combine it with other navigation controls that let the user move down the site map hierarchy.

Customizing the SiteMapPath

The SiteMapPath control is also thoroughly customizable. Table 11-3 lists some of its most commonly configured properties.

Table 11-3. *SiteMapPath Appearance-Related Properties*

Property	Description
ShowToolTips	Set this to false if you don't want the description text to appear when the user hovers over a part of the site map path.
ParentLevelsDisplayed	Sets the maximum number of levels above the current page that will be shown at once. By default, this setting is –1, which means all levels will be shown.
RenderCurrentNodeAsLink	If true, the portion of the page that indicates the current page is turned into a clickable link. By default, this is false because the user is already at the current page.
PathDirection	You have two choices: RootToCurrent (the default) and CurrentToRoot (which reverses the order of levels in the path).
PathSeparator	Indicates the characters that will be placed between each level in the path. The default is the greater-than symbol (>). Another common path separator is the colon (:).

Using SiteMapPath Styles and Templates

For even more control, you can configure the SiteMapPath control with styles or even redefine the controls and HTML with templates (see Table 11-4).

Table 11-4. *SiteMapPath Styles and Templates*

Style	Template	Applies To
NodeStyle	NodeTemplate	All parts of the path except the root and current node.
CurrentNodeStyle	CurrentNodeTemplate	The node representing the current page.
RootNodeStyle	RootNodeTemplate	The node representing the root. If the root node is the same as the current node, the current node template or styles are used.
PathSeparatorStyle	PathSeparatorTemplate	The separator in between each node.

Styles are easy enough to grasp—they define formatting settings that apply to one part of the SiteMapPath control. Templates are a little trickier, because they rely on data binding expressions. Essentially, a *template* is a bit of HTML (that you create) that will be shown for a specific part of the SiteMapPath control. For example, if you want to configure how the root node displays in a site map, you could create this template:

```
<asp:SiteMapPath ID="SiteMapPath1" runat="server">
  <RootNodeTemplate>
    <b>Root</b>
  </RootNodeTemplate>
</asp:SiteMapPath>
```

This template ignores the information for the root node and simply displays the word *Root* in bold.

Usually, you'll use a data binding expression to retrieve some site map information—chiefly, the description, text, or URL that's defined for the current node in the site map file. Chapter 14 covers data binding expressions in detail, but this section will present a simple example that shows you all you need to know to use them with the SiteMapPath.

Imagine you want to change how the current node is displayed so that it's shown in italics. To get the name of the current node, you need to write a data binding expression that retrieves the title. This data binding expression is bracketed between <%# and %> characters and uses a method named Eval(). Here's what it looks like:

```
<asp:SiteMapPath ID="SiteMapPath1" runat="server">
  <CurrentNodeTemplate>
    <i><%# Eval("title") %></i>
  </CurrentNodeTemplate>
</asp:SiteMapPath>
```

Data binding also gives you the ability to retrieve other information from the site map node, such as the description. Consider the following example:

```
<asp:SiteMapPath ID="SiteMapPath1" runat="server">
  <PathSeparatorTemplate>
    <asp:Image ID="Image1" ImageUrl="~/arrowright.gif"
     runat="server" />
  </PathSeparatorTemplate>
  <RootNodeTemplate>
    <b>Root</b>
  </RootNodeTemplate>
  <CurrentNodeTemplate>
    <%# Eval("title") %> <br />
    <small><i><%# Eval("description") %></i></small>
  </CurrentNodeTemplate>
</asp:SiteMapPath>
```

This SiteMapPath uses several templates. First, it uses the PathSeparatorTemplate to define a custom arrow image that's used between each part of the path. This template uses an Image control instead of an ordinary HTML <img> tag because only the Image control understands the ~/ characters in the image URL, which represent the application's root folder. If you don't include these characters, the image won't be retrieved successfully if you place your page in a subfolder.

Next, the SiteMapPath uses the RootNodeTemplate to supply a fixed string of bold text for the root portion of the site map path. Finally, the CurrentNodeTemplate uses two data binding expressions to show two pieces of information—both the title of the node and its description (in smaller text, underneath). Figure 11-9 shows the final result.

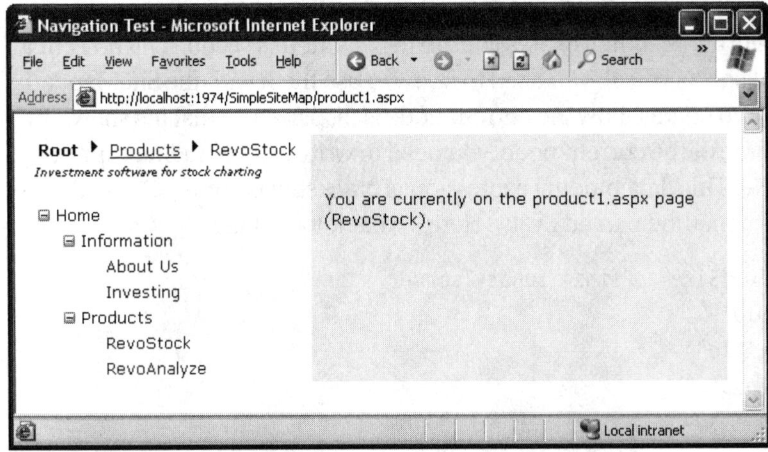

Figure 11-9. *A SiteMapPath with templates*

Adding Custom Site Map Information

In the site maps you've seen so far, the only information that's provided for a node is the title, description, and URL. This is the bare minimum of information you'll want to use. However, the schema for the XML site map is open, which means you're free to insert custom attributes with your own data.

You might want to insert additional node data for a number of reasons. This additional information might be descriptive information that you intend to display or contextual information that describes how the link should work. For example, you could add attributes that specify a target frame or indicate that a link should open in a pop-up window. The only catch is that it's up to you to act on the information later. In other words, you need to configure your user interface so it uses this extra information.

For example, the following code shows a site map that uses a target attribute to indicate the frame where the link should open. This technique is useful if you're using frames-based navigation. In this example, one link is set with a target of _blank so it will open in a new (pop-up) browser window.

```
<siteMapNode title="RevoStock"
  description="Investment software for stock charting"
  url="~/product1.aspx" target="_blank" />
```

Now in your code, you have several options. If you're using a template in your navigation control, you can bind directly to the new attribute. Here's an example with the SiteMapPath from the previous section:

```
<NodeStyle>
  <a href='<%# Eval("url") %>'
   target='<%# Eval("[target]") %>'><%# Eval("Title") %></a>
</NodeStyle>
```

This creates a link that uses the node URL (as usual) but also uses the target information. The one trick in this example is that you need to put square brackets around the attribute name to indicate that the value is being looked up (by name) in the data item's indexer.

If your navigation control doesn't support templates (or you don't want to create one), you'll need to find another approach. Both the TreeView and Menu classes expose an event that fires when an individual item is bound (TreeNodeDataBound and MenuItemDataBound). You can then customize the current item. To apply the new target, you use this code:

```
protected void TreeView1_TreeNodeDataBound(object sender, TreeNodeEventArgs e)
{
    e.Node.Target = ((SiteMapNode)e.Node.DataItem)["target"];
}
```

Notice that you can't retrieve the custom attribute from a strongly typed property. Instead, you retrieve it by name using the SiteMapNode indexer.

The TreeView Control

You've already seen the TreeView at work for displaying navigational information. As you've learned, the TreeView can show a portion of the full site map or the entire site map. Each node becomes a link that, when clicked, takes the user to the new page. If you hover over a link, you'll see the corresponding description information appear in a tooltip.

In the following sections, you'll learn how to change the appearance of the TreeView. In later chapters, you'll learn how to use the TreeView for other tasks, such as displaying data from a database.

■ **Note** The TreeView is one of the most impressive controls in ASP.NET. Not only does it allow you to show site maps, but it also supports showing information from a database and filling portions of the tree on demand (and without refreshing the entire page). But most important, it supports a wide range of styles that can transform its appearance.

TreeView Properties

The TreeView has a slew of properties that let you change how it's displayed on the page. Table 11-5 describes some of the most useful properties.

Table 11-5. *Useful TreeView Properties*

Property	Description
MaxDataBindDepth	Determines how many levels the TreeView will show. By default, MaxDataBindDepth is –1, and you'll see the entire tree. However, if you used a value such as 2, you'd see two only levels under the starting node. This can help you pare down the display of long, multileveled site maps.
ExpandDepth	Ordinarily, when you first request a page that contains a TreeView, every level in the TreeView is expanded, which means all the nodes are visible on the page. If this isn't the behavior you want, you can set the ExpandDepth to a specific number. If you use 0, the TreeView begins completely closed. If you use 1, only the first level is expanded, and so on.
NodeIndent	Sets the number of pixels between each level of nodes in the TreeView. Set this to 0 to create a nonindented TreeView, which saves space.
CollapseImageUrl, ExpandImageUrl, and NoExpandImageUrl	Sets the pictures that are shown next to nodes for collapsing and expanding a node (which are usually represented by plus and minus icons). The NoExpandImageUrl is used if the node doesn't have any children (in which case no image is shown by default).
NodeWrap	Set this to true to let node text wrap over more than one line.
ShowExpandCollapse	Set this to false to hide the expand/collapse boxes. This isn't recommended, because the user won't have a way to expand or collapse a level without clicking it (which causes the browser to navigate to the page).
ShowLines	Set this to true to add lines that connect every node.
ShowCheckBoxes	Set this to true to show a check box next to every node. This isn't terribly useful for site maps, but it is useful with other types of trees.

For example, Figure 11-10 shows a TreeView with a NodeIndent of 0 and shows custom images next to each node set through the CollapseImageUrl, ExpandImageUrl, and NoExpandImageUrl properties.

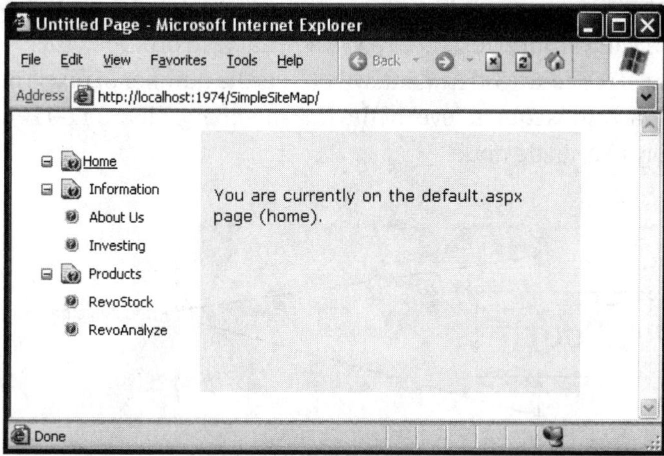

Figure 11-10. *A no-indent TreeView with custom node icons*

Properties give you a fair bit of customizing power, but without a doubt the most interesting and powerful formatting features come from styles.

TreeView Styles

Styles are represented by the TreeNodeStyle class, which derives from the more conventional Style class. As with other rich controls, the styles give you options to set background and foreground colors, fonts, and borders. Additionally, the TreeNodeStyle class adds the node-specific style properties shown in Table 11-6. These properties deal with the node image and the spacing around a node.

Table 11-6. *TreeNodeStyle-Added Properties*

Property	Description
ImageUrl	The URL for the image shown next to the node
NodeSpacing	The space (in pixels) between the current node and the node above and below
VerticalPadding	The space (in pixels) between the top and bottom of the node text and border around the text
HorizontalPadding	The space (in pixels) between the left and right of the node text and border around the text
ChildNodesPadding	The space (in pixels) between the last child node of an expanded parent node and the following sibling node

Because a TreeView is rendered using an HTML table, you can set the padding of various elements to control the spacing around text, between nodes, and so on. One other property that comes into play is TreeView.NodeIndent, which sets the number of pixels of indentation (from the left) in each subsequent level of the tree hierarchy. Figure 11-11 shows how these settings apply to a single node.

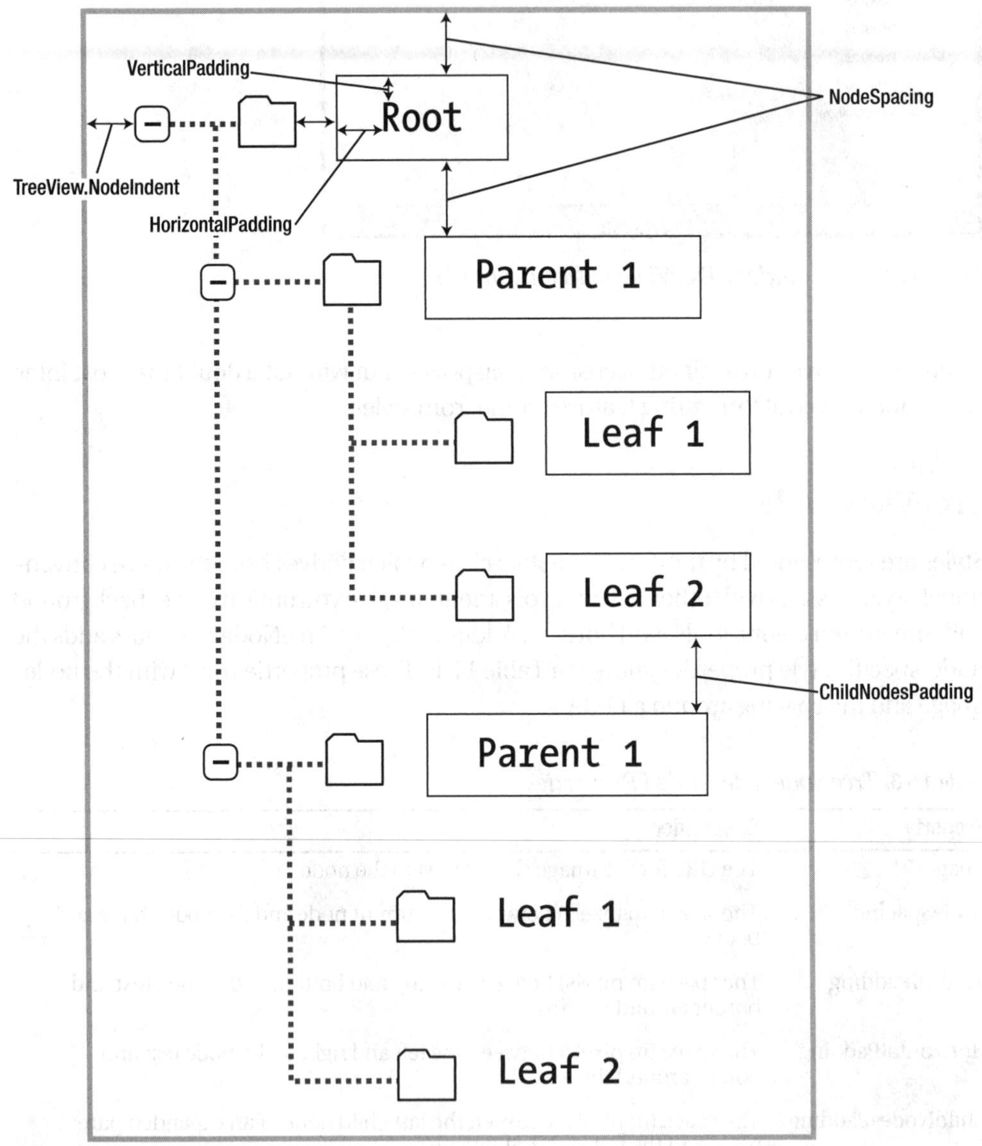

Figure 11-11. *Node spacing*

Clearly, styles give you a lot of control over how different nodes are displayed. To make a change that affects every node in the TreeView, you can modify the TreeNodeStyle object that's provided by the TreeView.NodeStyle property. But if you want to tweak a specific part of the tree, you need to understand how different styles apply to different nodes, as described in the following sections.

Applying Styles to Node Types

The TreeView allows you to individually control the styles for types of nodes—for example, root nodes, nodes that contain other nodes, selected nodes, and so on. Table 11-7 lists different TreeView styles and explains what nodes they affect.

Table 11-7. *TreeView Style Properties*

Property	Description
NodeStyle	Applies to all nodes.
RootNodeStyle	Applies only to the first-level (root) nodes.
ParentNodeStyle	Applies to any node that contains other nodes, except root nodes.
LeafNodeStyle	Applies to any node that doesn't contain child nodes and isn't a root node.
SelectedNodeStyle	Applies to the currently selected node.
HoverNodeStyle	Applies to the node the user is hovering over with the mouse. These settings are applied only in up-level clients that support the necessary dynamic script.

Styles are listed in this table in order of most general to most specific. This means the SelectedNodeStyle style settings override any conflicting settings in a RootNodeStyle, for example. (If you don't want a node to be selectable, set the TreeNode.SelectAction to None.) However, the RootNodeStyle, ParentNodeStyle, and LeafNodeStyle settings never conflict, because the definitions for root, parent, and leaf nodes are mutually exclusive. You can't have a node that is simultaneously a parent and a root node, for example—the TreeView simply designates this as a root node.

Applying Styles to Node Levels

Being able to apply styles to different types of nodes is interesting, but often a more useful feature is being able to apply styles based on the node *level*. That's because many trees use a rigid hierarchy. (For example, the first level of nodes represents categories, the second level represents products, the third represents orders, and so on.) In this case, it's not so important to determine whether a node has children. Instead, it's important to determine the node's depth.

The only problem is that a TreeView can have a theoretically unlimited number of node levels. Thus, it doesn't make sense to expose properties such as FirstLevelStyle,

SecondLevelStyle, and so on. Instead, the TreeView has a LevelStyles collection that can have as many entries as you want. The level is inferred from the position of the style in the collection, so the first entry is considered the root level, the second entry is the second node level, and so on. For this system to work, you must follow the same order, and you must include an empty style placeholder if you want to skip a level without changing the formatting.

For example, here's a TreeView that differentiates levels by applying different amounts of spacing and different fonts:

```
<asp:TreeView runat="server" HoverNodeStyle-Font-Underline="true"
 ShowExpandCollapse="false" NodeIndent="3" DataSourceID="SiteMapDataSource1">
  <LevelStyles>
    <asp:TreeNodeStyle ChildNodesPadding="10" Font-Bold Font-Size="12pt"
     ForeColor="DarkGreen"/>
    <asp:TreeNodeStyle ChildNodesPadding="5" Font-Bold Font-Size="10pt" />
    <asp:TreeNodeStyle ChildNodesPadding="5" Font-UnderLine Font-Size="10pt" />
  </LevelStyles>
</asp:TreeView>
```

If you apply this to the category and product list shown in earlier examples, you'll see a page like the one shown in Figure 11-12.

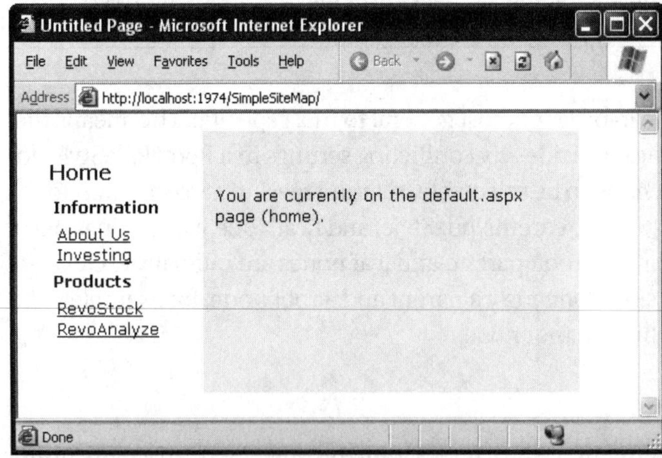

Figure 11-12. *A TreeView with styles*

Using TreeView Themes

Using the right combination of style settings can dramatically transform your TreeView. However, for those less artistically inclined (or those who don't have the right set of images handy), it's comforting to know that Microsoft has made many classic designs available in a skin file. This skin file includes formatting settings and links to graphics that allow you to implement many common TreeView designs. Using these themes, you can easily adapt the TreeView to display anything from logged errors to an MSN Messenger contact list.

As with any skin file, you can apply these settings to a TreeView simply by attaching the skin file to the page and setting the TreeView.SkinID property to the skin you want to use. (See Chapter 11 for the full details.) Visual Studio makes this even easier—just click the Auto Format link in the smart tag, and you'll be able to choose from one of several built-in skins. Figure 11-13 shows some of your options.

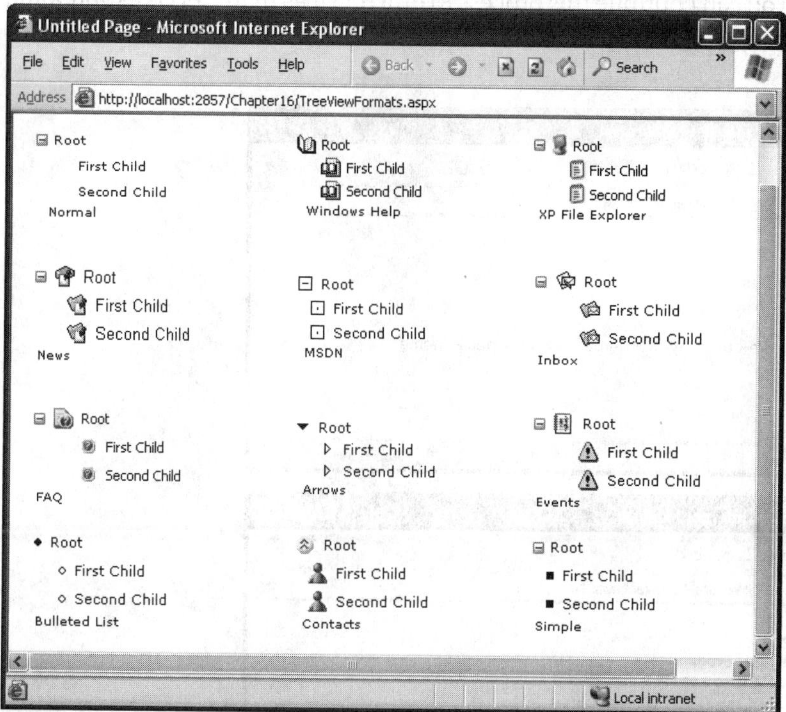

Figure 11-13. *Different looks for a TreeView*

The Menu Control

The new ASP.NET 2.0 Menu control is another rich control that supports hierarchical data. Like the TreeView, you can bind the Menu control to a data source, or you can fill it by hand using MenuItem objects.

To try the Menu control, remove the TreeView from your master page, and add the following Menu control tag:

```
<asp:Menu ID="Menu1" runat="server" DataSourceID="SiteMapDataSource1" />
```

Notice that this doesn't configure any properties—it uses the default appearance. The only step you need to perform is setting the DataSourceID property to link the menu to the site map information.

When the Menu first appears, you'll see only the starting node, with an arrow next to it. However, when you move your mouse over the starting node, the next level of nodes will pop into display. You can continue this process to drill down as many levels as you want, until you find the page you want to click (see Figure 11-14).

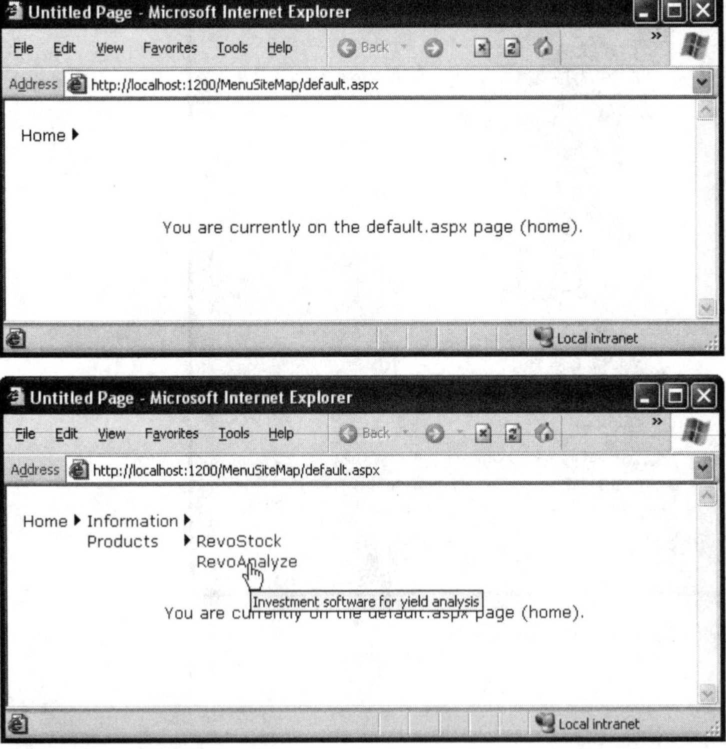

Figure 11-14. *Navigating through the menu*

Overall, the Menu and TreeView controls expose strikingly similar programming models, even though they render themselves quite differently. They also have a similar style-based formatting model. But a few noteworthy differences exist:

- The Menu displays a single submenu. The TreeView can expand an arbitrary number of node branches at a time.
- The Menu displays a root level of links in the page. All other items are displayed using fly-out menus that appear over any other content on the page. The TreeView shows all its items inline in the page.
- TreeView supports on-demand filling and client callbacks. The Menu does not.
- The Menu supports templates. The TreeView does not.
- The TreeView supports check boxes for any node. The Menu does not.
- The Menu supports horizontal and vertical layouts, depending on the Orientation property. The TreeView supports only vertical layout.

Menu Styles

The Menu control provides an overwhelming number of styles. Like the TreeView, the Menu derives a custom class from the Style base class—in fact, it derives two (MenuStyle and MenuItemStyle). These styles add spacing properties (ItemSpacing, HorizontalPadding, and VerticalPadding). However, you can't set menu item images through the style, because it doesn't have an ImageUrl property.

Much like the TreeView, the Menu supports defining different menu styles for different menu levels. However, the key distinction that the Menu control encourages you to adopt is between *static* items (the root-level items that are displayed in the page when it's first generated) and *dynamic* items (the items in fly-out menus that are added when the user moves the mouse over a portion of the menu). Most websites have a definite difference in the styling of these two elements. To support this, the Menu class defines two parallel sets of styles, one that applies to static items and one that applies to dynamic items, as shown in Table 11-8.

Table 11-8. *Menu Styles*

Static Style	Dynamic Style	Description
StaticMenuStyle	DynamicMenuStyle	Sets the appearance of the overall "box" in which all the menu items appear. In the case of StaticMenuStyle, this box appears on the page, and with DynamicMenuStyle it appears as a pop-up.
StaticMenuItemStyle	DynamicMenuItemStyle	Sets the appearance of individual menu items.
StaticSelectedStyle	DynamicSelectedStyle	Sets the appearance of the selected item. Note that the selected item isn't the item that's currently being hovered over; it's the item that was previously clicked (and that triggered the last postback).
StaticHoverStyle	DynamicHoverStyle	Sets the appearance of the item that the user is hovering over with the mouse.

Along with these styles, you can set level-specific styles so that each level of menu and submenu is different. You do this using three collections: LevelMenuItemStyles, LevelSubMenuStyles, and LevelSelectedStyles. These collections apply to ordinary menus, menus that contain other items, and selected menu items, respectively.

It might seem like you have to do a fair bit of unnecessary work when separating dynamic and static styles. The reason for this model becomes obvious when you consider another remarkable feature of the Menu control—it allows you to choose the number of static levels. By default, only one static level exists, and everything else is displayed as a fly-out menu when the user hovers over the corresponding parent. But you can set the Menu.StaticDisplayLevels property to change all that. If you set it to 2, for example, the first two levels of the menu will be rendered in the page, using the static styles. (You can control the indentation of each level using the StaticSubMenuIndent property.)

Figure 11-15 shows the previous example with this change (and some styles applied through the Auto Format link). Note that the items still change as you hover over them, and selection works in the same way. If you want, you can make your entire menu static.

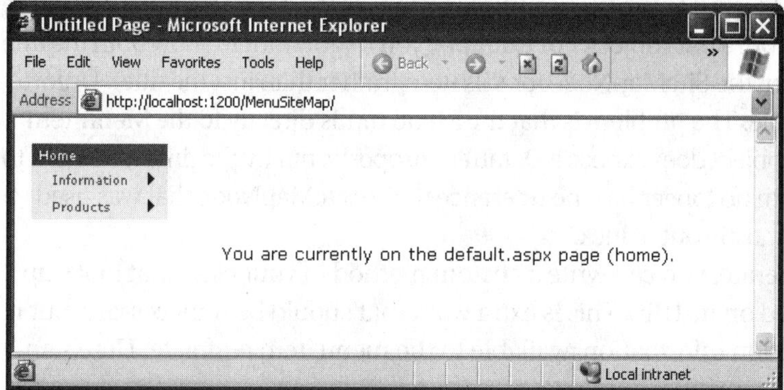

Figure 11-15. *A menu with two static levels*

■ **Tip** The Menu control exposes many more top-level properties for tweaking specific rendering aspects. For example, you can set the delay before a pop-up menu disappears (DisappearAfter), the default images used for expansion icons and separators, the scrolling behavior (which kicks into gear when the browser window is too small to fit a pop-up menu), and much more. Consult MSDN for a full list of properties.

Menu Templates

The Menu control also supports templates through the StaticItemTemplate and DynamicItemTemplate properties. These templates determine the HTML that's rendered for each menu item, giving you complete control.

Interestingly, whether you fill the Menu class declaratively or programmatically, you can still use a template. From the template's point of view, you're always binding to a MenuItem object. This means your template always needs to extract the value for the item from the MenuItem.Text property, as shown here:

```
<asp:Menu ID="Menu1" runat="server">
  <StaticItemTemplate>
    <%# Eval("Text") %>
  </StaticItemTemplate>
</asp:Menu>
```

One reason you might want to use the template features of the Menu is to show multiple pieces of information from a data object. For example, you might want to show both the title and the description from the SiteMapNode for this item (rather than just the title). Unfortunately, that's not possible. The problem is that the Menu binds directly to the MenuItem object. The MenuItem object does expose a DataItem property, but by the time it's added to the menu, that DataItem no longer has the reference to the SiteMapNode that was used to populate it. So, you're mostly out of luck.

If you're really desperate, you can write a custom method in your class that looks up the SiteMapNode based on its URL. This is extra work that should be unnecessary, but it does make the description information available to the menu item template. Here's an example:

```
private string matchingDescription = "";

protected string GetDescriptionFromTitle(string title)
{
    // This assumes there's only one node with this title.
    SiteMapNode node = SiteMap.RootNode;
    SearchNodes(node, title);
    return matchingDescription;
}

private void SearchNodes(SiteMapNode node, string title)
{
    if (node.Title == title)
    {
        matchingDescription = node.Description;
        return;
    }
    else
    {
        foreach (SiteMapNode child in node.ChildNodes)
        {
            // Perform recursive search.
            SearchNodes(child, title);
        }
    }
}
```

Now you can use the GetDescriptionFromTitle() method in a template:

```
<asp:Menu ID="Menu1" runat="server" DataSourceID="SiteMapDataSource1">
  <StaticItemTemplate>
    <%# Eval("Text") %><br />
    <small>
    <%# GetDescriptionFromTitle(((MenuItem)Container.DataItem).Text) %>
    </small>
  </StaticItemTemplate>
  <DynamicItemTemplate>
    <%# Eval("Text") %><br />
    <small>
    <%# GetDescriptionFromTitle(((MenuItem)Container.DataItem).Text) %>
    </small>
  </DynamicItemTemplate>
</asp:Menu>
```

Figure 11-16 shows the new, more descriptive menu.

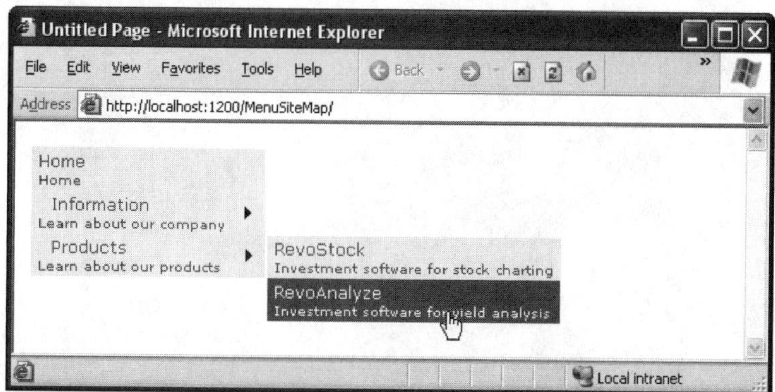

Figure 11-16. *Showing node descriptions in a menu*

The Last Word

In this chapter, you explored the new navigation model and learned how to define site maps and bind the navigation data. You then considered three controls that are specifically designed for navigation data: the SiteMapPath, TreeView, and Menu. Using these controls, you can add remarkably rich site maps to your websites with very little coding. But before you begin, make sure you've finalized the structure of your website. Only then will you be able to create the perfect site map and choose the best ways to present the site map information in the navigation controls.

CHAPTER 12

■ ■ ■

Deploying ASP.NET Applications

The .NET Framework makes it almost painless to deploy any type of application, including ASP.NET websites. Often, you won't need to do much more than copy your web application directory to the web server and then configure it as a virtual directory. The headaches of the past—registering components and troubleshooting version conflicts—are gone. This simplicity makes it practical to deploy websites by manually copying files, rather than relying on a dedicated setup tool.

In this chapter, you'll begin by learning about IIS (Internet Information Services), the Windows operating system component that acts as a web server. You'll explore how to create virtual directories for your web applications, making them available to other clients on the network or on the Internet. Finally, you'll consider the tools in Visual Studio 2005 that simplify website deployment.

ASP.NET Applications and the Web Server

ASP.NET applications always work in conjunction with a web server—a specialized piece of software that accepts requests over HTTP (Hypertext Transport Protocol) and serves content. Web servers run special software to support mail exchange, FTP and HTTP access, and everything else clients need in order to access web content. Before you can go any further, you need to understand a little more about how web servers work.

How Web Servers Work

The easiest job a web server has is to provide ordinary HTML pages. When you request such a file, the web server simply reads it off the hard drive (or retrieves it from an in-memory cache) and sends the complete document to the browser, which displays it. In this case, the web server is just a glorified file server that waits for network requests and dishes out the corresponding documents.

When you use a web server in conjunction with dynamic content such as an ASP.NET page, something more interesting takes place. On its own, the web server has no idea how to process ASP.NET tags or run C# code. However, it's able to enlist the help of the ASP.NET engine to perform all the heavy lifting. Figure 12-1 diagrams how this process works for ASP and ASP.NET pages. For example, when you request the page Default.aspx, the web server sends the request over the ASP.NET engine (which starts automatically if needed). The ASP.NET engine loads the requested page, runs the code it contains, and then creates the final HTML document, which it passes back to IIS. IIS then sends the HTML document to the client.

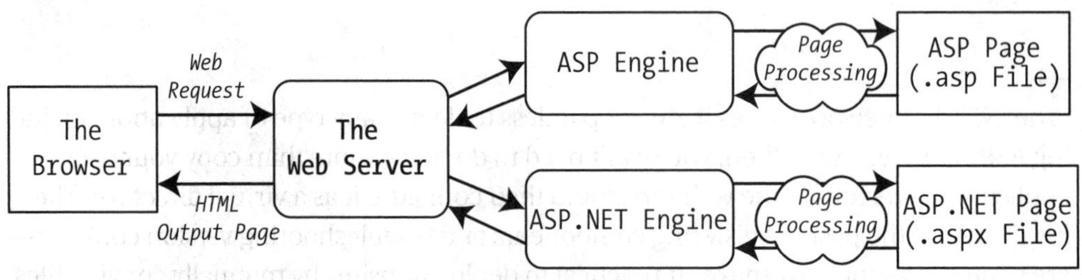

Figure 12-1. *How IIS handles an ASP file request*

At this point, you might be wondering how the web server knows when it needs to get the ASP or ASP.NET engine involved. Essentially, the web server looks at the file extension of the requested page (such as .asp or .aspx) to determine the type of content. The web server compares this extension against a list to determine what program owns this file type. For example, the web server's list indicates that the .aspx extension is owned by the aspnet_isapi.dll component in the c:\[WinDir]\Microsoft.NET\Framework\[Version] directory. The aspnet_isapi.dll component is known as an *ISAPI extension,* because it uses the ISAPI (Internet Server API) model to plug into the web server.

■ **Note** In theory, you can tweak the file type registrations differently for each application. This way, you can have an application in one directory use the ASP.NET 1.1 engine while another application uses ASP.NET 2.0. You'll see how to do this in the "Registering the ASP.NET File Mappings" section.

All web servers perform the same task as that shown in Figure 12-1. However, when you run an ASP.NET application in Visual Studio, you don't need to worry about deployment and file type registration. That's because Visual Studio 2005 includes a component that acts like a built-in web server. It receives the requests for the pages in your web application and then runs the corresponding code.

But to run your web application outside the development environment, you need something more—you need a web server. The web server software runs continuously on your computer (or, more likely, a dedicated web server computer). This means it's ready to handle HTTP requests at any time and provide your pages to clients who connect from the same network or over the Internet. On Microsoft Windows operating systems, the web server you'll use is IIS.

■ **Note** IIS is available only if your computer is running Windows 2000, Windows 2000 Server, Windows XP Professional, or Windows Server 2003. Each version of Windows has a slightly different version or configuration of IIS. As a general rule, when you want to publish your website, you should use a server version of Windows to host it. Desktop versions, like Windows 2000 and Windows XP Professional, are fine for development testing, but they implement a connection limit of ten simultaneous users, which makes them less suitable for real-world use.

In most cases, you won't be developing on the same computer you use to host your website. If you do, you will hamper the performance of your web server by tying it up with development work. You will also frustrate clients if a buggy test application crashes the computer and leaves the website unavailable or if you accidentally overwrite the deployed web application with a work in progress! Generally, you'll perfect your web application on another computer and then copy all the files to the web server.

Web Application URLs

You can use ASP.NET applications in a variety of different environments, including LANs (local area networks) and over the Internet. To understand the difference, it helps to review a little about how web servers work with networks and the Internet.

A *network* is defined simply as a group of devices connected by communication links. A traditional LAN connects devices over a limited area, such as within a company site or an individual's house. Multiple LANs are connected into a WAN (wide area network) using a variety of technologies. In fact, the Internet is nothing more than a high-speed backbone that joins millions of LANs.

The cornerstone of the Internet is IP (Internet Protocol). On an IP network, each computer is given a unique 32-bit number called an *IP address*. An IP address is typically written as four numbers from 0 to 255 separated by periods (as in 192.145.0.1). To access another computer over a network, you need to use its IP address.

Of course, IP addresses aren't easy to remember and don't make for great marketing campaigns. To make life easier, web servers on the Internet usually register unique *domain names* such as www.amazon.com. This domain name is mapped to the IP address by a special catalog, which is maintained by a network of servers on the Internet.

This network, called the DNS (Domain Name Service), is a core part of the infrastructure of the Internet. When you type `http://www.microsoft.com` in a web browser, the browser contacts a DNS server, looks up the IP address that's mapped to `www.microsoft.com`, and contacts it.

So, what effect does all this have on the accessibility of your website? To be easily reached over the Internet, the web server you use needs to be in the DNS registry. To get in the DNS registry, you must have a fixed IP address. Commercial Internet service providers won't give you a fixed IP address unless you're willing to pay a sizable fee. In fact, most will place you behind a firewall or some type of NAT (network address translation), which will hide your computer's IP address. The same is true in most company networks, which are shielded from the outside world.

However, ASP.NET applications don't *need* to be accessible over the Internet. Many are useful within an internal network. In this case, you don't need to worry about the DNS registry. Other computers can access your website using either the IP address of your machine or, more likely, the network computer name.

For example, imagine you deploy an application to a virtual directory named MyWebApp. On the web server, you can access it like this:

```
http://localhost/MyWebApp
```

■ **Tip** Remember, `localhost` is a special part of the URL called a *loopback alias*. It always points to the current computer, whatever its name it. Technically, the loopback alias is mapped to something called the *loopback address*, which is the number 127.0.0.1. You can use the alias or the numeric address interchangeably.

Assuming the computer is named MyWebServer, here's how you can access the virtual web directory on another computer on the same LAN:

```
http://MyWebServer/MyWebApp
```

■ **Tip** If you don't know the name of your computer, right-click the My Computer icon either on your desktop or in Windows Explorer, and select Properties. Then, choose the Computer Name tab. Look for Full Computer Name.

Now, assume that MyWebServer is registered in the DNS as `www.MyWebServer.com` and is exposed to the Internet. You could then use the following URL:

```
http://www.MyWebServer.com/MyWebApp
```

Finally, you can always use the computer's IP address, provided the computer is on the same network or visible on the Internet. Assuming the IP address is 123.5.123.4, here's the URL you would use:

```
http://123.5.123.4/MyWebApp
```

Internal networks often use dynamic IP addresses, and DNS registration changes. For these reasons, using the computer name or domain name is usually the best approach for accessing a website.

If you study the URLs that the built-in web server in Visual Studio uses, you'll notice they're a little different than what you usually see when surfing the Internet. Namely, they include a port number. That means instead of requesting a page like this:

```
http://localhost/MyWebApp/Default.aspx
```

you might request a page like this:

```
http://localhost:2040/MyWebApp/Default.aspx
```

That's because the Visual Studio web server watches requests on a dynamically chosen port number. (In this example, the port number is 2040, but you'll see that it changes each time you run Visual Studio.) By using a dynamic port number, Visual Studio makes sure its built-in web server doesn't infringe on any other web server software you have on the computer.

Real web servers are almost always configured to monitor port 80 (and port 443 for encrypted traffic). If you don't type in a port number for a URL, the browser assumes you're using port 80.

Web Farms

Some applications run on *web farms*, a group of server computers that share the responsibility of handling requests. Usually web farms are reserved for high-powered web applications that need to be able to handle heavy loads, because multiple computers can deal with more simultaneous surfers than a single web server. However, web farms are overkill for many small- and mid-sized websites.

The way a web farm works is deceptively simple. Essentially, instead of placing web application files on a single web server, you place a copy on several separate web servers. When a request is received for your website, it's directed to one of these web servers (based on which one has the lightest load). That web server then deals with the request. Obviously, if you decide to update your application, you need to make sure you update each web server in the web farm with the same version to prevent discrepancies.

Some web hosting companies use web farms to host multiple websites. For example, your website might be running on more than one web server, but each of these web servers might also host multiple websites. This provides a flexible deployment model that lets different web applications share resources.

Web farms pose a few new challenges. For example, if you decide to use session state, it's important you use StateServer or SqlServer mode, as described in Chapter 9. Otherwise, a user's session information might get trapped on one server. If a subsequent request is directed to another server, the information will be lost, and a new session will be created.

Another wrinkle occurs with view state (discussed in Chapter 9) and forms authentication (Chapter 18). The problem in both cases is the same—ASP.NET encodes some information to prevent tampering and verifies the information later. For example, with view state ASP.NET adds a hash code, which double-checks the next time the page is posted back to make sure the user hasn't changed the hidden view state field (in which case the request is rejected). The problem that can happen with web farms is that the hash code one web server creates might not match the hash code expected by another web server that uses a different secret key. As a result, if a page is posted back to a web farm and a different web server gets involved, an error can occur.

To resolve this problem, you can disable view state hash codes (as described in Chapter 9). This isn't recommended. A better solution is to configure each web server in the web farm to use the same key. In a web hosting provider, this step will have already been performed. However, if you have your own web farm, it won't be—instead, the default is for every server to create its own random key. Obviously, these keys won't match.

To configure web servers to use the same key, head to the c:\Windows\Microsoft.NET\Framework\[Version]\Config directory, and crack open the machine.config file in a text editor. In the <system.web> section, add a <machineKey> element, like this:

```
<machineKey validationKey="DE4C0C8F69E34EFC93F2FD3C04484A184A6FF124BFD14504..."
 decryptionKey="0A335689ABD7F3EB3BB79826861359E08..." validation="SHA1" />
```

This key explicitly sets a validation key and a decryption key. As long as you set all the servers in the web farm to use the same key, they can share view state (and use other features, such as forms authentication). Of course, you can't create the key string on your own and have it sufficiently random. Instead, you should use a tool (such as the key generator at `http://www.aspnetresources.com/tools/keycreator.aspx`).

IIS (Internet Information Services)

As you've probably guessed by now, deploying a web application is just the process of copying your web application files to a web server. By taking this step, you accomplish three things:

- You ensure your web applications are available even when Visual Studio isn't running.
- You allow users on other computers to run your web applications. (The Visual Studio web server handles only local requests.)
- Your web application URLs will no longer need a port number.

Depending on your organization, you may be in charge of deploying web applications, or a dedicated web administrator may handle the process. Either way, it's worth learning the deployment process, which is quite straightforward. But before you can deploy a web application, you need to make sure the target computer has the required IIS web server software.

If you're running Windows 2000, Windows Server 2000, or Windows XP Professional, you need IIS 5. If you're running Windows Server 2003, you need IIS 6. The following sections explain how to get set up.

■ **Tip** As a quick test to find out whether IIS is installed, try firing up a browser and requesting `http://localhost/localstart.asp` on the current computer. If IIS is installed, this request should retrieve a help page from the default website.

Installing IIS 5

Installing IIS is easy Here are the steps you follow on a Windows 2000, Windows Server 2000, or Windows XP Professional computer:

1. Click Start, and select Settings ➤ Control Panel.
2. Choose Add or Remove Programs.
3. Click Add/Remove Windows Components.

4. If Internet Information Services (ISS) is checked (see Figure 12-2), you already have this component installed. Otherwise, click it, and then click Next to install the required IIS files. You'll probably need to have your Windows setup CD handy.

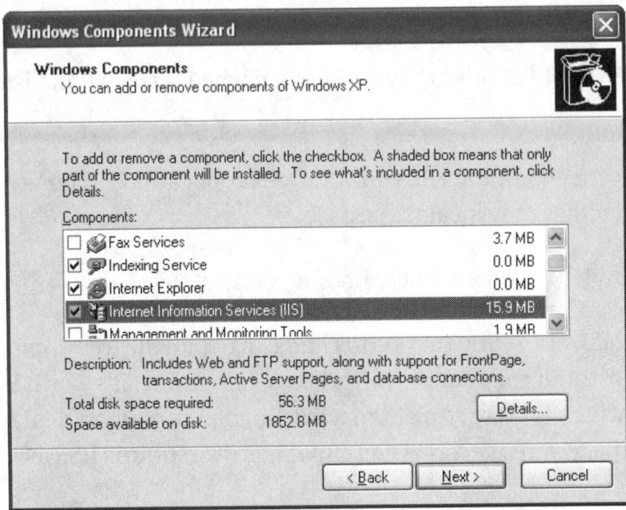

Figure 12-2. *Installing IIS*

5. Now it's time to install ASP.NET (if you haven't already). You have several ways to install ASP.NET, but one of the easiest is to choose it from the list of optional downloads available through the Windows Update feature. Just select Windows Update from the Start menu.

■ **Note** You can also install ASP.NET through the free SDK (available for download at `http://www.asp.net`), or you can install Visual Studio 2005, which includes it. However, best security practices encourage you not to include any development tools on the web server but to install only the .NET runtime (which includes the ASP.NET engine).

Installing IIS 6

If you're using Windows Server 2003, you can install IIS through the Add/Remove Windows Components dialog box, but it's more likely you'll use the Manage Your Server Wizard. Here's how it works:

1. Select Add or Remove a Role from the main Manage Your Server window. This launches the Configure Your Server Wizard.

2. Click Next to continue past the introductory window. The setup wizard will test your available and enabled network connections and then continue to the next step.

3. Now you choose the roles to enable. Select Application Server (IIS, ASP.NET) from the list, as shown in Figure 12-3, and click Next.

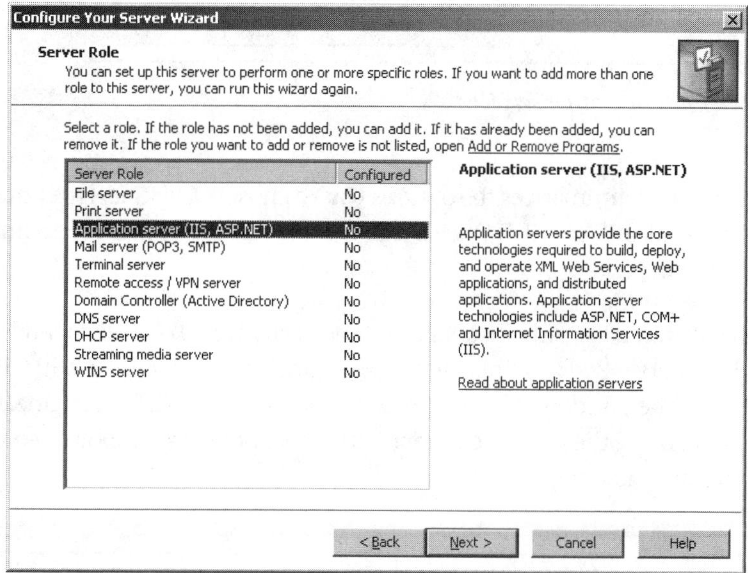

Figure 12-3. *Choosing an application server role*

4. Check the Enable ASP.NET box on the next window (shown in Figure 12-4). If you don't, IIS will be enabled, but it will be able to serve only static content such as ordinary HTML pages. Click Next to continue.

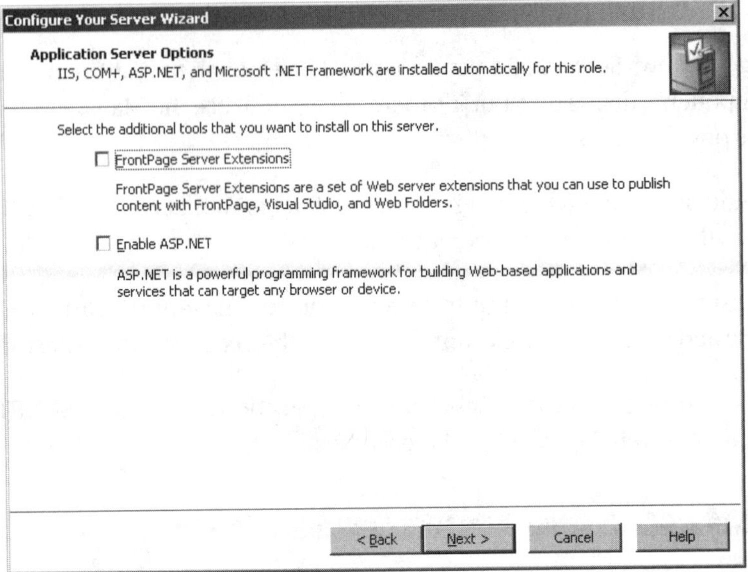

Figure 12-4. *Enabling other services*

5. The next window summarizes the options you've chosen. Click Next to continue by installing IIS 6.0 and ASP.NET. Once the process is complete, you'll see a final confirmation message.

At this point, you may have extra installation steps to go through—it all depends which release of Windows Server 2003 you're using. The original release includes ASP.NET 1.1, so you'll need to use the Windows Update feature to add the ASP.NET 2.0 engine. On the other hand, if you're using the more recent minor update known as Windows Server 2003 R2, you'll already have the right version.

■ **Note** The rest of this chapter uses IIS 5 as an example. If you're working with IIS 6, you'll still be able to use most of the instructions in this chapter, but you may want to supplement your knowledge with the online help for IIS 6 or a dedicated book about IIS 6 administration.

Registering the ASP.NET File Mappings

Ideally, you'll install IIS *before* you install ASP.NET. That's because when you perform the ASP.NET setup, it configures IIS to recognize all the right file types (such as .aspx). If you install ASP.NET before IIS, you'll run into a problem because IIS won't recognize your

ASP.NET files and won't hand them off to the ASP.NET worker process to execute your code. Instead, it sends the raw text of the page (the .aspx tags) directly to the requesting browser. The next section demonstrates this problem.

Fortunately, it's easy to correct this problem by repairing your IIS file mappings. You need to use the aspnet_regiis.exe command-line utility. Here's the syntax you'll need:

```
c:\[WinDir]\Microsoft.NET\Framework\[Version]\aspnet_regiis.exe -i
```

At this point, ASP.NET will check all your virtual directories and register the ASP.NET file types.

■ **Note** If you have more than one version of ASP.NET installed on the computer, make sure you run the correct version of aspnet_regiis (the one in the latest version's directory). If you use the version of aspnet_regiis included with an older version of ASP.NET, like 1.1, you'll reset all your web applications to use ASP.NET 1.1.

In some cases, this approach is more drastic than what you really want, because it affects every web application on the web server. In some cases, you might have more than one version of ASP.NET on the same web server, and you might want some applications to execute with the older ASP.NET 1.1 and others to use ASP.NET 2.0. (This might occur if you're in the process of updating several web applications and the migration isn't yet tested.) In this case, you need to use aspnet_regiis carefully so that it applies its magic to individual applications only.

To change file mappings for a single web application, you use the -s parameter, followed by the full path to your web application. This path always starts with W3SVC/1/ROOT/ followed by the application folder name, as shown here:

```
aspnet_regiis -s W3SVC/1/ROOT/SampleApp1
```

Remember, if you want to register an application to use a different version of ASP.NET, you need to use the version of aspnet_regiis that's included with that version, along with the -s parameter.

Every version of aspnet_regiis is able to give you a list of all the versions of ASP.NET that are installed on the computer (and where they are). Just use the -lv option, as shown here:

```
aspnet_regiis -lv
```

You can get more information about aspnet_regiis.exe from the MSDN Help, and you can see all the parameters by using the -? parameter. Later in this chapter (in the "Managing Websites with IIS Manager" section), you'll learn how you can configure virtual directories using the graphical IIS Manager tool. One of the features it provides is a way to set the ASP.NET version for each web application, without requiring you to run aspnet_regiis.

Verifying That ASP.NET Is Correctly Installed

After installing ASP.NET, it's a good idea to test that it's working. All you need to do is create a simple ASP.NET page, request it in a browser, and make sure it's processed successfully.

To perform this test, create a text file in the c:\Inetpub\wwwroot directory. Name this file test.aspx. The file name isn't that important, but the extension is. It's the .aspx extension that tells IIS this file needs to be processed by the ASP.NET engine.

Inside the test.aspx file, paste the following code:

```
<html>
    <body>
        <h1>The date is <% Response.Write(DateTime.Now.ToLongDateString()) %>
        </h1>
    </body>
</html>
```

When you request this file in a browser, ASP.NET will load the file, execute the embedded code statement (which retrieves the current date and inserts it into the page), and then return the final HTML page. This example isn't a full-fledged ASP.NET web page, because it doesn't use the web control model. However, it's still enough to test that ASP.NET is working properly. When you enter `http://localhost/test.aspx` in the browser, you should see a page that looks like the one shown in Figure 12-5.

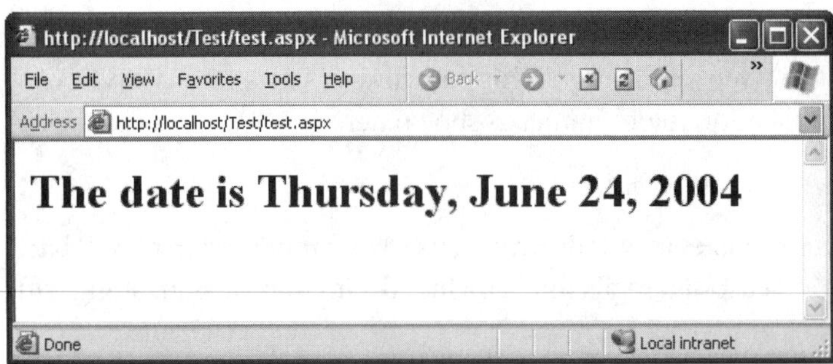

Figure 12-5. *ASP.NET is correctly installed.*

If you see only the plain text, as in Figure 12-6, ASP.NET isn't installed correctly. This problem commonly occurs if ASP.NET is installed but the ASP.NET file types aren't registered in IIS. In this case, ASP.NET won't actually process the request. Instead, the raw page will be sent directly to the user, and the browser will display only the content that isn't inside a tag or script block.

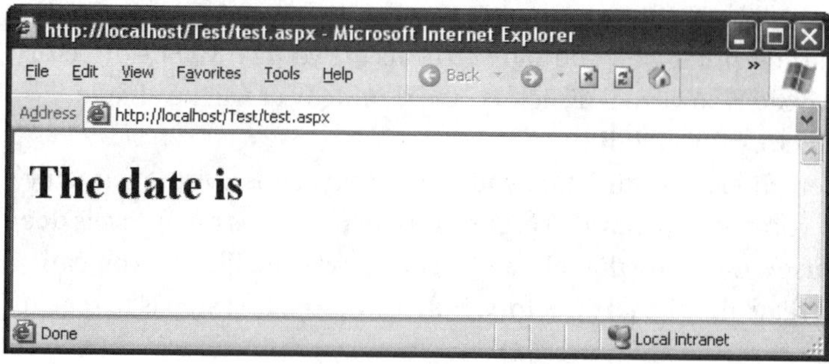

Figure 12-6. *ASP.NET isn't installed or configured correctly.*

To solve this problem, use the aspnet_regiis.exe tool described in the previous section to register the ASP.NET file mappings.

Managing Websites with IIS Manager

When IIS is installed, it automatically creates a directory named c:\Inetpub\wwwroot, which represents your website. Any files in this directory will appear as though they're in the root of your web server.

To add more pages to your web server, you can copy HTML, ASP, or ASP.NET files directly to the c:\Inetpub\wwwroot directory. For example, if you add the file TestFile.html to this directory, you can request it in a browser through the URL `http://localhost/TestFile.html`. You can even create subdirectories to group related resources. For example, you can access the file c:\Inetpub\wwwroot\MySite\MyFile.html through a browser using the URL `http://localhost/MySite/MyFile.html`. If you're using Visual Studio 2005 to create new web projects, you'll find that it automatically generates new subdirectories in the wwwroot directory. So, if you create a web application named WebApplication1, the files will be stored in c:\Inetpub\wwwroot\WebApplication1 and made available through `http://localhost/WebApplication1`.

Using the wwwroot directory is straightforward, but it makes for poor organization. To properly use ASP or ASP.NET, you need to make your own *virtual directory* for each web application you create. With a virtual directory, you can expose any physical directory (on any drive on your computer) on your web server as though it were located in the c:\Inetpub\wwwroot directory.

Creating a Virtual Directory

When you're ready to create a new website, the first step you'll usually take is to create the physical directory where the pages will be stored (for example, c:\MySite). The second step is to expose this physical directory as a virtual directory through IIS. This means the website becomes publicly visible to other computers that are connected to your computer. Ordinarily, a remote computer won't be allowed to access your c:\MySite directory. However, if you map c:\MySite to a virtual directory, the remote user will be able to request the files in the directory through IIS.

Before going any further, choose the directory you want to expose as a virtual directory. You can use any directory you want, on any drive, and you can place it as many levels deep as makes sense. You can use a directory that already has your website files, or you can copy these files after you create the virtual directory. Either way, the first step is to register this directory with IIS.

The easiest and most flexible way to create a virtual directory is to use the IIS Manager utility. Here's how it works:

1. To start IIS Manager, select Settings ➤ Control Panel ➤ Administrative Tools ➤ Internet Information Services from the Start menu.

2. To create a new virtual directory for an existing physical directory, right-click the Default Website item in the IIS tree, and choose New ➤ Virtual Directory from the context menu. A wizard will start to manage the process. As you step through the wizard, you'll need to provide three pieces of information: an alias, a directory, and a set of permissions.

3. Choose an *alias* (see Figure 12-7). The alias is the name a remote client will use to access the files in this virtual directory. For example, if your alias is MyApp and your computer is MyServer, you can request pages using URLs such as `http://MyServer/MyApp/MyPage.aspx`.

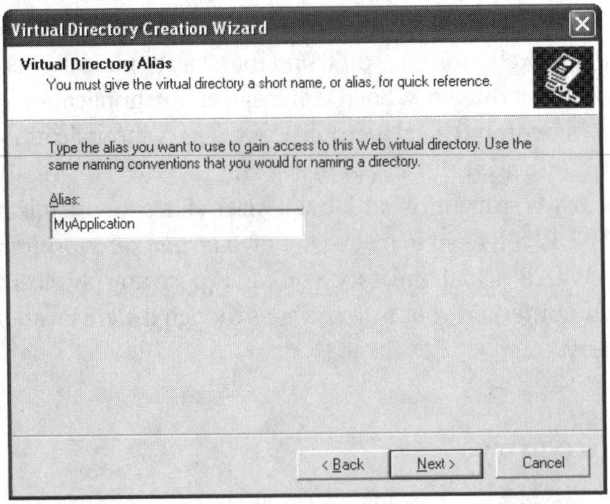

Figure 12-7. *Choosing an alias*

4. Click Next.

5. Choose a directory (see Figure 12-8). The directory is the physical directory on your hard drive that will be exposed as a virtual directory. For example, c:\Inetpub\wwwroot is the physical directory that is used for the root virtual directory of your web server. IIS will provide access to all the allowed file types in this directory.

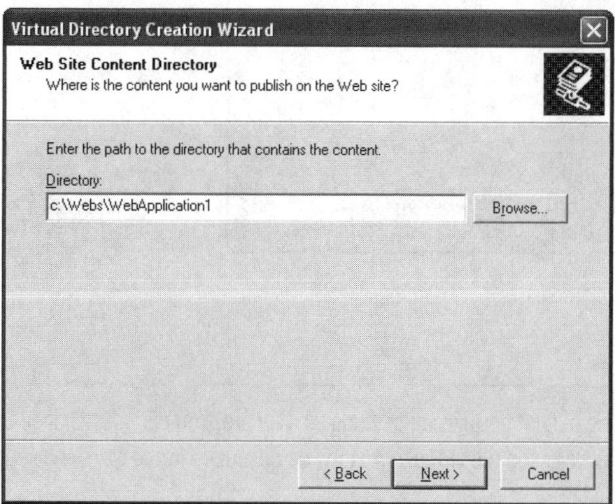

Figure 12-8. *Choosing a physical directory*

6. Click Next.

7. Choose your permissions (see Figure 12-9). To host an ASP.NET application, you need only to enable the read and execute permissions (the first two check boxes). If you're using a development computer that will never act as a live web server, you can allow additional permissions. (Keep in mind, however, that this could allow other users on a local network to access and modify files in the virtual directory.)

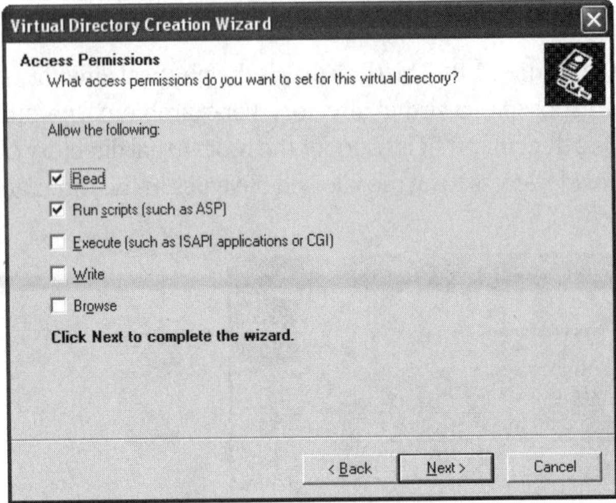

Figure 12-9. *Setting permissions*

■ **Note** If you're unsure, leave the default permission settings as they are. You can also change the virtual directory permissions after you have created the virtual directory, as described in the following sections.

---

8. Click Next and then Finish to create the virtual directory.

When you finish these steps, you'll see your new virtual directory appear in the list in IIS Manager. You can remove an existing virtual directory by selecting it and pressing the Delete key, or you can change its settings by right-clicking it and choosing Properties.

Once you've created your virtual directory, fire up a browser to make sure it works. For example, if you've created the virtual directory with the alias MyApplication and it contains the page MyPage.aspx, you should be able to request `http://localhost/MyApplication/MyPage.aspx`.

Virtual Directories and Web Applications

You can manage all the virtual directories on your computer in the Internet Information Services utility by expanding the tree under the Default Website item. You'll notice that items in the tree use different types of icons, as shown in Figure 12-10.

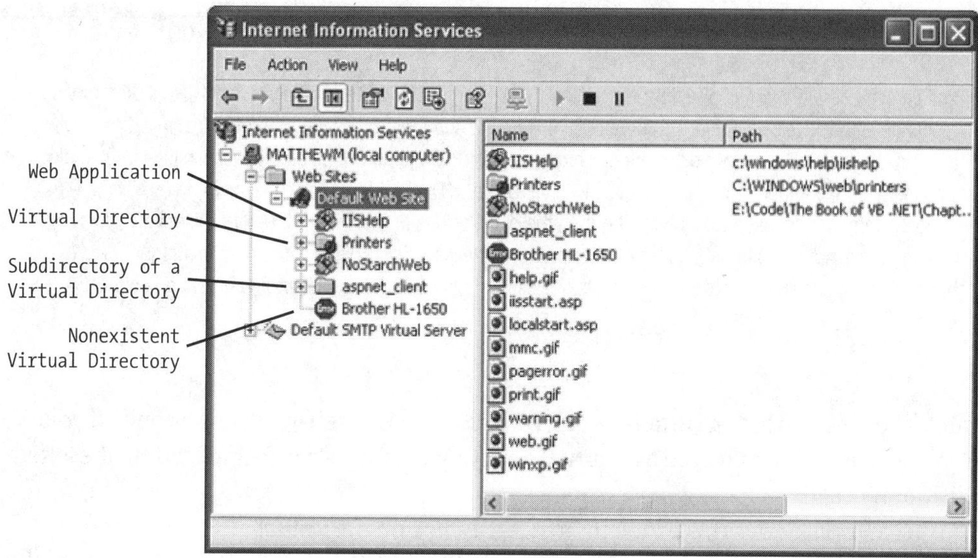

Figure 12-10. *Web folders*

Different icons have different meanings:

- *An ordinary folder*: This represents a subdirectory inside another virtual directory. For example, if you create a virtual directory and then add a subdirectory to the physical directory, it will be displayed here.
- *A folder with a globe*: This represents a virtual directory.
- *A package folder*: This represents a virtual directory that is also a web application. By default, when you use the wizard to create a virtual directory, it's also configured as a web application. This means it will share a common set of resources and run in its own application domain. Chapter 5 explained web applications.
- *An error icon*: This indicates a virtual directory for a physical directory that no longer exists. You can delete these virtual directories and re-create them with the correct information.

When you create a virtual directory with the Virtual Directory Creation Wizard, it's also configured as a web application. This is almost always what you want.

If your virtual directory *isn't* a web application, you won't be able to control its ASP.NET configuration settings. This leads to a common problem—when you try to run the application, you receive an error page informing you that the settings in the web.config file aren't

> **VIRTUAL DIRECTORIES ALLOW ACCESS TO SUBDIRECTORIES**
>
> Imagine you create a virtual directory called MyApp on a computer called MyServer. The virtual directory corresponds to the physical directory c:\MyApp. If you add the subdirectory c:\MyApp\MoreFiles, this directory will automatically be included in the IIS tree as an ordinary folder. Clients will be able to access files in this folder by specifying the folder name, as in `http://MyServer/MyApp/MoreFiles/SomeFile.html`.
>
> By default, the subdirectory will inherit all the permissions of the virtual directory. However, you can change these settings using the Internet Information Services utility. This is a common technique used to break a single application into different parts (for example, if some pages require heightened security settings).

valid. The problem is that certain settings are restricted to web applications only. If your web application is configured as a virtual directory but not as a web application, these settings aren't valid.

You can easily solve this problem. Just right-click on the virtual directory, choose Properties, and select the Virtual Directory tab. Finally, click the Create button next to the Application Name box.

Configuring an Existing Virtual Directory

IIS makes it easy to configure virtual directories after you've created them. Simply right-click the virtual directory in the list, and choose Properties. The Properties window will appear, with its information divided into several tabs.

The following sections briefly explain the most important settings you'll want to configure. Many other settings are designed specifically for classic ASP and have no effect on ASP.NET, and others are rarely changed (and can have performance implications if they are). For more information, consult a dedicated IIS book.

■ **Note** Any changes you make in the Properties window are automatically applied to all subdirectories. If your change conflicts with the custom settings you have set for a virtual directory, IIS will warn you. It will present a list of the directories that will be affected and give you the chance to specify exactly which ones you want to change and which ones you want to leave as is. If you want to make a change that will affect all the virtual directories on your server, right-click the Default Website item, and choose Properties.

Virtual Directory

The Virtual Directory tab contains basic information about your virtual directory (see Figure 12-11).

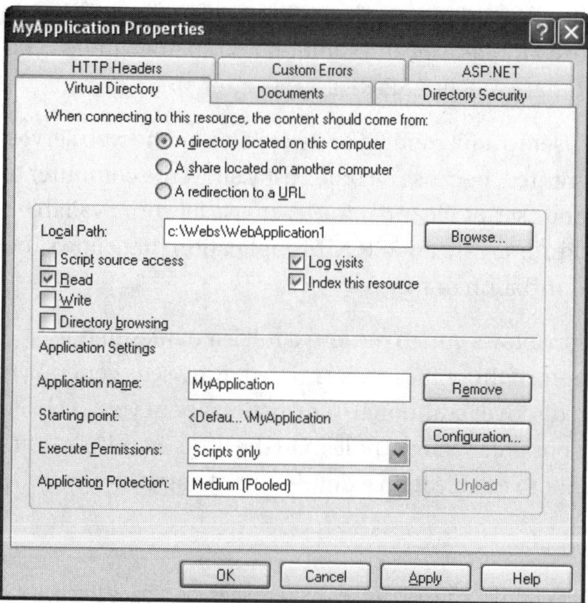

Figure 12-11. *Web directory properties*

At the top of the tab is information about the physical path for this virtual directory. If you're looking at the root of a virtual directory, you can set the local path to point to a different physical directory by clicking the Browse button. If you're looking at an ordinary subdirectory *inside* a virtual directory, the local path will be read-only.

Underneath the path are several options that control the permissions of this virtual directory. IIS consider these permissions when deciding how to handle an incoming request. They include:

Read: This is the most basic permission—it's required in order for IIS to provide any requested files to the user. If this is disabled, the client will not be able to access ASP or ASP.NET pages or static files such as HTML and images. Note that even when you enable read permissions, you have several other layers of possible security in IIS. For example, some file types (such as those that correspond to ASP.NET configuration files) are automatically restricted, even if they're in a directory that has read permission.

Run scripts: This permission allows the user to request an ASP or ASP.NET page. If you enable read but don't allow script permission, the user will be restricted to static file types such as HTML documents. ASP and ASP.NET pages require a higher permission because they could conceivably perform operations that would damage the web server or compromise security.

Execute: This permission allows the user to run an ordinary executable file or CGI application. This is a possible security risk as well and shouldn't be enabled unless you require it (which you won't for ordinary ASP or ASP.NET applications).

Write: This permission allows the user to add, modify, or delete files on the web server. This permission should never be granted, because it could easily allow the computer to upload and then execute a dangerous script file (or at the least, use all your available disk space). Instead, use an FTP site, or create an ASP.NET application that allows the user to upload specific types of information or files.

Directory Browsing: This permission allows you to retrieve a full list of files in the virtual directory, even if the contents of those files are restricted. Browse is generally disabled because it allows users to discover additional information about your website and its structure as well as exploit possible security holes. On the other hand, it's quite useful for testing, so you might want to enable it on a development computer.

■ **Note** Remember, virtual directory permissions are used only when you're requesting a page through IIS. If you can directly access the computer's hard drive using Windows Explorer or some other tool, these permissions won't come into effect.

Further down is the information about the application name for your virtual directory. Remember, when you create a virtual directory with the wizard, it's also configured as a web application. You can change this by clicking the Remove button next to the application name. Similarly, you can click the Create button to transform an ordinary virtual directory into a full-fledged application. Usually you won't need to perform these tasks, but it's nice to know they are available if you need to make a change.

Documents

This tab allows you to specify the default documents for a virtual directory. For example, consider the virtual directory `http://localhost/MySite`. A user can request a specific page in this directory using a URL such as `http://localhost/MySite/MyPage1.aspx`. But what happens if the user simply types `http://localhost/MySite` into a web browser?

In this case, IIS will examine the list of default documents defined for that virtual directory. It will scan the list from top to bottom and return the first matching page. Using the list in Figure 12-12, IIS will check first for a Default.htm file, then for Default.asp, index.htm, iisstart.asp, and Default.aspx.

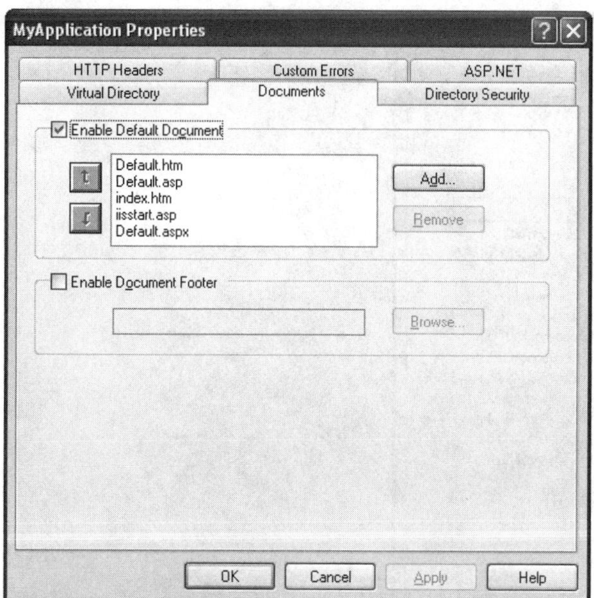

Figure 12-12. *The default document list*

If IIS doesn't find any of these pages, it will either return an error message or, if you've enabled the Browse permission (which usually you won't), provide a file list.

You can configure the default document list by removing entries or adding new ones. Most ASP.NET applications simply use Default.aspx as their home page.

Custom Errors

The Custom Errors tab allows you to specify an error page that will be displayed for specific types of HTTP errors (see Figure 12-13). As you learned, you can use various ASP.NET features to replace HTTP errors or application errors with custom messages. However, these techniques won't work if the web request never makes it to the ASP.NET service (for example, if the user requests an HTML file that doesn't exist). In this case, you may want to supplement custom ASP.NET error handling with the appropriate IIS error pages for other generic error conditions.

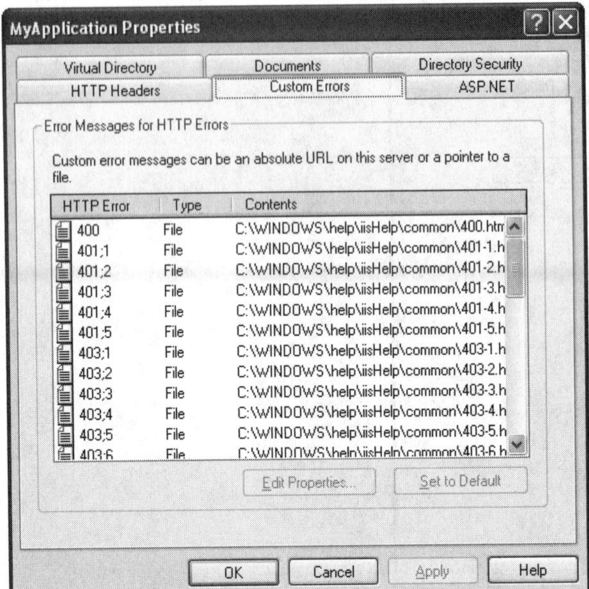

Figure 12-13. *IIS custom errors*

File Mappings

As explained earlier in this chapter, IIS hands off requests for ASP pages to the ASP service and requests for ASP.NET pages to the ASP.NET service. However, both ASP and ASP.NET support a variety of file types. How does IIS know which files belong to ASP.NET and which ones belong to ASP?

You can find the answer in the application file mappings. To view file mappings, click the Configuration button on the Virtual Directory tab. You'll see the dialog box shown in Figure 12-14.

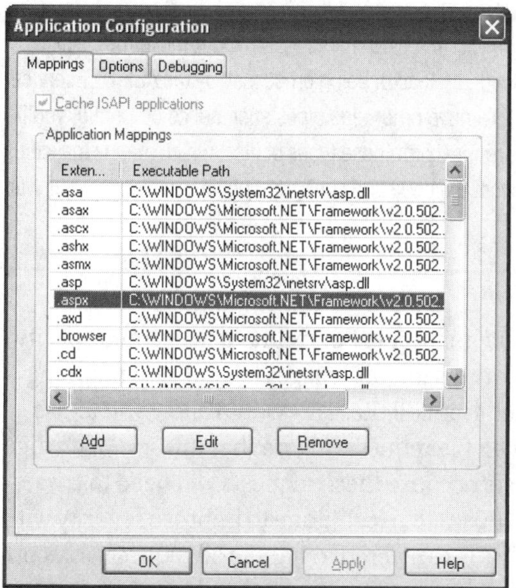

Figure 12-14. *File mappings*

You'll notice that ASP files are mapped differently than ASP.NET files. For example, .asp requests are handled by c:\[WinDir]\System32\inetsrv\asp.dll, and .aspx requests are handled by c:\[WinDir]\Microsoft.NET\Framework\[Version]\aspnet_isapi.dll. Every version of ASP.NET uses a different version of aspnet_isapi.dll (which is stored in a different directory), which allows a single web server to host many different types and versions of website. If a file type isn't mapped (such as .html), its contents are sent directly to the user as plain text, without any processing.

One reason you might want to work with file mapping is to explicitly remove file mappings you don't need or mappings that could be security risks. For example, if you don't want to support classic ASP files, you may choose to remove the .asp file mapping. However, keep in mind that when you remove a mapping, you simply prevent it from being processed in its usual program. You don't prevent the user from requesting it. In other words, if you remove the mapping for ASP files, a user who requests an .asp page will receive the text that's stored in that file, which may include sensitive code that users shouldn't be allowed to see.

■ **Caution** You should never remove any of the ASP.NET file type mappings! If you remove the .aspx or .asmx file types, web pages and web services won't work. Instead of being processed by the ASP.NET service, the raw file will be sent directly to the browser. If you remove other files types such as .cs or .config, you'll compromise security. ASP.NET will no longer process requests for these types of files, which means malicious users will be able to request them through IIS and inspect the code and configuration information for your web application.

In other cases, you might want to add a file mapping. For example, you could specify that the ASP.NET service will handle any requests for GIF images by adding a mapping for the GIF file type that points to the aspnet_isapi.dll file. This would allow you to use ASP.NET security services and logging for GIF file requests. (Note that this sort of change can slow down performance for GIF requests because these requests will need to trickle through more layers on the server.) ASP.NET uses this technique to improve security with configuration and source code files. ASP.NET is registered to handle all requests for .config, .cs, and .vb files so that it can explicitly deny these requests, regardless of the IIS security settings.

ASP.NET

The ASP.NET tab provides several useful features (as shown in Figure 12-15):

- It gives you at-a-glance information about the current version of ASP.NET you're using for this application.
- It allows you to choose any version of ASP.NET that's installed on the computer just by selecting it from a drop-down list. This is an easy way to configure different applications to use different versions of ASP.NET, without using the aspnet_regiis.exe tool described earlier.
- It provides an Edit Configuration button that, when clicked, launches another set of tabs that you can use to tweak the settings in the web.config file. There's no difference between changing settings through this window and changing them by hand. However, harried website administrators might find this approach makes it easier to monitor and tweak the configuration of different applications without hunting for files.

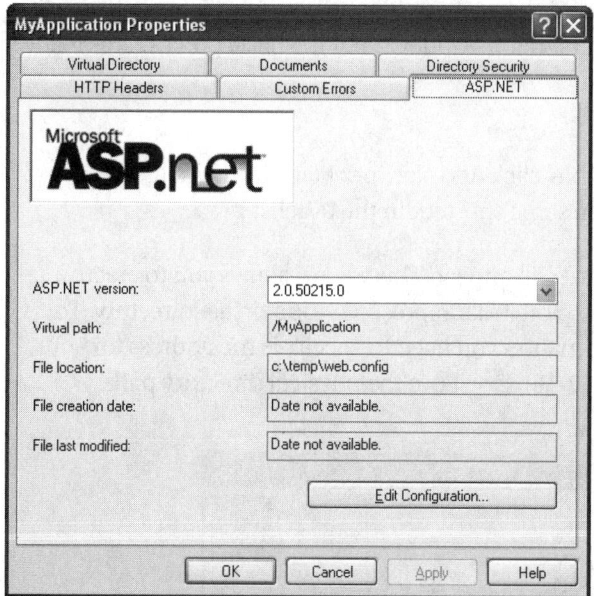

Figure 12-15. *The ASP.NET configuration tab*

Directory Security

The Directory Security tab allows you to set security settings that restrict your virtual directory to specific Windows users. You'll learn about this technique, and other types of ASP.NET authentication, in Chapter 18.

Adding a Virtual Directory to Your Neighborhood

Working with a web application can sometimes be a little awkward. If you use Windows Explorer and look at the physical directory for the website, you can see the full list of files, but you can't execute any of them directly. On the other hand, if you use your browser and go through the virtual directory, you can run any page, but you have no way to browse through a directory listing because virtual directories almost always have directory browsing permission disabled.

While you're developing an application, you may want to circumvent this limitation. That way you can examine exactly what your web application comprises and run several different pages easily, without needing to constantly type a full file name or dart back and forth between Internet Explorer and Windows Explorer. All you need to do is enable directory browsing for your virtual directory. You can easily enable or disable this setting from inside IIS Manager.

To make life even easier, you can add a virtual directory to your My Network Places list. This task varies slightly in different versions of Windows, but the basic process is as follows:

1. First, open Windows Explorer.
2. Then click Network, and double-click Add Network Place from the file list. (In Windows XP, you can click the same shortcut in the task list.)
3. The Add Network Place Wizard will appear. This wizard allows you to create a network folder in Windows Explorer that represents your virtual directory. The only important piece of information you need to specify is the address for your virtual directory (see Figure 12-16). Don't use the physical directory path.

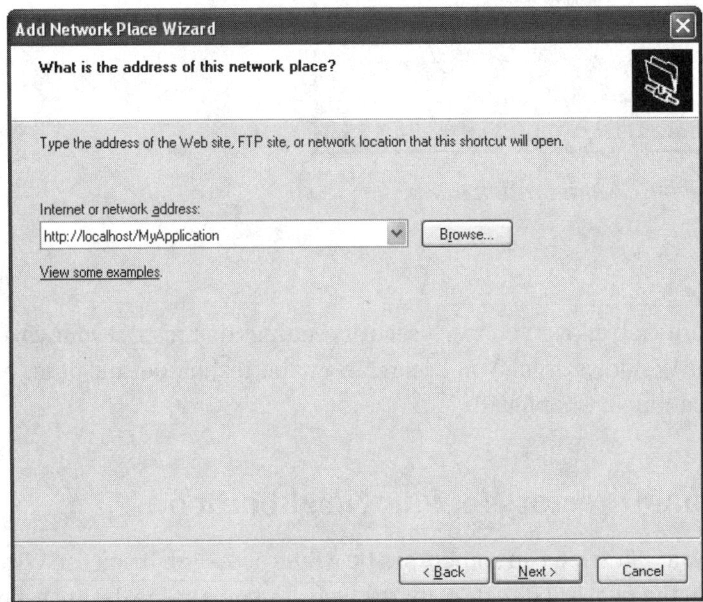

Figure 12-16. *Specify the virtual directory*

4. Now choose the name that will be used for this virtual directory.

Once you finish the wizard, the directory will appear in your Network Neighborhood, and you can browse through the remote files (see Figure 12-17). Interestingly, when you browse this directory, you're actually receiving all the information you need over HTTP. You can also execute an ASP or ASP.NET file by double-clicking—which you can't do directly from the physical directory.

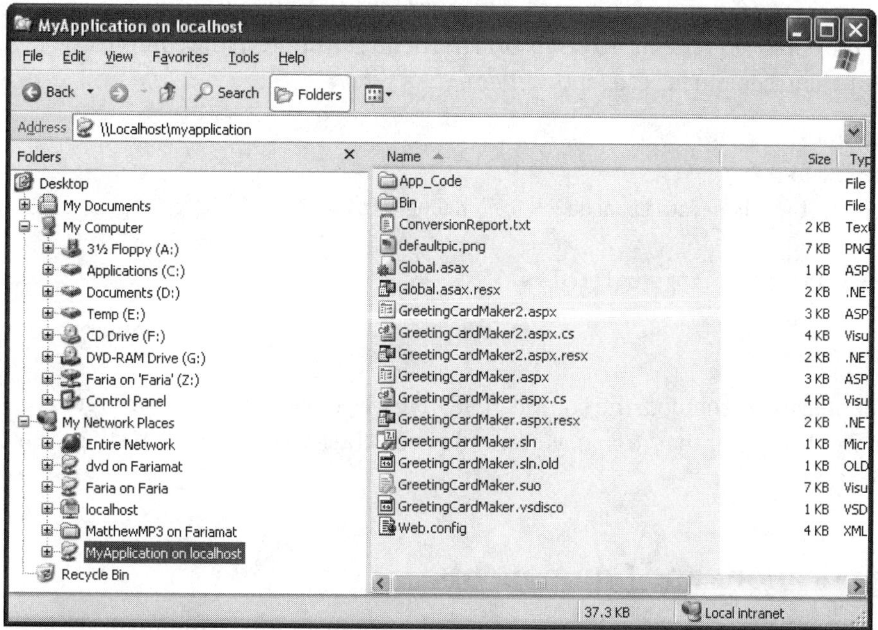

Figure 12-17. *The mapped virtual directory*

Deploying a Simple Site

You now know enough to deploy an ordinary ASP.NET website. All you need to do is follow these two simple steps:

1. Create the virtual directory on the web server.

2. Copy the entire site (including subdirectories) to the virtual directory.

How you transfer these files depends on the Internet hosting service you're using. Usually, you'll need to use an FTP program to upload the files to a designated area. However, if both your computer and the web server are on the same internal network, you might just use Windows Explorer or the command prompt to copy files.

If you're using a commercial web host, the virtual directory will already be created for you, and you'll simply need to transfer the files.

Before you transfer your application files, you should make sure debug mode isn't enabled in the deployed version. To do so, find the debug attribute in the compilation tag, if it is present, and set it to false, as shown here:

```
<configuration>
    <system.web>
        <compilation defaultLanguage="cs" debug="false" />

        <!-- Other settings omitted. -->
    </system.web>
<configuration>
```

When debugging is enabled, the compiled ASP.NET web page code will be larger and execute more slowly. For that reason, you should use debugging only while testing your web application.

Web Applications and Components

It's just as straightforward to deploy web applications that use other components. That's because any custom components your website uses are copied into the Bin subdirectory when you add a reference in Visual Studio. No additional steps are required to register assemblies or to copy them to a specific system directory.

■ Note Private assemblies are quite a boon for web hosting companies that need to host dozens, hundreds, or thousands of web applications on the same computer. Their web servers can't install risky components into a system directory just because one website requires it—especially when the version that one site requires might conflict with the version needed by another site on the same computer.

Of course, this principle doesn't hold true if you're using *shared assemblies*, which are stored in a special system location called the GAC (global assembly cache). Usually, you won't store components in this location, because it complicates development and offers few benefits. The core .NET assemblies are located in the GAC because they're large and likely to be used in almost every .NET application. It doesn't make sense to force you to deploy the .NET assemblies with every website you create. However, this means it's up to the administrator of the web server to install the version of the .NET Framework you require. This detail just isn't in your website's control.

Other Configuration Steps

The simple model of deployment you've seen so far is often called *zero-touch deployment,* because you don't need to manually configure web server resources. (It's also sometimes called *XCopy deployment,* because transferring websites is as easy as copying directories.) However, some applications are more difficult to set up on a web server. Here are some common factors that will require additional configuration steps:

Databases: If your web application uses a database, you'll need to transfer the database to the web server. You can do this by generating an SQL script that will automatically create the database and load it with data. Alternately, you could back up the database and then restore it on the web server. In either case, an administrator needs to use a database management tool.

Alternate machine.config settings: You can control the settings for your web application in the web.config file that you deploy. However, problems can occur if your web application relies on settings in the machine.config file that aren't present on the web server.

Windows account permissions: Usually, a web server will run web page code under a restricted account. This account might not be allowed to perform the tasks you rely on, such as writing to files or the Windows event log. In this case, an administrator needs to specifically grant the permissions you need to the account that runs the ASP.NET engine for your website.

IIS security settings: If your website uses SSL encryption or Windows authentication (as described in Chapter 18), the virtual directory settings will need to be tweaked. This also requires the help of an administrator.

To solve these problems in the most effective way, it helps to work with an experienced Windows administrator. That's especially true if the web server is using IIS 6 (the version of IIS provided with Windows 2003). IIS 6 provides a number of configuration options and allows every web application on a server to run under a different Windows account. This ensures that your website can be granted the exact permission set it requires, without affecting any other web application.

The ASPNET Account

Some of the subtlest issues with ASP.NET deployment involve security. When the web server launches the aspnet_isapi.dll for the first time, it loads under a specific Windows user account. The actual account that's used depends on the version of IIS you're using:

- If you're using IIS 5, the account is ASPNET (which is created automatically when you install the .NET Framework).
- If you're using IIS 6 (the version that's included with Windows Server 2003), it's the local *network service* account.
- If you're using the integrated test server in Visual Studio, the server runs under your account. That means it has all your permissions, and as a result you generally won't run into permission problems while you're testing your application.

When you're running your website through IIS, this setting is just a default, and you can change it. Under IIS 5, you change the account by editing the machine.config file that defines settings for the entire web server. In IIS 6, you configure this account in IIS Manager.

■ **Note** You might wonder how virtual directory permissions and the ASP.NET account settings interact. Essentially, the virtual directory permissions determine what files a user can request. If the user successfully requests an ASP.NET file, the ASP.NET engine will then execute the corresponding web page code. The ASP.NET account settings determine what this code is allowed to do.

New ASP.NET programmers often ask why ASP.NET code doesn't run under another account—say, the account of the user who is making the request from the browser. However, if you consider this situation, you'll quickly realize the problems. It's almost certain that the end user doesn't have a Windows account defined on the web server. Even if the user has a corresponding user account, that account shouldn't have the same rights as the ASP.NET engine.

The trick is to use an account that's limited enough that it can't be abused by attackers but still has the required permissions to run your code. Both the ASPNET account and the network account achieve that goal, because they have a set of carefully limited privileges.

By default, the ASPNET account won't be allowed to perform tasks such as reading the Windows registry, retrieving information from a database, or writing to most locations on the local hard drive. On the other hand, it will have the permissions that are essential for normal functioning. For example, the ASPNET account *is* allowed to access the c:\[WinDir]\Microsoft.NET\[Version]\Temporary ASP.NET Files directory so that it can compile and cache web pages.

The limited security settings of the ASPNET and network service accounts are designed to prevent attacks on your web server. In most cases, the goal is to prevent any attacks that could exploit flaws in your application and trick it into undertaking actions that it's technically allowed to do (such as deleting a file) but should never perform. Although this is a worthwhile goal, you'll probably find that your applications require some additional permissions beyond those given to the ASPNET and network service accounts. For example, you might need access to a specific file or a database. To make this possible, you grant additional permissions to these account in the same way you would grant them to any other Windows user account. However, the process isn't always obvious—so you might want to consult a good handbook about Windows system administration before you take these steps.

Alternatively, you might want to change the account that's used to run the worker process to a different account with the required permissions. The following sections explain how.

Note Before changing the account used to run ASP.NET code, make sure you fully understand the effects. If you use an account with more permissions than you need, you open the door to a wide range of potential hacks and attacks. It's always best to use a dedicated user for running ASP.NET code and to restrict what it can do to the bare minimum.

Changing the Account in IIS 5

To change the ASP.NET settings to use a different account, you need to perform the following steps:

1. Open the machine.config file in the c:\[WinDir]\Microsoft.NET\[Version]\Config directory using Notepad.

2. Search for the setting userName="Machine". You'll find this setting in the processModel tag, which looks something like this:

```
<processModel enable="true" ...
 userName="Machine" password="AutoGenerate" ... />
```

3. The userName="Machine" instruction tells ASP.NET to run using the special ASPNET account. You can modify userName and password to use any other account that's defined on the web server. Alternatively, you can modify this attribute to be userName="System" and leave the password as AutoGenerate. This tells ASP.NET to use the local system account, which is a local account with wide-ranging permissions.

Note It's tempting to use the local system account, because it has complete power to perform any task on the computer. Although this may make sense for test web server scenarios, it's a dangerous habit. First, using the local system account makes developers less conscious of security while they program, which is never a good approach in the threat-conscious world of modern programming. Second, it also means you are less aware of the minimum permissions the application requires, which can complicate your life when you need to deploy the application to a production server.

4. Now you must restart the ASP.NET service. To do this, either you can reboot the computer or you can use Task Manager to manually terminate the ASP.NET service. In the latter case, look for the process named aspnet_wp.exe. Select it, and click End Process.

Note The ASP.NET account is a global setting that affects all web applications on the computer.

Changing the Account in IIS 6

If you're using Windows Server 2003, you must use configure the IIS 6 application pool settings using IIS Manager. Editing the machine.config file (as described in the previous section) will have no effect.

Here's what you need to do:

1. In IIS Manager, right-click the pool, and select Properties.
2. Select the Identity tab.
3. You can choose one of the predefined account types from the drop-down list, including Network Service (the default), Local Service (which is essentially the same as ASPNET), or Local System. Alternatively, you can supply the user name and password for a specific user. If you take this approach, the information you enter is encrypted for the current computer (unlike with IIS 5, where it's stored in ordinary text in the machine.config file.
4. Finally, you must restart the ASP.NET service or reboot the computer so that the application pool starts with the new identity.

Code Compilation

By default, when you deploy an application you've created with Visual Studio 2005, you deploy the uncompiled source files. The first time a web server requests a page, it's compiled dynamically and cached in a temporary directory for reuse. The advantage of this approach is that it's easy to make last-minute changes directly to your files without needing to go through any compilation steps. However, this approach has some clear disadvantages:

- The first request for a page is slow. Once each page has been requested at least once, this problem disappears.
- The web server contains all your source code and is clearly visible to anyone who has access to the server. Even though visitors can't see your code, website administrators can (and they could even change it).

To improve performance and prevent other people from seeing your code, you have another option—you can use ASP.NET's *precompilation* feature. Essentially, you use a command-line tool named aspnet_compiler.exe, which is stored in the familiar c:\[WinDir]\Microsoft.NET\Framework\[Version] directory. You use this compiler on your development machine before you deploy the application. It compiles the entire website into binary files.

Here's the syntax for the aspnet_compiler tool:

```
aspnet_compiler -m metabasePath targetDirectory
```

Essentially, you need to specify the source (where the web application currently resides) and the target directory (where the compiled version of the application should be copied).

To specify the source, you use the -m option and specify the metabase path in the form W3SVC/1/ROOT/[VirtualDirectoryName], just as you would with aspnet_regiis. Here's an example:

```
aspnet_compiler -m W3SVC/1/ROOT/MyApp C:\MyAppDeploy
```

You can then copy the files from the target directory to your web server (or if you're really crafty, you can use aspnet_compiler to send the compiled files straight to the target directory as part of your build process).

If you use the command line shown previously, the c:\MyAppDeploy directory will contain all the .aspx files but no .cs files—meaning all the source code is compiled into assemblies in the Bin directory and hidden. Even more interestingly, the information in the .aspx files has also been removed. If you open a web page, you'll find that it doesn't contain any tags. Instead, it just contains the statement "This is a marker file generated by the precompilation tool and should not be deleted!" All the tags have been moved into the compiled files in the Bin directory, along with the source code. The aspnet_compiler just keeps the .aspx files so you can remember what web pages actually exist in your web page.

■ **Note** In all these examples, the aspnet_compiler is compiling a web application to prepare it for deployment. However, you have another option—you can compile a website *after* it's transferred to the web server. This is called an *in-place compilation*, and it won't remove your code. Instead, it simply creates and caches the compiled versions of your web pages so that there won't be any delay for the first set of requests. In-place compilation is useful when you want to optimize performance but don't want to (or need to) hide the code. To perform an in-place compilation, omit the target directory when you use aspnet_compiler.

Deploying with Visual Studio 2005

Visual Studio 2005 aims to simplify web application deployment in the same way it simplifies the task of designing rich web pages. Although you need to understand how IIS works in order to manage virtual directories effectively (and fix the inevitable configuration problems), Visual Studio includes features that integrate with IIS and allow you to create virtual directories without leaving the comfort of your design-time environment.

Visual Studio has three key deployment-related features:

- You can create a virtual directory when you create a new project.
- You can use the Copy Web Site feature to transfer an existing website to a virtual directory.
- You can use the Publish feature to compile your website and transfer it to another location.

Creating a Virtual Directory for a New Project

When you create a website in Visual Studio, you can simultaneously create a virtual directory for that website. If you choose to do so, Visual Studio won't use its built-in web server. Instead, all your requests will flow through IIS. (Happily, you'll still see the same behavior and have access to the same debugging tools.)

To try this, select File ➤ New Web Site. In the New Web Site dialog box, choose HTTP for the location (instead of File System). You can then supply a URL. For example, if you supply `http://localhost/MyWebSite`, Visual Studio will create the virtual directory MyWebSite on the current computer. Figure 12-18 shows an example.

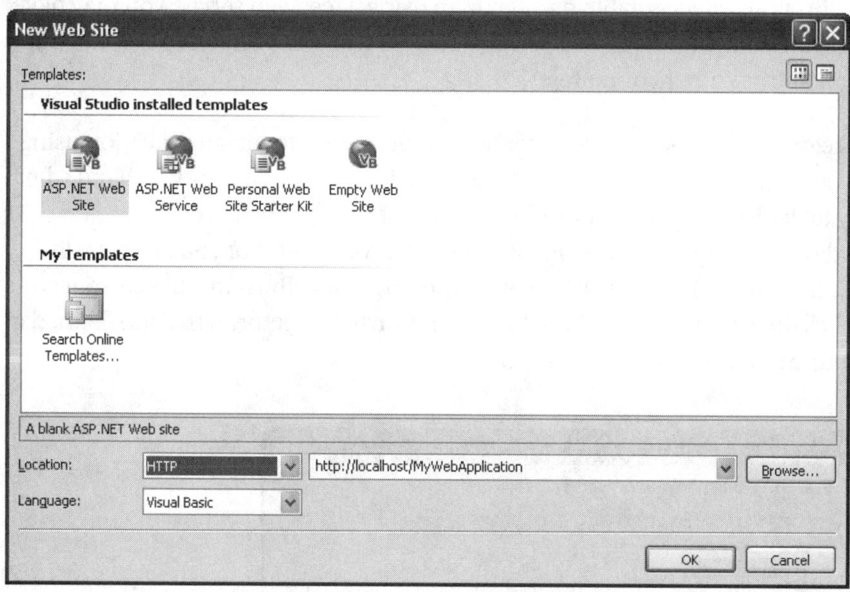

Figure 12-18. *Creating a virtual directory to hold a new project*

■ **Note** If you specify a virtual directory that already exists, Visual Studio won't create it—it will just use the existing directory. This is convenient, because it allows you to set up the virtual directory ahead of time with exactly the options you want and then create the website in it.

This approach often isn't the best way to create a virtual directory. It has several limitations:

- It forces you to set the virtual directory up when you first create the application. If you've already created an application, this option isn't available.
- The virtual directory is always created in the c:\Inetpub\wwwroot directory. This can make it hard to keep track of where your files are. (As you'll discover shortly, you can work around this limitation.)

- You can configure other settings, such as default pages, custom errors, and virtual directory permissions.
- Any change you make and debugging you perform act on the live version of your application that's running on the web server. If you're using a production web server, this is an unacceptable risk. If you're using a test web server, you may have opened potential security issues because remote users can request pages in your application from other computers.

For these reasons, it's more common for developers to create their application using the built-in web server in Visual Studio and then create a virtual directory by hand when they're ready to deploy it to a test or production web server.

Visual Studio doesn't give you the full options of IIS Manager, but you can get a little more control. In the New Web Site dialog box, type **http://localhost** (for the current computer), and click the Browse button. You'll see all the virtual directories that are defined in IIS, just as in IIS Manager (see Figure 12-19).

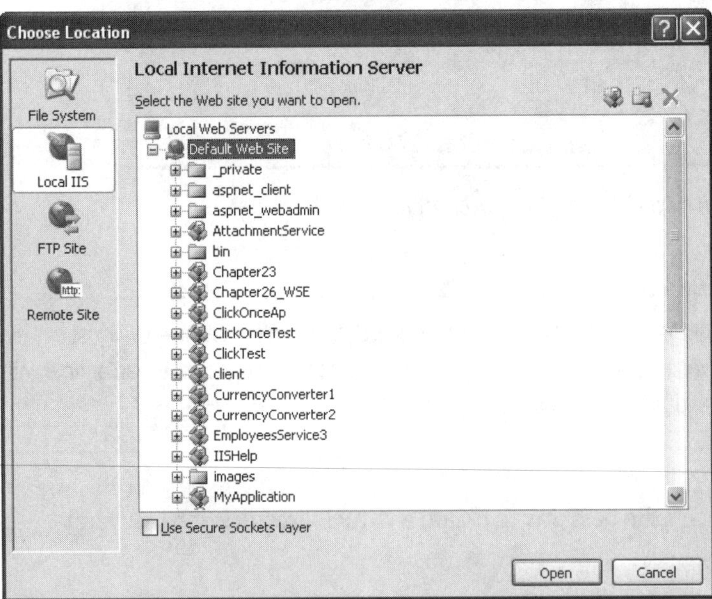

Figure 12-19. *Viewing virtual directories in Visual Studio*

You can't view or change their properties, but you can choose an existing virtual directory where you want to create your application. You can also use the Create New Virtual Directory button in the top-right corner of the window (it appears as a folder icon). Click this button, and you'll get the chance to supply the virtual directory alias *and* its physical file path (see Figure 12-20).

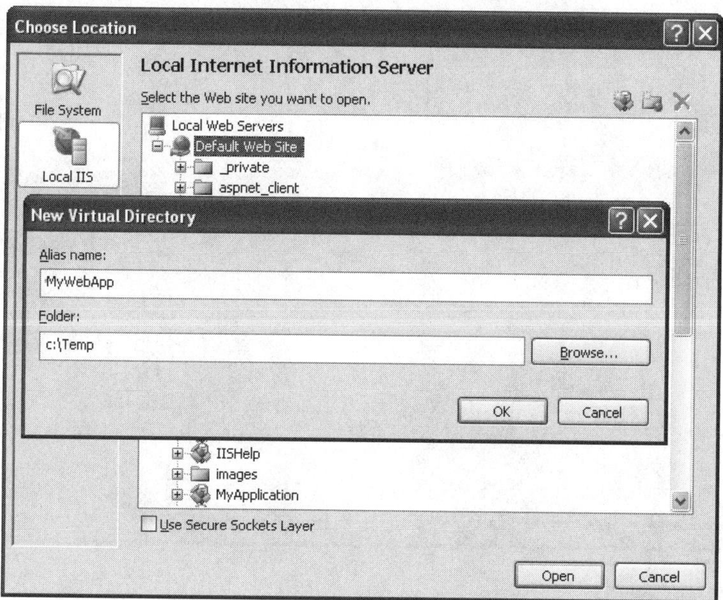

Figure 12-20. *Creating a virtual directory in a specific location*

Copying a Website

Visual Studio also includes a quick and easy way to transfer your web application files without using a separate program or leaving the design environment. You simply need to open your web project and select Project ➤ Copy Web Site from the menu. This opens a new Visual Studio dialog box that will be familiar to anyone who has used Microsoft FrontPage (see Figure 12-21).

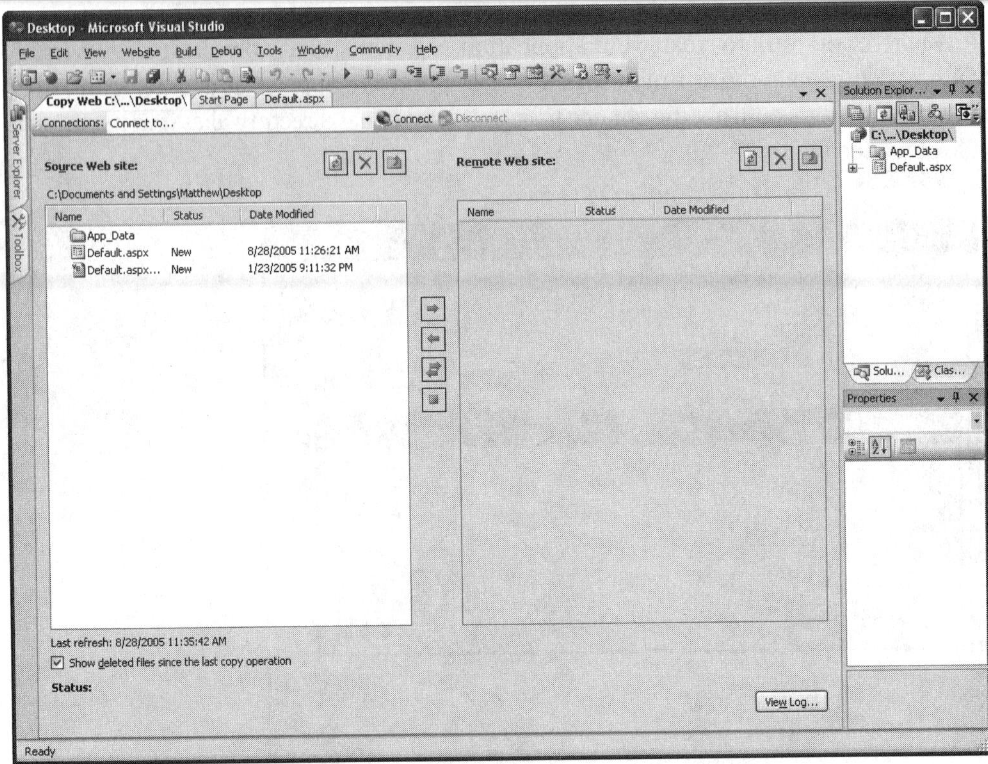

Figure 12-21. *Copying a website*

This window includes two file lists. On the left are the files in the current project (on your local hard drive). On the right are the files on the target location (the remote web server). When you first open this window, you won't see anything on the right, because you haven't specified the target. You need to click the Connect button at the top of the window to supply this information.

When you click Connect, Visual Studio shows a familiar dialog box—it looks almost the same as what you see when you create a virtual directory for a new project. Using this window, you can specify one of the following types of locations:

File System: This is the easiest choice—you simply need to browse through a tree of drives and directories or through the shares provided by other computers on the network. If you want to create a new directory for your application, just click the Create New Folder icon above the top-right corner of the directory tree.

Local IIS: This choice allows you to browse the virtual directories made available on the local computer through IIS. You can create a new virtual directory by clicking the Create New Web Application icon at the top-right corner of the virtual directory tree.

FTP Site: This option isn't quite as convenient as browsing for a directory—instead, you'll need to enter all the connection information, including the FTP site, port, directory, and a user name and password before you can connect (see Figure 12-22).

Remote Web Server: This option accesses a website at a specified URL using HTTP. For this to work, the web server must have the FrontPage Extensions installed. When you connect, you'll be prompted for a user name and password.

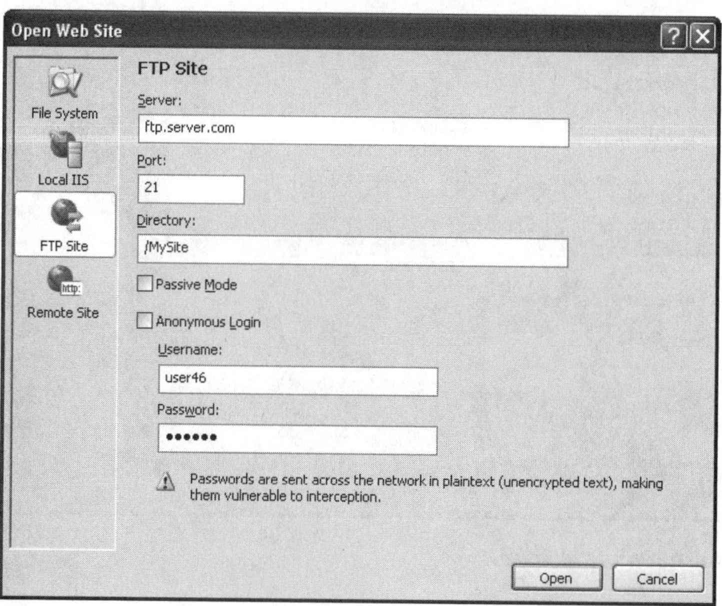

Figure 12-22. *Setting the target site*

Once you choose the appropriate destination, click Open. Visual Studio will attempt to connect to the remote site and retrieve a list of its files.

The Copy Web Site feature is particularly useful for updating a web server. That's because Visual Studio compares the file list on the local and remote websites, and it flags files that exist in one location only (with the status New) or those that are newer versions (with the status Changed). You can then select the files you want to transfer and click one of the arrow buttons to transfer them from one location to the other (see Figure 12-23).

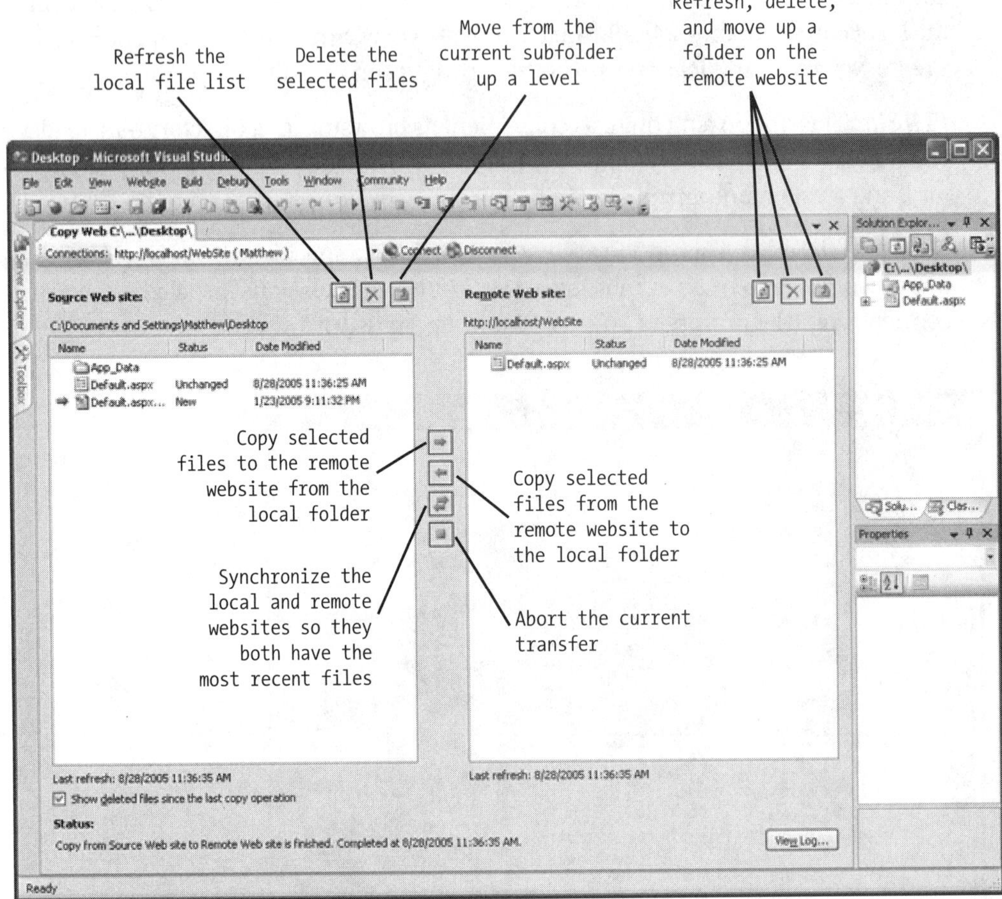

Figure 12-23. *Synchronizing a remote website*

Publishing a Website

The website copying feature is great for transferring files to a test server. However, it doesn't give you the option of precompiling your code. If you're deploying your application to a live web server and you want to keep the source code tightly locked down, you'll want something more.

As described earlier in this chapter, you can use the aspnet_compiler command-line utility to compile ASP.NET applications. This functionality is also available in Visual Studio through the website publishing feature. While the website copying feature is designed to let you update individual files (which is ideal when updating a test server), the publishing feature is intended to transfer your entire website in compiled form with a couple of clicks.

Here's what you need to do:

1. Select Build ➤ Publish from the menu. The Publish Web Site dialog box will appear (see Figure 12-24).

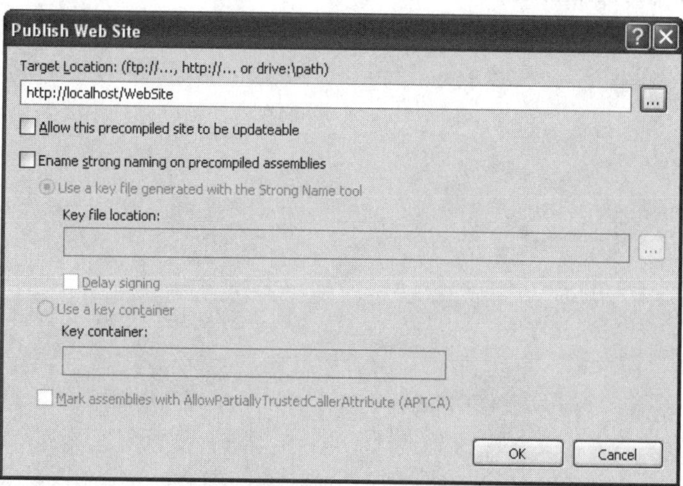

Figure 12-24. *Publishing a website*

2. Enter a file path or a URL for an FTP site or FrontPage-enabled site in the Target Location text box. To get some help, click the ellipsis (...) next to the Target Location text box. This opens the familiar dialog box with options for choosing (or creating) a virtual directory, file path, FTP site, or remote server.

3. Leave the other check boxes unselected. You can choose to allow updates, in which case the code-behind files are compiled, but the .aspx files with the HTML and tags aren't compiled. This option allows you to make only limited changes (and it increases the potential for accidental changes or tampering), so it isn't terribly useful.

4. Click OK. Your website files will be compiled with aspnet_compiler and then transferred to the target location.

The Last Word

This chapter covered IIS (the web server that powers ASP.NET websites) and the deployment model for ASP.NET. You also considered the tools that Visual Studio includes to make deployment easier. This rounds out Part 2 of this book, and you now have all the fundamentals you need to create a basic ASP.NET website. In the next part, you'll dive into practical database programming with ADO.NET.

PART 3

Working with Data

CHAPTER 13

ADO.NET Fundamentals

So far, you've learned that ASP.NET isn't just a new way to create modern web applications—it's also part of an ambitious multilayered strategy called .NET. ASP.NET is only one component in Microsoft's .NET platform, which includes new languages, a new philosophy for cross-language integration, a new way of looking at components and deployment, and a shared class library with components that allow you to do everything from handling errors to analyzing XML documents. In this chapter, you'll discover that the .NET Framework has yet another surprise in store: ADO.NET, Microsoft's latest data access model.

ADO.NET allows you to interact with relational databases and other data sources. Quite simply, ADO.NET is the technology that ASP.NET applications use to communicate with a database, whether they need to add a new customer record, log a purchase, or display a product catalog.

In this chapter, you'll learn about ADO.NET and the family of objects that provides its functionality. You'll also learn how to put these objects to work by creating simple pages that use ADO.NET to retrieve information from a database and apply changes.

Note ASP.NET 2.0 includes a new data binding framework that can hide the underlying ADO.NET plumbing in your web pages. You can skip to Chapter 14 to start learning about these features right away. However, to build scalable, high-performance web applications, you'll need to write custom database code. That means you'll need a thorough understanding of the concepts presented in this chapter.

ADO.NET and Data Management

Almost every piece of software ever written works with data. In fact, a typical Internet application is often just a thin user interface shell on top of a sophisticated database program that reads and writes information from a database on the web server. At its simplest, a database program might allow a user to perform simple searches and display results in a formatted table. A more sophisticated ASP.NET application might use a database behind the scenes to retrieve information, which is then processed and displayed in the appropriate format and location in the browser. The user might not even be aware (or care) that the displayed information originates from a database. Using a database is an excellent way to start dividing the user interface logic from the content, which allows you to create a site that can work with dynamic, easily updated data.

The Role of the Database

The most common way to manage data is to use a database. Database technology is particularly useful for business software, which typically requires hierarchical sets of related information. For example, a typical database for a sales program consists of a list of customers, a list of products, and a list of sales that draws on information from the other two tables. This type of information is best described using a relational model, which is the philosophy that underlies all modern database products, including SQL Server, Oracle, and even Microsoft Access. (In a relational model, information is broken down into its smallest and most concise units. For example, a sales record doesn't store all the information about the products that were sold. Instead, it stores just a product ID that refers to a full record in a product table, as shown in Figure 13-1.)

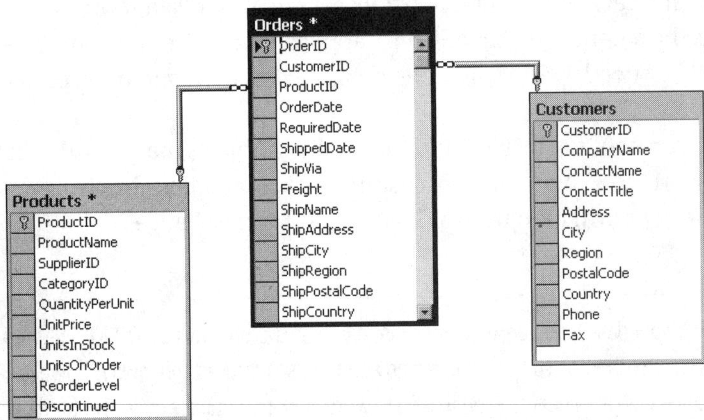

Figure 13-1. *Basic table relationships*

Although it's technically possible to organize data into tables and store it on the hard drive as an XML file, this wouldn't be very flexible. Instead, a web application needs a full relational database management system (RDBMS), such as SQL Server. The RDBMS handles the data infrastructure, ensuring optimum performance and reliability. These products take the responsibility of providing data to multiple users simultaneously and making sure that certain rules are followed (for example, disallowing conflicting changes or invalid data types).

In most ASP.NET applications, you'll need to use a database for some tasks. Here are some basic examples of data-driven ASP.NET applications:

- E-commerce sites involve managing sales, customers, and inventory information. This information might be displayed directly on the screen (as with a product catalog) or used unobtrusively to record transactions or customer information.
- Online knowledge bases and customized search engines involve less structured databases that store vast quantities of information or links to various documents and resources.
- Information-based sites such as web portals can't be easily scalable or manageable unless all the information they use is stored in a consistent, strictly defined format. Typically, a site like this is matched with another ASP.NET program that allows an authorized user to add or update the displayed information by modifying the corresponding database records through a browser interface.

You probably won't have any trouble thinking about where you need to use database technology in an ASP.NET application. What Internet application couldn't benefit from a guest book that records user comments or a simple e-mail address submission form that uses a back-end database to store a list of potential customers or contacts? This is where ADO.NET comes into the picture. ADO.NET is a technology designed to let an ASP.NET program (or any other .NET program, for that matter) access data.

Database Access in the Internet World

Accessing a database in an Internet application is a completely different scenario than accessing a database in a typical desktop or client/server program. Most developers hone their database skills in the desktop world and run into serious problems when they try to apply what they have learned with stand-alone applications in the world of the Web. Quite simply, web applications raise a whole new set of considerations and potential problems.

Problems of Scale

A web application has the potential to be used by hundreds of simultaneous users. This means it can't be casual about using server memory or limited resources such as database connections. If you design an ASP application that acquires a database connection and holds it for even a few minutes, other users may notice a definite slowdown or even be locked out of the database completely. And if you don't carefully consider database concurrency issues, problems such as locked records and conflicting updates can make it difficult to provide consistent data to all users.

All of these problems are possible with traditional client/server database development. The difference is that they are far less likely to have any negative effect because the typical load (the number of simultaneous users) is dramatically lower. Database practices that might slightly hamper the performance of a client/server application can multiply rapidly and cause significant problems in a web application.

Problems of State

As you already know, HTTP is a stateless protocol. When a user browses to a page in an ASP.NET application, a connection is made, the code is processed, an HTML page is returned, and the connection is immediately severed. Although users may have the illusion that they are interacting with a continuously running application, they are really just receiving a string of static pages. (ASP.NET makes this illusion so convincing that it's worth asking if it can really be considered an illusion at all.)

With data-driven web applications, the stateless nature of HTTP can be a thorny problem. The typical approach is to connect to a database, read information, display it, and then close the database connection. This approach runs into difficulties if you want the user to be able to modify the retrieved information. In this scenario, the application requires a certain amount of intelligence in order to be able to identify the original record, build a SQL statement to select it, and update it with the new values.

Introducing ADO.NET

ADO.NET has a few characteristics that make it different from previous data access technologies (such as ADO, the database library that was used in classic ASP pages).

The DataSet

Many ADO.NET tasks revolve around a new object called the DataSet. The DataSet is a cache of information that has been queried from your database. The innovative features of the DataSet are that it's disconnected (see the next section) and can store more than one table. For example, a DataSet could store a list of customers, a list of products, and a list of customer orders. You can even define all these relationships in the DataSet to prevent invalid data and make it easier to answer questions such as "What products did Joe Smith order?"

Disconnected Access

Disconnected access is the one of the most important characteristics of ADO.NET and perhaps the single best example of the new .NET philosophy for accessing data.

With previous database access technologies, it's easy to hold open a connection with the database server while your code does some work. This live connection allows you to make immediate updates, and you can even see the changes made by other users in real time. Unfortunately, database servers can provide only a limited number of connections

DISCONNECTED ACCESS RAISES NEW ISSUES

Disconnected access is a key requirement for Internet applications, and it's also an approach that often requires additional consideration and precautions. Disconnected access makes it easy for users to create inconsistent updates, a problem that won't be resolved (or even identified) until the update is committed to the original data source. Disconnected access can also require special considerations because changes aren't applied in the order they were entered. This design can cause problems when you modify related records.

Fortunately, ADO.NET provides a rich set of features to deal with all these possibilities. However, you do need to be aware that the new disconnected model may introduce new considerations and require extra care.

before they reject connection requests. The longer you keep a connection open, the greater the chance becomes that another user will be prevented from accessing the database. In a poorly written program, the database connection is kept open while other tasks are being performed. But even in a well-written program using an old data access technology such as ADO, the connection must be kept open until all the data is processed and the query results are no longer needed.

ADO.NET has an entirely different philosophy. In ADO.NET you still create a connection to a database, but you're able to close the connection much faster. That's because you're able to fill a DataSet object with a *copy* of the information drawn from the database. You can then close the connection before you start processing the data. This means you can easily process and manipulate the data without worrying, because you aren't using a valuable database connection. (Of course, if you change the information in the DataSet, the information in the corresponding table in the database isn't changed. You'll need to reconnect to commit any changes.)

XML Integration

ADO.NET has deep support for XML. This fact isn't immediately obvious when you're working with a DataSet object, because you'll usually use the built-in methods and properties of the DataSet to perform all the data manipulation you need. But if you delve a little deeper, you'll discover that you can access the information in the DataSet as an XML document. You can even modify values, remove rows, and add new records by modifying the XML, and the DataSet will be updated automatically.

SQL Server 2005 Express Edition

This chapter includes code that works with SQL Server 7 or later. If you don't have a test database server handy, you may want to use SQL Server 2005 Express Edition, the free data engine included with some versions of Visual Studio and downloadable separately. SQL Server 2005 Express Edition is a scaled-down version of SQL Server 2005 that's free to distribute. SQL Server 2005 Express Edition has certain limitations—for example, it can use only one CPU and a maximum of 1GB of RAM, databases can't be larger than 4GB, and graphical tools aren't included. However, it's still remarkably powerful and suitable for many mid-scale websites. Even better, you can easily upgrade from SQL Server 2005 Express Edition to a for-fee version of SQL Server 2005 if you need more features later. For more information about SQL Server 2005 Express Edition, refer to the MSDN Help or the white paper at `http://msdn.microsoft.com/library/en-us/dnsse/html/sseoverview.asp`.

■ **Note** This part uses examples drawn from the pubs and Northwind databases, which are sample databases included with many versions of Microsoft SQL Server. If you aren't using SQL Server, or if you're using SQL Server 2005, you won't have these databases preinstalled. However, you can easily install them using the scripts provided with the online samples. See the readme for full instructions.

Browsing and Modifying Databases in Visual Studio

As an ASP.NET developer, you may have the responsibility of creating the database required for a web application. Alternatively, it may already exist, or it may be the responsibility of a dedicated database administrator. If you're using a full version of SQL Server, you'll probably use a graphical tool such as Enterprise Manager to create and manage your databases. If you're using SQL Server 2005 Express Edition, you won't have any dedicated tools, so you'll need to use the support that's built into Visual Studio.

Here's how you can get started: First, choose View ➤ Server Explorer to show the Server Explorer window. Then, using the Data Connections node in the Server Explorer, you can connect to existing databases or create new ones. Assuming you've installed the pubs database (see the readme file for instructions), you can create a connection to it by following these steps:

1. Right-click the Data Connections node, and choose Add Connection.
2. If you're using a full version of SQL Server, enter **localhost** as your server name. This indicates the database server is the default instance on the local computer. (Replace this with the name of a remote computer if needed.) If you're using SQL Server Express Edition, you'll need to use the server name localhost\SQLEXPRESS instead, as shown in Figure 13-2. The second part indicates that you're connecting to a *named instance* of SQL Server, with the name SQLEXPRESS. This is the default for SQL Server 2005 Express Edition.

Figure 13-2. *Creating a connection in Visual Studio*

3. Click Test Connection to verify that this is the location of your database. If you haven't installed a database product yet, and you didn't choose to install SQL Server 2005 Express Edition when you installed Visual Studio, this step will fail. Otherwise, you'll know that your database server is installed and running.

4. In the Select or Enter a Database Name list, choose the pubs database. If you're using SQL Server 2005 Express Edition, you'll begin with no databases at all, and you'll need to install the pubs database using the script that's included with the sample code. Similarly, the full version of SQL Server 2005 doesn't include the pubs database.

■ **Tip** Alternatively, you can choose to create a new database by right-clicking the Data Connections node and choosing Create New SQL Server Database.

---

5. Click OK. The database connection will appear in the Server Explorer window. You can now explore its groups to see and edit tables, stored procedures, and more. For example, if you right-click a table and choose Show Table Data, you'll see a grid of records that you can browse and edit, as shown in Figure 13-3.

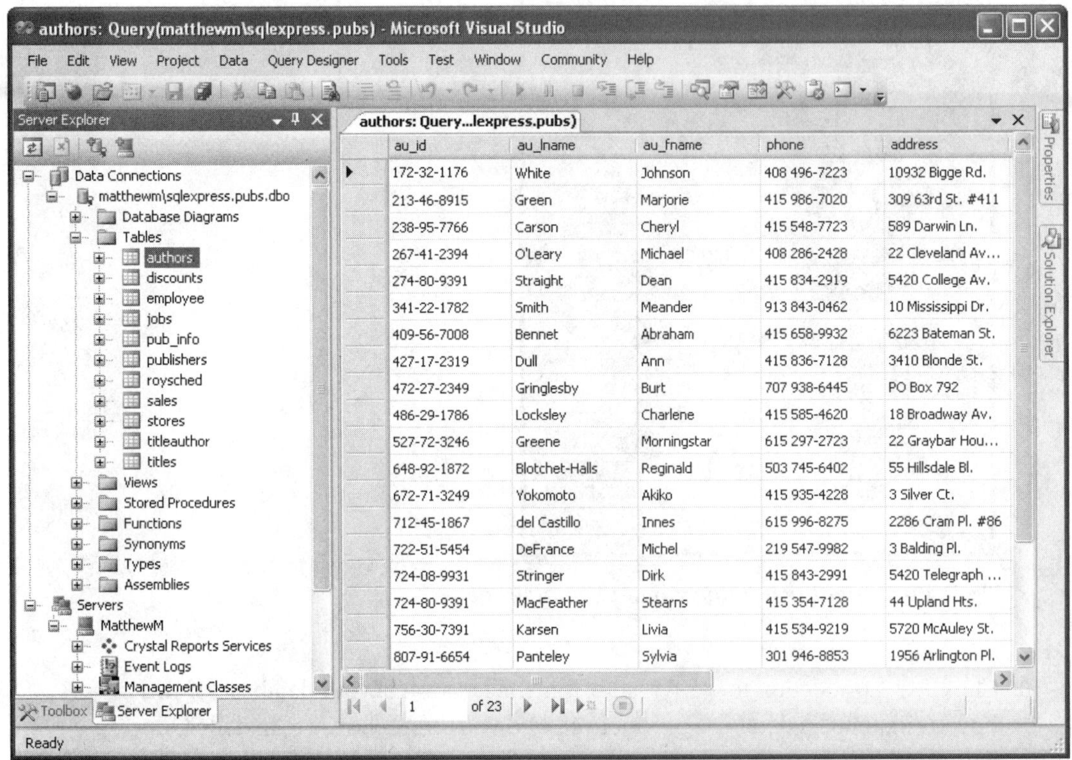

Figure 13-3. *Editing table data in Visual Studio*

SQL Basics

When you interact with a data source through ADO.NET, you use SQL to retrieve, modify, and update information. In some cases, ADO.NET will hide some of the details for you or even generate required SQL statements automatically. However, to design an efficient database application with a minimal amount of frustration, you need to understand the basic concepts of SQL.

SQL (Structured Query Language) is a standard data access language used to interact with relational databases. Different databases differ in their support of SQL or add other features, but the core commands used to select, add, and modify data are common. In a database product such as SQL Server, it's possible to use SQL to create fairly sophisticated SQL scripts for stored procedures and triggers (although they have little of the power of a full object-oriented programming language). When working with ADO.NET, however, you'll probably use only the following standard types of SQL statements:

- A Select statement retrieves records.
- An Update statement modifies existing records.
- An Insert statement adds a new record.
- A Delete statement deletes existing records.

If you already have a good understanding of SQL, you can skip the next few sections. Otherwise, read on for a quick tour of SQL fundamentals.

■ **Tip** To learn more about SQL, use one of the SQL tutorials available on the Internet, such as the one at `http://www.w3schools.com/sql`. If you're working with SQL Server, you can use Microsoft's thorough Books Online reference to become a database guru.

Running Queries in Visual Studio

If you've never used SQL before, you may want to play around with it and create some sample queries before you start using it in an ASP.NET site. Most database products provide some sort of tool for testing queries. If you're using a full version of SQL Server, you can try the SQL Query Analyzer. If you're using SQL Server 2005, or you just don't want to use the design environment, you can use the Server Explorer feature described earlier. Just follow these steps:

1. Right-click your connection, and choose New Query.
2. Choose the table (or tables) you want to use in your query from the Add Table dialog box (as shown in Figure 13-4), and then click Close.

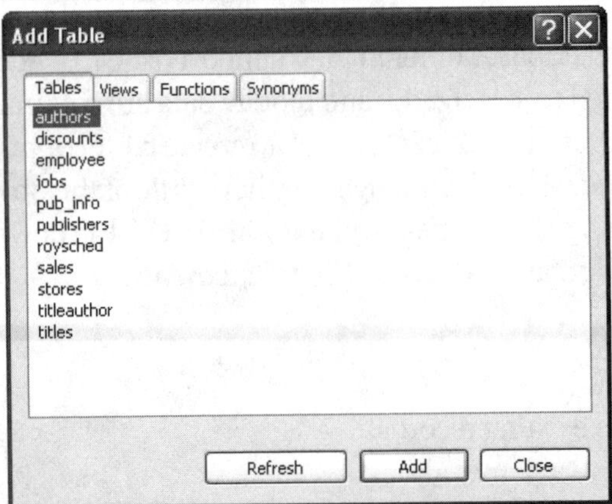

Figure 13-4. *Adding tables to a query*

3. You'll now see a handy query-building window. You can create your query by adding check marks next to the fields you want, or you can edit the SQL by hand in the lower portion of the window. Best of all, if you edit the SQL directly, you can type in anything—you don't need to stick to the tables you selected in step 2, and you don't need to restrict yourself to Select statements.

4. When you're ready to run the query, select Query Designer ➤ Execute SQL. Assuming your query doesn't have any errors, you'll get one of two results. If you're selecting records, the results will appear at the bottom of the window (see Figure 13-5). If you're deleting or updating records, a message box will appear informing you how many records were affected.

■ **Tip** When programming with ADO.NET, it always helps to know your database. If you have information on hand about the data types it uses, the stored procedures it provides, and the user account you need to use, you'll be able to work more quickly and with less chance of error.

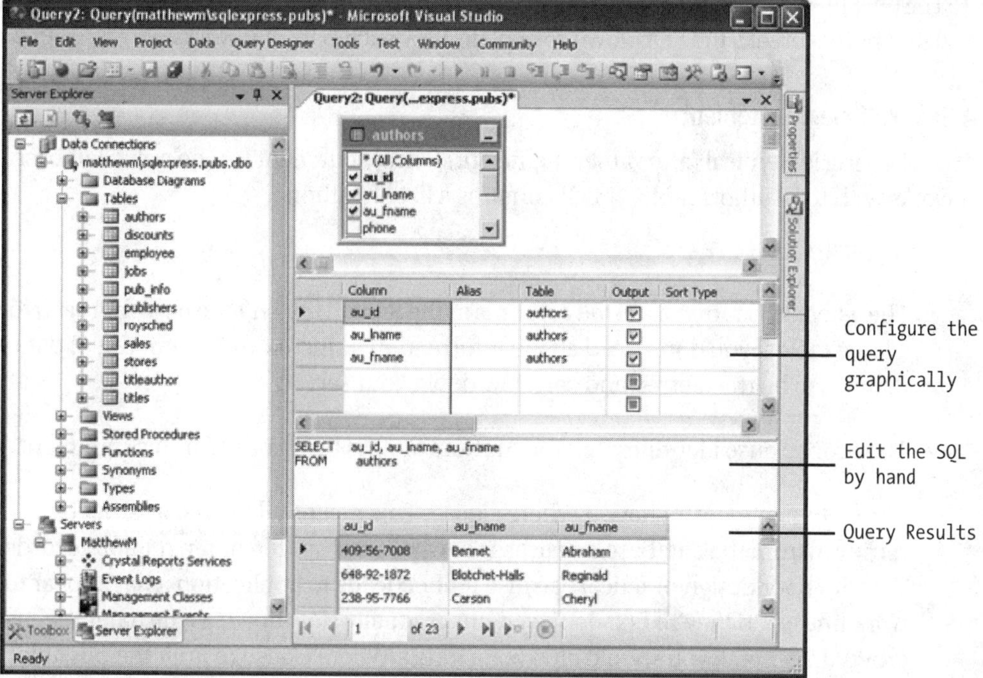

Figure 13-5. *Executing a query*

The Select Statement

To retrieve one or more rows of data, you use a Select statement. A basic SQL statement has the following structure:

```
SELECT [columns] FROM [tables] WHERE [search_condition]
       ORDER BY [order_expression ASC | DESC]
```

This format really just scratches the surface of SQL. If you want, you can create more sophisticated queries that use subgrouping, averaging and totaling, and other options (such as setting a maximum number of returned rows). By performing this work in a query (instead of in your application), you can often create far more efficient applications.

The next few sections present sample Select statements. After each example, a series of bulleted points breaks the SQL down to explain how each part of it works.

A Sample Select Statement

The following is a typical (and rather inefficient) Select statement for the pubs database. It works with the Authors table, which contains a list of authors:

```
SELECT * FROM Authors
```

- The asterisk (*) retrieves all the columns in the table. This isn't the best approach for a large table if you don't need all the information. It increases the amount of data that has to be transferred and can slow down your server.

- The From clause identifies that the Authors table is being used for this statement.

- The statement doesn't have a Where clause. This means all the records will be retrieved from the database, regardless of whether it has ten or ten million records. This is a poor design practice, because it often leads to applications that appear to work fine when they're first deployed but gradually slow down as the database grows. In general, you should always include a Where clause to limit the possible number of rows (unless you absolutely need them all). Often, queries are limited by a date field (for example, including all orders that were placed in the last three months).

- The statement doesn't have an Order By clause. This is a perfectly acceptable approach, especially if order doesn't matter or you plan to sort the data on your own using the tools provided in ADO.NET.

Improving the Select Statement

Here's another example that retrieves a list of author names:

```
SELECT au_lname, au_fname FROM Authors WHERE State='MI' ORDER BY au_lname ASC
```

- Only two columns are retrieved (au_lname and au_fname). They correspond to the first and last names of the author.

- A Where clause restricts results to those authors who live in the specified state. Note that the Where clause requires apostrophes around the value you want to match (unless it is a numeric value).

- An Order By clause sorts the information alphabetically by the author's last name.

An Alternative Select Statement

Here's one last example:

```
SELECT TOP 100 * FROM Sales ORDER BY ord_date DESC
```

- This example uses the Top clause instead of a Where statement. The database rows will be sorted, and the first 100 matching results will be retrieved. In this case, it's the 100 most recent orders. You could also use this type of statement to find the most expensive items you sell or the best-performing employees.
- This example uses an Order By expression that sorts orders by the order date, with the most recent orders first.

The Where Clause

In many respects, the Where clause is the most important part of the Select statement. You can combine multiple conditions with the And keyword, and you can specify greater-than and less-than comparisons by using the greater-than (>) and less-than (<) operators.

The following is an example with a different table and a more sophisticated Where statement:

```
SELECT * FROM Sales WHERE ord_date < '2000/01/01' AND ord_date > '1987/01/01'
```

- This example uses the international date format to compare date values. Although SQL Server supports many date formats, yyyy/mm/dd is recommended to prevent ambiguity.
- If you were using Microsoft Access, you would need to use the U.S. date format mm/dd/yyyy and replace the apostrophes around the date with the number (#) symbol.

String Matching with the Like Operator

The Like operator allows you to perform partial string matching to filter records where a particular field starts with, ends with, or contains a certain set of characters. For example, if you wanted to see all store names that start with *B*, you could use the following statement:

```
SELECT * FROM Stores WHERE stor_name LIKE 'B%'
```

To see a list of all stores *ending* with *B*, you would put the percent sign *before* the B, like this:

```
SELECT * FROM Stores WHERE stor_name LIKE '%B'
```

The third way to use the Like operator is to return any records that contain a certain character or sequence of characters. For example, suppose you want to see all stores that have the word *BOOK* somewhere in the name. In this case, you could use a SQL statement like this:

```
SELECT * FROM Stores WHERE stor_name LIKE '%book%'
```

By default, SQL is not case-sensitive, so this syntax finds instances of *BOOK*, *book*, or any variation of mixed case.

Finally, you can indicate one of a set of characters, rather than just any character, by listing the allowed characters within square brackets. Here's an example:

```
SELECT * FROM Stores WHERE stor_name LIKE '[abcd]%'
```

This SQL statement will return stores with names starting with *a*, *b*, *c*, or *d*.

Aggregate Queries

The SQL language also defines special *aggregate functions*. Aggregate functions work with a set of values but return only a single value. For example, you can use an aggregate function to count the number of records in a table or to calculate the average price of a product. Table 13-1 lists the most commonly used aggregate functions

Table 13-1. *SQL Aggregate Functions*

Command	Description
Avg(fieldname)	Calculates the average of all values in a given numeric field
Sum(fieldname)	Calculates the sum of all values in a given numeric field
Min(fieldname) and Max(fieldname)	Finds the minimum or maximum value in a number field
Count(*)	Returns the number of rows in the result set
Count(DISTINCT fieldname)	Returns the number of unique (and non-null) rows in the result set for the specified field

For example, here's a query that returns a single value—the number of records in the Authors table:

```
SELECT COUNT(*) FROM Authors
```

And here's how you could calculate the total quantity of all sales by adding together the qty field in each record:

```
SELECT SUM(qty) FROM Sales
```

The SQL Update Statement

The SQL Update statement selects all the records that match a specified search expression and then modifies them all according to an update expression. At its simplest, the Update statement has the following format:

```
UPDATE [table] SET [update_expression] WHERE [search_condition]
```

Typically, you'll use an Update statement to modify a single record. The following example adjusts the phone column in a single author record. It uses the unique author ID to find the correct row.

```
UPDATE Authors SET phone='408 496-2222' WHERE au_id='172-32-1176'
```

This statement returns the number of affected rows. (See Figure 13-6 for an example in Visual Studio.) However, it won't display the change. To do that, you need to request the row by performing another SQL statement:

```
SELECT phone FROM Authors WHERE au_id='172-32-1176'
```

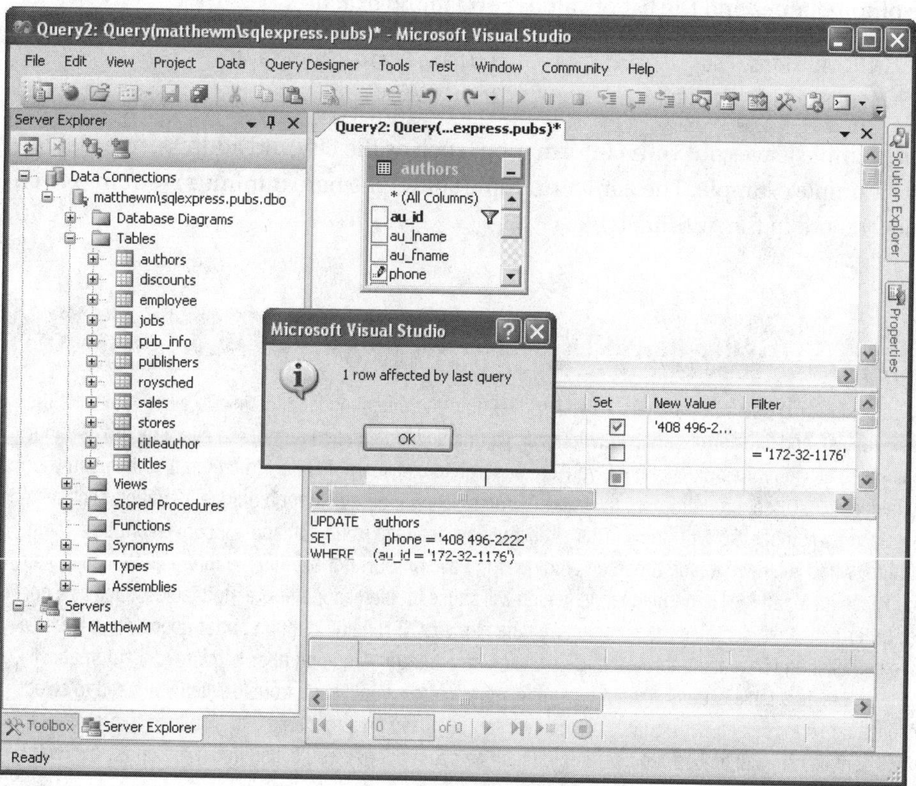

Figure 13-6. *Executing an update query in Visual Studio*

As with a Select statement, you can use an Update statement with several criteria:

```
UPDATE Authors SET au_lname='Whiteson', au_fname='John'
    WHERE au_lname='White' AND au_fname='Johnson'
```

You can even use the Update statement to update an entire range of matching records. The following example modifies the phone number for every author who lives in California:

```
UPDATE Authors SET phone='408 496-2222' WHERE state='CA'
```

The SQL Insert Statement

The SQL Insert statement adds a new record to a table with the information you specify. It takes the following form:

```
INSERT INTO [table] ([column_list]) VALUES ([value_list])
```

You can provide the information in any order you want, as long as you make sure the list of column names and the list of values correspond exactly.

```
INSERT INTO Authors (au_id, au_lname, au_fname, zip, contract)
       VALUES ('998-72-3566', 'Khan', 'John' 84152, 0)
```

This example leaves out some information, such as the city and address, in order to provide a simple example. The earlier example shows the bare minimum required to create a new record in the Authors table.

AUTO-INCREMENT FIELDS ARE INDISPENSABLE

If you're designing a database, make sure you add an auto-incrementing identity field to every table. It's the fastest, easiest, and least error-prone way to assign a unique identification number to every record. Without an automatically generated identity field, you'll need to go to considerable effort to create and maintain your own unique field. Often, programmers fall into the trap of using a data field for a unique identifier, such as a Social Security number (SSN) or name. This almost always leads to trouble at some inconvenient time far in the future, when you need to add a person who doesn't have an SSN (for example, a foreign national) or you need to account for an SSN or name change (which will cause problems for other related tables, such as a purchase order table that identifies the purchaser by the name or SSN field). A much better approach is to use a unique identifier and have the database engine assign an arbitrary unique number to every row automatically.

If you create a table without a unique identification column, you'll have trouble when you need to select that specific row for deletion or updates. Selecting records based on a text field can also lead to problems if the field contains special embedded characters (such as apostrophes). You'll also find it extremely awkward to create table relationships.

Remember, database tables often have requirements that can prevent you from adding a record unless you fill in all the fields with valid information. Alternatively, some fields may be configured to use a default value if left blank. In the Authors table, some fields are required, and a special format is defined for the ZIP code and author ID.

One feature the Authors table doesn't use is an automatically incrementing identity column. This feature, which is supported in most relational database products, assigns a unique value to a specified column when you perform an insert operation. When you insert a record into a table that has a unique incrementing ID, you shouldn't specify a value for the ID. Instead, allow the database to choose one automatically.

The SQL Delete Statement

The Delete statement is even easier to use. It specifies criteria for one or more rows that you want to remove. Be careful: once you delete a row, it's gone for good!

```
DELETE FROM [table] WHERE [search_condition]
```

The following example removes a single matching row from the Authors table:

```
DELETE FROM Authors WHERE au_id='172-32-1176'
```

The Delete and Update commands return a single piece of information: the number of affected records. You can examine this value and use it to determine whether the operation was successful or executed as expected.

The rest of this chapter shows how you can combine SQL with the ADO.NET objects to retrieve and manipulate data in your web applications.

ADO.NET Basics

ADO.NET relies on the functionality in a small set of core objects. You can divide these objects into two groups: those that are used to contain and manage data (such as DataSet, DataTable, DataRow, and DataRelation) and those that are used to connect to a specific data source (such as Connection, Command, and DataReader).

The data container objects are completely generic. No matter what data source you use, once you extract the data, it's stored using the same DataSet class. Think of the DataSet as playing the same role as a collection or an array—it's a package for data. The difference is that the DataSet is customized for relational data, which means it understands concepts such as rows, columns, and table relationships natively.

The second group of objects exists in several different flavors. Each set of data interaction objects is called an ADO.NET *data provider*. Data providers are customized so that each one uses the best-performing way of interacting with its data source. For example, the SQL Server data provider is designed to work with SQL Server 7 or later. Internally, it uses SQL Server's TDS (tabular data stream) protocol for communicating, thus guaranteeing the best possible performance. If you're using Oracle, you'll need to use the Oracle provider objects instead.

It's important to understand that you can use any data provider in almost the same way, with almost the same code. The provider objects derive from the same base classes, implement the same interfaces, and expose the same set of methods and properties. In some cases, a data provider object will provide custom functionality that's available only with certain data sources, such as SQL Server's ability to perform XML queries. However, the basic members used for retrieving and modifying data are identical.

Microsoft includes the following four providers:

SQL Server provider: Provides optimized access to a SQL Server database (version 7.0 or later).

OLE DB provider: Provides access to any data source that has an OLE DB driver.

Oracle provider: Provides optimized access to an Oracle database (version 8i or later).

ODBC provider: Provides access to any data source that has an ODBC (Open Database Connectivity) driver.

In addition, third-party developers and database vendors have released their own ADO.NET providers, which follow the same conventions and can be used in the same way as those that are included with the .NET Framework.

When choosing a provider, you should first try to find one that's customized for your data source. If you can't find a suitable provider, you can use the OLE DB provider, as long as you have an OLE DB driver for your data source. The OLE DB technology has been around for many years as part of ADO, so most data sources provide an OLE DB driver (including SQL Server, Oracle, Access, MySQL, and many more). In the rare situation that you can't find a full provider or an OLE DB driver, you can fall back on the ODBC provider, which works in conjunction with an ODBC driver.

■ **Tip** Microsoft includes the OLE DB provider with ADO.NET so that you can use your existing OLE DB drivers. However, if you can find a provider that's customized specifically for your data source, you should use it instead. For example, you can connect to SQL Server database using either the SQL Server provider or the OLE DB provider, but the first approach will perform best.

To help understand the different layers that come into play with ADO.NET, refer to Figure 13-7.

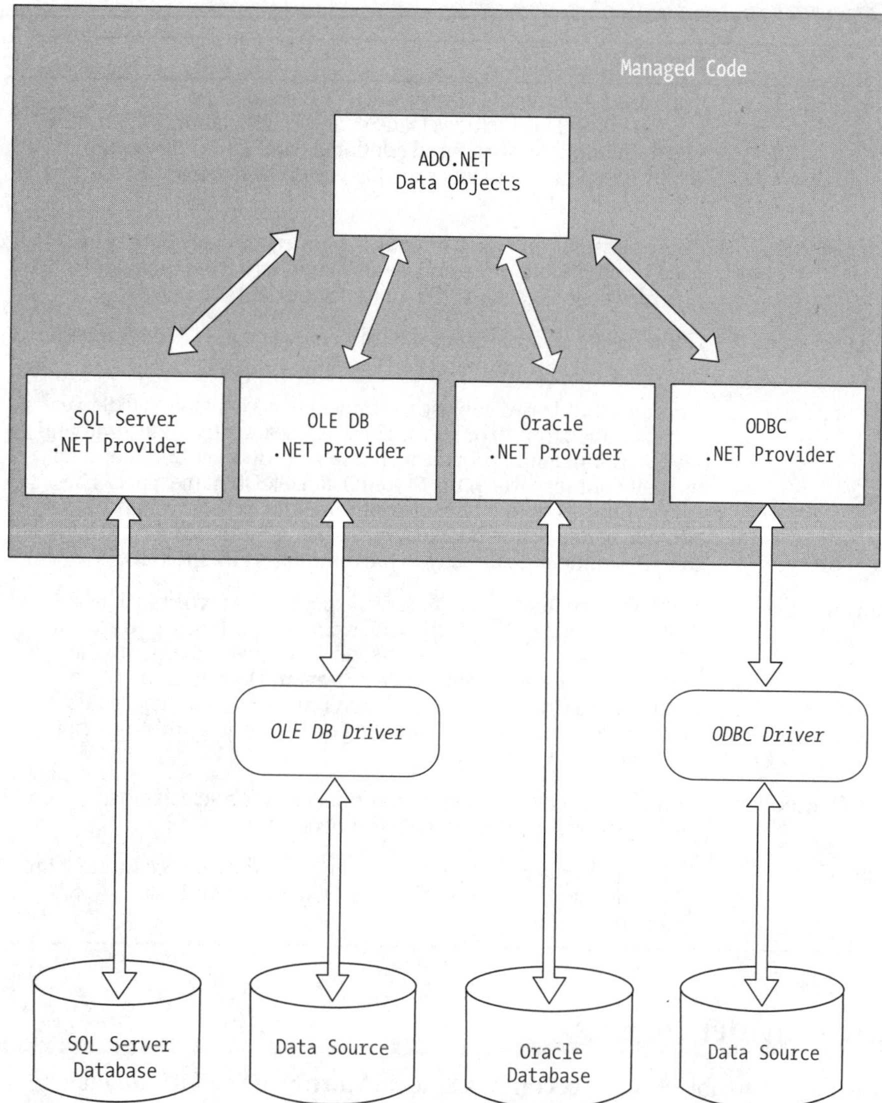

Figure 13-7. *The layers between your code and the data source*

Data Namespaces

The ADO.NET components live in seven namespaces in the .NET class library. Together, these namespaces hold all the functionality of ADO.NET. Table 13-2 describes each data namespace.

Table 13-2. *ADO.NET Namespaces*

Namespace	Purpose
System.Data	Contains fundamental classes with the core ADO.NET functionality. This includes DataSet and DataRelation, which allow you to manipulate structured relational data. These classes are totally independent of any specific type of database or the way you use to connect to it.
System.Data.Common	These classes aren't used directly in your code. Instead, they are used by other data provider classes that inherit from them and provide versions customized for a specific data source.
System.Data.OleDb	Contains the classes you use to connect to an OLE DB data source, including OleDbCommand and OleDbConnection.
System.Data.SqlClient	Contains the classes you use to connect to a Microsoft SQL Server database (version 7.0 or later). These classes, such as SqlCommand and SqlConnection, provide all the same properties and methods as their counterparts in the System.Data.OleDb namespace. The only difference is that they are optimized for SQL Server and provide better performance by eliminating the extra OLE DB layer (and by connecting directly to the optimized TDS interface).
System.Data.SqlTypes	Contains structures for SQL Server–specific data types such as SqlMoney and SqlDateTime. You can use these types to work with SQL Server data types without needing to convert them into the standard .NET equivalents (such as System.Decimal and System.DateTime). These types aren't required, but they do allow you to avoid any potential rounding or conversion problems that could adversely affect data.
System.Data.OracleClient	Contains the classes you use to connect to an Oracle database, such as OracleCommand and OracleConnection.
System.Data.Odbc	Contains the classes you use to connect to a data source through an ODBC driver. These classes include OdbcCommand and OdbcConnection.

The Data Provider Objects

On their own, the data objects can't accomplish much. You might want to add tables, rows, and data by hand, but in most cases, the information you need is located in a data source such as a relational database. To access this information, extract it, and insert it into the appropriate data objects, you need the objects described in this section. Remember, each one of these objects has a database-specific implementation. That means you use a different, but essentially equivalent, object depending on whether you're interacting with SQL Server, Oracle, or the OLE DB provider.

The goal of the data source objects is to create a connection and move information into a DataSet or into a DataReader.

Regardless of which provider you use, your code will look almost the same. Often, the only differences will be the namespace that's used and the name of the ADO.NET data access objects (as listed in Table 13-3).

Each provider designates its own prefix for naming objects. Thus, the SQL Server provider includes SqlConnection and SqlCommand objects, and the Oracle provider includes OracleConnection and OracleCommand objects. Internally, these objects work quite differently, because they need to connect to different databases using different low-level protocols. Externally, however, these objects look quite similar and provide an identical set of basic methods because they implement the same common interfaces. This means your application is shielded from the complexity of different standards and can use the SQL Server provider in the same way the Oracle provider uses it. In fact, you can often translate a block of code for interacting with a SQL Server database into a block of Oracle-specific code just by renaming the objects.

Table 13-3. *The ADO.NET Data Provider Objects*

	SQL Server .NET Provider	OLE DB .NET Provider	Oracle .NET Provider	ODBC .NET Provider
Connection	SqlConnection	OleDbConnection	OracleConnection	OdbcConnection
Command	SqlCommand	OleDbCommand	OracleCommand	OdbcCommand
DataReader	SqlDataReader	OleDbDataReader	OracleDataReader	OdbcDataReader
DataAdapter	SqlDataAdapter	OleDbDataAdapter	OracleDataAdapter	OdbcDataAdapter

The examples in this chapter make note of any differences between the OLE DB and SQL Server providers. Remember, though the underlying technical details differ, the objects are almost identical. The only real differences are as follows:

- The names of the Connection, Command, DataReader, and DataAdapter classes are different in order to help you distinguish them.
- The connection string (the information you use to connect to the database) differs depending on what data source you're using, where it's located, and what type of security you're using.
- Occasionally, a provider may choose to add features, such as methods for specific features or classes to represent specific data types. For example, the SQL Server Command class includes a method for executing XML queries that aren't part of the SQL standard. In this chapter, you'll focus on the standard functionality, which is shared by all providers and used for the majority of data access operations.

In the rest of this chapter, you'll consider two ways to program web pages with ADO.NET. First, you'll consider the most straightforward approach—direct data access. Next, you'll consider disconnected data access, which allows you to retrieve data in the DataSet and cache it for longer periods of time. Both approaches complement each other, and in most web applications you'll use a combination of the two.

Direct Data Access

The easiest way to access data is to perform all your database operations directly and not worry about maintaining disconnected information. This model is closest to traditional ADO programming, and it allows you to sidestep potential concurrency problems, which occur when multiple users try to update information at once. It's also well suited to ASP.NET web pages, which don't need to store disconnected information for long periods of time. Remember, an ASP.NET web page is loaded when the page is requested and shut down as soon as the response is returned to the user. That means a page typically has a lifetime of only a few seconds.

With simple data access, a disconnected copy of the data isn't retained. This means that data selection and data modifications are performed separately. Your program must keep track of the changes that need to be committed to the data source. For example, if a user deletes a record, you need to explicitly specify that record using a SQL Delete statement.

Simple data access is ideal if you need only to read information or if you need to perform only simple update operations, such as adding a record to a log or allowing a user to modify values in a single record (for example, the customer information for an e-commerce site). Simple data access may not be as useful if you want to modify several different records or tables at the same time.

To retrieve information with simple data access, follow these steps:

1. Create Connection, Command, and DataReader objects.

2. Use the DataReader to retrieve information from the database, and display it in a control on a web form.

3. Close your connection.

4. Send the page to the user. At this point, the information your user sees and the information in the database no longer have any connection, and all the ADO.NET objects have been destroyed.

To add or update information, follow these steps:

1. Create new Connection and Command objects.

2. Execute the Command (with the appropriate SQL statement).

This chapter demonstrates both of these approaches. Figure 13-8 shows a high-level look at how the ADO.NET objects interact to make direct data access work.

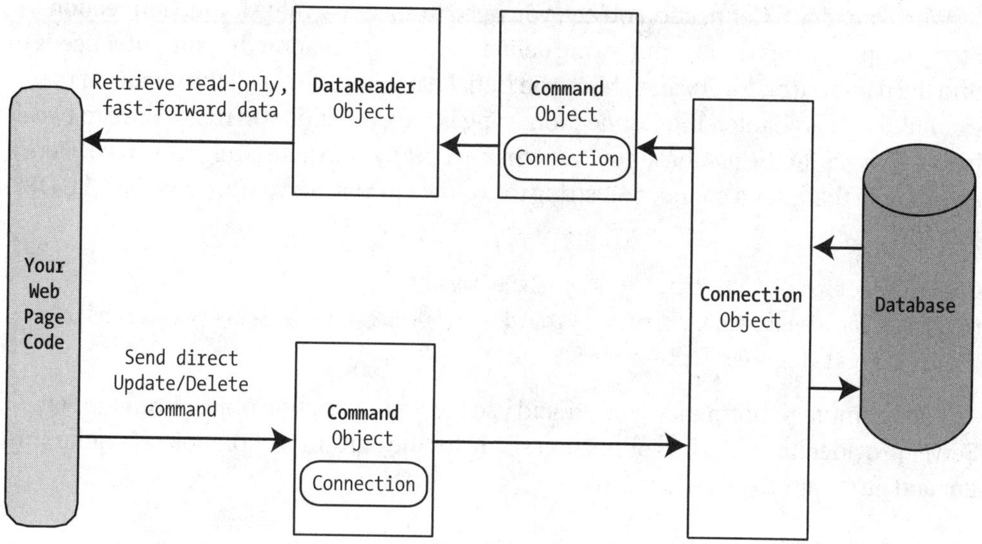

Figure 13-8. *Direct data access with ADO.NET*

Importing the Namespaces

Before continuing, make sure you import the ADO.NET namespaces. In this chapter, we assume you're using the SQL Server provider, in which case you need these two namespace imports:

```
using System.Data;
using System.Data.SqlClient;
```

If you're using Visual Studio, you'll find that the using statement for the System.Data namespace is automatically added to your web page files. However, you'll still need to import the namespace for your specific provider (in this case, System.Data.SqlClient).

Creating a Connection

Before you can retrieve or update data, you need to make a connection to the data source. Generally, connections are limited to some fixed number, and if you exceed that number (either because you run out of licenses or because your database server can't accommodate the user load), attempts to create new connections will fail. For that reason, you should try to hold a connection open for as short a time as possible. You should also write your database code inside a try/catch error handling structure so that you can respond if an error does occur and make sure you close the connection even if you can't perform all your work.

When creating a Connection object, you need to specify a value for its ConnectionString property. This ConnectionString defines all the information the computer needs to find the data source, log in, and choose an initial database. Out of all the details in the examples in this chapter, the ConnectionString is the one value you might have to tweak before it works for the database you want to use. Luckily, it's quite straightforward. Here's an example that uses a connection string to connect to SQL Server through the OLE DB provider:

```
OleDbConnection myConnection = new OleDbConnection();
myConnection.ConnectionString = "Provider=SQLOLEDB.1;Data Source=localhost;" +
 "Initial Catalog=Pubs;Integrated Security=SSPI";
```

For optimum performance, you should use the SqlConnection object from the SQL Server provider instead. The connection string for the SqlConnection object is quite similar and just omits the Provider setting:

```
SqlConnection myConnection = new SqlConnection();
myConnection.ConnectionString = "Data Source=localhost;" +
 "Initial Catalog=Pubs;Integrated Security=SSPI";
```

And if you're using SQL Server 2005 Express Edition, your connection string will include an instance name, as shown here:

```
SqlConnection myConnection = new SqlConnection();
myConnection.ConnectionString = "Data Source=localhost\\SQLEXPRESS;" +
 "Initial Catalog=Pubs;Integrated Security=SSPI";
```

■ Note When you add the instance name in C#, you must add two backslash characters, as in localhost\\SQLEXPRESS. This is because a single backslash is interpreted as a special character. However, if you define the connection string in a configuration file, as described in the next section, you need only one backslash, because you're no longer dealing with pure C# code.

The Connection String

The connection string is actually a series of distinct pieces of information separated by semicolons (;). In the preceding example, the connection string identifies the following pieces of information:

Data source: This indicates the name of the server where the data source is located. If the server is on the same computer that hosts the ASP.NET site, localhost is sufficient. The only exception is if you're using a named instance of SQL Server. For example, if you've installed SQL Server 2005 Express Edition, you'll need to use the data source localhost\SQLEXPRESS, because the instance name is SQLEXPRESS.

Initial catalog: This is the name of the database that this connection will be accessing. It's only the "initial" database because you can change it later by using the Connection.ChangeDatabase() method.

Integrated security: This indicates you want to connect to SQL Server using the Windows user account that's running the web page code. Alternatively, you can supply a user ID and password that's defined in the database for SQL Server authentication.

ConnectionTimeout: This determines how long your code will wait, in seconds, before generating an error if it cannot establish a database connection. Our example connection string doesn't set the ConnectionTimeout, so the default of 15 seconds is used. You can use 0 to specify no limit, but this is a bad idea. This means that, theoretically, the code could be held up indefinitely while it attempts to contact the server.

You can set some other, lesser-used options for a connection string. For more information, refer to the .NET Help files. Look under the appropriate Connection object (such as SqlConnection or OleDbConnection).

Windows Authentication

The previous example uses *integrated Windows authentication*, which is the default security standard for new SQL Server installations. You can also use *SQL Server authentication*. In this case, you will explicitly place the user ID and password information in the connection string. However, SQL Server authentication is disabled by default in SQL Server 2000 and SQL Server 2005, because it's not considered to be as secure.

Here's the lowdown on both types of authentication:

- With SQL Server authentication, SQL Server maintains its own user account information in the database. It uses this information to determine whether you are allowed to access specific parts of a database.
- With integrated Windows authentication, SQL Server automatically uses the Windows account information for the currently logged-in process. In the database, it stores information about what database privileges each user should have.

■ Tip You can set what type of authentication your SQL Server uses using a tool such as Enterprise Manager. Just right-click your server in the tree, which will be named (local), and select Properties. Choose the Security tab to change the type of authentication. You can choose either Windows Only or SQL Server and Windows, which allows both Windows authentication and SQL Server authentication. This option is also known as *mixed-mode authentication*.

For Windows authentication to work, the currently logged-on Windows user must have the required authorization to access the SQL database. This isn't a problem while you test your websites, because Visual Studio launches your web applications using your user account. However, when you deploy your application to a web server running IIS, you might run into trouble. In this situation, all ASP.NET code is run by a more limited user account that might not have the rights to access the database. (See Chapter 12 for the full details.) In this case, you'll need to grant database access to this account, or your web pages will receive a security error whenever they try to connect to the database.

Connection String Tips

Typically, all the database code in your application will use the same connection string. For that reason, it usually makes the most sense to store a connection string in a class member variable or, even better, a configuration file:

```
string connectionString = "...";
```

You can also create a Connection object and supply the connection string in one step by using a different constructor:

```
SqlConnection myConnection = new SqlConnection(connectionString);
// myConnection.ConnectionString is now set to connectionString.
```

You don't need to hard-code a connection string. The <connectionStrings> section of the web.config file is a handy place to store your connection strings. Here's an example:

```
<configuration xmlns="http://schemas.microsoft.com/.NetConfiguration/v2.0">
  <connectionStrings>
    <add name="Pubs" connectionString=
"Data Source=localhost;Initial Catalog=Pubs;Integrated Security=SSPI"/>
  </connectionStrings>
  ...
</configuration>
```

You can then retrieve your connection string by name from the WebConfigurationManager.ConnectionStrings collection, like so:

```
string connectionString =
  WebConfigurationManager.ConnectionStrings["Pubs"].ConnectionString;
```

This approach helps to ensure all your web pages are using the same connection string. It also makes it easy for you to change the connection string for an application, without needing to edit the code in multiple pages. The examples in this chapter all store their connection strings in the web.config file in this way.

Making the Connection

Before you can use a connection, you have to explicitly open it, as shown here:

```
myConnection.Open();
```

To verify that you have successfully connected to the database, you can try displaying some basic connection information. The following example writes some basic information to a Label control named lblInfo (see Figure 13-9).

Here's the code using a try/catch error handling block:

```
// Define the ADO.NET Connection object.
string connectionString = "Data Source=localhost\\SQLEXPRESS;Initial
Catalog=Pubs;";
SqlConnection myConnection = new SqlConnection(connectionString);

try
{
    // Try to open the connection.
    myConnection.Open();
    lblInfo.Text = "<b>Server Version:</b> " + myConnection.ServerVersion;
    lblInfo.Text += "<br /><b>Connection Is:</b> " +
      myConnection.State.ToString();
}
catch (Exception err)
{
    // Handle an error by displaying the information.
    lblInfo.Text = "Error reading the database. ";
    lblInfo.Text += err.Message;
}
finally
{
    // Either way, make sure the connection is properly closed.
    // (Even if the connection wasn't opened successfully,
    //  calling Close() won't cause an error.)
    myConnection.Close();
    lblInfo.Text += "<br /><b>Now Connection Is:</b> ";
    lblInfo.Text +=  myConnection.State.ToString();
}
```

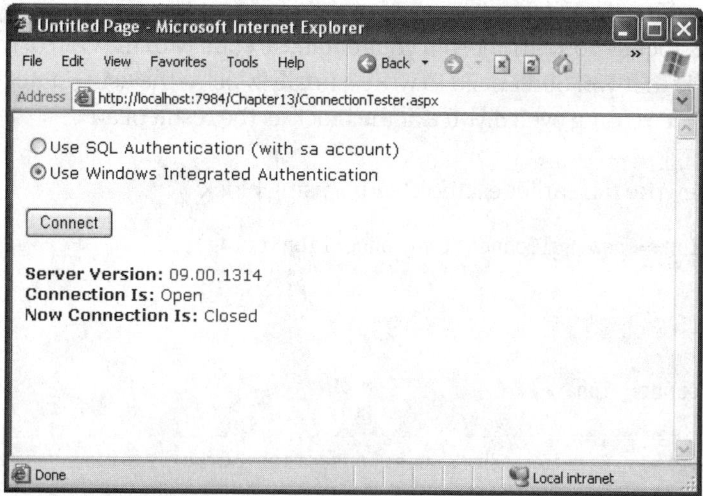

Figure 13-9. *Testing your connection*

Once you use the Open() method, you have a live connection to your database. One of the most fundamental principles of data access code is that you should reduce the amount of time you hold a connection open as much as possible. Imagine that as soon as you open the connection, you have a live, ticking time bomb. You need to get in, retrieve your data, and throw the connection away as quickly as possible in order to ensure your site runs efficiently.

Closing a connection is just as easy, as shown here:

```
myConnection.Close();
```

Another approach is to use the C# using statement. The using statement declares that you are using a disposable object for a short period of time. As soon as you finish using that object and the using block ends, the common language runtime will release it immediately by calling the Dispose() method. Here's the basic structure of the using block:

```
using (object)
{
    ...
}
```

It just so happens that calling the Dispose() method of a connection object is equivalent to calling Close(). That means you can shorten your database code with the help of a using block. The best part is that you don't need to write a finally block—the using statement releases the object you're using even if you exit the block as the result of an unhandled exception.

Here's how you could rewrite the earlier example with a using block:

```
SqlConnection myConnection = new SqlConnection(connectionString);

using (myConnection)
{
    // Try to open the connection.
    myConnection.Open();
    lblInfo.Text = "<b>Server Version:</b> " + myConnection.ServerVersion;
    lblInfo.Text += "<br /><b>Connection Is:</b> " +
      myConnection.State.ToString();
}
lblInfo.Text += "<br /><b>Now Connection Is:</b> ";
lblInfo.Text +=  myConnection.State.ToString();
```

Defining a Select Command

The Connection object provides a few basic properties that supply information about the connection, but that's about all. To actually retrieve data, you need a few more ingredients::

- A SQL statement that selects the information you want
- A Command object that executes the SQL statement
- A DataReader or DataSet object to catch the retrieved records

Command objects represent SQL statements. To use a Command, you define it, specify the SQL statement you want to use, specify an available connection, and execute the command.

You can use one of the earlier SQL statements, as shown here:

```
SqlCommand myCommand = new SqlCommand();
myCommand.Connection = myConnection;
myCommand.CommandText = "SELECT * FROM Authors";
```

Or you can use the constructor as a shortcut:

```
SqlCommand myCommand = new SqlCommand("SELECT * FROM Authors", myConnection);
```

The process is identical for the SqlCommand:

```
SqlCommand myCommand = new SqlCommand("SELECT * FROM Authors", myConnection);
```

■Note It's also a good idea to dispose of the Command object when you're finished, although it isn't as critical as closing the Connection object.

Using a Command with a DataReader

Once you've defined your command, you need to decide how you want to use it. The simplest approach is to use a DataReader, which allows you to quickly retrieve all your results. The DataReader uses a live connection and should be used quickly and then closed. The DataReader is also extremely simple. It supports fast-forward-only read-only access to your results, which is generally all you need when retrieving information. Because of the DataReader's optimized nature, it provides better performance than the DataSet. It should always be your first choice for simple data access.

Before you can use a DataReader, make sure you've opened the connection:

```
myConnection.Open();
```

To create a DataReader, you use the ExecuteReader() method of the command object, as shown here:

```
// You don't need the new keyword, as the Command will create the DataReader.
SqlDataReader myReader;
myReader = myCommand.ExecuteReader();
```

These two lines of code define a DataReader object and then create it by executing your command. Once you have the reader, you retrieve a single row at a time using the Read method:

```
myReader.Read();    // The first row in the result set is now available.
```

You can then access the values in the current row using the corresponding field names. The following example adds an item to a list box with the first name and last name for the current row:

```
lstNames.Items.Add(myReader["au_lname"] + ", " + myReader["au_fname"]);
```

To move to the next row, use the Read() method again. If this method returns true, a row of information has been successfully retrieved. If it returns false, you've attempted to read past the end of your result set. There is no way to move backward to a previous row.

Each field is stored as a generic object. This means you'll often need to explicitly cast fields to the data type you need. In the preceding code statement, no problem occurs because the C# compiler realizes that you're joining strings because it sees the snippet of literal text (", ") in the expression. If this hint wasn't provided, you'd receive a compile-time error, which you could easily correct using casting syntax or the ToString() method, as shown here:

```
lstNames.Items.Add(myReader["au_lname"].ToString());
```

As soon as you've finished reading all the results you need, close the DataReader and Connection:

```
myReader.Close();
myConnection.Close();
```

Putting It All Together

The next example demonstrates how you can use all the ADO.NET ingredients together to create a simple application that retrieves information from the Authors table. You can select an author record by last name using a drop-down list box, as shown in Figure 13-10.

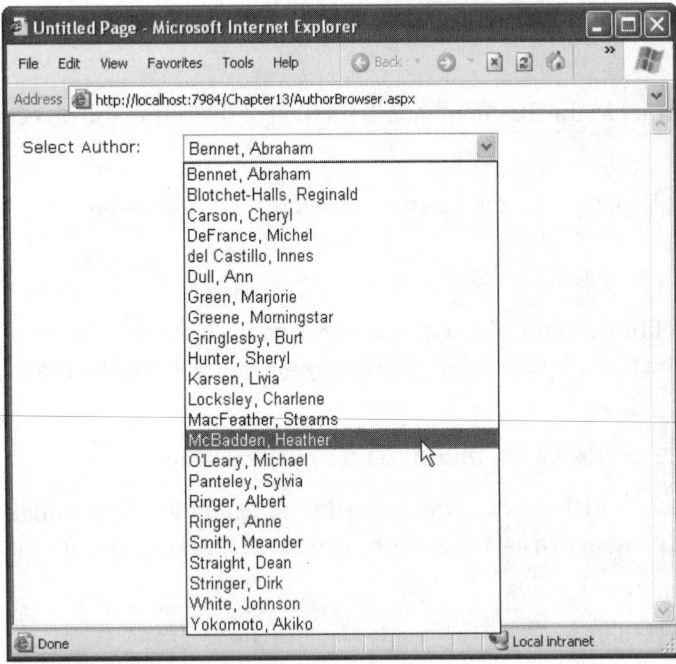

Figure 13-10. *Selecting an author*

The full record is then retrieved and displayed in a simple label, as shown in Figure 13-11.

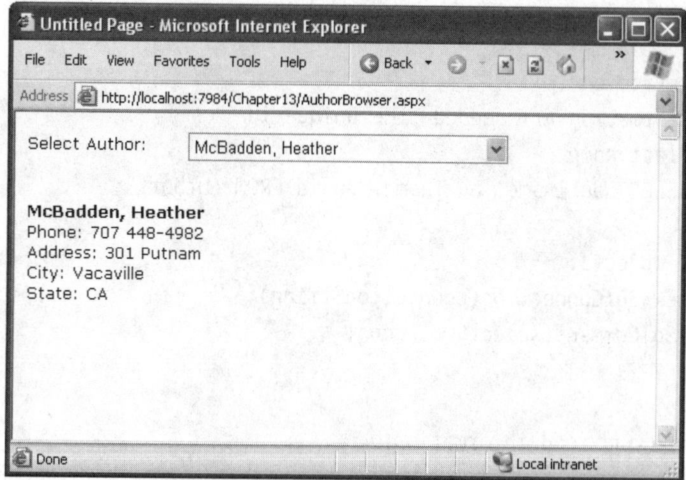

Figure 13-11. *Author information*

Filling the List Box

To start, the connection string is defined as a private variable for the page class and retrieved from the connection string:

```
private string connectionString =
  WebConfigurationManager.ConnectionStrings["Pubs"].ConnectionString;
```

The list box is filled when the Page.Load event occurs. Because the list box is set to persist its view state information, this information needs to be retrieved only once, the first time the page is displayed. It will be ignored on all postbacks.

Here's the code that fills the list from the database:

```
protected void Page_Load(Object sender, EventArgs e)
{
    if (!this.IsPostBack)
    {
        FillAuthorList();
    }
}
```

```
private void FillAuthorList()
{
    lstAuthor.Items.Clear();

    // Define the Select statement.
    // Three pieces of information are needed: the unique id
    // and the first and last name.
    string selectSQL = "SELECT au_lname, au_fname, au_id FROM Authors";

    // Define the ADO.NET objects.
    SqlConnection con = new SqlConnection(connectionString);
    SqlCommand cmd = new SqlCommand(selectSQL, con);
    SqlDataReader reader;

    // Try to open database and read information.
    try
    {
        con.Open();
        reader = cmd.ExecuteReader();

        // For each item, add the author name to the displayed
        // list box text, and store the unique ID in the Value property.
        while (reader.Read())
        {
            ListItem newItem = new ListItem();
            newItem.Text = reader["au_lname"] + ", " + reader["au_fname"];
            newItem.Value = reader["au_id"].ToString();
            lstAuthor.Items.Add(newItem);
        }
        reader.Close();
    }
    catch (Exception err)
    {
        lblResults.Text = "Error reading list of names. ";
        lblResults.Text += err.Message;
    }
```

```
    finally
    {
        con.Close();
    }
}
```

This example looks more sophisticated than the previous bite-sized snippets in this chapter, but it really doesn't introduce anything new. It uses the standard Connection, Command, and DataAdapter objects. The Connection is opened inside an error handling block so that your page can handle any unexpected errors and provide information. A finally block makes sure the connection is properly closed, even if an error occurs.

The actual code for reading the data uses a loop. With each pass, the Read() method is called to get another row of information. When the reader has read all the available information, this method will return false, the while condition will evaluate to false, and the loop will end gracefully.

The unique ID (the value in the au_id field) is stored in the Value property of the list box for reference later. This is a crucial ingredient that is needed to allow the corresponding record to be queried again. If you tried to build a query using the author's name, you would need to worry about authors with the same name. You would also have the additional headache of invalid characters (such as the apostrophe in O'Leary) that would invalidate your SQL statement.

Retrieving the Record

The record is retrieved as soon as the user changes the selection in the list box. To make this possible, the AutoPostBack property of the list box is set to true so that its change events are detected automatically.

```
protected void lstAuthor_SelectedIndexChanged(Object sender, EventArgs e)
{
    // Create a Select statement that searches for a record
    // matching the specific author ID from the Value property.
    string selectSQL;
    selectSQL = "SELECT * FROM Authors ";
    selectSQL += "WHERE au_id='" + lstAuthor.SelectedItem.Value + "'";

    // Define the ADO.NET objects.
    SqlConnection con = new SqlConnection(connectionString);
    SqlCommand cmd = new SqlCommand(selectSQL, con);
    SqlDataReader reader;
```

```
    // Try to open database and read information.
    try
    {
        con.Open();
        reader = cmd.ExecuteReader();
        reader.Read();
        lblResults.Text = "<b>" + reader["au_lname"];
        lblResults.Text += ", " + reader["au_fname"] + "</b><br />";
        lblResults.Text += "Phone: " + reader["phone"] + "<br />";
        lblResults.Text += "Address: " + reader["address"] + "<br />";
        lblResults.Text += "City: " + reader["city"] + "<br />";
        lblResults.Text += "State: " + reader["state"] + "<br />";
        reader.Close();
    }
    catch (Exception err)
    {
        lblResults.Text = "Error getting author. ";
        lblResults.Text += err.Message;
    }
    finally
    {
        if (reader != null) reader.Close();
        con.Close();
    }
}
```

The process is similar to the procedure used to retrieve the last names. There are only a couple of differences:

- The code dynamically creates a SQL statement based on the selected item in the drop-down list box. It uses the Value property of the selected item, which stores the unique identifier. This is a common (and useful) technique.
- Only one record is read. The code assumes that only one author has the matching au_id, which is reasonable as this field is unique.

■ **Note** This example shows how ADO.NET works to retrieve a simple result set. Of course, ADO.NET also provides handy controls that go beyond this generic level and let you provide full-featured grids with sorting and editing. These controls are described in Chapter 14 and Chapter 15. For now, you should concentrate on understanding the fundamentals about ADO.NET and how it works with data.

Updating Data

Now that you understand how to retrieve data, it isn't much more complicated to perform simple delete and update operations. Once again, you use the Command object, but this time you don't need a DataReader because no results will be retrieved. You also don't use a SQL Select command. Instead, you use one of three new SQL commands: Update, Insert, or Delete.

To execute an Update, Insert, or Delete statement, you need to create a Command object. You can then execute the command with the ExecuteNonQuery() method. This method returns the number of rows that were affected, which allows you to check your assumptions. For example, if you attempt to update or delete a record and are informed that no records were affected, you probably have an error in your Where clause that is preventing any records from being selected. (If, on the other hand, your SQL command has a syntax error or attempts to retrieve information from a nonexistent table, an exception will occur.)

Enhancing the Author Page

To demonstrate how to Update, Insert, and Delete simple information, the previous example has been enhanced. Instead of being displayed in a label, the information from each field is added to a separate text box. Two additional buttons allow you to update the record (Update) or delete it (Delete). You can also insert a new record by clicking Create New, entering the information in the text boxes, and then clicking Insert New. Figure 13-12 shows the updated web page.

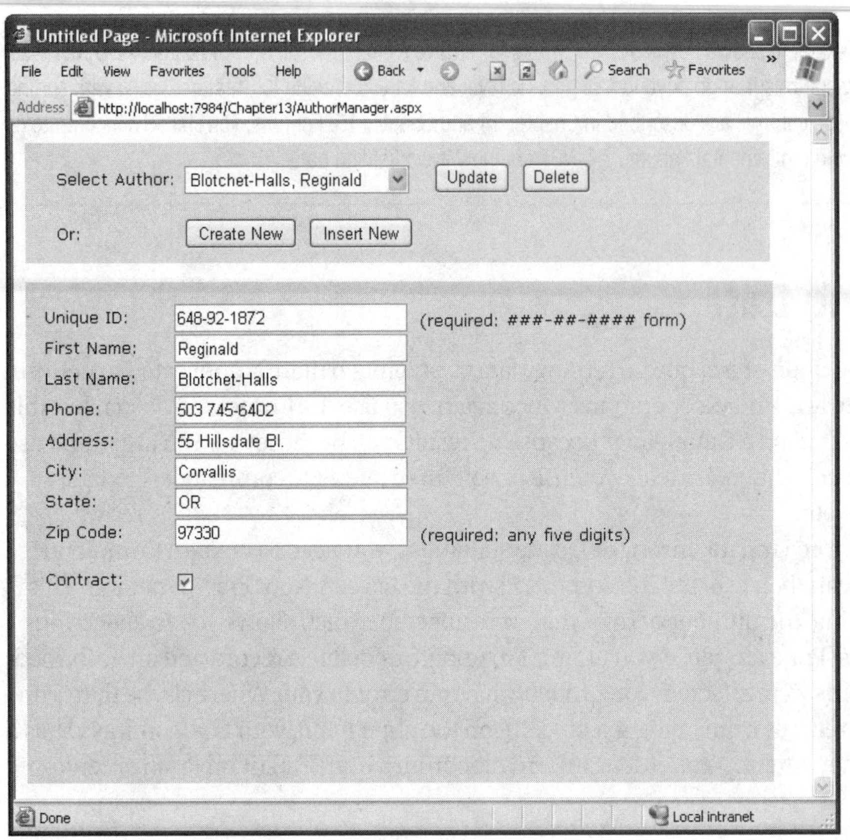

Figure 13-12. *A more advanced author manager*

The record selection code is identical from an ADO.NET perspective, but it now uses the individual text boxes:

```
protected void lstAuthor_SelectedIndexChanged(Object sender, EventArgs e)
{
    // Define ADO.NET objects.
    string selectSQL;
    selectSQL = "SELECT * FROM Authors ";
    selectSQL += "WHERE au_id='" + lstAuthor.SelectedItem.Value + "'";
    SqlConnection con = new SqlConnection(connectionString);
    SqlCommand cmd = new SqlCommand(selectSQL, con);
    SqlDataReader reader;
```

```
    // Try to open database and read information.
    try
    {
        con.Open();
        reader = cmd.ExecuteReader();
        reader.Read();

        // Fill the controls.
        txtID.Text = reader["au_id"].ToString();
        txtFirstName.Text = reader["au_fname"].ToString();
        txtLastName.Text = reader["au_lname"].ToString();
        txtPhone.Text = reader["phone"].ToString();
        txtAddress.Text = reader["address"].ToString();
        txtCity.Text = reader["city"].ToString();
        txtState.Text = reader["state"].ToString();
        txtZip.Text = reader["zip"].ToString();
        chkContract.Checked = (bool)reader["contract"];
        reader.Close();
        lblStatus.Text = "";
    }
    catch (Exception err)
    {
        lblStatus.Text = "Error getting author. ";
        lblStatus.Text += err.Message;
    }
    finally
    {
        con.Close();
    }
}
```

To see the full code, refer to the online samples for this chapter. If you play with the example at length, you'll notice that it lacks a few niceties that would be needed in a professional website. For example, when creating a new record, the name of the last selected user is still visible, and the Update and Delete buttons are still active, which can lead to confusion or errors. A more sophisticated user interface could prevent these problems by disabling inapplicable controls (perhaps by grouping them in a Panel control) or by using separate pages. In this case, however, the page is useful as a quick way to test some basic data access code.

Adding a Record

To start adding a new record, click Create New to blank the fields. Technically speaking, this step isn't required, but it simplifies the user's life.

```
protected void cmdNew_Click(Object sender, EventArgs e)
{
    txtID.Text = "";
    txtFirstName.Text = "";
    txtLastName.Text = "";
    txtPhone.Text = "";
    txtAddress.Text = "";
    txtCity.Text = "";
    txtState.Text = "";
    txtZip.Text = "";
    chkContract.Checked = false;

    lblStatus.Text = "Click Insert New to add the completed record.";
}
```

The Insert New button performs the actual ADO.NET code to insert the finished record using a dynamically generated Insert statement:

```
protected void cmdInsert_Click(Object sender, EventArgs e)
{
    // Perform user-defined checks.
    // Alternatively, you could use RequiredFieldValidator controls.
    if (txtID.Text == "" || txtFirstName.Text == "" || txtLastName.Text == "")
    {
        lblStatus.Text = "Records require an ID, first name, and last name.";
        return;
    }

    // Define ADO.NET objects.
    string insertSQL;
    insertSQL = "INSERT INTO Authors (";
    insertSQL += "au_id, au_fname, au_lname, ";
    insertSQL += "phone, address, city, state, zip, contract) ";
    insertSQL += "VALUES ('";
    insertSQL += txtID.Text + "', '";
    insertSQL += txtFirstName.Text + "', '";
    insertSQL += txtLastName.Text + "', '";
```

```
    insertSQL += txtPhone.Text + "', '";
    insertSQL += txtAddress.Text + "', '";
    insertSQL += txtCity.Text + "', '";
    insertSQL += txtState.Text + "', '";
    insertSQL += txtZip.Text + "', '";
    insertSQL += Convert.Int16(chkContract.Checked) + "')";

    SqlConnection con = new SqlConnection(connectionString);
    SqlCommand cmd = new SqlCommand(insertSQL, con);

    // Try to open the database and execute the update.
    int added = 0;
    try
    {
        con.Open();
        added = cmd.ExecuteNonQuery();
        lblStatus.Text = added.ToString() + " records inserted.";
    }
    catch (Exception err)
    {
        lblStatus.Text = "Error inserting record. ";
        lblStatus.Text += err.Message;
    }
    finally
    {
        con.Close();
    }

    // If the insert succeeded, refresh the author list.
    if (added > 0)
    {
        FillAuthorList();
    }
}
```

If the insert fails, the problem will be reported to the user in a rather unfriendly way (see Figure 13-13). This is typically the result of not specifying valid values. In a more polished application, you would use validators (as shown in Chapter 8) and provide more useful error messages. If the insert operation is successful, the page is updated with the new author list.

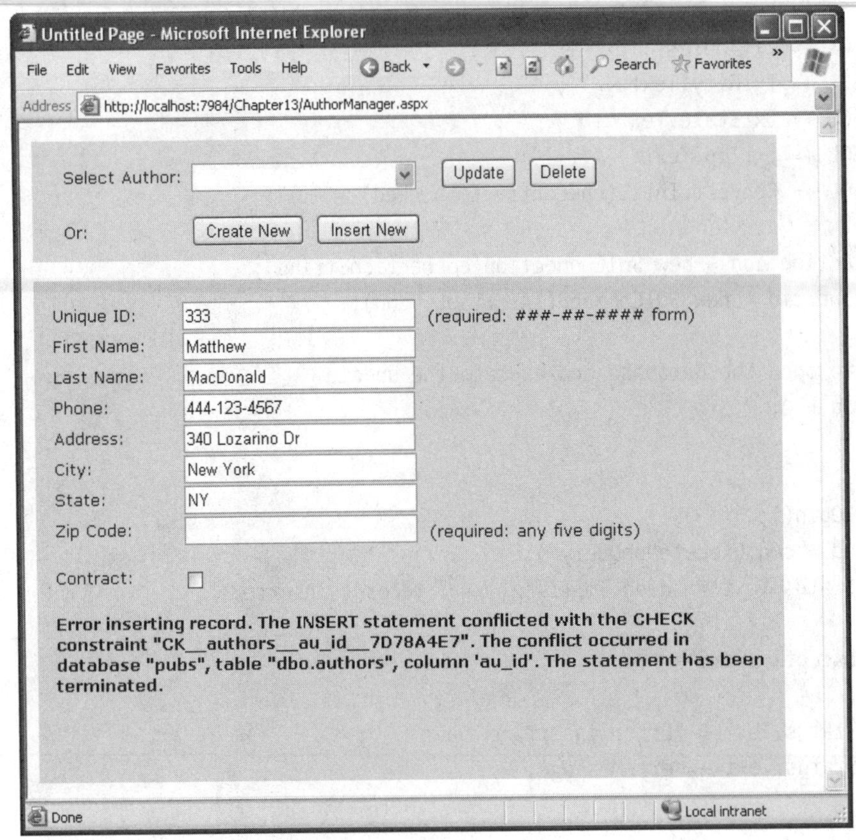

Figure 13-13. *A failed insertion*

Creating More Robust Commands

The previous example performed its database work using a dynamically pasted-together SQL string. This off-the-cuff approach is great for quickly coding database logic, and it's easy to understand. However, it has two potentially serious drawbacks:

- Users may accidentally enter characters that will affect your SQL statement. For example, if a value contains an apostrophe ('), the pasted-together SQL string will no longer be valid.
- Users might *deliberately* enter characters that will affect your SQL statement. Examples include using the single apostrophe to close a value prematurely and then following the value with additional SQL code.

The second of these is known as *SQL injection attack*, and it facilitates an amazingly wide range of exploits. Crafty users can use SQL injection attacks to do anything from returning additional results (such as the orders placed by other customers) or even executing additional SQL statements (such as deleting every record in another table in the same database). In fact, SQL Server includes a special system stored procedure that allows users to execute arbitrary programs on the computer, so this vulnerability can be extremely serious!

You could address these problems by carefully validating the supplied input and checking for dangerous characters such as apostrophes. One approach is to sanitize your input by doubling all apostrophes in the user input (in other words, replace ' with ''). Here's an example:

```
string authorID = txtID.Text.Replace("'", "''");
```

A much more robust and convenient approach is to use a *parameterized command*. A parameterized command is one that replaces hard-coded values with placeholders. The placeholders are then added separately and automatically encoded.

For example, this SQL statement:

```
SELECT * FROM Customers WHERE CustomerID = 'ALFKI'
```

would become this:

```
SELECT * FROM Customers WHERE CustomerID = @CustomerID
```

The syntax used for parameterized commands differs from provider to provider. For the SQL Server provider, parameterized commands used named placeholders, with unique names. You can use any name you want, as long as it begins with the @ character. Usually, you'll choose a parameter name that matches the field name (such as @CustomerID for the CustomerID value in the previous example). The OLE DB provider uses a different syntax. It requires that each hard-coded value is replaced with a question mark. Parameters aren't identified by name but by their position in the SQL string.

```
SELECT * FROM Customers WHERE CustomerID = ?
```

In either case, you need to supply a Parameter object for each parameter, which you insert in the Command.Parameters collection. In OLE DB, you must make sure you add the parameters in the same order they appear in the SQL string. In SQL Server this isn't a requirement, because the parameters are matched to the placeholders based on their name.

The following example rewrites the insert code of the record author manager example with a parameterized command:

```
protected void cmdInsert_Click(Object sender, EventArgs e)
{
    // Perform user-defined checks.
    if (txtID.Text == "" || txtFirstName.Text == "" || txtLastName.Text == "")
```

```
    {
        lblStatus.Text = "Records require an ID, first name, and last name.";
        return;
    }

    // Define ADO.NET objects.
    string insertSQL;
    insertSQL = "INSERT INTO Authors (";
    insertSQL += "au_id, au_fname, au_lname, ";
    insertSQL += "phone, address, city, state, zip, contract) ";
    insertSQL += "VALUES (";
    insertSQL += "@au_id, @au_fname, @au_lname, ";
    insertSQL += "@phone, @address, @city, @state, @zip, @contract)";

    SqlConnection con = new SqlConnection(connectionString);
    SqlCommand cmd = new SqlCommand(insertSQL, con);

    // Add the parameters.
    cmd.Parameters.AddWithValue("@au_id", txtID.Text);
    cmd.Parameters.AddWithValue("@au_fname", txtFirstName.Text);
    cmd.Parameters.AddWithValue("@au_Lname", txtLastName.Text);
    cmd.Parameters.AddWithValue("@phone", txtPhone.Text);
    cmd.Parameters.AddWithValue("@address", txtAddress.Text);
    cmd.Parameters.AddWithValue("@city", txtCity.Text);
    cmd.Parameters.AddWithValue("@state", txtState.Text);
    cmd.Parameters.AddWithValue("@zip", txtZip.Text);
    cmd.Parameters.AddWithValue("@contract",
      Convert.ToInt16(chkContract.Checked));

    // Try to open the database and execute the update.
    int added = 0;
    try
    {
        con.Open();
        added = cmd.ExecuteNonQuery();
        lblStatus.Text = added.ToString() + " records inserted.";
    }
    catch (Exception err)
    {
        lblStatus.Text = "Error inserting record. ";
        lblStatus.Text += err.Message;
    }
```

```
    finally
    {
        con.Close();
    }

    // If the insert succeeded, refresh the author list.
    if (added > 0)
    {
        FillAuthorList();
    }
}
```

For basic security, it's recommended that you always use parameterized commands. In fact, many of the most infamous attacks on e-commerce websites weren't fueled by hard-core hacker knowledge but were made using simple SQL injection by modifying values in web pages or query strings.

Updating a Record

When the user clicks the Update button, the information in the text boxes is applied to the database as follows:

```
protected void cmdUpdate_Click(Object sender, EventArgs e)
{
    // Define ADO.NET objects.
    string updateSQL;
    updateSQL = "UPDATE Authors SET ";
    updateSQL += "au_id=@au_id, au_fname=@au_fname, au_lname=@au_lname, ";
    updateSQL += "phone=@phone, address=@address, city=@city, state=@state, ";
    updateSQL += "zip=@zip, contract=@contract";
    updateSQL += "WHERE au_id=@au_id_original";

    SqlConnection con = new SqlConnection(connectionString);
    SqlCommand cmd = new SqlCommand(updateSQL, con);

    // Add the parameters.
    cmd.Parameters.AddWithValue("@au_id", txtID.Text);
    cmd.Parameters.AddWithValue("@au_fname", txtFirstName.Text);
    cmd.Parameters.AddWithValue("@au_Lname", txtLastName.Text);
    cmd.Parameters.AddWithValue("@phone", txtPhone.Text);
    cmd.Parameters.AddWithValue("@address", txtAddress.Text);
    cmd.Parameters.AddWithValue("@city", txtCity.Text);
    cmd.Parameters.AddWithValue("@state", txtState.Text);
    cmd.Parameters.AddWithValue("@zip", txtZip.Text);
```

```
    cmd.Parameters.AddWithValue("@contract",
      Convert.ToInt16(chkContract.Checked));
    cmd.Parameters.AddWithValue("@au_id_original",
      lstAuthor.SelectedItem.Value);

    // Try to open database and execute the update.
    try
    {
        con.Open();
        int updated = cmd.ExecuteNonQuery();
        lblStatus.Text = updated.ToString() + " records updated.";
    }
    catch (Exception err)
    {
        lblStatus.Text = "Error updating author. ";
        lblStatus.Text += err.Message;
    }
    finally
    {
        con.Close();
    }
}
```

The update code is similar to the record selection code. The main differences are as follows:

- No DataReader is used, because no results are returned.
- A dynamically generated Update command is used for the Command object. It selects the corresponding author records, and changes all the fields to correspond to the values entered in the text boxes.
- The ExecuteNonQuery() method returns the number of affected records. This information is displayed in a label to confirm to the user that the operation was successful.

Deleting a Record

When the user clicks the Delete button, the author information is removed from the database. The number of affected records is examined, and if the Delete operation was successful, the FillAuthorList() function is called to refresh the page.

```
protected void cmdDelete_Click(Object sender, EventArgs e)
{
    // Define ADO.NET objects.
    string deleteSQL;
    deleteSQL = "DELETE FROM Authors ";
    deleteSQL += "WHERE au_id=@au_id";

    SqlConnection con = new SqlConnection(connectionString);
    SqlCommand cmd = new SqlCommand(deleteSQL, con);
    cmd.Parameters.AddWithValue("@au_id ", lstAuthor.SelectedItem.Value);

    // Try to open the database and delete the record.
    int deleted = 0;
    try
    {
        con.Open();
        deleted = cmd.ExecuteNonQuery();
    }
    catch (Exception err)
    {
        lblStatus.Text = "Error deleting author. ";
        lblStatus.Text += err.Message;
    }
    finally
    {
        con.Close();
    }

    // If the delete succeeded, refresh the author list.
    if (deleted > 0)
    {
        FillAuthorList();
    }
}
```

Interestingly, delete operations rarely succeed with the records in the pubs database, because they have corresponding child records linked in another table of the pubs database. Specifically, each author can have one or more related book titles. Unless the author's records are removed from the TitleAuthor table first, the author cannot be deleted. Because of the careful error handling used in the previous example, this problem is faithfully reported in your application (see Figure 13-14) and doesn't cause any real problems.

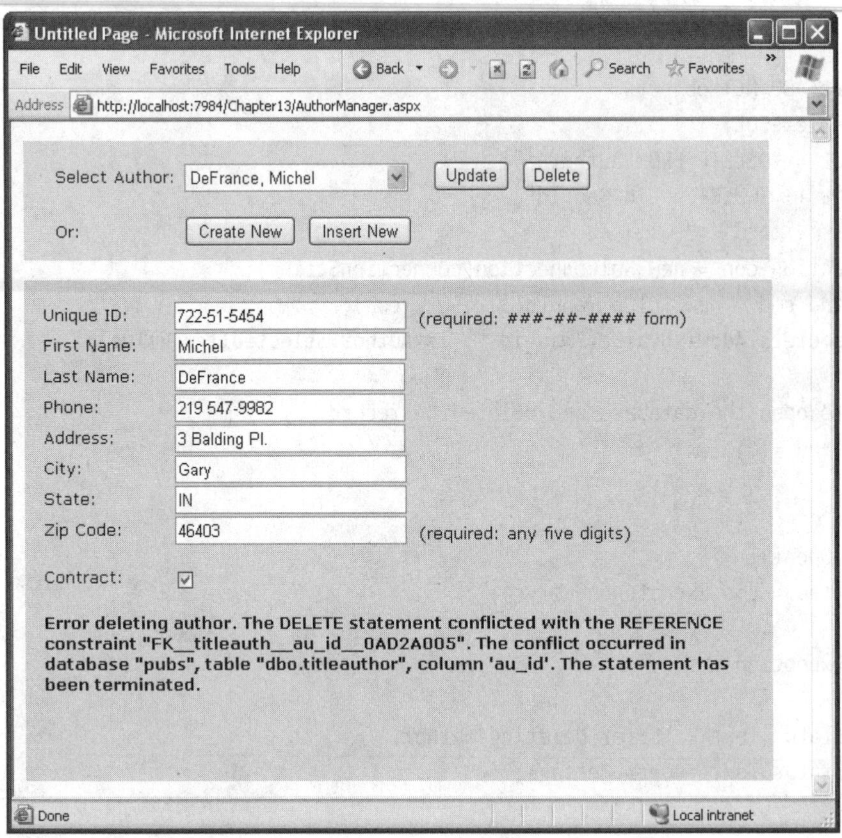

Figure 13-14. *A failed delete attempt*

To get around this limitation, you can use the Create New and Insert New buttons to add a new record and then delete this record. Because this new record won't be linked to any other records, its deletion will be allowed.

Disconnected Data Access

With disconnected data, you need to code a little differently. First, you'll make your changes through the DataSet rather than with direct commands. Also, you'll need to watch for the problems that can occur if more than one user attempts to make conflicting changes at the same time or if you need to commit changes to multiple tables. In this simple one-page scenario, disconnected data access won't present much of a problem. If, however, you use disconnected data access to make a number of changes and commit them all at once, you're more likely to run into trouble.

With disconnected data access, a copy of the data is retained in memory while your code is running. Changes are tracked automatically using the built-in features of the DataSet object. Figure 13-15 shows a model of the DataSet.

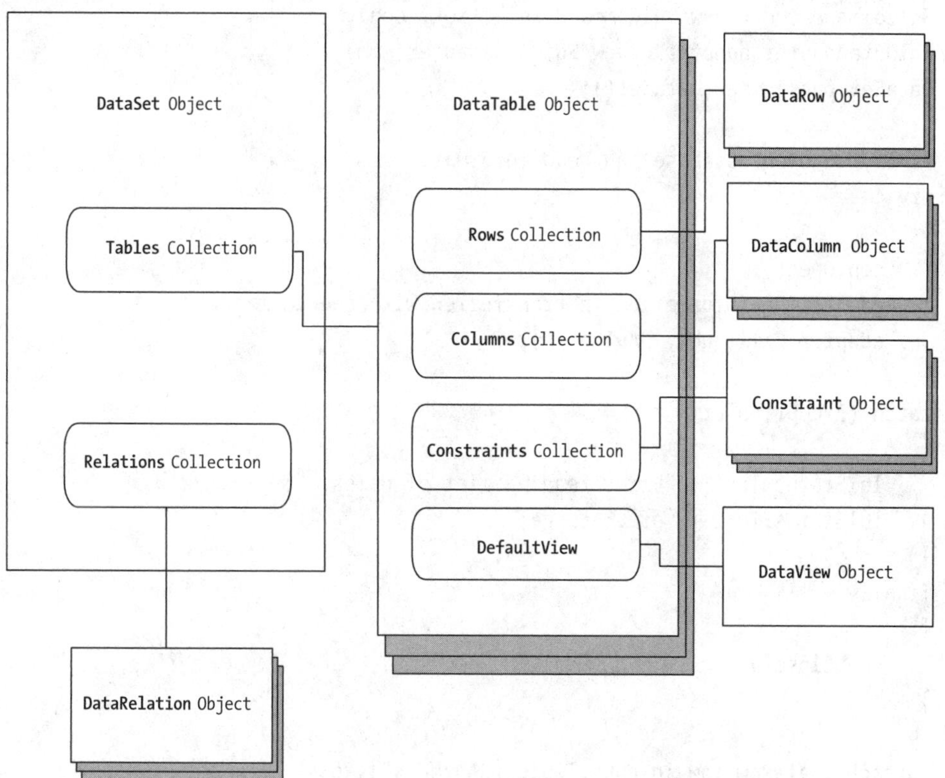

Figure 13-15. *The data modeling objects*

You fill the DataSet in much the same way that you connect a DataReader. However, although the DataReader holds a live connection, information in the DataSet is always disconnected.

Selecting Disconnected Data

The following example shows how you could rewrite the FillAuthorList() subroutine to use a DataSet instead of a DataReader. The changes are highlighted in bold.

```
private void FillAuthorList()
{
    lstAuthor.Items.Clear();
```

```
    // Define ADO.NET objects.
    string selectSQL;
    selectSQL = "SELECT au_lname, au_fname, au_id FROM Authors";
    SqlConnection con = new SqlConnection(connectionString);
    SqlCommand cmd = new SqlCommand(selectSQL, con);
    SqlDataAdapter adapter = new SqlDataAdapter(cmd);
    DataSet pubs = new DataSet();

    // Try to open database and read information.
    try
    {
        con.Open();
        // All the information in transferred with one command.
        adapter.Fill(pubs, "Authors");
    }
    catch (Exception err)
    {
        lblStatus.Text = "Error reading list of names. ";
        lblStatus.Text += err.Message;
    }
    finally
    {
        con.Close();
    }

    foreach (DataRow row in pubs.Tables["Authors"].Rows)
    {
        ListItem newItem = new ListItem();
        newItem.Text = row["au_lname"] + ", " +
          row["au_fname"];
        newItem.Value = row["au_id"].ToString();
        lstAuthor.Items.Add(newItem);
    }
}
```

To fill a DataSet, you always use a DataAdapter. Every DataAdapter can hold four commands: SelectCommand, InsertCommand, UpdateCommand, and DeleteCommand. This allows you to use a single DataAdapter object for multiple tasks. The Command object supplied in the constructor is automatically assigned to the DataAdapter.SelectCommand property. Figure 13-16 shows how the DataAdapter interacts with your web application.

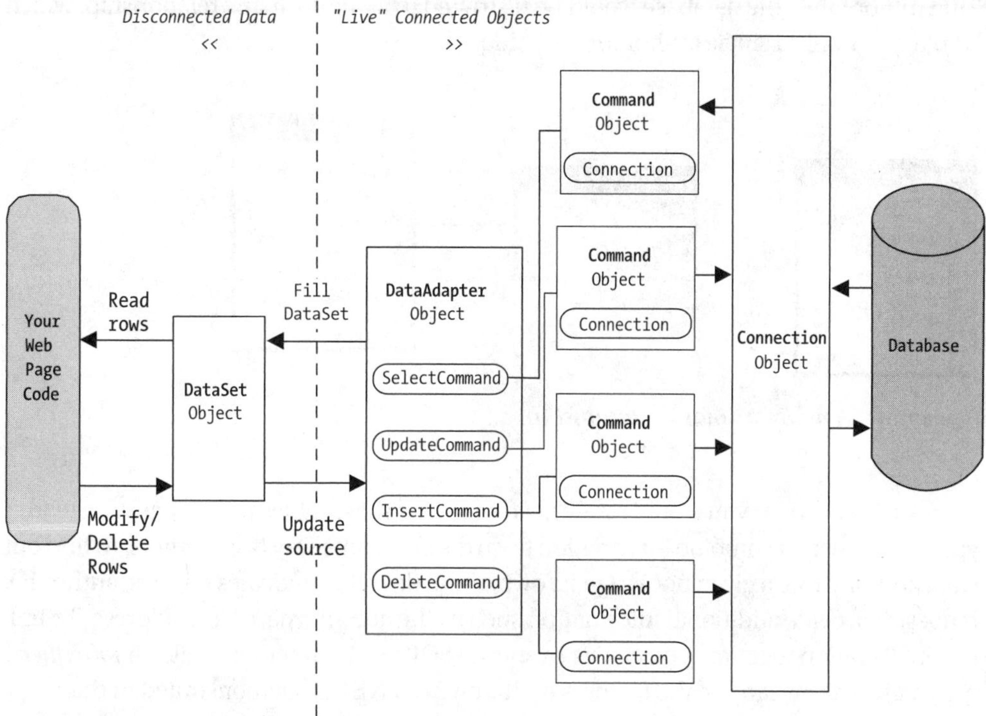

Figure 13-16. *Using a DataSet with ADO.NET*

The DataAdapter.Fill() method takes a DataSet and inserts one table of information. In this case, the table is named Authors, but any name could be used. That name is used later to access the appropriate table in the DataSet.

To access the individual DataRows, you can loop through the Rows collection of the appropriate table. Each piece of information is accessed using the field name, as it was with the DataReader.

Selecting Multiple Tables

A DataSet can contain as many tables as you need, and you can even add relationships between the tables to better emulate the underlying relational data source. Unfortunately, you have no way to connect tables together automatically based on relationships in the underlying data source. However, you can add relations with a few extra lines of code, as shown in the next example.

In the pubs database, authors are linked to titles using three tables. This arrangement (called a *many-to-many* relationship, shown in Figure 13-17) allows several authors to be related to one title and several titles to be related to one author. Without the intermediate

TitleAuthor table, the database would be restricted to a one-to-many relationship, which would allow only a single author for each title.

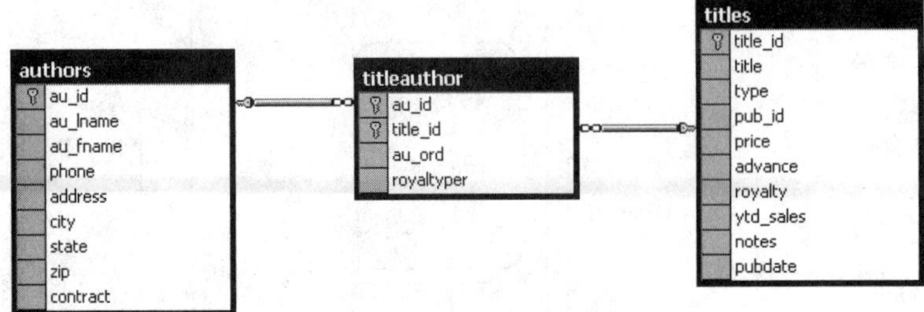

Figure 13-17. *A many-to-many relationship*

In an application, you would rarely need to access these tables individually. Instead, you would need to combine information from them in some way (for example, to find out what author wrote a given book). On its own, the Titles table indicates only the author ID. It doesn't provide additional information such as the author's name and address. To link this information together, you can use a special SQL Select statement called a *Join query*. Alternatively, you can use the features built into ADO.NET, as demonstrated in this section.

The next example provides a simple page that lists authors and the titles they have written. The interesting thing about this page is that it's generated using ADO.NET table linking.

To start, the standard ADO.NET data access objects are created, including a DataSet. All these steps are performed in a custom CreateList() method, which is called from the Page.Load event handler so that the output is created when the page is first generated.

```
// Define ADO.NET objects.
string selectSQL = "SELECT au_lname, au_fname, au_id FROM Authors";
SqlConnection con = new SqlConnection(connectionString);
SqlCommand cmd = new SqlCommand(selectSQL, con);
SqlDataAdapter adapter = new SqlDataAdapter(cmd);
DataSet dsPubs = new DataSet();
```

Next, the information for all three tables is pulled from the database and placed in the DataSet. This task could be accomplished with three separate Command objects, but to make the code a little leaner, this example uses only one and modifies the CommandText property as needed.

```
try
{
    con.Open();
    adapter.Fill(dsPubs, "Authors");

    // This command is still linked to the data adapter.
    cmd.CommandText = "SELECT au_id, title_id FROM TitleAuthor";
    adapter.Fill(dsPubs, "TitleAuthor");

    // This command is still linked to the data adapter.
    cmd.CommandText = "SELECT title_id, title FROM Titles";
    adapter.Fill(dsPubs, "Titles");
}
catch (Exception err)
{
    lblList.Text = "Error reading list of names. ";
    lblList.Text += err.Message;
}
finally
{
    con.Close();
}
```

Now that all the information is in the DataSet, you can create two DataRelation objects to make it easier to navigate through the linked information. In this case, these DataRelation objects match the foreign key restrictions that are defined in the database.

To create a DataRelation, you need to specify the linked fields from two different tables, and you need to give your DataRelation a unique name. The order of the linked fields is important. The first field is the parent, and the second field is the child. (The idea here is that one parent can have many children, but each child can have only one parent. In other words, the *parent-to-child* relationship is another way of saying a *one-to-many* relationship.) In this example, each book title can have more than one entry in the TitleAuthor table. Each author can also have more than one entry in the TitleAuthor table.

```
DataRelation Titles_TitleAuthor = new DataRelation("Titles_TitleAuthor",
  dsPubs.Tables["Titles"].Columns["title_id"],
  dsPubs.Tables["TitleAuthor"].Columns["title_id"]);
DataRelation Authors_TitleAuthor = new DataRelation("Authors_TitleAuthor",
  dsPubs.Tables["Authors"].Columns["au_id"],
  dsPubs.Tables["TitleAuthor"].Columns["au_id"]);
```

Once you've create these DataRelation objects, you must add them to the DataSet:

```
dsPubs.Relations.Add(Titles_TitleAuthor);
dsPubs.Relations.Add(Authors_TitleAuthor);
```

The remaining code loops through the DataSet. However, unlike the previous example, which moved through one table, this example uses the DataRelation objects to branch to the other linked tables. It works like this:

1. Select first record from the Author table.
2. Using the Authors_TitleAuthor relationship, find the child records that correspond to this author. This step uses the GetChildRows method of the DataRow.
3. For each matching record in TitleAuthor, look up the corresponding Title record to get the full text title. This step uses the GetParentRows method of the DataRow.
4. Move to the next Author record, and repeat the process.

The code is lean and economical:

```
foreach (DataRow rowAuthor in dsPubs.Tables["Authors"].Rows)
{
    lblList.Text += "<br /><b>" + rowAuthor["au_fname"];
    lblList.Text += " " + rowAuthor["au_lname"] + "</b><br />";

    foreach (DataRow rowTitleAuthor in
     rowAuthor.GetChildRows(Authors_TitleAuthor))
    {
        foreach (DataRow rowTitle in
         rowTitleAuthor.GetParentRows(Titles_TitleAuthor))
        {
            lblList.Text += "  ";
            lblList.Text += rowTitle["title"] + "<br />";
        }
    }
}
```

Figure 13-18 shows the final result.

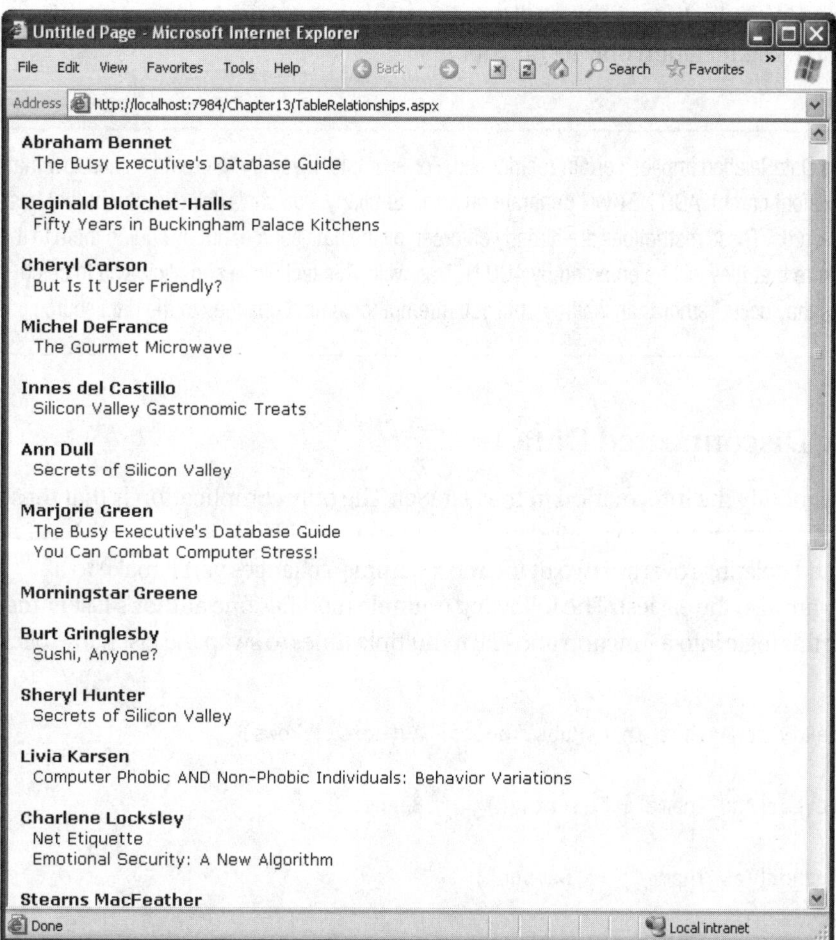

Figure 13-18. *Hierarchical information from two tables*

If authors and titles have a simple one-to-many relationship, you could leave out the inner foreach statement and use simpler code, as follows:

```
foreach (DataRow rowAuthor in dsPubs.Tables["Authors"].Rows
{
    // Display author.
    foreach (DataRow rowTitle in rowAuthor.GetChildRows(Authors_Titles)
    {
        // Display title.
    }
}
```

However, having seen the more complicated example, you're ready to create and manage multiple DataRelation objects on your own.

■ **Note** Using a DataRelation implies certain restrictions. For example, if you try to create a child row that refers to a nonexistent parent, ADO.NET will generate an error. Similarly, you can't delete a parent that has linked children records. These restrictions are already enforced by the data source, but by adding them to the DataSet, you ensure that they will be enforced by ADO.NET as well. This technique can allow you to catch errors as soon as they occur rather than waiting until you attempt to commit changes to the data source.

Modifying Disconnected Data

You can easily modify the information in the DataSet. The only complication is that these changes aren't committed until you update the data source with a DataAdapter object.

Updating and deleting rows are two of the most common changes you'll make to a DataSet. They are also the easiest. The following example modifies one author's last name. You can place this logic into a function and call it multiple times to swap the last name back and forth.

```
foreach (DataRow rowAuthor in dsPubs.Tables["Authors"].Rows)
{
    if (rowAuthor["au_lname"].ToString() == "Bennet")
    {
        rowAuthor["au_lname"] = "Samson";
    }
    else if (rowAuthor["au_lname"].ToString() == "Samson")
    {
        rowAuthor["au_lname"] = "Bennet";
    }
}
```

Deleting a record is just as easy:

```
foreach (DataRow rowAuthor in dsPubs.Tables["Authors"].Rows)
{
    if (rowAuthor["au_fname"] == "Cheryl")
    {
        rowAuthor.Delete();
    }
}
```

Alternatively, if you know the exact position of a record, you can modify or delete it using the index number rather than enumerating through the collection:

```
dsPubs.Tables["Authors"].Rows[3].Delete();
```

The DataSet is always disconnected. Any changes you make will appear in your program but won't affect the original data source unless you take additional steps. In fact, when you use the Delete method, the row isn't actually removed, only marked for deletion. (If the row were removed entirely, ADO.NET would be unable to find it and delete it from the original data source when you reconnect later.)

If you use the Delete() method, you need to be aware of this and take steps to avoid trying to use deleted rows, as follows:

```
foreach (DataRow row in dsPubs.Tables["Authors"].Rows)
{
    if (row.RowState != DataRowState.Deleted)
    {
        // It's OK to display the row value, modify it, or use it.
    }
    else
    {
        // This record is scheduled for deletion.
        // You should just ignore it.
    }
}
```

If you try to read a field of information from a deleted item, an error will occur. As warned earlier, life with disconnected data isn't always easy.

■ **Note** You can use the DataSet.Rows.Remove() method to delete a record completely. However, if you use this method, the record won't be deleted from the data source when you reconnect and update it with your changes. Instead, it will just be eliminated from your DataSet.

Adding Information to a DataSet

You can also add a new row using the Add() method of the Rows collection. Before you can add a row, however, you need to use the NewRow() method first to get a blank copy. The following example uses this technique with the original web page for viewing and adding authors:

```
DataRow rowNew;
rowNew = dsPubs.Tables["Authors"].NewRow();
```

```
rowNew["au_id"] = txtID.Text;
rowNew["au_fname"] = txtFirstName.Text;
rowNew["au_lname"] = txtLastName.Text;
rowNew["phone"] = txtPhone.Text;
rowNew["address"] = txtAddress.Text;
rowNew["city"] = txtCity.Text;
rowNew["state"] = txtState.Text;
rowNew["zip"] = txtZip.Text;
rowNew["contract"] = Conver.ToInt16(chkContract.Checked);
dsPubs.Tables["Authors"].Rows.Add(rowNew);
```

The full code needed to update the data source with these changes is included a little later in this chapter, in the "A Disconnected Update Example" section.

Updating Disconnected Data

Earlier, you saw how the DataAdapter object allows you to retrieve information. Unlike the DataReader, DataAdapter objects can transfer data in both directions.

Updating the data source is a more complicated operation than reading from it. Depending on the changes that have been made, the DataAdapter may need to perform Insert, Update, or Delete operations. Luckily, you don't need to create these Command objects by hand. Instead, you can use ADO.NET's special utility class: the CommandBuilder object. Each provider includes its own CommandBuilder. SqlCommandBuilder is the class used with the SQL Server provider, and SqlCommandBuilder is used with the OLE DB provider.

The CommandBuilder

The CommandBuilder examines the DataAdapter object you used to create the DataSet, and it adds the additional Command objects for the InsertCommand, DeleteCommand, and UpdateCommand properties. The process works like this:

```
// Create the CommandBuilder.
SqlCommandBuilder cb = new SqlCommandBuilder(adapter);

// Retrieve an updated DataAdapter.
adapter = cb.DataAdapter;
```

■ **Note** Using a CommandBuilder is a convenient approach, but it's not always ideal. That's because you have no real control over the commands that the CommandBuilder generates. If you want to tweak these commands to optimize performance (for example, using a stored procedure) or to enforce different types of concurrency, you'll need to create your Command objects by hand. For more information about getting into the nitty-gritty details of ADO.NET, consult one of the books referenced at the end of this chapter.

Updating a DataTable

With the correctly configured DataAdapter, you can update the data source using the Update() method. Here's the code to commit the changes for the Authors table:

```
con.Open();
int rowsAffected = adapter.Update(dsPubs, "Authors");
con.Close();
```

If you need to update more than one table, you'll need to create a separate DataAdapter for each table. You must then use the CommandBuilder to configure the DataAdapter so that it has the commands required to update the given table. You can then open the connection, use the Update() method of each DataAdapter, and close the connection.

The DataSet stores information about the current state of all the rows and their original state. This allows ADO.NET to find the changed rows. It adds every new row (rows with the state DataRowState.Added) with the DataAdapter.InsertCommand. It removes every deleted row (DataRowState.Deleted) using the DataAdapter.DeleteCommand. It also updates every changed row (DataRowState.Modified) with the DataAdapter.UpdateCommand. There is no guaranteed order in which these operations will take place. Once the update is successfully completed, all rows will be reset to DataRowState.Unchanged.

■ **Tip** If you use the DataAdapter.Update() method without opening the connection, the connection will be opened automatically and closed once the update is complete. However, it's usually best to explicitly control when the connection is opened and closed. That allows you more flexibility. For example, you could open the connection once and perform two operations, rather than opening the connection separately for each table you want to update.

Controlling Updates

If you used linked tables, the standard way of updating the data source can cause some problems, particularly if you've deleted or added records. These problems occur because changes usually aren't committed in the same order they were made. (To provide this type of tracking, the DataSet object would need to store much more information and waste valuable memory on the server.)

You can control the order in which tables are updated, but that's not always enough to prevent a conflict. For example, if you update the Authors table first, ADO.NET might try to delete an Author record before it deletes the TitleAuthor record that is still using it. It you update the TitleAuthor table first, ADO.NET might try to create a TitleAuthor that references a nonexistent Title. At some point, ADO.NET may be enhanced with the intelligence needed to avoid these problems, provided you use DataRelations. Currently, you need to resort to other techniques for more fine-grained control.

Using features built into the DataSet, you can pull out the rows that need to be added, modified, or deleted into separate DataSets and choose an update order that will not place the database into an inconsistent state at any point. A safe update orders is as follows. Begin with the inserts. When inserting records, make sure you insert the parent records first. That's because some of the new child records may link to one of the new parent records. Once the insertions are complete, it's safe to commit updates. Finally, you can perform the record deletions. Start by deleting any child records, and then delete parents, so that you won't be prevented from removing a child record because it's linked to a still-existing parent.

By using the DataSet.GetChanges() method, you can implement this exact pattern:

```
// Create three DataSets, and fill them from dsPubs.
DataSet dsNew = dsPubs.GetChanges(DataRowState.Added);
DataSet dsModify = dsPubs.GetChanges(DataRowState.Modified);
DataSet dsDelete = dsPubs.GetChanges(DataRowState.Delete);

// Update these DataSets separately. Remember, each DataSet has three tables!
// Also note that the add operation for the Authors and Titles tables
// must be carried out before the add operation for the TitleAuthor table.
AuthorsAdapter.Update(dsNew, "Authors");
TitlesAdapter.Update(dsNew, "Titles");
TA_Adapter.Update(dsNew, "TitleAuthor");
AuthorsAdapter.Update(dsModify, "Authors");
TitlesAdapter.Update(dsModify, "Titles");
TA_Adapter.Update(dsModify, "TitleAuthor");
AuthorsAdapter.Update(dsDelete, "Authors");
TitlesAdapter.Update(dsDelete, "Titles");
TA_Adapter.Update(dsDelete, "TitleAuthor");
```

This adds a layer of complexity and a significant amount of extra code. However, in cases where you make many different types of modifications to several different tables at once, this is the only solution. To avoid these problems, you can commit changes earlier (rather than committing an entire batch of changes at once), or you can use Command objects directly instead of relying on the disconnected data features of the DataSet. Batched updates are almost always more trouble than they're worth in a web application. (On the other hand, they are indispensable in some desktop applications that need to work with data even when a network connection isn't present.)

A Disconnected Update Example

The next example rewrites the code for adding a new author in the update page with equivalent DataSet code. You can find this example in the online samples as AuthorManager_Disconnected.aspx. (AuthorManager.aspx is the original, command-based version.)

```
protected void cmdInsert_Click(Object sender, EventArgs e)
{
    // Define ADO.NET objects.
    string selectSQL;
    selectSQL = "SELECT * FROM Authors";
    SqlConnection con = new SqlConnection(connectionString);
    SqlCommand cmd = new SqlCommand(selectSQL, con);
    SqlDataAdapter adapter = new SqlDataAdapter(cmd);
    DataSet dsPubs = new DataSet();

    // Get the schema information.
    try
    {
        con.Open();
        adapter.FillSchema(dsPubs, SchemaType.Mapped, "Authors");
    }
    catch (Exception err)
    {
        lblResults.Text = "Error reading schema. ";
        lblResults.Text += err.Message;
    }
    finally
    {
        con.Close();
    }
```

```
    DataRow rowNew;
    rowNew = dsPubs.Tables["Authors"].NewRow();
    rowNew["au_id"] = txtID.Text;
    rowNew["au_fname"] = txtFirstName.Text;
    rowNew["au_lname"] = txtLastName.Text;
    rowNew["phone"] = txtPhone.Text;
    rowNew["address"] = txtAddress.Text;
    rowNew["city"] = txtCity.Text;
    rowNew["state"] = txtState.Text;
    rowNew["zip"] = txtZip.Text;
    rowNew["contract"] = Convert.ToInt16(chkContract.Checked);
    dsPubs.Tables["Authors"].Rows.Add(rowNew);

    // Insert the new record.
    int added = 0;
    try
    {
        // Create the CommandBuilder.
        SqlCommandBuilder cb = new SqlCommandBuilder(adapter);
        // Retrieve an updated DataAdapter.
        adapter = cb.DataAdapter;

        // Update the database using the DataSet.
        con.Open();
        added = adapter.Update(dsPubs, "Authors");
    }
    catch (Exception err)
    {
        lblResults.Text = "Error inserting record. ";
        lblResults.Text += err.Message;
    }
    finally
    {
        con.Close();
    }

    // If the insert succeeded, refresh the author list.
    if (added > 0)
    {
        FillAuthorList();
    }
}
```

In this case, the example is quite, inefficient. To add a new record, a DataSet needs to be created, with the required tables and a valid row. To retrieve information about what this row should look like, the DataAdapter. FillSchema() method is used. The FillSchema() method creates a table with no rows but with other information about the table, such as the name of each field and the requirements for each column (the data type, the maximum length, any restriction against null values, and so on). If you wanted, you could use the FillSchema() method followed by the Fill() method.

After this step, the information is entered into a new row in the DataSet, the DataAdapter is updated with the CommandBuilder, and the changes are committed to the database. The whole operation took two database connections and required the use of a DataSet that was then abruptly abandoned. In this scenario, disconnected data is probably an extravagant solution to a problem that would be better (and more efficiently) solved with ordinary Command objects.

■ **Tip** Many database tables use identity columns that increment automatically. For example, an alternate design of the Authors table might use au_id as an auto-incrementing column. In this case, the database would automatically assign a unique ID to each inserted author record. When adding new authors, you wouldn't specify any value for the au_id field; instead, this number would be generated when the changes are committed to the database.

Concurrency Problems

As you discovered earlier, ADO.NET maintains information in the DataSet about the current and the original value of every piece of information in the DataSet. When updating a row, ADO.NET searches for a row that matches every "original" field exactly and then updates it with the new values. If another user changes even a single field in that record while your program is working with the disconnected data, an exception is thrown. The update operation is then halted, potentially preventing other valid rows from being updated.

You can handle these potential problems in an easier way: using the DataAdapter.RowUpdated event. This event occurs after every individual insert, update, or delete operation, but before an exception is thrown. It gives you the chance to examine the results, note any errors, and prevent an error from occurring.

The first step is to create an appropriate event handler for the DataAdapter.RowUpdated event, as follows:

```
protected void OnRowUpdated(Object sender, SqlRowUpdatedEventArgs e)
{
    // Check whether any records were affected.
    // If no records were affected, the statement didn't execute as expected.
```

```
        if (e.RecordsAffected < 1)
        {
            // Find out the type of failed error.
            switch (e.StatementType)
            {
                case StatementType.Delete:
                    lstErrors.Items.Add("Not deleted: " + e.Row["au_id"]);
                    break;
                case StatementType.Insert:
                    lstErrors.Items.Add("Not inserted: " + e.Row["au_id"]);
                    break;
                case StatementType.Update:
                    lstErrors.Items.Add("Not updated: " + e.Row["au_id"]);
                    break;
            }

            // Using the OledDbRowUpdatedEventArgs class, you can tell ADO.NET
            // to ignore the problem and keep updating the other rows.
            e.Status = UpdateStatus.SkipCurrentRow;
        }
    }
```

The SqlRowUpdatedEventArgs object provides this event handler with information about the row that ADO.NET just attempted to modify (e.Row), the type of modification (e.StatementType), and the result (e.RecordsAffected). In this example, errors are detected, and information about the unsuccessfully updated rows is added to a list control. Now that the problem has been noted, the e.Status property can be used to instruct ADO.NET to continue updating other changed rows in the DataSet.

Remember, this event occurs while the DataAdapter is in mid-update and using a live database connection. For that reason, you should not try to perform anything too complicated or time-consuming in this event handler. Instead, quickly log or display the errors and continue.

Now that the event handler has been created, you need to attach it to the DataSet before your perform the update. You connect this event the same way you connect the web control events:

```
// Connect the event handler.
adapter.RowUpdated += new SqlRowUpdatedEventHandler(OnRowUpdated);

// Perform the update.
int rowsAffected = adapter.Update(dsPubs, "Authors");
```

A Concurrency Example

It can be hard to test the code you write to deal with concurrency problems, because it's executed only in specific circumstances. These circumstances may be common for a fully deployed large-scale application, but they're more difficult to re-create when a single developer is doing the testing.

The ConcurrencyHandler.aspx file in the online samples simulates a concurrency problem by making invalid changes to a database using two separate DataSets. When the code attempts to commit these changes, the OnRowUpdated code springs into action and reports the problem (see Figure 13-19).

The full-page code is as follows:

```
public partial class ConcurrencyHandler : Page
{
    // Connection string used for all connections.
    private connectionString =
      WebConfigurationManager.ConnectionStrings["Pubs"].ConnectionString;

    public void OnRowUpdated(Object sender, SqlRowUpdatedEventArgs e)
    {
        // Check whether any records were affected.
        if (e.RecordsAffected < 1)
        {
            // Find out the type of failed error.
            switch (e.StatementType)
            {
                case StatementType.Delete:
                    lblResult.Text += "<br />Not deleted: ";
                    break;
                case StatementType.Insert:
                    lblResult.Text += "<br />Not inserted: ";
                    break;
                case StatementType.Update:
                    lblResult.Text += "<br />Not updated: ";
                    break;
            }

            lblResult.Text += "(" + e.Row["au_id"] + " " + e.Row["au_lname"];
            lblResult.Text += ", " + e.Row["au_fname"] + ")";
```

```
            // Continue processing.
            e.Status = UpdateStatus.SkipCurrentRow;
        }
    }

    protected void cmdTest_Click(Object sender, EventArgs e)
    {
        lblResult.Text = "";

        // Define ADO.NET objects.
        string selectSQL = "SELECT * FROM Authors";
        SqlConnection con = new SqlConnection(connectionString);
        SqlCommand cmd = new SqlCommand(selectSQL, con);
        SqlDataAdapter adapter = new SqlDataAdapter(cmd);

        // Create the CommandBuilder.
        SqlCommandBuilder cb = new SqlCommandBuilder(adapter);
        // Retrieve an updated DataAdapter.
        adapter = cb.DataAdapter;

        // Connect the event handler.
        adapter.RowUpdated += new SqlRowUpdatedEventHandler(OnRowUpdated);

        // Create two DataSets...perfect for conflicting data.
        DataSet dsPubs1 = new DataSet();
        DataSet dsPubs2 = new DataSet();

        try
        {
            con.Open();

            // Fill both DataSets with the same table.
            adapter.Fill(dsPubs1, "Authors");
            adapter.Fill(dsPubs2, "Authors");

            // "Flip" the contract field in the first row of dsPubs1.
            if ((bool)dsPubs1.Tables[0].Rows[0]["contract"] == true)
            {
                dsPubs1.Tables[0].Rows[0]["contract"] = false;
            }
```

```
            else
            {
                dsPubs1.Tables[0].Rows[0]["contract"] = true;
            }

            // Update the database.
            adapter.Update(dsPubs1, "Authors");

            // Make a change in the second DataSet.
            dsPubs2.Tables[0].Rows[0]["au_fname"] = "Bill";
            dsPubs2.Tables[0].Rows[0]["au_lname"] = "Gates";

            // Try to update this row. Even though these changes don't conflict,
            // the update will fail because the row has been changed.
            adapter.Update(dsPubs2, "Authors");
        }
        catch (Exception err)
        {
            lblResult.Text += "Error reading schema. ";
            lblResult.Text += err.Message;
        }
        finally
        {
            con.Close();
        }
    }
}
```

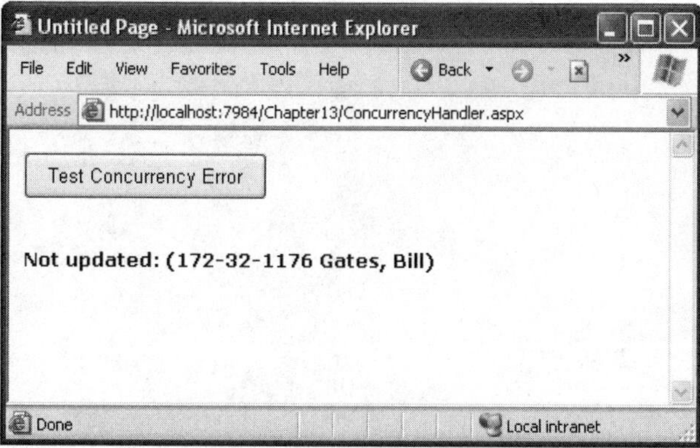

Figure 13-19. *Reporting concurrency problems*

DIRECT COMMANDS OR THE DATASET—WHICH WORKS BEST?

As you've seen in this chapter, ADO.NET gives you two ways to solve the same problems. Direct commands are the leanest, most straightforward approach, and they sidestep some of the headaches you'll face with disconnected data. On the other hand, DataSets really shine when you need to work with more than one related table, and they also work well with the data binding techniques you'll use in Chapter 14 and Chapter 15. Which one you use depends on the situation, but in many cases, both approaches will work equally well.

The key fact you should realize is that the simpler approach—using direct commands—often makes perfect sense. Overeager .NET converts sometimes try to use the DataSet everywhere, needlessly complicating life. But if you're happy with forward-only, read-only data and you don't need to convert your data to XML or send it to another component, there's no embarrassment in using ADO.NET's DataReader.

The Last Word

The chapter gave you a comprehensive introduction to ADO.NET and its new disconnected data model. Although you've seen all the core concepts, you still have much more to learn. For a comprehensive book that focuses exclusively on ADO.NET, you may be interested in a book such as *Microsoft ADO.NET 2.0: Core Reference* (Microsoft Press, 2005), which investigates some of the techniques you can use to optimize ADO.NET data access code.

In the next two chapters, you'll learn about ASP.NET's new data binding features and see how you can use them with a little ADO.NET code to write practical data-driven pages.

CHAPTER 14

Data Binding

In the previous chapter, you learned how to use ADO.NET to retrieve information from a database, how to work with an ASP.NET application, and how to apply your changes to the original data source. These techniques are flexible and powerful, but they aren't always convenient.

For example, you can use the DataSet or the DataReader to retrieve rows of information, format them individually, and add them to an HTML table on a web page. Conceptually, this isn't too difficult. However, it still requires a lot of repetitive code to move through the data, format columns, and display it in the correct order. Repetitive code may be easy, but it's also error-prone, difficult to enhance, and unpleasant to read. Fortunately, ASP.NET adds a feature that allows you to skip this process and pop data directly into HTML elements and fully formatted controls. It's called *data binding*.

Introducing Data Binding

The basic principle of data binding is this: you tell a control where to find your data and how you want it displayed, and the control handles the rest of the details. Data binding in ASP.NET is superficially similar to data binding in the world of desktop or client/server applications, but in truth, it's fundamentally different. In those environments, data binding involves creating a direct connection between a data source and a control in an application window. If the user changes a value in the on-screen control, the data in the linked database is modified automatically. Similarly, if the database changes while the user is working with it (for example, another user commits a change), the display can be refreshed automatically.

This type of data binding isn't practical in the ASP.NET world, because you can't effectively maintain a database connection over the Internet. This "direct" data binding also severely limits scalability and reduces flexibility. In fact, data binding has acquired a bad reputation for exactly these reasons.

ASP.NET data binding, on the other hand, has little in common with direct data binding. ASP.NET data binding works in one direction only. Information moves *from* a data object *into* a control. Then the data objects are thrown away, and the page is sent to the client. If the user modifies the data in a data-bound control, your program can update the corresponding record in the database, but nothing happens automatically.

ASP.NET data binding is much more flexible than traditional data binding. Many of the most powerful data binding controls, such as the Repeater, DataList, and GridView, allow you to configure formatting options and even add repeating controls and buttons for each record. This is all set up through special templates, which are a new addition to ASP.NET. Templates are examined in detail in the next chapter.

Types of ASP.NET Data Binding

Two types of ASP.NET data binding exist: single-value binding and repeated-value binding. Single-value data binding is by far the simpler of the two, whereas repeated-value binding provides the foundation for the most advanced ASP.NET data controls.

Single-Value, or "Simple," Data Binding

You can use *single-value data binding* to add information anywhere on an ASP.NET page. You can even place information into a control property or as plain text inside an HTML tag. Single-value data binding doesn't necessarily have anything to do with ADO.NET. Instead, single-value data binding allows you to take a variable, property, or expression and insert it dynamically into a page. Single-value binding also helps you create templates for the rich data controls you'll study in Chapter 15.

Repeated-Value, or "List," Binding

Repeated-value data binding allows you to display an entire table or all the values from a single field in a table. Unlike single-value data binding, this type of data binding requires a special control that supports it. Typically, this will be a list control such as CheckBoxList or ListBox, but it can also be a much more sophisticated control such as the GridView (which is described in Chapter 15). You'll know a control supports repeated-value data binding if it provides a DataSource property. As with single-value binding, repeated-value binding doesn't necessarily need to use data from a database, and it doesn't have to use the ADO.NET objects. For example, you can use repeated-value binding to bind data from a collection or an array.

How Data Binding Works

Data binding works a little differently depending on whether you're using single-value or repeated-value binding. In single-value binding, a data binding expression is inserted into the HTML markup in the .aspx file (not the code-behind file). In repeated-value binding, data binding is configured by setting the appropriate control properties (typically in the Page.Load event handler). You'll see specific examples of both these techniques later in this chapter.

Once you specify data binding, you need to activate it. You accomplish this task by calling the DataBind() method. The DataBind() method is a basic piece of functionality supplied in the Control class. It automatically binds a control and any child controls that it contains. With repeated-value binding, you can use the DataBind() method of the specific list control you're using. Alternatively, you can bind the whole page at once by calling the DataBind() method of the current Page object. Once you call this method, all the data binding expressions in the page are evaluated and replaced with the specified value.

Typically, you call the DataBind() method in the Page.Load event handler. If you forget to use it, ASP.NET will ignore your data binding expressions, and the client will receive a page that contains empty values.

This is a general description of the whole process. To really understand what's happening, you need to work with some specific examples.

Single-Value Data Binding

Single-value data binding is really just a different approach to dynamic text. To use it, you add special data binding expressions into your .aspx files. These expressions have the following format:

```
<%# expression_goes_here %>
```

This may look like a script block, but it isn't. If you try to write any code inside this tag, you will receive an error. The only thing you can add is a valid data binding expression. For example, if you have a public or protected variable on your page named Country, you could write the following:

```
<%# Country %>
```

When you call the DataBind() method for the page, this text will be replaced with the value for Country (for example, Spain). Similarly, you could use a property or a built-in ASP.NET object as follows:

```
<%# Request.Browser.Browser %>
```

This would substitute a string with the current browser name (for example, IE). In fact, you can even call a public or protected function defined on your page or execute a simple expression, provided it returns a result that can be converted to text and displayed on the page. Thus, the following data binding expressions are all valid:

```
<%# GetUserName(ID) %>
<%# 1 + (2 * 20) %>
<%# "John " + "Smith" %>
```

Remember, you place these data binding expressions in the HTML tags of your .aspx file. This means if you're relying on Visual Studio to manage your HTML code automatically, you may have to venture into slightly unfamiliar territory. To examine how you can add a data binding expression, and see why you might want to, it helps to review a simple example.

A Simple Data Binding Example

This section shows a simple example of single-value data binding. The example has been stripped to the bare minimum amount of detail needed to illustrate the concept.

You start with a special variable defined in your Page class, which is called TransactionCount:

```
public partial class SimpleDataBinding : Page
{
    protected int TransactionCount;

    // (Additional code omitted.)
}
```

Note that this variable must be designated as public or protected, not private. Otherwise, ASP.NET will not be able to access it when it's evaluating the data binding expression.

Now, assume that this value is set in the Page.Load event handler using some database lookup code. For testing purposes, the example skips this step and hard-codes a value:

```
protected void Page_Load(object sender, EventArgs e)
{
    // (You could use database code here
    // to look up a value for TransactionCount.)
    TransactionCount = 10;

    // Now convert all the data binding expressions on the page.
    this.DataBind();
}
```

Two actions actually take place in this event handler: the TransactionCount variable is set to 10, and all the data binding expressions on the page are bound. Currently, no data binding expressions exist, so this method has no effect. Notice that this example uses the this keyword to refer to the current page. You could just write DataBind() without the this keyword, because the default object is the current Page object. However, using the this keyword makes it a bit clearer what object is being used.

To make this data binding accomplish something, you need to add a data binding expression. Usually, it's easiest to add this value directly to the presentation code in the .aspx file. If you're using Notepad to create your ASP.NET pages, you won't have any trouble with this approach. If, on the other hand, you're using Visual Studio to create your controls, you can add a Label control and then configure the data binding expression in the HTML view by clicking the Source button at the bottom of the web page design window (see Figure 14-1).

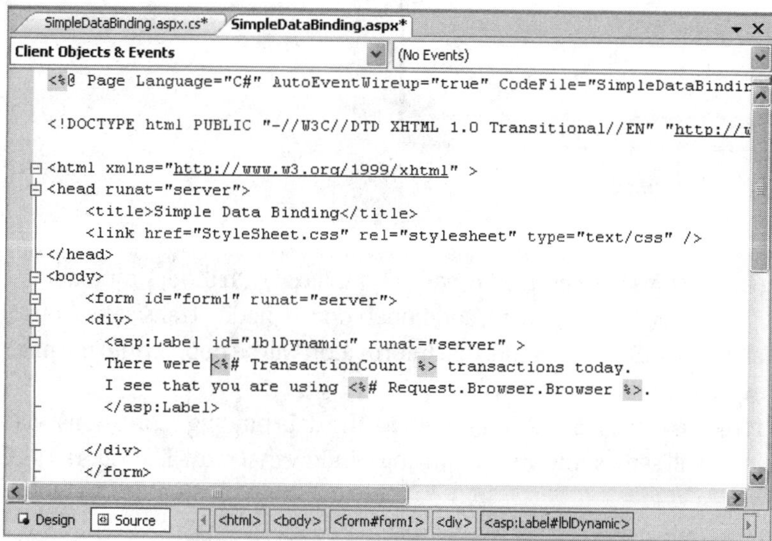

Figure 14-1. *Source view in the web page designer*

To add your expression, find the tag for the Label control. Modify the Text property as shown in the following code.

```
<asp:Label id="lblDynamic" runat="server" Font-Size="X-Large">
There were <%# TransactionCount %> transactions today.
I see that you are using <%# Request.Browser.Browser %>.
</asp:Label>
```

This example uses two separate data binding expressions, which are inserted along with the normal static text. The first data binding expression references the TransactionCount variable, and the second uses the built-in Request object to determine some information about the user's browser. When you run this page, the output looks like Figure 14-2.

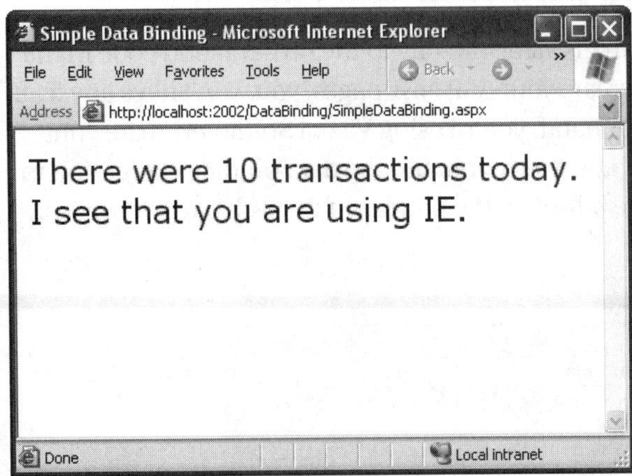

Figure 14-2. *The result of data binding*

The data binding expressions have been automatically replaced with the appropriate values. If the page is posted back, you could use additional code to modify TransactionCount, and as long as you call the DataBind() method, that information will be popped into the page in the data binding expression you've defined.

If, however, you forget to call the DataBind() method, the data binding expressions will be ignored, and the user will see a somewhat confusing window that looks like Figure 14-3.

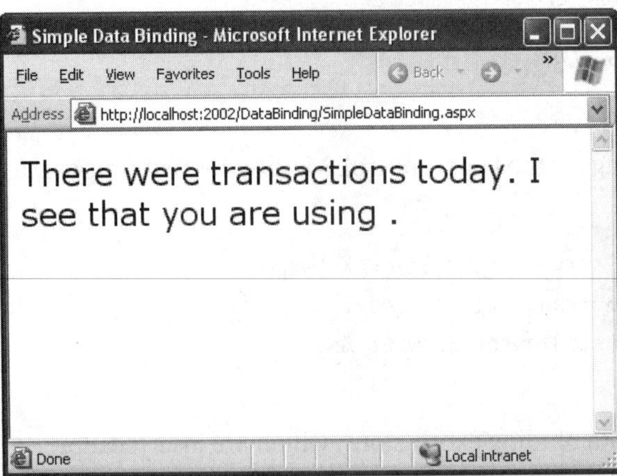

Figure 14-3. *The non-data-bound page*

You also need to be a little careful with your data-bound control in the design environment so that you don't inadvertently clear a data binding expression by entering different values in the Properties window.

Note When using single-value data binding, you need to consider when you should call the DataBind() method. For example, if you made the mistake of calling it before you set the TransactionCount variable, the corresponding expression would just be converted to 0. Remember, data binding is a one-way street. This means changing the TransactionCount variable after you've used the DataBind() method won't produce any visible effect. Unless you call the DataBind() method again, the displayed value won't be updated.

Simple Data Binding with Properties

The previous example uses a data binding expression to set static text information inside a label tag. However, you can also use single-value data binding to set other types of information on your page, including control properties. To do this, you simply have to know where to put the data binding expression.

For example, consider the following page, which defines a variable named URL and uses it to point to a picture in the application directory:

```
public partial class DataBindingUrl : Page
{
    public string URL;

    protected void Page_Load(Object sender, EventArgs e)
    {
        URL = Server.MapPath("picture.jpg");
        this.DataBind();
    }
}
```

You can now use this URL to create a label, as shown here:

```
<asp:Label id="lblDynamic" runat="server"><%# URL %></asp:Label>
```

You can also use it for a check box caption:

```
<asp:CheckBox id="chkDynamic" Text="<%# URL %>" runat="server" />
```

Or you can use it for a target for a hyperlink:

```
<asp:Hyperlink id="lnkDynamic" Text="Click here!" NavigateUrl="<%# URL %>"
 runat="server" />
```

You can even use it for a picture:

```
<asp:Image id="imgDynamic" Src="<%# URL %>" runat="server" />
```

The only trick is that you need to edit these control tags manually. Figure 14-4 shows what a page that uses all these elements would look.

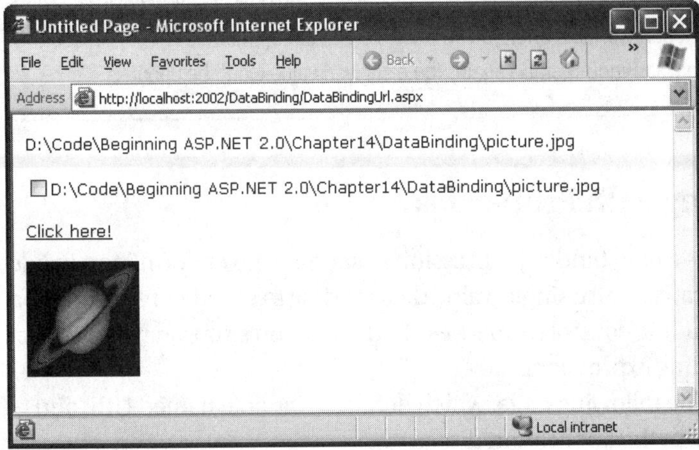

Figure 14-4. *Multiple ways to bind the same data*

To examine this example in more detail, try the sample code for this chapter.

Problems with Single-Value Data Binding

Before you start using single-value data binding techniques in every aspect of your ASP.NET programs, you should consider some of the serious drawbacks this approach can present:

Putting code into a page's user interface: One of ASP.NET's great advantages is that it finally allows developers to separate the user interface code (the HTML and control tags in the .aspx file) from the actual code used for data access and all other tasks (in the code-behind file). However, overenthusiastic use of single-value data binding can encourage you to disregard that distinction and start coding function calls and even operations into your page. If not carefully managed, this can lead to complete disorder.

Fragmenting code: When using data binding expressions, it may not be obvious to other developers where the functionality resides for different operations. This is particularly a problem if you blend both approaches (modifying the same control using a data binding expression and then directly in code). Even worse, the data binding code may have certain dependencies that aren't immediately obvious. If the page code changes, or a variable or function is removed or renamed, the corresponding data binding expression could stop providing valid information without any explanation or even an obvious error.

Of course, some developers love the flexibility of single-value data binding and use it to great effect, making the rest of their code more economical and streamlined. It's up to you to be aware of (and avoid) the potential drawbacks.

■ **Note** In one case, single-value data binding is quite useful—when building *templates*. Templates declare a block of HTML that's reused for each record in an entire table. However, they work only with certain rich data controls, such as the GridView. You'll learn more about this control in Chapter 15.

Using Code Instead of Simple Data Binding

If you decide not to use single-value data binding, you can accomplish the same thing using code. For example, you could use the following event handler to display the same output as the first label example:

```
protected void Page_Load(Object sender, EventArgs e)
{
    TransactionCount = 10;
    lblDynamic.Text = "There were " + TransactionCount.ToString();
    lblDynamic.Text += "transactions today. ";
    lblDynamic.Text += "I see that you are using " + Request.Browser.Browser;
}
```

This code dynamically fills in the label without using data binding. The trade-off is more code. Instead of importing ASP.NET code into the .aspx file, you end up doing the reverse: importing the user interface (the specific text) into your code file!

■ **Tip** As much as possible, stick to one approach for using dynamic text. If you decide to use data binding, try to reduce the number of times you modify a control's text in code. If you do both, you may end up confusing others or just canceling your own changes! For example, if you call the DataBind() method on a control that uses a data expression after changing its values in code, your data binding expression will not be used.

Repeated-Value Data Binding

Although using simple data binding is optional, repeated-value binding is so useful that almost every ASP.NET application will want to use it somewhere. Repeated-value data binding uses one of the special list controls included with ASP.NET. You link one of these controls to a data list source (such as a field in a data table), and the control automatically creates a full list using all the corresponding values. This saves you from having to write code that loops through the array or data table and manually adds elements to a control. Repeated-value binding can also simplify your life by supporting advanced formatting and template options that automatically configure how the data should look when it's placed in the control.

To create a data expression for list binding, you need to use a list control that explicitly supports data binding. Luckily, ASP.NET provides a whole collection, many of which you've probably already used in other applications or examples:

ListBox, DropDownList, CheckBoxList, and RadioButtonList: These web controls provide a list for a single-column of information.

HtmlSelect: This server-side HTML control represents the HTML <select> element and works essentially the same way as the ListBox web control. Generally, you'll use this control only for backward compatibility or when upgrading an existing ASP page.

GridView, DetailsView, and FormView: These rich web controls allow you to provide repeating lists or grids that can display more than one column (or field) of information at a time. For example, if you were binding to a Hashtable (a special type of collection), you could display both the key and the value of each item. If you were binding to a full-fledged table in a DataSet, you could display multiple fields in any combination. These controls offer the most powerful and flexible options for data binding.

With repeated-value data binding, you can write a data binding expression in your .aspx file, or you can apply the data binding by setting control properties. In the case of the simpler list controls, you'll usually just set properties. Of course, you can set properties in many ways, such as by using code in a code-behind file or by modifying the control tag in the .aspx file, possibly with the help of Visual Studio's Properties window. The approach you take doesn't matter. The important detail is that you don't use any <%# expression %> data binding expressions.

To continue any further with data binding, it helps to divide the subject into a few basic categories. You'll start by looking at data binding with the list controls.

Data Binding with Simple List Controls

In some ways, data binding to a list control is the simplest kind of data binding. You need to follow only three steps:

1. Create and fill some kind of data object. You have numerous options, including an Array, ArrayList, Collection, Hashtable, DataTable, and DataSet. Essentially, you can use any type of collection that supports the IEnumerable interface, although you'll discover each class has specific advantages and disadvantages.

2. Link the object to the appropriate control. To do this, you need to set only a couple of properties, including DataSource. If you're binding to a full DataSet, you'll also need to set the DataMember property to identify the appropriate table you want to use.

3. Activate the binding. As with single-value binding, you activate data binding by using the DataBind() method, either for the specific control or for all contained controls at once by using the DataBind() method for the current page.

This process is the same whether you're using the ListBox, the DropDownList, the CheckBoxList, the RadioButtonList, or even the HtmlSelect control. All these controls provide the same properties and work the same way. The only difference is in the way they appear on the final web page.

A Simple List Binding Example

To try this type of data binding, add a ListBox control to a new web page. Use the Page.Load event handler to create an ArrayList collection to use as a data source as follows:

```
ArrayList fruit = new ArrayList();
fruit.Add("Kiwi");
fruit.Add("Pear");
fruit.Add("Mango");
fruit.Add("Blueberry");
fruit.Add("Apricot");
fruit.Add("Banana");
fruit.Add("Peach");
fruit.Add("Plum");
```

Now, you can link this collection to the ListBox control:

```
lstItems.DataSource = fruit;
```

Because an ArrayList is a straightforward, unstructured type of object, this is all the information you need to set. If you were using a DataTable (which has more than one field) or a DataSet (which has more than one DataTable), you would have to specify additional information.

To activate the binding, use the DataBind() method:

```
this.DataBind();
```

You could also use lstItems.DataBind() to bind just the ListBox control. Figure 14-5 shows the resulting web page.

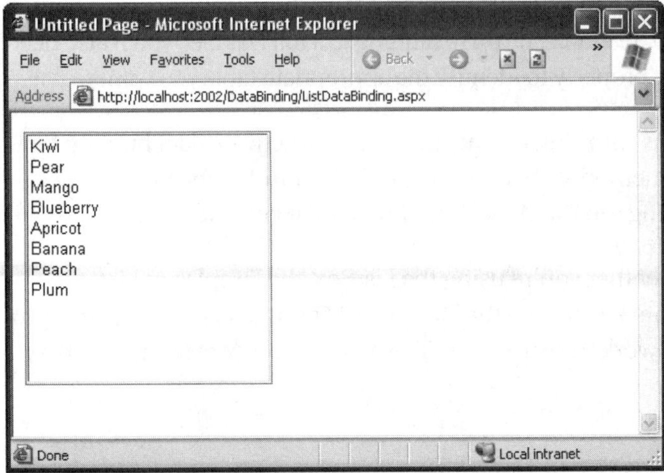

Figure 14-5. *A data-bound list*

This technique can save quite a few lines of code. This example doesn't offer a lot of savings because the collection is created just before it's displayed. In a more realistic application, however, you might be using a function that returns a ready-made collection to you:

```
ArrayList fruit;
fruit = GetFruitsInSeason("Summer");
```

In this case, it's extremely simple to add the extra two lines needed to bind and display the collection in the window:

```
lstItems.DataSource = fruit;
this.DataBind();
```

Or you could even change it to the following, even more compact, code:

```
lstItems.DataSource = GetFruitsInSeason("Summer");
this.DataBind();
```

On the other hand, consider the extra trouble you would have to go through if you didn't use data binding. This type of savings compounds rapidly, especially when you start combining data binding with multiple controls, advanced objects such as DataSets, or advanced controls that apply formatting through templates.

Generic Collections

You can use data binding with the Hashtable and ArrayList, two of the more useful collection classes in the System.Collections namespace. However, as you learned in Chapter 3, .NET 2.0 adds a new set of collections in another namespace—System.Collections.Generic.

These collections are ideal in cases where you want your collection to hold just a single type of object (such as a string or an instance of a specific class). When you use the generic collections, you choose the item type you want to use, and the collection object is "locked in" to your choice (similar to how an array works). This means if you try to add another type of object in your code, it results in a compile-time error. Similarly, when you pull an item from the collection, you don't need to write casting code to convert it to the right type, because the compiler already knows what type of objects you're using. This behavior is safer and more convenient, and it's what you'll want most of the time.

To use a generic collection, you must import the right namespace:

```
using System.Collections.Generic;
```

The generic version of the ArrayList class is named List. Here's how you create a List collection object that can only store strings:

```
List<string> fruit = new List<string>();
fruit.Add("Kiwi");
fruit.Add("Pear");
```

All you need to do is specify the type you want to use in angled brackets after the class name when you declare and create the collection object. The List collection provides the same basic methods as the ArrayList.

Multiple Binding

You can bind the same data list object to multiple different controls. Consider the following example, which compares all the types of list controls at your disposal by loading them with the same information:

```
protected void Page_Load(Object sender, EventArgs e)
{
    // Create and fill the collection.
    List<string> fruit = new List<string>();
    fruit.Add("Kiwi");
    fruit.Add("Pear");
    fruit.Add("Mango");
    fruit.Add("Blueberry");
    fruit.Add("Apricot");
    fruit.Add("Banana");
    fruit.Add("Peach");
    fruit.Add("Plum");
```

```
    // Define the binding for the list controls.
    MyListBox.DataSource = fruit;
    MyDropDownListBox.DataSource = fruit;
    MyHTMLSelect.DataSource = fruit;
    MyCheckBoxList.DataSource = fruit;
    MyRadioButtonList.DataSource = fruit;

    // Activate the binding.
    this.DataBind();
}
```

Figure 14-6 shows the rendered page.

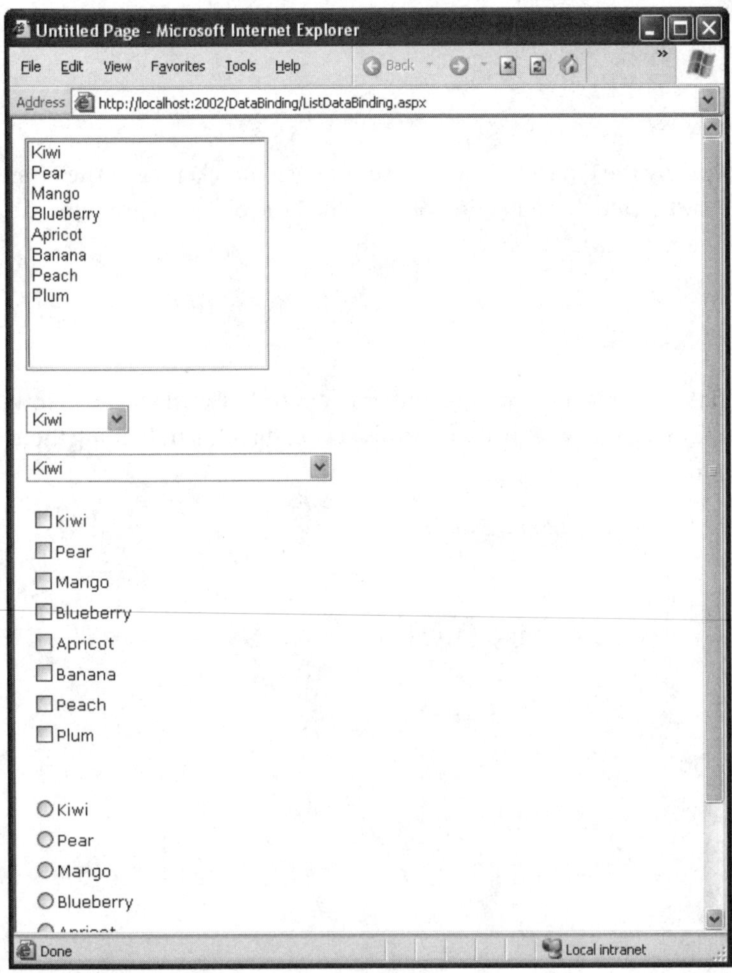

Figure 14-6. *Multiple bound lists*

This is another area where ASP.NET data binding may differ from what you have experienced in a desktop application. In traditional data binding, all the different controls are sometimes treated like "views" on the same data source, and you can work with only one record from the data source at a time. In this type of data binding, when you select Pear in one list control, the other list controls automatically refresh so that they too have Pear selected (or the corresponding information from the same row). This isn't how ASP.NET uses data binding.

Data Binding and View State

Remember, the original collection is destroyed as soon as the page is completely processed into HTML and sent to the user. However, the information will remain in the controls if you've set their EnableViewState properties to true. This means you don't need to re-create and rebind the control every time the Page.Load event occurs, and you should check the IsPostBack property first.

Of course, in many cases, especially when working with databases, you'll want to rebind on every pass. For example, if you presented information corresponding to values in a database table, you might want to let the user make changes or specify a record to be deleted. As soon as the page is posted back, you would execute a SQL command and rebind the control to show the new data (thereby confirming to the user that the data source was updated with the change). In this case, you'll rebind the data with every postback.

The important concept to realize now is that you need to be consciously evaluating state options. If you don't need view state for a data-bound list control, you should disable it, because it can slow down response times if a large amount of data is displayed on the screen. This is particularly, true for the multiple binding example, because each control will have its own view state and its own separate copy of the identical data.

Data Binding with a Dictionary Collection

A *dictionary collection* is a special kind of collection in which every item (or *definition*, to use the dictionary analogy) is indexed with a specific key (or dictionary *word*). This is similar to the way that built-in ASP.NET collections such as Session, Application, and Cache work.

Dictionary collections always need keys, which make them more efficient for retrieving and sorting. Ordinary collections, on the other hand, are like large canvas bags that accommodate anything. Generally, you need to go through every item in a generic collection to find what you need, which makes them ideal for cases where you always need to display or work with all the items at the same time.

You can use two basic dictionary-style collections in .NET. The Hashtable collection (in the System.Collections namespace) allows you to store any type of object and use any type of object for the key values. The Dictionary collection (in the System.Collections.Generic namespace) uses generics to provide the same "locking in" behavior as the List collection. You choose the item type and the key type upfront to prevent errors and reduce the amount of casting code you need to write.

The following example uses the Dictionary collection class. You create a Dictionary object in much the same way you create an ArrayList or List collection. The only difference is that you need to supply a unique key for every item. This example uses the lazy practice of assigning a sequential number for each key:

```
protected void Page_Load(Object sender, EventArgs e)
{
    if (!this.IsPostBack)
    {
        // Use integers to index each item. Each item is a string.
        Dictionary<int, string> fruit = new Dictionary<int, string>();

        fruit.Add(1, "Kiwi");
        fruit.Add(2, "Pear");
        fruit.Add(3, "Mango");
        fruit.Add(4, "Blueberry");
        fruit.Add(5, "Apricot");
        fruit.Add(6, "Banana");
        fruit.Add(7, "Peach");
        fruit.Add(8, "Plum");

        // Define the binding for the list controls.
        MyListBox.DataSource = fruit;

        // Choose what you want to display in the list.
        MyListBox.DataTextField = "Value";

        // Activate the binding.
        this.DataBind();
    }
}
```

There's one new detail here. It's this line:

```
MyListBox.DataTextField = "Value";
```

Each item in a dictionary-style collection has both a key and a value associated with it. If you don't specify which property you want to display, ASP.NET simply calls the ToString() method on each collection item. This may or may not produce the result you want. However, by inserting this line of code you control exactly what appears in the list. The page will now appear as expected, with all the fruit names.

■ **Note** Notice that you need to enclose the property name in quotation marks. ASP.NET uses reflection to inspect your object and find the property that has the name Value at runtime.

You might want to experiment with what other types of collections you can bind to a list control. One interesting option is to use a built-in ASP.NET control such as the Session object. An item in the list will be created for every currently defined Session variable, making this trick a nice little debugging tool to quickly check current session information.

Using the DataValueField Property

Along with the DataTextField property, all list controls that support data binding also provide a DataValueField property, which adds the corresponding information to the value attribute in the control element. This allows you to store extra (undisplayed) information that you can access later. For example, you could use these two lines to define your data binding with the previous example:

```
MyListBox.DataTextField = "Value";
MyListBox.DataValueField = "Key";
```

The control will appear the same, with a list of all the fruit names in the collection. However, if you look at the rendered HTML that's sent to the client browser, you'll see that value attributes have been set with the corresponding numeric key for each item:

```
<select name="MyListBox" id="MyListBox" >
    <option value="8">Plum</option>
    <option value="7">Peach</option>
    <option value="6">Banana</option>
    <option value="5">Apricot</option>
    <option value="4">Blueberry</option>
    <option value="3">Mango</option>
    <option value="2">Pear</option>
    <option value="1">Kiwi</option>
</select>
```

You can retrieve this value later using the SelectedItem class to get additional information. For example, you could enable AutoPostBack for the list control and add the following code:

```
protected void MyListBox_SelectedIndexChanged(Object sender,
 EventArgs e)
{
    lblMessage.Text = "You picked: " + MyListBox.SelectedItem.Text;
    lblMessage.Text += " which has the key: " + MyListBox.SelectedItem.Value;
}
```

Figure 14-7 demonstrates the result. This technique is particularly useful with a database. You could embed a unique ID into the value property and be able to quickly look up a corresponding record depending on the user's selection by examining the value of the SelectedItem object.

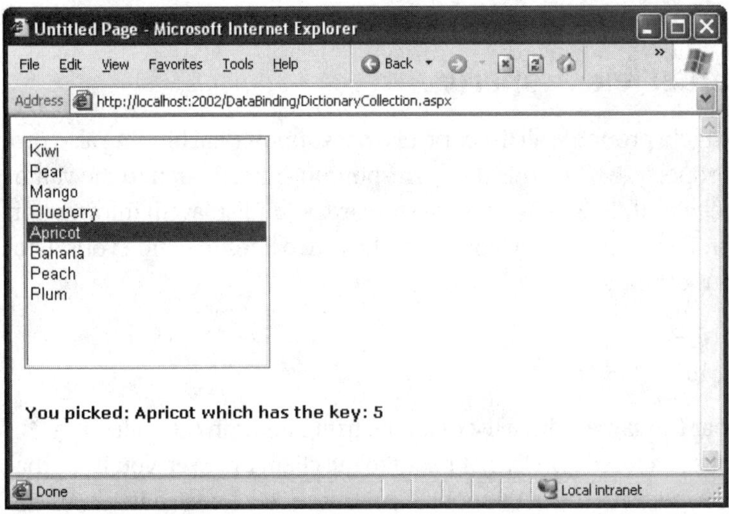

Figure 14-7. *Binding to the key and value properties*

Note that for this to work, you must not be regenerating the list with every postback. If you are, the selected item information will be lost, and an error will occur. The preceding example uses the Page.IsPostBack property to determine whether to build the list.

Data Binding with ADO.NET

So far the examples in this chapter have dealt with data binding that doesn't involve databases or any part of ADO.NET. Although this is an easy way to familiarize yourself with the concepts, and a useful approach in its own right, you get the greatest advantage of data binding when you use it in conjunction with a database.

The data binding process still takes place in the same three steps with a database. First you create your data source, which will be a DataReader or DataSet object. A DataReader generally offers the best performance, but it limits your data binding to a single control, so a DataSet is a more common choice. In the following example, the DataSet is filled by hand, but it could just as easily be filled using a DataAdapter object:

```
// Define a DataSet with a single DataTable.
DataSet dsInternal = new DataSet();
dsInternal.Tables.Add("Users");

// Define two columns for this table.
dsInternal.Tables["Users"].Columns.Add("Name");
dsInternal.Tables["Users"].Columns.Add("Country");

// Add some actual information into the table.
DataRow rowNew = dsInternal.Tables["Users"].NewRow();
rowNew["Name"] = "John";
rowNew["Country"] = "Uganda";
dsInternal.Tables["Users"].Rows.Add(rowNew);

rowNew = dsInternal.Tables["Users"].NewRow();
rowNew["Name"] = "Samantha";
rowNew["Country"] = "Belgium";
dsInternal.Tables["Users"].Rows.Add(rowNew);

rowNew = dsInternal.Tables["Users"].NewRow();
rowNew["Name"] = "Rico";
rowNew["Country"] = "Japan";
dsInternal.Tables["Users"].Rows.Add(rowNew);
```

Next, you bind a table from the DataSet to the appropriate control. In this case, you need to specify the appropriate field using the DataTextField property:

```
// Define the binding.
lstUser.DataSource = dsInternal.Tables["Users"];
lstUser.DataTextField = "Name";
```

Alternatively, you could use the entire DataSet for the data source, instead of just the appropriate table. In that case, you would have to select a table by setting the control's DataMember property. This is an equivalent approach, but the code is slightly different:

```
// Define the binding.
lstUser.DataSource = dsInternal;
lstUser.DataMember = "Users";
lstUser.DataTextField = "Name";
```

As always, the last step is to activate the binding:

```
this.DataBind();
```

The final result is a list with the information from the specified database field, as shown in Figure 14-8. The list box will have an entry for every single record in the table, even if it appears more than once, from the first row to the last.

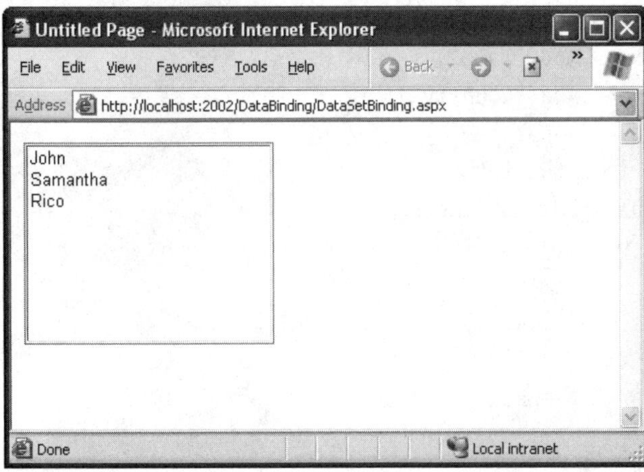

Figure 14-8. *DataSet binding*

■ **Tip** The simple list controls require you to bind their Text or Value property to a single data field in the data source object. However, much more flexibility is provided by the more advanced data binding controls examined in the next chapter. They allow fields to be combined in any way using templates.

Creating a Record Editor

The next example is more practical. It's a good example of how you might use data binding in a full ASP.NET application. This example allows the user to select a record and update one piece of information by using data-bound list controls.

The first step is to add the connection string to your web.config file. This example uses the Products table from the Northwind database included with many versions of SQL Server. Here's how you can define the connection string for SQL Server:

```
<configuration xmlns="http://schemas.microsoft.com/.NetConfiguration/v2.0">
  <connectionStrings>
    <add name="Northwind" connectionString=
"Data Source=localhost;Initial Catalog=Northwind;Integrated Security=SSPI" />
  </connectionStrings>
  ...
</configuration>
```

The next step is to retrieve the connection string and store it in a private variable in the Page class so that every part of your page code can access it easily:

```
private string connectionString =
  WebConfigurationManager.ConnectionStrings["Northwind"].ConnectionString;
```

The next step is to create a drop-down list that allows the user to choose a product for editing. The Page.Load event handler takes care of this task—retrieving the data, binding it to the drop-down list control, and then activating the binding:

```
protected void Page_Load(Object sender, EventArgs e)
{
    if (!this.IsPostBack)
    {
        // Define the ADO.NET objects for selecting Products.
        string selectSQL = "SELECT ProductName, ProductID FROM Products";
        SqlConnection con = new SqlConnection(connectionString);
        SqlCommand cmd = new SqlCommand(selectSQL, con);

        // Open the connection.
        con.Open();

        // Define the binding.
        lstProduct.DataSource = cmd.ExecuteReader();
        lstProduct.DataTextField = "ProductName";
        lstProduct.DataValueField = "ProductID";
```

```
        // Activate the binding.
        lstProduct.DataBind();

        con.Close();

        // Make sure nothing is currently selected.
        lstProduct.SelectedIndex = -1;
    }
}
```

The actual database code is similar to what was used in the previous chapter. The example uses a Select statement but carefully limits the returned information to just the ProductName field, which is the only piece of information it will use. The resulting window lists all the products defined in the database, as shown in Figure 14-9.

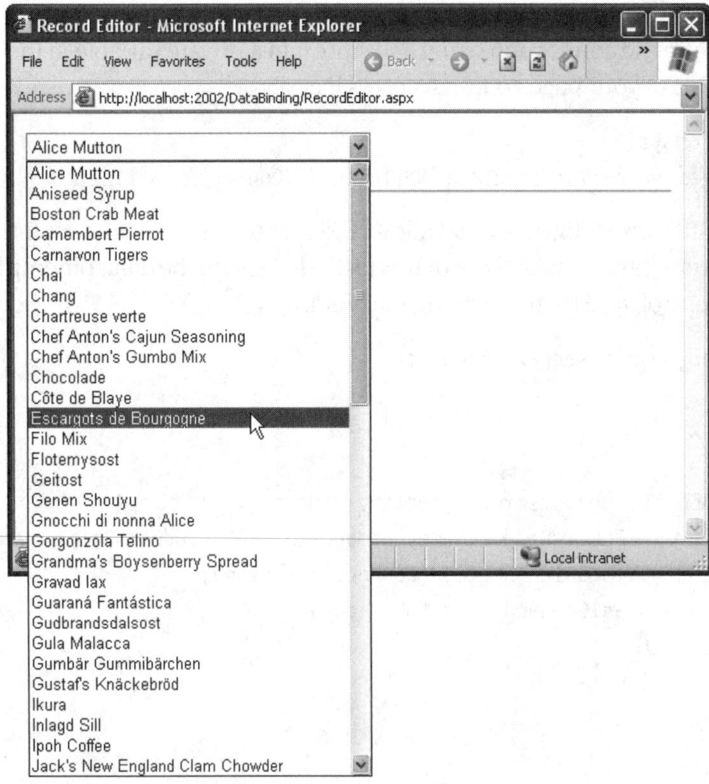

Figure 14-9. *Product choices*

The drop-down list enables AutoPostBack, so as soon as the user makes a selection, a lstProduct.SelectedItemChanged event fires. At this point, your code performs the following tasks:

- It reads the corresponding record from the Products table and displays additional information about it in a label. In this case, a special Join query links information from the Products and Categories tables. The code also determines what the category is for the current product. This is the piece of information it will allow the user to change.
- It reads the full list of CategoryNames from the Categories table and binds this information to a different list control.
- It highlights the row in the category list that corresponds to the current product. For example, if the current product is a Seafood category, the Seafood entry in the list box will be selected.

This logic appears fairly involved, but it's really just an application of what you've learned over the past two chapters. The full listing is as follows:

```
protected void lstProduct_SelectedIndexChanged(object sender, EventArgs e)
{
    // Create a command for selecting the matching product record.
    string selectProduct = "SELECT ProductName, QuantityPerUnit, " +
     "CategoryName FROM Products INNER JOIN Categories ON " +
     "Categories.CategoryID=Products.CategoryID " +
     "WHERE ProductID=@ProductID";

    // Create the Connection and Command objects.
    SqlConnection con = new SqlConnection(connectionString);
    SqlCommand cmdProducts = new SqlCommand(selectProduct, con);
cmdProducts.Parameters.AddWithValue("@ProductID", lstProduct.SelectedItem.Value);
    // Retrieve the information for the selected product.
    using (con)
    {
        con.Open()
        SqlDataReader reader = cmdProducts.ExecuteReader();
        reader.Read();
```

```
            // Update the display.
            lblRecordInfo.Text = "<b>Product:</b> " +
              reader["ProductName"] + "<br />";
            lblRecordInfo.Text += "<b>Quantity:</b> " +
              reader["QuantityPerUnit"] + "<br />";
            lblRecordInfo.Text += "<b>Category:</b> " + reader["CategoryName"];

            // Store the corresponding CategoryName for future reference.
            string matchCategory = reader["CategoryName"].ToString();

            // Close the reader.
            reader.Close();

            // Create a new Command for selecting categories.
            string selectCategory = "SELECT CategoryName, " +
              "CategoryID FROM Categories";
            SqlCommand cmdCategories = new SqlCommand(selectCategory, con);
            cmdProducts.Parameters.AddWithValue("@ProductID",
              lstProduct.SelectedItem.Value);

            // Retrieve the category information, and bind it.
            lstCategory.DataSource = cmdCategories.ExecuteReader();
            lstCategory.DataTextField = "CategoryName";
            lstCategory.DataValueField = "CategoryID";
            lstCategory.DataBind();

            // Highlight the matching category in the list.
            lstCategory.Items.FindByText(matchCategory).Selected = true;
        }

        lstCategory.Visible = true;
        cmdUpdate.Visible = true;
    }
```

You could improve this code in several ways. It probably makes the most sense to remove these data access routines from this event handler and put them into more generic functions. For example, you could use a function that accepts a ProductName and returns a single DataRow with the associated product information. Another improvement would be to use a stored procedure to retrieve this information, rather than a full-fledged DataReader.

The end result is a window that updates itself dynamically whenever a new product is selected, as shown in Figure 14-10.

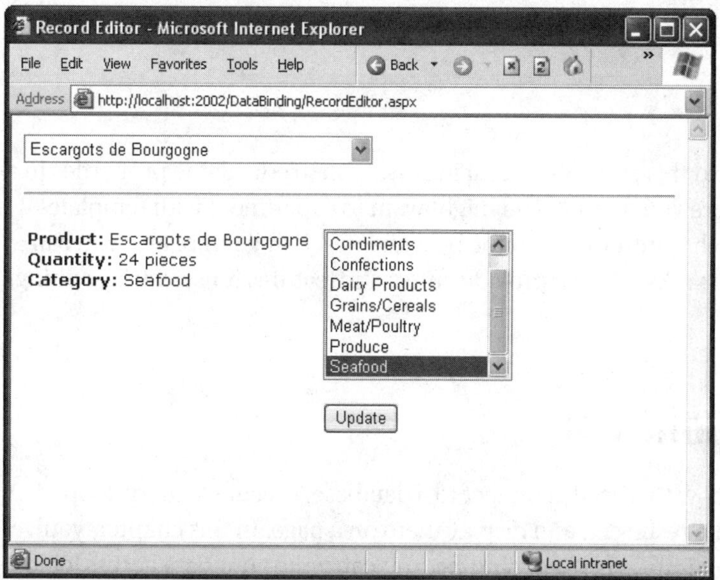

Figure 14-10. *Product information*

This example still has one more trick in store. If the user selects a different category and clicks Update, the change is made in the database. Of course, this means creating new Connection and Command objects, as follows:

```
protected void cmdUpdate_Click(object sender, EventArgs e)
{
    // Define the Command.
    string updateCommand = "UPDATE Products " +
     "SET CategoryID=@CategoryID WHERE ProductID=@ProductID";

    SqlConnection con = new SqlConnection(connectionString);
    SqlCommand cmd = new SqlCommand(updateCommand, con);

    cmd.Parameters.AddWithValue("@CategoryID", lstCategory.SelectedItem.Value);
    cmd.Parameters.AddWithValue("@ProductID", lstProduct.SelectedItem.Value);
```

```
        // Perform the update.
        using (con)
        {
            con.Open();
            cmd.ExecuteNonQuery();
        }
    }
```

You could easily extend this example so that it allows you to edit all the properties in a product record. But before you try that, you might want to experiment with template-based data binding, which is introduced in the next chapter. Using templates, you can create sophisticated lists and grids that provide automatic features for selecting, editing, and deleting records.

Data Source Controls

In Chapter 13, you saw how to directly connect to a database, execute a query, loop through the records in the result set, and display them on a page. In this chapter, you've already seen a simpler option—with data binding, you can write your data access logic and then show the results in the page with no looping or control manipulation required. Now, it's time to introduce *another* convenience—data source controls. Amazingly enough, data source controls allow you to create data-bound pages without writing any data access code.

■ **Note** As you'll soon see, often a gap exists between what you *can* do and what you *should* do. In most professional applications, you'll need to write and fine-tune your data access code for optimum performance or access to specific features. That's why you've spent so much time learning how ADO.NET works, rather than jumping straight to the data source controls.

The data source controls include any control that implements the IDataSource interface. The .NET Framework includes the following data source controls:

SqlDataSource: This data source allows you to connect to any data source that has an ADO.NET data provider. This includes SQL Server, Oracle, and OLE DB or ODBC data sources. When using this data source, you don't need to write the data access code.

ObjectDataSource: This data source allows you to connect to a custom data access class. This is the preferred approach for large-scale professional web applications, but it forces you to write much more code. You'll tackle the ObjectDataSource in Chapter 24.

XmlDataSource: This data source allows you to connect to an XML file. You'll learn more in Chapter 17.

SiteMapDataSource: This data source allows you to connect to a .sitemap file that describes the navigational structure of your website. You saw this data source in Chapter 11.

You can find all the data source controls in the Data tab of the Toolbox in Visual Studio. Data source controls are new in ASP.NET 2.0, and it's expected that more will become available, both from Microsoft and from third-party vendors.

When you drop a data source control onto your web page, it shows up as a gray box in Visual Studio. However, this box won't appear when you run your web application and request the page (see Figure 14-11).

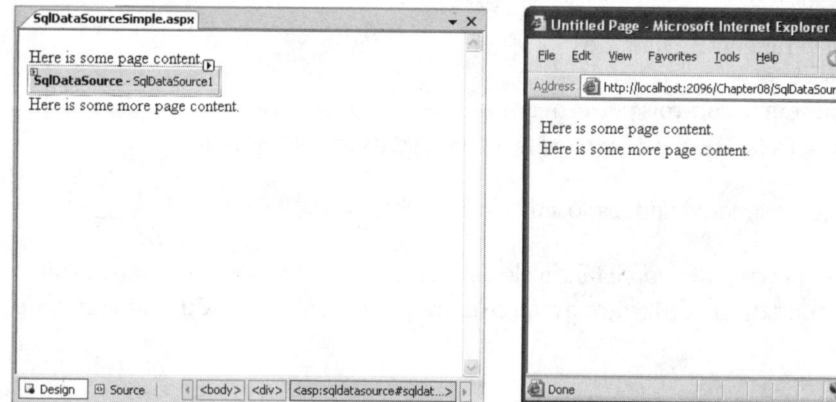

Figure 14-11. *A data source control at design time and runtime*

If you perform more than one data access task in the same page (for example, you need to be able to query two different tables), you'll need more than one data access control. If you find that the clutter of data source controls is disturbing your page layout at design time, just select View ➤ Non Visual Controls from the menu to hide them. You can still select each data source control from the Properties window when you want to configure it.

The Page Life Cycle with Data Binding

Data source controls can perform two key tasks:

- They can retrieve data from a data source and supply it to linked controls.
- They can update the data source when edits take place in linked controls.

To use the data source controls, you need to understand the page life cycle. The following steps explain the sequence of stages your page goes through in its lifetime. The two steps in bold (4 and 6) are the steps where the data source controls will spring into action.

1. The page object is created (based on the .aspx file).
2. The page life cycle begins, and the Page.Init and Page.Load events fire.
3. All other control events fire.
4. The data source controls perform any updates. If a row is being updated, the Updating and Updated events fire. If a row is being inserted, the Inserting and Inserted events fire. If a row is being deleted, the Deleting and Deleted events fire.
5. The Page.PreRender event fires.
6. The data source controls perform any queries and insert the retrieved data in the linked controls. The Selecting and Selected events fire at this point.
7. The page is rendered and disposed.

In the rest of this chapter, you'll take a closer look at the SqlDataSource control, and you'll use it to build the record editor example demonstrated earlier—with a lot less code.

The SqlDataSource

Data source controls turn up in the .aspx markup portion of your web page like ordinary controls. Here's an example:

```
<asp:SqlDataSource ID="SqlDataSource1" runat="server" ... />
```

The SqlDataSource represents a database connection that uses an ADO.NET provider. However, this has a catch. The SqlDataSource needs a generic way to create the Connection, Command, and DataReader objects it requires. The only way this is possible is if your data provider includes something called a *data provider factory*. The factory has the responsibility of creating the provider-specific objects that the SqlDataSource needs to access the data source. Fortunately, .NET includes a data provider factory for each of its four data providers:

- System.Data.SqlClient
- System.Data.OracleClient

- System.Data.OleDb
- System.Data.Odbc

These are registered in the machine.config file, and as a result you can use any of them with the SqlDataSource. You choose a data source by setting the provider name. Here's a SqlDataSource that connects to a SQL Server database using the SQL Server provider:

```
<asp:SqlDataSource ProviderName="System.Data.SqlClient" ... />
```

■ **Tip** Technically, you can omit this piece of information, because the System.Data.SqlClient provider factory is the default.

The next step is to supply the required connection string—without it, you cannot make any connections. Although you can hard-code the connection string directly in the SqlDataSource tag, it's always better to keep it in the <connectionStrings> section of the web.config file to guarantee greater flexibility and ensure you won't inadvertently change the connection string.

To refer to a connection string in your .aspx markup, you use a special syntax in this format:

```
<%$ ConnectionStrings:[NameOfConnectionString] %>
```

This looks like a data binding expression, but it's slightly different. (For one thing, it begins with the character sequence <%$ instead of <%#.)

For example, if you have a connection string named Northwind in your web.config file that looks like this:

```
<configuration>
  <connectionStrings>
    <add name="Northwind" connectionString=
"Data Source=localhost;Initial Catalog=Northwind;Integrated Security=SSPI" />
  </connectionStrings>
  ...
</configuration>
```

you would specify it in the SqlDataSource using this syntax:

```
<asp:SqlDataSource ConnectionString="<%$ ConnectionStrings:Northwind %>" ... />
```

Once you've specified the provider name and connection string, the next step is to add the query logic that the SqlDataSource will use when it connects to the database.

Selecting Records

You can use each SqlDataSource control you create to retrieve a single query. Optionally, you can also add corresponding commands for deleting, inserting, and updating rows. For example, one SqlDataSource is enough to query and update the Customers table in the Northwind database. However, if you need to independently retrieve or update Customers and Orders information, you'll need two SqlDataSource controls.

The SqlDataSource command logic is supplied through four properties—SelectCommand, InsertCommand, UpdateCommand, and DeleteCommand—each of which takes a string. The string you supply can be inline SQL (in which case the corresponding SelectCommandType, InsertCommandType, UpdateCommandType, or DeleteCommandType property should be Text, the default) or the name of a stored procedure (in which case the command type is StoredProcedure). You need to define commands only for the types of actions you want to perform. In other words, if you're using a data source for read-only access to a set of records, you need to define only the SelectCommand property.

■ **Note** If you configure a command in the Properties window, you'll see a property named SelectQuery instead of SelectCommand. The SelectQuery is actually a virtual property that's displayed as a design-time convenience. When you edit the SelectQuery (by clicking the ellipsis next to the property name), you can use a special designer to write the command text (the SelectCommand) and add command parameters (the SelectParameters) at the same time.

Here's a complete SqlDataSource that defines a Select command for retrieving product information from the Products table:

```
<asp:SqlDataSource ID="sourceProducts" runat="server"
  ProviderName="System.Data.SqlClient"
  ConnectionString="<%$ ConnectionStrings:Northwind %>"
  SelectCommand="SELECT ProductName, ProductID FROM Products"
/>
```

■ **Tip** You can write the data source logic by hand or by using a design-time wizard that lets you create a connection and create the command logic in a graphical query builder. To launch this tool, select the data source control, and choose Configure Data Source from the smart tag.

This is enough to build the first stage of the record editor example shown earlier—namely, the drop-down list box that shows all the products. All you need to do is set the ListBox.DataSourceID property to point to the SqlDataSource you've created. The easiest way to do this is using the Properties window, which provides a drop-down list of all the data sources on your current web page. At the same time, make sure you set the DataTextField and DataValueField properties. Once you make these changes, you'll wind up with a control tag like this:

```
<asp:DropDownList ID="lstProduct" runat="server" AutoPostBack="true"
  DataSourceID="sourceProducts" DataTextField="ProductName"
  DataValueField="ProductID" />
```

The best part about this example is that you don't need to write any code. When you run the page, the ListBox asks the SqlDataSource for the data it needs. At this point, the SqlDataSource executes the query you defined, fetches the information, and binds it to the ListBox. The whole process unfolds automatically.

How the Data Source Controls Work

As you learned earlier in this chapter, you can bind to a DataReader or a DataSet. So it's worth asking—which approach does the SqlDataSource control use? It's actually in your control, based on whether you set the DataSourceMode to SqlDataSourceMode.DataSet (the default) or to SqlDataSourceMode.DataReader. The DataSet mode is almost always better, because it supports advanced sorting, filtering, and caching settings that depend on the DataSet. All these features are disabled in DataReader mode. However, you can use the DataReader mode with extremely large grids, because it's more memory-efficient. That's because the DataReader holds only one record in memory at a time—just long enough to copy the record's information to the linked control.

Another important fact to understand about the data source controls is that when you bind more than one control to the same data source, you cause the query to be executed multiple times. For example, if two controls are bound to the same data source, the data source control performs its query twice—once for each control. This is somewhat inefficient—after all, if you wrote the data binding code yourself by hand, you'd probably choose to perform the query once and then bind the returned DataSet twice. Fortunately, this design isn't quite as bad as it seems at first.

First, you can avoid this multiple-query overhead using caching, which allows you to store the retrieved data in a temporary memory location where it will be reused automatically. The SqlDataSource supports automatic caching if you set EnableCaching to true. Chapter 26 provides a full discussion of how caching works and how you can use it with the SqlDataSource.

Second, contrary to what you might expect, most of the time you *won't* be binding more than one control to a data source. That's because the rich data controls you'll learn about in Chapter 15—the GridVew, DetailsView, and FormsView—have the ability to present multiple pieces of data in a flexible layout. If you use these controls, you'll need to bind only one control, which allows you to steer clear of this limitation.

It's also important to note that data binding is performed at the end of your web page processing, just before the page is rendered. This means the Page.Load event will fire, followed by any control events, followed by the Page.PreRender event, and only then will the data binding take place. The data binding is performed on every postback (unless you redirect to another page). If you need to write code that springs into action *after* the data binding is complete, you need to override the Page.OnPreRenderComplete() method. This method is called immediately after the PreRender stage but just before the view state is serialized and the final HTML is rendered.

Parameterized Commands

In the previous example, the complete query was hard-coded. Often, you won't have this flexibility. Instead, you'll want to retrieve a subset of data, such as all the products in a given category or all the employees in a specific city.

The record editor offers an ideal example. Once you select a product, you want to execute another command to get the full details for that product. (You might just as easily execute another command to get records that are related to this product.) To make this work, you need two data sources. You've already created the first SqlDataSource, which fetches limited information about every product. Here's the second SqlDataSource, which gets more extensive information about a single product (the query is split over several lines to fit the printed page):

```
<asp:SqlDataSource ID="sourceEmployees" runat="server"
  ProviderName="System.Data.SqlClient"
  ConnectionString="<%$ ConnectionStrings:Northwind %>"
  SelectCommand="SELECT * FROM Products WHERE ProductID=@ProductID"
/>
```

But this example has a problem. It defines a parameter (@ProductID) that identifies the ID of the product you want to retrieve. How do you fill in this piece of information? It turns out you need to add a <SelectParameters> section to the SqlDataSource tag. Inside this section, you must define each parameter that's referenced by your SelectCommand and tell the SqlDataSource where to find the value it should use. You do that by *mapping* the parameter to a value in a control.

Here's the corrected command:

```
<asp:SqlDataSource ID="sourceProductDetails" runat="server"
  ProviderName="System.Data.SqlClient"
  ConnectionString="<%$ ConnectionStrings:Northwind %>"
  SelectCommand="SELECT * FROM Products WHERE ProductID=@ProductID">
  <SelectParameters>
    <asp:ControlParameter ControlID="lstProduct" Name="ProductID"
     PropertyName="SelectedValue" />
  </SelectParameters>
</asp:SqlDataSource>
```

You always indicate parameters with an @ symbol, as in @City. You can define as many symbols as you want, but you must map each provider to another value. In this example, the value for the @ProductID parameter comes from the lstProduct.SelectedValue property. In other words, you are binding a value that's currently in a control to place it into a database command. (You could also use the SelectedText property to get the currently displayed text.)

Now all you need to do is bind this to the remaining controls where you want to display information. This is where the example takes a slightly different turn. In the previous version of the record editor, you took the information and used a combination of values to fill in details in a label and a list control. This type of approach doesn't work well with data source controls. First, you can bind only a single data field to most simple controls such as lists. Second, each bound control makes a separate request to the SqlDataSource, triggering a separate database query. This means if you bind a dozen controls, you'll perform the same query a dozen times, with terrible performance. You can alleviate this problem with data source caching (see Chapter 26), but it indicates you aren't designing your application in a way that lends itself well to the data source control model.

The solution is to use one of the rich data controls, such as the GridView, DetailsView, or FormView. These controls have the smarts to show multiple fields at once, in a highly flexible layout. You'll learn about these three controls in detail in the next chapter, but the following example shows a simple demonstration of how to use the DetailsView.

The DetailsView is a rich data control that's designed to show multiple fields in a data source. As long as AutoGenerateRows is true (the default), it creates a separate row for each field, with the field caption and value. Figure 14-12 shows the result.

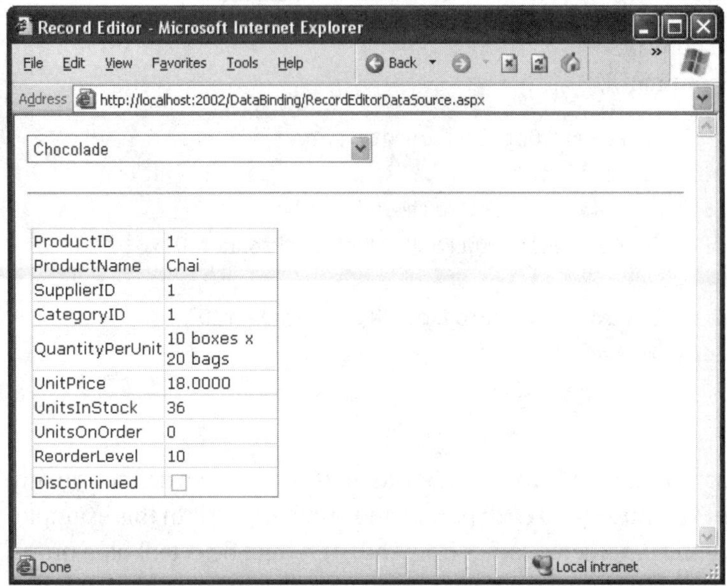

Figure 14-12. *Displaying full product information in a DetailsView*

Here's the basic DetailsView tag that makes this possible:

```
<asp:DetailsView ID="DetailsView1" runat="server"
  DataSourceID="sourceProductDetails" />
```

As you can see, the only property you need to set is DataSourceID. That binds the DetailsView to the SqlDataSource you created earlier. This SqlDataSource gets the full product information for a single row, based on the selection in the list control. Best of all, this whole example still hasn't required a line of code.

Other Types of Parameters

In the previous example, the @ProductID parameter in the second SqlDataSource is configured based on the selection in a drop-down list. This type of parameter, which links to a property in another control, is called a *control parameter*. But parameter values aren't necessarily drawn from other controls. You can map a parameter to any of the parameter types defined in Table 14-1.

Table 14-1. *Parameter Types*

Source	Control Tag	Description
Control property	<asp:ControlParameter>	A property from another control on the page.
Query string value	<asp:QueryStringParameter>	A value from the current query string.

Source	Control Tag	Description
Session state value	<asp:SessionParameter>	A value stored in the current user's session.
Cookie value	<asp:CookieParameter>	A value from any cookie attachedt to the current request.
Profile value	<asp:ProfileParameter>	A value from the current user's profile (see Chapter 20 for more about profiles).
A form variable	<asp:FormParameter>	A value posted to the page from an input control. Usually, you'll use a control property instead, but you might need to grab a value straight from the Forms collection if you've disabled view state for the corresponding control.

For example, you could split the earlier example into two pages. In the first page, define a list control that shows all the available products:

```
<asp:SqlDataSource ID="sourceProducts" runat="server"
  ProviderName="System.Data.SqlClient"
  ConnectionString="<%$ ConnectionStrings:Northwind %>"
  SelectCommand="SELECT ProductName, ProductID FROM Products"
/>
<asp:DropDownList ID="lstProduct" runat="server" AutoPostBack="true"
  DataSourceID="sourceProducts" DataTextField="ProductName"
  DataValueField="ProductID" />
```

Now, you'll need a little extra code to copy the selected city to the query string and redirect the page. Here's a button that does just that:

```
protected void cmdGo_Click(object sender, EventArgs e)
{
    Response.Redirect("QueryParameter2.aspx?prodID=" + lstCities.SelectedValue);
}
```

Finally, the second page can bind the DetailsView according to the ProductID value that's supplied in the query string:

```
<asp:SqlDataSource ID="sourceProductDetails" runat="server"
  ProviderName="System.Data.SqlClient"
  ConnectionString="<%$ ConnectionStrings:Northwind %>"
  SelectCommand="SELECT * FROM Products WHERE ProductID=@ProductID">
  <SelectParameters>
    <asp:QueryStringParameter Name="Product" QueryStringField="prodID" />
  </SelectParameters>
</asp:SqlDataSource>
```

Handling Errors

When you deal with an outside resource such as a database, you need to protect your code with a basic amount of error-handling logic. Even if you've avoided every possible coding mistake, you still need to defend against factors outside your control—for example, if the database server isn't running or the network connection is broken.

You can count on the SqlDataSource to properly release any resources (such as connections) if an error occurs. However, the underlying exception won't be handled. Instead, it will bubble up to the page and derail your processing. As with any other unhandled exception, the user will receive a cryptic error message or an error page. This design is unavoidable—if the SqlDataSource suppressed exceptions, it could hide potential problems and make debugging extremely difficult. However, it's a good idea to handle the problem in your web page and show a more suitable error message.

To do this, you need to handle the data source event that occurs immediately *after* the error. If you're performing a query, that's the Selected event. If you're performing an update, delete, or insert operation, you would handle the Updated, Deleted, or Inserted event instead. (If you don't want to offer customize error messages, you could handle all these events with the same event handler.)

In the event handler, you can access the exception object through the SqlDataSourceStatusEventArgs.Exception property. If you want to prevent the error from spreading any further, simply set the SqlDataSourceStatusEventArgs.ExceptionHandled property to true. Then, make sure you show an appropriate error message on your web page to inform the user that the command was not completed.

Here's an example:

```
protected void sourceEmployees_Selected(object sender,
 SqlDataSourceStatusEventArgs e)
{
    if (e.Exception != null)
    {
        lblError.Text = "An exception occurred performing the query.";

        // Consider the error handled.
        e.ExceptionHandled = true;
    }
}
```

Updating Records

Selecting data is only half the equation. The SqlDataSource can also apply changes. The only catch is that not all controls support updating. For example, the humble ListBox doesn't provide any way for the user to edit values, delete existing items, or insert new ones. Fortunately, ASP.NET's rich data controls—including the GridView, DetailsView, and FormView—all have editing features you can switch on.

Before you can switch on the editing features in a given control, you need to define suitable commands for the operations you want to perform in your data source. That means supplying commands for inserting (InsertQuery), deleting (DeleteQuery), and updating (UpdateQuery). If you know you will allow the user to perform only certain operations (such as updates) but not others (such as insertions and deletions), you can safely omit the commands you don't need.

You define the InsertCommand, DeleteCommand, and UpdateCommand in the same way you define the command for the SelectCommand property—by using a parameterized query. For example, here's a revised version of the SqlDataSource for product information that defines a basic update command to update every field:

```
<asp:SqlDataSource ID="sourceProductDetails" runat="server"
  ProviderName="System.Data.SqlClient"
  ConnectionString="<%$ ConnectionStrings:Northwind %>"
  SelectCommand="SELECT ProductID, ProductName, UnitPrice, UnitsInStock,
UnitsOnOrder, ReorderLevel, Discontinued FROM Products WHERE
ProductID=@ProductID"
  UpdateCommand="UPDATE Products SET ProductName=@ProductName,
UnitPrice=@UnitPrice,
UnitsInStock=@UnitsInStock, UnitsOnOrder=@UnitsOnOrder,
ReorderLevel=@ReorderLevel,
Discontinued=@Discontinued WHERE ProductID=@ProductID">
  <SelectParameters>
    <asp:ControlParameter ControlID="lstProduct" Name="ProductID"
     PropertyName="SelectedValue" />
  </SelectParameters>
</asp:SqlDataSource>
```

■ Note In this chapter, the text for some of the commands is too long to a fit on a single line. In this case, it appears on several lines to fit the dimensions of the page. However, in your .aspx page, you need to place the entire text of an individual command on one line.

In this example, the parameter names aren't chosen arbitrarily. As long as you give each parameter the same name as the field it affects and preface it with the @ symbol (so ProductName becomes @ProductName), you don't need to define the parameter. That's because the ASP.NET data controls automatically submit a collection of parameters with the new values before triggering the update. Each parameter in the collection uses this naming convention, which is a major timesaver.

You also need to give the user a way to enter the new values. Most rich data controls make this fairly easy—with the DetailsView, it's simply a matter of setting the AutoGenerateEditButton property to true, as shown here:

```
<asp:DetailsView ID="DetailsView1" runat="server"
  DataSourceID="sourceProductDetails" AutoGenerateEditButton="true" />
```

Now when you run the page, you'll see an edit link. When clicked, this link switches the DetailsView into edit mode. All fields are changed to edit controls (typically text boxes), and the Edit link is replaced with an Update link and a Cancel link (see Figure 14-13).

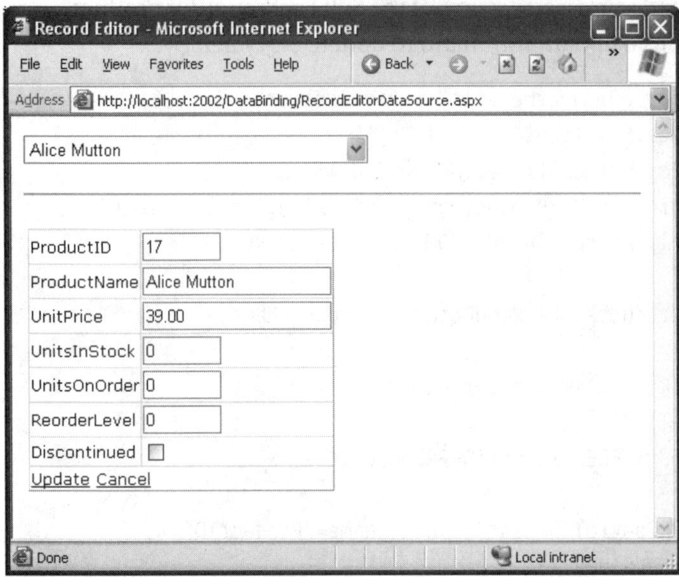

Figure 14-13. *Editing with the DetailsView*

The Cancel link returns the row to its initial state. The Update link passes the values to the SqlDataSource.UpdateParameters collection (using the field names) and then triggers the SqlDataSource.Update() method to apply the change to the database. Once again, you don't have to write any code.

You can create similar parameterized commands for the DeleteCommand and InsertCommand. To enable deleting and inserting, you need to set the AutoGenerateDeleteButton and AutoGenerateInsertButton properties of the DetailsView to true.

Strict Concurrency Checking

The update command in the previous example matches the record based on its ID. You can tell this by examining the Where clause:

```
UpdateCommand="UPDATE Products SET ProductName=@ProductName,
UnitPrice=@UnitPrice,
 UnitsInStock=@UnitsInStock, UnitsOnOrder=@UnitsOnOrder,
ReorderLevel=@ReorderLevel,
 Discontinued=@Discontinued WHERE ProductID=@ProductID"
```

The problem with this approach is that it opens the door to an update that overwrites the changes of another user, if these changes are made between the time your page is requested and the time your page commits its updated.

For example, imagine Chen and Lucy are viewing the same table of product records. Lucy commits a change to the price of a product. A few seconds later, Chen commits a name change to the same product record. However, that update command not only applies the new name but it also overwrites every field with the values in Chen's page—effectively replacing the price Lucy entered with the old price.

This is the same sort of concurrency problem you considered in Chapter 13 with the DataSet. The difference is that the DataSet used automatically generated updating commands that were created with the CommandBuilder. The CommandBuilder uses a different approach. It always attempts to match every field. As a result, if the original has been changed, the update command won't find it, and the update won't be performed at all. So in the scenario described previously, Chen will receive an error when he attempts to apply the new product name, and he'll need to edit the record and apply the change again.

You can use the same approach that the CommandBuilder uses with the SqlDataSource. All you need to do is write your commands a little differently so that the Where clause tries to match every field. Here's what the modified command would look like:

```
UpdateCommand="UPDATE Products SET ProductName=@ProductName,
UnitPrice=@UnitPrice,
 UnitsInStock=@UnitsInStock, UnitsOnOrder=@UnitsOnOrder,
ReorderLevel=@ReorderLevel,
 Discontinued=@Discontinued WHERE ProductID=@ProductID AND
 ProductName=@original_ProductName AND UnitPrice=@original_UnitPrice AND
 UnitsInStock=@original_UnitsInStock AND UnitsOnOrder=@original_UnitsOnOrder AND
 ReorderLevel=@original_ReorderLevel AND Discontinued=@original_Discontinued"
```

Although this makes sense conceptually, you're not finished yet. Before this command can work, you need to tell the SqlDataSource to maintain the old values from the data source and to give them parameter names that start with original_. You do this by setting to properties. First, set the SqlDataSource.ConflictDetection property to ConflictOptions.CompareAllValues instead of ConflictOptions.OverwriteChanges (the default). Next, set the long-winded OldValuesParameterFormatString property to the text "original_{0}". This tells the SqlDataSource to insert the text original_ before the field name to create the parameter that stores the old value. Now your command will work as written.

The SqlDataSource doesn't raise exception to notify you if no update is performed. So, if you use the command shown in this example, you need to handle the SqlDataSource.Updated event and check the SqlDataSourceStatusEventArgs.AffectedRows property. If it's 0, no records have been updated, and you should notify the user about the concurrency problem so the update can be attempted again, as shown here:

```
protected void sourceProductDetails_Updated(object sender,
  SqlDataSourceStatusEventArgs e)
{
    if (e.AffectedRows == 0)
    {
        lblInfo.Text = "No update was performed. " +
"A concurrency error is likely, or the command is incorrectly written.";
    }
    else
    {
        lblInfo.Text = "Record successfully updated.";
    }
}
```

The Last Word

This chapter presented a thorough overview of data binding in ASP.NET. First, you learned an interesting way to create dynamic text with simple data binding. Although this is a reasonable approach to get information into your page, it doesn't surpass what you can already do with pure code. However, you also learned how ASP.NET builds on this infrastructure with much more useful features, including repeated-value binding for quick-and-easy data display in a list control and the data source controls, which let you create code-free bound pages.

Using the techniques in this chapter, you can create a wide range of data-bound pages. However, if you want to create a page that incorporates record editing, sorting, and other more advanced tricks, the data binding features you've learned about so far are just the first step. You'll also need to turn to specialized controls, such as the DetailsView and GridView, which build upon these data binding features. You'll learn how to master these controls in the next chapter. You'll also learn how to extend your data binding skills to work with data access components in Chapter 24.

CHAPTER 15

■ ■ ■

The Data Controls

When it comes to data binding, not all ASP.NET controls are created equal. In the previous chapter, you saw how data binding could help you automatically insert single values and lists into all kinds of common controls. In this chapter, you'll concentrate on three more advanced controls—the GridView, DetailsView, and FormView—that allow you to bind entire tables of data.

The rich data controls are quite a bit different from the simple list controls—for one thing, they are designed exclusively for data binding. They also have the ability to display more than one field at a time, often in a table-based layout or according to what you've defined. They also support higher-level features such as selecting, editing, and sorting.

The rich data controls include the following:

GridView: The GridView is an all-purpose grid control for showing large tables of information. The GridView is the heavyweight of ASP.NET data controls—it's also the successor to the ASP.NET 1.*x* DataGrid.

DetailsView: The DetailsView is ideal for showing a single record at a time, in a table that has one row per field. The DetailsView also supports editing.

FormView: Like the DetailsView, the FormView shows a single record at a time and supports editing. The difference is that the FormView is based on templates, which allow you to combine fields in a much more flexible layout that doesn't need to be table-based.

In this chapter, you'll explore the rich data controls in detail.

The GridView

The GridView is an extremely flexible grid control that displays a multicolumn table. Each record in your data source becomes a separate row. Each field in the record becomes a separate column.

The GridView is the most powerful of the three rich data controls you'll learn about in this chapter, because it comes equipped with the most ready-made functionality. This functionality includes features for automatic paging, sorting, selecting, and editing. The GridView is also the only data control that you'll consider in this chapter that can show more than one record at a time.

Automatically Generating Columns

The GridView provides a DataSource property for the data object you want to display, much like the list controls you saw in Chapter 14. Once you've set the DataSource property, you call the DataBind() method to perform the data binding and display each record in the GridView. However, the GridView doesn't provide properties, such as DataTextField and DataValueField, that allow you to choose what column you want to display. That's because the GridView automatically generates a column for *every* field, as long as the AutoGenerateColumns property is true (which is the default).

Here's all you need to create a basic grid with one column for each field:

```
<asp:GridView ID="GridView1" runat="server" />
```

Once you've added this GridView tag to your page, you can fill it with data. Here's an example that performs a query using the ADO.NET objects and binds the retrieved DataSet:

```
protected void Page_Load(object sender, EventArgs e)
{
    // Define the ADO.NET objects.
    string connectionString =
      WebConfigurationManager.ConnectionStrings["Northwind"].ConnectionString;
    string selectSQL = "SELECT ProductID, ProductName, UnitPrice FROM Products";
    SqlConnection con = new SqlConnection(connectionString);
    SqlCommand cmd = new SqlCommand(selectSQL, con);
    SqlDataAdapter adapter = new SqlDataAdapter(cmd);

    // Fill the DataSet
    DataSet ds = new DataSet();
    adapter.Fill(ds, "Products");

    // Perform the binding.
    GridView1.DataSource = ds;
    GridView1.DataBind();
}
```

Figure 15-1 shows the GridView this code creates.

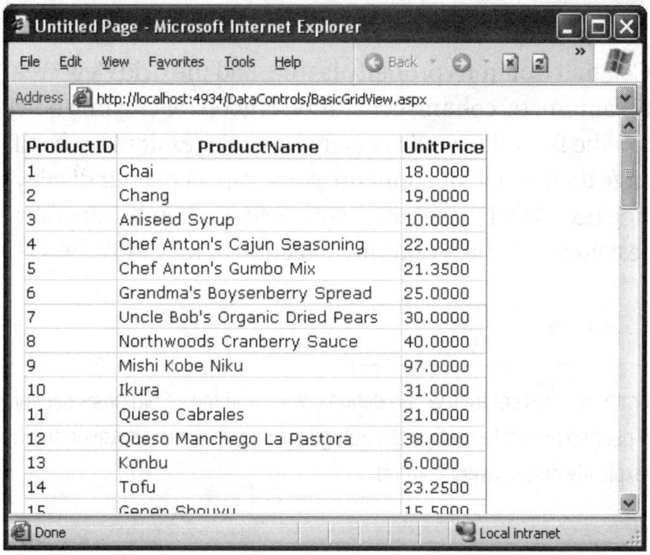
Untitled Page - Microsoft Internet Explorer
File Edit View Favorites Tools Help
Back
Address http://localhost:4934/DataControls/BasicGridView.aspx
ProductID ProductName UnitPrice
1 Chai 18.0000
2 Chang 19.0000
3 Aniseed Syrup 10.0000
4 Chef Anton's Cajun Seasoning 22.0000
5 Chef Anton's Gumbo Mix 21.3500
6 Grandma's Boysenberry Spread 25.0000
7 Uncle Bob's Organic Dried Pears 30.0000
8 Northwoods Cranberry Sauce 40.0000
9 Mishi Kobe Niku 97.0000
10 Ikura 31.0000
11 Queso Cabrales 21.0000
12 Queso Manchego La Pastora 38.0000
13 Konbu 6.0000
14 Tofu 23.2500
Done
Local intranet

Figure 15-1. *The bare-bones GridView*

Of course, you don't need to write this data access code by hand. As you learned in the previous chapter, you can use the SqlDataSource control to define your query. You can then link that query directly to your data control, and ASP.NET will take care of the entire data binding process.

Here's how you would define a SqlDataSource to perform the query shown in the previous example:

```
<asp:SqlDataSource ID="sourceProducts" runat="server"
  ConnectionString="<%$ ConnectionStrings:Northwind %>"
  SelectCommand="SELECT ProductID, ProductName, UnitPrice FROM Products" />
```

Next, set the GridView.DataSourceID property to link the data source to your grid:

```
<asp:GridView ID="GridView1" runat="server" DataSourceID="sourceProducts" />
```

These two tags duplicate the example in Figure 15-1 but with significantly less effort. Now you don't have to write any code to execute the query and bind the DataSet.

Using the SqlDataSource has positive and negative sides. Although it gives you less control, it streamlines your code quite a bit, and it allows you to remove all the database details from your code-behind class. In this chapter, we'll focus on the data source approach, because it's much simpler when creating complex data-bound pages that support features such as editing. In Chapter 24, you'll learn how to adapt these examples to use the ObjectDataSource instead of the SqlDataSource. The ObjectDataSource is a great compromise—it allows you to write customized data access code in a database component without giving up the convenient design-time features of the data source controls.

Defining Columns

By default, the GridView.AutoGenerateColumns property is true, and the GridView creates a column for each field. This automatic column generation is good for creating quick test pages, but it doesn't give you the flexibility you'll usually want. For example, what if you want to hide columns, change their order, or configure some aspect of their display, such as the formatting or heading text? In all these cases, you need to set AutoGenerateColumns to false and define the columns in the <Columns> section of the GridView control tag.

■ **Tip** It's possible to have AutoGenerateColumns set to true and define columns in the <Columns> section. In this case, the columns you explicitly defined are added before the autogenerated columns. However, for the most flexibility you'll usually want to explicitly define every column.

Each column can be any of several types, as described in Table 15-1. The order of your column tags determines the left-to-right order of columns in the GridView.

Table 15-1. *Column Types*

Column	Description
BoundField	This column displays text from a field in the data source.
ButtonField	This column displays a button for each item in the list.
CheckBoxField	This column displays a check box for each item in the list. It's used automatically for true/false fields (in SQL Server, these are fields that use the bit data type).
CommandField	This column provides selection or editing buttons.
HyperlinkField	This column displays its contents (a field from the data source or static text) as a hyperlink.
ImageField	This column displays image data from a binary field (providing it can be successfully interpreted as a supported image format).
TemplateField	This column allows you to specify multiple fields, custom controls, and arbitrary HTML using a custom template. It gives you the highest degree of control but requires the most work.

The most basic column type is BoundField, which binds to one field in the data object. For example, here's the definition for a single data-bound column that displays the ProductID field:

```
<asp:BoundField DataField="ProductID" HeaderText="ID" />
```

This tag demonstrates how you can change the header text at the top of a column from ProductID to just ID.

Here's a complete GridView declaration with explicit columns:

```
<asp:GridView ID="GridView1" runat="server" DataSourceID="sourceProducts"
 AutoGenerateColumns="false">
  <Columns>
    <asp:BoundField DataField="ProductID" HeaderText="ID" />
    <asp:BoundField DataField="ProductName" HeaderText="Product Name" />
    <asp:BoundField DataField="UnitPrice" HeaderText="Price" />
  </Columns>
</asp:GridView>
```

Explicitly defining columns has several advantages:

- You can easily fine-tune your column order, column headings, and other details by tweaking the properties of your column object.
- You can hide columns you don't want to show by removing the column tag. (However, don't overuse this technique, because it's better to reduce the amount of data you're retrieving if you don't intend to display it.)
- You'll see your columns in the design environment (in Visual Studio). With automatically generated columns, the GridView simply shows a few generic placeholder columns.
- You can add extra columns to the mix for selecting, editing, and more.

This example shows how you can use this approach to change the header text. However, the HeaderText property isn't the only column property you can change in a column. In the next section, you'll learn about a few more.

Configuring Columns

When you explicitly declare a bound field, you have the opportunity to set other properties. Table 15-2 lists these properties.

Table 15-2. *BoundField Properties*

Property	Description
DataField	The name of the field you want to display in this column.
DataFormatString	A format string that formats the field. This is useful for getting the right representation of numbers and dates.
ApplyFormatInEditMode	If true, the format string will be used to format the value even when it appears in a text box in edit mode. The default is false, which means the underlying value will be used (such as 1143.02 instead of $1,143.02).
FooterText, HeaderText, and HeaderImageUrl	Sets the text in the header and footer region of the grid, if this grid has a header (ShowHeader is true) and Footer (ShowFooter is true). The header is most commonly used for a descriptive label such as the field name; the footer can contain a dynamically calculated value such as a summary. To show an image in the header *instead* of text, set the HeaderImageUrl property.
ReadOnly	If true, the value for this column can't be changed in edit mode. No edit control will be provided. Primary key fields are often read-only.
InsertVisible	If false, the value for this column can't be set in insert mode. If you want a column value to be set programmatically or based on a default value defined in the database, you can use this feature.
Visible	If false, the column won't be visible in the page (and no HTML will be rendered for it). This property gives you a convenient way to programmatically hide or show specific columns, changing the overall view of the data.
SortExpression	An expression that can be applied to your results to sort them based on one or more columns. You'll learn about sorting later in the "Sorting and Paging the GridView" section of this chapter.
HtmlEncode	If true (the default), all text will be HTML encoded to prevent special characters from mangling the page. You could disable HTML encoding if you want to embed a working HTML tag (such as a hyperlink), but this approach isn't safe. It's always a better idea to use HTML encoding on all values and provide other functionality by reacting to GridView selection events.
NullDisplayText	The text that will be displayed for a null value. The default is an empty string, although you could change this to a hard-coded value, such as "(not specified)".
ConvertEmptyStringToNull	If this is true, before an edit is committed, all empty strings will be converted to null values.
ControlStyle, HeaderStyle, FooterStyle, and ItemStyle	Configures the appearance for just this column, overriding the styles for the row. You'll learn more about styles throughout this chapter.

Generating Columns with Visual Studio

When you first create a GridView, the AutoGenerateColumns property is set to false. When you bind it to a data source control, nothing changes. However, Visual Studio also allows you to create all the column tags you need automatically using a nifty trick.

Here's how it works: Select the GridView control, and click Refresh Schema in the smart tag. At this point, Visual Studio will retrieve the basic schema information from your data source (for example, the names and data type of each column) and then add one <BoundField> tag for each field.

■ **Tip** If you modify the data source so it returns a different set of columns, you can regenerate the GridView columns. Just select the GridView, and click the Refresh Schema link in the smart tag. This step will wipe out any custom columns you've added (such as editing controls).

Once you've created your columns, you can also use some helpful design-time support to configure the properties of each column (rather than editing the column tag by hand). To do this, select the GridView, and click the ellipsis (...) next to the Columns property in the Properties window. You'll see a Fields dialog box that lets you add, remove, and refine your columns (see Figure 15-2).

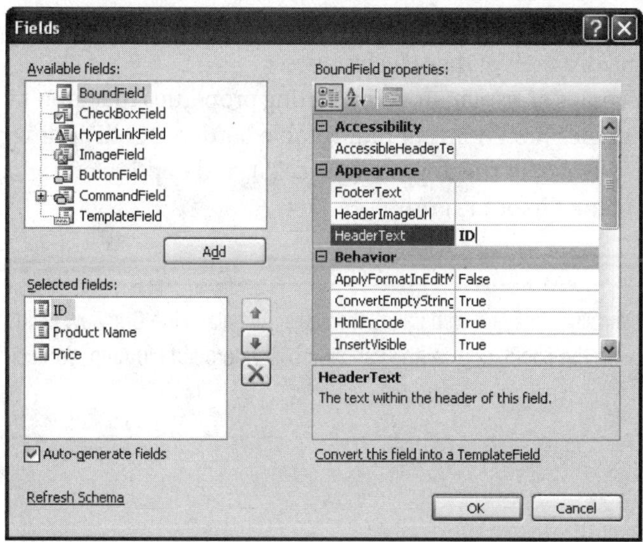

Figure 15-2. *Configuring columns in Visual Studio*

Now that you understand the underpinnings of the GridView, you've still only started to explore its higher-level features. In the following sections, you'll tackle these topics:

Formatting: How to format rows and data values

Selecting: How to let users select a row in the GridView and respond accordingly

Editing: How to let users commit record updates, inserts, and deletes

Sorting: How to dynamically reorder the GridView in response to clicks on a column header

Paging: How to divide a large result set into multiple pages of data

Templates: How to take complete control of designing, formatting, and editing by defining templates

Formatting the GridView

Formatting consists of several related tasks. First, you want to ensure that dates, currencies, and other number values are presented in the appropriate way. You handle this job with the DataFormatString property. Next, you'll want to apply the perfect mix of colors, fonts, borders, and alignment options to each aspect of the grid, from headers to data items. The GridView supports these features through styles. Finally, you can intercept events, examine row data, and apply formatting to specific values programmatically. In the following sections, you'll consider each of these techniques.

The GridView also exposes several self-explanatory formatting properties that aren't covered here. These include GridLines (for adding or hiding table borders), CellPadding and CellSpacing (for controlling the overall spacing between cells), and Caption and CaptionAlign (for adding a title to the top of the grid).

■ **Tip** Want to create a GridView that scrolls—inside a web page? It's easy. Just place the GridView inside a Panel control, set the appropriate size for the panel, and set the Panel.Scrollbars property to Auto, Vertical, or Both.

Formatting Fields

Each BoundField column provides a DataFormatString property you can use to configure the appearance of numbers and dates using a *format string*.

Format strings generally consist of a placeholder and format indicator, which are wrapped inside curly brackets. A typical format string looks something like this:

```
{0:C}
```

In this case, the 0 represents the value that will be formatted, and the letter indicates a predetermined format style. In this case, C means currency format, which formats a number as a dollar figure (so 3400.34 becomes $3,400.34). Here's a column that uses this format string:

```
<asp:BoundField DataField="UnitCost" HeaderText="Price"
  DataFormatString="{0:C}" HtmlEncode="false" />
```

■ **Note** Because of a bug in the way the GridView uses HTML encoding, you may need to set the HtmlEncode property of the column to false. (Refer to Table 15-2 for more information about this property.) Otherwise, the encoding will be performed before the formatting, which can cause the formatting to fail. If you attempt to use a format string but the value doesn't appear to be changed in the grid, this is the most likely problem.

Table 15-3 shows some of the other formatting options for numeric values.

Table 15-3. *Numeric Format Strings*

Type	Format String	Example
Currency	{0:C}	$1,234.50 Brackets indicate negative values: ($1,234.50). The currency sign is locale-specific: (¢1,234.50).
Scientific (Exponential)	{0:E}	1.234.50E+004
Percentage	{0:P}	45.6%
Fixed Decimal	{0:F?}	Depends on the number of decimal places you set. {0:F3} would be 123.400. {0:F0} would be 123.

You can find other examples in the MSDN Help. For date or time values, you'll find an extensive list. For example, if you want to write the BirthDate value in the format month/day/year (as in 12/30/05), you use the following column:

```
<asp:BoundField DataField="BirthDate" HeaderText="Birth Date"
 DataFormatString="{0:MM/dd/yy}" HtmlEncode="False"/>
```

Table 15-4 shows some more examples.

Table 15-4. *Time and Date Format Strings*

Type	Format String	Syntax	Example
Short Date	{0:d}	M/d/yyyy	10/30/2005
Long Date	{0:D}	dddd, MMMM dd, yyyy	Monday, January 30, 2005
Long Date and Short Time	{0:f}	dddd, MMMM dd, yyyy HH:mm aa	Monday, January 30, 2005 10:00 AM
Long Date and Long Time	{0:F}	dddd, MMMM dd, yyyy HH:mm:ss aa	Monday, January 30, 2005 10:00:23 AM
ISO Sortable Standard	{0:s}	yyyy-MM-dd HH:mm:ss	2005-01-30 10:00:23
Month and Day	{0:M}	MMMM dd	January 30
General	{0:G}	M/d/yyyy HH:mm:ss aa (depends on locale-specific settings)	10/30/2002 10:00:23 AM

The format characters are not specific to the GridView. You can use them with other controls, with data-bound expressions in templates (as you'll see later in the "GridView Templates" section), and parameters for many methods. For example, the Decimal and DateTime types expose their own ToString() methods that accept a format string, allowing you to format values manually.

Using Styles

The GridView exposes a rich formatting model that's based on *styles*. Altogether, you can set eight GridView styles, as described in Table 15-5.

Table 15-5. *GridView Styles*

Style	Description
HeaderStyle	Configures the appearance of the header row that contains column titles, if you've chosen to show it (if ShowHeader is true).
RowStyle	Configures the appearance of every data row.
AlternatingRowStyle	If set, applies additional formatting to every other row. This formatting acts in addition to the RowStyle formatting. For example, if you set a font using RowStyle, it is also applied to alternating rows, unless you explicitly set a different font through AlternatingRowStyle.
SelectedRowStyle	Configures the appearance of the row that's currently selected. This formatting acts in addition to the RowStyle formatting.
EditRowStyle	Configures the appearance of the row that's in edit mode. This formatting acts in addition to the RowStyle formatting.

Style	Description
EmptyDataRowStyle	Configures the style that's used for the single empty row in the special case where the bound data object contains no rows.
FooterStyle	Configures the appearance of the footer row at the bottom of the GridView, if you've chosen to show it (if ShowFooter is true).
PagerStyle	Configures the appearance of the row with the page links, if you've enabled paging (set AllowPaging to true).

Styles are not simple single-value properties. Instead, each style exposes a Style object that includes properties for choosing colors (ForeColor and BackColor), adding borders (BorderColor, BorderStyle, and BorderWidth), sizing the row (Height and Width), aligning the row (HorizontalAlign and VerticalAlign), and configuring the appearance of text (Font and Wrap). These style properties allow you to refine almost every aspect of an item's appearance.

Here's an example that changes the style of rows and headers in a GridView:

```
<asp:GridView ID="GridView1" runat="server" DataSourceID="sourceProducts"
  AutoGenerateColumns="false">
    <RowStyle BackColor="#E7E7FF" ForeColor="#4A3C8C" />
    <HeaderStyle BackColor="#4A3C8C" Font-Bold="True" ForeColor="#F7F7F7" />
    <Columns>
      <asp:BoundField DataField="ProductID" HeaderText="ID" />
      <asp:BoundField DataField="ProductName" HeaderText="Product Name" />
      <asp:BoundField DataField="UnitPrice" HeaderText="Price" />
    </Columns>
</asp:GridView>
```

In this example, every column is affected by the formatting changes. However, you can also define column-specific styles. To create a column-specific style, you simply need to rearrange the control tag so that the formatting tag becomes a nested tag *inside* the appropriate column tag. Here's an example that formats just the ProductName column:

```
<asp:GridView ID="GridView2" runat="server" DataSourceID="sourceProducts"
  AutoGenerateColumns="false" >
    <Columns>
      <asp:BoundField DataField="ProductID" HeaderText="ID" />
      <asp:BoundField DataField="ProductName" HeaderText="Product Name">
        <ItemStyle BackColor="#E7E7FF" ForeColor="#4A3C8C" />
        <HeaderStyle BackColor="#4A3C8C" Font-Bold="True" ForeColor="#F7F7F7" />
      </asp:BoundField>
      <asp:BoundField DataField="UnitPrice" HeaderText="Price" />
    </Columns>
</asp:GridView>
```

Figure 15-3 compares these two examples. You can use a combination of ordinary style settings and column-specific style settings (which override ordinary style settings if they conflict).

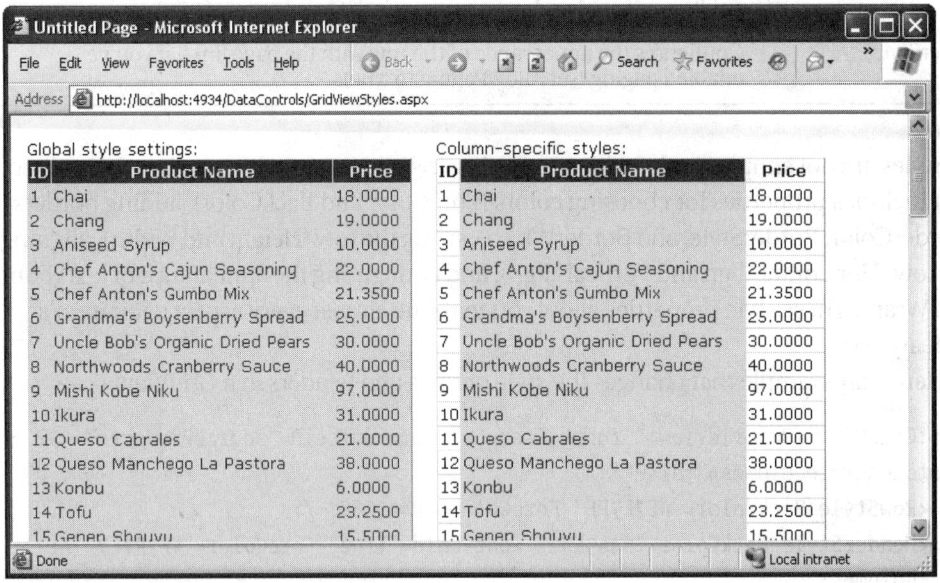

Global style settings:

ID	Product Name	Price
1	Chai	18.0000
2	Chang	19.0000
3	Aniseed Syrup	10.0000
4	Chef Anton's Cajun Seasoning	22.0000
5	Chef Anton's Gumbo Mix	21.3500
6	Grandma's Boysenberry Spread	25.0000
7	Uncle Bob's Organic Dried Pears	30.0000
8	Northwoods Cranberry Sauce	40.0000
9	Mishi Kobe Niku	97.0000
10	Ikura	31.0000
11	Queso Cabrales	21.0000
12	Queso Manchego La Pastora	38.0000
13	Konbu	6.0000
14	Tofu	23.2500
15	Genen Shouyu	15.5000

Column-specific styles:

ID	Product Name	Price
1	Chai	18.0000
2	Chang	19.0000
3	Aniseed Syrup	10.0000
4	Chef Anton's Cajun Seasoning	22.0000
5	Chef Anton's Gumbo Mix	21.3500
6	Grandma's Boysenberry Spread	25.0000
7	Uncle Bob's Organic Dried Pears	30.0000
8	Northwoods Cranberry Sauce	40.0000
9	Mishi Kobe Niku	97.0000
10	Ikura	31.0000
11	Queso Cabrales	21.0000
12	Queso Manchego La Pastora	38.0000
13	Konbu	6.0000
14	Tofu	23.2500
15	Genen Shouyu	15.5000

Figure 15-3. *Formatting the GridView*

One reason you might use column-specific formatting is to define specific column widths. If you don't define a specific column width, ASP.NET makes each column just wide enough to fit the data it contains (or, if wrapping is enabled, to fit the text without splitting a word over a line break). If values range in size, the width is determined by the largest value or the width of the column header, whichever is larger. However, if the grid is wide enough, you might want to expand a column so it doesn't appear to be crowded against the adjacent columns. In this case, you need to explicitly define a larger width.

Configuring Styles with Visual Studio

There's no reason to code style properties by hand in the GridView control tag, because the GridView provides rich design-time support. To set style properties, you can use the Properties window to modify the style properties. For example, to configure the font of the header, expand the HeaderStyle property to show the nested Font property, and set that. The only limitation of this approach is that it doesn't allow you to set the style for individual columns—if you need that trick, you must first call up the Fields dialog box (shown in the earlier Figure 15-2) by editing the Columns property. Then, select the appropriate column, and set the style properties accordingly.

You can even set a combination of styles using a preset theme by clicking the Auto Format link in the GridView smart tag. Figure 15-4 shows the Auto Format dialog box with some of the preset styles you can choose. Select Remove Formatting to clear all the style settings.

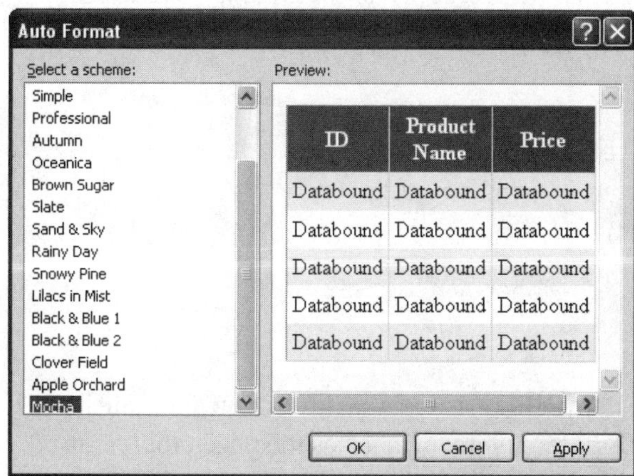

Figure 15-4. *Automatically formatting a GridView*

Once you've chosen a theme, the style settings are inserted into your GridView tag, and you can tweak them by hand or by using the Properties window.

Formatting-Specific Values

The formatting you've learned so far isn't that fine-grained. At its most specific, this formatting applies to a single column of values. But what if you want to change the formatting for a specific row or even just a single cell?

The solution is to react to the GridView.RowCreated event. This event is raised when a part of the grid (the header, footer, pager, or a normal, alternate, or selected item) is being created. You can access the current row as a GridViewRow control. The GridViewRow.DataItem property provides the data object for the given row, and the GridViewRow.Cells collection allows you to retrieve the row content. You can use the GridViewRow to change colors and alignment, add or remove child controls, and so on.

The following example handles the RowCreated event and changes the background color to highlight high prices (those more expensive than $50):

```
protected void GridView1_RowCreated(object sender, GridViewRowEventArgs e)
{
    if (e.Row.RowType == DataControlRowType.DataRow)
    {
        // Get the price for this row.
        decimal price = (decimal)DataBinder.Eval(e.Row.DataItem, "UnitPrice");

        if (price > 50)
        {
            e.Row.BackColor = System.Drawing.Color.Maroon;
            e.Row.ForeColor = System.Drawing.Color.White;
            e.Row.Font.Bold = true;
        }
    }
}
```

First, the code checks whether the item being created is an item or an alternate item. If neither, it means the item is another interface element, such as the pager, footer, or header, and the procedure does nothing. If the item is the right type, the code extracts the UnitPrice field from the data-bound item.

To get a value from the bound data object (provided through the GridViewRowEventArgs.Row.DataItem property), you need to cast the data object to the correct type. The trick is that the type depends on the way you're performing your data binding. In this example, you're binding to the SqlDataSource in DataSet mode, which means each data item will be a DataRowView object. (If you were to bind in DataReader mode, a DbDataRecord represents each item instead.) To avoid coding these details, which can make it more difficult to change your data access code, you can rely on the DataBinder.Eval() helper method, which understands all these types of data objects. That's the techniques used in this example.

Figure 15-5 shows the resulting page.

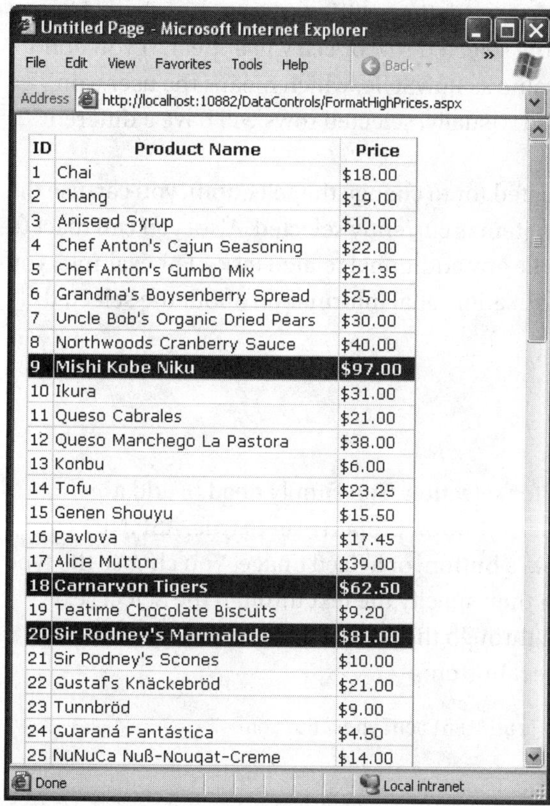

ID	Product Name	Price
1	Chai	$18.00
2	Chang	$19.00
3	Aniseed Syrup	$10.00
4	Chef Anton's Cajun Seasoning	$22.00
5	Chef Anton's Gumbo Mix	$21.35
6	Grandma's Boysenberry Spread	$25.00
7	Uncle Bob's Organic Dried Pears	$30.00
8	Northwoods Cranberry Sauce	$40.00
9	Mishi Kobe Niku	$97.00
10	Ikura	$31.00
11	Queso Cabrales	$21.00
12	Queso Manchego La Pastora	$38.00
13	Konbu	$6.00
14	Tofu	$23.25
15	Genen Shouyu	$15.50
16	Pavlova	$17.45
17	Alice Mutton	$39.00
18	Carnarvon Tigers	$62.50
19	Teatime Chocolate Biscuits	$9.20
20	Sir Rodney's Marmalade	$81.00
21	Sir Rodney's Scones	$10.00
22	Gustaf's Knäckebröd	$21.00
23	Tunnbröd	$9.00
24	Guaraná Fantástica	$4.50
25	NuNuCa Nuß-Nougat-Creme	$14.00

Figure 15-5. *Formatting individual rows based on values*

Selecting a GridView Row

Selecting an item refers to the ability to click a row and have it change color (or become highlighted) to indicate that the user is currently working with this record. At the same time, you might want to display additional information about the record in another control. With the GridView, selection happens almost automatically once you set up a few basics.

Before you can use item selection, you must define a different style for selected items. The SelectedRowStyle determines how the selected row or cell will appear. If you don't set this style, it will default to the same value as RowStyle, which means the user won't be able to tell which row is currently selected. Usually, selected rows will have a different BackColor property.

To find out what item is currently selected (or to change the selection), you can use the SelectedIndex property. It will be –1 if no item is currently selected. Also, you can react to the SelectedIndexChanged event to handle any additional related tasks. For example, you might want to update another control with additional information about the selected record.

Adding a Select Button

The GridView provides built-in support for selection. You simply need to add a CommandField column with the ShowSelectButton property set to true. ASP.NET can render the CommandField as a hyperlink, a button, or a fixed image. You choose the type using the ButtonType property. You can then specify the text through the SelectText property or specify the link to the image through the SelectImageUrl property.

Here's an example that displays a select button:

```
<asp:CommandField ShowSelectButton="True" ButtonType="Button"
 SelectText="Select" />
```

And here's an example that shows a small clickable icon:

```
<asp:CommandField ShowSelectButton="True" ButtonType="Image"
 SelectImageUrl="select.gif" />
```

Figure 15-6 shows a page with a text select button (and product 14 selected).

When you click a select button, the page is posted back, and a series of steps unfolds. First, the GridView.SelectedIndexChanging event fires, which you can intercept to cancel the operation. Next, the GridView.SelectedIndex property is adjusted to point to the selected row. Finally, the GridView.SelectedIndexChanged event fires, which you can handle if you want to manually update other controls to reflect the new selection. When the page is rendered, the selected row is given the selected row style.

■ **Tip** Rather than add the select button yourself, you can choose Enable Selection from the GridView's smart tag, which adds a basic select button for you.

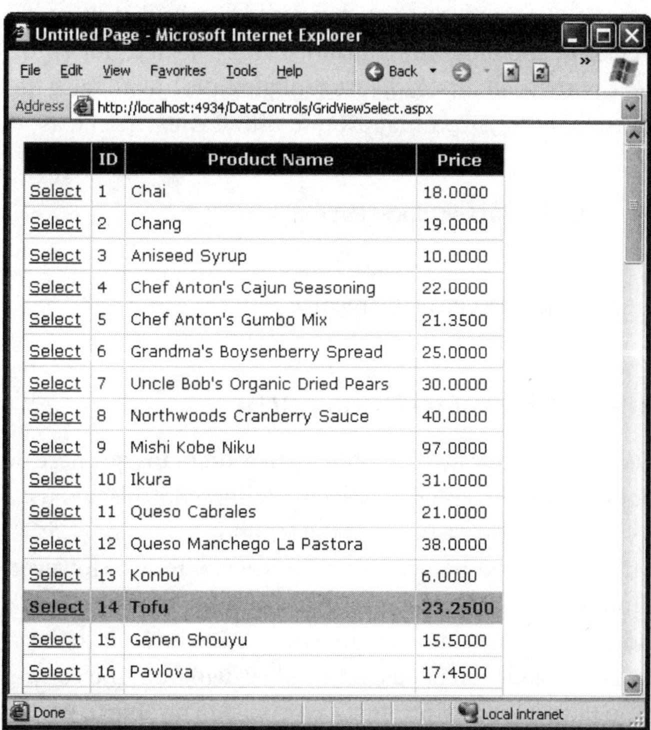

Figure 15-6. *GridView selection*

Using a Data Field As a Select Button

You don't need to create a new column to support row selection. Instead, you can turn an existing column into a link. This technique is commonly used to allow users to select rows in a table by the unique ID value.

To use this technique, remove the CommandField column, and add a ButtonField column instead. Then, set the DataTextField to the name of the field you want to use.

```
<asp:ButtonField ButtonType="Button" DataTextField="ProductID" />
```

This field will be underlined and turned into a Button that, when clicked, will post back the page and trigger the GridView.RowCommand event. You could handle this event, determine which row has been clicked, and programmatically set the SelectedIndex property. However, you can use an easier method. Instead, just configure the link to raise the SelectedIndexChanged event by specifying a CommandName with the text Select, as shown here:

```
<asp:ButtonField CommandName="Select" ButtonType="Button"
 DataTextField="ProductID" />
```

Now clicking the data field automatically selects the record.

Using Selection to Create a Master-Details Form

As demonstrated in the previous chapter, you can bind other data sources to a property in a control using parameters. For example, you could add two GridView controls and use information from the first GridView to perform a query in the second.

In the case of the GridView, the property you need to bind is SelectedIndex. However, this has one problem. SelectedIndex returns a zero-based index number representing where the row occurs in the grid. This isn't the information you need to insert into the query that gets the related records. Instead, you need a unique key field from the corresponding row. For example, if you have a table of products, you need to be able to get the ProductID for the selected row. Unfortunately, you have no way to pull this information out of the original data object, because all the data objects are discarded the moment the grid is filled. However, the GridView has the ability to track important fields—fields that represent unique key values—if you tell it to do so.

The trick is to set the DataKeyNames property for the GridView. This property requires a comma-separated list of one or more key fields. Each name you supply must match one of the fields in the bound data source. Usually, you'll have only one key field, as shown here:

```
<asp:GridView ID="gridEmployees" runat="server" DataSourceID="sourceProducts"
 DataKeyNames="ProductID">
```

Once you've established this link, the GridView is nice enough to keep track of the key fields for the selected record. It allows you to retrieve this information at any time through the SelectedDataKey property.

The following example puts it all together. It defines two GridView controls. The first shows a list of categories. The second shows the products that fall into the currently selected category. (Or, if no category has been selected, this GridView doesn't appear at all.)

Here's the page markup for this example:

```
Categories:<br />
<asp:GridView ID="gridCategories" runat="server" DataSourceID="sourceCategories"
  DataKeyNames="CategoryID">
    <Columns>
      <asp:CommandField ShowSelectButton="True" />
    </Columns>
    <SelectedRowStyle BackColor="#FFCC66" Font-Bold="True" ForeColor="#663399" />
</asp:GridView>
<asp:SqlDataSource ID="sourceCategories" runat="server"
  ConnectionString="<%$ ConnectionStrings:Northwind %>"
  SelectCommand="SELECT * FROM Categories"></asp:SqlDataSource>
<br />

Products in this category:<br />
<asp:GridView ID="gridProducts" runat="server" DataSourceID="sourceProducts">
  <SelectedRowStyle BackColor="#FFCC66" Font-Bold="True" ForeColor="#663399" />
</asp:GridView>
<asp:SqlDataSource ID="sourceProducts" runat="server"
  ConnectionString="<%$ ConnectionStrings:Northwind %>"
  SelectCommand="SELECT ProductID, ProductName, UnitPrice FROM Products WHERE
CategoryID=@CategoryID">
    <SelectParameters>
      <asp:ControlParameter Name="CategoryID" ControlID="gridCategories"
        PropertyName="SelectedDataKey.Value" />
    </SelectParameters>
</asp:SqlDataSource>
```

As you can see, you need two data sources, one for each GridView. The second data source uses a ControlParameter that links it to the SelectedDataKey property of the first GridView. Best of all, you still don't need to write any code or handle the SelectedIndexChanged event on your own.

Figure 15-7 shows this example in action.

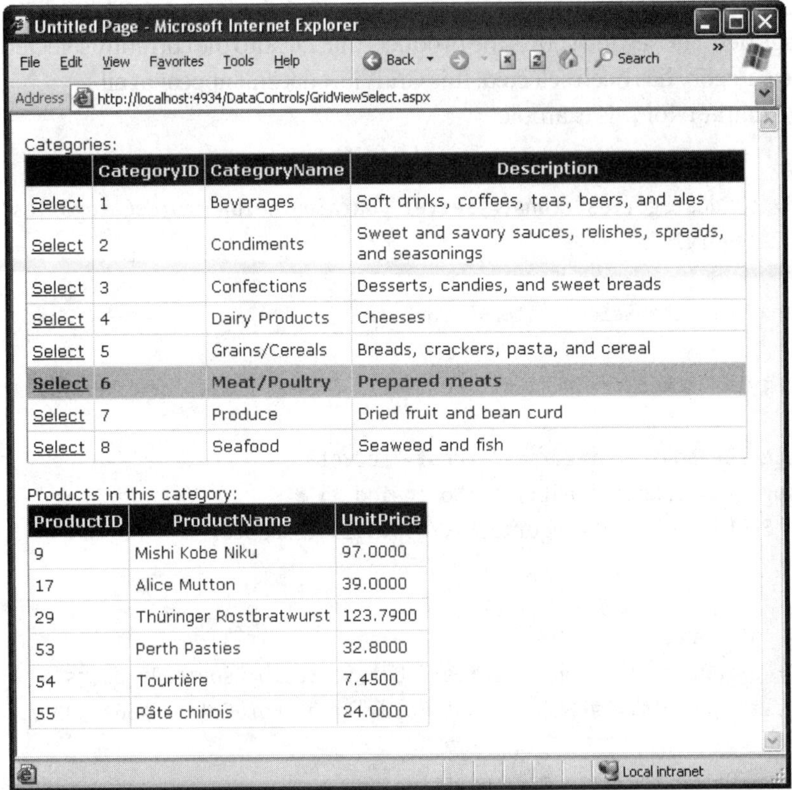

Figure 15-7. *A master-details page*

Editing with the GridView

The GridView provides support for editing that's almost as convenient as its support for selection. To switch a row into select mode, you simply set the SelectedIndex property to the corresponding row number. To switch a row into edit mode, you set the EditIndex property in the same way.

Of course, both of these tasks can take place automatically if you use specialized button types. For selection, you use a CommandField column with the ShowSelectButton property set to true. To add edit controls, you follow almost the same step—once again, you use the CommandField column, but now you set ShowEditButton to true.

Here's an example of a GridView that supports editing:

```
<asp:GridView ID="gridProducts" runat="server" DataSourceID="sourceProducts"
  AutoGenerateColumns="False" DataKeyNames="ProductID" >
```

```
    <Columns>
      <asp:BoundField DataField="ProductID" HeaderText="ID" ReadOnly="True" />
      <asp:BoundField DataField="ProductName" HeaderText="Product Name"/>
      <asp:BoundField DataField="UnitPrice" HeaderText="Price" />
      <asp:CommandField ShowEditButton="True" />
    </Columns>
</asp:GridView>
```

And here's a revised data source control that can commit your changes:

```
<asp:SqlDataSource id="sourceProducts" runat="server"
  ConnectionString="<%$ ConnectionStrings:Northwind %>"
  SelectCommand="SELECT ProductID, ProductName, UnitPrice FROM Products"
  UpdateCommand="UPDATE Products SET ProductName=@ProductName,
UnitPrice=@UnitPrice WHERE ProductID=@ProductID" />
```

Remember, you don't need to define the update parameters, as long as you make sure they match the field names (with an at sign [@] at the beginning). Chapter 14 has more information about using update commands with the SqlDataSource control.

When you add a CommandField with the ShowEditButton property set to true, the GridView editing controls appear in an additional column. When you run the page and the GridView is bound and displayed, the edit column shows an Edit link next to every record (see Figure 15-8).

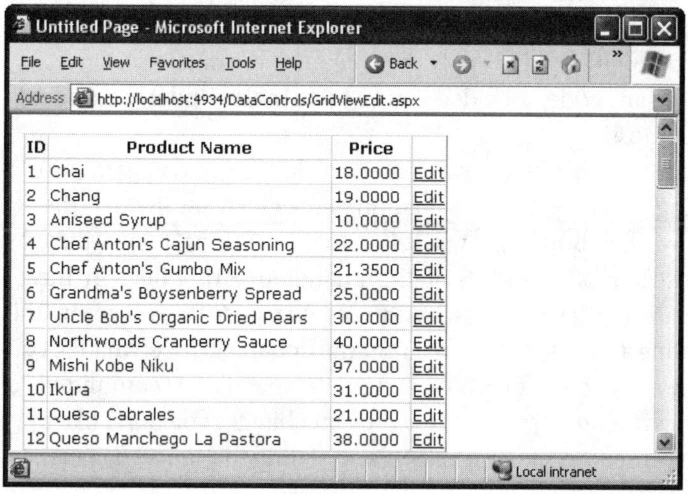

Figure 15-8. *The editing controls*

When clicked, this link switches the corresponding row into edit mode. All fields are changed to text boxes, with the exception of read-only fields (which are not editable) and true/false bit fields (which are shown as check boxes). The Edit link is replaced with an Update link and a Cancel link (see Figure 15-9).

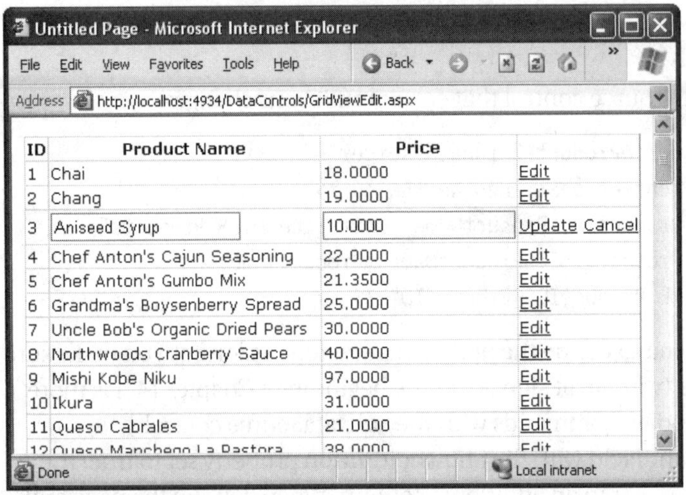
Untitled Page - Microsoft Internet Explorer
File Edit View Favorites Tools Help
Back
Address http://localhost:4934/DataControls/GridViewEdit.aspx
ID
Product Name
Price
1 Chai 18.0000 Edit
2 Chang 19.0000 Edit
3 Aniseed Syrup 10.0000 Update Cancel
4 Chef Anton's Cajun Seasoning 22.0000 Edit
5 Chef Anton's Gumbo Mix 21.3500 Edit
6 Grandma's Boysenberry Spread 25.0000 Edit
7 Uncle Bob's Organic Dried Pears 30.0000 Edit
8 Northwoods Cranberry Sauce 40.0000 Edit
9 Mishi Kobe Niku 97.0000 Edit
10 Ikura 31.0000 Edit
11 Queso Cabrales 21.0000 Edit
Done
Local intranet

Figure 15-9. *Editing a record*

The Cancel link returns the row to its initial state. The Update link passes the values to the SqlDataSource.UpdateParameters collection (using the field names) and then triggers the SqlDataSource.Update() method to apply the change to the database. Once again, you don't have to write any code, provided you've filled in the UpdateCommand for the linked data source control.

You can use a similar approach to add support for record deleting and inserting. To enable deleting and inserting, you need to add a column to the GridView that has the ShowInsertButton and ShowDeleteButton properties set to true. As long as your linked SqlDataSource has the InsertCommand and DeleteCommand properties filled in, these operations will work automatically. If you want to write your own code that plugs into this process (for example, updating a label to inform the user the update has been made), consider reacting to the GridView event that fires after an update operation is committed, such as RowDeleted and RowUpdated. You can also prevent changes you don't like by reacting to the RowDeleting and RowUpdating events and setting the cancel flag in the event arguments.

■ **Note** The basic built-in updating features of the GridView don't give you a lot of flexibility. You can't change the types of controls that are used for editing, format these controls, or add validation. However, you can add all these features by building your own editing templates, a topic you'll consider later in the "GridView Templates" section.

Sorting and Paging the GridView

The GridView is a great all-in-one solution for displaying all kinds of data, but it becomes a little unwieldy as the number of fields and rows in your data source grows. Dense grids contribute to large pages that are slow to transmit over the network and difficult for the user to navigate. The GridView has two features that address these issues and make data more manageable: sorting and paging.

Both sorting and paging can be performed by the database server, provided you craft the right SQL using the Order By and Where clauses. In fact, sometimes this is the best approach for performance. However, the sorting and paging provided by the GridView and SqlDataSource is easy to implement and thoroughly flexible. These techniques are particularly useful if you need to show the same data in several ways and you want to let the user decide how the data should be ordered.

Sorting

The GridView sorting features allow the user to reorder the results in the GridView by clicking a column header. It's convenient—and easy to implement.

Although you may not realize it, when you bind to a DataTable, you actually use another object called the DataView. The DataView sits between the ASP.NET web page binding and your DataTable. Usually it does little aside from providing the information from the associated DataTable. However, you can customize the DataView so it applies its own sort order. That way, you can customize the data that appears in the web page, without needing to actually modify your data.

You can create a new DataView object by hand and bind the DataView directly to a data control such as the GridView. However, the GridView and SqlDataSource controls make it even easier. They provide several properties you can set to control sorting. Once you've configured these properties, the sorting is automatic, and you still won't need to write any code in your page class.

To enable sorting, you must set the GridView AllowSorting property to true. Next, you need to define a SortExpression for each column that can be sorted. In theory, a sort expression can use any syntax that's understood by the data source control. In practice, a sort expression almost always takes the form used in the ORDER BY clause of a SQL query. This means the sort expression can include a single field or a list of comma-separated fields, optionally with the word *ASC* or *DESC* added after the column name to sort in ascending or descending order.

Here's how you could define the ProductName column so it sorts by alphabetically ordering rows:

```
<asp:BoundField DataField="ProductName" HeaderText="Product Name"
 SortExpression="ProductName"/>
```

Note that if you don't want a column to be sort-enabled, you simply don't set its SortExpression property. Figure 15-10 shows an example with a grid sorted by product name.

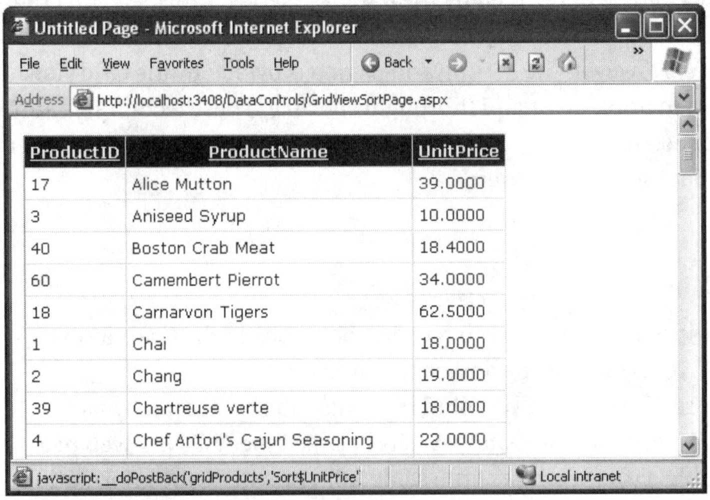

Figure 15-10. *Sorting the GridView*

Once you've associated a sort expression with the column and set the AllowSorting property to true, the GridView will render the headers with clickable links, as shown in Figure 15-10. However, it's up to the data source control to implement the actual sorting logic. How the sorting is implemented depends on the data source you're using. Not all data sources support sorting, but the SqlDataSource does. Essentially, when the user clicks a column link, the SqlDataSource sets the DataView.Sort property behind the scenes by using the sorting expression for that column. The end result is a perfectly sorted, code-free grid.

With DataView sorting, the data is retrieved unordered from the database, and the results are sorted in memory. This is not the speediest approach (sorting in memory requires more overhead and is slower than having SQL Server do the same work), but it is more scalable when you add caching to the mix. That's because you can cache a single copy of the data and sort it dynamically in several ways. (Chapter 26 has much more about this technique.) Without DataView sorting, you need a separate query to retrieve the newly sorted data.

■ **Note** The sort is according to the data type of the column. Numeric and date columns are ordered from smallest to largest. String columns are sorted alphanumerically without regard to case. Columns that contain binary data cannot be sorted.

Sorting and Selecting

If you use sorting and selection at the same time, you'll discover another issue. To see this problem in action, select a row, and then sort the data by any column. You'll see that the selection will remain, but it will shift to a new item that has the same index as the previous item. In other words, if you select the second row and perform a sort, the second row will still be selected in the new page, even though this isn't the record you selected. The only way to solve this problem is to programmatically change the selection every time a header link is clicked.

The simplest option is to react to the GridView.Sorted event to clear the selection, as shown here:

```
protected void GridView1_Sorted(object sender, GridViewSortEventArgs e)
{
    // Clear selected index.
    GridView1.SelectedIndex = -1;
}
```

In some cases you'll want to go even further and make sure a selected row remains selected when the sorting changes. The trick here is to store the selected value of the key field in view state each time the selected index changes:

```
protected void GridView1_SelectedIndexChanged(object sender, EventArgs e)
{
    // Save the selected value.
    if (GridView1.SelectedIndex != -1)
    {
        ViewState["SelectedValue"] = GridView1.SelectedValue.ToString();
    }
}
```

Now, when the grid is bound to the data source (for example, after a sort operation), you can reapply to the last selected index:

```
protected void GridView1_DataBound(object sender, EventArgs e)
{
    if (ViewState["SelectedValue"] != null)
    {
        string selectedValue = (string)ViewState["SelectedValue"];

        // Reselect the last selected row.
        foreach (GridViewRow row in GridView1.Rows)
        {
            string keyValue = GridView1.DataKeys[row.RowIndex].Value.ToString();
            if (keyValue == selectedValue)
            {
                GridView1.SelectedIndex = row.RowIndex;
                return;
            }
        }
    }
}
```

Keep in mind that this approach can be confusing if you also have enabled paging (which is described in the next section). This is because a sorting operation might move the current row to another page, rendering it not visible but keeping it selected. This makes sense but is quite confusing in practice.

Paging

Often, a database search will return too many rows to be realistically displayed in a single page. If the client is using a slow connection, sending an extremely large GridView can take a frustrating amount of time to arrive. Once the data is retrieved, the user may find out it doesn't contain the right content anyway or that the search was too broad and they can't easily wade through all the results to find the important information.

The GridView handles this scenario with an automatic paging feature. When you use automatic paging, the full results are retrieved from the data source and placed into a DataSet. Once the DataSet is bound to the GridView, however, the data is subdivided into smaller groupings (for example, with 20 rows each), and only a single batch is sent to the user. The other groups are abandoned when the page finishes processing. To allow the user to skip from one page to another, the GridView automatically displays a group of pager controls at the bottom of the grid. These pager controls could be previous/next links (often displayed as < and >) or number links (1, 2, 3, 4, 5, …) that lead to specific pages. If you've ever used a search engine, you've seen paging at work.

PAGING AND PERFORMANCE

When you use paging, every time a new page is requested, the full DataSet is queried from the database. This means paging does not reduce the amount of time required to query the database. In fact, because the information is split into multiple pages and you need to repeat the query every time the user moves to a new page, the database load actually *increases*. However, the client will see an improvement. Because any given page contains only a subset of the total data, the page size is smaller and will be transmitted faster, reducing the client's wait. The end result is a more responsive and manageable page.

You can use paging in certain ways without increasing the amount of work the database needs to perform. One option is to cache the entire DataSet in server memory. That way, every time the user moves to a different page, you simply need to retrieve the data from memory and rebind it, avoiding the database altogether. You'll learn how to use this technique in Chapter 26.

By setting a few properties, you can make the GridView control manage the paging for you. Table 15-6 describes the key properties.

Table 15-6. *Paging Members of the GridView*

Property	Description
AllowPaging	Enables or disables the paging of the bound records. It is false by default.
PageSize	Gets or sets the number of items to display on a single page of the grid. The default value is 10.
CurrentPageIndex	Gets or sets the zero-based index of the currently displayed page, if paging is enabled.
PagerSettings	Provides a PagerSettings object that wraps a variety of formatting options for the pager controls. These options determine where the paging controls are shown and what text or images they contain. You can set these properties to fine-tune the appearance of the pager controls, or you can use the defaults.
PagerStyle	Provides a style object you can use to configure fonts, colors, and text alignment for the paging controls.
PageIndexChanged event	Occurs when one of the page selection elements is clicked.

To use automatic paging, you need to set AllowPaging to true (which shows the page controls), and you need to set PageSize to determine how many rows are allowed on each page.

Here's an example of a GridView control declaration that sets these properties:

```
<asp:GridView ID="GridView1" runat="server" DataSourceID="sourceProducts"
 PageSize="10" AllowPaging="True" ...>
  ...
</asp:GridView>
```

This is enough to start using paging. Figure 15-11 shows an example with ten records per page (for a total of eight pages).

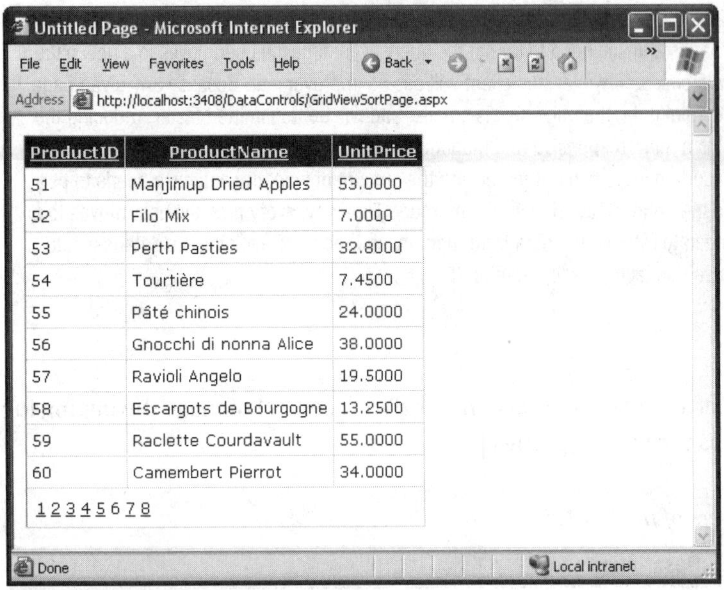

Figure 15-11. *Paging the GridView*

Using GridView Templates

So far, the examples have used the GridView control to show data using separate bound columns for each field. If you want to place multiple values in the same cell, or you have the unlimited ability to customize the content in a cell by adding HTML tags and server controls, you need to use a TemplateField.

The TemplateField allows you to define a completely customized *template* for a column. Inside the template you can add control tags, arbitrary HTML elements, and data binding expressions. You have complete freedom to arrange everything the way you want.

For example, imagine you want to create a column that combines the in stock, on order, and reorder level information for a product. To accomplish this trick, you can construct an ItemTemplate like this:

```
<asp:TemplateField HeaderText="Status">
  <ItemTemplate>
    <b>In Stock:</b>
    <%# Eval("UnitsInStock") %><br />
    <b>On Order:</b>
```

```
    <%# Eval("UnitsOnOrder") %><br />
    <b>Reorder:</b>
    <%# Eval("ReorderLevel") %>
  </ItemTemplate>
</asp:TemplateField>
```

To create the data binding expressions, the template uses the Eval() method, which is a static method of the System.Web.UI.DataBinder class. Eval() is an indispensable convenience—it automatically retrieves the data item that's bound to the current row, uses reflection to find the matching field, and retrieves the value.

■Tip The Eval() method also adds the extremely useful ability to format data fields on the fly. To use this feature, you must implement the overloaded version of the Eval() method that accepts an additional format string parameter. Here's an example:

```
<%# Eval("BirthDate", "{0:MM/dd/yy}") %>
```

You can use any of the format strings defined in Table 15-3 and Table 15-4 with the Eval() method.

You'll notice that this example template includes three data binding expressions. These expressions get the actual information from the current row. The rest of the content in the template defines static text, tags, and controls.

You also need to make sure the data source provides these three pieces of information. If you attempt to bind a field that isn't present in your result set, you'll receive a runtime error. If you retrieve additional fields that are never bound to any template, no problem will occur.

Here's the revised data source with these fields:

```
<asp:SqlDataSource ID="sourceProducts" runat="server"
  ConnectionString="<%$ ConnectionStrings:Northwind %>"
  SelectCommand="SELECT ProductID, ProductName, UnitPrice, UnitsInStock,
UnitsOnOrder,ReorderLevel FROM Products"
  UpdateCommand="UPDATE Products SET ProductName=@ProductName,
UnitPrice=@UnitPrice WHERE ProductID=@ProductID">
</asp:SqlDataSource>
```

When you bind the GridView, the GridView fetches the data from the data source and walks through the collection of items. It processes the ItemTemplate for each item, evaluates the data binding expressions, and adds the rendered HTML to the table. You're free to mix template columns with other column types. Figure 15-12 shows an example with several normal columns and the template column at the end.

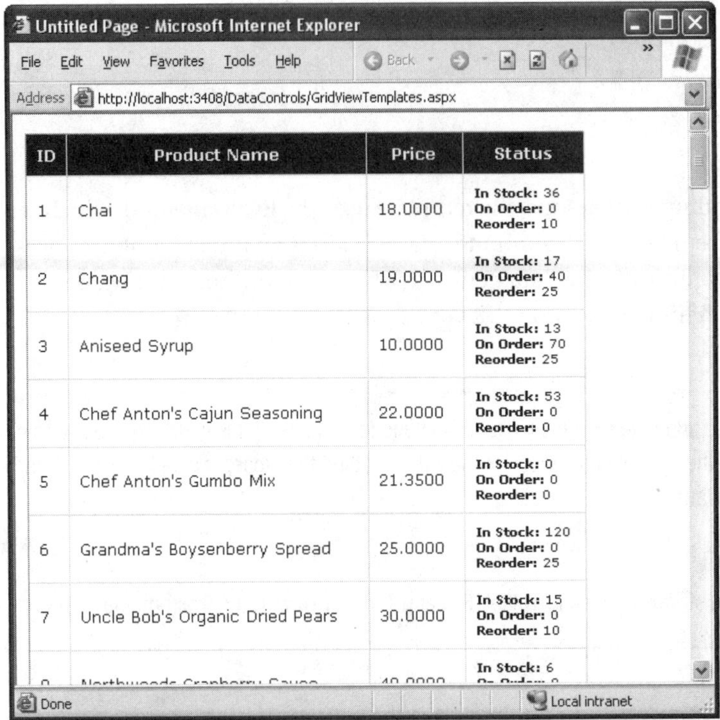

Figure 15-12. *A GridView with a template column*

Using Multiple Templates

The previous example used a single template to configure the appearance of data items. However, the ItemTemplate isn't the only template that the GridView provides. In fact, the GridView allows you to configure various aspects of its appearance with a number of templates. Inside every template column, you can use the templates listed in Table 15-7.

Table 15-7. *GridView Templates*

Mode	Description
HeaderTemplate	Determines the appearance and content of the header cell
FooterTemplate	Determines the appearance and content of the footer cell
ItemTemplate	Determines the appearance and content of each data cell (if you aren't using the AlternatingItemTempalte) or every odd-numbered data cell (if you are)
AlternatingItemTemplate	Used in conjunction with the ItemTemplate to format even-numbered and odd-numbered rows differently
EditItemTemplate	Determines the appearance and controls used in edit mode

Of the templates listed in Table 15-7, the EditItemTemplate is one of the most useful, because it gives you the ability to control the editing experience for the field. If you don't use template fields, you're limited to ordinary text boxes, and you won't have any validation. The GridView also defines two templates you can use outside any column. These are the PagerTemplate, which lets you customize the appearance of pager controls, and the EmptyDataTemplate, which lets you set the content that should appear if the GridView is bound to an empty data object.

Editing Templates in Visual Studio

Visual Studio 2005 includes greatly improved support for editing templates in the web page designer. To try this, follow these steps:

1. Create a GridView with at least one template column.
2. Select the GridView, and click Edit Templates in the smart tag. This switches the GridView into template edit mode.
3. In the smart tag, use the Display drop-down list to choose the template you want to edit (see Figure 15-13). You can choose either of the two templates that apply to the whole GridView (EmptyDataTemplate or PagerTemplate), or you can choose a specific template for one of the template columns.

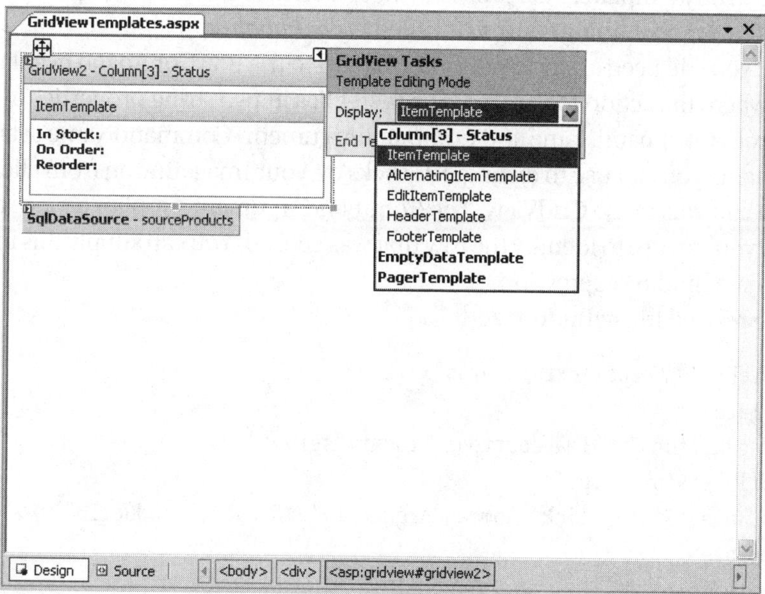

Figure 15-13. *Editing a template in Visual Studio*

4. Enter your content in the control. You can enter static content, drag and drop controls, and so on.

5. When you're finished, choose End Template Editing from the smart tag.

Handling Events in a Template

In some cases, you might need to handle events that are raised by the controls you add to a template column. For example, imagine you wanted to add a clickable image link by adding an ImageButton control. This is easy enough to accomplish:

```
<asp:TemplateField HeaderText="Status">
  <ItemTemplate>
    <asp:ImageButton ID="ImageButton1" runat="server"
     ImageUrl="statuspic.gif" />
  </ItemTemplate>
</asp:TemplateField>
```

The problem is that if you add a control to a template, the GridView creates multiple copies of that control, one for each data item. When the ImageButton is clicked, you need a way to determine which image was clicked and to which row it belongs.

The way to resolve this problem is to use an event from the GridView, *not* the contained button. The RowCommand event serves this purpose, because it fires whenever any button is clicked in any template. This process, where a control event in a template is turned into an event in the containing control, is called *event bubbling*.

Of course, you still need a way to pass information to the RowCommand event to identify the row where the action took place. The secret lies in two string properties of all button controls: CommandName and CommandArgument. CommandName sets a descriptive name you can use to distinguish clicks on your ImageButton from clicks on other button controls in the GridView. The CommandArgument supplies a piece of row-specific data you can use to identify the row that was clicked. You can supply this information using a data binding expression.

Here's the revised ImageButton tag:

```
<asp:TemplateField HeaderText="Status">
  <ItemTemplate>
    <asp:ImageButton ID="ImageButton1" runat="server"
     ImageUrl="statuspic.gif"
     CommandName="StatusClick" CommandArgument='<%# Eval("ProductID") %>' />
  </ItemTemplate>
</asp:TemplateField>
```

And here's the code you need in order to respond when an ImageButton is clicked:

```
protected void GridView1_RowCommand(object sender, GridViewCommandEventArgs e)
{
    if (e.CommandName == "StatusClick")
      lblInfo.Text = "You clicked product #" + e.CommandArgument;
}
```

This example simply displays the ProductID in a label.

Editing with a Template

One of the best reasons to use a template is to provide a better editing experience. In the previous chapter, you saw how the GridView provides automatic editing capabilities—all you need to do is switch a row into edit mode by setting the GridView.EditItemIndex property. The easiest way to make this possible is to add a CommandField column with the ShowEditButton set to true. Then, the user simply needs to click a link in the appropriate row to begin editing it. At this point, every label in every column is replaced by a text box (unless the field is read-only).

The standard editing support has several limitations:

It's not always appropriate to edit values using a text box: Certain types of data are best handled with other controls (such as drop-down lists), large fields need multiline text boxes, and so on.

You get no validation: It would be nice to restrict the editing possibilities so that currency figures can't be entered as negative numbers, and so on. You can do that by adding validator controls to an EditItemTemplate.

The visual appearance is often ugly: A row of text boxes across a grid takes up too much space and rarely seems professional.

In a template column, you don't have these issues. Instead, you explicitly define the edit controls and their layout using the EditItemTemplate. This can be a somewhat laborious process.

Here's the template column used earlier for stock information with an editing template:

```
<asp:TemplateField HeaderText="Status">
  <ItemStyle Width="100px" />
    <ItemTemplate>
      <b>In Stock:</b> <%# Eval("UnitsInStock") %><br />
      <b>On Order:</b> <%# Eval("UnitsOnOrder") %><br />
      <b>Reorder:</b> <%# Eval("ReorderLevel") %>
    </ItemTemplate>
```

```
    <EditItemTemplate>
      <b>In Stock:</b> <%# Eval("UnitsInStock") %><br />
      <b>On Order:</b> <%# Eval("UnitsOnOrder") %><br /><br />
      <b>Reorder:</b>
      <asp:TextBox Text='<%# Bind("ReorderLevel") %>' Width="25px"
       runat="server" id="txtReorder" />
    </EditItemTemplate>
  </asp:TemplateField>
```

Figure 15-14 shows the row in edit mode.

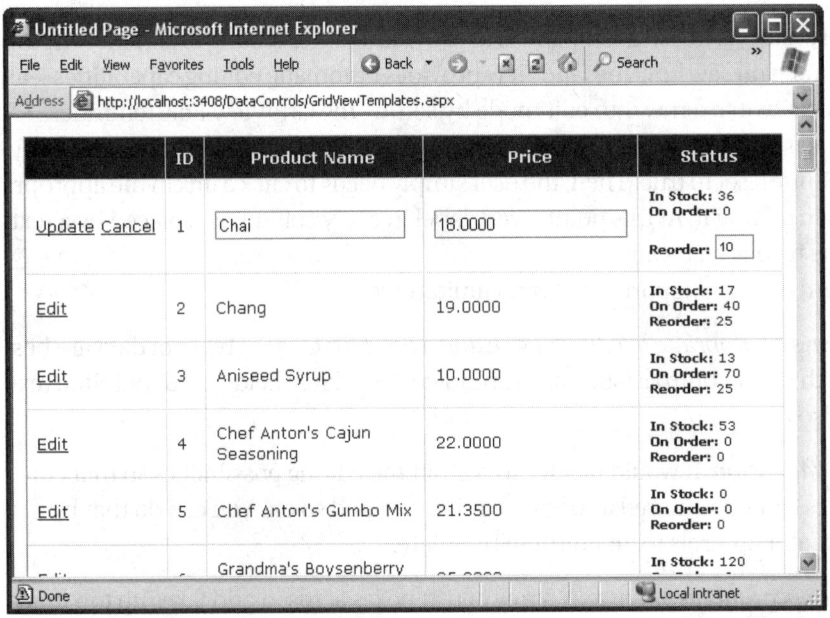

Figure 15-14. *Using an edit template*

When binding an editable value to a control, you must use the Bind() method in your data binding expression instead of the ordinary Eval() method. Only the Bind() method creates the two-way link, ensuring that updated values will be returned to the server.

One interesting detail here is that even though the item template shows three fields, the editing template allows only one of these to be changed. When the GridView commits an update, it will submit only the bound, editable parameters. In the previous example, this means the GridView will pass back a @ReorderLevel parameter but *not* a @UnitsInStock or

@UnitsOnOrder parameter. This is important, because when you write your parameterized update command, it must use only the parameters you have available. Here's the correct command:

```
<asp:SqlDataSource ID="sourceProducts" runat="server"
  ConnectionString="<%$ ConnectionStrings:Northwind %>"
  SelectCommand="SELECT ProductID, ProductName, UnitPrice, UnitsInStock,
UnitsOnOrder,ReorderLevel FROM Products"
  UpdateCommand="UPDATE Products SET ProductName=@ProductName,
UnitPrice=@UnitPrice,
ReorderLevel=@ReorderLevel WHERE ProductID=@ProductID">
</asp:SqlDataSource>
```

Editing with Validation

Now that you have your template ready, why not add an extra fill, such as a validator, to catch editing mistakes? In the following example, a RangeValidator prevents changes that put the ReorderLevel at less than 0 or more than 100:

```
<asp:TemplateField HeaderText="Status">
  <ItemStyle Width="100px" />
    <ItemTemplate>
      <b>In Stock:</b> <%# Eval("UnitsInStock") %><br />
      <b>On Order:</b> <%# Eval("UnitsOnOrder") %><br />
      <b>Reorder:</b> <%# Eval("ReorderLevel") %>
    </ItemTemplate>
  <EditItemTemplate>
    <b>In Stock:</b> <%# Eval("UnitsInStock") %><br />
    <b>On Order:</b> <%# Eval("UnitsOnOrder") %><br /><br />
    <b>Reorder:</b>
    <asp:TextBox Text='<%# Bind("ReorderLevel") %>' Width="25px"
     runat="server" id="txtReorder" />
    <asp:RangeValidator id="rngValidator" MinimumValue="0" MaximumValue="100"
     ControlToValidate="txtReorder" runat="server"
     ErrorMessage="Value out of range." Type="Integer"/>
  </EditItemTemplate>
</asp:TemplateField>
```

Figure 15-15 shows the validation at work.

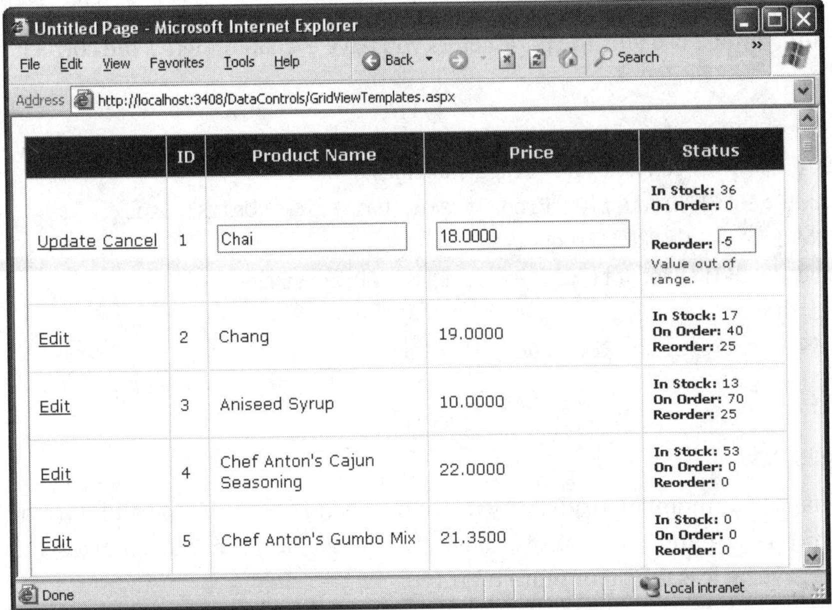

Figure 15-15. *Creating an edit template with validation*

Editing Without a Command Column

So far, all the examples you've seen have used a CommandField that automatically generates edit controls. However, now that you've made the transition over to a template-based approach, it's worth considering how you can add your own edit controls.

It's actually quite easy. All you need to do is add a button control to the item template and set the CommandName to Edit. This automatically triggers the editing process, which fires the appropriate events and switches the row into edit mode.

```
<ItemTemplate>
  <b>In Stock:</b> <%# Eval("UnitsInStock") %><br />
  <b>On Order:</b> <%# Eval("UnitsOnOrder") %><br />
  <b>Reorder:</b> <%# Eval("ReorderLevel") %>
  <br /><br />
  <asp:LinkButton runat="server" Text="Edit"
   CommandName="Edit" ID="Linkbutton1" />
</ItemTemplate>
```

In the edit item template, you need two more buttons with CommandName values of "Update" and "Cancel":

```
<EditItemTemplate>
  <b>In Stock:</b> <%# Eval("UnitsInStock") %><br />
  <b>On Order:</b> <%# Eval("UnitsOnOrder") %><br /><br />
  <b>Reorder:</b>
  <asp:TextBox Text='<%# Bind("ReorderLevel") %>' Width="25px"
   runat="server" id="txtReorder" />
  <br /><br />
  <asp:LinkButton runat="server" Text="Update"
   CommandName="Update" ID="Linkbutton1" />
  <asp:LinkButton runat="server" Text="Cancel"
   CommandName="Cancel" ID="Linkbutton2" />
</EditItemTemplate>
```

As long as you use these names, the GridView editing events will fire and the data source controls will react in the same way as if you were using the automatically generated editing controls. Figure 15-16 shows the custom edit buttons.

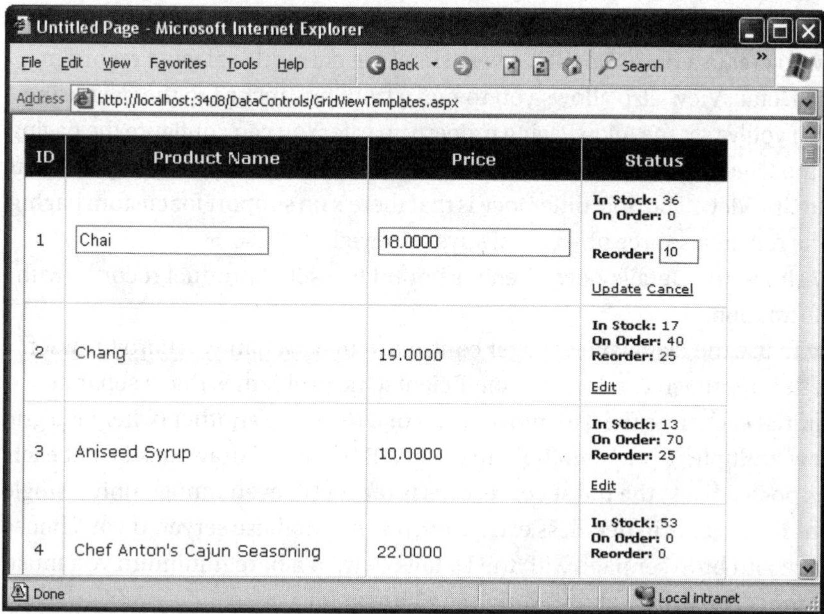

Figure 15-16. *Custom edit controls*

The DetailsView and FormView

The GridView excels at showing a dense table with multiple rows of information. However, sometimes you want to provide a detailed look at a single record. Although you could work out a solution using a template column in a GridView, ASP.NET also includes two controls that are tailored for this purpose: the DetailsView and FormView. Both show a single record at a time but can include optional pager buttons that let you step through a series of records (showing one per page). The difference between the DetailsView and the FormView is their support for templates. The DetailsView is built from field objects, in the same way the GridView is built from column objects. On the other hand, the FormView is based on templates that work in the same way as a GridView template column, which requires a little more work but gives you much more flexibility.

Now that you understand the features of the GridView, you can get up to speed with the DetailsView and FormView quite quickly. That's because both the DetailsView and the FormView borrow a portion of the GridView model.

The DetailsView

The DetailsView displays a single record at a time. It places each field in a separate row of a table.

You saw how to create a basic DetailsView to show the currently selected record in Chapter 14. The DetailsView also allows you to move from one record to the next using paging controls, if you've set the AllowPaging property to true. You can configure the paging controls using the PagerStyle and PagerSettings properties in the same way as you tweak the pager for the GridView. The only difference is that there's no support for custom paging, which means the full data source object is always retrieved.

Figure 15-17 shows the DetailsView when it's bound to a set of product records, with full product information.

It's tempting to use the DetailsView pager controls to make a handy record browser. Unfortunately, this approach can be quite inefficient. One problem is that a separate postback is required each time the user moves from one record to another (whereas a grid control can show multiple records on the same page). But the real drawback is that each time the page is posted back, the full set of records is retrieved, even though only a single record is shown. This results in needless extra work for the database server. If you choose to implement a record browser page with the DetailsView, at a bare minimum you must enable caching to reduce the database work (see Chapter 26).

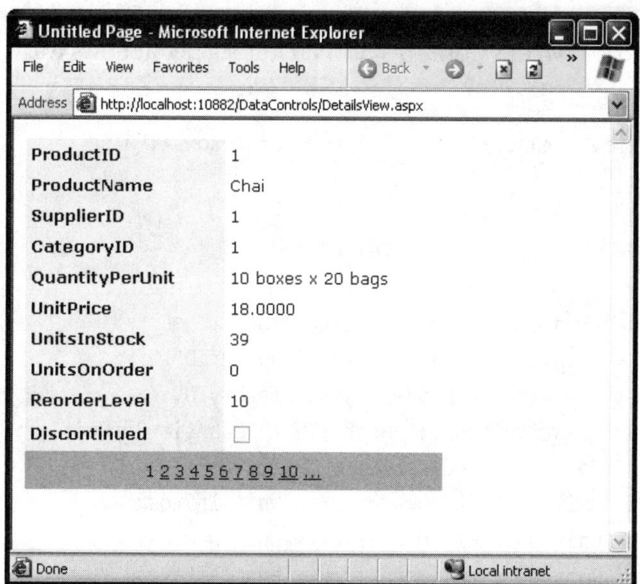

Figure 15-17. *The DetailsView with paging*

■ **Tip** It's almost always a better idea to use another control to let the user choose a specific record (for example, by choosing an ID from a list box) and then show the full record in the DetailsView using a parameterized command that matches just the selected record. Chapter 14 demonstrates this technique.

Defining Fields

The DetailsView uses reflection to generate the fields it shows. This means it examines the data object and creates a separate row for each field it finds, just like the GridView. You can disable this automatic row generation by setting AutoGenerateRows to false. It's then up to you to declare information you want to display.

Interestingly, you use the same field tags to build a DetailsView as you use to design a GridView. For example, fields from the data item are represented with the BoundField tag, buttons can be created with the ButtonField, and so on. For the full list, refer to the earlier Table 15-1.

The following code defines a DetailsView that shows product information. This tag creates the same grid of information shown in Figure 15-17, when AutoGenerateRows was set to true.

```
<asp:DetailsView ID="DetailsView1" runat="server" AutoGenerateRows="False"
 DataSourceID="sourceProducts">
  <Fields>
    <asp:BoundField DataField="ProductID" HeaderText="ProductID"
     ReadOnly="True" />
    <asp:BoundField DataField="ProductName" HeaderText="ProductName" />
    <asp:BoundField DataField="SupplierID" HeaderText="SupplierID" />
    <asp:BoundField DataField="CategoryID" HeaderText="CategoryID" />
    <asp:BoundField DataField="QuantityPerUnit" HeaderText="QuantityPerUnit" />
    <asp:BoundField DataField="UnitPrice" HeaderText="UnitPrice" />
    <asp:BoundField DataField="UnitsInStock" HeaderText="UnitsInStock" />
    <asp:BoundField DataField="UnitsOnOrder" HeaderText="UnitsOnOrder" />
    <asp:BoundField DataField="ReorderLevel" HeaderText="ReorderLevel" />
    <asp:CheckBoxField DataField="Discontinued" HeaderText="Discontinued" />
  </Fields>
  ...
</asp:DetailsView>
```

You can use the BoundField tag to set properties such as header text, formatting string, editing behavior, and so on (refer to Table 15-2). In addition, you can use the ShowHeader property. When it's false, the header text is left out of the row, and the field data takes up both cells.

■ **Tip** Rather than coding each field by hand, you can use the same shortcut you used with the GridView. Simply select the control at design time, and select Refresh Schema from the smart tag.

The field model isn't the only part of the GridView that the DetailsView control adopts. It also uses a similar set of styles, a similar set of events, and a similar editing model. The only difference is that instead of creating a dedicated column for editing controls, you simply set Boolean properties such as AutoGenerateDeleteButton, AutoGenerateEditButton, and AutoGenerateInsertButton. The links for these tasks are added to the bottom of the DetailsView. When you add or edit a record, the DetailsView always uses standard text box controls such as the GridView (see Figure 15-18). For more editing flexibility, you'll want to use the FormView control.

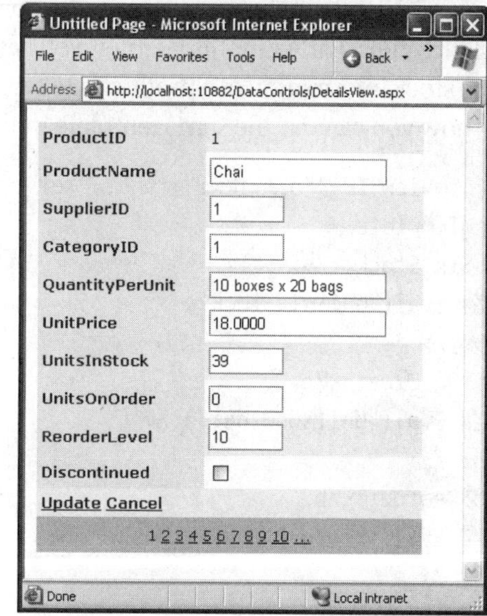

Figure 15-18. *Editing in the DetailsView*

The FormView

If you need the ultimate flexibility of templates, the FormView provides a template-only control for displaying and editing a single record.

The beauty of the FormView template model is that it matches the model of the TemplateField in the GridView quite closely. This means you can work with the following templates:

- ItemTemplate
- EditItemTemplate
- InsertItemTemplate
- FooterTemplate
- HeaderTemplate
- EmptyDataTemplate
- PagerTemplate

You can use the same template content you use with a TemplateField in a GridView in the FormView. Earlier in this chapter, you saw how you can use a template field to combine the stock information of a product into one column (shown in the earlier Figure 15-12). Here's how you can use the same template in the FormView:

```
<asp:FormView ID="FormView1" runat="server" DataSourceID="sourceProducts">
  <ItemTemplate>
    <b>In Stock:</b>
    <%# Eval("UnitsInStock") %>
    <br />
    <b>On Order:</b>
    <%# Eval("UnitsOnOrder") %>
    <br />
    <b>Reorder:</b>
    <%# Eval("ReorderLevel") %>
    <br />
  </ItemTemplate>
</asp:FormView>
```

Like the DetailsView, the FormView can show only a single record at a time. (If the data source has more than one record, you'll see only the first one.) You can deal with this issue by setting the AllowPaging property to true so that paging links are automatically created. These links allow the user to move from one record to the next, as in the previous example with the DetailsView.

Another option is to bind to a data source that returns just one record. Figure 15-19 shows an example where a drop-down list control lets you choose a product, and a second data source shows the matching record in the FormView control. The FormView uses the template from the previous example (it's the shaded region on the page).

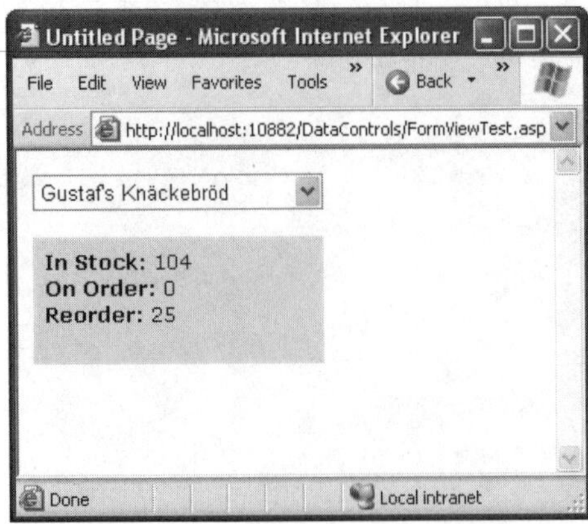

Figure 15-19. *A FormView that shows a single record*

■ **Note** If you want to support editing with the FormView, you need to add button controls that trigger the edit and update processes, as described in the "Editing with a Template" section.

The Last Word

In this chapter, you considered everything you need to build rich data-bound pages. You took a detailed tour of the GridView and considered its support for formatting, selecting, sorting, paging, using templates, and editing. You also considered the DetailsView and FormView, which allow you to display and edit individual records. Using these three controls, you can build all-in-one pages that display and edit data, without needing to write pages of ADO.NET code. Best of all, every data control is thoroughly configurable, which means you can tailor it to fit just about any web application.

CHAPTER 16

■ ■ ■

Files and Streams

You examined ADO.NET before considering simpler data access techniques such as writing and reading to ordinary files for good reason. Traditional file access is generally much less useful in a web application than it is in a desktop program. Databases, on the other hand, are designed from the ground up to support a large load of simultaneous users with speed, safety, and efficiency. Most web applications will rely on a database for some features, but many won't have any use for straight file access.

Of course, enterprising ASP.NET developers can find a use for almost any technology. If this book didn't cover file access, no doubt many developers would be frustrated when they designed web applications with legitimate (and innovative) uses for ordinary files. In fact, file access is so easy and straightforward in .NET that it may be perfect for simple, small-scale solutions that don't need a full external database.

This chapter explains how you can use the input/output classes in .NET to read and change file system information and even build a simple file browser. You'll also learn how to create simple text and binary files of your own. Finally, you'll consider how you can allow users to upload their own files to your web server.

Files and Web Applications

Why is it that most web applications don't use files? There are several limitations to files:

File naming limitations: Every file you create needs to have a unique name (or it will overwrite another file). Unfortunately, no easy way exists to ensure that a file's name is unique. Although relational databases provide an auto-increment data type that automatically fills the field with a unique number when you create the record, files have no such niceties. Usually, you need to let the user specify the file name or fall back on some random number system. For example, you might create a file name based on a random number combined with the current date and time or create a file name that uses a GUID (globally unique identifier). With both of these approaches, file names would be statistically unique, which means duplicates would be extremely unlikely.

Multiuser limitations: As you've seen in the ADO.NET chapters, relational databases provide features to manage locking, inconsistent updates, and transactions. Comparatively, the web server's file system is woefully backward. Although you can allow multiple users to read a file at once, it's almost impossible to let multiple users update the same file at the same time without catastrophe.

Scalability problems: File operations suffer from some overhead. In a simple scenario, file access may be faster than connecting to a database and performing a query. But when multiple users are working with files at the same time, these advantages disappear, and your web server may slow down dramatically.

Security risks: If you allow the user to specify a file or path name, the user could devise a way to trick your application into accessing or overwriting a protected system file. Even without this ability, a malicious or careless user might use an ASP.NET page that creates or uploads files to fill up your web server hard drive and cause it to stop working.

Of course, file access does have its uses. Maybe you need to access information that's already stored in a specific file and directory structure by another application (and you can't change that organization). Or maybe you don't have a local database, and you need to create only a small internal application (such as one hosted on an intranet). In this situation, you may be able to assume a smaller number of simultaneous users, as well as a set of trusted users who are less likely to try to battle your web server.

File System Information

Many of the considerations mentioned previously apply to web applications that create their own files. However, the simplest level of file access just involves retrieving information about existing files and directories and performing typical file system operations such as copying files and creating directories.

ASP.NET provides five basic classes for retrieving this sort of information. They are all located in the System.IO namespace (and, incidentally, can be used in desktop applications in exactly the same way they are used in web applications).

- The Directory and File classes provide static methods that allow you to retrieve information about any files and directories visible from your server.
- The DirectoryInfo and FileInfo classes use similar instance methods and properties to retrieve the same sort of information.
- The DriveInfo class provides static methods that allow you to retrieve information about a drive and the amount of free space it provides.

In Chapter 3, you saw how a class can provide two types of members. Static members are always available—you just use the name of the class. To access an instance member, you need to create an object first and then access the property or method through the object's variable name.

With the file access classes, static methods are more convenient to use because they don't require you to create an instance of the class. On the other hand, if you need to retrieve several pieces of information, it's easier to use an instance of the class. That way, you don't need to keep specifying the name of the directory or file each time you call a method. It's also faster. That's because the FileInfo and DirectoryInfo classes perform their security checks once—when you create the object instance. The Directory and File classes perform a security check every time you invoke a method.

The Directory and File Classes

The Directory and File classes provide a number of useful methods. Table 16-1 and Table 16-2 tell the whole story. Note that every method takes the same parameter: a fully qualified path name identifying the directory or file you want the operation to act on. A few methods, such as Delete(), have optional parameters.

Table 16-1. *Directory Class Members*

Method	Description
CreateDirectory()	Creates a new directory. If you specify a directory inside another nonexistent directory, ASP.NET will thoughtfully create *all* the required directories.
Delete()	Deletes the corresponding empty directory. To delete a directory along with its contents (subdirectories and files), add the optional second parameter of true.
Exists()	Returns true or false to indicate whether the specified directory exists.
GetCreationTime(), GetLastAccessTime(), and GetLastWriteTime()	Returns a DateTime object that represents the time the directory was created, accessed, or written to. Each "Get" method has a corresponding "Set" method, which isn't shown in this table.
GetDirectories(), GetFiles(), and GetLogicalDrives()	Returns an array of strings, one for each subdirectory, file, or drive in the specified directory (depending on which method you're using). This method can accept a second parameter that specifies a search expression (such as ASP*.*). Drive letters are in this format: c:\.
GetParent()	Parses the supplied directory string and tells you what the parent directory is. You could do this on your own by searching for the \ character (or, more generically, the Path.DirectorySeparatorChar), but this function makes life a little easier.

Continued

Table 16-1. *Continued*

Method	Description
GetCurrentDirectory() and SetCurrentDirectory()	Allows you to set and retrieve the current directory, which is useful if you need to use relative paths instead of full paths. Generally, these functions shouldn't be relied on and aren't necessary.
Move()	Accepts two parameters: the source path and the destination path. The directory and all its contents can be moved to any path, as long as it's located on the same drive.
GetAccessControl()	Returns a System.Security.AccessControl.DirectorySecurity object. You can use this object to examine the Windows ACLs (access control lists) that are applied to this directory and even change them programmatically.

Table 16-2. *File Class Members*

Method	Description
Copy()	Accepts two parameters: the fully qualified source file name and the fully qualified destination file name. To allow overwriting, use the version that takes a Boolean third parameter and set it to true.
Delete()	Deletes the specified file but doesn't throw an exception if the file can't be found.
Exists()	Indicates true or false whether a specified file exists.
GetAttributes() and SetAttributes()	Retrieves or sets an enumerated value that can include any combination of the values from the FileAttributes enumeration.
GetCreationTime(), GetLastAccessTime(), and GetLastWriteTime()	Returns a DateTime object that represents the time the file was created, accessed, or last written to. Each "Get" method has a corresponding "Set" method, which isn't shown in this table.
Move()	Accepts two parameters: the fully qualified source file name and the fully qualified destination file name. You can move a file across drives and even rename it while you move it (or rename it without moving it).
GetAccessControl()	Returns a System.Security.AccessControl.DirectorySecurity object. You can use this object to examine the Windows ACLs that are applied to this file and even change them programmatically.

The File class also includes some methods that allow you to create and open files as streams. You'll explore these features in the "Reading and Writing with Streams" section. The only feature the File class lacks (and the FileInfo class provides) is the ability to retrieve the size of a specified file.

The File and Directory methods are completely intuitive. For example, consider the code for a simple page that displays some information about the files in a specific directory. You might use this code to create a simple admin page that allows you to review the contents of an FTP directory (see Figure 16-1). Clients could use this page to review their documents and remove suspicious files.

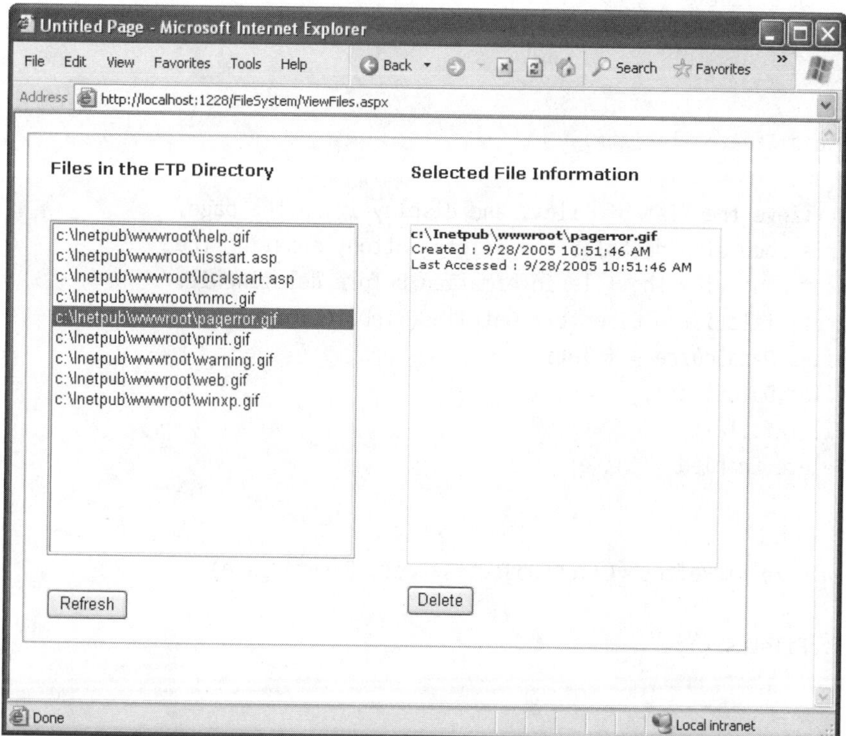

Figure 16-1. *An admin page with file information*

Begin by importing the namespace that has the IO classes:

```
using System.IO;
```

The code for this page is as follows:

```
public partial class ViewFiles : Page
{
    private string ftpDirectory = @"c:\Inetpub\wwwroot";

    protected void Page_Load(Object sender, EventArgs e)
    {
        if (!this.IsPostBack)
        {
            CreateFileList();
        }
    }

    private void CreateFileList()
    {
        // Retrieve the list of files, and display it in the page.
        // This code also disables the delete button, ensuring the
        // user must view the file information before deleting it.
        string[] fileList = Directory.GetFiles(ftpDirectory);
        lstFiles.DataSource = fileList;
        lstFiles.DataBind();
        lblFileInfo.Text = "";
        cmdDelete.Enabled = false;
    }

    protected void cmdRefresh_Click(Object sender, EventArgs e)
    {
        CreateFileList();
    }

    protected void lstFiles_SelectedIndexChanged(Object sender,
      EventArgs e)
    {
        // Display the selected file information.
        // Use the StringBuilder for the fastest way to build the string
        // that will be displayed.
```

```
        StringBuilder displayText = new StringBuilder();
        string fileName = lstFiles.SelectedItem.Text;
        displayText.Append("<b>");
        displayText.Append(fileName);
        displayText.Append("</b><br />Created : ");
        displayText.Append(File.GetCreationTime(fileName).ToString());
        displayText.Append("<br />Last Accessed : ");
        displayText.Append(File.GetLastAccessTime(fileName).ToString());
        displayText.Append("<br />");

        // Show attribute information. GetAttributes() can return a combination
        // of enumerated values, so you need to evaluate it with the
        // bitwise and (&) operator.
        FileAttributes attributes = File.GetAttributes(fileName);
        if ((attributes & FileAttributes.Hidden) == FileAttributes.Hidden)
        {
            displayText.Append("This is a hidden file.<br />");
        }
        if ((attributes & FileAttributes.ReadOnly) == FileAttributes.ReadOnly)
        {
            displayText.Append("This is a read-only file.<br />");
            cmdDelete.Enabled = false;
        }
        else
        {
            cmdDelete.Enabled = true;
        }

        // Show the generated text in a label.
        lblFileInfo.Text = displayText.ToString();
    }

    protected void cmdDelete_Click(Object sender, EventArgs e)
    {
        File.Delete(lstFiles.SelectedItem.Text);
        CreateFileList();
    }
}
```

Dissecting the Code...

- The string with the file path c:\Inetpub\wwwroot is preceded by a special at sign (@) character. This tells C# to interpret the string exactly as written. Without this character, C# would assume the directory separation character (\) indicates the start of a special character sequence. Another option is to use the special character sequence \\, which C# reads as a single literal slash. In this case, the path would become c:\\Inetpub\\wwwroot.

- The CreateFileList() procedure is easy to code, because it uses the data binding feature of the ListBox. The array returned from the GetFiles() methods can be attached to the list with no extra code.

- When the user chooses an item in the list, the control posts the page back immediately and allows your code to refresh the file information.

- When evaluating the FileAttributes enumeration, you need to use the & operator to perform *bitwise arithmetic*. This is because the value returned from GetAttributes() can actually contain a combination of more than one attribute.

- The code that gets the file information builds a long string of text, which is then displayed in a label. For optimum performance, the System.Text.StringBuilder is used. Without the StringBuilder, every time you added a piece of text to the string, you would be creating a new string object, which takes longer.

- The code that displays file information could benefit from a switch to the FileInfo class (as shown in the next section) . As it is, every method needs to specify the file, which requires a separate security check.

One ingredient this code lacks is error handling. It's always a good idea to wrap your file access code in a try/catch block, in case the file isn't accessible or the account running the code doesn't have the required permissions to access the file. When you're testing your application in Visual Studio, you're unlikely to run into file permission errors. However, when you deploy your application, life gets more complicated. As you learned in Chapter 12, in a deployed website ASP.NET runs under an account with carefully limited privileges. (If you're using IIS 5, this is the ASPNET account.) If you attempt to access a file without the required permissions, you'll receive a SecurityException.

To solve problems like these, you can modify the permissions for a file or an entire directory. To do so, right-click the file or directory, select Properties, and choose the Security tab. Here you can add or remove users and groups and configure what operations they're allowed to do. Alternatively, you might find it easier to modify the account ASP.NET uses. For more information, refer to Chapter 12, which explains how to configure the account used for ASP.NET applications.

The DirectoryInfo and FileInfo Classes

The DirectoryInfo and FileInfo classes mirror the functionality in the Directory and File classes. In addition, they make it easy to walk through directory and file relationships. For example, you can easily retrieve the FileInfo objects of files in a directory represented by a DirectoryInfo object.

Note that while the Directory and File classes expose only methods, DirectoryInfo and FileInfo provide a combination of properties and methods. For example, while the File class had separate GetAttributes and SetAttributes methods, the FileInfo class exposes a read-write Attributes property.

Another nice thing about the DirectoryInfo and FileInfo classes is that they share a common set of properties and methods because they derive from the common FileSystemInfo base class. Table 16-3 describes the members they have in common.

Table 16-3. *DirectoryInfo and FileInfo Members*

Member	Description
Attributes	Allows you to retrieve or set attributes using a combination of values from the FileAttributes enumeration.
CreationTime, LastAccessTime, and LastWriteTime	Allows you to set or retrieve the creation time, last-access time, and last-write time using a DateTime object.
Exists	Returns true or false depending on whether the file or directory exists. In other words, you can create FileInfo and DirectoryInfo objects that don't actually correspond to current physical directories, although you obviously won't be able to use properties such as CreationTime and methods such as MoveTo().
FullName, Name, and Extension	Returns a string that represents the fully qualified name, the directory or file name (with extension), or the extension on its own, depending on which property you use.
Delete()	Removes the file or directory, if it exists. When deleting a directory, it must be empty, or you must specify an optional parameter set to true.
Refresh()	Updates the object so it's synchronized with any file system changes that have happened in the meantime (for example, if an attribute was changed manually using Windows Explorer).
Create()	Creates the specified directory or file.
MoveTo()	Copies the directory and its contents or the file. For a DirectoryInfo object, you need to specify the new path; for a FileInfo object, you specify a path and file name.

In addition, the FileInfo and DirectoryInfo classes have a couple of unique members, as indicated in Table 16-4 and Table 16-5.

Table 16-4. *Unique DirectoryInfo Members*

Member	Description
Parent and Root	Returns a DirectoryInfo object that represents the parent or root directory.
CreateSubdirectory()	Creates a directory with the specified name in the directory represented by the DirectoryInfo object. It also returns a new DirectoryInfo object that represents the subdirectory.
GetDirectories()	Returns an array of DirectoryInfo objects that represent all the subdirectories contained in this directory.
GetFiles()	Returns an array of FileInfo objects that represent all the files contained in this directory.

Table 16-5. *Unique FileInfo Members*

Member	Description
Directory	Returns a DirectoryInfo object that represents the parent directory.
DirectoryName	Returns a string that identifies the name of the parent directory.
Length	Returns a Long with the file size in bytes.
CopyTo()	Copies a file to the new path and file name specified as a parameter. It also returns a new FileInfo object that represents the new (copied) file. You can supply an optional additional parameter of true to allow overwriting.

When you create a DirectoryInfo or FileInfo object, you specify the full path in the constructor:

```
DirectoryInfo myDirectory = new DirectoryInfo(@"c:\Temp");
FileInfo myFile = new FileInfo(@"c:\Temp\readme.txt");
```

This path may or may not correspond to a real physical file or directory. If it doesn't, you can always use the Create() method to create the corresponding file or directory:

```
// Define the new directory and file.
DirectoryInfo myDirectory = new DirectoryInfo(@"c:\Temp\Test");
FileInfo myFile = new FileInfo(@"c:\Temp\Test\readme.txt");

// Now create them. Order here is important.
// You can't create a file in a directory that doesn't exist yet.
myDirectory.Create();
myFile.Create();
```

The DriveInfo Class

The DriveInfo class allows you to retrieve information about a drive on your computer. Just a few pieces of information will interest you—typically, the DriveInfo class is merely used to retrieve the total amount of used and free space.

Table 16-6 shows the DriveInfo members. Unlike the FileInfo and DriveInfo classes, no Drive class provides instance versions of these methods.

Table 16-6. *DriveInfo Members*

Member	Description
TotalSize	Gets the total size of the drive, in bytes. This includes allocated and free space.
TotalFreeSpace	Gets the total amount of free space, in bytes.
AvailableFreeSpace	Gets the total amount of available free space, in bytes. Available space may be less than the total free space if you've applied disk quotas limiting the space the ASP.NET process can use.
DriveFormat	Returns the name of the file system used on the drive (such as NTFS or FAT32).
DriveType	Returns a value from the DriveType enumeration, which indicates whether the drive is a Fixed, Network, CDRom, Ram, or Removable drive (or Unknown if the drive's type cannot be determined).
IsReady	Returns whether the drive is ready for reading or writing operations. Removable drives are considered "not ready" if they don't have any media. For example, if there's no CD in a CD drive, IsReady will return false. In this situation, it's not safe to query the other DriveInfo properties. Fixed drives are always read.
Name	Returns the drive letter name of the drive (such as C: or E:).
VolumeLabel	Returns the descriptive volume label for the drive. In an NTFS-formatted drive, the volume label can be up to 32 characters. If not set, this property returns null.
RootDirectory	Returns a DirectoryInfo object for the root directory in this drive.
GetDrives()	Retrieves an array of DriveInfo objects, representing all the logical drives on the current computer.

■ **Tip** Attempting to read from a drive that's not ready (for example, a CD drive that doesn't currently have a CD in it) will throw an exception. To avoid this problem, check the DriveInfo.IsReady property, and attempt to read other properties only if it returns true.

A Sample File Browser

You can use methods such as DirectoryInfo.GetFiles() and DirectoryInfo.GetDirectories() to create a simple file browser. Be warned that although this code is a good example of how to use the DirectoryInfo and FileInfo classes, it isn't a good example of security. Generally, you wouldn't want a user to find out so much information about the files on your web server.

The sample file browser program allows the user to see information about any file in any directory in the current drive, as shown in Figure 16-2.

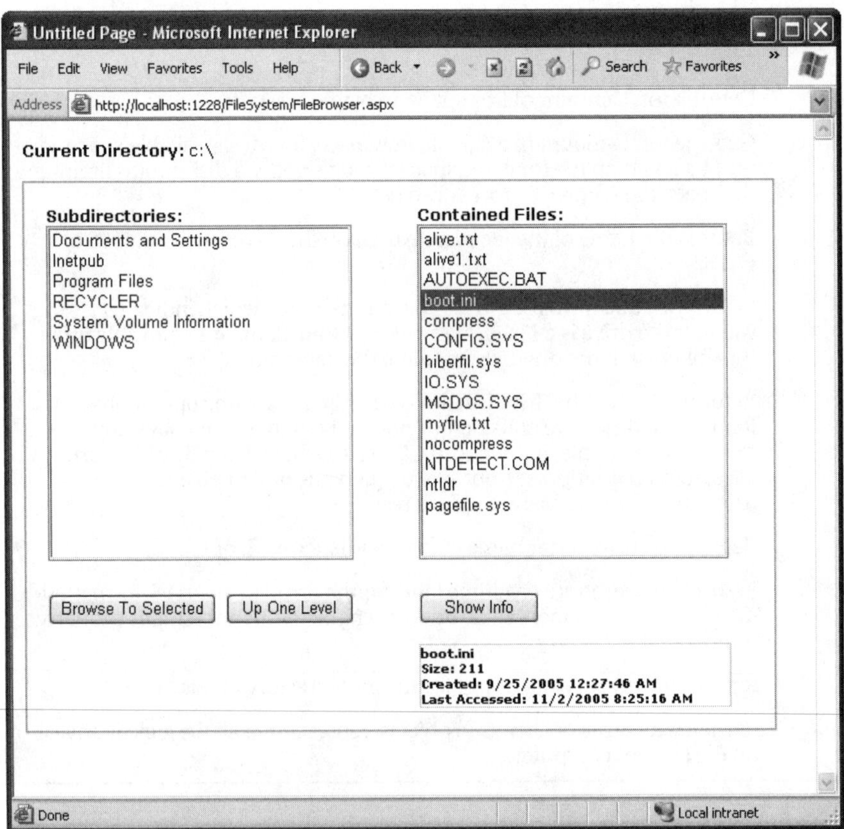

Figure 16-2. *A web server file browser*

The code for the file browser page is as follows:

```
public partial class FileBrowser : Page
{
    protected void Page_Load(object sender, EventArgs e)
    {
        if (!this.IsPostBack)
        {
            string startingDir = @"c:\";
            lblCurrentDir.Text = startingDir;
            ShowFilesIn(startingDir);
            ShowDirectoriesIn(startingDir);
        }
    }

    private void ShowFilesIn(string dir)
    {
        DirectoryInfo dirInfo = new DirectoryInfo(dir);

        lstFiles.Items.Clear();
        foreach (FileInfo fileItem in dirInfo.GetFiles())
        {
            lstFiles.Items.Add(fileItem.Name);
        }
    }

    private void ShowDirectoriesIn(string dir)
    {
        DirectoryInfo dirInfo = new DirectoryInfo(dir);

        lstDirs.Items.Clear();
        foreach (DirectoryInfo dirItem in dirInfo.GetDirectories())
        {
            lstDirs.Items.Add(dirItem.Name);
        }
    }
```

```
protected void cmdBrowse_Click(Object sender, EventArgs e)
{
    // Browse to the currently selected subdirectory.
    if (lstDirs.SelectedIndex != -1)
    {
        string newDir = Path.Combine(lblCurrentDir.Text,
          lstDirs.SelectedItem.Text);
        lblCurrentDir.Text = newDir;
        ShowFilesIn(newDir);
        ShowDirectoriesIn(newDir);
    }
}

protected void cmdParent_Click(object sender, EventArgs e)
{
    // Browse up to the current directory's parent.
    // The Directory.GetParent() method helps us out.
    if (Directory.GetParent(lblCurrentDir.Text) == null)
    {
        // This is the root directory; there are no more levels.
    }
    else
    {
        string newDir = Directory.GetParent(lblCurrentDir.Text).FullName;
        lblCurrentDir.Text = newDir;
        ShowFilesIn(newDir);
        ShowDirectoriesIn(newDir);
    }
}

protected void cmdShowInfo_Click(object sender, EventArgs e)
{
    // Show information for the currently selected file.
    if (lstFiles.SelectedIndex != -1)
    {
        string fileName = Path.Combine(lblCurrentDir.Text,
          lstFiles.SelectedItem.Text);
        FileInfo selFile = new FileInfo(fileName);
```

```
            StringBuilder displayText = new StringBuilder();
            displayText.Append("<b>");
            displayText.Append(selFile.Name);
            displayText.Append("</b><br />Size: ");
            displayText.Append(selFile.Length);
            displayText.Append("<br />");
            displayText.Append("Created: ");
            displayText.Append(selFile.CreationTime.ToString());
            displayText.Append("<br />Last Accessed: ");
            displayText.Append(selFile.LastAccessTime.ToString());
            lblFileInfo.Text = displayText.ToString();
        }
    }
}
```

Dissecting the Code...

- The list controls in this example don't post back immediately. Instead, the web page relies on the Browse to Selected and Show Info buttons.
- By default, directory names don't end with a trailing backslash (\) character. (For example, c:\Temp is used instead of c:\Temp\.) However, when referring to the root drive, a slash is required. This is because only c:\ refers to the root drive; c: refers to the current directory, whatever it may be. This can cause problems when you're manipulating strings that contain file names, because you don't want to add an extra trailing slash to a path (as in the invalid path c:\\myfile.txt). To solve this problem, the page uses the dedicated Path class in the System.IO namespace, which provides a static Combine() method that correctly joins any file and path name together.
- The ShowFilesIn() and ShowDirectoriesIn() subroutines loop through the file and directory collections to build the lists. Another approach is to use data binding instead, as shown in the following code sample. Just remember that when you bind a collection of objects, you need to specify which property will be used for the list. In this case, it's the DirectoryInfo.Name or FileInfo.Name property.

```
// Another way to fill lstFiles.
lstFiles.DataSource = DirInfo.GetFiles();
lstFiles.DataMember = "Name";
lstFiles.DataBind();
```

Reading and Writing with Streams

The .NET Framework makes it easy to create simple "flat" files in text or binary format. Unlike a database, these files don't have any internal structure (that's why they're called *flat*). Instead, these files are really just a list of whatever information you want.

Text Files

You can write to a file and read from a file using a StreamWriter and a StreamReader—dedicated classes that abstract away the process of file interaction. There really isn't much to it. You can create the StreamWriter and StreamReader classes on your own, or you can use one of the helpful static methods included in the File class, such as CreateText() or OpenText().

Here's an example that gets a StreamWriter for writing data to the file c:\myfile.txt:

```
// Define a StreamWriter (which is designed for writing text files).
StreamWriter w;

// Create the file, and get a StreamWriter for it.
w = File.CreateText(@"c:\myfile.txt");
```

Once you have the StreamWriter, you can use the WriteLine() method to add information to the file. The WriteLine method is overloaded so it can write many simple data types, including strings, integers, and other numbers. These values are essentially all converted into strings when they're written to a file and must be converted back into the appropriate types manually when you read the file.

```
w.WriteLine("This file generated by ASP.NET");  // Write a string.
w.WriteLine(42);                                // Write a number.
```

When you finish with the file, you must make sure to close it. Otherwise, the changes may not be properly written to disk, and the file could be locked open. At any time, you can also call the Flush() method to make sure all data is written to disk, as the StreamWriter will perform some in-memory caching to optimize performance.

```
// Tidy up.
w.Flush();
w.Close();
```

Finally, it's always a good idea to look at what you wrote in Notepad while debugging an application that writes to files. Figure 16-3 shows the contents that are created in c:\myfile.txt with the simple code you've considered.

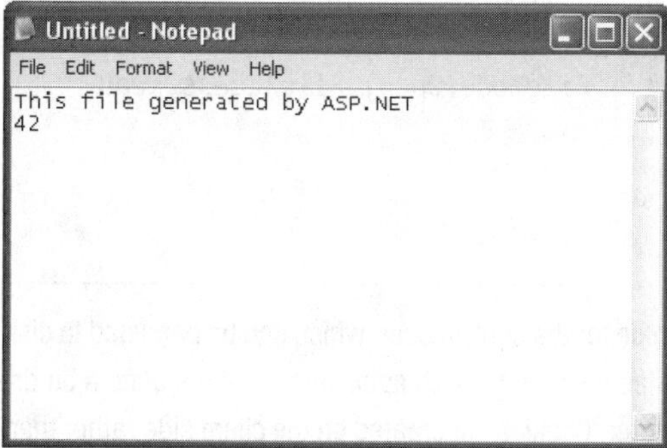

Figure 16-3. *A sample text file*

To read the information, you use the corresponding StreamReader class. It provides a ReadLine() method that gets the next available value and returns it as a string. ReadLine() starts at the first line and advances the position to the end of the file, one line at a time.

```
StreamReader r = File.OpenText(@"c:\myfile.txt");
string inputString;
inputString = r.ReadLine();     // = "This file generated by ASP.NET"
InputString = r.ReadLine();     // = "42"
```

ReadLine() returns a null reference when there is no more data in the file. This means you can read all the data in a file using code like this:

```
// Read and display the lines from the file until the end
// of the file is reached.
string line;
do
{
    line = r.ReadLine();
    if (line != null)
    {
        // (Process the line here.)
    }
} while (line != null);
```

The code you've seen so far opens a file in single-user mode. If a second user tries to access the same file at the same time, an exception will occur. You can reduce this problem when opening files using the more generic four-parameter version of the File.Open() method instead of File.OpenText(). You must specify FileShare.Read for the final parameter. Unlike the OpenText() method, the Open() method returns a FileStream object, and you must manually create a StreamReader that wraps it.

Here's the complete code you need to create a multiuser-friendly StreamReader:

```
FileStream fs = File.Open(@"c:\myfile.txt", FileMode.Open, FileAccess.Read,
  FileShare.Read);
StreamReader r = new StreamReader(fs);
```

■Tip In Chapter 9, you saw how you can create a cookie for the current user, which can be persisted to disk as a simple text file. This is probably a more common technique for a web application, but it's quite a bit different from the file access code you've seen in this chapter. Cookies are created on the client side rather than on the server. This means your ASP.NET code may be able to use them on subsequent requests, but they aren't useful for tracking other information you need to retain.

Binary Files

You can also write to a binary file. Binary data uses space more efficiently but also creates files that aren't human-readable. If you open a file in Notepad, you'll see a lot of extended ASCII characters (politely known as *gibberish*).

To open a file for binary writing, you need to create a new BinaryWriter Object. The class constructor accepts a stream, which you can retrieve using the File.OpenWrite() method. Here's the code to open the file c:\binaryfile.bin for binary writing:

```
BinaryWriter w = new BinaryWriter(File.OpenWrite(@"c:\binaryfile.bin"));
```

.NET concentrates on stream objects, rather than the source or destination for the data. This means you can write binary data to any type of stream, whether it represents a file or some other type of storage location, using the same code. In addition, writing to a binary file is almost the same as writing to a text file.

```
string str = "ASP.NET Binary File Test";
int integer = 42;
w.Write(str);
w.Write(integer);

w.Flush();
w.Close();
```

Unfortunately, you need to know the data type you want to retrieve. To retrieve a string, you use the ReadString() method. To retrieve an integer, you must use ReadInt32(). That's why the preceding code example writes variables instead of literal values. If the value 42 were hard-coded as the parameter for the Write() method, it wouldn't be clear if the value would be written as a 16-bit integer, 32-bit integer, decimal, or something else. Unfortunately, you may need to micromanage binary files in this way to prevent errors.

```
BinaryReader r = new BinaryReader(File.OpenRead(@"c:\binaryfile.bin"));
string str;
int integer;
str = r.ReadString();
integer = r.ReatInt32();
```

Once again, if you want to use file sharing, you need to use File.Open() instead of File.OpenRead(). You can then create a BinaryReader by hand, as shown here:

```
FileStream fs = File.Open(@"c:\binaryfile.bin", FileMode.Open, FileAccess.Read,
  FileShare.Read);
BinaryReader r = new BinaryReader(fs);
```

■ **Note** You have no easy way to jump to a location in a text or binary file without reading through all the information in order. Although you can use methods such as Seek() on the underlying stream, you need to specify an offset in bytes, which involves some fairly involved calculations to determine variable sizes. If you need to store a large amount of information and move through it quickly, you need a dedicated database, not a binary file.

Shortcuts for Reading and Writing Files

.NET includes functionality for turbo-charging your file writing and reading. This functionality comes from several static methods in the File class that let you read or write an entire file in a single line of code.

For example, here's a quick code snippet that writes a three-line file and then retrieves it into a single string:

```
string[] lines = new string[]{"This is the first line of the file.",
  "This is the second line of the file.",
  "This is the third line of the file."}
```

```
// Write the file in one shot.
File.WriteAllLines(@"c:\testfile.txt", lines);

// Read the file in one shot (into a variable named content).
string content = File.ReadAllText(@"c:\testfile.txt");
```

Table 16-7 describes the full set of quick file access methods.

Table 16-7. *File Methods for Quick Input/Output*

Method	Description
ReadAllText()	Reads the entire contents of a file and returns it as a single string.
ReadAllLines	Reads the entire contents of a file and returns it as an array of strings, one for each line.
ReadAllBytes	Reads the entire file and returns its contents as an array of bytes.
WriteAllText	Creates a file, writes a supplied string to the file, and closes it. If the file already exists, it is overwritten.
WriteAllLines	Creates a file, writes a supplied array of strings to the file (separating each line with a hard return), and closes the file. If the file already exists, it is overwritten.
WriteAllBytes	Creates a file, writes a supplied bytes array to the file, and closes it. If the file already exists, it is overwritten.

The quick file access methods are certainly convenient for creating small files. They also ensure a file is kept only for as short a time as possible, which is always the best approach to minimize concurrency problems. But are they really practical? It all depends on the size of the file. If you have a large file (say, one that's several megabytes), reading the entire content into memory at once is a terrible idea. It's much better to read one piece of data at a time and process the information bit by bit. Even if you're dealing with medium-sized files (say, several hundreds of kilobytes), you might want to steer clear of the quick file access methods. That's because in a popular website you might have multiple requests dealing with files at the same time, and the combined overhead of keeping every user's file data in memory might reduce the performance of your application.

A Simple Guest Book

The next example demonstrates the file access techniques described in the previous sections to create a simple guest book. The page actually has two parts. If there are no current guest entries, the client will see only the controls for adding a new entry, as shown in Figure 16-4.

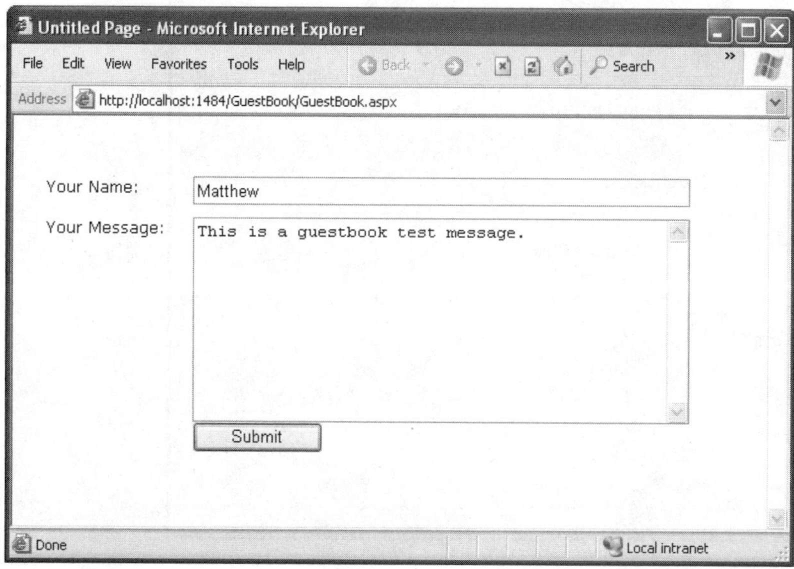

Figure 16-4. *The initial guest book page*

When the user clicks Submit, a file will be created for the new guest book entry. As long as at least one guest book entry exists, a GridView control will appear at the top of the page, as shown in Figure 16-5.

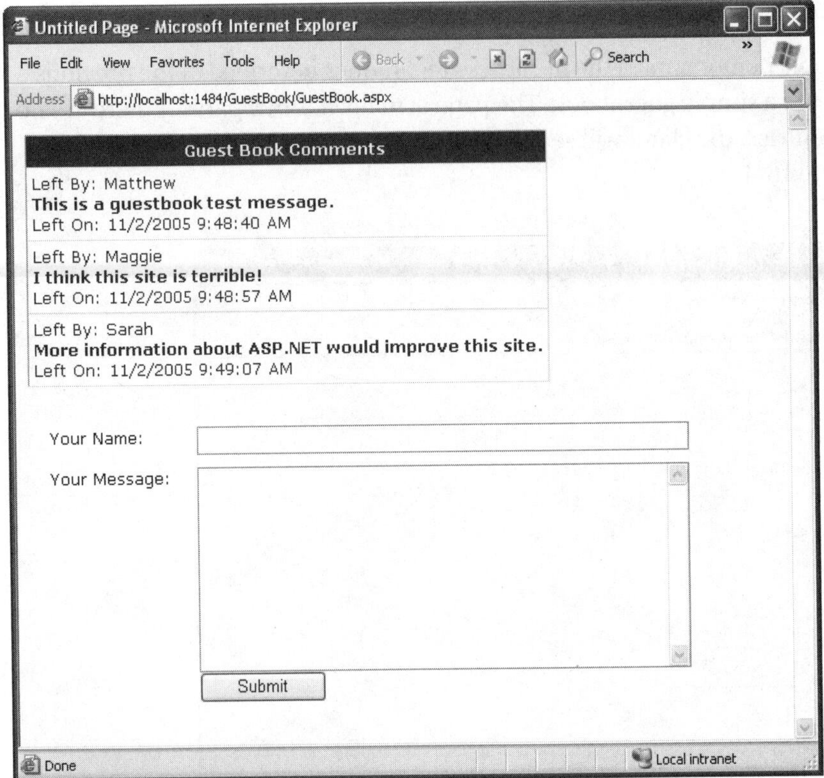

Figure 16-5. *The full guest book page*

The GridView that represents the guest book is constructed using data binding, which you explored in Chapters 14 and 15. Technically speaking, the GridView is bound to a collection that contains instances of the BookEntry class. The BookEntry class definition is included in the code-behind file for the web page and looks like this:

```
public class BookEntry
{
    private string author;
    public string Author
    {
        get { return author; }
        set { author = value; }
    }
```

```
    private DateTime submitted;
    public DateTime Submitted
    {
        get { return submitted; }
        set { submitted = value; }
    }

    private string message;
    public string Message
    {
        get { return message; }
        set { message = value; }
    }
}
```

The GridView uses a single template column, which fishes out the values it needs to display. Here's what the template looks like:

```
<ItemTemplate>
    Left By:
    <%# Eval("Author") %>
    <br />
    <b><%# Eval("Message") %></b>
    <br />
    Left On:
    <%# Eval("Submitted") %>
</ItemTemplate>
```

It also adds some style information that isn't included here, because it isn't necessary to understand the logic of the program. In fact, these styles were applied in Visual Studio using the GridView's Auto Format feature.

As for the entries, the guest book page uses a special directory (GuestBook) to store a collection of files. Each file represents a separate entry in the guest book. A better approach would usually be to create a GuestBook table in a database and make each entry a separate record.

The code for the web page is as follows:

```
public partial class GuestBook : Page
{
    private string guestBookName;
```

```
protected void Page_Load(Object sender, EventArgs e)
{
    guestBookName = Server.MapPath("GuestBook");

    if (!this.IsPostBack)
    {
        GuestBookList.DataSource = GetAllEntries();
        GuestBookList.DataBind();
    }
}

protected void cmdSubmit_Click(Object sender, EventArgs e)
{
    // Create a new BookEntry object.
    BookEntry newEntry = new BookEntry();
    newEntry.Author = txtName.Text;
    newEntry.Submitted = DateTime.Now;
    newEntry.Message = txtMessage.Text;

    // Let the SaveEntry procedure create the corresponding file.
    SaveEntry(newEntry);

    // Refresh the display.
    GuestBookList.DataSource = GetAllEntries();
    GuestBookList.DataBind();

    txtName.Text = "";
    txtMessage.Text = "";
}

private List<BookEntry> GetAllEntries()
{
    // Return an ArrayList that contains BookEntry objects
    // for each file in the GuestBook directory.
    // This function relies on the GetEntryFromFile function.
    List<BookEntry> entries = new List<BookEntry>();
    DirectoryInfo guestBookDir = new DirectoryInfo(guestBookName);
```

```
        foreach (FileInfo fileItem in guestBookDir.GetFiles())
        {
            entries.Add(GetEntryFromFile(fileItem));
        }
        return entries;
    }

    private BookEntry GetEntryFromFile(FileInfo entryFile)
    {
        // Turn the file information into a Book Entry object.
        BookEntry newEntry = new BookEntry();
        StreamReader r = entryFile.OpenText();
        newEntry.Author = r.ReadLine();
        newEntry.Submitted = DateTime.Parse(r.ReadLine());
        newEntry.Message = r.ReadLine();
        r.Close();

        return newEntry;
    }

    private void SaveEntry(BookEntry entry)
    {
        // Create a new file for this entry, with a file name that should
        // be statistically unique.
        Random random = new Random();
        string fileName = guestBookName + @"\";
        fileName += DateTime.Now.Ticks.ToString() + random.Next(100).ToString();
        FileInfo newFile = new FileInfo(fileName);
        StreamWriter w = newFile.CreateText();

        // Write the information to the file.
        w.WriteLine(entry.Author);
        w.WriteLine(entry.Submitted.ToString());
        w.WriteLine(entry.Message);
        w.Flush();
        w.Close();
    }
}
```

Dissecting the Code...

- The code uses text files so that you can easily review the information on your own with Notepad. You could use binary files just as easily, which would save a small amount of space.
- The file name for each entry is generated using a combination of the current date and time (in ticks) and a random number. Practically speaking, this makes it impossible for a file to be generated with a duplicate file name.
- This program doesn't use any error handling, which is an obvious limitation. Whenever you try to access a file, you should use a try/catch block, because all kinds of unexpected events can occur and cause problems.
- Careful design makes sure this program isolates file writing and reading code in separate functions, such as SaveEntry(), GetAllEntries(), and GetEntryFromFile(). For even better organization, you could move these routines in a separate class or even a separate component. This would allow you to use the ObjectDataSource to reduce your data binding code. For more information, read Chapter 24.

Allowing File Uploads

Although you've seen detailed examples about how to work with files and directories on the web server, you haven't yet considered the question of how to allow file uploads. The problem with file uploading is that you need some way to retrieve information from the client—and as you already know, all ASP.NET code executes on the server.

Fortunately, ASP.NET includes a control that allows website users to upload files to the web server. Once the web server receives the posted file data, it's up to your application to examine it, ignore it, or save it to a back-end database or a file on the web server. The FileUpload control does this work, and it represents the <input type="file"> HTML tag.

Declaring the FileUpload control is easy. It doesn't expose any new properties or events you can use through the control tag.

```
<asp:FileUpload ID="Uploader" runat="server" />
```

The <input type="file"> tag doesn't give you much choice as far as user interface is concerned (it's limited to a text box that contains a file name and a Browse button). When the user clicks Browse, the browser presents an Open dialog box and allows the user to choose a file. This part is hard-wired into the browser, and you can't change this behavior. Once the user selects a file, the file name is filled into the corresponding text box. However, the file isn't uploaded yet—that happens later, when the page is posted back. At this point, all the data from all input controls (including the file data) is sent to the server. For that reason, it's common to add a button to post back the page.

To get information about the posted file content, you can access the FileUpload.PostedFile object. You can save the content by calling the PostedFile.SaveAs() method:

```
Uploader.PostedFile.SaveAs(@"c:\newfile");
```

ASP.NET also includes an HTML server control that represents the <input type="file"> HTML tag. The only real difference is that the FileUpload control takes care of automatically setting the encoding of the form to multipart/form-data. If you use the HtmlInputFile control, it's up to you to make this change using the enctype attribute of the <form> tag—if you don't, the HtmlInputFile control won't work. That means you need to make sure your form tag has this information:

```
<form id="Form1" enctype="multipart/form-data" runat="server">
  <!-- Server controls go here, including the HtmlInput control. -->
</form>
```

The only real reason you'll use HtmlInputFile is for backward compatibility, because previous versions of ASP.NET didn't include the FileUpload control.

Figure 16-6 shows a complete web page that demonstrates how to upload a user-specified file. This example introduces a twist—it allows the upload of only those files with the extensions .bmp, .gif, and .jpg.

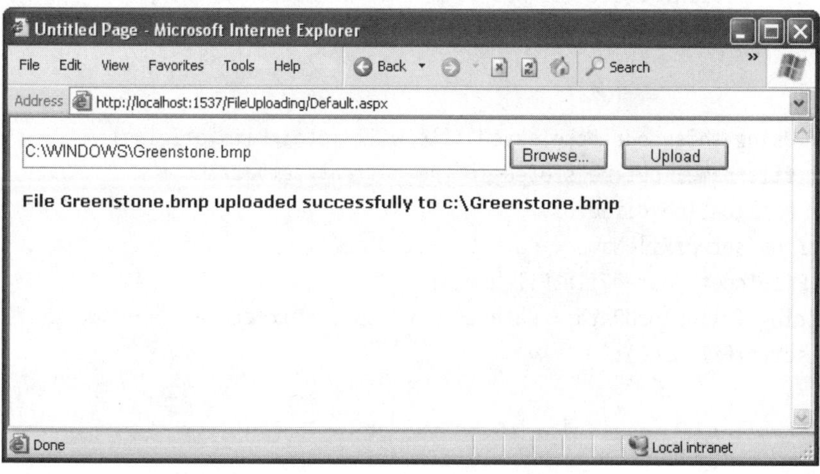

Figure 16-6. *A simple file uploader*

Here's the code for the upload page:

```
public partial class UploadFile : Page
{
    private string uploadDirectory = @"c:\";

    protected void cmdUpload_Click(object sender, EventArgs e)
    {
        // Check that a file is actually being submitted.
        if (FileInput.PostedFile.FileName == "")
        {
            lblInfo.Text = "No file specified.";
        }
        else
        {
            // Check the extension.
            string extension = Path.GetExtension(FileInput.PostedFile.FileName);
            switch (extension.ToLower())
            {
                case ".bmp":
                case ".gif":
                case ".jpg":
                    break;
                default:
                    lblInfo.Text = "This file type is not allowed.";
                    return;
            }

            // Using this code, the saved file will retain its original
            // file name, but be stored in the current server
            // application directory.
            string serverFileName = Path.GetFileName(
              FileInput.PostedFile.FileName);
            string fullUploadPath = Path.Combine(uploadDirectory,
              serverFileName);

            try
            {
                FileInput.PostedFile.SaveAs(fullUploadPath);
```

```
                lblInfo.Text = "File " + serverFileName;
                lblInfo.Text += " uploaded successfully to";
                lblInfo.Text += fullUploadPath;
            }
            catch (Exception err)
            {
                lblInfo.Text = err.Message;
            }
        }
    }
}
```

Dissecting the Code...

- The saved file keeps its original (client-side) name. The code uses the Path.GetFileName() static method to transform the fully qualified name provided by FileUpload.PostedFile.FileName and retrieve just the file, without the path.
- The FileUpload.PostedFile object contains only a few properties. One interesting property is ContentLength, which returns the size of the file in bytes. You could examine this setting and use it to prevent a user from uploading excessively large files.

THE MAXIMUM SIZE OF A FILE UPLOAD

By default, ASP.NET will reject a request that's larger than 4MB. However, you can alter this maximum by modifying the maxRequestLength setting in the web.config file. This sets the largest allowed file in kilobytes. The following sample setting configures the server to accept files up to 8MB:

```
<?xml version="1.0" encoding="utf-8" ?>
<configuration>
  <system.web>
    <!-- Other settings omitted for clarity. -->
    <httpRuntime maxRequestLength="8192"
    />
  </system.web>
</configuration>
```

Be careful, though. When you allow an 8MB upload, your code won't run until that full request has been received. This means a malicious server could cripple your server by sending large request messages to your application. Even if your application ultimately rejects these messages, the ASP.NET worker process threads will still be tied up waiting for the requests to complete. This type of attack is called a *denial-of-service attack*, and the larger your allowed request size is, the more susceptible your website becomes.

The Last Word

Although databases and websites make a perfect fit, nothing is preventing you from using the classes in the .NET Framework to access other types of data, including files. In fact, the code you use to interact with the file system is the same as what you would use in a desktop application or any .NET program. Thanks to the .NET Framework, you can finally solve common programming problems in the same way, regardless of the type of application you're creating.

CHAPTER 17

XML

XML is woven right into the fabric of .NET, and it powers key parts of the ASP.NET technology. In this chapter, you'll learn why XML comes into play in every ASP.NET web application—whether you realize it or not.

You'll also learn how you can create and read XML documents on your own by using the classes of the .NET library. Along the way, you'll sort through some of the near-hysteric XML hype and consider what practical role XML can play in a web application. You may find that ASP.NET's built-in XML support is all you need and decide you don't want to manually create and manipulate XML data. On the other hand, you might want to use the XML classes to communicate with other applications and components, or just as a convenient replacement for simple text files. This chapter assesses all these issues realistically—which is a departure from many of today's ASP.NET articles, seminars, and books. The chapter starts with a whirlwind introduction to XML that explains how it works and why it exists.

XML's Hidden Role in .NET

The most useful place for XML isn't in your web applications but in the infrastructure that supports them. Microsoft has taken this philosophy to heart with ASP.NET. Instead of providing separate components that allow you to add a basic XML parser or similar functionality, ASP.NET uses XML quietly behind the scenes to accomplish a wide range of tasks. If you don't know much about XML yet, the first thing you should realize is that you're already using it.

Configuration Files

ASP.NET stores settings in a human-readable XML format using configuration files such as machine.config and web.config, which were first introduced in Chapter 5. Arguably, a plain-text file could be just as efficient. However, that would force the designers of the ASP.NET platform to create their own proprietary format, which developers would then need to learn. XML provides an all-purpose syntax for storing any data in a customized yet consistent and standardized way using tags. Anyone who understands XML will immediately understand how the ASP.NET configuration files are organized.

ADO.NET Data Access

The ADO.NET DataSet can represent any data as an XML document, without requiring an error-prone conversion step. This has a number of interesting consequences. For example, it allows you to easily save the information you've retrieved from the database in an XML file so you can retrieve it for later use. This feature is particularly useful for client applications that aren't always connected to the network, but you may choose to use it occasionally in a web application.

Web Services

Web services, which are described in Part 5 of this book, are one of the best examples of integrated XML in ASP.NET. To create or use a web service in a .NET program, you don't actually have to understand anything about XML, because the .NET Framework handles all the details for you. However, because web services are built on these accepted standards, other programmers can develop clients for your web services in completely different programming languages, operating systems, and computer platforms with little extra work. In fact, they can even use a competitor's toolkit to create a web service that you can call from a .NET application! Cross-platform programming is clearly one of XML's key selling points.

Anywhere Miscellaneous Data Is Stored

Just when you think you've identified everywhere XML markup is used, you'll find it appearing somewhere new. You'll find XML when you write an advertisement file defining the content for the AdRotator control or when you use .NET serialization to write an object to a file. That these formats use XML probably won't change the way they work, but it does open up other possibilities for integrating the data with other applications and tools. It's also one more example that the developers of the .NET Framework have embraced XML in unprecedented ways, abandoning Microsoft's traditional philosophy of closed standards and proprietary technologies.

XML Explained

The basic premise of XML is fairly simple, although the possible implementations of it (and the numerous extensions to it) can get quite complex. XML is designed as an all-purpose format for organizing data. In many cases, when you decide to use XML, you're deciding to store data in a standardized way, rather than creating your own new (and to other developers, unfamiliar) format conventions. The actual location of this data—in memory, in a file, in a network stream—is irrelevant.

The best way to understand the role XML plays is to consider the evolution of a simple file format *without* XML. For example, consider a simple program that stores product items as a list in a file. Say when you first create this program, you decide it will store three pieces of product information (ID, name, and price), and you'll use a simple text file format for easy debugging and testing. The file format you use looks like this:

```
1
Chair
49.33
2
Car
43399.55
3
Fresh Fruit Basket
49.99
```

This is the sort of format you might create by using .NET classes such as the StreamWriter. It's easy to work with—you just write all the information, in order, from top to bottom. Of course, it's a fairly fragile format. If you decide to store an extra piece of information in the file (such as a flag that indicates whether an item is available), your old code won't work. Instead, you might need to resort to adding a header that indicates the version of the file:

```
SuperProProductList
Version 2.0
1
Chair
49.33
true
2
Car
43399.55
true
3
Fresh Fruit Basket
49.99
false
```

Now, you could check the file version when you open it and use different file reading code appropriately. Unfortunately, as you add more and more possible versions, the file reading code will become incredibly tangled, and you may accidentally break compatibility with one of the earlier file formats without realizing it. A better approach would be to create a file format that indicates where every product record starts and stops. Your code would then just set some appropriate defaults if it finds missing information in an older file format.

Here's a relatively crude solution that improves the SuperProProductList by adding a special sequence of characters (##Start##) to show where each new record begins:

```
SuperProProductList
Version 3.0
##Start##
1
Chair
49.33
true
3
##Start##
2
Car
43399.55
true
3
##Start##
3
Fresh Fruit Basket
49.99
false
4
```

All in all, this isn't a bad effort. Unfortunately, you may as well use the binary file format at this point—the text file is becoming hard to read, and it's even harder to guess what piece of information each value represents. On the code side, you'll also need some basic error checking abilities of your own. For example, you should make your code able to skip over accidentally entered blank lines, detect a missing ##Start## tag, and so on, just to provide a basic level of protection.

The central problem with this homegrown solution is that you're reinventing the wheel. While you're trying to write basic file access code and create a reasonably flexible file format for a simple task, other programmers around the world are creating their own private, ad hoc solutions. Even if your program works fine and you can understand it, other programmers will definitely not find it easy.

Improving the List with XML

This is where XML comes into the picture. XML is an all-purpose way to identify any type of data using tags. These tags use the same sort of format found in an HTML file, but while HTML tags indicate formatting, XML tags indicate content. (Because an XML file is just about data, there is no standardized way to display it in a browser, although Internet Explorer shows a collapsible view that lets you show and hide different portions of the document.)

The SuperProProductList could use the following, clearer XML syntax:

```
<?xml version="1.0"?>
<SuperProProductList>
    <Product>
        <ID>1</ID>
        <Name>Chair</Name>
        <Price>49.33</Price>
        <Available>true</Available>
        <Status>3</Status>
    </Product>
    <Product>
        <ID>2</ID>
        <Name>Car</Name>
        <Price>43399.55</Price>
        <Available>true</Available>
        <Status>3</Status>
    </Product>
    <Product>
        <ID>3</ID>
        <Name>Fresh Fruit Basket</Name>
        <Price>49.99</Price>
        <Available>false</Available>
        <Status>4</Status>
    </Product>
</SuperProProductList>
```

This format is clearly understandable. Every product item is enclosed in a <Product> tag, and every piece of information has its own tag with an appropriate name. Tags are nested several layers deep to show relationships. Essentially, XML provides the basic tag syntax, and you (the programmer) define the tags you want to use. That's why XML is often described as a *metalanguage*—it's a language you use to create your own language. In the SuperProProductList example, this custom XML language defines tags such as <Product>, <ID>, <Name>, and so on.

XML FILES VS. DATABASES

You can perform many tasks with XML—perhaps including some things it was never designed to do. This book is not intended to teach you XML programming but good ASP.NET application design. For most ASP.NET programmers, XML file processing is an ideal replacement for custom file access routines and works best in situations where you need to store a small amount of data for relatively simple tasks.

XML files aren't a good substitute for a database, because they have the same limitations as any other type of file access. In a web application, only a single user can access a file at a time without causing an error, regardless of whether the file contains an XML document or binary content. Database products provide a far richer set of features for managing multiuser concurrency and providing optimized performance. Of course, nothing is stopping you from storing XML data *in* a database, which many database products actively encourage. In fact, the newest versions of leading database products such as SQL Server and Oracle even included extended XML features that support some of the standards you'll see in this chapter.

Best of all, when you read this XML document in most programming languages (including those in the .NET Framework), you can use XML parsers to make your life easier. In other words, you don't need to worry about detecting where a tag starts and stops, collapsing whitespace, and identifying attributes (although you do need to worry about capitalization, because XML is case-sensitive). Instead, you can just read the file into some helpful XML data objects that make navigating the entire document much easier.

XML Basics

Part of XML's popularity is a result of its simplicity. When creating your own XML document, you need to remember only a few rules. The following two considerations apply to both XML and HTML markup:

- Whitespace is ignored, so you can freely use tabs and hard returns to properly align your information. To add a real space, you need to use the   entity equivalent, as in HTML.
- You can use only valid characters. You can't enter special characters, such as the angle brackets (< >) and the ampersand (&), as content. Instead, you'll have to use the entity equivalents (such as < and > for angle brackets, and & for the ampersand). These equivalents are the same as in HTML coding and will be automatically converted to the original characters when you read them into your program with the appropriate .NET classes.

In addition, XML imposes rules not found in ordinary HTML:

- XML tags are case-sensitive, so <ID> and <id> are completely different tags.

- Every start tag must have an end tag, or you must use the special "empty tag" format, which includes a forward slash at the end. For example, you can use <Name>Content</Name> or <Name />, but you cannot use <Name> on its own. This is similar to the syntax for ASP.NET controls.

- All tags must be nested in a root tag. In SuperProProductList example, the root tag is <SuperProProductList>. As soon as the root tag is closed, the document is finished, and you cannot add any more content. In other words, if you omit the <SuperProProductList> tag and start with a <Product> tag, you'll be able to enter information for only one product; this is because as soon as you add the closing </Product>, the document is complete. (HTML has a similar rule and requires that all page content be nested in a root <html> tag, but most browsers let you get away without following this rule.)

- Every tag must be fully enclosed. In other words, when you open a subtag, you need to close it before you can close the parent. <Product><ID></ID></Product> is valid, but <Product><ID></Product></ID> isn't. As a general rule, indent when you open a new tag, because this will allow you to see the document's structure and notice if you accidentally close the wrong tag first.

If you meet these requirements, your XML document can be parsed and displayed as a basic tree. This means your document is well formed, but it doesn't mean it is valid. For example, you may still have your elements in the wrong order (for example, <ID><Product></Product></ID>), or you may have the wrong type of data in a given field (for example, <ID>Chair</ID><Name>2</Name>). You can impose these additional rules on your XML documents, as you'll see later in this chapter when you consider XML schemas.

The combination of an XML starting and ending tag and its data is known as an *element*. These elements are the primary units for organizing information (as demonstrated with the SuperProProductList example), but they aren't the only option. You can also use *attributes*.

■ **Note** XHTML is a new standard that aims to replace HTML with a revised markup language enforcing many of these rules. For the most part, XHTML pages look like HTML pages, but they require closing tags, proper nesting, and so on. They also don't tolerate any deviance from these rules. Although XHTML hasn't yet gained enough widespread standardization in client browsers to replace HTML, you can read about it at `http://www.w3.org/TR/xhtml1`.

Attributes

Attributes add extra information to an element. Instead of putting information into a subelement, you can use an attribute. In the XML community, deciding whether to use subtags or attributes—and what information should go into an attribute—is a matter of great debate, with no clear consensus.

Here's the SuperProProductList example with an ID and Name attribute instead of an ID and Name subtag:

```
<?xml version="1.0"?>
<SuperProProductList>
    <Product ID="1" Name="Chair">
        <Price>49.33</Price>
        <Available>true</Available>
        <Status>3</Status>
    </Product>
    <Product ID="2" Name="Car">
        <Price>43399.55</Price>
        <Available>true</Available>
        <Status>3</Status>
    </Product>
    <Product ID="3" Name="Fresh Fruit Basket">
        <Price>49.99</Price>
        <Available>false</Available>
        <Status>4</Status>
    </Product>
</SuperProProductList>
```

Of course, you've already seen this sort of syntax with HTML tags and ASP.NET server controls:

```
<asp:DropDownList id="lstBackColor" AutoPostBack="true"
  runat="server" Width="194px" Height="22px"/>
```

Attributes are also common in the configuration file:

```
<sessionState mode="Inproc" cookieless="false" timeout="20" />
```

Note that using attributes in XML is more stringent than in HTML. In XML, attributes must always have values, and these values must use quotation marks. For example, <Product Name="Chair" /> is acceptable, but <Product Name=Chair /> or <Product Name /> isn't. (ASP.NET control tags don't need to follow these rules.)

■ **Tip** Order is not important when dealing with attributes. XML parsers treat attributes as a collection of unordered information relating to an element. On the other hand, the order of elements often *is* important. Thus, if you need a way of arranging information and preserving its order, or if you have repeated items with the same name, then use elements, not attributes.

Comments

You can also add comments to an XML document. Comments go just about anywhere and are ignored for data processing purposes. Comments are bracketed by the <!-- and --> character sequences. The following listing includes three valid comments:

```
<?xml version="1.0"?>
<SuperProProductList>
<!-- This is a test file. -->
    <Product ID="1" Name="Chair">
        <Price>49.33<!-- Why so expensive? --></Price>
        <Available>true</Available>
        <Status>3</Status>
    </Product>
    <!-- Other products omitted for clarity. -->
</SuperProProductList>
```

The only place you can't put a tag is embedded within a start or end tag (as in <myData <!-- A comment should not go here --></myData>).

The XML Classes

.NET provides a rich set of classes for XML manipulation in several namespaces that start with System.Xml. One of the most confusing aspects of using XML with .NET is deciding which combination of classes you should use. Many of them provide similar functionality in a slightly different way, optimized for specific scenarios or for compatibility with specific standards.

The majority of the examples you'll explore use the types in the core System.Xml namespace. The classes here allow you to read and write XML files, manipulate XML data in memory, and even validate XML documents.

In this chapter, you'll look at the following options for dealing with XML data:

- Reading and writing XML directly, just like you read and write text files using XmlTextWriter and XmlTextReader
- Dealing with XML as a collection of in-memory objects, such as XmlDocument and XmlNode
- Binding to the XmlDataSource to display XML information with minimum fuss
- Dealing with XML as an interface to relational data using the XmlDataDocument class

The XML TextWriter

One of the simplest ways to create or read any XML document is to use the basic XmlTextWriter and XmlTextReader classes. These classes work like their StreamWriter and StreamReader relatives, except that they write and read XML documents instead of ordinary text files. This means you follow the same process you saw in Chapter 16 for creating a file. First, you create or open the file. Then, you write to it or read from it, moving from top to bottom. Finally, you close it and get to work using the retrieved data in whatever way you'd like.

Before beginning this example, you'll need to import the namespaces for file handling and XML processing:

```
using System.IO;
using System.Xml;
```

Here's an example that creates a simple version of the SuperProProductList document:

```
FileStream fs = new FileStream(@"c:\SuperProProductList.xml",
  FileMode.Create);
XmlTextWriter w = new XmlTextWriter(fs, null);

w.WriteStartDocument();
w.WriteStartElement("SuperProProductList");
w.WriteComment("This file generated by the XmlTextWriter class.");

// Write the first product.
w.WriteStartElement("Product");
w.WriteAttributeString("ID", "", "1");
w.WriteAttributeString("Name", "", "Chair");
```

```
w.WriteStartElement("Price");
w.WriteString("49.33");
w.WriteEndElement();

w.WriteEndElement();

// Write the second product.
w.WriteStartElement("Product");
w.WriteAttributeString("ID", "", "2");
w.WriteAttributeString("Name", "", "Car");

w.WriteStartElement("Price");
w.WriteString("43399.55");

w.WriteEndElement();

w.WriteEndElement();

// Write the third product.
w.WriteStartElement("Product");
w.WriteAttributeString("ID", "", "3");
w.WriteAttributeString("Name", "", "Fresh Fruit Basket");

w.WriteStartElement("Price");
w.WriteString("49.99");
w.WriteEndElement();

w.WriteEndElement();

// Close the root element.
w.WriteEndElement();
w.WriteEndDocument();
w.Close();
```

This code is similar to the code used for writing a basic text file. It does have a few advantages, however. You can close elements quickly and accurately, the angle brackets (< >) are included for you automatically, and some errors (such as closing the root element too soon) are caught automatically, thereby ensuring a well-formed XML document as the final result.

To check that your code worked, open the file in Internet Explorer, which automatically provides a collapsible view for XML documents (see Figure 17-1).

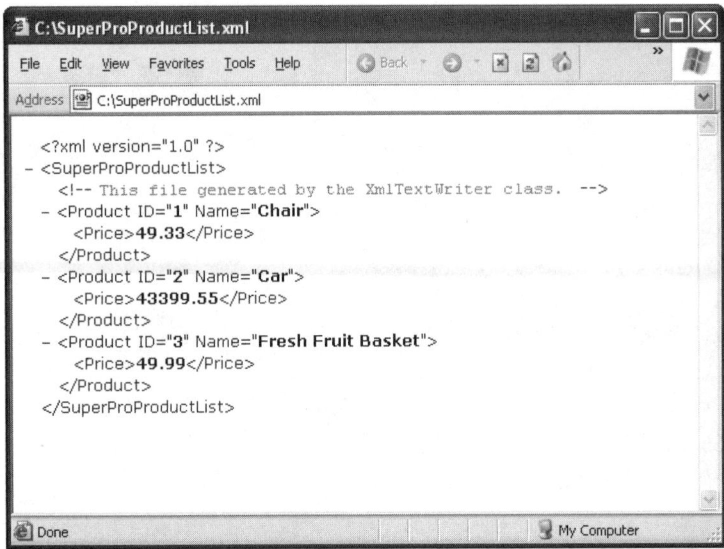

Figure 17-1. *SuperProProductList.xml*

The XML Text Reader

Reading the XML document in your code is just as easy with the corresponding XmlTextReader class. The XmlTextReader moves through your document from top to bottom, one node at a time. You call the Read() method to move to the next node. This method returns true if there are more nodes to read or false once it has read the final node. The current node is provided through the properties of the XmlTextReader class, such as NodeType and Name.

FORMATTING YOUR XML

By default, the XmlTextWriter will create an XML file that has all its tags lumped together in a single line without any helpful carriage returns or indentation. Although additional formatting isn't required (and doesn't change how the data will be processed), it can make a significant difference if you want to read your XML files in Notepad or another text editor. Fortunately, the XmlTextWriter supports formatting; you just need to enable it, as follows:

```
// Set it to indent output.
w.Formatting = Formatting.Indented;

// Set the number of indent spaces.
w.Indentation = 5;
```

A node is a designation that includes comments, whitespace, opening tags, closing tags, content, and even the XML declaration at the top of your file. To get a quick understanding of nodes, you can use the XmlTextReader to run through your entire document from start to finish and display every node it encounters. The code for this task is as follows:

```
FileStream fs = new FileStream(@"c:\SuperProProductList.xml", FileMode.Open);
XmlTextReader r = new XmlTextReader(fs);

// Store the whole file in a StringWriter (much quicker than using
// string operations).
StringWriter writer = new StringWriter();

// Parse the file, and read each node.
while (r.Read())
{
    writer.Write("<b>Type:</b> ");
    writer.Write(r.NodeType.ToString());
    writer.Write("<br>");

    if (r.Name != "")
    {
        writer.Write("<b>Name:</b> ");
        writer.Write(r.Name);
        writer.Write("<br>");
    }

    if (r.Value != "")
    {
        writer.Write("<b>Value:</b> ");
        writer.Write(r.Value);
        writer.Write("<br>");
    }

    if (r.AttributeCount > 0)
    {
        writer.Write("<b>Attributes:</b> ");
        for (int i = 0; i < r.AttributeCount; i++)
        {
            writer.Write("  ");
            writer.Write(r.GetAttribute(i));
            writer.Write("  ");
```

```
            }
            writer.Write("<br>");
        }
        writer.Write("<br>");
    }
    r.Close();

    // Copy the string content into a label to display it.
    lblXml.Text = writer.ToString();
```

To test this, try the XmlText.aspx page included with the online samples (as shown in Figure 17-2).

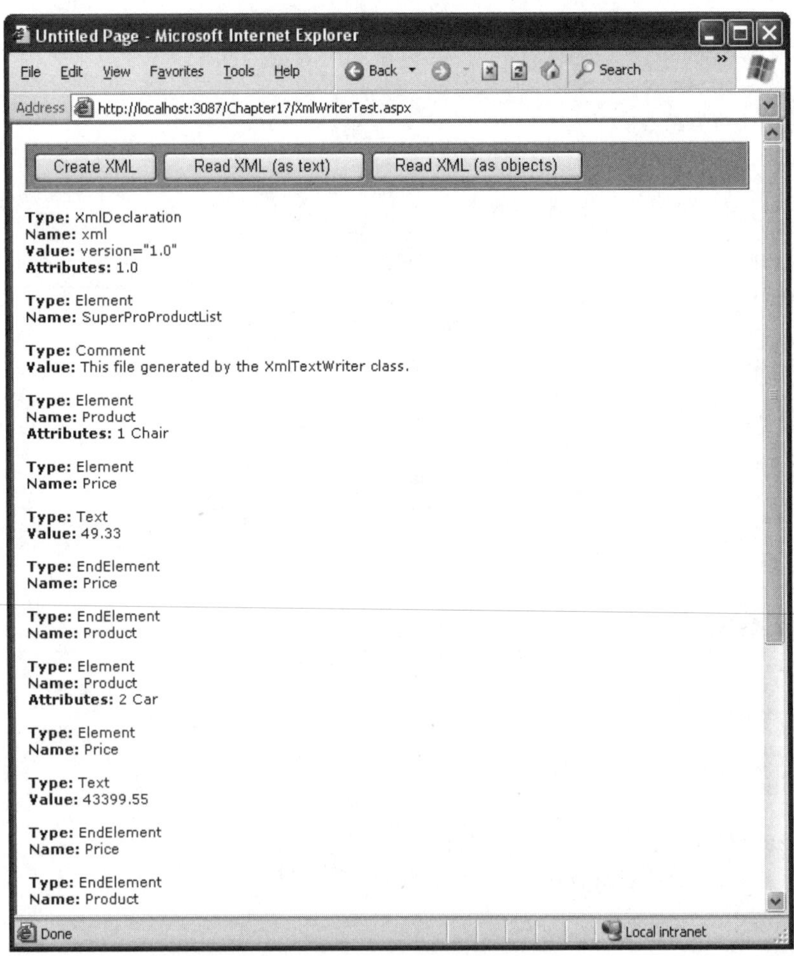

Figure 17-2. *Reading XML structure*

The following is a list of all the nodes that are found, shortened to include only one product:

```
Type: XmlDeclaration
Name: xml
Value: version="1.0"
Attributes: 1.0

Type: Element
Name: SuperProProductList

Type: Comment
Value: This file generated by the XmlTextWriter class.

Type: Element
Name: Product
Attributes: 1, Chair

Type: Element
Name: Price

Type: Text
Value: 49.33

Type: EndElement
Name: Price

Type: EndElement
Name: Product

Type: EndElement
Name: SuperProProductList
```

In a typical application, you would need to go fishing for the elements that interest you. For example, you might read information from an XML file such as SuperProProductList.xml and use it to create Product objects based on the Product class shown here:

```
public class Product
{
    private int id;
    private string name;
    private decimal price;
```

```
    public int ID
    {
        get { return id; }
        set { id = value; }
    }

    public string Name
    {
        get { return name; }
        set { name = value; }
    }

    public decimal Price
    {
        get { return price; }
        set { price = value; }
    }
}
```

Nothing is particularly special about this class—all it does is allow you to store three related pieces of information (a price, name, and ID). Note that this class uses property procedures and so is eligible for data binding.

A typical application might read data from an XML file and place it directly into the corresponding objects. The next example (also a part of the XmlWriterTest.aspx page) shows how you can easily create a group of Product objects based on the SuperProProductList.xml file:

```
// Open a stream to the file.
FileStream fs = new FileStream(@"c:\SuperProProductList.xml", FileMode.Open);
XmlTextReader r = new XmlTextReader(fs);

// Create a generic collection of products.
List<Product> products = new List<Product>();
```

```
// Loop through the products.
while (r.Read())
{
    if (r.NodeType == XmlNodeType.Element && r.Name == "Product")
    {
        Product newProduct = new Product();
        newProduct.ID = Int32.Parse(r.GetAttribute(0));
        newProduct.Name = r.GetAttribute(1);

        // Get the rest of the subtags for this product.
        while (r.NodeType != XmlNodeType.EndElement)
        {
            r.Read();

            // Look for Price subtags.
            if (r.Name == "Price")
            {
                while (r.NodeType != XmlNodeType.EndElement)
                {
                    r.Read();
                    if (r.NodeType == XmlNodeType.Text)
                    {
                        newProduct.Price = Decimal.Parse(r.Value);
                    }
                }
            }

            // You could check for other Product nodes
            // (such as Available, Status, etc.) here.
        }

        // Add the product to the list.
        products.Add(newProduct);
    }
}
```

```
r.Close();

// Display the retrieved document.
gridResults.DataSource = products;
gridResults.DataBind();
```

Dissecting the Code...

- This code uses a nested looping structure. The outside loop iterates over all the products, and the inner loop searches through all the product tags (in this case, there is only a possible Price tag). This keeps the code well organized. The EndElement node alerts you when a node is complete and the loop can end. Once all the information is read for a product, the corresponding object is added into the collection.

- All the information is retrieved from the XML file as a string. Thus, the Int32.Parse() method is used to convert this text to a numeric value.

- Data binding is used to display the contents of the collection. A GridView set to generate columns automatically creates the table shown in Figure 17-3.

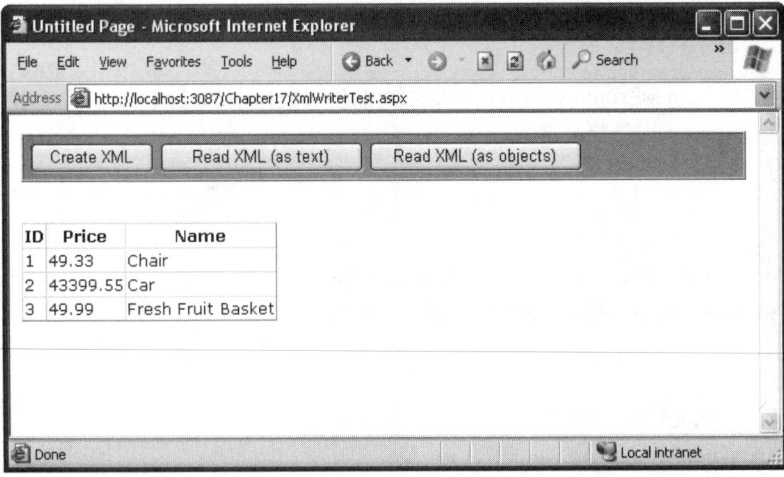

Figure 17-3. *Reading XML content*

■Note The XmlTextReader provides many more properties and methods. These additional members don't add new functionality; they allow for increased flexibility. For example, you can read a portion of an XML document into a string using methods such as ReadString(), ReadInnerXml(), and ReadOuterXml(). These members are all documented in the MSDN class library reference. Generally, the most straightforward approach is just to work your way through the nodes, as shown in the SuperProProductList example.

Working with XML Documents

The XmlTextReader and XmlTextWriter use XML as a *backing store*. These classes are streamlined for getting XML data into and out of a file quickly. You don't actually work with the XML data in your program. Instead, you open the file, use the data to create the appropriate objects or fill the appropriate controls, and close it soon after. This approach is ideal for storing simple blocks of data. For example, you could slightly modify the guest book page in the previous chapter to store data in an XML format, which would provide greater standardization but wouldn't change how the application works.

The XmlDocument class provides a different approach to XML data. It provides an in-memory model of an entire XML document. You can then browse through the document, reading, inserting, or removing nodes at any location. You can load the content from a file into an XML document and save it to the file later, but the XmlDocument class doesn't maintain a direct connection to the file. In this respect, the XmlDocument is analogous to the DataSet in ADO.NET programming: it's always disconnected. The XmlTextWriter and XmlTextReader, on the other hand, are always connected to a stream, which is usually a file.

When you use the XmlDocument class, your XML file is created as a series of linked .NET objects in memory. Figure 17-4 shows the object model.

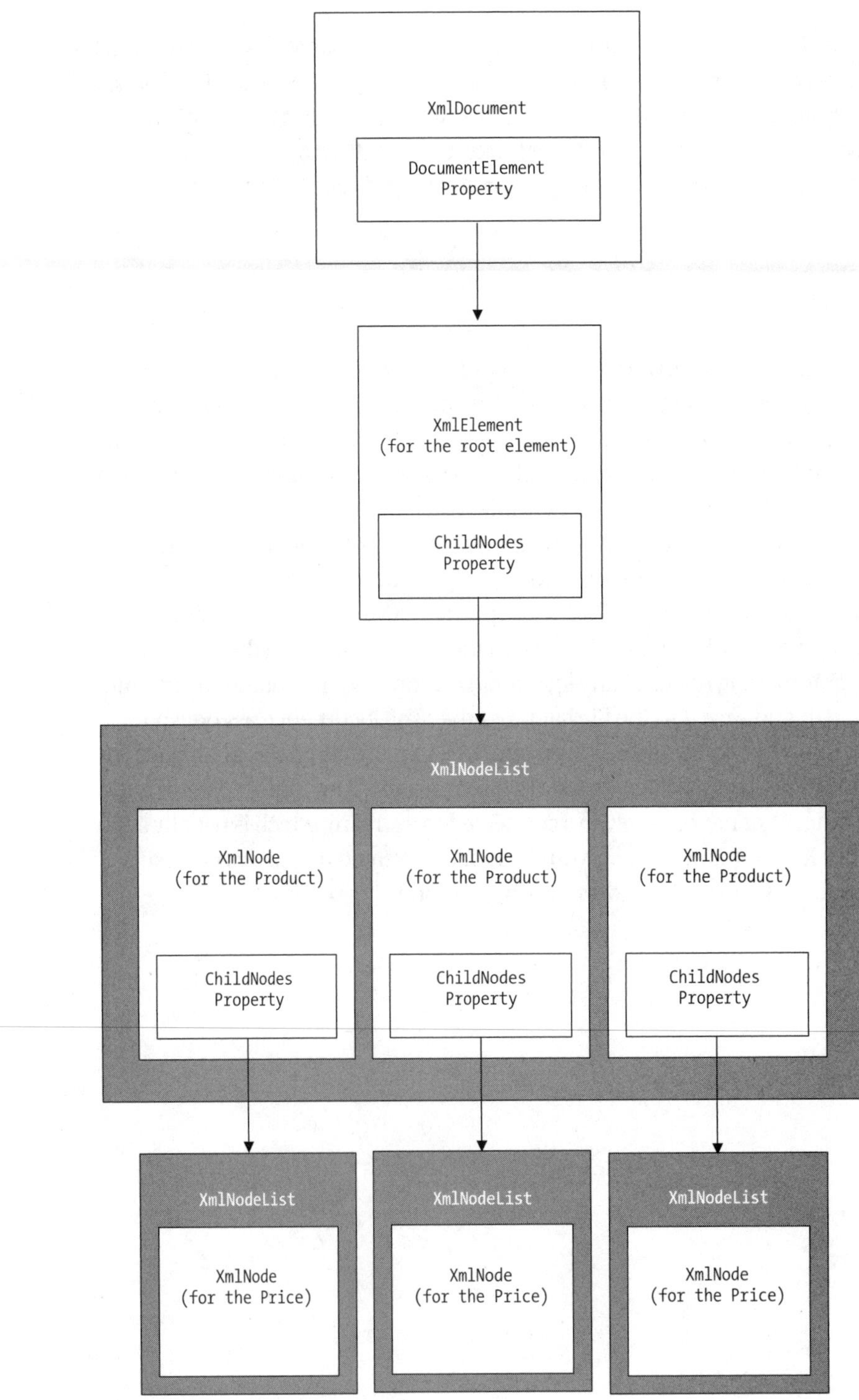

Figure 17-4. *An XML document in memory*

The following is an example that creates the SuperProProductList in memory, using an XmlDocument class. When it's finished, the XML document is transferred to a file using the XmlDocument.Save() method.

```
// Start with a blank in-memory document.
XmlDocument doc = new XmlDocument();

// Create some variables that will be useful for
// manipulating XML data.
XmlElement rootElement, productElement, priceElement;
XmlAttribute productAttribute;
XmlComment comment;

// Create the declaration.
XmlDeclaration declaration;
declaration = doc.CreateXmlDeclaration("1.0", null, "yes");

// Insert the declaration as the first node.
doc.InsertBefore(declaration, doc.DocumentElement);

// Add a comment.
comment = doc.CreateComment("Created with the XmlDocument class.");
doc.InsertAfter(comment, declaration);

// Add the root node.
rootElement = doc.CreateElement("SuperProProductList");
doc.InsertAfter(rootElement, comment);

// Add the first product.
productElement = doc.CreateElement("Product");
rootElement.AppendChild(productElement);

// Set and add the product attributes.
productAttribute = doc.CreateAttribute("ID");
productAttribute.Value = "1";
productElement.SetAttributeNode(productAttribute);
productAttribute = doc.CreateAttribute("Name");
productAttribute.Value = "Chair";
productElement.SetAttributeNode(productAttribute);
```

```
// Add the price node.
priceElement = doc.CreateElement("Price");
priceElement.InnerText = "49.33";
productElement.AppendChild(priceElement);

// (Code to add two more products omitted.)

// Save the document.
doc.Save(@"c:\SuperProProductList.xml");
```

One of the best features of the XmlDocument class is that it doesn't rely on any underlying file. When you use the Save() method, the file is created, a stream is opened, the information is written, and the file is closed, all in one line of code. This means this is probably the only line you need to put inside a try/catch error handling block.

While you're manipulating data with the XML objects, your text file isn't being changed. Once again, this is conceptually similar to the ADO.NET DataSet.

Dissecting the Code...

- Every separate part of the XML document is created as an object. Elements (tags) are created as XmlElement objects, comments are created as XmlComment objects, and attributes are represented as XmlAttribute objects.

- To create a new element, comment, or attribute for your XML document, you need to use one of the XmlDocument class methods, such as CreateComment(), CreateAttribute(), or CreateElement(). This ensures the XML is generated correctly for your document, but it doesn't actually place any information into the XmlDocument.

- Once you have created the appropriate object and entered any additional inner information, you need to add it to your document. You can do so using XmlDocument methods such as InsertBefore() or InsertAfter(). To add a child element (such as the Product element inside the SuperProProductList element), you need to find the appropriate parent object and use its AppendChild() method. In other words, you need to keep track of some object references; you can't write a child element directly to the document in the same way you could with the XmlTextWriter.

- You can insert nodes anywhere. While the XmlTextWriter and XmlTextReader forced you to read every node, from start to finish, the XmlDocument is a much more flexible collection of objects.

Figure 17-5 shows the file written by this code (as displayed by Internet Explorer).

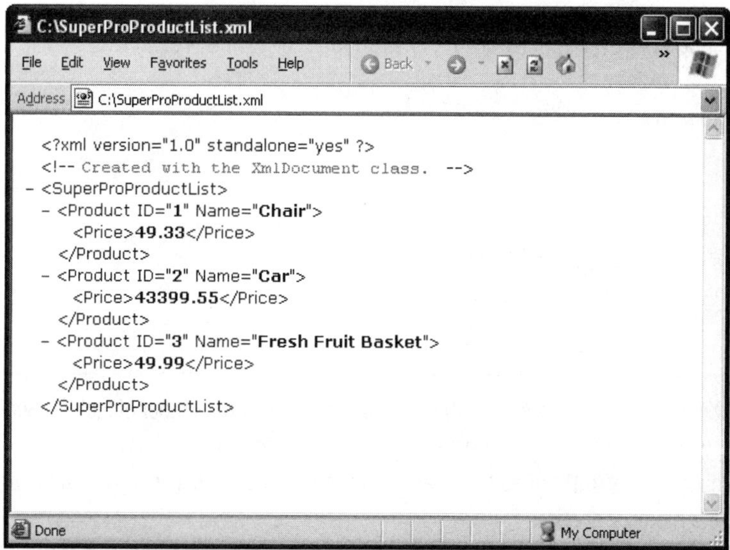

Figure 17-5. *The XML file*

Reading an XML Document

To read information from your XML file, all you need to do is create an XmlDocument object and use its Load() method. Depending on your needs, you may want to keep the data in its XML form, or you can extract by looping through the collection of linked XmlNode objects. This process is similar to the XmlTextReader example, but the code is noticeably cleaner.

```
// Create the document.
XmlDataDocument doc = new XmlDataDocument();
doc.Load(@"c:\SuperProProductList.xml");

// Loop through all the nodes, and create the ArrayList.
ArrayList products = new ArrayList();
foreach (XmlElement element in doc.DocumentElement.ChildNodes)
{
    Product newProduct = new Product();
    newProduct.ID = Int32.Parse(element.GetAttribute("ID"));
    newProduct.Name = element.GetAttribute("Name");
```

```
        // If there were more than one child node, you would probably use
        // another For Each loop here and move through the
        // Element.ChildNodes collection.
        newProduct.Price = Decimal.Parse(element.ChildNodes[0].InnerText);

        products.Add(newProduct);
    }

    // Display the results.
    gridResults.DataSource = products;
    gridResults.DataBind();
```

■ **Tip** Whether you use the XmlDocument or the XmlTextReader class depends on a number of factors. Generally, you use XmlDocument when you want to deal directly with XML, rather than just use XML as a way to persist some information. In general, the XmlTextReader is best for large XML files, because it won't attempt to load the entire document into memory at once.

You have a variety of other options for manipulating your XmlDocument and extracting or changing pieces of data. Table 17-1 provides an overview.

Table 17-1. *XmlNode Manipulation*

Technique	Description	Example
Finding a node's relative	Every XmlNode leads to other XmlNode objects. You can use properties such as FirstChild, LastChild, PreviousSibling, NextSibling, and ParentNode to return a reference to a related node.	ParentNode = MyNode.ParentNode;
Cloning a portion of an XmlDocument	You can use the CloneNode() method with any XmlNode to create a duplicate copy. You need to specify true or false to indicate whether you want to clone all children (true) or just the single node (false).	NewNode = MyNode.Clone(true);
Removing or adding nodes	Find the parent node, and then use one of its node-adding methods. You can use AppendChild() to add the child to the end of the child list and PrependChild() to add the node to the start of the child list. You can also remove nodes with RemoveChild(), ReplaceChild(), and RemoveAll(), which deletes all the children and all the attributes for the current node.	MyNode.RemoveChild(NodeToDelete);

Technique	Description	Example
Adding inner content	Find the node, and add a NodeType.Text child node. One possible shortcut is just to set the InnerText property of your node, but that will erase any existing child nodes.	
Manipulating attributes	Every node provides an XmlAttributeCollection of all its attributes through the XmlNode.Attributes property. To add an attribute, you must create an XmlAttribute object and use methods such as Append(), Prepend(), InsertBefore(), or InsertAfter(). To remove an attribute, you can use Remove() and RemoveAll().	MyNode.Attributes.Remove(AttributeToDelete);
Working with content as string data	You can retrieve or set the content inside a node using properties such as InnerText, InnerXml, and OuterXml. Be warned that the inner content of a node includes all child nodes. Thus, setting this property carelessly could wipe out other information, such as subtags.	

The XmlDocument class provides a rich set of events that fire before and after nodes are inserted, removed, and changed. The likelihood of using these events in an ordinary ASP.NET application is fairly slim, but it represents an interesting example of the features .NET puts at your fingertips.

THE DIFFERENCE BETWEEN XMLNODE AND XMLELEMENT

You may have noticed that the XmlDocument is created with specific objects such as XmlComment and XmlElement but read back as a collection of XmlNode objects. The reason is that XmlComment and XmlElement are customized classes that inherit their basic functionality from XmlNode.

The ChildNodes collection allows you to retrieve all the content contained inside any portion of an XML document. Because this content could include comments, elements, and any other types of node, the ChildNodes collection uses the lowest common denominator. Thus, it provides child nodes as a collection of standard XmlNode objects. Each XmlNode has basic properties similar to what you saw with the XmlTextReader, including NodeType, Name, Value, and Attributes. You'll find that you can do all your XML processing with XmlNode objects.

Searching an XML Document

One of the pleasures of the XmlDocument is its support of searching, which allows you to find nodes when you know they are there—somewhere—but you aren't sure how many matches exist or where the elements are.

To search an XmlDocument, all you need to do is use the GetElementById() or GetElementsByTagName() method. The following code example puts the GetElementsByTagName() method to work and creates the output shown in Figure 17-6:

```
XmlDataDocument doc = new XmlDataDocument();
doc.Load(@"c:\SuperProProductList.xml");

// Find the matches.
XmlNodeList results = doc.GetElementsByTagName("Price");

// Display the results.
lblXml.Text = "<b>Found " + results.Count.ToString() + " Matches ";
lblXml.Text += " for the Price tag: </b><br><br>";
foreach (XmlNode result in results)
{
    lblXml.Text += result.FirstChild.Value + "<br>";
}
```

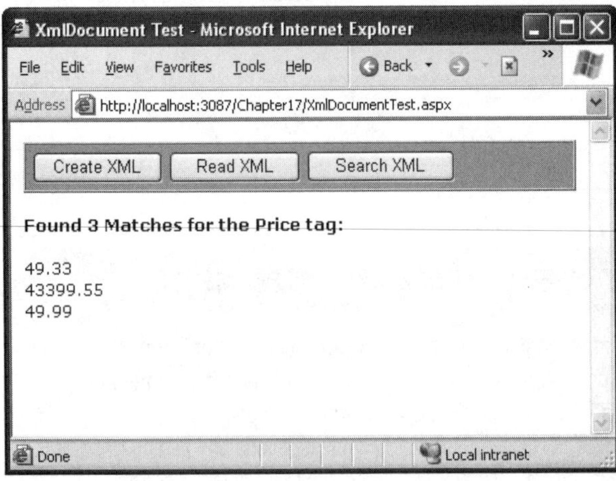

Figure 17-6. *Searching an XML document*

This technique works well if you want to find an element based on its name. If you want to use more sophisticated searching, match only part of a name, or examine only part of a document, you'll have to fall back on the traditional standard: looping through all the nodes in the XmlDocument.

■ **Tip** The search method provided by the XmlDocument class is relatively primitive. For a more advanced tool, you might want to learn the XPath language, which is a W3C recommendation (defined at `http://www.w3.org/TR/xpath`) designed for performing queries on XML data. .NET provides XPath support through the classes in the System.Xml.XPath namespace, which include an XPath parser and evaluation engine. Of course, these aren't much use unless you learn the syntax of the XPath language.

XML Validation

XML has a rich set of supporting standards, many of which are far beyond the scope of this book. One of the most useful in this family of standards is XSD (XML Schema Definition). XSD defines the rules to which a specific XML document should conform. When you're creating an XML file on your own, you don't need to create a corresponding XSD file—instead, you might just rely on the ability of your code to behave properly. While this is sufficient for tightly controlled environments, if you want to open your application to other programmers or allow it to interoperate with other applications, you should create an XSD document. Think of it this way: XML allows you to create a custom language for storing data, and XSD allows you to define the syntax of the language you create.

XML Namespaces

Before you can create an XSD document, you'll need to understand one other XML standard, called XML namespaces. XML namespaces uniquely identify different XML-based languages. For example, you could tell the difference between your SuperProProductList standard and another organization's product catalog because they would use different namespaces. Namespaces are particularly important for applications, which need an easy way to determine what type of XML file they're processing. By examining the namespace, your code can determine whether it will be able to process a given XML file.

■ **Note** XML namespaces aren't directly related to .NET namespaces. XML namespaces identify different XML languages. .NET namespaces are a code construct used to organize types.

To specify that an element belongs to a specific namespace, you simply need to add the xmlns attribute to the start tag and indicate the namespace. For example, here's how you could put all the elements in an XML document into the namespace SuperProProductList:

```
<?xml version="1.0"?>
<SuperProProductList xmlns="SuperProProductList">
    <Product>
        <ID>1</ID>
        <Name>Chair</Name>
        <Price>49.33</Price>
        <Available>true</Available>
        <Status>3</Status>
    </Product>

    <!-- Other products omitted. -->
</SuperProProductList>
```

This code example defines a default namespace. All elements, including the Product, ID, and Name elements, are automatically placed in this namespace.

■ **Tip** Many XML namespaces use URIs (universal resource identifiers). Typically, these URIs look like a web page URL. For example, `http://www.mycompany.com/mystandard` is a typical name for a namespace. Though the namespace looks like it points to a valid location on the Web, this isn't required (and shouldn't be assumed). The reason URIs are used for XML namespaces is because they're more likely to be unique. Typically, if you create a new XML markup, you'll use a URI that points to a domain or website you control. That way, you can be sure no one else is likely to use that URI. For example, the namespace `http://www.mycompany.com/SuperProProductList` is much more likely to be unique than just SuperProProductList if you own the domain `www.mycompany.com`.

Another approach is to use namespace prefixes. A namespace prefixes a short character sequence that you can insert in front of a tag name to indicate its namespace. You define the prefix in the xmlns attribute by inserting a colon (:) followed by the characters you want to use for the prefix. Here's how the SuperProProductList would look using this commonly used technique:

```
<?xml version="1.0"?>
<super:SuperProProductList xmlns:super="SuperProProductList">
    <super:Product>
        <super:ID>1</super:ID>
        <super:Name>Chair</super:Name>
        <super:Price>49.33</super:Price>
```

```
        <super:Available>true</super:Available>
        <super:Status>3</super:Status>
    </super:Product>

    <!-- Other products omitted. -->
</super:SuperProProductList>
```

Namespace prefixes simply map an element to a namespace. The actual prefix you use isn't important as long as it remains consistent. It also doesn't matter whether you use namespace prefixes or a default namespace, provided the namespaces match.

■ **Tip** Namespace names must match exactly. If you change the capitalization in part of a namespace, add a trailing / character, or modify any other detail, the XML parser will interpret it as a different namespace.

XSD Documents

An XSD document, or *schema*, defines what elements a document should contain and the way these elements are organized (the structure). It can also identify the appropriate data types for all the content. XSD documents are written using an XML syntax with special tag names. All the XSD tags are placed in the `http://www.w3.org/2001/XMLSchema` namespace. Often, this namespace uses the prefix xsd: or xs:, as in the following example.

The full XSD specification is out of the scope of this chapter, but you can learn a lot from a simple example. The following is the slightly abbreviated SuperProProductList.xsd file. All it does is define the elements and attributes used in the SuperProProductList.xml document and their data types. It indicates the file is a list of Product elements, which are a complex type made up of a string (Name), a decimal value (Price), and an integer (ID). This example uses the second version of the SuperProProductList.xsd document to demonstrate how to use attributes in a schema file.

```
<?xml version="1.0"?>
<xs:schema id="SuperProProductList"
    targetNamespace="SuperProProductList"
    xmlns:xs=" http://www.w3.org/2001/XMLSchema" >
  <xs:element name="SuperProProductList">
    <xs:complexType>
      <xs:choice maxOccurs="unbounded">
        <xs:element name="Product">
          <xs:complexType>
            <xs:sequence>
              <xs:element name="Price" type="xs:decimal"
                  minOccurs="0" />
```

```
            </xs:sequence>
            <xs:attribute name="ID" form="unqualified"
                type="xs:string" />
            <xs:attribute name="Name" form="unqualified"
                type="xs:int" />
          </xs:complexType>
        </xs:element>
      </xs:choice>
    </xs:complexType>
  </xs:element>
</xs:schema>
```

In the XSD file, you need to specify the namespace for the documents you want to validate. You do this by adding the targetNamespace attribute to the first element in the XSD document:

```
<xs:schema id="SuperProProductList"
    targetNamespace="SuperProProductList"
    xmlns:xs=" http://www.w3.org/2001/XMLSchema" >
```

Validating an XML File

To validate an XML document against a schema, you need to create an XmlReader that has validation features built in.

The first step when performing validation is to import the System.Xml.Schema namespace, which contains types such as XmlSchema and XmlSchemaCollection:

```
using System.Xml.Schema;
```

You must perform two steps to create the validating reader. First, you create an XmlReaderSettings object that specifically indicates you want to perform validation. You do this by setting the ValidationType property and loading your XSD schema file into the Schemas collection, as shown here:

```
XmlReaderSettings settings = new XmlReaderSettings();
settings.ValidationType = ValidationType.Schema;
settings.Schemas.Add("SuperProProductList",
  Request.PhysicalApplicationPath + @"\SuperProProductList.xsd");
```

Second, you need to create the validating reader using the static XmlReader.Create() method. This method has several overloads, but the version used here requires a FileStream (with the XML document) and the XmlReaderSettings object that has your validation settings:

```
// Open the XML file.
FileStream fs = new FileStream(filePath, FileMode.Open);

// Create the validating reader.
XmlReader r = XmlReader.Create(fs, settings);
```

This XmlReader in this example works in the same way as the XmlTextReader you've been using up until now, but it adds the ability to verify that the XML document follows the schema rules. This reader throws an exception (or raises an event) to indicate errors as you move through the XML file.

The following example shows how you can create an XmlValidatingReader that uses the SuperProProductList.xsd file and use it to verify that the XML in SuperProProductList.xml is valid:

```
// Set the validation settings.
XmlReaderSettings settings = new XmlReaderSettings();
settings.Schemas.Add("SuperProProductList",
  Request.PhysicalApplicationPath + @"\SuperProProductList.xsd");
settings.ValidationType = ValidationType.Schema;

// Open the XML file.
FileStream fs = new FileStream(filePath, FileMode.Open);

// Create the validating reader.
XmlReader r = XmlReader.Create(fs, settings);

// Read through the document.
while (r.Read())
{
    // Process document here.
    // If an error is found, an exception will be thrown.
}
r.Close();
```

Using the current file, this code will succeed, and you'll be able to access the current node through the XmlValidatingReader object in the same way you could with the XmlTextReader. However, consider what happens if you make the minor modification shown here:

```
<Product ID="A" Name="Chair">
```

Now when you try to validate the document, an XmlSchemException (from the System.Xml.Schema namespace) will be thrown, alerting you to the invalid data type, as shown in Figure 17-7.

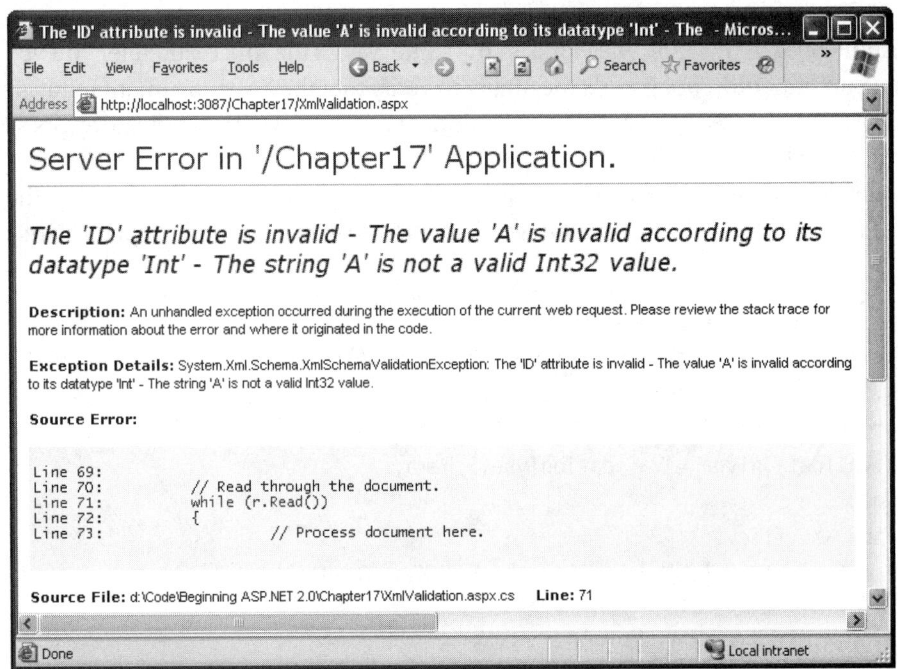

Figure 17-7. *An XMLSchemaException*

Instead of catching errors, you can react to the ValidationEventHandler event. If you react to this event, you'll be provided with information about the error, but no exception will be thrown. To connect an event handler to this event, create a new ValidationEventHandler delegate, and assign it to the XmlReaderSettings.ValidationEventHandler event before you create the reader:

```
// Connect to the method named ValidateHandler.
settings.ValidationEventHandler += new ValidationEventHandler(ValidateHandler);
```

The event handler receives a ValidationEventArgs class, which contains the exception, a message, and a number representing the severity:

```
private void ValidateHandler(Object sender, ValidationEventArgs e)
{
    lblStatus.Text += "Error: " + e.Message + "<br>";
}
```

To test the validation, you can use the XmlValidation.aspx page in the online samples. It allows you to validate a valid SuperProProductList, as well as two other versions, one with incorrect data and one with an incorrect tag (see Figure 17-8).

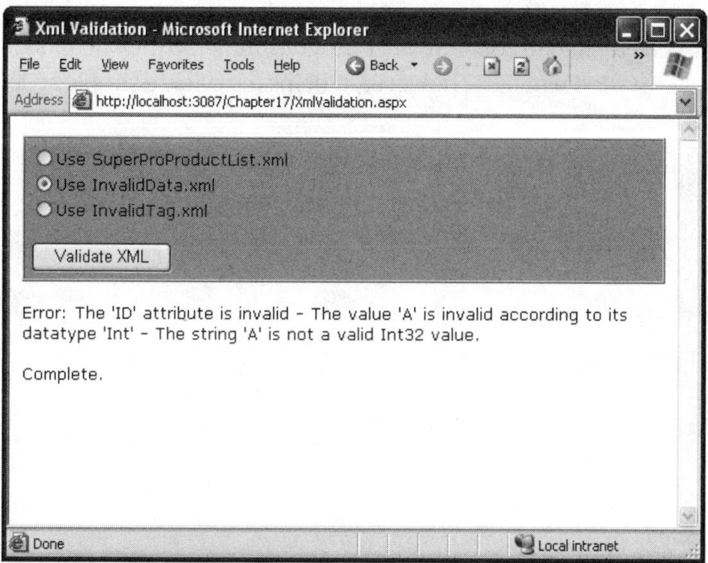

Figure 17-8. *The validation test page*

XML Display and Transforms

Another standard associated with XML is XSL, which uses a style sheet to transform an XML document. XSL can extract a portion of an XML document or convert an XML document into another type of XML document. An even more popular use of XSL transformations is to convert an XML document into an HTML document that can be displayed in a browser.

XSL is easy to use from the point of view of the .NET class library. All you need to understand is how to create an XmlTransform object (found in the System.Xml.Xsl namespace).

You use its Load() method to specify a style sheet and its Transform() method to output the result to a file or stream:

```
XmlTransform transformer = new XmlTransform;

// Load the XSL style sheet.
transformer.Load("SuperProProductList.xslt");

// Create a transformed XML file.
// SuperProProductList.xml is the starting point.
transformer.Transform("SuperProProductList.xml", "New.xml");
```

However, this doesn't spare you from needing to learn the XSL syntax. Once again, the intricacies of XSL aren't directly related to core ASP.NET programming, so they're outside the scope of this book. To get started with XSL, however, it helps to review a simple style sheet example:

```
<?xml version="1.0" encoding="UTF-8" ?>
<xsl:stylesheet xmlns:xsl="http://www.w3.org/1999/XSL/Transform"
    version="1.0" >

  <xsl:template match="SuperProProductList">
    <html><body><table border="1">
    <xsl:apply-templates select="Product"/>
    </table></body></html>
  </xsl:template>

  <xsl:template match="Product">
    <tr>
    <td><xsl:value-of select="@ID"/></td>
    <td><xsl:value-of select="@Name"/></td>
    <td><xsl:value-of select="Price"/></td>
    </tr>
  </xsl:template>

</xsl:stylesheet>
```

Every XSL file has a root xsl:stylesheet element. The style sheet can contain one or more templates (the sample file SuperProProductList.xslt has two). In this example, the first template searches for the root SuperProProductList element. When it finds it, it outputs the tags necessary to start an HTML table and then uses the xsl:apply-templates command to branch off and perform processing for any contained Product elements.

```
<xsl:template match="SuperProProductList">
  <html><body><table border="1">
  <xsl:apply-templates select="Product"/>
```

When that process is complete, the HTML tags for the end of the table will be written:

```
</table></body></html>
```

When processing each Product element, information about the ID, Name, and Price is extracted and written to the output using the xsl:value-of command. The at sign (@) indicates that the value is being extracted from an attribute, not a subtag. Every piece of information is written inside a table row. For more advanced formatting, you could use additional HTML tags to format some text in bold or italics:

```
<xsl:template match="Product">
  <tr>
  <td><xsl:value-of select="@ID"/></td>
  <td><xsl:value-of select="@Name"/></td>
  <td><xsl:value-of select="Price"/></td>
  </tr>
</xsl:template>
```

The final result of this process is the HTML file shown here:

```
<html>
  <body>
    <table border="1">
      <tr>
        <td>1</td>
        <td>Chair</td>
        <td>49.33</td>
      </tr>
      <tr>
        <td>2</td>
        <td>Car</td>
        <td>43398.55</td>
      </tr>
      <tr>
        <td>3</td>
        <td>Fresh Fruit Basket</td>
        <td>49.99</td>
      </tr>
    </table>
  </body>
</html>
```

In the next section, you'll look at how this output appears in an Internet browser.

Generally speaking, if you aren't sure you need XSL, you probably don't. The .NET Framework provides a rich set of tools for searching and manipulating XML files using objects and code, which is the best approach for small-scale XML use.

■**Tip** To learn more about XSL, consider Jeni Tennison's excellent book *Beginning XSLT 2.0: From Novice to Professional* (Apress, 2005).

The Xml Web Control

If you use an XLST transform such as the one demonstrated in the previous example, you might wonder what your code should do with the generated HTML. You could try to write it directly to the browser or save it to the hard drive, but these approaches are awkward, especially if you want to display the generated HTML inside a normal ASP.NET web page that contains other controls. The XmlTransform object just converts XML files—it doesn't provide any way to insert the output into your web page.

ASP.NET includes an Xml web control that fills this gap and can display XML content. You can specify the XML content for this control in several ways: by assigning an XmlDocument object to the Document property, by assigning a string containing the XML content to the DocumentContent property, or by specifying a string that refers to an XML file using the DocumentSource property.

```
// Display the information from an XML file in the Xml control.
Xml.DocumentSource = Request.PhysicalApplicationPath +
  @"\SuperProProductList.xml";
```

If you assign the SuperProProductList.xml file to the Xml control, you're likely to be disappointed. The result is just a string of the inner text (the price for each product), bunched together without a space (see Figure 17-9).

However, you can also apply an XSL transformation, either by assigning an XslTransform object to the Transform property or by using a string that refers to the XSLT file with the TransformSource property:

```
// Specify a XSLT file.
Xml.TranformSource = Request.PhysicalApplicationPath +
  @"\SuperProProductList.xslt";
```

Now the output is automatically formatted according to your style sheet (see Figure 17-10).

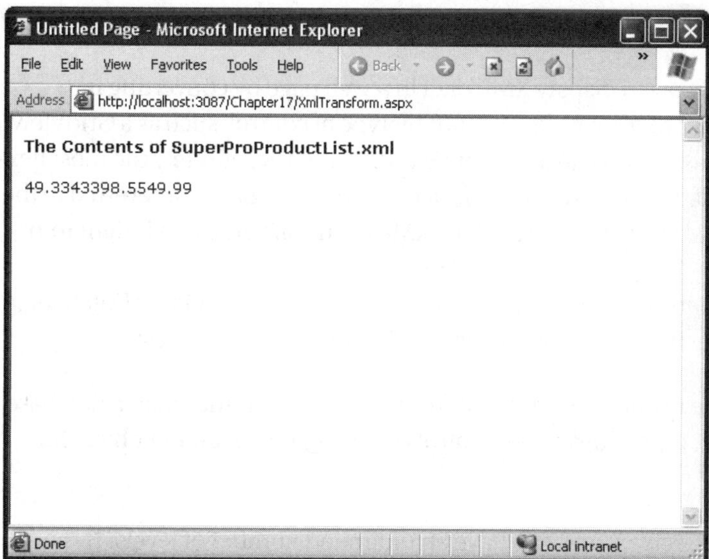

Figure 17-9. *Unformatted XML content*

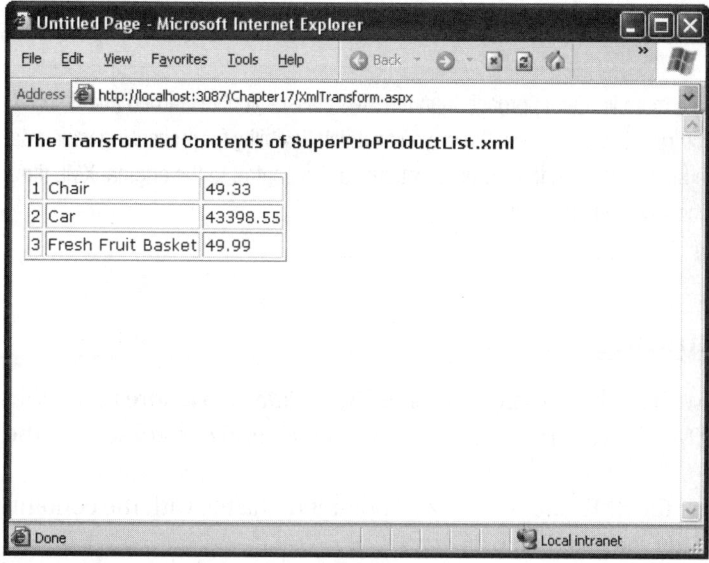

Figure 17-10. *Transformed XML content*

XML Data Binding

The Xml control is a great way to display XML data in a web page by converting it to HTML. But what if you want to display data in another type of control, such as a GridView? You could use the XML classes you learned about earlier, which is definitely the most flexible approach. However, if you don't need that much control, you may be interested in the XmlDataSource control, which allows you to take XML from a file and feed it right into another control.

The XmlDataSource control works much like the SqlDataSource and ObjectDataSource controls you learned about in Chapter 14. However, it has two key differences:

- The XmlDataSource extracts information from an XML file, rather than a database or data access class. It provides other controls with an XmlDocument object for data binding.
- XML content is hierarchical and can have an unlimited number of levels. By contrast, the SqlDataSource and ObjectDataSource return flat tables of data.

The XmlDataSource also provides a few features in common with the other data source controls, including caching.

■ **Note** The XmlDataSource is a more limited approach than the XML classes you've learned about so far. The XmlDataSource assumes you're using files, doesn't give you as much flexibility for processing your data, and doesn't support updateable binding (saving the changes you make in a control to the original XML file). However, it also makes some scenarios much simpler.

Nonhierarchical Binding

The simplest way to deal with the hierarchical nature of XML data is to ignore it. In other words, you can bind the XML data source directly to an ordinary grid control such as the GridView.

The first step is to define the XML data source and point it to the file with the content you want to implement using the DataFile property:

```
<asp:XmlDataSource ID="sourceXml" runat="server"
 DataFile="SuperProProductList.xml" />
```

Now you can bind the GridView with automatically generated columns, in the same way you bind it to any other data source:

```
<asp:GridView ID="GridView1" runat="server" AutoGenerateColumns="True"
 DataSourceID="sourceXml" />
```

■ **Note** Remember, you don't need to use automatically generated columns. If you refresh the schema at design time, Visual Studio will read the linked XML file, determine its structure, and define the corresponding GridView columns explicitly.

Now, when you run the page, the XmlDataSource will extract the data from the SuperProProductList.xml file, provide it to the GridView as an XmlDocument object, and call DataBind(). However, this approach has a catch. As explained earlier, the XmlDocument.Nodes collection contains only the first level of nodes. Each node can contain nested nodes through its own XmlNode.Nodes collection. However, the XmlDataSource doesn't take this into account. It walks over the upper level of XmlNode objects, and as a result you'll see only the top level of nodes. This works fine for the SuperProProductList (as shown in Figure 17-11). However, it doesn't work as well for an XML document with a deep, multilayered structure.

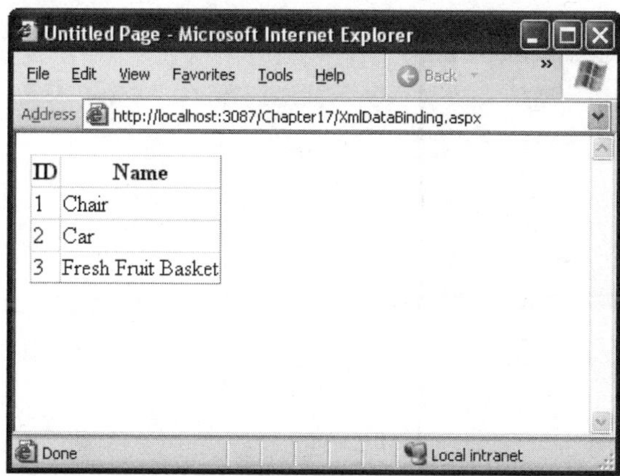

Figure 17-11. *XML data binding (attributes only)*

For example, imagine you use the following XML that divides its products into categories:

```
<?xml version="1.0" standalone="yes"?>
<SuperProProductList xmlns="SuperProProductList" >
  <Category Name="Hardware">
    <Product ID="1" Name="Chair">
      <Price>49.33</Price>
    </Product>
    <Product ID="2" Name="Car">
      <Price>43398.55</Price>
    </Product>
  </Category>
  <Category Name="Produce">
    <Product ID="3" Name="Fresh Fruit Basket">
      <Price>49.99</Price>
    </Product>
  </Category>
</SuperProProductList>
```

Now all you'll see is the list of categories, because these make up the first level of nodes (see Figure 17-12).

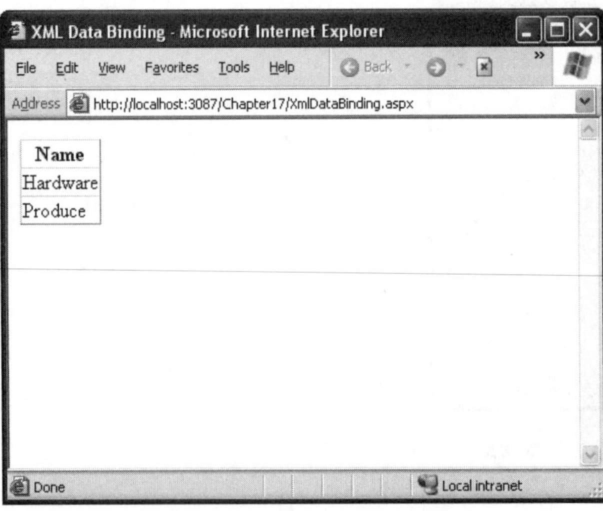

Figure 17-12. *XML data binding (top-level nodes only)*

Clearly, the XmlDataSource has two significant limitations. First, it displays only attribute values, not the text inside elements (in this case, the product price). Second, it shows only the top level of nodes, which may not be what you want. To solve these problems, you need to return to the XML classes, or you need to use one of the following approaches:

- You can use XPath to filter out the important elements, even if they're several layers deep.
- You can use an XSL transformation to flatten the XML into exactly the structure you want. Just make sure all the information is in the top level of nodes and in attributes only.
- You can nest one data control inside another (however, this can get quite complex).
- You can use a control that supports hierarchical data. The only ready-made .NET control that fits is the TreeView.

All of these options require considerably more work. In the next section, you'll see how to use the TreeView.

Hierarchical Binding with the TreeView

Some controls have the built-in smarts to show hierarchical data. In .NET, the principal example is the TreeView. When you bind the TreeView to an XmlDataSource, it uses the XmlDataSource.GetHierarchcialView() method and displays the full structure of the XML document (see Figure 17-13).

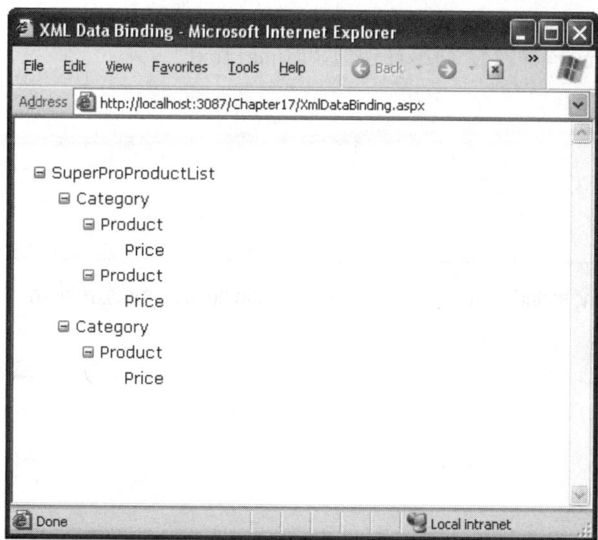

Figure 17-13. *Automatically generated TreeView bindings*

The TreeView's default XML representation still leaves a lot to be desired. It shows only the document structure (the element names), not the document content (the element text). It also ignores attributes. To improve this situation, you need to set the TreeView.AutomaticallyGenerateDataBindings property to false, and you then need to explicitly map different parts of the XML document to TreeView nodes.

```
<asp:TreeView ID="TreeView1" runat="server" DataSourceID="sourceDVD"
 AutoGenerateDataBindings="False">
  ...
</asp:TreeView>
```

To create a TreeView mapping, you need to add <TreeNodeDataBinding> elements to the <DataBinding> section. You must start with the root element and then add a binding for each level you want to show. You cannot skip any levels.

Each <TreeNodeDataBinding> must name the node it binds to (through the DataMember property), the text it should display (DataField), and the hidden value for the node (ValueField). Unfortunately, both DataField and ValueField are designed to bind to attributes. If you want to bind to element content, you can use an ugly hack and specify the #InnerText code. However, this shows *all* the inner text, including text inside other, more deeply nested nodes.

The next example defines a basic set of nodes to show the product information:

```
<asp:TreeView ID="TreeView1" runat="server" DataSourceID="sourceXml"
 AutoGenerateDataBindings="False">
  <DataBindings>
    <asp:TreeNodeBinding DataMember="SuperProProductList" Text="Product List" />
    <asp:TreeNodeBinding DataMember="Category" TextField="Name" />
    <asp:TreeNodeBinding DataMember="Product" TextField="Name" />
    <asp:TreeNodeBinding DataMember="Price" TextField="#InnerText" />
  </DataBindings>
</asp:TreeView>
```

Figure 17-14 shows the result.

Tip To learn how to format the TreeView, including how to tweak gridlines and node pictures, refer to Chapter 11.

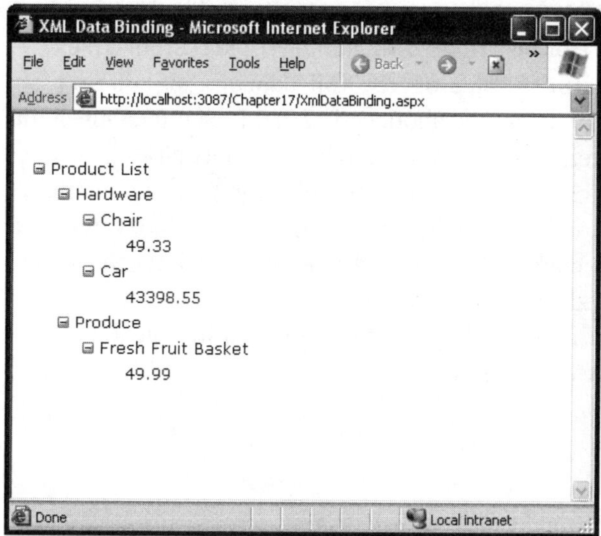

Figure 17-14. *Binding to specific content*

Binding to XML Content from Other Sources

So far, all the examples you've seen have bound to XML content in a file. This is the standard scenario for the XmlDataSource control, but it's not your only possibility. The other option is to supply the XML as text through the XmlDataSource.Data property.

You can set the Data property at any point before the binding takes place. One convenient time is during the Page.Load event:

```
protected void Page_Load(object sender, EventArgs e)
{
    string xmlContent;
    // (Retrieve XML content from another location.)
    sourceXml.Data = xmlContent;
}
```

■ **Tip** If you use this approach, you may find it's still a good idea to set the XmlDataSource.DataFile property at design time in order for Visual Studio to load the schema information about your XML document and make it available to other controls. Just remember to remove this setting when you're finished developing.

This allows you to read XML content from another source (such as a database) and still work with the bound data controls. However, it requires adding some custom code.

Even if you do use the XmlDataSource.Data property, XML data binding still isn't nearly as flexible as the XML classes you learned about earlier in this chapter. One of the key limitations is that the XML content needs to be loaded into memory all at once as a string object, which isn't all that efficient. If you're dealing with large XML documents, or you just need to ensure the best possible scalability for your web application, you might be able to reduce the overhead considerably by using the XmlTextReader instead, even though it will require much more code. Handling the XML parsing process yourself also gives you unlimited flexibility to rearrange and aggregate your data into a meaningful summary, which isn't always easy using XSLT alone.

XML in ADO.NET

The integration between ADO.NET and XML is straightforward and effortless, but it isn't likely to have a wide range of usefulness. Probably the most interesting feature is the ability to serialize a DataSet to an XML file (with or without a corresponding XSD schema file). The following code example demonstrates this technique:

```
// Save a DataSet.
myDataSet.WriteXml(Request.PhysicalApplicationPath + @"\datasetfile.xml");

// Save a DataSet schema that defines the structure of the DataSet tables.
myDataSet.WriteSchema(Request.PhysicalApplicationPath + @"\datasetfile.xsd");

// Retrieve the DataSet with its schema. Using the schema
// means no data types are corrupted and no structural information is lost.
DataSet myDataSet2 = new DataSet();
myDataSet2.ReadXmlSchema(Request.PhysicalApplicationPath + @"\datasetfile.xsd");
myDataSet2.ReadXml(Request.PhysicalApplicationPath + @"\datasetfile.xml");
```

This technique could be useful for permanently storing the results of a slow-running query. A web page that needs this information could first check for the presence of the file before trying to connect to the database. This type of system is similar to many home-grown solutions used in traditional ASP programming. It's useful, but it raises additional issues. For example, every web page that needs the data must check the file's age to determine whether it's still valid. Presumably, the XML file will need to be refreshed at periodic intervals, but if more than one executing web page finds that the file needs to be refreshed and tries to create it at the same time, a file access problem will occur. You can solve all these problems with a little painful coding, although caching provides a more streamlined and elegant solution. It also offers much better performance, because the data is stored in memory. Chapter 26 describes caching.

■ **Tip** You can also use the ReadXml(), WriteXml(), ReadXmlSchema(), and WriteXmlSchema() methods on DataTable objects to read or write XML for a single table in a DataSet.

Of course, sometimes you may need to exchange the results of a query with an application on another platform, or you may need to store the results permanently (caching information will be automatically removed if it isn't being used or the server memory is becoming scarce). In these cases, the ability to save a DataSet can come in handy. But whatever you do, don't try to work with the retrieved DataSet and commit changes back to the data source. Handling concurrency issues is difficult enough without trying to use stale data from a file!

Accessing a DataSet As XML

Another option provided by the DataSet is the ability to access it through an XML interface. This allows you to perform XML-specific tasks (such as hunting for a tag or applying an XSL transformation) with the data you've extracted from a database. To do so, you create an XmlDataDocument that wraps the DataSet. When you create the XmlDataDocument, you supply the DataSet you want as a parameter:

```
XmlDataDocument dataDocument = new XmlDataDocument(myDataSet);
```

Now you can look at the DataSet in two ways. Because XmlDataDocument inherits from XmlDocument class, it provides all the same properties and methods for examining nodes and modifying content. You can use this XML-based approach to deal with your data, or you can manipulate the DataSet through the XmlDataDocument.DataSet property. In either case, the two views are kept automatically synchronized—when you change the DataSet, the XML is updated immediately, and vice versa.

For example, consider the pubs database, which includes a table of authors. Using the XmlDataDocument, you could examine a list of authors as an XML document and even apply an XSL transformation with the help of the Xml web control. Here's the complete code you'd need:

```
string connectionString =
  WebConfigurationManager.ConnectionStrings["Pubs"].ConnectionString;
string SQL = "SELECT * FROM authors WHERE city='Oakland'";

// Create the ADO.NET objects.
SqlConnection con = new SqlConnection(connectionString);
SqlCommand cmd = new SqlCommand(SQL, con);
SqlDataAdapter adapter = new SqlDataAdapter(cmd);
DataSet ds = new DataSet("AuthorsDataSet");
```

```
// Retrieve the data.
con.Open();
adapter.Fill(ds, "AuthorsTable");
con.Close();

// Create the XmlDataDocument that wraps this DataSet.
XmlDataDocument dataDoc = new XmlDataDocument(ds);

// Display the XML data (with the help of an XSLT) in the XML web control.
XmlControl.Document = dataDoc;
XmlControl.TransformSource = "authors.xslt";
```

Figure 17-15 shows the processed data.

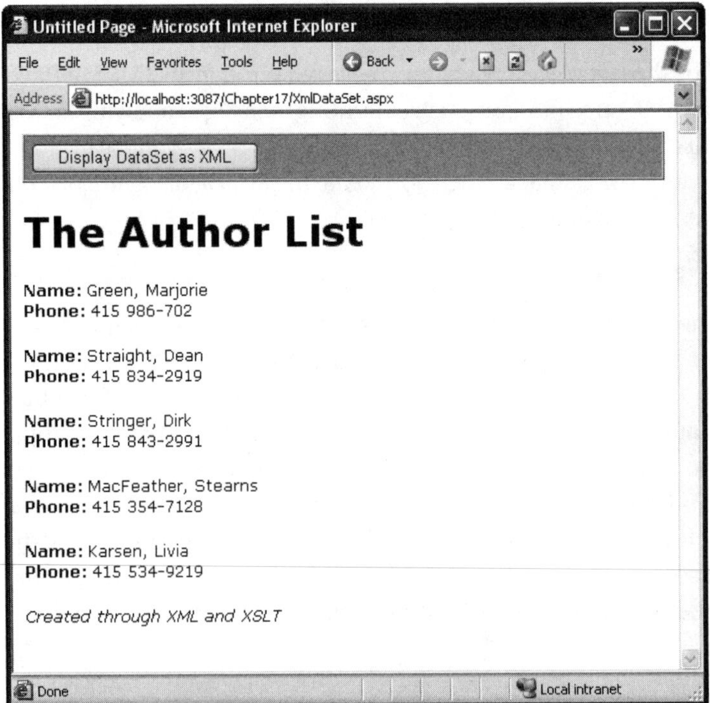

Figure 17-15. *Displaying the results of a query through XML and XSLT*

Remember, when you interact with your data as XML, all the customary database-oriented concepts such as relationships and unique constraints go out the window. The only reason you should interact with your DataSet as XML is if you need to perform an XML-specific task, not to replace the ADO.NET approach for updating data. In most cases, you'll find it easier to use advanced controls such as the DataList and DataGrid, rather than creating a dedicated XSL transform to transform data into the HTML you want to display.

Accessing XML Through the DataSet

Often, a more useful way to implement the XmlDataDocument is to access an ordinary XML file as though it were one or more tables. This means you don't need to work with the XML syntax you've explored, and you don't need to go to the work of extracting all the information and creating the appropriate objects and collections. Instead, you can use the familiar ADO.NET objects to manipulate the underlying XML document.

Consider these few remarkable lines of code:

```
XmlDataDocument dataDoc = new XmlDataDocument();

// Set the schema, and retrieve the data.
dataDoc.DataSet.ReadXmlSchema(Request.PhysicalApplicationPath +
  @"\SuperProProductList.xsd");
dataDoc.Load(Request.PhysicalApplicationPath + @"\SuperProProductList.xml");

// Display the retrieved data.
gridData.DataSource = dataDoc.DataSet;
gridData.DataBind();
```

In this example, a new XmlDataDocument is created, an XML file is loaded into it, and the information is automatically provided through a special DataSet "attached" to the XmlDataDocument. This allows you to use the ADO.NET objects to work with data (such as the DataTable and DataRow objects), as well as the standard XmlDocument members (such as the GetTagsByElementName() method and the ChildNodes property). You could even use both approaches at the same time, because both the XML and the ADO.NET interface access the same underlying data.

Figure 17-16 shows the retrieved data.

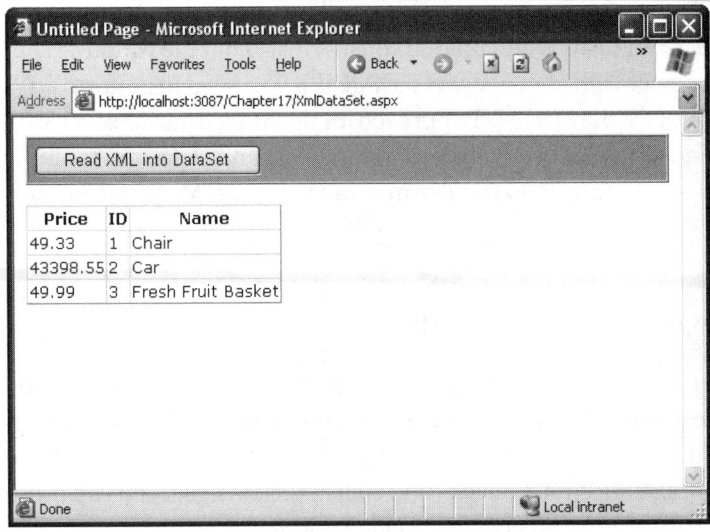

Figure 17-16. *Accessing XML data through ADO.NET*

The only catch is that your XML file must have a schema for ASP.NET to be able to determine the proper structure of your data. Before you retrieve the XML file, you must use the XmlDataDocument.DataSet.ReadXmlSchema() method. Otherwise, you won't be able to access the data through the DataSet. In addition, the structure of your XML document must conform to the table-based and row-based structure used by ADO.NET. You'll find that some XML files can be loaded into an XmlDataDocument more successfully than others.

Clearly, if you need to store hierarchical data in an XML file and are willing to create an XSD schema, the XmlDataDocument is a great convenience. It also allows you to bridge the gap between ADO.NET and XML—some clients can look at the data as XML, and others can access it through the database objects without losing any information or requiring an error-prone conversion process.

The Last Word

Now that your lightning tour of XML and ASP.NET is drawing to a close, you should have a basic understanding of what XML is, how it looks, and why you might use it in a web page. XML represents a new tool for breaking down the barriers between businesses and platforms—it's nothing less than a universal model for storing and communicating all types of information.

XML on its own is a remarkable innovation. However, to get the most out of XML, you need to embrace other standards that allow you to validate XML, transform it, and search it for specific information. The .NET Framework provides classes for all these tasks in the System.Xml namespaces. To continue your exploration, start with a comprehensive review of XML standards (such as the one provided at `http://www.w3schools.com/xml`) and then dive into the class library.

PART 4

Website Security

CHAPTER 18

Security Fundamentals

By default your ASP.NET applications are available to any user who can connect to your server (whether it's over a local network or the Internet). Although this is ideal for many web applications (and it suits the original spirit of the Internet), it isn't always appropriate. For example, an e-commerce site needs to provide a secure shopping experience to win customers. A subscription-based site needs to limit content or site access to extract a fee. Even a wide-open public site may provide some resources or features (such as an administrative report or configuration page) that shouldn't be available to all users.

ASP.NET provides a multilayered security model that makes it easy to protect your web applications. Although this security is powerful and profoundly flexible, it can appear somewhat confusing because of, in large part, the number of layers where security can be applied. Much of the work in applying security to your application doesn't come from writing code but from determining the appropriate places to implement your strategy.

In this chapter, you'll sort out the different security subsystems and consider how you can use Windows, IIS, and ASP.NET services to protect your application. You'll also look at some examples that use ASP.NET forms-based security, which provides a quick and easy model for adding a database-backed user authentication system.

Determining Security Requirements

The first step in securing your applications is deciding where you need security and what it needs to protect. For example, you may need to block access in order to protect private information, or maybe you just need to enforce a subscription policy. Perhaps you don't need any sort of security at all, but you want a login system to provide personalization for frequent visitors. These requirements will determine the approach you use.

Security doesn't need to be complex, but it does need to be wide-ranging. For example, even if you force users to log into a part of your site, you still need to make sure the information is stored in the database under a secure account with a password that couldn't easily be guessed by a user on your local network. You also need to guarantee your application can't be tricked into sending private information (a possibility if the user modifies a page or a query string to post back different information than you expect).

Restricted File Types

ASP.NET automatically provides a basic level of security by blocking requests for certain file types (such as configuration and source code files). To accomplish this, ASP.NET registers the file types with IIS but specifically assigns them to the HttpForbiddenHandler class. This class has a single role in life—it denies every request it receives.

Some of the restricted file types include the following:

```
.asax
.ascx
.config
.cs
.csproj
.vb
.vbproj
.resx
.resources
```

To see the full list, refer to the web.config.default file in the c:\[WindowsDir]\Microsoft.NET\Framework\[version]\Config folder, and search for the text *System.Web.HttpForbiddenHandler.*

Security Concepts

Three concepts form the basis of any discussion about security:

Authentication: This is the process of determining a user's identity and forcing users to prove they are who they claim to be. Usually, this involves entering credentials (typically a user name and password) into some sort of login page or window. These credentials are then authenticated against the Windows user accounts on the computer, a list of users in a file, or a back-end database.

Authorization: Once a user is authenticated, authorization is the process of determining whether that user has sufficient permissions to perform a given action (such as viewing a page or retrieving information from a database). Windows imposes some authorization checks (for example, when you open a file), but your code will probably want to impose its own checks (for example, when a user performs a task in your web application such as submitting an order, assigning a project, or giving a promotion).

Impersonation: In ASP.NET, all code runs under a fixed account defined in the machine.config file. Impersonation allows a portion of your code to run under a different identity, with a different set of Windows permissions.

Authentication and authorization are the two cornerstones of creating a secure user-based site. The Windows operating system provides a good analogy. When you first boot up your computer, you supply a user ID and password, thereby authenticating yourself to the system. After that point, every time you interact with a restricted resource (such as a file, database, registry key, and so on), Windows quietly performs authorization checks to ensure your user account has the necessary rights.

The ASP.NET Security Model

As you've seen in previous chapters, web requests are fielded first by IIS, which then passes the request to ASP.NET if the file type is registered with the ASP.NET service. Figure 18-1 shows how these levels interact.

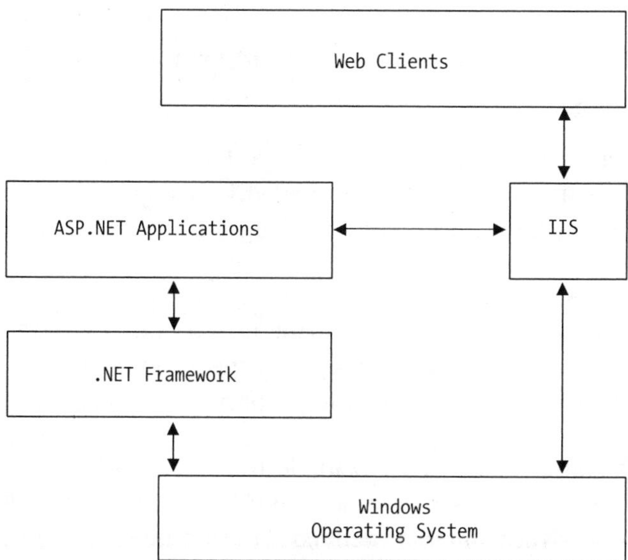

Figure 18-1. *IIS and ASP.NET interaction*

You can apply security at several places in this chain. First, consider the process for an ordinary (non-ASP.NET) web page request:

1. IIS attempts to authenticate the user. Generally, IIS allows requests from all anonymous users and automatically logs them in under the IUSR_[ServerName] account. IIS security settings are configured on a per-directory basis.

2. If IIS authenticates the user successfully, it attempts to send the user the appropriate HTML file. The operating system performs its own security checks to verify that the authenticated user (typically IUSR_[ServerName]) is allowed access to the specified file and directory.

An ASP.NET request requires several additional steps (as shown in Figure 18-2). The first and last steps are similar, but the process has intermediary layers:

1. IIS attempts to authenticate the user. Generally, IIS allows requests from all anonymous users and automatically logs them in under the IUSR_[ServerName] account.

2. If IIS authenticates the user successfully, it passes the request to ASP.NET with additional information about the authenticated user. ASP.NET can then use its own security services, depending on the settings in the web.config file and the page that was requested.

3. If ASP.NET authenticates the user, it allows requests to the .aspx page or .asmx web service. Your code can perform additional custom security checks (for example, manually asking for another password before allowing a specific operation).

4. When the ASP.NET code requests resources (for example, tries to open a file or connect to a database), the operating system performs its own security checks. All ASP.NET code runs under a fixed account that's defined in the machine.config file. However, if you enable impersonation, these system operations will be performed under the account of the authenticated user (or a different account you specify).

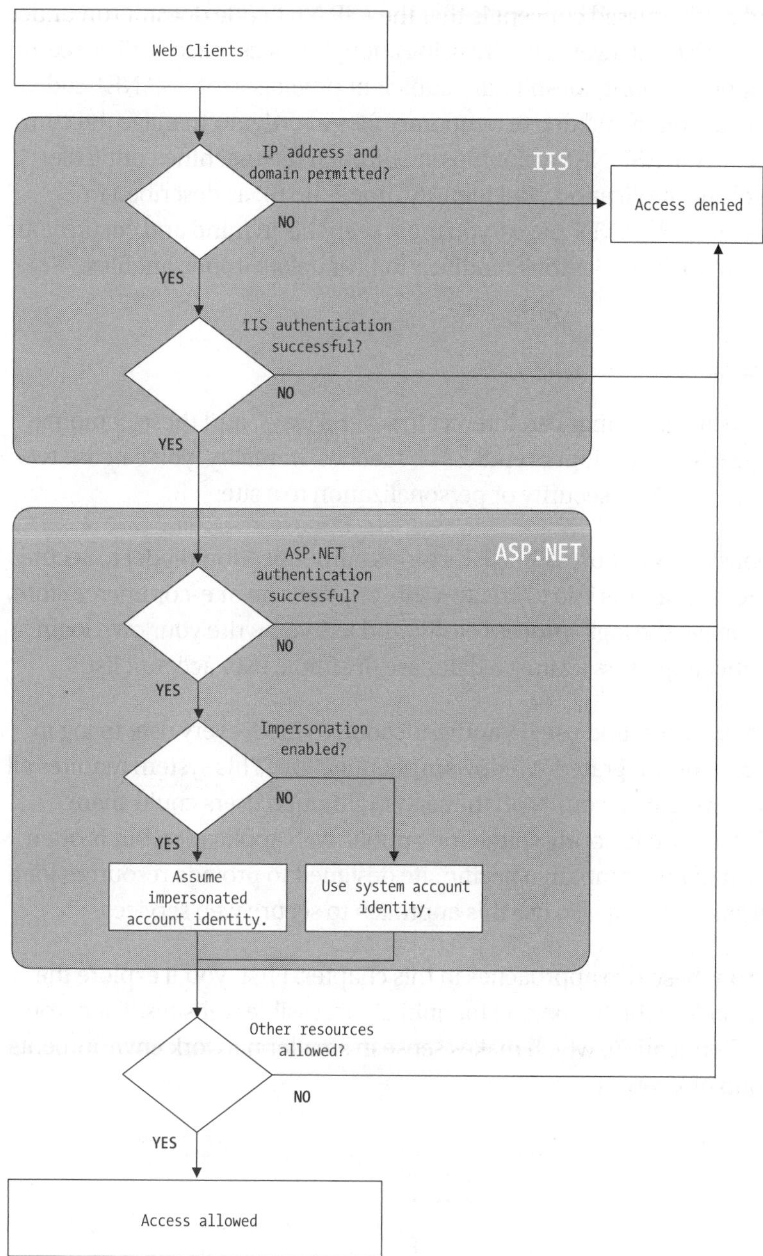

Figure 18-2. *Authenticating a request*

One important and easily missed concept is that the ASP.NET code doesn't run under the IUSR_[ServerName] account, even if you're using anonymous user access. The reason is the IUSR_[ServerName] account doesn't have sufficient privileges for ASP.NET code, which needs to be able to create and delete temporary files in order to manage the compilation process. Instead, the ASP.NET account is set through the machine.config file (if you're using IIS 5) or the application pool identity (under IIS 6), as described in Chapter 12. When designing ASP.NET pages, you must keep this in mind and ensure your program can't be used to make dangerous modifications or delete important files.

Security Strategies

The IIS and ASP.NET security settings can interact in several ways, and these combinations often give new ASP.NET developers endless headaches. In reality, you can use two central strategies to add ASP.NET security or personalization to a site:

- Allow anonymous users but use ASP.NET's forms authentication model to secure parts of your site. This allows you to create a subscription site or e-commerce store, allows you to manage the login process easily, and lets you write your own login code for authenticating users against a database or simple user account list.

- Forbid anonymous users, and use IIS authentication to force every user to log in using Basic, Digest, or Integrated Windows authentication. This system requires all users have Windows user accounts on the server (although users could share accounts). This scenario is poorly suited for a public web application but is often ideal with an intranet or company-specific site designed to provide resources for a limited set of users. You can also use this approach to secure web services.

You'll concentrate on these two approaches in this chapter. First, you'll explore the forms authentication model, which is perfect for publicly accessible websites. Then, you'll consider Windows authentication, which makes sense in smaller network environments where you have a group of known users.

Certificates

One topic this chapter doesn't treat in detail is certificates and SSL (Secure Sockets Layer) connections. These technologies are supported by IIS and are really independent from ASP.NET programming. However, they are an important ingredient in creating a secure website.

Essentially, certificates allow you to demonstrate that your site and your organization information are registered and verified with a certificate authority. This generally encourages customer confidence, although it doesn't guarantee the company or organization acts responsibly or fairly. A certificate is a little like a driver's license—it doesn't prove you can drive, but it demonstrates that a third party (in this case, a department of the government) is willing to attest to your identity and your qualifications. Your web server requires a certificate in order to use SSL, which automatically encrypts all the information sent between the client and server.

To add a certificate to your site, you first need to purchase one from a certificate authority. These are some well-known certificate authorities:

- VeriSign (`http://www.verisign.com`)
- GeoTrust (`http://www.geotrust.com`)
- GlobalSign (`http://www.globalsign.com`)
- Thawte (`http://www.thawte.com`)

The first step in this process of getting a certificate is to e-mail a certificate request for your web server. IIS Manager allows you to create a certificate request automatically. In IIS 5, begin by launching IIS Manager (select Settings ➤ Control Panel ➤ Administrative Tools ➤ Internet Information Services from the Start menu). Expand the Web Sites group, right-click your website item (usually titled Default Web Site), and choose Properties. Under the Directory Security tab, you'll find a Server Certificate button (see Figure 18-3). Click this button to start a Web Server Certificate Wizard that requests some basic organization information and generates a request file. You'll also need to supply a bit length for the key—the higher the bit length, the stronger the key.

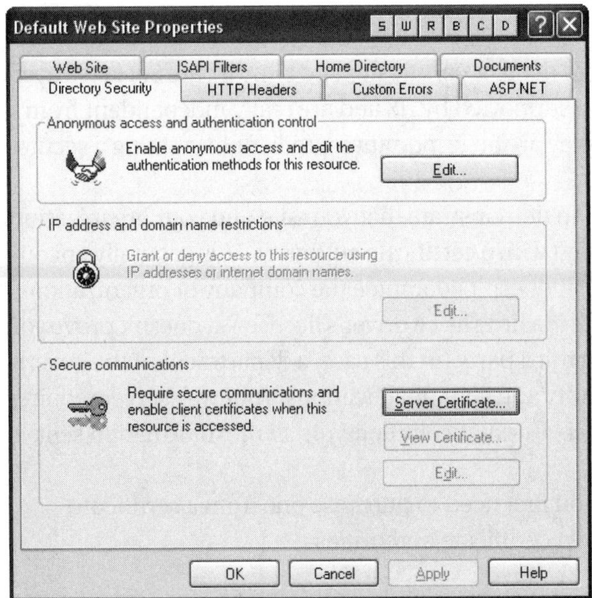

Figure 18-3. *Directory security settings*

You can save the generated file as a text file, but you must ultimately e-mail it to a certificate authority. The following is a sample (slightly abbreviated) request file:

```
Webmaster: administrator@certificatecompany.com
Phone: (555) 555-5555
Server: Microsoft Key Manager for IIS Version 4.0

Common-name: www.yourcompany.com
Organization: YourOrganization
```


```
-----BEGIN NEW CERTIFICATE REQUEST-----
MIIB1DCCAToCAQAwgZMxCzAJBgNVBAYTAlVTMREwDwYDVQQIEwhOZXcgWW9yazEQ
MA4GA1UEBxMHQnVmZmFsbzEeMBwGA1UEChMVVW5pdmVyc2l0eSBhdCBCdWZmYWxv
MRwwGgYDVQQLExNSZXNlYXJjaCBGb3VuZGF0aW9uMSEwHwYDVQQDExh3d3cucmVz
ZWFyY2guYnVmZmFsby5lZHUwgZ8wDQYJKoZIhvcNAQEBBQADgYOAMIGJAoGBALJO
hbsCagHN4KMbl7uzOGwvcjJeWH8JqIUFVFi352tnoA15PZfCxW18KNtFeBtrbOpf
-----END NEW CERTIFICATE REQUEST-----
```


The certificate authority will return a certificate that you can install according to its instructions.

Secure Sockets Layer

SSL technology encrypts communication between a client and a website. Although it slows performance, it's often used when private or sensitive information needs to be transmitted between an authenticated user and a web application. Without SSL, any information that's sent over the Internet, including passwords, credit card numbers, and employee lists, is easily viewable to an eavesdropper with the right network equipment. This is also true with web services, which send their information in plain-text SOAP messages.

Even with the best encryption, you have another problem to wrestle with—just how can a client be sure a web server is who it claims to be? For example, consider a clever attacker who uses some sort of IP spoofing to masquerade as Amazon.com. Even if you use SSL to transfer your credit card information, the malicious web server on the other end will still be able to decrypt all your information seamlessly. To prevent this type of deception, SSL uses certificates. The certificate establishes the identity, and SSL protects the communication. If a malicious user abuses a certificate, the certificate authority can revoke it.

To use SSL, you need to install a valid certificate. You can then set IIS directory settings specifying that individual folders require an SSL connection. To access this page over SSL, the client simply types the URL with a preceding *https* instead of *http* at the beginning of the request.

In your ASP.NET code, you can check whether a user is connecting over a secure connection using code like this:

```
protected void Page_Load(Object sender, EventArgs e)
{
    if (Request.IsSecureConnection)
    {
        lblStatus.Text = "This page is running under SSL.";
    }
    else
    {
        lblStatus.Text = "This page isn't secure.<br />";
        lblStatus.Text += "Please request it with the ";
        lblStatus.Text += "prefix https:// instead of http://";
    }
}
```

HOW DOES SSL WORK?

With SSL, the client and web server start a secure session before they communicate any information. This secure session uses a randomly generated encryption key.

Here's how the process works:

1. The client requests an SSL connection.
2. The server signs its digital certificate and sends it to the client.
3. The client verifies the certificate was issued by a certificate authority it trusts, matches the web server it wants to communicate with, and has not expired or been revoked. If the certificate is valid, the client continues to the next step.
4. The client tells the server what encryption key sizes it supports.
5. The server chooses the strongest key length that is supported by both the client and server. It then informs the client what size this is.
6. The client generates a session key (a random string of bytes). It encrypts this session key using the server's public key (which was provided through the server's digital certificate). It then sends this encrypted package to the server.
7. The server decrypts the session key using its private key. Both the client and server now have the same random session key, which they can use to encrypt communication for the duration of the session.

Forms Authentication

In traditional ASP programming, developers often had to create their own security systems. A common approach was to insert a little snippet of code at the beginning of every secure page. This code would check for the existence of a custom cookie. If the cookie didn't exist, the user would be redirected to a login page, where the cookie would be created after a successful login.

ASP.NET uses the same approach in its forms authentication model. You are still responsible for writing the code for your login page. However, you no longer have to create or check for the cookie manually, and you don't need to add any code to secure pages. You also benefit from ASP.NET's support for sophisticated validation algorithms, which make it all but impossible for users to spoof their own cookies or try other hacking tricks to fool your application into giving them access.

Figure 18-4 shows a simplified security diagram of the forms authentication model in ASP.NET.

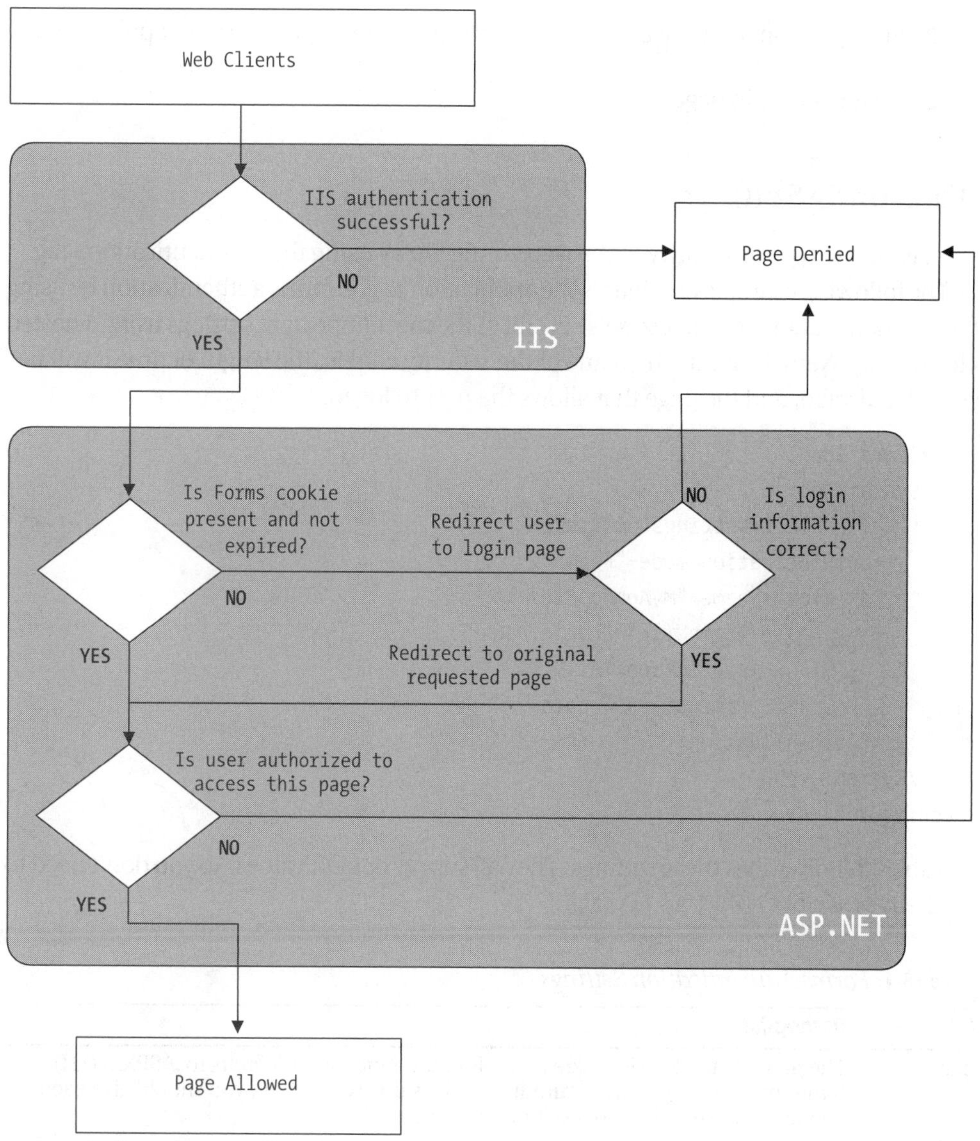

Figure 18-4. *ASP.NET forms authentication*

To implement forms-based security, you need to follow three steps:

1. Set the authentication mode in the web.config file (or use the WAT).
2. Restrict anonymous users from a specific page or directory in your application.
3. Create the login page.

Web.config Settings

You define the type of security in the web.config file by using the <authentication> tag.

The following example configures the application to use forms authentication by using the <authentication> tag. It also sets several of the most important settings using a nested <forms> tag. Namely, it sets the name of the security cookie, the length of time it will be considered valid, and the page that allows the user to log in.

```
<configuration>
    <system.web>
        <!-- Other settings omitted. -->
        <authentication mode="Forms">
            <forms name="MyAppCookie"
                   loginUrl="~/Login.aspx"
                   protection="All"
                   timeout="30" path="/" />
        </authentication>
    </system.web>
</configuration>
```

Table 18-1 describes these settings. They all supply default values, so you don't need to set them explicitly.

Table 18-1. *Forms Authentication Settings*

Attribute	Description
name	The name of the HTTP cookie to use for authentication (defaults to .ASPXAUTH). If multiple applications are running on the same web server, you should give each application's security cookie a unique name.
loginUrl	Your custom login page, where the user is redirected if no valid authentication cookie is found. The default value is default.aspx.
protection	The type of encryption and validation used for the security cookie (can be All, None, Encryption, or Validation). Validation ensures the cookie isn't changed during transit, and encryption (typically Triple-DES) is used to encode its contents. The default value is All.

Attribute	Description
timeout	The number of minutes before the cookie expires. ASP.NET will refresh the cookie when it receives a request, as long as half of the cookie's lifetime has expired. The default value is 30.
path	The path for cookies issued by the application. The default value (/) is recommended, because case mismatches can prevent the cookie from being sent with a request.

For a complete list of supported attributes, consult the MSDN reference.

Authorization Rules

If you make these changes to an application's web.config file and request a page, you'll notice that nothing unusual happens, and the web page is served in the normal way. This is because even though you have enabled forms authentication for your application, you have not restricted anonymous users. In other words, you've chosen the system you want to use for authentication, but none of your pages needs authentication!

To control who can and can't access your website, you need to add access control rules to the <authorization> section of your web.config file. Here's an example that duplicates the default behavior:

```
<configuration>
    <system.web>
        <!-- Other settings omitted. -->
        <authorization>
            <allow users="*" />
        </authorization>
    </system.web>
</configuration>
```

The asterisk (*) is a wildcard character that explicitly permits all users to use the application, even those who haven't been authenticated. Even if you don't include this line in your application's web.config file, this is the still the behavior you'll see, because the default settings inherited from the machine.config file allow all users. To change this behavior, you need to explicitly add a more restrictive rule, as shown here:

```
<configuration>
    <system.web>
        <!-- Other settings omitted. -->
        <authorization>
            <deny users="?" />
        </authorization>
    </system.web>
</configuration>
```

The question mark (?) is a wildcard character that matches all anonymous users. By including this rule in your web.config file, you specify that anonymous users are not allowed. Every user must be authenticated, and every user request will require the security cookie. If you request a page in the application directory now, ASP.NET will detect that the request isn't authenticated and attempt to redirect the request to the login page (which will probably cause an error, unless you've already created this file).

Now consider what happens if you add more than one rule to the authorization section:

```
<authorization>
    <allow users="*" />
    <deny users="?" />
</authorization>
```

When evaluating rules, ASP.NET scans through the list from top to bottom and then continues with the settings in any .config file inherited from a parent directory, ending with the settings in the base machine.config file. As soon as it finds an applicable rule, it stops its search. Thus, in the previous case, it will determine that the rule <allow users="*"> applies to the current request and will not evaluate the second line. This means these rules will allow all users, including anonymous users.

But consider what happens if these two lines are reversed:

```
<authorization>
    <deny users="?" />
    <allow users="*" />
</authorization>
```

Now these rules will deny anonymous users (by matching the first rule) and allow all other users (by matching the second rule).

Controlling Access to Specific Directories

A common application design is to place files that require authentication in a separate directory. With ASP.NET configuration files, this approach is easy. Just leave the default <authorization> settings in the normal parent directory, and add a web.config file that specifies stricter settings in the secured directory. This web.config simply needs to deny anonymous users (all other settings and configuration sections can be omitted).

```
<configuration>
    <system.web>
        <authorization>
            <deny users="?" />
        </authorization>
    </system.web>
</configuration>
```

■ **Note** You cannot change the <authentication> tag settings in the web.config file of a subdirectory in your application. Instead, all the directories in the application must use the same authentication system. However, each directory can have its own authorization rules.

Controlling Access to Specific Files

Generally, setting file access permissions by directory is the cleanest and easiest approach. However, you also have the option of restricting specific files by adding <location> tags to your web.config file.

The location tags sit outside the main <system.web> tag and are nested directly in the base <configuration> tag, as shown here:

```
<configuration>
    <system.web>
        <!-- Other settings omitted. -->
        <authorization>
            <allow users="*" />
        </authorization>
    </system.web>

    <location path="SecuredPage.aspx">
        <system.web>
            <authorization>
                <deny users="?" />
            </authorization>
        </system.web>
    </location>

    <location path="AnotherSecuredPage.aspx">
        <system.web>
            <authorization>
                <deny users="?" />
            </authorization>
        </system.web>
    </location>

</configuration>
```

In this example, all files in the application are allowed, except SecuredPage.aspx and AnotherSecuredPage.aspx, which have an additional access rule denying anonymous users.

■ **Tip** You can also use the location tags to set rules for a specific subdirectory. It's up to you whether you want to use this approach or you prefer to create separate web.config files for each subdirectory, as described in the previous section.

Controlling Access for Specific Users

The <allow> and <deny> rules don't need to use the asterisk or question mark wildcards. Instead, they can specifically identify a user name or a list of comma-separated user names. For example, the following list specifically restricts access from three users. These users will not be able to access the pages in this directory. All other authenticated users will be allowed.

```
<authorization>
    <deny users="?" />
    <deny users="matthew,sarah" />
    <deny users="john" />
    <allow users="*" />
</authorization>
```

You'll notice that the first rule in this example denies all anonymous users. Otherwise, the following rules won't have any effect, because users won't be forced to authenticate themselves.

The following rules explicitly allow two users. All other user requests will be denied access, even if they are authenticated.

```
<authorization>
    <deny users="?" />
    <allow users="matthew,sarah" />
    <deny users="*" />
</authorization>
```

■ **Tip** Your application assigns the user names when a user logs in through the login page. These names might correspond to a name or ID in a database—it's up to you. They won't correspond to a Windows user account.

The WAT

You have another way to set up your authentication and authorization rules. Rather than edit the web.config file by hand, you can use the WAT (website administration tool) from inside Visual Studio. The WAT guides you through the process, although you'll find it's still important to understand what changes are actually being made to your web.config file. It's also often quicker to enter a list of authorization rules by hand rather than use the WAT.

To use the WAT for this type of configuration, select Website ➤ ASP.NET Configuration from the menu. Next, click the Security tab. You'll see the window shown in Figure 18-5, which gives you links to set the authentication type, define authorization rules (using the Access Rules section), and enable role-based security. (Role-based security is an optional higher-level feature you can use with forms authentication. You'll learn more about how it works and how to enable it in the next chapter.)

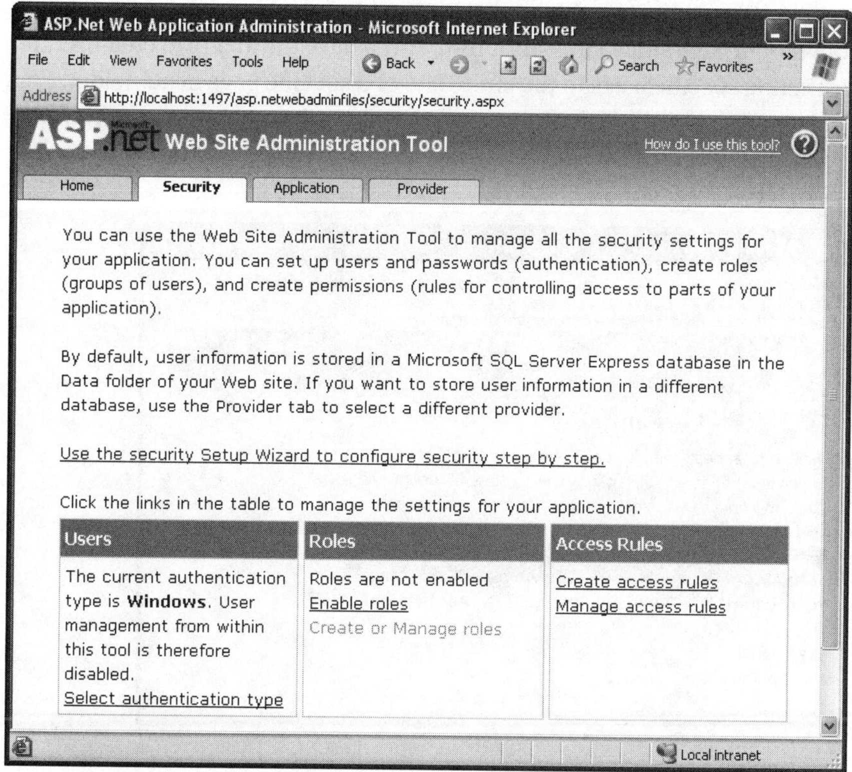

Figure 18-5. *The Security tab in the WAT*

To set an application to use forms authentication, follow these steps:

1. Click the Select authentication type link.
2. Choose the From the Internet option. (If you chose From a Local Network instead, you'd wind up using the built-in Windows authentication approach described later in the "Windows Authentication" section.)
3. Click Done. The appropriate <authorization> tag will be created in the web.config file.

■ **Tip** The Select Authentication options are worded in a slightly misleading way. It's true applications that have users connecting from all over the Internet are sure to use forms authentication. However, applications that run on a local network might also use forms authentication—it all depends on how they connect and whether you want to use the information in existing accounts. The truth is, a local intranet gives you the option to use Windows authentication but doesn't require it.

Next, it's time to define the authorization rules. To do so, click the Create Access Rules link. (You can also change existing rules by clicking the Manage Access Rules link.) Using the slightly convoluted page shown in Figure 18-6, you'll have the ability to create a rule allowing or restricting specific users to the entire site or a specific page or subfolder. For example, the rule in Figure 18-6 will deny the user jenny from the entire site once you click OK to add it. This takes you to the Security tab.

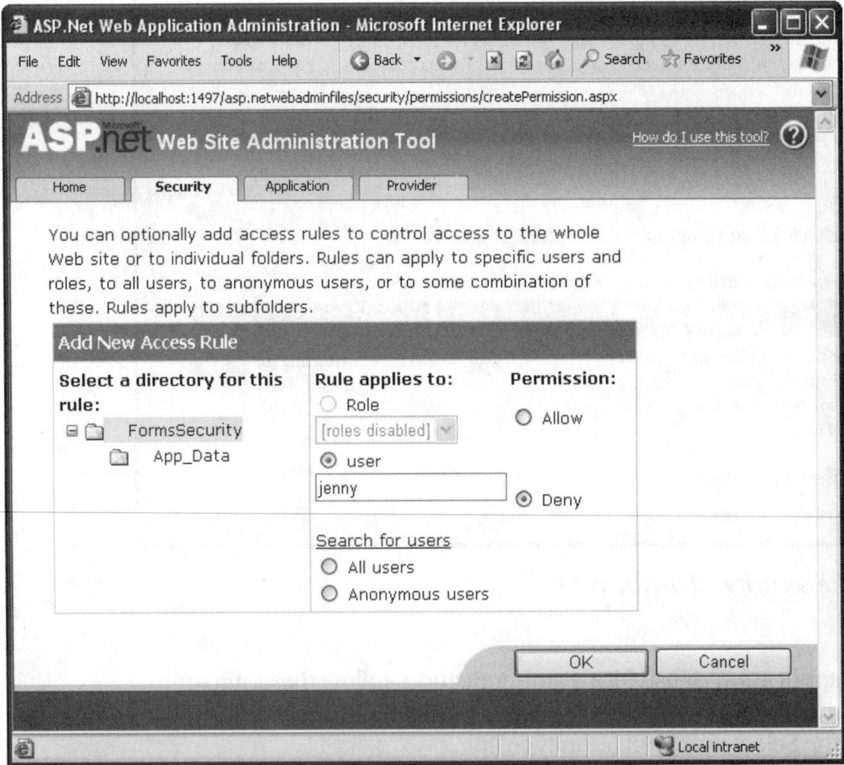

Figure 18-6. *Adding an authorization rule*

To manage multiple rules, you'll need to click the Manage Access Rules link. Now you'll have the chance to change the order of rules (and hence the priority, as described earlier), as shown in Figure 18-7. If you have a large number of rules to create, you may find it's easier to edit the web.config file by hand. You might just want to create one initial rule to make sure it's in the right place and then copy and paste your way to success.

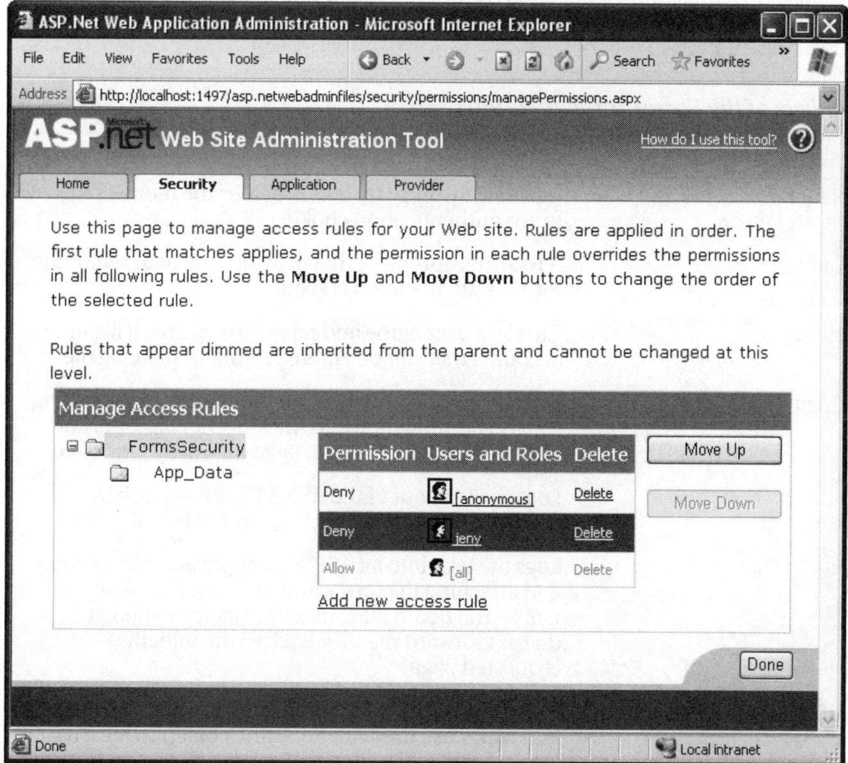

Figure 18-7. *Ordering authorization rules*

The Security tab is a little overwhelming at first glance because it includes a few features you haven't been introduced to yet. For example, the Security tab also allows you to create and manage user records and roles, as long as you're willing to use the prebuilt database structure that ASP.NET requires. You'll learn more about these details, which are a part of a broad feature called *membership*, in the next chapter. For now, you'll concentrate on the authentication and authorization process.

The Login Page

Once you've specified the authentication mode and the authorization rules, you need to build the actual login page, which is an ordinary .aspx page that requests information from the user and decides whether the user should be authenticated.

ASP.NET provides a special FormsAuthentication class in the System.Web.Security namespace, which provides static methods that help manage the process. Table 18-2 describes the most important methods of this class.

Table 18-2. *Members of the FormsAuthentication Class*

Member	Description
FormsCookieName	A read-only property that provides the name of the forms authentication cookie.
FormsCookiePath	A read-only property that provides the path set for the forms authentication cookie.
Authenticate()	Checks a user name and password against a list of accounts that can be entered in the web.config file.
RedirectFromLoginPage()	Logs the user into an ASP.NET application by creating the cookie, attaching it to the current response, and redirecting the user to the page originally requested.
SignOut()	Logs the user out of the ASP.NET application by removing the current encrypted cookie.
SetAuthCookie()	Logs the user into an ASP.NET application by creating and attaching the forms authentication cookie. Unlike the RedirectFromLoginPage() method, it doesn't forward the user back to the initially requested page.
GetRedirectUrl()	Provides the URL of the originally requested page. You could use this with SetAuthCookie() to log a user into an application and make a decision in your code whether to redirect to the requested page or use a more suitable default page.
GetAuthCookie()	Creates the authentication cookie but doesn't attach it to the current response. You can perform additional cookie customization and then add it manually to the response, as described in Chapter 10.
HashPasswordForStoringInConfigFile()	Encrypts a string of text using the specified algorithm (SHA1 or MD5). This hashed value provides a secure way to store an encrypted password in a file or database.

A simple login page can put these methods to work with little code. For example, consider the Login.aspx page in Figure 18-8.

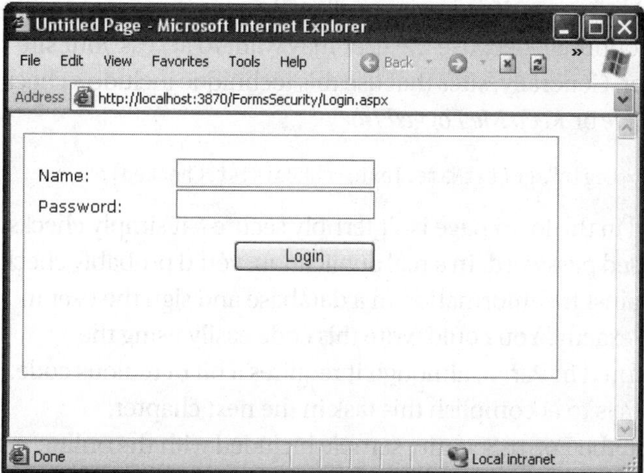

Figure 18-8. *A typical login page*

This page checks whether the user has typed in the password *Secret* and then uses the RedirectFromLoginPage() method to log the user in. Here's the complete page code:

```
public partial class Login : Page
{
    protected void cmdLogin_Click(Object sender, EventArgs e)
    {
        if (txtPassword.Text.ToLower() == "secret")
        {
            FormsAuthentication.RedirectFromLoginPage(
              txtName.Text, false);
        }
        else
        {
            lblStatus.Text = "Try again.";
        }
    }
}
```

The RedirectFromLoginPage() method requires two parameters. The first sets the name of the user. The second is a Boolean variable that creates a persistent forms authentication cookie when set to true or an ordinary forms authentication cookie when set to false. A persistent cookie will be stored on the user's hard drive with an expiration date set to 50 years in the future. This is a convenience that's sometimes useful when you're using the forms authentication login for personalization instead of security. It's also a security risk because another user could conceivably log in from the same computer, acquiring the cookie and the access to the secured pages. If you want to allow the user to create a persistent cookie, you should make it optional, because the user may want to access your site from a public or shared computer. Generally, sites that use this technique include a check box with text such as *Persist Cookie* or *Keep Me Logged In.*

```
FormsAuthentication.RedirectFromLoginPage(txtName.Text, chkPersist.Checked);
```

Obviously, the approach used in the login page isn't terribly secure—it simply checks that the user supplies a hard-coded password. In a real application, you'd probably check the user name and password against the information in a database and sign the user in only if the information matches exactly. You could write this code easily using the ADO.NET programming you learned in Part 3, although it requires a bit of tedious code. You'll consider more practical ways to accomplish this task in the next chapter.

You can test this example with the FormsSecurity sample included with the online code. If you request the SecuredPage.aspx file, you'll be redirected to Login.aspx. After entering the correct password, you'll return to SecuredPage.aspx. As the user is logged in, you can retrieve the identity through the built-in User object, as shown in Figure 18-9.

```
protected void Page_Load(Object sender, EventArgs e)
{
    lblMessage.Text = "You have reached the secured page, ";
    lblMessage.Text += User.Identity.Name + ".";
}
```

Figure 18-9. *Accessing a secured page*

Your application should also feature a prominent logout button that destroys the forms authentication cookie:

```
private void cmdSignOut_Click(Object sender, EventArgs e)
{
    FormsAuthentication.SignOut();
    Response.Redirect("~/Login.aspx");
}
```

■ **Tip** In the next chapter, you'll learn how to simplify life with the login controls. These controls allow you to build login pages (and other types of security-related user interfaces) with no code. However, they require another feature—membership—in order to work.

Windows Authentication

With Windows authentication, IIS takes care of the authentication process. ASP.NET simply uses the authenticated IIS user and makes this identity available to your code for your security checks.

If your virtual directory uses the default settings, users will be authenticated under the anonymous IUSER_[ServerName] account. But when you use Windows authentication, you'll force users to log into IIS before they're allowed to access secure content in your website. The user login information can be transmitted in several ways, but the end result is that the user is authenticated using a local Windows account. Typically, this makes Windows authentication best suited to intranet scenarios, in which a limited set of known users is already registered on a network server.

The advantages of Windows authentication are that it can be performed transparently (depending on the client's operating system and browser) and your ASP.NET code can examine all the account information. For example, you can use the User.IsInRole() method to check which groups a user belongs to.

To implement Windows-based security with known users, you need to follow three steps:

1. Set the authentication mode in the web.config file (or use the WAT).

2. Disable anonymous access for a directory by using an authorization rule (or by disabling access in IIS Manager). You can also choose the protocol that will be used to transmit the user name and password information with IIS Manager.

3. Configure the Windows user accounts on your web server (if they aren't already present).

■Note Most of the discussion in this chapter describes how IIS behaves with Windows authentication. However, when you're testing a web application, you're probably not using IIS. Instead, you're using the built-in web server that's included with Visual Studio. For the most part, this web server works the same as IIS but has one important distinction—it doesn't support anonymous use. This means Visual Studio always logs you into the web server using your Windows account. In IIS, you need to force the user to log in by explicitly denying anonymous access to a page or subdirectory with authorization rules. To see the difference, you may want to test your application with IIS (as explained in Chapter 12).

IIS Settings

To disable anonymous access, start IIS Manager (select Settings ➤ Control Panel ➤ Administrative Tools ➤ Internet Information Services). Then right-click a virtual directory or a subdirectory inside a virtual directory, and choose Properties. Select the Directory Security tab, which is shown in Figure 18-10.

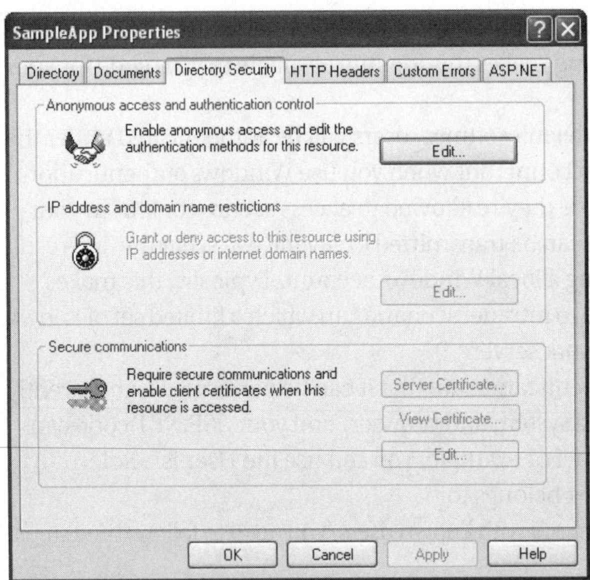

Figure 18-10. *Directory security settings*

Click the Edit button to modify the directory security settings (see Figure 18-11). In the bottom half of the window, you can enable one of the Windows authentication methods. However, none of these methods will be used unless you explicitly clear the Anonymous Access check box. Table 18-3 describes the authentication methods.

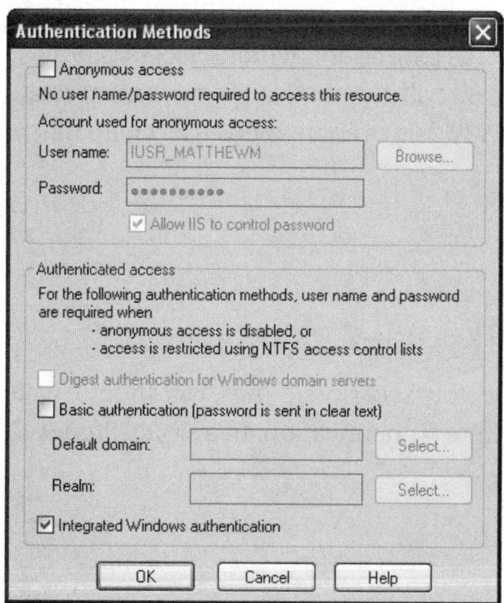

Figure 18-11. *Directory authentication methods*

Table 18-3. *Windows Authentication Methods*

Mode	Description
Anonymous	Anonymous authentication is technically not a true authentication method, because the client isn't required to submit any information. Instead, users are given free access to the website under a special user account, IUSR_[ServerName]. Anonymous authentication is the default.
Basic	Basic authentication is a part of the HTTP 1.0 standard, and almost all browsers and web servers support it. When using Basic authentication, the browser presents the user with a login box with a user name and password field. This information is then transmitted to IIS, where it's matched with a local Windows user account. The disadvantage of Basic authentication is that the password is transmitted in clear text and is visible over the Internet (unless you combine it with SSL technology).
Digest	Digest authentication remedies the primary weakness of Basic authentication: sending passwords in plain text. Digest authentication sends a digest (also known as a *hash*) instead of a password over the network. The primary disadvantage is that Digest authentication is supported only by Internet Explorer 5.0 and later. Your web server also needs to use Active Directory or have access to an Active Directory server.
Integrated	Integrated Windows authentication (formerly known as NTLM authentication and Windows NT Challenge/Response authentication) is the best choice for most intranet scenarios. When using Integrated authentication, Internet Explorer can send the required information automatically using the currently logged-in Windows account on the client, provided it's on a trusted domain. Integrated authentication is supported only on Internet Explorer 2.0 and later and won't work across proxy servers.

You can enable more than one authentication method. In this case, the client will use the strongest authentication method it supports, as long as anonymous access is *not* enabled. If anonymous access is enabled, the client will automatically access the website anonymously, unless the web application explicitly denies anonymous users with this rule in the web.config file:

```
<deny users="?" />
```

Web.config Settings

Once you've enabled the appropriate virtual directory security settings, you should make sure your application is configured to use Windows authentication. In a Visual Studio project, this is the default.

```
<configuration>
    <system.web>
        <!-- Other settings omitted. -->
        <authentication mode="Windows" />
    </system.web>
</configuration>
```

Next, you can add <allow> and <deny> elements to specifically allow or restrict users from specific files or directories. You can also restrict certain types of users, provided their accounts are members of the same Windows group, by using the roles attribute:

```
<authorization>
    <deny users="?" />
    <allow roles="Administrator,SuperUser" />
    <deny users="matthew" />
</authorization>
```

In this example, all users who are members of the Administrator or SuperUser group will be automatically authorized to access ASP.NET pages in this directory. Requests from the user matthew will be denied, unless he is a member of the Administrator or SuperUser group. Remember, ASP.NET examines rules in the order they appear and stops when it finds a match. Reversing these two authorization lines would ensure that the user matthew was always denied, regardless of group membership.

If you using Windows authentication, you must use the more explicit syntax shown here, which precedes the user name with the name of the domain or server:

```
<allow users="MyDomainName\matthew" />
```

You can also examine a user's group membership programmatically in your code. Since the string includes a backslash, you need to remember to double it, or you can turn off C# escaping with a preceding at sign (@), as shown here:

```
protected void Page_Load(Object sender, EventArgs e)
{
    if (User.IsInRole(@"MyDomainName\SalesAdministrators"))
    {
        // Do nothing; the page should be accessed as normal because
        // the user has administrator privileges.
    }
    else
    {
        // Don't allow this page. Instead, redirect to the home page.
        Response.Redirect("default.aspx");
    }
}
```

In this example, the code checks for membership in a custom Windows group called SalesAdministrators. If you want to check whether a user is a member of one of the built-in groups, you don't need to specify a computer or domain name. Instead, you use this syntax:

```
if (User.IsInRole(@"BUILTIN\Administrators"))
{
    // (Code goes here.)
}
```

For more information about the <allow> and <deny> rules and configuring individual files and directories, refer to the discussion in the "Authorization Rules" section earlier in this chapter.

Note that you have no way to retrieve a list of available groups on the web server (that would violate security), but you can find out the names of the default built-in Windows roles using the System.Security.Principal.WindowsBuiltInRole enumeration. Table 18-4 describes these roles. Not all will apply to ASP.NET use, although Administrator, Guest, and User probably will.

Table 18-4. *Default Windows Roles*

Role	Description
AccountOperator	Users with the special responsibility of managing the user accounts on a computer or domain.
Administrator	Users with complete and unrestricted access to the computer or domain.
BackupOperator	Users who can override certain security restrictions only as part of backing up or restore operations.
Guest	Like the User role but even more restrictive.
PowerUser	Similar to Administrator but with some restrictions.
PrintOperator	Like User but with additional privileges for taking control of a printer.
Replicator	Like User but with additional privileges to support file replication in a domain.
SystemOperator	Similar to Administrator with some restrictions. Generally, system operators manage a computer.
User	Users are prevented from making systemwide changes and can run only *certified applications* (see `http://www.microsoft.com/windows2000/server/evaluation/business/certified.asp` for more information).

A Windows Authentication Test

One of the nice features of Windows authentication is that no login page is required. Once you enable it in IIS, your web application can retrieve information directly from the User object. You can access some additional information by converting the generic Identity object to a WindowsIdentity object (which is defined in the System.Security.Principal namespace).

The following is a sample test page that uses Windows authentication (see Figure 18-12):

```
public partial class SecuredPage : Page
{
    protected void Page_Load(Object sender, EventArgs e)
    {
        StringBuilder displayText = new StringBuilder();
        displayText.Append("You have reached the secured page, ");
        displayText.Append(User.Identity.Name);

        WindowsIdentity winIdentity = (WindowsIdentity)User.Identity;
        displayText.Append(".<br /><br />Authentication Type: ");
        displayText.Append(winIdentity.AuthenticationType);
        displayText.Append("<br />Anonymous: ");
```

```
        displayText.Append(winIdentity.IsAnonymous);
        displayText.Append("<br />Authenticated: ");
        displayText.Append(winIdentity.IsAuthenticated);
        displayText.Append("<br />Guest: ");
        displayText.Append(winIdentity.IsGuest);
        displayText.Append("<br />System: ");
        displayText.Append(winIdentity.IsSystem);
        displayText.Append("<br />Administrator: ");
        displayText.Append(User.IsInRole(@"BUILTIN\Administrators"));

        lblMessage.Text = displayText.ToString();
    }
}
```

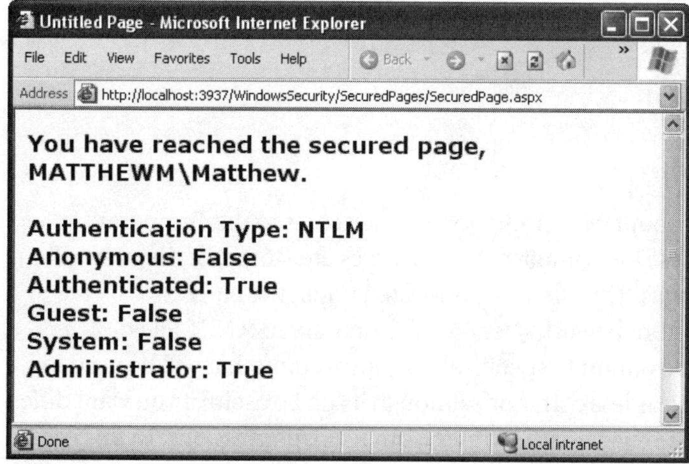

Figure 18-12. *Retrieving Windows authentication information*

Impersonation

Impersonation is an additional option that's available in Windows or forms authentication, although it's most common with Windows users in an intranet scenario. For impersonation to work, the authenticated user account must correspond to a Windows account, which isn't guaranteed (or even likely) with forms authentication.

With impersonation, your ASP.NET code interacts with the system under the identity of the authenticated user—not the normal system account. You'll usually choose this technique when you don't want to worry about authorization details in your code.

For example, if you have a simple application that displays XML files, you can set specific permissions for each XML file, restricting them from some users and allowing them to others. Unfortunately, your ASP.NET XML viewer utility always executes under the ASPNET or local system account, which probably has the authority to view all these files. Thus, any authenticated user can view any file. To remedy this situation, you can specifically add user verification checks in your code and refuse to open files that aren't allowed. However, this will typically result in a lot of extra code. On the other hand, if impersonation is enabled, your ASP.NET code will be prevented from accessing any XML files the current user isn't allowed to view. Of course, this means your application will encounter an error when you try to read the file—so you'll need to use exception handling code to deal with the situation gracefully.

To enable impersonation, you simply add an <identity> tag to the web.config file, as shown here:

```
<configuration>
    <system.web>
        <!-- Other settings omitted. -->
        <identity impersonate="true" >
    </system.web>
</configuration>
```

Keep in mind the user account will require read-write access to the Temporary ASP.NET Files directory where the compiled ASP.NET files are stored, or the user will not be able to access any pages. This directory is located under the path C:\[WinDir]\Microsoft.NET\Framework\[Version]\Temporary ASP.NET Files.

ASP.NET also provides the option to specifically set an account that will be used for running code. This technique is less common, although it can be useful if you want different ASP.NET applications to execute with different, but fixed, permissions. In this case, the user's authenticated identity isn't used by the ASP.NET code.

```
<configuration>
    <system.web>
        <!-- Other settings omitted. -->
        <identity impersonate="true" userName="matthew" password="secret" >
    </system.web>
</configuration>
```

This approach is more flexible than changing the machine.config account setting. The machine.config setting determines the default account that will be used for all web applications on the computer. The impersonation settings, on the other hand, override the machine.config setting for individual websites.

Unfortunately, the password for the impersonated account cannot be encrypted in the web.config file. This may constitute a security risk if other users have access to the computer and can read the password.

Programmatic Impersonation

Sometimes it's more useful to use impersonation programmatically through the WindowsIdentity.Impersonate() method. This allows you to execute some code in the identity of a specific user (such as your file access routine) but allows the rest of your code to run under the local system account, guaranteeing it won't encounter any problems.

To use programmatic impersonation, you need to use Windows authentication by disabling anonymous access for the virtual directory. You also need to make sure impersonation is disabled for your web application. (In other words, make sure you do *not* add the <identity> tag to your web.config file.) This way, the standard account defined in the machine.config file will be used by default, but the authenticated Windows identity will be available for you to use when you need it.

The following code shows how your code can use the Impersonate() method to switch identities:

```
if (User.GetType() == typeof(WindowsPrincipal))
{
    WindowsIdentity id;
    id = (WindowsIdentity)User.Identity;
    WindowsImpersonationContext impersonateContext;
    impersonateContext = id.Impersonate();

    // Now perform tasks under the impersonated ID.
    // This code will not be able to perform any task
    // (such as reading a file) that the user would not be allowed to do.

    // Revert to the original ID as shown below.
    impersonateContext.Undo();
}
else
{
    // User isn't Windows authenticated.
    // Throw an error or take other steps.
}
```

The Last Word

In this chapter, you learned about the multilayered security architecture in ASP.NET and IIS and how you can safeguard your web pages and web services by using a custom login page or Windows authentication. You also learned the basics about certificates and SSL.

In the next chapter, you'll continue to build on your knowledge by considering some add-on features that can simplify your life and enhance your security. You'll learn how to get ASP.NET to create a basic user database for your site (complete with password encryption), saving you from creating it yourself or writing any ADO.NET code. You'll also extend your authorization rules by learning how you can group forms-authenticated users into logical groups, each of which can be assigned its own permissions.

CHAPTER 19

Membership

In the previous chapter, you learned how you can use ASP.NET forms authentication as the cornerstone of your website security. With forms authentication, you can identify users and restrict them from pages they shouldn't access. Best of all, ASP.NET manages the whole process for you by creating and checking the forms authentication cookie.

As convenient as forms authentication is, it isn't a complete solution. It's still up to you to take care of a variety of related tasks. For example, you need to maintain a user list and check it during the authentication process. You also need to create the login page, decide how to separate public from private content, and decide what each user should be allowed to do. These tasks aren't insurmountable, but they can be tedious. That's why Microsoft decided to add another layer of features to its authentication framework in ASP.NET 2.0. This extra layer is known as *membership*.

The membership features fall into three broad categories:

User record management: Rather than create your own user database, if you use the membership features, ASP.NET can create and maintain this catalog of user information. It can even implement advanced rules (such as requiring e-mail addresses, asking security questions, and implementing strong passwords).

Security controls: Every secure website needs a login page. With ASP.NET's security controls, you don't need to design your own—instead, you can use a ready-made version straight from the Toolbox. And along with the basic Login control are other controls for displaying secure content, creating new users, and changing passwords. Best of all, you can customize how every security control works by setting properties and reacting to events.

Role-based security: In many websites, you need to give different permissions to different users. Of course, life would be far too complex if you had to maintain a different set of settings for each user, so instead it's useful to assemble users into groups that define certain permissions. These groups are called *roles*, and ASP.NET's membership features include tools for automatically creating a database with role information.

In this chapter, you'll explore all three of these feature areas and see how you can create secure sites with surprisingly little code.

The Membership Data Store

The key membership feature is the ability of ASP.NET to store user credentials in a database. The idea is that you make a few choices about the information that will be stored and the security policy that will be used. From that point on, ASP.NET manages the user database for you—adding new user information, checking credentials when users try to log in, and so on.

Clearly, the membership data store has the ability to greatly reduce the amount of code you need to write. You can create a secure website with much less code and hence much less work. You also don't need to worry about inevitable bugs, because the ASP.NET membership module is a well-known, carefully tested component.

So, why *wouldn't* you want to use the membership data store? A few possible reasons exist:

You don't want to store your data in a database: In theory, you can store your user list in any type of data store, from an XML file to an Oracle database. Technically, each data store requires a different *membership provider*. However, ASP.NET includes only two providers—the SQL Server provider you'll use in this chapter and a provider for Active Directory. If you want to use another data store, such as a different relational database, you'll need to find a corresponding membership, or you'll need to forgo membership altogether.

You need backward compatibility: If you've already created a table to store user information, it may be too much trouble to switch over to the membership data store. That's because the SQL Server membership provider expects a specific table structure. It won't work with existing tables, because they'll have a subtly different combination of fields and data types. And even if you don't need to keep the current table structure, you might find it's just too much work to re-create all your user records in the membership data store.

You want to manage user information in non-ASP.NET applications: As you'll see in this chapter, ASP.NET gives you a powerful set of objects for interacting with membership data. For example, you can update user records, delete user records, retrieve user records based on certain criteria, and so on. However, if you're creating another application outside ASP.NET that needs to perform these tasks, you might find it's not as easy, because you'll need to understand the membership table structure. In this case, you may find that it's easier to manage users with straight SQL statements that work with your own user table.

If you decide not to use the membership data store, it's up to you to write ADO.NET code to retrieve user records and check user credentials. Using these techniques, you can create your own login pages the hard way, as explained in Chapter 18.

Before continuing any further, you should set up your website to use forms authentication by adding the <forms> tag. Here's what you need to add:

```
<configuration>
    <system.web>
        <authentication mode="Forms" />
    </system.web>
</configuration>
```

Optionally, you can define additional details such as the location of the login page and the time before the security cookie times out, as described in Chapter 18. You may also want to add an authorization rule that prevents anonymous users from accessing a specific page or subfolder so that you can better test your website security.

Membership with SQL Server 2005 Express

Assuming you do decide to use membership, you need to create the membership database. However, if you're using SQL Server 2005 Express Edition, the task is a lot easier than you might expect. In fact, it all happens automatically.

By default, membership is enabled for every new website you create. The default membership provider makes the following assumptions:

- You want to store your membership database using SQL Server 2005 Express Edition.
- SQL Server 2005 Express Edition is installed on the current computer, with the instance name SQLEXPRESS.
- Your membership data store will be a file named aspnetdb.mdf, which will be stored in the App_Data subdirectory of the web application.

These assumptions make a lot of sense. They allow you to create as many web applications as you want while still keeping the user databases separate. That's because each website will have its own aspnetdb.mdf file. These files are never registered in SQL Server, which means when you open a connection in another application, you won't see dozens of user databases. Instead, the only way to connect to them is to specify the file path in the connection string, which ASP.NET does.

Another advantage of this setup is that it's potentially easier to deploy your website. Assuming the web server where you'll deploy your application has SQL Server 2005 Express Edition, you won't need to change the connection string. You also don't need to perform any extra steps to install the database—you simply copy the aspnetdb.mdf file with your website. If the target server is using the full version of SQL Server 2005, your application will still work, provided the default connection string in the machine.config file has been adjusted accordingly. You still won't need to worry about installing the database manually. This is clearly a great advantage for large web hosting companies, because it's otherwise quite complex to support multiple websites, each with its own custom database that needs to be installed and maintained.

To see how this works, it helps to create a new web project with a simple test page. Drag the CreateUserWizard control onto your page from the Login section of the Toolbox. Now run the page (shown in Figure 19-1), without adding any code or configuring the control.

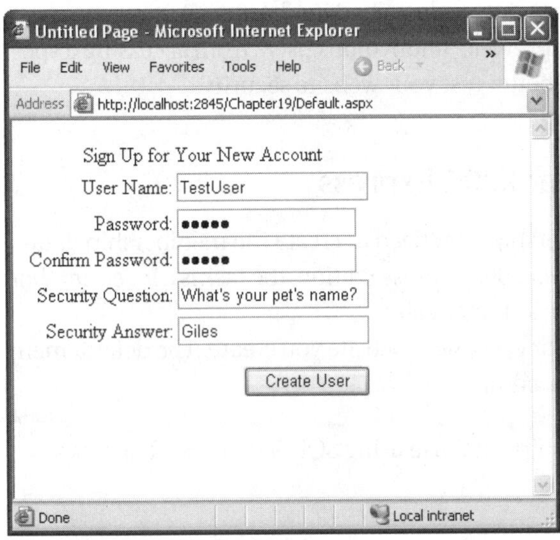

Figure 19-1. *The CreateUserWizard control*

Fill in all the text boxes with user information. Note that by default you need to supply a password that includes at least one character that isn't a number or letter (such as an underscore or asterisk). Once you've filled in all the information, click Create User.

At this point, the CreateUserWizard control uses the ASP.NET Membership class behind the scenes to create a new user. The default membership provider creates the aspnetdb.mdf file (if it doesn't exist already) and then adds the new user record. Once this process is complete, the CreateUserWizard control shows a message informing you that the user was created. Miraculously, all of this takes place automatically even though you haven't configured anything in the web.config file and you didn't create the database file in advance.

To reassure yourself that the user really was created, you can check for the aspnetdb.mdf file. In the Solution Explorer, right-click the App_Data folder, and select Refresh Folder. You'll see the aspnetdb.mdf file appear immediately. Using Visual Studio, you can even dig into the contents of the aspnetdb.mdf file. To do so, double-click the file in the Solution Explorer. Visual Studio will configure a new connection and add it to the

Server Explorer on the left. Using the Server Explorer, you can roam freely through the database, examining its tables and stored procedures.

Check the aspnet_Users table to find the user record you created. Just right-click the table name, and choose Show Table Data. You'll see something like the record shown in Figure 19-2. Among other details, you'll find a randomly generated GUID that uniquely identifies the user and the date the user last used your web application. You won't see the password and password question—that's stored in a linked record in the aspnet_Membership table, and it's encrypted to prevent casual snooping.

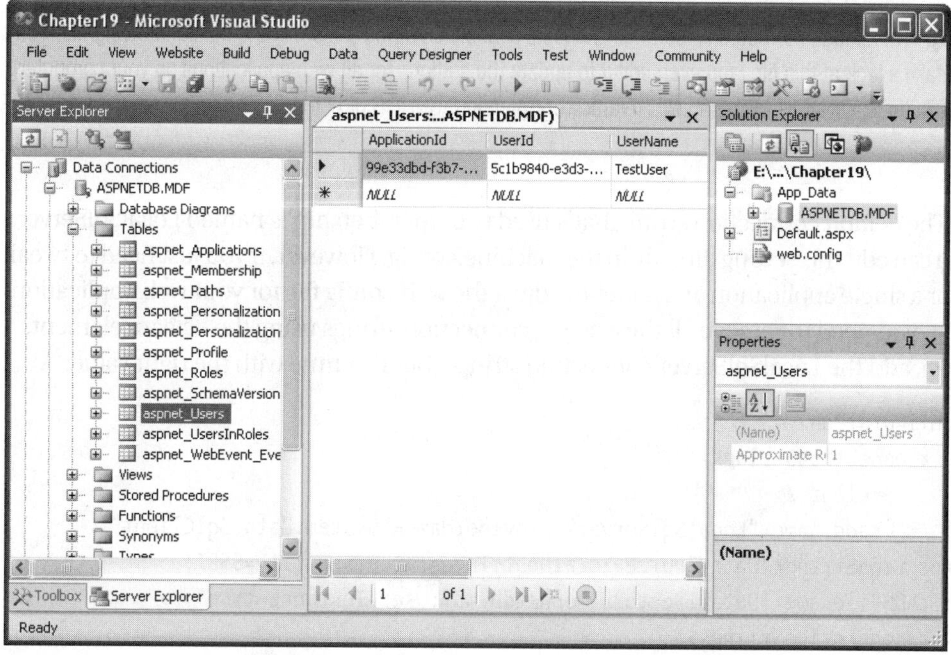

Figure 19-2. *A user record in the aspnetdb.mdf database*

Note At first glance, you'll find the membership database includes a dizzying number of tables. Some of these tables are for other related features you may or may not use, such as role-based security (discussed later in the "Role-Based Security" section) and profiles (discussed in Chapter 20).

Before diving into the rest of ASP.NET's membership features in detail, it's important to consider what you should do if you don't want the default membership data store. For example, you might decide to store your membership tables in a different database, or you might want to configure one of the many options for the membership provider. You'll learn how to do so in the next two sections.

Configuring the Membership Provider

If you're using the automatically generated database for SQL Server 2005 Express Edition, you don't need to touch the web.config file. In any other case, you'll need to do a bit of configuration tweaking.

The simplest case is if you are using the full version of SQL Server 2005. In this case, you can still use the default membership settings. However, you need to change the connection string.

■ **Tip** The default membership settings and local connection string are set in the machine.config file. You can take a look at this file (and even edit it to update the settings for all web applications on your computer). Look in the C:\[WinDir]\Microsoft.NET\Framework\[Version]\CONFIG directory.

The default connection string that's used with membership is named LocalSqlServer. You can edit this setting directly in the machine.config. However, if you just need to tweak it for a single application, it's better to adjust the web.config file for your web application. First, you need to remove all the existing connection strings using the <clear> element. Then, add the LocalSqlServer connection string—but this time with the right value:

```
<configuration>
    <connectionStrings>
        <clear />
        <add name="LocalSqlServer" providerName="System.Data.SqlClient"
connectionString="Data Source=localhost;Integrated Security=SSPI;
AttachDBFilename=|DataDirectory|aspnetdb.mdf;User Instance=true" />
    </connectionStrings>
    ...
</configuration>
```

This <connectionStrings> section removes all connection strings and then creates a new connection string. This new connection string is almost identical to the version in the machine.config file—the only difference is that it specifies the Data Source value of localhost rather than localhost\SQLEXPRESS. This means the connection string connects to the default instance of SQL Server. By default, the full edition of SQL Server installs itself as a named instance, and SQL Server 2005 Express Edition installs itself as a named instance with the instance name SQLEXPRESS. The changed connection string still uses the AttachDBFileName parameter, which allows it to connect directly to a database file in the

App_Data directory. As with the default settings, this file will be named aspnetdb.mdf, and it will be created automatically if required. If you want, you could change the file name by modifying the AttachDBFilename parameter.

If you're an older version of SQL Server, such as SQL Server 2000, you need to go to a little more work. SQL Server 2000 doesn't support the AttachDBFilename option, so you'll need to supply the name of a database on your server. By convention, this database usually has the name aspnetdb (although you will probably change this if you want to support several distinct web applications with the same database server).

Here's a connection string that uses the aspnetdb database and is suitable for SQL Server 2000:

```
<configuration>
    <connectionStrings>
        <clear />
        <add name="LocalSqlServer" providerName="System.Data.SqlClient"
        connectionString=
"Data Source=localhost;Integrated Security=SSPI; Initial Catalog=aspnetdb"
        />
    </connectionStrings>
    ...
</configuration>
```

The only catch is that the aspnetdb database won't be created automatically. Instead, you'll need to perform the steps in the following section to generate it with the aspnet_regsql.exe command-line tool.

Configuring the connection string is the simplest change you can make when setting up the membership data store. However, you may also want to tweak other membership settings. For example, you can change the default password policy.

■ **Note** As with the connection string, the default membership provider is defined in the machine.config file. You can edit the machine.config file to change these defaults for all applications on the computer, but you shouldn't, because it will complicate your life when you deploy the application. Instead, you should make the changes by configuring a new membership provider in your application's web.config file.

To configure your membership provider, you need to add the <membership> element to your web application. Inside the <membership> element, you define a new membership provider with your custom settings. Then, you set the defaultProvider attribute of the <membership> element so it refers to your membership provider by name.

Here's the basic structure you need to follow:

```
<configuration>
    ...
    <system.web>
        <membership defaultProvider="MyMembershipProvider">
            <providers>
                <!-- Clear any existing providers. -->
                <clear />

                <!-- Define your provider, with custom settings. -->
                <add name="MyMembershipProvider" ... />
            </providers>
        </membership>
        ...
    </system.web>
</configuration>
```

Of course, the interesting part is the attributes you use in the <add> tag to configure your membership provider. Here's an example that defines a membership provider with relaxed password settings. The first three attributes supply required settings (the name, type, and connection string for the membership provider). The remaining settings remove the requirement for a security question and allow a password to be as short as one character and contain only letters.

```
<membership defaultProvider="MyMembershipProvider">
    <providers>
        <clear/>
        <add
          name="MyMembershipProvider"
          type="System.Web.Security.SqlMembershipProvider"
          connectionStringName="LocalSqlServer"
          requiresQuestionAndAnswer="false"
          minRequiredPasswordLength="1"
          minRequiredNonalphanumericCharacters="0" />
    </providers>
</membership>
```

Table 19-1 describes the most commonly used membership settings.

Table 19-1. *Attributes for Configuring a Membership Provider*

Attribute	Description
name*	Specifies a name for the membership provider. You can choose any name you want. This is the name you use later to reference the provider (for example, when you set the defaultProvider attribute). You can also use it to get provider information programmatically.
type*	The type of membership provider. In this chapter, you will always be using the System.Web. Security.SqlMembershipProvider. ASP.NET also includes an ActiveDirectoryMembershipProvider, which allows you to use the membership features with Windows authentication through an Active Directory server. (For more information on this topic, consult the MSDN Help.) Finally, you can use a custom membership provider that you or a third-party developer creates.
applicationName	The name of the web application. This setting is primarily useful if you have several web applications using the same membership database. If you give each one a separate application name, all the information (including user, profiles, and so on) is completely separated so it's usable only in the appropriate application.
connectionStringName*	The name of the connection string setting. This must correspond to a connection string defined in the <connectionStrings> section of web.config or machine.config.
description	An optional description for the membership provider.
passwordFormat	Sets the way passwords are stored in the database. You can use Clear (passwords are stored as is, with no encryption), Encrypted (passwords are encrypted using a computer-specific key), or Hash (passwords are hashed, and the hash value is stored in the database). Hashing passwords offers similar protection to encrypting them (namely, if you look at the hash you'll have a difficult time reverse-engineering the password). However, when passwords are hashed, they can never be retrieved—only reset.
minRequiredPasswordLength	Specifies the minimum length of a password. If the user enters fewer characters, it will be rejected with an error message.

Continued

Table 19-1. *Continued*

Attribute	Description
minRequiredNonAlphanumericCharacters	Specifies the number of nonalphanumeric characters (characters other than numbers and letters) the password needs to have. If the user enters fewer, it will be rejected with an error message. Although requiring nonalphanumeric characters makes for stronger (less guessable) passwords, it also can confuse users, causing them to forget their passwords more often or (worse) write them down in a conspicuous place, where they might be stolen.
maxInvalidPasswordAttempts	Specifies the number of times a user can supply an invalid password for their login before the user account is locked and made inaccessible.
passwordAttemptWindow	The internal time in which maxInvalidPasswordAttempts is measured. For example, if you set a window of 30 minutes, after 30 minutes the number of invalid password attempts is reset. If the user surpasses the maxInvalidPasswordAttempts within passwordAttemptWindow, the account is locked.
enablePasswordReset	Determines whether a password can be reset, which is useful if a password is forgotten.
enablePasswordRetrieval	Determines whether a password can be requested (and e-mailed to the user), which is useful if a user forgets a password. This feature is never supported if passwordFormat is set to Hash, because the password isn't stored in that case.
requiresQuestionAndAnswer	Determines whether the membership security answer will be required when you request or reset a user password.
requiresUniqueEmail	If false, more than one user can have the same e-mail address. The e-mail address information is always optional.

* *This setting is required.*

Now that you've seen the settings you can tweak, it's worth asking what the defaults are. If you look at the <membership> section in the machine.config file, here's what you'll find:

```
<membership>
    <providers>
        <add name="AspNetSqlMembershipProvider"
            type="System.Web.Security.SqlMembershipProvider"
            connectionStringName="LocalSqlServer"
```

```
            enablePasswordRetrieval="false" enablePasswordReset="true"
            requiresQuestionAndAnswer="true" applicationName="/"
            requiresUniqueEmail="false" passwordFormat="Hashed"
            minRequiredPasswordLength="7"
            minRequiredNonalphanumericCharacters="1"
            passwordAttemptWindow="10" maxInvalidPasswordAttempts="5" />
    </providers>
</membership>
```

As you can see, the default membership provider is AspNetSqlMembershipProvider. It connects using the LocalSqlServer connection string and supports password resets but not password retrieval. Accounts require a security question but not a unique e-mail. The passwords themselves are hashed in the database for security, so they can't be retrieved. Passwords must be seven characters long with one nonalphanumeric character. Finally, if a user makes five invalid password attempts in ten minutes, the account is disabled.

Manually Creating the Membership Tables

If you don't want to use the automatically created SQL Server 2005 database, you'll need to create the membership data tables on your own. ASP.NET includes a tool for this purpose, aspnet_regsql. Rather than hunt around for this file, the easiest way to launch it is to fire up the Visual Studio command prompt (choose Programs ➤ Visual Studio 2005 ➤ Visual Studio Tools ➤ Visual Studio 2005 Command Prompt from the Start menu) and then type it in.

You can use aspnet_regsql in two ways. If you use it without adding any command-line parameters, a Windows wizard will appear that leads you through the process. You'll be asked to supply the connection information for your database server. The database will be named aspnetdb, which is the recommended default. The contents of aspnetdb will be the same as the contents of the aspnetdb.mdf file demonstrated in the previous section.

Your other option is to specify exactly what you want to happen using command-line switches. This is particularly useful when deploying your application—you can use aspnet_regsql as part of a setup batch file, which will then create the membership data store automatically. This is the option you'll use if you want to choose the database name or if you want to install only some of the database tables. By default, the aspnet_regsql tool installs tables that can be used for user authentication, role-based authorization, profiles, and Web Parts personalization. This gives you maximum flexibility, but you may feel it's overkill if you aren't planning to use some of these features.

Table 19-2 describes all the command-line options. Here's an example command line that connects to an unnamed SQL Server instance on the current computer (using the -S parameter), connects with the current Windows account (using the -E parameter), installs all tables (using the -A parameter), and places them all in a database named AspDatabase (with the -d parameter):

```
aspnet_regsql -S (local) -E -A all -d AspDatabase
```

■ **Tip** It's a good idea to install all the tables at once (using the -A all option). This way, your database will be ready for the profile feature discussed in the next chapter. Once you've finished testing your application and you're ready to create the final database, you can create a database that just has the options you've decided to use. (For example, use -A mr to use membership and role management but nothing else.)

Table 19-2. *Command-Line Switches for aspnet_regsql.exe*

Switch	Description
-S ServerName	Specifies the location of the SQL Server instance where you want to install the database.
-E	Connects to the server through Windows authentication, using the currently logged-in Windows account.
-U UserName and -P Password	Specifies the user name and password you need to connect to the SQL Server database. Usually, you'll use -E instead.
-A	Specifies the features that you want to use (and determines the database tables that are created). Valid options for this switch are all, m (membership), r (role-based security), p (profiles), c (Web Part personalization), and w (for database cache dependencies with SQL Server 2000).
-R	Removes the databases specified by the -A switch.
-d DatabaseName	Allows you to specify the name of the database in which the tables will be created. If you don't specify this parameter, a database named aspnetdb is created automatically.
-sqlexportonly	Creates SQL scripts for the specified options but doesn't actually create the tables in the database. Instead, you can run the script afterward. This is useful technique for deploying your application.

Of course, once you've taken this step, you'll need to configure the membership provider so it knows where to find the membership data store, or it will simply continue trying to use an autogenerated SQL Server 2005 Express Edition database. You do this by tweaking the connection string, as described in the previous section.

Creating Users with the WAT

Once you've created the membership data store and (optionally) configured the membership provider, you're ready to use membership-backed security in your web application. As you've already seen, you can create new users with the CreateUserWizard control. You'll consider the CreateUserWizard control and the other security controls later in this chapter. First, it's worth considering your other options for setting up your user list.

One option is to use the WAT. Choose Website ➤ ASP.NET Web Configuration to launch this tool. Next, click the Security tab. In the bottom-left corner, a box indicates how many users are currently in the database (see Figure 19-3). This box also provides links that allow you to examine the existing user records or add new ones.

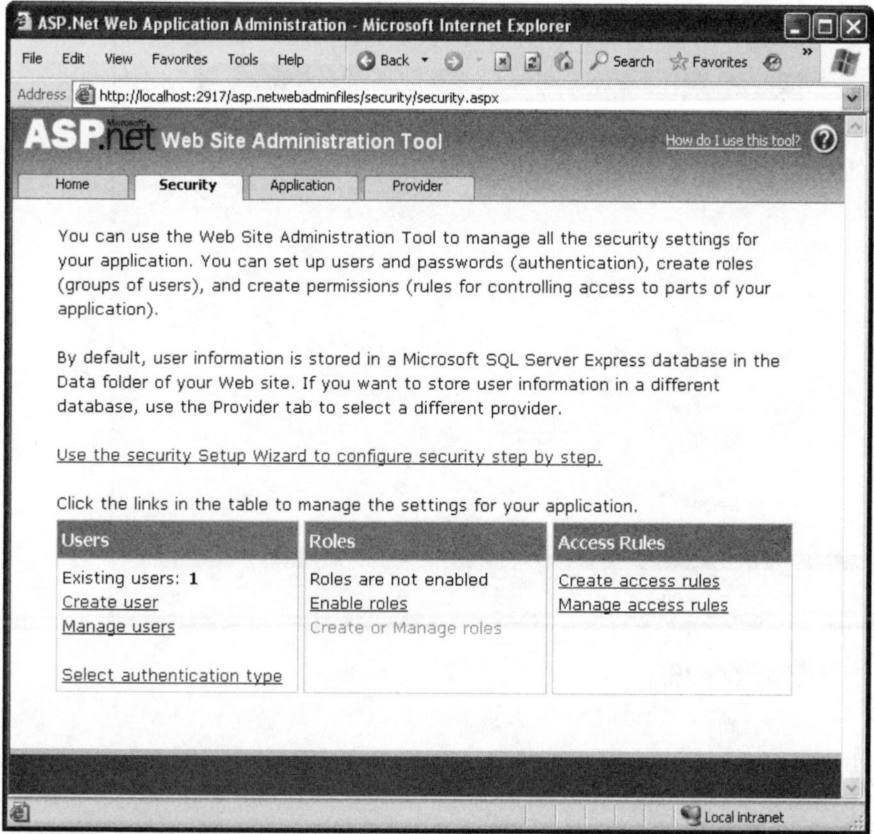

Figure 19-3. *Managing website security with the WAT*

If you want to browse the current user list or update an existing user record, click the Manage Users link. To add new users, click Create User. You'll see a set of controls that are similar to the CreateUserWizard control used in the test page earlier (see Figure 19-4). After you've created a few users, you may want to take another look at the aspnet_Users and aspnet_Membership tables in your database to see what the user records look like.

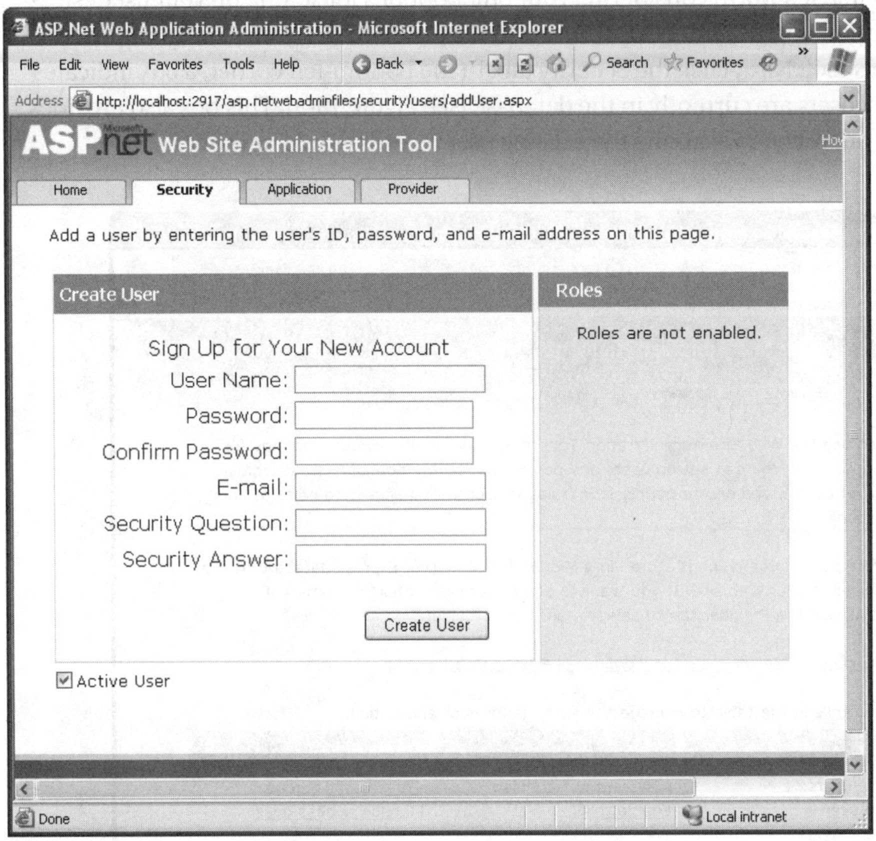

Figure 19-4. *Creating a new user*

Although the WAT is a perfectly sensible way to add user records, you might find the web interface is a little sluggish if you have a large number of users to create. Another option is to use the Membership class, as shown here:

```
// Create a user record based with user name, password, and e-mail information.
Membership.CreateUser(userName, password, email);
```

Here's an example with hard-coded values:

```
Membership.CreateUser("joes", "ignreto12__", "joes@domains.com");
```

This creates a new user with just a single line of code. Of course, the CreateUser() method has multiple overloads, which you can use to supply details such as the password question and answer. If you haven't changed the default membership settings, you won't be able to create an account unless you provide these details. Instead, you'll need to use this more complex overload:

```
MembershipCreateStatus createStatus;
Membership.CreateUser("joes", "ignreto12__", "joes@domains.com",
  "What is your favorite restaurant?", "Saigon", true, out createStatus);
```

The first few parameters are self-explanatory—they take the user name, password, e-mail address, password question, and password answer. The second-to-last parameter takes a Boolean value that determines whether the account is given the IsApproved flag. If you supply false, the account won't be usable until you modify it using the Membership.UpdateUser() method. In the simpler overload that doesn't include this parameter, accounts are always marked as approved.

The last parameter returns a value from the MembershipCreateStatus enumeration. If this value isn't MembershipCreateStatus.Success, an error occurred when creating the record. The value indicates the exact error condition (for example, a password that wasn't strong enough, a duplicate e-mail address when your membership provider doesn't allow duplicates, and so on). In the simpler overload that doesn't include the MembershipCreateStatus, any error results in an exception object being thrown that has the same information.

■ **Tip** Clearly, if you needed to transfer a large number of user accounts from a custom database into the membership data store, the quickest option would be to write a routine that loops through the existing records and use the CreateUser() method to insert the new ones.

The Membership and MembershipUser Classes

There wouldn't be much point to using the membership data store if you still needed to write handcrafted ADO.NET code to retrieve or modify user information. That's why ASP.NET offers a more convenient, higher-level model with the Membership class.

Membership is a useful class that's full of practical static methods such as CreateUser(). You can find it in the System.Web.Security namespace. Table 19-3 provides a snapshot of its most useful methods.

Table 19-3. *Membership Methods*

Method	Description
CreateUser()	Adds a new user to the database.
DeleteUser()	Deletes an existing user from the database. You specify the user by the user name. You can also choose whether you want to delete all related data in other tables (the default is to remove it).
GetUser()	Gets a specific user from the database, by user name.
GetUserNameByEmail()	Retrieves a user name for the user that matches a given e-mail address. Keep in mind that duplicate e-mail addresses are allowed by default, in which case this method will find only the first match.
FindUsersByName()	Gets users from the membership database that match a given user name. This supports partial matches, so User will match TestUser, User001, and so on.
FindUsersByEmail()	Gets users from the membership database that match a specific e-mail address. You can also supply part of an e-mail address (such as the domain name), in which case you'll get every user who has an e-mail address that contains this text.
GetAllUsers()	Gets a collection that represents all the users in the database. An overloaded version of this method allows you to get just a portion of the full user list (a single page of users, based on a starting index and length).
GetNumberOfUsersOnline()	Gets the number of logged-in users currently accessing an application. This calculation assumes a user is online if that user's last activity time stamp falls within a set time limit (such as 20 minutes).
GeneratePassword()	Generates a random password of the specified length. This is useful when programmatically creating new user records.
UpdateUser()	Updates the database with new information for a specific user.
ValidateUser()	Tests whether the supplied user name and password are valid.

The Membership class also provides static read-only properties that let you retrieve information about the configuration of your membership provider, as set in the configuration file. For example, you can retrieve the required password length, the maximum number of password attempts, and all the other details described in Table 19-1.

Many of these methods use the MembershipUser class, which represents a user record. For example, when you call GetUser(), you receive the information as a MembershipUser object. If you want to update that user, you can change its properties and then call Membership.UpdateUser() with the modified MembershipUser object.

■ **Note** The MembershipUser object combines the details from the aspnet_Users table and the linked aspnet_Membership table. For example, it includes the password question. However, the password answer and the password itself aren't available.

The MembershipUser class also provides its own smaller set of methods, as detailed in Table 19-4.

Table 19-4. *Membership User Methods*

Method	Description
UnlockUser()	Reactivates a user account that was locked out for too many invalid login attempts.
GetPassword()	Retrieves a user password. If requiresQuestionAndAnswer is true in the membership configuration (which is the default), you must supply the answer to the password question in order to retrieve a password. Note that this method won't work at all if the passwordFormat setting is Hash, which is also the default.
ResetPassword()	Resets a user password using a new, randomly generated password, which this method returns. If requiresQuestionAndAnswer is true in the membership configuration (which is the default), you must supply the answer to the password question in order to reset a password. You can display the new password for the user or send it in an e-mail.
ChangePassword()	Changes a user password. You must supply the current password in order to apply a new one.
ChangePasswordQuestionAndAnswer()	Changes a user password question and answer. You must supply the current password in order to change the security question.

To get a sense of how the Membership class works, you can create a simple test page that displays a list of all the users in the membership database. Figure 19-5 shows this page.

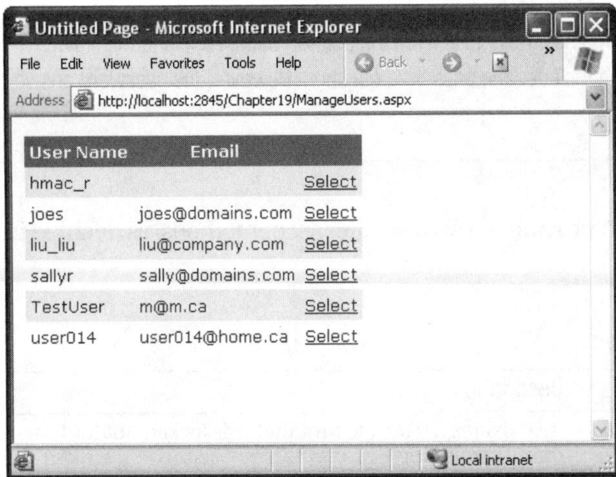

Figure 19-5. *Getting a list of users*

To create this page, you simply need to call the Membership.GetAllUsers() method and bind the results to a GridView, as shown here:

```
protected void Page_Load(object sender, EventArgs e)
{
    GridView1.DataSource = Membership.GetAllUsers();
    GridView1.DataBind();
}
```

To make the example more interesting, when a record is selected, the corresponding MembershipUser object is retrieved. This object is then added to a collection so it can be bound to the DetailsView for automatic display:

```
protected void GridView1_SelectedIndexChanged(object sender, EventArgs e)
{
    List<MembershipUser> list = new List<MembershipUser>();
    list.Add(Membership.GetUser(GridView1.SelectedValue.ToString()));
    DetailsView1.DataSource = list;
    DetailsView1.DataBind();
}
```

Figure 19-6 shows the information that's available in a single record. Among other details, you can use the MembershipUser object to check whether a user is online, when they last accessed the system, and what their e-mail address is.

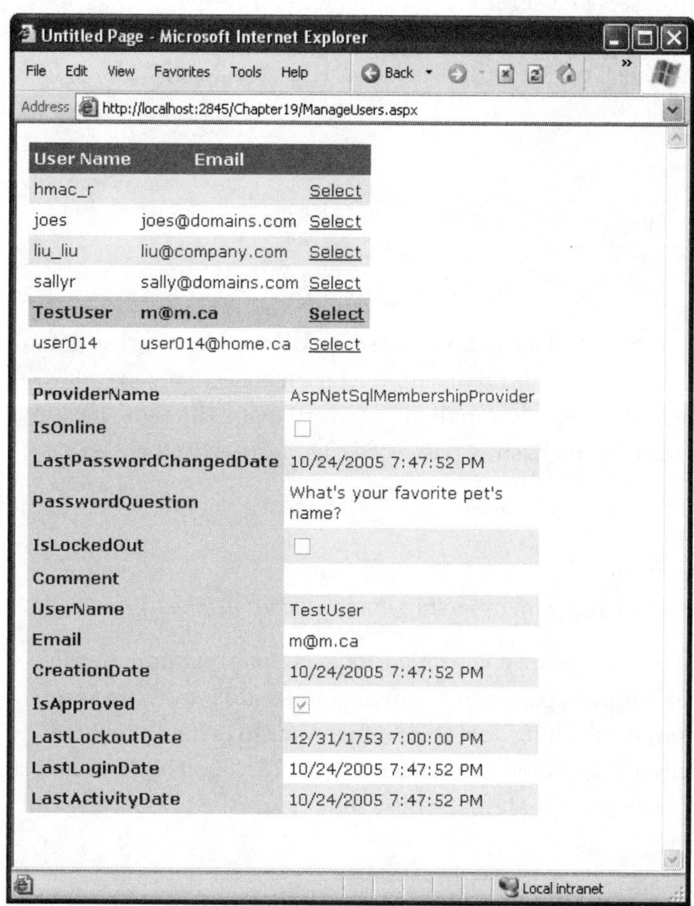

Figure 19-6. *The information in a MembershipUser object*

Authentication with Membership

Now that you've switched to membership, and all your users are stored in the membership data store, you need to change the way your login page works. Life now gets a lot simpler—rather than create ADO.NET objects to query a database and see whether a matching user record exists, you can let the Membership class perform all the work for you. The method you need is Membership.ValidateUser(). It takes a user name and password and returns true if there's a valid match in the database.

Here's the new login page you need:

```
protected void cmdLogin_Click(object sender, EventArgs e)
{
    if (Membership.ValidateUser(txtUsername.Text, txtPassword.Text))
    {
        FormsAuthentication.RedirectFromLoginPage(txtUsername.Text, false);
    }
    else
    {
        lblStatus.Text = "Invalid username or password.";
    }
}
```

Actually, a fair bit of work is taking place behind the scenes. If you're using the default membership provider settings, passwords are hashed. That means when you call ValidateUser(), ASP.NET hashes the newly supplied password using the same hashing algorithm and then compares it to the hashed password that's stored in the database.

Disabled Accounts

An account can become disabled in the membership database in two ways:

The account isn't approved: This occurs if you create an account programmatically and supply false for the isApproved parameter. You might take this step if you want to create an account automatically but allow an administrator to review it before it becomes live. To make this account active, you need to get a MembershipUser object for the corresponding user record, set MembershipUser.IsApproved to true, and call Membership.UpdateUser().

The account is locked out: This occurs if the user makes multiple attempts to access a user account with an invalid password. In this case, you need to get a MembershipUser object for the user, and call MembershipUser.UnlockUser(). You may also want to call MembershipUser.ResetPassword() to prevent another lockout.

To help you with these tasks, you might want to create an administrative page like the one shown in Figure 19-6. For example, you can allow a user to review all accounts that aren't yet approved and approve them by clicking a button.

Similarly, if you want to disable an account at any time, you can retrieve a MembershipUser object for that user and set the IsApproved property to false. However, you have no way to programmatically lock a user account.

You're probably already thinking of a wide range of pages you can create using the Membership and MembershipUser classes. For example, you can build pages that allow users to request a password reset or check whether they are locked out. However, you might not need to create all these pages, because ASP.NET includes a rich set of security controls that automate many common tasks. You'll learn more about the security controls in the next section.

The Security Controls

The basic membership features are a remarkable time-saver. They allow you to concentrate on programming your web application, without worrying about managing security and crafting the perfect database or user information. Instead, you can use the higher-level Membership and MembershipUser classes to do everything you need.

However, the ASP.NET membership feature doesn't stop there. Not only does the Membership class simplify common security tasks, it also standardizes them. As a result, other components and controls can user the Membership class to integrate themselves with the ASP.NET security model, without worrying about the specifics of each web application. You can find the best example of this new flexibility in ASP.NET's security controls. These controls interact with the membership provider using the methods of the Membership and MembershipUser classes to implement common bits of user interfaces such as a login page, a set of user creation controls, and a password recovery wizard.

Table 19-5 lists all the ASP.NET security controls that work with membership. In Visual Studio, you can find these controls in the Login section of the Toolbox.

Table 19-5. *Security Controls*

Control	Description
Login	Displays the familiar user name and password text boxes, with a login button.
LoginStatus	A simple control that varies itself based on whether the user is logged in. If not, the control shows a login button that redirects the user to the configured login page. Otherwise, it displays a sign-out button. You can choose the test used for the login and sign-out buttons, but that's about it.
LoginName	A simple control that displays the user name of the logged-in user.
LoginView	A powerful control that displays different content depending on whether the user is logged in. You can even use this control to show different content for different groups of users, or *roles.*
PasswordRecovery	Allows the user to request a password via e-mail or reset it. Typically, the user must supply the answer to the security question to get the password.
ChangePassword	Allows the user to set a new password (as long as the user can supply the current password).
CreateUserWizard	Allows a user to create a new record, complete with e-mail address and a password question and answer.

A simple way and a complex way to use most of these controls exist. At their simplest, you merely drop the control on a page, without writing a line of code. (You saw this approach with the CreateUserWizard control at the beginning of this chapter.) You can also modify properties, handle events, and even create templates to customize these controls.

In the following sections, you'll take a closer look at the Login, PasswordRecovery, and CreateUserWizard controls. And later in the "Role-Based Security" section, you'll put the LoginView control to work to show different content to users in different roles.

The Login Control

So far, the secure websites you've seen have used handmade login pages. In many websites this is what you'll want—after all, it gives you complete control to adjust the user interface exactly the way you want it. However, a login page is standard, so it makes sense for ASP.NET to give developers some extra shortcuts that can save them work.

Along these lines, ASP.NET includes a Login control that pairs a user name and password text box with a login button. The Login control also adds a few features:

- It includes validator controls that prevent the page from being posted back until a user name and password have been entered.
- It automatically handles the signing in and redirection process when the user logs in successfully. If invalid login credentials are entered, it shows an error message.
- It provides a Remember Me check box that, if selected, stores a persistent cookie that remains indefinitely on the user's computer; therefore, the user doesn't need to log back in at the beginning of each visit.

In other words, if the basic Login control is right for your needs (in other words, it gives the user interface you want), you won't need to write a line of code.

To try this, drop the Login control onto a new page. Make sure this page is named Login.aspx so it's used as the default login page for forms authentication (or edit the <forms> tag to choose a different login page, as explained in the previous chapter). Then, run the page. You'll see the basic interface shown in Figure 19-7.

Although the Login control takes care of the login process for you automatically, you can step in with your own custom code. To do so, you must react to one of the Login control events, as listed in Table 19-6.

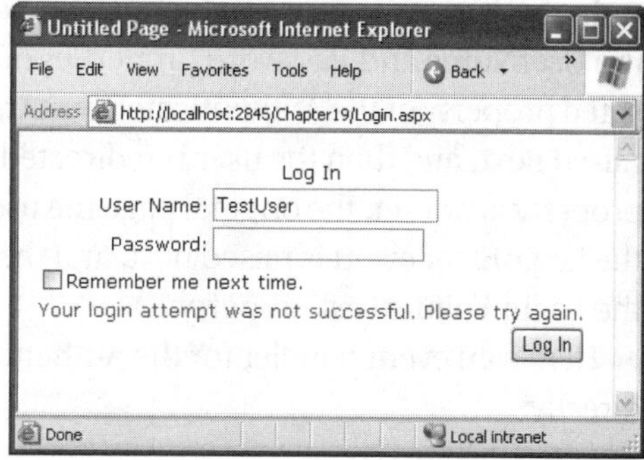

Figure 19-7. *The Login control and a failed login attempt*

Table 19-6. *Events of the Login control*

Event	Description
LoggingIn	Raised before the user is authenticated.
LoggedIn	Raised after the user has been authenticated by the control.
LoginError	Raised when the login attempt fails (for example, if the user enters the wrong password).
Authenticate	Raised to authenticate the user. If you handle this event, it's up to you to supply the login code—the Login control won't perform any action.

The LoggingIn, LoggedIn, and LoginError events are primarily useful if you want to update other controls to display certain information based on the login process. For example, after the first login failure, you might choose to show a link that redirects the user to a password retrieval page:

```
protected void Login1_LoginError(object sender, EventArgs e)
{
    lblStatus.Text = "Have you forgotten your password?";
    lnkRedirectToPasswordRetrieval.Visible = true;
}
```

However, the Authenticate event is the most important event. It allows you to write your own authentication logic, as you did in the previous chapter. This is typically useful in two situations. First, you might want to supplement the default checking in the Login control with other requirements (for example, prevent any users from logging in at specific times of day, allow users to log in only if they've entered information in another control, and so on). The other reason you might handle the Authenticate event is if you aren't using the membership provider at all. In this case, you can still use the Login control, as long as you provide the authentication logic.

In the Authenticate event handler, you can check the user name and password using the UserName and Password properties of the Login control. You then set the Authenticated property of the AuthenticateEventArgs to true or false. If true, the LoggedIn event is raised next, and then the user is redirected to the Login.DestinationPageUrl, or if that property is not set, the original page the user came from. If you set Authenticated to false, the LoginError event is raised next, and the control displays the error message defined by the Login.FailureText property.

Here's an event handler for the Authenticated event that uses the membership classes directly:

```
protected void Login1_Authenticate(object sender, AuthenticateEventArgs e)
{
    if (Membership.ValidateUser(Login1.UserName, Login1.Password))
    {
        e.Authenticated = true;
    }
    else
    {
        e.Authenticated = false;
    }
}
```

That covers everything you need to know about interacting with the Login control, but you can tweak many properties to configure the appearance of the Login control. There's even an Auto Format link you can choose from the Properties window to give the Login control a face-lift with a single click.

The most powerful formatting properties for the Login control are style properties, which allow you to tweak fonts, coloring, and alignment for individual parts of the control. You've already seen styles at work with several other controls, including the Calendar (Chapter 8) and the GridView (Chapter 15), and they work in the same way with the security controls. Table 19-7 details the style properties of the Login control.

Table 19-7. *Style Properties of the Login Control*

Style	Description
TitleTextStyle	Defines a style for the title text of the Login control.
LabelStyle	Defines the style for the Username and Password labels.
TextBoxStyle	Defines the style for the user name and password text boxes.
LoginButtonStyle	Defines the style for the login button.
FailureStyle	Defines the style for the text displayed if the login attempt fails.

Style	Description
CheckBoxStyle	Defines the style properties for the Remember Me check box.
ValidatorTextStyle	Defines styles for RequiredFieldValidator controls that validate the user name and password information. These style properties tweak how the error text looks. (By default, the error text is simply an asterisk that appears next to the empty text box.)
HyperLinkStyle	The Login control provides properties that allow you to show several additional links (such as links for creating a new user record, retrieving a password, and so on). This property configures them all.
InstructionTextStyle	The Login control allows you to add some helpful instructions under the title, by setting the Login.InstructionText property. This style formats this text. By default, the Login control has no instruction text.

Of course, styles aren't the only feature you can change in the Login control. You can adjust several properties to change the text it uses and to add links. For example, the following tag for the Login control adjusts the formatting and uses the CreateUserUrl and PasswordRecoveryUrl properties to add links to a page for registering a new user and another for recovering a lost password. (Obviously, you'll need to create both of these pages in order for the links to work.)

```
<asp:Login ID="Login1" runat="server" BackColor="#EFF3FB" BorderColor="#B5C7DE"
  BorderPadding="4" BorderStyle="Solid" BorderWidth="1px" Font-Names="Verdana"
  ForeColor="#333333" Height="256px" Width="368px"
  CreateUserText="Register for the first time" CreateUserUrl="Register.aspx"
  PasswordRecoveryText="Forgot your password?"
  PasswordRecoveryUrl="PasswordRecovery.aspx"
  InstructionText=
   "Please enter your username and password for logging into the system.">

    <TitleTextStyle BackColor="#507CD1" Font-Bold="True" Font-Size="Large"
      ForeColor="White" Height="35px" />
    <InstructionTextStyle Font-Italic="True" ForeColor="Black"  />
    <LoginButtonStyle BackColor="White"
      BorderColor="#507CD1" BorderStyle="Solid"
      BorderWidth="1px" Font-Names="Verdana" ForeColor="#284E98" />

</asp:Login>
```

Figure 19-8 shows the revamped Login control. Table 19-8 explains the other properties of the Login control.

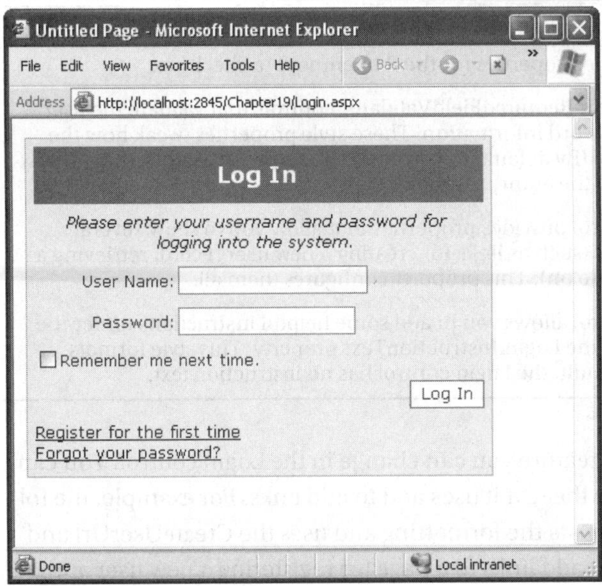

Figure 19-8. *A formatted Login control*

Table 19-8. *Useful Properties of the Login Control*

Property	Description
TitleText	The text that's displayed in the heading of the control.
InstructionText	The text that's displayed just below the heading but above the login controls. By default, the Login control has no instruction text.
FailureText	The text that's displayed when a login attempt fails.
UserNameLabelText	The text that's displayed before the user name text box.
PasswordLabelText	The text that's displayed before the password text box.
UsernameRequiredErrorMessage	The error message that's shown by the RequiredFieldValidator if the user doesn't type in a user name. By default, this is simply an asterisk (*).
PasswordRequiredErrorMessage	The error message that's shown by the RequiredFieldValidator if the user doesn't type in a password. By default, this is simply an asterisk (*).
LoginButtonText	The text displayed for the login button.
LoginButtonType	The type of button control that's used as the login button. It can be displayed as Link, Button, or Image.

Property	Description
LoginButtonImageUrl	If you display the login button as an image (by tweaking the LoginButtonStyle), you must provide a URL that points to the button image you want to use.
DestinationPageUrl	The page to which the user is redirected if the login attempt is successful. This property is blank by default, which means the Login control uses the forms infrastructure and redirects the user to the originally requested page (or to the defautlUrl configured in web.config file).
DisplayRememberMe	Determines whether the Remember Me check box will be shown. You may want to remove this option to ensure stricter security so that malicious users can't gain access to your website through another user's computer.
RememberMeSet	Sets the default value for the Remember Me check box. By default, this option is set to false, which means the check box is not checked initially.
VisibleWhenLoggedIn	If set to false, the Login control automatically hides itself if the user is already logged in. If set to true (the default), the Login control is displayed even if the user is already logged in.
CreateUserUrl	Supplies a URL to a user registration page. This property is used in conjunction with the CreateUserText.
CreateUserText	Sets the text for a link to the user registration page. If this text is not supplied, this link is not displayed in the Login control.
CreateUserIconUrl	Supplies a URL to an image that will be displayed alongside the CreateUserText for the user registration link.
HelpPageUrl	Supplies a URL to a page with help information.
HelpPageText	Sets the text for the link to the help page. If this text is not supplied, this link is not displayed in the Login control.
HelpPageIconUrl	Supplies a URL to an image that will be displayed alongside the HelpPageText for the help page link.
PasswordRecoveryUrl	Supplies a URL to a password recovery page.
PasswordRecoveryText	Sets the text for the link to the password recovery page. If this text is not supplied, this link is not displayed in the Login control.
PasswordRecoveryIconUrl	Supplies a URL to an image that will be displayed alongside the PasswordRecoveryText for the password recovery page link.

To round out the example in Figure 19-8, you must create the Register.aspx and PasswordRecovery.aspx pages. In the next sections, you'll learn how you can do this easily using two more of the ASP.NET security controls.

The CreateUserWizard Control

You already used the CreateUserWizard control to create a basic user record at the beginning of this chapter. Now that you've seen the flexibility of the Login control, it should come as no surprise to learn that you have just as many options for tweaking the appearance and behavior of the CreateUserWizardControl.

The CreateUserWizard control operated in two steps. The first step collects the user information that's needed to generate the user record. The second step displays a confirmation message once the account is created.

Overall, the CreateUserWizard provides a dizzying number of properties you can adjust. However, it helps to understand that really only three types of properties exist:

Style properties that format just a section of the control: For example, TitleTextStyle configures how the text heading is formatted.

Properties that set the text for the control: For example, you can configure each label, the success text, and the messages shown under different error conditions. You can also retrieve or set the values in each text box.

Properties that hide or show a part of the control: For example, you can use DisplaySidebar, DisplayCancelButton, and RequireEmail to show or hide the sidebar, cancel button, and e-mail text box, respectively.

The CreateUserWizard control also provides a familiar set of events, including CreatingUser, CreatedUser, and CreateUserError. Once again, these events are handy for synchronizing other controls on the page or for overriding the user creation process if you decide not to use the membership features.

■ **Tip** By default, newly created users are automatically logged in. You can change this behavior by setting the CreateUserWizard.LoginCreatedUser property to false. You also set the ContinueDestinationPage property to set the URL where the user should be redirected once the new record is created.

Interestingly enough, the CreateUserWizard control inherits from the Wizard control you explored in Chapter 8. As a result, you can add as many extra steps as you want, just as you can with the Wizard control. These steps might perform other tasks, such as signing the user up to receive a regular newsletter. However, the actual user creation process must always take place in a single step.

For example, consider the markup for the basic CreateUserWizard (with style tags omitted):

```
<asp:CreateUserWizard ID="CreateUserWizard1" runat="server" ... >
    <WizardSteps>
        <asp:CreateUserWizardStep runat="server" Title="Create User">
        </asp:CreateUserWizardStep>
        <asp:CompleteWizardStep runat="server">
        </asp:CompleteWizardStep>
    </WizardSteps>
</asp:CreateUserWizard>
```

Essentially, the CreateUserWizard is a Wizard control that supports two specialized step types: a CreateUserWizardStep where the user information is collected and the user record is created and a CompleteWizardStep where the confirmation message is shown.

The following example shows how you can add an ordinary WizardStep into this sequence. In this case, the extra step simply provides some additional options for the newly created user (namely, the choice to subscribe to automatic e-mail newsletters).

```
<asp:CreateUserWizard ID="CreateUserWizard1" runat="server" ... >
    <WizardSteps>
        <asp:CreateUserWizardStep runat="server" Title="Create User">
        </asp:CreateUserWizardStep>

        <asp:WizardStep runat="server" Title="Subscribe">
            Would you like to sign up for the following newsletters?<br />
            <br />
            <asp:CheckBoxList ID="CheckBoxList1" runat="server">
                <asp:ListItem>MSN Today</asp:ListItem>
                <asp:ListItem>C# Planet</asp:ListItem>
                <asp:ListItem>The High-Tech Herald</asp:ListItem>
            </asp:CheckBoxList>
        </asp:WizardStep>

        <asp:CompleteWizardStep runat="server">
        </asp:CompleteWizardStep>
    </WizardSteps>
</asp:CreateUserWizard>
```

Figure 19-9 shows the first two steps. Notice that the sidebar appears (by setting CreateUserWizard.DisplaySidebar to true) to show the order of steps.

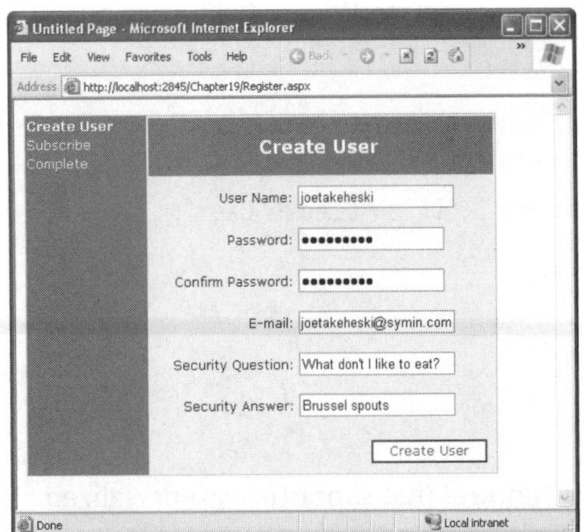

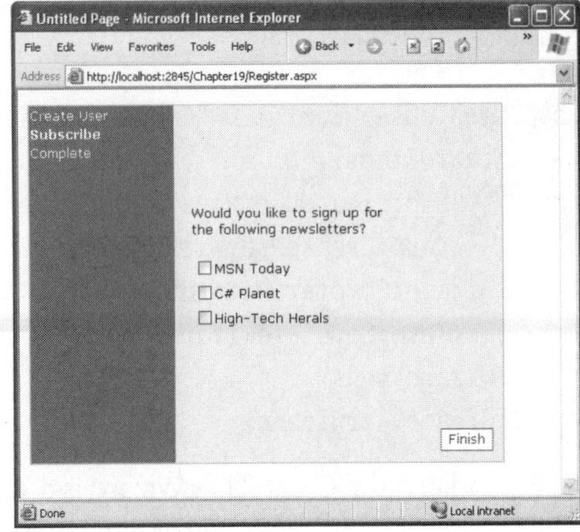

Figure 19-9. *A CreateUserWizard with a custom step*

It's still up to you to take the appropriate action in your code by reacting to one of the CreateUserWizard events. In this case, you use the FinishButtonClick event, because it occurs on the last step before the completion message. If you place your step earlier in the sequence, you'll need to react to NextButtonClick. In the current example, you might want to add this information to the user's profile table. You'll learn how to use profiles in the next chapter.

For complete layout and formatting power, you can convert one of the CreateUserWizard steps into a template. You're then free to rearrange the existing content and add new controls and HTML content. However, be careful not to remove any of the required elements. The CreateUserWizard will throw an exception if you try to use it but you're missing one of the required text boxes for account information.

The easiest way to convert a step into a template is to use the smart tag links. First, select the CreateUserControl in Visual Studio. Then, select the Customize Create User Step link or the Customize Complete Step link, depending on which step you want to modify. ASP.NET will then insert the controls into a template in the CreateUserWizard control tag.

For example, imagine you want to show the options the user selected in your custom step in the final summary. In this case, you might want to add a new Label control, as shown here:

```
<asp:CompleteWizardStep runat="server">
    <ContentTemplate>
        <table border="0" style="...">
            <tr>
```

```
            <td align="center" colspan="2" style="...">
                Complete
            </td>
        </tr>
        <tr>
            <td>
                Your account has been successfully created.<br /><br />
                You subscibed to:
                <asp:Label ID="lblSubscriptionList" runat="server">
                </asp:Label>
            </td>
        </tr>
        <tr>
            <td align="right" colspan="2">
                <asp:Button ID="ContinueButton" runat="server"
                 BackColor="White"
                 BorderColor="#507CD1" BorderStyle="Solid" BorderWidth="1px"
                 CausesValidation="False" CommandName="Continue"
                 Font-Names="Verdana" ForeColor="#284E98" Text="Continue"
                 ValidationGroup="CreateUserWizard1" />
            </td>
        </tr>
    </table>
  </ContentTemplate>
</asp:CompleteWizardStep>
```

Now, when the user moves to the last step, you can fill in the label with the information from the CheckBoxList control. However, because the Label and CheckBoxList controls are placed inside a template, you can't access them directly by name. Instead, you need to extract them using the FindControl() method:

```
protected void CreateUserWizard1_FinishButtonClick(object sender,
  WizardNavigationEventArgs e)
{
    Label lbl = (Label)CreateUserWizard1.CompleteStep.Controls[0].FindControl(
      "lblSubscriptionList");
    CheckBoxList chk = (CheckBoxList)CreateUserWizard1.FindControl(
    "chkSubscription");
    string selection = "";
    foreach (ListItem item in chk.Items)
```

```
    {
        if (item.Selected) selection += "<br />" + item.Text;
    }
    lbl.Text = selection;
}
```

Figure 19-10 shows the final step.

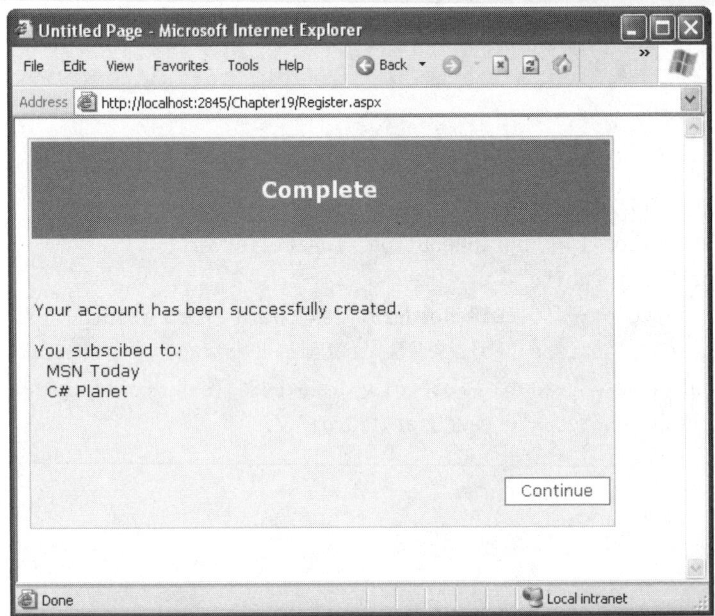

Figure 19-10. *Enhancing the complete step with extra content*

The PasswordRecovery Control

The PasswordRecovery comes in handy when users forget their passwords. The PasswordRecovery control leads the user through a short wizard that begins by asking for a user name and then showing the relevant security question. If the user correctly provides the matching security answer, the password is automatically mailed to the e-mail that's configured for the user.

The PasswordRecovery control has three steps. First, it requests the user name. Next, it shows the security questions and requests the answer. Finally, if the correct answer was provided, the PasswordRecovery sends an e-mail to the user's e-mail address. If you use a password format of Encrypted or Clear (refer to Table 19-1), the e-mail contains the original password. If you are using the default password format Hash, a new, random password is generated, and that password is sent in the e-mail. Either way, the last step shows a confirmation message informing you that the e-mail was sent.

Figure 19-11 shows the PasswordRecovery control in action.

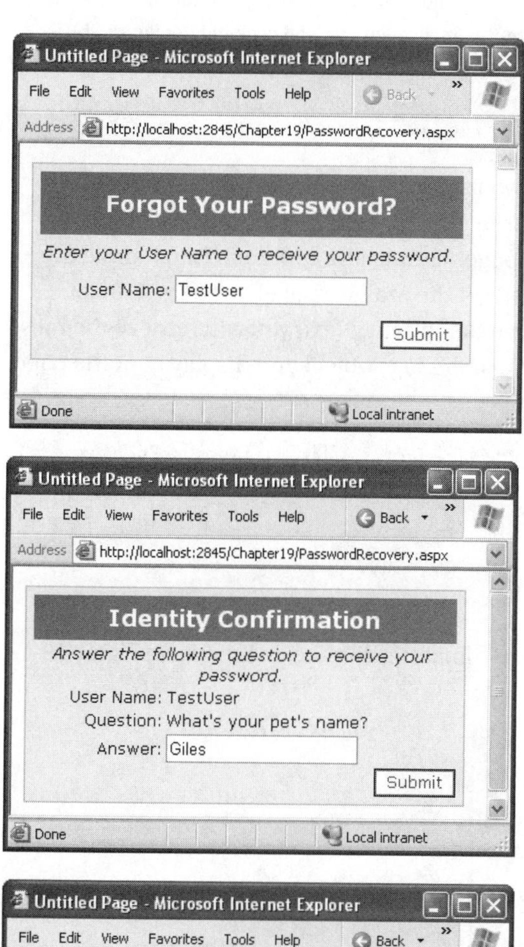

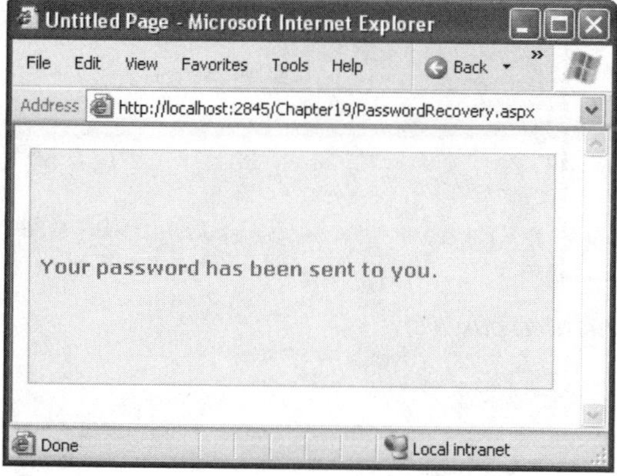

Figure 19-11. *Requesting a password*

For the PasswordRecovery control to do its work, your computer must have a correctly configured SMTP server, and the user must have an e-mail address in the user record.

■ **Note** You can configure your SMTP server by selecting the PasswordRecovery control and choosing Administer Website from the smart tag. Then, choose the Application tab, and click the Configure SMTP E-mail Settings link.

If your application doesn't meet these two requirements—either you're not able to send e-mail messages or users aren't guaranteed to have an e-mail address—you can display the newly password directly in the page. The easiest approach is to handle the PasswordRecovery.SendingMail event. First, set the MailMessageEventArgs.Cancel property to true to prevent the message from being sent. Next, you can retrieve the message content from the MailMessageEventArgs.Message object and display it on the page. Here's an example:

```
protected void PasswordRecovery1_SendingMail(object sender,MailMessageEventArgs e)
{
    e.Cancel = true;
    PasswordRecovery1.SuccessText = e.Message.Body;
}
```

When you use this event handler, you'll see a final step like the one shown in Figure 19-12.

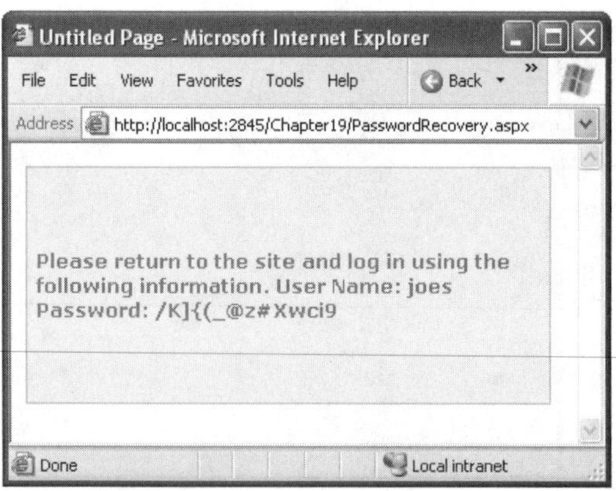

Figure 19-12. *Displaying the retrieved or regenerated password*

Of course, for complete flexibility you can create your own page that resets passwords. You just need to use the methods of the Membership and MembershipUser classes described earlier.

Role-Based Security

The authentication examples you've examined so far provide an all-or-nothing approach that either forbids or allows a user. In many cases, however, an application needs to recognize different levels of users Some users will be provided with a limited set of capabilities, and other users might be allowed to perform potentially dangerous changes or use the administrative portions of a website.

To allow this type of multitiered access, you need ASP.NET's *role-based authorization* feature. As with membership, ASP.NET takes care of storing the role information and making it available to your code. All you need to do is create the roles, assign users to each role, and then test for role membership in your code.

Before you can use role-based authorization, you need to enable it. Although you can perform this step using the WAT (just click the Enable Roles link in the Security tab), it's easy enough just to add the required line to your web.config file directly:

```
<configuration>
    <system.web>
        <roleManager enabled="true" />
        ...
    </system.web>
</configuration>
```

As with the membership data store, ASP.NET will automatically create the role information in the aspnetdb.mdf file using SQL Server 2005. If you want to use a different database, you need to follow the steps earlier in this chapter to create the database using aspnet_regsql.exe and modify the connection string.

Creating and Assigning Roles

Once you've enable role management, you need to create a basic set of roles (for example, User, Administrator, Guest, and so on). You can then assign users to one or more groups.

You can create roles in two ways. You can do so programmatically, or you can do so by hand using the WAT.

To use the WAT, follow these steps:

1. Launch the WAT by selecting Website ➤ ASP.NET Configuration.
2. Click the Security tab.
3. Click the Create or Manage Roles link.
4. To add a new role, type it into the provided text box, and click Add Role (see Figure 19-13). Or, use the Manage and Delete links in the role list to modify or delete an existing role record.

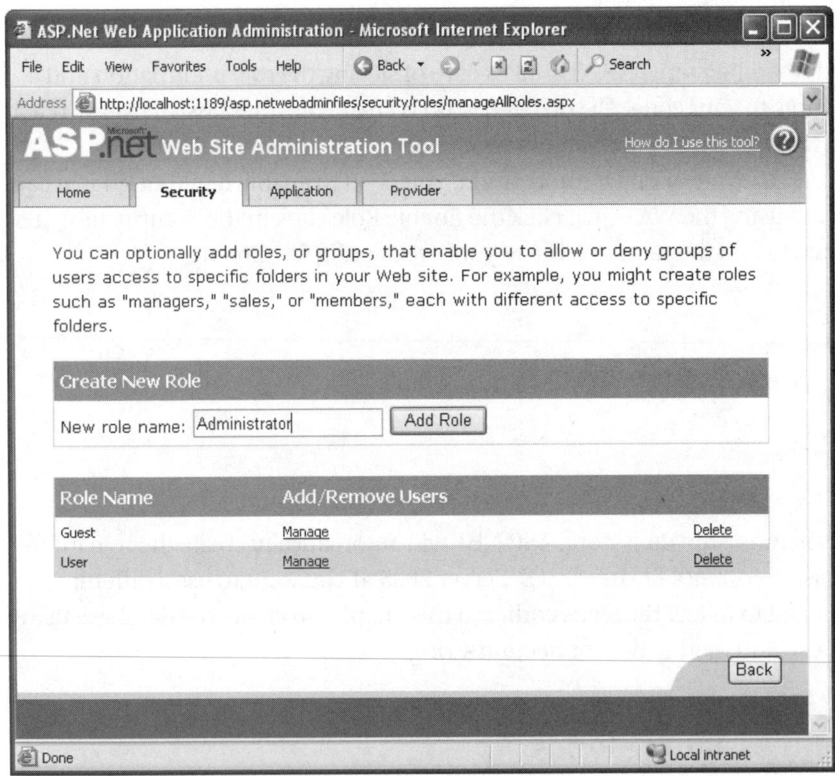

Figure 19-13. *Creating roles*

To place a user into a role, you'll need to head back to the main security page (click the Back button in the role management page). Then follow these steps:

1. Select Manage Users from the Security tab. You'll see the full list of users for your website (subdivided into pages).

2. Find the user you want to change, and click the Edit Roles link next to that user.

3. Fill in the check box for each role you want to assign to that user.

Figure 19-14 shows an example where the user joes is being given the User role.

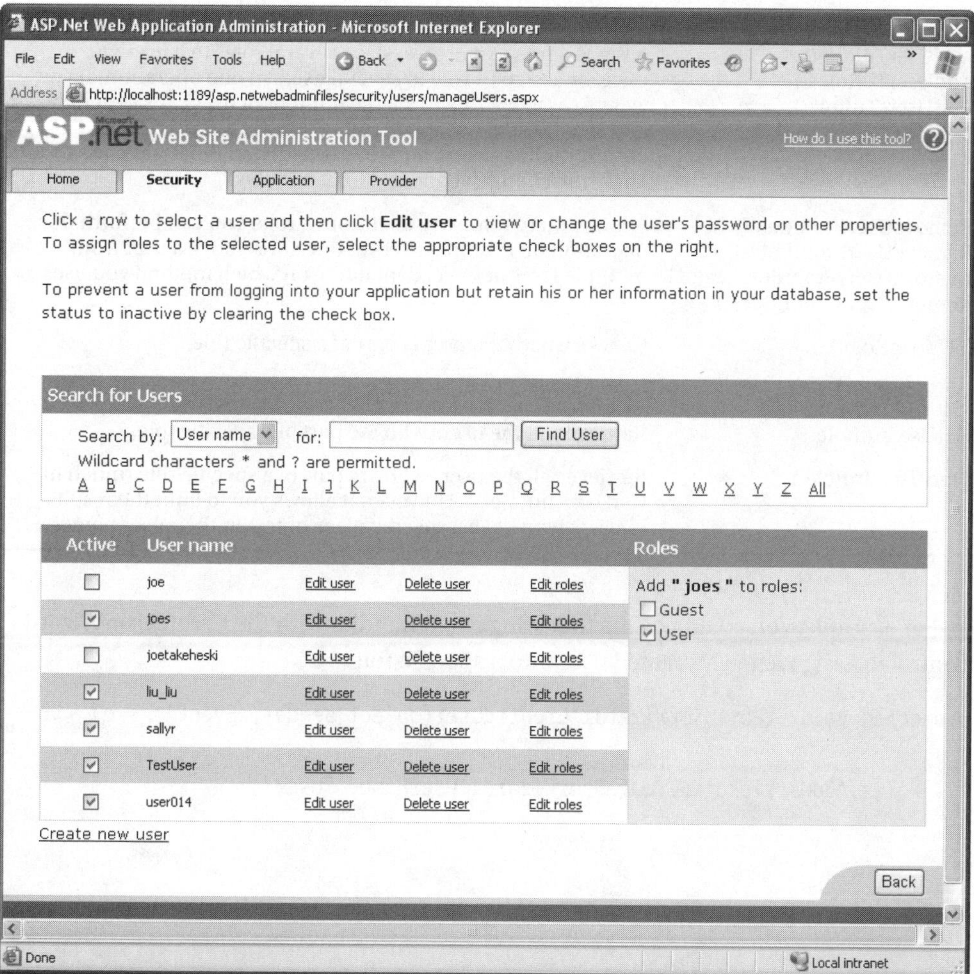

Figure 19-14. *Applying roles*

Of course, you don't need to use the WAT. You can also use the Roles class. The Roles class serves the same purpose for role management as the Membership class did for membership—it provides a number of static utility methods that let you modify role information. Table 19-9 lists the methods you can use.

Table 19-9. *Methods of the Roles class*

Method	Description
CreateRole()	Adds a new role to the database.
DeleteRole()	Deletes an existing role from the database.
RoleExists()	Checks whether a specific role name exists in the database.
GetAllRoles()	Retrieves a list of all the roles for this application.
AddUserToRole(), AddUserToRoles(), AddUsersToRole()	Assigns a role to a user, assigns several roles to a user at once, or assigns a role to several users in one operation. If you want to assign a role to a large number of users, it's generally much quicker to use the Membership class to retrieve the corresponding user names (if needed) and the Roles class to apply the change at once.
RemoveUserFromRole(), RemoveUserFromRoles(), RemoveUsersFromRole(), and RemoveUsersFromRoles()	Allows you to remove a user from a role. You can perform this operation on multiple users at once or remove a user from multiple roles at once, depending on which method you use.
IsUserInRole()	Checks whether a user is part of a specific role.
GetRolesForUser()	Retrieves all the roles for a specific user.
GetUsersInRole()	Retrieves all the users who are part of a specific role.
FindUsersInRole()	Retrieves all the users who are part of a specific role (much like GetUsersInRole()). However, it allows you to limit the results to users who have a specific piece of text in their user names.

For example, you could use the following event handler with the CreateUserWizard control to assign a newly created user into a specific role:

```
protected void CreateUserWizard1_CreatedUser(object sender, EventArgs e)
{
    Roles.AddUserToRole(CreateUserWizard1.UserName, "User");
}
```

Restricting Access Based on Roles

Once you've created and assigned your roles, you need to adjust your application to take the role information into account. You can use several techniques:

- You can write authorization rules that specifically deny certain roles from specific pages or subfolders. You can write these rules by hand by adding the <authorization> section to your web.config file, or you can define them with the help of the WAT by clicking the Manage Access Rules link.
- You can use the User.IsInRole() method in your code to test whether the user belongs to a specific role and then decide whether to allow an action or show certain content accordingly.
- You can use the LoginView control to set different content for different roles.

You already learned how to use the first two techniques in the previous chapter. For example, you already know how to write web.config rules that restrict a specific group, like this:

```
<authorization>
    <deny users="?" />
    <deny roles="Guest" />
</authorization>
```

These rules deny all anonymous users and any users in the Guest role. Remember, a user may be part of more than one role, so the order of the <deny> tags matters. The first rule that matches determines whether the user is allowed or denied.

Similarly, you know how to use the User.IsInRole() method to make a programmatic authorization decision:

```
private void Page_Load(Object sender, EventArgs e)
{
    lblMessage.Text = "You have reached the secured page, ";
    lblMessage.Text += User.Identity.Name + ".";

    if (User.IsInRole("Administrator"))
    {
        lblMessage.Text += "<br /><br />Congratulations:";
        lblMessage.Text += "you are an administrator.";
    }
}
```

The only remaining technique is to consider the LoginView control.

The LoginView Control

The LoginView is a view control like the Panel or MultiView control you learned about in Chapter 8. The difference is that the user doesn't choose which view is used. Instead, the view is set based on the authentication status of the user.

The simplest way to use the LoginView is to show separate content for authenticated and anonymous users. To use this design, you simply fill some content in the <AnonymousTemplate> and <LoggedInTemplate> sections of the control. Here's an example:

```
<asp:LoginView ID="LoginView1" runat="server">
    <AnonymousTemplate>
        <h1>You are anonymous</h1>
         Why don't you <a href="Login.aspx">log in</a>?
    </AnonymousTemplate>
    <LoggedInTemplate>
        <h1>You are logged in</h1>
        <p>You are now ready to see this super-secret content.</p>
    </LoggedInTemplate>
</asp:LoginView>
```

Figure 19-15 shows the two ways this control can appear, depending on whether the user is currently logged in.

Figure 19-15. *Showing different content with the LoginView*

■Tip You can also react to the ViewChanging and ViewChanged events of the LoginView control to initialize the controls that are shown in a specific view when it becomes the current view. This approach is faster than initializing all the controls every time the page is served.

The LoginView also supports one other tag—the RoleGroups tag. Inside the RoleGroups tag, you add one or more RoleGroup controls. Each role group is specifically mapped to one or more roles. In other words, when you use the RoleGroups template, you can show different content for authenticated users, depending to which role they belong.

Here's an example:

```
<asp:LoginView ID="LoginView1" runat="server">
    <AnonymousTemplate>
        <h1>You are anonymous</h1>
         Why don't you <a href="Login.aspx">log in</a>?
    </AnonymousTemplate>
    <RoleGroups>
        <asp:RoleGroup Roles="User, Guest">
            <ContentTemplate>
                <p>If you can see this, you are a member of the
                   User or Guest roles.</p>
            </ContentTemplate>
        </asp:RoleGroup>
        <asp:RoleGroup Roles="Administrator">
            <ContentTemplate>
                <p>Congratulations, you are an administrator.</p>
            </ContentTemplate>
        </asp:RoleGroup>
    </RoleGroups>
</asp:LoginView>
```

Remember, a user can belong to more than one role. However, only one template can display at a time. When matching the role to a RoleGroup, the LoginView control steps through the RoleGroup tags in order and uses the first match. If it can't find a match, it uses the ordinary <LoggedInTemplate>, if provided.

The LoginView is a fairly powerful control. It gives you an effective way to separate secure content from ordinary content declaratively—that is, without writing custom code to hide and show labels. This approach is clearer, more concise, and less error-prone.

The Last Word

ASP.NET's membership features give you several high-level services that work with the basic form authentication and Windows authentication systems you learned about in Chapter 18.

In this chapter, you saw how to use membership to maintain a database of users, either with the free SQL Server 2005 Express Edition or with another version of SQL Server. You also learned how to use the prebuilt security controls, which give you a convenient and flexible way to add user management features and organize secure content. Finally, you considered how you can use role management in conjunction with membership to determine exactly what actions a user should—and shouldn't—be allowed to perform in your applications.

CHAPTER 20

Profiles

You can store information for the users of your website in a variety of ways. In Chapter 9, you learned how to use techniques such as view state, session state, and cookies to keep track of information for a short period of time. However, if you need to store information between visits, the only realistic option is a server-side database. Using the ADO.NET skills you've learned so far, it's fairly easy to save information such as customer addresses and user preferences in a database and retrieve it later.

The only problem with the database approach is that it's up to you to write all the code for retrieving information and updating records. This code isn't terribly complex—Chapter 13 covers everything you need to know—but it can be tedious. ASP.NET includes a feature that allows you to avoid this tedium, if you're able to work within certain limitations. This feature is called *profiles,* and it's designed to keep track of user-specific information automatically.

When you use profiles, ASP.NET handles the unglamorous work of retrieving the information you need and updating the database when it changes. You don't need to write any ADO.NET code, or even design the appropriate database tables, because ASP.NET takes care of all the details. Best of all, the profiles feature integrates with ASP.NET authentication so that the information for the currently logged-in user (referred to as that user's *profile*) is always available to your web page code.

The only drawback to the profiles feature is that it forces you to use a preset database structure. This limits your ability to use tables you've already created to store user-specific details, and it poses a new challenge if you want to use the same information in other applications or reporting tools. If the locked-in structure is too restricting, your only choice is to create a custom profile provider that extends the profiles feature (which is a more challenging task outside the scope of this book) or forgo profiles altogether and write your own ADO.NET code by hand.

In this chapter, you'll learn how to use profiles, how the profile system works, and when profiles make the most sense.

Understanding Profiles

One of the most significant differences between profiles and other types of state management is that profiles are designed to store information permanently, using a back-end data source such as a database. Most other types of state management are designed to maintain information for a series of requests occurring in a relatively short space of time (such as session state) or in the current browser session (such as cookies and view state) or to transfer information from one page to another (such as cross-page posting and the query string). If you need to store information for the longer term in a database, profiles simply provide a convenient model that manages the retrieval and persistence of this information for you.

Before you begin using profiles, you need to assess them carefully. In the following sections, you'll learn how they stack up.

Profile Performance

The goal of ASP.NET's profiles feature is to provide a transparent way to manage user-specific information, without forcing you to write custom data access code using the ADO.NET data classes. Unfortunately, many features that seem convenient suffer from poor performance or scalability. This is particularly a concern with profiles, because they involve database access, and database access can easily become a scalability bottleneck for any web application.

So, do profiles suffer from scalability problems? This question has no simple answer. It all depends on how much data you need to store and how often you plan to access it. To make an informed decision, you need to know a little more about how profiles work.

Profiles plug into the page life cycle in two ways:

- The first time you access the Profile object in your code, ASP.NET retrieves the complete profile data for the current user from the database. From this point on, you can read the profile information in your code without any database work.

- If you change any profile data, the update is deferred until the page processing is complete. At that point (after the PreRender, PreRenderComplete, and Unload events have fired for the page), the profile is written back to the database. This way, multiple changes are batched into one operation. If you don't change the profile data, no extra database work is incurred.

Overall, the profiles feature could result in two extra database trips for each request (in a read-write scenario) or one extra database trip (if you are simply reading profile data). The profiles feature doesn't integrate with caching, so every request that uses profile data requires a database connection.

From a performance standpoint, profiles work best when the following is true:

- You have a relatively small number of pages accessing the profile data.
- You are storing small amounts of data.

They tend to work less well when the following is true:

- You have a large number of pages needing to use profile information.
- You are storing large amounts of data. This is particularly inefficient if you need to use only some of that data in a given request (because the profile model always retrieves the full block of profile data).

Of course, you can combine profiles with another type of state management. For example, imagine your website includes an order wizard that walks the user through several steps. At the beginning of this process, you could retrieve the profile information and store it in session state. You could then use the Session collection for the remainder of the process. Assuming you're using the in-process or out-of-process state server to maintain session data, this approach is more efficient because it saves you from needing to connect to the database repeatedly.

How Profiles Store Data

The most significant limitation with profiles doesn't have anything to do with performance—instead, it's a limitation of how the profiles are serialized. The default profile provider included with ASP.NET serializes profile information into a block of data that's inserted into a single field in a database record. For example, if you serialize address information, you'll end up with something like this:

```
Marty Soren315 Southpart DriveLompocCalifornia93436U.S.A.
```

Another field indicates where each value starts and stops, using a format like this:

```
Name:S:0:11:Street:S:11:19:City:S:30:6:State:S:36:10:ZipCode:S:46:5:Country:S:51:6
```

Essentially, this string identifies the value (Name, Street, City, and so on), the way it's stored (S for string), the starting position, and the length. So the first part of this string:

```
Name:S:0:11
```

indicates that the first profile property is Name, which is stored as a string, starts at position 0, and is 11 characters long.

Although this approach gives you the flexibility to store just about any combination of data, it makes it more difficult to use this data in other applications. You can write custom code to parse the profile data to find the information you want, but depending on the amount of data and the data types you're using, this can be an extremely tedious process. And even if you do this, you're still limited in the ways you can reuse this information. For example, imagine you use profiles to store customer address information. Because of the proprietary format, it's no longer possible to generate customer lists in an application such as Microsoft Word or perform queries that filter or sort records using this profile data. (For example, you can't easily perform a query to get all the customers living in a specific city.)

This problem has two solutions:

- Use your own custom ADO.NET code instead of profiles.
- Create a custom profile provider that's designed to store information using your database schema.

Of the two options, creating a custom data access component is easier, and it gives you more flexibility. You can design your data component to have any interface you want, and you can then reuse that component with other .NET applications. Currently, ASP.NET developers are more likely to use this approach because it has been around since .NET 1.0 and is well understood.

The second option is interesting because it allows your page to keep using the profile model. In fact, you could create an application that uses the standard profile serialization with the SqlProfileProvider and then switch it later to use a custom provider. To make this switch, you don't need to change any code. Instead, you simply modify the profile settings in the web.config file. As it becomes more common for websites to use the profiles features, custom profile providers will become more attractive.

■ **Note** It's also important to consider the type of data that works best in a profile. As with many other types of state management, you can store any serializable types into a profile, including simple types and custom classes.

One significant difference between profiles and other types of state management is that profiles are stored as individual records, each of which is uniquely identified by user name. This means profiles require you to use some sort of authentication system. It makes no difference what type of authentication system you use (Windows, forms, or a custom authentication system)—the only requirement is that authenticated users are assigned a unique user name. That user name is used to find the matching profile record in the database.

■ **Note** Later in this chapter (in the section "Anonymous Profiles"), you'll also learn how the anonymous identification feature lets you temporarily store profile information for users who haven't logged in.

When deciding whether to use profiles, it's natural to compare the profiles feature with the kind of custom data access code you wrote in Chapter 13 (and the database components you'll learn to build in Chapter 24). Clearly, writing your own ADO.NET code is far more flexible. It allows you to store other types of information and perform more complex business tasks. For example, an e-commerce website could realistically use profiles to maintain customer address information (with the limitations discussed in the previous section). However, you wouldn't use a profile to store information about previous orders. Not only is it far too much information to store efficiently, it's also awkward to manipulate.

■ **Tip** In general, use a profile to store only the same sort of information you'd place in the user table. Don't use it to store related data that you'd place in separate tables.

Using the SqlProfileProvider

The SqlProfileProvider allows you to store profile information in a SQL Server 7.0 (or later) database (including SQL Server 2005 Express Edition). You can choose to create the profile tables in any database. However, you can't change any of the other database schema details, which means you're locked into specific table names, column names, and serialization format.

From start to finish, you need to perform the following steps to use profiles:

1. Enable authentication for a portion of your website.
2. Configure the profile provider. (This step is optional if you're using SQL Server 2005 Express Edition. Profiles are enabled by default.)
3. Create the profile tables. (This step isn't required if you're using SQL Server 2005 Express Edition.)
4. Define some profile properties.
5. Use the profile properties in your web page code.

You'll tackle these steps in the following sections.

Enabling Authentication

Because profiles are stored in a user-specific record, you need to authenticate the current user before you can read or write profile information. You can use any type of authentication system, including Windows- and forms-based authentication. The profile system doesn't care—it simply stores the user-specific information in a record that's identified based on the user ID. Seeing as every authentication system identifies users uniquely by user ID, any authentication system will work.

The following web.config file uses Windows authentication. This way, you don't need to create any user records, because you'll use your existing Windows user account. You also don't need to create a login page.

```
<configuration>
  ...
  <system.web>
    <authentication mode="Windows"/>
    <authorization>
      <deny users="?"/>
    </authorization>
    ...
  </system.web>
</configuration>
```

If you decide to use forms authentication instead, you'll need to decide whether you want to perform the authentication using your own custom user list (Chapter 18) or in combination with the membership features (Chapter 19). In most cases, the membership and profiles features are used in conjunction—after all, if you're using the profiles feature to store user-specific information automatically, why not also store the list of user credentials (user names and passwords) automatically in the same database?

■ **Tip** The downloadable examples for this chapter show profiles in action in one site that uses forms authentication and in another site that uses Windows authentication.

Once you've chosen your authentication system (and taken care of any other chores that may be necessary, such as creating a user list and generating your login page), you're ready to use profiles. Remember, profiles store user-specific information, so the user needs to be authenticated before their profile is available. In the web.config file shown previously, an authorization rule ensures this by denying all anonymous users.

Profiles with SQL Server 2005 Express Edition

In the previous chapter, you learned that no special steps are required to configure a web application to use membership with SQL Server 2005 Express Edition. The same is true of profiles. As with the membership details, profile information is stored in the automatically generated aspnetdb.mdf file. If this file doesn't exist, it's created the first time you use any membership or profiles features, and it's placed in the App_Data subdirectory of your web application.

If you're happy using this automatic support, you can skip ahead to the "Defining Profile Properties" section. However, sometimes this might not be enough. Here are two examples:

- If you want to use the full version SQL Server 2005, you need to configure the profile connection string, as described in the next section ("Configuring the Profile Provider to Use a Different Database").
- If you want to use an older version of SQL Server, such as SQL Server 2000, you need to change the connection string (see "Configuring the Profile Provider to Use a Different Database") and create the database tables you need (see "Manually Creating the Profile Tables").

■ **Tip** Keep in mind that the profiles feature uses the same database as the membership feature. That means if you followed the steps in Chapter 19, you may have already created the database you need.

Configuring the Profile Provider to Use a Different Database

If you're using a different database, the first step is to change the connection string.

By default, the connection strings are set using a connection string named LocalSqlServer. You can edit this file directly in the machine.config file.

■ **Tip** The default membership settings and local connection string are set in the machine.config file. You can look at this file (and even edit it to update the settings for all web applications on your computer). Look in the C:\[WinDir]\Microsoft.NET\Framework\[Version]\CONFIG directory.

However, if you just need to tweak a single application, it's better to adjust the web.config file for your web application. First, you need to remove all the existing connection strings using the <clear> element. Then, add the LocalSqlServer connection string again—but this time with the right value:

```
<configuration>
    <connectionStrings>
        <clear />
        <add name="LocalSqlServer" providerName="System.Data.SqlClient"
connectionString="Data Source=localhost;Integrated Security=SSPI;
AttachDBFilename=|DataDirectory|aspnetdb.mdf;User Instance=true" />
    </connectionStrings>
    ...
</configuration>
```

This is the same process you used in Chapter 19, because both the membership feature and the profiles feature use the LocalSqlServer connection string. In this example, the new connection string is for the full version of SQL Server 2005. It uses the same database (a file named aspnetdb.mdf in the App_Data directory), but it sets the data source to localhost instead of localhost\SQLEXPRESS. If you're using SQL Server 2000, you can use the same basic approach, but the AttachDBFilename option isn't supported. Instead, you need to supply the Initial Catalog option with the database name, as shown here:

```
<configuration>
    <connectionStrings>
        <clear />
        <add name="LocalSqlServer" providerName="System.Data.SqlClient"
connectionString="Data Source=localhost;Integrated Security=SSPI;
Initial Catalog=aspnetdb" />
    </connectionStrings>
    ...
</configuration>
```

You'll then need to create the aspnetdb database in your database server by following the steps in the next section ("Manually Creating the Profile Tables").

You have one other option. Instead of modifying the LocalSqlServer connection string, you can explicitly reregister the profile provider. You might take this approach in the unlikely case that you want the profile provider to use a different connection string than the membership provider.

To pull this off, start by defining a connection string for the profile database. Then, use the <profile> section to remove any existing providers (with the <clear> element), and add a new instance of the System.Web.Profile.SqlProfileProvider (with the <add> element). Here are the configuration settings you need:

```
<configuration>
  <connectionStrings>
    <add name="SqlServices" connectionString=
    "Data Source=localhost;Integrated Security=SSPI;Initial Catalog=aspnetdb;"
/>
  </connectionStrings>

  <system.web>
    <profile defaultProvider="SqlProvider">
      <providers>
        <clear />
        <add name="SqlProvider"
          type="System.Web.Profile.SqlProfileProvider"
          connectionStringName="SqlServices"
          applicationName="TestApplication" />
      </providers>
    </profile>
    ...
  </system.web>
</configuration>
```

When you define a profile provider, you need to supply a name (which the <profile> element can then reference as the default provider), the exact type name, a connection string, and a web application name. Use different application names to separate the profile information between web applications (or use the same application name to share it).

Manually Creating the Profile Tables

If you're using SQL Server 2005, ASP.NET will create the profile database automatically, as long as you use the AttachDBFilename option in the connection string. However, if you're using an older version of SQL Server, or you want to share a single database between several web applications, you'll need to create it yourself.

To create the profile tables, you use the aspnet_regsql.exe command-line utility, the same tool that allows you to generate databases for other ASP.NET features, such as SQL Server–based session state, membership, roles, database cache dependencies, and Web Parts personalization. You can find the aspnet_regsql.exe tool in the c:\[WinDir]\Microsoft.NET\Framework\[Version] folder.

To create the tables, views, and stored procedures required for profiles, you use the -A p command-line option. The only other detail you need to supply is the server location (-S), database name (-d), and authentication information for connecting to the database (use -U and -P to supply a password and user name, or use -E to use the current Windows account). If you leave out the server location and database name, aspnet_regsql.exe uses the default instance on the current computer and creates a database named aspnetdb.

To try this with SQL Server 2005 Express, select Programs ➤ Visual Studio 2005 ➤ Visual Studio Tools ➤ Visual Studio 2005 Command Prompt from the Start menu. (The exact location of the Visual Studio 2005 Command Prompt shortcut may vary depending on the edition of Visual Studio you're using.)

Now you can create the profile database with aspnet_regsql. The following is an example that creates a database named AspDatabase with the default name on the current computer by logging into the database using the current Windows account:

```
aspnet_regsql.exe -S (local) -E -A all -d AspDatabase
```

Even if you don't use the default database name (aspnetdb), you should use a new, blank database that doesn't include any other custom tables. That's because aspnet_regsql.exe creates several tables for profiles (see Table 20-1 in the next section), and you shouldn't risk confusing them with business data.

■ **Note** This command line uses the -A all option to create tables for all of ASP.NET's database features, including profiles and membership. You can also choose to add tables for just one feature at a time. For more information about -A and the other command-line parameters you can use with aspnet_regsql, refer to Table 19-2 in Chapter 19.

The Profile Databases

Whether you use aspnet_regsql to create the profile databases on your own or use SQL Server 2005 and let ASP.NET create them automatically, you'll wind up with the same tables. Table 20-1 briefly describes them. (The rather unexciting views aren't included.) If you want to look at these tables, you can use a tool that's included with the database (such as Enterprise Manager) or the Server Explorer in Visual Studio.

Table 20-1. *Database Tables Used for Profiles*

Table Name	Description
aspnet_Applications	Lists all the web applications that have records in this database. It's possible for several ASP.NET applications to use the same aspnetdb database. In this case, you have the option of separating the profile information so it's distinct for each application (by giving each application a different application name when you register the profile provider) or of sharing it (by giving each application the same application name).
aspnet_Profile	Stores the user-specific profile information. Each record contains the complete profile information for a single user. The PropertyNames field lists the property names, and the PropertyValuesString and PropertyValuesBinary fields list all the property data, although you'll need to do some work if you want to parse this information for use in other non-ASP.NET programs. Each record also includes the last update date and time (LastUpdatedDate).
aspnet_SchemaVersions	Lists the supported schemas for storing profile information. In the future, this could allow new versions of ASP.NET to provide new ways of storing profile information without breaking support for old profile databases that are still in use.
aspnet_Users	Lists user names and maps them to one of the applications in aspnet_Applications. Also records the last request date and time (LastActivityDate) and whether the record was generated automatically for an anonymous user (IsAnonymous). You'll learn more about anonymous user support later in this chapter (in the section "Anonymous Profiles").

Figure 20-1 shows the relationships between the most important profile tables.

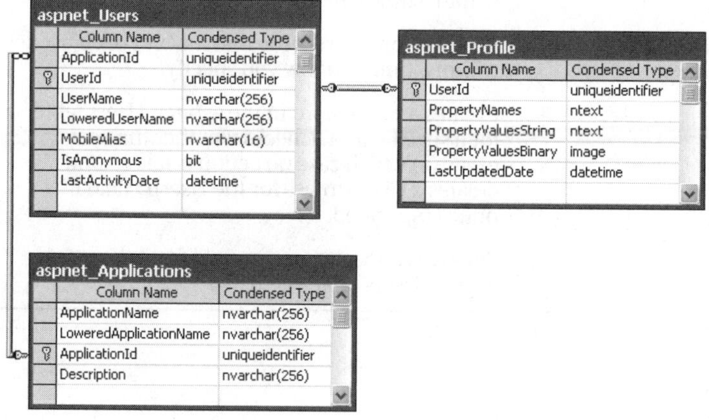

Figure 20-1. *The profile tables*

ASP.NET also creates several stored procedures that allow it to manage the information in these tables more easily. Table 20-2 lists the most noteworthy stored procedures.

Table 20-2. *Database Stored Procedures Used for Profiles*

Stored Procedure	Description
aspnet_Applications_CreateApplications	Checks whether a specific application name exists in the aspnet_Applications table and creates the record if needed.
aspnet_CheckSchemaVersion	Checks for support of a specific schema version for a specific feature (such as profiles) using the aspnet_SchemaVersions table.
aspnet_Profile_GetProfiles	Retrieves the user name and update times for all the profile records in the aspnet_Profile table for a specific web application. This doesn't return the actual profile data.
aspnet_Profile_GetProperties	Retrieves the profile information for a specific user (which you specify by user name). The information is not parsed in any way—instead, this stored procedure simply returns the underlying fields (PropertyNames, PropertyValuesString, and PropertyValuesBinary).
aspnet_Profile_SetProperties	Sets the profile information for a specific user (which you specify by user name). This stored procedure requires values for the PropertyNames, PropertyValuesStrings, and PropertyValuesBinary fields. You have no way to update just a single property in a profile.
aspnet_Profile_GetNumberOfInactiveProfiles	Returns profile records that haven't been used within a time window you specify.
aspnet_Profile_DeleteInactiveProfiles	Removes profile records that haven't been used within a time window you specify.
aspnet_Users_CreateUser	Creates a new record in the aspnet_Users table for a specific user. Checks whether the user exists (in which case no action is taken) and creates a GUID to use for the UserID field if none is specified.
aspnet_Users_DeleteUser	Removes a specific user record from the aspnet_Users table.

Defining Profile Properties

Before you can store anything in the aspnet_Profile table, you need to define it specifically. You do this by adding the <properties> element inside the <profile> section of the web.config file. Inside the <properties> element, you place one <add> tag for each user-specific piece of information you want to store. At a minimum, the <add> element supplies the name for the property, like this:

```
<profile defaultProvider="SqlProvider">
  <providers>
    ...
  </providers>
  <properties>
    <add name="FirstName"/>
    <add name="LastName"/>
  </properties>
</profile>
```

Usually, you'll also supply the data type. (If you don't, the property is treated as a string.) You can specify any serializable .NET class as the type, as shown here:

```
<add name="FirstName" type="String"/>
<add name="LastName" type="String"/>
<add name="DateOfBirth" type="DateTime"/>
```

You can set a few more property attributes to create the more advanced properties shown in Table 20-3.

Table 20-3. *Profile Property Attributes*

Attribute (for the <add> Element)	Description
name	The name of the property.
type	The fully qualified class name that represents the data type for this property. By default, this is String.
serializeAs	Indicates the format to use when serializing this value (String, Binary, Xml, or ProviderSpecific). You'll look more closely at the serialization model in the section "Profile Serialization."

Continued

Table 20-3. *Continued*

Attribute (for the <add> Element)	Description
readOnly	Add this attribute with a value of true to create a property that can be read but not changed. (Attempting to change the property will cause a compile-time error.) By default, this is false.
defaultValue	A default value that will be used if the profile doesn't exist or doesn't include this particular piece of information. The default value has no effect on serialization—if you set a profile property, ASP.NET will commit the current values to the database, even if they match the default values.
allowAnonymous	A Boolean value that indicates whether this property can be used with the anonymous profiles feature discussed later in this chapter. By default, this is false.
Provider	The profile provider that should be used to manage just this property. By default, all properties are managed using the provider specified in the <profile> element, but you can assign different properties to different providers.

Using Profile Properties

With these details in place, you're ready to access the profile information using the Profile property of the current page. When you run your application, ASP.NET creates a new class to represent the profile by deriving from System.Web.Profile.ProfileBase, which wraps a collection of profile settings. ASP.NET adds a strongly typed property to this class for each profile property you've defined in the web.config file. These strongly typed properties simply call the GetPropertyValue() and SetPropertyValue() methods of the ProfileBase base class to retrieve and set the corresponding profile values.

For example, if you've defined a string property named FirstName, you can set it in your page like this:

```
Profile.FirstName = "Henry";
```

Figure 20-2 presents a complete test page that allows the user to display the profile information for the current user or set new profile information.

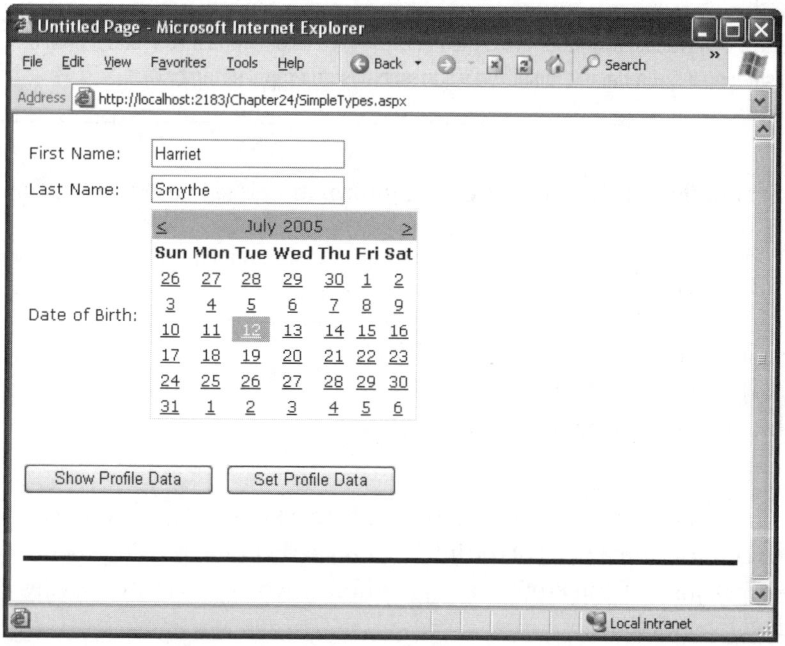

Figure 20-2. *Testing profiles*

The first time this page runs, no profile information is retrieved, and no database connection is used. However, if you click the Show Profile Data button, the profile information is retrieved and displayed on the page:

```
protected void cmdShow_Click(object sender, EventArgs e)
{
    lbl.Text = "First Name: " + Profile.FirstName + "<br />" +
      "Last Name: " + Profile.LastName + "<br />" +
      "Date of Birth: " + Profile.DateOfBirth.ToString();
}
```

At this point, an error will occur if the profile database is missing or the connection can't be opened. Otherwise, your page will run without a hitch, and you'll see the newly retrieved profile information. Technically, the complete profile is retrieved when your code accesses the Profile.FirstName property in the first line and is used for the subsequent code statements.

■ **Note** Profile properties behave like any other class member variable. This means if you read a profile value that hasn't been set, you'll get a default initialized value (such as an empty string or 0).

If you click the Set Profile Data button, the profile information is set based on the current control values:

```
protected void cmdSet_Click(object sender, EventArgs e)
{
    Profile.FirstName = txtFirst.Text;
    Profile.LastName = txtLast.Text;
    Profile.DateOfBirth = Calendar1.SelectedDate;
}
```

Now the profile information is committed to the database when the page request finishes. If you want to commit some or all of the information earlier (and possibly incur multiple database trips), just call the Profile.Save() method. As you can see, the profiles feature is unmatched for simplicity.

■ **Tip** The Profile object doesn't just include the properties you've defined. It also provides LastActivityDate and LastUpdatedDate properties with information drawn from the database.

Profile Serialization

Earlier, you learned how properties are serialized into a single string. For example, if you save a FirstName of Harriet and a LastName of Smythe, both values are crowded together in the PropertyValuesString field, saving space:

```
HarrietSmythe
```

The PropertyNames field gives the information you need to parse each value from the PropertyValuesString field. Here's what you'll see in the PropertyNames field in this example:

```
FirstName:S:0:7:LastName:S:7:6:
```

The colons (:) are used as delimiters. The basic format is as follows:

```
PropertyName:StringOrBinarySerialization:StartingCharacterIndex:Length:
```

Something interesting happens if you create a profile with a DateTime data type. When you look at the PropertyValuesString field, you'll see something like this:

```
<?xml version="1.0" encoding="utf-16"?><dateTime>2005-07-12T00:00:00-04:00
</dateTime>HarrietSmythe
```

Initially, it looks like the profile data is serialized as XML, but the PropertyValuesString clearly doesn't contain a valid XML document (because of the text at the end). What has actually happened is that the first piece of information, the DateTime, is serialized (by default) as XML. The following two profile properties are serialized as ordinary strings.

The ProperyNames field makes it slightly clearer:

```
DateOfBirth:S:0:87:FirstName:S:87:7:LastName:S:94:6:
```

Interestingly, you have the ability to change the serialization format of any profile property by adding the serializeAs attribute to its declaration in the web.config file. Table 20-4 lists your choices.

Table 20-4. *Serialization Options*

SerializeAs	Description
String	Converts the type to a string representation. Requires a type converter that can handle the job.
Xml	Converts the type to an XML representation, which is stored in a string, using the System.Xml.XmlSerialization.XmlSerializer (the same class that's used with web services).
Binary	Converts the type to a proprietary binary representation that only .NET understands using the System.Runtime.Serialization.Formatters.Binary. BinaryFormatter. This is the most compact option but the least flexible. Binary data is stored in the PropertyValuesBinary field instead of the PropertyValues.
ProviderSpecific	Performs customized serialization that's implemented in a custom provider.

For example, here's how you can change the serialization for the profile settings:

```
<add name="FirstName" type="String" serializeAs="Xml"/>
<add name="LastName" type="String" serializeAs="Xml"/>
<add name="DateOfBirth" type="DateTime" serializeAs="String"/>
```

Now the next time you set the profile, the serialized representation in the PropertyValuesString field will take this form:

```
7/12/2005<?xml version="1.0" encoding="utf-16"?><string>Harriet</string>
<?xml version="1.0" encoding="utf-16"?><string>Smythe</string>
```

If you use the binary serialization mode, the property value will be placed in the PropertyValuesBinary field instead of the PropertyValuesString field. The only indication of this shift is the use of the letter *B* instead of *S* in the PropertyNames field. Here's an example where the FirstName property is serialized in the PropertyValuesBinary field:

```
DateOfBirth:S:0:9:FirstName:B:0:31:LastName:S:9:64:
```

All of these serialization details raise an important question—what happens when you change profile properties or the way they are serialized? Profile properties don't have any support for versioning. However, you can add or remove properties with relatively minor consequences. For example, ASP.NET will ignore properties that are present in the aspnet_Profile table but not defined in the web.config file. The next time you modify part of the profile, these properties will be replaced with the new profile information. Similarly, if you define a profile in the web.config file that doesn't exist in the serialized profile information, ASP.NET will just use the default value. However, more dramatic changes—such as renaming a property, changing its data type, and so on, are likely to cause an exception when you attempt to read the profile information. Even worse, because the serialized format of the profile information is proprietary, you have no easy way to migrate existing profile data to a new profile structure.

■ **Tip** Not all types are serializable in all ways. For example, classes that don't provide a parameterless constructor can't be serialized in Xml mode. Classes that don't have the [Serializable] attribute can't be serialized in Binary mode. You'll consider this distinction when you consider how to use custom types with profiles (see the "Profiles and Custom Data Types" section), but for now just keep in mind that you may run across types that can be serialized only if you choose a different serialization mode.

Profile Groups

If you have a large number of profile settings, and some settings are logically related to each other, you may want to use profile groups to achieve better organization.

For example, you may have some properties that deal with user preferences and others that deal with shipping information. Here's how you could organize these profile properties using the <group> element:

```
<profile defaultProvider="SqlProvider">
  <properties>
    <group name="Preferences">
      <add name="LongDisplayMode" defaultValue="true" type="Boolean" />
      <add name="ShowSummary" defaultValue="true" type="Boolean" />
    </group>
```

```
    <group name="Address">
      <add name="Name" type="String" />
      <add name="Street" type="String" />
      <add name="City" type="String" />
      <add name="ZipCode" type="String" />
      <add name="State" type="String" />
      <add name="Country" type="String" />
    </group>
  </properties>
</profile>
```

Now you can access the properties through the group name in your code. For example, here's how you retrieve the country information:

```
lblCountry.Text = Profile.Address.Country;
```

Groups are really just a poor man's substitute for a full-fledged custom structure or class. For example, you could achieve the same effect as in the previous example by declaring a custom Address class. You'd also have the ability to add other features (such as validation in the property procedures). The next section shows how.

Profiles and Custom Data Types

Using a custom class with profiles is easy. You need to begin by creating the class that wraps the information you need. In your class, you can use public member variables or full-fledged property procedures. The latter choice, though longer, is the preferred option because it ensures your class will support data binding, and it gives you the flexibility to add property procedure code later.

Here's a slightly abbreviated Address class that ties together the same information you saw in the previous example:

```
[Serializable()]
public class Address
{
    private string name;
    public string Name {...}

    private string street;
    public string Street {...}

    private string city;
    public string City {...}
```

```
    private string zipCode;
    public string ZipCode {...}

    private string state;
    public string State {...}

    private string country;
    public string Country {...}

    public Address(string name, string street, string city,
      string zipCode, string state, string country)
    {
        Name = name;
        Street = street;
        City = city;
        ZipCode = zipCode;
        State = state;
        Country = country;
    }
    public Address()
    { }
}
```

You can place this class in the App_Code directory (or compile it and place the DLL assembly in the Bin directory). The final step is to add a property that uses it:

```
<properties>
  <add name="Address" type="Address" />
</properties>
```

Now you can create a test page that uses the Address class. Figure 20-3 shows a simple example that simply allows you to load, change, and save the address information in a profile.

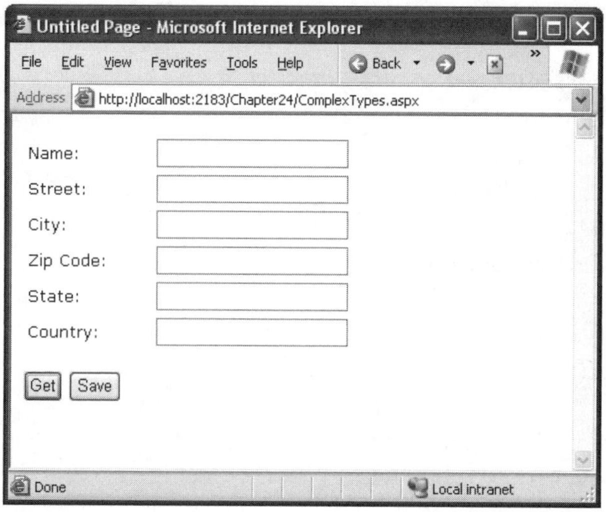

Figure 20-3. *Editing complex information in a profile*

Here's the page class that makes this possible:

```
public partial class ComplexTypes : System.Web.UI.Page
{
    protected void Page_Load(object sender, EventArgs e)
    {
        if (!Page.IsPostBack)
          LoadProfile();
    }

    protected void cmdGet_Click(object sender, EventArgs e)
    {
        LoadProfile();
    }
```

```
    private void LoadProfile()
    {
        txtName.Text = Profile.Address.Name;
        txtStreet.Text = Profile.Address.Street;
        txtCity.Text = Profile.Address.City;
        txtZip.Text = Profile.Address.ZipCode;
        txtState.Text = Profile.Address.State;
        txtCountry.Text = Profile.Address.Country;
    }

    protected void cmdSave_Click(object sender, EventArgs e)
    {
        Profile.Address = new Address(txtName.Text,
          txtStreet.Text, txtCity.Text, txtZip.Text,
          txtState.Text, txtCountry.Text);
    }

}
```

Dissecting the Code...

- When the page loads (and when the user clicks the Get button), the profile information is copied from the Profile.Address object into the various text boxes. A private LoadProfile() method handles this task.
- The user can make changes to the address values in the text boxes. However, the change isn't committed until the user clicks the Save button.
- When the Save button is clicked, a new Address object is created using the constructor that accepts name, street, city, zip code, state, and country information. This object is then assigned to the Profile.Address property. Instead of using this approach, you could modify each property of the current Profile.Address object to match the text values.
- The content of the Profile object is saved to the database automatically when the request ends. No extra work is required.

Custom Type Serialization

You need to keep in mind a few points, depending on how you decide to serialize your custom class. By default, all custom data types use XML serialization with the XmlSerializer.

This class is relatively limited in its serialization ability. It simply copies the value from every public property or member variable into a straightforward XML format like this:

```
<Address>
  <Name>...</Name>
  <Street>...</Street>
  <City>...</City>
  <ZipCode>...</ZipCode>
  <State>...</State>
  <Country>...</Country>
</Address>
```

When deserializing your class, the XmlSerializer needs to be able to find a parameterless public constructor. In addition, none of your properties can be read-only. If you violate either of these rules, the deserialization process will fail.

If you decide to use binary serialization instead of XmlSerialization, .NET uses a completely different approach:

```
<add name="Address" type="Address" serializeAs="Binary"/>
```

In this case, ASP.NET enlists the help of the BinaryFormatter. The BinaryFormatter can serialize the full public and private contents of any class, provided the class is decorated with the [Serializable] attributes. Additionally, any class it derives from or references must also be serializable.

Automatic Saves

The ProfileModule that saves profile information isn't able to detect changes in complex data types (anything other than strings, simple numeric types, Boolean values, and so on). This means if your profile includes complex data types, ASP.NET saves the profile information at the end of every request that accesses the Profile object.

This behavior obviously adds unnecessary overhead. To optimize performance when working with complex types, you have several choices. One option is to set the corresponding profile property to be read-only (if you know it never changes). Another approach is to disable the autosave behavior completely by adding the automaticSaveEnabled attribute on the <profile> element and setting it to false, as shown here:

```
<profile defaultProvider="SqlProvider" automaticSaveEnabled="false">...</profile>
```

If you choose this approach, it's up to you to call Profile.Save() to explicitly commit changes. Generally, this approach is the most convenient, because it's easy to spot the places in your code where you modify the profile. Just add the Profile.Save() call at the end:

```
Profile.Address = new Address(txtName.Text, txtStreet.Text, txtCity.Text,
  txtZip.Text, txtState.Text, txtCountry.Text);
Profile.Save();
```

For example, you could modify the earlier example (shown in Figure 20-3) to save address information only when it changes. The easiest way to do this is to disabled automatic saves but call Profile.Save() when the Save button is clicked. You could also handle the TextBox.TextChanged event to determine when changes are made and save the profile immediately at this point.

The Profile API

Although your page automatically gets the profile information for the current user, this doesn't prevent you from retrieving and modifying the profiles of other users. In fact, you have two tools to help you—the ProfileBase class and the ProfileManager class.

The ProfileBase object (provided by the Page.Profile property) includes a useful GetProfile() function that retrieves the profile information for a specific user by user name. Figure 20-4 shows an example with a Windows-authenticated user.

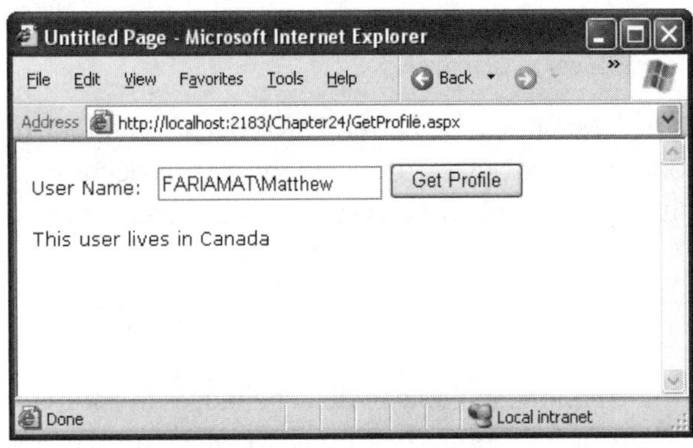

Figure 20-4. *Retrieving a profile manually*

Here's the code that gets the profile:

```
protected void cmdGet_Click(object sender, EventArgs e)
{
    ProfileCommon profile = Profile.GetProfile(txtUserName.Text);
    lbl.Text = "This user lives in " + profile.Address.Country;
}
```

Notice that once you have a Profile object, you can interact with it in the same way you interact with the profile for the current user. You can even make changes. The only difference is that changes aren't saved automatically. If you want to save a change, you need to call the Save() method of the Profile object.

■ **Note** If you try to retrieve a profile that doesn't exist, you won't get an error. Instead, you'll simply end up with blank data. If you change and save the profile, a new profile record will be created.

If you need to perform other tasks with profiles, you can use the ProfileManager class in the System.Web.Profile namespace, which exposes the useful static methods described in Table 20-5. Many of these methods work with a ProfileInfo class, which provides information about a profile. The ProfileInfo includes the user name (UserName), last update and last activity dates (LastActivityDate and LastUpdateDate), the size of the profile in bytes (Size), and whether the profile is for an anonymous user (IsAnonymous). It doesn't provide the actual profile values.

Table 20-5. *ProfileManager Methods*

Method	Description
DeleteProfile()	Deletes the profile for the user you specify.
DeleteProfiles()	Deletes multiple profiles at once. You supply an array of user names.
DeleteInactiveProfiles()	Deletes profiles that haven't been used since a time you specify. You also must supply a value from the ProfileAuthenticationOption enumeration to indicate what type of profiles you want to remove (All, Anonymous, or Authenticated).
GetNumberOfProfiles()	Returns the number of profile records in the data source.
GetNumberOfInactiveProfiles()	Returns the number of profiles that haven't been used since the time you specify.
GetAllInactiveProfiles()	Retrieves profile information for profiles that haven't been used since the time you specify. The profiles are returned as ProfileInfo objects.
GetAllProfiles()	Retrieves all the profile data from the data source as a collection of ProfileInfo objects. You can choose what type of profiles you want to retrieve (All, Anonymous, or Authenticated). You can also use an overloaded version of this method that uses paging and retrieves only a portion of the full set of records based on the starting index and page size you request.

Continued

Table 20-5. *Continued*

Method	Description
FindProfilesByUserName()	Retrieves a collection of ProfileInfo objects matching a specific user name. The SqlProfileProvider uses a LIKE clause when it attempts to match user names, which means you can use wildcards such as the % symbol. For example, if you search for the user name user%, you'll return values such as user1, user2, user_guest, and so on. You can use an overloaded version of this method that uses paging.
FindInactiveProfilesByUserName()	Retrieves profile information for profiles that haven't been used since the time you specify. You can also filter out certain types of profiles (All, Anonymous, or Authenticated) or look for a specific user name (with wildcard matching). The return value is a collection of ProfileInfo objects.

For example, if you want to remove the profile for the current user, you need only a single line of code:

```
ProfileManager.DeleteProfile(User.Identity.Name);
```

And if you want to display the full list of users in a web page (not including anonymous users), just add a GridView with AutoGenerateColumns set to true and use this code:

```
protected void Page_Load(object sender, EventArgs e)
{
    GridView1.DataSource = ProfileManager.GetAllProfiles(
      ProfileAuthenticationOption.Authenticated);
    GridView1.DataBind();
}
```

Figure 20-5 shows the result.

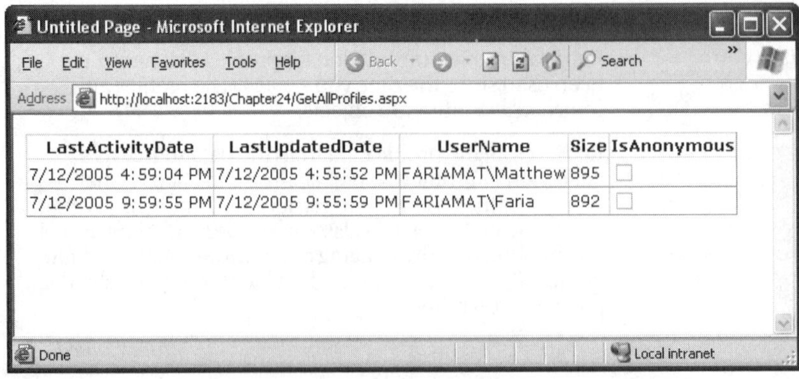

Figure 20-5. *Retrieving information about all the profiles in the data source*

Anonymous Profiles

So far, all the examples have assumed that the user is authenticated before any profile information is accessed or stored. Usually, this is the case. However, sometimes it's useful to create a temporary profile for a new, unknown user. For example, most e-commerce websites allow new users to begin adding items to a shopping cart before registering. If you want to provide this type of behavior and you choose to store shopping cart items in a profile, you'll need some way to uniquely identify anonymous users.

ASP.NET provides an anonymous identification feature that fills this gap. The basic idea is that the anonymous identification feature automatically generates a random identifier for any anonymous user. This random identifier stores the profile information in the database, even though no user ID is available. The user ID is tracked on the client side using a cookie (or in the URL, if you've enabled cookieless mode). Once this cookie disappears (for example, if the anonymous user closes and reopens the browser), the anonymous session is lost and a new anonymous session is created.

Anonymous identification has the potential to leave a lot of abandoned profiles, which wastes space in the database. For that reason, anonymous identification is disabled by default. However, you can enable it using the <anonymousIdentification> element in the web.config file, as shown here:

```
<configuration xmlns="http://schemas.microsoft.com/.NetConfiguration/v2.0">
  ...
  <system.web>
    <anonymousIdentification enabled="true" />
    ...
  </system.web>
</configuration>
```

You also need to flag each profile property that will be retained for anonymous users by adding the allowAnonymous attribute and setting it to true. This allows you to store just some basic information and restrict larger objects to authenticated users.

```
<properties>
  <add name="Address" type="Address" allowAnonymous="true" />
  ...
</properties>
```

The <anonymousIdentification> element also supports numerous optional attributes that let you set the cookie name and timeout, specify whether the cookie will be issued only over an SSL connection, control whether cookie protection (validation and encryption) is used to prevent tampering and eavesdropping, and configure support for cookieless ID tracking. Here's an example:

```
<anonymousIdentification enabled="true" cookieName=".ASPXANONYMOUS"
  cookieTimeout="43200" cookiePath="/" cookieRequireSSL="false"
```

```
cookieSlidingExpiration="true" cookieProtection="All"
cookieless="UseCookies"/>
```

For more information, refer to the MSDN Help.

■ **Tip** If you use anonymous identification, it's a good idea to delete old anonymous sessions regularly using the aspnet_Profile_DeleteInactiveProfiles stored procedure, which you can run at scheduled intervals using the SQL Server Agent. You can also delete old profiles using the ProfileManager class, as described in the previous section.

Migrating Anonymous Profiles

One challenge that occurs with anonymous profiles is what to do with the profile information when a previously anonymous user logs in. For example, in an e-commerce website a user might select several items and then register or log in to complete the transaction. At this point, you need to make sure the shopping cart information is copied from the anonymous user's profile to the appropriate authenticated (user) profile.

Fortunately, ASP.NET provides a solution through the ProfileModule.MigrateAnonymous event. This event (which can be handled in the global.asax file) fires whenever an anonymous identifier is available (either as a cookie or in the URL if you're using cookieless mode) *and* the current user is authenticated.

The basic technique when handling the MigrateAnonymous event is to load the profile for the anonymous user by calling Profile.GetProfile() and passing in the anonymous ID, which is provided to your event handler through the ProfileMigrateEventArgs.

Once you've loaded this data, you can then transfer the settings to the new profile manually. You can choose to transfer as few or as many settings as you want, and you can perform any other processing that's required. Finally, your code should remove the anonymous profile data from the database and clear the anonymous identifier so the MigrateAnonymous event won't fire again. For example:

```
void Profile_OnMigrateAnonymous(Object sender, ProfileMigrateEventArgs pe)
{
    // Get the anonymous profile.
    ProfileCommon anonProfile = Profile.GetProfile(pe.AnonymousID);

    // Copy information to the authenticated profile
    // (but only if there's information there).
    if (anonProfile.Address.Name != null || anonProfile.Address.Name != "")
    {
        Profile.Address = anonProfile.Address;
    }
```

```
    // Delete the anonymous profile from the database.
    // (You could decide to skip this step to increase performance
    //  if you have a dedicated job scheduled on the database server
    //  to remove old anonymous profiles.)
    System.Web.Profile.ProfileManager.DeleteProfile(pe.AnonymousID);

    // Remove the anonymous identifier.
    AnonymousIdentificationModule.ClearAnonymousIdentifier();
}
```

You need to handle this task with some caution. If you've enabled anonymous identification, the MigrateAnonymous event fires every time a user logs in, even if the user hasn't entered any information into the anonymous profile. That's a problem—if you're not careful, you could easily overwrite the real (saved) profile for the user with the blank anonymous profile. The problem is further complicated by the fact that complex types (such as the Address object) are created automatically by ASP.NET, so you can't just check for a null reference to determine whether the user has anonymous address information.

In the previous example, the code tests for a missing Name property in the Address object. If this information isn't part of the anonymous profile, no information is migrated. A more sophisticated example might test for individual properties separately or might migrate an anonymous profile only if the information in the user profile is missing or outdated.

The Last Word

In this chapter, you learned how to use profiles and how they store information in the database. Many ASP.NET developers will prefer to write their own ADO.NET code for retrieving and storing user-specific information. Not only does this allow you to use your own database structure, but it also allows you to add your own features, such as caching, logging, validation, and encryption. However, profiles are handy for quickly building modest applications that don't store a lot of user-specific information and don't have special requirements for how this information is stored.

PART 5

Web Services

CHAPTER 21

Web Services Architecture

Microsoft has promoted ASP.NET web services more than almost any other part of the .NET Framework. But despite Microsoft's efforts, confusion is still widespread about what web services are and, more important, what they're meant to accomplish. This chapter introduces web services and explains their role in Microsoft's vision of the programmable Web. Along the way, you'll learn about the open-standards plumbing that allows web services to work, including technical standards such as WSDL (Web Services Description Language) and SOAP.

Internet Programming Then and Now

To understand the place of web services, you have to understand the shortcomings of the current architecture of Internet applications. In many respects, Internet applications are at the same point in their development that client/server desktop applications were several years ago—the monolithic era. Today's Internet is dominated by full-featured websites that are written entirely from scratch and aren't able to share functionality between each other.

The Era of Monolithic Applications

Most of the applications you use over the Internet today can be considered "monolithic" because they combine a variety of services behind a single proprietary user interface. For example, you may already use your bank's website to do everything from checking exchange rates and reviewing stock quotes to paying bills and transferring funds. This is a successful model of development, but it has the following unavoidable shortcomings:

- Monolithic applications take a great deal of time and resources to create. They are often tied to a specific platform or to specific technologies, and they can't be easily extended and enhanced.

- Getting more than one application to work together is a full project of its own. Usually, an integration project involves a lot of custom work that's highly specific to a given scenario. And what's worse, every time you need to interact with another business, you need to start the integration process all over again. Currently, most websites limit themselves to extremely simple methods of integration. For example, you might be provided with a link that opens another website in an existing frame on the current web page.

- Most important, units of application logic can't easily be reused between one application and another. With ASP.NET, source code can be shared using .NET classes, but this isn't possible for applications created by different companies or written using different programming languages. And if you want to perform more sophisticated or subtle integration, such as between a website and a Windows application, or between applications hosted on different platforms, no easy solutions are available.

- Sometimes, you might want to get extremely simple information from a web application, such as an individual stock quote. To get this information, you usually need to access and navigate through the entire web application, locate the correct page, and then perform the required task. You have no way to access information or perform a task without working through the graphical user interface, which can be cumbersome over a slow connection or unworkable on a portable device such as a cell phone.

Components and the COM Revolution

This state of affairs may sound familiar if you know the history of the Windows platform. A similar situation existed in the world of desktop applications many years ago. Developers found they were spending the majority of their programming time solving problems they had already solved. Programmers needed to structure in-house applications carefully with DLLs or source code components in order to have any chance of reusing their work. Third-party applications usually could be integrated only through specific pipelines. For example, one program might need to export to a set file format, which would then be manually imported into a different application. Companies focused on features and performance but had no easy way to share data or work together.

The story improved dramatically when Microsoft introduced its COM technology (parts of which also go by the more market-friendly name ActiveX). With COM, developers found they could develop components in their language of choice and reuse them in a variety of programming environments, without needing to share source code. Similarly, less need existed to export and import information using proprietary file formats. Instead, COM components allowed developers to package functionality into succinct and reusable chunks with well-defined interfaces.

COM helped end the era of monolithic applications. Even though we all still use database and office productivity applications, such as Microsoft Word, that seem to be monolithic, integrated applications, much of the functionality in these applications is delegated to separate components behind the scenes. As with all object-oriented programming, this makes code easier to debug, alter, and extend.

Web Services and the Programmable Web

Web services enable the same evolution that COM did, with a twist. Web services are individual units of programming logic that exist on a web server. They can be easily integrated into all sorts of applications, including everything from other ASP.NET applications to simple command-line applications. The twist is that, unlike COM, which is a platform-specific standard, web services are built on a foundation of open standards. These standards allow web services to be created with .NET but consumed on other platforms—or vice versa. In fact, the idea of web services didn't originate at Microsoft. Other major computer forces such as IBM helped to develop the core standards that Microsoft uses natively in ASP.NET.

The root standard for all the individual web service standards is XML. Because XML is text-based, web service invocations can pass over normal HTTP channels. Other distributed object technologies, such as DCOM, are much more complex, and as a result, they are exceedingly difficult to configure correctly, especially if you need to use them over the Internet. So not only are web services governed by cross-platform standards, but they're also easier to use.

You can look at web services in two ways. Application programmers (and the .NET Framework) tend to treat a web service as a set of methods that you can call over the Internet. Of course, these methods have all the capabilities that ASP.NET programmers are used to, such as the automatic security and session state facilities discussed in other parts of this book. XML gurus take a different perspective. They prefer to treat web services as a way to exchange XML messages.

Which perspective you take depends to some extent on the type of web service you are creating. For example, if you need to pass messages through several intermediaries as part of a long-running business-to-business transaction, you'll have an easier time looking at your web service as a message-passing system. On the other hand, if you're calling a web service just to get some information—such as a product catalog or stock quote—you'll probably treat it like any other useful function.

When Web Services Make Sense

With the overbearing web services hype, developers sometimes forget to ask tough questions about when web services should and should *not* be used. Although web services are an impressive piece of technology, they aren't the best choice for all applications.

Microsoft recommends you use web services when your application needs to cross *platform boundaries* or *trust boundaries*. You cross a platform boundary when your system incorporates a non-.NET application. In other words, web services are a perfect choice if you need to provide data to a Java client running on a Unix computer. Because web services are based on open standards, Java developers simply need to use a web service toolkit that's designed for the Java platform. They can then call your .NET web services seamlessly, without worrying about any conversion issues.

You cross a trust boundary when your system incorporates applications from more than one company or organization. In other words, web services work well if you need to provide some information from a database (such as a product catalog or customer list) to an application written by other developers. If you use web services, you won't need to supply the third-party developers with any special information—instead, they can get all the information using an automated tool that reads the WSDL document. You also won't need to give them access to privileged resources. For example, instead of connecting directly to your database or to a proprietary component, they can interact with the web service, which will retrieve the data for them. In fact, you can even use some of the same security settings that you use with web pages to protect your web services.

If you aren't crossing platform or trust boundaries, web services might not be a great choice. For example, web services are generally a poor way to share functionality between two web applications on your web server or to share functionality between different types of applications in your company. Instead, it's a much better idea to develop and share a dedicated .NET component. This technique ensures optimum performance, because you do not need to translate data into XML or send messages over the network. You'll find more details of this technique in Chapter 24, which tackles component-based development.

The Open-Standards Plumbing

Before using web services, it helps to understand a little about the architecture that makes it all possible. Strictly speaking, this knowledge isn't required to work with web services. In fact, you can skip to the next chapter and start creating your first web service right now. However, understanding a little bit about the way web services work can help you determine how to use them best.

Remember, web services are designed from the ground up with open-standard compatibility in mind. To ensure the greatest possible compatibility and extensibility, the web service architecture has been made as generic as possible. This means few assumptions are made about the format and encoding used to send information to and from a web service. Instead, all these details are explicitly defined, in a flexible way, using standards such as SOAP and WSDL. And as you'll see, in order for a client to be able to connect to a web service, a lot of mundane work has to go on behind the scenes to process and interpret this SOAP and WSDL information. This mundane work does exert a bit of a performance overhead, but it won't hamper most well-designed web services.

Table 21-1 summarizes the standards this chapter examines.

Table 21-1. *Web Service Standards*

Standard	Description
WSDL	Tells a client what methods are present in a web service, what parameters and return values each method uses, and how to communicate with them.
SOAP	The preferred way to encode information (such as data values) before sending it to a web service.
HTTP	The protocol over which all web service communication takes place. For example, SOAP messages are sent over HTTP channels.
DISCO	The discovery standard that contains links to web services or that can be used to provide a dynamic list of web services in a specified path.
UDDI	A standard for creating business registries that list information about companies, the web services they provide, and the corresponding URLs for DISCO file or WSDL contracts. Unfortunately, UDDI is still too new to be widely accepted and useful.

Web Services Description Language

WSDL is an XML-based standard that specifies how a client can interact with a web service, including details such as how parameters and return values should be encoded in a message and what protocol should be used for transmission over the Internet. Currently, three standards are supported for the actual transmission of web service information: HTTP GET, HTTP POST, and SOAP (over HTTP).

You can find the full WSDL standard at `http://www.w3.org/TR/wsdl`. The standard is fairly complex, but its underlying logic is hidden from the developer in ASP.NET programming, just as ASP.NET web controls abstract away the messy details of HTML tags and attributes. As you'll see in the next chapter, ASP.NET creates WSDL documents for your web services automatically. ASP.NET can also create a proxy class based on a WSDL document. This proxy class allows a client to call a web service without worrying about networking or formatting issues. Many non-.NET platforms provide similar tools to make these chores relatively painless. For example, Visual Basic 6 or C++ developers can use Microsoft's SOAP Toolkit (To find the download, surf to `http://msdn.microsoft.com` and search for "SOAP Toolkit.").

In the next few sections, you'll examine a sample WSDL document for a simple web service, consisting of a single method called GetStockQuote(). This method accepts a string specifying a stock ticker and returns a numeric value that represents a current price quote. The web service is called StockQuote, and you'll peer into its actual ASP.NET code in the next chapter.

■ **Note** The WSDL document contains information for communication between a web service and client. It doesn't contain information that has anything to do with the code or implementation of your web service methods—that is unnecessary and would compromise security.

The <definitions> Element

The WSDL document is quite long, so the next few sections will consider it section by section, in order. Don't worry about understanding it in detail—the .NET Framework will handle that—but do use it to get an idea about how web services communicate.

The header and root namespace look like this:

```
<?xml version="1.0" encoding="utf-8" ?>
<definitions xmlns:s="http://www.w3.org/2001/XMLSchema"
  xmlns:http="http://schemas.xmlsoap.org/wsdl/http/"
  xmlns:mime="http://schemas.xmlsoap.org/wsdl/mime/"
  xmlns:tm="http://microsoft.com/wsdl/mime/textMatching/"
  xmlns:soap="http://schemas.xmlsoap.org/wsdl/soap/"
  xmlns:soapenc="http://schemas.xmlsoap.org/soap/encoding/"
  xmlns:s0="http://tempuri.org/" targetNamespace="http://tempuri.org/"
  xmlns="http://schemas.xmlsoap.org/wsdl/">

  <!-- This is where all the rest of the WSDL document goes.
  I've snipped it into the individual pieces shown in the
  rest of the chapter. -->

</definitions>
```

Looking at the WSDL document, you'll notice that all the information appears in a root <definitions> element.

The <types> Element

The first element contained inside the <description> element is a <types> element that defines information about the data types of the return value and parameters your web service method uses. If your web service returns an instance of a custom class, ASP.NET will add an entry to define your class (although only data members will be preserved, not methods, which can't be converted into an XML representation).

The following code shows the <types> element for StockQuote. By looking at it, you can tell that the function GetStockQuote() uses a string parameter, called Ticker, and a decimal return value (shown in bold).

```
<types>
  <s:schema attributeFormDefault="qualified" elementFormDefault="qualified"
     targetNamespace="http://www.prosetech.com/Stocks/">
    <s:element name="GetStockQuote">
      <s:complexType>
        <s:sequence>
          <s:element minOccurs="1" maxOccurs="1" name="Ticker"
             nillable="true" type="s:string"/>
        </s:sequence>
      </s:complexType>
    </s:element>
    <s:element name="GetStockQuoteResponse">
      <s:complexType>
        <s:sequence>
          <s:element minOccurs="1" maxOccurs="1"
             name="GetStockQuoteResult" type="s:decimal"/>
        </s:sequence>
      </s:complexType>
    </s:element>
    <s:element name="decimal" type="s:decimal"/>
  </s:schema>
</types>
```

Here's the corresponding method in the web service:

```
public decimal GetStockQuote(string ticker)
{
    // (Code goes here.)
}
```

Incidentally, the information in the <types> section is defined using the XML schema standard (XSD). Chapter 17 introduced this standard when covering XML validation. Web services use the same technique to validate the messages that are exchanged between a web service and a client, although the process is completely seamless.

The <message> Elements

Messages represent the information exchanged between a web service method and a client. When you request a stock quote from the simple web service, ASP.NET sends a message, and the web service returns a different message. You can find the definition for these messages in the <message> section of the WSDL document. Here's an example:

```
<message name="GetStockQuoteSoapIn">
  <part name="parameters" element="s0:GetStockQuote"/>
</message>
<message name="GetStockQuoteSoapOut">
  <part name="parameters" element="s0:GetStockQuoteResponse"/>
</message>
```

In this example, you'll notice that ASP.NET creates both a GetStockQuoteSoapIn and a GetStockQuoteSoapOut message. The naming is a matter of convention, but it underscores that a separate message is required for input (sending parameters and invoking a web service method) and output (retrieving a return value from a web service method).

The data used in these messages is defined in terms of the information in the <types> section. For example, the GetStockQuoteSoapIn request message sends the GetStockQuote element, which is defined in the <types> section as a string named Ticker.

Similar message definitions are used for the other two types of communication, HTTP POST and HTTP GET. These are simpler communication methods that are primarily used for testing. Instead of using a full-fledged SOAP message, they just send simple XML:

```
<message name="GetStockQuoteHttpGetIn">
  <part name="Ticker" type="s:string"/>
</message>
<message name="GetStockQuoteHttpGetOut">
  <part name="Body" element="s0:decimal"/>
</message>
<message name="GetStockQuoteHttpPostIn">
  <part name="Ticker" type="s:string"/>
</message>
<message name="GetStockQuoteHttpPostOut">
 <part name="Body" element="s0:decimal"/>
</message>
```

Remember, StockQuote contains only one method. The three versions of it that you see in WSDL are provided and supported by ASP.NET automatically to give the client a chance to choose a preferred method of communication.

The <portType> Elements

The information in the <portType> section of the WSDL document provides an overview of all the methods available in the web service. Each method is defined as an <operation>, and each operation includes the request and response messages.

For example, you'll see that for the SOAP port type (StockQuoteSoap), the GetStockQuote() method requires an input message called GetStockQuoteIn and a matching output message called GetStockQuoteOut:

```
<portType name="StockQuoteSoap">
  <operation name="GetStockQuote">
    <input message="s0:GetStockQuoteSoapIn"/>
    <output message="s0:GetStockQuoteSoapOut"/>
  </operation>
</portType>
<portType name="StockQuoteHttpGet">
  <operation name="GetStockQuote">
    <input message="s0:GetStockQuoteHttpGetIn"/>
    <output message="s0:GetStockQuoteHttpGetOut"/>
  </operation>
</portType>
<portType name="StockQuoteHttpPost">
  <operation name="GetStockQuote">
    <input message="s0:GetStockQuoteHttpPostIn"/>
    <output message="s0:GetStockQuoteHttpPostOut"/>
  </operation>
</portType>
```

The <binding> Elements

The <binding> elements link the abstract data format to the protocol used for transmission over an Internet connection. So far, the WSDL document has specified the data type used for various pieces of information, the required messages used for an operation, and the structure of each message. With the <binding> element, the WSDL document specifies the low-level communication protocol you can use to talk to a web service.

For example, the StockQuote WSDL document specifies that the SOAP-specific GetStockQuote operation communicates using SOAP messages. The HTTP POST and HTTP GET operations receive information as an XML document (type mimeXML) and send it encoded either as a query string argument (type http:urlEncoded) or in the body of a posted form (type application/x-www-form-urlencoded).

```
<binding name="StockQuoteSoap" type="s0:StockQuoteSoap">
  <soap:binding transport="http://schemas.xmlsoap.org/soap/http"
   style="document"/>
  <operation name="GetStockQuote">
    <soap:operation soapAction="http://www.prosetech.com/Stocks/GetStockQuote"
     style="document"/>
    <input>
      <soap:body use="literal"/>
    </input>
    <output>
      <soap:body use="literal"/>
    </output>
  </operation>
</binding>
<binding name="StockQuoteHttpGet" type="s0:StockQuoteHttpGet">
  <http:binding verb="GET"/>
  <operation name="GetStockQuote">
    <http:operation location="/GetStockQuote"/>
    <input>
      <http:urlEncoded/>
    </input>
    <output>
      <mime:mimeXml part="Body"/>
    </output>
  </operation>
</binding>
<binding name="StockQuoteHttpPost" type="s0:StockQuoteHttpPost">
  <http:binding verb="POST"/>
  <operation name="GetStockQuote">
    <http:operation location="/GetStockQuote"/>
    <input>
      <mime:content type="application/x-www-form-urlencoded"/>
    </input>
    <output>
      <mime:mimeXml part="Body"/>
    </output>
  </operation>
</binding>
```

■ Note You'll actually see two versions of the same binding information for a .NET web service. That's because .NET web services support two versions of SOAP (the original SOAP 1.1 and the similar but less common SOAP 1.2). The WSDL document includes binding information for both, with similar instructions.

The <service> Element

The <service> element defines the entry points into your web service. This is how a client accesses the web service.

An ASP.NET web service defines three different <port> elements in the <service> element, one for each protocol. Inside each <port> element is another element that identifies the Internet address (URL) needed to access the web service. Most web services (and all ASP.NET web services) use the same URL address for all types of communication.

```
<service name="StockQuote">
  <port name="StockQuoteSoap" binding="s0:StockQuoteSoap">
    <soap:address
          location="http://localhost/WebServices/StockQuote.asmx"/>
  </port>
  <port name="StockQuoteHttpGet" binding="s0:StockQuoteHttpGet">
    <http:address
          location="http://localhost/WebServices/StockQuote.asmx"/>
  </port>
  <port name="StockQuoteHttpPost" binding="s0:StockQuoteHttpPost">
    <http:address
          location="http://localhost/WebServices/StockQuote.asmx"/>
  </port>
</service>
```

■ Tip Here's a neat trick: any ASP.NET service will display its corresponding WSDL document if you add ?WSDL to the query string. For example, you could look at the WSDL document for the preceding web service example by navigating to `http://localhost/WebServices/StockQuote.asmx?WSDL`. The greatest benefits of web services are their autodiscovery and self-description features.

SOAP

A client can use three protocols to communicate with a web service in .NET:

- HTTP GET, which communicates with a web service by encoding information in the query string and retrieves information as a basic XML document.
- HTTP POST, which places parameters in the request body (as form values) and retrieves information as a basic XML document.
- SOAP, which uses XML for both request and response messages. Like HTTP GET and HTTP POST, SOAP works over HTTP, but it uses a more detailed XML-based language for bundling information. SOAP messages are widely supported by many platforms.

Although .NET has the ability to support all three of these protocols, it restricts the first two for better security. By default, it disables HTTP GET, and it restricts HTTP POST to the local computer. This means you can use it to test a web service (as you'll see in the next chapter), but you can't use it to call a web service from a remote computer. You can change this setup by modifying the web.config file, but that's not recommended.

A Sample SOAP Message

Essentially, when you use SOAP, you're simply using the SOAP standard to encode the information in your messages. SOAP messages follow an XML-based standard and look something like this:

```
<?xml version="1.0" encoding="UTF-8" standalone="no"?>
<soap:Envelope xmlns="http://schemas.xmlsoap.org/soap/envelope/">
  <soap:Body>
    <GetStockQuote xmlns ="http://www.prosetech.com/Stocks/">
      <Ticker>MSFT</Ticker>
    </GetStockQuote>
  </soap:Body>
</soap:Envelope>
```

Looking at the preceding SOAP message, you can see that the root element is a <soap:envelope>, which contains the <soap:body> of the request. Inside the body is information indicating that the GetStockQuote() method is being called with a Ticker parameter of MSFT. Although this is a fairly straightforward method call, SOAP messages can easily contain entire structures representing custom objects or DataSets.

In response to this request, a SOAP output message will be returned. Here's an example of what you can expect:

```
<?xml version="1.0" encoding="utf-8"?>
<soap:Envelope xmlns="http://schemas.xmlsoap.org/soap/envelope/">
  <soap:Body>
    <GetStockQuoteResponse xmlns="http://www.prosetech.com/Stocks">
      <GetStockQuoteResult>29.23</GetStockQuoteResult>
    </GetStockQuoteResponse>
  </soap:Body>
</soap:Envelope>
```

This example demonstrates why the SOAP message format is superior to HTTP GET and HTTP POST. When using SOAP, both request and response messages are formatted using XML. When using HTTP GET and HTTP POST, the response messages use XML, but the request messages use simple : name/value pairs to supply the parameter information. This means HTTP GET and HTTP POST won't allow you to use complex objects as parameters and won't be natively supported on most non-.NET platforms. HTTP GET and HTTP POST are primarily included for testing purposes.

Remember, your applications won't directly handle SOAP messages. Instead, .NET will translate the information in a SOAP message into the corresponding .NET data types before the data reaches your code. This allows you to interact with web services in the same way you interact with any other object.

For information about the SOAP standard, you can read the full specification at `http://www.w3.org/TR/SOAP`. (Once again, these technical details explain a lot about how SOAP works but are rarely implemented in day-to-day programming.)

Communicating with a Web Service

The WSDL and SOAP standards enable the communication between web services and clients, but they don't show how it happens. The following three components play a role:

- A custom web service class that provides some piece of functionality.
- A client application that wants to use this functionality.
- A proxy class that acts as the interface between the two. The proxy class contains a representation of all the web service methods and takes care of the details involved in communicating with the web service by the chosen protocol.

The actual process works like this (see Figure 21-1):

1. The client creates an instance of a proxy class.

2. The client invokes the method on the proxy class, exactly as though it were using a normal, local class.

3. Behind the scenes, the proxy class sends the information to the web service in the appropriate format (usually SOAP) and receives the corresponding response, which is converted to the corresponding data or object.

4. The proxy class returns the result to the calling code.

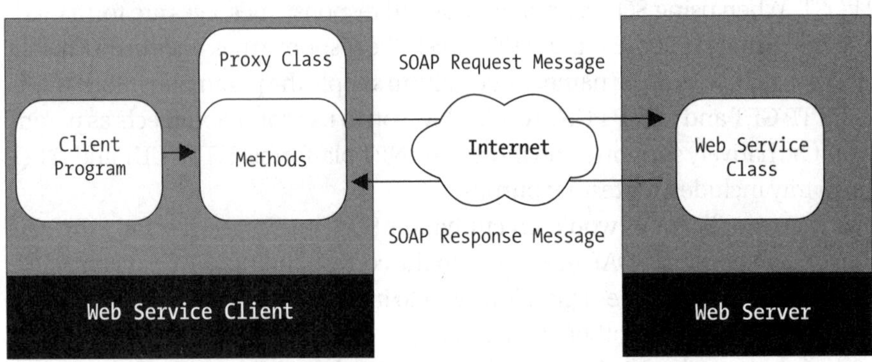

Figure 21-1. *Web service communication*

Perhaps the most significant detail is that the client doesn't need to be aware that a remote function call to a web service is taking place. The process is completely transparent and works as though you were calling a function in your own local code!

Of course, the following additional limitations and considerations apply:

- Not all data types are supported for method parameters and return values. For example, you can't pass many .NET class library objects (the DataSet is one important exception).

- The network call takes a short but measurable amount of time. If you need to use several web service methods in a row, this delay can start to add up.

- Unless the web service takes specific steps to remember its state information, this data will be lost. Basically, this means you should treat a web service like a stateless utility class, composed of as many independent methods as you need. You shouldn't think of a web service as an ordinary object with properties and member variables.
- A variety of new errors can occur and interrupt your web method (for example, network problems). You may need to take this into account when building a robust application.

You'll examine all these issues in detail throughout the next two chapters.

Web Service Discovery

Imagine you've created a web service that uses WSDL to describe how it works and transmits information in SOAP packets. Inevitably, you'll start to ask how clients can find your web services. At first thought, it seems to be a trivial question. Clearly, a web service is available at a specific URL address. Once clients have this address, they can retrieve the WSDL document by adding ?WSDL to the URL, and all the necessary information is available. So why is a discovery standard required at all?

The straightforward process described earlier works great if you need to share a web service only with specific clients or inside a single organization. However, as web services become more and more numerous and eventually evolve into a common language for performing business transactions over the Web, this manual process seems less practical. For instance, if a company provides 12 web services, how does it communicate each of these 12 URLs to prospective clients? E-mailing them to individual developers is sure to take time and create inefficiency. Trying to recite them over the telephone is worse. Providing an HTML page that consolidates all the appropriate links is a start, but it will still force client application developers to manually enter information into their programs. If this information changes later, it will result in painstaking minor changes that could cause countless headaches. Sometimes, trivial details aren't so trivial.

The DISCO Standard

The DISCO standard picks up where the "HTML page with links" concept ends. When following the DISCO standard, you provide a .disco file that specifies where a web service is located. Tools such as Visual Studio can read the .disco file and automatically provide you with the list of corresponding web services.

Here is a sample .disco file:

```
<disco:discovery  xmlns:disco="http://schemas.xmlsoap.org/disco"
  xmlns:wsdl="http://schemas.xmlsoap.org/disco/wsdl">
    <wsdl:contractRef
          ref="http://localhost/WebServices/StockQuote.asmx?WSDL"/>
</disco:discovery>
```

The benefit of a .disco file is that it is clearly used for web services (while .html and .aspx files can contain any kind of content). The other advantage is that you can insert <disco> elements for as many web services as you want, including ones that reside on other web servers. In other words, a .disco file provides a straightforward way to create a repository of web service links that can be used automatically by .NET. However, you don't need to create a .disco file to use a web service.

■ **Note** The DISCO standard is Microsoft-specific, and it's a bit of a dead end. It's slated for eventual replacement by WS-Inspection, a similar standard that's backed by all web service vendors.

Universal Description, Discovery, and Integration

UDDI is one of the youngest and most rapidly developing standards in the web service family. UDDI is an initiative designed to make it easier for you to locate web services on any server.

With discovery files, the client still needs to know the specific URL location of the discovery file. Discovery files may make life easier by consolidating multiple web services into one document, but they don't provide any obvious way to examine the web services offered by a company without navigating to its website and looking for a .disco hyperlink. The goal of UDDI, on the other hand, is to provide repositories where businesses can advertise all the web services they have. For example, a company might list the services it has for business document exchange, which describe how purchase orders can be submitted and tracking information can be retrieved. To submit this information, a business must be registered with the service.

In some ways, UDDI is the equivalent of Google for web services, with one significant difference. Most web search engines attempt to catalog the entire Internet. Setting up a UDDI registry with all the web services of the world doesn't have much point, because different industries have different needs, and a single disorganized collection won't please anyone. Instead, it's much more likely that groups of companies and consortiums will band together to set up their own UDDI registries organized into specific industries. In all likelihood, many of these registries will be restricted so that they aren't publicly available.

WHERE ARE WEB SERVICES TODAY?

Currently, first-generation web services are being used to bridge the gap between modern applications and older technologies. For example, an organization might use a web service to provide access to a legacy database. Internal applications can then contact the web service instead of needing to interact directly with the database, which could be much more difficult. Similar techniques are being used to allow different applications to interact. For example, web services can act as a kind of "glue" that allows a payroll system to interact with another type of financial application in the same company. Second-generation web services are those that allow partnering companies to work together. For example, an e-commerce company might need to submit orders or track parcels through the web service provided by a shipping company. Second-generation web services require two companies to work closely together to devise a strategy for exposing the functionality they each need. Second-generation web services are in their infancy but are gaining ground quickly.

The third generation of web services will allow developers to create much more modular applications by aggregating many different services into one application. For example, you might add a virtual hard drive to your web applications using a third-party web service. You would pay a subscription fee to the web service provider, but the end user wouldn't be aware of what application functionality is provided by you and what functionality relies on third-party web services. This third generation of web services will require new standards and enhancements that will allow web services to better deal with issues such as reliability, discovery, and performance. These standards are constantly evolving, and it's anyone's guess how long it will be before third-generation web services begin to flourish, but it's probably just a matter of time.

Already, you can use third-party web services from companies such as eBay, Amazon, and Google. These web services act as part of a value-added proposition and may eventually evolve into separate cost-based services. But if you're curious, you can seek these web services out today and use them in your own .NET applications.

Interestingly enough, the UDDI registry defines a complete programming interface that specifies how SOAP messages can be used to retrieve information about a business or register the web services for a business. In other words, the UDDI registry is itself a web service! This standard is still not in widespread use, but you can find detailed specifications at `http://uddi.microsoft.com`.

WS-Interoperability

Web services have developed rapidly, and standards such as SOAP and WSDL are still evolving. In early web service toolkits, different vendors interpreted parts of these standards in different ways, leading to interoperability headaches. Adding to the confusion is that some features from the original standards are now considered obsolete.

Negotiating these subtle differences is a small minefield, especially if you need to create web services that will be accessed by clients using other programming platforms and web service toolkits. Fortunately, another standard has appeared recently that sets out a broad range of rules and recommendations designed to guarantee interoperability across the web service implementations of different vendors. This document is the WS-Interoperability Basic Profile (see `http://www.ws-i.org`). It specifies a recommended subset of the full SOAP 1.1 and WSDL 1.1 specifications and lays out a few ground rules. WS-Interoperability is strongly backed by all web service vendors (including Microsoft, IBM, Sun, and Oracle).

Ideally, as a developer, you shouldn't need to worry about the specifics of WS-Interoperability. However, you'll be happy to learn that ASP.NET 2.0 web services follow its guidelines automatically.

■ **Note** With a fair bit of work, you can configure your web service to break these rules, but by default .NET won't let you. Instead, your web service will throw an exception when it's compiled. In the next chapter, you'll learn how to turn WS-Interoperability checking on and off.

The Last Word

This chapter introduced web services, explained the role they play in distributed applications, and dissected the standards and technologies they rely on to provide their magic. In the next chapter, you'll see just how easy .NET makes it to create your own web services.

CHAPTER 22

Creating Web Services

Web services have the potential to dramatically simplify the way distributed applications are built. They might even lead to a new generation of applications that seamlessly integrate multiple remote services into a single web page or desktop interface. However, the greatest programming concept in the world is doomed to fail if it isn't supported by powerful, flexible tools that make its use not only possible but also convenient. Fortunately, ASP.NET doesn't disappoint. It provides classes that allow you to create a web service quickly and easily.

In the previous chapter, you looked at the philosophy that led to the creation of web services and the XML infrastructure that makes it all possible. This chapter delves into the practical side of web services, leading you through the process of creating and using a basic service.

Web Service Basics

As you've already seen in this book, ASP.NET is based on object-oriented principles. Instead of dealing with a slew of miscellaneous functions, you work with discrete classes that wrap code into neat, reusable objects. Web services follow that pattern—in fact, every web service is really an ordinary class. Even better, a client can create an instance of your web service and use its methods just as though it were any other locally defined class. The underlying HTTP transmission and data type conversion that has to happen takes place behind the scenes.

How does this magic work? It's made possible by the .NET Framework and the types in the System.Web.Services namespace.

A typical web service consists of a few basic ingredients:

- *An .asmx file*: This is the web service end point—the URL where the client sends its request messages. The .asmx file plays the same role with web services as the .aspx file plays with web pages.
- *The web service class*: This contains the functionality (the code) for the web service. As with web pages, you can place the web service class directly in the .asmx file or in a separate code-behind file. Typically, your web service class will inherit from System.Web.Services.WebService, but it doesn't need to do so.
- *One or more web service methods*: These are ordinary methods in the web service class that are marked with the WebMethod attribute. This attribute indicates that the corresponding method should be made available though ASP.NET.

As long as you have these basic ingredients in place, ASP.NET will manage the lower-level details for you. For example, you never need to create a WSDL document or a SOAP message. ASP.NET automatically generates the WSDL document for your web service when it's requested and converts ordinary .NET method calls to SOAP messages transparently.

The only layer you need to worry about is the business-specific code that actually performs the task (such as inserting data into a database, creating a file, performing a calculation, and so on). You write this code like any other C# method.

Configuring a Web Service Project

You can add web services to any web application. In fact, the only difference between the ASP.NET Web Site and ASP.NET Web Service project types in Visual Studio is that the Web Site project type starts off with one web page, while the Web Service project type has one default web service. Other than that, the project types (and their configurations) are identical.

However, if you want to use web services in a client application (which you usually do), you need to take some extra steps to set up your project. The problem is that you can't rely on the built-in Visual Studio web server to host your web services. The Visual Studio web server dynamically chooses a new port each time you run it, which means your client application would have serious difficulties tracking down the web service. Instead, you need to create a virtual directory for your web application (as described in Chapter 12). Once you've taken this step, you can create the web project in this location. That way, your web application is hosted by IIS at a fixed location, which allows clients to connect to it.

Chapter 12 contains a great deal of information about IIS and web services. However, here's a quick series of steps that will get you started. (These steps assume you're using Windows 2000 or Windows XP—consult Chapter 12 for information about Windows 2003.)

1. First, create the virtual directory for your application. For example, create the directory c:\ASP.NET\WebServices using Windows Explorer.

2. The next step is to turn this folder into a virtual directory and a web application. Start IIS Manager (select Start ➤ Programs ➤ Administrative Tools ➤ Internet Information Services), right-click the Default Website item, and select New Virtual Directory.

3. Follow the Virtual Directory Creation Wizard, choosing WebServices for the virtual folder alias and supplying the physical path you created in step 1. Use the default security settings.

4. Now fire up Visual Studio. Select File ➤ New Web Site, and choose the ASP.NET Web Site or ASP.NET Web Service project type (either one works for web services).

5. In the Location box, choose HTTP. Then, supply the virtual path to your web service, which is `http://localhost/` followed by the virtual directory alias, as in `http://localhost/WebServices`.

6. Click OK to create your web service project in the virtual directory.

7. To add a web service to your project, right-click the project in the Solution Explorer, and choose Add ➤ Add New Item. In the Add New Item dialog box, pick Web Service (see Figure 22-1). You can choose to place the code in a separate code-behind file (which is the usual approach) or directly in the web service file. Click OK to add the file.

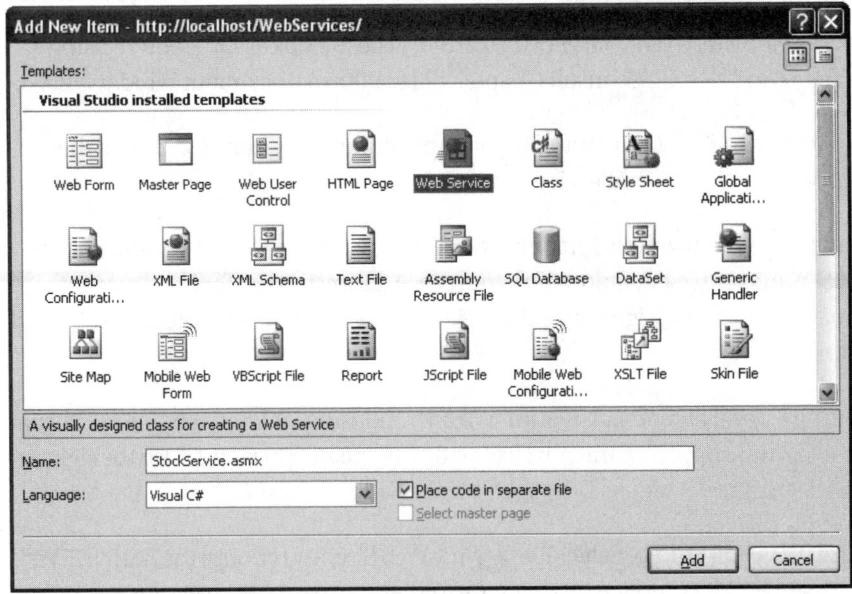

Figure 22-1. *Adding a web service to any project*

■ **Tip** You need to use a similar approach to use the web service examples included with the book. You can place the folder with the web services wherever you want, as long as you create the correct virtual directory (`http://localhost/WebServices`). The readme file has complete instructions.

In the following sections, you'll look at the code for a simple web service and learn how it works.

The StockQuote Web Service

The previous chapter examined the WSDL document generated for a simple web service that contained only one method. Now you'll get a chance to look at the actual code and see how it works.

The following listing shows the StockQuote web service code. In this simple example, all the code is placed in a single .asmx file (so no code-behind file is used).

```
<%@ WebService Language="C#" Class="StockQuote" %>

using System;
using System.Web;
using System.Web.Services;

public class StockQuote : WebService
{
    [WebMethod]
    public decimal GetStockQuote(string ticker)
    {
        // (Perform database lookup here.)
    }
}
```

As you can see, the StockQuote class looks more or less the same as any .NET class. The two differences—inheriting from WebService and using the WebMethod attribute—are highlighted in bold in the example.

An .asmx file is similar to the standard .aspx file used for graphical ASP.NET pages. As with .aspx files, .asmx files start with a directive that specifies the language and are compiled the first time they are requested in order to increase performance. You can create them with Notepad or any other text editor, but professional developers use Visual Studio. The letter *m* indicates "method" because all web services are built from one or more web methods that provide the actual functionality.

Understanding the StockQuote Service

The code for the StockQuote web service is quite straightforward. The first line specifies the file is used for a web service and is written in C#. The next line imports the web service namespace so all the classes you need are at your fingertips. As with other core pieces of ASP.NET technology, web service functionality is provided through prebuilt types in the .NET class library.

The remainder of the code is the actual web service, which is built from a single class that derives from WebService. In the previous example, the web service class contains a method called GetStockQuote(). This is a normal C# function with a [WebMethod] attribute before its definition.

.NET attributes are used to *describe* code. The WebMethod attribute doesn't change how your function works, but it does tell ASP.NET that this is one of the procedures it must make available over the Internet. Methods that don't have this attribute won't be accessible (or even visible) to remote clients, regardless of whether they are defined with the private or public keyword.

The best way to understand a web service is to think of it as a business object. Business objects support your programs but don't take part in creating any user interface. For example, business objects might have helper functions that retrieve information from a database, perform calculations, or process custom data. Your code creates business objects whenever it needs to retrieve or store specific information, such as report information from a database. Sometimes business objects are called *service providers* because they perform a task (a service), but they rarely retain any information in memory.

The most remarkable part of this example is that the StockQuote web service is already complete. All you need to do is place this .asmx file on your web server in a virtual directory that other clients can access, as you would with an .aspx page. Other clients can then start creating instances of your class and can call the GetStockQuote() method as though it were a locally defined procedure. All they need to do is use .NET to create a proxy class.

Web Services with Code-Behind

As you've seen with web pages, Visual Studio uses code-behind files so you can separate design and code. In the case of .asmx files, this feature isn't really necessary because web service files consist entirely of code and don't contain any user interface elements. However, it's still usually done as a matter of convention.

Visual Studio presents web service code files a little differently than web page code files. Web service code files are automatically placed in the App_Code subfolder (see Figure 22-2). This is because of a minor difference in the way ASP.NET compiles web services. If you don't place the web service code file here, it won't be compiled.

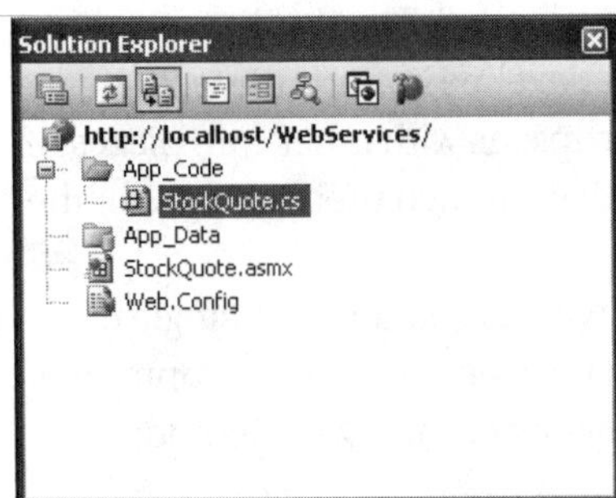

Figure 22-2. *A web service with a code-behind file*

The code-behind version of the StockQuote web service is almost identical. Listing 22-1 shows StockQuote.asmx, and Listing 22-2 shows StockQuote.asmx.cs.

Listing 22-1. *StockQuote.asmx*

```
<%@ WebService Language="C#"
  CodeBehind="~/App_Code/StockService.cs" Class="StockService" %>
```

Listing 22-2. *StockQuote.asmx.cs*

```
using System;
using System.Web;
using System.Web.Services;

public class StockQuote : WebService
{
    [WebMethod()]
    public decimal GetStockQuote(string ticket)
    {
        // (Perform database lookup here.)
    }
}
```

Note that the client always connects to web service using a URL that points to the .asmx file, much as a client requests a web page using a URL that points to an .aspx file. That means clients find the StockQuote service at `http://localhost/WebServices/StockQuote.asmx`.

The ASP.NET Intrinsic Objects

When you inherit from System.Web.Services.WebService, you gain access to several of the standard built-in ASP.NET objects that you can use in an ordinary Web Forms page. These include the following:

Application: Used to store data globally so that it's available to all clients (as described in Chapter 9).

Server: Used for utility functions, such as encoding strings, so they can be safely displayed on a web page (as described in Chapter 5).

Session: Used for client-specific state information. However, you'll need to take some extra steps to make it work with web services. Chapter 23 has the full details.

User: Used to retrieve information about the current client, if the client has been authenticated. Chapter 23 discusses web services and security.

Context: Provides access to Request and Response and, more usefully, the Cache object (described in Chapter 26).

On the whole, these built-in objects won't often be used in web service programming, with the exception of the Cache object. Generally, a web service should look and work like a business object and not rely on retrieving or setting additional information through a built-in ASP.NET object. However, if you need to use per-user security or state management, these objects will be useful. For example, you could create a web service that requires the client to log on and subsequently stores important information in the Session collection. Or you could create a web service that retrieves a large object (such as a DataSet), stores it in server memory using the Session collection, and returns whatever information you need through other web methods that can be invoked as required.

Documenting Your Web Service

Web services are self-describing, which means ASP.NET automatically provides all the information the client needs about what methods are available and what parameters they require. This is all accomplished through the WSDL document. However, although the WSDL document describes the mechanics of the web service, it doesn't describe its purpose or the meaning of the information supplied to and returned from each method. Most web services will provide this information in separate developer documents. However, you can (and should) include a bare minimum of information with your web service by using attributes.

YOU DON'T NEED TO INHERIT FROM WEBSERVICE

Remember, inheriting from WebService is just a convenience for accessing a few common ASP.NET objects. If you don't need to use any of these objects (or if you're willing to go through the static HttpContext.Current property to access them), you don't need to inherit.

Here's how you would access application state in a web service if you derive from the base WebService class:

```
// Store a number in session state.
Application["Counter"] += 1;
```

Here's the equivalent code you would need to use if your web service class doesn't derive from WebService:

```
// Store a number in session state.
HttpContext.Current.Application["Counter"] += 1;
```

■ **Tip** Attributes are a special language construct that's built into the .NET Framework. Essentially, attributes describe your code to the .NET runtime by adding extra metadata. The attributes you use for web service description are recognized by the .NET Framework and provided to clients in automatically generated description documents and through the browser test page. Attributes are used in many other situations, and even if you haven't encountered them before, you're sure to encounter them again in .NET programming.

Descriptions

You can add descriptions to each function through the WebMethod attribute and to the entire web service as a whole using a WebService attribute. For example, you could describe the StockQuote service like this:

```
[WebService(Description="Methods to get information about a stock.")]
public class StockQuote : WebService
{
    [WebMethod(Description="Gets a quote for a NASDAQ stock.")]
    public decimal GetStockQuote(string ticker)
    {
        // (Perform database lookup here.)
    }
}
```

In this example, the Description property is added as a named argument using the = operator.

These custom descriptions will appear in two important places. First, they will be added to the WSDL document that ASP.NET generates automatically. The descriptive information is added as <documentation> tags:

```
<service name="StockQuote">
  <documentation>Methods to get information about a stock.
</documentation>
  ...
</service>
```

Second, the descriptive information will also appear in the automatically generated browser test page, which is more likely to be viewed by the programmer who is designing the client application. The test page is described later in this chapter (in the "Testing Your Web Service" section).

The XML Namespace

You should specify a unique namespace for your web service that can't be confused with the namespaces used for other web services on the Internet. Note that this is an XML namespace, not a .NET namespace. It doesn't affect how your code works or how the client uses your web service. Instead, this namespace uniquely identifies your web service in the WSDL document. XML namespaces look like URLs, but they don't need to correspond to a valid Internet location. For more information, refer to the XML overview in Chapter 17.

■ **Tip** Think of XML namespaces as one of the ways that an application or a web service catalog can distinguish between different web services.

Ideally, the namespace you use will refer to a URL address that you control. Often, this will incorporate your company's Internet domain name as part of the namespace. For example, if your company uses the website `http://www.mycompany.com`, you might give the stock quote web service a namespace like `http://www.mycompany.com/StockQuote`. If you don't specify a namespace, the default (`http://tempuri.org/`) will be used. This is fine for development, but you'll see a warning message in the test page advising you to use something more distinctive.

You specify the namespace through the WebService attribute, as shown here:

```
[WebService(Description="Gets a quote for a NASDAQ stock.",
 Namespace="http://www.prosetech.com/Stocks")]
public class StockQuote : WebService
{ ... }
```

Conformance Claims

As you learned in Chapter 21, web services have developed rapidly, and the standards web services use (such as SOAP and WSDL) are still evolving. To deal with the confusion, web gurus created yet another standard: WS-Interoperability, which sets out a series of guidelines and recommendations web services must follow. If the web services and web clients follow the same WS-Interoperability rules, they shouldn't have any trouble communicating.

When you create a new web service, Visual Studio adds a [WebServiceBinding] attribute to your web service declaration. This attribute indicates the level of compatibility you're targeting. Currently, the only option is WsiProfiles.BasicProfile1_1, which represents the

WS-Interoperability Basic Profile 1.1. However, as standards evolve, you'll see newer versions of SOAP and WSDL, as well as newer versions of the WS-Interoperability profile to go along with them.

```
[WebServiceBinding(ConformsTo = WsiProfiles.BasicProfile1_1)]
[WebService(Description="Retrieve information about a stock.")]
public class StockQuote : WebService
{ ... }
```

Once you have the WebServiceBinding attribute in place, .NET will warn you with a compile error if your web service strays outside the bounds of allowed behavior. By default, all .NET web services are compliant, but you can inadvertently create a noncompliant service by adding certain attributes. For example, it's possible to create two web methods with the same name, as long as their signatures differ and you give them different message names using the MessageName property of the WebMethod attribute. This strange feature isn't recommended, and this behavior isn't allowed according to the WS-Interoperability profile. If you use this feature and try to run your web service, you'll get a compilation error explaining that you've violated the standard.

You can also choose to advertise your conformance with the EmitConformanceClaims property, as shown here:

```
[WebServiceBinding(ConformsTo=WsiProfiles.BasicProfile1_1,
 EmitConformanceClaims=true)]
[WebService(Description="Retrieve information about a stock.")]
public class StockQuote : WebService
{ ... }
```

In this case, additional information is inserted into the WSDL document to indicate that your web service is conformant. It's important to understand that this is for informational purposes only—your web service can be conformant without explicitly stating that it is.

In rare cases you might choose to violate one of the WS-Interoperability rules in order to create a web service that can be consumed by an older, noncompliant application. In this situation, your first step is to turn off compliance by removing the WebServiceBinding attribute. Alternatively, you can disable compliance checking and document this by using the WebServiceBinding attribute without a profile:

```
[WebServiceBinding(ConformsTo=WsiProfiles.None)]
[WebService(Description="Retrieve information about a stock.")]
public class StockQuote : WebService
{ ... }
```

Testing Your Web Service

Even without creating a client for your web service, you can use the built-in features of the .NET Framework to view information about your web service and perform a rudimentary test.

The most useful testing feature is the ASP.NET test page: an automatically generated HTML page that lets you execute the methods in a web service and review its WSDL document. You don't have to perform any special steps to see this page—ASP.NET generates it automatically when you request an .asmx web service file.

Before continuing, you should modify the GetStockQuote() method in the same web service so it returns a hard-coded value. This will allow you to test that it's working with the test page. For example, you could use the statement Return Ticker.Length. That way, the return value will be the number of characters you supplied in the Ticker parameter.

```
[WebMethod(Description="Gets a quote for a NASDAQ stock.")]
public decimal GetStockQuote(string ticker)
{
    return ticker.Length;
}
```

The Web Service Test Page

To view the web service test page, you can have one of two options:

- Seeing as you're using IIS to host your web service project, you don't need to run Visual Studio to get the test page. Just fire up a browser, and request the web service URL (such as `http://localhost/WebServices/StockQuote.asmx`).
- Inside Visual Studio you can quickly launch the current web service in the same way you launch a web page—just click the Run button.

Either way, you'll see a simple web page (shown in Figure 22-3) that lists all the available web service methods. (In this case, only one, GetStockQuote(), is available.) The test page also lists whatever description information you may have added through the WebMethod and WebService attributes.

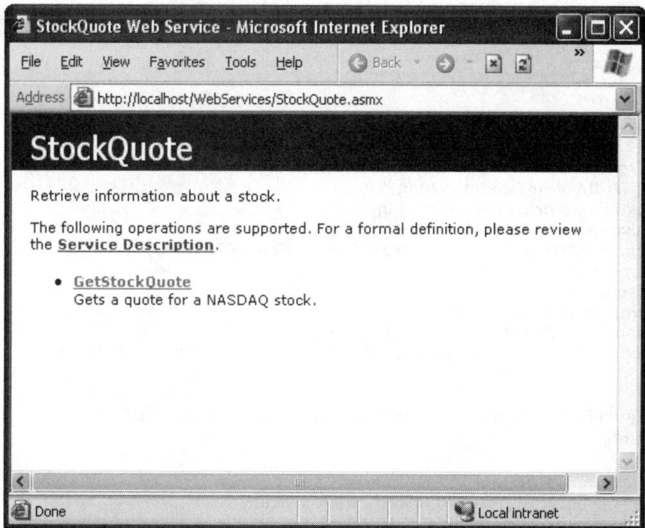

Figure 22-3. *The web service test page*

Remember, you don't need to write any special code to make this page appear, and you can make the request using any browser. ASP.NET generates the page for you automatically, and the page is intended purely as a testing convenience. Clients using your web service won't browse to this page to interact with your web service, but they might use it to find out some basic information about how to use it.

Service Description

You can also click the Service Descriptions link to display the WSDL description of your web service (see Figure 22-4), which you examined in detail in Chapter 21.

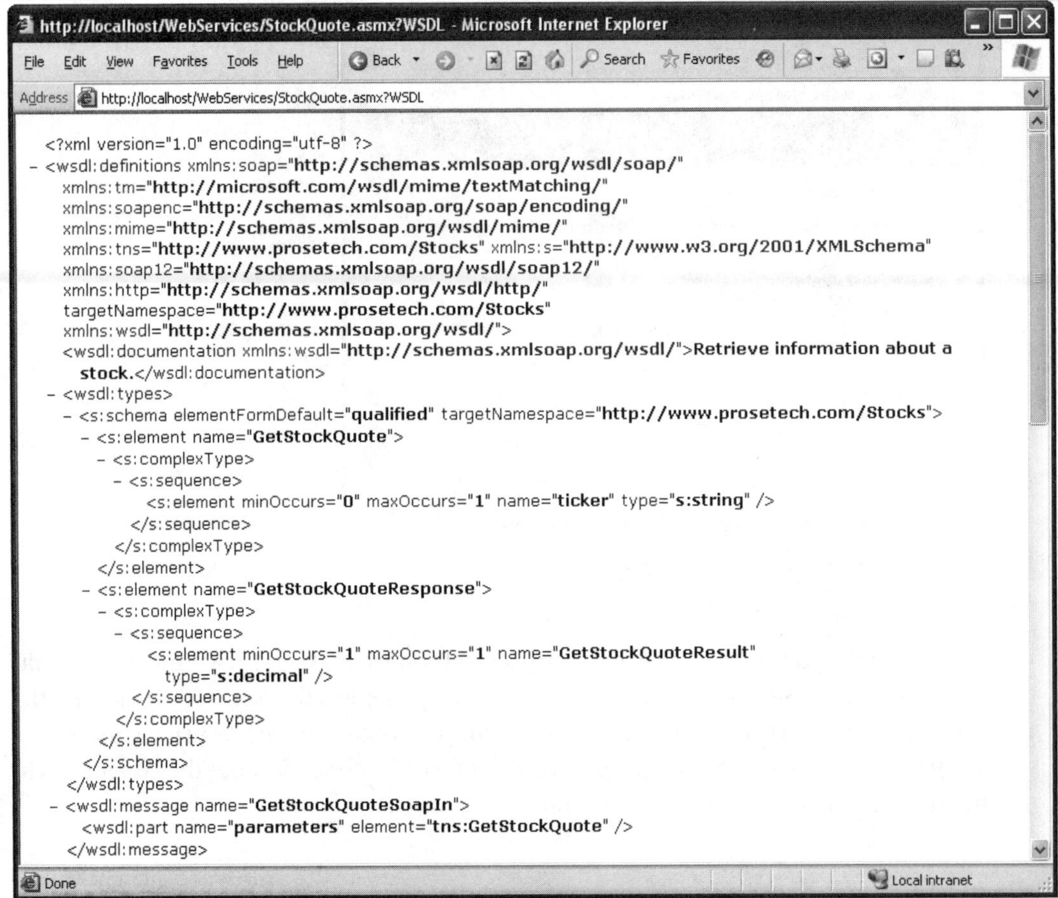

Figure 22-4. *A portion of the StockQuote WSDL document*

When you click this link, the browser makes a request to the .asmx file with a WSDL parameter in the query string:

```
http://localhost/WebServices/StockQuote.asmx?WSDL
```

If you know the location of an ASP.NET web service file, you can always retrieve its WSDL document by adding ?WSDL to the URL. This provides a standard way for a client to find all the information it needs to make a successful connection. Whenever ASP.NET receives a URL in this format, it generates and returns the WSDL document for the web service.

Method Description

You can find out information about the methods in your web service by clicking the corresponding link. For example, in the StockQuote web service, you can click the GetStockQuote link (see Figure 22-5).

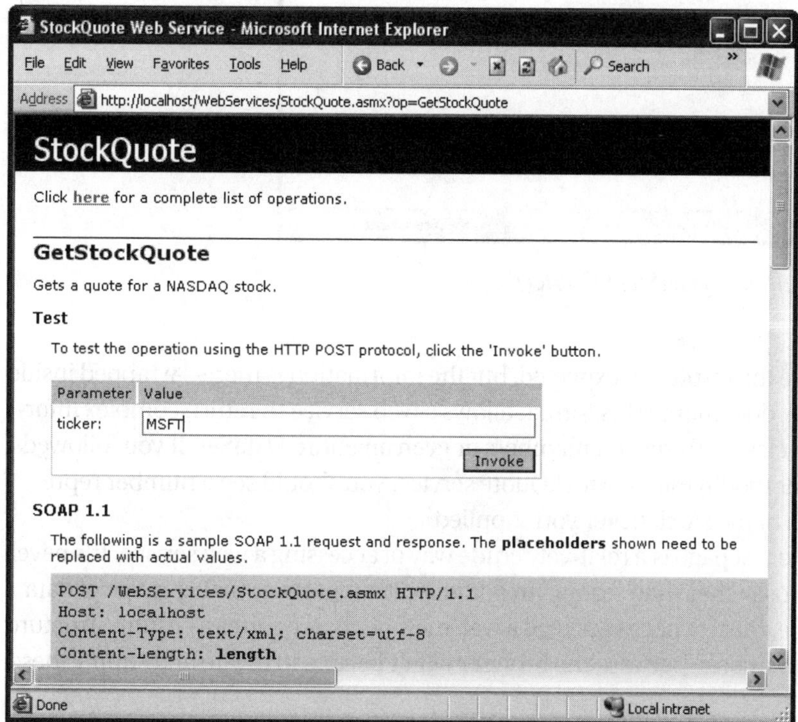

Figure 22-5. *The GetStockQuote() method description*

This window provides two sections. The first part consists of a text box and Invoke button that allows you to run the function without needing to create a client. The second part is a list of the different protocols you can use to connect with the web service (HTTP POST, HTTP GET, and SOAP) and a technical description of the message format for each one.

Testing a Method

To test your method, enter a ticker, and click the Invoke button. The result will be returned to you as an HTML page (see Figure 22-6).

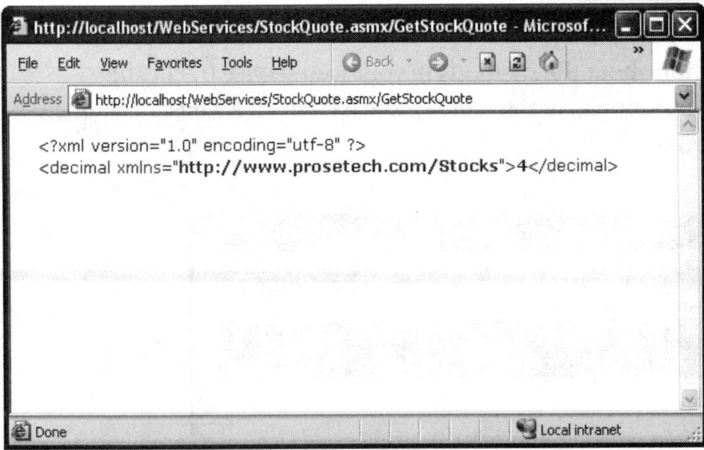

Figure 22-6. *The result from GetStockQuote()*

This may not be the result you expected, but the information is there—wrapped inside the tags of an XML document. This format allows a web service to return complex information, such as a class with several members or even an entire DataSet. If you followed the suggestions for modifying the StockQuote service, you should see a number representing the length of the stock ticker you supplied.

The web service test page is a relatively crude way of accessing a web service. It's never used for any purpose other than testing. In addition, it supports a smaller range of data types. For example, the test page can't call a web method that requires a custom structure or DataSet as a parameter, because the browser won't be able to create and supply these objects.

One question that many users have after seeing this page is, where does this functionality come from? For example, you might wonder whether the test page has additional script code for running your method or whether it relies on features built into the latest version of Internet Explorer. In fact, all that happens when you click the Invoke button is a normal HTTP operation. In version 1.1 of the .NET Framework, this operation is an HTTP POST that submits the parameters you supply. If you look at the URL for the result page, you'll see something like this:

```
http://localhost/WebServices/StockQuote.asmx/GetStockQuote
```

The request URL follows this format:

```
http://localhost/[VirtualDirectory]/[AsmxFile]/[Method]
```

The actual parameter values are posted to this URL in the body of the request (similar to a web page postback), so you won't see them in the URL. The results are sent back to your browser as an XML document.

The clients that use your web service will almost never use this HTTP POST approach Instead, they will send full SOAP messages over HTTP. The actual physical connection (also known as the *transport protocol*) remains the same. The only difference is in the data you send (otherwise known as the *message protocol*). With HTTP POST, you send the values in a simple name/value collection, according to the HTML standard. With SOAP over HTTP, you post the data in an XML package called a SOAP message.

SOAP allows for more flexibility. Because it was designed with web services in mind, it lets you send custom objects or DataSets as parameters. But the fact that you can access your web method through a simple HTTP request demonstrates the simplicity of web services. Surely, if you can run your code this easily in a basic browser, true cross-platform integration can't be that much harder.

Web Service Data Types

Although the client can interact with a web service method as though it were a local function or subroutine, some differences exist. The most significant of these are the restrictions on the data types you can use. Table 22-1 lists the data types that are supported for web service parameters and return values.

■ **Tip** These limitations are designed to ensure cross-platform compatibility. There's no reason .NET couldn't create a way to convert objects to XML and back and then use that to allow you to send complex objects to a web service. However, this "extension" would limit the ability of non-.NET clients to use the web services.

Table 22-1. *Web Service Data Types*

Data Type	Description
The basics	Standard types such as integers and floating-point numbers, Boolean variables, dates and times, and strings are fully supported.
Enumerations	Enumeration types (defined in C# with the enum keyword) are fully supported.
DataSet and DataTable	This gives you an easy package to send information drawn from a relational database. For this to work, the web service actually converts the DataSet or DataTable into an XML document. The client converts it back into an object (if it's a .NET client) or just works with the XML (if it's a client on another platform). The DataRow class isn't supported.

Continued

Table 22-1. *Continued*

Data Type	Description
XmlNode	Objects based on System.Xml.XmlNode are representations of a portion of an XML document. Under the hood, all web service data is passed as XML. This class allows you to directly support a portion of XML information whose structure may change.
Custom objects	You can pass any object you create based on a custom class or structure. The only limitation is that only public data members are transmitted. If you use a class with defined methods, these methods will not be transmitted to the client, and they will not be accessible to the client. You won't be able to successfully use most other .NET classes.
Arrays and collections	You can use arrays of any supported type, including DataSets, XmlNodes, and custom objects. You can also use many collection types, such as the ArrayList and generic lists.

The full set of objects is supported for return values and for parameters when you're communicating through SOAP. If you're communicating through HTTP GET or HTTP POST, you'll be able to use only basic types, enumerations, and arrays of basic types or enumerations. This is because complex classes and other types cannot be represented in the query string (for HTTP GET) or form body (for an HTTP POST operation).

The StockQuote Service with a Data Object

If you've ever used a stock quote service over the Internet, you've probably noticed that the example so far is somewhat simplified. The GetStockQuote() function returns one piece of information—a price quote—whereas popular financial sites usually produce a full quote with a 52-week high and 52-week low and other information about the volume of shares traded on a particular day. You could add more methods to the web service to supply this information, but that would require multiple similar function calls, which would slow down performance, because more time would be spent sending messages back and forth over the Internet. The client code would also become more tedious.

A better solution is to use a data object that encapsulates all the information you need. You can define the class for this object in the same file and then use it as a parameter or return value for any of your functions. The data object is a completely ordinary C# class, and it shouldn't derive from System.Web.Services.WebService. It can contain public member variables that use any of the data types supported for web services. It can't contain methods—if it does, they will simply be ignored and won't be available to the client.

The client will receive the data object and be able to work with it exactly as though it were defined locally. In fact, it will be—the automatically generated proxy class will contain a copy of the class definition.

Here's how the StockQuote service would look with the addition of a convenient data object:

```
[WebServiceBinding(ConformsTo=WsiProfiles.None)]
[WebService(Description="Methods to get stock information.",
 Namespace="http://www.prosetech.com/Stocks")]
public class StockQuote_DataObject : WebService
{
    [WebMethod(Description="Gets a price quote for a stock.")]
    public StockInfo GetStockQuote(string ticker)
    {
        StockInfo quote = new StockInfo();
        quote.Symbol = ticker;
        quote = FillQuoteFromDB(quote);
        return quote;
    }

    private StockInfo FillQuoteFromDB(StockInfo lookup)
    {
        // You can add the appropriate database code here.
        // For test purposes this function hard-codes
        // some sample information.
        lookup.CompanyName = "Trapezoid";
        lookup.Price = 400;
        lookup.High_52Week = 410;
        lookup.Low_52Week = 20;
        return lookup;
    }
}

public class StockInfo
{
    public decimal Price;
    public string Symbol;
    public decimal High_52Week;
    public decimal Low_52Week;
    public string CompanyName;
}
```

Dissecting the Code...

Here's what happens in the GetStockQuote() function:

1. A new StockInfo object is created.
2. The corresponding Symbol is specified for the StockInfo object.
3. The StockInfo object is passed to another function that fills it with information. This function is called FillQuoteFromDB().

The FillQuoteFromDB() function isn't visible to remote clients because it lacks the WebMethod attribute. It isn't even visible to other classes or code modules, because it's defined with the Private keyword. Typically, this function will perform some type of database lookup. It might return information that is confidential and should not be made available to all clients. By putting this logic into a separate function, you can separate the code that determines what information the client should receive and still have the ability to retrieve the full record if your web service code needs to examine or modify other information. Generally, most of the work that goes into creating a web service—once you understand the basics—will be spent trying to decide the best way to divide its functionality into separate procedures.

You might wonder how the client will understand the StockInfo object. In fact, the object is really just returned as a blob of XML or SOAP data. If you invoke this method through the test page, you'll see the result shown in Figure 22-7.

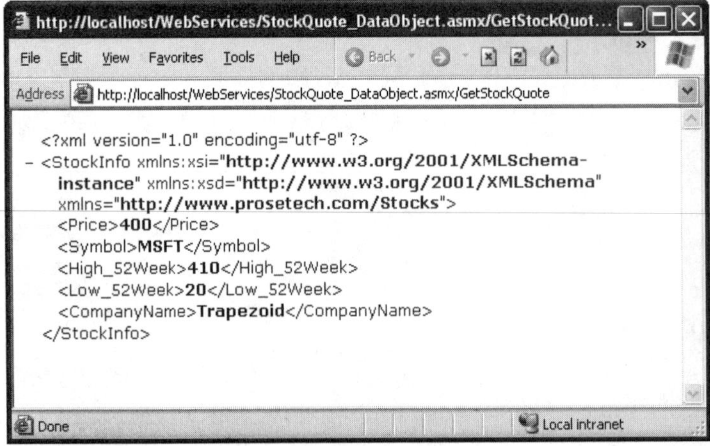
http://localhost/WebServices/StockQuote_DataObject.asmx/GetStockQuot...
File Edit View Favorites Tools Help
Back
Address http://localhost/WebServices/StockQuote_DataObject.asmx/GetStockQuote
<?xml version="1.0" encoding="utf-8" ?>
- <StockInfo xmlns:xsi="http://www.w3.org/2001/XMLSchema-instance" xmlns:xsd="http://www.w3.org/2001/XMLSchema" xmlns="http://www.prosetech.com/Stocks">
<Price>400</Price>
<Symbol>MSFT</Symbol>
<High_52Week>410</High_52Week>
<Low_52Week>20</Low_52Week>
<CompanyName>Trapezoid</CompanyName>
</StockInfo>
Done
Local intranet

Figure 22-7. *The result from GetStockQuote() as a data object*

But ASP.NET is extremely clever about custom objects. When you use a class like StockInfo in your web service, it adds the definition directly into the WSDL document:

```
<types>
  ...
  <s:complexType name="StockInfo">
    <s:sequence>
      <s:element minOccurs="1" maxOccurs="1" name="Price"
         type="s:decimal" />
      <s:element minOccurs="1" maxOccurs="1" name="Symbol"
         nillable="true" type="s:string" />
      <s:element minOccurs="1" maxOccurs="1" name="High_52Week"
         type="s:decimal" />
      <s:element minOccurs="1" maxOccurs="1" name="Low_52Week"
         type="s:decimal" />
      <s:element minOccurs="1" maxOccurs="1" name="CompanyName"
         nillable="true" type="s:string" />
    </s:sequence>
  </s:complexType>
</types>
```

When you generate a client for this web service, a proxy class will be created automatically. It will define the StockInfo class and convert the XML data into a StockInfo object. The end result is that all the information will return to your application in the form you expect, just as if you had used a local function. You'll see an example in the next chapter.

Incidentally, it's up to you whether you use full property procedures or just public variables—the effect is the same. This means you could just as easily rewrite the StockInfo class using property procedures like this:

```
public class StockInfo
{
    private decimal price;
    private string symbol;
    private decimal high_52Week;
    private decimal low_52Week;
    private string companyName;
```

```
    public decimal Price
    {
        get {return price;}
        set {value = price;}
    }
    public string Symbol;
    {
        get {return symbol;}
        set {value = symbol;}
    }
    // (Remainder of property procedures omitted.)
}
```

From the standpoint of the web service client, this version of the StockInfo class is completely equivalent to the version shown earlier. That's because any code you place in a property procedure (other than the code that sets or gets the value) is ignored when the class is generated on the client side. If you think about it, this makes sense. The StockInfo class definition is used to create the WSDL definition, and the client code is generated based on the WSDL document. The WSDL document never contains code.

RETURNING HISTORICAL DATA FROM STOCKQUOTE

It may interest you to model a class for a web service that returns historical information that is used to create a price graph. You could implement this in a few ways. For example, you might use a function that requires the starting and ending dates and returns an array that contains a number of chronological price quotes. Your client code would then determine how much information was returned by checking the upper bound of the array. The web method definition would look something like this:

```
[WebMethod()]
public decimal[] GetHistory(string ticker,
 DateTime start, DateTime end)
```

Alternatively, you might use a function that accepts a parameter specifying the number of required entries and the time span:

```
[WebMethod()]
public decimal[] GetHistory(string ticker,
  TimeSpan period, int numberOfEntries)
```

In either case, it's up to you to find the best way to organize a web service. The process is a long and incremental one that often involves performance tuning and usability concerns. Of course, it also gives you a chance to put everything you've learned into practice and get into the fine details of ASP.NET programming.

Consuming a Web Service

Microsoft has repeatedly declared that its ambition with programming tools such as Visual Studio, the CLR, and the .NET class library is to provide a common infrastructure for application developers, who will then need to create only the upper layer of business-specific logic. Web services hold true to that promise. In the following sections, you'll see how you can call a web service method as easily as a method in a local class.

Configuring a Web Service Client in Visual Studio

When developing and testing a web service in Visual Studio, it's often easiest to add both the web service and the client application to the same solution. This allows you to test and change both pieces at the same time. You can even use the integrated debugger to set breakpoints and step through the code in both the client and the server as though they were really a single application!

To work with both projects at once in Visual Studio, follow these steps:

1. Open the web service application (in this case, the StockQuote service).
2. Select File ➤ Add ➤ New Web Site (assuming you want to create a web client).
3. Choose ASP.NET Web Site, give it a title (for example, enter **StockQuoteClient**), and click OK.
4. You should set the new project as the start-up project (otherwise, you'll just see the web service test page when you click the Start button). To make this adjustment, right-click the new project in the Solution Explorer, and choose Set As StartUp Project.

Your Solution Explorer should now look like Figure 22-8.

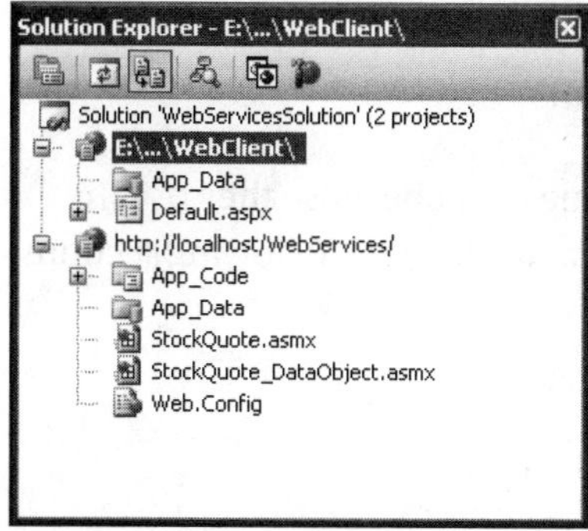

Figure 22-8. *Two projects in Solution Explorer*

Once you've created a solution that has both the web service and the client, you might want to save a solution file so you can quickly load this combination again. To do this, select the first item in the Solution Explorer (the solution name). Then, choose File ➤ Save [SolutionName].sln As.

By default, Visual Studio saves the solution file in a user-specific temporary location. However, you can save it somewhere that's more easily accessible for future use. Once you've saved the .sln solution file, you can double-click it in Windows Explorer to launch Visual Studio with both projects.

■ **Note** You don't need to create a virtual directory in advance for your web client project. You do need to create a virtual directory for your web service project (as described in the previous chapter), because the client needs to know where to find the web service.

The Role of the Proxy Class

Web services communicate with other .NET applications through a special ingredient called the *proxy class*. The proxy class sits between the code in your client application and the web service.

When you (the client) want to call a web method, you call the corresponding method of the proxy object. The proxy class then silently fetches the results for you using SOAP calls. Strictly speaking, you don't need to use a proxy class—you could create and receive the SOAP messages on your own. However, this process is quite difficult and involves a degree of low-level understanding and complexity that would make web services much less useful. The proxy class simplifies life because it takes care of details such as communicating over the network, waiting for a response, parsing the result out of the SOAP message that's returned from the web service, and so on.

You can create a proxy class in .NET in two ways:

- You can use the WSDL.exe command-line tool.
- You can use the Visual Studio web reference feature.

Both of these approaches produce essentially the same result because they use the same classes in the .NET Framework to perform the actual work. In the following sections, you'll try both approaches.

Creating a Web Reference in Visual Studio

Even when two projects are added to the same solution, they still have no way to communicate with each other. To set up this layer of interaction, you need to create a special proxy class. In Visual Studio, you create this proxy class by adding a web reference. Web references are similar to ordinary references, but instead of pointing to assemblies with ordinary .NET types, they point to a URL with a WSDL contract for a web service.

■ **Note** Before you can add a web reference, you should save and compile the web service application (right-click the project, and choose Build Web Site in Visual Studio). Otherwise, the client might get outdated information about the web services you provide or be unable to see them.

To create a web reference, follow these steps:

1. Right-click the client project in the Solution Explorer, and select Add Web Reference.

2. The Add Web Reference dialog box opens, as shown in Figure 22-9. This dialog box provides options for searching web registries or entering a URL directly.

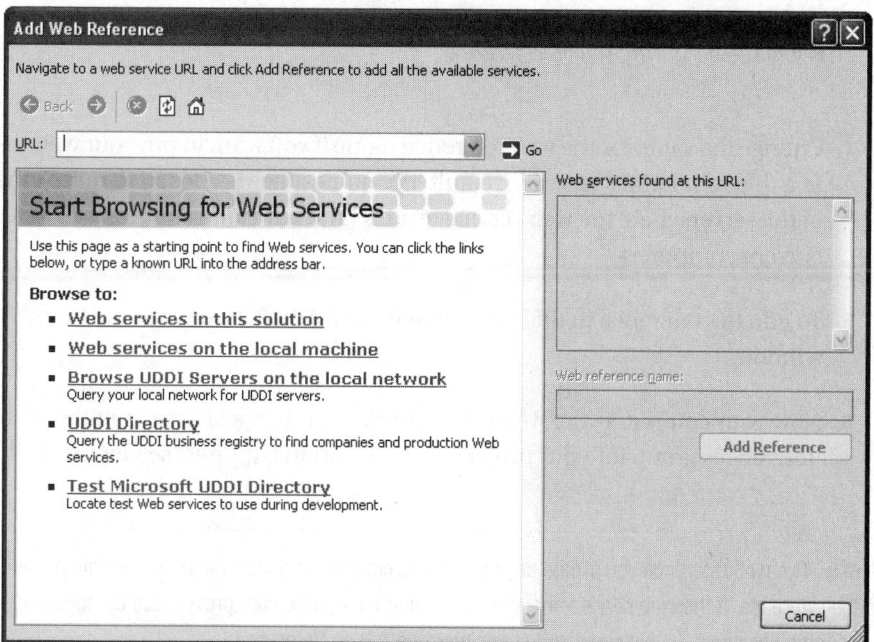

Figure 22-9. *The Add Web Reference dialog box*

3. You can browse directly to your web service by entering a URL that points to the .asmx file. The test page will appear in the preview window (as shown in Figure 22-10), and the Add Reference button will be enabled.

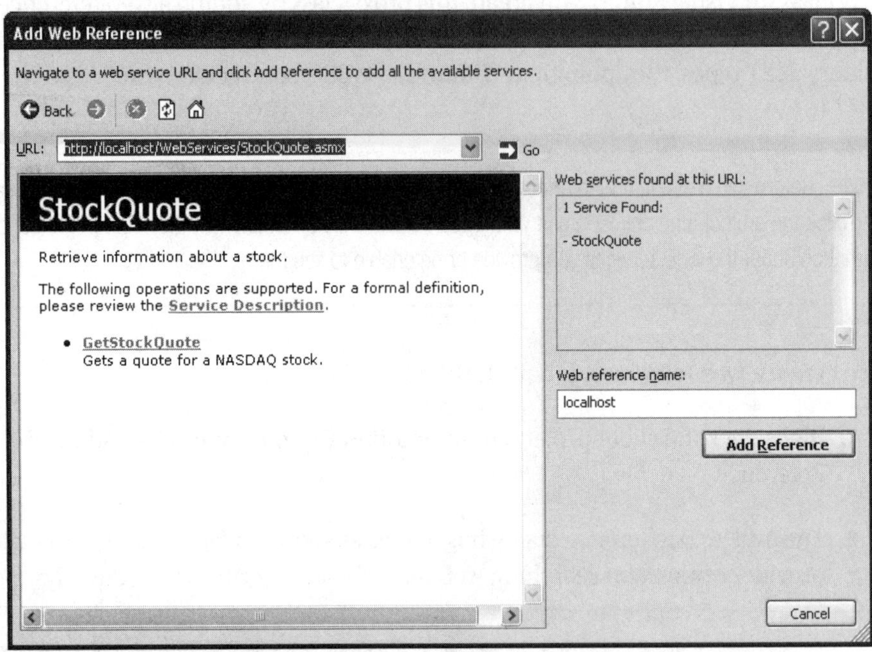

Figure 22-10. *Adding a web reference*

4. Change the value for the web reference name if you want to put your web reference in a different namespace. By default, the namespace is chosen to match the name of the server where the web service resides (and is localhost for web services on the current computer).

5. To add the reference to this web service, click Add Reference at the bottom of the window.

6. Now your computer (the web server for this service) will appear in the Web References group for your project in the Solution Explorer (see Figure 22-11).

Note The web reference you create uses the WSDL contract and information that exists at the time you add the reference. If the web service changes, you'll need to update your proxy class by right-clicking the server name (localhost, in this case) and choosing Update Web Reference.

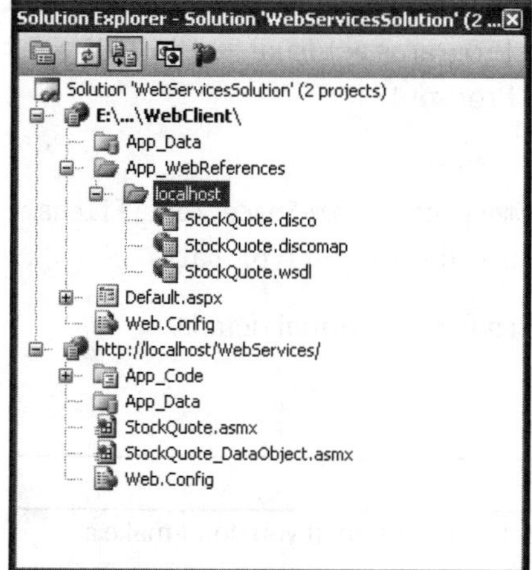

Figure 22-11. *The web reference*

You can add a web reference only to a single .asmx file at a time. If you have more than one web service in the same web application, you need to add a separate web service for each one you want to use. For example, the downloadable examples have two versions of the StockQuote web service—one that uses a data object and one that doesn't. If you decide to use both, you'll need to add two web references.

Creating a Proxy with WSDL.exe

You can also generate the proxy class by hand; you just use a utility called WSDL.exe that is included with the .NET Framework. (You can find this file in the .NET Framework directory, which is typically in a path similar to c:\Program Files\Microsoft.NET\SDK\v2.0\Bin. Visual Studio users have the WSDL.exe utility in the C:\Program Files\Microsoft Visual Studio 8\SDK\v2.0\Bin directory.)

In most cases, you'll use the Visual Studio web reference feature instead of WSDL.exe. But sometimes WSDL.exe makes more sense:

- You need to configure advanced options that Visual Studio doesn't provide. For example, you can use WSDL.exe to generate proxies for different web services that use the same set of objects.

- You want to look at the proxy class code. With an ASP.NET client, the proxy class code is created when the application executes for the first time, and you never get to see it.

- You aren't using Visual Studio.

WSDL.exe is a command-line utility, so it's easiest to use by opening a command prompt window. (Click the Start button, and choose Programs ➤ Visual Studio 2005 ➤ Visual Studio Tools ➤ Visual Studio 2005 Command Prompt.)

The syntax for WSDL.exe is as follows:

```
wsdl /language:language  /protocol:protocol /namespace:myNameSpace /out:filename
    /username:username /password:password /domain:domain <url or path>
```

Table 22-2 describes these parameters, along with a few additional details.

Table 22-2. *WSDL.exe Command-Line Parameters*

Parameter	Meaning
language	This is the language in which the class is written. If you don't make a choice, the default is C#.
protocol	Usually, you'll omit this option and use the default (SOAP). However, you could also specify HttpGet and HttpPost for slightly more limiting protocols.
namespace	This is the .NET namespace that your proxy class will use. If you omit this parameter, no namespace is used, and the classes in this file are available globally. For better organization, you should probably choose a logical namespace.
out	This allows you to specify the name for the generated file. By default, this is the name of the service followed by an extension indicating the language (such as StockQuote.cs). You can always rename this file after it's generated.
username, password, and domain	You should specify these values if the web server requires authentication to access the discovery and WSDL documents.
url or path	This is the last portion of the WSDL.exe command line, and it specifies the location of the WSDL file for the web service.
appsettingurlkey	The is the configuration setting that's used to store the web service URL. You can change this configuration setting if your web service moves to another server.
fields	If you use this option, any data objects that the web service uses will be generated with public member variables instead of public properties.
sharetypes	This allows you to add a reference to two or more web services that use the same data objects. This ensures that any data object classes are created only once. More important, you can use the same data objects with both web services.

A typical WSDL.exe command might look something like this:

```
wsdl /namespace:localhost http://localhost/WebServices/StockQuote.asmx?WSDL
```

In this case, a StockQuote.cs file is created with the proxy class code. You can add this class to your ASP.NET application (in the App_Code folder) and use it to communicate with the web service.

■ **Note** You can use a web service without WSDL.exe or Visual Studio. In fact, you don't even need a proxy class. All you need is a program that can send and receive SOAP messages. After all, web services are designed to be cross-platform. However, unless you have significant experience with another tool (such as the Microsoft SOAP Toolkit), the details are generally frustrating and unpleasant. .NET provides the prebuilt infrastructure you need to guarantee easy, error-free operation.

Dissecting the Proxy Class

On the surface, Visual Studio makes it seem like all you need is a simple link to your web service. In reality, whenever you add a web reference, Visual Studio creates a proxy class for you automatically. To really understand how web service clients work, you need to take a look at this class.

Unfortunately, you won't see the file for the proxy class in your client project. That's because ASP.NET generates it automatically when you run your application. If you want to study the proxy class code, you'll need to create the proxy class using WSDL.exe (as described in the previous section), or you'll need to add a web reference to another type of application that doesn't use the same compile-on-demand model (such as a Windows application).

■ **Note** You'll learn how to create a Windows client in Chapter 23. For now, you can experiment with the WSDL.exe tool or just review the code that's shown next.

The proxy class has the same name as the web service class. It inherits from SoapHttpClientProtocol, which has a fair bit of built-in functionality. Here's the declaration for the proxy class that provides communication with the StockQuote service:

```
public class StockQuote :
 System.Web.Services.Protocols.SoapHttpClientProtocol
{ ... }
```

The StockQuote class contains the same methods as the StockQuote web service. This class acts as a stand-in for the remote StockQuote web service. When you call a StockQuote method, you're really calling a method of this local class. This class then performs the SOAP communication as required to contact the "real" remote web service. The proxy class acquires its ability to communicate in SOAP through the .NET class library. It inherits from the SoapHttpClientProtocol class and binds its local methods to web service methods with prebuilt .NET attributes. In other words, the low-level SOAP details are hidden not only from you but also from the proxy class, which relies on ready-made .NET components from the System.Web.Services.Protocols namespace.

For example, here's the GetStockQuote() method as it's defined in the proxy class:

```
[System.Web.Services.Protocols.SoapDocumentMethodAttribute()]
public decimal GetStockQuote(string ticker)
{
     object[] results = this.Invoke("GetStockQuote",
       new object[] {ticker});
    return ((decimal)(results[0]));
}
```

You'll notice that this method doesn't contain any of the business code you created in the web service. (In fact, the client has no way to get any information about the internal workings of your web service code—if it could, this would constitute a serious security breach.) Instead, the proxy class contains the code needed to query the remote web service and convert the results. In this case, the method calls the base SoapHttpClientProcotol.Invoke() to create the SOAP message and start waiting for the response. The final line of code converts the returned object into a decimal value.

If you're using the version, of the StockService that uses the StockInfo data object, you'll see a similar version of the GetStockQuote() method, with one key difference:

```
[System.Web.Services.Protocols.SoapDocumentMethodAttribute()]
public StockInfo GetStockQuote(string ticker)
{
     object[] results = this.Invoke("GetStockQuote",
       new object[] {ticker});
    return ((StockInfo)(results[0]));
}
```

As you can see, the proxy class not only handles the SOAP communication layer but also handles the conversion from XML to .NET objects and data types as needed. If .NET types were used directly with web services, it would be extremely difficult to use them from other non-Microsoft platforms.

Of course, you might wonder how the client can manipulate a StockInfo object—after all, you defined this object in the web service, *not* the client. This is another web service trick. When Visual Studio builds the proxy class, it automatically checks the parameter and return types of each method that's defined in the WSDL document. If it determines that a custom class is required, it creates a definition for that class in the proxy file.

You'll see this class definition after the proxy class in the same file:

```
public partial class StockInfo
{
    private decimal priceField;
    private string symbolField;
    private decimal high_52WeekField;
    private decimal low_52WeekField;
    private string companyNameField;

    public decimal Price
    {
        get { return this.priceField; }
        set { this.priceField = value; }
    }

    public string Symbol
    {
        get { return this.symbolField; }
        set { this.symbolField = value; }
    }

    public decimal High_52Week
    {
        get { return this.high_52WeekField; }
        set { this.high_52WeekField = value; }
    }

    public decimal Low_52Week
    {
        get { return this.low_52WeekField; }
        set { this.low_52WeekField = value; }
    }

    public string CompanyName
    {
        get { return this.companyNameField; }
        set { this.companyNameField = value; }
    }
}
```

Because you now have a definition for the StockInfo class, you can create your own StockInfo objects directly and work with them locally. Unlike the StockQuote proxy class, the StockInfo class doesn't participate in any SOAP messages or Internet communication; it's just a simple data class.

■ **Note** Remember, the data class on the client won't necessarily match the data class in the web service. Visual Studio simply looks for all public properties and member variables in the web service version and creates a client-side version that consists entirely of public properties. (Visual Studio uses properties instead of public variables because that gives you support for data binding.) Any code you've placed in the web service version of the class (whether it's in methods, property procedures, or constructors) is ignored completely.

The proxy class also contains some additional code you haven't seen for implementing asynchronous functionality, which allows a client to initiate a web service request and continue working, without waiting for the response. The client will be notified later when the response is received.

This is a useful technique in desktop applications where you don't want to become bogged down waiting for a slow Internet connection. However, the examples in this chapter focus on ASP.NET clients, which don't benefit as much from asynchronous consumption because the page isn't returned to the client until all the code has finished processing.

Dynamic Web Service URLs

When you create a web reference with Visual Studio, the location is stored in a configuration file. This is useful because it allows you to change the location of the web service when you deploy the application, without forcing you to regenerate the proxy class.

The exact location of this setting depends on the type of application. If the client is a web application, this information will be added to the web.config file, as shown here:

```
<?xml version="1.0" encoding="utf-8"?>
<configuration>
  <appSettings>
    <add key="localhost.StockQuoteService"
     value="http://localhost/WebServices1/StockQuoteService.asmx"/>
  </appSettings>
  ...
</configuration>
```

If you're creating a different type of client application, such as a Windows application, the configuration file will have a name in the format [AppName].exe.config.

For example, if your application is named SimpleClient.exe, the configuration file will be SimpleClient.exe.config. You must follow this naming convention.

■ **Tip** Visual Studio uses a little sleight of hand with named configuration files. In the design environment, the configuration file will have the name App.config. However, when you build the application, this file will be copied to the build directory and given the appropriate name (to match the executable file). The only exception is if the client application is a web application. All web applications use a configuration file named web.config, no matter what filenames you use. That's what you'll see in the design environment as well.

If you use WSDL.exe to generate your proxy class, the default URL isn't stored in a configuration file—it's hard-coded in the constructor. To change this behavior, just use /appsettingurlkey. For example, you could use this command line:

```
wsdl http://localhost/WebServices/StockQuote.asmx /appsettingurlkey:WsUrl
```

In this case, the key is stored with the key WsUrl in the <appSettings> section.

Using the Proxy Class

Using the proxy class is easy. In most respects, it isn't any different from using a local class. The following sample page uses the StockQuote service and displays the information it retrieves in a label. You could place this snippet of code into a Page.Load event handler.

```
// Create a StockInfo object for your results.
localhost.StockInfo wsInfo;

// Create the actual web service proxy class.
localhost.StockQuote ws = new localhost.StockQuote();

// Call the web service method.
wsInfo = ws.GetStockQuote("MSFT");

lblResult.Text = wsInfo.CompanyName + " is at: " + wsInfo.Price.ToString();
```

The whole process is quite straightforward. First, the code creates a StockInfo object to hold the results. Then the code creates an instance of the proxy class, which allows access to all the web service functionality. Finally, the code calls the web service method using the proxy class and catches the returned data in the StockInfo object. Notice that the proxy class is placed in the localhost namespace, because this proxy class was created through the Visual Studio web reference feature with a web reference name of localhost. If you create a proxy class using WSDL.exe, this isn't the case—in fact, the proxy class isn't placed into any namespace, which means it's in the global namespace and is always available.

Figure 22-12 shows the result in a test web page.

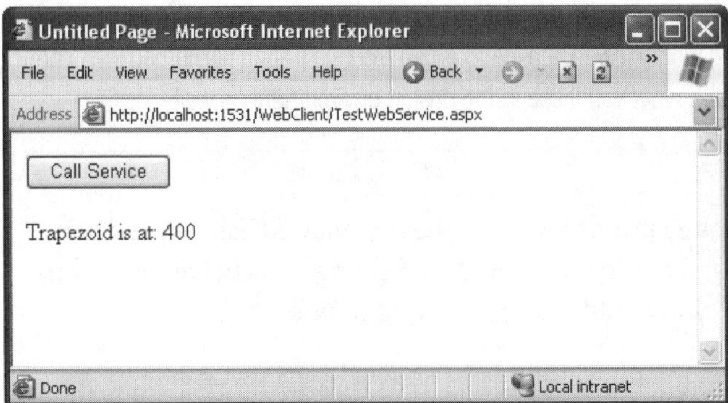

Figure 22-12. *Calling a web service in a web page*

As you experiment with your project, remember that it doesn't have a direct connection to your web service. Whenever you change the web service, you'll have to rebuild it (right-click the web service project, and select Build), and then update the web reference (right-click the client project's localhost reference, and select Update Web Reference). Until you perform these two steps, your client will not be able to access any new methods or methods that have modified signatures (different parameter lists).

Waiting and Timeouts

You might have noticed that the proxy class (StockQuote) really contains many more members than just the three methods shown in the source code. In fact, it acquires a substantial amount of extra functionality because it inherits from the SoapHttpClientProtocol class. In many scenarios, you won't need to use any of these additional features. In some cases, however, they will become useful. One example is with the Timeout property.

The Timeout property allows you to specify the maximum amount of time you're willing to wait, in milliseconds. The default (–1) indicates that you'll wait as long as it takes, which could make your web application unacceptably slow if you attempt to perform a number of operations with an unresponsive web service.

When using the Timeout property, you need to include error handling. If the Timeout period expires without a response, an exception will be thrown, giving you the chance to notify the user about the problem. By default, the timeout is 100,000 milliseconds (10 seconds).

In the following example, the simple StockQuote client has been rewritten to use a timeout:

```
localhost.StockQuote_DataObject ws = new localhost.StockQuote_DataObject();

// This timeout will apply to all web method calls until it's changed.
ws.Timeout = 3000;  // 3,000 milliseconds is 3 seconds.

try
{
    // Call the web service method.
    localhost.StockInfo wsInfo = ws.GetStockQuote("MSFT");
    lblResult.Text = wsInfo.CompanyName + " is at: " + wsInfo.Price.ToString();
}
catch (System.Net.WebException err)
{
    if (err.Status == WebExceptionStatus.Timeout)
    {
        lblResult.Text = "Web service timed out after 3 seconds.";
    }
    else
    {
        lblResult.Text = "Another type of problem occurred.";
    }
}
```

Web Service Errors

Of course, a typical web service call could lead to other types of errors. For example, the code in your web method could generate an error. To try this, you can create the following error-prone web method:

```
[WebMethod]
public void CauseAnError()
{
    throw new DivideByZeroException();
}
```

You might assume (quite reasonably) that when the client calls this method, it will receive a DivideByZeroException. However, this actually isn't the case. That's because web services are designed to be thoroughly interoperable, and as a result they don't support the idea of .NET exceptions. And that makes sense—after all, you might call a .NET web service, or you might call a web service created with some other programming framework with a different set of exception objects or a different way of handling errors. (And even if ASP.NET supported .NET exceptions in SOAP messages, you can imagine how a problem could occur if a web method threw a custom exception. The client might not have the required custom exception class, leaving it unable to process the error.)

Instead, when an unhandled exception occurs in a web method, ASP.NET catches the exception and sends a SOAP fault message to the client. When the proxy class receives this fault message, it throws a System.Web.Services.Protocols.SoapException. In other words, no matter what caused the error condition, your code will receive a SoapException. The SoapException.Message property will reveal more details, including the original exception name.

Here's how you can catch this exception on the client:

```
localhost.ErrorService ws = new localhost.ErrorService;

try
{
    // Call the web service method.
    ws.CauseAnError();
}
catch (System.Web.Services.Protocols.SoapException err)
{
    lblResult.Text = "An error occurred in the web method code.<br />";
    lblResult.Text += "The error is " + err.Message;
}
```

■ **Tip** Whenever you make a web service call, you should add exception handlers for WebException and SoapException.

Connecting Through a Proxy

The proxy class also has some built-in intelligence that allows you to reroute its HTTP communication with special Internet settings. By default, the proxy class uses the Internet settings on the current computer. In some networks, this may not be the best approach. You can override these settings by using the Proxy property of the web service proxy class.

■ **Tip** In this case, the term *proxy* is being used in two ways: as a proxy that manages communication between a client and a web service and as a proxy server in your organization that manages communication between a computer and the Internet.

For example, if you need to connect through a computer called ProxyServer using port 80, you could use the following code before you called any web service methods:

```
WebProxy connectionProxy = new WebProxy("ProxyServer", 80);

localhost.StockQuote ws = new localhost.StockQuote();
ws.Proxy = connectionProxy;
```

The WebProxy class has many other options that allow you to configure connections in more complicated scenarios.

The Last Word

In ASP.NET, designing a web service is almost as easy as creating an ordinary business class. But to use web services *well,* you need to understand the role they play in enterprise applications. Web services aren't the best way to share functionality between different web pages or web applications on a web server, because of the overhead needed to send SOAP messages over the network. However, they are an excellent way to connect different software packages or glue together the internal systems of separate companies.

In the next chapter, you'll learn how to go further with web services. You'll use more advanced features such as state management, security, and transactions, and you'll learn how to call a web service from Windows application.

CHAPTER 23

Enhancing Web Services

The past couple of chapters examined how to create and consume basic web services. You learned how to code the StockQuote web service and how to call it from an ASP.NET web client. In this chapter, you'll add a few more frills to the mix, including state management, security, and transactions. As you'll see, not all of these features lend themselves easily to the web services model. Although these features are available, some complicate your web service and don't keep to the cross-platform ideal of SOAP. In many cases the best web services are the simplest web services.

Finally, for a little more fun, you'll see how to access a real, mature web service on the Internet: Microsoft's TerraService, which exposes a vast library of millions of satellite pictures from a database that is 1.5 terabytes in size. You'll build both a web client and a Windows client that perform a few basic tasks with TerraService.

State Management

Web services are usually designed as *stateless* classes. This means a web service provides a collection of utility functions that don't need to be called in any particular order and don't retain any information between requests.

This design is used for a number of reasons. First, retaining any kind of state uses memory on the web server, which reduces performance as the number of clients grows. Another problem is that contacting a web service takes time. If you can retrieve all the information you need at once and process it on the client, it's generally faster than making several separate calls to a web service that maintains state.

Several kinds of state management are available in ASP.NET, including using the Application and Session collections or using custom cookies. All of these techniques are also applicable to web services. However, with web services, session management is disabled by default. Otherwise, the server needs to check for session information each time a request is received, which imposes a slight overhead.

You can enable session state management for a specific method by using the EnableSession property of the WebMethod attribute:

```
[WebMethod(EnableSession=true)]
```

Before you implement state management, make sure you review whether you can accomplish your goal in another way. Many ASP.NET gurus believe that maintaining state is, at best, a performance drag and is, at worse, a contradiction to the philosophy of lightweight stateless web services. For example, instead of using a dedicated function to submit client preferences, you could add extra parameters to all your functions to accommodate the required information. Similarly, instead of allowing a user to manipulate a large DataSet stored in the Session collection on the server, you could return the entire object to the client and then clear it from memory.

■ **Tip** When evaluating state management, you have to consider many application-specific details. But in general, it's always a good idea to reduce the amount of information stored in memory on the web server, especially if you want to create a web service that can scale to serve hundreds of simultaneous users.

What happens when you have a web service that enables session state management for some methods but disables it for others? Essentially, disabling session management just tells ASP.NET to ignore any in-memory session information and withhold the Session collection from the current procedure. It doesn't cause existing information to be cleared from the collection (that will happen only when the session times out). The only performance benefit you're receiving is from not having to look up session information when it isn't required.

The StockQuote Service with State Management

The following example introduces state management into the StockQuote web service:

```
[WebService(Description="Methods to get stock information.",
 Namespace="http://www.prosetech.com/Stocks")]
public class StockQuote_SessionState : WebService
{
 [WebMethod(EnableSession=true)]
    public decimal GetStockQuote(string ticker)
    {
        // Increment counters. This function locks the application
        // collection to prevent synchronization errors.
        Application.Lock();
        if (Application[ticker] == null)
```

```
            {
                Application[ticker] = 1;
            }
            else
            {
                Application[ticker] = (int)Application[ticker] + 1;
            }
            Application.UnLock();

            if (Session[ticker] == null)
            {
                Session[ticker] = 1;
            }
            else
            {
                Session[ticker] = (int)Session[ticker] + 1;
            }

            // Return a value representing the length of the ticker.
            return ticker.Length;
        }

        [WebMethod(EnableSession=true)]
        public CounterInfo GetStockUsage(string ticker)
        {
            CounterInfo result = new CounterInfo();
            result.GlobalRequests = (int)Application[ticker];
            result.SessionRequests = (int)Session[ticker];
            return result;
        }
    }

    public class CounterInfo
    {
        public int GlobalRequests;
        public int SessionRequests;
    }
```

This example allows the StockQuote service to record how much it has been used. Every time the GetStockQuote() method is called, two counters are incremented. One is a global counter that tracks the total number of requests for that stock quote from all clients. The other one is a session-specific counter that represents how many times the current client has requested a quote for the specified stock. The Ticker string is used to name the stored item. This means if a client requests quotes for 50 different stocks, 50 different counter variables will be created. Clearly, this system wouldn't be practical for large-scale use. One practice that this example does follow correctly is that of locking the Application collection before updating it. This can cause a significant performance slowdown, but it guarantees that the value will be accurate even if multiple clients are accessing the web service simultaneously.

To view the counter information, you can call the GetStockUsage() function with the ticker for the stock you're interested in. A custom object, CounterInfo, is returned to you with both pieces of information.

It's unlikely that you'd design an application to store this much usage information in memory, but it gives you a good indication of how you can use session and application state management in a web service just as easily as in an ASP.NET page. Note that session state automatically expires after a preset amount of time, and both the Session and Application collections will be emptied when the application is stopped. For more information about ASP.NET state management, refer to Chapter 9.

Consuming a Stateful Web Service

If you try to use a stateful web service, you're likely to be frustrated. Every time you re-create the proxy class, a new session ID is automatically assigned, which means you won't be able to access the session information from the previous request. To counter this problem, you need to take extra steps to preserve the cookie that has the session ID.

In a web client, you'll need to store the session ID between requests and then reapply it to the proxy object just before you make a call to the web service. You can use just about any type of storage: a database, a local cookie, view state, or even the Session collection for the current web page. In other words, you could store information for your web service session in your current (local) page session.

If the previous discussion seems a little confusing, it's because you need to remind yourself that this example really has two active sessions. The web service client has one session, which is maintained as long as the user reading your site doesn't close the browser. The web service itself also has its own session. (In fact, the web service could even be hosted on a different web server.) The web service session can't be maintained automatically because you don't communicate with it directly. Instead, the proxy class bears the burden of holding the web service session information. Figure 23-1 illustrates the difference.

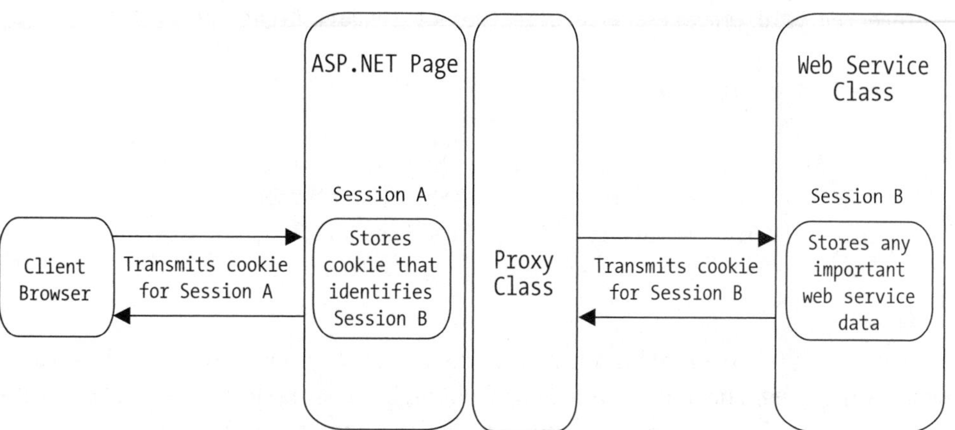

Figure 23-1. *Session cookies with a web client*

The next example sheds some light on this situation. It uses the same web service, but it takes additional steps to maintain the cookie with the session ticket, allowing session state to remain between calls..

Your client is a simple web page with two buttons and a label. Every time the Call Service button is clicked, the GetStockQuote() method is invoked with a default parameter. When the Get Usage Info button is clicked, the GetStockUsage() method is called, which returns the current usage statistics. Information is added to the label, creating a log that records every action.

```
public partial class FailedSessionServiceTest : Page
{
    private localhost.StockQuote_SessionState ws =
     new localhost.StockQuote_SessionState();

    protected void cmdGetCounter_Click(Object sender, EventArgs e)
    {
        localhost.CounterInfo wsInfo;
        wsInfo = ws.GetStockUsage("MSFT");

        // Add usage information to the label.
        lblResult.Text += "<b>Global: " + wsInfo.GlobalRequests.ToString();
        lblResult.Text += "<br />Session: ";
        lblResult.Text += wsInfo.SessionRequests.ToString() + "<br /></b>";
    }
```

```
    protected void cmdCallService_Click(Object sender, EventArgs e)
    {
        decimal result = ws.GetStockQuote("MSFT");

        // Add confirmation message to the label.
        lblResult.Text += "GetStockQuote With MSFT Returned ";
        lblResult.Text += result.ToString() + "<br />";
    }
}
```

Unfortunately, every time this button is clicked, the proxy class is re-created, and a new session is used. The output on the page tells an interesting story: after clicking cmdCallService four times and cmdGetCounter once, the web service reports the right number of global application requests but the wrong number of session requests, as shown in Figure 23-2.

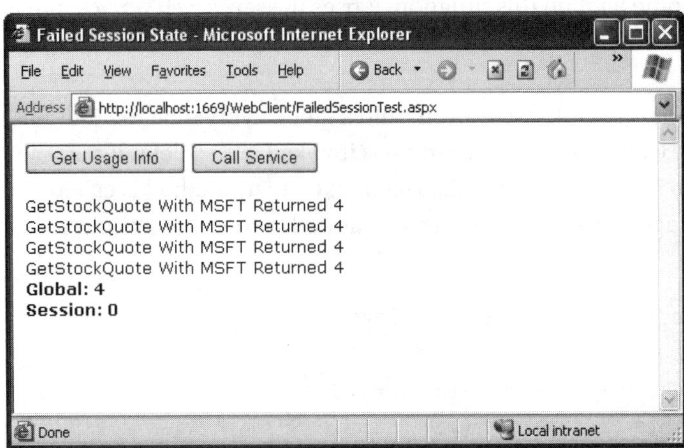

Figure 23-2. *A failed attempt to use session state*

To fix this problem, you need to set the CookieContainer property of the proxy class. First be sure to import the System.Net class, which has the cookie classes this example needs:

```
using System.Net;
```

The next step is to modify the event handlers. In the following example, the event handlers call two private functions: GetCookie() and SetCookie(). These methods are called immediately before and after the web method call.

```
protected void cmdGetCounter_Click(Object sender, EventArgs e)
{
    localhost.CounterInfo wsInfo;
```

```
    GetCookie();
    wsInfo = ws.GetStockUsage("MSFT");
    SetCookie();

    // Add usage information to the label.
    lblResult.Text += "<b>Global: " + wsInfo.GlobalRequests.ToString();
    lblResult.Text += "<br />Session: ";
    lblResult.Text += wsInfo.SessionRequests.ToString() + "<br /></b>";
}

protected void cmdCallService_Click(Object sender, EventArgs e)
{
    GetCookie();
    decimal result = ws.GetStockQuote("MSFT");
    SetCookie();

    // Add confirmation message to the label.
    lblResult.Text += "GetStockQuote With MSFT Returned ";
    lblResult.Text += result.ToString() + "<br />";
}
```

The GetCookie() method initializes the CookieContainer for the proxy class, enabling it to send and receive cookies. It also tries to retrieve the cookie from the current session.

```
private void GetCookie()
{
    // Initialize the proxy class CookieContainer so it can receive cookies.
    ws.CookieContainer = new CookieContainer();

    // If a cookie is found, place it in the proxy class.
    // The only reason it won't be found is if this is the first time the
    // button has been clicked.
    if (Session["WebServiceCookie"] != null)
    {
        // Create a cookie object, and try to retrieve it from session state.
        Cookie sessionCookie;
        sessionCookie = (Cookie)Session["WebServiceCookie"];
        ws.CookieContainer.Add(sessionCookie);
    }
}
```

DOES SESSION STATE MANAGEMENT MAKE SENSE WITH A WEB SERVICE?

Because web services are destroyed after every method call, they don't provide a natural mechanism for storing state information. You can use the Session collection to compensate for this limitation, but this approach raises the following complications:

- Session state will disappear when the session times out. The client will have no way of knowing when the session times out, which means the web service may behave unpredictably.
- Session state is tied to a specific user, not to a specific class or object. This can cause problems if the same client wants to use the same web service in two different ways or creates two instances of the proxy class at once.
- Session state is maintained only if the client preserves the session cookie. The state management you use in a web service won't work if the client fails to take these steps.

The SetCookie() method explicitly stores the web service session cookie in session state:

```
private void SetCookie()
{
    // Retrieve and store the current cookie for next time.
    // The session is always stored in a special cookie
    // called ASP.NET_SessionId.
    Uri wsUri = new Uri("http://localhost");

    CookieCollection cookies = ws.CookieContainer.GetCookies(wsUri);
    Session["WebServiceCookie"] = cookies["ASP.NET_SessionId"];
}
```

The code could have been simplified somewhat if it stored the whole cookie collection instead of just the session cookie, but this approach is more controlled.

Now the page works correctly, as shown in Figure 23-3.

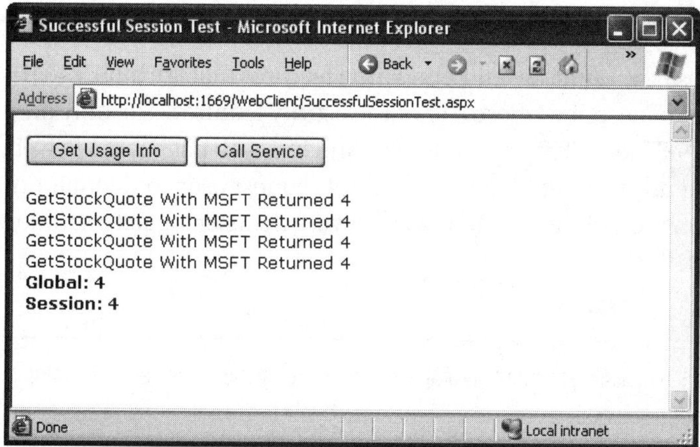

Figure 23-3. *A successful use of session state*

Web Service Security

Most of the security issues that relate to web pages also affect web services. For example, web services transmit messages using clear text, which means a malicious user with access to the network could easily spy on confidential information or even modify a message as it's transmitted. To prevent both of these possibilities in a web service that requires complete confidentiality, your best bet is SSL, as described in Chapter 18. SSL doesn't mesh perfectly with the world of web services—it's a little more heavyweight than is ideal, and it complicates business-to-business transactions with multiple web services—but it's the safest choice for today's web services. Other SOAP-based encryption and signing standards that address these problems are evolving, but they're still in flux. You can get more information and even try them in your web services by downloading Microsoft's WSE (Web Services Enhancements) toolkit at `http://msdn.microsoft.com/webservices/building/wse`. Just expect to adapt as the standards of today continue to change.

Along with the issue of encryption, web services may also need the same ability to authenticate users as web pages. For example, you may want to verify that a user is allowed to access a web service (or a particular web method) before you perform a task.

You have two options for setting up authentication with a web service:

- Your first option is to use the Windows authentication features that are built into IIS and ASP.NET. Chapter 18 describes these standard security features. The only difference between ASP.NET security in a web service and in a web page is that a web service doesn't present any user interface, so it cannot request user credentials on its own. It has to rely on the calling code or rely on having the user logged on under an authorized account.

■ **Note** Windows authentication is a realistic solution only if all your users are on the same network, running Windows, and have preexisting user accounts.

- For maximum flexibility, you can create and use your own login and authentication code. Sadly, forms authentication won't help you here—its reliance on cookies and its assumption that end user will log in through a web page mean it won't work in a web service scenario. However, you can use the membership features discussed in Chapter 19 to reduce the code you write for the login process.

In the following sections, you'll consider both approaches.

Windows Authentication with a Web Service

Windows authentication works with a web service in much the same way it works with a web page. The difference is that a web service is executed by another application, not directly by the browser. For that reason, a web service has no built-in way to prompt the user for a user name and password. Instead, the application that's using the web service needs to supply this information. The application might read this information from a configuration file or database, or it might prompt the user for this information before contacting the web service.

For example, consider the following web service, which provides a single TestAuthenticated() method. This method checks whether the user is authenticated. If the user is authenticated, it returns the full user name.

```
public class SecureService : System.Web.Services.WebService
{
    [WebMethod()]
    public string TestAuthenticated()
    {
        if (!User.Identity.IsAuthenticated)
```

```
        {
            return "Not authenticated.";
        }
        else
        {
            return "Authenticated as: " + User.Identity.Name;
        }
    }
}
```

Note To use this approach, you also need to ensure the <authentication> tag is set to use Windows authentication (the default), and you need to configure the authentication protocols you want to support using IIS Manager. Chapter 18 has the full details about configuring a web application to use Windows authentication.

The first time you test this web service, you'll find that the user isn't authenticated. As with a web page, authentication springs into action only when you explicitly deny anonymous users. To do this, you can configure the virtual directory in IIS Manager (as described in Chapter 18) or add an authorization rule that targets a specific page or folder. For example, here's what you need to require authentication for the SecureService.asmx method:

```
<configuration>
    <location path="SecureService.asmx">
        <system.web>
            <authorization>
                <deny users="?"/>
            </authorization>
        </system.web>
    </location>

    <system.web>
      ...
    </system.web>
</configuration>
```

It's not possible to turn authentication on or off for individual methods. As a result, if you want some methods to use authentication and others to not require it, you'll need to code these methods in separate web services.

If you request this page in a browser, you'll get the expected result. The browser will authenticate you, and the web service will return your full user name, which is a string in the form [DomainName]\[UserName] or [ComputerName]\[UserName]).

However, if you try to call your web service from a client, you won't be as lucky. Instead, you'll receive an Access Denied error message. This indicates that authentication was required but the client didn't supply the correct authentication credentials.

The problem is that, by default, the proxy class won't supply any authentication information (unlike a browser, which prompts the user to log in). To submit user credentials to this service, the client needs to modify the NetworkCredential property of the proxy class. You have two options:

- You can create a new NetworkCredential object and attach this to the NetworkCredential property of the proxy object. When you create the NetworkCredential object, you'll need to specify the user name and password you want to use. This approach works with all forms of Windows authentication.

- If the web service is using Integrated Windows authentication, you can automatically submit the credentials of the current user by using the static DefaultCredentials property of the CredentialCache class and applying that to the NetworkCredential property of the proxy object.

Both the CredentialCache and NetworkCredential classes are found in the System.Net namespace. Thus, before continuing, you should import this namespace:

```
using System.Net;
```

You'll also need to add a reference to the System.Security.dll assembly that defines the credential classes. To do this, choose Website ➤ Add Reference, and select the System.Security entry in the .NET tab.

The following code shows a web page with two buttons. One button performs an unauthenticated call, while the user submits some user credentials. The unauthenticated call will fail if you've disabled anonymous users for the web application. Otherwise, the unauthenticated call will succeed, but the TestAuthenticated() method will return a string informing you that authentication wasn't performed. The authenticated call will always succeed as long as you submit credentials that correspond to a valid user on the web server.

```
public partial class TestSecuredService : Page
{
    protected void cmdUnauthenticated_Click(Object sender, EventArgs e)
```

```
    {
        localhost.SecureService ws = new localhost.SecureService();
        lblInfo.Text = ws.TestAuthenticated();
    }

    protected void cmdAuthenticated_Click(Object sender, EventArgs e)
    {
        localhost.SecureService ws = new localhost.SecureService();

        // Specity some user credentials for the web service.
        // This example uses the user account "GuestAccount" with the password
        // "Guest".
        NetworkCredential credentials = new NetworkCredential(
          "GuestAccount", "Guest");
        ws.Credentials = credentials;

        lblInfo.Text = ws.TestAuthenticated();
    }
}
```

Figure 23-4 shows what the web page looks like after a successfully authenticated call to the computer fariamat.

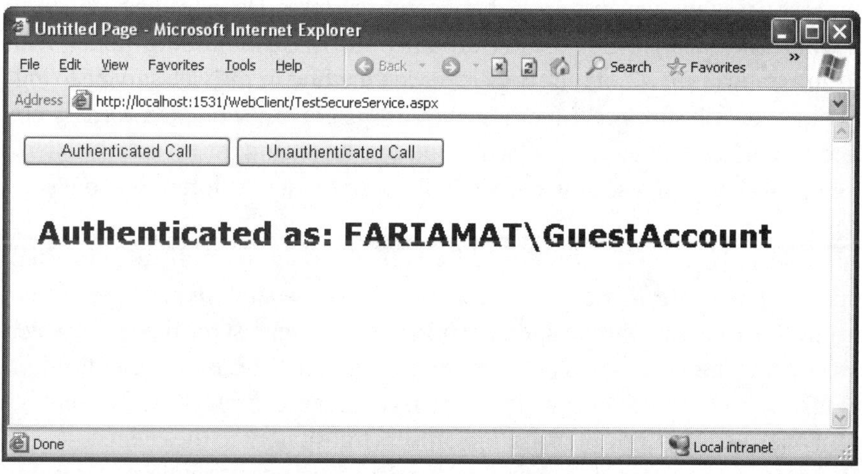

Figure 23-4. *Successful authentication through a web service*

If you wanted to use the credentials of the currently logged-in account with Integrated Windows authentication, you would use this code instead:

```
localhost.SecureService ws = new localhost.SecureService();
ws.Credentials = CredentialCache.DefaultCredentials;
lblInfo.Text = ws.TestAuthenticated();
```

Keep in mind that this probably won't have the result you want in a deployed web application. On a live web server, the current user account is always the account that ASP.NET is using, not the user account of the remote user who is requesting the web page. (For example, if you're using IIS 5, the ASPNET account runs all ASP.NET code.) However, this technique makes sense in a Windows application. In this case, when you retrieve the default credentials, you'll submit the account information of the user who is running the application.

■ **Note** Forms authentication won't work with a web service because there's no way for a web service to direct the user to a web page. In fact, the web service might not even be accessed through a browser—it might be used by a Windows application or even an automated Windows service.

Ticket-Based Authentication

Many web services use their own custom authentication systems. Usually, they use a form of *ticket-based authentication* to increase performance and make the coding model. With ticked-based authentication, clients call a specific web method in the web service to log in, at which point they will supply credentials (such as a user name and password combination). The login method will then create a new, unique ticket and return it to the client. From this point, the client can use any method in the web service, as long the client supplies the ticket.

The benefit of ticket-based authentication is that you need only one authentication step, which is properly separated from the rest of your code. On subsequent requests, your web service can verify the ticket rather than authenticating the user against the database, which is always faster (in a properly designed ticket system). Finally, ticket-based authentication allows you to take advantage of SOAP headers (which you'll see shortly). SOAP headers make the ticket management and authorization process transparent to the client.

Fortunately, you can get most of the benefits of a ticked-based authentication system without writing your own authentication logic. Instead, you can use the membership and role management features that ASP.NET provides (as discussed in Chapter 19). It's still up to you to transfer the user credentials and keep track of who has logged in by issuing and verifying tickets. However, you don't need to write the authentication code that checks whether a user and password combination is valid.

The following example shows how you could adapt the StockQuote service to use ticked-based authentication:

```
[WebService(Description="Methods to get stock information.",
 Namespace="http://www.prosetech.com/Stocks")]
public class StockQuote_Security : WebService
{
    [WebMethod]
    public LicenseKey Login(string userName, string password)
    {
        if (Membership.ValidateUser(userName, password))
        {
            // Generate a license key made up of
            // some random sequence of characters.
            LicenseKey key = new LicenseKey();
            key.Ticket = Guid.NewGuid().ToString();

            // Add the key object to application state.
            Application[key.Ticket] = key;

            return key;
        }
        else
        {
            // Cause an error that will be returned to the client.
            throw new SecurityException("Unauthorized.");
        }
    }

    [WebMethod]
    public int GetStockQuote(string ticker, LicenseKey key)
    {
        if (!VerifyKey(key.Ticket))
        {
            throw new SecurityException("Unauthorized.");
        }
        else
        {
            // Normal GetStockQuote code goes here.
            return ticker.Length;
        }
    }
```

```
    private bool VerifyKey(string ticket)
    {
        // Look up this key to make sure it's valid.
        LicenseKey key = Application[ticket] as LicenseKey;
        return (ticket != null);
    }
}

public class LicenseKey
{
    public string Ticket;
}
```

Dissecting the Code...

- Before using any method in this class, the client must call the Login() method and store the received license key. Every other web method will require that license key.

- The Login() method uses the Membership class, which performs the user authentication for you. To use membership in a web application, you need to configure the membership database. However, if you're using SQL Server 2005 Express Edition, the default settings will create the required database for you in the App_Data directory automatically. Chapter 19 has the full details.

- The LicenseKey class uses a GUID. This is a randomly generated 128-bit number that is guaranteed to be statistically unique. (In other words, the chance of generating two unique GUIDs in a web service or guessing another user's GUID is astronomically small.) You could also add other information to the LicenseKey class about the current user to retrieve later as needed. For example, you could keep track of the date when the license was issued.

- The same private function—VerifyKey()—is used regardless of what web method is invoked. This ensures that the license verification code is written in only one place and is used consistently.

- The Login() method stores the key in server memory using application state. The Application collection has certain limitations, including no support for multiple web servers (web farms). The tickets will also be lost if the web application restarts.

■ **Note** You could add data caching to this design to get around the limitations of the Application class. With data caching, you would store every key in two places—in the database, which would be used as a last resort, and duplicated in the in-memory cache. The VerifyKey() function would perform the database lookup only if the cached item was not found. For more information about caching, refer to Chapter 26. However, even if you make this enhancement, the essential design of this web service remains the same. The only difference is how the LicenseKey is stored and retrieved in between requests.

Ticket-Based Authentication with SOAP Headers

The potential problem with this example is that it requires a license key to be submitted with each method call as a parameter. This can be a bit tedious. To streamline this process, you can use a custom SOAP header.

SOAP headers are separate pieces of information that are sent, when required, in the header section of a SOAP message. These headers can contain all the same data types you use for method parameters and return values. The advantage of SOAP headers is just the convenience. The client specifies a SOAP header once, and the header is automatically sent to every method that needs it, making the coding clearer and more concise. You can also change the header details without being forced to edit the signature of every web method.

To create a custom SOAP header, you first need to define a class that inherits from the SoapHeader class (which is found in the System.Web.Services.Protocols namespace). You can then add all the additional pieces of information you want it to contain as member variables. In the following example, the SOAP header simply stores the license key:

```
public class LicenseKeyHeader : System.Web.Services.Protocols.SoapHeader
{
    public string Ticket;

    public LicenseKeyHeader(string ticket)
    {
        Ticket = ticket;
    }

    public LicenseKeyHeader()
    {
        Ticket = Guid.NewGuid().ToString()
    }
}
```

Notice that this class is slightly enhanced over the previous version. The default constructor now generates a random ticket value automatically.

Next, your web service needs a public member variable to receive the SOAP header:

```
public class StockQuote_SoapSecurity : WebService
{
    public LicenseKeyHeader KeyHeader;

    // (Other web service code goes here.)
}
```

The web service requires one last ingredient. Each web service method that wants to access the LicenseKeyHeader must explicitly indicate this requirement with a SoapHeader attribute. The attribute indicates the web service member variable where the header should be placed.

```
[WebMethod]
[SoapHeader("KeyHeader", Direction=SoapHeaderDirection.In)]
public int GetStockQuote(string ticker)
{ ... }
```

The Direction parameter indicates that this method *receives* the header with the ticket information. That's different from the Login() method, which creates the header and returns it to the client.

The complete web service is quite similar to the earlier example. The chief difference is that when the client calls the Login() method, no information is provided as a return value. Instead, a LicenseKeyHeader is created and sent silently to the client. The next time the client calls any methods, this header is transmitted automatically, which means those methods don't need to accept key information through their parameters.

Here's the full code:

```
[WebService(Description="Methods to get stock information.",
 Namespace="http://www.prosetech.com/Stocks")]
public class StockQuote_Security : WebService
{
    public LicenseKeyHeader KeyHeader;

    [WebMethod]
    [SoapHeader("KeyHeader", Direction=SoapHeaderDirection.Out)]
    public void Login(string userName, string password)
```

```
        {
            if (Membership.ValidateUser(userName, password))
            {
                // Generate a license key, and store it in the SOAP header.
                KeyHeader = new LicenseKey();

                // Store the KeyHeader object in application state.
                Application[KeyHeader.Ticket] = KeyHeader;
            }
            else
            {
                // Cause an error that will be returned to the client.
                throw new SecurityException("Unauthorized.");
            }
        }

        [WebMethod]
        [SoapHeader("KeyHeader", Direction=SoapHeaderDirection.In)]
        public int GetStockQuote(string ticker)
        {
            // Get the key from the SOAP header.
            if (!VerifyKey(KeyHeader))
            {
                throw new System.Security.SecurityException("Unauthorized.");
            }
            else
            {
                // Normal GetStockQuote code goes here.
                return ticker.Length;
            }
        }

        private bool VerifyKey(string ticket)
        {
            // Look up this key to make sure it's valid.
            LicenseKeyHeader key = Application[ticket] as LicenseKeyHeader;
            return (ticket != null);
        }
    }
```

■ **Caution** SOAP messages are sent over the network as ordinary text. This means if you create an authentication system like this, malicious users could watch network traffic and intercept passwords as they are sent from the client to the web service. To solve this problem, you can use SSL with your web service to encrypt all the messages that are exchanged. Refer to Chapter 18 for more information.

Using SOAP Headers in the Client

Some web services allow information to be specified once and used for multiple methods automatically. This technique works through SOAP headers. The previous example showed a web service that used a SOAP header to receive and maintain security credentials. When you create a client for this service, the custom SoapHeader class is copied into the proxy file.

Using this web service is remarkably easy. First you call the login method and supply your user credentials:

```
// Create the web service proxy class.
localhost.StockQuote_SoapSecurity ws = new localhost.StockQuote_SoapSecurity();

// Log in.
ws.Login("testUser", "openSesame");
```

If this test succeeds, the web service issues a new ticket, which is attached to the proxy object. From this point, whenever you call a web method that needs the LicenseKeyHeader, it will be transmitted automatically.

```
decimal price = ws.GetStockQuote("MSFT");
```

In other words, you set the header once and don't need to worry about supplying any additional security information, as long as you use the same instance of the proxy class. The online examples include a simple example of a web service client that uses a SOAP header for authentication.

Web Service Transactions

Transactions are an important feature in many business applications. They ensure that a series of operations either succeeds or fails as a unit. Transactions also prevent the possibility of inconsistent or corrupted data that can occur if an operation fails midway through after committing only some of its changes. The most common example of a transaction is a bank account transfer. When you move $100 from one account to another, two actions take place: a withdrawal in the first account and a deposit in the second. If these two tasks are a part of a single transaction, they will either both succeed or both fail. It will be impossible for one account to be debited if the other isn't credited.

Web services can participate in COM+ transactions but in a somewhat limited way. Because of the stateless nature of HTTP, web service methods can act only as the root object in a transaction. This means a web service method can start a transaction and use it to perform a series of related tasks, but multiple web services cannot be grouped into one transaction. As a result, you may have to put in some extra thought when you're creating a transactional web service. For example, it won't make sense to create a financial web service with separate DebitAccount() and CreditAccount() methods, because they won't be able to be grouped into a transaction. Instead, you can make sure both tasks execute as a single unit using a transactional TransferFunds() method.

To use a transaction in a web service, you first have to add a reference to the System.EnterpriseServices.dll assembly. To do this, choose Website ➤ Add Reference, and select the System.EnterpriseServices entry on the .NET tab.

You can now import the corresponding namespace so the types you need (TransactionOption and ContextUtil) are at your fingertips:

```
using System.EnterpriseServices;
```

To start a transaction in a web service method, set the TransactionOption property of the WebMethod attribute. TransactionOption is an enumeration providing several values that allow you to specify whether a code component uses or requires transactions. Because web services must be the root of a transaction, most of these options don't apply. To create a web service method that starts a transaction automatically, use the following attribute:

```
[WebMethod(TransactionOption=TransactionOption.RequiresNew)]
```

The transaction is automatically committed when the web method completes. The transaction is rolled back if any unhandled exception occurs or if you explicitly instruct the transaction to fail using the following code:

```
ContextUtil.SetAbort();
```

Most databases support COM+ transactions. The moment these databases are used in a transactional web method, they will automatically be enlisted in the current transaction. If the transaction is rolled back, the operations you perform with these databases (such as adding, modifying, or removing records) will be automatically reversed. However, some operations (such as writing a file to disk) aren't inherently transactional. That means these operations will not be rolled back if the transaction fails.

Now consider the following web method, which takes two actions: it deletes records in a database and then tries to read from a file. However, if the file operation fails and the exception isn't handled, the entire transaction will be rolled back, and the deleted records will be restored.

```
[WebMethod(TransactionOption=TransactionOption.RequiresNew)]
public void UpdateDatabase()
{
    // Create ADO.NET objects.
    string connectionString =
      WebConfigurationManager.ConnectionStrings["Northwind"].ConnectionString;
    SqlConnection con = new SqlConnection(connectionString);
    SqlCommand cmd = new SqlCommand("DELETE * FROM authors", con);

    // Apply the update. This will be registered as part of the transaction.
    using (con)
    {
        con.Open();
        cmd.ExecuteNonQuery();
    }

    // Try to access a file. This generates an exception that isn't handled.
    // The web method will be aborted, and the changes will be rolled back.
    FileStream fs = new FileStream("does_not_exist.bin", FileMode.Open);

    // (If no errors have occurred, the database changes
    // are committed here when the method ends).
}
```

Another way to handle this code is to catch the error, perform any cleanup that's required, and then explicitly roll back the transaction if necessary:

```
[WebMethod(TransactionOption=TransactionOption.RequiresNew)]
public void UpdateDatabase()
{
    // Create ADO.NET objects.
    string connectionString =
      WebConfigurationManager.ConnectionStrings["Northwind"].ConnectionString;
    SqlConnection con = new SqlConnection(connectionString);
    SqlCommand cmd = new SqlCommand("DELETE * FROM authors", con);

    // Apply the update.
    try
    {
        con.Open();
        cmd.ExecuteNonQuery();
```

```
        FileStream fs = new FileStream("does_not_exist.bin", FileMode.Open);
    }
    catch
    {
        ContextUtil.SetAbort();
    }
    finally
    {
        con.Close();
    }
}
```

Does a web service need to use COM+ transactions? It all depends on the situation. If multiple updates are required in separate data stores, you may need to use transactions to ensure your data's integrity. If, on the other hand, you're modifying values only in a single database, you can probably use the data provider's built-in transaction features instead.

An Example with TerraService

Now that you know how to use a web service, you aren't limited just to using the web services that you create. In fact, the Internet is brimming with sample services you can use to test your applications or to try new techniques. In the future, you'll even be able to buy prebuilt functionality you can integrate into your ASP.NET applications by calling a web service. Typically, you'll pay for these services using some kind of subscription model. Because they're implemented through .NET web services and WSDL contracts, you won't need to install anything extra on your web server.

The next sections cover how to use one of the more interesting web services: Microsoft's TerraService. TerraService is based on the hugely popular TerraServer site where web surfers can view topographic maps and satellite photographs of most of the globe. The site was developed by Microsoft's research division to test SQL Server and increase Microsoft's boasting ability. Under the hood, a 1.5TB SQL Server 2000 database stores all the pictures that are used as a collection of millions of different tiles. You can find out more about TerraServer at `http://terraservice.net`.

To promote .NET, Microsoft has equipped TerraServer with a web service interface that allows you to access the TerraServer information. Using this interface (called TerraService) isn't difficult, but creating a polished application with it is. Before you can really understand how to stitch together different satellite tiles to create a large picture, you need to have some basic understanding of geography and projection systems. You can find plenty of additional information about it at the TerraServer site. However, because this book is about .NET and not geography, your use of TerraService will be fairly straightforward. Once you understand the basics, you can continue experimenting with additional web methods and create a more extensive application based on TerraService.

Adding the Reference

The first step is to create a new ASP.NET application and add a web reference. In Visual Studio, you start by returning to the Add Web Reference dialog box. The TerraService web service is located at `http://terraservice.net/TerraService.asmx`. Type it into the Address text box, and press Enter. The TerraService text page will appear (see Figure 23-5).

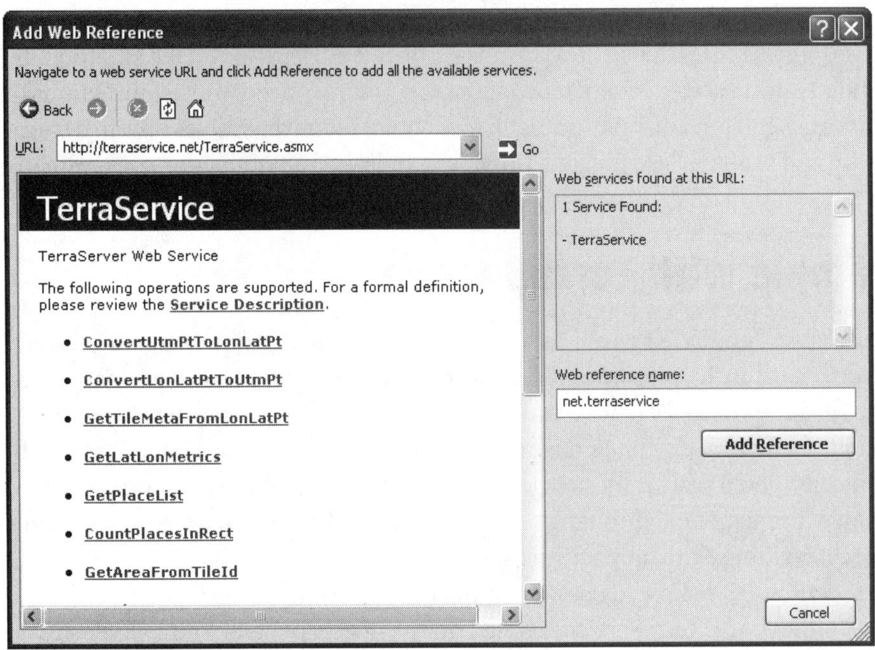

Figure 23-5. *Adding a TerraService web reference*

You can see from the displayed test page that there are approximately 15 functions. At the time of this writing, no additional information is provided on the test page (indicating that Microsoft doesn't always follow its own recommendations). To read about these methods, you'll have to browse the site on your own.

Click Add Reference to create the Web Reference. The WSDL document and discovery files will be created under the namespace net.terraservice, as shown in Figure 23-6.

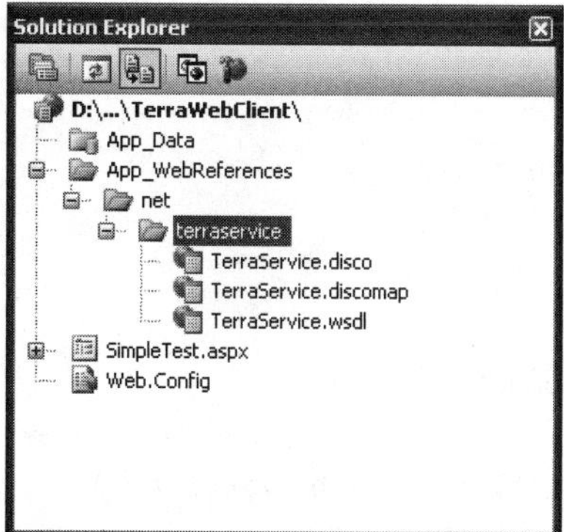

Figure 23-6. *The TerraService files in Visual Studio*

Testing the Client

Before continuing too much further, it makes sense to try a simple method to see whether the web service works as expected. A good choice to start is the simple GetPlaceFacts() method, which retrieves some simple information about a geographic location that you supply. In this case, the TerraService documentation (and the Visual Studio IntelliSense) informs you that this method requires the use of two special classes: a Place class (which specifies what you're searching for) and a PlaceFacts class (which provides you with the information about your place). These classes are available in the net.terraservice namespace.

The following example retrieves information about a place named Seattle when a button is clicked and displays it in a label. The process is split into two separate subroutines for better organization, although this isn't strictly required.

```
private net.terraservice.TerraService ts = new net.terraservice.TerraService();

protected void cmdShow_Click(Object sender, EventArgs e)
{
    // Create the Place object for Seattle.
    net.terraservice.Place searchPlace = new net.terraservice.Place();
    searchPlace.City = "Seattle";
    searchPlace.State = "Washington";
    searchPlace.Country = "US";

    // Define the PlaceFacts objects to retrieve your information.
    net.terraservice.PlaceFacts facts;
```

```
        // Call the web service method.
        facts = ts.GetPlaceFacts(searchPlace);

        // Display the results with the help of a subroutine.
        ShowPlaceFacts(facts);
    }

    private void ShowPlaceFacts(net.terraservice.PlaceFacts facts)
    {
        lblResult.Text += "<b>Place: " + facts.Place.City + "</b><br /><br />";
        lblResult.Text += facts.Place.State + ", " + facts.Place.Country;
        lblResult.Text += "<br /> Lat: " + facts.Center.Lat.ToString();
        lblResult.Text += "<br /> Long: " + facts.Center.Lon.ToString();
        lblResult.Text += "<br /><br />";
    }
```

The result is a successful retrieval of information about the city of Seattle, including its longitude, latitude, and country, as shown in Figure 23-7.

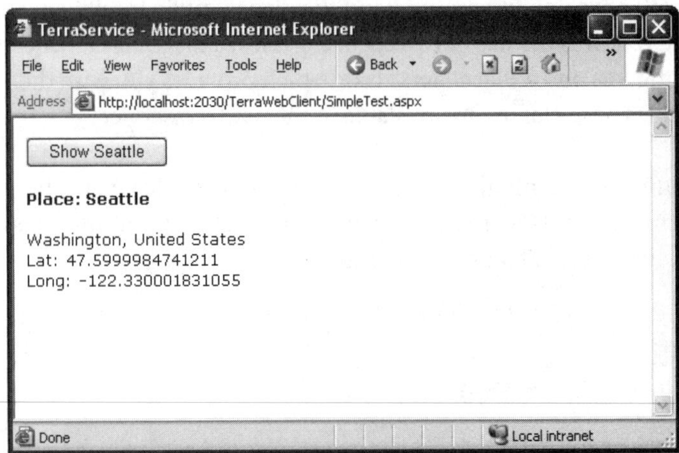

Figure 23-7. *Retrieving information from TerraService*

Searching for More Information

The TerraService documentation doesn't recommend relying on the GetPlaceFacts() method, because it's able to retrieve information only about the first place with the matching name. Typically, many locations share the same name. Even in the case of Seattle, several landmark locations are stored in the TerraServer database along with the city itself. All these places start with the word *Seattle*.

The GetPlaceList() method provides a more useful approach, because it returns an array with all the matches. When using GetPlaceList(), you have to specify a maximum number of allowed matches to prevent your application from becoming tied up with an extremely long query. You also have a third parameter, which you can set to true to retrieve only results that have corresponding picture tiles in the database or to false to return any matching result. Typically, you would use true if you were creating an application that displays the satellite images for searched locations. You'll also notice that the GetPlaceList() function accepts a place name directly and doesn't use a Place object.

To demonstrate this method, add a second button to the test page, and use the following code:

```
protected void cmdShowAll_Click(Object sender, EventArgs e)
{
    // Retrieve the matching list (for the city Kingston).
    net.terraservice.PlaceFacts[] factsArray;
    factsArray = ts.GetPlaceList("Kingston", 100, false);

    // Loop through all the results, and display them.
    foreach (net.terraservice.PlaceFacts facts in factsArray)
    {
        ShowPlaceFacts(facts);
    }
}
```

The result is a list of about 50 matches for places with the name Kingston, as shown in Figure 23-8.

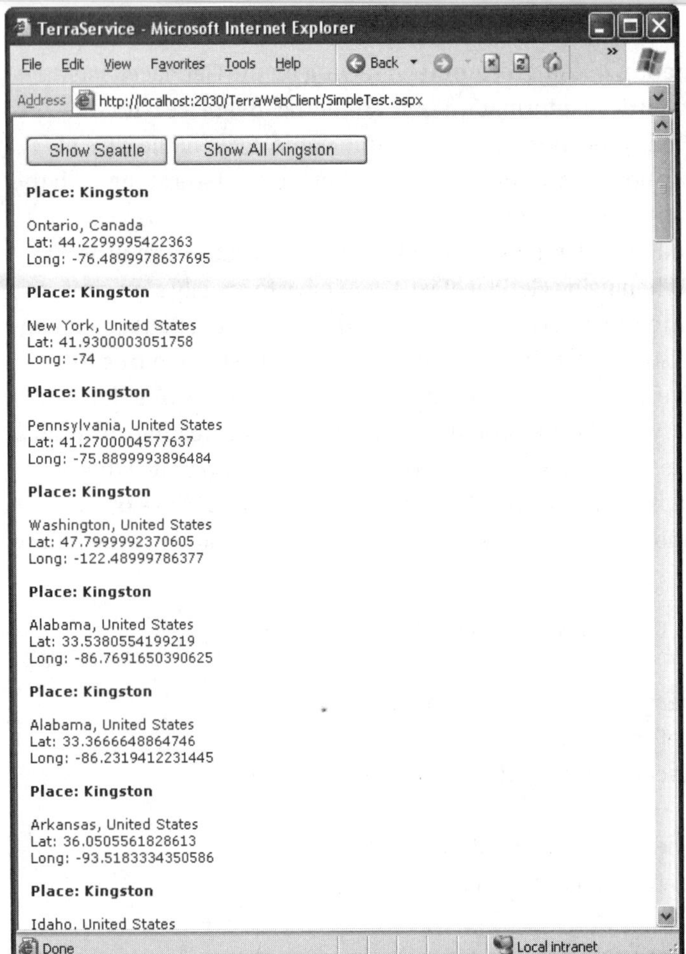

Figure 23-8. *Retrieving place matches*

Displaying a Tile

By this point, you've realized that using TerraService isn't really different from using any other DLL or code library. The only difference is that you're accessing it over the Internet. In this case, it's no small feat: the TerraServer database contains so much information that it would be extremely difficult to download over the Internet. Providing an organized, carefully limited view through a web service interface solves all these problems.

The next example shows your last trick for a web service. It retrieves the closest matching tile for the city of Seattle and displays it. To display the tile, the example takes the low-level approach of using Response.WriteBinary(). In a more advanced application, a significant amount of in-memory graphical manipulation might be required to get the result you want. Figure 23-9 shows the retrieved tile.

```
protected void cmdShowPic_Click(Object sender, EventArgs e)
{
    // Define the search.
    net.terraservice.Place searchPlace = new net.terraservice.Place();
    searchPlace.City = "Seattle";
    searchPlace.State = "Washington";
    searchPlace.Country = "US";

    // Get the PlaceFacts for Seattle.
    net.terraservice.PlaceFacts facts;
    facts = ts.GetPlaceFacts(searchPlace);

    // Retrieve information about the tile at the center of Seattle, using
    // the Scale and Theme enumerations from the terraservice namespace.
    net.terraservice.TileMeta tileData;
    tileData = ts.GetTileMetaFromLonLatPt(facts.Center,
     net.terraservice.Theme.Photo, net.terraservice.Scale.Scale16m);

    // Retrieve the image.
    byte[] image = ts.GetTile(tileData.Id);

    // Display the image.
    Response.BinaryWrite(image);
}
```

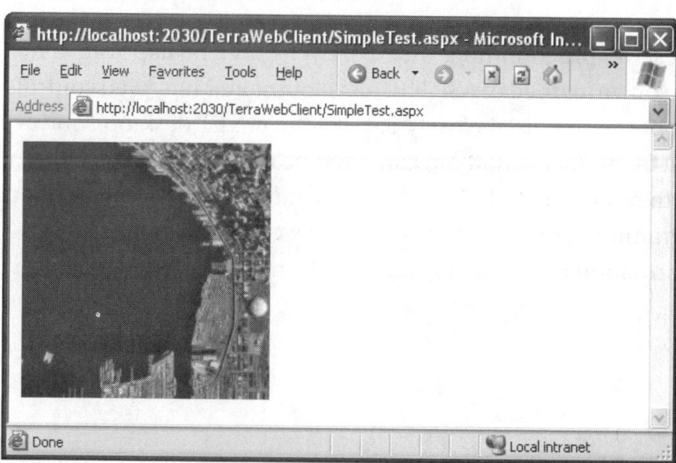

Figure 23-9. *A tile from TerraService*

This example uses two additional TerraService methods. GetTileMetaFromLonLatPt() retrieves information about the tile at a given point. This function finds out what tile contains the center of Seattle. The GetTile() method retrieves the binary information representing the tile by using the TileID provided by GetTileMetaFromLonLatPt().

You'll probably also want to combine several tiles, which requires the use of other TerraService methods. You can find the full set of supported methods documented at `http://terraservice.net/`. Once again, using these methods requires an understanding of graphics and geography, but the method don't require any unusual use of web services. The core concept—remote method calls through SOAP communication—remains the same.

Windows Clients

Because this book focuses on ASP.NET, you haven't had the chance to see one of the main advantages of web services. Quite simply, they allow desktop applications to use pieces of functionality from the Internet. This allows you to provide a rich, responsive desktop interface that periodically retrieves any real-time information it needs from the Internet. The process is almost entirely transparent. As high-speed access becomes more common, you may not even be aware of which portions of functionality depend on the Internet and which ones don't.

You can use web service functionality in a Windows application in the same way you would use it in an ASP.NET application. First, you create the proxy class using Visual Studio or the WSDL.exe utility. Then, you add code to create an instance of your proxy class and call a web method. The only difference is the upper layer: the user interface the application uses.

If you haven't explored desktop programming with .NET yet, you'll be happy to know you can reuse much of what you've learned in ASP.NET development. Many web controls (such as labels, buttons, text boxes, and lists) closely parallel their .NET desktop equivalents, and the code you write to interact with them can often be transferred from one environment to the other with few changes. In fact, the main difference between desktop programming and web programming in .NET is the extra steps you need to take in web applications to preserve information between postbacks and when transferring the user from one page to another.

The following example shows the form code for a simple Windows TerraService client that uses the GetPlaceList() web method. It has been modified to search for a place that the user enters in a text box and display the results in a list box. The basic designer code, which creates the controls and sets their initial properties, has been omitted. (This plays the same role as the control tags in the .aspx web page file.)

```
public partial class WindowsTerraClient : System.Windows.Forms.Form
{
    // (Initialization code omitted.)

    private net.terraservice.TerraService ts = new
      net.terraservice.TerraService();

    private void cmdShow_Click(Object sender, EventArgs e)
    {
        // Retrieve the matching list.
        net.terraservice.PlaceFacts[] factsArray;
        factsArray = ts.GetPlaceList(txtPlace.Text, 100, false);

        // Loop through all the results, and display them.
        foreach (net.terraservice.PlaceFacts facts in factsArray)
        {
            ShowPlaceFacts(facts);
        }
    }

    private void ShowPlaceFacts(net.terraservice.PlaceFacts facts)
    {
        string newItem;
        newItem = "Place: " + facts.Place.City + ", ";
        newItem += facts.Place.State + ", " + facts.Place.Country;
        lstPlaces.Items.Add(newItem);
    }
}
```

Figure 23-10 shows the interface for this application.

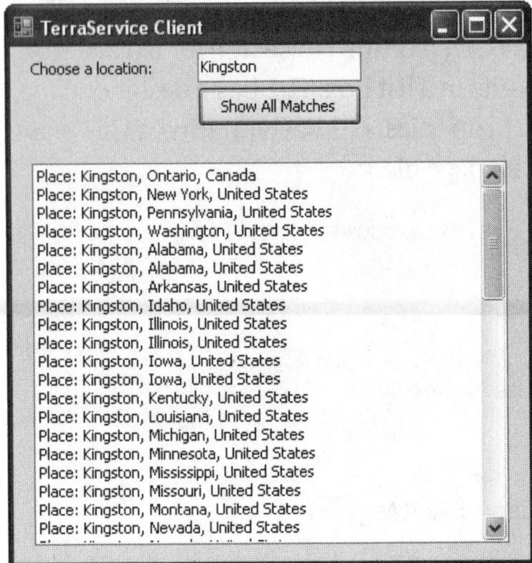

Figure 23-10. *A Windows client for TerraService*

Of course, Windows development contains many other possibilities, which are covered in many other excellent books. The interesting part from your vantage point is that a Windows client can interact with a web service just like an ASP.NET application does. This raises a world of new possibilities for integrated Windows and web applications.

The Last Word

This chapter explored some more ideas for developing your web services. You took an in-depth look at web service security and considered when (and if) it makes sense to use session state and transactions in a web service.

To keep learning about web services, it helps to look at examples on the Web, such as TerraService. For even more experimentation, consider some of the following web services:

- XMethods (`http://www.xmethods.com`) is a more general web service catalog. It includes many web services you can use in .NET applications, such as a currency exchange reporter and a delayed stock quote. Even though most of these web services run on non-.NET platforms, you can use them in your .NET applications seamlessly.

- Microsoft's MapPoint (`http://msdn.microsoft.com/library/en-us/dnanchor/html/anch_mappointmain.asp`) is an interesting example that enables you to access high-quality maps and geographical information. MapPoint isn't free, but you can use a free trial of the web service.

PART 6

Advanced ASP.NET

CHAPTER 24

Component-Based Programming

Component-based programming is a simple, elegant idea. When used properly, it allows your code to be more organized, consistent, and reusable. It's also incredibly easy to implement in a .NET application, because you never need to use the Windows registry or perform any special configuration.

A component, at its simplest, is one or more classes that are compiled into a separate DLL assembly file. These classes provide some unit of logically related functionality. You can access a component in a single application, or you can share the component between multiple applications. Your web pages (or any other .NET application) can use the classes in your components in the same way they use any other .NET class. Best of all, your component provides exactly the features your code requires and hides all the other messy details.

When combined with careful organization, component-based programming is the basis of good ASP.NET application design. In this chapter, you'll examine how you can create components (and why you should) and consider examples that show you how to encapsulate database functionality with a well-written business object. You'll also learn how to bind your database component to the web controls on a page using the ObjectDataSource.

Why Use Components?

To master ASP.NET development, you need to become a skilled user of the .NET class library. So far, you've learned how to use .NET components designed for storing user sessions, reading files, and interacting with databases. Though these class library ingredients are powerful, they aren't customizable, which is both an advantage and a weakness.

For example, if you want to retrieve data from a SQL Server database, you need to weave database details (such as SQL queries) directly into your code-behind class or (if you're using the SqlDataSource) into the .aspx markup portion of your web page file. Either way if the structure of the database changes even slightly, you could be left with dozens of pages to update and retest. To solve these problems, you need to create an extra layer between your web page code and the database. This extra layer takes the form of a custom component.

This database scenario is only one of the reasons you might want to create your own components. Component-based programming is really just a logical extension of good code-organizing principles, and it offers a long list of advantages:

Safety: Because the source code isn't contained in your web page, you can't modify it. Instead, you're limited to the functionality your component provides. For example, you could configure a database component to allow only certain operations with specific tables, fields, or rows. This is often easier than setting up complex permissions in the database. Because the application has to go through the component, it needs to play by its rules.

Better organization: Components move the clutter out of your web page code. It also becomes easier for other programmers to understand your application's logic when it's broken down into separate components. Without components, commonly used code has to be copied and pasted throughout an application, making it extremely difficult to change and synchronize.

Easier troubleshooting: It's impossible to oversell the advantage of components when testing and debugging an application. Component-based programs are broken down into smaller, tighter blocks of code, making it easier to isolate exactly where a problem is occurring.

More manageability: Component-based programs are much easier to enhance and modify because the component and web application code can be modified separately. That means you don't necessarily have to recompile your web application to use an updated data access routine.

Code reuse: Components can be shared with any ASP.NET application that needs the component's functionality. Even better, any .NET application can use a component, meaning you could create a common "backbone" of logic that's used by a web application and an ordinary Windows application.

Simplicity: Components can provide multiple related tasks for a single client request (writing several records to a database, opening and reading a file in one step, or even starting and managing a database transaction). Similarly, components hide details—an application programmer can use a database component without worrying about the database name, the location of the server, or the user account needed to connect. Even better, you can perform a search using certain criteria, and the component itself can decide whether to use a dynamically generated SQL statement or stored procedure.

Performance: If you need to perform a long, time-consuming operation, you can create a component that works asynchronously. That allows you to perform other tasks with the web page code and return to pick up the result later.

■ **Note** Some of these advantages are possible just by using separate classes in your web application. However, separate components offer a higher level of code separation and reuse, including the ability to manage and compile different code units separately and even write them in different .NET languages.

Component Jargon

Component-based programming is sometimes shrouded in a fog of specialized jargon. Understanding these terms helps sort out exactly what a component is supposed to do, and it also allows you to understand MSDN articles about application design. If you're already familiar with the fundamentals of components, feel free to skip ahead.

Three-Tier Design

The idea of *three-tier* design is that the functionality of most complete applications can be divided into three main levels (see Figure 24-1). The first level is the user interface (or presentation tier), which displays controls and receives and validates user input. All the event handlers in your web page are in this first level. The second level is the business tier, where the application-specific logic takes place. For an e-commerce site, application-specific logic includes rules such as how shipping charges are applied to an order, when certain promotions are valid, and what customer actions should be logged. It doesn't involve generic .NET details such as how to open a file or connect to a database. The third level is the data tier, where the application's information is stored in files or a database. The third level contains logic about how to retrieve and update data, such as SQL queries or stored procedures.

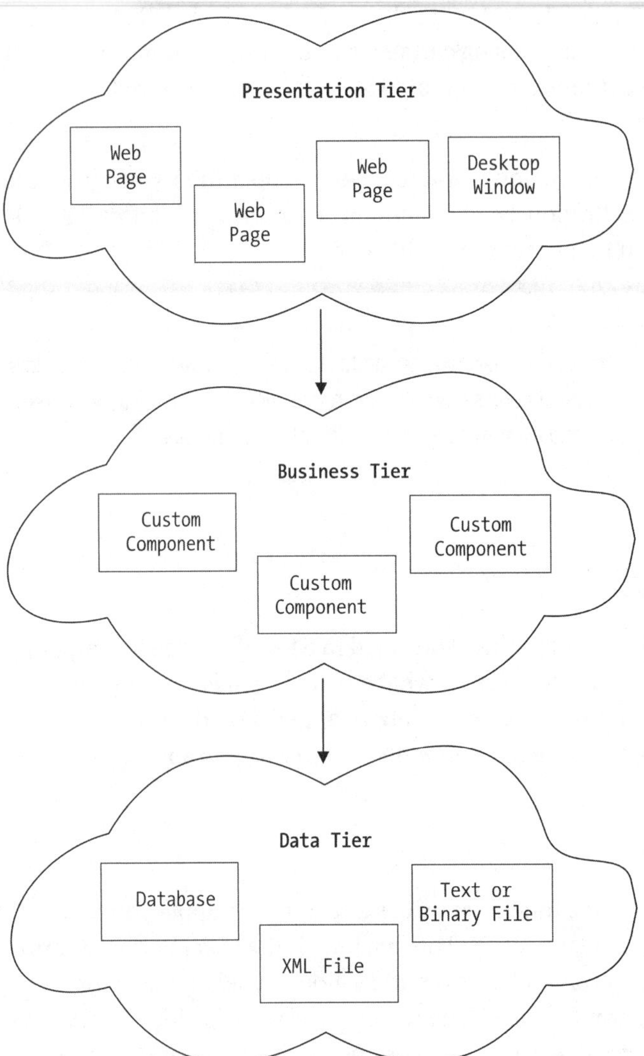

Figure 24-1. *Three-tier design*

The important detail about three-tier design is that information travels from only one level to an adjacent level. In other words, your user interface code shouldn't try to directly access the database and retrieve information. Instead, it should go through the second level and then arrive at the database.

This basic organization principle can't always be adhered to, but it's a good model to follow. When you create a component it's almost always used in the second level to bridge the gap between the data and the user interface. In other words, if you want to fill a list of product categories in a list box, your user interface code calls a component, which gets the list from the database and then returns it to your code. Your web page code is isolated from the database—and if the database structure changes, you need to change one concise component instead of every page on your site.

Encapsulation

If three-tier design is the overall goal of component-based programming, *encapsulation* is the best rule of thumb. Encapsulation is the principle that you should create your application out of "black boxes" that hide information. So, if you have a component that logs a purchase on an e-commerce site, that component handles all the details and allows only the essential variables to be specified.

For example, this component might accept a user ID and an order item ID and then handle all the other details. The calling code doesn't need to worry about how the component works or where the data is coming from—it just needs to understand how to use the component. (This principle is described in a lot of picturesque ways. For example, you know how to drive a car because you understand its component interface—the steering wheel and pedals—not because you understand the low-level details about internal combustion and the engine. As a result, you're able to transfer your knowledge to many different types of automobiles, even if they have dramatically different internal workings.)

Data Objects

Data objects are used in a variety of ways. In this book, the term refers to a custom object that you make that represents a certain grouping of data. For example, you could create a Person class that has properties such as Height, Age, and EyeColor. Your code can then create data objects based on this class. You might want to use a data object to pass information from one portion of code to another. (Note that data objects are sometimes used to describe objects that handle data management. This isn't the way you'll see me use them in this book.)

Business Objects

The term *business object* often means different things to different people. Generally, business objects are the components in the second level of your application that provide the extra layer between your code and the data source. They are called business objects because they enforce *business rules*. For example, if you try to submit a purchase order without any items, the appropriate business object would throw an exception and refuse to continue. In this case, no .NET error has occurred—instead, you've detected the presence of a condition that shouldn't be allowed according to your application's logic.

WEB SERVICES VS. COMPONENTS

Web services provide some of the same opportunities for code reuse as custom components. However, web services are primarily designed as an easy way to share functionality across different computers and platforms. A component, on the other hand, isn't nearly as easy to share with the wide world of the Internet, but it is far more efficient for sharing internally (for example, between different applications in the same company or different websites on the same server). For that reason, web services and components don't directly compete—in fact, a web service could even use a component (or vice versa). In some cases, you might find yourself programming a site with a mixture of the two, putting the code that needs to be reused in-house into components and putting the functionality that needs to be made publicly available into web services.

In this chapter's examples, business objects are also going to contain data access code. In an extremely complicated, large, and changeable system, you might want to further subdivide components and actually have your user interface code talking to a business object, which in turn talks to a data object that interacts with the data source. However, for most programmers, this extra step is overkill, especially with the increased level of consistency ADO.NET provides.

Creating a Simple Component

Technically, a component is just a collection of one or more classes that are compiled together as a unit. For example, Microsoft's System.Web.dll is a single (but very large) component that provides the objects found in many of the System.Web namespaces.

So far, the code examples in this book have used only a few types of classes—mainly custom web page classes that inherit from System.Web.UI.Page and contain mostly event handling procedures. Component classes, on the other hand, usually won't include any user interface logic (which would limit their use unnecessarily) and don't need to inherit from an existing class. They are more similar to the custom web service classes described in Part 4 of this book, which collect related features together in a series of utility methods.

The Component Class

To create a component, you create a new class library project in Visual Studio. Just select File ➤ New Project, and choose the Class Library project template in the Add New Project dialog box (see Figure 24-2). You'll need to choose a file location and project name.

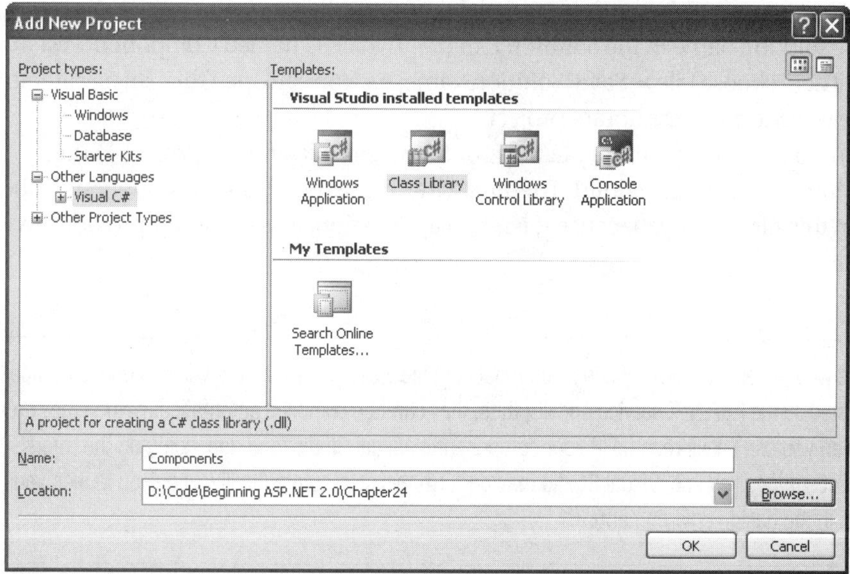

Figure 24-2. *Creating a component in Visual Studio*

Rather than just choosing File ➤ New Project to create the class library, you can add it to the same solution as your website. This makes it easy to debug the code in your component while you're testing it with a web page. (On its own, there's no way to run a component, so there's no way to test it.) To create a new class library in an existing web solution, start by opening your website, and then choose File ➤ Add ➤ New Project. Specify the directory and project name in the Add New Project dialog box.

Figure 24-3 shows a solution with both a website and a class library named Components. The website is in bold in the Solution Explorer to indicate that it runs on start-up (when you click the Start button).

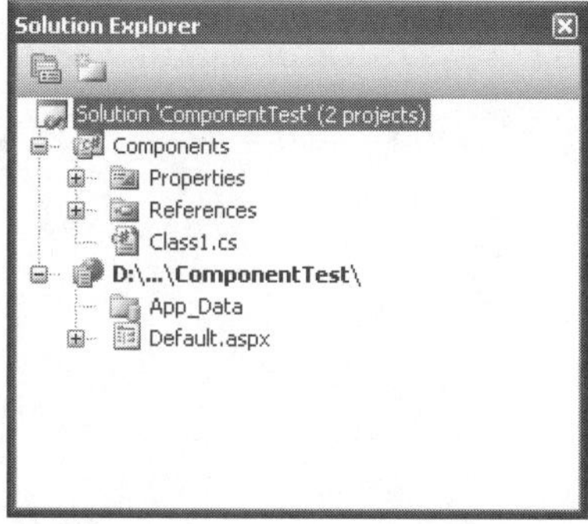

Figure 24-3. *A solution with a website and class library project*

To make it easy to open this solution, you might want to take a moment to save your solution. Click the solution name in the Solution Explorer (which is named ComponentTest in Figure 24-3). Then, choose File ➤ Save [SolutionName] As. You can open this .sln file later to load both the website and class library project.

You can compile your class library at any point by right-clicking the project in the Solution Explorer and choosing Build. This creates a DLL assembly file (Components.dll). You can't run this file directly, because it isn't an application, and it doesn't provide any user interface.

■ **Note** Unlike web pages and web services, you must compile a component before you can use it. Components aren't hosted by the ASP.NET service and IIS; thus, they can't be compiled automatically when they are needed. However, you can easily recompile your component in Visual Studio (and depending on the references and project settings you use, Visual Studio may perform this step automatically when you launch your web application in the design environment).

Classes and Namespaces

Once you've created your class library project, you're ready to add a class in a .cs file. Here's an example that creates a class named SimpleTest:

```
public class SimpleTest
{
    // (Code goes here, inside one or more methods.)
}
```

Remember, a component can contain more than one class. You can create these other classes in the same file, or you can use separate files for better organization. In either case, all the classes and source code files are compiled together into one assembly:

```
public class SimpleTest
{ ... }

public class SimpleTest2
{ ... }
```

To add functionality to your class, add public methods or properties. The web page code calls these methods to retrieve information or perform a task. The following example shows one of the simplest possible components, which does nothing more than return a string to the calling code:

```
public class SimpleTest
{
    public string GetInfo(string param)
    {
        return "You invoked SimpleTest.GetInfo() with '" +
              param + "'";
    }
}

public class SimpleTest2
{
    public string GetInfo(string param)
    {
        return "You invoked SimpleTest2.GetInfo() with '" +
              param + "'";
    }
}
```

Usually, these classes are organized in a namespace. In the following example, the classes are accessed in other applications such as Components.SimpleTest and Components.SimpleTest2:

```
namespace Components
{
    public class SimpleTest
    {
        // (Class code omitted.)
    }

    public class SimpleTest2
    {
        // (Class code omitted.)
    }
}
```

If you need to do so, you can create multiple levels of nested namespaces. In Visual Studio, every time you add a new class file, your code is automatically placed in a namespace block with the default namespace for your project. You can then edit this namespace if you want, and you can even change the default project namespace. To do so, right-click the project in the Solution Explorer, and select Properties. Look for the Default Namespace text box. You can also use this window to configure the name that is given to the compiled assembly file (the assembly name).

■ **Tip** The general rule for naming namespaces is to use the company name followed by the technology name and optionally followed by a feature-specific division, as in CompanyName.TechnologyName.Feature. Example namespaces that follow this syntax include Microsoft.Media and Microsoft.Media.Audio. These namespace conventions dramatically reduce the possibility that more than one company might release components in the same namespaces, which would lead to naming conflicts. The only exception to the naming guidelines is in the base assemblies that are part of .NET. They use namespaces that begin with *System*.

Adding a Reference to the Component

Using the component in an actualASP.NET page is easy. Essentially, your website needs a copy of your component in its Bin directory. ASP.NET automatically monitors this directory and makes all of its classes available to any web page in the application. To create this copy, you use a Visual Studio feature called *project references*.

Here's how it works: First, select your website in the Solution Explorer. Then, select Website ➤ Add Reference from the menu. This brings you to the Add Reference dialog box. You can take two approaches here:

- If your class library project is in the same solution, use the Projects tab. This shows you a list of all the class library projects in your assembly (see Figure 24-4). Select the class library, and click OK.
- If your class library is in a different solution, or you have the compiled DLL file only (perhaps the component was created by another developer), use the Browse tab (see Figure 24-5). Browse through your directories until you find the DLL file, select it, and click OK.

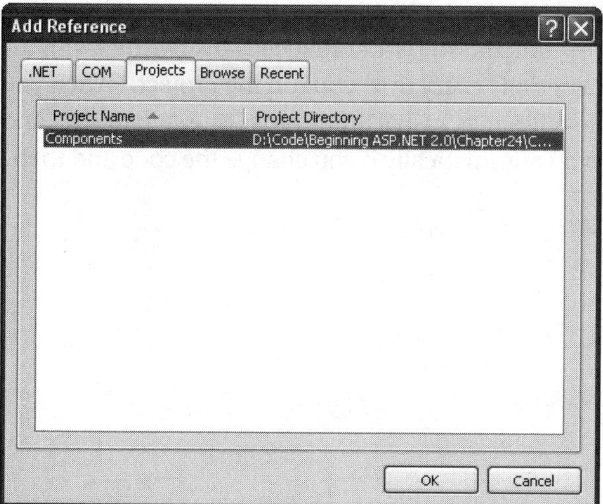

Figure 24-4. *Adding a project reference*

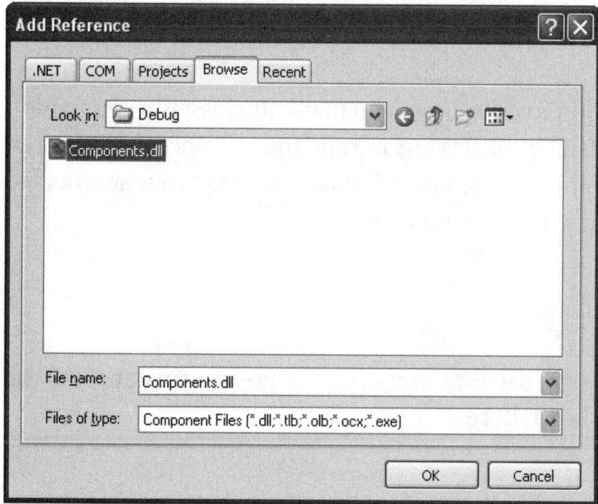

Figure 24-5. *Adding a file reference*

Either way, .NET copies the compiled DLL file to the Bin directory of your web application (see Figure 24-6). The nice feature is that this file is automatically overwritten with the most recent compiled version of the assembly every time you run the project. (When you use a project reference instead of a file reference, Visual Studio goes one step further and compiles the class library project for you automatically if you change the code and then run the web application that uses it.)

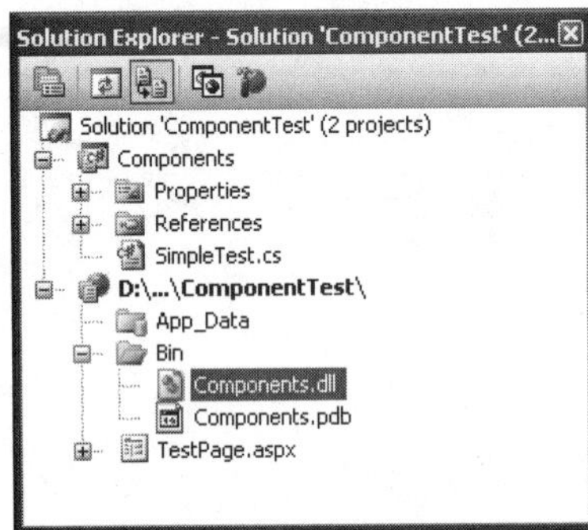

Figure 24-6. *A component in the Bin directory*

When you add a reference, Visual Studio also allows you to use its classes in your code with the usual syntax checking and IntelliSense. If you don't add the reference, you won't be able to use the component classes (and if you try, Visual Studio interprets your attempts to use the class as mistakes and refuses to compile your code).

Using the Component

Once you've added the reference, you can use the component by creating instances of the SimpleTest or SimpleTest2 class, as shown here:

```
using Components;

public partial class TestPage : Page
{
    protected void Page_Load(Object sender, EventArgs e)
    {
        SimpleTest testComponent = new SimpleTest();
        SimpleTest2 testComponent2 = new SimpleTest2();
        lblResult.Text = testComponent.GetInfo("Hello") + "<br><br>";
        lblResult.Text += testComponent2.GetInfo("Bye");
    }
}
```

The output for this page, shown in Figure 24-7, combines the return value from both GetInfo() methods.

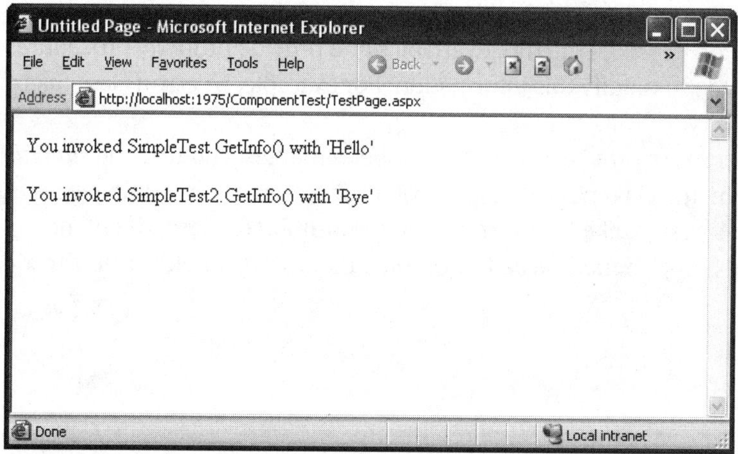

Figure 24-7. *The SimpleTest component output*

To make this code slightly simpler, you can choose to use static methods so that you don't need to create an object before using the method. A static GetInfo() method looks like this:

```
public class SimpleTest
{
    public static string GetInfo(string param)
    {
        return "You invoked SimpleTest.GetInfo() with '" +
               param + "'";
    }
}
```

In this case, the web page accesses the static GetInfo() method through the class name and doesn't need to create an object:

```
protected void Page_Load(Object sender, EventArgs e)
{
    lblResult.Text = SimpleTest.GetInfo("Hello");
}
```

Properties and State

The SimpleTest classes provide functionality through public methods. If you're familiar with class-based programming (as described in Chapter 4), you'll remember that classes can also store information in private member variables and provide property procedures that allow the calling code to modify this information. For example, a Person class might have a FirstName property.

When you use properties to provide access to member variables, you're using *stateful design.* In stateful design, the class has the responsibility of maintaining certain pieces of information. In stateless design, like the one found in the SimpleTest component, no information is retained between method calls. Compare that to the stateful SimpleTest class shown here:

```
public class SimpleTest
{
    private string data;
    public string Data
    {
        get
        { return data; }
        set
        { data = value; }
    }

    public string GetInfo()
    {
        return "You invoked SimpleTest.GetInfo()," +
               "and data is '" + data + "'";
    }
}
```

In the programming world, great debates have occurred about whether stateful or stateless programming is best. Stateful programming is the most natural, object-oriented approach, but it also has a few disadvantages. To accomplish a common task, you might need to set several properties before calling a method. Each of these steps adds a little bit of unneeded overhead. A stateless design, on the other hand, often performs all its work in a single method call. However, because no information is retained in state, you may need to specify several parameters, which can make for tedious programming. A good example of stateful versus stateless objects is shown by the FileInfo and File classes, which are described in Chapter 17.

There is no short answer about whether stateful or stateless design is best, and it often depends on the task at hand. Components that are high-performance, components that use transactions, or components that need to be invoked remotely (such as web services) usually use stateless design, which is the simplest and most reliable approach. Because no information is retained in memory, fewer server resources are used, and no danger exists of losing valuable data if a software or hardware failure occurs. The next example illustrates the difference with two ways to design an Account class.

A Stateful Account Class

Consider a stateful account class that represents a single customer account. Information is read from the database when it's first created in the constructor method, and this information can be updated using the Update() method.

```
public class CustomerAccount
{
    private int accountNumber;
    private decimal balance;

    public decimal Balance
    {
        get
        { return balance; }
        set
        { balance = value; }
    }

    public CustomerAccount(int accountNumber)
    {
        // (Code to read account record from database goes here.)
    }

    public void Update()
    {
        // (Code to update database record goes here.)
    }
}
```

If you have two CustomerAccount objects that expose a Balance property, you need to perform two separate steps to transfer money from one account to another. Conceptually, the process works like this:

```
// Create an account object for each account,
// using the account number.
CustomerAccount accountOne = new CustomerAccount(122415);
CustomerAccount accountTwo = new CustomerAccount(123447);
decimal amount = 1000;

// Withdraw money from one account.
accountOne.Balance -= amount;

// Deposit money in the other account.
accountTwo.Balance += amount;

// Update the underlying database records using an Update method.
accountOne.Update();
accountTwo.Update();
```

The problem here is that if this task is interrupted halfway through by an error, you'll end up with at least one unhappy customer.

A Stateless AccountUtility Class

A stateless object, on the other hand, might expose only a static method called FundTransfer(), which performs all its work in one method:

```
public class AccountUtility
{
    public static void FundTransfer(int accountOne,
      int accountTwo, decimal amount)
    {
        // (The code here retrieves the two database records,
        //  changes them, and updates them.)
    }
}
```

The calling code can't use the same elegant CustomerAccount objects, but it can be assured that account transfers are protected from error. Because all the database operations are performed at once, they can use a database stored procedure for greater performance and can use a transaction to ensure that the withdrawal and deposit either succeed or fail as a whole:

```
// Set the account and transfer details.
decimal amount = 1000;
int accountIDOne = 122415;
int accountIDTwo = 123447;

AccountUtility.FundTransfer(accountIDOne, accountIDTwo,
  amount);
```

In a mission-critical system, transactions are often required. For that reason, classes that retain little state information are often the best design approach, even though they aren't quite as satisfying from an object-oriented perspective.

■ **Tip** There is one potential compromise. You can create stateful classes to represent common items such as accounts, customers, and so on, without adding *any* functionality. Then, you can use these classes as data packages to send information to and from a stateless utility class.

Database Components

Clearly, components are extremely useful. But if you're starting a large programming project, you may not be sure what features are the best candidates for being made into separate components. Learning how to break an application into components and classes is one of the great arts of programming, and it takes a good deal of practice and fine-tuning.

One of the most common types of components is a database component. Database components are an ideal application of component-based programming for several reasons:

Databases require extraneous details: These details include connection strings, field names, and so on, all of which can distract from the application logic and can easily be encapsulated by a well-written component.

Databases change frequently: Even if the underlying table structure remains constant and additional information is never required (which is far from certain), queries may be replaced by stored procedures, and stored procedures may be redesigned.

Databases have special connection requirements: You may even need to change the database access code for reasons unrelated to the application. For example, after profiling and testing a database, you might discover that you can replace a single query with two queries or a more efficient stored procedure. In either case, the returned data remains constant, but the data access code is dramatically different.

Databases are used repetitively in a finite set of ways: In other words, a common database routine should be written once and is certain to be used many times.

A Simple Database Component

To examine the best way to create a database component, you'll consider a simple application that provides a classifieds page that lists items that various individuals have for sale. The database uses two tables: one is an Items table that lists the description and price of a specific sale item, and the other is a Categories table that lists the different groups you can use to categorize an item. Figure 24-8 shows the relationship.

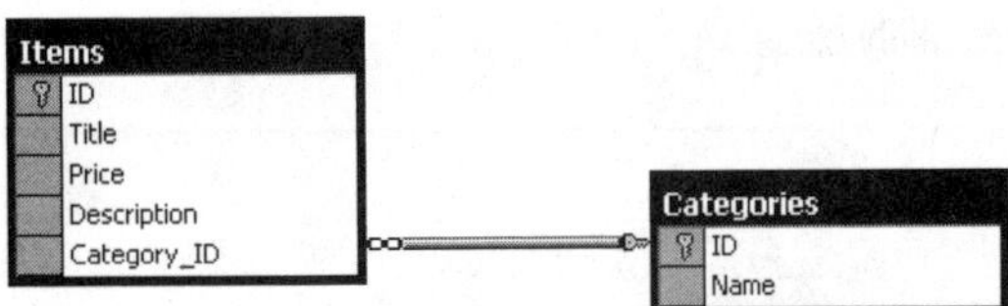

Figure 24-8. *The AdBoard database relationships*

In this example, you're connecting with a SQL Server database using the OLE DB part of the class library. You can create this database yourself, or you can refer to the online samples, which include a SQL script that generates it automatically. To start, the Categories table is preloaded with a standard set of allowed categories.

The database component is simple. It's an instance class that retains some basic information (such as the connection string to use), but it doesn't allow the client to change this information. Therefore, it doesn't need any property procedures. Instead, it performs most of its work in methods such as GetCategories() and GetItems(). These methods return DataSets with the appropriate database records. This type of design creates a fairly thin layer over the database—it handles some details, but the client is still responsible for working with familiar ADO.NET classes such as the DataSet.

```
using System;
using System.Data;
using System.Data.SqlClient;
using System.Web.Configuration;
```

```
namespace DatabaseComponent
{
    public class DBUtil
    {
        private string connectionString;

        public DBUtil()
        {
            connectionString =
              WebConfigurationManager.ConnectionStrings[
              "AdBoard"].ConnectionString;
        }

        public DataSet GetCategories()
        {
            string query = "SELECT * FROM Categories";
            SqlCommand cmd = new SqlCommand(query);
            return FillDataSet(cmd, "Categories");
        }

        public DataSet GetItems()
        {
            string query = "SELECT * FROM Items";
            SqlCommand cmd = new SqlCommand(query);
            return FillDataSet(cmd, "Items");
        }

        public DataSet GetItems(int categoryID)
        {
            // Create the Command.
            string query = "SELECT * FROM Items WHERE Category_ID=@CategoryID";
            SqlCommand cmd = new SqlCommand(query);
            cmd.Parameters.AddWithValue("@CategoryID", categoryID);

            // Fill the DataSet.
            return FillDataSet(cmd, "Items");
        }

        public void AddCategory(string name)
        {
            SqlConnection con = new SqlConnection(connectionString);
```

```
        // Create the Command.
        string insertSQL = "INSERT INTO Categories ";
        insertSQL += "(Name) VALUES @Name";
        SqlCommand cmd = new SqlCommand(insertSQL, con);
        cmd.Parameters.AddWithValue("@Name", "name");

        try
        {
            con.Open();
            cmd.ExecuteNonQuery();
        }
        finally
        {
            con.Close();
        }
    }

    public void AddItem(string title, string description,
                        decimal price, int categoryID)
    {
        SqlConnection con = new SqlConnection(connectionString);

        // Create the Command.
        string insertSQL = "INSERT INTO Items ";
        insertSQL += "(Title, Description, Price, Category_ID)";
        insertSQL += "VALUES (@Title, @Description, @Price, @CategoryID)";
        SqlCommand cmd = new SqlCommand(insertSQL, con);
        cmd.Parameters.AddWithValue("@Title", title);
        cmd.Parameters.AddWithValue("@Description", description);
        cmd.Parameters.AddWithValue("@Price", price);
        cmd.Parameters.AddWithValue("@CategoryID", categoryID);

        try
        {
            con.Open();
            cmd.ExecuteNonQuery();
        }
        finally
        {
            con.Close();
        }
    }
```

```
        private DataSet FillDataSet(SqlCommand cmd, string tableName)
        {
            SqlConnection con = new SqlConnection(connectionString);
            cmd.Connection = con;
            SqlDataAdapter adapter = new SqlDataAdapter(cmd);

            DataSet ds = new DataSet();
            try
            {
                con.Open();
                adapter.Fill(ds, tableName);
            }
            finally
            {
                con.Close();
            }
            return ds;
        }
    }
}
```

Dissecting the Code...

- This code automatically retrieves the connection string from the web.config file when the class is created, as described in Chapter 5. This trick enhances encapsulation, but if the client web application doesn't have the appropriate setting, the component doesn't work.

- This class uses an overloaded GetItems() method. This means the client can call GetItems() with no parameters to return the full list or with a parameter indicating the appropriate category. (Chapter 3 provides an introduction to overloaded functions.)

- Each method that accesses the database opens and closes the connection. This is a far better approach than trying to hold a connection open over the lifetime of the class, which is sure to result in performance degradation in multiuser scenarios.

- The code uses its own private FillDataSet() function to make the code more concise. This isn't made available to clients. Instead, the GetItems() and GetCategories() methods use the FillDataSet() function.

■ **Note** To use this example as written, you need to add a reference to the System.Configuration and System.Web assemblies in the class library. Otherwise, you can't use the WebConfigurationManager to dig up the connection string you need. To add this reference, select Project ➤ Add Reference, and look in the .NET tab.

Consuming the Database Component

To use this component in a web application, you first have to make sure the appropriate connection string is configured in the web.config file, as shown here:

```
<?xml version="1.0" encoding="utf-8" ?>
<configuration>

  <connectionStrings>
    <add name="AdBoard" connectionString=
"Data Source=localhost;Initial Catalog=AdBoard;Integrated Security=SSPI" />
  </connectionStrings>
  ...
</configuration>
```

Next, compile and copy the component DLL file, or add a reference to it if you're using Visual Studio. The only remaining task is to add the user interface.

To test this component, you can create a simple test page. In the example shown in Figure 24-9, this page allows users to browse the current listing by category and add new items. When the user first visits the page, it prompts the user to select a category.

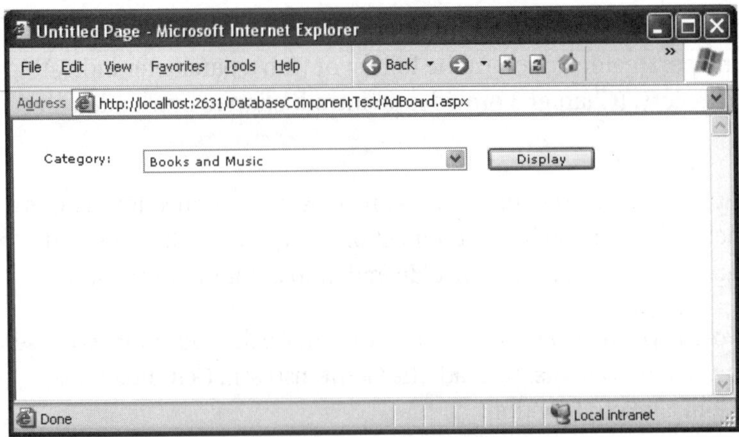

Figure 24-9. *The AdBoard categories*

Once a category is chosen, the matching items display, and a panel of controls appears, which allows the user to add a new entry to the AdBoard under the current category, as shown in Figure 24-10.

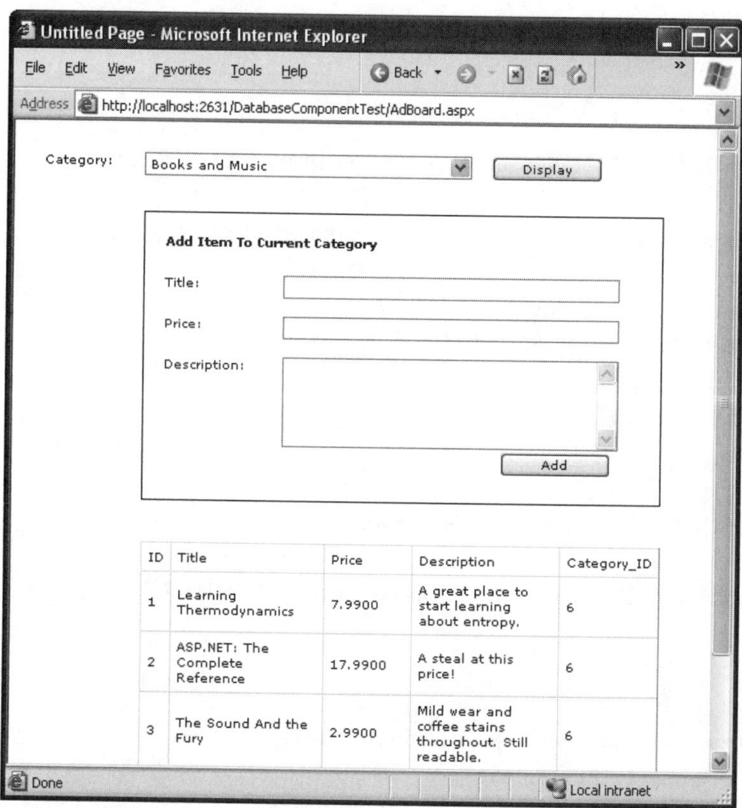

Figure 24-10. *The AdBoard listing*

The page code creates the component to retrieve information from the database and displays it by binding the DataSet to the drop-down list or GridView control:

```
public partial class AdBoard : Page
{
    protected void Page_Load(Object sender, EventArgs e)
    {
        if (!this.IsPostBack)
        {
            DatabaseComponent.DBUtil DB = new DatabaseComponent.DBUtil();
```

```
            lstCategories.DataSource = DB.GetCategories();
            lstCategories.DataTextField = "Name";
            lstCategories.DataValueField = "ID";
            lstCategories.DataBind();
            pnlNew.Visible = false;
        }
    }

    protected void cmdDisplay_Click(Object sender, EventArgs e)
    {
        DatabaseComponent.DBUtil DB = new DatabaseComponent.DBUtil();

        gridItems.DataSource = DB.GetItems(
          Int32.Parse(lstCategories.SelectedItem.Value));
        gridItems.DataBind();
        pnlNew.Visible = true;
    }

    protected void cmdAdd_Click(Object sender, EventArgs e)
    {
        DatabaseComponent.DBUtil DB = new DatabaseComponent.DBUtil();

        try
        {
            DB.AddItem(txtTitle.Text, txtDescription.Text,
              Decimal.Parse(txtPrice.Text),
              Int32.Parse(lstCategories.SelectedItem.Value));

            gridItems.DataSource = DB.GetItems(
              Int32.Parse(lstCategories.SelectedItem.Value));
            gridItems.DataBind();
        }
        catch (FormatException err)
        {
            // An error occurs if the user has entered an
            // invalid price (non-numeric characters).
            // In this case, take no action.
            // Another option is to add a validator control
            // for the price text box to prevent invalid input.
        }
    }
}
```

Dissecting the Code...

- Not all the functionality of the component is used in this page. For example, the page doesn't use the AddCategory() method or the version of GetItems() that doesn't require a category number. This is completely normal. Other pages may use different features from the component.
- The page is free of data access code. It does, however, need to understand how to use a DataSet, and it needs to know specific field names to create a more attractive GridView with custom templates for layout (instead of automatically generated columns).
- The page could be improved with error handling code or validation controls. As it is, no validation is performed to ensure that the price is numeric or even to ensure that the required values are supplied.

Enhancing the Component with Error Handling

One way you could enhance the component is with better support for error reporting. As it is, any database errors that occur are immediately returned to the calling code. In some cases (for example, if there is a legitimate database problem), this is a reasonable approach, because the component can't handle the problem.

However, the component fails to handle one common problem properly. This problem occurs if the connection string isn't found in the web.config file. Though the component tries to read the connection string as soon as it's created, the calling code doesn't realize a problem exists until it tries to use a database method.

A better approach is to notify the client as soon as the problem is detected, as shown in the following code example:

```
public class DBUtil
{
    private string connectionString;

    public DBUtil()
    {
        if (WebConfigurationManager.ConnectionStrings["AdBoard"] == null)
        {
            throw new ApplicationException(
              "Missing ConnectionString variable in web.config.");
        }
        else
```

```
            {
                connectionString =
                  WebConfigurationManager.ConnectionStrings[
                  "AdBoard"].ConnectionString;
            }
        }

        // (Other class code omitted.)
}
```

This code throws an ApplicationException with a custom error message that indicates the problem. To provide even better reporting, you could create your own exception class that inherits from ApplicationException, as described in Chapter 11.

■ Tip If you're debugging your code in Visual Studio, you'll find you can single-step from your web page code right into the code for the component, even if it isn't a part of the same solution. The appropriate source code file is loaded into your editor automatically, as long as it's available (and you've compiled the component in debug mode).

Enhancing the Component with Aggregate Information

The component doesn't have to limit the type of information it provides to DataSets. Other information is also useful. For example, you might provide a read-only property called ItemFields that returns an array of strings representing the names for fields in the Items table. Or you might add another method that retrieves aggregate information about the entire table, such as the average cost of an item or the total number of currently listed items, as shown here:

```
public class DBUtil
{
    // (Other class code omitted.)

    public decimal GetAveragePrice()
    {
        string query = "SELECT AVG(Price) FROM Items";
```

```
        SqlConnection con = new SqlConnection(connectionString);
        SqlCommand cmd = new SqlCommand(query, con);

        con.Open();
        decimal average = (decimal)cmd.ExecuteScalar();
        con.Close();

        return average;
    }

    public int GetTotalItems()
    {
        string query = "SELECT Count(*) FROM Items";

        SqlConnection con = new SqlConnection(connectionString);
        SqlCommand cmd = new SqlCommand(query, con);

        con.Open();
        int count = (int)cmd.ExecuteScalar();
        con.Close();

        return count;
    }
}
```

These commands use some customized SQL that may be new to you (namely, the Count and AVG functions). However, these methods are just as easy to use from the client's perspective as GetItems() and GetCategories():

```
DatabaseComponent.DBUtil DB = new DatabaseComponent.DBUtil();
decimal averagePrice = DB.GetAveragePrice();
int totalItems = DB.GetTotalItems();
```

It may have occurred to you that you can return information such as the total number of items through a read-only property procedure (such as TotalItems) instead of a method (in this case, GetTotalItems). Though this does work, property procedures are better left to information that is maintained with the class (in a private variable) or is easy to reconstruct. In this case, it takes a database operation to count the number of rows, and this database operation can cause an unusual problem or slow down performance if used frequently. To help reinforce that fact, a method is used instead of a property.

The ObjectDataSource

Using a dedicated database component is a great way to keep your code efficient and well organized. It also makes it easy for you to apply changes later. However, this has a drawback—namely, you need to write quite a bit of code to create a web page *and* a separate database component. In Chapter 14, you saw that you could simplify your life by using components such as the SqlDataSource to encapsulate all your data access details. Unfortunately, that code-free approach won't work if you're using a separate component—or will it?

It turns out there is a way to get the best of both worlds and use a separate database component and easier web page data binding. Instead of using the SqlDataSource, you use the ObjectDataSource, which defines a link between your web page and your component. This won't save you from writing the actual data access code in your component, but it will save you from writing the tedious code in your web page to call the methods in your component, extract the data, format it, and display it in the page.

■ **Note** The ObjectDataSource allows you to create code-free web pages, but you still need to write the code in your component. You shouldn't view this as a drawback—after all, you need to write this code to get fine-grained control over exactly what's taking place and thereby optimize the performance of your data access strategy.

In the following sections, you'll learn how to take the existing DBUtil component presented earlier and use it in a data-bound web page. You'll learn how to replicate the example shown in Figure 24-9 and Figure 24-10 without writing any web page code.

Making Classes the Object Data Source Can Understand

Essentially, the ObjectDataSource allows you to create a declarative link between your web page controls and a data access component that queries and updates data. Although the ObjectDataSource is remarkably flexible, it can't support every conceivable component you could create. In fact, for your data component to be usable with the ObjectDataSource, you need to conform to a few rules:

- Your class must be stateless. That's because the ObjectDataSource will create an instance only when needed and destroy it at the end of every request.
- Your class must have a default, no-argument constructor.

- All the logic must be contained in a single class. (If you want to use different classes for selecting and updating your data, you'll need to wrap them in another higher-level class.)
- Your class must provide the query results when a single method is called.
- None of the methods you want to use can be static.
- The query results must be provided as a DataSet, DataTable, or some sort of collection of objects. (If you decide to use a collection of objects, each data object needs to expose all the data fields as public properties.)

Fortunately, many of these rules are best practices that you should be already following. Even though the DBUtil class wasn't expressly designed for the ObjectDataSource, it meets all these criteria.

Selecting Records

You can learn a lot about the ObjectDataSource by building the page shown in Figure 21-10. In the following sections, you'll tackle this challenge.

The first step is to create the list box with the list of categories. For this list, you need an ObjectDataSource that links to the DBUtil class and calls the GetCategories() method to retrieve the full list of category records.

The first step is to define the ObjectDataSource and indicate the name of the class that contains the data access methods. You do this by specifying the fully qualified class name with the TypeName property, as shown here:

```
<asp:ObjectDataSource ID="sourceCategories" runat="server"
 TypeName="DatabaseComponent.DBUtil" ... />
```

Once you've attached the ObjectDataSource to a class, the next step is to point it to the methods it can use to select and update records.

The ObjectDataSource defines SelectMethod, DeleteMethod, UpdateMethod, and InsertMethod properties that you use to link your data access class to various tasks. Each property takes the name of the method in the data access class. In this example, you simply need to enable querying, so you need to set the SelectMethod property so it calls the GetCategories() method:

```
<asp:ObjectDataSource ID="sourceCategories" runat="server"
 TypeName="DatabaseComponent.DBUtil" SelectMethod="GetCategories" />
```

Once you've set up the ObjectDataSource, you can bind your web page controls in the same way you do with the SqlDataSource. Here's the tag you need for the list box:

```
<asp:DropDownList ID="lstCategories" runat="server"
  DataSourceID="sourceCategories" DataTextField="Name" DataValueField="ID">
</asp:DropDownList>
```

This tag shows a list of category names (thanks to the DataTextField property) and also keeps track of the category ID (using the DataValueField property).

This example works fine so far. You can run the test web page and see the list of categories in the list box (as in Figure 24-9).

Using Method Parameters

The next step is to show the list of items in the current category in the GridView underneath. As with the SqlDataSource, the ObjectDataSource can be used only for a single query. That means you'll need to create a second ObjectDataSource that's able to retrieve the list of items by calling GetItems().

The trick here is that the GetItems() method requires a single parameter (named categoryID). That means you need to create an ObjectDataSource that includes a single parameter. You can use all the same types of parameters used with the SqlDataSource to get values from the query string, other controls, and so on. In this case, the category ID is provided by the SelectedValue property of the list box, so you can use a control parameter that points to this property.

Here's the ObjectDataSource definition you need:

```
<asp:ObjectDataSource ID="sourceItems" runat="server" SelectMethod="GetItems"
 TypeName="DatabaseComponent.DBUtil" >
  <SelectParameters>
      <asp:ControlParameter ControlID="lstCategories" Name="categoryID"
        PropertyName="SelectedValue" Type="Int32" />
  </SelectParameters>
</asp:ObjectDataSource>
```

Again, you use the DBUtil component, but this time it's the GetItems() method you need. Even though the GetItems() method has two methods (one that takes a categoryID parameter and one that doesn't), don't worry. The ObjectDataSource automatically uses the correct overload by looking at the parameters you've defined.

In this case, you use a single parameter that extracts the selected category ID from the list box and passes it to the GetItems() method. Notice that the name defined in the ControlParameter tag matches the parameter name of the GetItems() method. This is an absolute requirement. When the ObjectDataSource calls the method, it uses reflection to examine the method and find the corresponding method. If you have several parameters, you can put them in any order, as the ObjectDataSource will determine the order of arguments based on the order of the parameters as defined in the method. If the ObjectDataSource can't find the method, or the method has a different name, an exception is raised at this point.

■ **Tip** If you're ever in doubt what method is being called in your database component, place a breakpoint on the possible methods, and use Visual Studio's debugging features (as described in Chapter 4).

The final step is to link the GridView to the new ObjectDataSource using the DataSourceID. Here's the tag that does it:

```
<asp:GridView ID="GridView1" runat="server" DataSourceID="sourceItems"/>
```

This is all you need. You should keep the Display button, because it triggers a page postback and allows the ObjectDataSource to get to work. (If you don't want to use this button, set the AutoPostback property on the list box to true so it posts back whenever you change the selection.) You don't need to write any event handling code to react when the button is clicked. The queries are executed automatically, and the controls are bound automatically.

Updating Records

The final step is to provide a way for the user to add new items. The easiest way to make this possible is to use a rich data control that deals with individual records—either the DetailsView or the FormsView. The DetailsView is the simpler of the two, because it doesn't require a template. It's the one used in the following example.

Ideally, you'd define the DetailsView using a tag like this and let it generate all the fields it needs based on the bound data source:

```
<asp:DetailsView ID="DetailsView1" runat="server" DataSourceID="sourceItems"/>
```

Unfortunately, this won't work in this example. The problem is that this approach creates too many fields. In this example, you don't want the user to specify the item ID (that's set by the database automatically) or the category ID (that's based on the currently selected category). So neither of these details should appear. The only way to make sure this is the case is to turn off automatic field generation and define each field you want explicitly, as shown here:

```
<asp:DetailsView ID="DetailsView1" runat="server"
  DataSourceID="sourceItems" AutoGenerateRows="false">
  <Fields>
    <asp:BoundField DataField="Title" HeaderText="Title" />
    <asp:BoundField DataField="Price" HeaderText="Price"/>
```

```
    <asp:BoundField DataField="Description" HeaderText="Description" />
  </Fields>
</asp:DetailsView>
```

You need to make a couple of other changes. To allow inserting, you need to set the AutoGenerateInsertButton to true. This way, the DetailsView creates the links that allow you to start entering a new record and then insert it. At the same time, you can set the DefaultMode property to Insert. This way, the DetailsView is always in insert mode and is used exclusively for adding records (not displaying them), much like the non-data-bound page shown earlier.

```
<asp:DetailsView ID="DetailsView1" runat="server"
  DefaultMode="Insert" AutoGenerateInsertButton="True"
  DataSourceID="sourceItems" AutoGenerateRows="false">
  ...
</asp:DetailsView>
```

The ObjectDataSource provides the same type of support for updatable data binding as the SqlDataSource. The first step is to specify the UpdateMethod, which needs to be a public instance method in the same class:

```
<asp:ObjectDataSource ID="sourceEmployees" runat="server"
 TypeName="DatabaseComponent.DBUtil"
 SelectMethod="GetItems" UpdateMethod="AddItem" >
</asp:ObjectDataSource>
```

The challenge is in making sure the UpdateMethod has the right signature. As with the SqlDataSource, updates, inserts, and deletes automatically receive a collection of parameters from the linked data control. These parameters have the same names as the corresponding field names. So in this case, the fields are Title, Price, and Description, which exactly match the parameter names in the AddItem() method. (The capitalization is not the same, but the ObjectDataSource is not case-sensitive, so this isn't a problem.)

This still has a problem, however. When the user commits an edit, the GridView submits the three parameters you expect (Title, Price, and Description). However, the AddItem() method needs a *fourth* parameter—CategoryID. We've left that parameter out of the DetailsView fields, because you don't want the user to be able to set the category ID. However, you still need to supply it to the method.

So where can you get the current category ID from? The easiest choice is to extract it from the list box, just as you did for the GetItems() method. All you need to do is add a

ControlParameter tag that defines a parameter named CategoryID and binds it to the SelectedValue property of the list box. Here's the revised tag for the ObjectDataSource:

```
<asp:ObjectDataSource ID="sourceItems" runat="server" SelectMethod="GetItems"
 TypeName="DatabaseComponent.DBUtil" InsertMethod="AddItem" >
  <SelectParameters>
    ...
  </SelectParameters>
  <InsertParameters>
    <asp:ControlParameter ControlID="lstCategories" Name="categoryID"
     PropertyName="SelectedValue" Type="Int32" />
  </InsertParameters>
</asp:ObjectDataSource>
```

Now you have all the parameters you need—the three from the DetailsView and the one extra from the list box. When the user attempts to insert a new record, the ObjectDataSource collects these four parameters, makes sure they match the signature for the AddItem() method, puts them in order, and then calls the method.

Figure 24-11 shows an insert in progress.

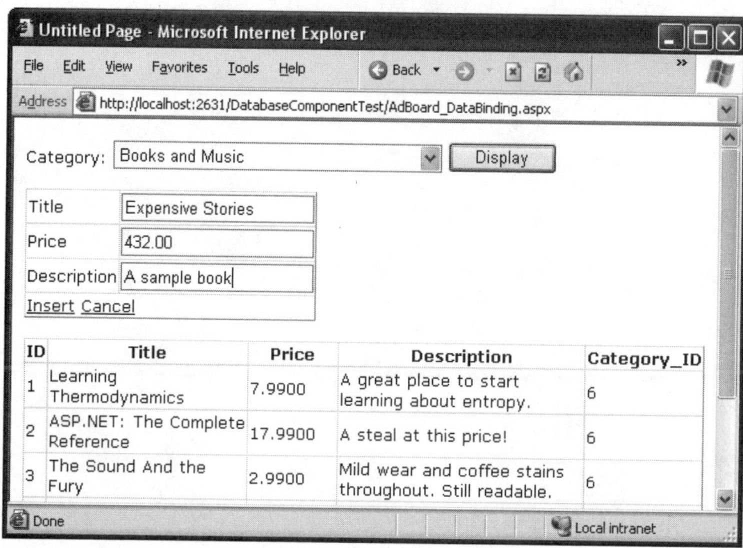

Figure 24-11. *Inserting with the DetailsView*

■ **Note** In some cases, you might need to supply an extra parameter that you need to set programmatically. In this case, you need to define a plain-vanilla Parameter tag (instead of a ControlParameter tag), with a name and data type but no value. Then, you can respond to the ObjectDataSource.Updating event to fill in the value you need just in time. It's a little messy (and it forces you to write code in your web page), but it's sometimes a necessity.

The Last Word

The components used in this chapter are business objects. They perform a service such as querying a database. Generally, business components return data but don't get involved in how this data is formatted or displayed to the user.

The next chapter shows how you can use the same component-oriented approach to reuse a user interface in multiple web pages with custom controls.

CHAPTER 25

Custom Controls

Component-based development encourages you to divide the logic in your application into discrete, independent blocks. Once you've made the jump to custom classes and objects, you can start creating modular web applications that are built with reusable units of code. But while these objects help work out thorny data access procedures or custom business logic, they don't offer much when it comes to simplifying your user interface code. If you want to create web applications that reuse a customized portion of user interface, you're still stuck rewriting control tags and reconfiguring page initialization code in several places.

It doesn't have to be this way. ASP.NET includes tools for modularizing and reusing portions of user interface code that are just as powerful as those that allow you to design custom business objects. You have two main tools at your fingertips, both of which you'll explore in this chapter:

- User controls allow you to reuse a portion of a page by placing it in a special .ascx file. ASP.NET also allows you to make smart user controls that provide methods and properties and configure their contained controls automatically.

- Custom-derived controls allow you to build a new control by inheriting from an ASP.NET control class. With custom controls, there is no limit to what you can do, whether it's adding a new property or tweaking the rendered HTML output.

User Controls

User controls look pretty much the same as ASP.NET web forms. Like web forms, they are composed of an HTML-like portion with control tags (the .ascx file) and can optionally use a .cs code-behind file with event handling logic. They can also include the same range of HTML content and ASP.NET controls, and they experience the same events as the Page object (such as Load and PreRender). The only differences between user controls and web pages are as follows:

- User controls begin with a <%@ Control %> directive instead of a <%@ Page %> directive.
- User controls use the file extension .ascx instead of .aspx, and their code-behind files inherit from the System.Web.UI.UserControl class. In fact, the UserControl class and the Page class both inherit from the same base classes, which is why they share so many of the same methods and events, as shown in the inheritance diagram in Figure 25-1.
- User controls can't be requested directly by a client. Instead, they are embedded inside other web pages.

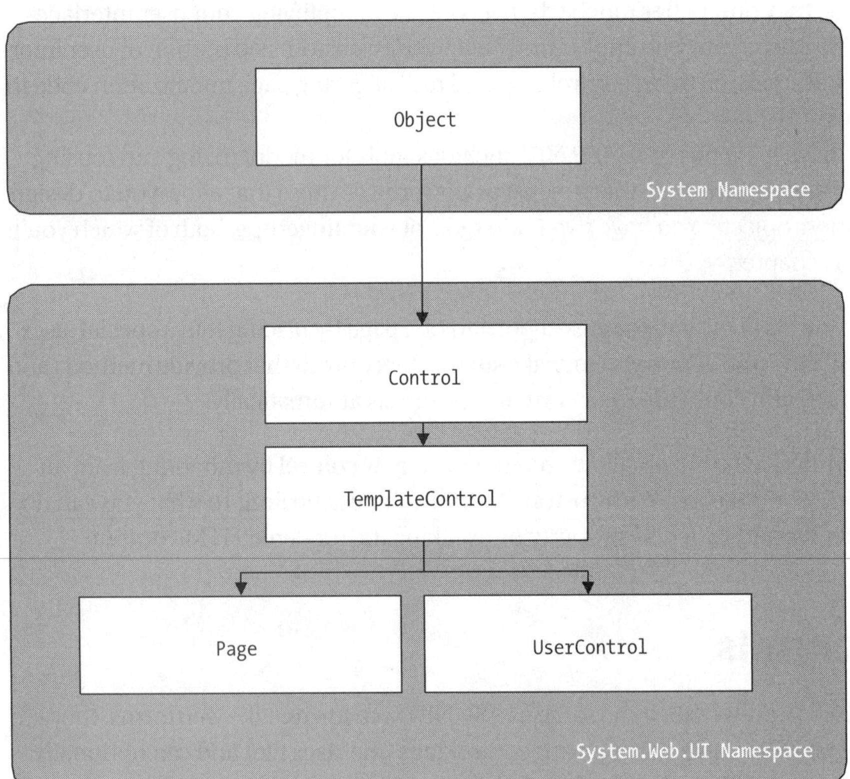

Figure 25-1. *The Page and UserControl inheritance chain*

Creating a Simple User Control

You can create a user control in Visual Studio in much the same way you add a web page. Just select Website ➤ Add New Item, and choose Web User Control from the list.

The following user control contains a single Label control:

```
<%@ Control Language="C#" AutoEventWireup="true"
    CodeFile="Footer.ascx.cs"  Inherits="Footer" %>


<asp:Label id="lblFooter" runat="server" />
```

Note that the Control directive uses the same attributes used in the Page directive for a web page, including Language, AutoEventWireup, and Inherits.

The code-behind class for this sample user control is similarly straightforward. It uses the UserControl.Load event to add some text to the label:

```
public partial class Footer : UserControl
{
    protected void Page_Load(Object sender, EventArgs e)
    {
        lblFooter.Text = "This page was served at ";
        lblFooter.Text += DateTime.Now.ToString();
    }
}
```

To test this user control, you need to insert it into a web page. This is a two-step process. First, you need to add a <%@ Register %> directive to identify the control you want to use and associate it with a unique control prefix:

```
<%@ Register TagPrefix="apress" TagName="Footer" Src="Footer.ascx" %>
```

The Register directive specifies a tag prefix and name. Tag prefixes group sets of related controls (for example, all ASP.NET web controls use the tag prefix *asp*). Tag prefixes are usually lowercase—technically, they are case-insensitive—and should be unique for your company or organization. The Src directive identifies the location of the user control template file, not the code-behind file.

Second, you can now add the user control whenever you want (and as many times as you want) by inserting its control tag. Consider this page example:

```
<%@ Page Language="C#" AutoEventWireup="true"
    CodeFile="FooterHost.aspx.cs" Inherits="FooterHost"%>
<%@ Register TagPrefix="apress" TagName="Footer" Src="Footer.ascx" %>
```

```
<html xmlns="http://www.w3.org/1999/xhtml" >
<head runat="server">
    <title>Footer Host</title>
</head>
<body>
    <form id="form1" runat="server">
    <div>
      <h1>A Page With a Footer</h1><hr />
      Static Page Text<br /><br />
      <apress:Footer id="Footer1" runat="server" />
    </div>
    </form>
</body>
</html>
```

This example (shown in Figure 25-2) demonstrates a simple way that you can create a header or footer and reuse it in all the pages in your website just by adding a user control. In the case of your simple footer, you won't save much code. However, this approach will become much more useful for a complex control with extensive formatting or several contained controls.

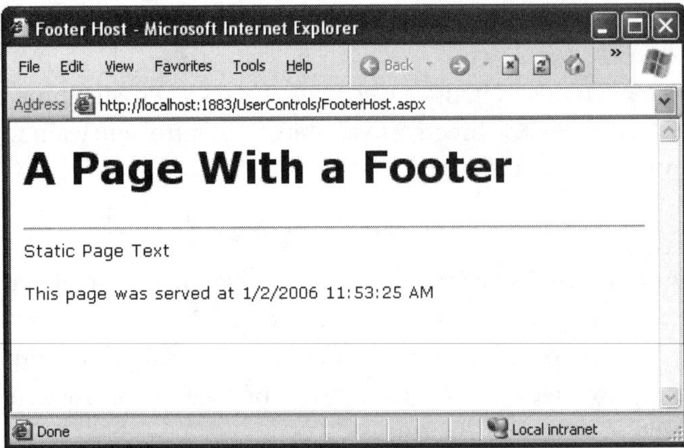

Figure 25-2. *A page with a user control footer*

Of course, this only scratches the surface of what you can do with a user control. In the following sections, you'll learn how to enhance a control with properties, methods, and events—transforming it from a simple "include file" into a full-fledged object.

■Note The Page class provides a special LoadControl() method that allows you to create a user control dynamically at runtime from an .ascx file. The user control is returned to you as a control object, which you can then add to the Controls collection of a container control on the web page (such as PlaceHolder or Panel) to display it on the page. This technique isn't a good substitute for declaratively using a user control, because it's more complex. However, it does have some interesting applications if you want to generate a user interface dynamically.

In Visual Studio, you have a few shortcuts available when working with user controls. Once you've created your user control, simply build your project, and then drag the .ascx file from the Solution Explorer and drop it onto the drawing area of a web form. Visual Studio automatically adds the Register directive for you, as well as an instance of the user control tag.

Independent User Controls

Conceptually, two types of user controls exist: independent and integrated. *Independent* user controls don't interact with the rest of the code on your form. The Footer user control is one such example. Another example might be a LinkMenu control that contains a list of buttons offering links to other pages. This LinkMenu user control can handle the events for all the buttons and then run the appropriate Response.Redirect() code to move to another web page. Or it can just be an ordinary HyperLink control that doesn't have any associated server-side code. Every page in the website can then include the same LinkMenu user control, enabling painless website navigation with no need to worry about frames.

The following sample defines a simple control that presents an attractively formatted list of links. Note that the style attribute of the <div> tag (which defines fonts and formatting) has been omitted for clarity.

```
<%@ Control Language="C#" AutoEventWireup="true"
    CodeFile="LinkMenu.ascx.cs" Inherits="LinkMenu" %>

<div>
  Products:
  <asp:HyperLink id="lnkBooks" runat="server"
    NavigateUrl="MenuHost.aspx?product=Books">Books
  </asp:HyperLink><br />
  <asp:HyperLink id="lnkToys" runat="server"
    NavigateUrl="MenuHost.aspx?product=Toys">Toys
  </asp:HyperLink><br />
```

```
  <asp:HyperLink id="lnkSports" runat="server"
    NavigateUrl="MenuHost.aspx?product=Sports">Sports
  </asp:HyperLink><br />
  <asp:HyperLink id="lnkFurniture" runat="server"
    NavigateUrl="MenuHost.aspx?product=Furniture">Furniture
  </asp:HyperLink>
</div>
```

The links don't actually trigger any server-side code—instead, they render themselves as ordinary HTML anchor tags with a hard-coded URL.

To test this menu, you can use the following MenuHost.aspx web page. It includes two controls: the Menu control and a Label control that displays the product query string parameter. Both are positioned using a table.

```
<%@ Page Language="C#" AutoEventWireup="true"
    CodeFile="MenuHost.aspx.cs" Inherits="MenuHost"%>
<%@ Register TagPrefix="apress" TagName="LinkMenu" Src="LinkMenu.ascx" %>

<html xmlns="http://www.w3.org/1999/xhtml" >
<head runat="server">
    <title>Menu Host</title>
</head>
<body>
    <form id="form1" runat="server">
    <div>
      <table>
        <tr>
          <td><apress:LinkMenu id="Menu1" runat="server" /></td>
        </tr>
        <tr>
          <td><asp:Label id="lblSelection" runat="server" /></td>
        </tr>
      </table>
    </div>
    </form>
</body>
</html>
```

When the MenuHost.aspx page loads, it adds the appropriate information to the lblSelection control:

```
protected void Page_Load(Object sender, EventArgs e)
{
    if (Request.Params["product"] != null)
    {
        lblSelection.Text = "You chose: ";
        lblSelection.Text += Request.Params["product"];
    }
}
```

Figure 25-3 shows the end result. Whenever you click a button, the page is posted back, and the text is updated.

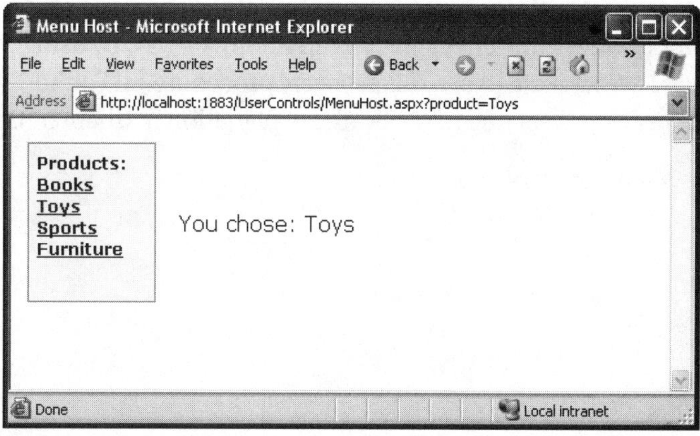

Figure 25-3. *The LinkMenu user control*

You could use the LinkMenu control to repeat the same menu on several pages. This is particularly handy in a situation where you can't use master pages to standardize layout (possibly because the pages are too different).

Integrated User Controls

Integrated user controls interact with the web page that hosts them in one way or another. When you're designing these controls, the class-based design tips you learned in Chapter 4 really become useful.

A typical example is a user control that allows some level of configuration through properties. For example, you can create a footer that supports two different display formats: long date and short time. To add a further level of refinement, the Footer user control allows the web page to specify the appropriate display format using an enumeration.

The first step is to create an enumeration in the custom Footer class. Remember, an enumeration is simply a type of constant that is internally stored as an integer but is set in code by using one of the allowed names you specify. Variables that use the FooterFormat enumeration can take the value FooterFormat.LongDate or FooterFormat.ShortTime:

```
public enum FooterFormat
{ LongDate, ShortTime }
```

The next step is to add a property to the Footer class that allows the web page to retrieve or set the current format applied to the footer. The actual format is stored in a private variable called *format*, which is set to the long date format by default when the object is first created. (You can accomplish the same effect, in a slightly sloppier way, by using a public member variable named Format instead of a full property procedure.) If you're hazy on how property procedures work, feel free to review the explanation in Chapter 3.

```
private FooterFormat format = FooterFormat.LongDate;

public FooterFormat Format
{
    get { return format; }
    set { format = value; }
}
```

Finally, the UserControl.Load event handler needs to take account of the current footer state and format the output accordingly. The following is the full Footer class code:

```
public partial class Footer : UserControl
{
    protected Label lblFooter;

    public enum FooterFormat
    { LongDate, ShortTime }

    private FooterFormat format = FooterFormat.LongDate;
    public FooterFormat Format
    {
        get
        { return format; }
```

```
        set
        { format = value; }
    }

    protected void Page_Load(Object sender, EventArgs e)
    {
        lblFooter.Text = "This page was served at ";

        if (format == FooterFormat.LongDate)
        {
            lblFooter.Text += DateTime.Now.ToLongDateString();
        }
        else if (format == FooterFormat.ShortTime)
        {
            lblFooter.Text += DateTime.Now.ToShortTimeString();
        }
    }
}
```

To test this footer, you need to create a page that modifies the Format property of the Footer user control. Figure 25-4 shows an example page, which automatically sets the Format property for the user control to match a radio button selection whenever the page is posted back.

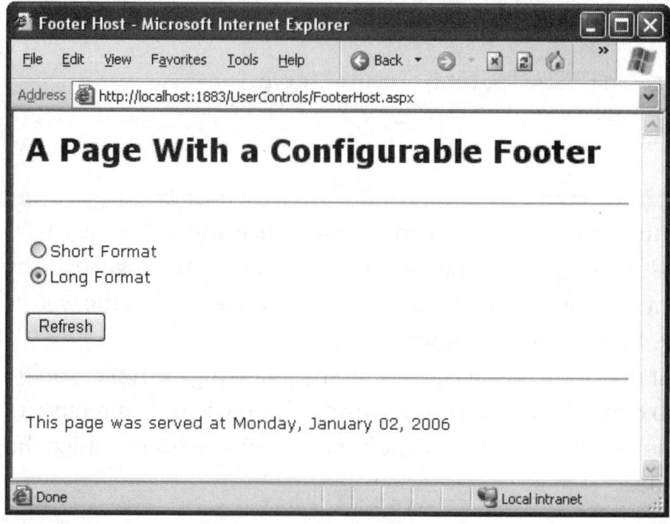

Figure 25-4. *The modified footer*

Note that the user control property is modified in the Page.Load event handler, not the cmdRefresh.Click event handler. The reason is that the Load event occurs before the user control has been rendered each time the page is created. The Click event occurs after the user control has been rendered, and though the property change is visible in your code, it doesn't affect the user control's HTML output, which has already been added to the page.

```
public partial class FooterHost : Page
{
    protected void Page_Load(Object sender, EventArgs e)
    {
        if (optLong.Checked)
        {
            Footer1.Format = Footer.FooterFormat.LongDate;
        }
        else if (optShort.Checked)
        {
            Footer1.Format = Footer.FooterFormat.ShortTime;
        }
        else
        {
            // The default value in the Footer class will apply.
        }
    }
}
```

You can also set the initial appearance of the footer in the control tag:

```
<apress:Footer Format="ShortTime" id="Footer1" runat="server" />
```

User Control Events

Another way that communication can occur between a user control and a web page is through events. With methods and properties, the user control reacts to a change made by the web page code. With events, the story is reversed: the user control notifies the web page about an action, and the web page code responds.

Creating a web control that uses events is fairly easy. In the following example, you'll see a version of the LinkMenu control that uses events. Instead of navigating directly to the appropriate page when the user clicks a button, the control raises an event, which the web page can choose to handle.

The first step to create this control is to define the events. Remember, to define an event, you use the event keyword and specify a delegate that represents the signature of the event. The .NET standard for events specifies that every event should use two parameters. The first one provides a reference to the control that sent the event, while the second incorporates any additional information. This additional information is wrapped into a custom EventArgs object, which inherits from the System.EventArgs class. (If your event doesn't require any additional information, you can just use the generic EventArgs object, which doesn't contain any additional data. Many events in ASP.NET, such as Page.Load or Button.Click, follow this pattern.) You can refer to Chapter 4 for a quick overview of how to use events in .NET.

The LinkMenu2 control uses a single event, which indicates when a link is clicked:

```
public event EventHandler LinkClicked;
```

This statement defines an event named LinkClicked, with the signature specified by the System.EventHandler delegate. This is the most basic event definition you can create. It includes two parameters—the event sender and the EventArgs class. That means any event handler you create to handle the LinkClicked event must look like this:

```
protected void LinkMenu_LinkClicked(object sender, EventArgs e)
{ ... }
```

This takes care of creating the event, but what about raising it? This part is easy. To fire the event, the LinkMenu2 control simply uses the event name and passes in the two parameters, like this:

```
// Raise the LinkClicked event, passing a reference to
// the current object (the sender) and an empty EventArgs object.
LinkClicked(this, EventArgs.Empty);
```

The LinkMenu2 control actually needs a few more changes. The original version used the HyperLink control. This won't do, because the HyperLink control doesn't fire an event when the link is clicked. Instead, you'll need to use the LinkButton. The LinkButton fires the Click event, which the LinkMenu2 control can intercept, and then raises the LinkClicked event to the web page.

The following is the full user control code:

```
public abstract class LinkMenu2 : UserControl
{
    public event EventHandler LinkClicked;
```

```
    protected void lnk_Click(object sender, EventArgs e)
    {
        // One of the LinkButton controls has been clicked.
        // Raise an event to the page.
        if (LinkClicked != null)
        {
            LinkClicked(this, EventArgs.Empty);
        }
    }
}
```

Notice that before raising the LinkClicked event, the LinkMenu2 control needs to test for a null reference. A null reference exists if no event handlers are attached to the event. In this case, you shouldn't try to raise the event, because it would only cause an error.

You can create a page that uses the LinkMenu2 control and add an event handler. Unfortunately, you won't be able to connect these event handlers using the Visual Studio Properties window, because the Properties window won't show the custom events that the user control provides. Instead, you'll need to modify the LinkMenu2 tag directly, as shown here:

```
<apress:LinkMenu2 id="Menu1" runat="server" OnLinkClicked="LinkClicked" />
```

And here's the event handler that responds in the web page:

```
protected void LinkClicked(object sender, EventArgs e)
{
    lblClick.Text = "Click detected.";
}
```

Figure 25-5 shows the result.

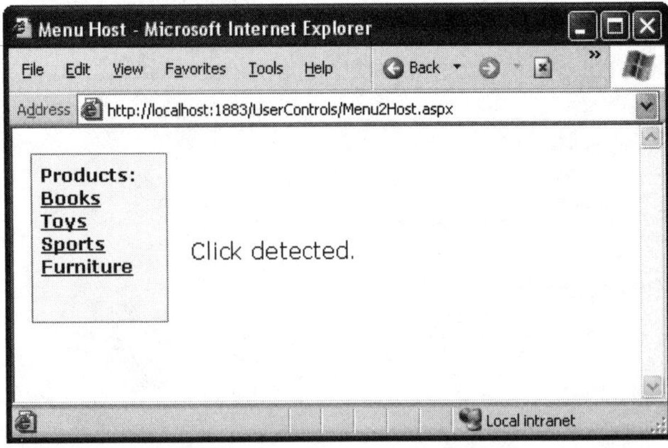

Figure 25-5. *Using the LinkMenu2 user control*

Conceptually, this approach should give your web page more power to customize how the user control works. Unfortunately, that's not the case at the moment, because a key piece of information is missing. When the LinkClicked event occurs, the web page has no way of knowing what link was clicked, which prevents it from taking any kind of reasonable action. The only way to solve this problem is to create a more intelligent event that can transmit some information through event arguments. You'll see how in the next section.

Using Events with Parameters

In the current LinkMenu2 example, no custom information is passed along with the event. In many cases, however, you want to convey additional information that relates to the event. To do so, you need to create a custom class that derives from EventArgs.

The EventArgs class that follows allows the LinkMenu2 user control to pass the URL that the user selected through a Url property. It also provides a Cancel property. If set to true, the user control will stop its processing immediately. But if Cancel remains false (the default), the user control will send the user to the new page. This way, the user control still handles the task of redirecting the user, but it allows the web page to plug into this process and change or stop it (for example, if there's unfinished work left on the current page).

```
public class LinkClickedEventArgs : EventArgs
{
    private string url;
    public string Url
    {
        get { return url; }
        set { url = value; }
    }

    private bool cancel = false;
    public bool Cancel
    {
        get { return cancel; }
        set { cancel = value; }
    }

    public LinkClickedEventArgs(string url)
    {
        Url = url;
    }
}
```

To use this EventArgs class, you need to create a new delegate that represents the LinkClicked event signature. Here's what it looks like:

```
public delegate void LinkClickedEventHandler(object sender,
  LinkClickedEventArgs e);
```

Both the LinkClickedEventArgs and LinkClickedEventHandler delegate must be placed in the App_Code directory. That way, these classes will be compiled automatically and made available to all web pages.

Now you can modify the LinkClicked event to use the LinkClickedEventHandler delegate:

```
public event LinkClickedEventHandler LinkClicked;
```

Next, your user control code for raising the event needs to submit the required information when calling the event. But how does the user control determine what link was clicked? The trick is to switch from the LinkButton.Click event to the LinkButton.Command event. The Command event automatically gets the CommandArgument that's defined in the tag. So if you define your LinkButton controls like this:

```
<asp:LinkButton ID="lnkBooks" runat="server"
  CommandArgument="Menu2Host.aspx?product=Books" OnCommand="lnk_Command">Books
</asp:LinkButton><br />
<asp:LinkButton ID="lnkToys" runat="server"
  CommandArgument="Menu2Host.aspx?product=Toys" OnCommand="lnk_Command">Toys
</asp:LinkButton><br />
<asp:LinkButton ID="lnkSports" runat="server"
  CommandArgument="Menu2Host.aspx?product=Sports" OnCommand="lnk_Command">Sports
</asp:LinkButton><br />
<asp:LinkButton ID="lnkFurniture" runat="server"
  CommandArgument="Menu2Host.aspx?product=Furniture" OnCommand="lnk_Command">
Furniture</asp:LinkButton>
```

you can pass the link along to the web page like this:

```
LinkClickedEventArgs args = new LinkClickedEventArgs((string)e.CommandArgument);
LinkClicked(this, args);
```

Here's the complete user control code. It implements one more feature. After the event is raised (as has been handled by the web page), it checks the Cancel property. If it's false, it goes ahead and performs the redirect using Reponse.Redirect().

```
public partial class LinkMenu2 : System.Web.UI.UserControl
{
    public event LinkClickedEventHandler LinkClicked;
```

```
    protected void lnk_Command(object sender, CommandEventArgs e)
    {
        // One of the LinkButton controls has been clicked.
        // Raise an event to the page.
        if (LinkClicked != null)
        {
            // Pass along the link information.
            LinkClickedEventArgs args =
              new LinkClickedEventArgs((string)e.CommandArgument);
            LinkClicked(this, args);

            // Perform the redirect.
            if (!args.Cancel)
            {
                // Notice we use the Url from the LinkClickedEventArgs
                // object, not the original link. That means the web page
                // can change the link if desired before the redirect.
                Response.Redirect(args.Url);
            }
        }
    }
}
```

Finally, your receiving code needs to update its event handler to use the new signature. In the following code, it checks the URL and allows it in all cases except one:

```
protected void LinkClicked(object sender, LinkClickedEventArgs e)
{
    if (e.Url == "Menu2Host.aspx?product=Furniture")
    {
        lblClick.Text = "This link is not allowed.";
        e.Cancel = true;
    }
    else
    {
        // Allow the redirect, and don't make any changes to the URL.
    }
}
```

If you click the Furniture link, you'll see the message shown in Figure 25-6.

Figure 25-6. *Handling a user control event in the page*

User Control Limitations

User controls provide a great deal of flexibility when you want to combine several web controls (and additional HTML content) in a single unit and possibly add some higher-level business logic. However, they are less useful when you want to modify or extend individual web controls.

For example, imagine you want to create a custom text box–like control that adds a few convenient features. This text box resembles the ordinary TextBox control that's included in ASP.NET, but it adds some new features. For example, you might add some new methods that automate common tasks for parsing or reformatting the text in the text box.

To create this sort of custom control with the user control model, you need to design a user control that contains a single TextBox control. You can then add the methods you need to your user control. This is called a model of *containment*, because the user control contains the text box.

The problem is that this model often raises more problems than it solves. Although you can easily add your custom methods to the user control (which is good), you end up hiding the control inside the user control (which is bad). That means when a developer drops your new user control into a web page, they'll have access to all your new features, but they won't be able to access the original text box properties and methods. For example, they won't be able to set the text box font, colors, or size. In other words, you can create a specialized text box, but even as you add new features, you end up obscuring the existing ones.

To deal with these problems, you can add more properties to your user control that duplicate the properties of the control inside. In the text box user control example, you could add a ForeColor property that exposes the TextBox.ForeColor property. This strategy works, but it's tedious. Web controls are complex and have a lot of properties. Trying to duplicate these details in every user control you create is a lot of extra work.

The next section describes a better, more fine-grained approach for extending or fine-tuning individual controls. Instead of using containment to wrap a control, you'll use *inheritance* to extend it.

Derived Custom Controls

Thanks to the class-based .NET Framework, you can create specialized controls using inheritance in an easier way. All you need to do is find the control you want to extend in the .NET class library and derive a new class from it that adds the additional functionality you need.

You can create a derived custom control for an ASP.NET application in two ways:

- You can create the custom control as a part of the web application. In this case, you must put the custom control class in the App_Code directory so that it's compiled automatically and made available to all your pages.

- You can create the custom control in a separate project and compile it into a DLL component. That way, you can keep your control code separate, and you can reuse it in a variety of different web applications.

In the following sections, you'll start with the simpler approach (creating the control in the current project) and then graduate to creating a complete, separate, custom control library.

Creating a Simple Derived Control

Imagine you want to create a control that looks and acts like a text box but adds some new features that are tailored for working with names (such as Smith, Joe). Thanks to inheritance, this is easier than you'd expect.

Consider the following example—a NameTextBox that adds GetFirstName() and GetLastName() methods. These methods examine the entered text and parse it into a first and last name using one of two recognized formats: space-separated (FirstName LastName) or comma-separated (LastName, FirstName). This way, the user can enter a name in either format, and your code doesn't have to go through the work of parsing the text. Instead, the NameTextBox control handles it automatically.

```
public class NameTextBox : TextBox
{
    private string firstName;
    private string lastName;
```

```
    public string GetFirstName()
    {
        UpdateNames();
        return firstName;
    }

    public string GetLastName()
    {
        UpdateNames();
        return lastName;
    }

    private void UpdateNames()
    {
        int commaPos = this.Text.IndexOf(',');
        int spacePos = this.Text.IndexOf(' ');

        string[] nameArray;
        if (commaPos != -1)
        {
            nameArray = this.Text.Split(',');
            firstName = nameArray[1];
            lastName = nameArray[0];
        }
        else if (spacePos != -1)
        {
            nameArray = this.Text.Split(' ');
            firstName = nameArray[0];
            lastName = nameArray[1];
        }
        else
        {
            // The text has no comma or space.
            // It cannot be converted to a name.
            throw new InvalidOperationException();
        }
    }
}
```

You should place this class in the App_Code folder.

In this example, the custom NameTextBox class inherits from the TextBox class (which is found in the System.Web.UI.WebControls namespace). Because the NameTextBox class extends the TextBox class, all the original TextBox members (such as Font and ForeColor) are still available to the web page programmer and can be set in code or through the control tag. The NameTextBox works directly with the Text property, which it inherits from the TextBox class.

Using a Derived Control

You can't use a derived control in the same way as a user control. Dragging and dropping it onto a page won't have any effect. Instead, you need to first compile your project by selecting Build ➤ Build Website from the menu. When you perform this step, Visual Studio scans your assembly looking for any web control classes (quite simply, classes that derive directly or indirectly from System.Web.UI.Control). When it finds one, it adds it to the Toolbox automatically, as shown in Figure 25-7.

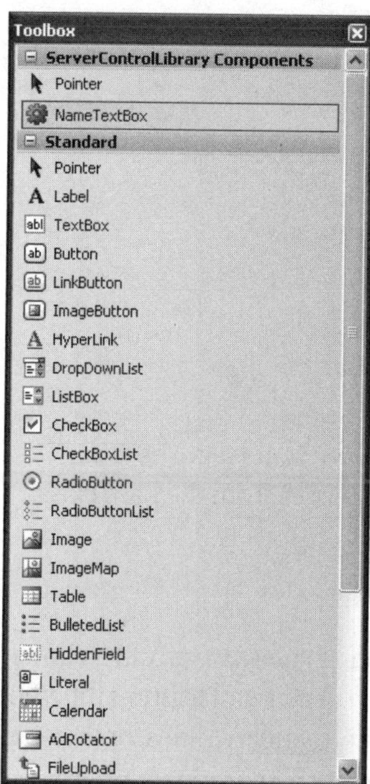

Figure 25-7. *A custom control in the Toolbox*

You can now add this control to any web page. When you do, ASP.NET adds a Register directive that looks something like this:

```
<apress:NameTextBox id="NameTextBox1" runat="server" />
```

Figure 25-8 shows a simple page that allows you to test the NameTextBox control. It retrieves the first and last name entered in the text box when the user clicks a button.

```
protected void cmdGetNames_Click(Object sender, EventArgs e)
{
    lblNames.Text = "<b>First name:</b> ";
    lblNames.Text += NameTextBox1.GetFirstName();
    lblNames.Text += "<br /><b>Last name:</b> ";
    lblNames.Text += NameTextBox1.GetLastName();
}
```

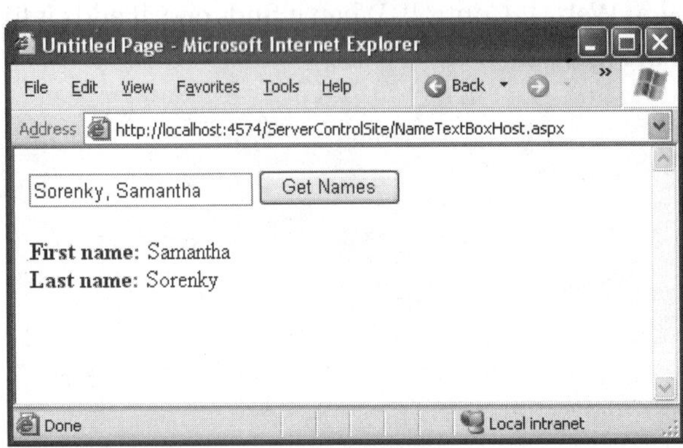

Figure 25-8. *A derived control based on the text box*

You can set properties of the NameTextBox in code or through the tag. These can include any additional properties you've defined or the properties from the base class:

```
<apress:NameTextBox id="NameTextBox1" BackColor="LightYellow"
    Font="Verdana" Text="Enter Name Here" runat="server" />
```

The technique of deriving custom control classes is known as *subclassing*, and it allows you to easily add the functionality you need without losing the basic set of features inherent in a control. Subclassed controls can add new properties, events, and methods, or they can override the existing ones. For example, you could add a ReverseText() or EncryptText() method to the NameTextBox class that loops through the text contents and modifies them.

The process of defining and using custom control events, methods, and properties is the same as with user controls.

Creating a Custom Control Library

For better organization, it's best to develop custom controls in a separate class library project. You can then compile the assembly into a DLL file and add a reference to the assembly in any website. This approach allows you to manage the custom control code separately from the rest of your website, and it enhances the design-time support for your controls.

■ **Tip** To simplify your life a little, choose the web control library project. A web control library project is identical to an ordinary class library project, except that it includes references to some of the assemblies you'll need to use, such as System.Web.dll.

To try this, follow these steps:

1. Create a new website as you would ordinarily.
2. Select File ➤ Add ➤ New Project.
3. Choose the Web Control Library project type.
4. Choose a name and a location for your control assembly. Keep in mind that this location is *separate* from your web application. When you use your control library with a web application, the compiled DLL file is automatically copied into that website's Bin directory. As a result, you don't need to deploy the control library separately—it's always deployed as a part of the web application that uses it.
5. Click OK to create your project. Now, in the Solution Explorer you'll see two projects: your website and your custom control library (see Figure 25-9).
6. To make it easy to open these two projects in combination again, you should save a solution (.sln) file that points to both projects. To do this, select the name of the solution in the Solution Explorer (it's the first item at the top of the tree), and choose File ➤ Save [SolutionName] As. You can choose the exact directory where you want to store this file so you can find it easily later.

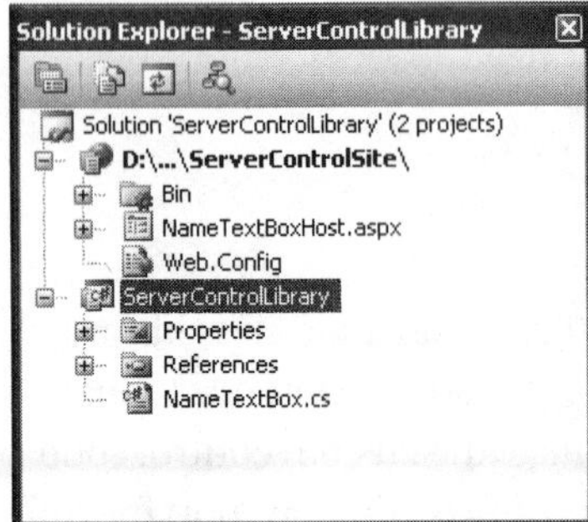

Figure 25-9. *A solution with a website and custom control library*

■ **Tip** Remember, the solution file is a small file that simply points to the website and control library projects. If you move these projects to a different location on your hard drive, the solution file won't work any longer. You'll need to create a new solution and add the website and the custom control project to that solution.

To place an instance of your custom control page, you use the same approach described earlier. Compile your solution (choose Build ➤ Build Solution), and then use the Toolbox to drop the control onto a web page. The first time you do, Visual Studio will copy the custom control library to your web application's Bin directory. From that point on, it will check for a newer version every time you compile the website and update your website by copying the latest control library automatically.

You'll notice that when you use this approach, the Register directive has a slightly different set of attributes than the directive you used for user controls. Here's an example:

```
<%@ Register TagPrefix="apress" Namespace="ServerControlLibrary"
    Assembly="CustomCtrls" %>
```

This register directive identifies the compiled assembly file and the namespace that holds the custom control. When you register a custom control assembly in this fashion, you gain access to all the control classes in it. You can insert a control by using the tag prefix followed by a colon (:) and the class name.

```
<apress:NameTextBox id="NameTextBox1" runat="server" />
```

Custom Controls and Default Values

One common reason for subclassing a control is to add default values. For example, you might create a custom Calendar control that automatically modifies some properties in its constructor. When you first create the control, these default properties are applied automatically.

```
public class FormattedCalendar : Calendar
{
    public FormattedCalendar()
    {
        // Configure the appearance of the calendar table.
        this.CellPadding = 8;
        this.CellSpacing = 8;
        this.BackColor = Color.LightYellow;
        this.BorderStyle = BorderStyle.Groove;
        this.BorderWidth = Unit.Pixel(2);
        this.ShowGridLines = true;

        // Configure the font.
        this.Font.Name = "Verdana";
        this.Font.Size = FontUnit.XXSmall;

        // Configure calendar settings.
        this.FirstDayOfWeek = FirstDayOfWeek.Monday;
        this.PrevMonthText = "<--";
        this.NextMonthText = "-->";

        // Select the current date by default.
        this.SelectedDate = DateTime.Today;
    }
}
```

You can even add event handling logic to this class that uses the Calendar's DayRender event to configure a custom date display. This way, the Calendar class itself handles all the required formatting and configuration; your page code doesn't need to work at all!

```
protected void FormattedCalendar_DayRender(Object sender,
  DayRenderEventArgs e)
{
    if (e.Day.IsOtherMonth)
    {
        e.Day.IsSelectable = false;
        e.Cell.Text = "";
    }
```

```
    else
    {
        e.Cell.Font.Bold = true;
    }
}
```

The preferred way to handle this is actually to override the OnDayRender() method, which is automatically called just before the event is fired. That way, you don't need to write delegate code to connect your event handlers. When you override a method like this, make sure you call the base method using the base keyword. This ensures that any basic tasks (such as firing the event) are performed.

The effect of the following code is equivalent to the event-based approach:

```
protected override void OnDayRender(TableCell cell, CalendarDay day)
{
    // Call the base Calendar.OnDayRender method.
    base.OnDayRender(cell, day);

    if (day.IsOtherMonth)
    {
        day.IsSelectable = false;
        cell.Text = "";
    }
    else
    {
        cell.Font.Bold = true;
    }
}
```

Figure 25-10 contrasts two Calendar controls: the normal one and the custom FormattedCalendar control class.

■ **Tip** Even though you set these defaults in the custom class code, this doesn't prevent you from modifying them in your web page code. The constructor code runs when the Calendar control is created, after which the control tag settings are applied. Finally, the event handling code in your web page also has the chance to modify the FormattedCalendar properties.

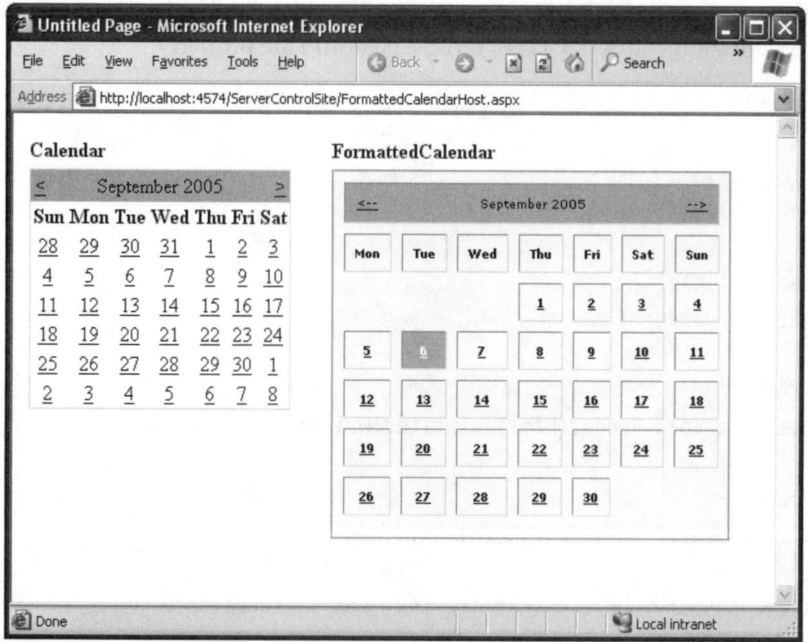

Figure 25-10. *A subclassed Calendar control*

Changing Control Rendering

You can also subclass a control and add low-level refinements by manually configuring the HTML that is generated from the control. To do this, you need to follow only a few basic guidelines:

- Override one of the render methods (Render(), RenderContents(), RenderBeginTag(), and so on) from the base control class. To override the method successfully, you need to specify the same access level as the original method (such as public or protected). Visual Studio helps you out on this account by warning you if you make a mistake.
- Use the base keyword to call the base method. In other words, you want to make sure you're adding functionality to the method, not replacing it with your code. The original method may perform some required cleanup task that you aren't aware of, or it may raise an event that the web page could be listening for.
- Add the code to write out any additional HTML. Usually, this code uses the HtmlWriter class, which supplies a helpful Write() method for direct HTML output.

The following is an example of a TextBox control that overrides the Render() method to add a title. The content for this title is taken from the custom Title property.

```
public class TitledTextBox : TextBox
{
    private string title;
    public string Title
    {
        get { return title; }
        set { title = value; }
    }

    protected override void Render(HtmlTextWriter writer)
    {
        // Add new HTML.
        writer.Write("<h1>" + title + "</h1>");

        // Call the base method (so that the text box is rendered).
        base.Render(writer);
    }
}
```

Figure 25-11 shows what the TitledTextBox control looks like in the design environment.

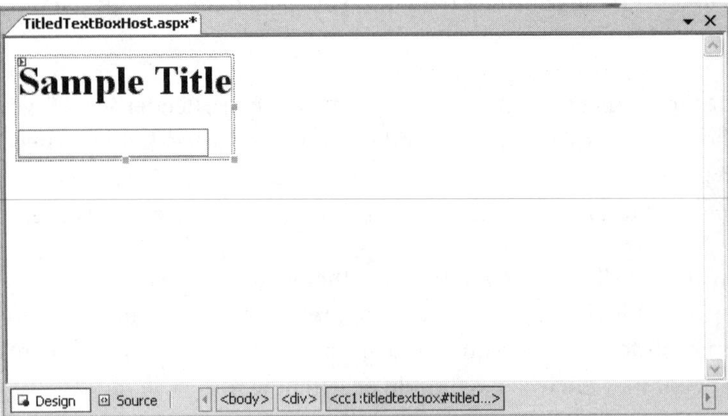

Figure 25-11. *A subclassed text box with a title*

Remember, ASP.NET creates a page by moving through the list of controls and instructing each one to render itself (by calling the Render() method). It collects the total HTML output and sends it as a complete page.

The only limitation in this approach is that you lose the ability to use the control-based style model. For example, if you want to create a heading with a specific font, specific alignment, and specific color characteristics, you need to render all the style code. On the other hand, if you create a user control or a composite control (a special type of server control discussed in the "Creating a Composite Control" section later in this chapter), the heading would be represented by a separate Label control, and you'd be able to tweak all of its properties.

You can use a similar technique to add attributes to the HTML text box tag. For example, you might want to link a little JavaScript code to the OnBlur attribute to make a message box appear when the control loses focus. No TextBox property exposes this attribute, but you can add it manually in the AddAttributesToRender() method. The code you need is as follows:

```
public class LostFocusTextBox : TextBox
{
    protected override void AddAttributesToRender(
      HtmlTextWriter writer)
    {
        base.AddAttributesToRender(writer);
        writer.AddAttribute("OnBlur",
          "javascript:alert('You Lost Focus')");
    }
}
```

The resulting HTML for the LostFocusTextBox looks something like this:

```
<input type="text" id="LostFocusTextBox2"
      OnBlur="javascript:alert('You Lost Focus')" />
```

Figure 25-12 shows what happens when the text box loses focus. You can extend the usefulness of this control by making the alert message configurable, as shown here:

```
public class LostFocusTextBox : TextBox
{
    private string alert;
    public string AlertMessage
    {
        get { return alert; }
        set { alert = value; }
    }
```

```
    protected override void AddAttributesToRender(
      HtmlTextWriter writer)
    {
        base.AddAttributesToRender(writer);
        writer.AddAttribute("OnBlur",
          "javascript:alert('" + alert + "')");
    }
}
```

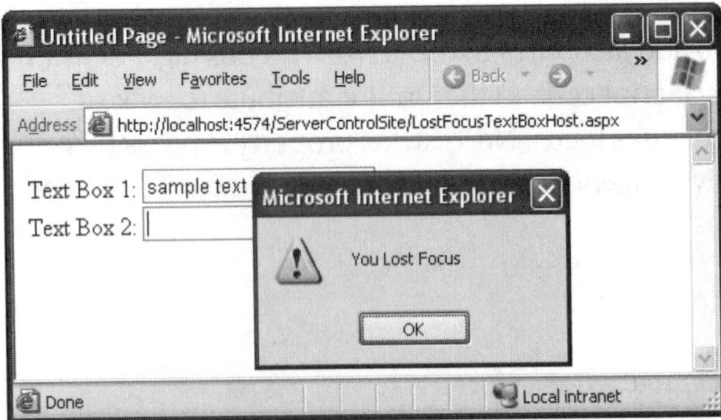

Figure 25-12. *The LostFocusTextBox control*

Creating a Web Control from Scratch

Once you start experimenting with altering the TextBox control's HTML, it might occur to you to design a control entirely from scratch. This is an easy task in ASP.NET—all you need to do is inherit from the System.Web.UI.WebControls.WebControl class, which is the base of all ASP.NET web controls. Figure 25-13 shows the inheritance hierarchy for web controls.

■ **Note** Technically, you can inherit from the base System.Web.UI.Control class instead, but it provides fewer features. The main difference with the WebControl class is that it provides a basic set of formatting properties such as Font, BackColor, and ForeColor. These properties are automatically implemented by adding the appropriate HTML attributes to your HTML tag and are also persisted in view state for you automatically. If you inherit from the more basic Control class, you need to provide your own style-based properties, add them as attributes using the HtmlTextWriter, and store the settings in view state so they'll be remembered across postbacks.

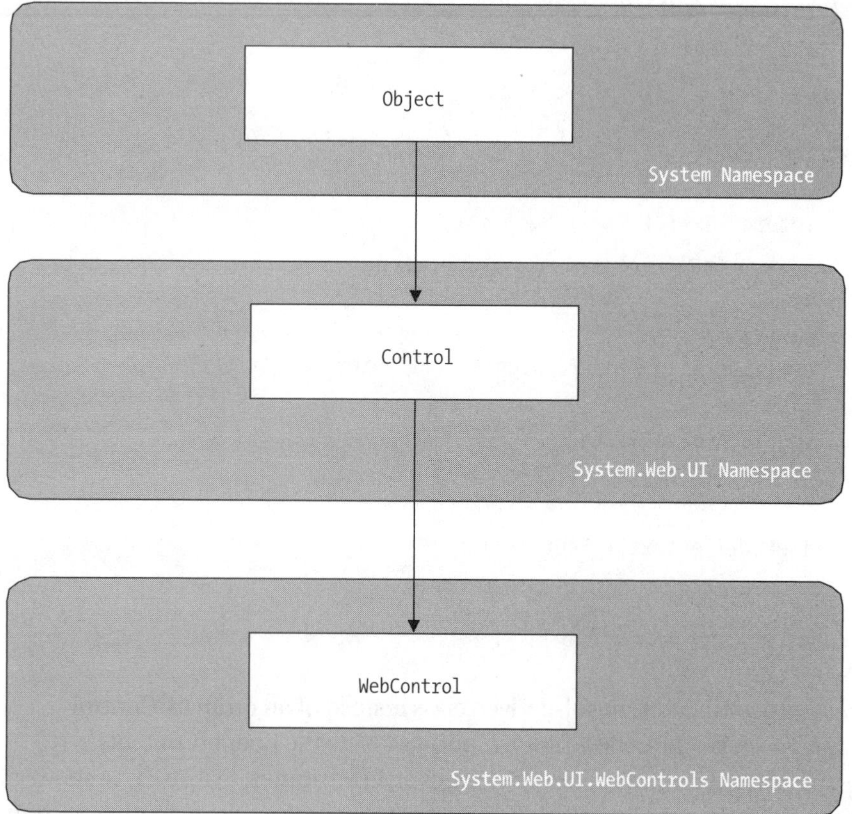

Figure 25-13. *Web control inheritance*

To create your own control from scratch, you need to do little more than add the appropriate properties and implement your own custom RenderContents() or Render() method, which writes the HTML output using the HtmlTextWriter class. The RenderContents() method takes place after the Render() method, which means the formatting attributes have already been applied.

The code is quite similar to the earlier TextBox examples. It creates a repeater type of control that lists a given line of text multiple times. The RepeatTimes property sets the number of repeats.

```
public class ConfigurableRepeater : WebControl
{
    private int repeatTimes = 3;
    private string text = "Text";

    public int RepeatTimes
    {
```

```
        get { return repeatTimes; }
        set { repeatTimes = value; }
    }

    public string Text
    {
        get { return text; }
        set { text = value; }
    }

    protected override void RenderContents(HtmlTextWriter writer)
    {
        base.RenderContents(writer);
        for (int i = 0; i < repeatTimes; i++)
        {
            writer.Write(text + "<br />");
        }
    }
}
```

Because you've used a WebControl-derived class instead of an ordinary Control-derived class and because the code writes the output inside the RenderContents() method, the web page programmer can set various style attributes. Figure 25-14 shows a sample formatted ConfigurableRepeater. If you want to include a title or another portion that you don't want rendered with formatting, add it to the Render method.

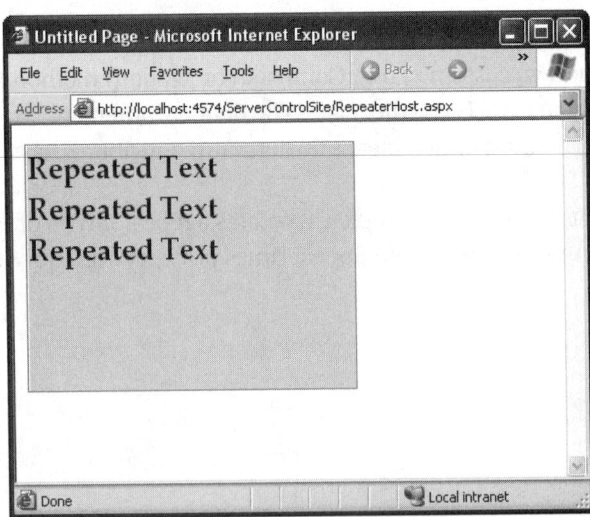

Figure 25-14. *WebControl formatting for repeating control*

Maintaining State Information

Currently, the repeater control provides an EnableViewState property, but it doesn't actually abide by it. You can test this by creating a simple page with two buttons (see Figure 25-15). One button changes the RepeatTimes to 5, while the other button simply triggers a postback. You'll find that every time you click the Postback button, RepeatTimes is reset to the default of 3. If you change the Text property in your code, you'll also find that it reverts to the value specified in the control tag.

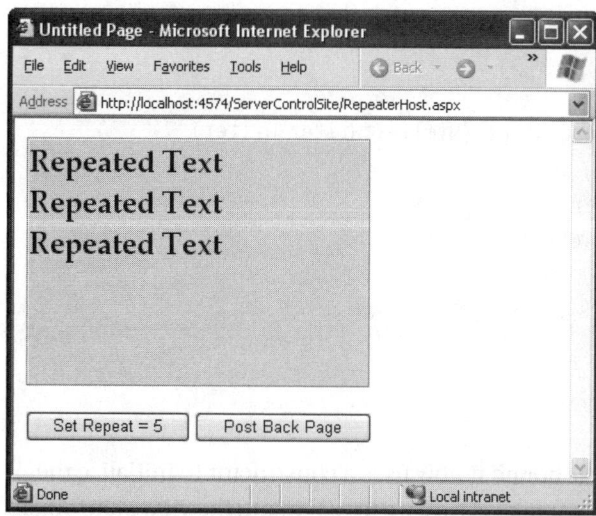

Figure 25-15. *Testing view state*

This problem has an easy solution: store the value in the control's view state. As with web pages, the values in the member variables in a custom web control class are automatically abandoned after the page is returned to the client.

Here's a rewritten control that uses a variable stored in view state instead of a member variable:

```
public class ConfigurableRepeater : WebControl
{
    public ConfigurableRepeater()
    {
        RepeatTimes = 3;
        Text = "";
    }
```

```
    public int RepeatTimes
    {
        get { return (int)ViewState["RepeatTimes"]; }
        set { ViewState["RepeatTimes"] = value; }
    }

    public string Text
    {
        get { return (string)ViewState["Text"]; }
        set { ViewState["Text"] = value; }
    }

    protected override void RenderContents(HtmlTextWriter writer)
    {
        base.RenderContents(writer);
        for (int i = 0; i < RepeatTimes; i++)
        {
            writer.Write(Text + "<br />");
        }
    }
}
```

The code is essentially the same, although it now uses a constructor to initialize the RepeatTimes and Text values. You must take extra care to make sure the view state object is converted to the correct data type. Performing this conversion manually ensures that you won't end up with difficult-to-find bugs or quirks. Note that although the code looks the same as the code used to store a variable in a Page object's view state, the collections are different. This means the web page programmer won't be able to access the control's view state directly.

You'll find that if you set the EnableViewState property to false, changes aren't remembered, but no error occurs. When view state is disabled, ASP.NET still allows you to write items to view state, but they won't persist across postbacks.

If the EnableViewState property of your control is set to false, the view state collection isn't maintained. Your code will still work, but the values you attempt to store will actually be ignored. With the ConfigurableRepeater, you'll see the same behavior you saw without view state—at the start of each postback, the property values will be reset to their defaults.

Although this sounds inconvenient, it's actually the behavior you want. For example, the web page developer may decide to set certain properties at the beginning of every postback, in which case there's no point in maintaining them in view state. You should ensure that your control should still work when view state is switched off, even if changes won't persist.

■ **Note** In some advanced control scenarios, you may need to retain a bare minimum of state information just to make your control functional. In this scenario, you can use a control state feature that ASP.NET provides. The basic idea is that you override the SaveControlState() method to store the information you need and the LoadControlState() method to retrieve it. The information is still placed in the page's view state, but it won't be removed even if EnableViewState is set to false. Microsoft recommends you use this feature with caution and only when it is absolutely required. To learn more about this feature, consult the documentation for the SaveControlState() and LoadControlState() methods in the MSDN Help.

Design-Time Support

Any properties you add for the custom control automatically appear in the Properties window under the Misc heading. You can further customize the design-time behavior of your control by using various attributes from the System.ComponentModel namespace:

```
using System.ComponentModel;
```

For example, the property defined next will always appear in the Layout category of the Properties window. It indicates this to Visual Studio through the System.ComponentModel.Category attribute.

```
[Category("Layout")]
public int RepeatTimes
{
    get { return repeatTimes; }
    set { repeatTimes = value; }
}
```

Note that attributes are always enclosed in square brackets and must appear in front of the code element they refer to. (You may remember that .NET attributes were also used when programming web services. In that case, the attributes were named WebMethod and WebService.)

You can specify more than one attribute at a time, as long as you separate them using commas. The example here includes a Category attribute and a Description attribute. Figure 25-16 shows the result in the Properties window.

```
[Description("The number of times Text will be repeated"), Category("Layout")]
```

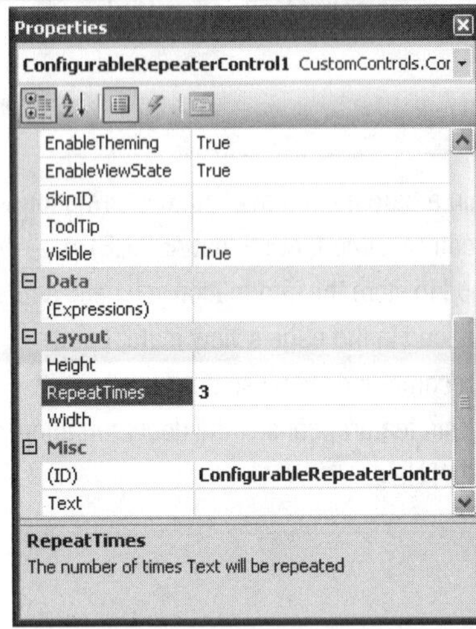

Figure 25-16. *Custom control design-time support*

Table 25-1 lists some useful attributes for configuring a control's design-time support.

Table 25-1. *Attributes for Design-Time Support*

<table>
<tr><th>Attribute</th><th>Description</th></tr>
<tr><td>[Browsable(true|false)]</td><td>If false, this property doesn't appear in the Properties window (although the programmer can still modify it in code or by manually adding the control tag attribute, as long as you include a Set property procedure).</td></tr>
<tr><td>[Category("")]</td><td>A string that indicates the category under which the property appears in the Properties window.</td></tr>
<tr><td>[Description("")]</td><td>A string that indicates the description the property has when selected in the Properties window.</td></tr>
<tr><td>[DefaultValue()]</td><td>Sets the default value that is displayed for the property in the Properties window.</td></tr>
<tr><td>[ParenthesizePropertyName(true|false)]</td><td>If true, Visual Studio displays parentheses around this property in the Properties window (as it does with the ID property).</td></tr>
<tr><td>[ToolboxData("")]</td><td>Lets you control what the control tag looks like when you drop the control into a page from the Toolbox. Usually, the tag takes the format <TagPrefix:ClassName> as in <apress:NameTextBox>. However, you can tweak this so the tag name is different from the class name. To do so, use this attribute and a string in the format "<{0}:NameTextBox runat=server> </{0}:NameTextBox>" where {0} represents the tag prefix and everything else is entered as is.</td></tr>
</table>

Creating a Composite Control

So far, you've seen how user controls are generally used for aggregate groups of controls with some added higher-level business logic, while custom controls allow you to create the final HTML output from scratch. You'll also find that user controls are generally quicker to create, easier to work with in a single project, and simpler to program. Custom controls, on the other hand, provide extensive low-level control features you haven't even considered in this chapter, such as templates and data binding.

One technique you haven't considered is *composite controls*—custom controls that are built from other controls. Composite controls are a little bit closer to user controls, because they render their user interface at least partly from other controls. For example, you might find that you need to generate a complex user interface using an HTML table. Rather than write the entire block of HTML manually in the Render() method (and try to configure it based on various higher-level properties), you could dynamically create and insert a Table web control. This pattern is quite common with ASP.NET server controls—for example, it's logical to expect that advanced controls such as the Calendar and DataGrid rely on simpler table-based controls such as Table to generate their user interfaces.

Generating composite controls is quite easy. All you need to do is derive from a control class such as Control or WebControl, override the CreateChildControls() method, create the control objects you want to use, and add them to the Controls collection of your custom control.

The following example creates a grid of buttons, based on the Rows and Cols properties. Figure 25-17 shows a simple test page for this control.

```
public class ButtonGrid : Control
{
    public ButtonGrid()
    {
        Rows = 2;
        Cols = 2;
    }

    public int Cols
    {
        get { return (int)ViewState["Cols"]; }
        set { ViewState["Cols"] = value; }
    }

    public int Rows
    {
        get { return (int)ViewState["Rows"]; }
        set { ViewState["Rows"] = value; }
    }
```

```
    protected override void CreateChildControls()
    {
        int count = 0;
        for (int row = 0; row < Rows; row++)
        {
            for (int col = 0; col < Cols; col++)
            {
                count++;

                // Create and configure a button.
                Button ctrlB = new Button();
                ctrlB.Width = Unit.Pixel(60);
                ctrlB.Text = count.ToString();

                // Add the button.
                this.Controls.Add(ctrlB);
            }

            // Add a line break.
            LiteralControl ctrlL = new LiteralControl("<br />");
            this.Controls.Add(ctrlL);
        }
    }
}
```

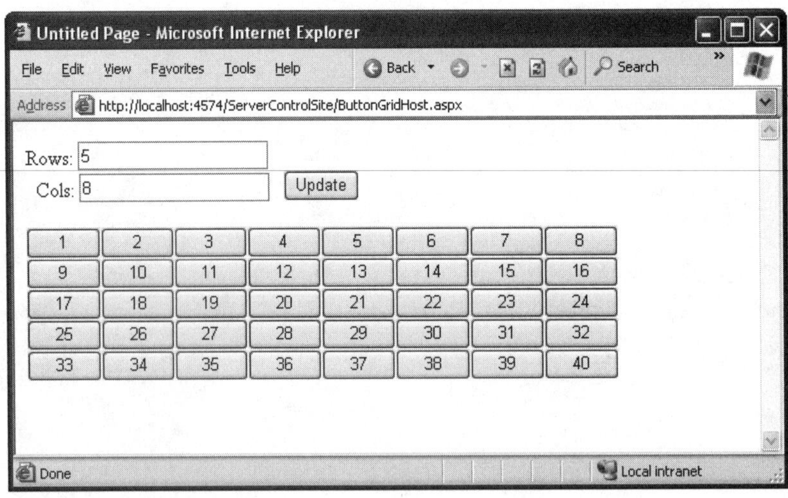

Figure 25-17. *A composite control using buttons*

Custom Control Events and Postbacks

Raising an event from a control is just as easy as it was with a user control. All you need to do is define the event (and any special EventArgs class) and then fire it with the RaiseEvent statement.

However, to raise an event, your code needs to be executing—and for your code to be triggered, the web page needs to be posted back to the server. If you need to create a control that reacts to user actions instantaneously and then refreshes itself or fires an event to the web page, you need a way to trigger and receive a postback.

In an ASP.NET web page, web controls fire postbacks by calling a special JavaScript function called __doPostBack(). This function was described in Chapter 7. The __doPostBack() function accepts two parameters: the name of the control that triggered the postback and a string representing additional postback data. You can retrieve a reference to the __doPostBack() function using the special Page. GetPostBackEventReference() method in your rendering code. (Every control provides the Page property, which provides a reference to the web page where the control is situated.)

The GetPostBackEventReference() method allows you to perform an interesting trick—namely, creating a control or HTML link that invokes the __doPostBack function. The easiest way to perform this magic is usually to add a JavaScript onClick attribute to an HTML element. Anchors, images, and buttons all support the onClick attribute.

Consider the ButtonGrid control. Currently, the buttons are created, but there is no way to receive their events. You can change this by setting each button's onClick attribute to refer to the __doPostBack() function. The added lines are highlighted in bold in the following code:

```
protected override void CreateChildControls()
{
    int k = 0;
    for (int i = 0; i < Rows; i++)
    {
        for (int j = 0; j < Cols; j++)
        {
            k++;

            // Create and configure a button.
            Button ctrlB = new Button();
            ctrlB.Width = Unit.Pixel(60);
            ctrlB.Text = k.ToString();
```

```
                // Set the onClick attribute with a reference to
                // __doPostBack. When clicked, ctrlB will cause a
                // postback to the current control and return
                // the assigned text of ctrlB.
                ctrlB.Attributes["onClick"] =
                  Page.ClientScript.GetPostBackEventReference(this, ctrlB.Text);

                // Add the button.
                this.Controls.Add(ctrlB);
            }

            // Add a line break.
            LiteralControl ctrlL = new LiteralControl("<br />");
            this.Controls.Add(ctrlL);
        }
}
```

To handle the postback, your custom control also needs to implement the IPostBackEventHandler interface, as shown here:

```
public class ButtonGrid : Control, IPostBackEventHandler
{
    // (Control code goes here.)
}
```

You then need to create a method that implements the IPostBackEventHandler.RaisePostBackEvent() method. This method is triggered when your control fires the postback, and it receives any additional information that is submitted through the GetPostBackEventReference() method. In the ButtonGrid control, this extra information is the text of the button that was clicked.

```
public virtual void RaisePostBackEvent(string eventArgument)
{
    // (Respond to postback here.)
}
```

Once you receive the postback, you can modify the control or even raise another event to the web page. To enhance the ButtonGrid example to use this method, you'll define an additional EventArgs class, delegate, and event:

```
public class GridClickEventArgs : EventArgs
{
    public string ButtonName;
```

```
    public GridClickEventArgs(string buttonName)
    {
        ButtonName = buttonName;
    }
}

public delegate void GridClickEventHandler(object sender,
  GridClickEventArgs e);

public event GridClickEventHandler GridClick;
```

This event handler raises an event to the web page, with information about the selected button.

The RaisePostBackEvent() method can then trigger the GridClick event. Here's the complete, revised code for the ButtonGrid:

```
public class ButtonGrid : Control, IPostBackEventHandler
{
    public event GridClickEventHandler GridClick;

    public ButtonGrid()
    {
        Rows = 2;
        Cols = 2;
    }

    public int Cols
    {
        get { return (int)ViewState["Cols"]; }
        set { ViewState["Cols"] = value; }
    }

    public int Rows
    {
        get { return (int)ViewState["Rows"]; }
        set { ViewState["Rows"] = value; }
    }

    public virtual void RaisePostBackEvent(string eventArgument)
    {
        if (GridClick != null)
```

```
        {
            GridClick(this, new GridClickEventArgs(eventArgument));
        }
    }

    protected override void CreateChildControls()
    {
        int k = 0;
        for (int i = 0; i < Rows; i++)
        {
            for (int j = 0; j < Cols; j++)
            {
                k++;

                // Create and configure a button.
                Button ctrlB = new Button();
                ctrlB.Width = Unit.Pixel(60);
                ctrlB.Text = k.ToString();

                ctrlB.Attributes["onClick"] =
                  Page.ClientScript.GetPostBackEventReference(this, ctrlB.Text);

                // Add the button.
                this.Controls.Add(ctrlB);
            }

            // Add a line break.
            LiteralControl ctrlL = new LiteralControl("<br />");
            this.Controls.Add(ctrlL);
        }
    }
}
```

Figure 25-18 shows a web page that allows you to test the ButtonGrid. It handles the GridClick event and displays a message indicating which button was clicked. It also allows the user to specify the number of rows and columns that should be added to the grid.

■ **Note** One of the nice things about compiling controls in a separate assembly is that it gives you enhanced design-time support. Not only can you add these controls to the Toolbox, but you can also create event handlers for any of their custom events (such as the ButtonGrid.GridClick event) using the Properties window. Unfortunately, the same feat isn't possible with user controls.

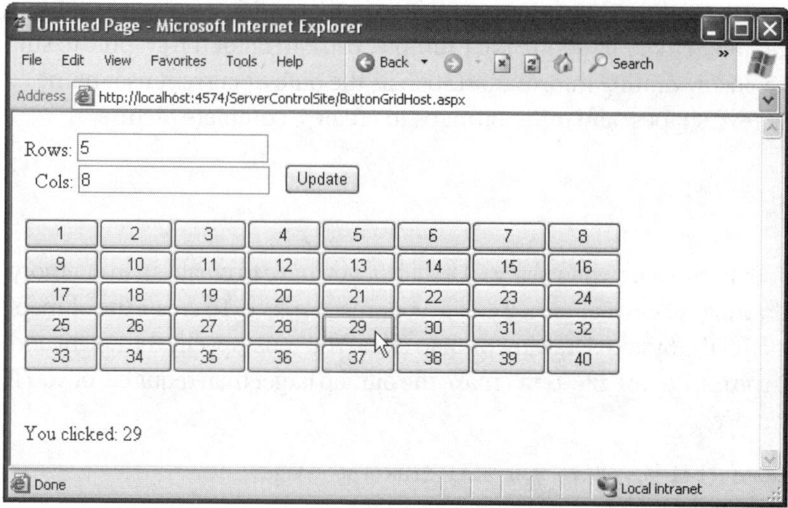

Figure 25-18. *Handling custom control events*

Here's the web page code:

```
public partial class ButtonGridHost : Page
{
    protected void cmdUpdate_Click(Object sender, EventArgs e)
    {
        ButtonGrid1.Rows = Int32.Parse(txtRows.Text);
        ButtonGrid1.Cols = Int32.Parse(txtCols.Text);
    }

    protected void ButtonGrid1_GridClick(object sender,
      CustomControls.GridClickEventArgs e)
    {
        lblInfo.Text = "You clicked: " + e.ButtonName;
    }
}
```

Dynamic Graphics

One of the features of the .NET Framework is GDI+, a set of classes designed for creating bitmaps. You can use GDI+ in a Windows or an ASP.NET application to draw dynamic graphics. In a Windows application, the graphics you draw would be copied to a window for display. In ASP.NET, the graphics can be rendered right into the HTML stream and be sent directly to the client browser.

In general, using GDI+ code to draw a graphic is slower than using a static image file. However, it gives you much more freedom. For example, you can tailor the graphic to suit a particular purpose, incorporating information such as the date or current user name. You can also mingle text, shapes, and other bitmaps to create a complete picture.

Basic Drawing

You need to follow four basic steps when using GDI+. First, you have to create an in-memory bitmap. This is the drawing space where you'll create your masterpiece. To create the bitmap, declare a new instance of the System.Drawing.Bitmap class. You must specify the height and width of the image in pixels. Be careful—don't make the bitmap larger than required, or you'll needlessly waste memory.

```
// Create an in-memory bitmap where you will draw the image.
// The Bitmap is 300 pixels wide and 50 pixels high.
Bitmap image = new Bitmap(300, 50);
```

The next step is to create a GDI+ graphics context for the image, which is represented by the System.Drawing.Graphics object. This object provides the methods that allow you to render content to the in-memory bitmap. To create a Graphics object from an existing Bitmap object, you just use the static Graphics.FromImage() method, as shown here:

```
Graphics g = Graphics.FromImage(image);
```

Now comes the interesting part. Using the methods of the Graphics class, you can draw text, shapes, and images on the bitmap. Table 25-2 lists some of the most fundamental Graphics class methods. The methods that begin with the word *Draw* draw outlines, while the methods that begin with the word *Fill* draw solid regions. The only exceptions are the DrawString() method, which draws filled-in text using a font you specify, and the methods for copying bitmap images, such as DrawIcon() and DrawImage().

Table 25-2. *Graphics Class Methods for Drawing*

Method	Description
DrawArc()	Draws an arc representing a portion of an ellipse specified by a pair of coordinates, a width, and a height
DrawBezier() and DrawBeziers()	Draws the infamous and attractive Bezier curve, which is defined by four control points
DrawClosedCurve()	Draws a curve and then closes it off by connecting the end points
DrawCurve()	Draws a curve (technically, a cardinal spline)
DrawEllipse()	Draws an ellipse defined by a bounding rectangle specified by a pair of coordinates, a height, and a width
DrawIcon() and DrawIconUnstreched()	Draws the icon represented by an Icon object and (optionally) stretches it to fit a given rectangle

Method	Description
DrawImage() and DrawImageUnscaled()	Draws the image represented by an Image-derived object and (optionally) stretches it to fit a given rectangle
DrawLine() and DrawLines()	Draws a line connecting the two points specified by coordinate pairs
DrawPie()	Draws a "piece of pie" shape defined by an ellipse specified by a coordinate pair, a width, a height, and two radial lines
DrawPolygon()	Draws a multisided polygon defined by an array of points
DrawRectangle() and DrawRectangles()	Draws an ordinary rectangle specified by a starting coordinate pair and width and height
DrawString()	Draws a string of text in a given font
FillClosedCurve()	Draws a curve, closes it off by connecting the end points, and fills it
FillEllipse()	Fills the interior of an ellipse
FillPie()	Fills the interior of a "piece of pie" shape
FillPolygon()	Fills the interior of a polygon
FillRectangle() and FillRectangles()	Fills the interior of a rectangle
FillRegion()	Fills the interior of a Region object

When calling the Graphics class methods, you need to specify several parameters to indicate the pixel coordinates for what you want to draw. For example, when drawing a rectangle, you need to specify the location of the top-left corner and its width and height. Here's an example of how you might draw a solid rectangle in yellow:

```
// Draw a rectangle starting at location (0, 0)
// that is 300 pixels wide and 50 pixels high.
g.FillRectangle(Brushes.Yellow, 0, 0, 300, 50);
```

When measuring pixels, the point (0, 0) is the top-left corner of your image in (x, y) coordinates. The x coordinate increases as you go farther to the right, and the y coordinate increases as you go farther down. In the current example, the image is 300 pixels wide and 50 pixels high, which means the point (300, 50) is the bottom-right corner.

You'll also notice you need to specify either a Brush or a Pen object when you create any graphic. Methods that draw shape outlines require a Pen, while methods that draw filled-in regions require a Brush. You can create your own custom Pen and Brush objects, but .NET provides an easier solution with the Brushes and Pens classes. These classes expose static properties that provide various Brushes and Pens for different colors. For example, Brushes.Yellow returns a Brush object that fills regions using a solid yellow color.

Once the image is complete, you can send it to the browser using the Image.Save() method. Conceptually, you "save" the image to the browser's response stream. It then gets sent to the client and displayed in the browser.

```
// Render the image to the HTML output stream.
image.Save(Response.OutputStream,
  System.Drawing.Imaging.ImageFormat.Gif);
```

■ **Tip** You can save an image to any valid stream, including a FileStream. This technique allows you to save dynamically generated images to disk so that you can use them later in other web pages.

Finally, you should explicitly release your image and graphics context when you're finished, because both hold onto some unmanaged resources that might not be released right away if you don't:

```
g.Dispose();
image.Dispose();
```

GDI+ is a specialized approach, and its more advanced features are beyond the scope of this book. However, you can learn a lot by considering a couple of simple examples.

Drawing Custom Text

Using the techniques you've learned, it's easy to create a simple web page that uses GDI+. The next example uses GDI+ to render some text in a bordered rectangle with a happy-face graphic next to it.

Here's the code you'll need:

```
protected void Page_Load(Object sender, EventArgs e)
{
    // Create an in-memory bitmap where you will draw the image.
    // The Bitmap is 300 pixels wide and 50 pixels high.
    Bitmap image = new Bitmap(300, 50);

    // Get the graphics context for the bitmap.
    Graphics g = Graphics.FromImage(image);

    // Draw a solid yellow rectangle with a red border.
    g.FillRectangle(Brushes.LightYellow, 0, 0, 300, 50);
    g.DrawRectangle(Pens.Red, 0, 0, 299, 49);

    // Draw some text using a fancy font.
    Font font = new Font("Alba Super", 20, FontStyle.Regular);
    g.DrawString("This is a test.", font, Brushes.Blue, 10, 0);
```

```
    // Copy a smaller gif into the image from a file.
    Image icon = Image.FromFile(Server.MapPath("smiley.gif"));
    g.DrawImageUnscaled(icon, 240, 0);

    // Render the entire bitmap to the HTML output stream.
    image.Save(Response.OutputStream,
      System.Drawing.Imaging.ImageFormat.Gif);

    // Clean up.
    g.Dispose();
    image.Dispose();
}
```

Figure 25-19 shows the resulting web page.

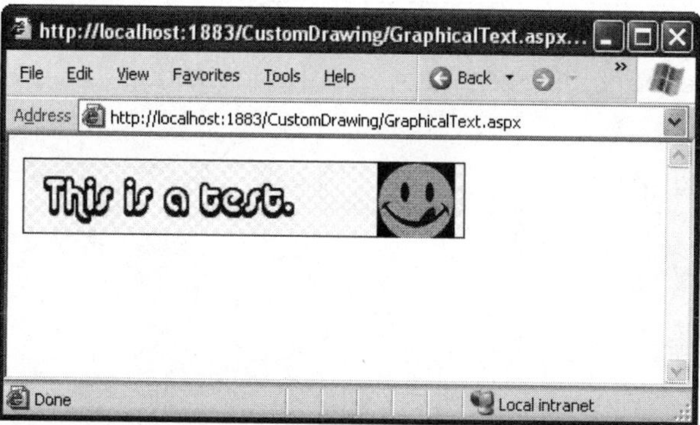

Figure 25-19. *Drawing a custom image*

■ **Tip** Because this image is generated on the server, you can use any font that the server has installed when it's creating the graphic. The client doesn't need to have the same font, because the client receives the text as a rendered image.

Placing Custom Images Inside Web Pages

The Image.Save() approach demonstrated so far has one problem. When you save an image to the response stream, you overwrite whatever information ASP.NET would otherwise use. If you have a web page that includes other static content and controls, this content won't appear at all in the final web page. Instead, the dynamically rendered graphics replace it.

Fortunately, this has a simple solution: you can link to a dynamically generated image using the HTML <img> tag or the Image web control. But instead of linking your image to a static image file, link it to the .aspx file that generates the picture.

For example, you could create a file named GraphicalText.aspx that writes a dynamically generated image to the response stream. In another page, you could show the dynamic image by adding an Image web control and setting the ImageUrl property to GraphicalText.aspx. In fact, you'll even see the image appear in Visual Studio's design-time environment before you run the web page!

When you use this technique to embed dynamic graphics in web pages, you also need to think about how the web page can send information to the dynamic graphic. For example, what if you don't want to show a fixed piece of text, but instead you want to generate a dynamic label that incorporates the name of the current user? (In fact, if you do want to show a static piece of text, it's probably better to create the graphic ahead of time and store it in a file, rather than generating it using GDI+ code each time the user requests the page.) One solution is to pass the information using the query string. The page that renders the graphic can then check for the query string information it needs.

Here's how you'd rewrite the dynamic graphic generator with this in mind:

```
// Get the user name.
if (Request.QueryString["Name"] == null)
{
    // No name was supplied.
    // Don't display anything.
}
else
{
    string name = Request.QueryString["Name"];

    // Create an in-memory bitmap where you will draw the image.
    Bitmap image = new Bitmap(300, 50);

    // Get the graphics context for the bitmap.
    Graphics g = Graphics.FromImage(image);

    g.FillRectangle(Brushes.LightYellow, 0, 0, 300, 50);
    g.DrawRectangle(Pens.Red, 0, 0, 299, 49);

    // Draw some text based on the query string.
    Font font = new Font("Alba Super", 20, FontStyle.Regular);
    g.DrawString(name, font, Brushes.Blue, 10, 0);
```

```
        // Render the entire bitmap to the HTML output stream.
        image.Save(Response.OutputStream,
          System.Drawing.Imaging.ImageFormat.Gif);

        g.Dispose();
        image.Dispose();
}
```

Figure 25-20 shows a page that uses this dynamic graphic page, along with two Label controls. The page passes the query string argument Joe Brown to the page. The full Image.ImageUrl thus becomes GraphicalText.aspx?Name=Joe%20Brown.

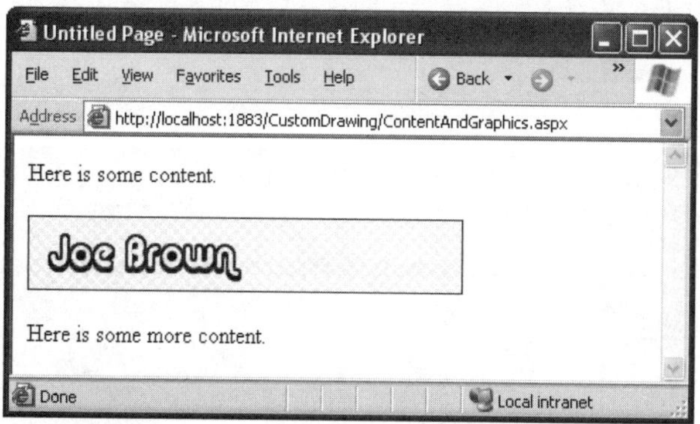

Figure 25-20. *Mingling custom images and controls on the same page*

The Last Word

ASP.NET custom control creation could be a book in itself. To master it, you'll want to experiment with the online samples for this chapter. Once you've perfected your controls, pay special attention to the attributes described in Table 25-1. These are the key to making your control behave properly and work conveniently in design environments such as Visual Studio.

CHAPTER 26

Caching and Performance Tuning

ASP.NET applications are a bit of a contradiction. On the one hand, because they're hosted over the Internet, they have unique requirements—namely, they need to be able to serve hundreds of clients as easily and quickly as they deal with a single user. On the other hand, ASP.NET includes some remarkable tricks that let you design and code a web application in the same way you program a desktop application. These tricks are useful, but they can lead developers into trouble. The problem is that ASP.NET makes it easy to forget you're creating a web application—so easy that you might introduce programming practices that will slow or cripple your application when it's used by a large number of users in the real world.

Fortunately, middle ground exists. You can use the incredible timesaving features such as view state, web controls, and session state that you've spent the last 20-odd chapters learning about and still create a robust web application. But to finish the job properly, you'll need to invest a little extra time to profile and optimize your website's performance.

This chapter discusses the strategies you can use to ensure performance. They fall into three main categories:

Design for performance: A few key guidelines, if you keep them in mind, can steer you toward efficient, scalable designs.

Profile your application: One problem with web applications is that it's sometimes hard to test them under the appropriate conditions and really get an idea of what their problems may be. However, Microsoft provides several useful tools that allow you to benchmark your application and put it through a rigorous checkup.

Implement caching: A little bit of caching may seem like a novelty in a single-user test, but it can make a dramatic improvement in real-world scenarios. You can easily incorporate output and fragment caching into most pages and use data caching to replace less memory-friendly approaches such as state management.

Designing for Performance

The chapters throughout this book have combined practical how-to information with tips and insight about the best designs you can use (and the possible problems you'll face). Now that you're a more accomplished ASP.NET programmer, it's a good idea to review a number of considerations—and a few minor ways that you can tune all aspects of your application.

ASP.NET Code Compilation

ASP.NET provides dramatically better performance than ASP, although it's hard to quote a hard statistic because the performance increases differ widely depending on the ways you structure your pages and the type of operations you perform. The greatest performance increase results from ASP.NET's automatic code compilation. With traditional ASP pages, the script code in a web page was processed for every client request. With ASP.NET, each page class is compiled to native code the first time it's requested; then it's cached for future requests.

This system has one noticeable side effect. The very first time a user accesses a particular web page (or the first time a user accesses it after it has been modified), they will see a longer delay while the page compiles. To remove this delay, you can use the precompilation technique described in Chapter 12. This way, pages are ready to go from the moment you upload them to the web server.

Server Controls

Most of the examples in this book use server controls extensively. Server controls are the basic ingredient in an ASP.NET page, and they don't carry a significant performance overhead—in fact, they usually provide better performance than dynamically writing a page with tricks such as the Response.Write() method.

However, ASP.NET server controls can be unnecessary in some situations. For example, if you have static text that never needs to be accessed or modified in your code, you don't need to use a Label web control. Instead, you can enter the text as static HTML in your .aspx layout file. In Visual Studio, you can choose the Div control from the HTML section of the Toolbox. The Div control is just an ordinary <div> tag. Unless you specifically check the Run As Server Control option, it will be created as a static element rather than a full server control.

Another potential refinement involves view state. If you don't need view state for a control, you should disable it by setting the control's EnableView state to false. Two cases in which you don't need view state are when the control is set at design time and never changes and when the control is refreshed with every postback and doesn't need to keep track of its previous set of information. The latter case has one catch: if you need to retrieve the user's selection when the page is posted back, you'll still need to enable view state for the control. For example, this is why you use view state with data-bound web pages, even though the controls are refilled from the data source after every postback. View state won't materially slow down your server, but it will increase the page size and hence the time required to send the page to the client. From the user's point of view, the application will feel less responsive, particularly if connecting over a slow connection.

Generally, view state becomes most significant when dealing with large controls that can contain large amounts of data. The problem is that this data exerts a greater toll on your application because it's added to the web page twice: directly in the HTML for the control and again in the hidden label used for view state. It's also sent both to the client and then back to the server with each postback. To get a handle on whether view state could be an issue, use page tracing (as described in Chapter 7) to see how many bytes the current page's view state is consuming.

■ **Tip** Both of these issues (static text and view state) are fairly minor refinements. They can speed up download times, particularly if your application is being used by clients with slow Internet connections. However, these issues will almost never cause a serious problem in your application the way poor database or session state code can. Don't spend too much time tweaking your controls, but do keep these issues in mind while programming so that you can optimize your pages when the opportunity presents itself.

ADO.NET Database Access

The rules for accessing a database are relatively straightforward, but they can't be overemphasized. Open a connection to the database only at the point where you need it, and close it properly as soon as possible. Database connections are a limited resource and represent a potential bottleneck if you don't design your web pages carefully.

In addition to making sure you treat your database with this basic degree of respect, you can take a number of additional steps to improve performance:

Improve your database with stored procedures: Relational database management systems such as SQL Server are remarkably complex products. They provide a number of configuration options that have nothing to do with ASP.NET but can make a substantial difference in performance. For example, a database that uses intelligently designed stored procedures instead of dynamically generated queries will often perform much better because stored procedures can be compiled and optimized in advance. This is particularly true if a stored procedure needs to perform several related operations at once.

Improve your database with profiling and indexes: Defining indexes that match the types of searches you need to perform can result in much quicker row-lookup capabilities. To perfect your database, you'll need to examine it with a profiling tool (such as

SQL Server Profiler). These tools record database activity into a special log that can be reviewed, analyzed, and replayed. The profiling utility can usually identify problem areas (such as slow executing queries) and even recommend a new set of indexes that will provide better performance. However, to properly profile the database, you'll need to simulate a typical load by running your application.

Get only the information you need: One of the simplest ways to improve any database code is to reduce the amount of information it retrieves, which will reduce the network load, the amount of time the connection needs to be open, and the size of the final page. For example, all searches should be limited to present a small set of rows at a time (perhaps by filtering by date) and should include only the fields that are truly important. Note, however, that while this is an excellent rule of thumb, it isn't always the right solution. For example, if you're providing a page that allows a user to edit a database record, it's often easier to retrieve all the information for all the rows at once rather than requery the database every time the user selects a record to get additional information.

Use connection pooling: In a typical web application, your RDBMS receives requests on behalf of countless clients from several web pages. Generally, these connections are open and active for only a short amount of time, and creating them is the most time-consuming step. However, if every web page uses the same connection string, database products such as SQL Server will be able to use their built-in connection pooling to reuse a connection for more than one consecutive client, speeding up the process dramatically. This happens transparently and automatically, provided you always use the same connection string (even a minor difference such as the order of settings will prevent a connection from being reused). To ensure that the connection string is the same, centralize it in the web.config file.

Use data binding: The fastest way to get information out of a database and into a page is to use a DataReader or DataSet and bind it directly to a data control. This approach may involve a little more work with custom templates, but it's better than moving through the rows manually and writing to the page yourself.

Use caching: If a certain set of data is frequently requested and changes slowly, it's an ideal candidate for caching. With caching, the information will be read from the database and loaded into temporary memory the first time a client requests it, and it will be made directly available to future requests without any database access required. Output and data caching are discussed in detail throughout the second half of this chapter.

Session State

Session state was the single greatest restriction on performance in traditional ASP development. Although ASP.NET introduces some features that make session state more scalable, it still needs to be used carefully.

Generally, you won't run into problems if you're just storing a customer's ID in session state. You can create a simple shopping basket by storing a list of currently selected products. However, if you plan to store large amounts of information such as a DataSet, you need to tread carefully and consider the multiplying effect of a successful application. If each session reserves about 1MB of information, 100 simultaneous sessions (not necessarily all corresponding to users who are still at your site) can easily chew up more than 100MB of memory. To solve this sort of problem, you have two design choices:

- Store everything in a database record, and store the ID for that database in session state. When the client returns, look up the information. Nothing is retained in memory, and the information is durable—it won't expire until you remove the record. Of course, this option can reclaim server memory, but it slows down the application with database access, which is the other vulnerable part of your application.

- Often a better solution is to store information in a database record and then cache some of the information in memory. Then you can still retrieve the information quickly when needed, but ASP.NET can reclaim the memory if the server's performance is suffering. You'll learn much more about data caching throughout this chapter.

Also keep in mind that with session state, the best state facility is almost always the default in-process session state store. The other options (such as storing session state in a SQL database) impose additional performance overhead and are necessary only when hosting your website in a web farm with multiple web servers.

Profiling

To judge the success of an attempted performance improvement, you need to be able to measure the performance of your application. In cases where performance is lagging, you also need enough information to diagnose the possible bottleneck so that you can make a meaningful change.

Stress Testing

You can use many testing tools and .NET Framework features to profile your ASP.NET applications. Being able to bridge the gap from test results to application insight is often not as easy. You may be able to record important information such as TTFB and TTLB (the time taken to serve the first byte and the time taken to deliver the last byte and complete the delivery), but without a way to gauge the meaning of these settings, it isn't clear whether your application is being held back by a slow hard drive, a poor choice of ASP.NET settings, an overtasked database, or bad application design. In fact, performance testing is an entire science of its own.

Most basic tests use a dedicated web server, a set of dedicated client machines that are interacting with your web server over a fast isolated network, and a load-generating tool that runs on each client. The load-generating tool automatically requests a steady stream of pages, simulating a heavy load. You might use a utility such as Microsoft's ACT (Application Center Test), which is included with some versions of Visual Studio, or the ASP favorite, WAST (Web Service Applications Stress Tool), which is available for free download from `http://www.microsoft.com/technet/archive/itsolutions/intranet/downloads/webstres.mspx`. (With ACT, you can create tests directly in Visual Studio simply by adding the appropriate project type to your solution.) Note that if you try to test the server using a load-testing tool running from the same computer, you'll retrieve data that is much less accurate and much less useful.

Both ACT and WAST simulate real-world conditions by continuously requesting pages through several connections simultaneously. You can configure how many requests are made at once and what files are requested. You can even use a wizard that records typical browser activity while you use the site and then replays it later.

Most load-generating tools record some kind of report as they work. Both ACT and WAST create text summaries. Additionally, you can record results using Windows performance counters, which you'll examine in the next section.

Performance Counters

Windows performance counters are the basic unit of measurement for gauging the performance of your application. You can add or configure counters from a testing utility such as WAST, or you can monitor performance directly from the system Performance dialog box. To do so, choose Settings ➤ Control Panel ➤ Administrative Tools ➤ Performance from the Start menu. Figure 26-1 shows the Performance dialog box.

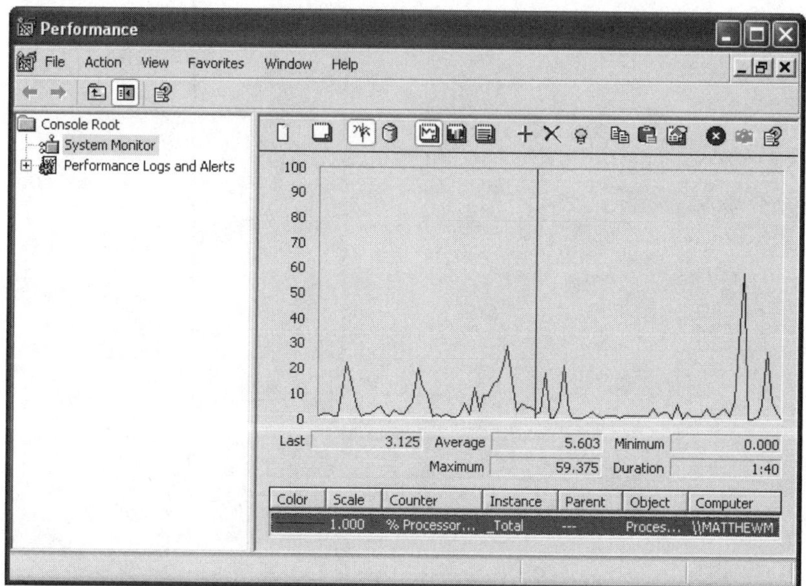

Figure 26-1. *Monitoring performance counters*

By default, you'll see performance counters only for measuring basic information such as the computer's CPU and disk drive use. However, ASP.NET installs much more useful counters for tracking web application performance. To add these counters, right-click the counter list, and choose Properties. You can configure numerous options (such as changing the appearance of the graph and logging information to a report), but the most important tab is Data, which allows you to add and remove counters from the current list. To start, remove the default counters, and click Add to choose more useful ones, as shown in Figure 26-2.

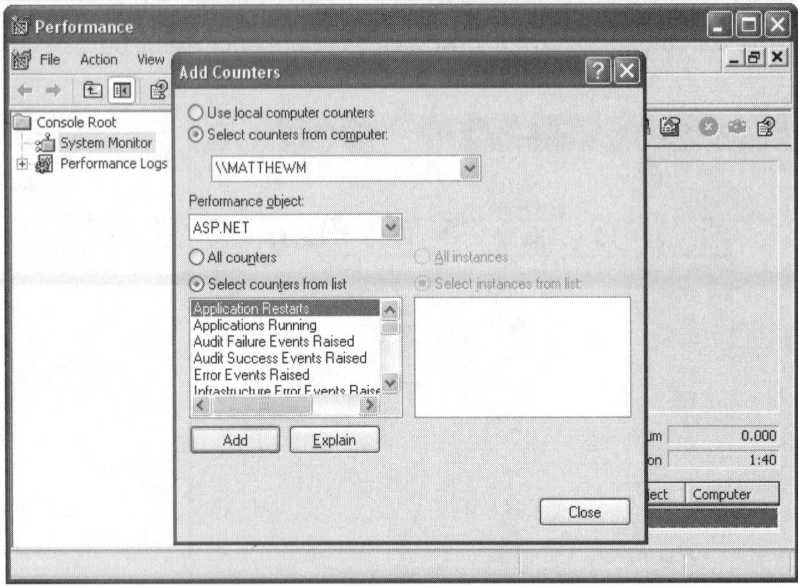

Figure 26-2. *Adding ASP.NET performance counters*

You'll notice several important features in the Add Counters dialog box. First, you can specify a computer name—in other words, you can monitor the performance of a remote computer. Monitoring the web server's performance on a client computer is ideal, because it ensures that the act of monitoring doesn't have as much of an effect on the server. The next important feature of this window is the performance object, which allows you to choose a performance counter category. You can use dozens of different categories.

For ASP.NET, you'll find four main categories. The ASP.NET category provides information about the overall performance of ASP.NET, while the ASP.NET Applications category provides information about a single specified web application. Also, two similar categories include the version number (such as ASP.NET [Version] and ASP.NET Apps [Version]). These categories provide the same list of counters as the corresponding categories that don't indicate the version. This design supports the side-by-side execution features of .NET, which allow you to install two (or more) versions of the .NET Framework at the same time and use them to host different websites. In this case, you would find one ASP.NET [Version] category and one ASP.NET Apps [Version] category for each version of ASP.NET that is installed on your server. The ASP.NET and ASP.NET Application categories automatically map to the most recent version.

Table 26-1 lists some of the most useful counter types by category and name. The asterisked rows indicate counters that can help you diagnose a problem, while the other rows represent counters that are always useful.

Table 26-1. *Useful Performance Counters*

Category	Counter	Description
Processor	% CPU Utilization	The percentage of the CPU's processing time that is being used. If your CPU use remains consistently low regardless of the client load, your application may be trapped waiting for a limited resource.
ASP.NET	Requests Queued	The number of requests waiting to be processed. Use this counter to gain an idea about the maximum load that your web server can support. The default machine.config setting specifies a limit of 5,000 queued requests.
ASP.NET Applications	Requests/Sec	The throughput of the web application.
ASP.NET Applications	* Errors Total	This counter should remain at or close to zero. If a web application generates errors, it can exert a noticeable performance slowdown (required for handling the error), which will skew performance results.
ASP.NET	* Application Restarts, Worker Process Restarts	The ASP.NET process may restart based on a fatal crash or automatically in response to recycling options set in the machine.config file. These counters can give you an idea about how often the ASP.NET process is being reset and can indicate unnoticed problems.
System	* Context Switches/sec	Indicates the rate at which thread contexts are switched. A high number may indicate that various threads are competing for a limited resource.
ASP.NET Applications	Pipeline Instance Count	The number of request pipelines for an application. This gives an idea of the maximum number of concurrent requests being served. If this number is low under a load, it often signifies that the CPU is being used well.
.NET	* CLR Exceptions, # of Exceps Thrown	The number of exceptions thrown in a .NET application. This can indicate that unexpected errors are occurring (as with the ErrorsTotal counter), but it can also indicate the normal operation of error handling code in response to a missing file or invalid user action.

.NET provides some interesting features that let you interact with the system performance counters programmatically. For example, you can add new performance counters, or retrieve the current value of a performance counter in your code, and then display the relevant information in a web page or desktop application. To use these features, you simply need to explore the types in the System.Diagnostics namespace. Table 26-2 gives an overview of the .NET classes you can use to interact with performance counters. For more information, refer to the MSDN class library reference.

Table 26-2. *Performance Counter Classes*

Class	Description
PerformanceCounter	Represents an individual counter, which includes information such as the counter name and the type of data it records. You can create your own counter to represent application-specific performance measures (such as number of purchases per second).
PerformanceCounterCategory	Represents a counter category, which will contain one or more counters.
CounterCreationData	Represents the data required to create a new counter. It can be used for more control or as a shortcut when creating PerformanceCounter objects.
CounterSample	Represents a single piece of information recorded by the counter. It provides a RawValue (the recorded number), a TimeStamp (when the value was recorded), and additional information about the type of counter and how frequently the counter is read. A typical performance counter might create samples several times per second.

Caching

ASP.NET has taken some dramatic steps forward with caching. Many developers who first learn about caching see it as a bit of a frill, but nothing could be further from the truth. Used intelligently, caching could provide a twofold, threefold, or even tenfold performance improvement by retaining important data for just a short period of time.

ASP.NET really has two types of caching. Your applications can and should use both types, because they complement each other:

- *Output caching*: This is the simplest type of caching. It stores a copy of the final rendered HTML page that is sent to the client. The next client that submits a request for this page doesn't actually run the page. Instead, the final HTML output is sent automatically. The time that would have been required to run the page and its code is completely reclaimed.

- *Data caching*: This is carried out manually in your code. To use data caching, you store important pieces of information that are time-consuming to reconstruct (such as a DataSet retrieved from a database) in the cache. Other pages can check for the existence of this information and use it, thereby bypassing the steps ordinarily required to retrieve it. Data caching is conceptually the same as using application state, but it's much more server-friendly because items will be removed from the cache automatically when it grows too large and performance could be affected. Items can also be set to expire automatically.

Also, two specialized types of caching build on these models:

- *Fragment caching*: This is a specialized type of output caching—instead of caching the HTML for the whole page, it allows you to cache the HTML for a portion of it. Fragment caching works by storing the rendered HTML output of a user control on a page. The next time the page is executed, the same page events fire (and so your page code will still run), but the code for the appropriate user control isn't executed.
- *Data source caching*: This is the caching that's built into the data source controls, including the SqlDataSource, ObjectDataSource, and XmlDataSource. Technically, data source caching uses data caching. The difference is that you don't need to handle the process explicitly. Instead, you simply configure the appropriate properties, and the data source control manages the caching storage and retrieval.

In the remainder of this chapter, you'll consider every caching option. You'll begin by learning the basics of output caching and data caching. Next, you'll examine the caching in the data source controls. Finally, you'll explore one of ASP.NET's hottest new features—linking cached items to tables in a database with SQL cache dependencies.

Output Caching

With output caching, the final rendered HTML of the page is cached. When the same page is requested again, the control objects are not created, the page life cycle doesn't start, and none of your code executes. Instead, the cached HTML is served. Clearly, output caching gets the theoretical maximum performance increase, because all the overhead of your code is sidestepped.

To see output caching in action, you can create a simple page that displays the current time of day. Figure 26-3 shows this page.

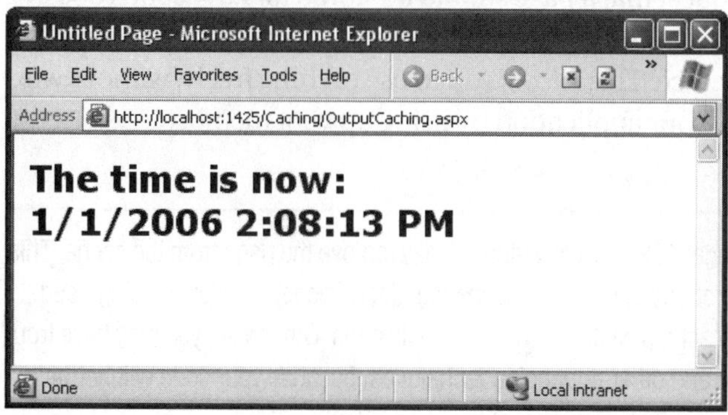

Figure 26-3. *Displaying the time a page is served*

The code for this task is elementary:

```
public partial class OutputCaching : Page
{
    protected void Page_Load(Object sender, EventArgs e)
    {
        lblDate.Text = "The time is now:<br />";
        lblDate.Text += DateTime.Now.ToString();
    }
}
```

You can cache an ASP.NET page in two ways. The most common approach is to insert the OutputCache directive at the top of your .aspx file, as shown here:

```
<%@ OutputCache Duration="20" VaryByParam="None" %>
```

The Duration attribute instructs ASP.NET to cache the page for 20 seconds. The VaryByParam attribute is also required—but you'll learn about its effect in the "Caching and the Query String" section.

When you run the test page, you'll discover some interesting behavior. The first time you access the page, you will see the current time displayed. If you refresh the page a short time later, however, the page will not be updated. Instead, ASP.NET will automatically send the cached HTML output to you, until it expires in 20 seconds. When the cached page expires, ASP.NET will run the page code again, generate a new cached copy, and use that for the next 20 seconds.

Twenty seconds may seem like a trivial amount of time, but in a high-volume site, it can make a dramatic difference. For example, you might cache a page that provides a list of products from a catalog. By caching the page for 20 seconds, you limit database access for this page to three operations per minute. Without caching, the page will try to connect to the database once for each client and could easily make dozens of requests in the course of 20 seconds.

Of course, just because you request that a page should be stored for 20 seconds doesn't mean that it actually will be. The page could be evicted from the cache early if the system finds that memory is becoming scarce. This allows you to use caching freely, without worrying too much about hampering your application by using up vital memory.

■Tip When you recompile a cached page, ASP.NET will automatically remove the page from the cache. This prevents problems where a page isn't properly updated, because the older, cached version is being used. However, you might still want to disable caching while testing your application. Otherwise, you may have trouble using variable watches, breakpoints, and other debugging techniques, because your code will not be executed if a cached copy of the page is available.

Caching on the Client Side

Another option is to cache the page exclusively on the client side. In this case, the browser stores a copy and will automatically use this page if the client browses back to the page or retypes the page's URL. However, if the user clicks the Refresh button, the cached copy will be abandoned, and the page will be rerequested from the server, which will run the appropriate page code once again. You can cache a page on the client side using the Location attribute, which specifies a value from the System.Web.UI.OutputCache-Location enumeration. Possible values include Server (the default), Client, None, and All.

```
<%@ OutputCache Duration="20" VaryByParam="None" Location="Client" %>
```

Client-side caching is less common than server-side caching. Because the page is still re-created for every separate user, it won't reduce code execution or database access nearly as dramatically as server-side caching (which shares a single cached copy among all users). However, client-side caching can be a useful technique if your cached page uses some sort of personalized data. Even though each user is in a separate session, the page will be created only once and reused for all clients, ensuring that most will receive the wrong greeting. Instead, you can either use fragment caching to cache the generic portion of the page or use client-side caching to store a user-specific version on each client's computer.

Caching and the Query String

One of the main considerations in caching is deciding when a page can be reused and when information must be accurate up to the latest second. Developers, with their love of instant gratification (and lack of patience), generally tend to overemphasize the importance of real-time information. You can usually use caching to efficiently reuse slightly stale data without a problem and with a considerable performance improvement.

Of course, sometimes information needs to be dynamic. One example is if the page uses information from the current user's session to tailor the user interface. In this case, full page caching just isn't appropriate (although fragment caching may help). Another example is if the page is receiving information from another page through the query string. In this case, the page is too dynamic to cache—or is it?

The current example sets the VaryByParam attribute to None, which effectively tells ASP.NET that you need to store only one copy of the cached page, which is suitable for all scenarios. If the request for this page adds query string arguments to the URL, it makes no difference—ASP.NET will always reuse the same output until it expires. You can test this by adding a query string parameter manually in the browser window. For example, try tacking on ?a=b to the end of your URL. The cached output is still used.

Based on this experiment, you might assume that output caching isn't suitable for pages that use query string arguments. But ASP.NET actually provides another option. You can set the VaryByParam attribute to * to indicate that the page uses the query string and to instruct ASP.NET to cache separate copies of the page for different query string arguments:

```
<%@ OutputCache Duration="20" VaryByParam="*" %>
```

Now when you request the page with additional query string information, ASP.NET will examine the query string. If the string matches a previous request and a cached copy of that page exists, it will be reused. Otherwise, a new copy of the page will be created and cached separately.

To get a better idea of how this process works, consider the following series of requests:

1. You request a page without any query string parameter and receive page copy A.
2. You request the page with the parameter ProductID=1. You receive page copy B.
3. Another user requests the page with the parameter ProductID=2. That user receives copy C.
4. Another user requests the page with ProductID=1. If the cached output B has not expired, it's sent to the user.
5. The user then requests the page with no query string parameters. If copy A has not expired, it's sent from the cache.

You can try this on your own, although you might want to lengthen the amount of time that the cached page is retained to make it easier to test.

■ **Note** Output caching works well with pages that vary only based on server-side data (for example, the data in a database) and the data in query string. However, output caching doesn't work if the page output depends on user-specific information such as session data or cookies. Output caching also won't work with event-driven pages that use forms. In these cases, events will be ignored, and a static page will be re-sent with each postback, effectively disabling the page. To avoid these problems, use fragment caching instead to cache a portion of the page or use data caching to cache specific information.

Caching with Specific Parameters

Setting VaryByParam to the wildcard asterisk (*) is unnecessarily vague. It's usually better to specifically identify an important query string variable by name. Here's an example:

```
<%@ OutputCache Duration="20" VaryByParam="ProductID" %>
```

In this case, ASP.NET will examine the query string looking for the ProductID parameter. Requests with different ProductID parameters will be cached separately, but all other parameters will be ignored. This is particularly useful if the page may be passed additional query string information that it doesn't use. ASP.NET has no way to distinguish the "important" query string parameters without your help.

You can specify several parameters as long as you separate them with semicolons:

```
<%@ OutputCache Duration="20" VaryByParam="ProductID;CurrencyType" %>
```

In this case, ASP.NET will cache separate versions provided the query string differs by ProductID or CurrencyType.

A Multiple Caching Example

The following example uses two web pages to demonstrate how multiple versions of a web page can be cached separately. The first page, QueryStringSender.aspx, isn't cached. It provides three buttons, as shown in Figure 26-4.

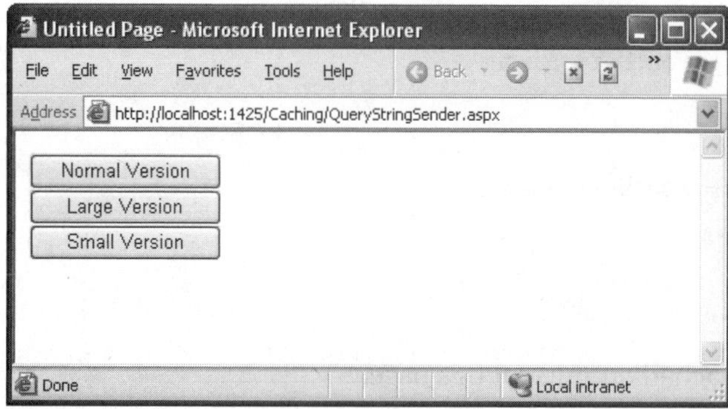

Figure 26-4. *Three page options*

A single event handler handles the Click event for all three buttons. The event handler navigates to the QueryStringRecipient.aspx page and adds a Version parameter to the query string to indicate which button was clicked—cmdNormal, cmdLarge, or cmdSmall:

```
protected void cmdVersion_Click(Object sender, EventArgs e)
{
    Response.Redirect("QueryStringRecipient.aspx" + "?Version=" +
      ((Control)sender).ID);
}
```

The QueryStringRecipient.aspx destination page displays the familiar date message. The page uses an OutputCache directive that looks for a single query string parameter (named Version):

```
<%@ OutputCache Duration="60" VaryByParam="Version" %>
```

In other words, this has three separately maintained HTML outputs: one where Version equals cmdSmall, one where Version equals cmdLarge, and one where Version equals cmdNormal.

Although it isn't necessary for this example, the Page.Load event handler tailors the page by changing the font size of the label accordingly. This makes it easy to distinguish the three versions of the page and verify that the caching is working as expected.

```
protected void Page_Load(Object sender, EventArgs e)
{
    lblDate.Text = "The time is now:<br />" + DateTime.Now.ToString();

    switch (Request.QueryString["Version"])
    {
        case "cmdLarge":
            lblDate.Font.Size = FontUnit.XLarge;
            break;
        case "cmdNormal":
            lblDate.Font.Size = FontUnit.Large;
            break;
        case "cmdSmall":
            lblDate.Font.Size = FontUnit.Small;
            break;
    }
}
```

Figure 26-5 shows one of the cached outputs for this page.

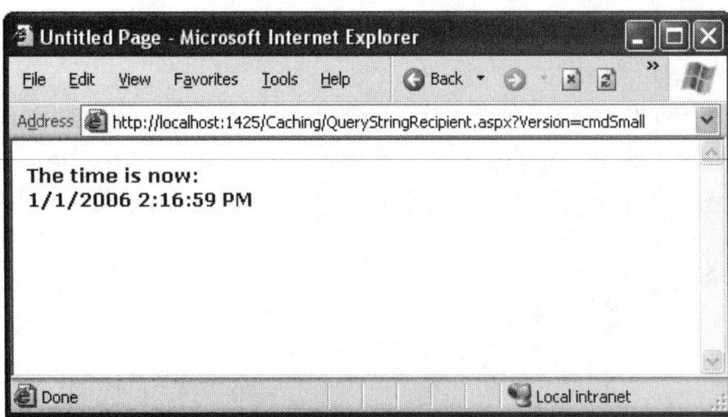

Figure 26-5. *One page with three cached outputs*

Custom Caching Control

Varying by query string parameters isn't the only option when storing multiple cached versions of a page. ASP.NET also allows you to create your own procedure that decides whether to cache a new page version or reuse an existing one. This code examines whatever information is appropriate and then returns a string. ASP.NET uses this string to implement caching. If your code generates the same string for different requests, ASP.NET will reuse the cached page. If your code generates a new string value, ASP.NET will generate a new cached version and store it separately.

One way you could use custom caching is to cache different versions of a page based on the browser type. That way, Netscape browsers will always receive Netscape-optimized pages, and Internet Explorer users will receive IE-optimized HTML. To set up this sort of logic, you start by adding the OutputCache directive to the pages that will be cached. Use the VaryByCustom attribute to specify a name that represents the type of custom caching you're creating. The following example uses the name Browser because pages will be cached based on the client browser:

```
<%@ OutputCache Duration="10" VaryByParam="None" VaryByCustom="Browser" %>
```

Next, you need to create the procedure that will generate the custom caching string. This procedure must be coded in the global.asax application file (or its code-behind file) and must use the following syntax:

```
public override string GetVaryByCustomString(
  HttpContext context, string arg)
{
    // Check for the requested type of caching.
    if (arg == "browser")
    {
       // Determine the current browser.
       string browserName;
       browserName = Context.Request.Browser.Browser;

       // Indicate that this string should be used to vary caching.
       return browserName;
    }
    else
    {
        // For any other type of caching, use the default logic.
        return base.GetVaryByCustomString(context, arg);
    }
}
```

The GetVaryByCustomString() function passes the VaryByCustom name in the arg parameter. This allows you to create an application that implements several types of custom caching in the same function. Each type would use a different VaryByCustom name (such as Browser, BrowserVersion, or DayOfWeek). Your GetVaryByCustomString() function would examine the VaryByCustom name and then return the appropriate caching string. If the caching strings for different requests match, ASP.NET will reuse the cached copy of the page. Or to look at it another way, ASP.NET will create and store a separate cached version of the page for each caching string it encounters.

The OutputCache directive has a third attribute that you can use to define caching. This attribute, VaryByHeader, allows you to store separate versions of a page based on the value of an HTTP header received with the request. You can specify a single header or a list of headers separated by semicolons. Multilingual sites could use this technique to cache different versions of a page based on the client browser language.

```
<%@ OutputCache Duration="20" VaryByParam="None"
    VaryByHeader="Accept-Language" %>
```

Interestingly, the base implementation of the GetVaryByCustomString() method already includes the logic for browser-based caching. That means you don't need to code the method shown previously. The base implementation of GetVaryByCustomString() creates the cached string based on the browser name and major version number. If you want to change how this logic works (for example, to vary based on name, major version, and minor version), you could override the GetVaryByCustomString() method, as in the previous example.

Fragment Caching

In some cases, you may find that you can't cache an entire page, but you would still like to cache a portion that is expensive to create and doesn't vary. One way to implement this sort of scenario is to use data caching to store just the underlying information used for the page. You'll examine this technique in the next section. Another option is to use fragment caching.

To implement fragment caching, you need to create a user control for the portion of the page you want to cache. You can then add the OutputCache directive to the user control. The result is that the page will not be cached, but the user control will.

Fragment caching is conceptually the same as page caching. It has only one catch—if your page retrieves a cached version of a user control, it cannot interact with it in code. For example, if your user control provides properties, your web page code cannot modify or access these properties. When the cached version of the user control is used, a block of HTML is simply inserted into the page. The corresponding user control object is not available.

Cache Profiles

One problem with output caching is that you need to embed the instruction into the page—either in the .aspx markup portion or in the code of the class. Although the first option (using the OutputCache) is relatively clean, it still produces management problems if you create dozens of cached pages. If you want to change the caching for all these pages (for example, moving the caching duration from 30 to 60 seconds), you need to modify every page. ASP.NET also needs to recompile these pages.

ASP.NET 2.0 introduces a new option that's suitable if you need to apply the same caching settings to a group of pages. This feature, called *cache profiles*, allows you to define the caching settings in a web.config file, associate a name with these settings, and then apply these settings to multiple pages using the name. That way, you have the freedom to modify all the linked pages at once simply by changing the caching profile in the web.config file.

To define a cache profile, you use the <add> tag in the <outputCacheProfiles> section, as follows. You assign a name and a duration.

```
<configuration>
  <system.web>
    <caching>
      <outputCacheSettings>
        <outputCacheProfiles>
          <add name="ProductItemCacheProfile" duration="60" />
        </outputCacheProfiles>
      </outputCacheSettings>
    </caching>
  ...
  </system.web>
</configuration>
```

You can now use this profile in a page through the CacheProfile attribute:

```
<%@ OutputCache CacheProfile="ProductItemCacheProfile" VaryByParam="None" %>
```

Interestingly, if you want apply other caching details, such as the VaryByParam behavior, you can set it either as an attribute in the OutputCache directive or as an attribute of the <add> tag for the profile. Just make sure you start with a lowercase letter if you use the <add> tag, because the property names are camel cased, as are all configuration settings, and case is important in XML.

Output Caching in a Web Service

You can also use output caching for individual methods in a web service. To do so, you need to add the CacheDuration value to the WebMethod before the appropriate method declaration. The following example caches a web method's result for 30 seconds:

```
[WebMethod(CacheDuration=30)]
private string MyMethod(int myParameter)
{
    // (Code goes here.)
}
```

When using output caching with a web service, you don't need to enable any type of cache varying. Responses are reused only for requests that supply an identical set of parameters. For example, if three clients invoke MyMethod(), each with a different value of myParameter, three separate strings will be stored in the cache. If another client calls MyMethod() with a matching myParameter value before the 30-second time limit elapses, that client will receive the cached data, and the web method code will not be executed.

Data Caching

Data caching is the most flexible type of caching, but it also forces you to take specific additional steps in your code to implement it. The basic principle of data caching is that you add items that are expensive to create to a built-in collection object called Cache. This object works much like the Application object you saw in Chapter 11. It's globally available to all requests from all clients in the application. But it has three key differences:

The Cache object is thread-safe: This means you don't need to explicitly lock or unlock the Cache collection before adding or removing an item. However, the objects in the Cache collection will still need to be thread-safe themselves. For example, if you create a custom business object, more than one client could try to use that object at once, which could lead to invalid data. You can code around this limitation in various ways—one easy approach that you'll see in this chapter is to just make a duplicate copy of the object if you need to work with it in a web page.

Items in the Cache collection are removed automatically: ASP.NET will remove an item if it expires, if one of the objects or files it depends on changes, or if the server becomes low on memory. This means you can freely use the cache without worrying about wasting valuable server memory, because ASP.NET will remove items as needed. But because items in the cache can be removed, you always need to check whether a cache object exists before you attempt to use it. Otherwise, you could generate a null reference exception.

Items in the cache support dependencies: You, can link a cached object to a file, a database table, or another type of resource. If this resource changes, your cached object is automatically deemed invalid and released.

Adding Items to the Cache

You can insert an object into the cache in several ways. You can simply assign it to a new key name (as you would with the Session or Application collection), but this approach is generally discouraged because it does not allow you to have any control over the amount of time the object will be retained in the cache. A better approach is to use the Insert() method.

The Insert() method has four overloaded versions. The most useful and commonly used one requires four parameters:

```
Cache.Insert(key, item, dependencies, absoluteExpiration, slidingExpiration);
```

Table 26-3 describes these parameters.

Table 26-3. *Cache.Insert() Parameters*

Parameter	Description
key	A string that assigns a name to this cached item in the collection and allows you to look it up later.
item	The actual object you want to cache.
dependencies	A CacheDependency object that allows you to create a dependency for this item in the cache. If you don't want to create a dependent item, just specify null for this parameter.
absoluteExpiration	A DateTime object representing the time at which the item will be removed from the cache.
slidingExpiration	A TimeSpan object represents how long ASP.NET will wait between requests before removing a cached item. For example, if this value is 20 minutes, ASP.NET will evict the item if it isn't used by any code for a 20-minute period.

Typically, you won't use all of these parameters at once. Cache dependencies, for example, are a special tool you'll consider a little later in the "Caching with Dependencies" section. Also, you cannot set both a sliding expiration and an absolute expiration policy at the same time. If you want to use an absolute expiration, set the slidingExpiration parameter to TimeSpan.Zero:

```
Cache.Insert("MyItem", obj, null,
  DateTime.Now.AddMinutes(60), TimeSpan.Zero);
```

Absolute expirations are best when you know the information in a given item can be considered valid only for a specific amount of time (such as a stock chart or weather report). Sliding expiration, on the other hand, is more useful when you know that a cached item will always remain valid (such as with historical data or a product catalog) but should still be allowed to expire if it isn't being used. To set a sliding expiration policy, set the absoluteExpiration parameter to DateTime.Max, as shown here:

```
Cache.Insert("MyItem", obj, null,
  DateTime.MaxValue, TimeSpan.FromMinutes(10));
```

A Simple Cache Test

The following page presents a simple caching test. An item is cached for 30 seconds and reused for requests in that time. The page code always runs (because the page itself isn't cached), checks the cache, and retrieves or constructs the item as needed. It also reports whether the item was found in the cache.

```
public partial class SimpleDataCache : Page
{
    protected void Page_Load(Object sender, EventArgs e)
    {
        if (this.IsPostBack)
        {
            lblInfo.Text += "Page posted back.<br />";
        }
        else
        {
            lblInfo.Text += "Page created.<br />";
        }

        if (Cache["TestItem"] == null)
        {
            lblInfo.Text += "Creating TestItem...<br />";
            DateTime testItem = DateTime.Now;

            lblInfo.Text += "Storing TestItem in cache ";
            lblInfo.Text += "for 30 seconds.<br />";
            Cache.Insert("TestItem", testItem, null,
              DateTime.Now.AddSeconds(30), TimeSpan.Zero);
        }
```

```
        else
        {
            lblInfo.Text += "Retrieving TestItem...<br />";
            DateTime testItem = (DateTime)Cache["TestItem"];
            lblInfo.Text += "TestItem is '" + testItem.ToString();
            lblInfo.Text += "'<br />";
        }

        lblInfo.Text += "<br />";
    }
}
```

Figure 26-6 shows the result after the page has been loaded and posted back several times in the 30-second period.

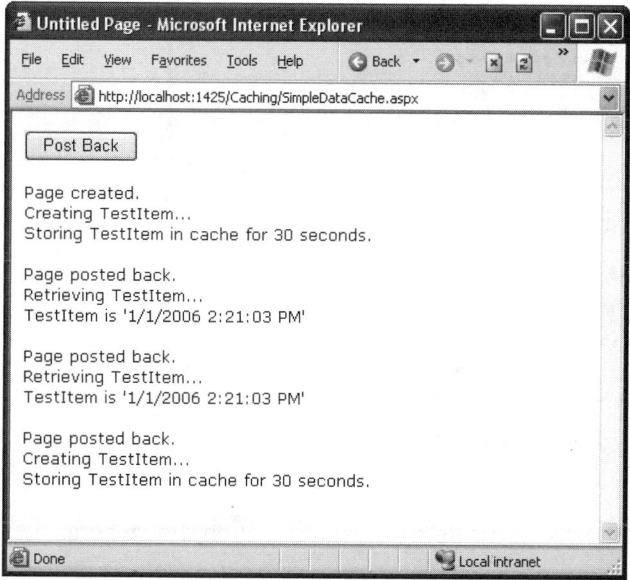

Figure 26-6. *A simple cache test*

Caching to Provide Multiple Views

The next example shows a more interesting demonstration of caching, which includes retrieving information from a database and storing it in a DataSet. This information is then displayed in a GridView. However, the output for the web page can't be efficiently cached because the user is given the chance to customize the display by hiding any combination of columns. Note that even with just ten columns, you can construct more than a thousand different possible views by hiding and showing various columns. These are far too many columns for successful output caching!

Figure 26-7 shows the page.

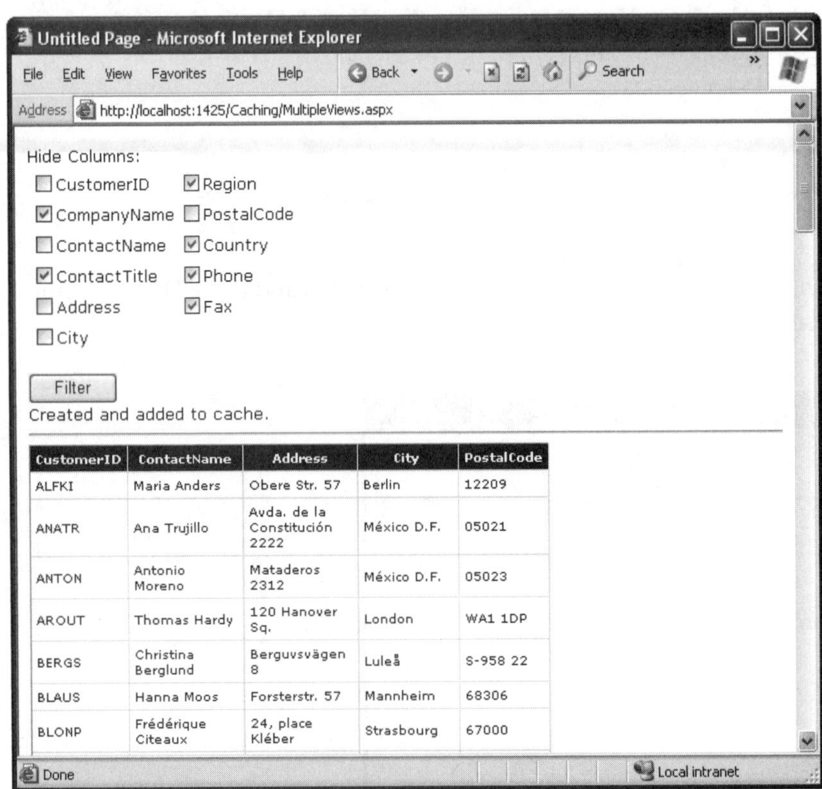

Figure 26-7. *Filtering information from a cached DataSet*

The DataSet is constructed in the dedicated RetrieveData() function shown here:

```
private DataSet RetrieveData()
{
    string connectionString =
      WebConfigurationManager.ConnectionStrings["Northwind"].ConnectionString;
    string SQLSelect = "SELECT * FROM Customers";
    SqlConnection con = new SqlConnection(connectionString);
    SqlCommand cmd = new SqlCommand(SQLSelect, con);
    SqlDataAdapter adapter = new SqlDataAdapter(cmd);
    DataSet ds = new DataSet();
```

```
    try
    {
        con.Open();
        adapter.Fill(ds, "Customers");
    }
    finally
    {
        con.Close();
    }

    return ds;
}
```

When the page is first loaded, the check box list of columns is filled:

```
chkColumns.DataSource = ds.Tables[0].Columns;
chkColumns.DataMember = "Item";
chkColumns.DataBind();
```

The DataSet is inserted into the cache with a sliding expiration of two minutes when the page is loaded:

```
Cache.Insert("DataSet", ds, null, DateTime.MaxValue,
  TimeSpan.FromMinutes(2));
```

Every time the Filter button is clicked, the page attempts to retrieve the DataSet from the cache. If it cannot retrieve the DataSet, it calls the RetrieveData function and then adds the DataSet to the cache. It then reports on the page whether the DataSet was retrieved from the cache or generated manually.

To provide the configurable grid, the code actually loops through the DataTable, removing all the columns that the user has selected to hide before binding the data. Many other alternatives are possible (another approach is just to hide columns), but this strategy demonstrates an important fact about the cache. When you retrieve an item, you actually retrieve a reference to the cached object. If you modify that object, you're actually modifying the cached item as well. For the page to be able to delete columns without affecting the cached copy of the DataSet, the code needs to create a duplicate copy before performing the operations using the DataSet.Copy() method.

The full code for the Filter button is as follows:

```
protected void cmdFilter_Click(Object sender, EventArgs e)
{
    DataSet ds;
    if (Cache["DataSet"] == null)
```

```
    {
        ds = RetrieveData();
        Cache.Insert("DataSet", ds, null, DateTime.MaxValue,
                     TimeSpan.FromMinutes(2));
        lblCacheStatus.Text = "Created and added to cache.";
    }
    else
    {
        ds = (DataSet)Cache["Titles"];
        ds = ds.Copy();
        lblCacheStatus.Text = "Retrieved from cache.";
    }

    foreach (ListItem item in chkColumns.Items)
    {
        if (item.Selected)
        {
            ds.Tables[0].Columns.Remove(item.Text);
        }
    }

    gridPubs.DataSource = ds.Tables[0];
    gridPubs.DataBind();
}
```

Data Caching in a Web Service

A web service can use data caching just as easily as a web page. In fact, you can store data in a web method and retrieve it in a web page, or vice versa. The only difference is that to access the Cache object in a web service, you need to use the HttpContext.Current.Cache property. It isn't provided as a property of the web service class.

The following web service presents a simple example of caching at work. It provides two web methods: GetAuthorData() and GetAuthorNames(). Both of these web methods call the same private GetAuthorDataSet() method, which returns a DataSet with the full customer table. GetAuthorData() returns this DataSet directly, while the GetAuthorNames() retrieves this DataSet, extracts just the author names, and returns it as an array of strings.

```
[WebService()]
public class DataCachingTest : WebService
```

```
{
    string connectionString =
      WebConfigurationManager.ConnectionStrings["Pubs"].ConnectionString;

    [WebMethod()]
    public DataSet GetAuthorData()
    {
        // Return the full author DataSet (from the cache if possible).
        return GetAuthorDataSet();
    }

    [WebMethod()]
    public string[] GetAuthorNames()
    {
        // Get the customer DataSet (from the cache if possible).
        DataTable dt = GetAuthorDataSet().Tables[0];

        // Create an array that will hold the name of each customer.
        string[] names = new string[dt.Rows.Count];

        // Fill the array.
        int i = 0;
        foreach (DataRow row in dt.Rows)
        {
            names[i] = row["au_fname"] + " " + row["au_lname"];
            i++;
        }
        return names;
    }

    private DataSet GetAuthorDataSet()
    {
        System.Web.Caching.Cache cache;
        cache = HttpContext.Current.Cache ;

        // Check for cached item.
        DataSet ds = cache["DataSet"] as DataSet;
        if (ds == null)
```

```
        {
            // Re-create the item.
            ds = new DataSet("DataSet");
            SqlConnection con = new SqlConnection(connectionString);
            SqlCommand cmd = new SqlCommand("SELECT * FROM Authors", con);
            SqlDataAdapter adapter = new SqlDataAdapter(cmd);
            try
            {
                con.Open();
                adapter.Fill(ds, "Authors");
            }
            finally
            {
                con.Close();
            }

            // Store the item in the cache (for 60 seconds).
            cache.Insert("DataSet", ds, null,
              DateTime.Now.AddSeconds(60), TimeSpan.Zero);
        }
        return ds;
    }
}
```

The GetCustomerDataSet() method includes all the caching logic. If the DataSet is in the cache, it returns it immediately. Otherwise, it queries the database, creates the DataSet, and inserts it in the cache. The end result is that both web methods can use the same cached data.

Caching with the Data Source Controls

The SqlDataSource (Chapter 15), ObjectDataSource (Chapter 24), and XmlDataSource (Chapter 17) all support built-in data caching. Using caching with these controls is highly recommended, because unlike your own custom data code, the data source controls always requery the data source in every postback. They also query the data source once for every bound control, so if you have three controls bound to the same data source, three separate queries are executed against the database just before the page is rendered. Even a little caching can reduce this overhead dramatically.

■ **Note** Although many data source controls support caching, it's not a required data source control feature, and you'll run into data source controls that don't support it or for which it may not make sense (such as the SiteMapDataSource).

To support caching, the data source controls all use the same properties, which are listed in Table 26-4.

Table 26-4. *Values for the CacheItemRemovedReason Enumeration*

Property	Description
EnableCaching	If true, caching is switched on. It's false by default.
CacheExpirationPolicy	Uses a value from the DataSourceCacheExpiry enumeration—Absolute for absolute expiration (which times out after a fixed interval of time) or Sliding for sliding expiration (which resets the time window every time the data object is retrieved from the cache).
CacheDuration	The number of seconds to cache the data object. If you are using sliding expiration, the time limit is reset every time the object is retrieved from the cache. The default, DataSourceCacheExpiry. Infinite, keeps cached items perpetually.
CacheKeyDependency and SqlCacheDependency	Allows you to make a cached item dependent on another item in the data cache (CacheKeyDependency) or on a table in your database (SqlCacheDependency). Dependencies are discussed in the "Cache Dependencies" section.

Caching with SqlDataSource

When you enable caching for the SqlDataSource control, you cache the results of the SelectQuery. However, if you create a select query that takes parameters, the SqlDataSource will cache a separate result for every set of parameter values.

For example, imagine you create a page that allows you to view employees by city. The user selects the desired city from a list box, and you use a SqlDataSource control to fill in the matching employee records in a grid (see Figure 26-8).

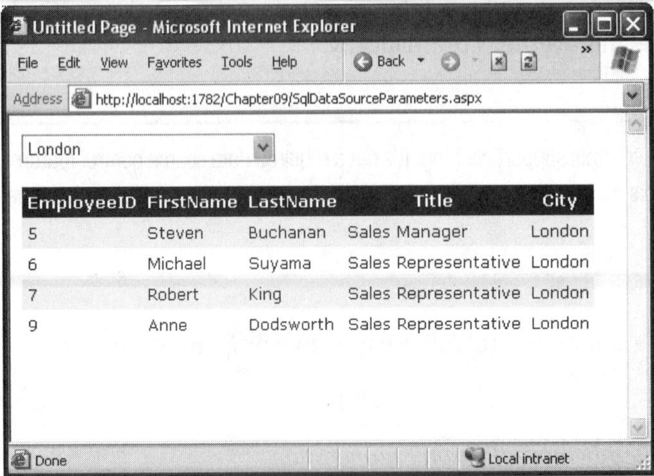

Figure 26-8. *Retrieving data from the cache*

To fill the grid, you use the following SqlDataSource:

```
<asp:SqlDataSource ID="sourceEmployees" runat="server"
 ProviderName="System.Data.SqlClient"
 ConnectionString="<%$ ConnectionStrings:Northwind %>"
 SelectCommand="SELECT EmployeeID, FirstName, LastName, Title, City FROM
Employees WHERE City=@City">
  <SelectParameters>
    <asp:ControlParameter ControlID="lstCities" Name="City"
     PropertyName="SelectedValue" />
  </SelectParameters>
</asp:SqlDataSource>
```

In this example, each time you select a city, a separate query is performed to get just the matching employees in that city. The query is used to fill a DataSet, which is then cached. If you select a different city, the process repeats, and the new DataSet is cached separately. However, if you pick a city that you or another user has already requested, the appropriate DataSet is fetched from the cache (provided it hasn't yet expired).

■ **Note** SqlDataSource caching works only when the DataSourceMode property is set to DataSet (the default). That's because the DataReader object can't be efficiently cached, because it represents a live connection to the database.

Caching separate results for different parameter values works well if some parameter values are used much more frequently than others. For example, if the results for London are requested much more often than the results for Redmond, this ensures that the London results stick around in the cache even when the Redmond DataSet has been released. Assuming the full set of results is extremely large, this may be the most efficient approach.

On the other hand, if the parameter values are all used with similar frequency, this approach isn't as suitable. One of the problems it imposes is that when the items in the cache expire, you'll need multiple database queries to repopulate the cache (one for each parameter value), which isn't as efficient as getting the combined results with a single query.

If you fall into the second situation, you can change the SqlDataSource so that it retrieves a DataSet with all the employee records and caches that. The SqlDataSource can then extract just the records it needs to satisfy each request from the DataSet. This way, a single DataSet with all the records is cached, which can satisfy any parameter value.

To use this technique, you need to rewrite your SqlDataSource to use *filtering*. First, the select query should return all the rows and not use any SELECT parameters:

```
<asp:SqlDataSource ID="sourceEmployees" runat="server"
 SelectCommand=
"SELECT EmployeeID, FirstName, LastName, Title, City FROM Employees"
 ...>
</asp:SqlDataSource>
```

Second, you need to define the filter expression. This is the portion that goes in the WHERE clause of a typical SQL query, and you write it in the same as you used the DataView.RowFilter property in Chapter 9. (In fact, the SqlDataSource uses the DataView's row filtering abilities behind the scenes.) However, this has a catch—if you're supplying the filter value from another source (such as a control), you need to define one or more placeholders, using the syntax {0} for the first placeholder, {1} for the second, and so on. You then supply the filter values using the <FilterParameters> section, in much the same way you supplied the select parameters in the first version.

Here's the completed SqlDataSource tag:

```
<asp:SqlDataSource ID="sourceEmployees" runat="server"
 ProviderName="System.Data.SqlClient"
 ConnectionString="<%$ ConnectionStrings:Northwind %>"
 SelectCommand=
"SELECT EmployeeID, FirstName, LastName, Title, City FROM Employees"
 FilterExpression="City='{0}'" EnableCaching="True">
  <FilterParameters>
    <asp:ControlParameter ControlID="lstCities" Name="City"
     PropertyName="SelectedValue" />
  </FilterParameters>
</asp:SqlDataSource>
```

■**Tip** Don't use filtering unless you are using caching. If you use filtering without caching, you are essentially retrieving the full result set each time and then extracting a portion of its records. This combines the worst of both worlds—you have to repeat the query with each postback, and you fetch far more data than you need each time.

Caching with ObjectDataSource

The ObjectDataSource caching works on the data object returned from the SelectMethod. If you are using a parameterized query, the ObjectDataSource distinguishes between requests with different parameter values and caches them separately. Unfortunately, the ObjectDataSource caching has a significant limitation—it works only when the select method returns a DataSet or DataTable. If you return any other type of object, you'll receive a NotSupportedException.

This limitation is unfortunate, because there's no technical reason you can't cache custom objects in the data cache. If you want this feature, you'll need to implement data caching inside your method by manually inserting your objects into the data cache and retrieving them later. In fact, caching inside your method can be more effective, because you have the ability to share the same cached object in multiple methods. For example, you could cache a DataTable with a list of product categories and use that cached item in both the GetProductCategories() and GetProductsByCategory() methods.

■**Tip** The only consideration you should keep in mind is to make sure you use unique cache key names that aren't likely to collide with the names of cached items that the page might use. This isn't a problem when using the built-in data source caching, because it always stores its information in a hidden slot in the cache.

If your custom class returns a DataSet or DataTable, and you do decide to use the built-in ObjectDataSource caching, you can also use filtering as discussed with the SqlDataSource control. Just instruct your ObjectDataSource to call a method that gets the full set of data, and set the FilterExpression to retrieve just those items that match the current view.

Caching with Dependencies

As time passes, the data source may change in response to other actions. However, if your code uses caching, you may remain unaware of the changes and continue using out-of-date information from the cache. To help mitigate this problem, ASP.NET supports *cache dependencies*. Cache dependencies allow you to make a cached item dependent on another resource so that when that resource changes, the cached item is removed automatically.

ASP.NET includes three types of dependencies:

- Dependencies on other cached items
- Dependencies on files or folders
- Dependencies on a database query

To create a cache dependency, you need to create a CacheDependency object and then use it when adding the dependent cached item. For example, the following code creates a cached item that will automatically be evicted from the cache when an XML file is changed:

```
// Create a dependency for the ProductList.xml file.
CacheDependency prodDependency = new CacheDependency(
  Server.MapPath("ProductList.xml"));

// Add a cache item that will be dependent on this file.
Cache.Insert("ProductInfo", prodInfo, prodDependency);
```

CacheDependency monitoring begins as soon as the object is created. If the XML file changes before you have added the dependent item to the cache, the item will expire immediately once it's added.

The CacheDependency object provides several constructors. You've already seen how it can make a dependency based on a file by using the file name constructor. You can also specify a directory that needs to be monitored for changes, or you can use a constructor that accepts an array of strings that represent multiple files and directories.

Yet another constructor accepts an array of file names and an array of cache keys. The following example uses this constructor to create an item that is dependent on another item in the cache:

```
Cache("Key 1") = "Cache Item 1";

// Make Cache("Key 2") dependent on Cache("Key 1").
string[] dependencyKey = new string[1];
dependencyKey[0] = "Key 1";
CacheDependency dependency = new CacheDependency(null, dependencyKey);

Cache.Insert("Key 2", "Cache Item 2", dependency);
```

Now, when Cache("Key 1") changes or is removed from the cache, Cache("Key 2") will automatically be dropped.

Figure 26-9 shows a simple test page that is included with the online samples for this chapter. It sets up a dependency, modifies the file, and allows you to verify that the cached item has been dropped from the cache.

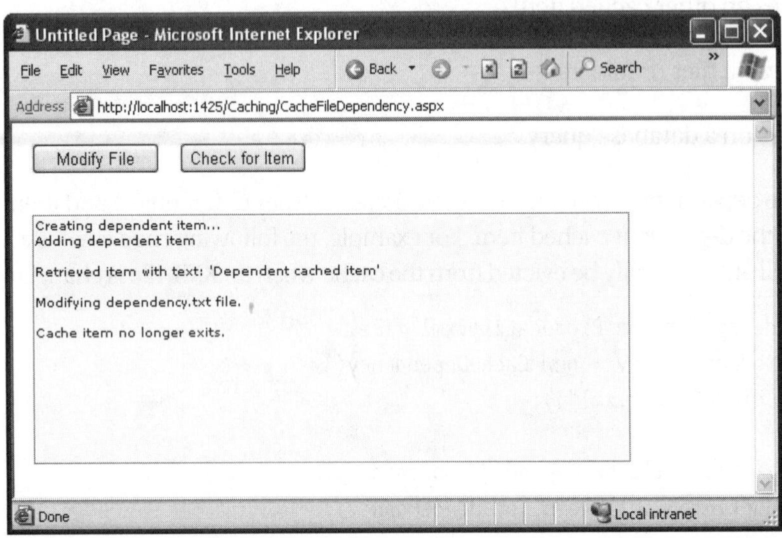

Figure 26-9. *Testing cache dependencies*

A more complex kind of cache dependency is the SQL Server cache dependency. It's one of the most widely touted new ASP.NET 2.0 features. In a nutshell, SQL cache dependencies provide the ability to automatically invalidate a cached data object (such as a DataSet) when the related data is modified in the database. This feature is supported in both SQL Server 2005 (including the Express Edition) and in SQL Server 2000, although the underlying plumbing is quite a bit different.

■ **Tip** Using SQL cache dependencies still entails more complexity than just using a time-based expiration policy. If it's acceptable for certain information to be used without reflecting all the most recent changes (and developers often overestimate the importance of up-to-the-millisecond live information), you may not need it at all.

Cache Notifications in SQL Server 2000 or SQL Server 7

ASP.NET uses a polling model for SQL Server 2000 and SQL Server 7. Older versions of SQL Server and other databases aren't supported (although third parties can implement their own solutions by creating a custom dependency class).

With the polling model, ASP.NET keeps a connection open to the database and checks periodically whether a table has been updated. The effect of tying up one connection in this way isn't terribly significant, but the extra database work involved with polling does add some database overhead. For the polling model to be effective, the polling process needs to be quicker and lighter than the original query that extracts the data.

You must take several steps to enable notification with SQL Server 2000. Here's an overview of the process:

1. The first step is to determine which tables need notification support.

2. Next, use the aspnet_regsql.exe command-line utility to create the notification tables for your database.

3. Then, you need to register each table that requires notification support. You also use the aspnet_regsql.exe command for this step.

4. Finally, you enable ASP.NET polling through a web.config file. You're now ready to create SqlCacheDependency objects.

The following sections describe these steps.

Enabling Notifications

Before you can use SQL Server cache invalidation, you need to enable notifications for the database. This task is performed with the aspnet_regsql.exe command-line utility, which is located in the c:\[WinDir]\Microsoft.NET\Framework\[Version] directory. To enable notifications, you need to use the -ed command-line switch. You also need to identify the server (use -E for a trusted connection and -S to choose a server other than the current computer) and the database (use -d). Here's an example that enables notifications for the Northwind database on the current server:

```
aspnet_regsql -ed -E -d AspNet
```

When you take this step, a new table named SqlCacheTablesForChangeNotification is added to the database named AspNet (which must already exist). The SqlCacheTablesForChangeNotification table has three columns: tableName, notificationCreated, and changeId. This table is used to track changes. Essentially, when a change takes place, SQL Server writes a record to this table. ASP.NET's polling service queries this table.

This design achieves a number of benefits:

- Because the change notification table is much smaller than the table with the cached data, it's much faster to query.
- Because the change notification table isn't used for other tasks, reading these records won't risk locking and concurrency issues.
- Because multiple tables in the same database will use the same notification table, you can monitor several tables at once without increasing the polling overhead.

Figure 26-10 shows an overview of how SQL Server 2000 cache invalidation works.

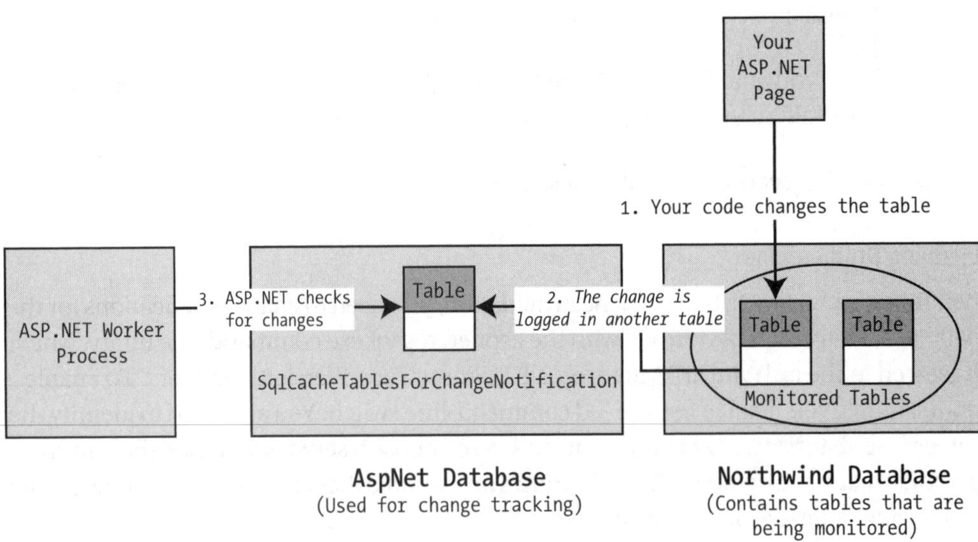

Figure 26-10. *Monitoring a database for changes in SQL Server 2000*

Even once you've created the SqlCacheTablesForChangeNotification table, you still need to enable notification support for each table. You can do this manually using the SqlCacheRegisterTableStoredProcedure, or you can rely on aspnet_regsql by using the -et parameter to turn on the notifications and the -t parameter to name the table. Here's an example that enables notifications for the Employees table:

```
aspnet_regsql -et -E -d Northwind -t Employees
```

This step generates the notification trigger for the Employees table.

How Notifications Work

Now you have all the ingredients in place to use the notification system. For example, imagine you cache the results of a query like this:

```
SELECT * FROM Employees
```

This query retrieves records from the Employees table. To check for changes that might invalidate your cached object, you need to know whether any record in the Employees table is inserted, deleted, or updated. You can watch for these operations using triggers. For example, here's the trigger on the Employees table that aspnet_regsql creates:

```
CREATE TRIGGER dbo.[Employees_AspNet_SqlCacheNotification_Trigger]
  ON [Employees]
  FOR INSERT, UPDATE, DELETE AS BEGIN

  SET NOCOUNT ON
  EXEC dbo.AspNet_SqlCacheUpdateChangeIdStoredProcedure N'Employees'
END
```

In other words, when a change takes place on the table that's being monitored, that change triggers the AspNet_SqlCacheUpdateChangeIdStoredProcedure stored procedure. This stored procedure simply increments the changeId of the corresponding row in the change notification table:

```
CREATE PROCEDURE dbo.AspNet_SqlCacheUpdateChangeIdStoredProcedure
  @tableName NVARCHAR(450)
AS
  BEGIN
  UPDATE dbo.AspNet_SqlCacheTablesForChangeNotification WITH (ROWLOCK)
    SET changeId = changeId + 1
    WHERE tableName = @tableName
  END
GO
```

The AspNet_SqlCacheTablesForChangeNotification contains a single record for every table you're monitoring. As you can see, when you make a change in the table (such as inserting a record), the changeId column is incremented by 1. ASP.NET queries this table repeatedly and keeps track of the most recent changeId values for every table. When this value changes in a subsequent read, ASP.NET knows that the table has changed.

This hints at one of the major limitations of cache invalidation as implemented in SQL Server 2000 and SQL Server 7. *Any* change to the table is deemed to invalidate *any* query for that table. In other words, if you use this query:

```
SELECT * FROM Employees WHERE City='London'
```

the caching still works in the same way. That means if any employee record is touched, even if the employee resides in another city (and therefore isn't one of the cached records), the notification is still sent and the cached item is considered invalid. Keeping track of what changes do and do not invalidate a cached data object is simply too much work for SQL Server 2000 (although it is possible in SQL Server 2005).

■ **Tip** The implementation of cache invalidation with SQL Server 2000 has more overhead than the implementation with SQL Server 2005 and isn't as fine-grained. As a result, it doesn't make sense for tables that change frequently or for narrowly defined queries that retrieve only a small subset of records from a table.

Enabling ASP.NET Polling

The next step is to instruct ASP.NET to poll the database. You do this on a per-application basis. In other words, every application that uses cache invalidation will hold a separate connection and poll the notification table on its own.

To enable the polling service, you use the <sqlCacheDepency> element in the web.config file. You set the enabled attribute to true to turn it on, and you set the pollTime attribute to the number of milliseconds between each poll. (The higher the poll time, the longer the potential delay before a change is detected.) You also need to supply the connection string information.

For example, this web.config file checks for updated notification information every 15 seconds:

```
<configuration xmlns="http://schemas.microsoft.com/.NetConfiguration/v2.0">
  <connectionStrings>
    <add name="Northwind" connectionString=
"Data Source=localhost;Initial Catalog=Northwind;Integrated Security=SSPI"/>
  </connectionStrings>

  <system.web>
    <caching>
      <sqlCacheDependency enabled="true" pollTime="15000" >
```

```
        <databases>
          <add name="Northwind" connectionStringName="Northwind" />
        </databases>
      </sqlCacheDependency>
    </caching>
    ...
  </system.web>
</configuration>
```

Creating the Cache Dependency

Now that you've seen how to set up your database to support SQL Server notifications, the only remaining detail is the code, which is quite straightforward. You can use your cache dependency with programmatic data caching, a data source control, and output caching.

For programmatic data caching, you need to create a new SqlCacheDependency and supply that to the Cache.Insert() method, much as you did with file dependencies. In the SqlCacheDependency constructor, you supply two strings. The first is the name of the database you defined in the <add> element in the <sqlCacheDependency> section of the web.config file. The second is the name of the linked table.

Here's an example:

```
// Create a dependency for the Employees table.
SqlCacheDependency empDependency = new SqlCacheDependency(
  "Northwind", "Employees");

// Add a cache item that will be invalidated if this table changes.
Cache.Insert("Employees", dsEmployees, empDependency);
```

To perform the same trick with output caching, you simply need to set the SqlCacheDependency property with the database dependency name and the table name, separated by a colon:

```
<%@ OutputCache Duration="600" SqlDependency="Northwind:Employees"
    VaryByParam="none" %>
```

You can also set the dependency using programmatic output caching with the Response.AddCacheDependency() method:

```
Response.AddCacheDependency(empDependency);

// Use output caching for this page (for 60 seconds or until the table changes).
Response.Cache.SetCacheability(HttpCacheability.Public);
Response.Cache.SetExpires(DateTime.Now.AddSeconds(60));
Response.Cache.SetValidUntilExpires(true);
```

Finally, the same technique works with the SqlDataSource and ObjectDataSource controls:

```
<asp:SqlDataSource EnableCaching="True"
 SqlCacheDependency="Northwind:Employees" ... />
```

To try a complete example, you can use the downloadable code for this chapter.

Cache Notifications in SQL Server 2005

SQL Server 2005 gets closest to the ideal notification solution, because the notification infrastructure is built into the database with a messaging system called the *Service Broker*. The Service Broker manages *queues*, which are database objects that have the same standing as tables, stored procedures, or views.

Essentially, you can instruct SQL Server 2005 to send notifications for specific events using the CREATE EVENT NOTIFICATION command. ASP.NET offers a higher-level model—you register a query, and ASP.NET automatically instructs SQL Server 2005 to send notifications for any operations that would affect the results of that query. This mechanism works in a similar way to indexed views. Every time you perform an operation, SQL Server determines whether your operation affects a registered command. If it does, SQL Server sends a notification message and stops the notification process.

When using notification with SQL Server, you get the following benefits over SQL Server 2000:

Notification is much more fine-grained: Instead of invalidating your cached object when the table changes, SQL Server 2005 invalidates your object only when a row that affects your query is inserted, updated, or deleted.

Notification is more intelligent: A notification message is sent the first time the data is changed but not if the data is changed again (unless you reregister for notification messages by adding an item back to the cache).

No special steps are required to set up notification: You do not run aspnet_regsql or add polling settings to the web.config file. However, you do need to call the SqlDependency.Start() method somewhere in your code to start the polling service.

Notifications work with SELECT queries and stored procedures. However, some restrictions exist for the SELECT syntax you can use. To properly support notifications, your command must adhere to the following rules:

- You must fully qualify table names in the form [Owner].table, as in dbo.Employees (not just Employees).
- Your query cannot use an aggregate function, such as COUNT(), MAX(), MIN(), or AVERAGE().
- You cannot select all columns with the wildcard * (as in SELECT * FROM Employees). Instead, you must specifically name each column so that SQL Server can properly track changes that do and do not affect the results of your query.

Here's an acceptable command:

```
SELECT EmployeeID, FirstName, LastName, City FROM dbo.Employees
```

These are the most important rules, but the SQL Server Books Online has a lengthy list of caveats and exceptions. If you break one of these rules, you won't receive an error. However, the notification message will be sent as soon as you register the command, and the cached item will be invalidated immediately.

Initializing the Caching Service

Before you can use SQL cache dependencies with SQL Server 2005, you need to call the static SqlDependency.Start() method. This initializes the listening service on the web server.

```
string connectionString = WebConfigurationManager.ConnectionStrings[
  "Northwind"].ConnectionString;
SqlDependency.Start(connectionString)
```

You need to call the Start() method only once over the lifetime of your web application, so it often makes sense to place the call in the Application_Start() method of the global.asax file so it's triggered automatically. It's safe to call the Start() method even if the listener is already started, as this won't cause an error. You can also use the Stop() method to halt the listener.

FAILED NOTIFICATIONS

If your cached item never expires, the ASP.NET polling service is not receiving the invalidation message. This has several possible causes. The most common is that you haven't enabled the CLR for SQL Server. The procedure that sends notification messages is a .NET procedure, so it requires this support.

To enable CLR support, fire up the Visual Studio 2005 Command Prompt window, and run the SqlCmd.exe command-line utility:

```
SqlCmd -S localhost\SQLEXPRESS
```

You may need to change the server name, depending where your database is installed. The previous command line is for SQL Server 2005 Express Edition on the local computer.

Next, enter the following SQL statements:

```
EXEC sp_configure 'show advanced options', '1'
GO
RECONFIGURE
GO
EXEC sp_configure 'clr enabled', 1
GO
RECONFIGURE
```

Then type **quit** to exit the SqlCmd tool.

If your cached item expires immediately, the most likely problem is that you've broken one of the rules for writing commands that work with notifications, as described earlier.

Creating the Cache Dependency

You need a different syntax to use SQL cache dependencies with SQL Server 2005. That's because it's not enough to simply identify the database name and table—instead, SQL Server needs to know the exact command.

If you use programmatic caching, you must create the SqlCacheDependency using the constructor that accepts a SqlCommand object. Here's an example:

```
// Create the ADO.NET objects.
SqlConnection con = new SqlConnection(connectionString);
string query =
 "SELECT EmployeeID, FirstName, LastName, City FROM dbo.Employees";
SqlCommand cmd = new SqlCommand(query, con);
SqlDataAdapter adapter = new SqlDataAdapter(cmd);

// Fill the DataSet.
DataSet ds = new DataSet();
adapter.Fill(ds, "Employees");
```

```
// Create the dependency.
SqlCacheDependency empDependency = new SqlCacheDependency(cmd);

// Add a cache item that will be invalidated if one of its records changes
// (or a new record is added in the same range).
Cache.Insert("Employees", ds, empDependency);
```

If you're using the OutputCache directive or a data source control, ASP.NET takes care of the registration for you. You simply need to supply the string value CommandNotification, as shown here:

```
<%@ OutputCache Duration="600" SqlDependency="CommandNotification"
    VaryByParam="none" %>
```

The Last Word

The most performance-critical area in most web applications is the data layer. But many ASP.NET developers don't realize that you can dramatically reduce the burden on your database and increase the scalability of all your web applications with just a little caching code.

However, with any performance-optimization strategy, the only way to gauge the value of a change is to perform stress testing and profiling. Without this step, you might spend a great deal of time perfecting code that will achieve only a minor improvement in performance or scalability, at the expense of more effective changes.

CHAPTER 27

■ ■ ■

Web Parts

There has been a growing interest in *portals,* sites that let users customize one or more pages to suit their needs and tastes. You've seen a fully customizable portal if you've ever used My MSN (see Figure 27-1), and several other major sites, including Yahoo and Google, are also moving toward full customization.

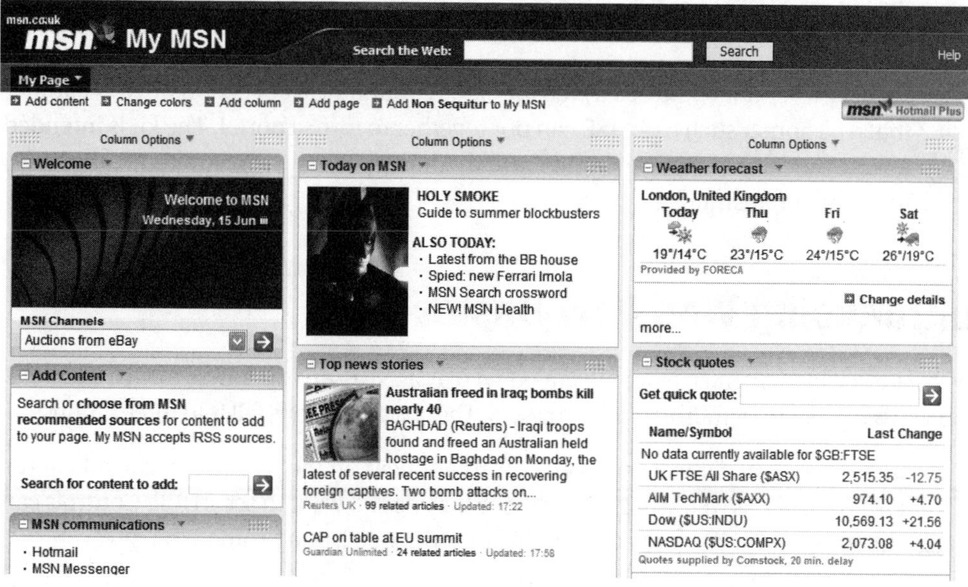

Figure 27-1. *The My MSN customizable portal page*

Portals aggregate content, pulling in information from various sources and letting users choose what they want to see, whether it is weather reports, news headlines, sports results, or the content of their inboxes.

You may also have seen portals in action in Microsoft SharePoint Portal Server, a Microsoft server product especially designed to host portal applications. SharePoint introduced the concept of *Web Parts*: building blocks that are used to create portal pages and that users of the page could pick and choose and then customize to suit their own uses. Web Parts could be written as ASP.NET custom controls, which were then hosted within SharePoint server and served to browsers as HTML. Because Web Parts were ASP.NET controls, they could operate in a typical, interactive ASP.NET manner, so users could interact with the web page to customize its appearance and content.

With ASP.NET 2.0, the idea of building portals using Web Parts is now a core part of ASP.NET. You no longer need SharePoint Portal Server to host portal pages, so the development of portals is now within the reach of every ASP.NET developer. The intention is that ASP.NET Web Parts will in the future be able to interoperate seamlessly with SharePoint.

What could you do with Web Parts? Here are two suggestions:

- First, you could create a company, department, or project website that users can customize. Do you want the company phone list on your page, a stock price ticker, or your to-do list? Developers may want information on builds and bug counts and the latest headlines from Slashdot or the Register, while sales and marketing people may be more interested in share prices and PR announcements. Using Web Parts makes it possible for all users to customize their own experience and use of the site.

- Second, a vendor could sell a website "kit," containing a collection of Web Parts that a customer such as an ISP can put together to form a portal. The kit is intended for use by the customer, so in this case modification may be restricted to the customer's administrators.

Introducing Web Part Basics

Web Parts are implemented as an integrated set of ASP.NET server controls that let users customize web pages directly from their browsers. The customizations fall into three groups:

Content: Users can determine which controls appear on the page. They can add and remove controls, as well as minimize those they do not want to see in full. Controls can also be imported and exported via XML files, which helps to promote reuse.

Appearance: Users can change fonts and colors and drag controls to where they want them on the page.

Behavior: Connections can be established between controls, such that events fired by one control will cause a change in a dependent control. The ability to fire and handle events is built into the controls themselves, but the user can wire them together at runtime.

Customization relies heavily on personalization: when a user modifies a page, the modifications are saved as personalization data. This means that to use Web Parts to their fullest, you will need to start with a website that supports membership.

Note Several important concepts are peculiar to the Web Parts technology. This section introduces the concepts, and you'll get a fuller idea of what they are and how they work as you progress through the chapter.

Web Parts are the building blocks of portal pages. A Web Part can be any ASP.NET server control, which means you can use any of the following:

- Standard ASP.NET server controls
- ASP.NET user controls
- ASP.NET custom controls

For maximum flexibility, you can also write custom Web Part controls by deriving from the System.Web.UI.WebControls.WebParts.WebPart class.

Zones are containers for Web Parts, and four zone types exist:

- A WebPartZone holds the visible parts on the page, and it defines the default layout and behavior of the Web Parts it contains. Customizable pages may allow users to drag Web Parts between zones, thus altering the layout of the page. WebPartZones don't have formatting properties of their own, and it is common to use HTML tables to place the zones exactly where you want them on the page.
- An EditorZone contains editor Web Parts that are used for interacting with page content. EditorZones aren't visible until the page is put into edit mode.
- A CatalogZone is used to manage the "catalog" of parts that aren't visible on the page. These can include parts that are not displayed by default, parts that the user has elected to close, and parts imported from outside the application. Like the EditorZone, a CatalogZone isn't visible until the page is put into catalog mode.
- The fourth zone type, ConnectionsZone, edits dynamic connections between Web Parts. It too is invisible until the user chooses to edit connections.

The WebPartManager control orchestrates the operation of Web Parts and zones. It knows exactly what is on the page, it maintains page state, and it fires events when page state changes. It also manages personalization of pages and handles communication between Web Parts.

Note You can have only one WebPartManager object per page. It has no UI, and so it appears as a gray rectangle in the Visual Studio designer.

You can view pages in several *modes*:

- Browse mode, which (as the name implies) is used for normal browsing
- Design mode, which allows you to play with the content on the page, rearranging and hiding parts
- Editor mode, which allows you to edit the properties of parts
- Connect mode, which allows the editing of dynamic connections between parts
- Catalog mode, which you use to display a catalog of hidden or extra parts, so that you can add content to the page

Just which modes clients can use will depend on what access they're granted. For a company website, everyone may be able to customize the home page, while an ISP creating a portal with Web Parts may not allow much customization at all.

Verbs are the buttons, links, and menu items on the title bar of a Web Part, which you use to interact with the part. Exactly what verbs you'll see depends on how much you're allowed to customize the page.

And finally, *chrome* refers to the UI elements that frame Web Parts, such as the border, icons, title bar, and text; it's probable that the term comes from the chrome used to decorate automobiles. You set the chrome at zone level, so all the parts within a zone share the same chrome.

Using Web Parts

The following sections will show you how to use Web Parts: how to create them, place them on a page, edit them, and connect them.

■ **Note** This introduction to Web Parts concentrates on using them declaratively. It is also possible to interact with Web Parts from code, and a full object model comes with .NET that supports this.

Getting Started

You'll need to start with a website that has personalization and membership set up. Although you can create Web Part pages without personalization, users won't be able to customize them—or save their customizations—without being logged in.

Note You will find details on how membership works in Chapter 19.

A typical site will have a LoginStatus control on the main page. This will tell users when they need to log in and will display their status when they are logged in. To use Web Parts, add a new Web Form to the project, and then add a link to it from the LoggedInTemplate of the LoginStatus control, as shown in Figure 27-2.

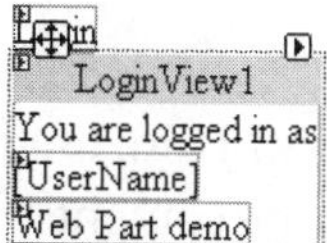

Figure 27-2. *A LoginStatus control with a link to the Web Part page*

Adding the link to the LoggedInTemplate means the user will see the link only once they are logged in. Make sure that login works before going further.

Adding Web Parts to a Page

To use Web Parts on a page, you need to add a WebPartManager, which you'll find in the WebParts section of the Toolbox. Because this control doesn't have a runtime representation, it will display as a gray rectangle in the designer. The default HTML for the WebPartManager is simple:

```
<asp:WebPartManager ID="WebPartManager1" runat="server"></asp:WebPartManager>
```

The next step is to create the zones to contain the parts. You're responsible for laying out the parts on the page, and you can use an HTML table or CSS positioning. We've created a simple table with three cells, and in Figure 27-3 we've dragged three WebPartZone controls from the Toolbox and dropped them into the cells of the table. We've changed the IDs of the controls to describe their location.

Figure 27-3. *A Web Part page showing an HTML table containing WebPartZone controls*

Now we'll start adding some Web Parts to the zones. To add a simple piece of text, drag a Label control from the Standard section in the Toolbox, and drop it onto the content area of the LeftZone control. To set the text in the label, switch to Source view, and enter a string such as **<h3>Here's a web part</h3>** as content for the <asp:Label> element. Each Web Part displays as a mini-window with a title bar, so it is useful to add the title attribute for the label, which will show up in the title bar of the part.

When you've added the Label control to the zone, you'll see that in the designer it has a title, with a tiny, black downward-pointing arrow to the right of it. This arrow displays editing commands at runtime.

GENERICWEBPART

If you use a standard server control as a Web Part, you'll often want to use the title attribute to set the title for the part. When you add this into the HTML, you'll find that the HTML editor objects, because title isn't an attribute for a server control.

So that server controls and user controls can be used as Web Parts, they get wrapped in a GenericWebPart wrapper at runtime. It is this object that provides the necessary mechanism to allow the control to function as a Web Part, and it is also this object that uses the title attribute.

The WebPartZone and its new Web Part are represented in the HTML like this:

```
<asp:WebPartZone ID="LeftZone" runat="server" HeaderText="Left Zone">
  <ZoneTemplate>
    <asp:Label ID="Label1" runat="server" Text="Label" title="A Label">
        <h3>Here's a web part</h3></asp:Label>
  </ZoneTemplate>
</asp:WebPartZone>
```

You can see that the control being used as a Web Part is enclosed in a ZoneTemplate element: all the Web Parts in a zone must be in a ZoneTemplate, but apart from that, they are simply references to ASP.NET controls.

You can add user controls just as easily as standard ASP.NET server controls. If you add a user control to the project, simply drag it from Solution Explorer, and drop it into the content area of a WebPartZone to add it to the zone. Figure 27-4 shows the completed simple design, with Label and Calendar controls in the top two WebPartZones, and a simple To Do List user control in the bottom zone.

Figure 27-4. *WebPartZone controls hosting Web Parts*

Running the Page

Save all files, and run the application. When you have logged in, use the link to navigate to the demo page. Figure 27-5 shows what you should see: the three Web Parts display with the default formatting, and each has a title with an arrow next to it.

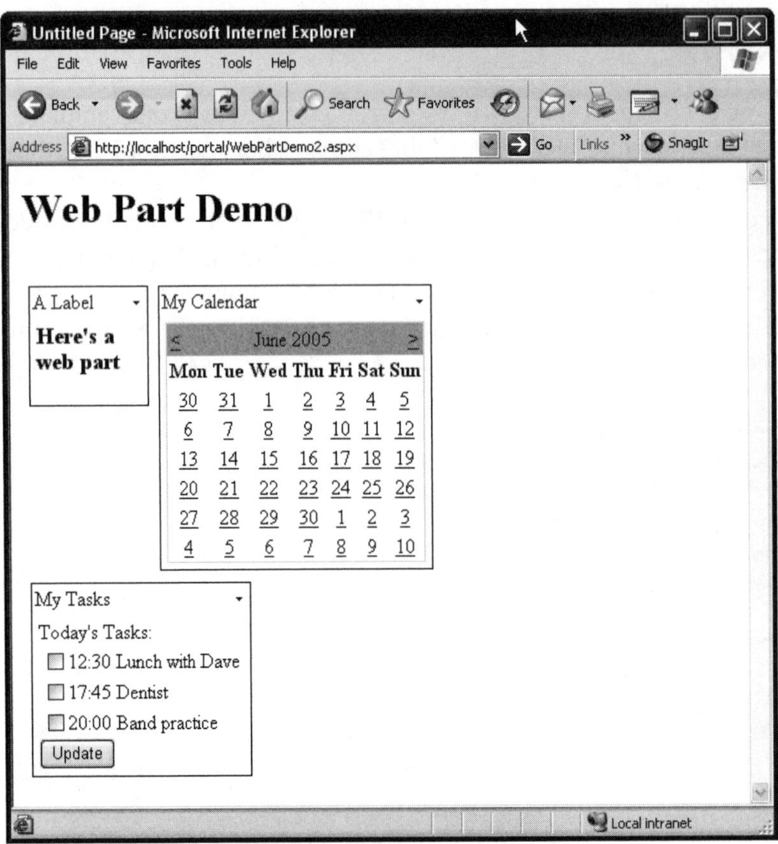

Figure 27-5. *A page containing Web Parts, with default formatting*

You can now start to see some of the power of Web Parts. Click the arrow next to one of the parts, and you'll see a small menu appear. The two options on this menu let you minimize the part or remove it from display altogether; try minimizing the parts and then restoring them again. Figure 27-6 shows the page with two of the parts minimized.

Figure 27-6. *The page with minimized Web Parts.*

Here's the really neat bit. Exit the application, and then start it up, and log in again. You'll find that the page displays just as you left it, because personalization has saved the changes you made to the page.

■ **Caution** By all means try closing a part, but for now there's no easy way to get it back! It will still be there in the project, but ASP.NET will remember that you didn't want to see it, so it won't appear whenever you view the page. For this reason, you may want to leave closing parts alone until we cover editing later in the "Making Pages Editable" section.

Formatting Parts

The default formatting for Web Parts is rather boring, and as you might expect, you can control their appearance in many ways. The simplest way is to use *autoformat*. If you've ever used tables in Word or a DataGrid in ASP.NET, you'll be familiar with the idea of autoformat. Select one of the zone controls in the Designer, and click the small right-facing arrow that appears at the top-right of the control. This will display a context menu entitled WebPartZone Tasks, which has a single item, Autoformat. Select this, and a familiar autoformat dialog box will appear. Figure 27-7 shows the context menu along with an autoformatted control:

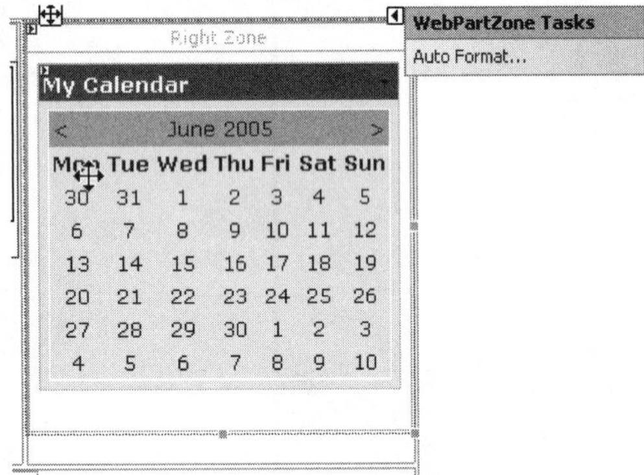

Figure 27-7. *Autoformatting Web Parts*

■ **Note** Formatting is applied to zones, so all Web Parts placed in a zone will display with that zone's formatting.

When you format a control, style information is added to the HTML. You can control the appearance of all aspects of the zone using style elements, from the color used for pop-up menus to the font used for the titles of Web Parts. Although the autoformat styles define preset selections of style elements, you can also modify and define your own styles by using the appropriate elements. Table 27-1 shows some of the commonly used style elements; if you want to explore all of them, you'll find them documented as properties of the WebPartZoneBase class.

Table 27-1. *Common Style Elements for WebPartZones*

Element	Description
EmptyZoneTextStyle	The style elements for the placeholder text in an empty zone
HeaderStyle	The style elements for a zone's header area

Element	Description
MenuLabelStyle	The style elements for the verb menu label
MenuPopupStyle	The style elements for pop-up menus in this zone
MenuVerbHoverStyle	The style elements for verb menu items when the mouse hovers over them
MenuVerbStyle	The style elements for verb menu items
PartChromeStyle	The style elements for the chrome of Web Parts within the zone
PartStyle	The style elements for Web Parts within the zone
PartTitleStyle	The style elements for the title of a Web Part in the zone

Here's how a typical formatted WebPartZone looks in HTML:

```
<asp:WebPartZone ID="WebPartZone2" runat="server" BorderColor="#CCCCCC"
      Font-Names="Verdana" Padding="6">
  <PartChromeStyle BackColor="#F7F6F3" BorderColor="#E2DED6"
      Font-Names="Verdana" ForeColor="White"/>
  <MenuLabelHoverStyle ForeColor="#E2DED6" />
  <EmptyZoneTextStyle Font-Size="0.8em" />
  <MenuLabelStyle ForeColor="White" />
  <MenuVerbHoverStyle BackColor="#F7F6F3" BorderColor="#CCCCCC"
      BorderStyle="Solid" BorderWidth="1px" ForeColor="#333333" />
  <HeaderStyle Font-Size="0.7em" ForeColor="#CCCCCC"
      HorizontalAlign="Center" />
  <MenuVerbStyle BorderColor="#5D7B9D" BorderStyle="Solid"
      BorderWidth="1px" ForeColor="White" />
  <PartStyle Font-Size="0.8em" ForeColor="#333333" />
  <TitleBarVerbStyle Font-Size="0.6em" Font-Underline="False"
      ForeColor="White" />
  <MenuPopupStyle BackColor="#5D7B9D" BorderColor="#CCCCCC"
      BorderWidth="1px" Font-Names="Verdana" Font-Size="0.6em" />
  <PartTitleStyle BackColor="#5D7B9D" Font-Bold="True"
      Font-Size="0.8em" ForeColor="White" />
  <ZoneTemplate>
     <apress:tempdisplaywebpart runat="server"
         id="TempDisplaywebpart1"/>
  </ZoneTemplate>
</asp:WebPartZone>
```

Each of these elements is represented in code by a style object. For example, the PartTitleStyle element is implemented by a System.Web.UI.WebControls.WebParts.TitleStyle object, which has more than a dozen properties, including BackColor, ForeColor,

HorizontalAlign, VerticalAlign, and Wrap. You can easily find the details of what properties are supported by a given element by consulting the documentation, and it is easy to use them as HTML attributes.

Controlling Page Modes

Now that you can display a simple Web Part page, you can explore how to allow users to control the page by editing the behavior and appearance of parts, using a catalog to add and remove parts, and creating connections between parts.

Before you get there, however, you need to do one job first. You need to provide a way for the user to switch between the various display modes available for the page. For example, if you allow editing, the page will have browse and edit modes. If you then add the ability to select parts from the catalog, the page will have browse, edit, and catalog modes.

Beta 1 provided a WebPartPageMenu control that provided a simple way to switch between page modes using a simple drop-down menu. This provided limited functionality and has been removed from Beta 2. As a result, you need to code your own way of switching between page modes, and you can easily do this using a user control.

You can make this control work any way you like, but this example uses a simple menu. Start by creating a user control called PageMode.ascx.

Figure 27-8 shows the UI for the control:

- The top combo box displays the page modes and allows the user to select one.
- The bottom combo box controls the scope of personalization (that is, whether the personalization is going to be for this user only or for all users). If shared personalization is not enabled for the current user, there will be only one entry in this drop-down list.

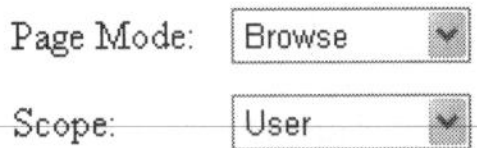

Figure 27-8. *A user control for controlling page modes*

■ **Note** Shared scope means the changes this user makes will affect everyone using the page. This obviously isn't something you want every user to be able to do, so you have to grant permission in the web.config file. We discuss this further in the "Editing Behavior with BehaviorEditorPart" section.

In the code-behind page, you'll need a field to represent the current WebPartManager for the page on which the control is being used. You also need to add a handler for the Init event for the control and implement it to hook the InitComplete event for the hosting page. This will ensure that the InitComplete handler will be called when the host page has finished initializing:

```
// The WebPartManager for the current page.
private WebPartManager _mgr;

// Handler for the Page_Init event.
void Page_Init(object sender, EventArgs ev)
{
  // Add a handler so we're notified when page initialization is complete.
  Page.InitComplete +=new EventHandler(Page_InitComplete);
}
```

The Page_InitComplete method initializes the state of the controls. This method first gets a reference to the WebPartManager for the page and then asks it for the current set of supported display modes. What modes are supported will depend on the zones that have been added to the page. For example, if a ConnectionsZone appears on the page, then Connect mode will be supported. Each mode has a name, but since modes can be enabled and disabled from code, the name is added to the list only after ensuring that it is enabled.

```
// Called when the page has finished initializing. This handler is used
// to set up the content of the controls on the page.
void Page_InitComplete(object sender, EventArgs ev)
{
  // Get the manager for the page.
  _mgr = WebPartManager.GetCurrentWebPartManager(Page);

  // Ask the manager for the list of page modes. If a mode is enabled,
  // add it to the list of supported modes.
  foreach (WebPartDisplayMode wpdm in _mgr.SupportedDisplayModes)
  {
    if (wpdm.IsEnabled(_mgr))
    {
      string modeName = wpdm.Name;
      cbMode.Items.Add(new ListItem(modeName, modeName));
    }
  }
```

```
  // Add the allowed scopes to the list. Everyone has 'user' scope.
  cbScope.Items.Add("User");
  // If the user can use shared scope, add that.
  if (_mgr.Personalization.CanEnterSharedScope)
    cbScope.Items.Add("Shared");
  // Select the item for the current scope.
  if (_mgr.Personalization.Scope == PersonalizationScope.Shared)
    cbScope.SelectedIndex = 1;
  else
    cbScope.SelectedIndex = 0;
}
```

A handler for the PreRender event sets the selected item in the combo box equal to the current mode of the host page:

```
// Make sure the control is displaying the current mode.
void Page_PreRender(object sender, EventArgs ev)
{
  // Set the selected item in the mode drop-down list to the manager's
  // current mode.
  cbMode.SelectedIndex =
       cbMode.Items.IndexOf(
           cbMode.Items.FindByText(_mgr.DisplayMode.Name));
}
```

The handler for the SelectedIndexChanged event on the combo box named Page Mode changes the page mode to the one selected:

```
// Called when the user changes the mode.
protected void cbMode_SelectedIndexChanged(object sender, EventArgs e)
{
  WebPartDisplayMode wpdm =
          _mgr.SupportedDisplayModes[cbMode.SelectedValue];
  if (wpdm != null)
    _mgr.DisplayMode = wpdm;
}
```

In the same way, the handler for the combo box named Scope changes the personalization scope:

```
// Called when the user changes the scope. You can't change to user
// or shared scope explicitly, so it is necessary to check where
// you are and toggle the scope between the two settings.
protected void cbScope_SelectedIndexChanged(object sender, EventArgs e)
{
```

```
    if (cbScope.SelectedValue.Equals("Shared") &&
        _mgr.Personalization.Scope == PersonalizationScope.User)
    {
      _mgr.Personalization.ToggleScope();
    }
    if (cbScope.SelectedValue.Equals("User") &&
        _mgr.Personalization.Scope == PersonalizationScope.Shared)
    {
      _mgr.Personalization.ToggleScope();
    }
}
```

Once you've completed the control, you can drag on onto the page, placing it just below the WebPartManager control.

You can test this immediately: run the page, and choose Design from the page mode combo box. The page layout will change to show the outline of the zones, and you'll be able to drag items from one zone to another. Figure 27-9 shows a Web Part being dragged from the left zone on a page to the right zone.

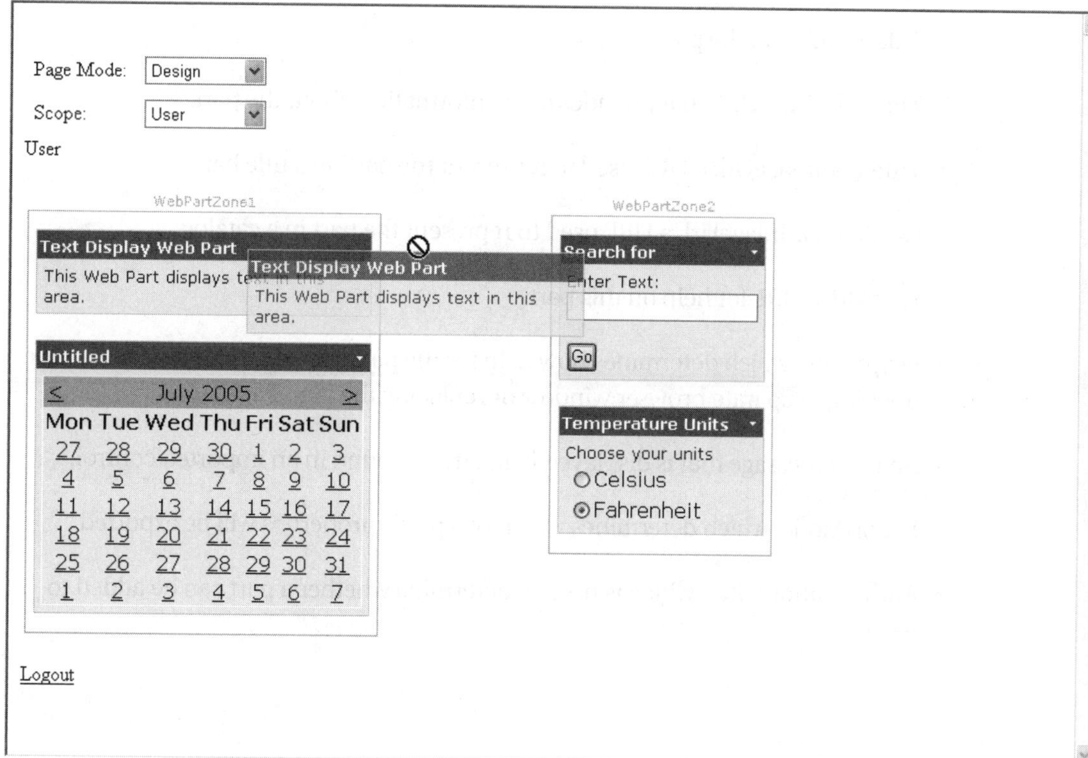

Figure 27-9. *A Web Part being dragged between zones*

Making Pages Editable

Four editor Web Parts enable editing behavior for the page: AppearanceEditorPart, BehaviorEditorPart, LayoutEditorPart, and PropertyGridEditorPart.

The AppearanceEditorPart lets the user edit the following UI properties of a control:

- The title of the Web Part.
- The height and width of the part.
- The ChromeType, which defines the border type for the control.
- Whether the control is hidden or displayed.
- The direction in which the part's content is displayed, which will affect (for example) on which side of radio buttons the text is displayed. For English text, the value will be left to right.

The BehaviorEditorPart lets the user edit the following UI properties that relate to behavior:

- A description of the part.
- The TitleUrl, a URL that provides extra information about the part.
- TitleIconImageUrl, a URL used to represent the part on a title bar.
- CatalogIconImageUrl, a URL used to represent the part in a catalog.
- HelpUrl, a URL for help on this part.
- HelpMode, which determines how help for the part is displayed. This can include opening a separate browser window or replacing the Web Parts page.
- An error message that is displayed if an error is found in an imported control.
- ExportMode, which determines which of a part's properties will be exported.
- AuthorizationFilter, which is used to determine whether a part can be added to a page.

- Whether the part can be closed.
- Whether the part allows other parts to connect to it.
- Whether the part can be edited.
- Whether the part can be hidden by the user.
- Whether the part can be minimized.
- Whether the part can be moved between zones.

The LayoutEditorPart lets the user edit UI attributes that control layout:

- The ChromeState, that is, whether the part is in minimized or normal state
- The zone the part is in
- The ZoneIndex, which gives the index of the part within the zone

The PropertyGridEditorPart lets users edit custom properties, if those properties were declared in the source code with a WebBrowsable attribute.

Editing controls are held in an EditorZone, and you add one of these to a page exactly as you did for WebPartZones. Typically, an EditorZone is placed in an HTML table cell and is not visible until the user selects edit mode.

Note Although these four controls let you modify the most commonly used control properties, you can also derive your own editor controls by inheriting from the EditorPart class.

Figure 27-10 shows an EditorZone containing an AppearanceEditorPart and a LayoutEditorPart.

Note EditorPart controls can be placed only in EditorZones, and EditorZones will not host any controls except EditorParts.

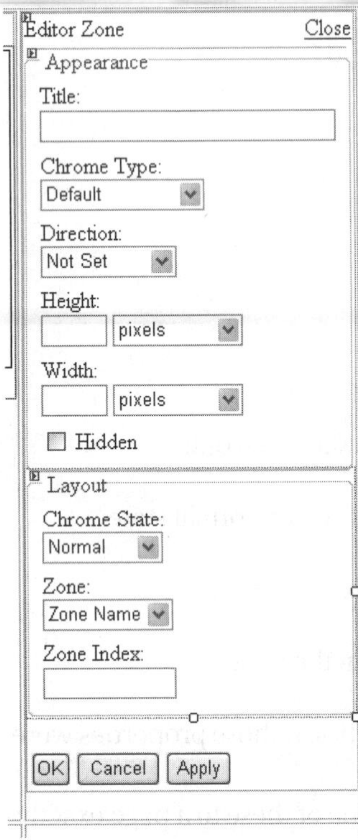

Figure 27-10. *An EditorZone containing editing Web Parts*

If you look at the source for the web page, you'll see the editor parts inside the zone:

```
<asp:EditorZone ID="EditorZone1" runat="server">
  <ZoneTemplate>
    <asp:AppearanceEditorPart ID="AppearanceEditorPart1" runat="server" />
    <asp:LayoutEditorPart ID="LayoutEditorPart1" runat="server" />
  </ZoneTemplate>
</asp:EditorZone>
```

As with standard Web Parts, editor parts are placed in a ZoneTemplate element and can have styles applied to them to alter their appearance on the page.

Here's how editing works: when you run the page, the mode change combo box will display three modes. Because the page now contains an EditorZone, one of these will be Edit. When you select this mode, the page display will change to show all the parts and outline the zones. If you select the menu for one of the parts, you'll see that it now contains an Edit entry; select it, and the EditorZone will appear, with its fields filled in with values for the part you're editing. You can see this in Figure 27-11.

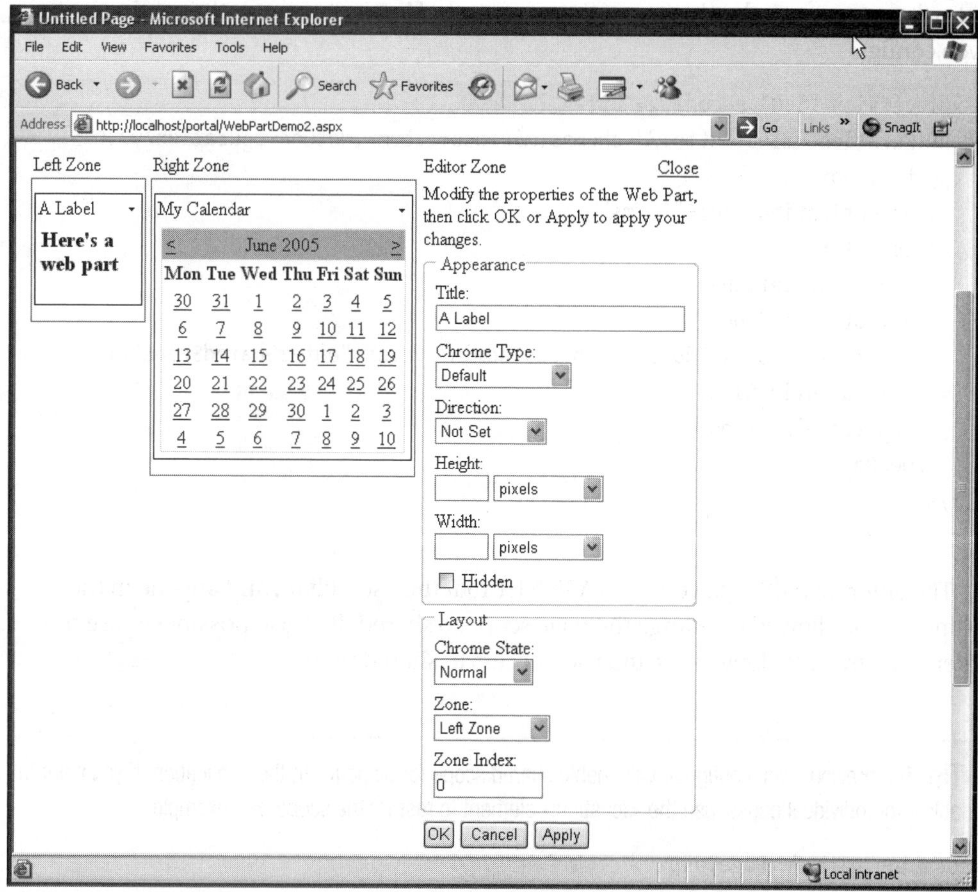

Figure 27-11. *The EditorZone in action*

Edit the properties as required, and then hit OK to apply them. The page will reflect the new appearance of the part, and the changes will be saved in the personalization database.

Editing Behavior with BehaviorEditorPart

You can use the LayoutEditorPart and AppearanceEditorPart controls by simply including them on a page, but the BehaviorEditorPart control needs some special setup. This editor control appears only when the page is in shared mode, so you need to switch the page mode before it will appear. The user control presented earlier will let you change to and from shared mode.

In addition, because you can use a BehaviorEditorPart to change the characteristics of a control for all users, it isn't something that you want enabled by default. So before you can use one on a page, you need to edit web.config to give permission to the users and roles that you want to be able to configure controls. Here's how the authorization looks in web.config:

```
<?xml version="1.0" encoding="utf-8"?>
<configuration xmlns="http://schemas.microsoft.com/.NetConfiguration/v2.0">
  <system.web>
    <authentication mode="Forms" />
    <webParts>
      <personalization>
        <authorization>
          <allow users="julian" roles="admin" verbs="enterSharedScope"/>
        </authorization>
      </personalization>
    </webParts>
  </system.web>
</configuration>
```

The enterSharedScope verb tells ASP.NET that the user julian, and anyone in the admin role is allowed to change the page scope to shared. It is also possible to use the <deny> element to deny users and roles access to shared scope.

■ **Tip** The previous web.config file will enable shared scope for all pages in the application. If you want to enable it for individual pages, use the <location> element to restrict the scope. For example:

```
<location path="MyPage.aspx">
  <system.web>
    ...
  </system.web>
</location>
```

Using Catalogs

You can maintain a catalog of Web Parts that aren't being used on the page currently. This makes it possible to provide optional content for the page and also provides somewhere for the user to store parts that they currently don't want to see but without losing access to them.

As you might expect by now, a catalog is implemented by a collection of Web Parts, held in a CatalogZone. As with the EditorZone, a CatalogZone is displayed only when the page is switched to display in catalog mode.

You can use three types of parts in a CatalogZone. A DeclarativeCatalogPart holds a set of parts that users may later choose to add to the page and is a useful way to provide optional content. Developers can provide a set of parts declaratively as part of the HTML, and users can add them to the page with no extra coding required.

A PageCatalogPart holds the parts that the user may have closed on the page, so that they can add them back later. Only closed controls are added to the catalog: when a control is closed, it isn't visible on the page, it isn't rendered, and it doesn't participate in the page lifecycle. It is also possible that a part may be configured so that it cannot be closed, in which case it will never be added to the catalog.

■ **Caution** Closing a control is not the same as deleting it. If a control is deleted from the page, it isn't added to the catalog and cannot be retrieved later.

An ImportCatalogPart allows the user to import the settings for a control so that settings can easily be shared. Note that this doesn't import a control itself, only the settings; the control, as an assembly in a DLL or a user control in an .ascx file, must be accessible from the server.

Using the PageCatalogPart

Figure 27-12 shows a CatalogZone on a page, configured with a single PageCatalogPart. At runtime, the PageCatalogPart will display a list of parts that have been deleted from the page; checking the box next to a part will let you add it back to the page again.

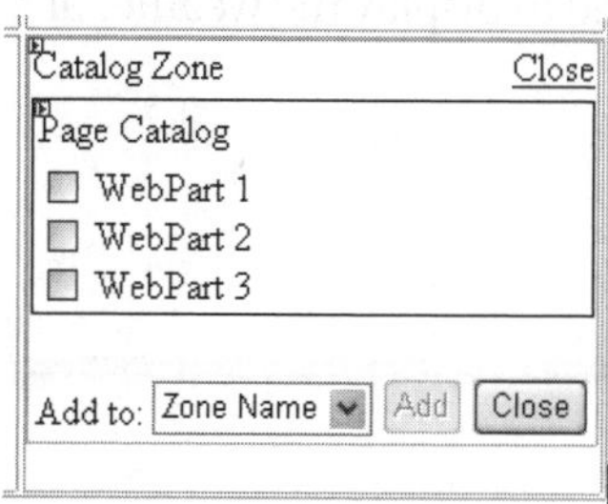

Figure 27-12. *A CatalogZone containing a PageCatalogPart*

When you run the application, you'll see that a Catalog has been added to the page mode drop-down list. When you select this, the CatalogZone will appear on the page. Figure 27-13 shows part of a page: the My Tasks part has been closed so that it appears in the PageCatalogPart, and now nothing is in the Bottom Zone area. Checking the box next to the part name and pressing Add will add the part back into the selected zone.

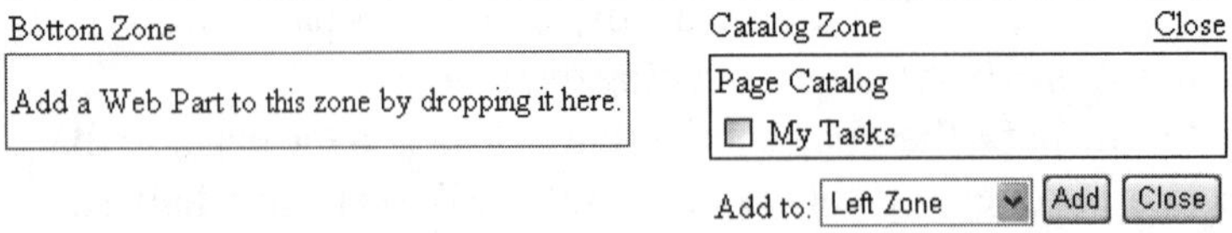

Bottom Zone
Add a Web Part to this zone by dropping it here.
Catalog Zone Close
Page Catalog
My Tasks
Add to: Left Zone Add Close

Figure 27-13. *Closed parts are listed in the PageCatalogPart*

Using the DeclarativeCatalogPart

A DeclarativeCatalogPart holds optional parts that the user can add to the page as required.

To use a DeclarativeCatalogPart, drag one and drop it onto the CatalogZone. Click the arrow at its top-right corner to display the tasks menu, and select Edit Templates. You can now use the designer in Visual Studio to add any controls to the catalog that you want. If you look at the source, you will see that the catalog is represented by a WebPartsTemplate element; you can manually add references to Web Parts and other ASP.NET server controls if you don't want to use the designer.

```
<asp:DeclarativeCatalogPart ID="DeclarativeCatalogPart1" runat="server">
  <WebPartsTemplate>
    <uc3:WeatherControl ID="WeatherControl1" runat="server" />
  </WebPartsTemplate>
</asp:DeclarativeCatalogPart>
```

Figure 27-14 shows a DeclarativeCatalogPart open for editing in the designer. It currently contains one user control, a WeatherControl that is used to display the weather at a selected location.

Figure 27-14. *A DeclarativeCatalogPart*

The CatalogZone on this page now contains a DeclarativeCatalogPart and a PagePartCatalog. When you view the page in catalog mode, the zone displays one catalog, along with a link to allow you to view the other one (see Figure 27-15).

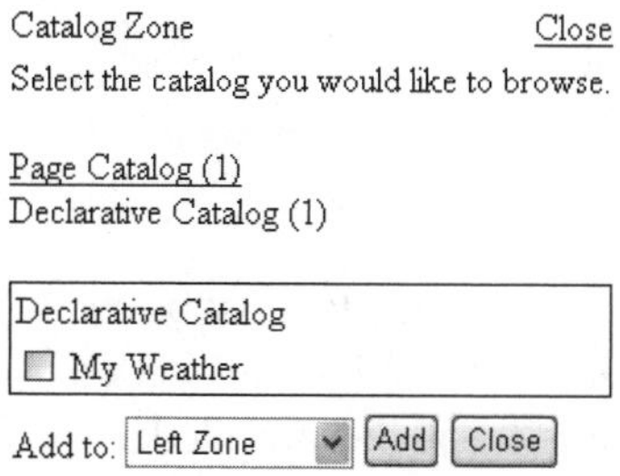

Catalog Zone Close
Select the catalog you would like to browse.

Page Catalog (1)
Declarative Catalog (1)

Declarative Catalog
My Weather

Add to: Left Zone Add Close

Figure 27-15. *A CatalogZone containing two CatalogParts at runtime*

As with the PageCatalog, select a part by checking the box, and then click Add to add it to the selected zone. Unlike the PageCatalog, however, adding a part from a declarative catalog doesn't remove it from the catalog listing, so you could add more than one to a page.

Creating Custom Web Parts

You can create custom Web Parts in two ways: as user controls and as code-based custom controls. Which one you use depends on the functionality you require: it is easier to create user controls, but custom controls can provide more functionality.

You create custom Web Part controls by deriving from the System.Web.UI.WebControls.WebParts.WebPart class, an abstract class that provides the base functionality for all Web Parts. You will probably want to create a custom control for three reasons:

- You want to specify the content of the control.
- You want to expose custom properties at runtime.
- You want to provide connections for other controls to use.

This section covers the first two topics here, and the "Connecting Parts" section covers connections. The simple control used in this section displays a set of possible temperature units (that is, Celsius and Fahrenheit) as radio buttons, along with an explanatory string. Later in the chapter you'll see how to connect to this control so that changing the unit selection causes a change in other parts on the page. Figure 27-16 shows the control in the designer: you can see the RadioButtonList with two options and the Label control displaying Choose Your Units.

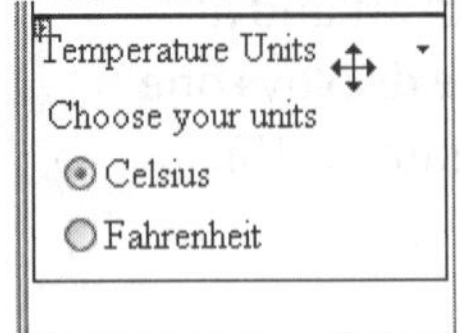

Figure 27-16. *A custom Web Part control*

A custom server control is simply created as a source file, and the code must be available when the page is run. In ASP.NET 2.0, the App_Code directory holds code needed by a web application; you place source code in this directory, and it will be compiled as needed.

Note In Visual Studio 2005, you can create this directory by right-clicking the solution name in the Solution Explorer. Choose Add Folder and then App_Code Folder from the context menu. You can then create the control class within App_Code by right-clicking the folder and choosing Add Item from the context menu.

Before starting on content, you may want to specify how the control can be used as a Web Part. The WebPart class has a number of properties controlling how it acts when on a page, and these can conveniently be set in the constructor:

```
public class TempUnitWebPart : WebPart
{
  // Constructor.
  public TempUnitWebPart()
  {
    // Allow minimizing, closing, and editing for this part.
    this.AllowClose = true;
    this.AllowMinimize = true;
    this.AllowEdit = true;

    // Supply a title.
    this.Title = "Temperature Units";

    ...
  }
```

Table 27-2 describes the most commonly used properties for the WebPart class.

Table 27-2. *Common Properties of the WebPart Class*

Property	Description
AllowClose	If true, the control can be closed.
AllowConnect	If true, other controls can connect to this one.
AllowEdit	If true, the control can be edited through parts in an EditorZone.
AllowHide	If true, the control can be hidden.
AllowMinimize	If true, the control can be minimized.
AllowZoneChange	If true, the user can drag the control to another zone.
BackColor	Specifies the background color for the Web Part.
BorderColor	Specifies the border color for the Web Part.
BorderStyle	Specifies the border style for the Web Part.
ChromeState	Specifies whether a control and its border are in a normal or collapsed state.
ChromeType	Specifies the kind of border that surrounds the part.
Enabled	If true, the control is enabled.
ForeColor	Gets or sets the foreground color of the page.
Hidden	Returns true if the control is hidden.
IsClosed	Returns true if the control is closed on the page.
IsShared	Returns true if the control is shared, that is, visible to all users of the page.
IsStatic	Returns true if the control is static, that is, it has been declared in the HTML and not added dynamically.
Page	Gets a reference to the page that contains this control.
Title	Gets or sets a string representing the title displayed for this part.
Verbs	Represents the collection of custom verbs for this control.
Zone	At runtime, gets the zone in which the control is located.

The content of a custom Web Part control is commonly provided in one of two ways. The control developer can override the RenderControl method in order to write HTML directly. Alternatively, if the control is composed of a set of child controls, the developer can override the CreateChildControls method.

The following code shows how to create the child controls:

```
protected override void CreateChildControls()
{
  // Clear the current set of controls.
  Controls.Clear();
```

```
    // Create a Label, and set its content.
    // _textString will be exposed as an editable property.
    _text = new Label();
    _text.Text = _textString;
    // Add the Label to the control set
    this.Controls.Add(_text);

    // Create the RadioButtonList, and add two items.
    _rbList = new RadioButtonList();
    _liCelsius = new ListItem("Celsius");
    _liFahr = new ListItem("Fahrenheit");
    _rbList.Items.Add(_liCelsius);
    _rbList.Items.Add(_liFahr);

    // Add the RadioButtonList to the control set.
    this.Controls.Add(_rbList);

    // Select the enabled item.
    // (See below)

    // Signal that we're done.
    ChildControlsCreated = true;
}
```

The control's _useCelsius field determines the currently selected item; this is maintained by an event handler that is called when the selection changes:

```
// Select the enabled item.
if (_useCelsius)
  _liCelsius.Selected = true;
else
  _liFahr.Selected = true;

_rbList.SelectedIndexChanged += new EventHandler(rbList_SelectedIndexChanged);
```

You've already seen how the appearance and behavior of Web Parts can be edited at runtime using the EditorZone. You can add custom properties to a control, and these can then be edited using a PropertyGridEditorPart in an EditorZone.

For a property to be editable at runtime, it needs to be marked with two attributes, as shown in the following code fragment:

```
[Personalizable(), WebBrowsable]
public string TextString
{
  get { return _textString; }
  set { _textString = value; }
}
```

The Personalizable attribute ensures that this property will be persisted when the control is used as a Web Part. For a property to be personalizable, it must meet the following criteria:

- It must be public, with public get/set accessors.
- It must be read/write.
- It must not have parameters.
- It cannot be indexed.

The WebBrowsable attribute enables the property for runtime editing by the user, and it will appear in a PropertyGridEditorPart if one is added to the page.

To use custom controls on a page, you can simply drag the control name from the Solution Explorer and drop it onto a zone in the designer. This will add a Register directive to the top of the page source, establishing a prefix for the control's namespace:

```
<%@ Register TagPrefix="apress" Namespace="Apress.WebParts" %>
```

An element representing the control itself will be added to the WebPartZone:

```
<asp:WebPartZone ID="WebPartZone2" Runat="server">
  <ZoneTemplate>
    <uc1:textinputcontrol runat="server" id="TextInputControl1" />
    <apress:tempunitwebpart runat="server" id="TempUnitwebpart1"/>
  </ZoneTemplate>
</asp:WebPartZone>
```

Figure 27-17 shows the TextString property being edited using a PropertyGridEditorPart.

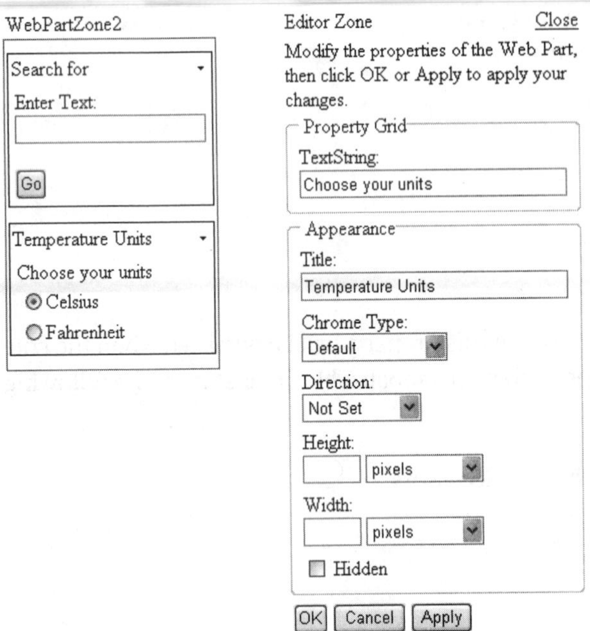

Figure 27-17. *A PropertyGridEditorPart control editing custom properties on a Web Part*

You can see that the grid displays the name of the property, plus displays a textbox to edit its value. The editor control will display text boxes for scalar properties (in other words, string, int, float, Unit, DateTime), check boxes for Boolean properties, and DropDownLists for enumerations.

Connecting Parts

For Web Parts to be truly useful, you need some way for them to interact. For example, if the user chooses a city from a Location part, the other parts on the page, such as news or weather displays, may want to change their contents to reflect the chosen location. Web Part connections make this possible.

A part (also known as a *provider*) can make data available for other parts (*consumers*) to use. It is a pull model, because the consumer queries the provider to get the data.

Two types of connections exist. *Static connections* are set up in the HTML of the hosting page within a *ConnectionsZone* and are created during the prerendering of the page. *Dynamic connections* use the ConnectionsZone to display a UI with which the user can create and destroy connections at runtime. As you would expect, connections are personalized.

How Do Connections Work?

Communication between parts is defined by interfaces: a provider exposes methods, properties, and events by defining and implementing an interface, and consumers use the interface. A consumer obviously has to know about the interfaces it wants to use, although it doesn't have to implement any specific interfaces itself.

How does the WebPartManager know that a Web Part is a provider? After all, the fact that a class defines and implements an interface doesn't necessarily mean anything particular.

The WebPartManager can connect controls that implement *connection points.* Both providers and consumers can implement connection points, and the WebPartManager uses them to connect controls together. You can think of connection points as plugs (for the consumers) and sockets (for the providers). But note that just because one part implements a consumer connection point and another implements a provider connection point doesn't necessarily mean that they can be connected; the consumer has to be expecting to work with the provider and know what methods to call. The connection points just provide the mechanism.

■ **Note** f you've ever worked with ActiveX controls, you may have come across the term *connection point* before. The concept here is the same, although the implementation is very different.

Creating Providers

Here's an example of an interface that the temperature unit part might define in order to make information on the current units available to consumers:

```
interface ITempUnits
{
  bool IsCelsius { get; }
}
```

The class would implement the interface in the normal way:

```
public class TempUnitWebPart : WebPart, ITempUnits
{
  ...
  public bool IsCelsius
  {
     get
```

```
      {
        return _useCelsius;
      }
    }
    ...
  }
```

You can create a provider connection point in several ways, but the simplest is to use the ConnectionProvider attribute, like this:

```
[ConnectionProvider("TempUnits", "TempUnits")]
private ITempUnits ProvideTempUnits()
{
  return this;
}
```

The method—its name is not important—has a return type matching the provider interface, and it returns a reference to the object. You can see that this gives the caller access to the interface methods on the object, without giving access to any other functionality.

The ConnectionProvider attribute takes two parameters, which are often identical. The first is a display name to label the connection, and the second is a unique ID to identify this connection.

■ **Note** If a class exposes more than one interface via connection points, you have to specify a third parameter that gives the type of the interface, for example typeof(ITempUnits). This is not necessary when you expose only one interface.

Creating Consumers

A Web Part that is going to act as a consumer has to implement a consumer connection point for the interface it wants to use. It goes without saying that a consumer can connect to a number of interfaces if necessary, defining a connection point for each. Here's what a consumer might implement to use the ITempUnits interface:

```
[ConnectionConsumer("TempUser", "TempUser")]
private void GetTempUnits(ITempUnits itu)
{
  // If the reference is null, there's no connection.
  if (itu == null)
    throw new Exception("No connection");
```

```
    // Query the provider, and do something.
    if (itu.IsCelsius == true)
      _labelText = _strText + _strCelsius;
    else
      _labelText = _strText + _strFahr;
}
```

The runtime creates a consumer connection point as a callback. If the property on the ITempUnits interface changes, the runtime will invoke this method, so the consumer will instantly see—and respond to—the change in the provider.

Setting Up Static Connections

Static connections are declared in the HTML as part of the WebPartManager element. Here's an example:

```
<asp:WebPartManager ID="WebPartManager1" runat="server">
  <StaticConnections>
    <asp:WebPartConnection ID="connection1"
       ProviderID="TempUnitwebpart1" ProviderConnectionPointID="TempUnits"
       ConsumerID="TempDisplaywebpart1" ConsumerConnectionPointID="TempUser" />
  </StaticConnections>
</asp:WebPartManager>
```

Static connections are set up using a StaticConnections element, which in turn contains one or more WebPartConnection elements. Each connection has to have an ID attribute, along with ProviderID and ConsumerID attributes that define the Web Parts acting as the provider and consumer; these IDs must obviously match those of two controls elsewhere on the page. If the parts expose only a single producer or consumer connection point, you can omit the ProviderConnectionPointID and ConsumerConnectionPointID attributes; if either end implements more than one connection point, you must use these attributes to specify which one is taking part in the connection.

■ **Note** Static connections are not personalized, because they are a property of the page rather than a preference of any one user. They can therefore be used on pages that don't support personalization.

Using Dynamic Connections

Static connections cannot be made or broken at runtime. If you want to allow users to connect and disconnect parts, you will need to use dynamic connections instead. You can implement them by adding a ConnectionsZone part to the page, as shown in Figure 27-18. Unlike some of the other Zone controls, the ConnectionsZone has no content.

Figure 27-18. *A ConnectionsZone Web Part on a page in design mode*

Adding a ConnectionsZone to a page adds another possible page display mode. When you select Connect mode, the Connect verb will appear on the menus of all connectable controls. When you choose this verb, the ConnectionsZone part will appear. If there is no connection to the control, the ConnectionsZone will prompt you to make a selection, as shown in Figure 27-19.

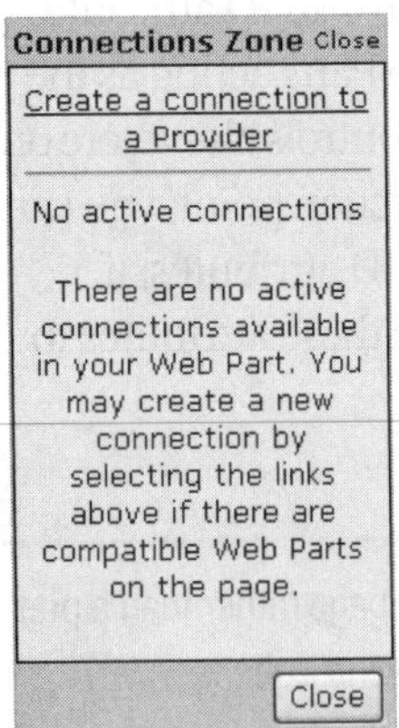

Figure 27-19. *The ConnectionsZone in Connect mode*

Clicking the link will show you the parts that your chosen control can interact with; in other words, those parts that implement the same provider/consumer interface contract. Figure 27-20 shows this in action, choosing the Temperature Units part as the provider for the TempUnits connection point.

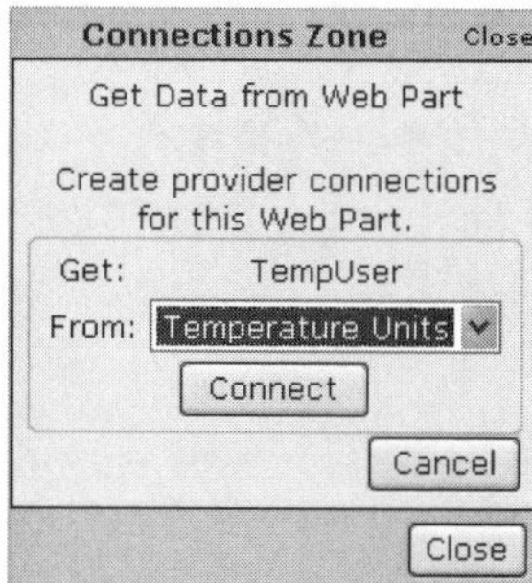

Figure 27-20. *Using the ConnectionsZone to choose a provider*

Once you have made a connection between two parts, they will work together automatically. Since a user can choose which parts to connect or disconnect, dynamic connections are personalized so that each user's choices will be saved.

If you execute the Connect verb on a part that already has connections, the ConnectionsZone will list the connections and allow you to disconnect any that you no longer need.

The Last Word

In this chapter, you saw how Web Part technology makes is possible to create highly customizable pages. The support for editing part behavior and appearance, together with the ability to add and remove parts to give a personal view of the page, makes it possible to produce complex, personalized pages with little effort.

And if a website has been set up for personalization, any changes that a user makes to their view of the Web Parts on a page will be saved and reapplied when they next log on.

Index

E

F

H

I

P

T

U

V

Y

Z